Principles of Marketing

STUDENT ACCESS KIT – DON'T THROW IT AWAY!

With your purchase of this textbook, you received a Student Access Kit for MyMarketingLab: an online learning environment that produces a personalised Study Plan for each student.

 When you see this icon in the margin of the text, go to **www.pearsoned.co.uk/kotler**. There you will find a quiz, the results of which will indicate your understanding of each key concept.
MyMarketingLab uses your results to diagnose individual strengths and weaknesses, and builds a customised Study Plan to help improve your grades.

Puts You in Control!

MyMarketingLab gives you access to an unrivalled suite of online resources:

- Practice tests for each key concept in marketing that assess your understanding.
- A personalised Study Plan, which adapts to your strengths and weaknesses.
- Interactive exercises that break key concepts into component steps, allowing you to actively engage with each issue.
- Pages from an e-book version of this text, which allow convenient study on the go.
- A wealth of video clips demonstrate how top marketing managers from a wide range of companies (including IKEA, Land Rover, HSBC, VSO and many more) refer to marketing theory in their day-to-day lives.
- Audio MP3 clips, recorded by a marketing professional, briefly outline how a key concept relates to contemporary practice.
- An online Glossary defines key terms and provides examples.

To activate your pre-paid subscription go to **www.pearsoned.co.uk/kotler** and follow the instructions on-screen to register as a new user, and see your grades improve.

PEARSON
Education

We work with leading authors to develop the
strongest educational materials in marketing,
bringing cutting-edge thinking and best learning
practice to a global market.

Under a range of well-known imprints, including
Financial Times Prentice Hall, we craft high quality
print and electronic publications which help readers to
understand and apply their content, whether studying
or at work.

To find out more about the complete range of our
publishing, please visit us on the World Wide Web at:
www.pearsoned.co.uk/marketing

FIFTH EUROPEAN EDITION

Principles of Marketing

PHILIP KOTLER

GARY ARMSTRONG

VERONICA WONG

JOHN SAUNDERS

Prentice Hall
FINANCIAL TIMES

An imprint of **Pearson Education**
Harlow, England • London • New York • Boston • San Francisco • Toronto • Sydney • Singapore • Hong Kong
Tokyo • Seoul • Taipei • New Delhi • Cape Town • Madrid • Mexico City • Amsterdam • Munich • Paris • Milan

Dedication

To Peng Chow and Jack

Pearson Education Limited
Edinburgh Gate
Harlow
Essex CM20 2JE
England

and Associated Companies throughout the world

Visit us on the World Wide Web at:
www.pearsoned.co.uk

First European edition published 1996 by Prentice Hall Europe
Second European edition published 1999
Third European edition published 2001 by Pearson Education
Fourth European edition published 2005
Fifth European edition published 2008

© Prentice Hall Europe 1996, 1999
© Pearson Education Limited 2008

The rights of Philip Kotler, Gary Armstrong, Veronica Wong and John Saunders to be identified as authors of this work have been asserted by them in accordance with the Copyright, Designs and Patents Act 1988.

ISBN: 978-0-273-71156-8

British Library Cataloguing-in-Publication Data
A catalogue record for this book is available from the British Library

Library of Congress Cataloging-in-Publication Data
Principles of marketing / Philip Kotler ... [et al.]. -- 5th European ed.
    p. cm.
 Edition for U.S. published under: Principles of marketing / Philip Kotler, Gary Armstrong. 12th ed., c2008.
 ISBN 978-0-273-71156-8 (pbk.)
1. Marketing.   I. Kotler, Philip.
 HF5415.K6314 2008
 658.8--dc22

                              2008003309

10 9 8 7 6 5 4 3 2
12 11 10 09

Typeset in 10/12.5pt Minion by 73
Printed and bound by Rotolito Lombarda, Italy

The publisher's policy is to use paper manufactured from sustainable forests.

BRIEF CONTENTS

v

Principles of Marketing

Supporting resources

Visit **www.pearsoned.co.uk/kotler** to find premium online resources.

MyMarketingLab for students

- Online video documentaries referred to at the start of each part.
- Practice tests for each key concept in marketing that assess your understanding.
- A personalised Study Plan, which adapts to your strengths and weaknesses.
- Interactive exercises that break key concepts into component steps, allowing you to actively engage with each issue.
- Pages from an e-book version of this book, allowing for convenient study on the go.
- A wealth of additional video clips demonstrating how top marketing managers from a wide range of companies (including IKEA, Land Rover, HSBC, VSO and many more) refer to Marketing theory in their day-to-day lives.
- Audio MP3 clips, recorded by a marketing professional, briefly outlining how a key concept relates to contemporary practice.
- Annotated links to relevant, specific sites on the web.
- A searchable online Glossary defining key terms and providing examples.
- Flashcards to help you when revising, testing your knowledge of key terms and definitions.

For instructors

- A DVD containing full versions of the video documentaries within the book, plus three unseen cases.
- Media-rich PowerPoint slides, including animated key figures from the book, video clips, audio and direct links to the web
- Extensive Instructor's Manual, with sample answers for all the case study question material including the extra case studies on the book's website.
- Sample answers to the questions in the book that accompany the video case studies integrated with the book.
- A testbank of over 2500 multiple choice questions.
- Classic extra case studies for use in class or in seminars.

Also: The Companion Website provides the following features:

- Search tool to help locate specific items of content.
- E-mail results and profile tools to send results of quizzes to instructors.
- Online help and support to assist with website usage and troubleshooting.

For more information please contact your local Pearson Education sales representative or visit **www.pearsoned.co.uk/marketing**

CONTENTS

Contents

Part three Core strategy 365

Chapter eight Relationship marketing 367

Chapter nine Segmentation and positioning 407

GUIDED TOUR

Navigation and setting the scene

Chapter openers concisely introduce the themes and issues explored in the chapter. They include a **mini contents list** so you can see at a glance what major topics are covered and **learning objectives** that highlight what you should have learnt by the end of the chapter.

CHAPTER **two**

Sustainable marketing: marketing ethics and social responsibility

Mini Contents List

- Prelude case – NSPCC: Full Stop to child cruelty
- Introduction
- Social criticisms of marketing
- Real Marketing 2.1 – The Dove Campaign for Real Beauty
- Marketing's impact on other businesses
- Citizen and public actions to regulate marketing
- Business actions towards socially responsible marketing
- Real Marketing 2.2 – From Plato's Republic to supermarket slavery
- Company case 2 – Nestlé: singled out again and again

Prelude case Big food has a lot on its plate

I will always remember the first time I tried to buy a packet of crisps – or potato chips, if you prefer – in a New York supermarket. In vain, I searched for the single-portion packets which a European may find familiar: all I could see on the shelves were rows and rows of what appeared to be party-sized bags. Then suddenly, I noticed the slogan on Frito-Lay's Ruffles: 'Bet your own bag', it screamed, and I realised with amazement and some awe that, in the land of plenty, these enormous bags were intended for a party of one!

> Fat, salt and sugar have been the building blocks of success for most of the world's big brand owners.

The Frito-Lay's website gives the crisps' calorie content as 160 calories to the ounce (28 g). On that basis, an 8 oz got-your-own bag would contain 1,280 calories, more than half the 2,500 RDA (Recommended Daily Allowance) average of calories for men and close to 65 per cent of the 2,000 RDA for women. And that is without 120 calories for a soft drink or 180 calories for a can of lager.

Fat, salt and sugar have been the building blocks of success for most of the world's big brand owners. It is not surprising that Unilever plans cuts in its sales targets. As food companies go, Unilever is better than most: a lot of its products are reasonably nutritious and some, such as its cholesterol-busting spreads, can improve people's health. But even Unilever has been caught up in the sudden panic over obesity. Their simultaneous acquisition of SlimFast Foods, the slimming company, and Ben & Jerry's Homemade, the fattening ice-cream company, looked like a clever each-way bet. However, as people have become fatter and more desperate for a miracle remedy, Atkins has replaced SlimFast as the diet of choice, while Ben & Jerry's high-fat, premium ice-creams have begun to look gross.

Still, things could be worse. Coca-Cola, PepsiCo, McDonald's, Burger King, Cadbury Schweppes, Mars, Hershey – all are founded on products now blamed for causing obesity; and most of the rest – Kraft Foods, Nestlé, HJ Heinz, Kellogg, General Mills, Campbell Soup – make an unhealthily large contribution to the output of fatty, salty or sugary foods that are accused of contributing to the problem.

Perhaps the food industry's enthusiasm for fattening products mattered less when people's limited means restricted their ability to gorge on them. Evolutionary theory suggests we are programmed to overeat because, through most of human history, food was scarce and over-consumption was an insurance policy against lean times. So, as disposable incomes have risen, it has been hard for us to resist the temptation to binge on the food companies' heavily marketed output.

An odd result from international studies of food intake and income shows a contrast between poor and wealthy countries. In poor countries rich people are healthier than their less well-off residents because they can afford nutritious food. In wealthy countries, people with high incomes are also healthier than those on low incomes. In this case it is because wealthy people have a healthier diet than people on low incomes who have a much higher protein intake.

Despite all the media coverage and political posturing over obesity, a recent National Opinion Poll (NOP) survey found that relatively few respondents regularly buy reduced-fat food, with the exception of dairy products. The regular purchase of all types of diet and low-fat foods has actually fallen since 2000.

Some people attempt to limit their calorie intake by choosing natural foods wisely. However, demand for convenience is such that the market for processed, reduced-fat, reduced-sugar products and calorie-counted food is large. Such foods appeal to people opting for a healthy alternative and also to slimmers, who may be tempted to buy products they may previously have considered out-of-bounds. According to McVitie's, owned by United Biscuits, this latter category has significantly contributed to increased sales of its 'Go Ahead!' brand.

Weight Watchers and Nestlé's Lean Cuisine brands are other leading brands benefiting from consumer desire for processed healthy food. Supermarket own-label brands have moved upmarket to challenge the leading brands. 'Be Good to Yourself', a low-fat range promoted as indulgent as well as healthy, is Sainsbury's biggest in-store brand. Other own-brand healthy options include 'Count on Us' from Marks & Spencer and the newly introduced 'Perfectly Balanced' range from Waitrose.

So, what happens now? Even among anti-obesity campaigners, few would advocate measures as illiberal as banning undesirable food products or taxing them out of existence, though doubtless we could think of some prime candidates (Velveeta? Spam? fish and chips?).

On the other hand, the industry seems unlikely to get away with the idea that people should simply take more exercise. Even large amounts of physical activity burn off relatively few calories: you would have to do three hours' downhill skiing or spend more than five hours on the golf course to burn off an 8 oz bag of Ruffles.

177

PART **two**

A **prelude case** gives you an insight into how the major themes in each chapter are applied in practice, by looking at well known products, brands and organisations.

NEW to this edition! A **video case** opens each part of the book. These fascinating documentaries include interviews with top management teams from a variety of European companies, who discuss how the products or services offered by their organisations are marketed. Represented are multinational corporations such as Electrolux to small enterprises such as Acme Whistles and not-for-profit entities, such as VSO. Access these documentaries online at **www.pearsoned.co.uk/kotler**.

Video Case Marketing Birmingham

Birmingham, Britain's second city, has had to transform itself in recent years. The city grew during the Industrial Revolution becoming a powerhouse known as the 'workshop of the world' and the 'city of a thousand trades'. With the decline of manufacturing, the city has had to transform itself into a centre for commercial and consumer services. Birmingham has many assets, such as being Europe's youngest city – based on the average age of its residents, a multicultural population and a maker of things as diverse as Cadbury's chocolate, Jaguar cars and more than half of Britain's jewellery. It also boasts that the it has more canals than Venice and more acres of parks than any other city in the world. Birmingham is also the home of heavy metal music (Led Zeppelin, Judas Priest, Black Sabbath/Ozzy Osbourne, etc.) and Tolkien (Gandalf, hobbits, orcs, etc.).

Birmingham's 'thousand' trades means those marketing the city have a lot to talk about, but its diversity also makes the city complex to market. Gain some idea about the city from the its own website [www.birmingham.gov.uk]. Visit Birmingham guide [www.birmingham.gov.uk], Cadbury World [www.cadburyworld.co.uk], the Balti Triangle [www.birmingham.gov.uk/balti.bcc], Jewellery Quarter [the-quarter.com] or surf the city's canals [www.canaljunction.com/canal/birmingham_navigations.html].

After viewing the video, you may address the following questions:

1. Does the marketing of cities, such as Birmingham, Lyon or Munich, differ to that of goods and services?
2. Why is market research important? How does it help marketing decision-makers in their efforts to [a] build and sustain a brand's image and positioning; [b] develop effective marketing and communications campaigns; and [c] to determine marketing effectiveness?
3. Why must an organisation measure the economic and non-economic impacts of its marketing activities and identify ways in which new web-based technologies enable marketers to evaluate the returns on their firm's marketing spend?

> Let the great world spin for ever down the ringing grooves of change.
> ALFRED LORD TENNYSON

Markets

Chapter 4 The marketing environment ● Chapter 5 Consumer markets ● Chapter 6 Business-to-business marketing ● Chapter 7 Marketing research

PART TWO OF PRINCIPLES OF MARKETING examines markets. The marketing setting has undergone dramatic change in the past decade. Technological advances, globalisation, changing values, lifestyles and demographics have compelled marketers to rethink their marketing strategies and processes. In Part Two, we address how marketing is affected by changes in the market environment, changes in consumer and business-to-business markets and how these can be analysed, and finally market research – how to gather and use information about markets.

Chapter 4 looks at the marketing environment in two parts: the microenvironment that is specific to an organisation's operation, such as suppliers and competitors; and the macroenvironment of wider forces that shape society, such as the natural and political environment.

Chapter 5 explores ways of understanding consumer markets: individuals and households who buy goods and services for final consumption. The many ways of doing this give insights that can help in the design of marketing research and guide marketing decision making.

Chapter 6 looks at the business-to-business markets that account for most of the world's transactions. Although consumer marketing is the most visible, the majority of marketing is to other organisations. These include suppliers selling to retailers that sell on to final consumers, and sellers of capital equipment – such as trucks, raw materials, components or business services.

As Gunther Grass recognised, 'Information networks straddle the world. Nothing remains concealed. But the sheer volume of information dissolves the information. We are unable to take it all in.' **Chapter 7** shows how marketing research and marketing information systems help sift through this information, gather further information, and process and present results to support marketing decision making.

Understanding the concepts

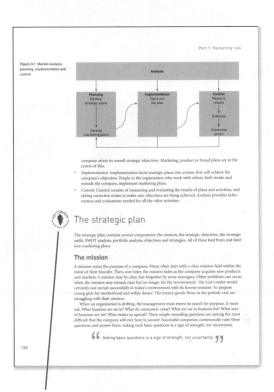

Key terms are highlighted in the text with a brief explanation in the margin where they first appear. These terms are also included in the **Glossary** at the end of the book and on the Companion Website. For your revision, you can test your understanding of these key terms using **flashcards** on the website.

Key concept icons in the text direct you to a range of valuable online resources at MyMarketingLab such as self-assessment questions, interactive exercises, audio and video clips and an e-book. These resources can support your study by testing your understanding, devising a personalised Study Plan, and reinforcing the key concepts of marketing.

Marketing in context

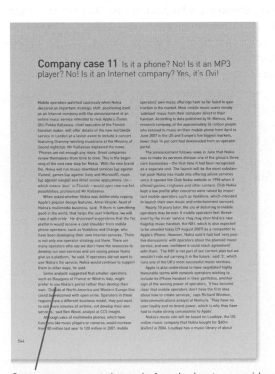

Real marketing boxes explore concepts in the chapter further by including short examples and company cases.

Company cases at the end of each chapter provide a broad view of the topics discussed in the chapter in the context of a wide range of global organisations to encourage you to apply what you have learnt to a real life marketing situation.

Critical thinking and further study

Reviewing the concept recaps and reinforces the key points to take away from the chapter whilst linking back to the learning objectives so you can check that you have understood all the major points.

At the end of every chapter **applying the concept** includes useful assessment questions for you to test your knowledge.

Discussing the concept includes thought provoking questions for debates and discussions if you want to explore the topics in the text further.

There is an extensive **list of references** at the end of each chapter, directing you to other relevant text and web sources so that you can read and research further into the key topics discussed in the chapter.

MyMarketingLab puts you in control

New to this fifth European edition of *Principles of Marketing* is the powerful learning environment **MyMarketingLab**. This is a premium online resource that helps you test your knowledge, identify the areas that need further study and creates a personalised Study Plan.

Go to **www.pearsoned.co.uk/kotler** to register and create your own account using the access code supplied with this book.

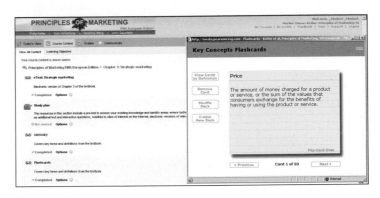

Self-assessment **practice tests** for each key concept in the textbook enable you to check your understanding and identify the areas in which you need to improve.

Based on your performance on a practice test, MyMarketingLab generates a personal **Study Plan** that shows you where to focus your studies. This study plan consists of a series of additional learning resources, including an e-book, interactive exercises, video and audio clips and much, much more!

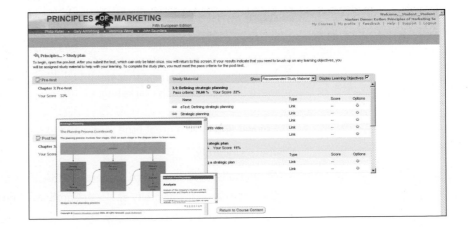

A MESSAGE FROM THE AUTHORS

Welcome to the fifth European edition of *Principles of Marketing*! With each new edition, we work to bring you the freshest and most authoritative insights into the fascinating world of marketing. As we present this new edition, we want to again thank you and the millions of other marketing students and professors who have used our text over the years. You've been our inspiration. With your help, this book remains a market leader and international best seller. Thank you.

The goal of every marketer is to create more value for customers. So it makes sense that our goal for the fifth edition is to create more value for you – *our customer*. How does this text bring you more value? First, it builds on a unique, integrative, and intuitive marketing framework: Simply put, marketing is art and science of creating value *for* customers in order to capture value *from* customers in return. Marketers lead the way in developing and managing profitable, value-based customer relationships. We introduce this customer-value framework in the first two chapters and then build upon it throughout the book.

Beyond the strengthened customer-relationships framework, we emphasize four additional customer value themes. First, we expand our emphasis on *sustainable marketing*. Marketing is about caring for customers so there is nothing more important than not destroying the environment in which customers and their children will have to exist. Second, we focus on the importance of *measuring and managing return on marketing* – of capturing value in return for the customer value that the company creates. Third, we present all of the latest developments in the *marketing technologies* that are rapidly changing how marketers create and communicate customer value. Finally, we emphasise the importance of *marketing around the world*. As the world becomes an increasingly smaller place, marketers must be good at marketing their brands globally and in socially responsible ways that create long-term value to society as a whole.

Beyond providing all the latest marketing thinking, to add even more value, we have worked to make learning about and teaching marketing easier and more exciting for both students and instructors. The fifth edition presents marketing in a complete yet practical, exciting, and easy-to-digest way. For example, to help bring marketing to life, we have filled the text with interesting examples and stories about real companies and their marketing practices. Moreover, the integrated, cutting-edge teaching and learning package lets you customise your learning and teaching experience. We highlight the fifth edition's many new features and enhancements in the pages that follow.

So, the fifth edition *creates more value for you* – more value in the content, more value in the supplements, more value in learning, and more value in YOUR classroom. We think that it's the best edition yet. We hope that you'll find *Principles of Marketing* the very best text from which to learn about and teach marketing.

Enjoy it and have a great time marketing to the world.

Yours sincerely,

Philip Kotler, Northwestern University, USA

Gary Armstrong, University of North Carolina – Chapel Hill, USA

Veronica Wong, Aston University, UK

John Saunders, Aston University, UK

PREFACE

The fifth edition – creating more value for you!

The goal of *Principles of Marketing*, Fifth Edition, is to introduce people to the fascinating world of modern marketing in an innovative, practical and enjoyable way. Like any good marketer, we're out to create more value for you, *our* customer. We have perused every page, table, figure, fact, and example in an effort to make this the best text from which to learn about and teach marketing.

Today's marketing is all about creating customer value and building profitable customer relationships. It starts with understanding consumer needs and wants, deciding which target markets the organisation can serve best, and developing a compelling value proposition by which the organisation can win, keep, and grow targeted consumers. If an organisation does these things well, it will reap the rewards in terms of market share, profits, and customer equity.

Marketing is much more than just an isolated business function – it is a philosophy that guides the entire organisation. The marketing department cannot create customer value and build profitable customer relationships by itself. This is a companywide undertaking that involves broad decisions about who the company wants as its customers, which needs to satisfy, what products and services to offer, what prices to set, what communications to send, and what partnerships to develop. Marketing must work closely with other company departments and with other organisations throughout its entire value-delivery system to delight customers by creating superior customer value.

Marketing: creating customer value and relationships

From beginning to end, *Principles of Marketing* develops an innovative customer-value and customer-relationships framework that captures the essence of today's marketing. That means not just providing for the immediate gratification of customers but taking a long term view of the welfare of today's and tomorrow's customers.

Five major value themes

The fifth edition builds on five major value themes:

1. **Sustainable marketing to strive for the long run survival of customers and the businesses that provide for them.** Marketing has been hugely successful in helping shape the modern

world in providing affordable goods to wealthy customers when and where they want them. Businesses and not for profit organisations fail by ignoring the immediate needs and wants of customers and succeed by responding to them. However, the sustainability of a strategy is limited fulfilling a customers needs and wants is against their long term interests or that of society as a whole. For instance, our evolution has led to craving for sweet things, salt and fatty foods that served us well as stimuli to search for the food we needed to sustain us in the jungle or savannah millions of years ago. With the success of modern manufacturing and supply chains these craving that are too easily fulfilled and so damage the health of nations. Increased global wealth also means increased competition for raw materials and basic food stuffs as well as the environmental impact of fulfilling that demand and the noxious waste of consumption.

The evolution of business orientations from that of production orientation to *sustainable marketing* is traced in Chapter 1. *Sustainable marketing* then becomes the subject of Chapter 2 that looks beyond buying and selling to examine marketing's role and *responsibilities in society*. These themes of *sustainability* and *social responsibility* reoccur throughout the text as real life examples, discussion questions and case studies. These range from airlines trying to resolve their position on global warming to market as sustainable alternative to cod.

2. **Creating value for customers in order to capture value from customers in return.** Today's marketers must be good at *creating customer value* and *managing customer relationships*. They must attract targeted customers with strong value propositions. Then, they must keep and grow customers by delivering superior customer value and effectively managing the company-customer interface. Today's outstanding marketing companies understand the marketplace and customer needs, design value-creating marketing strategies, development integrated marketing programs that deliver customer value and delight, and build strong customer relationships. In return, they capture value from customers in the form of sales, profits, and customer loyalty.

    This innovative customer value *framework* is introduced at the start of Chapter 1 in a five-step marketing process model, which details how marketing *creates* customer value and *captures* value in return. The framework is carefully explained in the first two chapters, providing students with a solid foundation. The framework is then integrated throughout the remainder of the text.

3. **Managing return on marketing to recapture value.** In order to capture value from customers in return, marketing managers must be good at measuring and managing the return on their marketing investments. They must ensure that their marketing dollars are being well spent. In the past, many marketers spent freely on big, expensive marketing programs, often without thinking carefully about the financial and customer response returns on their spending. But all that is changing rapidly. Measuring and managing return on marketing investments has become an important part of strategic marketing decision making.

4. **Harnessing new marketing technologies.** New digital and other high-tech marketing developments are dramatically changing how marketers create and communication customer value. Today's marketers must know how to leverage new computer, information, communication, and distribution technologies to connect more effectively with customers and marketing partners in this digital age.

5. **Marketing in a socially responsible way around the globe.** As technological developments make the world an increasingly smaller place, marketers must be good at marketing their brands globally and in socially responsible ways that create not just short-term value for individual customers but also long-term value for society as a whole.

Important changes and additions

We have thoroughly revised the fifth European edition of *Principles of Marketing* to reflect the major trends and forces impacting marketing in this era of customer value and relationships. Here are just some of the major changes you'll find in this edition.

- We have always taken social responsibility and marketing very seriously but, reflecting heightened concerns about the environment, we have introduced the concept **sustainable marketing.**
- This new edition builds on and extends the innovative **customer-value framework** from previous editions. No other marketing text presents such a clear and comprehensive customer-value approach.
- The integrated marketing communications chapters have been completely restructured to reflect sweeping shifts in how today's marketers communicate value to customers.
  - A newly revised Chapter 15: Communicating customer value, addresses today's **shifting integrated marketing communications model**. It tells how marketers are now adding a host new-age media – everything from interactive TV and the Internet to iPods and mobile phones – to reach targeted customers with more personalized messages.
  - Advertising and public relations are now combined in Chapter 16, which includes important new discussions on the merging of advertising and entertainment to break through the clutter, return on advertising, and other important topics. A restructured Chapter 17 now combines personal selling and sales promotion.
  - The new Chapter 18: Direct and online marketing – provides focused new coverage of direct marketing and its fastest growing arm, marketing on the Internet. The new chapter includes a section on new digital direct marketing technologies, such as mobile phone marketing, podcasts and vodcasts, and interactive TV. Direct and online marketing involves the distributing and order taking as well as communications so has been moved to along-side the *PLACE* section of the book that looks at the physical market place, the electronic market place and the global market place.
- We have revised the pricing discussions in Chapter 14: Pricing. It now focuses on **customer-value-based pricing** – on understanding and capturing customer value as the basis for setting and adjusting prices. The revised chapter includes new discussions of 'good-value' and 'value-added' pricing strategies, dynamic pricing, and competitive pricing considerations.
- In line with the text's emphasis on **measuring and managing return on marketing**, we have added 'The return on marketing' section in Chapter 3 has also been revised, and we have added return on advertising and return on selling discussions in later chapters.
- Chapter 12 contains a new section on managing new-product development, covering new **customer-driven, team-based, holistic new-product development** approaches.
- Chapter 5: Consumer behaviour, provides a new discussion on '**online social networks**' that tells how marketers are tapping digital online networks such as YouTube, MySpace, and others to build stronger relationships between their brands and customers.

The fifth edition also includes new and expanded material on a wide range of other topics, including managing customer relationships and CRM, brand strategy and positioning, SWOT analysis, data mining and data networks, ethnographic consumer research, marketing and diversity, generational marketing, buzz marketing, services marketing, supplier satisfaction and partnering, environmental sustainability, cause-related marketing, socially responsible marketing, global marketing strategies, and much, much more.

Countless new examples have been added within the running text. All tables, examples, and references throughout the text have been thoroughly updated. The fifth edition of *Principles of*

Marketing contains mostly new photos and advertisements that illustrate key points and make the text more effective and appealing. All new or updated company cases and many new video cases help to bring the real world directly into the classroom. The text even has a new look, with freshly designed figures. We don't think you'll find a fresher, more current, or more approachable text anywhere.

Real value through real marketing

Principles of Marketing features in-depth, real-world examples and stories that show concepts in action and reveal the drama of modern marketing. In the fifth edition, every chapter opening vignette and Real Marketing highlight has been updated or replaced to provide fresh and relevant insights into real marketing practices. Learn how:

- Tesco plans to take on the mighty Wal-Mart in the US;
- the Arctic Monkeys's use social networking signalled the end of the music industry as it was known;
- Nestlé responds to the continuous campaigning that followed a baby milk concerns decades ago;
- market research and marketing is helping tackle AIDS in Africa;
- leading companies have been caught sorting 'trash diving' in the waste bins of their competitors;
- many businesses sometimes forget how to KISS;
- 'big food' companies are doing about people getting too big for their own good;
- you respond to smells even though you do not know it;
- consumers are so confused about what food is good for them;
- Lexus leads the luxury car market by with the philosophy that if you 'delight the customer, and continue to delight the customer, you will have a customer for life';
- Sony came to shoot their cute little dog while an aggressive dinosaur survives;
- Proctor and Gamble sends it global marketing officer to sit among teenagers in Seoul's PC Bang;
- Staples held back its now familiar 'Staples: That was easy' repositioning campaign for more than a year. First, it had to *live* the slogan;
- Ryanair – Europe's original, largest, and most profitable low-fares airline – appears to have found a radical new pricing solution: Fly free!
- Dove – with its Campaign for Real Beauty campaign featuring candid and confident images of real women of all types – is on a bold mission to create a broader and healthier view of beauty;
- To sell to the super rich who already have it all.

These and countless other examples and illustrations throughout each chapter reinforce key concepts and bring marketing to life.

Valuable learning aids

A wealth of chapter-opening, within-chapter, and end-of-chapter learning devices help students to learn, link, and apply major concepts:

- *Great quotes* – lines by famous authors, politicians or marketers that capture the essence and humour of marketing.
- *Rock references* – songs or line from songs that introduce ideas in most chapters.

- *Previewing the concepts* – a section at the beginning of each chapter briefly previews chapter concepts, links them with previous chapter concepts, outlines chapter learning objectives, and introduces the chapter-opening vignette.
- *Chapter-opening marketing stories* – each chapter begins with an engaging marketing, deeply developed marketing story that introduces the chapter material and sparks student interest.
- *Extracted headlines* – headlined key statements or comments extracted from each chapter.
- *Real marketing highlights* – each chapter contains two highlight features that provide an in-depth look at real marketing practices of large and small companies.
- *Reviewing the concepts* – a summary at the end of each chapter reviews major chapter concepts and chapter objectives.
- *Reviewing the key terms* – key terms are highlighted within the text, clearly defined in the margins of the pages in which they appear, and listed at the end of each chapter.
- *Discussing the concepts* and *Applying the concepts* – each chapter contains a set of discussion questions and application exercises covering major chapter concepts.
- *References* – up to date and comprehensive lists references and further readings upon which the marketing theory, examples and cases are based.
- *Company cases* – all new or revised company cases for class or written discussion are provided at the end of each chapter. These cases challenge students to apply marketing principles to real companies in real situations.
- *Video shorts* – short vignettes and discussion questions appear at the end of every chapter, to be used with the set of 4- to 7-minute videos that accompany this edition.

More than ever before, the fifth edition of *Principles of Marketing* creates value for you – it gives you all you need to know about marketing in an effective and enjoyable total learning package!

CUSTOM PUBLISHING

Custom publishing allows academics to pick and choose content from one or more texts for their course and combine it into a definitive course text.

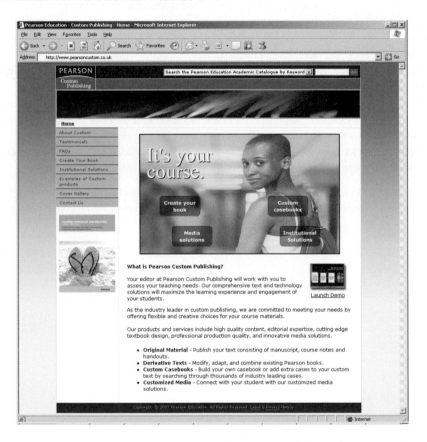

Here are some common examples of custom solutions which have helped over 500 courses across Europe:

- different chapters from across our publishing imprints combined into one book;
- lecturer's own material combined together with textbook chapters or published in a separate booklet;
- third party cases and articles that you are keen for your students to read as part of the course;
- or any combination of the above.

The Pearson Education custom text published for your course is professionally produced and bound – just as you would expect from a normal Pearson Education text. You can even choose your own cover design and add your university logo. Since many of our titles have online resources accompanying them we can even build a custom website that matches your course text.

Whatever your choice, our dedicated editorial and production teams will work with you throughout the process, right until you receive a copy of your custom text.

Some adopters of Kotler, Armstrong, Wong and Saunders, *Principles of Marketing* have found that the flexibility of custom publishing has allowed them to include additional material on certain aspects of their course.

To give you an idea of combinations which have proved popular, here is a list of subject areas in which Pearson Education publish one or more key texts that could provide extra chapters to match the emphasis of your course:

- Branding
- Innovation management
- Internet marketing
- Marketing strategy
- Marketing planning
- Public sector marketing
- Services marketing

For more details on any of these books or to browse other material from our Marketing portfolio, please visit: **www.pearsoned.co.uk/marketing**.

If, once you have had time to review this title, you feel custom publishing might benefit you and your course, please do get in contact. However minor, or major the change – we can help you out.

You can contact us at: www.pearsoncustom.co.uk or via your local representative at: www.pearsoned.co.uk/replocator.

ACKNOWLEDGEMENTS

No book is the work only of its authors. Our thanks go to our colleagues at the J. L. Kellogg Graduate School of Management, Northwestern University; the Kenan-Flagler Business School, University of North Carolina at Chapel Hill; and Aston Business School, for ideas, encouragement and suggestions. Also thanks to all our friends in the Academy of Marketing, European Marketing Academy, Informs, the American Marketing Association, the Chartered Institute of Marketing and the European Foundation for Management Development who have stimulated and advised us over the years. It has been an honour to work with so many people who have helped pioneer marketing in Europe. Also many thanks to Alexandra Muresan for her expertise in updating and expanding the robust supplements package.

We were aided in our revision of this edition by many reviewers from universities and colleges throughout Europe who responded to Pearson Education's questionnaires and to whom we extend our thanks.

We also owe a great deal to the people at Pearson Education who have done a wonderful job in helping us develop and produce this book: David Cox, acquisitions editor; Alex Gay, marketing manager; Emma Travis, development editor; Julian Partridge, editorial director; David Harrison, media development editor; and Andrew Harrison, assistant editor. We also thank Rhian McKay and Joe Vella, desk editors; Patrick Bonham, copyeditor, Sue Gard, proofreader and Kay Altwegg, freelance picture researcher. A special mention should also go to Maggie Wells for producing the text and cover design.

ABOUT THE AUTHORS

Philip Kotler is S.C. Johnson & Son Distinguished Professor of International Marketing at the J.L. Kellogg School of Management, Northwestern University. He received his master's degree at the University of Chicago and his PhD at MIT, both in Economics. Dr Kotler is author of *Marketing Management*, Thirteenth Edition (Prentice Hall). He has authored over 30 books and he has written over 100 articles for leading journals. He is the only three-time winner of the Alpha Kappa Psi Award for the best annual article in the *Journal of Marketing*. Dr Kotler's numerous honours include the Paul D. Converse Award given by the American Marketing Association to honour 'outstanding contributions to the science of marketing' and the Stuart Henderson Brit Award as Marketer of the Year. In 1985, he was named the first recipient of two major awards: the Distinguished Marketing Educator of the Year Award, given by the American Marketing Association, and the Philip Kotler Award for Excellence in Health Care Marketing. He has consulted on many US and foreign companies on marketing strategy. He has received over ten honorary doctorates from abroad.

Gary Armstrong is Blackwell Distinguished Professor of Undergraduate Education in the Kenan-Flagler Business School at the University of North Carolina at Chapel Hill. He received his PhD in marketing from Northwestern University. Dr Armstrong has contributed articles to leading research journals and consulted with many companies on marketing strategy. However, his first love is teaching. He has been very active in Kenan-Flagler's undergraduate business programme and he has received several campus-wide and business schools teaching awards. In 2004, Dr Armstrong received the UNC Board of Governors Award for Excellence in Teaching, the highest teaching honour bestowed at the University of North Carolina at Chapel Hill.

Veronica Wong, BSc, MBA (Bradford), PhD (Manchester), Fellow of the Royal Society of Arts, Fellow of the Chartered Institute of Marketing, is Professor of Marketing and Director of the Diversity Knowledge and Innovation Research Programme at Aston Business School (ABS). Dr Wong has also been Research Convenor (2002–03) and Head (2003–07) of the Marketing Group at ABS. She is also a Visiting Professor at Audencia Nantes Ecole de Management, France. Dr Wong was born in Malaysia where she studied until her first degree. Previously, she worked at the Universities of Loughborough and Warwick. She has also taught in Malaysia and worked for Ciba Laboratories, UK. Dr Wong is an active member of the European Marketing Academy (EMAC) and the Product Development and Management Association (PDMA) and has served as Vice-President of Conferences and Committee Member of the UK/Ireland Chapter respectively. She has worked with a wide range of international companies as well as public sector and nonprofit organisations on innovation and marketing strategy, including Britain's Department of Trade and Industry (DTI), the Marketing Council and Home Office. She has also published over sixty articles for leading journals, including publications in the *Journal of International Business Studies*, *Research Policy*, the *Journal of Product Innovation Management*, *Technovation* and *Industrial Marketing Management*.

John Saunders, BSc (Loughborough), MBA (Cranfield), PhD (Bradford) is Professor of Marketing at Aston Business School and Audencia Nantes Ecole de Management, France. He is past Dean of Loughborough and Aston Business Schools. He has held the posts of editor of the *International Journal of Research in Marketing*, President of the European Marketing Academy (EMAC) and Dean of the Academic Senate of the Chartered Institute of Marketing (CIM). He is fellow of the CIM, Royal Society of Arts, the EMAC, the British Academy of Management and a member of the Worshipful Company of Marketers. His academic work has appeared in the *Journal of Marketing Research*, *Journal of Marketing*, *Journal of Advertising Research*, *Marketing Science*, *International Journal of Research in Marketing*, *Journal of Product Innovation Management*, *Journal of International Business Studies* and many other leading journals. He has consulted and run programmes for many leading organisations including the Association of Business Schools, Nestle, Unilever, Rolls-Royce, Ford, The European Commission, the Asian Development Bank and the Singapore government.

PUBLISHER'S ACKNOWLEDGEMENTS

We are grateful to the following for permission to reproduce copyright material:

Figures and tables

Figure 1.6: Adapted from Werner Reinartz and V. Kumar, 'Mismanagement of customer loyalty', *Harvard Business Review* (July 2002), p. 93. Copyright © 2002 by the Harvard Business School Publishing Corporation. All rights reserved. Reprinted with permission; Figure 2.1: From Stuart Hart, 'Beyond greening: strategies for a sustainable world', *Harvard Business Review* (January–February 1997). Copyright © 1997 by the Harvard Business School Publishing Corporation. All rights reserved. Reprinted with permission; Table 3.1: Market-oriented business definitions reproduced with kind permission of Royal Dutch Shell, Nestlé S.A., EDF Energy and Unilever; Figure 3.5: Adapted from Roland T. Rust, Katherine N. Lemon and Valerie A. Zeithamal, 'Return on marketing: Using consumer equity to focus marketing strategy', *Journal of Marketing* (January 2004), p. 112. Reprinted with permission from the American Marketing Association; Figure 4.6: World Advertising Research Center, *The European Marketing Pocket Book 2007* (www.warc.com); Table 5.1: From Office for National Statistics (ONS) Socioeconomic Classification. Crown copyright material is reproduced with permission of the Controller of HMSO under the terms of the Click-Use Licence; Table 5.2: From European Commission, *Task Force on Core Social Variables, Final Report* (Brussels: Eurostat, 2007). Copyright © European Communities, 2007; Figure 5.3: Adapted from William O. Bearden and M. J. Etzel, 'Reference group influence on product and brand purchase decisions', *Journal of Consumer Research*, (September 1982), p. 185. Copyright © 1982 Journal of Consumer Research, Inc. Reproduced with permission from the University of Chicago Press; Table 5.3: Adapted from Patrick E. Murphy and William A. Staples, 'A modernised family life cycle', *Journal of Consumer Research* (June 1979), p. 16. Copyright © 1979 Journal of Consumer Research, Inc. Reproduced with permission from the University of Chicago Press; Figure 5.4: Adapted from Abraham H. Maslow, *Motivation and Personality*, 2nd edn. (Prentice-Hall, Inc., 1970). Reprinted by permission of Ann Kaplan; Table 5.4: From Joseph T. Plummer, 'The concept and application of lifestyle segmentation', *Journal of Marketing* (January 1974), p. 34. Reprinted with permission from the American Marketing Association; Figure 5.5: Adapted from Henry Assael, *Consumer Behaviour and Marketing Action*, 6th edn. (Boston, Massachusetts, Kent Publishing Company, 1988). Reprinted by permission of the author; Figure 5.8: From Everett M. Rogers, *Diffusion of Innovations*, 4th edn. (New York: The Free Press). Copyright © 1962, 1971, 1983 by The Free Press. Copyright © 1995 by Everett M. Rogers. Reprinted with the permission of The Free Press, a Division of Simon & Schuster Adult Publishing Group; Exhibit 6.1: Adapted from Transparency International (TI) (www.transparency.org/policy_research/surveys_indices/cpi/2007). Copyright © 2007 Transparency International: the global coalition against corruption. Used with permission. For more information, visit www.transparency.org; Table 7.2: Adapted from Del I. Hawkins and Marjorie A. Tull, *Marketing Research: Measurement and Method*, 7th edn. (Macmillan Publishing Company, 1993). Reprinted by permission; Figure 8.2: From M. E. Porter, *Competitive Advantage: Creating and Sustaining Superior Performance* (New York: The Free Press, 1998). Reprinted with the permission of The Free Press, a Division of Simon & Schuster Adult Publishing Group; Figure 8.3: From R. Luchs, 'Quality as a strategic weapon: measuring relative quality, value and market differentiation', *European Business Journal*, Vol. 2, No. 4 (1990). Whurr Publishers Ltd. Table 9.3: Adapted from T. V. Bonoma and B. P. Shapiro, *Segmenting the Industrial Market* (Lexington Books, 1983); Exhibits 9.3 and 9.4: From National

Food Survey (UK Ministry of Agriculture, Fisheries and Foods [now DEFRA]). Crown copyright material is reproduced with permission of the Controller of HMSO under the terms of the Click-Use Licence; Figure 10.2: Adapted from J. F. Rayport and B. J. Jaworski, *e-Commerce* (The McGraw-Hill Companies, Inc., 2001); Table 12.2: From P. Kotler, *Marketing Management: Analysis, Planning, Implementation, and Control*, 12th edn. (Upper Saddle River, New Jersey: Prentice Hall, 2006), p. 332. Copyright © 2003. Reprinted with permission of Pearson Education, Inc.; Figure 14.2: From T. T. Nagle and R. K. Holden, *The Strategy and Tactics of Pricing*, 3rd edn. (Upper Saddle River, New Jersey: Prentice Hall, 1995). Copyright © 1995. Reprinted with permission of Pearson Education, Inc.; Table 17.1: Adapted from Sam T. Johnson, 'Sales compensation: In search of a better solution', *Compensation and Benefits Review* (November–December), pp. 53–60. Copyright © 1993 by Sage Publications, Inc. Journals. Reproduced with permission of Sage Publications, Inc. Journals in the format Textbook via Copyright Clearance Center; Figure 17.2: By permission of Proudfoot Consulting; Table 18.1: From '2007 marketing fact book', *Marketing News* (15 July 2007), p. 28. Reprinted with permission from American Marketing Association, Ovum Ltd; Table 18.3: From '2007 marketing fact book', Marketing News (15 July 2007). American Marketing Association (ZenithOptimedia Group Ltd., December 2006, via eMarketer Inc. 2007); Table 18.4: Reprinted by permission of DBT Database and Internet Solutions, (www.dbt.co.uk); Table 20.1: Adapted from P. Douglas, C. S. Craig and W. Keegan, 'Approaches to assessing international opportunities for small and medium-sized businesses', *Columbia Journal of World Business*, 17(3), Fall, pp. 26–32. Copyright © 1982 Elsevier. Reproduced with permission.

Advertisements and photos

Page 2: The Advertising Archives; 15: Red Bull North America, Inc.; 27: ING Direct; 31: npower; 34: Bear Design Ltd; 45: Samaritans (www.samaritans.org); 48: The Advertising Archives; 62: The Advertising Archives; 66: NSPCC. Photographer: Matt Harris. The Advertising Archives; 68: Reprinted by permission of Pearson Education, Inc. From Philip Kotler and Gary Armstrong, *Principles of Marketing*, 12th edn. (Upper Saddle River, New Jersey: Pearson), p. 571. Copyright © 2008 Pearson Education, Inc.; 72: The Advertising Archives; 73: Ruby Washington / The New York Times / Redux Pictures; 80: The Advertising Archives; 88: The Advertising Archives; 89: Reproduced with permission of Aviva (www.aviva.com); 95 (image only): Stockbyte / Getty Images; 99: The Advertising Archives; 101: Creative; 125: The Advertising Archives; 131: eBay, Inc. These materials have been reproduced with the permission of eBay, Inc. Copyright © 2008 EBAY INC. All rights reserved; 133: Michelin and Hjemmet Mortensen AS; 139: Mont Blanc and The Advertising Archives; 140: Breitling; 147, 148 and 190: The Advertising Archives; 200: Volkswagen and Arnold Worldwide; 208: Joseph Van Os, Getty Images, Inc. / Image Bank; 215: Marks & Spencer; 224: Shell International. Agency: J. Walter Thompson; 234: The Advertising Archives; 246: adidas International Marketing B.V. adidas and adicolor are registered trademarks of the adidas group, used with permission; 249, 250: The Advertising Archives; 257: Michelle Pedone / Photonica / Getty Images; 258: Justin Sullivan / Getty Images News / Getty Images; 262: Ronald Grant Archive: 264: PatekPhilippe, Agency: Geneva/Leagas Delaney, Photographer: Peggy Sirota (represented by E. M. Managed); 266: Copyright © 2008 The LEGO Group. Reproduced with permission; 287: The Advertising Archives; 289: NetJets Management; 293: INVISTA, McCann Erikson; 296: Hans-Jürgen Burkard / Bilderberg Archiv der Fotografen GmbH; 301: British Airways / M&C Saatchi, Photographer: Gary Simpson; 306, 321, 328: The Advertising Archives; 329: Andy Reynolds / Stone / Getty Images; 330: Infineon, agency: J. Walter Thompson; 337: Cereal Partners, UK / Courtesy of Société des Produits Nestlé S.A., trademark owners; 346: Douglas A. Fidaleo; 348: Copyright © 2007 SAS Institute, Inc. All rights reserved. Reproduced with permission of SAS Institute, Inc., Cary, North Carolina, USA; 352: Greg Kahn / Kahn Research; 371: Triumph International Ltd (www.triumph.com); 375 The Advertising Archives; 394: People Soft UK & Ireland; 406: The Advertising Archives; 409: P1 International Limited 2007; 411: The Advertising Archives; 413: Duck Head Apparel Co.; 416, 419, 425: The Advertising Archives; 430: Copyright © 2008 The LEGO Group, used with permission; 432: Reprinted by permission of Porsche cars North America, Inc.; 437: Staples The Office Superstore, LLC; 456: The Advertising Archives; 475: Eurex. Photographer: Karin Hieronymi; 477, 478: The Advertising

Archives; 480: Virgin Atlantic; 485: Lofthouse of Fleetwood Ltd; 498: The Advertising Archives; 505: Reprinted with permission of Rockwell Corporation. Agency: Chilworth Communications; 509: Omega / SA / Photo copyright © NASA; 524: The Advertising Archives; 526: Interbrand; 531, 537, 547: The Advertising Archives; 552: New Product Showcase and Learning Centre. NewProductWorks; 553: The Advertising Archives; 558: Daimler AG; 562 (left): Peter Cade / Stone / Getty Images; 562 (right): Steve Krongard / Stone / Getty Images; 568: Electrolux AB; 575: Copyright © H.J. Heinz Company 2008. All rights reserved; 576, 577, 579, 592: The Advertising Archives; 600: Chewton Glen; 606: Shangri-La International Hotel Management Limited / TBWA Hong Kong; 620: The Advertising Archives; 622: Save the Children; 634: Surf / bbh; 650: The Advertising Archives; 651: Steinway & Sons; 664: Photo by Jim Whitmer; 669: www.priceline. com; 686, 700: The Advertising Archives; 704: Savoir Beds. Agency: Large, Smith and Walford Partnership; 705: Reproduced with kind permission of Volkswagen of America, Inc. and Arnold Worldwide, Photgrapher: © Steve Bronstein; 728: ABSOLUT MAGIC under permission of V&S Vin & Sprit (publ). ABSOLUT country of Sweden vodka and logo, ABSOLUT, ABSOLUT bottle design and ABSOLUT calligraphy are trademarks owned by V&S Vin & Sprit (publ). Copyright © 2004 V&S Vin & Sprit (publ); 732: Carlsberg, the official beer of Glastonbury; 741: Reproduced with permission from V&S Vin & Sprit (publ). ABSOLUT country of Sweden vodka and logo, ABSOLUT, ABSOLUT bottle design and ABSOLUT calligraphy are trademarks owned by V&S Vin & Sprit (publ). Copyright © 2003 V&S Vin & Sprit (publ); 743, 744: The Advertising Archives; 746: Daimler AG, Stuttgart, Germany; 758: HSBC Holdings plc. Agency: Lowe Worldwide. Photographer: Richard Pullar; 764: The Image Works; 781: The Advertising Archives; 787: Digital Vision Limited; 791: Javier Pierini / Photodisc / Getty Images; 796: Jon Feingersh / Stock Boston; 803: Iceland Foods plc. The Advertising Archives; 818: The Advertising Archives; 822: cooldiamonds.com Ltd. Molly McKellar Public Relations, London; 828: SAP Global Marketing. Agency: OgilvyOne Worldwide Ltd; 836: Toru Yamanaka / AFP / Getty Images; 841, 843: The Advertising Archives; 847: planetfeedback.com; 848: The Advertising Archives; 850: Copyright © 2008 MINI, a division of North America, LLC. All rights reserved. The MINI and BMW trademarks, model names and logos are registered trademarks; 883: Ralph Orlowski / Getty Images; 888: Copyright © Inditex; 889: The Advertising Archives; 902 (top and bottom): Birmingham Picture Library / Jonathan Berg (www.bplphoto.co.uk); 907: Michael Beway, Bentley Houston; 913: Robocom Systems International (www.robocom.com); 914: Dirk Kruell / laif / Redux; 921: DHL Worldwide Network / Jung van Matt / Spree; 936: The Advertising Archives; 944: Stockbyte / Getty Images; 946: Fritz Hoffmann; 961: Pirelli & C. SpA; 962: HSBC Holdings Plc. Agency: Lowe Worldwide. Photographer: Richard Pullar; 968: Courtesy of Bernard Matussiere.

Text

Page 11: Extract from Hewlett-Packard advertisement, reprinted by permission of Hewlett Packard (www.hp.com/personal); 26: Extract adapted from Denny Hatch, 'Delight your customers', *Target Marketing* (April 2002). North American Publishing Company; 70: Extract from Lane Jennings, 'Hype, spin, puffery and lies: Should we be scared?', originally published in *The Futurist* (January–February 2004). Used with permission from the World Future Society, 7910 Woodmont Avenue, Suite 450, Bethesda, MD 20814 USA. Telephone: +1-301-656-8274, url: www.wfs.org; 93: Extract adapted from 'The Top 3 in 2005' *The Global 100 Most Sustainable Corporations in the World* (www.global100.org/2005/top3.asp) by Corporate Knights Inc. and Innovest Strategic Value Advisors; 160: Extract from Diane Brady, 'Making marketing measure up', *BusinessWeek* (13 December 2004), pp. 112–13. Reprinted by permission of BusinessWeek; 187: Extract from Gregg Bennett and Tony Lachowitz, 'Marketing to lifestyles: Action sports and generation Y', *Sport Marketing Quarterly* 13, 4 (2004), pp. 239–43. Copyright © 2004 Fitness Information Technology, Inc. Reproduced with permission in the format textbook via the Copyright Clearance Center; 191: Extract from 'The grey market. Hey, big-spender', *The Economist*, (3 December 2005), pp. 79–80. Copyright © The Economist Newspaper Limited, London; 218: Extracts from Yankelovich Monitor about 'At capacity individuals' and 'Driven individuals' by kind permission of Yankelovich (www.yankelovich.com); 219: Extract adapted from Ronald Grover, 'Trading the bleachers for the couch', *BusinessWeek*, (22 August 2005), p. 32.

Reprinted by permission of BusinessWeek; 245: Extract adapted from Michael Witte, 'Buzz-z-z marketing', *BusinessWeek*, (30 July 2001). Reprinted by permission of BusinessWeek; 297: Extract from IKEA website (www.ikea.com). Copyrightb © Inter IKEA Systems B. V. 2008. Reprinted by permission of IKEA Ltd; 307: Extract from Kate Maddox, '#1 Hewlett-Packard Co.: www.hp.com', *BtoB Magazine* (11 August 2003). Copyright © Crain Communications Inc., reprinted with permission. 325: Extract from 'Tesco: fresh, but far from easy', *The Economist* (21 June 2007). Copyright © The Economist Newspaper Limited, London; 336: Extracts adapted from Spencer E. Ante, 'The science of desire', *BusinessWeek* (5 June 2006). Reprinted by permission of BusinessWeek; 336 and 342: Extracts and adapted extracts from David Kiley, 'Shoot the focus group, *BusinessWeek*, (14 November 2005). Reprinted by permission of BusinessWeek; 403: Extracts from the Abel & Cole website (www.abel-cole.co.uk). Reprinted by permission of Abel & Cole Ltd; 403: Extracts from Janice Turner, 'Perfect delivery', *The Guardian* (30 May 2005). Reprinted by permission of the author; 415–16: Extracts from the Rohan Designs website (www.rohan.co.uk). Reprinted by permission of Rohan Designs Ltd; 472: Extract adapted from M. Der Hovanesian, 'The black card that gives you carte blanche', *BusinessWeek* (9 August 2004). Reprinted by permission of BusinessWeek; 511: Extract from T. Kontiokari, K. Sundqvist, M. Nuutinen, T. Pokka, M. Koskela and M. Uhari, 'Randomised trial of cranberry-lingonberry juice and Lactobacillus GG drink for the prevention of urinary tract infections in women', *British Medical Journal* (30 June 2001). Reproduced with permission from the BMJ Publishing Group; 562: Extract from C. Matlock, 'The Vuitton machine', *BusinessWeek* (22 March 2004). Reprinted by permission of BusinessWeek; 568–70: Quotes and extracts adapted from *Acceleration . . . Electrolux Annual Report* (7 April 2006). Reprinted by permission of AB Electrolux; 581: Extract adapted from 'Leica refocuses', *The Economist* (30 September 2006). Copyright © The Economist Newspaper Limited, London; 618: Extract adapted from Jenny Davey, 'Oxfam stores get touch of Topshop', *The Sunday Times* (24 June 2007). Copyright © Jenny Davey / NI Syndication Limited; 619: Extract abridged from R. Smithers, 'Oxfam to launch online shop for donated goods', *Society Guardian* (14 September 2007). Copyright © Guardian News & Media Ltd. 2007; 642: Extract adapted from 'For whom the Dell tolls', *The Economist* (13 May 2006). Copyright © The Economist Newspaper Limited, London; 670–1: Extract adapted from Charles Dublow, 'Where do iPods cost most – or least?', *BusinessWeek* (17 May 2006). Reprinted by permission of BusinessWeek; 692: Adapted from P.D. Bennett, *The AMA Dictionary of Marketing Terms*, 2nd edn. (American Marketing Association, 1995); 694–6: Adapted from 'Murdoch's space', *The Economist* (1 April 2006). Copyright © The Economist Newspaper Limited, London; 708–9: Extract from 'Building buzz', *The Economist* (1 April 2007). Copyright © The Economist Newspaper Limited, London; 719–21: Adapted from Claire Forbes, 'Be careful what you promise', *The Marketer* (Issue 17, October 2005) and Louella Miles 'Playing the game by', *The Marketer* (Issue 17, October 2005). Reprinted by permission of The Chartered Institute of Marketing, (www.cim.co.uk/themarketer); 762–3: From G. Fouché, 'Norwegians queue for chance to stay at Ikea', *The Guardian* (14 July 2007). Copyright © Guardian News & Media Ltd. 2007; 772–3: Based on David Bowen, 'In search of a mission', *Financial Times* (5 February 2004). Copyright © David Bowen. Reprinted by permission of the author; 777–8: Based on Mogéns Bjerre, 'MD Foods AMBA: a new world of sales and marketing', in Celia Philips, Ad Pruynet and Marie-Paule Kestemont (eds.) *Understanding Marketing: A European Casebook* (Chichester: Wiley, 2000). Copyright © John Wiley & Sons Limited. Reproduced with permission; 783: Extract from Charles Fleming and Leslie Lopez, 'The corporate challenge – no boundaries: ABB's dramatic plan is to recast its structure along global lines', *Wall Street Journal* (28 September 1998). Reproduced with permission of Dow Jones & Company, Inc. conveyed through Copyright Clearance Center, Inc.; 805-7: Adapted from Jeremy Stern, 'Promotions under siege?', *Sales Promotion* (26 April 2007). Sales Promotion Publishing Ltd; 821–2: Based on company data provided by Cool Diamonds, CoolDiamonds.com Ltd; 852–3: Based on David Bowen, 'How well are we being served?', *Financial Times* (28 March 2007) and David Bowen, 'Digital Business: Time to seize control' *FT Report* (4 October 2006). Reprinted by permission of the author; 856–7: Extract adapted from K. Allen, 'Spending on internet advertising "to double"', *The Guardian* (13 July 2007). Copyright © Guardian News & Media Ltd. 2007; 861: Extract from the Quelle website (www.quelle.com). Reprinted by permission of Primondo

Publisher's acknowledgements

Management Service GmbH; 917: Adapted from Sarah Murray, 'The green way to keep trucking', *Financial Times* (13 March 2007) and 'It's good to go green', *Financial Times* (17 March 2007). Reproduced with permission from Sarah Murray; 938: Extract from lyrics to 'Deadworld' from Shadows Fall album *Fallout from the War*, reprinted by permission of The Bicycle Music Company; 949: Extract abridged from G. Edmondson, 'L'Oreal: The beauty of global branding', *BusinessWeek*, International Edition (28 June 1999). reprinted by permission of BusinessWeek; 972: Extract from Sarah Ellison, 'Revealing price disparities, the Euro aids bargain-hunters', *Wall Street Journal* (30 January 2002). Reproduced with permission of Dow Jones & Company, Inc. conveyed through Copyright Clearance Center, Inc.

We are grateful to the Financial Times Limited for permission to reprint the following material:

Page 5: Roger Blitz, 'Tourism chiefs face green guilt trip', *Financial Times* (13 May 2007). Copyright © 2007 Financial Times Limited; 76: Tobias Buck, 'Brussels get teeth into food groups 'misleading' claims, *Financial Times* (1–2 February 2003). Copyright © 2003 Financial Times Limited; 96: Carlos Grande, 'Ethical consumption makes mark on branding, *Financial Times* (20 February 2007). Copyright © 2007 Financial Times Limited; 128: Haig Simonian, 'Tag Heuer CEO Interview: This is what we're made of' *Financial Times* (8 June 2007); Copyright © 2007 Financial Times Limited; 177: Richard Tompkins, 'Big food has a lot on its plate', *Financial Times* (12 February 2004). Copyright © 2004 Financial Times Limited; 191: Dan Roberts, 'The ageing business', *Financial Times* (20 January 2004). Copyright © 2004 Financial Times Limited; 197: Catherine Moye, 'Thank goodness, the gays are here' *FT Weekend – House & Home* (4 September 2004). Copyright © 2004 Financial Times Limited; 217: Fiona Harvey and Jenny Wiggins, 'Companies cash in on environment awareness', *Financial Times* (14 September 2006); Copyright © 2006 Financial Times Limited; 474 (Table 10.1): *FT Global 500*. Copyright © 2007 Financial Times Limited; 517: Sathnam Sanghera, 'Plain and simple truth about good customer service', *Financial Times* (22 June 2006). Copyright © 2006 Financial Times Limited; 528: Sophy Buckley, 'Co-op to bring all own-brand coffee under Fairtrade label', *Financial Times* (13 November 2003). Copyright © 2006 Financial Times Limited; 544: Maija Palmer, 'Nokia set to strike a fresh strategic note' and 'Nokia's Ovi opens door to the internet', *Financial Times* (29 August 2007). Copyright © 2007 Financial Times Limited; 580: Ian Chapman, 'A camera focused on luxury', *Financial Times* (31 March 2003). Copyright © 2003 Financial Times Limited; 645: Nicholas George, 'Brio's toy train hits the buffers', *Financial Times* (29 August 2003). Copyright © 2003 Financial Times Limited; 689: John Reed 'Rolls works hard on its soft sell', *Financial Times* (6 February 2007). Copyright © 2007 Financial Times Limited; 694: Aline van Duyn and Jonathan Birchall 'Wal-Mart's amateur advertisers', *Financial Times* (21 July 2006). Copyright © 2006 Financial Times Limited; 750: Ross Tieman, 'Mobile marketing: Volunteers sign up for adverts', *Financial Times* (18 April 2007). Copyright © 2007 Financial Times Limited; 832: Tom Braithwaite, '"Flick to Click" shoppers turn to a new page', *Financial Times* (9 August 2007). Copyright © 2007 Financial Times Limited; 879: James Wilson, 'Secrets behind a good hair day', *Financial Times* (18 January 2007). Copyright © 2007 Financial Times Limited; 920: Simon Brooke, 'It's different for guys', *Financial Times* (28–29 April 2007). Copyright © 2007 Financial Times Limited; 922: Andrew Ward, 'Where winners are fast rather than large', *Financial Times* (27 March 2007). Copyright © 2007 Financial Times Limited; 939: Bettina Wassener. 'Schnapps goes to college', *Financial Times* (4 September 2003). Copyright © 2003 Financial Times Limited; 942: Bertrand Benoit and Richard Milne, 'Germany's best-kept secret: how its exporters are beating the world', *Financial Times* (19 May 2006). Copyright © 2006 Financial Times Limited; 959: Neil Buckley, 'Pet foods overtake sweet success', *Financial Times* (10 October 2006). Copyright © 2006 Financial Times Limited; 963: Jenny Wiggins, 'Burger, fries and shake-up', *Financial Times* (27 February 2007). Copyright © 2007 Financial Times Limited; 967: Beatrice Aidin, 'Big brands are watching you', *Financial Times* (4–5 November 2007). Copyright © 2007 Financial Times Limited; 970: Hugh Williams, 'Advertisers try to bridge Germany's consumers divide', *Financial Times* (27 July 2007). Copyright © 2007 Financial Times Limited.

In some instances we have been unable to trace the owners of copyright material, and we would appreciate any information that would enable us to do so.

Video Case Land Rover

Colin Green
Marketing Director

Like Hummer and Jeep, Land Rover is a car maker whose roots are in off-road utility vehicles rather than passenger cars. For a long while, Land Rover only made their pioneering, multi-purpose, all-terrain utility vehicle but in 1970 their completely radical all-terrain luxury Range Rover created the sports utility vehicle (SUV). When launched in the United States, it proved so popular among the rich and wealthy that it became known as the 'Hollywood Jeep'. The company's narrow focus on large 4 × 4 vehicles seems ill-fitting to a world of high fuel prices and concerns for global warming.

Nevertheless, Land Rover remains profitable and successful, partly because Land Rover 4 × 4s are real all-terrain vehicles, the products' cult status with magazines and off-the-road experiences being dedicated to the brand.

To learn more about Land Rover, visit their website (www.landrover.com) and some of the websites for Land Rover fans: the Internet Land Rover Club (www.landroverclub.net), Land Rover Magazines (www.landroverenthusiast.com) or the Land Rover Experience (www.landroverexperience.com).

After viewing the video, you may address the following questions:

1. What is the company doing in response to the challenges of globalisation and environmental sustainability?
2. As a relatively small manufacturer of passenger vehicles, what is the company's strategy to remain successful and to compete with the global, volume car manufacturers and the numerous new competitors in the SUV segment originally pioneered by Land Rover?
3. How and why does the company position the Land Rover brand across global markets such as North America, Africa and emerging countries like China?

No profit grows where is no pleasure taken.

WILLIAM SHAKESPEARE

Marketing now

Chapter 1 Marketing ● **Chapter 2** Sustainable marketing ● **Chapter 3** Strategic marketing

PART ONE OF *PRINCIPLES OF MARKETING* examines marketing's role in an organisation, society and the activities that constitute marketing, and how the parts are integrated into a marketing strategy.

Chapter 1 shows how marketing is everywhere. It also tells how marketing has grown with the belief that organisations do best by caring for their customers. It then looks at the marketing activities appearing elsewhere in *Principles of Marketing* and shows how they combine to make modern marketing.

Chapter 2 looks beyond buying and selling to examine marketing's role and responsibilities in society. Sustainability is critical to our planet. Environmental concerns are changing markets, and marketing makes a vital contribution to ensuring that today's production and consumption do not damage tomorrow's.

Chapter 3 shifts from what marketing does to how marketing is done. In developing the strategic marketing planning process, it looks at how marketing fits with other business activities, the making of a marketing plan and how the plans become actions. Together these opening chapters examine marketing as recognised by advertising guru David Ogilvy: 'the place where the selfish interests of the manufacturer coincide with the interest of society'.

PART one

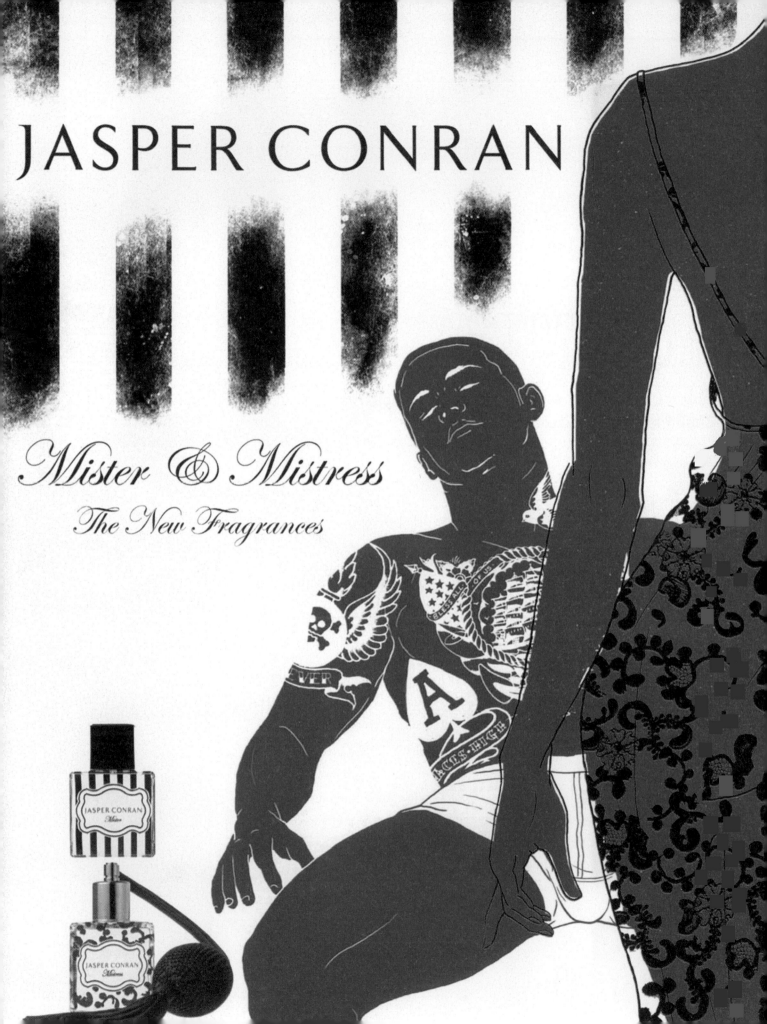

Marketing is to selling what seduction is to abduction.

Marketing

Mini Contents List

◄ SOURCE: The Advertising Archives.

Previewing the concepts

Welcome to the exciting and challenging world of marketing. In this chapter we first introduce you to the basic concepts. We start with a simple question: What *is* marketing? Simply
put, marketing is managing profitable customer relationships. The aim of marketing is to
create value for customers and to capture value in return. Sustainable marketing implies
creating long-term value that is in the interest of the customer and society in general.
Chapter 1 is organised around five steps in the marketing process – from understanding
customer needs, to designing customer-driven marketing strategies and programmes, to
building customer relationships and capturing value for the firm.

After reading this chapter, you should be able to:

1. Define *marketing* and outline the steps in the marketing process.
2. Explain the importance of understanding customers and the marketplace and identify the
   core marketplace concepts.
3. Identify the key elements of a customer-driven marketing strategy and discuss the
   marketing management orientations that guide marketing strategy.
4. Discuss customer relationship management and identify strategies for creating value *for*
   customers and capturing value *from* customers in return.
5. Describe sustainable marketing and the major trends and forces that are changing the
   marketing landscape.

Understanding these basic concepts, and forming your own ideas about what they really
mean to you, will give you a solid foundation for all that follows. To set the stage, let's first
look at the prelude case: Bye-bye Ryanair.

Prelude case Bye-bye Ryanair

Hotel, airline and hospitality chief executives provided no clear way ahead at the 2007 Annual Global Travel and Tourism Summit in Lisbon. The tourism industry has never had it so good, but its senior executives are feeling strangely guilty about their success and fearful of a green backlash.

Expected to grow by 4.3 per cent a year over the next decade, the industry's bosses are fretting over climate change, worried that flying is seen as the most polluting activity, and falling over themselves to champion schemes that allow the travelling public to go on clocking up air miles. 'There is a real conundrum with how we grow in a way we feel good about,' said Andrew Cosslett, the chief executive of InterContinental Hotels Group. 'We need to find ways of making people feel very good about how they feel about these things.'

Some wanted to rally governments to provide the infrastructure to meet the demand of the emerging middle classes of China, India and Mexico, who are readying themselves for global travel. Others were worried about fuel prices, security, visa problems, technological innovation and the armies of hospitality staff needed to cope with demand which, according to the World Travel and Tourism Council, will this year generate about $7bn of economic activity. But no one could escape the dark shadow of climate change, even though they wished it. 'We look at climate change as an image issue,' said Armin Meier, chief executive of Kuoni Travel, the luxury tour operator.

Maurice Flanagan, vice-chairman of Emirates Airline, was quite happy to share his trenchant view that global warming was 'an argument'. At the World Economic Forum in Davos earlier this year, he said he was taken aback at the way airlines were being 'demonised as the cause of all this'. More worrying to him than the apparent threat to the planet was the real threat to the existence of low-cost carriers such as easyJet and Ryanair. 'If extremists get their way, thousands and thousands of jobs in travel and tourism will be lost,' Mr Flanagan said. Others were more philosophical. 'The debate is over,' said Sir Stelios Haji-Ioannou, founder of easyJet. Airlines had to replace their fleets with modern fuel-efficient engines, he said, 'but the replacement process is slow.'

Airlines, hotels and other sectors in the industry will be pooling resources in a public campaign to demonstrate that they are taking climate change seriously. They have given up trying to argue the technical niceties of aviation's contribution to carbon emissions. Whether it is 2, 3 or 5 per cent, it has to do something, they have concluded.

'At the end of the day, it is the developer, the capital-provider, who is going to be making the investment decision,' said Arthur de Haast, chief executive of Jones Lang LaSalle Hotels. 'And the majority of them are still very focused on shareholder returns and maximising those returns,' he added.

For all the talk, practical meaningful solutions were little in evidence. It fell to James Russell of the Clinton Global Initiative to tell the industry what was expected of it. 'Don't be an Exxon,' he told the airlines, 'work out what you can do to drive down energy consumption. Travel agents should push hotels for carbon disclosure. The message to chief executives is that perceptions are changing and you have between 12 and 24 months to get on that route.'

How much and for how long is arguable. 'It's flavour of the month,' said Charles Petruccelli, the president of global travel services at American Express. 'The problem will realise its way beyond the industry soon.'

> 'We look at climate change as an image issue.'

> 'Don't be an Exxon . . . work out what you can do to drive down energy consumption.'

Questions

1. Are the marketing skills that drove the huge growth of Emirates Airline, Ryanair and easyJet the same as those that will be needed to address the environmental challenge they currently face?
2. How would marketing be undertaken by long-haul holiday specialist Kuoni, if it took the view that climate change is not just 'an image issue' but one that demanded the industry to reduce its carbon footprint?
3. How could an agile company in the tourist industry take advantage of the environmental concerns of consumers?

SOURCE: Based on Roger Blitz, 'Tourism chiefs face green guilt trip,' Financial Times (13 May 2007), p. 1.

Introduction

Today's successful companies have one thing in common. Like Ryanair, easyJet and Emirates Airline, their success comes from a strong customer focus and heavy commitment to marketing and change. These companies share a passion for satisfying customer needs in their well-defined target markets. They motivate everyone in the organisation to build lasting customer relationships through superior customer satisfaction. These organisations know that if they take care of their customers, market share and profits will follow.

What is marketing?

Marketing, more than any other business function, deals with customers. Customers are an essential component of a marketing system. Each one of us is a customer in every area of human interrelation, from consumption of education and healthcare and the queue in the post office to flying with a budget airline, and in every financial transaction, from the buying of soft drinks to the purchase of a music download. Creating customer value and satisfaction is at the very heart of modern marketing thinking and practice. Although we will explore more detailed definitions of marketing, perhaps the simplest definition is this one: marketing is managing profitable customer relationships. The twofold goal of marketing is to attract new customers by promising superior value and to keep and grow current customers by delivering satisfaction.

Many people think that only large companies operating in developed economies use marketing, but sound marketing is critical to the success of every organisation. Large profit-making firms such as Nokia, Unilever, Toyota, Philips and Apple use marketing. But so do not-for-profit organisations such as schools, charities, churches, hospitals, museums and even police services.

You already know a lot about marketing – it is all around you. You see the results of marketing in the abundance of products in your nearby shopping centre. You see marketing in the advertisements that fill your TV screen, spice up your magazines, stuff your mailbox or enliven your web pages. At home, at college, where you work, where you play – you see marketing in almost everything you do. Yet, there is much more to marketing than meets the consumer's casual eye. Behind it all is a massive network of people and activities competing for your attention and purchases.

 You already know a lot about marketing – it is all around you.

This book will give you a complete introduction to the basic concepts and practices of today's marketing. In this chapter, we begin by defining marketing and the marketing process.

Marketing defined

What does the term *marketing* mean? Many people think of marketing only as advertising and selling. And no wonder, for every day we are bombarded with television commercials, newspaper ads, direct mail offers, telephone sales calls and Internet pitches. Although they are important, they are only the tip of the marketing iceberg.

Today, marketing must be understood not in the old sense of making a sale – 'telling and selling' – but in the new sense of *satisfying customer needs*. Selling occurs only after a product is produced. By contrast, marketing starts long before a company has a product. Marketing is the homework that managers undertake to assess needs, measure their extent and intensity and determine whether a profitable opportunity exists. Marketing continues throughout the product's life, trying to find new customers and keep current customers by improving product appeal and performance, learning from product sales results and managing repeat performance. If the marketer understands consumer needs, develops products and services that provide superior customer value, and prices, distributes and promotes them effectively, these products will sell easily. In fact, according to management guru Peter Drucker, 'The aim of marketing is to make selling unnecessary.' The aim is to 'know and understand the customer so well that the product or service fits . . . and sells itself.'[1] This does not mean that selling and advertising are unimportant. Rather, it means that they are part of a larger marketing mix – a set of marketing tools that work together to satisfy customer needs and build customer relationships.

> ❝ The aim of marketing is to make selling unnecessary. ❞

Broadly defined, marketing is *a social and managerial process by which individuals and groups obtain what they need and want through creating and exchanging products and value with others.* In a narrower business context, marketing involves building profitable, value-laden exchange relationships with customers. Hence, we define **marketing** as *the process by which companies create value for customers and build strong customer relationships in order to capture value from customers in return.*

Marketing—A social and managerial process by which individuals and groups obtain what they need and want through creating and exchanging products and value with others.

The marketing process

Figure 1.1 presents a five-step model of the marketing process. In the first four steps, companies work to understand consumers, create customer value and build strong customer relationships. In the final step, companies reap the rewards of creating superior customer value. By creating value *for* consumers, they in turn capture value *from* consumers in the form of sales, profits and long-term customer equity.

In this and the next two chapters, we will examine the steps of this simple model of marketing. In this chapter, we will review each step but focus more on the customer relationship steps – understanding customers, building customer relationships and capturing value from customers. In Chapter 2, we will examine marketing in a broader social context. This means sustainable marketing in considering the impact of marketing on society as a whole as well as a means of building relationships with customers. In Chapter 3, we look at integrating and coordinating marketing by designing marketing strategies and constructing integrated marketing programmes.

Each part of the marketing definition defines what marketing is and how it is practised. In business-to-business marketing, often referred to as B2B marketing, professional organisations *exchange products of value to each other.* In this case marketing is an *exchange* between similar *individuals and groups.* This contrasts with business-to-consumer (or B2C) markets where marketing is not an *exchange* between similar *individuals and groups.* In B2C markets, for

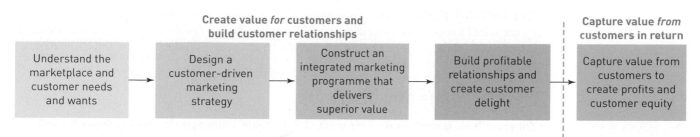

Figure 1.1 A simple model of the marketing process

businesses which may or may not be profit-making organisations, marketing is a *managerial process* pursued to fulfil their *needs and wants*, while the consumer is trying to fulfil their *needs and wants* while just living their life. With this difference in mind, the definition of marketing identifies marketing's unique contribution to an organisation and the demands it imposes.

What is marketing?	A *managerial process* deployed by an organisation (*individual or group*).
What is its objective?	To fulfil the *needs and wants* of the deploying organisation. These could be anything. They could be to maximise profits, although the objective of commercial marketers is usually to achieve sales targets or market share objectives. More generally, the objective for a profit or non-profit organisation could be to change the *needs and wants* of *other individuals or groups*, for example to increase the *want* of *individuals* for protection against sexually transmitted diseases or to vote for a political candidate.
How is this achieved?	A *social process* whereby *other individuals or groups obtain needs and wants* by *creating and exchanging products and value*. This limits how the deploying organisation behaves. It has to understand the *needs and wants* of *other individuals or groups* and changes itself so that it can *create products and value* that it can *exchange*.

The essence of marketing is a very simple idea that extends to all walks of life. Success comes from understanding the needs and wants of others and creating ideas, services or products that fulfil those needs and wants. Most failing organisations, from Boo.com to WorldCom, fail because they do what they want to do rather than fulfil the wants and needs of others.

> " Organisations . . . fail because they do what they want to do rather than fulfil the wants and needs of others. "

Understanding the marketplace and customer needs

As a first step, marketers need to understand customer needs and wants and the marketplace within which they operate. We now examine the five core customer and marketplace concepts in Figure 1.1: (1) *needs, wants and demands*; (2) *market offerings (products, services and experiences)*; (3) *value, satisfaction and quality*; (4) *exchanges, transactions and relationships*; and (5) *markets and the marketing system*.

Needs, wants and demands

Needs—States of felt deprivation.

The most basic concept underlying marketing is that of human needs. Human **needs** are states of felt deprivation. They include basic *physical* needs for food, clothing, warmth and safety; *social* needs for belonging and affection; and *individual* needs for knowledge and self-expression. Marketers did not invent these needs; they evolved as a basic part of our human make-up.

Wants are the form human needs take as they are shaped by culture and individual personality. We all *need* food but *want* to eat different dishes to fulfil our hunger. A person in Mauritius may want a mango, rice, lentils and beans. A person in Hong Kong may want a bowl of noodles, 'char-siu' pork and jasmine tea. A British drinker may want an Indian curry after leaving the pub. Wants are shaped by one's society and are described in terms of objects that will satisfy needs.

People have narrow, basic needs (e.g. for food or shelter) but almost unlimited wants. However, they also have limited resources. Thus, they want to choose products that provide the most satisfaction for their money. When backed by an ability to pay – that is, buying power – wants become **demands**. Consumers view products as bundles of benefits and choose products that give them the best bundle for their money. Thus, a Fiat Grande Punto Multijet is a great budget buy that is very fuel efficient, while the comfort and reliability of a Mercedes E-series make it a best buy as a luxury saloon. Given their wants and resources, people demand products with the benefits that add up to the most value and satisfaction.

Outstanding marketing companies go to great lengths to learn about and understand their customers' needs, wants and demands. They conduct consumer research and analyse mountains of customer data – complaints, enquiries, warranties and service data. They observe customers using their own and competing products and train salespeople to be on the lookout for unfulfilled customer needs. Understanding customer needs, wants and demands in detail provides important input for designing value-laden marketing strategies.

The market offering – products, services and experiences

Companies address needs by putting forth a *value proposition*, a set of benefits that they promise to consumers to satisfy their needs. The value proposition is fulfilled through a **market offering** – some combination of products, services, information or experiences offered to a market to satisfy a need or want. Marketing offers are not limited to physical *products*. They also include *services*, activities or benefits offered for sale that are essentially intangible and do not result in the ownership of anything. Examples include banking, airline, hotel, tax preparation and home appliance repair services. More broadly, marketing offers also include other entities, such as *persons*, *places*, *organisations*, *information* and *ideas*.

Many sellers make the mistake of paying more attention to the specific products they offer than to the benefits and experiences produced by these products. They see themselves as selling a product rather than providing a solution to a need. These sellers may suffer from 'marketing myopia'. They are so taken with their products that they focus only on existing wants and lose sight of underlying customer needs.[2] They forget that a product is only a tool to solve a consumer problem. A manufacturer of 8 mm drill bits may think that the customer needs a drill bit. But what the customer *really* needs is an 8 mm hole. Or, more likely, the real *need* is to fix things together. These sellers will have trouble if a new product comes along that serves the customer's need better or less expensively. The customer will have the same *need* but will *want* the new product.

Thus, smart marketers look beyond the attributes of the products and services they sell. They create brand *meaning* and brand *experiences* for consumers. For example, Absolut Vodka means much more to consumers than just white alcoholic spirit – it has become an icon rich in style and meaning. A Fender is more than just a guitar, it is B.B. King, Jimi Hendrix, Eric Clapton, Keith Richards – it is Rock'n'Roll.

By orchestrating several services and products, companies can create, stage and market brand experiences. Disneyworld is an experience; so is driving a Porsche. You experience a visit to a West End show in London, browsing in Galeries Lafayette or delving into YouTube. As products

Wants—The form that human needs take as shaped by culture and individual personality.

Demands—Human wants that are backed by buying power.

Market offering—Some combination of products, services, information or experiences offered to a market to satisfy a need or want.

Market offerings are not limited to physical products. For example, LaSalle Bank runs ads asking people to donate used or old winter clothing to the Salvation Army. In this case, the 'marketing offer' is helping to keep those who are less fortunate warm.
SOURCE: LaSalle Bank.

and services increasingly become commodities, experiences have emerged for many firms as the next step in differentiating the company's offer. Consider Whole Foods Market, a grocery store that targets young graduates:

Whole Foods Market's 7,500 m^2 food extravaganza in Kensington High Street, London, is more like Harrods' food hall than a supermarket but with the added attraction of an oyster and champagne bar, sushi counter, a DJ, poetry corner, massage centre, meditation classes and speed dating on singles nights when 'like-minded people can meet like-minded people'. The grocer aims at the top end of the food market where people will pay a lot more for food that they think is fresher and healthier. There will not be a lot of these emporiums for good produce. The firm estimates there is need for about forty in a large European country. Their location? Only in areas where there are lots of rich graduates.[3]

'What consumers really want is [offers] that dazzle their senses, touch their hearts, and stimulate their minds,' declares one expert. 'They want [offers] that deliver an experience.'[4] HP and Apple recognise that a personal computer is much more than just a collection of wires and electrical components.

> An HP ad captures this relationship between a person and their computer: 'There is hardly anything that you own that is *more* personal. Your personal computer is your backup brain. It's your life . . . It's your astonishing strategy, staggering proposal, dazzling calculation. It's your autobiography, written in a thousand daily words.'[5]

Value, satisfaction and quality

Consumers usually face a broad array of products and services that might satisfy a given need. How do they choose among these many market offerings? Customers form expectations about the value and satisfaction that various market offerings will deliver and buy accordingly. Satisfied customers buy again and tell others about their good experiences. Dissatisfied customers often switch to competitors and disparage the product or service to others.

Marketers must be careful to set the right level of expectations. If they set expectations too low, they may satisfy those who buy but fail to attract enough buyers. If they raise expectations too high, buyers will be disappointed. Customer value and customer satisfaction are key building blocks for developing and managing customer relationships. We will revisit these core concepts later in the chapter.

The guiding concept is **customer value**. Customer value is the difference between the values the customer gains from owning and using a product and the costs of obtaining the product. For example, Volvo S40 customers gain a number of benefits. Among these are reliability and outstanding safety and security. However, customers may also receive some status and image values. Owning or driving a Volvo may make them feel more important, sensible and safe. When deciding whether to buy the desired model, customers will weigh these and other values against what it costs to buy the car. Moreover, they will compare the value of owning a Volvo against the value of owning other comparable manufacturers' models – Mercedes, Jaguar, BMW – and select the one that gives them the greatest delivered value.

> *Smart companies aim to delight customers by promising only what they can deliver, then delivering more than they promise.*

Customers often do not judge product values and costs accurately or objectively. They act on *perceived* value. Customers perceive Jaguars to provide superior performance, and are hence prepared to pay the higher prices that the company charges. **Customer satisfaction** depends on a product's perceived performance in delivering value relative to a buyer's expectations. If the product's performance falls short of the customer's expectations, the buyer is dissatisfied. If performance matches expectations, the buyer is satisfied. If performance exceeds expectations, the buyer is delighted. Outstanding marketing companies go out of their way to keep their customers satisfied. They know that satisfied customers make repeat purchases and tell others about their good experiences with the product. The key is to match customer expectations with company performance. Smart companies aim to delight customers by promising only what they can deliver, then delivering more than they promise.[6]

Exchanges, transactions and relationships

Marketing occurs when people decide to satisfy needs and wants through exchange relationships. **Exchange** is the act of obtaining a desired object from someone by offering something in return. Exchange is only one of many ways people can obtain a desired object. For example, hungry people can find food by hunting, fishing or gathering fruit. They could beg for food or take food from someone else. Finally, they could offer money, another good or a service in return for food.

As a means of satisfying needs, exchange has much in its favour. People do not have to prey on others or depend on donations. Nor must they possess the skills to produce every necessity for

Customer value—The consumer's assessment of the product's overall capacity to satisfy his or her needs.

Customer satisfaction—The extent to which a product's perceived performance matches a buyer's expectations. If the product's performance falls short of expectations, the buyer is dissatisfied. If performance matches or exceeds expectations, the buyer is satisfied or delighted.

Exchange—The act of obtaining a desired object from someone by offering something in return.

themselves. They can concentrate on making things they are good at making and trade them for needed items made by others. Thus, exchange allows a society to produce much more than it would with any alternative system.

Exchange is the core concept of marketing. For an exchange to take place, several conditions must be satisfied. Of course, at least two parties must participate and each must have something of value to offer the other. Each party must also want to deal with the other party and each must be free to accept or reject the other's offer. Finally, each party must be able to communicate and deliver.

These conditions simply make exchange *possible*. Whether exchange actually *takes place* depends on the parties coming to an agreement. If they agree, we must conclude that the act of exchange has left both of them better off or, at least, not worse off. After all, each was free to reject or accept the offer. In this sense, exchange creates value just as production creates value. It gives people more consumption choices or possibilities.

Transaction—A trade between two parties that involves at least two things of value, agreed-upon conditions, a time of agreement and a place of agreement.

Whereas exchange is the core concept of marketing, a transaction is marketing's unit of measurement. A **transaction** consists of a trading of values between two parties: one party gives X to another party and gets Y in return. For example, you pay a retailer €2,000 for a plasma TV or a hotel €120 a night for a room. This is a classic monetary transaction, but not all transactions involve money. In a barter transaction, you might trade your old refrigerator in return for a neighbour's second-hand television set. Or a lawyer writes a will for a vet in return for neutering his dog.

In the broadest sense, the marketer tries to bring about a response to some market offering. The response may be more than simply buying or trading products and services. A political candidate, for instance, wants votes, a church wants membership, an orchestra wants an audience and a social action group wants idea acceptance.

Relationship marketing— The process of creating, maintaining and enhancing strong, value-laden relationships with customers and other stakeholders.

Marketing consists of actions taken to build and maintain desirable exchange *relationships* with target audiences involving a product, service, idea or other object. Transaction marketing is part of the larger idea of **relationship marketing**. Beyond simply attracting new customers and creating short-term transactions, the goal is to retain customers and grow their business with the company. Marketers want to build strong relationships by consistently delivering superior customer value. We will expand on the important concept of managing customer relationships later in the chapter.

In order to fulfil their relationships with customers, marketers also have to work at building long-term relationships with distributors, dealers and suppliers. They build strong economic and social connections by promising and consistently delivering high-quality products, good service and fair prices. Increasingly, marketing is shifting from trying to maximise the profit on each individual transaction to maximising mutually beneficial relationships with consumers and other parties. Ultimately, a company wants to build a unique company asset called a marketing network that consists of the company and all of its supporting stakeholders. These include customers, employees, suppliers, distributors, retailers, ad agencies, and others with whom it has built mutually profitable business relationships. Increasingly, competition is not between companies but rather between whole networks, with the prize going to the company that has built the best network. The operating principle is simple: build a good network of relationships with key stakeholders and returns will follow.[7] For example, food retailer Sainsbury's has SpecSavers, Fuji Film and Persil Service dry cleaning concessions within their stores. Persil and Fuji have an even closer relationship since they share the same counter and operators. Sainsbury's, SpecSavers, Fuji, Persil and other partners cooperate and the customer benefits from having a more convenient shopping experience.[8] Chapter 8 will further explore relationship marketing and its role in creating and maintaining customer satisfaction.

Markets and the marketing system

Market—The set of all actual and potential buyers of a product or service.

The concepts of exchange and relationships lead to the concept of a market. A **market** is the set of actual and potential buyers of a market offering. These buyers share a particular need or want that can be satisfied through exchanges and relationships. Thus, the size of a market depends on the number of people who exhibit the need, have resources to engage in exchange, and are

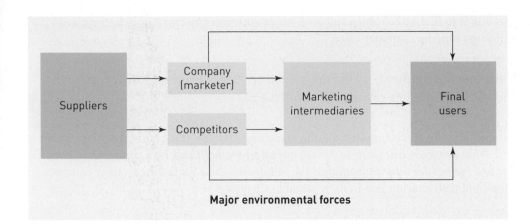

Figure 1.2 Elements of a modern marketing system

willing to offer these resources in exchange for what they want. Markets need not be physical locations where buyers and sellers interact. With modern communications and transportation, a merchant can easily advertise a product on the Internet or a late evening television programme, take orders from thousands of customers over the phone or online, and mail the goods to the buyers on the following day, without having had any physical contact with them.

Marketing means managing markets to bring about profitable customer relationships through creating value and satisfying needs and wants. However, creating these relationships takes work. Sellers must search for buyers, identify their needs, design good market offerings, set prices for them, promote them and store and deliver them. Activities such as product development, research, communication, distribution, pricing and service are core marketing activities.

Although we normally think of marketing as being carried out by sellers, buyers also carry out marketing. Consumers do marketing when they search for the goods they need at prices they can afford. Company purchasing agents do marketing when they track down sellers and bargain for good terms. A *sellers' market* is one in which sellers have more power and buyers must be the more active 'marketers'. In a *buyers' market*, buyers have more power and sellers have to be more active 'marketers'.

Figure 1.2 shows the main elements in a modern marketing system. In the usual situation, marketing involves serving a market of final consumers in the face of competitors. The company and the competitors send their respective offers and messages to consumers, either directly or through marketing intermediaries. All of the actors in the system are affected by major environmental forces – demographic, economic, physical, technological, political/legal and social/cultural. These forces that affect marketing decisions will be examined in greater detail in Chapter 4.

Each party in the system adds value for the next level. All of the arrows represent relationships that must be developed and managed. Thus, a company's success at building profitable relationships depends not only on its own actions but also on how well the entire system serves the needs of final consumers. Tesco or Carrefour cannot fulfil their promise of low prices unless their suppliers provide merchandise at low costs, and Mercedes and BMW cannot deliver high quality to car buyers unless their dealers provide outstanding sales and service.

Designing a customer-driven marketing strategy

Marketing management— The art and science of choosing target markets and building profitable relationships with them.

Once it fully understands consumers and the marketplace, marketing management can design a customer-driven marketing strategy. We define **marketing management** as the art and science of choosing target markets and building profitable relationships with them. The marketing manager's aim is to find, attract, keep and grow target customers by creating, delivering and communicating superior customer value.

> **"** Marketing management . . . [is] the art and science of choosing target markets and building profitable relationships with them. **"**

To design a winning marketing strategy, the marketing manager must answer two important questions: *What customers will we serve (what's our target market)?* and *How can we serve these customers best (what's our value proposition)?* We will discuss these marketing strategy concepts briefly here, and then look at them in more detail in Chapter 3.

Selecting customers to serve

The company must first decide *who* it will serve. It does this by dividing the market into segments of customers (*market segmentation*) and selecting which segments it will go after (*target marketing*). Some people think of marketing management as finding as many customers as possible and increasing demand. But marketing managers know that they cannot serve all customers in every way. By trying to serve all customers, they may not serve any customers well. Instead, the company wants to select only customers that it can serve well and profitably.

For example, Four Seasons Hotels profitably targets affluent travellers expecting 'the highest standards of hospitality', while Holiday Inn Express is successfully expanding across Europe offering 'a refreshing night's sleep at a price that won't break the bank' for more price-sensitive travellers.

The organisation also has a desired level of demand for its products. At any point in time, there may be no demand, adequate demand, irregular demand or too much demand, and marketing management must find ways to deal with these different demand states. Marketing management is concerned not only with finding and increasing demand, but also with changing or even reducing it. For example:

The Eden Project is an ecologically appealing attraction in south-west England that has a series of huge 'biomes' with climates and plants from deserts to rainforests. Unfortunately, in summertime it has trouble meeting demand during peak usage periods that typically occur when holidaymakers try to escape a rainy day at the coast. In these and other cases of excess demand, the needed marketing task, called **demarketing**, is to reduce demand temporarily or permanently. The aim of demarketing is not to destroy demand, but only to reduce or shift it.

Demarketing—Marketing to reduce demand temporarily or permanently – the aim is not to destroy demand, but only to reduce or shift it.

Thus, marketing managers must decide which customers they want to target, and the level, timing and nature of their demand. Simply put, marketing management is *customer management* and *demand management*.

Choosing a value proposition

The company must also decide how it will serve targeted customers – how it will *differentiate and position* itself in the marketplace. A company's *value proposition* is the set of benefits or values it promises to deliver to consumers to satisfy their needs. Saab promises driving performance and excitement, reminding Japanese consumers that 'You don't need flying lessons to take off in a Saab'. By contrast, Škoda Roomster is 'roomy by nature'. Propel Fitness Water by Gatorade is 'made for bodies in motion'. Red Bull Energy Drink, on the other hand, helps you fight mental and physical fatigue. It captures 70 per cent of the energy drinks market by promising it 'gives you wiiings!'

Such value propositions differentiate one brand from another. They answer the customer's question 'Why should I buy your brand rather than a competitor's?' Companies must design strong value propositions that give them the greatest advantage in their target markets. Chapter 9 explores market segmentation, the choice of target markets and how to differentiate offerings.

Marketing management orientations

Marketing management wants to design strategies that will build profitable relationships with target consumers. But what *philosophy* should guide these marketing strategies? What weight should be given to the interests of customers, the organisation and society? Very often, these interests conflict.

Value propositions: Red Bull Energy Drink 'gives you wiiings' and 'vitalizes both body and mind.'
SOURCE: Red Bull North America, Inc.

There are six alternative concepts under which organisations design and carry out their marketing strategies: the *production, product, selling, marketing, societal marketing* and *sustainable marketing* concepts.

The production concept

Production concept—The philosophy that consumers will favour products that are available and highly affordable, and that management should therefore focus on improving production and distribution efficiency.

The **production concept** holds that consumers will favour products that are available and highly affordable. Therefore, management should focus on improving production and distribution efficiency. This concept is one of the oldest orientations that guides sellers.

The production concept is still a useful philosophy in some situations. When the product's cost is too high, improved productivity is needed to bring it down to enable sellers to charge competitive prices. Or, when the demand for a product exceeds the supply, it makes sense for management to look for ways to increase production. For example, computer maker Lenovo dominates the highly competitive, price-sensitive Chinese PC market through low labour costs, high production efficiency and mass distribution. However, although useful in some situations, the production concept can lead to marketing myopia. Companies adopting this orientation run a major risk of focusing too narrowly on their own operations and losing sight of the real objective – satisfying customer needs and building customer relationships.

The product concept

Product concept—The idea that consumers will favour products that offer the most quality, performance and features, and that the organisation should therefore devote its energy to making continuous product improvements.

The **product concept** holds that consumers will favour products that offer the most in quality, performance and innovative features. Under this concept, marketing strategy focuses on making continuous product improvements.

Product quality and improvement are important parts of most marketing strategies. However, focusing *only* on the company's products can lead to obsession with technology, because managers believe that technical superiority is the key to business success. It can also lead to marketing myopia. For example, some manufacturers believe that if they can 'build a better mousetrap, the world will beat a path to their door'. But they are often rudely shocked. Buyers may well be looking for a better solution to a mouse problem but not necessarily for a better mousetrap. The better solution might be a chemical spray, an extermination service or something that works better than a mousetrap. Furthermore, a better mousetrap will not sell unless the manufacturer designs, packages and prices it attractively, places it in convenient distribution channels, brings it to the attention of people who need it, and convinces buyers that it is a better product.

Europe's multinational consortium that built Galileo is looking increasingly like a very expensive better mousetrap. With development cost increased to €2bn and launch delayed, the 20-satellite system is designed to compete with America's GPS system that is free to users – unless the Americans switch off access. The European Commission is trying to think of ways to commercialise the project but, as one observer quipped, 'Why sell Pepsi-Cola when you can get Coca-Cola free?'[9]

The selling concept

Selling concept—The idea that consumers will not buy enough of the organisation's products unless the organisation undertakes a large-scale selling and promotion effort.

Many companies follow the **selling concept**, which holds that consumers will not buy enough of the firm's products unless it undertakes a large-scale selling and promotion effort. Most firms practise the selling concept when they have overcapacity. The concept is also typically practised with unsought goods – those that buyers do not normally think of buying, such as insurance or blood donations. These industries must be good at tracking down prospects and selling them on product benefits. The selling concept is also practised in the non-profit area. A political party, for example, will vigorously sell its candidate to voters as a fantastic person for the job. The candidate works hard at selling him or herself – shaking hands, kissing babies, meeting supporters and making speeches. Much money also has to be spent on radio and television advertising, posters and mailings. Candidate flaws are often hidden from the public because the aim is to get the sale, not to worry about consumer satisfaction afterwards.

Such aggressive selling, however, carries high risks. It focuses on creating sales transactions rather than on building long-term, profitable customer relationships. The aim often is to sell what the company makes rather than making what the market wants. It assumes that customers who are coaxed into buying the product will like it. Or, if they don't like it, they will possibly forget their disappointment and buy it again later. These are usually poor assumptions. Most studies show that dissatisfied customers do not buy again. Worse yet, while the average satisfied customer tells three others about good experiences, the average dissatisfied customer tells 10 others of his or her bad experiences.[10]

The marketing concept

The **marketing concept** holds that achieving organisational goals depends on knowing the needs and wants of target markets and delivering the desired satisfactions better than competitors do. Under the marketing concept, customer focus and value are the *paths* to sales and profits. Instead of a product-centred 'make and sell' philosophy, the marketing concept is a customer-centred 'sense and respond' philosophy. It views marketing not as 'hunting', but as 'gardening'. The job is not to find the right customers for your product, but to find the right products for your customers.

Figure 1.3 contrasts the selling concept and the marketing concept. The selling concept takes an *inside-out* perspective. It starts with the factory, focuses on the company's existing products, and calls for heavy selling and promotion to obtain profitable sales. It focuses primarily on customer conquest – getting short-term sales with little concern about who buys or why.

> " The marketing concept . . . views marketing not as 'hunting', but as 'gardening'. "

In contrast, the marketing concept takes an *outside-in* perspective. The marketing concept starts with a well-defined market, focuses on customer needs, and integrates all the marketing activities that affect customers. In turn, it yields profits by creating lasting relationships with the right customers based on customer value and satisfaction.

Many successful and well-known global companies have adopted the marketing concept. IKEA, Procter & Gamble, Tesco, Marriott and Toyota take a customer- and marketing-oriented view of their business.

Marketing concept—The marketing management philosophy which holds that achieving organisational goals depends on determining the needs and wants of target markets and delivering the desired satisfactions more effectively and efficiently than competitors do.

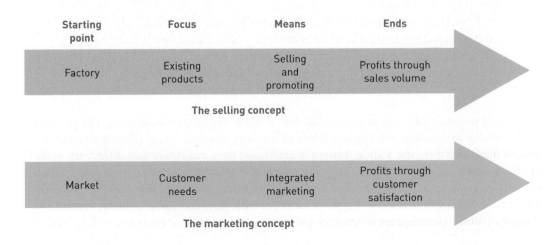

Figure 1.3 The selling and marketing concepts contrasted

For example, Toyota gets deep into the hearts and minds of its customers, to establish precisely what they want and subsequently find ways to fulfil their wishes. In Japan, Toyota's Amlux building, resembling a blue and black striped rocket, attracts millions of visitors. These could be potential customers or people with ideas on how the company should respond to consumers' vehicle requirements. These visitors can spend as much time as they want designing their own vehicles on computer/TV screens in the vehicle-design studio. Visitors can gather specific information about the company, its dealers or products. They are also allowed to expound, at length, on what they think Toyota should be doing or making. Meanwhile, Toyota's attentive note-taking staff ensure that the entire Amlux complex is dedicated to involving potential customers who can give them close insights into how their car needs can be satisfied.

Many companies claim to practise the marketing concept but do not. They have the *forms* of marketing – such as a marketing director, product managers, marketing plans and marketing research – but this does not mean that they are *market-focused* and *customer-driven* companies. The question is whether they are finely tuned to changing customer needs and competitor strategies. Great companies – Philips, Marks & Spencer, Ford, Sony, IBM – have lost substantial market share in the past because they failed to adjust their marketing strategies to the changing marketplace.

In marketing-led organisations, real customer focus works from the top down and the bottom up. The organisation-wide belief in delivering value and desired satisfactions becomes a priority and all staff are committed to building lasting customer relationships. To achieve a marketing orientation, the organisation has to channel the knowledge and understanding, the motivation, the inspiration and the imagination of all staff to deliver products and services that meet exactly what the customer requires from the organisation.

Implementing the marketing concept often means more than simply responding to customers' stated desires and obvious needs. *Customer-driven* companies research current customers deeply to learn about their desires, gather new product and service ideas, and test proposed product improvements. Such customer-driven marketing usually works well when a clear need exists and when customers know what they want.

 Our goal is to lead customers where they want to go before *they* know where they want to go.

In many cases, however, customers *don't* know what they want or even what is possible. For example, even 20 years ago, how many consumers would have thought to ask for now-commonplace products such as mobile phones, notebook computers, iPods, digital cameras and satellite navigation systems in their cars? Such situations call for *customer-driving* marketing – understanding customer needs even better than customers themselves do and creating products and services that meet existing and latent needs, now and in the future. As an executive at 3M puts it: 'Our goal is to lead customers where they want to go before *they* know where they want to go'.

It is hard to turn a sales-oriented company into a marketing-oriented company. The goal is to build customer satisfaction into the very fabric of the firm. However, the marketing concept does not also mean that a company should try to give *all* consumers *everything* they want, even at the expense of losing money for the business. The purpose of marketing is not to *maximise* customer satisfaction, but to meet customer needs profitably. Marketers must therefore seek to achieve the very delicate balance between creating more value for customers and making profits for the company. We will examine how this is achieved later in the chapter.

The societal marketing concept

The **societal marketing concept** questions whether the pure marketing concept overlooks possible conflicts between consumer *short-run wants* and consumer *long-run welfare*. Is a firm that satisfies the immediate needs and wants of target markets always doing what's best for consumers in the long run? The societal marketing concept holds that marketing strategy should deliver value to customers in a way that maintains or improves both the consumer's *and society's* well-being.

> Consider the aviation industries that figure in the Bye-bye Ryanair prelude case. Low-cost air travel has revolutionised lives, not just for main holidays but for an increasing number of people shuttling between two homes in the north and south of Europe. More affluent people are likely to have second homes on other continents, Florida and South Africa being particularly popular with Northern Europeans. Malaysia and Thailand are the latest boom places in the second-home lifestyle. The airline industry is hugely successful in bringing people of the world together by cutting prices to make frequent international travel accessible to almost everyone. Unleashed with successful business models that fulfil customer needs, the industry projects continued growth for decades to come, partly fuelled by the new wealth in China and India.
>
> The industry was gung-ho with its success, then suddenly 'more and more often environmentalists are calling aviation a "rogue industry", lumped together alongside Big Tobacco,' says Marion Blakey, head of the US Federal Aviation Administration. In Europe 34 per cent of airline executives viewed the environment as the key challenge. Ms Blakey explains further: 'Along with congested airspace, aircraft emissions may be the most serious barrier to aviation growth, at least in the long term.' Only 5 per cent of US aviation executives view the environment as a key challenge but some European airlines are putting the issue centre stage. According to Rod Eddington, chief executive of British Airways, 'Technology and market mechanisms have driven massive economic progress during the past two centuries. Now we need to harness them to tackle the environmental challenges that the world faces. It is vital that the aviation industry plays its part.'[11]

Such concerns and conflicts led to the societal marketing concept. As Figure 1.4 shows, the societal marketing concept calls upon marketers to balance three considerations in setting their marketing strategies: company profits, consumer wants and society's interests. Originally, most

Societal marketing concept—A principle of enlightened marketing which holds that an organisation should make good marketing decisions by considering consumers' wants, the company's requirements, consumers' long-run interests and society's long-run interests.

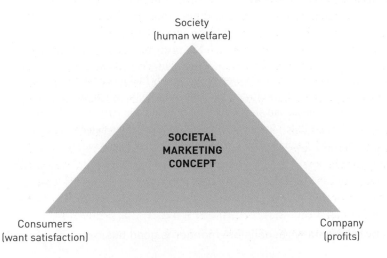

Society
(human welfare)

SOCIETAL MARKETING CONCEPT

Consumers
(want satisfaction)

Company
(profits)

Figure 1.4 Three considerations underlying the societal marketing concept

companies based their marketing decisions largely on short-run company profit. Eventually, they began to recognise the long-run importance of satisfying consumer wants, and the marketing concept emerged. Now many companies have to think of society's interests when making their marketing decisions.

The sustainable marketing concept

The Brundtland Report on the findings of the 1987 World Commission on Environment and Development said 'sustainable development meets the needs of the present without compromising the ability of future generations to meet their own need.' Although this statement has become widely publicised as defining sustainability, sustainability is not limited to this one definition. The term captures the concerns being expressed of the aviation sector. Whether the aviation sector contributes 2, 3 or 5 per cent of the world's carbon emissions, scientists uniformly predict that this output is a contributor to global warming that is already having an impact on the world.[12] Unfairly, the worst contributors to global warming, the United States (30 per cent) and Europe (28 per cent), have so far suffered little, while the greatest impact is in poor African nations that contribute only 2.5 per cent of the damage.

> The attitude of marketers towards the threat of global warming is not uniform. The prelude case encapsulates how marketers respond to the issue. Some, such as Emirates Airlines' Maurice Flanagan, see global warming as an inconvenient but unproven issue. Others are concerned about the immediate consumer backlash or, like Kuoni Travel's Armin Meier, see climate change as 'an image issue'. Others, such as easyJet's founder Sir Stelios Haji-Ioannou, think 'the debate is over' and aim to forge ahead in a more energy efficient way. Many businesses try to act themselves but also call upon governments to take the lead. Among this latter group is British Airways' Rod Eddington who wants carbon trading to be introduced for European airlines. Other competitors are making sustainability a platform of their strategy. Virgin Atlantic's Sir Richard Branson has declared he will invest all the airline's profits ($3bn) to fight global warming, proclaiming 'We must rapidly wean ourselves off our dependence on coal and fossil fuels.'

Sustainable marketing concept—A principle of marketing that holds that an organisation should meet the needs of its present consumers without compromising the ability of future generations to fulfil their own needs.

The difference between societal marketing and the **sustainable marketing concept** is a time shift. Societal marketing is concerned with the conflict between supplying consumers' wants with the impact upon others. Sustainable marketing counters today's consumption against that of future consumers and future society as a whole. Sustainable marketing also recognises the future of tomorrow's organisation.

> BP's restated its initials as meaning 'Beyond Petroleum' to identify that its own future is not tied to burning fossil fuels. Equally Shell is cultivating a dialogue with the wider community, questioning the structure of their business, and seeks 'real energy solutions for the real world'. As Jeroen van de Veer, the CeO of Royal Dutch Shell, explains: 'Sure, companies need to make a profit. At the same time Shell knows that acting in an environmentally responsible manner is good business.'

 Acting in an environmentally responsible manner is good business.

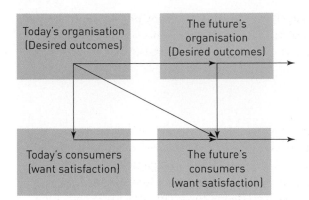

Figure 1.5 Four considerations of the sustainable marketing concept

Sustainable marketing is not a retreat in the face of pressure groups or a public relations gambit to counter negative publicity. It is founded on the recognition that the best strategy is to serve the long-term needs of customers and to pursue strategies that are consistent with the long-term survival of a business. It is not a cost that has to be borne but a means of increasing brand value and profits. A survey by the Economics Intelligence Unit gives an indication of the outcomes businesses are experiencing from carbon reduction. One third of the executives said carbon reduction would enhance their image. One in six companies said carbon reduction had already boosted their profits, while another third expected to do so within three years. In contrast only a tenth of companies complained of higher costs now or in the future.[13] Figure 1.5 shows four considerations of the sustainable marketing concept.

Increasingly, firms also have to meet the expectations of society as a whole and be seen to be doing so. For example, society expects businesses genuinely to uphold basic ethical and environmental standards. Not only should they have ethics and environmental policies, they must also back these with actions. Many of tomorrow's successful firms will succeed not by adjusting to environmental and social pressures but by responding to the market opportunities created by these changes.

Building profitable customer relationships

Managing demand means managing customers. A company's demand comes from two groups: new customers and repeat customers. Traditional marketing theory and practice have focused on attracting new customers and creating transactions – making the sale. In today's marketing environment, however, changing demographic, economic and competitive factors mean that there are fewer new customers to go around. The costs of attracting new customers are rising. In fact, it costs five times as much to attract a new customer as it does to keep a current customer satisfied. Thus, although finding new customers remains very important, the emphasis is shifting towards retaining profitable customers and building lasting relationships with them.

Companies have also discovered that losing a customer means losing not just a single sale, but also a lifetime's worth of purchases and referrals. For example, the customer lifetime value of a supermarket customer might well exceed €1,000,000. Thus, working to retain customers makes good economic sense. A company can lose money on a specific transaction, but still benefit greatly from a long-term relationship. The key to customer retention is superior customer value and satisfaction.

Marketing management practice

All kinds of organisations use marketing, and they practise it in widely varying ways. Many large firms apply standard marketing practices in a formalised way. However, other companies use marketing in a less formal and orderly fashion. Companies such as easyJet and YouTube achieved success by seemingly breaking all the rules of marketing. Instead of commissioning expensive

real marketing

'Whatever people say I am, that's what I'm not'

Arctic Monkeys, Domino: B000BTDMDC, 2006

The Arctic Monkeys' 'Whatever people say I am, that's what I'm not' is the fastest-selling debut album ever. The achievement is amazing given the advent of music downloads and bootlegging causing collapse of CD sales to a fraction of their level a decade ago. On top of that, the album was released in January, a month that is usually slow after the Christmas surge.

Seemingly, out of nowhere the band's first album outsold all other albums in the UK album charts in the week of its release. The sales came on the back of sell-out gigs where wildly enthusiastic fans sang along to every song sung by Alex Turner, the band's inspired lead singer, even though they had never had the chance to learn the words from the album.

Their record company EMI and music stores like HMV are looking to the band's success to counter some of the decline they are facing elsewhere in the market. The band's strong sales have provided some comfort to music industry executives concerned about the ever-increasing quantity of music being made available for free on the Internet, through illegal peer-to-peer file-sharing services or community sites such as MySpace. The industry is making good money out of the band's success but the scale of the band's success, even before it signed a record deal, concerns some industry members. They fear it heralds fundamental changes in the way they find talent, the skills needed to market bands, and the way in which the proceeds will be shared out in the digital age. 'What will be interesting is when the talent bypasses the music companies,' said Patrick Parodi, chairman of the Mobile Entertainment Forum.

The teenage band from Sheffield, England, became famous via fans' Internet sites. Every song from the band's first album has been available for free on the Internet. Fans also loaded CDs that the band handed out at their early concerts on to websites, and then recommended them to friends. Social networks that bypass the industry are part of the digital age. A proliferation of specialist radio stations and websites such as MySpace and DrownedInSound also allowed users to rank new bands, providing music companies with a measure of a band's popularity at a very early stage. 'The Internet was word-of-mouth in the new generation,' comments Guy Moot of EMI Music Publishing.

It was not just the Internet that enabled this fan-based revolution. While music sales decline, live music is growing. In the early days of popular music, successful artists could be mediocre show-people, but now the excitement of live acts lights the fire.

Not only have the Arctic Monkeys used social networks to achieve success, they have spurned some easy money from the pop world to retain credibility with their followers. They rejected making ringtone recordings for mobile phones and an invitation to appear on pop-oriented TV programmes.

Since Elvis Presley at Sun Records, revolutionaries have upturned the music industry, be it the Beatles, punk or gangster rap. This time it is the Arctic Monkeys and social networks are the latest revolution. As with each revolutionary wave, people follow what looks like the easy pickings to be made. Not only is the recording industry trying to reproduce the Arctic Monkeys' marketing methods, but huge fortunes are being poured into trying to recreate another customer-driven social network like MySpace or YouTube. Not surprisingly, Rupert Murdoch's News Corporation recently paid $580m for YouTube, a site which generates $150m income a month! Now, so much money is chasing so few original ideas that some are predicting another 'dot-com crash'.

SOURCES: Andrew Edgecliffe-Johnson, 'Arctic Monkeys are the talk of the web generation', *Financial Times* (26 January 2006); 'Hanging with the in-crowd: Big media firms and investors are cosying up to social-networking websites', *The Economist* (14 September 2006); Greg Kot, 'Arctic Monkeys blast Riviera with 3-minute bursts', *Chicago Tribune*, Illinois – KRTBN (10 May 2007); Paul Lewis, 'Ibiza is dancing to new tune as Arctic Monkeys head for island', *The Guardian* (14 May 2007); Nic Fildes, 'HMV looks to magic of Arctic Monkeys and Harry Potter to help lift sagging sales', *The Independent* (4 May 2007); Tom Findlay and Rob Wood, 'Arctic Monkeys obey new laws of the jungle', *Financial Times* (27 January 2006).

...1.1

marketing research, spending huge sums on mass advertising and operating large marketing departments, these companies practised entrepreneurial marketing. Their founders, typically, live by their wits. They visualise an opportunity and do what it takes to gain attention. They build a successful organisation by stretching their limited resources, living close to their customers and creating more satisfying solutions to customer needs. It seems that not all marketing must follow in the footsteps of marketing giants such as Procter & Gamble.

However, entrepreneurial marketing often gives way to formulated marketing. As small companies achieve success, they inevitably move towards more formulated marketing. They begin to spend more on television advertising in selected markets. They may also expand their sales force and establish a marketing department that carries out market research. They embrace many of the tools used in so-called professionally run marketing companies. Before long, these companies grow to become large and, eventually, mature companies. They get stuck in formulated marketing, poring over the latest Nielsen numbers, scanning market research reports and trying to fine-tune dealer relations and advertising messages. These companies sometimes lose the marketing creativity and passion that they had at the start. They now need to re-establish within their companies the entrepreneurial spirit and actions that made them successful in the first place. They need to practise entrepreneurial marketing, that is, to encourage more initiative and 'entrepreneurship' at the local level. Their brand and product managers need to get out of the office, start living with their customers and visualise new and creative ways to add value to their customers' lives.

The bottom line is that effective marketing can take many forms. There will be a constant tension between the formulated side of marketing and the creative side. It is easier to learn the formulated side of marketing, which will occupy most of our attention in this book. However, we will also see how real marketing creativity and passion operate in many companies – whether small or large, new or mature – to build and retain success in the marketplace.

Preparing an integrated marketing plan and programme

The company's marketing strategy outlines which customers the company will serve and how it will create value for these customers. Next, the marketer develops an integrated marketing programme that will deliver the intended value to target customers. The marketing programme builds customer relationships by transforming the marketing strategy into action. It consists of the firm's *marketing mix*, the set of marketing tools the firm uses to implement its marketing strategy.

The major marketing mix tools are classified into four broad groups, called the *four Ps* of marketing: product, price, place and promotion. To deliver on its value proposition, the firm must first create a need-satisfying market offering (product). It must decide how much it will charge for the offer (price) and how it will make the offer available to target consumers (place). Finally, it must communicate with target customers about the offer and persuade them of its merits (promotion). The firm must blend all of these marketing mix tools into a comprehensive, *integrated marketing programme* that communicates and delivers the intended value to chosen customers. We will explore marketing programmes and the marketing mix in much more detail in later chapters.

Building customer relationships

The first three steps in the marketing process – understanding the marketplace and customer needs, designing a customer-driven marketing strategy and constructing marketing programmes – all lead up to the fourth and most important step: building profitable customer relationships.

Customer relationship management

Customer relationship management (CRM) is perhaps the most important concept of modern marketing. Until recently, CRM has been defined narrowly as a customer data management activity. By this definition, it involves managing detailed information about individual customers and carefully managing customer 'touchpoints' in order to maximise customer loyalty. We will discuss this narrower CRM activity in Chapter 8 dealing with marketing information.

More recently, however, customer relationship management has taken on a broader meaning. In this broader sense, customer relationship management is the overall process of building and maintaining profitable customer relationships by delivering superior customer value and satisfaction. It deals with all aspects of acquiring, keeping and growing customers.

Relationship building blocks: customer value and satisfaction

The key to building lasting customer relationships is to create superior customer value and satisfaction. Satisfied customers are more likely to be loyal customers and to give the company a larger share of their business.

Customer value

Attracting and retaining customers can be a difficult task. Customers often face a bewildering array of products and services from which to choose. A customer buys from the firm that offers the highest **customer perceived value** – the customer's evaluation of the difference between all the benefits and all the costs of a market offering relative to those of competing offers.

Customer relationship management (CRM)—The overall process of building and maintaining profitable customer relationships by delivering superior customer value and satisfaction.

Customer perceived value—The customer's evaluation of the difference between all the benefits and all the costs of a market offering relative to those of competing offers.

For example, Toyota Prius hybrid automobile owners gain a number of benefits. The most obvious benefit is fuel efficiency. However, by purchasing a Prius, the owners also may receive some status and image values. Driving a Prius makes owners feel and appear more environmentally responsible. When deciding whether to purchase a Prius, customers will weigh these and other perceived values of owning the car against the money, effort and psychic costs of acquiring it. Moreover, they will compare the value of owning a Prius against that of owning another hybrid or non-hybrid brand. They will select the brand that gives them the greatest perceived value.

Customers often do not judge product values and costs accurately or objectively. They act on *perceived* value. For example, is the Prius really the most economical choice? Renate Künast, German Green MP and former environment minister, thinks so and infuriated the German car industry by urging consumers to buy Japanese. 'I expect the German industry finally to produce modern cars, and if they can't do that, people must buy a Toyota Prius.'[14] In reality, it might take years to save enough in reduced fuel costs to offset the car's higher price. Germany's carmakers think not, protesting that their newest clean diesel cars match or even beat the carbon dioxide emissions of Toyota's hybrids. However, Toyota has captured people's imagination, with Prius buyers perceiving that they are getting real value. A recent survey of the ownership experiences of 69,000 new car

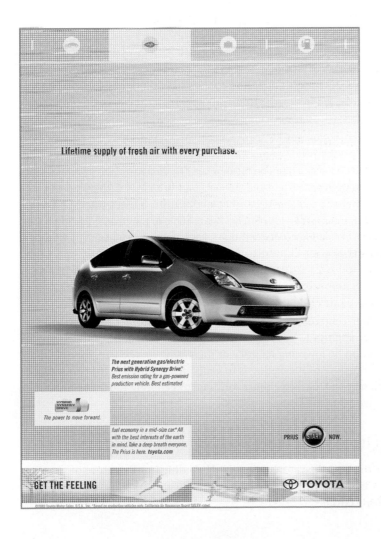

Perceived customer value: When deciding whether to purchase a Prius, customers will weigh its benefits against the benefits of owning another hybrid or non-hybrid brand.
SOURCE: Saatchi & Saatchi.

buyers showed that the Prius was rated as most 'delightful' in terms of fuel economy, and that Prius owners perceived more overall value for their money than buyers of any other hybrid car.[15]

Customer satisfaction

Customer satisfaction depends on the product's perceived performance relative to a buyer's expectations. If the product's performance falls short of expectations, the customer is dissatisfied. If performance matches expectations, the customer is satisfied. If performance exceeds expectations, the customer is highly satisfied or delighted.

Outstanding marketing companies go out of their way to keep important customers satisfied. Most studies show that higher levels of customer satisfaction lead to greater customer loyalty, which in turn results in better company performance. Smart companies aim to *delight* customers by promising only what they can deliver, then delivering *more* than they promise. Delighted customers not only make repeat purchases, they become 'customer evangelists' who tell others about their good experiences with the product.

For companies interested in delighting customers, exceptional value and service are more than a set of policies or actions – they are a company-wide attitude, an important part of the overall company culture. Consider the following example:[16]

> Erik bought his high-spec Lexus RS300 – a £36,000 toy. He could afford a Mercedes, a BMW or a Jaguar, but he bought the Lexus. He took delivery of his new 'toy' and drove it home, luxuriating in the smell of the leather interior and the glorious handling. On the motorway, he pushed the pedal down and felt a healthy surge of power. The lights, the windscreen washer, the gizmo cup holder that popped out of the centre console, the seat heater that warmed his bum on a cold winter's morning – he tried all of these with mounting pleasure. On a whim, he turned on the radio. His favourite station, Classic FM, came on in splendid quadraphonic sound. He pushed the second button; it was BBC Radio 4, his favourite speech radio station. The third button was his local FM station that he enjoyed each morning. The fourth button he did not enjoy; it was Galaxy, his daughter's R&B/Dance station. Every button was set to his family's tastes. Erik knew the car's electronics were smart, but was it psychic? No. The mechanic at Lexus had noted the radio settings on his trade-in vehicle and duplicated them on the new car. The customer was delighted. This was his car now – through and through! No one told the mechanic to do it. It's just part of the Lexus philosophy: delight a customer and continue to delight that customer, and you will have a customer for life. What the mechanic did cost Lexus nothing. Yet it solidified the relationship that could be worth six figures to Lexus in customer lifetime value. Such relationship-building passions in dealerships around the country have made Lexus the world's top-selling luxury vehicle.

However, although the customer-centred firm seeks to deliver high customer satisfaction relative to competitors, it does not attempt to *maximise* customer satisfaction. A company can always increase customer satisfaction by lowering its price or increasing its services. But this may result in lower profits. Thus, the purpose of marketing is to generate customer value profitably. This requires a very delicate balance: the marketer must continue to generate more customer value and satisfaction but not 'give away the house'.

Customer relationship levels and tools

Companies can build customer relationships at many levels, depending on the nature of the target market. At one extreme, a company with many low-margin customers may seek to develop *basic relationships* with them. For example:

Chapter 1 MarketingChapter 1 Marketing

 Nestlé does not phone or call on all of its Buitoni pasta customers to get to know them personally. Instead the company creates relationships through brand-building advertising, sales promotions and its series of Buitoni Clubs for customers, from Italy to Japan, who are keen on making authentic Italian meals.

At the other extreme, in markets with few customers and high margins, sellers want to create full partnerships with key customers.

In selling Buitoni through their distribution channel, Nestlé customer teams work closely with Carrefour, Metro, Tesco, Ahold and other large retailers.

In between these two extreme situations, other levels of customer relationships are appropriate. Dramatic changes are occurring in the ways in which companies are relating to their customers. Yesterday's companies focused on mass marketing to all customers at arm's length. Today's companies are building more direct and lasting relationships with more carefully selected customers. Chapter 18 will address direct forms of marketing and its fastest growing form – online marketing.

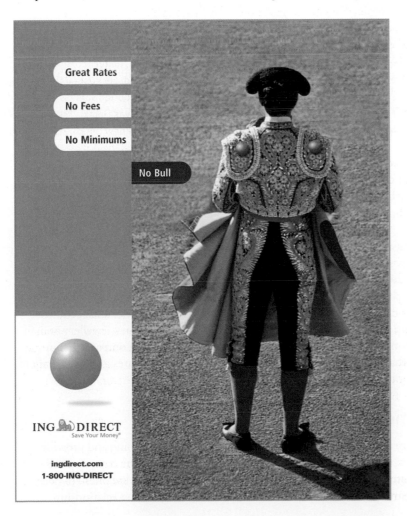

Selective relationship management: ING DIRECT seeks relationships with customers who don't need or want expensive pampering, routinely 'firing' overly demanding customers. The bank lures low-maintenance customers with high interest rates and no fees or minimums. 'No Bull!'
SOURCE: ING Direct.

Capturing value from customers

The first four steps in the marketing process involve building customer relationships by creating and delivering superior customer value. The final step involves capturing value in return, in the form of current and future sales, market share and profits. By creating superior customer value, the firm creates highly satisfied customers who stay loyal and buy more. This, in turn, means greater long-run returns for the firm. Here, we discuss the outcomes of creating customer value: customer loyalty and retention, share of market and share of customer, and customer equity.

Creating customer loyalty and retention

Good customer relationship management creates customer delight. In turn, delighted customers remain loyal and talk favourably to others about the company and its products. Studies show big differences in the loyalty of customers who are less satisfied, somewhat satisfied, and completely satisfied. Even a slight drop from complete satisfaction can create an enormous drop in loyalty. Thus, the aim of customer relationship management is to create not just customer satisfaction, but customer delight.[17]

Companies are realising that losing a customer means losing more than a single sale. It means losing the entire stream of purchases that the customer would make over a lifetime of patronage. For example, here is a dramatic illustration of **customer lifetime value**: Lexus estimates that a single satisfied and loyal customer is worth over €800,000 in lifetime sales. The customer lifetime value of a fast food outlet can exceed €16,000.[18] Thus, working to retain and grow customers makes good economic sense. A company can even lose money on a specific transaction but still benefit greatly from a long-term relationship. This means that companies must aim high in building customer relationships. Customer delight creates an emotional relationship with a product or service, not just a rational preference.

Customer lifetime value—The value of the entire stream of purchases that a customer would make over a lifetime of patronage.

Growing share of customer

Beyond simply retaining good customers to capture customer lifetime value, good customer relationship management can help marketers to increase their **share of customer** – the share they get of the customer's purchasing in their product categories. Thus, banks want to increase 'share of wallet'. Supermarkets and restaurants want to get more 'share of stomach'. Airlines want a greater 'share of travel'.

To increase share of customer, firms can offer greater variety to current customers, or they can train employees to cross-sell and up-sell in order to market more products and services to existing customers. For example, Amazon has leveraged relationships with its 50 million customers to increase its share of each customer's purchases. Originally an online bookseller, Amazon now offers customers music, videos, gifts, toys, consumer electronics, office products, home improvement items, lawn and garden products, clothing and accessories, jewellery and an online auction. In addition, based on each customer's purchase history, the company recommends related products that might be of interest. In this way, Amazon captures a greater share of each customer's spending budget.

Share of customer—The share of the customer's purchasing that a company gets in its product categories.

Building customer equity

We can now see the importance of not just acquiring customers, but of keeping and growing them as well. One marketing consultant puts it this way: 'The only value your company will ever create is the value that comes from customers – the ones you have now and the ones you will have in the future. Without customers, you don't have a business.'[19] Customer relationship management takes a long-term view. Companies want not only to create profitable customers, but to 'own' them for life, capture their customer lifetime value, and earn a greater share of their purchases.

 The only value your company will ever create is the value that comes from customers.

What is customer equity?

The ultimate aim of customer relationship management is to produce high **customer equity**.[20] Customer equity is the combined discounted customer lifetime values of all of the company's current and potential customers. Clearly, the more loyal the firm's profitable customers, the higher the firm's customer equity. Customer equity may be a better measure of a firm's performance than current sales or market share. Whereas sales and market share reflect the past, customer equity suggests the future. Consider Cadillac's demise and BMW's rise in America:

Customer equity—The total combined customer lifetime values of all of the company's customers.

In the 1970s and 1980s, GM's Cadillac had some of the most loyal customers in the industry. To an entire generation of car buyers, the name 'Cadillac' defined American luxury and was celebrated in numerous popular songs. Cadillac's share of the luxury car market topped 50 per cent in 1976. Based on market share and sales, the brand's future looked good. However, measures of customer equity would have painted a bleak picture. Cadillac customers averaged age 60 and average customer lifetime value was falling. Many Cadillac buyers were on their last car! Thus, although Cadillac's market share was good, its customer equity was not. BMW's youthful and vigorous image didn't win BMW the early market share war. However, it did win BMW younger customers with higher customer lifetime values. As a result, in the years that followed, BMW's market share and profits grew while Cadillac's fortunes declined. Thus, market share is not the answer. We should care not just about current sales but also about future sales. Customer lifetime value and customer equity are critical. Recognising this, GM is now taking the Cadillac brand to a younger generation of consumers with new high-performance models and its successful Break Through advertising campaign. Sales are up 37 per cent over the past four years but there are far more foreign luxury cars, from Europe and Japan, than there ever were in Cadillac's heyday.[21]

Building the right relationships with the right customers

Companies should manage customer equity carefully. They should view customers as assets that need to be managed and maximised. But not all customers, not even all loyal customers, are good investments. Surprisingly, some loyal customers can be unprofitable, and some disloyal customers can be profitable. Which customers should the company acquire and retain? 'Up to a point, the choice is obvious: keep the consistent big spenders and lose the erratic small spenders,' says one expert. 'But what about the erratic big spenders and the consistent small spenders? It's often unclear whether they should be acquired or retained, and at what cost.'[22]

The company can classify customers according to their potential profitability and manage its relationships with them accordingly. Figure 1.6 classifies customers into one of four relationship groups, according to their profitability and projected loyalty.[23] Each group requires a different relationship management strategy. 'Strangers' show low profitability and little projected loyalty. There is little fit between the company's offerings and their needs. The relationship management strategy for these customers is simple: don't invest anything in them.

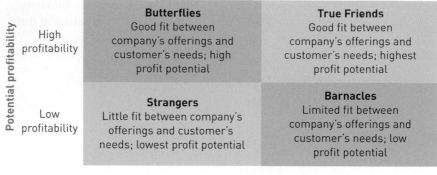

'Butterflies' are profitable but not loyal. There is a good fit between the company's offerings and their needs. However, like real butterflies, we can enjoy them for only a short while and then they're gone. An example is stock market investors who trade shares often and in large amounts, but who enjoy hunting out the best deals without building a regular relationship with any single brokerage company. Efforts to convert butterflies into loyal customers are rarely successful. Instead, the company should enjoy the butterflies for the moment. It should use promotional blitzes to attract them, create satisfying and profitable transactions with them, and then cease investing in them until the next time around.

'True friends' are both profitable and loyal. There is a strong fit between their needs and the company's offerings. The firm wants to make continuous relationship investments to delight these customers and nurture, retain and grow them. It wants to turn true friends into 'true believers', who come back regularly and tell others about their good experiences with the company.

'Barnacles' are highly loyal but not very profitable. There is a limited fit between their needs and the company's offerings. An example is smaller bank customers who bank regularly but do not generate enough returns to cover the costs of maintaining their accounts. Like barnacles on the hull of a ship, they create drag. Barnacles are perhaps the most problematic customers. The company might be able to improve their profitability by selling them more, raising their fees or reducing service to them. However, if they cannot be made profitable, they should be 'fired'.

The point here is an important one: different types of customer require different relationship management strategies. The goal is to build the *right relationships* with the *right customers*.

The new marketing landscape

As the world spins on, dramatic changes are occurring in the marketplace. Richard Love of Hewlett-Packard observes, 'The pace of change is so rapid that the ability to change has now become a competitive advantage.' Marketers are surrounded with change, in the customers, their competitors, technology, political landscape, everywhere. The graveyard of business is littered with companies that failed to recognise the need for continuous change. But marketers cannot just change with markets; the winners will be the change makers. In this section, we examine the major trends and forces that are changing the marketing landscape and challenging marketing strategy. We look at four major developments: sustainability, the growth in not-for-profit marketing, the electronic market place and globalisation.

"
The graveyard of business is littered with companies that failed to recognise the need for continuous change.
"

Sustainability

Marketers are re-examining their relationships with social values and responsibilities and with the very Earth that sustains us. At one time, they were responding to consumerism and environmentalism movements, but a tipping point has occurred and sustainability has taken centre stage politically and strategically.[24] Sustainable marketing moves on from concerns with ethics in business and the need for business to behave with social responsibility as entities separable from

As npower recognises, 2006 saw climate change shift from being someone else's problem, maybe, to being a major business opportunity or a business imperative.
SOURCE: npower.

sustainability. All are part of marketing in a way that enables today's business and consumers to survive to become tomorrow's business and consumers.

Social responsibility and concerns for the environment place strict demands on companies. In the last decade a renewed focus on business ethics occurred after the catastrophic failure of Enron, WorldCom and the likes. In these cases the strategy and ethics of the organisations were not sustainable, destroying the wealth and lives of many people.

Numerous other companies have faced campaigns based upon their lack of social responsibility. Much attention has focused upon the production of expensive Western goods in Third World sweatshops. Among these are campaigns to boycott McDonald's/Disney because of their Happy Meal toys made by Vietnamese girls earning 6 cents an hour, or Chevron and Shell's 'drilling and killing in Nigeria'.[25] In these cases the sustainability of a company's ability to serve its current customers can be damaged, whether the foundations of a boycott campaign are true or not.

Of direct concern to current consumers are products that damage the well-being of customers or other humans. The tobacco industry is a clear case although the sale of the product is not illegal. But social responsibility is not black and white. How about makers of fatty foods, such as typically British fish and chips, an innocent-looking croissant, Belgian chocolates, or beer with all its social and health implications? Of increasing concern now is sustaining the world for future organisations, customers and the wider community. The very nature of some sectors, such as the auto or travel industry, has a direct impact upon climate change. Should makers of private cars be demonised or just the makers of gas-guzzling 4 × 4, luxury saloons and high performance cars? Sustainability is not an easy or straightforward issue to address.

Some companies resist environmental movements, budging only when forced by legislation or organised consumer outcries. More forward-looking companies, however, readily accept their responsibilities to the world around them. They view socially responsible actions as an opportunity to do well by doing good. They seek ways to profit by serving the best long-run interests of their customers and communities.

Some companies – such as Body Shop, Ben & Jerry's and others – practise 'caring capitalism', setting themselves apart by being civic-minded and responsible. They are building sustainability, social responsibility and action into their company value and mission statements. We revisit the critical topic of sustainable marketing in greater detail in Chapter 2.

Not-for-profit marketing

In the past, marketing has been most widely applied in the for-profit business sector. In recent years, however, marketing also has become a major part of the strategies of many not-for-profit organisations, such as colleges, hospitals, museums, zoos, symphony orchestras, political parties and even churches. Sound marketing can help them to attract membership and support.

Facing declining numbers of school-age children, private schools increasingly use marketing to compete for students and funds. With relatively miniscule budgets they are succeeding in persuading parents to pay high fees for an education that they could get free in the public sector. Many performing arts groups – even the state-funded Royal Shakespeare Company in Stratford-upon-Avon and London, which has seasonal sell-outs – face huge operating deficits that they must cover by targeting potential donors, corporate sponsors and members. Finally, many long-standing not-for-profit organisations – the YMCA, the Salvation Army, the Girl Guides – have lost members and are now modernising their missions and 'products' to attract more members and donors.[26]

Government agencies have also shown an increased interest in marketing. For example, where military service is voluntary, the armed forces have marketing plans to attract recruits to its different services. Other government agencies and charities are designing *social marketing campaigns* to encourage energy conservation and concern for the environment or to discourage smoking, excessive drinking and drug use. Across Europe the old utilities monopolies are being broken up and forced to compete within the European Union. Throughout Europe also there is a mish-mash of increasingly global companies competing with state-owned businesses to supply the services that are central to our everyday life. Chapter 13 focuses on not-for-profit marketing along with the marketing of services generally.

The electronic marketplace

The recent technology boom has created a new digital age. The explosive growth in computer, telecommunications, information, transportation and other technologies has had a major impact on the ways companies bring value to their customers.

Now, more than ever before, we are all connected to each other and to things near and far in the world around us. Where it once took weeks or months to travel across the world's oceans, we can now travel around the globe in hours. Where it once took days or weeks to receive news about important world events, we now see them live by satellite. Where it once took weeks to correspond with others in distant places, they are now only moments away by phone or the Internet.

The technology boom has created exciting new ways to learn about and track customers, and to create products and services tailored to individual customer needs. Technology is also helping companies to distribute products more efficiently and effectively, and to communicate with customers in large groups or one-to-one.

Through videoconferencing, marketing researchers at a company's headquarters in London can look in on focus groups in Chicago, Paris or Tokyo without ever stepping onto a plane. With only a few clicks of a mouse button, a direct marketer can tap into online data services to learn anything from what car you drive to what you read to what flavour of ice cream you prefer. Or, using today's powerful computers, marketers can create their own detailed customer databases and use them to target individual customers with offers designed to meet their specific needs.

Technology has also brought a new wave of communication and advertising tools – ranging from mobile phones, iPods, DVRs, websites and personal video recorders to satellite navigation, and much more. Marketers can use these tools to zero in on selected customers with carefully targeted messages. Through the Internet, customers can learn about, design, order and pay for products and services, without ever leaving home. Then, through the marvels of express delivery, they can receive their purchases in less than 24 hours. From virtual reality displays that test new products to online virtual stores that sell them, the technology boom is affecting every aspect of marketing.

The Internet

Today, the Internet links individuals and businesses of all types to each other and to information all around the world. It allows connections to information, entertainment and communication anytime, anywhere. Companies are using the Internet to build closer relationships with customers and marketing partners. Beyond competing in traditional marketplaces, they now have access to exciting new marketspaces.

The Internet has now become a truly global phenomenon. The number of Internet users worldwide is expected to reach 1.8 billion by 2010.[27] This growing and diverse Internet population means that all kinds of people are now going to the Web for information and to buy products and services. Today, online consumer buying is growing at a healthy rate. The world's consumers are forecast to purchase over $300bn of products and services online in 2010 with 175 million European consumers spending €1,500 a year on average.[28]

These days, it's hard to find a company that doesn't use the Web in a significant way. E-commerce has not only changed the way we do business but also created new businesses. Three purely online retailers – Amazon, eBay and Google – now have sales of over €1bn. Other businesses have grown as e-marketing allows more convenient, low-cost means of distribution.

Gambling is one of many activities that is highly regulated or banned in many countries. The Internet is giving companies in countries with more relaxed laws global reach as well as using scale and operational economies to give the punters more of a chance of winning.
SOURCE: Bear Design Ltd.

Consumers across the world are benefiting from Ryanair and easyJet's pioneering of low-cost flying (see the prelude case) that uses Internet-only selling.

Meanwhile, innovative 'bricks-and-mortar' companies have embraced e-marketing. They have ventured online to attract new customers and build stronger relationships with existing ones. For example, Tesco's low-tech approach to e-retailing has allowed it to grow to become the world's largest online grocery retailer. In the US, supermarket chain Safeway has now licensed Tesco's low-tech approach. Business-to-business e-commerce is also booming. Giants such as Siemens, Microsoft, Philips and many others have moved quickly to exploit the B-to-B power of the Internet.

In fact, e-marketing is now so established that it does not seem new. It cuts across all four elements of the marketing mix, since the electronic marketplace has its own products, prices and promotions. It has gone through a life-cycle of excessive exuberance and investment, crashing decline and failure, to more staid maturity. This is true of dot.com bubble companies, such as boo.com and pet.com, though this shakeout in the early 2000s had little influence on the inexorable growth in e-business in recent years.

With penetration of online retailing well into double figures, growth will not remain as meteoric as in the early years, but the average growth rate of online business is 15 per cent compared with 3 per cent for conventional channel users. Whether a retailer adopts a purely online operation or not, consumers increasingly use the Internet to check out products, services and prices before they buy. Many people visit the Jamjar site to check out new car prices and discounts before seeing a car dealer, but increasing numbers of people also buy through such sites. Before going to a concert or the theatre, hiring a car, booking a hotel or a flight, increasing numbers of customers are recognising that lastminute.com is quicker, easier and cheaper than buying direct or through an agent. E-business and online retailing are still small compared with conventional trade, but for how long?[29] We will explore the impact of the new digital age in future chapters, especially Chapter 18.

The global marketplace

As they are redefining their relationships with customers and partners, marketers are also taking a fresh look at the ways in which they connect with the broader world around them. In an increasingly smaller world, many marketers are now connected *globally* with their customers and marketing partners.

Today, almost every company, large or small, is touched in some way by global competition. A neighbourhood florist buys its flowers from nurseries in Ghana, an electronics manufacturer competes in its home markets with giant Japanese rivals, and it is becoming rare to ring a computer helpdesk in the UK and not talk to a highly competent computer wiz in India. A fledgling Internet retailer finds itself receiving orders from all over the world at the same time that a consumer-goods producer in the developed world introduces new products into emerging markets abroad.

Globalisation influences the marketing environment in two ways: firstly, in the continued growth in the proportion of a country's trade that is traded internationally; and secondly, in the disquiet many people feel about globalisation. In the last decade, world trade in merchandise and services each increased by an average of 6.5 per cent per annum – close to doubling over 10 years! Simultaneously, each region's trade was becoming less concentrated. Over the 10-year period, the proportion of international trade between European Union partners increased in total, but declined from 72 per cent to 67 per cent of EU trade. The main regions taking up the increased proportion of EU trade were the USA, the ex-Soviet bloc countries and China.

Firms have been challenged at home by the skilful marketing of Japanese, Korean and now Indian and Chinese multinationals. Companies such as Toyota, Mattel, Sony and Samsung have often outperformed their local competitors in numerous markets. Similarly, some older companies in a wide range of industries have developed truly global operations, making and selling their products worldwide. Nestlé, HSBC, Shell and Unilever were born of an earlier global age when European countries dominated the world. HSBC even stands for the Hong Kong and Shanghai Banking Corporation, a reminder of a colonial age. New global leaders, such as Amazon, MySpace, Nokia, IKEA and Vodafone, almost emerged from the start as global players with little of their history being local. Increasingly it is almost impossible to guess where brands are made and designed, who owns the company and where their headquarters are, and who cares?

Today, companies are not only trying to sell more of their locally produced goods in international markets, they also are buying more supplies and components abroad. For example, a top Paris fashion designer may not be French and may choose fabrics from Australian wool with designs printed in Italy. Design a dress and e-mail the drawing to a Hong Kong agent, who will place the order with a Chinese factory, use a London-based ad agency and sell most products in New York and Tokyo.

The implications for marketers of this growing international trade are changed competition as marketers from the world's regions compete, emergence of global supply chains as producers chase low-cost suppliers, and an increase in the proportion of trade with people outside one's own culture. Advances in information and communications technology are also making marketing operations global as call centres and product development move abroad.

With the rate of change, it is no wonder that special-interest groups, from trade unions seeking to protect local jobs to eco-warriors seeking to save the world, find globalisation disturbing. Globalisation is shifting wealth across the world but not in the way that many people fear. The annual average growth per head of population in less developed economies that are 'more globalised' averaged 4 per cent plus between 1995 and 2005. This compares with growth rates averaging 2 per cent for rich countries and 1 per cent for 'less globalised', less developed countries. As a consequence, the proportion of the world's population in poverty has declined from 56 per cent in 1980 to 23 per cent in 2005. There remains a very large tail of 1.1 billion people in poverty (down from 1.9 billion in 1980), mostly in sub-Saharan Africa, but the world is developing a huge, technologically sophisticated middle class as world incomes even out.

The more even distribution of the world's income adds an extra globalisation pressure facing marketers. Since the colonial era, world trade involved selling sophisticated goods to less developed countries in exchange for raw materials. Increasingly, marketing success means selling to countries that are technological equals and who have their own enterprises and innovations.[30]

Thus, global marketers face many challenges. Managers are increasingly taking a global, not just local, view of the company's industry, competitors and opportunities. They are asking: What is global marketing? How does it differ from domestic marketing? How do global competitors and forces affect our business? To what extent should we 'go global'?

Marketing in the noughties

In the 1980s Japan was pre-eminent as the world champion marketer with its global manufacturing and consumer electronics. In the nineties Japan stumbled but Europe remained strong with its luxury brands and liberated East European markets. Through the two decades, the US remained strong, trading upon its technological leadership and global consumer products. Now, in the 'noughties', some of Europe's leading economies are stagnating, along with Japan, and the engines for growth are the economic giants at the extremes of the wealth spectrum. At one end, the wealthy US benefits from its leadership of the hardware (Dell and Intel), software (Microsoft), services (Amazon and eBay) and social networks (MySpace and YouTube) of the e-revolution. At the other end, freshly unshackled China and India achieve double-digit growth, becoming global leaders in services and manufacturing. Within a few years the huge Chinese economy will match the US or the EU in its output of goods and the pollution it creates in making them.[31]

> A company's winning formula for the last decade would probably be its undoing in the next decade.

As the world spins through the first decade of the twenty-first century, dramatic changes are occurring in the world of marketing. Business pundits and politicians are referring to a new economy (see Real Marketing 1.2) within which firms have to think afresh about their marketing objectives and practices. Rapid changes can quickly make yesterday's winning strategies out of date.

real marketing

1.2

A new dawn?

Western Europe's material prosperity has soared more in the past 250 years than in the previous 1,000 (see Exhibit 1.1), thanks to industrialisation. Arguably, this remarkable phenomenon will not go on forever, given that the frontiers of technology and science are moving closer. Or, natural or man-made environmental disasters may intervene. Nonetheless, scientific progress is certain to continue, harnessing technological progress that, in turn, sustains economic growth and improves living standards. For example, America's recent economic 'miracle' – rapid growth, subdued inflation and low unemployment – has been attributed to the information technology revolution. While America grew, Europe lagged. Will Western Europe now also partake of a 'new economy' and, if so, what is the shape of things to come?

Knowledge? Service? Digital? E-economy? M-economy?

Business pundits and politicians say that our countries' economic welfare will increasingly rely on wealth creation in knowledge-based, high value-added industries, such as automotive, technology hardware, software, electronics and pharmaceuticals, and those employing highly skilled knowledge workers, such as finance, the media and education. Many talk about the 'knowledge economy', driven by skyrocketing investment in knowledge. Witness the acceleration in the number of patents filed in the last decade. Thanks to landmark legal battles, businesses can now patent a raft of new areas of technology, from biotechnology, genes and financial services, to consulting, software, business methods and the Internet.

The EU's 2002 'Lisbon strategy' recognised the region lag in the Research and Development (R&D) that creates the discoveries upon which the knowledge-based industries survive. The aim was for the EU to increase investment in R&D to 3 per cent of Gross Domestic Product (GNP). Several years down the line Janez Potocnik, European commissioner for science and research, had good reason to be disappointed. At present growth rates the EU's public and private spending on R&D is set to crawl from 1.93 per cent of GDP in 2003 to a miserly 2.2 per cent in 2010, well short of the 'Lisbon strategy'. Mr Potocnik forecast that 'If current trends continue, Europe will lose the opportunity to become a leading global knowledge-based economy.' He also warned that China's R&D spending is increasing at a double-digit percentage rate and was set to overtake the EU in the percentage of GDP spent on R&D by 2009–10. With an R&D spend of 33 per cent of the world's total, Europe is second in R&D spend to the Americas (43 per cent) and ahead of the Asia Pacific region (24 per cent), but for how long? The European Commission argue for more EU direct investment in R&D, although European R&D is already more dependent upon state support than in other

...1.2

regions. Businesses finance 74 per cent of R&D in Japan, 63 per cent in the US and only 56 per cent in the EU.

Fortunately there are high spots. Sweden, which spends 3.8 per cent of GDP on R&D, tops the international league table, followed closely by Finland (3.7 per cent), then Japan (3.0), the US (2.7) and Germany (2.5). Austria, Britain, Denmark, France, Iceland and the Netherlands all spend close to the EU average of 2 per cent. This pattern follows the investment by leading high-tech businesses in the countries: Finland's Nokia, Sweden's Ericsson and Germany's Siemens, Mercedes, BMW and VW. The top 100 R&D spending companies together account for 61 per cent of all the world's R&D spend. Only in the US and UK have medium-sized businesses made a significant impact on overall R&D investment, but such businesses rarely stay medium-sized for long.

Europe looks better when examining the overall knowledge that includes services. By this measure, about 50 per cent of the EU's *total* business output is from its burgeoning knowledge economy. In spending on R&D, investment in software and both public and private spending on education, Sweden tops the list again, with an investment reaching 11 per cent of its GDP, followed by France (10 per cent), then Britain and the US (both 8 per cent). Japan's investment of 7 per cent is meagre compared to the EU's average spend of just under 8 per cent of GDP.

The OECD suggests that the proportion of business R&D spending accounted for by services rose nearly five-fold to 20 per cent over the past two decades. Moreover, nearly 20 per cent of global trade is now in services, rather than manufactured goods. According to the World Trade Organization (WTO), global exports of commercial services totalled $2.4 trillion in 2005, of which the EU accounted for some 46 per cent (an increase of 6 per cent in three years), compared to North America's decline

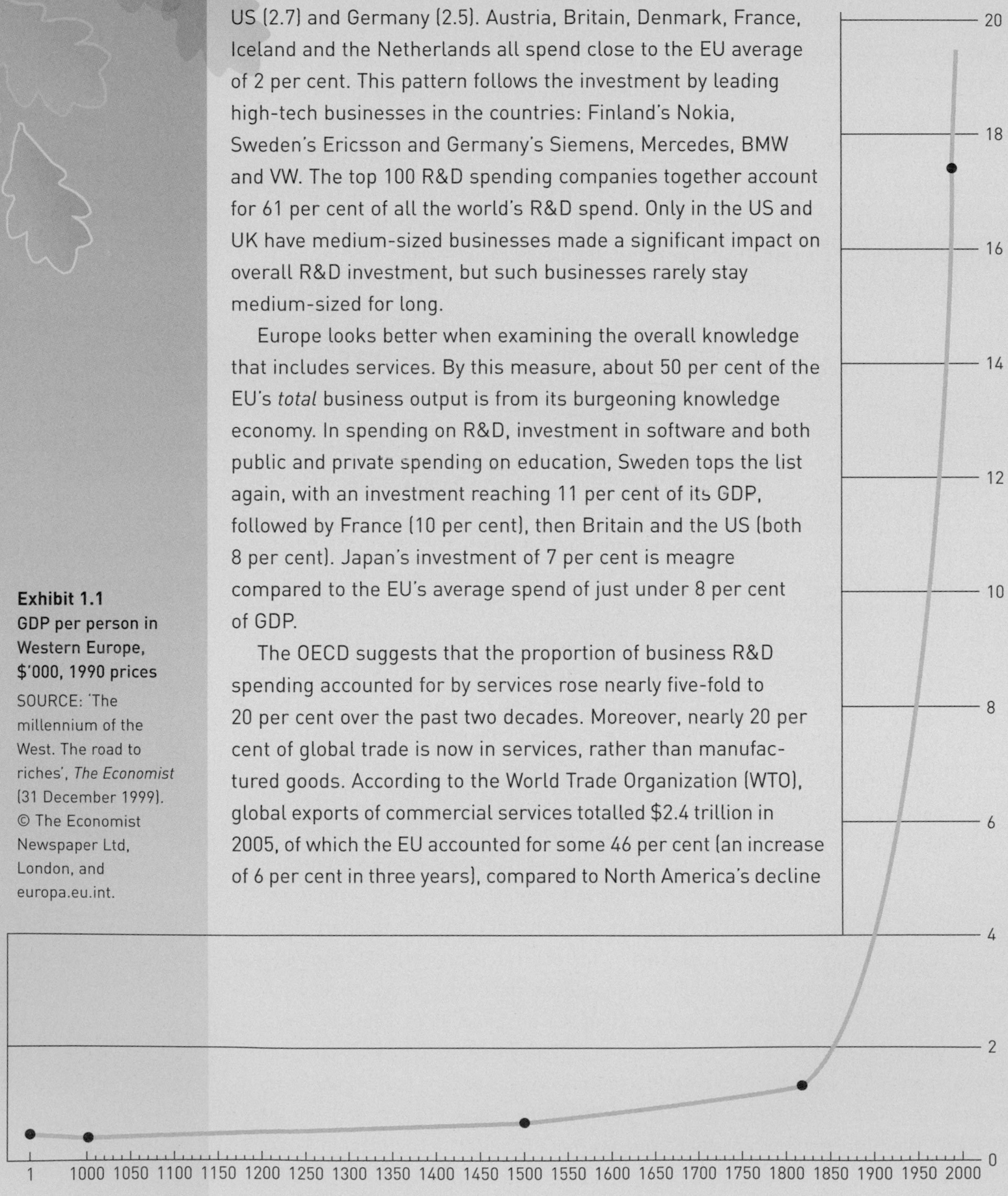

Exhibit 1.1
GDP per person in Western Europe, $'000, 1990 prices
SOURCE: 'The millennium of the West. The road to riches', *The Economist* (31 December 1999). © The Economist Newspaper Ltd, London, and europa.eu.int.

to 16 per cent share. Western Europe is advancing towards not only a knowledge economy, but also an increasingly dominant service economy.

What of the Internet and 'E'-economy? Although western European firms are increasing their investment in information technology (IT), the EU investment of nearly 4 per cent of GDP lags behind America's 5 per cent. However, Sweden at 7 per cent, the UK 6 per cent and Luxembourg outspend the US. At the end of the last decade the US had five times as many households per 1,000 population with access to the Internet. Now the gap is closing. Nevertheless, there is high variation across the EU. The EU is ahead of the US in 'wireless technology'. With a much higher use of mobile phones, which are touted to become the most widely used link to the Internet, M (mobile)-commerce is expected to flourish.

New digital products are showing signs of pulling Japan out of its long recession. World sales of DVD players and DVDs overtook those of VCRs in 2002, and satellite digital TV reception is already the dominant technology. Other substitutions are occurring. Digital camcorders and cameras overtook sales of their conventional brethren in 2004. HDTV and in-car GPS navigation are currently expensive but prices are coming down as production capacity rises and the products become less exclusive. Just breaking are digital radios and active GPS systems that warn drivers of hazards and speed restrictions. The question is, how many of these gizmos are made in the EU?

To reap the benefits of the E, M and digital economies, EU politicians have to make far-reaching structural, tax, labour market and capital market reforms. These will try to create flexible, open and efficient markets where business entrepreneurship and innovation can flourish. Europe itself is changing, for that matter. The euro zone creates a big single capital market, facilitating business's efforts to raise money for investment. *Slowly*, things are moving in the right direction: tax cuts in Germany, France and the Netherlands; deregulation of industries, such as utilities and telecommunications; and countries like Spain making their labour markets more flexible, although the effectiveness of these policies is not showing in the larger euro economies.

Many forces are working together to direct the EU's business revolution. From the Internet and information technology, to the pressures for restructuring and deregulation, responsive countries and businesses will emerge the winners. Whether in terms of knowledge, service, E, M or digital economy, Europe's economic transformation may hope to yield a capitalism that is more transparent, more efficient and, most importantly, more rewarding for all that partake in it. Europe is moving in the right direction but at a fraction of the speed of competing regions. The European commissioner Janez Potočnik's report on the EU so far might say 'could do better', or maybe 'must do better'.

SOURCES: Chris Anderson, 'The great crossover' in *The World in 2007, The Economist* (16 November 2006), London; Clive Cookson, Europe: 'R&D spending falls further behind target', *Financial Times* (24 October 2005); World News: Geoff Dyer, 'China overtakes Japan for R&D', *Financial Times* (4 December 2006); Raphael Minder, 'Chinese poised to outstrip Europe on R&D', *Financial Times* (10 October 2005); Clive Cookson, 'US widens gap with Europe on R&D', *Financial Times* (30 October 2006); also see www.wto.org (World Trade Organization); see www.europa.eu.int (European Union) and www.wto.org for regular updates on world trade.

As management thought-leader, the late Peter Drucker, observed, a company's winning formula for the last decade would probably be its undoing in the next decade. The rapid pace of change means that the firm's ability to change is an imperative rather than a competitive advantage.

From time immemorial people have seen their era as being one of uncertainty, discontinuity, turbulence and threat. 'Everything flows and nothing stays', said the Greek philosopher Heraclitus in 513 BC. Heraclitus also anticipated Peter Drucker's call for continuous change, explaining 'You can't step twice into the same river'. The popularity of retro-look products, such as the VW Beetle, Mini, Chrysler PT Cruiser and Ford Thunderbird, shows consumers have a yearning for the perceived security, simplicity and certainty of the past. A romantic view of the 1950s and 1960s forgets the Cold War, a Europe divided, Vietnam, Korea, race riots, and fear over the emergence of heroes who terrified the establishment: Elvis Presley, Chuck Berry, James Dean, The Rolling Stones, The Who, Jimi Hendrix, Muhammad Ali and Bob Dylan. In reality, times are always changing and marketing is the interface between organisations and that ever-changing environment.

Ever-changing markets are not a threat, but the lifeblood of marketing. They create opportunities for existing brands to refresh, opportunities for new products, new ways of communicating to customers and completely new markets:

- **An exciting brand**: rather than resisting change, the BBC championed digital radio, broadcasting an increased range of high sound quality digital channels to stimulate digital radio manufacture. Also, they have seen a huge rise in their overseas audience in the Middle East, where they are up against Al-Jazeera International, and in online news channels.[32]

- **New products**: seeing a market shift to small cars and retro appeal, BMW relaunched the Mini. With Europe's stagnant market, the Mini has become BMW's saviour in recent years. It is even succeeding in the USA where the 1960s Mini was never marketed.

- **Communications**: globalisation has allowed companies to keep in touch with their customers 24/7. Make an early morning telephone enquiry or book an airline ticket and the odds are you will be talking to someone in India. Do not expect a local accent to give you a clue; training takes care of that.

- **New markets**: not long ago few had heard of Nokia. The company grew with the emergence of mobile telecommunications and recognising mobile phones as a fashion accessory. Meanwhile, VW's dominant share (38 per cent) of China's motor vehicle market – growing at 40 per cent a year – is keeping it in profits while other car makers suffer.

The remainder of this chapter examines the components of marketing activity that link the world's changing environment to marketing strategies and actions that fulfil the needs of tomorrow's customers. It introduces each chapter of this book and shows how they follow a sequence that builds from an understanding of the environment surrounding marketing to creating marketing activities.

Marketing now (Part 1)

Marketing (Chapter 1)

'Business has only two basic functions – marketing and innovation', said Peter Drucker. Such claims can seduce marketers into seeing themselves as superior to or independent of other business functions. That view is incorrect. Marketing exists as part of an organisation whose parts are interdependent. Drucker emphasised the importance of selling and inventing what people want, rather than taking the production or sales concept of marketing and trying to sell what the producer wants. For an organisation to survive, all its parts must work together for the good of all.

 Business has only two basic functions – marketing and innovation.

Sustainable marketing: marketing ethics and social responsibility (Chapter 2)

Marketing is most often associated with capitalism, an often questioned socio-economic philosophy that took several knocks in the first few years of this millennium. In particular, the stock market collapse across the world, the flawed governance that allowed WorldCom, Enron and Vivendi to fail so catastrophically, and worldwide best-sellers such as *No Logo* and *Fast Food Nation*, question the foundation of modern business and marketing.[33]

The stock market collapse is not a marketing issue, although many small investors and savers probably suffered because of the overselling of risky investments. Similarly, marketing was not a central contributor to the most conspicuous corporate collapses. However, the business failures and the popular questioning of marketing make even more important an understanding of the relationship between business and society. The societal marketing concept starts to address the social dimensions of marketing. Additionally, the very definition of marketing, '*a social and managerial process by which individuals and groups obtain what they need and want through creating and exchanging products and value with others*', emphasises that the process should be an exchange that fulfils wants and needs. Furthermore, we know that the best marketing performance comes from satisfying customers so that they return to buy more and pass on the good news to their friends. Social responsibility is not just important to marketing: it is central to marketing.

Sustainable marketing draws attention to the need to think beyond the current needs of the organisation and its current customers. Past generations have passed on a great gift of wealth and health to an increasing proportion of those who live now. But what value is success and satisfaction now if it destroys the organisation and opportunities for our children, and our children's children? The forward-looking company must look towards its own future and tomorrow's customers, as well as today's. What is more, concern for the environment has created one of the fastest growing markets for energy-saving and alternatives to fossil fuels. The innovation that has fired success in the past has now turned its energy and creativity to a less damaged world.

A second dimension of marketing goes beyond commercial exchange. Marketing is increasingly used to achieve ends that are not commercial. Non-governmental organisations (NGOs) use marketing to draw attention to causes, to raise money to support their cause and to distribute to those in need. Both NGOs and government agencies use marketing to promote their activities. The Samaritans use advertising to alert those in need that there is someone to talk to and willing to help when they are desperate, and advertising is used to try to reduce accidents from drinking and driving. Besides reducing suffering, campaigns that reduce accidents are far more economical than the medical emergency and repair costs of accidents.

Strategic marketing (Chapter 3)

Marketing is one part of the strategy of an organisation where marketing of the strategic plan drives the company forward. The **marketing process** in Figure 1.7 shows marketing's role and activities in organisations and the forces influencing marketing strategy. The numbers in the figure refer to chapters covering the issues in this text.

The marketing activities that most people manage concern a small part of a large organisation with many other products and markets. For example, Anglo-Dutch Unilever has business units ranging from spreads and cooking products, marketing Rama, Flora Pro-activ and others, to prestige fragrances including Very Valentino and House of Curreti. All share the company's purpose: '. . . to serve consumers in a unique and effective way'. Subsidiary to Unilever's overall strategy are strategies for each business unit and each part of the world. Within those will be plans for 'I Can't Believe It's Not Butter' and Calvin Klein fragrances.

Marketing process—The process of (1) analysing marketing opportunities; (2) selecting target markets; (3) developing the marketing mix; and (4) managing the marketing effort.

41

Figure 1.7 Influences on marketing strategy, showing the numbers of the chapters in which they appear in this text

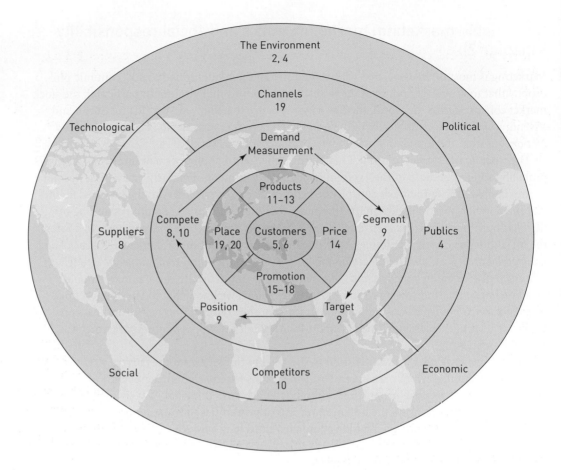

Chapter 3 starts by looking at the broad strategy of an organisation and works down from a company's overall strategy to the construction of marketing plans for individual products or brands. Marketing plans exist alongside an organisation's other plans. Operational plans set production levels for the mix of products made. Many marketing activities, such as 'buy one, get one free' price promotions, lead to hugely changed sales volumes and so need coordinating with production and distribution schedules so that shelves are stocked when campaigns run. Meeting increased production schedules will need extra staff and raw materials, hence influencing personnel plans and raw materials purchasing. More strategic marketing issues, such as developing new products to fit changing market needs, influence a company's research and development effort and financial strategy if a new product needs new production facilities or an expensive launch.

With limited resources and overlapping demand, the promotion of one product, such as cholesterol-reducing Flora Pro-activ, could influence the sales of Becel, another spread with a health appeal. These interactions form an important part of strategy, marketing and planning. Two particular issues are the relationship of marketing to other business functions and the various new ways in which marketing is organised.

Markets (Part 2)

Since marketing is about making and selling what people want to buy, the most important first stage in marketing planning understands the marketing environment: the setting where marketing takes place. This has two levels: first, the macroenvironment of broad societal forces that influence a business; and second, the microenvironment of forces closer to the company that affects its ability to serve its customers. These are the subject of Part 2 of this book.

The marketing environment (Chapter 4)

The macro- and microenvironment are largely issues that a company cannot control, but they can have a huge influence on an organisation's performance. They are the subject of Chapter 4 of this book. PEST analysis systematises an examination of the Political, Economic, Social and Technological elements of the macroenvironment. Marketers, like most groups of people, play a part in setting the PEST agenda, but in most cases their influence is small. The exception is organisations whose contributions to national economies are very large, such as food or extraction companies in the Third World, or lobby groups, such as French farmers or the American gun lobby.

Most organisations need to observe the macroenvironment to understand how they need to adjust to it. For example, the economic macroenvironment is causing many charities difficulties. Stock market declines are reducing their earnings from their investments and the economic pinch is influencing large donors, including governments, who arc less willing to give. This is throwing the charities back onto campaigns based on small donors or profits from charity shops whose contribution is less cyclical.

Several features of the PEST environment are having a huge influence on many markets. The economics of high house prices, available technology for planned parenting and a social change in the number of career women mean that people are setting up home later and having fewer children. The combined influence of these macroenvironmental factors will hugely change our world in the coming decades as populations age, children become rarer and dependency ratios increase. More immediately, many markets are changing as young adults are lingering with their parents until they are in their thirties and many people choose to be DINKYs (Double Income, No Kids Yet) rather than face the social and economic costs of parenting: big cars, big houses, child care fees, etc. This substitution of personal consumption for the costs of bringing up children is driving the demand for many luxury products (two-seat cars, designer clothes, clubs, loft living, restaurants, long-haul holidays).

As the macroenvironment shifts, so does the microenvironment. The media are changing in order to provide channels that serve young wealthy consumers; food retailers move into town to serve the YUPPY (Young Urban Professionals) market. In many cases, the huge, steady changes in the marketing environment are conspicuous but still too fast for those marketers who do not respond quickly to those changes. Hence the rapid decline of Toys 'R' Us and the steady decline of Mothercare. Other organisations such as Saga, which provides holidays, radio stations, insurance, etc. for older people, are doing well.

Consumer markets (Chapter 5)

To succeed in today's competitive marketplace, companies must be customer centred – winning customers from competitors by delivering greater value. However, before it can satisfy consumers, a company must first understand their needs and wants. Sound marketing requires analysis and understanding of customers' wants and needs.

> " To succeed in today's competitive marketplace, companies must be customer centred "

All marketing ends with consumers and the study of consumers is the subject of Chapter 5. Commercial organisations survive when enough people exchange enough of their assets for the product or service that an organisation offers. Often the asset is money, but it could also be debt to a credit company or products given in part exchange. This transaction gives suppliers the revenue they need to survive, and without it marketing has failed, but marketers are involved in streams of decisions, actions and behaviour before and after that transaction. The same is true for marketers in non-profit organisations, although in those cases an action, such as visiting a doctor or not drinking and driving, is the pivotal point.

To develop marketing strategies and plans, and to get ideas for new offerings, marketers explore the whole of consumer behaviour from well before to well after the pivotal transaction. Buyer behaviour starts with a consumer's social position, lifestyle and preferences even before there is a glimmer of a need or want for the product being marketed. Then, even if the purchase is as simple as a drink, there is a process of awareness of a product, interest in some more than others, desire for a particular form of need fulfilment, and only then, action. During this same process, consumers make decisions about where to get the drink – the cold water tap, the fridge, a convenience store or a bar? Marketers can fail anywhere in this process.

The richness of marketing stems from its central involvement in two of the most complex entities that we know of: the human brain and the society in which we live. In trying to understand consumers, marketers draw on all sources of knowledge: from psychology in understanding how we perceive objects to physics in understanding how we can make drink containers we can use on the move; from sociology in understanding how our friends influence our purchases to semiotics in understanding how we respond to symbols.

The result of this diversity is no one model of consumer behaviour but a vast wealth of ways of informing our thinking. Any of these can help us see why marketing campaigns are failing to reveal radical new marketing ideas. For example, recent years have seen two new products that invigorated orange drinks, a tired old commodity. Sunny Delight gave orange drinks a new sweeter, smoother taste that appealed to children and for a while outsold Coca-Cola in many markets. Tango's success came from advertising that made the product appealing to young men.

The study of consumer behaviour does not end with a purchase. What makes people satisfied or dissatisfied? Increasingly marketers are drawing on anthropology to understand how we relate to products.[34] We need to know how they are used. Gift purchases are very different from products purchased for self use. Companies want to know how to establish long-lasting relationships with consumers. This interest in the period after a purchase makes the study of consumers a circular rather than linear activity. People's attitudes and lifestyles are influenced by past purchases, and each passage through awareness, interest, desire and action influences all other purchase decisions.

Business-to-business marketing (Chapter 6)

All marketing ends with consumers, yet most marketing and sales are from business to business. Chapter 6 examines such markets. The reason why business-to-business markets are greater than consumer markets is the number of stages a product goes through from being a raw material or produce to the final consumer. Even a simple product, such as a magazine bought at a kiosk, has passed through several stages. Foresters sell logs to a paper maker; the paper maker sells to a printer working under contract to a publisher. The magazines then go to a specialist wholesaler who delivers them to the retailer. Until the final purchase, all the transactions are business-to-business. Moreover, the number of business-to-business transactions does not end there. The forester will hire contract loggers and pay a company to transport the logs to the paper maker; lawyers draw up contracts between the businesses involved. Each business will use commercial banks and maybe consultants to help them perform better.

Business-to-business marketing is not solely about commercial enterprise. Buyers and sellers are often governments and public-sector organisations, like schools or hospitals or charities. All share the same features in having complex buying processes involving many people with different motives who may come and go as the buying process continues. There are professional buyers and negotiators in the buying process, but many other actors play a role and the desires of the individuals concerned vary. Additionally, business-to-business markets are often international and involve overseas governments. Each person in a business-to-business market has the same emotions, needs and wants as a consumer, but they are overlaid with an extra layer of complexity.

An increasing proportion of marketing is social. Suicide is most common among young men. This ad in a music magazine could encourage those in need to call for help and raise awareness for fund raising.

SOURCE: www.samaritans.org.

Marketing research (Chapter 7)

Marketing research is a wide range of methods and tools used to help marketers understand markets. It is the subject of Chapter 7. Market research follows the breadth of consumer behaviour and business-to-business marketing in having a huge armoury of techniques to help with marketing questions. These range from anthropological studies where observers track a household's behaviour to routine mass surveys of thousands of retailers. The output can vary from descriptive analyses of a few customers' responses to a new product concept to mathematical models that forecast advertising effects or future demand.

Market research is such a specialised part of marketing that it is usually done by specialists, within either a marketer's organisation or an agency. Like advertising, market research is such a distinctive and important part of marketing that it has professional bodies, qualifications and an industry of its own. Within that industry, marketers can choose among a whole range of suppliers with different skills. Marketers may not conduct their own market research but they commission it and act upon its results. The quality of the marketing decisions depends upon the quality of the marketing research on which they are based and its interpretation. It is, therefore, essential that marketers appreciate market research and what it can do.

Core strategy (Part 3)

Strategic marketing, the process of aligning the strengths of an organisation with groups of customers it can serve, is the subject of Part 3 of this text. It affects the whole direction and future of an organisation, so knowledge of the macro- and microenvironments and the markets served needs to inform the process. Markets are also busy so that competitors are also trying to find ways of capturing more customers or retaining their own. Marketing strategy, therefore, has three interdependent parts: segmenting markets into groups that can be served, ways of developing advantageous relations with those customers, and strategies to handle competitors.

Relationship marketing (Chapter 8)

Marketing management's crucial task is to create profitable relationships with customers. Chapter 8 explores how to build those relationships. Until recently, customer relationship management was defined narrowly as a customer database management activity. By this definition, it involves managing detailed information about individual customers and carefully managing customer contacts in order to maximise customer loyalty. More recently, however, relationship management has taken on a broader meaning. In this broader sense, relationship management is the overall process of building and maintaining profitable customer relationships by delivering superior customer value and satisfaction. Thus, today's companies are going beyond designing strategies to *attract* new customers and create *transactions* with them. They are using customer relationship management to *retain* current customers and build profitable, long-term *relationships* with them. The new view is that marketing is the science and art of finding, retaining *and* growing profitable customers. Companies are also realising that losing a customer means losing more than a single sale. It means losing the entire stream of purchases that the customer would make over a lifetime of patronage.

The key to building lasting customer relationships is to create superior customer value and satisfaction. To gain an advantage, the company must offer greater value to chosen target segments, either by charging lower prices than competitors or by offering more benefits to justify higher prices. However, if the company positions the product as *offering* greater value, it must *deliver* greater value. Effective positioning begins with actually *differentiating* the company's marketing offer so that it gives consumers more value than is offered by the competition. Satisfied customers are more likely to be loyal customers, and loyal customers are more likely to give the company a larger share of their business.

Segmentation and positioning (Chapter 9)

Customers are people, so differ considerably. Companies know that they cannot satisfy all consumers in a given market – at least, not all consumers in the same way. There are too many kinds of consumer with too many kinds of need, and some companies are in a better position than others to serve some groups of customers better. Consequently, companies use **market segmentation** to divide the total market. They then choose **market segments** and design strategies for profitably serving chosen segments. This process involves market segmentation, targeting and positioning. These are the subject of Chapter 9.

From the complexity of humans, it follows that there are many ways in which markets segment, and finding a new way of segmenting markets or a new segment can be the breakthrough that creates a market success. Simple criteria, like age, gender and social class, do little to inform marketers, since even among middle-class teenage boys there is a huge variety in interest: sporty football fanatics, video junkies, punk musicians, etc. Only multi-criteria approaches reveal segments such as GUPPYs (gay urban professionals), high-spending groups who start and nurture many new trends in music, fashion and entertainment and whose presence in a community is a measure of its creative potential.

> ❝ Simple criteria, like age, gender and social class, do little to inform marketers. ❞

Market targeting involves evaluating each market segment's attractiveness and selecting one or more segments to enter. An organisation evaluates its strengths relative to the competition and considers how many segments it can serve effectively. **Market positioning** gives a product a clear, distinctive and desirable place in the minds of target consumers compared with competing products. A **product's position** is the place the product occupies in consumers' minds. If a product is perceived to be exactly like another product on the market, consumers would have no reason to buy it. Market positioning can be the key to success, such as a toy shop being marketed as the Early Learning Centre. Clearly, such an offering has to be more than just a name. To appeal to parents and their children, the store concentrates on educational toys and books, avoiding heavily merchandised products (such as Barbie or Disney) or electrical toys.

The company can position a product on only one important differentiating factor or on several. However, positioning on too many factors can result in consumer confusion or disbelief. Once the company has chosen a desired position, it must take steps to deliver and communicate that position to target consumers.

Competitive strategy (Chapter 10)

Providing excellent value and customer service is a necessary but not sufficient means of succeeding in the marketplace. Besides embracing the needs of consumers, marketing strategies must build an advantage over the competition. The company must consider its size and industry position, and then decide how to position itself to gain the strongest possible competitive advantage. Chapter 10 explains how to do this.

The design of competitive marketing strategies begins with competitor analysis. The company constantly compares the value and customer satisfaction delivered by its products, prices, channels and promotion with those of its close competitors. In this way, it can discern areas of potential advantage and disadvantage. The company must formally or informally monitor the competitive environment to answer these and other important questions: Who are our competitors? What are their objectives and strategies? What are their strengths and weaknesses? How will they react to different competitive strategies we might use?

Which competitive marketing strategy a company adopts depends on its industry position. A firm that dominates a market can adopt one or more of several **market leader** strategies.

Market segmentation—Dividing a market into distinct groups of buyers with different needs, characteristics or behaviour, who might require separate products or marketing mixes.

Market segment—A group of consumers who respond in a similar way to a given set of marketing stimuli.

Market targeting—The process of evaluating each market segment's attractiveness and selecting one or more segments to enter.

Market positioning—Arranging for a product to occupy a clear, distinctive and desirable place relative to competing products in the minds of target consumers. Formulating competitive positioning for a product and a detailed marketing mix.

Product's position—The way the product is defined by consumers on important attributes – the place the product occupies in consumers' minds relative to competing products.

Market leader—The firm in an industry with the largest market share; it usually leads other firms in price changes, new product introductions, distribution coverage and promotion spending.

There is an interesting dichotomy in the food market. Alongside the desire and increasing demand for organic and unadulterated food is a market for scientific functional foods, such as Danone Actimel.
SOURCE: The Advertising Archives.

Market challenger—A runner-up firm in an industry that is fighting hard to increase its market share.

Market follower—A runner-up firm in an industry that wants to hold its share without rocking the boat.

Market nicher—A firm in an industry that serves small segments that the other firms overlook or ignore.

Well-known leaders include Nescafé, Perrier, Swatch, Chanel, Johnnie Walker, Coca-Cola, McDonald's, Marlboro, Komatsu (large construction equipment), Sony, Nokia, Lego and Shell.

Market challengers are runner-up companies that aggressively attack competitors to get more market share. For example, Lexus challenges Mercedes, adidas challenges Nike, and Airbus challenges Boeing. The challenger might attack the market leader, other firms of its own size, or smaller local and regional competitors. Some runner-up firms will choose to follow rather than challenge the market leader. Firms using **market follower** strategies seek stable market shares and profit by following competitors' product offers, prices and marketing programmes. Smaller firms in a market, or even larger firms that lack established positions, often adopt **market nicher** strategies. They specialise in serving market niches that large competitors overlook or ignore.

Market nichers avoid direct confrontations with the big companies by specialising along market, customer, product or marketing-mix lines. Through clever niching, low-share firms in an industry can be as profitable as their large competitors. Two regions of Europe are particularly strong in cultivating strong niche players: Germany for medium-sized specialist engineering firms and northern Italy's fashion industry.

The marketing mix (Parts 4 to 7)

Once the company has chosen its overall competitive marketing strategy, it is ready to begin planning the details of the marketing mix. The marketing mix, one of the dominant ideas in modern marketing, is covered in Parts 4 to 7 of this book.

The **marketing mix** is the set of controllable tactical marketing tools that the firm blends to produce the response it wants in the target market. The marketing mix consists of everything the firm can do to influence the demand for its product. The many possibilities gather into four groups of variables known as the 'four Ps': product, price, place and promotion.[35] Figure 1.8 shows the marketing tools under each P.

Product means the totality of 'goods and services' that the company offers the target market. The product is the subject of the three chapters in Part 4 of this book.

> The Renault Clio 'product' is nuts, bolts, spark plugs, pistons, headlights and many other parts. Renault offers several Clio styles and dozens of optional features. The car comes fully serviced, with a comprehensive warranty and financing that is as much a part of the product as the exhaust pipe. Increasingly, the most profitable part of the business for car companies is the loan that they offer to car buyers.

Price is what customers pay to get the product. It is covered in this book's Part 5.

> Renault suggests retail prices that its dealers might charge for each car, but dealers rarely charge the full asking price. Instead, they negotiate the price with each customer. They offer discounts, trade-in allowances and credit terms to adjust for the current competitive situation and to bring the price into line with the buyer's perception of the car's value.

Marketing mix—The set of controllable tactical marketing tools – product, price, place and promotion – that the firm blends to produce the response it wants in the target market.

Product—Anything that can be offered to a market for attention, acquisition, use or consumption that might satisfy a want or need. It includes physical objects, services, persons, places, organisations and ideas.

Price—The amount of money charged for a product or service, or the sum of the values that consumers exchange for the benefits of having or using the product or service.

Figure 1.8 The four Ps: the marketing mix

Marketing mix			
Product	Price	Promotion	Place
Variety	List price	Advertising	Channels
Quality	Discounts	Promotions	Coverage
Design	Allowances	Personal selling	Assortments
Features	Payment period	Publicity	Locations
Brand name	Credit terms		Inventory
Packaging			Transport
Services			
Warranties			

Target market

Promotion—Activities that communicate the product or service and its merits to target customers and persuade them to buy.

Promotion means activities that communicate the merits of the product and persuade target customers to buy it. The communications landscape is changing rapidly. Technological advances including the Internet and new digital technologies are spawning new 'market spaces' where companies can create and communicate customer value and sustain long-lasting customer relationships. While they do not replace traditional promotion tools, such as mass advertising, sales promotions or personal selling, online and new media channels are forming an increasing proportion of marketing communications. Part 6 of this book devotes four chapters to marketing communications.

Renault spends millions on advertising each year to tell consumers about the company and its products. Its website provides further information about the company and is designed to communicate with diverse target audiences, from customers and suppliers to analysts and the media. Dealership salespeople assist potential buyers and persuade them that a Renault is the car for them. Renault and its dealers offer special promotions – sales, cash rebates, low financing rates – as added purchase incentives.

Although most cars are still bought from dealers, an increasing proportion of car manufacturers' promotional expenditure is on e-marketing. Visit any car manufacturer's web pages and you see why. A customer who visits the Clio's web pages is already well down the buying cycle. At this stage of readiness to buy, an interaction with an entertaining and appropriate website is far more involving than any conventional ad and will certainly engage a customer's interest for more time than a single TV commercial, poster or press advert.

Place—All the company activities that make the product or service available to target customers.

Place includes company activities that make the product available to target consumers. Place is covered in the final Part 7 of this book and covers two dimensions of place. Firstly, it discusses place in terms of physical distribution and conventional retailing in channelling products from the producer to the consumer. And secondly, we examine the special challenges facing marketers who compete in the global marketplace.

Most customers still go to dealers to see, consider and test the car they want to buy. The Renault Clio may be the exact car a customer wants but lack of care at the dealers can cause hard-won enquirers to switch. Also critical is delivering the customer's treasured acquisition with speed and in a pristine condition. For Renault, like all manufacturers of products with high development costs, global marketing is essential to achieve the level of sales to recoup development costs. Equally, Renault no longer competes with other French, or even European, cars but with the best in the world. Today, every day is like an Olympic final.

An effective marketing programme blends the marketing mix elements into a coordinated programme designed to achieve the company's marketing objectives. The marketing mix constitutes the company's tactical toolkit for establishing strong positioning in target markets. However, note that the four Ps represent the sellers' view of the marketing tools available for influencing buyers. From a consumer viewpoint, each marketing tool must deliver a customer benefit. One marketing expert suggests that companies should view the four Ps as the customer's four Cs:[36]

Four Ps	Four Cs
Product	Customer needs and wants
Price	Cost to the customer
Promotion	Communication
Place	Convenience

Winning companies are those that meet customer needs economically and conveniently and with effective communication.

So, what is marketing? Pulling it all together

At the start of this chapter, Figure 1.1 presented a simple model of the marketing process. Now that we have discussed all of the steps in the process, Figure 1.9 presents an expanded model that will help you pull it all together. What is marketing? Simply put, marketing is the process of building profitable customer relationships by creating value for customers and capturing value in return.

The first four steps of the marketing process focus on creating value for customers. The company first gains a full understanding of the marketplace by researching customer needs and managing marketing information. It then designs a customer-driven marketing strategy based on the answers to two simple questions. The first question is 'What customers will we serve?' (market segmentation and targeting). Good marketing companies know that they cannot serve all customers in every way. Instead, they need to focus their resources on the customers they can serve best and most profitably. The second marketing strategy question is 'How can we best serve targeted customers?' (differentiation and positioning). Here, the marketer outlines a value proposition that spells out what values the company will deliver in order to win target customers.

With its marketing strategy decided, the company now constructs an integrated marketing programme – consisting of a blend of the four marketing mix elements, or the four Ps – that transforms the marketing strategy into real value for customers. The figure above presents this most famous of marketing acronyms. The company develops product offers and creates strong brand identities for them. It prices these offers to create real customer value and distributes the offers to make them available to target consumers. Finally, the company designs promotion programmes that communicate the value proposition to target consumers and persuade them to act on the market offering.

Perhaps the most important step in the marketing process involves building value-laden, profitable relationships with target customers. Throughout the process, marketers practise customer relationship management to create customer satisfaction and delight. In creating customer value and relationships, however, the company cannot go it alone. It must work closely with marketing

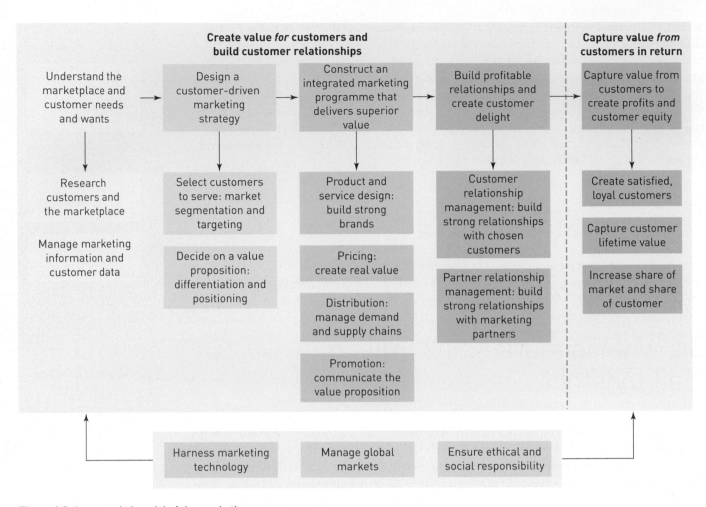

Figure 1.9 An expanded model of the marketing process

partners both inside the company and throughout the marketing system. Thus, beyond practising good customer relationship management, firms must also practise good partner relationship management.

The first four steps in the marketing process create value *for* customers. In the final step, the company reaps the rewards of its strong customer relationships by capturing value *from* customers. Delivering superior customer value creates highly satisfied customers who will buy more and will buy again. This helps the company to capture customer lifetime value and greater share of customer. The result is increased long-term customer equity for the firm.

Finally, in the face of today's changing marketing landscape, companies must take into account three additional factors. In building customer and partner relationships, they must harness marketing technology, take advantage of global opportunities, and ensure that they act in an ethical and socially responsible way.

Figure 1.9 provides a good roadmap to future chapters of the text. Chapters 1, 2 and 3 introduce the marketing process, with a focus on sustainability and building customer relationships and capturing value from customers now and into the future. Chapters 4, 5, 6 and 7 address the first step of the marketing process – understanding the marketing environment, frameworks for analysing consumer and business buyer behaviour and marketing research. Chapters 8 to 10 then look deeply into three major marketing strategy decisions: establishing customer relationships, selecting which customers to serve (segmentation and targeting) and deciding on a value proposition (differentiation and positioning) and, finally, how to compete in markets.

Finally, Chapters 11 through 20 develop the four Ps. Product and service marketing are the subject of Chapters 11 to 13. These include branding, product development and services marketing. Chapter 14 covers pricing principles and practice while Chapters 15 to 18 examine promotion in its many guises: advertising, public relations, personal selling, sales promotions and the increasingly important area of direct and online marketing. Lastly, place is the subject of Chapters 19 and 20. The former covers marketing channel decisions and examines in detail the role of channel members in creating and adding value for customers in traditional (physical) marketplaces. The final chapter addresses the growing influence of the global marketplace and the special considerations facing marketers.

Reviewing the concepts

Today's successful companies – whether large or small, for-profit or not-for-profit, domestic or global – share a strong customer focus and a heavy commitment to marketing. The goal of marketing is to build and manage profitable customer relationships. Marketing seeks to attract new customers by promising superior value and to keep and grow current customers by delivering satisfaction. Marketing operates within a dynamic global environment, which can quickly make yesterday's winning strategies obsolete. To be successful, companies will have to be strongly market focused.

1. Define marketing and outline the steps in the marketing process

Marketing is the process by which companies create value for customers and build strong customer relationships in order to capture value from customers in return.

The marketing process involves five steps. The first four steps create value for customers. First, marketers need to understand the marketplace and customer needs and wants. Next, marketers design a customer-driven marketing strategy with the goal of getting, keeping and growing target customers. In the third step, marketers construct a marketing programme that actually delivers superior value. All of these steps form the basis for the fourth step, building profitable customer relationships and creating customer delight. In the final step, the company reaps the rewards of strong customer relationships by capturing value from customers.

2. Explain the importance of understanding customers and the marketplace, and identify the five core marketplace concepts

Outstanding marketing companies go to great lengths to learn about and understand their customers' needs, wants and demands. This understanding helps them to design want-satisfying market offerings and build value-laden customer relationships by which they can capture customer lifetime value and greater share of customer. The result is increased long-term customer equity for the firm.

The core marketplace concepts are needs, wants and demands; market offerings (products, services and experiences); value and satisfaction; exchange and relationships; and markets. Wants are the form taken by human needs when shaped by culture and individual personality. When backed by buying power, wants become demands. Companies address needs by putting forth a value proposition, a set of benefits that they promise to consumers to satisfy their needs. The value proposition is fulfilled through a market offering, which delivers customer value and satisfaction, resulting in long-term exchange relationships with customers.

3. Identify the key elements of a customer-driven marketing strategy and discuss marketing management orientations that guide marketing strategy

To design a winning marketing strategy, the company must first decide *who* it will serve. It does this by dividing the market into segments of customers (*market segmentation*) and selecting which segments it will cultivate (*target marketing*). Next, the company must decide *how* it will serve targeted customers (how it will *differentiate and position* itself in the marketplace).

Marketing management can adopt one of six competing market orientations. The *production concept* holds that management's task is to improve production efficiency and bring down prices. The *product concept* holds that consumers favour products that offer the most in quality, performance and innovative features; thus, little promotional effort is required. The *selling concept* holds that consumers will not buy enough of the organisation's products unless it undertakes a large-scale selling and promotion effort. The *marketing concept* holds that achieving organisational goals depends on determining the needs and wants of target markets and delivering the desired satisfactions more effectively and efficiently than competitors do. The *societal marketing concept* holds that generating customer satisfaction *and* long-run societal well-being are the keys to both achieving the company's goals and fulfilling its responsibilities. The *sustainable marketing concept* holds that an organisation should meet the needs of its present consumers without compromising the ability of future generations to fulfil their own needs.

4. Discuss customer relationship management and identify strategies for creating value *for* customers and capturing value *from* customers in return

Broadly defined, *customer relationship management* is the process of building and maintaining profitable customer relationships by delivering superior customer value and satisfaction. The aim of customer relationship management is to produce high *customer equity*, the total combined customer lifetime values of all of the company's customers. The key to building lasting relationships is the creation of superior *customer value* and *satisfaction*.

Companies want not only to acquire profitable customers, but to build relationships that will keep them and grow 'share of customer'. Different types of customer require different customer relationship management strategies. The marketer's aim is to build the *right relationships* with the *right customers*. In return for creating value *for* targeted customers, the company captures value *from* customers in the form of profits and customer equity.

5. Describe sustainable marketing and the major trends and forces that are changing the marketing landscape

As the world spins on, dramatic changes are occurring in the marketing arena. The boom in computer, telecommunications, information, transportation and other technologies has created exciting new ways to learn about and track customers, and to create products and services tailored to individual customer needs. Gobal warming and the sustainability of business activities and the actions of consumers is of increasing importance. The sustainable marketing concept is an approach to marketing that holds that an organisation should meet the needs of their present consumers without compromising the ability of future generations to fulfil their own needs.

In an increasingly smaller world, many marketers are now connected *globally* with their customers and marketing partners. Today, almost every company, large or small, is touched in some way by global competition. Today's marketers are also re-examining their ethical and societal responsibilities. Marketers are being called upon to take greater responsibility for the social and environmental impact of their actions. Finally, in the past, marketing has been most widely applied in the for-profit business sector. In recent years, however, marketing also has become a major part of the strategies of many not-for-profit organisations, such as colleges, hospitals, museums, zoos, symphony orchestras and even churches.

Pulling it all together, as discussed throughout the chapter, the major new developments in marketing can be summed up in a single word: *relationships*. Today's marketers of all kinds are increasingly taking advantage of new opportunities for building relationships with their customers, their marketing partners and the world around them.

Discussing the concepts

1. Discuss why you should study marketing.

2. As the prelude case implies, the marketing efforts of organisations seek to fulfil consumer needs. How genuine are the needs targeted by the marketing efforts in the long-haul tourism industry? Critically evaluate the role that marketing plays in satisfying these human desires.

3. What is the single biggest difference between the marketing concept and the production, product and selling concepts? Which concepts are easiest to apply in the short run? Which concept can offer the best long-term success?

4. Using practical examples, discuss the key challenges facing companies in the twenty-first century. What actions might marketers take to ensure they continue to survive and thrive in the new connected world of marketing?

5. According to economist Milton Friedman, 'Few trends could so thoroughly undermine the very foundations of our free society as the acceptance by corporate officials of a social responsibility other than to make as much money for their stockholders as possible.' Do you agree or disagree with Friedman's statement? What are some drawbacks of the societal marketing concept?

Applying the concepts

1. Go to a fast food restaurant and order a meal. Note the questions you are asked and observe how special orders are handled. Next, go to a restaurant on your college or university campus and order a meal. Note the questions you are asked here and observe whether special orders are handled the same way as they are at the fast food restaurant. Did you observe any significant differences in how orders are handled?

   - Consider the differences you saw. Do you think the restaurants have different marketing management philosophies? Which is closest to the marketing concept? Is one closer to the selling or production concept?
   - What are the advantages of closely following the marketing concept? Are there any disadvantages?
   - Consider the fast food chains are profit-making organisations and the college operation is not-for-profit.

2. Visit a shopping centre. Choose a category of store, such as department stores, shoe shops, bookshops, clothing shops and so forth. List the competing shops in each category, walk past them and quickly observe their merchandise and style. Note how the shops are decorated and how well they are located. Note what other shops are close to them and how close they are to their competitors.

- Are the competing shops unique, or could one pretty much substitute for another? What does this say about the overall goals that the shopping centre is fulfilling?
- Consider the attitudes of the shoppers you saw. Did some apparently find shopping a pleasure, while others found it a bother?
- A major goal for marketing is to maximise consumer satisfaction. Discuss the extent to which the shopping centre serves this goal.

Now, visit online retailers in the same category as the bricks-and-mortar shop you chose.

- Note the categories of merchandise and store layout and comment on the overall goals that the online retailer is fulfilling. What are the major differences between a traditional and an electronic retailer?
- To what extent is the shopping experience similar or different across the traditional and online shopping environments?
- Contrast the ways in which the two shopping formats seek to maximise consumer satisfaction. What advantages have they over one another?
- Discuss the impacts of the growth in online shopping (a) on traditional retailing in the long run and (b) from a marketing sustainability perspective.

Web resources

For additional classic case studies and Internet exercises, visit **www. pearsoned.co.uk/ kotler**

References

1. Peter F. Drucker, *Management: Tasks, responsibilities, practices* (New York: Harper & Row, 1973), pp. 64–5.

2. See Theodore Levitt's classic article 'Marketing myopia', *Harvard Business Review* (July–August 1960), pp. 45–56. For more recent discussions, see Yves Doz, Jose Santos and Peter J. Williamson, 'Marketing myopia revisited: Why every company needs to learn from the world', *Ivey Business Journal* (January–February 2004), p. 1; Lon Zimmerman, 'Product positioning maps secure future', *Marketing News* (15 October 2005), p. 47.

3. Susie Mesure, 'Whole scale organic food invasion', *Independent on Sunday* (13 May 2007); 'Organic Albion', *The Economist* (26 May 2007), p. 30.

4. Ralph Waldo Emerson offered this advice: 'If a man . . . makes a better mousetrap . . . the world will beat a path to his door.' Several companies, however, have built better mousetraps yet failed. One was a laser mousetrap costing $1,500. Contrary to popular assumptions, people do not automatically learn about new products, believe product claims, or willingly pay higher prices.

5. From 'The computer is personal again', an HP ad appearing in *Business 2.0* (June 2006), p. 33. Also see www.hp.com/personal.

6. For more on customer satisfaction see Regina Fazio Marcuna, 'Mapping the world of customer satisfaction', *Harvard Business Review* (May–June), p. 30; David M. Szymanski, 'Customer satisfaction: a meta-analysis of the empirical evidence', *Academy of Marketing Science Journal* (Winter 2001), pp. 16–35; Claes Fornell, 'The science of satisfaction', *Harvard Business Review* (March–April 2001), pp. 120–1.

7. See Mary M. Long and Leon G. Schiffman, 'Consumption values and relationships', *Journal of Consumer Marketing* (2000), p. 241; Naras V. Eechambadi, 'Keeping your existing customers loyal', *Interaction Solutions* (February 2002).

8. Retail Technology, 'Sainsbury's picks Star for concessions', *Retail Technology Archive* 05/2006 (www.retailtechnology.co.uk/_private/fullstorydemo.asp?offset=176).

9. Andrew Bounds, 'Plans for European GPS break down', *Financial Times* (14 March 2007).

10. Barry Farber and Joyce Wycoff, 'Customer service: evolution and revolution', *Sales and Marketing Management* (May 1991), p. 47; Kevin Lawrence, 'How to profit from customer complaints', *The Canadian Manager* (Fall 2000), pp. 25, 29.

11. Doug Cameron, 'US airlines warned of emissions backlash', *Financial Times* (14 May 2007); Rod Eddington, Comment: 'How airlines can fight climate change', *Financial Times* (4 January 2005).

12. Al Gore, *An Inconvenient Truth* (New York: Penguin, 2006).

13. John Williams, 'Business opportunities "being missed"', *Financial Times* (15 May 2007), p. 12; Jeroen van der Veer, 'Energy v environment?', *Financial Times* (14 May 2007), p. 18; www.sustainablemarketing.com, a web community dedicated to sustainable marketing.

14. John Reed and Richard Milne, 'An embattled industry tries to engineer itself out of a hole', *Financial Times* (27 April 2007).

15. Paul A. Eisenstein, 'Strategic vision puts Toyota, Honda on top' (10 October 2005), accessed at www. thecarconnection.com; and Silvio Schindler, 'Hybrids and customers', *Automotive Design & Production* (June 2006), pp. 20–2.

16. Example adapted from Denny Hatch, 'Delight your customers', *Target Marketing* (April 2002), pp. 32–9, with additional information from 'Lexus earns best-selling brand title for sixth consecutive year', 4 January 2006, accessed at www.lexus.com/about/press_releases/index.html.

17. For more discussion of customer delight and loyalty, see Barry Berman, 'How to delight your customers', *California Management Review* (Fall 2005), pp. 129–51; Clara Agustin and Jagdip Singh, 'Curvilinear effects of consumer loyalty determinants in relational exchanges', *Journal of Marketing Research* (February 2005), pp. 96–108; Ben McConnell and Jackie Huba, 'Learning to leverage the lunatic fringe', *Point* (July–August 2006), pp. 14–15; and Fred Reichheld, *The Ultimate Question: Driving good profits and true growth* (Boston, MA: Harvard Business School Publishing, 2006).

18. For interesting discussions on assessing and using customer lifetime value, see Charlotte H. Mason, 'Tuscan lifestyles: Assessing customer lifetime value', *Journal of Interactive Marketing* (Autumn 2003), pp. 54–60; Erin Kinikin, 'How valuable are your customers?' (September 2001), accessed at www.advisor.com/articles.nsf/aid/KINIE01; Rajkumar Venkatesan and V. Kumar, 'A customer lifetime value framework for customer selection and resource allocation strategy', *Journal of Marketing* (October 2004), pp. 106–25; Rajkumar Venkatesan, V. Kumar and Timothy Bohling, 'Selecting valuable customers using a customer lifetime value framework', Marketing Science Institute, Report No. 05-121, 2005; and Lynette Ryals, 'Making customer relationships management work: The measurement and profitable management of customer relationships', *Journal of Marketing* (October 2005), pp. 252–61.

19. Don Peppers and Martha Rogers, 'Customers don't grow on trees', *Fast Company* (July 2005), p. 26.

20. See Roland T. Rust, Valerie A. Zeithaml and Katherine A. Lemon, *Driving Customer Equity* (New York: Free Press, 2000); Robert C. Blattberg, Gary Getz and Jacquelyn S. Thomas, *Customer Equity* (Boston, MA: Harvard Business School Press, 2001); Roland T. Rust, Katherine A. Lemon and Valerie A. Zeithaml, 'Return on marketing: Using customer equity to focus marketing strategy', *Journal of Marketing* (January 2004), pp. 109–27; James D. Lenskold, 'Customer-centered marketing ROI', *Marketing Management* (January/February 2004), pp. 26–32; Roland T. Rust, Valerie A. Zeithaml and Katherine A. Lemon, 'Customer-centered brand management', *Harvard Business Review* (September 2004), p. 110; Don Peppers and Martha Rogers, 'Hail to the customer', *Sales & Marketing Management* (October 2005), pp. 49–51; and Allison Enright, 'Serve them right', *Marketing News* (1 May 2006), pp. 21–2.

21. This example is adapted from information in Roland T. Rust, Katherine A. Lemon and Valerie A. Zeithaml, 'Where should the next marketing dollar go?', *Marketing Management* (September–October 2001), pp. 24–8. Also see David Welch and David Kiley, 'Can Caddy's driver make GM cool?', *BusinessWeek* (20 September 2004), pp. 105–6; John K. Teahen Jr, 'Cadillac kid: "gotta compete"', *Chicago Tribune* (7 May 2005), p. 1; and Jamie LaReau, 'Cadillac wants to boost sales, customer service', *Automotive News* (20 February 2006), p. 46.

22. Ravi Dhar and Rashi Glazer, 'Hedging customers', *Harvard Business Review* (May 2003), pp. 86–92. Also see Ian Gordon, 'Relationship marketing: Managing wasteful or worthless customer relationships', *Ivey Business Journal* (March/April 2006), pp. 1–4.

23. Werner Reinartz and V. Kumar, 'The mismanagement of customer loyalty', *Harvard Business Review* (July 2002), pp. 86–94. For more on customer equity management, see Sunil Gupta, Donald R. Lehman and Jennifer Ames Stuart, 'Valuing customers', *Journal of Marketing Research* (February 2004), pp. 7–18; Michael D. Johnson and Fred Selnes, 'Customer portfolio management: Toward a dynamic theory of

exchange relationships', *Journal of Marketing* (April 2004), pp. 1–17; Sunil Gupta and Donald R. Lehman, *Managing Customers as Investments* (Philadelphia: Wharton School Publishing, 2005); and Roland T. Rust, Katherine N. Lemon and Das Narayandas, *Customer Equity Management* (Upper Saddle River, NJ: Prentice Hall, 2005).

24. For the revolutionary introduction to the importance of tipping point, read Malcolm Gladwell, *The Tipping Point: How little things can make a big difference* (London: Abacus, 2000).

25. www.thirdworldtraveler.com/Boycotts/Boycotts_page.html

26. For other examples, and for a good review of non-profit marketing, see Philip Kotler and Alan R. Andreasen, *Strategic Marketing for Nonprofit Organizations*, 6th ed. (Upper Saddle River, NJ: Prentice Hall, 2003); Philip Kotler and Karen Fox, *Strategic Marketing for Educational Institutions* (Upper Saddle River, NJ: Prentice Hall, 1995); Norman Shawchuck, Philip Kotler, Bruce Wren and Gustave Rath, *Marketing for Congregations: Choosing to serve people more effectively* (Nashville, TN: Abingdon Press, 1993); Philip Kotler, John Bowen and James Makens, *Marketing for Hospitality and Tourism*, 3rd ed. (Upper Saddle River, NJ: Prentice Hall, 2003); and 'The nonprofit marketing landscape', special section, *Journal of Business Research* (June 2005), pp. 797–862.

27. 'Population explosion!', *ClickZ Stats* (12 April 2006), accessed at http://www.clickz.com/stats/sectors/geographics/article.php/151151.

28. 'The world in figures' in 'The World in 2007', *The Economist*, p. 112; Maija Palmer, 'Internet shopping tops £100bn', *Financial Times* (18 May 2007).

29. Susanna Voyle, 'Online, instore, in profit and now in the US', *Financial Times* (30 June 2001); Geoffrey Nain, 'Customers become a reality in web-based shopping malls', *Financial Times* (5 February 2003).

30. World Trade Organization (www.wto.com); 'Liberty's great advance – special supplement: a survey of capitalism and democracy', *The Economist* (28 June 2003), pp. 4–7.

31. 'More hot air: Asia's latest contribution to global warming', *The Economist* (12 January 2006); 'America's fear of China: China is a far-from-cuddly beast, but bashing it is a bad idea', *The Economist* (17 May 2007).

32. Andrew Edgecliffe-Johnson, 'Rise in BBC's overseas audience', *Financial Times* (21 May 2007), p. 2.

33. Naomi Klein, *No Logo: Taking aim at the brand bullies* (Flamingo, 2001); Eric Schlosser, *Fast Food Nation: What the all American meal is doing for the world* (Penguin, 2002).

34. Mark Ritson and Richard Elliott, 'Social issues of advertising: an ethnographic study of adolescent advertising audiences', *Journal of Consumer Research*, **24** (December 1999).

35. The four-P classification was first suggested by E. Jerome McCarthy, *Basic Marketing: A managerial approach* (Homewood, IL: Irwin, 1960). For more discussion of this classification scheme, see T.C. Melewar and John Saunders, 'Global corporate visual identity systems: using an extended marketing mix', *European Journal of Marketing*, **34**, 5/6 (2000), pp. 538–50; Christian Gronroos, 'Keynote paper: From marketing mix to relationship marketing – towards a paradigm shift in marketing', *Management Decision*, **35**, 4 (1997), pp. 322–39.

36. Robert Lauterborn, 'New marketing litany: four Ps passé; C-words take over', *Advertising Age* (1 October 1990), p. 26.

Company case 1 Build-A-Bear Workshop

Is all lost?

For Søren Lønne it was a glimmer of light: bears. He had just taken over as the third generation of a family business and all was not going well. His grandfather had set up his first toy shop in the early 1950s when the people of Denmark had little money to spare but there were many children. Success and expansion continued well into the 1990s with growing wealth and innovation in the industry. True, by then a lot of the toys sold were not as wonderful as the Corgi and Dinky toy cars that he still collected, not as absorbing as the train sets built over the years by father and son, the dolls' houses with all their intricate furniture, or as creative as Lego. The toy market was now all over the place, with each year bringing a hard-to-guess big winner: one year Furby from Tiger Electronics, the next year Pokémon, and then a golden oldie returned, everyone wanting new high-tech scooters. The following year Lego was back on top helped by their Harry Potter range, this year another mix of old and new with the Dr Who Cyberman Mask: like the Harry Potter Lego range, another media tie-up.

From work he did for his business school dissertation he new that toy sales did not tell the full story. For the last two years the top-grossing products for young teens were iPods, mobile phones and computer games consoles. His shop did sell games consoles but faced intense competition from electronic stores, specialist computer games shops and the Internet. He had also found out that the children and adults who accounted for the computer games sales found toy shops too childish for them. Not only was the number of children declining but the kids were maturing younger and spurning toys for adult gadgets.

The family business was also being squeezed by alternative distribution channels. Each year more and more people were buying more and more toys on the Internet. True to its reputation as a global category killer, Toys 'R' Us was making a real killing on www.toys-r-us.dk. Many small toy retailers had already disappeared, leaving his family firm with a larger and larger share of the declining high-street toy market.

He knew from the declining sales and from his business degree that he had to make big changes or he would have no business to pass on to his children. The glimmer of light came when talking to his MBA dissertation supervisor who mentioned that big money was moving into toys so it could not all be doom and gloom.

Billionaire hedge fund manager Steven Cohen had just said his company had taken a 5 per cent stake in Build-A-Bear Workshop, a cuddly animals business. Cohen's firm, SAC Capital, was not known for warm and fuzzy investments. Damien Hirst's 18-ft tiger shark, which was part of Cohen's art collection, seems closer to the spirit of SAC Capital than do teddy bears. If Steven Cohen saw opportunity in the toy market, there may also be a future for the Lønne toy business.

Next day, in his office above the Støget flagship store, Søren looked at Build-A-Bear's website and could see why Cohen was investing. Build-A-Bear had been a great success in the four markets where it currently operated: Canada, the US, the UK and Costa Rica. Nothing in continental Europe so far! What was even more exciting was that Build-A-Bear was looking to franchise their operation in new companies.

Mixing business with pleasure, he took his family for a weekend in Birmingham, England, to visit Build-A-Bear's store in the Bullring. He even bought a few bears. He also started looking into the background of Build-A-Bear. Maxine Clark founded Build-A-Bear Workshop in 1996; many critics thought that she was making a very poor decision. But as the company neared the end of its first decade, she had many fans. In 2005, a retail consultancy named Build-A-Bear one of the five hottest retailers as the company hit number 25 on *BusinessWeek's* Hot Growth list of fast-expanding small companies. Founder and CEO Maxine Clark also won Fast Company's Customer-Centered Leader Award.

Build-A-Bear

Since opening its first store in 1996 the company has opened more than 200 stores and has custom-made more than 30 million teddy bears and other stuffed animals. Annual revenues reached €262 million for 2005 and are growing at a steady and predictable 20 per cent annually. Annual sales per square metre are roughly double the retail average. The company plans to open approximately 30 new stores each year in the United States and Canada and to franchise an additional

20 stores per year internationally – there was Søren's chance. The company's share price had soared by 56 per cent since it went public in November 2004. No wonder Cohen was interested. On top of all this, the company's Internet sales were exploding.

What the numbers do not illustrate is *how* the company is achieving such success. That success comes not from the tangible object that children clutch as they leave a store. It comes from what Build-A-Bear is really selling: the experience of participating in the creation of personalised entertainment. When children enter a Build-A-Bear store, they step into a cartoon land, a fantasy world organised around a child-friendly assembly line comprised of clearly labelled work stations.

The process begins at the 'Choose Me' station where customers select an unstuffed animal from a bin. At the 'Stuff Me' station, the animal comes to life. A Build-A-Bear employee inserts a metal tube extending from a large tumbler-full of 'fluff' into the animal. The child operates a foot pedal that blows in the stuffing. She or he (25 per cent of Build-A-Bear customers are boys) decides how full the animal should be.

Other stations include 'Hear Me' (where customers decide whether or not to include a 'voice box'), 'Stitch Me' (where the child stitches the animal shut), 'Fluff Me' (where the child can give the animal a blow-dry spa treatment), 'Dress Me' (filled with accessories galore), and 'Name Me' (where a 'birth certificate' is created with the child-selected name). Unlike in most retail stores, queuing behind other customers is not unpleasant. Because the process is much of the fun, waiting actually enhances the experience. By the time a child leaves the store, they have a product unlike any they have ever bought or received before: one they created. More than just a stuffed animal that they can have and hold, it's entrenched with the memory created on their visit to the store.

Kids love Build-A-Bear. But parents love it too. The cost of the experience starts as low as €8. Although options and accessories can push that price up, the average bear leaves the store costing less than €20. It is more than an offshore-manufactured teddy but many parents consider this to be a bargain when they see their child's delight. It is educational too.

Why the concept works

Build-A-Bear is not competing with other toy companies. 'Our concept is based on customisation,' says Clark.

'Most things today are high-tech and hard-touch. We are soft-touch. We don't think of ourselves as a toy shop – we think of ourselves as an experience.' As evidence, Clark points out that, unlike the rest of the toy industry, Build-A-Bear sales do not peak during the holiday season but are evenly distributed throughout the year.

Product personalisation has long been popular in many industries. BMW's hugely successful Mini owes much of its success from people customising a car that has loads of personality. Dell has achieved industry leadership by doing the same. The Lego Factory now allows people to 'Custom Design Your Own Model' rather than sort among piles of bricks from old models. Jason Blair, research analyst for Rochdale Securities, says that the customisation is so satisfying that it 'builds fiercely loyal customers'. Although it is not very common in the toy industry, Maxine Clark asserts that personalisation is emerging because it lets customers be creative and express themselves. It provides far more value for the customer than they receive from mass-produced products. 'It's empowerment – it lets the customer do something in their control,' she adds. Build-A-Bear has capitalised on this concept not just by allowing for customisation, but by making it a key driver of customer value. The extensive customer involvement in the personalisation process is more of the 'product' than the resulting item.

Although Build-A-Bear has performed impressively, some analysts question whether or not it is just another toy industry fad, comparing the brand to Beanie Babies and Cabbage Patch Dolls. Maxine Clark has considered this, and she is confident that the Build-A-Bear product and experience will evolve as quickly as the fickle tastes of children. Although some outfits and accessories might be trendy (the company added Spiderman costumes to the bear-size clothing line at the peak of the movie's popularity), accessories assortments are changed 11 times each year.

Knowing the customer

Maxine Clark has been viewed as the visionary who has made the Build-A-Bear concept work. But her success as CEO derives from more than just business skills relating to strategy development and implementation. Clark attributes her success to 'never forgetting what it's like to be a customer'. Given that Clark has no children of her own, this is an amazing feat.

Understanding customers is certainly not a new concept, and Clark has employed both low-tech and high-tech methods for making Build-A-Bear a truly customer-centric organisation. To put herself in the customer's shoes, Clark walks where they walk. Every week, she visits two or three Build-A-Bear stores. She does not do this just to see how the stores are running but takes the opportunity of chatting with pre-teens and parents. She puts herself on the front line, assisting employees in serving customers. She even hands out business cards. As a result, Clark receives thousands of e-mails each week, and she's added to the buddy lists of pre-teens all over the world. Clark doesn't take this honour lightly, and she tries to respond to as many of those messages as possible using her BlackBerry.

To capitalise on these customer communications, she has created what she calls the 'Virtual Cub Advisory Council', a panel of children on her e-mail list. And what does Clark get in return from all this high-tech communication? 'Ideas,' she says. 'I used to feel like I had to come up with all the ideas myself, but it's so much easier relying on my customers for help.' From the location of stores to accessories that could be added to the Build-A-Bear line, Build-A-Bear actually puts customer ideas into practice. As the ideas come in, Clark polls the Cub Council to get real-time feedback from customers. Scooters, mascot bears at professional sports venues, and sequined purses are all ideas generated by customers that have become very successful additions. The future holds great potential as more ideas are being considered and implemented. Soon, Build-A-Bear Workshops will house in-store galleries of bear-sized furniture designed by children for children. The company will add sports licensing agreements and will give much more attention to a new line of stores called 'Friends 2B Made', a concept built around the personalisation of dolls rather than stuffed animals.

Although Maxine Clark may communicate with only a fraction of her customers, she sees this as the basis for a personal connection with all customers. 'With each child that enters our store, we have an opportunity to build a lasting memory,' she says. 'Any business can think that way, whether you're selling a screw, a bar of soap, or a bear.'

Søren was impressed but was Build-A-Bear a passing fad, like Tamagotchi, Beanie Babies or Cabbage Patch Dolls? Would the idea transfer to Denmark? Could his existing people handle something so different?

Questions

1. Which of the marketing management concepts covered in this chapter best describes Build-A-Bear Workshop?

2. How does Build-A-Bear contrast with traditional toy shops and what accounts for their sales growth in the face of declining toy sales generally? What new skills will Søren and his employees have to learn if they are to develop the Build-A-Bear operation?

3. In detail, describe all facets of Build-A-Bear's product. What is being exchanged in a Build-A-Bear transaction?

4. Is Build-A-Bear likely to be successful in continuing to build customer relationships? Why or why not?

5. Will Build-A-Bear transfer from the few markets in which it now operates into successful franchises across Europe? Why and how does Build-A-Bear need adapting to work in your national market?

SOURCES: Mark Dickens, 'The lollipop dollar', *Financial Times* (6 January 2004); Parija Bhatnagar, 'The next hot retailers?', *CNNMoney.com* (9 January 2006); Lucas Conley, 'Customer-centered leader: Maxine Clark', *Fast Company* (October 2005), p. 54; Ray Allegrezza, 'Kids today', *Kids Today* (1 April 2006), p. 10; 'The mini-me school of marketing', *Brand Strategy* (2 November 2005), p. 12; Michael O'Rourke, 'Build-A-Bear assembles dreams', *San Antonio Express-News* (4 February 2006), p. 1E; Dody Tsiantar, 'Not your average bear', *Time* (3 July 2005); Roger Crockett, 'Build-A-Bear Workshop: Retailing gets interactive with toys designed by tots', *BusinessWeek* (6 June 2005), p. 77; 'Build-A-Bear Workshop, Inc. reports strong sales and net income growth in Fiscal 2005 Fourth Quarter and Full Year', press release through *Business Wire* (16 February 2006); http://www.toyretailersassociation.co.uk/; 'Observer: Cohen's fuzzy side', *Financial Times* (10 January 2007).

We are in a system of fouling our own nest, so long as we behave as independent, rational, free-enterprises.

GARRETT HARDING

Sustainable marketing: marketing ethics and social responsibility

Mini Contents List

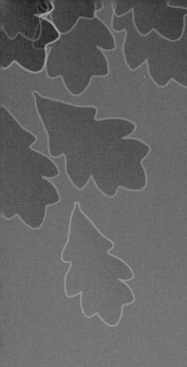

'Flash, love you, but we only have fourteen hours to save the world.'

From the film 'Flash Gordon' (1980) Dir. Mike Hodges, DEG.

Previewing the concepts

In this chapter, we will focus on sustainable marketing. First, we look at some common criticisms of marketing as it affects individual consumers, other businesses and society as a whole. Then, we'll examine consumerism, environmentalism and other citizen and public actions to keep marketing in check. Finally, we'll see how companies themselves can benefit from proactively pursuing socially responsible and ethical practices that bring value not just to individual customers, but to society as a whole and into the future. You'll see that sustainable marketing, social responsibility and ethical actions are more than just the right thing to do; they're also good for business.

After reading this chapter, you should be able to:

1. Identify the major social criticisms of marketing.
2. Define *consumerism* and *environmentalism* and explain how they affect marketing strategies.
3. Describe the principles of socially responsible marketing.
4. Explain the role of ethics in marketing.
5. Understand the dimensions of sustainable marketing.

First, we look at how marketing is being used to achieve social, not commercial ends. Formed in 1884, the NSPCC is an old charity controversially using modern marketing to achieve its objectives.

Prelude case NSPCC: Full Stop to child cruelty

The National Society for the Prevention of Cruelty to Children (NSPCC) Full Stop campaign has hardly ever been out of the headlines. Aimed to put a full stop to cruelty to children, the campaign was a call to children in need and people aware of them, to come forward so that the children could be helped.

At the start of the campaign, the charity's end-of-year 2000 accounts prompted condemnation. They revealed that the £43m (€63m) the charity spent on fundraising, publicity, campaigning and administration far exceeded the £32m it spent on services to children. It was 'a sign of complete incompetence', charged Conservative MP Gerald Howarth, who vowed to stop backing the NSPCC's high-profile Full Stop campaign. The furore was not helped by the NSPCC's use of pop icons, including Kylie Minogue, Ms Dynamite, David Beckham and Pelé to put their Full Stop message across.

After years sticking to the Full Stop campaign it believed in, the NSPCC again hit controversy. The celebrities supporting the campaign were more classy than they used to be, including artist Tracey Emin and actress Dame Judi Dench, but still attracted the anger of the charity's donors. Many donors were outraged over the revelations that £25,000 was spent producing 2,000 limited edition brochures for well-heeled NSPCC supporters to mark the end of the £250m Full Stop Appeal. Once again the charity's spending was under fire. The NSPCC spends 81p of every pound directly on ending cruelty to children. In comparison, 92p in every pound raised by the RSPCA (Royal Society for the Prevention of Cruelty to Animals) goes directly to animal welfare.

According to Quentin Anderson, chief executive of Addison, the corporate marketing arm of WPP Group, such criticism of the NSPCC strategy is unwise and failed to recognise the professional makeover many charities have undertaken in recent years. Charities are now highly organised operations and have adopted a more businesslike approach, which is essential if they are to survive in a crowded sector. When arguing how big the various components of the NSPCC's budget should be, detractors must remember that there is a multi-million pound budget to disburse. Charities need highly skilled staff to manage such funds.

According to Mr Anderson, the NSPCC's campaign makes sense. The charity has stated that its long-term objectives were to raise social awareness of child cruelty and to raise £250m through the 'Full Stop' initiative. On both these counts it had succeeded but the NSPCC needs to ensure that people understand what it is trying to achieve because it needs their help. It needs to show that it is awake, reacting to change and anticipating it.

Despite the furore, the NSPCC sticks to its guns and keeps campaigning. The advertising is central to NSPCC's mission: 'to end cruelty to children for ever'. With help from the campaign, 650,000 people pledged their support for their campaign to achieve a better future for all children.

Marketing is ideally suited to the task the charity has set itself. In crude terms, its route to market is not so obvious as those of other charities. For example, it is comparatively easy for 'Meals on Wheels' to identify the disabled and elderly to whom it provides hot food, so the charity can dedicate the majority of its expenditure to providing the service. By contrast, the NSPCC has defined its audience as the whole population. By communicating clearly with all communities, it hopes to enlist many more foot soldiers than direct action ever would.

The campaign has got a lot right. To achieve its aim, the NSPCC used celebrities to back its central message that to reduce cruelty to children you need to raise awareness of child cruelty and challenge social attitudes. To reach those at risk it focuses on teenage media: *Sugar*, *Cosmo Girl*, *Bliss*, *Shout* and *Mizz*. Boys are reached through music, football and games magazines, including *Hip-Hop Connection*, which offered a hip hop CD, 'Holla!', with a recent issue. Teen rock music fans are reached through *Kerrang!*. The charity's 2007 *Don't Hide It* campaign has a strong presence on teen websites, including Bebo.com, Piczo.com and Habbo.com. Donthideit.com is promoted as a place to access information about abuse. Anyone needing to speak out is encouraged to talk to ChildLine.

Matching your brand to stars is a successful marketing technique and need not be a cause for controversy, says the NSPCC. Nike pays Tiger Woods handsomely but obviously believes it gets value for money. The NSPCC would be foolish not to exploit celebrities willing to donate their time free of charge. Without celebrities, would the Full Stop campaign receive front-page exposure in the magazines teenagers read?

So, why should the NSPCC be criticised for spending money and talking about it? The charity understands that dissemination of better information creates confidence in the community. This leads to many benefits, including greater loyalty from donors and a more secure position in the sector. It also avoids the accusation of hoarding funds, a criticism that has been levelled at many charities.

The negative reaction to the NSPCC marketing campaign is a sign not that its marketing strategy is failing but that its communications policy is. A first principle for all good communicators is to evolve messages defining what the organisation does and what its aims are. The NSPCC should have explained better the rationale behind its spending on marketing.[1]

Questions

You should attempt these questions only after completing your reading of this chapter.

1. Who are the charity's target market and what are the main aspects of the service offered by a charity such as the NSPCC?
2. Assess the role of marketing in assisting the charity to achieve its goals. Should the charity spend more on fundraising, publicity, campaigning and administration than on direct services to children?
3. Evaluate the NSPCC's current marketing strategy. Has the charity got its current marketing strategy wrong? Or are the problems due to its communication policy?

Introduction

Responsible marketers discover what consumers want and respond with marketing offerings that create value for buyers in order to capture value in return. The *marketing concept* is a philosophy of customer value and mutual gain. Its practice leads the economy by an invisible hand to satisfy the many and changing needs of millions of consumers.

Not all marketers follow the marketing concept, however. In fact, some companies use questionable marketing practices, and some marketing actions that seem innocent in themselves strongly affect the larger society. Consider the sale of cigarettes. On the face of it, companies should be free to sell cigarettes and smokers should be free to buy them. But this transaction affects the public interest and involves larger questions of public policy. For example, the smokers are harming their health and may be shortening their own lives. Smoking places a financial burden on the smoker's family and on society at large. Other people around smokers may suffer discomfort and harm from secondary smoke. Finally, marketing cigarettes to adults might also influence young people to begin smoking. Thus, the marketing of tobacco products has sparked substantial debate and negotiation in recent years.[2]

Marketers face difficult decisions when choosing to serve customers profitably on the one hand, and seeking to maintain a close fit between consumers' wants or desires and societal welfare on the other. This chapter examines the social effects of private marketing practices. We address several questions: What are the most frequent social criticisms of marketing? What steps have private citizens taken to curb marketing ills? What steps have legislators and government agencies taken to curb marketing ills? What steps have enlightened companies taken to carry out

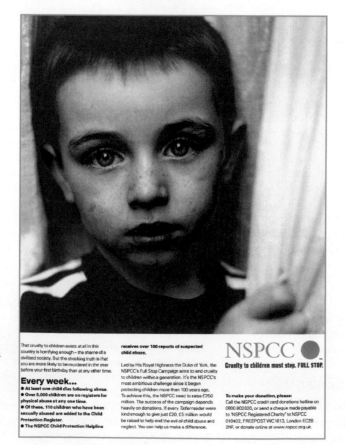

The NSPCC's 'Full Stop' campaign. To reach its various target audiences, the charity organisation has to spend huge sums on fundraising and marketing campaigns. Critics, however, question whether the organisation should spend more on marketing campaigns and administration than on direct services to children.
SOURCE: NSPCC. *Photographer*: Matt Harris. The Advertising Archives.

sustainable marketing that creates value for both individual customers and society as a whole, now and into the future? In addition, as the prelude case suggests, the issues of public accountability, social responsibility and ethical behaviour are also relevant for not-for-profit organisations.

Social criticisms of marketing

Marketing receives much criticism. Some of this criticism is justified; much is not. Social critics claim that certain marketing practices hurt individual consumers, society as a whole and other business firms. Malpractice may also endanger the survival of a company and the welfare of future consumers.

 Certain marketing practices hurt individual consumers, society as a whole and other business firms.

Marketing's impact on individual consumers

Consumers have many concerns about how well marketing and businesses, as a whole, serve their interests. Consumers, consumer advocates, government agencies and other critics have accused marketing of harming consumers through high prices, deceptive practices, high-pressure selling, shoddy or unsafe products, planned obsolescence and poor service to disadvantaged consumers.

High prices

Many critics charge that marketing practices raise the cost of goods and cause prices to be higher than they would be under more 'sensible' systems. They point to three factors: *high costs of distribution, high advertising and promotion costs* and *excessive mark-ups*.

High costs of distribution

A long-standing charge is that greedy intermediaries mark up prices beyond the value of their services. Critics charge either that there are too many intermediaries, or that intermediaries are inefficient and poorly run, or that they provide unnecessary or duplicated services. As a result, distribution costs too much and consumers pay for these excessive costs in the form of higher prices.

How do resellers answer these charges? They argue that intermediaries do work that would otherwise have to be done by manufacturers or consumers. Mark-ups reflect services that consumers themselves want – more convenience, larger stores and assortments, more service, longer store opening hours, return privileges and others. They argue that retail competition is so intense that margins are actually quite low. For example, after taxes, supermarket chains are typically left with barely 1 per cent profit on their sales. They survive by turning over their stock many times a year, so accumulating the 1 per cent. If some resellers try to charge too much relative to the value they add, other resellers will step in with lower prices. Low-price stores and other discounters pressure their competitors to operate efficiently and keep their prices down.

High advertising and promotion costs

Marketing is accused of pushing up prices because of heavy advertising and sales promotion. For example, a few dozen tablets of a heavily promoted brand of pain reliever sell for the same price as 100 tablets of less promoted (often termed 'generic') brands. Differentiated products – cosmetics,

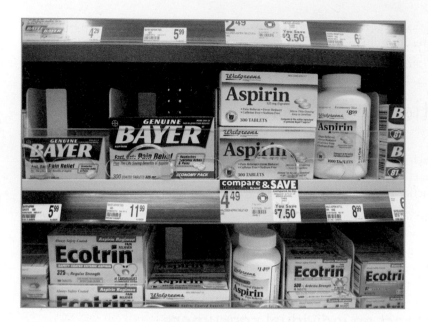

A heavily promoted brand of aspirin sells for much more than a virtually identical non-branded or store-branded product. Critics charge that promotion adds only psychological value to the product rather than functional value.

SOURCE: From Philip Kotler and Gary Armstrong, *Principles of Marketing*, 12th edn. (Upper Saddle River, New Jersey: Pearson), p. 571. Copyright © 2008 Pearson Education, Inc. Reprinted by permission of Pearson Education, Inc.

detergents, toiletries – include promotion and packaging costs that can amount to 40 per cent or more of the manufacturer's price to the retailer. Critics charge that much of the packaging and promotion adds only psychological value to the product rather than real functional value.

Marketers respond by saying that advertising does add to product costs, but it also adds value by informing potential buyers of the availability and merits of a brand. Brand name products may cost more, but branding gives buyers assurances of consistent quality. Moreover, consumers can usually buy functional versions of products at lower prices. However, they *want* and are willing to pay more for products that also provide psychological benefits – that make them feel wealthy, attractive or special. Also, heavy advertising and promotion may be necessary for a firm to match competitors' efforts – the business would lose 'share of mind' if it did not match competitive spending. At the same time, companies are cost-conscious about promotion and try to spend their money wisely.

Excessive mark-ups

Critics also charge that some companies mark up goods excessively. They point to the drug industry, where a pill costing 5 cents to make may cost the consumer €2 to buy. They point to the pricing tactics of perfume manufacturers, who take advantage of customers' ignorance of the true worth of a 50 ml bottle of Chanel perfume, while preying on their desire to satisfy emotional needs.

Marketers respond that most businesses try to deal fairly with consumers because they want to build customer relationships and repeat business. Most consumer abuses are unintentional. When shady marketers do take advantage of consumers, they should be reported to industry watchdogs and to other consumer-interest or consumer-protection groups. Marketers also stress that consumers often don't understand the reason for high mark-ups. For example, pharmaceutical mark-ups must cover the costs of purchasing, promoting and distributing existing medicines, plus the high research and development costs over many years of formulating and testing new drugs.

Deceptive practices

Marketers are sometimes accused of deceptive practices that lead consumers to believe they will get more value than they actually do. Deceptive marketing practices fall into three groups: *deceptive pricing, promotion* and *packaging.* Deceptive pricing includes inflationary price comparisons where 'factory' or 'wholesale' prices are falsely advertising a large price reduction from a falsely high retail list price. Deceptive promotion includes practices such as misrepresenting the product's features or performance, or 'bait and switch' where customers are lured to the store for a bargain that is out of stock, then sold a higher-priced item. Deceptive packaging includes exaggerating package contents through subtle design, not filling the package to the top, using misleading labelling or describing size in misleading terms. To be sure, questionable marketing practices do occur, as in the following example.

DFS sell well-designed sofas and armchairs at competitive prices. It has long been seen as one of the UK's most reliable financial performers in the retail sector, the retail sector's largest spender on advertising and the country's largest furniture retailer. Its advertising is bland, consistent and discount oriented. In spring 2007 DFS promoted '50% off the Eclipse collection'; 'designer sofas half price'; 'Bex, previous price £1698, half price £798; Opus, previous price £1155, half price £498'. Of course, not all the products on sale are half price, but there will be an equally generous-looking offer advertised all year round. As well as being well stocked with sofas, the warehouse-sized stores have enthusiastic salespeople who eagerly pounce on customers entering the store and are usually able to offer enticing financial deals to help them buy their living room suite. It is all legal but . . . . [3]

Deceptive practices have led to legislation and other consumer-protection actions, as in the following example.

European Council Directive 93/35/EEC paves the way for far-reaching changes to cosmetics laws. The legislation controls the constituents of cosmetic products and accompanying instructions and warnings about use. It also specifies requirements for marketing of cosmetic products, including product claims, labelling, information on packaging and details about the product's intended function. Where a product claims to remove 'unsightly cellulite' or make the user look '20 years younger', proofs must be documented and made available to the enforcement authorities. These laws also require clear details specifying where animal testing occurred on both the finished product and its ingredients. In recognition of the increased public resistance to animal testing, a limited EU ban on animal testing for cosmetic ingredients has been in force since 1998.

Despite regulations, some critics argue that deceptive claims are still the norm. The toughest problem is defining what is 'deceptive'. For instance, an advertiser's claim that its powerful laundry detergent 'makes your washing machine ten feet tall', showing a surprised home-maker watching her appliance burst through her laundry room ceiling, isn't intended to be taken literally. Instead, the advertiser might claim, it is 'puffery' – innocent exaggeration for effect. One noted marketing thinker, Theodore Levitt, claims that some advertising puffery is bound to occur – and that it may even be desirable:

> There is hardly a company that would not go down in ruin if it refused to provide fluff, because nobody will buy pure functionality . . . . Worse, it denies . . . people's honest needs and values. Without distortion, embellishment and elaboration, life would be drab, dull, anguished and at its existential worst.[4]

> " There is hardly a company that would not go down in ruin if it refused to provide fluff. "

However, others claim that puffery and alluring imagery can harm consumers in subtle ways, and that consumers must be protected through education. Lane Jennings talks of 'Hype, Spin, Puffery and Lies':

> The real danger to the public . . . comes not from outright lies – in most cases facts can ultimately be proven and mistakes corrected. But . . . advertising uses [the power of images and] emotional appeals to shift the viewer's focus away from facts. Viewers who do not take the trouble to distinguish between provable claims and pleasant but meaningless word play end up buying 'the sizzle, not the steak' and often paying high prices. The best defense against misleading ads . . . is not tighter controls on [advertisers], but more education and more critical judgment among . . . consumers. Just as we train children to be wary of strangers offering candy, to count change at a store, and to kick the tyres before buying a used car, we must make the effort to step back and judge the value of . . . advertisements, and then master the skills required to separate spin from substance.[5]

Marketers argue that most companies avoid deceptive practices because such practices harm their business in the long run. Profitable customer relationships are built upon a foundation of value and trust. If consumers do not get what they expect, they will switch to more reliable products. In addition, consumers usually protect themselves from deception. Most consumers recognise a marketer's selling intent and are careful when they buy, sometimes to the point of not believing completely true product claims.

High-pressure selling

Salespeople are sometimes accused of high-pressure selling that persuades people to buy goods they had no thought of buying. It is often said that cars, insurance and home improvement plans are *sold*, not *bought*. Salespeople are trained to deliver smooth, canned talks to entice purchase. They sell hard because commissions and sales contests promise big prizes to those who sell the most.

> Interested in buying a conservatory, a consumer contacted several local suppliers and Anglian Home Improvements, the market leader, who was promoting 'up to 25 per cent off conservatories plus free solar roof'. All the suppliers sent someone to discuss the project, sometimes the owner of the business. The local suppliers all supplied a plan and an estimate within a few days. Anglia sent a salesman who worked out an estimate on the spot, offered a loan at 1 per cent and tried to get a close. He even rang his boss, talking in a loud voice so that all could hear, to get a special deal if the customer's house could be a show house. The customer did not agree to buy on the spot and never did so because even with the '25 per cent off' the price was well over £20,000 (€30,000) while all the other estimates were well below that figure.

In most cases, marketers have little to gain from high-pressure selling. Such tactics may work in one-time selling situations for short-term gain. However, Anglian is the market leader.[6] Consumers are particularly vulnerable when making expensive purchases.

Holiday timeshare is one area. There are many reputable companies in this sector, such as Sunterra, that offer good-value products but still use high-pressure selling to achieve closure. The European Commission estimates holiday property rip-offs cost European consumers over €7bn a year and is extending the law protecting timeshare owners. The industry also wants political help in policing the sector. Sandy Grey, of the Timeshare Consumers' Association, says 'Nobody wants to buy because the reputation of the industry is so bad.'[7]

As these examples show, high-pressure selling abounds when selling high-cost services to vulnerable people. It also damages the prospects for legitimate marketers. Fortunately, most selling involves building long-term relationships with valued customers. High-pressure or deceptive selling can do serious damage to such relationships. For example, imagine a Unilever account manager trying to pressure a Tesco buyer, or an IBM salesperson trying to browbeat a Siemens information technology manager. It simply would not work.

Shoddy, harmful or unsafe products

Another criticism concerns poor product quality or function. One complaint is that, too often, products are not made well and services are not performed well. A second complaint is that many products deliver little benefit, or that they might even be harmful. For example, many critics have pointed out the dangers of today's fat-laden fast-food. McDonald's recently faced a class-action lawsuit charging that its fast food meals have contributed to the obesity epidemic.

Who's to blame for the nation's obesity problem? And what should responsible food companies do about it? As with most social responsibility issues, there are no easy answers. McDonald's has worked to improve its fare and make its menu and its customers healthier. However, other fast feeders seem to be going the other way. Burger King launched its Enormous Omelet breakfast sandwich, packing an unapologetic 47 grams of fat. Are these companies being socially irresponsible? Or are they simply serving customers choices they want?[8]

Once we laughed at the US as being the fast food nation. Now Europe is catching up. 'The last three decades have seen the levels of overweight and obesity in the EU population rise dramatically, particularly among children, where the estimated prevalence of overweight was 30 per cent', says Markos Kyprianou, the European Union health commissioner. He explained that in most EU countries more than half the adult population was either overweight or obese and 'today's overweight children will be tomorrow's heart attack victims'.

Governments in some countries have already acted. In some European countries, junk food is banned in schools and marketing restrictions are imposed on food companies, with the UK restricting television advertisements of junk food. Half the products of one in three European food companies had been 'reformulated' to make them healthier. Industry had also accepted voluntary curbs on advertising and modified their marketing to avoid further regulation. Soft drinks companies and some food companies are stopping advertisements to children under the age of 12.

The voluntary steps taken by the industry had persuaded the European Commission to give self-regulation a chance. Beuc, the European Consumers' Association, thinks the Commission has failed to tackle what the Commissioner himself called a 'top public health priority'. Beuc attacked the Commission's policy paper as a 'disappointing, unambitious and minimalist response to the problems of obesity and diet-related diseases'.[9]

For over 100 years consumers have worried about the 'goodness' of what they consume, hence the success of Marmite and Perrier. Dogs do not fret about food additives but their owners care for them.

SOURCE: The Advertising Archives.

At the opposite end of the spectrum to obesity, marketers and particularly the fashion industry are criticised for idolising images of beauty that are unrealistic, if not dangerous. Real Marketing 2.1 shows how Unilever have responded to this aspiration by trying to create a more realistic portrayal of womanhood.

real marketing 2.1

The Dove Campaign for Real Beauty

Unilever's Dove brand is on a mission. The Dove Campaign for Real Beauty aims to change the traditional definition of beauty.

SOURCE: Ruby Washington/The New York Times/Redux.

In a year when both 'skinny chic' and the size 00 – the waist of a typical seven-year-old – was the height of fashion, Ana Carolina Reston's death was poignant. She was the second model during 2006 to die from an eating disorder. In August, at a fashion show in Uruguay, 22-year-old Luisel Ramos suffered a heart attack thought to be the result of anorexia. Although anorexia is not the preserve of the fashion industry, it is not surprising that Reston's death has spotlighted how the fashion business treats its models and how destructive our current perception of female beauty can be.

How do you define beauty? Open the latest copy of a fashion magazine and check out the ads for cosmetics and beauty-care products. Look at the models in those ads – the classic beauties with incredibly lean, sexy figures with flawless features. Does anyone you know look like the women in those ads? Maybe not. They are supermodels, chosen to portray ideal beauty. The ads are aspirational. But real women, who compare themselves to these idealised images day in and day out, too often come away feeling diminished by thoughts that they could never really look like that.

...2.1

Unilever's Dove brand is on a mission to change all of this. Its Campaign for Real Beauty hopes to do more than just sell Dove beauty creams and lotions. It aims to change the traditional definition of beauty – to 'offer in its place a broader, healthier, more democratic view of beauty'. It tells women to be happy just the way they are. 'In Dove ads,' says one advertising expert, 'normal is the new beautiful.'

It all started with a Unilever study that examined the impact on women of a society that narrowly defines beauty by the images seen in entertainment, in advertising and on fashion catwalks. The startling result: only 2 per cent of 3,300 women and girls surveyed in 10 countries around the world considered themselves beautiful. Unilever's research revealed that among women ages 15 to 64 world-wide, 90 per cent want to change at least one aspect of their physical appearance and a staggering 67 per cent withdraw from some life-engaging activities because they are uncomfortable with their looks.

Unilever concluded: 'It is time to redefine beauty!' 'We believe that beauty comes in different shapes, sizes and ages,' says Dove marketing director Philippe Harousseau. 'Our mission is to make more women feel beautiful every day by broadening the definition of beauty.' Unilever launched the Dove Campaign for Real Beauty globally in 2004, with ads that featured candid and confident images of real women of all types (not just actresses or models) and headlines that prompted consumers to ponder their perceptions of beauty. Among others, it featured full-bodied women ('Oversized or Outstanding?'), older women ('Gray or Gorgeous?'; 'Wrinkled or Wonderful?') and a heavily freckled woman ('Flawed or Flawless?'). In 2005, the campaign's popularity skyrocketed as Dove introduced six new 'real beauties' of various ethnicities and proportions, in sizes ranging from 6 to 14. These women appeared in magazines and on billboards wearing nothing but their underwear and big smiles, with headlines proclaiming, 'Let's face it, firming the thighs of a size 2 supermodel is no challenge,' or 'New Dove Firming: As Tested on Real Curves.'

In 2006, Unilever took the Dove campaign to a new level, with a ground-breaking spot in the mother of all ad showcases, the US Super Bowl. This ad did not feature curvy, confident women. Instead, it presented young girls battling self-esteem issues – not models but real girls picked from schools, sports leagues and Girl Scout troops. In the ad, one dark-haired girl 'wishes she were a blond'. Another 'thinks she's ugly'. A pretty young redhead 'hates her freckles'. The ad also promoted the Dove Self-Esteem Fund, which supports, among other causes, the Girl Scouts' Uniquely Me programme. It urged viewers to 'get involved' at the campaignforrealbeauty.com website.

'We want to raise awareness of self-esteem being a real issue [for a young girl],' says Harousseau. 'Every single one of us can get engaged and can change the way we interact with her to increase self-esteem.' As the campaign has taken off, so have sales of Dove products. And calls to Unilever's consumer call centre have surged, as has traffic to the campaignforrealbeauty.com website. Women, girls and even men praise Dove for addressing a too-long-ignored social issue.

Debora Boyda, managing partner at Ogilvy & Mather, the ad agency that created the campaign, received a phone call from an emotional father. His teenage daughter had just recovered from a four-year battle with anorexia. The father thanked her and stressed how important he thought the ad was. 'That to me was the high point of what the ad achieved,' says Boyda.

In addition to the positive reactions, however, the Dove Campaign for Real Beauty has also received criticism. Critics argue that the 'real women' in the Dove ads are still head turners, with smooth skin, straight teeth and no cellulite. Although these unretouched beauties are more realistic than supermodels, they still represent a lofty standard of beauty. Fans of the campaign counter that, compared with typical ad-industry portrayals, the Dove women represent an image of beauty that is healthy, constructive and much closer to reality. For example, after seeing a Dove billboard, one young woman gushed, 'Most girls don't have that (supermodel) type of body and they know they won't get to that. But seeing this [Dove ad] they say, "I can do that."' Other critics claim that the campaign is hypocritical, celebrating less-than-perfect bodies while at the same time selling products designed to restore them, such as firming lotions.

'Any change in the culture of advertising that allows for a broader definition of beauty and encourages women to be more accepting and comfortable with their natural appearance is a step in the right direction,' says noted psychologist and author Mary Pipher. 'But embedded within this is a contradiction. They are still saying you have to use this product to be beautiful.' Still, she concedes, 'It's better than what we've had in the past.'

Yvonne, a woman featured in one of the Dove ads, takes issue with the criticism. 'That's like saying, why be into fashion? Women are women. We love to be the best we can be. It's not contradictory; it's just taking care of yourself.' Ad executive Boyda also defends Unilever's intentions: 'We are telling [women] we want them to take care of themselves, take care of their beauty,' she says. 'That's very different from sending them the message to look like something they're not.'

Still others criticise Unilever for capitalising on women's low self-esteem just to make a buck. But the company responds that it has created a lot more than just a

...2.1

series of ads. It is promoting a philosophy, supported by a substantial advertising budget, the Dove Self-Esteem Fund and a website full of resources designed to build the self-esteem of women and young girls.

Certainly, Unilever does have financial objectives for its Dove brand – most consumers understand and accept that. If women are not buying the message of Dove about the nature of real beauty, then they aren't buying its products either. But the people behind the Dove brand and the Campaign for Real Beauty have noble motives beyond sales and profits. According to Fernando Acosta, Dove vice-president of brand development, the bold and compelling mission of the Dove brand to redefine beauty and reassure women ranks well beyond the issues of money: 'You should see the faces of the people working on this brand now,' he says. 'There is a real love for the brand.'

SOURCES: Theresa Howard, 'Dove ad gets serious for super bowl', *USA Today* (23 January 2006), accessed at www.usatoday.com; Don Babwin, 'Dove ads with "real" women get attention', *Associated Press Financial Wire* (29 July 2005); Theresa Howard, 'Ad campaigns tell women to celebrate how they are', *USA Today* (7 August 2005), accessed at www.usatoday.com; Pallavi Gogoi, 'From reality TV to reality ads', *BusinessWeek Online* (17 August 2005), accessed at www.businessweek.com; 'Positioning: Getting comfy in their skin', *Brandweek* (19 December 2005), p. 16; Patricia Odell, 'Real girls', *Promo* (1 March 2006), p. 24; 'Beyond stereotypes: Rebuilding the foundation of beauty beliefs' (February 2006), accessed at www.campaignforrealbeauty.com; Jeani Read, 'Women modeling for Dove love challenging skinny stereotypes', *The Calgary Herald* (15 May 2006), p. C3; and information found at www.campaignforrealbeauty.com, December 2006; Tom Phillips, 'Everyone knew she was ill . . .', *The Observer* (14 January 2007).

In order to persuade customers to buy their brand rather than any other, manufacturers sometimes make claims that are not fully substantiated.

The recent spate of food scares and the increasing popularity of functional food products that claim to have beneficial effects on consumer health have spurred the European Commission into action. Planned legislation would ban companies from using claims 'that make reference to general, non-specific benefits to overall good health, well-being and normal functioning of the body'. So, slogans such as '90 per cent fat-free' and 'strengthens your body's natural defences' would be prohibited. According to the European Commission there is a need to ensure that consumers are not fooled by information provided on the products. A fundamental requirement is that consumers are protected. The food industry is less than enthusiastic. They welcome regulations that would allow companies to use the same labelling across the EU, but fear that the Commission may be overstepping the mark. It may be easy to see why. The new regulations would mean that Nestlé LCI yoghurts, Danone Actimel drinkable yoghurt range and Unilever's Latta margarine would not be able to claim to stimulate, help or strengthen your body's natural defences. Neither would Kellogg's be allowed to use the little symbols to indicate the health benefits that it puts on cereals in its range.[10]

A third complaint concerns product safety. Product safety has been a problem for several reasons, including manufacturer indifference, increased production complexity, poorly trained labour and poor quality control. Consider the following cases of costly and image-damaging crises brought upon several car manufacturers:

In 2004 Mercedes-Benz's quality image took a battering when it recalled almost one in three of the 4 million cars it had sold in the previous four years to fix electronic problems. Mercedes are far from alone among car makers in making recalls. VW recalled 350,000 of its models worldwide because of a potentially faulty electric cable, as well as some 950,000 Golfs, Jettas, Passats and Corrados because of problems, including a cooling system fault, which could potentially damage engines and injure passengers. In the same year Jaguar had to recall its top-of-the-range car after the manufacturer discovered the automatic gearbox could switch into reverse without warning. Such defects and recalls are an inevitable feature of mass-producing products as complicated as a car. The real issues occur when manufacturers resist or ignore problems. Ford and Firestone blamed each other for accidents following blowouts on their Ford Explorers Sports Utility Vehicle that were claimed to have caused 271 deaths and more than 800 injuries. And in Japan, Toyota executives faced a criminal investigation for failing to recall the company's Hi-Lux minivans for years.[11]

For years, consumer protection groups or associations in many countries have regularly tested products for safety, and have reported hazards found in tested products, such as electrical dangers in appliances, and injury risks from lawnmowers and faulty car design. The testing and reporting activities of these organisations have helped consumers make better buying decisions and have encouraged businesses to eliminate product flaws.

Marketers may sometimes face dilemmas when seeking to balance consumer needs and social responsibility. For example, no amount of test results can guarantee product safety in cars if consumers value speed and power more than safety features. Buyers might choose a less expensive chain-saw without a safety guard, although society or a government regulatory agency might deem it irresponsible and unethical for the manufacturer to sell it.

" No amount of test results can guarantee product safety. "

However, most responsible manufacturers *want* to produce quality goods. The way a company deals with product quality and safety problems can damage or help its reputation. Companies selling poor-quality or unsafe products risk damaging conflicts with consumer groups and regulators. Moreover, unsafe products can result in product liability suits and large awards for damages.

More fundamentally, consumers who are unhappy with a firm's products may avoid future purchases and talk other consumers into doing the same. Thus, quality missteps can have severe consequences. Today's marketers know that customer-driven quality results in customer value and satisfaction which, in turn, creates profitable customer relationships.

Planned obsolescence

Critics have charged that some producers follow a programme of **planned obsolescence**, causing their products to become obsolete before they should need replacement. For example, consider computer printer companies and their toner cartridges:

Planned obsolescence—A strategy of causing products to become obsolete before they actually need replacement.

Computer printer makers use a 'lamp and oil' pricing strategy adopted by Standard Oil to stimulate oil sales in the nineteenth century. Their Mei Foo, 'beautiful and trustworthy', lamp was sold very cheaply or given away with kerosene by the millions. Computer printer makers make their profits on ink cartridges that customers need to make the printer work. Kodak estimates that, as a consequence, consumers pay $4,000 per US gallon (about €800 per litre) for their ink. Not surprisingly, this high margin has attracted retailers, from local shops to large big-box stores, to now offer toner cartridge refill services. However, printer companies would prefer to sell their cartridges for €50 or more, rather than allow someone to refill one for half the price. So they make it hard for refill operations by continually introducing new models and tweaking inkjet cartridges and laser toner containers to make refillable ones obsolete. This leaves refill parts manufacturers struggling to keep up, jockeying with the printer companies that are working to thwart them.[12]

Critics charge that some producers continually change consumer concepts of acceptable styles in order to encourage more and earlier buying. An obvious example is constantly changing clothing fashions. Other producers are accused of holding back attractive functional features, then introducing them later to make older models obsolete. Critics claim that this practice is frequently found in the consumer electronics and computer industries. For example, Intel and Microsoft have been accused in recent years of holding back their next-generation computer chips or software until demand is exhausted for the current generation. Consumers have also expressed annoyance with kitchen appliances, cameras and consumer electronics companies' policy of rapid and frequent model replacement. Rapid obsolescence has created difficulties in obtaining spare parts for old models. Moreover, dealers refuse to repair outdated models and planned obsolescence rapidly erodes basic product values. Still other producers are accused of using materials and components that will break, wear, rust or rot sooner than they should.

Marketers respond that consumers *like* style changes; they get tired of the old goods and want a new look in fashion or a new design in cars. No one has to buy the new look, and if too few people like it, it will simply fail. For most technical products, customers *want* the latest innovations, even if older models still work. Companies that withhold new features run the risk that competitors will introduce the new feature first and steal the market. For example, consider personal computers. Some consumers grumble that the consumer electronics industry's constant push to produce 'faster, smaller, cheaper' models means that they must continually buy new machines just to keep up. Others, however, can hardly wait for the latest model to arrive.

Thus, companies rarely design their products to break down earlier, because they do not want to lose their customers to other brands. Instead, they seek constant improvement to ensure that products will consistently meet or exceed customer expectations. Much of so-called planned obsolescence is the working of the competitive and technological forces in a free society – forces that lead to ever-improving goods and services.

In addition, if exploited to excess consumers rebel and market opportunities arise. Miele, the top-of-the-range German kitchen appliance manufacturer, now offers a free 10-year warranty with its washing machines, and Kodak is launching computer printers that use inexpensive ink cartridges.

Poor service to disadvantaged consumers

Finally, marketing has been accused of serving disadvantaged consumers poorly. Critics claim that the urban poor often have to shop in smaller stores that carry inferior goods and charge higher prices. Others, particularly those in the countryside, are in retail deserts without access to main goods. The large grocery stores are doubly accused. First, they kill off local competitors and then, detractors say, they do not set up in low-income neighbourhoods and help to keep prices down. Furthermore, critics accuse major chain retailers of 'redlining', drawing a red line around disadvantaged neighbourhoods and avoiding placing stores there and so creating food deserts. The continued threat of the closure of small bank branches and local post offices creates a similar threat to less mobile people.[13]

Redlining charges have been levelled at the insurance, consumer lending, banking and healthcare industries. Home and motor car insurers have been accused of assigning higher premiums to people with poor credit ratings. The insurers claim that individuals with bad credit tend to make more insurance claims, and that this justifies charging them higher premiums. However, critics and consumer advocates have accused the insurers of a new form of redlining. Says one writer, 'This is a new excuse for denying coverage to the poor, elderly and minorities.'[14]

Marketing's eye on profits also means that disadvantaged consumers are not viable segments to target. The high-income consumer is the preferred target. Or, that corporations are not doing enough to enhance the quality of life or living conditions of the local communities their businesses depend on.

Marketing systems must be built to service disadvantaged consumers. In fact, many marketers profitably target such consumers with legitimate goods and services that create real value.

Many small retail chains survive in areas neglected by the majors. Multinationals such as Tesco are creating local Tesco Express convenience stores that give customers access to their goods and financial services in many countries. High-street banks deal with low-earners who want to open basic bank accounts into which state benefits can be paid. HBOS targets customers who are sub-prime or who have irregular incomes – such as contract workers. Capital One has a Classic MasterCard aimed at those rebuilding their credit record, at an annual percentage rate of up to 30 per cent. Provident Financial, a doorstep lender, is trialling a range of Vanquis credit cards that charge interest rates between 17 and 65 per cent. These are high but preferable to the threat of violence and extortion from loan sharks who live off people on low incomes.[15]

Having examined common criticisms of marketing as it impacts consumers, we now turn to social critics' assessment of how marketing affects society as a whole.

Marketing's impact on society as a whole

Marketing is accused of adding to the 'evils' in our society. Advertising has been a special target. It has been blamed for creating false wants, fostering greedy aspirations and urging too much materialism in our society. Marketing has also been blamed for working against the long-term interests of society and the well-being of its members. Here, we will examine the major societal concerns relating to marketing: the creation of false wants and too much materialism; overselling of private goods at the expense of social goods; cultural pollution and an excess of political power.

> " Advertising . . . has been blamed for creating false wants, fostering greedy aspirations and urging too much materialism. "

Businesses within immigrant communities often start by serving their own community. There are a range of ethnic companies supplying the Asian market – some from India and some from England.
SOURCE: The Advertising Archives.

False wants and too much materialism

Critics have charged that the marketing system urges too much interest in material possessions. People are judged by what they *own* rather than by who they *are*. To be considered successful, people must own a large home or smart-looking apartment in a prime residential area, expensive cars, the latest (or best) designer clothing and high-tech gadgets. This drive for wealth and possessions hit new highs in the 1980s and 1990s, when phrases such as 'greed is good' and 'shop till you drop' seemed to characterise the times. In the current decade, many social scientists have noted a reaction against the opulence and waste of the previous decades and a return to more basic values and social commitment. However, our infatuation with material things continues.

> Between 1960 and 2007 real GDP (inflation adjusted Gross Domestic Product) grew 400 per cent in the EU15 and close to 500 per cent in the US. The size of the typical new house has more than doubled. A family owning a car was once a goal, now it is hard to know where to put the multiple cars that families own. Designer everything, personal electronics and other items that didn't even exist a half-century ago are now affordable. Although our time spent shopping has dropped in recent years to just three hours a week, our rate of spend in that short time has exploded.[16]

The critics do not view this interest in material things as a natural state of mind, but rather as a matter of false wants created by marketing. Businesses spend huge sums of money to hire advertising agencies to stimulate people's desires for goods, and advertisers use the mass media to create materialistic models of the good life. People work harder to earn the necessary money. Their purchases increase the output of the nation's industry, and industry, in turn, uses the advertising industry to stimulate more desire for the industrial output. Thus marketing is seen as creating false wants that benefit industry more than they benefit consumers.

These criticisms overstate the power of business to create needs. People have strong defences against advertising and other marketing tools. Marketers are most effective when they appeal to existing wants rather than when they attempt to create new ones. Furthermore, people seek information when making important purchases and often do not rely on single sources. Even minor purchases that may be affected by advertising messages lead to repeat purchases only if the product delivers the promised customer value. Finally, the high failure rate of new products shows that companies are not able to control demand.

On a deeper level, our wants and values are influenced not only by marketers, but also by family, peer groups, religion, ethnic background, education and deep-seated needs that pre-date the modern age. The pre-industrial age 1660–69 diaries of Samuel Pepys, the writings of Dr Johnson (1709–84) and Jane Austen's (1775–1817) novels are littered with products that were desired and bestowed status. Also within Bronislaw Malinowski's seminal work on field anthropology is the realisation that people's status was based on jewellery traded across the Pacific islands. The roots of our modern materialistic societies are much deeper than business and mass media could produce alone. Dr Johnson even decoded and classified 'puff', meaning exaggeration, in advertising and selling.[17]

Too few social goods

Business is accused of overselling private goods at the expense of public goods. As private goods increase, they require more public services that are usually not forthcoming. For example, an increase in car ownership (private good) requires more roads, traffic control, parking spaces and police services (public goods). The overselling of private goods results in 'social costs'. For cars, the social costs include excessive traffic congestion, air pollution, fuel shortages and pedestrian injuries from car accidents.

A way must be found to restore a balance between private and public goods. One option is to make producers bear the full social costs of their operations. Governments are also requiring car manufacturers to build cars with even more safety features and better fuel efficiency. The European Commission's end-of-life vehicles (ELV) directive already makes manufacturers pay for the cost of scrapping the cars they make. Car makers raise their prices to cover extra costs. If buyers found the price of some cars too high, however, the production would decline, and demand would move to those producers that could support both the private and social costs.

A second option is to make consumers pay the social costs. For example, highway authorities around the world are starting to charge 'congestion charges' in an effort to reduce traffic congestion.

Countries such as Norway, the UK, France, Singapore and the US are managing traffic with varying tolls. For example, to unclog its streets, the city of London now levies a congestion charge of £10 (€15) per day per car to drive in an eight-square-mile area downtown. The charge has not only reduced traffic congestion by 30 per cent, it raises money to fund London's public transportation system. In southern California drivers are being charged premiums to travel in under-used car pool lanes. For example, San Diego has turned some of its HOV (high-occupancy vehicle) lanes into HOT (high-occupancy toll) lanes for drivers carrying too few passengers. Regular drivers can use the HOV lanes, but they must pay tolls ranging from $0.50 (€0.37) off-peak to $4.00 (€3) during rush hour. Peak surcharges are being studied for roads around other American cities. Economists point out that traffic jams are caused when drivers are not charged the costs they impose on others, such as delays. If the costs of driving rise high enough, consumers will travel at non-peak times or find alternative transportation modes. In Singapore, drivers are charged for every move they make in the city state's central business district and the licence to buy a car on taxes makes the cost of car ownership several times European levels, yet people still drive classy Mercedes. 'Make 'em pay' is part of making car drivers pay their full social cost but, whatever the price, people drive on.[18]

Cultural pollution

Critics charge the marketing system with creating *cultural pollution*. Our senses are assaulted constantly by advertising. Commercials interrupt serious programmes; pages of ads obscure printed matter; billboards mar beautiful scenery; spam fills our e-mail inboxes. These interruptions continuously pollute people's minds with messages of materialism, sex, power or status. Children's constant exposure to advertising, the protectionists argue, creates mercenary kids, experts in 'pester power', who force their downtrodden and beleaguered parents into spending enormous sums of money on branded goods and the latest crazes. Although not everyone may find advertising overly annoying (some even think it is the best part of television programming), a recent study noted that 65 per cent of consumers feel bombarded with too many marketing messages, and some critics call for sweeping changes.[19]

Marketers answer the charges of 'commercial noise' with these arguments. First, they hope that their ads reach primarily the target audience. But because of mass-communication channels, some ads are bound to reach people who have no interest in the product and are therefore bored or annoyed. People who buy magazines slanted towards their interests – such as *Vogue, Bliss, Loaded, Heat* or *Fortune* – rarely complain about the ads because the magazines advertise products of interest to them.

As for TV advertising's influence on children, free marketers point to European research that shows that parents and peers influence children more than advertising. Children are not empty vessels helplessly vulnerable to marketers' wiles. They are capable of absorbing and assimilating advertising messages, approaching commercials with a critical mind and drawing their own verdict.[20] Moreover, advertisers argue that parents are responsible for managing their children's exposure to marketing. Although children are hedonists, inclined to make impulse buys and less likely to make educated purchasing decisions, they have to start learning to distinguish truth from spin in advertising. Nevertheless, responsible marketers recognise that however hedonistic or naive they may be, children have long memories – deceive them and lose them as customers forever.

Second, ads make much of television and radio free, keep down the cost of magazines and newspapers and the cost of any place where advertising is allowed. Most people think commercials are a small price to pay for these benefits. Finally, consumers have alternatives: they can zip and zap TV commercials or avoid them altogether on many cable and satellite channels. Thus to hold consumer attention, advertisers are making their ads more entertaining and informative.

Excessive political power

Another criticism is that business wields too much political power. 'Oil', 'tobacco', 'pharmaceuticals', 'financial services' and 'alcohol' have the support of important politicians who look after an industry's interests against the public interest. Advertisers are accused of holding too much power over the mass media, limiting their freedom to report independently and objectively.

> '' 'Oil', 'tobacco', 'pharmaceuticals', 'financial services' and 'alcohol' have the support of important politicians who look after an industry's interests against the public interest. ''

The aerospace industries showed their particular cosiness to politicians when Tony Blair's government prematurely terminated a UK Serious Fraud Office investigation into allegations that BAE might have bribed officials in Saudi Arabia to secure defence contracts. British politicians were shocked and Washington issued a formal protest. However, the intensity of US scrutiny only increased after BAE boosted its US profile with the $4.1bn (€3bn) purchase of Armour Holdings – for the biggest maker of armour for Humvee transport vehicles. The scope of this investigation shows how many governments may be mixed up in dodgy arms deals. The US Congress is looking at the sale of two A-4N Skyhawk aircraft to the German Air Force, an agreement to upgrade Australian F/A-18 fighter jets, and an agreement between BAE and Japanese companies to make transporters. Swiss prosecutors are also investigating alleged money laundering relating to BAE Systems' Saudi Arabia arms sales, and the UK's Serious Fraud Office is still investigating the sale of BAE Hawk trainer aircraft and Saab Gripen fighters to South Africa.

BAE extricated themselves from troubled Airbus, but the French and German governments are at loggerheads over troubled EADS – Airbus's maker. Nicolas Sarkozy launched his presidency with a friendly dinner in Berlin with German chancellor Angela Merkel. According to the *Financial Times*, it went well until the new French president served up the tricky subject of EADS. Mr Sarkozy wants to resolve the infighting between the French and German camps at the European aerospace group. He appeared ready to talk tough to the Germans and unlikely to accept any more diplomatic dithering. The French themselves helped create the current crisis at EADS and its Airbus affiliate. The scandal surrounding the disgraced former French boss of EADS and Airbus – Noël Forgeard – was largely due to Paris political interference.[21]

Industries and other pressure groups have a right to representation in Parliament and the mass media, although their influence can become too great. Fortunately, many powerful business interests once thought to be untouchable have been tamed in the public interest. For example, in the EU and the US, consumerism campaigns have resulted in legislation requiring the car industry to build more safety into its cars and cigarette and food companies to put health warnings on their packages. Also, because the media receive advertising revenues from many different advertisers, it is easier to resist the influence of one or a few of them. As with politics, freedom of the press is an essential counterweight to powerful organisations. In a free society, too much power tends to result in counter-forces that check and offset these powerful interests.

Let us now take a look at the criticisms that business critics have levelled at companies' marketing practices.

Marketing's impact on other businesses

Critics charge that marketing practices can harm other companies and reduce competition. Three problems are involved: acquisition of competitors, marketing practices that create barriers to entry, and unfair competitive marketing practices.

Critics claim that firms are harmed and competition reduced when companies expand by acquiring competitors rather than by developing their own new products. The large number of acquisitions and the rapid pace of industry consolidation over the past two decades have caused concern that vigorous young competitors will be absorbed and that competition will be reduced. In virtually every major industry – retailing, financial services, utilities, transportation, motor vehicles, telecommunications, entertainment – the number of major competitors is shrinking.

Consider the recent feeding frenzy of acquisitions in the food industry – Unilever's buying Bestfoods, Philip Morris's snatching Nabisco, Nestlé buying Gerber, Danone buying 49 per cent of Denmark's Aqua d'Or and declaring it is placing 'more emphasis on acquisitions as a way of growing faster'.[22]

Acquisition is a complex subject. Acquisitions can sometimes be good for society. The acquiring company may gain economies of scale that lead to lower costs and lower prices.

A well-managed company may take over a poorly managed company and improve its efficiency. An industry that was not very competitive might become more competitive after the acquisition. But acquisitions can also be harmful and are therefore closely regulated by some governments and competition (or mergers and monopolies) commissions. Badly implemented, they can also damage the reputation of a well-respected company and write off a huge amount of wealth, as did the Daimler Chrysler merger.[23]

Critics have also claimed that marketing practices bar new companies from entering an industry. The use of patents and heavy promotion spending can tie up suppliers or dealers to keep out or drive out competitors. Those concerned with antitrust regulation recognise that some barriers are the natural result of the economic advantages of doing business on a large scale. Other barriers could be challenged by existing and new laws. For example, some critics have proposed a progressive tax on advertising spending to reduce the role of selling costs as a substantial barrier to entry.

Finally, some firms have in fact used unfair competitive marketing practices with the intention of hurting or destroying other firms. They may set their prices below costs, threaten to cut off business with suppliers, or discourage the buying of a competitor's products. Various laws work to prevent such predatory competition. It is difficult, however, to prove that the intent or action was really predatory.

> Recently, Microsoft felt the impact of EU antitrust regulators seeking to balance the interests of their scale and influence. The EU threatened Microsoft Corporation with fines of up to €3m a day, claiming the software giant had failed to live up to promises for providing information that could help rivals make servers compatible with Windows.[24]

Although competitors and governments charge that the actions of companies are predatory and illegal, others question whether this is unfair competition or the healthy competition of a more efficient company against the less efficient ones.[25]

Citizen and public actions to regulate marketing

Because some people view business as the cause of many economic and social ills, grassroots movements have arisen from time to time to keep business in line. The two main movements have been *consumerism* and *environmentalism*.

Consumer movements

Western business firms have been the targets of organised consumer movements on three occasions. The first has its origins in the early 1900s, fuelled by rising prices and Upton Sinclair's 1906 novel, *The Jungle*, that was an exposé of the dreadful conditions in the Chicago meat industry that provide branded canned food across the world. A drug scandal and price increases during the 1930s Great Depression sparked the second consumer movement. The third began in the 1960s. Consumers had become better educated, products had become more complex and potentially hazardous, and people were unhappy with Western institutions. Ralph Nader appeared on the scene in the 1960s to force many issues, and other well-known writers accused big business of wasteful and unethical practices. President John F. Kennedy and other Western politicians declared that consumers have the right to safety and to be informed, to choose and to be heard. The consumer movement has spread internationally and has become very strong in Europe.[26]

❝ . . . equating personal happiness with purchasing material possessions and consumption. **❞**

Consumerism—An organised movement of citizens and government agencies to improve the rights and power of buyers in relation to sellers.

But what is the consumer movement? Karl Marx and Thorstein Veblen used **consumerism** to describe the effects of equating personal happiness with purchasing material possessions and consumption. Consumerism is now more often used to describe an organised movement of citizens and government agencies to improve the rights and power of buyers in relation to sellers. Traditional sellers' rights include:

- The right to introduce any product in any size and style, provided it is not hazardous to personal health or safety; or, if it is, to include proper warnings and controls.
- The right to charge any price for the product, provided no discrimination exists among similar kinds of buyer.
- The right to spend any amount to promote the product, provided it is not defined as unfair competition.
- The right to use any product message, provided it is not misleading or dishonest in content or execution.
- The right to use any buying incentive schemes, provided they are not unfair or misleading.

Traditional buyers' rights include:

- The right not to buy a product that is offered for sale.
- The right to expect the product to be safe.
- The right to expect the product to perform as claimed.

Comparing these rights, many believe that the balance of power lies on the sellers' side. True, the buyer can refuse to buy. But critics feel that the buyer has too little information, education and protection to make wise decisions when facing sophisticated sellers. Consumer advocates call for the following additional consumer rights:

- The right to be well informed about important aspects of the product.
- The right to be protected against questionable products and marketing practices.
- The right to influence products and marketing practices in ways that will improve the 'quality of life'.

Each proposed right has led to more specific proposals by consumerists. The right to be informed includes the right to know the true interest on a loan (truth in lending), the true cost per unit of a brand (unit pricing), the ingredients in a product (ingredient labelling), the nutrition in foods (nutritional labelling), product freshness (open dating) and the true benefits of a product (truth in advertising). Proposals related to consumer protection include strengthening consumer rights in cases of business fraud, requiring greater product safety, ensuring information privacy and giving more power to government agencies. Proposals relating to quality of life include controlling the ingredients that go into certain products and packaging, reducing the level of advertising 'noise' and putting consumer representatives on company boards to protect consumer interests.

Consumers have not only the *right* but also the *responsibility* to protect themselves instead of leaving this function to someone else. Consumers who believe that they got a bad deal have several remedies available, including contacting the company or the media, contacting government or private consumer-interest/protection bodies or agencies, going to small-claims courts, or organising consumer boycotts.

Thomas Clarkson, a founder of the Society for Effecting the Abolition of Slavery in 1787, organised what was probably the first ever consumer boycott. It was against slave-grown sugar and aimed to bring home to Britons that they were paying a dreadful price in human cruelty for indulging a sweet tooth. At one time more than 300,000 people joined the boycott that was also designed to hit the profits of the plantation owners. It inspired a parliamentary movement against slavery, recruiting William Wilberforce, who brought bills before Parliament to abolish the slave trade until one was passed in 1807.

Over 200 years later Nike faced an anti-sweatshop protest. They initially denied responsibility at contractors' factories, but subsequently became a leader in an attempt to establish independent factory monitoring and promote labour rights, including the freedom for its 800,000 workers worldwide to form and join trade unions. Other companies, including Reebok and Levi Strauss, have since followed Nike's lead.[27]

The advent of electronic communication has made it possible for consumers to gain mass support and time their intervention powerfully. So powerful can these movements be that companies have rated reputation loss as the greatest risk they face.[28]

Environmentalism

Whereas consumerists consider whether the marketing system is efficiently serving consumer wants, environmentalists are concerned with marketing's effects on the environment and the costs of serving consumer needs and wants. **Environmentalism** is an organised movement of concerned citizens and government agencies to protect and improve people's living environment. Environmentalists are not against marketing and consumption; they simply want people and organisations to operate with more care for the environment. They assert that the marketing system's goal is not to maximise consumption, consumer choice or consumer satisfaction, but rather to maximise life quality. 'Life quality' means not only the quantity and quality of consumer goods and services, but also the quality of the environment. Environmentalists want environmental costs to be included in both producer and consumer decision making.

The first wave of modern environmentalism was driven by fringe environmental groups, such as Greenpeace, and concerned consumers in the 1960s and 1970s. They were concerned with damage to the ecosystem caused by strip mining, forest depletion, acid rain, loss of the atmosphere's ozone layer, toxic wastes, whaling and landfills. They were also concerned with the loss of recreational areas and with the increase in health problems caused by bad air, polluted water and chemically treated food.

The second wave was driven by governments, which passed laws and regulations during the 1970s and 1980s governing industrial practices impacting the environment. This wave hit some industries hard. Chemical and steel companies and utilities had to invest in pollution-control equipment and costlier (but cleaner) fuels. The car industry had to introduce expensive emission controls in cars. The packaging industry has had to find ways to reduce litter. These industries and others have often resented and resisted environmental regulations, especially when they have been imposed too rapidly to allow companies to make proper adjustments. Many of these companies claim they have had to absorb large costs that have made them less competitive.

Environmentalism—An organised movement of concerned citizens and government agencies to protect and improve people's living environment.

WHAT WILL IT TAKE TO MAKE YOU RECYCLE GLASS?

You don't have to do anything quite as strenuous as living in a tree to do your bit for the environment. Just recycle your glass bottles and jars at one of the 22,000 bottle bank sites in Britain. Every tonne of glass we recycle saves 1.2 tonnes of natural raw materials like sand and limestone. Which means less quarrying, less damage to our countryside, less pollution and valuable energy savings. Glass is one of the purest substances known to man. It can be recycled over and over again without any loss of quality, but only if we all play our part in the recycling chain. Please make the effort. After all, glass is recyclable. Our surroundings aren't.

GLASS
DON'T BIN IT. BANK IT.

Environmental campaigns are gaining popularity. This campaign urges the British public to make the effort to recycle their glass bottles and jars by disposing of them at bottle banks.

SOURCE: The Advertising Archives.

The first two environmentalism waves have now merged into a third and stronger wave in which companies are accepting responsibility for doing no harm to the environment. They are shifting from protest to prevention, and from regulation to responsibility. More and more companies are adopting **environmental sustainability**. Simply put, environmental sustainability is about generating profits while helping to save the planet. However, sustainability is a crucial but difficult goal.

Environmental sustainability—A management approach that involves developing strategies that both sustain the environment and produce profits for the company.

Savings Investments Insurance

Our strategy for the future is to make sure there is a future.

We're committed to becoming the first insurer to go carbon neutral worldwide.

AVIVA
Forward thinking

Aviva make themselves more attractive by 'becoming the first insurer to go carbon neutral worldwide'. It is good business logic 'to make sure there is a future' to do business.

SOURCE: Reproduced with permission of Aviva (www.aviva.com).

John Browne, chairman of giant oil company BP, asked this question: 'Is genuine progress still possible? Is development sustainable? Or is one strand of progress – industrialisation – now doing such damage to the environment that the next generation won't have a world worth living in? Browne sees the situation as an opportunity. BP broke ranks with the oil industry on environmental issues. BP once stood for British Petroleum. That changed to Beyond Petroleum. 'There are good commercial reasons to do right by the environment,' says Browne. Under his leadership, Beyond Petroleum has become active in public forums on global climate issues and has worked to reduce emissions in exploration and production. It has begun marketing cleaner fuels and invested significantly in exploring alternative energy sources, such as photovoltaic power and hydrogen. At the local level, BP recently opened 'the world's most environmentally friendly service station'.[29]

Some companies have responded to consumer environmental concerns by doing only what is required to avert new regulations or to keep environmentalists quiet. Enlightened companies, however, are taking action not because someone is forcing them to, or to reap short-run profits, but because it is the right thing to do – both for the company and for the planet's environmental future.

Figure 2.1 shows a grid that companies can use to gauge their progress towards environmental sustainability. At the most basic level, a company can practise *pollution prevention*. This involves more than pollution control – cleaning up waste after it has been created. Pollution prevention means eliminating or minimising waste *before* it is created. Companies emphasising prevention have responded with 'green marketing' programmes – developing ecologically safer products, recyclable and biodegradable packaging, better pollution controls and more energy-efficient operations.

Figure 2.1 The environmental sustainability grid

SOURCE: From Stuart Hart, 'Beyond greening: strategies for a sustainable world', *Harvard Business Review* (January–February 1997). Copyright © 1997 by the Harvard Business School Publishing Corporation. All rights reserved. Reprinted with permission.

	New environmental technology	**Sustainability vision**
Tomorrow	Is the environmental performance of our products limited by our existing technology base? Is there potential to realise major improvements through new technology?	Does our corporate vision direct us towards the solution of social and environmental problems? Does our vision guide the development of new technologies, markets, products and processes?
	Pollution prevention	**Product stewardship**
Today	Where are the most significant waste and emission streams from our current operations? Can we lower costs and risks by eliminating waste at the source or by using it as useful input?	What are the implications for product design and development if we assume responsibility for a product's entire life cycle? Can we add value or lower costs while simultaneously reducing the impact of our products?
	Internal	**External**

- Ricoh is aiming at zero waste in their plant and has cut waste to landfill by over 92 per cent since introducing a waste management system in 2001. Waste management costs fell by over 62 per cent, despite increases in landfill tax and waste carriage charges.
- Nike produces PVC-free shoes, recycles old sneakers and educates young people about conservation, reuse and recycling.
- VW is investing in low-emission diesels. Already their new Polo BlueMotion diesel model emits less carbon dioxide per kilometre than Toyota's top-selling Prius hybrid and costs a lot less to make.[30]

At the next level, companies can practise *product stewardship* – minimising not just pollution from production but all environmental impacts throughout the full product life cycle, and all the while reducing costs. Many companies are adopting design for environment (DFE) practices, which involve thinking ahead in the design stage to create products that are easier to recover, reuse or recycle. DFE not only helps to sustain the environment; it can be highly profitable for the company:

- Xerox Corporation's Equipment Remanufacture and Parts Reuse Programme converts end-of-life office equipment into new products and parts. Equipment returned to Xerox can be remanufactured reusing 70 to 90 per cent by weight of old machine components, while still meeting performance standards for equipment made with all new parts. The programme creates benefits for both the environment and the company. It prevents waste from entering landfills and reduces the amount of raw material and energy needed to produce new parts. Energy savings from parts reuse total an estimated 320,000 megawatt hours annually – enough energy to light more than 250,000 homes for a year.
- Among many other actions, the Tesco supermarket chain aims to give consumers clear information about the carbon cost of each product it sells – looking at its complete life cycle from production through distribution to consumption.[31]

At the third level of environmental sustainability, companies look to the future and plan for *new environmental technologies*. Many organisations that have made good headway in pollution prevention and product stewardship are still limited by existing technologies. To develop fully sustainable strategies, they will need to develop new technologies. For example, detergent manufacturers have developed laundry products for low-temperature washing. Some have embarked on a 'wash right' campaign which promotes the virtues of low-temperature washing by emphasising the benefits to the clothes as well as energy savings.

Wal-Mart is doing this too. It recently opened two experimental superstores designed to test dozens of environmentally friendly and energy-efficient technologies:[32]

A 143-foot-tall wind turbine stands outside one Wal-Mart Supercenter. Incongruous as it might seem, it is clearly a sign that something about the store is different. On the outside, the store's façade features row upon row of windows to allow in as much natural light as possible. The landscaping uses native, drought-tolerant plants cutting down on watering, mowing, and the amount of fertiliser and other chemicals needed. Inside the store, an efficient high-output linear fluorescent lighting system saves enough electricity annually from this store alone to supply the needs of 52 single-family homes. The store's heating system burns recovered cooking oil from the deli's fryers that is mixed with waste engine oil from the store's Tire and Lube Express. All organic waste, including produce, meats and paper, is placed in an organic waste compactor, which is then hauled off to a company that turns it into garden mulch. Wal-Mart's environmental goals are to use 100 per cent renewable energy, to create zero waste, and to sell products that sustain its resources and environment. Moreover, Wal-Mart is eagerly spreading the word by encouraging visitors – even from competing companies: 'This is not something we're keeping to ourselves. We want everyone to know about it.'

Finally, companies can develop a *sustainability vision*, which serves as a guide to the future. It shows how the company's products and services, processes and policies must evolve and what new technologies must be developed to get there. This vision of sustainability provides a framework for pollution control, product stewardship and environmental technology.

- Tesco aims to be leader in helping to create a low-carbon economy. Sir Terry Leahy, Tesco's CEO, champions a sustainable vision: 'I listen when the scientists say that, if we fail to mitigate climate change, the environmental, social and economic consequences will be stark and severe. This has profound implications for all of us, for our children, and for our children's children.'

- BSkyB decided to become carbon neutral in January 2007 and succeeded within six months through an effort across the whole organisation. But like Tesco, their aim is to educate as well as act: 'We saw the policy as part of a push to educate customers to reduce their impact on the environment.' Once sceptical Rupert Murdoch, chairman and chief executive of News Corporation which owns BSkyB, says that the rest of his media empire will now follow BSkyB's lead.

However, most companies today still focus on the lower-left quadrant of the grid in Figure 2.1, investing most heavily in pollution prevention. Some forward-looking companies practise product stewardship and are developing new environmental technologies. Few companies have well-defined sustainability visions. Emphasising only one or a few cells in the environmental sustainability grid in Figure 2.1 can be shortsighted. For example, investing only in the bottom half of the grid puts a company in a good position today but leaves it vulnerable in the future. In contrast, a heavy emphasis on the top half suggests that a company has good environmental vision but lacks the skills needed to implement it. Thus, companies should work at developing all four dimensions of environmental sustainability.

Alcoa, the world's leading producer of aluminium, is doing just that. For two years running, it has been one of three companies singled out by *Global 100* for superior sustainability excellence:

Alcoa has distinguished itself as a leader through its sophisticated approach to identifying and managing the material sustainability risks that it faces as a company. From pollution prevention via greenhouse gas emissions reduction programs to engaging stakeholders over new environmental technology, such as controversial hydropower projects, Alcoa has the sustainability strategies in place needed to meld its profitability objectives with society's larger environmental protection goals . . . . Importantly, Alcoa's approach to sustainability is firmly rooted in the idea that sustainability programs can indeed add financial value. Perhaps the best evidence is the company's efforts to promote the use of aluminum in transportation, where aluminum – with its excellent strength-to-weight ratio – is making inroads as a material of choice that allows automakers to build low-weight, fuel-efficient vehicles that produce fewer tailpipe emissions. This kind of forward-thinking strategy of supplying the market with the products that will help solve pressing global environmental problems shows a company that sees the future, has plotted a course, and is aligning its business accordingly. Says CEO Alain Belda, 'Our values require us to think and act not only on the present challenges, but also with the legacy in mind that we leave for those who will come after us . . . as well as the commitments made by those that came before us.'[33]

Environmentalism creates special challenges for global marketers. As international trade barriers come down and global markets expand, environmental issues will continue to have an ever-greater impact on international trade. Global companies have to operate in accordance with stringent environment regulations that are being developed in countries across North America, Western Europe and other developed regions.

For example, the EU has 'end-of-life' regulations affecting cars and consumer electronics products, and the EU's Eco-Management and Audit Scheme provides guidelines for environmental self-regulation. However, environmental policies still vary widely from country to country and uniform worldwide standards are not expected for many years. The EU wants to increase recycling, with landfill disposal 25 per cent lower in 2010 than it was in 1995 and 65 per cent lower by 2020. Across Europe the level of compliance varies hugely. The Netherlands is super-clean in already recycling more than 60 per cent of household waste, but Portugal and Greece manage less than 10 per cent.[34]

Although countries such as Denmark, Germany and Japan have fully developed environmental policies and high public expectations, major countries such as China, India, Brazil and Russia are only in the early stages of developing such policies. Moreover, environmental factors that motivate consumers in one country may have no impact on consumers in another. For example, PVC soft-drink bottles cannot be used in Switzerland or Germany. However, they are preferred in France, which has an extensive recycling process for them. Thus, international companies are finding it difficult to develop standard environmental practices that work around the world. Instead, they are creating general policies, and then translating these policies into tailored programmes that meet local regulations and expectations.

Marketers' lives will become more complicated. They must raise prices to cover environmental costs, knowing that the product will be harder to sell. Yet environmental issues have become so important in our society that there is no turning back to the time when few managers worried about the effects of product and marketing decisions on environmental quality.

Unforeseen consequences

The **Law of Unintended Consequences** encapsulates the recognition that almost all human actions have at least one unintended consequence. With its origins in the Scottish Enlightenment, it is not a law in the legal sense but the realisation that each cause has more than one effect, including *unforeseen consequences*. Global warming is an unforeseen consequence of our lifestyle – central heating, air-conditioning, lighting our homes, leaving electrical appliances on standby, gap years in Australia . . .

 Global warming is an unforeseen consequence of our lifestyle.

Our environment is complicated, so any intervention often has consequences we do not like. Early Australian settlers introduced rabbits to the continent as a familiar food source where the flora and fauna were unfamiliar. With no natural predators, rabbits multiplied uncontrollably and created deserts where they overgrazed on local plants. In response the settlers introduced foxes to keep down the rabbit population. Unfortunately the European fox found Australian marsupials easier meat than rabbits so, as the rabbit and fox populations soared, local plant and animal life declined.

It looked like a great improvement when, in the 1930s, it was realised that non-toxic, non-flammable chlorofluorocarbons (CFCs) were a substitute for the deadly refrigerants used in early refrigerators – and great stuff to power aerosols too. Not until the 1970s did scientists realise that the CFC release had the potential to destroy the ozone layer and therefore expose millions of people to higher levels of cancer-causing ultraviolet radiation.

We are now facing some of the unforeseen consequences of reacting to the dangers of global warming. Biofuels seem a green alternative to releasing the carbon dioxide tied up in fossil fuels, like oil. This appears to be true of ethanol produced from sugar cane grown in the tropics but less true of ethanol made from corn, as being promoted in the US. This uses so much energy in manufacture that it probably adds to global warming and the sudden allocation of corn to ethanol production is forcing up food prices. The price rises caused major riots in Mexico and commodity prices are pushing up food prices worldwide. Western economies can absorb the increased cost of food, but what of poor people in the Third World?

Biodiesel, a popular European solution to global warming, has its own unintended consequences. Rainforests in the tropics are being chopped down to create palm oil plantations. That was not the intention. Just as global warming is an unintended consequence of affluence, so intertwined are the global environment and economy that simple interventions designed to reduce the problem can have unforeseen consequences that bite back.[35]

Fortunately, not all unforeseen circumstances are bad. Pfizer found that a side-effect of using their anti-angina treatment UK-92480 for old people also treated impotence, hence Viagra. It has now been found that Viagra may accelerate recovery from jet-lag. Regain, which helps the hair growth of balding people, was also discovered as an unexpected benefit of taking a product to fend off heart attacks.[36]

Public actions to regulate marketing

Citizen concerns about marketing practices will usually lead to public attention and legislative proposals. New bills will be debated – many will be defeated, others will be modified and a few will become workable laws. Many laws affect marketing practices. As we will discuss in Chapter 3, companies operating within the EU are bound by several layers of laws and regulatory bodies. National laws are designed to regulate local marketing and business practices. In addition, businesses have to comply with EU competition and consumer laws enforced by the European Commission to ensure fair competition and to protect consumer rights. The task is to translate these laws into the language that marketing executives understand as they make decisions about competitive relations, products, price, promotion and channels of distribution. Figure 2.2 illustrates the principal legal issues facing marketing management.

'Ethical consumption is perhaps the biggest movement in branding today,' according to GfK NOP market research group. Its share of individual markets is relatively tiny although its influence is seen behind the sales of Toyota's hybrid, L'Oréal's €1bn acquisition of troubled Body Shop and the huge growth of organic food and drink sales. But the problem, GfK NOP concluded from their five-nation study, is that consumers are confused. The public is not sure what an ethical brand actually is. There are so many angles to being ethical. In food labelling, is it locally grown, organic or subject to fair trade agreements? In beauty, is it free from animal testing or produced from 'natural' ingredients? Or, maybe products that are fuel-efficient, recycled, produced in unionised work conditions or not linked to the tobacco or arms industries?

Figure 2.2 Legal issues facing marketing management
SOURCE: Stockbyte/Getty Images.

The study of 5,000 consumers found international differences:

- Germans felt that 'business ethics had worsened'.
- The more optimistic British thought that supporting ethical brands could help make companies more accountable but were wary that ethical brands were for 'people with money'.
- French were more likely than US respondents to prioritise environmental issues.
- Spaniards were enthusiastic about ethical food and beauty, but scoffed hype.[37]

" Consumers are confused. The public is not sure what an ethical brand actually is. "

Having discussed citizen and public actions to regulate marketing, we will next examine the business actions towards socially responsible marketing that lead to different philosophies of enlightened marketing and the fostering of marketing ethics.

Business actions towards socially responsible marketing

Enlightened marketing— A marketing philosophy holding that a company's marketing should support the best long-run performance of the marketing system; its five principles are consumer-oriented marketing, innovative marketing, value marketing, sense-of-mission marketing and societal marketing.

Consumer-oriented marketing—The philosophy of enlightened marketing that holds that the company should view and organise its marketing activities from the consumers' point of view.

At first, many companies opposed consumerism and environmentalism. They thought the criticisms were either unfair or unimportant. But, by now, most companies have grown to embrace the new consumer rights, at least in principle. They might oppose certain pieces of legislation as inappropriate ways to solve specific consumer problems, but they recognise the consumer's right to information and protection. Many of these companies have responded positively to consumerism and environmentalism in order to create greater customer value and to strengthen customer relationships.

Enlightened marketing

The philosophy of **enlightened marketing** holds that a company's marketing should support the best long-run performance of the marketing system. Enlightened marketing consists of five principles: consumer-oriented marketing, customer-value marketing, innovative marketing, sense-of-mission marketing and societal marketing.

Consumer-oriented marketing

Consumer-oriented marketing means that the company views and organises its marketing activities from the consumer's point of view. It works hard to sense, serve and satisfy the needs of a defined group of customers. Good marketing companies tend to have one thing in common – an all-consuming passion for delivering superior value to carefully chosen customers. Only by seeing the world through its customers' eyes can the company build lasting and profitable customer relationships.

Value marketing

According to the principle of **customer-value marketing**, the company should put most of its resources into value-building marketing investments. Many things marketers do – one-shot sales promotions, minor packaging changes, direct-response advertising – may raise sales in the short run, but add less *value* than would actual improvements in the product's quality, features or convenience. Enlightened marketing calls for building long-run consumer loyalty and relationships, by continually improving the value that consumers receive from the firm's market offering. By creating value *for* customers, the company can capture value *from* consumers in return.

Innovative marketing

The principle of **innovative marketing** requires that the company continuously seek real product and marketing improvements. The company that overlooks new and better ways to do things will eventually lose customers to another company that has found a better way.

An excellent example of an innovative marketer is Samsung Electronics:

Samsung Electronics, a subsidiary of South Korea's largest conglomerate, started as a copycat consumer electronics brand you bought off a shipping pallet at discount stores if you couldn't afford a Sony. But today, the brand holds a high-end, cutting-edge aura. In 1996, Samsung Electronics made an inspired decision. It turned its back on cheap knock-offs and set out to overtake rival Sony. The company hired fresh, young designers, who unleashed a torrent of new products – sleek, bold and beautiful products targeted to high-end users. Samsung called them 'lifestyle works of art' – from brightly coloured mobile phones and elegantly thin DVD players to flat-panel TV monitors. Every new product had to pass the 'Wow!' test: if it didn't get a 'Wow!' reaction during market testing, it went straight back to the design studio.

Samsung also changed its distribution to match its new caché. It initially abandoned low-end distributors, instead building strong relationships with speciality retailers. Interbrand calculates that Samsung is the world's fastest growing brand over the past five years. It's the world leader in CDMA cellphones and battling for the number-two spot in total handsets sold. It's also No. 1 worldwide in colour TVs, flash memory and LCD panels. 'Samsung's performance continues to astound brand watchers,' says one analyst. The company has become a model for others that 'want to shift from being a cheap supplier to a global brand.' Says a Samsung designer, 'We're not el cheapo anymore.'[38]

Sense-of-mission marketing

Sense-of-mission marketing means that the company should define its mission in broad *social* terms rather than narrow *product* terms. When a company defines a social mission, employees feel better about their work and have a clearer sense of direction. Brands linked with broader missions can serve the best long-run interests of both the brand and consumers. For example, Dove wants to do more than just sell its beauty-care products. It's on a mission to discover 'real beauty' and to help women be happy just the way they are.

Some companies define their overall corporate missions in broad societal terms.

For example, defined in narrow product terms, the mission of Unilever's Ben & Jerry's unit might be 'to sell ice cream'. However, Ben & Jerry's states its mission more broadly, as one of 'linked prosperity', including product, economic and social missions. From its beginnings, Ben & Jerry's championed a host of social and environmental causes, and it donated a whopping 7.5 per cent of pretax profits to support worthy causes. By the mid-1990s, Ben & Jerry's had become the [US] nation's number-two superpremium ice cream brand. However, having a 'double bottom line' of values and profits is no easy proposition. Throughout the 1990s, as

Customer-value marketing—A principle of enlightened marketing that holds that a company should put most of its resources into customer value-building marketing investments.

Innovative marketing—A principle of enlightened marketing which requires that a company seek real product and marketing improvements.

Sense-of-mission marketing—A principle of enlightened marketing which holds that a company should define its mission in broad social terms rather than narrow product terms.

competitors not shackled by 'principles before profits' missions invaded its markets, Ben & Jerry's growth and profits flattened. In 2000, after several years of less than stellar financial returns, Ben & Jerry's was acquired by giant food producer Unilever. Looking back, the company appears to have focused too much on social issues at the expense of sound business management. [Co-founder Ben] Cohen once commented, 'There came a time when I had to admit "I'm a businessman." And I had a hard time mouthing those words.'[39]

Such experiences taught the socially responsible business movement some hard lessons. The result is a new generation of activist entrepreneurs – not social activists with big hearts who hate capitalism, but well-trained business managers and company builders with a passion for a cause. For example, consider the US company Honest Tea:

Honest Tea has a social mission. 'We strive to live up to our name in the way we conduct our business,' states the company's 'philoso-tea'. 'We do this in every way we can – whether we are working with growers and suppliers, answering our customers' questions, or trying to leave a lighter environmental footprint.' It all starts with a socially responsible product, an 'Honest Tea' – tasty, barely sweetened, and made from all-natural ingredients, many purchased from poorer communities seeking to become more self-sufficient. But unlike old revolutionaries like Ben and Jerry, Honest Tea's founders are businesspeople – and proud of it – who appreciate solid business training. Co-founder Seth Goldman won a business-plan competition as a student at business school and later started the company with one of his professors.

Honest Tea's managers know that good deeds alone don't work. They are just as dedicated to building a viable, profitable business as to shaping a mission. For Honest Tea, social responsibility is not about marketing and hype. It goes about its good deeds quietly. A few years ago, Honest Tea became the first company to sell a Fair Trade bottled tea – every time the company purchases the tea for its Peach Oo-la-long tea, a donation is made to the workers who pick the tea leaves. The workers invest the money in their community for a variety of uses, including a computer lab for children in the village and a fund for families. Royalties from sales of Honest Tea's First Nation Peppermint tea go to I'tchik Herbal Tea, a small woman-owned company on the Crow Native Indian Reservation in Montana, USA, and the Pretty Shield Foundation, which includes foster care among its activities. However, 'when we first brought out our peppermint tea, our label didn't mention that we were sharing the revenues with the Crow Nation,' says Goldman. 'We didn't want people to think that was a gimmick.'[40]

Thus, today's new activist entrepreneurs are not social activists with big hearts, but well-trained business managers and company builders with a passion for a cause.

Societal marketing

Following the principle of societal marketing, an enlightened company makes marketing decisions by considering consumers' wants and long-run interests, the company's requirements and society's long-run interests. The company is aware that neglecting consumer and societal long-term interests is a disservice to consumers and society. Alert companies view societal problems as opportunities.

In many cases customer needs, customer wants and customer long-run interests are the same things, and customers are the best judges of what is good for them. However, customers do not invariably choose to do what's good for them. People want to eat fatty food, which is bad for their health; some people want to smoke cigarettes knowing that smoking can kill them and damage the environment for others; many enjoy drinking alcohol despite its ill-health effects. To control some of the potential evils of marketing, there has to be access to the media for the counter-argument – against smoking, against fatty foods, against alcohol. There is also a need for regulation – self if not statutory – to check unsavoury demand.

A second problem is that what consumers want is sometimes at odds with societal welfare. If marketing's job is to fulfil customers' wants, unsavoury desires leave marketers with a dilemma. Consumers want the convenience and prestige of hardwood window frames, doors and furniture, but society would also like to keep the Amazon rainforest; consumers want the comfort of central

Europeans now have the income, automobiles and access to cheap food that now allows them to challenge America's obesity. The lazy or indulgent lifestyle also creates market opportunities.

SOURCE: The Advertising Archives.

heating and air-conditioning, yet we need to conserve energy; the growing number of cars on the road, not least a fast-rising source of carbon emissions, overwhelm the benefits of improved fuel efficiency, but few bother to reduce car ownership per household. Marketing has to be more alert to the inconsistencies between consumer wants and society's welfare. Where there is insufficient drive from within the consumer movement and consumers' own sense of responsibility, marketers would do better to control or regulate their own behaviour in providing undesirable goods or services for society at large. If not, legislation is likely to do that for them.

> " What consumers want is sometimes at odds with societal welfare. "

A societally oriented marketer wants to design products that are not only pleasing but also beneficial. The difference is shown in Figure 2.3. Products can be classified according to their degree of immediate consumer satisfaction and long-run consumer benefit. **Deficient products**, such as bad-tasting and ineffective medicine, have neither immediate appeal nor long-run benefits. **Pleasing products** give high immediate satisfaction but may hurt consumers in the long run. Examples include cigarettes and junk food. **Salutary products** have low appeal but may benefit consumers in the long run – for instance, seat belts and air bags. **Desirable products** give both high immediate satisfaction and high long-run benefits, such as a tasty *and* nutritious breakfast food.

Examples of desirable products abound. Philips Lighting's Earth Light compact fluorescent light bulb provides good lighting while giving long life and energy savings. Toyota's hybrid Prius gives both a quiet ride and fuel efficiency. An interesting feature of economic development is that the energy needed to generate each unit of output declines as wealth increases. There are several reasons for this: the shift towards services, the use of more efficient manufacturing, the compression of more value into added-value products, and technological advance. The iPod is a wonderful example of a desirable product that has huge environmental benefits:

In World War II recorded music was not available because the shellac used in making short-lived 78 rpm discs was a strategic material. That is unsurprising given that shellac came from the secretion of the lac insect found only in the forests of Assam and Thailand! Shortly after the advent of rock'n'roll in the 1950s, the 5-inch 45 rpm and long-playing albums were made of much less expensive and longer lasting vinyl. Suddenly good recordings could be made for less. Then came unattractive cassette, everlasting streams of which often decorated roadsides. At last came almost indestructible and crackle-free CDs in their perfectly destructible cases. Now, the taste for a piece of music wore out before the record. Finally, with the MP3 player with electronic downloads comes the ability to carry around weeks of music that would have taken a truckload of 78s to store.

Deficient products—Products that have neither immediate appeal nor long-term benefits.

Pleasing products—Products that give high immediate satisfaction but may hurt consumers in the long run.

Salutary products—Products that have low appeal but may benefit consumers in the long run.

Desirable products—Products that give both high immediate satisfaction and high long-run benefits.

Figure 2.3 Societal classification of new products

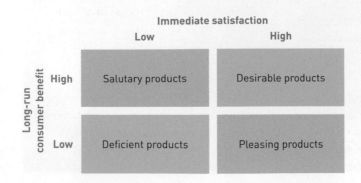

Some technological innovations can have huge environmental benefits. A Zen is produced with a fraction of the environmental impact of a boom box or even a CD Walkman; electronically stored music is more environmentally friendly than CD, tapes or vinyl and electronically stored photos do not consume paper or chemicals.
SOURCE: Creative.

Companies should try to turn all of their products into desirable products. The challenge posed by pleasing products is that they sell very well, but may end up hurting the consumer. The product opportunity, therefore, is to add long-run benefits without reducing the product's pleasing qualities. The challenge posed by salutary products is to add some pleasing qualities so that they will become more desirable in the consumers' minds.

Marketing ethics

Conscientious marketers, however, face many moral dilemmas. The best thing to do is often unclear. Because not all managers have fine moral sensitivity, companies need to develop *corporate marketing ethics policies* – broad guidelines that everyone in the organisation must follow. They cover distributor relations, advertising standards, customer service, pricing, product development and general ethical standards.

The finest guidelines cannot resolve all the difficult ethical situations the marketer faces. Table 2.1 lists some difficult ethical situations marketers could face during their careers. If marketers choose immediate sales-producing actions in all these cases, their marketing behaviour might well be described as immoral or even amoral. If they refuse to go along with *any* of the

Table 2.1 Some morally difficult situations in marketing

1. You work for a cigarette company. Public policy debates over many years leave no doubt in your mind that cigarette smoking and cancer are closely linked. Although your company currently runs an 'if you don't smoke, don't start' promotion campaign, you believe that other company promotions might encourage young (although legal age) non-smokers to pick up the habit. What would you do?

2. Your R&D department has changed one of your products slightly. It is not really 'new and improved', but you know that putting this statement on the package and in advertising will increase sales. What would you do?

3. You have been asked to add a stripped-down model to your line that could be advertised to pull customers into the store. The product won't be very good, but salespeople will be able to switch buyers up to higher-priced units. You are asked to give the green light for the stripped-down version. What would you do?

4. You are thinking of hiring a product manager who has just left a competitor's company. She would be more than happy to tell you all the competitor's plans for the coming year. What would you do?

5. One of your top dealers in an important territory recently has had family troubles and his sales have slipped. It looks like it will take him a while to straighten out his family trouble. Meanwhile you are losing many sales. Legally, on performance grounds, you can terminate the dealer's franchise and replace him. What would you do?

6. You have a chance to win a big account that will mean a lot to you and your company. The purchasing agent hints that a 'gift' would influence the decision. Your assistant recommends sending a fine colour television set to the buyer's home. What would you do?

7. You have heard that a competitor has a new product feature that will make a big difference in sales. The competitor will demonstrate the feature in a private dealer meeting at the annual trade show. You can easily send a snooper to this meeting to learn about the new feature. What would you do?

8. You have to choose between three ad campaigns outlined by your agency. The first (a) is a soft-sell, honest, straight-information campaign. The second (b) uses sex-loaded emotional appeals and exaggerates the product's benefits. The third (c) involves a noisy, somewhat irritating commercial that is sure to gain audience attention. Pretests show that the campaigns are effective in the following order: c, b, a. What would you do?

9. You are interviewing a capable female applicant for a job as salesperson. She is better qualified than the men that you just interviewed. Nevertheless, you know that some of your important customers prefer dealing with men and you will lose some sales if you hire her. What would you do?

actions, they might be ineffective as marketing managers and unhappy because of the constant moral tension. Managers need a set of principles that will help them figure out the moral importance of each situation and decide how far they can go in good conscience.

But *what* principle should guide companies and marketing managers on issues of ethics and social responsibility? One philosophy is that such issues are decided by the free market and legal system. Under this principle, companies and their managers are not responsible for making moral judgements. Companies can in good conscience do whatever the system allows.

A second philosophy puts responsibility not in the system, but in the hands of individual companies and managers. This more *enlightened philosophy* suggests that a company should have a 'social conscience'. Companies and managers should apply high standards of ethics and morality when making corporate decisions, regardless of 'what the system allows'. Each company must work out a philosophy of socially responsible and ethical behaviour. Under the societal marketing concept, each manager must look beyond what is legal and allowed, and develop standards based on personal integrity, corporate conscience and long-run consumer welfare. A clear and responsible philosophy will help the company deal with the many knotty questions posed by marketing and other human activities.

A clear and responsible philosophy will help the company deal with knotty issues such as the one faced recently by 3M:

In late 1997, a powerful new research technique for scanning blood kept turning up the same odd result: tiny amounts of a chemical 3M had made for nearly 40 years were showing up in blood drawn from people living all across the country. If the results held up, it meant that virtually everyone may be carrying some minuscule amount of the chemical, called perfluorooctane sulfonate (PFOS), in their systems. Even though at the time they had yet to come up with a definitive answer as to what harm the chemical might cause, the company reached a drastic decision. In mid-2000, although under no mandate to act, 3M decided to phase out products containing PFOS and related chemicals, including its popular Scotchgard fabric protector. This was no easy decision. Since there was as yet no replacement chemical, it meant a potential loss of about €400m in annual sales. 3M's voluntary actions drew praise from regulators. '3M deserves great credit for identifying the problem and coming forward,' says an Environmental Protection Agency administrator. 'It took guts,' comments another government scientist. 'The fact is that most companies . . . go into anger, denial, and the rest of that stuff. [We're used to seeing] decades-long arguments about whether a chemical is really toxic.' For 3M, however, it wasn't all that difficult a decision – it was simply the right thing to do.[41]

In searching for ethical standards for marketing, marketing managers may also draw upon postmodernist thinking and philosophies that date back well beyond marketing itself. Real Marketing 2.2 introduces some of this. As with environmentalism, the issue of ethics provides special challenges for international marketers. Business standards and practices vary a great deal from one country to the next.

Imagine you are trying to win a big public contract in a developing country. The minister in charge makes unmistakable references to the disgracefully low pay of local civil officials and the benefits his own children would enjoy if they could study abroad. The cost of providing this (concealed as a 'scholarship' paid for by your company) is minute compared with the value of the contract. Your competitors, given the chance, would assuredly find the money. Do you pull out, or pay up? Most businesspeople in such situations find that their scruples are soon swallowed. So do most governments.

2.2 real marketing

From Plato's *Republic* to supermarket slavery

There is good reason to search a long way back for the ethics to guide marketing. As the British philosopher Alfred North Whitehead (1861–1947) commented, 'All Western philosophy is really no more than a footnote to Plato's (428–354 BC) great work *The Republic.*' If that were true, our thinking on 'marketing ethics' is little more than a smudge on that footnote.

The ancients were also practical, as Plato's student explained:

> **Ethics is a rough and ready business determined by ordinary practical men of common sense, not by inbred ascetic 'experts' with their heads in a remote and austere world.**
>
> Aristotle (384–322 BC)

Thinking's the thing

A lot of thinking went on in ancient Athens, a city state of about 400,000 people. Socrates (469–399 BC) thought that the most important thing about human beings is that they ask questions. He also thought that real moral knowledge existed and was worth pursuing. He did not think morality could be tough, but said that it was more than just obeying the law. The newly democratic Athenians did not like this questioning of state morality, so they condemned him to death by poisoning.

Good for the state and good for you too

Plato thought that Athens' experiments with democracy were a shambles and left town. He believed in moral absolutes that were separate from the more sordid world. This led him to idealise regimes where right and wrong were well defined. He thought militaristic and disciplined Sparta was a much better place than freethinking Athens and that people should do what is good for the state. Lots of leaders have tried this and very nasty it is too.

Choosing the happy medium

Aristotle rejected his teachers' concern for absolute truths, suggesting that people take a middle road and learn how to behave from experience. People learn to become

...2.2

good citizens and from that achieve contentment. Well, most people! And how about being a good citizen of a gang of hooligans?

It was a long time before Western philosophy recovered from these Greeks, but the Renaissance got things going again. Machiavelli was born in another city state: Florence.

'He may be dung, but at least he's our dung'

Machiavelli (1469–1527) was an observer rather than a philosopher. After he saw what succeeded, he recognised that politics and morality mix badly. This is a convenient view for business leaders who think there should be two sets of moral standards: one for public life and one for private life. In political and business life it is necessary to be pragmatic and prudent – in other words, unethical – while retaining a different private ethic. As recent politicians have found, life does not always divide so easily.

Solitary, poor, nasty, brutish and short

The English Royalist Hobbes (1588–1678) is even more depressing than Machiavelli. People are awful and are prevented from degenerating into our natural brutish behaviour only by realising that everyone behaving that way would make life unbearable. People therefore establish a 'social contract' (which parents call 'bringing up') that has to be enforced by a neutral third party (government contract). Franco-Swiss Rousseau (1712–78) had the opposite view that humanity is essentially good, but is corrupted by society to want things like smart clothes, carriages and Nike trainers.

Sum happiness

English Utilitarians Bentham (1748–1832) and Mill (1806–73) invented a form of moral calculus. Bentham thought his country's laws were in a mess because they lacked a scientific foundation. He saw human beings as pleasure–pain machines, so he suggested that law makers should balance the sum of the pain and pleasure to achieve 'the greatest happiness of the greatest number'. This has two consequences: means justifying ends and problems for minority groups. Mills worried about this 'tyranny of the majority'. He preferred talking about happiness rather than pleasure, tolerated individual lifestyles and thought that the 'happiness sums' varied and were for individuals as well as law makers.

Bah, happiness

Kant (1724–1804) had little time for happiness. The German idealist's ethics had categorical imperatives. He believed that a moral action was one done out of a sense of duty. Ethics was about finding out our duties and living by them. Kant deduced a 'universality test' to find the compulsory rules. He asked people to imagine what it would be like if everybody did what they themselves wanted to do. Using this mind model, we deduce that if people sold shoddy goods habitually, life would be chaotic and, therefore, people have a duty not to sell shoddy goods.

And justice for all

The American John Rawls (1921–2002) has greatly influenced modern liberal thinking. He has a mind model based on imagining a group of people brought together with no knowledge of what place they will have in society. They have to invent a series of rules that will make their community just and fair. Then they have to live in it.

Don't know; can't know

This rationalist claim to understanding 'truths' started being undermined by Scotsman David Hume (1711–76). His 'meta-ethics' does not offer any advice, but recognises an 'is–ought gap' between what we experience (is) and the conclusion we try to draw from that (ought). Even though we know that bull bars on cars kill children (is), we can only produce a false argument that they should not be sold (ought). Developing similar insights, it follows that any moral argument between people is 'utterly futile, unsolvable and irrational' (A.J. Ayers, 1910–89).

The age of unreason

Postmodernists have pursued this ethical scepticism to new levels. Reason fails because of its dependence on language. What passed as reason in the past has caused so much human suffering. This level of ethical uncertainty is not new; it is close to the Sophist views that Plato argued against. Postmodernists despair at the society they see coming: a kaleidoscope of consumerist images that hypnotise citizens into accepting the morality of capitalism; where individual morality ceases to exist, where all that remains is supermarket slavery and where the only choice is by consumers between products – marketing.

...2.2

Meanwhile Alasdair MacIntyre looks back to the Aristotelian idea that we should concentrate less on the individual and more on people and what is good for society.

SOURCES: J. Ackrill, *Aristotle and the Philosophers* (Oxford, 1981); G. Kerner, *Three Philosophical Moralists* (Oxford, 1990); A. MacIntyre, *A Short History of Ethics* (Routledge, 1987); D. Robinson and C. Garratt, *Ethics for Beginners* (Icon, 1996); B. Russell, *A History of Western Philosophy* (Oxford, 1945); P. Singer, *Practical Ethics* (Oxford, 1993); Lynn Sharp Paine, *Value Shift* (McGraw-Hill, 2003).

Although bribes and kickbacks are illegal in many countries, they are standard business practice in many others. One recent study found that companies from some nations were much more likely to use bribes when seeking contracts in emerging-market nations. The most flagrant bribe-paying firms were from Russia and China, with Taiwan and South Korea close behind. Other countries where corruption is common include Turkmenistan, Bangladesh and Chad. The least corrupt were companies from Iceland, Finland, New Zealand and Denmark.[42]

" Although bribes and kickbacks are illegal in many countries, they are standard business practice in many others. "

Across the globe, national cultures naturally impose different standards of behaviour on individuals and organisations. In the EU, each market sector in each country is still characterised by a mixture of accepted commercial practices, codes of practice and formalised legislation. What is considered an acceptable practice in one country may be illegal in another. Although the EU seeks to move towards a pan-European business ethics policy and codes of conduct, that day is still some way off.

The question arises as to whether a company must lower its ethical standards to compete effectively in countries with lower standards. The answer: no. For the sake of all the company's stakeholders – customers, suppliers, employees, shareholders and the public – it is important to make a commitment to a common set of standards worldwide. For example, the ethical code of jeans manufacturer Levi Strauss forbids bribes, whether or not prevalent or legal in the foreign country involved.

Many industrial and professional associations have suggested codes of ethics and many companies are now adopting their own codes. Efforts have also been made to develop 'global' standards.

An example is the Social Accountability standard SA8000, an international certification standard that encourages organisations to develop, maintain and apply socially acceptable practices in the workplace. It was created in 1989 by Social Accountability International (SAI), an affiliate of the Council on Economic Priorities, and is viewed as the most globally acceptable independent workplace standard. It can be applied to any company, of any size, in any part of the world. The areas it addresses include forced and child labour, health and safety, freedom of association and collective bargaining, discrimination, disciplinary practices, working hours, compensation and management systems.[43]

Companies are also developing programmes, workshops and seminars to teach managers about important ethics issues and help them find the proper responses. They hold ethics workshops and seminars and set up ethics committees. Furthermore, many companies have appointed high-level ethics officers to champion ethics issues and to help resolve ethics problems and concerns facing employees.

PricewaterhouseCoopers (PwC) is a good example. In 1996, PwC established an ethics office and comprehensive ethics programme, headed by a high-level chief ethics officer. The ethics programme begins with a code of conduct, called 'The Way We Do Business'. PwC employees learn about the code of conduct and about how to handle thorny ethics issues in a comprehensive ethics training programme, called 'Navigating the Grey'. The programme also includes an ethics helpline and regular communications at all levels. 'It is obviously not enough to distribute a document,' says PwC's CEO, Samuel DiPiazza. 'Ethics is in everything we say and do.' Last year alone, the PwC training programme involved 40,000 employees, and the helpline received over 1,000 calls from people asking for guidance in working through difficult ethics dilemmas.[44]

Still, compliance rules, written codes and ethics training programmes do not guarantee ethical behaviour. Ethics and social responsibility require a total corporate commitment. They must be a component of the overall corporate culture. Ethics programmes or seminars for employees help to imbue corporate ethics and codes of conduct among staff, while ethical and social audits may be used to monitor and evaluate business conduct and to use the lessons to guide both policy and behaviour. In the final analysis, 'ethical behaviour' must be an integral part of the organisation, a way of life that is deeply ingrained in the collective corporate body.

The future holds many challenges and opportunities for marketing managers. In this chapter, we have examined many important concepts involving marketing's sweeping impact on individual consumers, other businesses, our ecological environment and society as a whole. Companies that are able to create new customer value in a socially responsible way will have a world to conquer.

Sustainable marketing

The concept of sustainable marketing holds that an organisation should meet the needs of its present consumers without compromising the ability of future generations to fulfil their own needs. Figure 2.4 shows how sustainable marketing and the marketing concept are linked by the dimension of time. The marketing concept recognises that organisations thrive from day to day

Figure 2.4 Sustainable marketing

Customer	The business	
	Now	Future
Now	Marketing concept	Strategic planning concept
Future	Societal marketing concept	Sustainable marketing concept

by determining the needs and wants of a target group of customers and fulfilling those needs and wants more effectively and efficiently than the competition. The focus is on what customers want now. Try to foist upon them what they do not want and they will buy elsewhere. That is why cars are getting larger and more powerful, why washing detergents still contain phosphates and why many breakfast meals contain more sugar or fat than is good for us. Marketers succeed by finding a need and fulfilling it. Sustainable marketing projects our focus on the long-run welfare of society.

Shoddy or defective goods

The first time dimension of sustainable marketing examines the welfare of customers now and in the future. This dimension has escalating levels of concern. The first is the provision of shoddy goods or defective goods.

This customer really did not want holes but needed them to fix a coat hook. He bought the appropriate-looking coat hooks from Focus, a DIY chain, and these came with screws for fixing. If they looked good, his aim was to fit out the whole corridor with these nifty hooks. Being handy, the customer recognised that it would be better to drill holes for the screws before fixing them. This he did, but when trying to fix the first screw it sheared, leaving an ugly bit of metal in a hole. He remeasured and tried a second screw. That also sheared, leaving a second ugly hole . . .

The customer had fulfilled his immediate need when buying the coat hooks, but ended up very annoyed. Focus had also fulfilled their immediate need by buying the coat hooks, as had the maker of the coat hooks in buying appropriately sized screws. At the same time, all lost because of the shoddy little component. For Focus, the defective goods had to be refunded, the follow-up order never came and the customer talked to others.

The marketing of shoddy ineffective goods is not sustainable because customers are likely to find out, stop buying and pass on information to their friends. Many companies make a living by knowingly fulfilling customer's immediate needs by mis-selling or selling shoddy goods. Probably the extreme case of this is the sale of bootlegged drugs that are, at their best, only theft but, at their worst, lethal. Bootlegging of music or books may seem a relatively harmless crime, but consider the long-run impact: what is the chance of a music industry or literature developing in a country where any creative output is immediately stolen?

Any company making anything can discover that the product is either defective or dangerous. 3M phased out products containing PFOS when they discovered the potential damage of the product without any legal action forcing them to do so. This contrasts with denial that sometimes occurs when dangers are uncovered.

Ford were aware of design flaws in their 1970s Ford Pinto but allegedly decided it would be cheaper to pay off possible lawsuits for resulting deaths than to change the car's design. A magazine obtained the cost-benefit analysis that it said Ford had used to compare the cost of an $11 (€7) repair against the cost of paying off potential lawsuits. Ford's reputation was hugely damaged by this disclosure as they were in the dispute with Firestone decades later over the Ford Explorer accidents.[45]

The sustainable marketing concept suggests that making defective goods, either knowingly or unknowingly, defies the basic marketing principle of customer care.

Intrinsically harmful goods

Some products, such as red wine, are harmful to customers if consumed to excess. Others, such as cigarettes, are harmful in any quantity. Yet others, such as asbestos, are harmful if ingested accidentally. How do products that kill those who consume them square with the marketing concept? Cigarettes certainly fulfil the needs and wants of those addicted to them, but is a strategy that depends upon killing customers by making them addicts sustainable? If you can keep the danger from the public, as big tobacco tried, then sales continue. But this form of denial, like that of Ford with the Pinto, had dire consequences once the cover-up was exposed. Cigarette smoking is declining, helped by the product being banned in public places. Even smokers agree with smoking being banned in the workplace.[46]

One sustainable marketing strategy pursued by tobacco companies is to diversify away from their cigarette base. With its Marlboro brand, Philip Morris is the world's largest tobacco producer, but it has also diversified away from that base to become Altria – a conglomerate that has among its assets Kraft, the foods and beverage giant, and Miller, America's second largest brewer.

In the eye of the storm over increased obesity, McDonald's has responded with a sustainable 'Plan to Win' strategy of diversifying from hamburgers into salads, sandwiches and fruit, which has continued to pay off. Aimed at broadening McDonald's appeal to health-conscious customers, the campaign helped sales increase 11 per cent and profits jump 22 per cent with European results being particularly strong. Also, after a seven-year search for an oil not containing dangerous trans fats without compromising the taste of its French fries, McDonald's is phasing out the traditional artery-clogging fats from its menu.[47]

Socially harmful goods

A driver of a large sports-utility vehicle (SUV) walked away from a crash with a small car whose occupant was killed. In response, the driver went out and bought an even larger SUV based on the thesis that they are safer. In reality roll-over crashes accounted for 3 per cent of car accidents in America but 32 per cent of deaths. Occupants of SUVs are three times more likely to die from their vehicle rolling over than are the occupants of saloon cars.

Similar consumption behaviour is displayed by drivers installing 'bull bars' on the front of their cars. Why? Few drivers encounter large wild animals on their school run or in their supermarket car park. Why do customers install them? Partly as a fashion accessory and partly because it protects their car in a bump or scrape. Unfortunately, these fashion items do have a large social cost. Experimental studies suggest that the collision effect on pedestrians and cyclists of adding bull bars is similar to doubling the actual speed of the vehicle. That trades off against 2 to 3 per cent more protection to the vehicle that the accessories provide.[48]

Externality—The effect of a purchase by one party on others who do not have a choice and whose interests are not taken into account.

In these cases the good bestows a fictional or marginal benefit to the buyer while imposing costs on others. These can be called third-person costs. This is a case of a negative **externality.**

Secondary smoking is another example of a negative externality, but not all externalities are negative. Where more than one in three people install anti-theft vehicle tracker systems in their cars, a positive externality occurs since the overall car crime rate goes down. Similarly, if more than one in ten install radar-controlled cruise control systems, the stop-start motor congestion on the roads declines for all drivers.

The social cost of goods such as SUVs or their bull bars may appear trivial to a buyer who is ignorant of the third-person costs, or because the events that incur the third-person costs, such as running over and killing a child, are rare.

The remoteness of negative externalities can lead to their neglect. In the nineteenth century, many people in England were ignorant of the squalor of working-class life until it was graphically illustrated in novels like Charles Dickens' *Oliver Twist*. Likewise, the cruelty of slavery was invisible to early generations, although not to later ones. In this century, it is not apparent that a pair of trainers that you buy was produced in a Third-World sweatshop or that a piece of hardwood furniture would involve destroying tribal areas in Borneo or the Amazon basin.

As the SUV examples show, marketers can achieve an immediate return from supplying goods where a third party pays the cost. Is the strategy sustainable? In the case of SUVs whose safety is illusory, it is akin to selling a dangerous good based on mythical safety claims. This flies in the face of the basic marketing concept. There is also a danger of a consumer backlash. In many countries SUVs and the perceived anti-social attitudes of their owners have become something of a joke. In other cases, banning the offending behaviour can wreck once-lucrative markets, as is occurring with bull bars and smoking in public places. Democratic governments have the ability to protect their own people from negative externalities, although it often takes pressure groups to stimulate action.

Where negative externalities are borne by distant peoples, the impulse for government action is diminished. Hence the emergence of campaigners who use all the skills of modern marketing to communicate their concerns – Live Aid and Live Eight, aimed at the G8 summit in Scotland, are global examples. Like Nike in sportswear and B&Q in wood, enlightened marketers also see the danger of reputation loss such as that which Nike faced or the opportunity to make their products more appealing to concerned customers, as did B&Q by making sure their wood came from renewable sources.

Many of the earlier concerns of environmentalists were the impact of pollution and other practices upon people who live now. Excessive use of private transport was a problem because of the environmental pollution and congestion it causes here and now. Global warming, however, implies that the true cost of our love of heating, air-conditioning, flying, power boats, electrical equipment that is instantly available and private motorised transport will be borne by future generations or even during the lifetime of current students.

Environmentally harmful consumption

Environmentally harmful behaviour is not new. The ancient Greek philosopher Aristotle recognised that: 'That which is common to the greatest number has the least care bestowed upon it.' For a long time this did not matter beyond the local community. Over-fishing may have destroyed the cod banks off North America's coast, London was smothered in its Dickensian smog, the Easter Islanders destroyed their lush tropical island, and the colonists of Greenland overgrazed their land, making its name seem oddly inappropriate, but elsewhere in the world it did not matter. These are all cases of **The Tragedy of the Commons**, a term derived originally from a parable published by William Forster Lloyd in 1833.[49] Over-exploitation occurs because consumption benefits individuals who are motivated to maximise their own use of the resource, while the costs of exploitation are distributed to all.

The Tragedy of the Commons—Free access to finite resource ultimately dooms the resource by over-exploitation.

> " That which is common to the greatest number has the least care bestowed upon it. "

The global tragedy of the commons now affects us all because the common good is the whole environment. Industrialisation means that our combined consumption can now destroy the air we all breathe and the atmosphere that protects us from the sun's rays. Marketing's endeavours that result in destroying our shared environment by fulfilling the immediate needs and wants of customers are clearly not sustainable. What does sustainable marketing offer?

The world's greatest generators of greenhouse gases are electricity and heat (26 per cent), deforestation (18), agriculture, industry and transport (14 each) and waste (4). In all sectors, some marketers have gained a strategic advantage, embracing the need to look to the needs of tomorrow's markets. Denmark's Vistas is growing fast as the world's leading producer of wind turbines but big money is catching up. GE has made 'green is green' their mantra. It has set up Ecomagination that brings together businesses, like wind turbines, that are intrinsically green, with its other businesses that are more environmentally sound than the competition. GE is generally highly successful but its Ecomagination businesses are growing by 12 per cent per annum compared with 9 per cent for GE as a whole. Likewise Bombardier, which makes planes as well as being a global leader in rail technology: the Pendolino trains they make for Virgin Trains already consume 76 per cent less fuel than road or local air travel, but Virgin Trains is now pioneering Europe's first biodiesel-powered Voyager trains that cut CO_2 by a further 14 per cent.

These companies, along with many others, including Alstom and Siemens, are in an increasingly strong position compared with those whose response to environmental concerns was denial. While Alstom, GE, Siemens, Vistas and the like were embracing sustainable marketing, the Global Climate Coalition (GCC) of big carbon emitters aimed to 'shoot the messengers', casting doubt on the science of global warning and greenhouse gas reductions. After GCC collapsed, the Competitive Enterprise Institute championed denial, running an ad proclaiming: 'Carbon dioxide: they call it pollution, we call it life.' Even Exxon has now broken from this alignment of doubters.[50]

These differing responses to sustainable marketing cut across industries. As a result, in the automotive industry Toyota, Nissan, PSA Peugeot Citroën and Renault are well positioned for a future cleaner-energy low-cost exposure to the changing market and strengths in low-carbon technologies. In contrast, BMW, Ford and GM, with their dependence on SUV and sporty cars, are highly exposed. As GM's vice-president of R&D now recognises: 'This industry is 98 per cent dependent on petroleum. GM has concluded that that's not sustainable.'[51]

Indications are that marketers cannot rely on the behaviour of today's consumers to provide the market signals to shift to sustainable marketing. A few people are committed to ethical consumption and many enjoy the warm glow of doing good when they buy, but consumers are confused and there is little sign that they will buy ethical products that cost more or perform less well than the norm. It is a free-rider problem: most wealthy consumers are enjoying being **free riders** where their immediate descendents and the world's poor pay.[52]

Free riders—People who consume more than their fair share of a resource, or shoulder less than a fair share of the costs of its production.

> " Consumers are enjoying being free riders where their immediate descendents and the world's poor pay. "

Today's free-riding consumers are benefiting from an externality that has a time dimension. The people who will pay are not born yet, so why bother? Environmentally damaging goods carry with them a double incentive not to act now. Besides, the negative externality is tomorrow's problem, so we can free-ride. If everyone else constrains their lifestyle or invests to cut back their environmental impact, we can benefit from a better environment without contributing anything. But what if we all free-ride? As an example, BA's customers have the chance to pay just £5 to offset the carbon emissions of a flight from London to Madrid but fewer than 1 per cent do. The link between our actions and the consequences are so remote that someone else can pick up the tab. Even when the economic benefits accrue directly to consumers, few respond.

The Green Car Congress promotes fuel-efficient driving by means that cost little to the consumers, such as switching off car engines when the car is stationary, holding a steady speed and removing unused roof racks. They also show the impact of speeding. The speed limit on UK motorways is 70 miles per hour (113 kph), although people in the fast lane often drive at 85 mph or more (138 kph). That speed difference worsens the fuel consumption of a typical family car, like an Opel Zafria, from 48 mpg (17 kpl) to 38 mpg (13.5 kpl), and that is without the accelerating and braking that fast driving involves. Drivers can save themselves a lot of money and be less damaging to the environment by driving legally.

Lighting accounts for 19 per cent of the world's electricity use, and one of the most effective ways of saving money and carbon emissions is changing a standard incandescent light bulb (costs €1 and uses €15 of electricity a year) for an energy-efficient light bulb (costs €5 and consumes €3 of electricity a year). Yet, according to Philips, only 30 per cent of the bulbs sold are of the energy-efficient variety.

Unless the carbon-efficient product bestows some status, such as a Toyota Prius, few consumers respond. As a result, companies are asking governments to act – even suggesting carbon taxes and targets. There is also more chance that consumers will act collectively as voters when everyone has to pay. It is already happening. The EU has a long-standing voluntary deal for car emissions to reduce the CO_2 to 120 g/km by 2012 but people so love big, fast cars that the requirement is likely to soon become mandatory. 'Not fair', shout BMW, Porsche and Mercedes, while Renault and PSA are strangely quiet as their investment in more sustainable vehicles pays off. The EU and Australia also intend to ban incandescent light bulbs on which consumers are so attached to wasting money.[53]

The sustainable company

At the foundation of marketing is the belief that a company that neglects the wants and needs of its customers will decline. The first dimension of sustainable marketing extends this view by suggesting the short-termism of marketing goods that harm customers, others in society or people in the future. Killing your customers, other people's customers or tomorrow's customers is not sustainable marketing.

> **Killing your customers, other people's customers or tomorrow's customers is not sustainable marketing.**

The second dimension of sustainable marketing is assuring the continuity of the business. This means looking beyond current markets to new ones as product life cycles fade. The music industry is doing this as recorded music sales decline by taking a greater interest in the growing demand for live music and investing in the copyright of songs. As the sale of digital cameras matures, Canon, the market leader, is moving into new-technology flat-screen TVs that fit with their digital imaging and hi-tech competences.

The long-term survival of a business also depends on socially responsible behaviour that does not risk the reputation of the company. The loss of reputation caused by poor **governance** and questionable business practices can go far beyond the direct financial loss. When author, magazine editor, TV host and domestic arts wizard Martha Stewart was convicted of insider trading and sentenced to prison, fined and barred from serving on a public company Board of Directors,

Governance—The action of developing and managing consistent and cohesive policies, processes, policies and decision rights for areas of responsibility within a business.

the shares in her company fell even faster than those of Enron. Similarly, recall the dissolution of the Arthur Andersen accounting firm, after its involvement with Enron, and the demise of Union Carbide after the death of thousands of people in the Bhopal disaster.

There are voluntary or legal codes designed to assure the governance of companies. Enron, Worldcom and Robert Maxwell's publishing empire all involved failures in governance that allowed the senior managers to hide their business's financial difficulties by ever more desperate means. Sustainable marketing, therefore, goes beyond caring for the needs and wants of today's customers. It means having concern for tomorrow's customers as well as the well-being of all those in assuring the survival of the business, the shareholders, the employees and the society in which they all live.

Reviewing the concepts

Responsible marketers discover what consumers want and respond with the right products, priced to give good value to buyers and profit to the company. A marketing system should sense, serve and satisfy consumer needs and improve the quality of consumers' lives. In working to meet consumer needs, marketers may take some actions that are not to everyone's liking or benefit. Marketing managers should be aware of the main *criticisms of marketing*.

1. Identify the major social criticisms of marketing

Marketing's *impact on individual consumer welfare* has been criticised for its *high prices, deceptive practices, high-pressure selling, shoddy or unsafe products, planned obsolescence* and *poor service to disadvantaged consumers*. Marketing's *impact on society* has been criticised for *creating false wants* and *too much materialism, too few social goods, cultural pollution* and *too much political power*. Critics have also criticised marketing's *impact on other businesses* for *harming competitors* and *reducing competition* through acquisitions, practices that create barriers to entry, and unfair competitive marketing practices. Some of these criticisms are justified, some are not.

2. Define consumerism and environmentalism and explain how they affect marketing strategies

Concerns about the marketing system have led to *citizen action movements*. *Consumerism* is an organised social movement intended to strengthen the rights and power of consumers relative to sellers. Alert marketers view it as an opportunity to serve consumers better by providing more consumer information, education and protection.

Environmentalism is an organised social movement seeking to minimise the harm done to the environment and quality of life by marketing practices. The first wave of modern environmentalism was driven by environmental groups and concerned consumers, whereas the second was driven by government, which passed laws and regulations governing practices impacting the environment. The first two environmentalism waves are now merging into a third and stronger wave in which companies are accepting responsibility for doing no environmental harm. Companies now are adopting policies of *environmental sustainability* – developing strategies that both sustain the environment and produce profits for the company.

3. Describe the principles of socially responsible marketing

Many companies originally opposed these social movements and laws, but most of them now recognise a need for positive consumer information, education and protection. Some companies have followed a policy of *enlightened marketing* which holds that a company's marketing should support the best long-run performance of the marketing system. Enlightened marketing consists of five principles: consumer-oriented marketing, customer-value marketing, innovative marketing, sense-of-mission marketing and societal marketing.

Because business standards and practices vary from country to country, the issue of ethics poses special challenges for international marketers. The growing consensus among today's marketers is that it is important to make a commitment to a common set of shared standards worldwide.

4. Explain the role of ethics in marketing

Increasingly, companies are responding to the need to provide company policies and guidelines to help their employees deal with questions of *marketing ethics*. Of course, even the best guidelines cannot resolve all the difficult ethical decisions that individuals and firms must make. However, there are some principles that marketers can choose among. One principle states that such issues should be decided by the free market and legal system. A second, and more enlightened, principle puts responsibility not in the system but in the hands of individual companies and managers. Each firm and marketing manager must work out a philosophy of socially responsible and ethical behaviour. Under the societal marketing concept, managers must look beyond what is legal and allowable and develop standards based on personal integrity, corporate conscience and long-term consumer welfare.

5. Understand the dimensions of sustainable marketing

Sustainable marketing recognises that the long-term survival of an organisation goes beyond serving the wants and needs of today's customers. It recognises the conflict between the short-term needs for profit and customer gratification to build an operation that enhances the lives of its current and future stakeholders. The first dimension of sustainable marketing looks to the needs of tomorrow's customers as well as today's and the need to address environmental issues that endanger the livelihood of all. This means concern for shoddy goods that unintentionally endanger customers (such as power motorcycles), intrinsically dangerous products (such as cigarettes), consumption that damages the lives of others (such as corn-based ethanol fuel that drives up the cost of the food of poor people) or consumption that endangers future generations (such as our appetite for energy to fuel our lifestyle). Sustainable marketing's second dimension means assuring the survival of a business in order that it can continue to serve future customers. That means a concern that the company has the agility to evolve as markets change and the governance to assure its well-being.

Discussing the concepts

1. Marketing receives much criticism, some justified and much not. Which of the major criticisms of marketing discussed in the chapter do you think are most justified? Which are least justified? Explain.

2. You have been invited to appear along with a sociologist on a panel assessing the marketing of video games. You are surprised when the economist opens the discussion with a long list of criticisms, focusing especially on the undesirable impacts of video gaming on society, such as lifelike depictions of violence and inclusion of hidden sex scenes, which steal children's innocence and make people violent. Abandoning your prepared comments, you set out to defend marketing in general, and the video gaming industry in particular. How would you respond to the sociologist's attack?

3. The issue of ethics provides special challenges for international marketers as business standards and practices vary a great deal from one country or cultural environment to the next. Imagine that you are a manager working for a global company. Select five moral dilemmas from Table 2.1. Propose an ethical response for each dilemma. Will these responses be the same irrespective of whether the company faces these dilemmas when operating in the UK, India or China? Discuss. Should the company adapt its ethical standards when operating in countries with different standards?

4. Can an organisation be focused on both their consumers and the environment at the same time? Explain, giving practical examples to support your answers.

5. How might companies benefit from practising the philosophy of sustainable marketing, and is the survival of a business guaranteed by fulfilling the wants and needs of customers?

Applying the concepts

1. Many corporations support worthy causes and contribute generously to their communities. Check out the websites of one of the following or some other company of your choice and report on its philanthropic and socially responsible activities: Nestlé (nestle.com), Virgin (virgin.com), Nike (nikebiz.com), Tesco (tesco.com), Saab (saab.com), Toyota (toyota.com) and BP (bp.com). How does philanthropy by corporations counter the social criticisms of marketing?

2. The growth of consumerism and environmentalism has led to marketing approaches that are *supposedly* good for society, but some are actually close to deception.

   - List three examples of marketing campaigns that you feel genuinely benefit society as a whole. If possible, find examples of corporate communications, including advertising, sponsorships, sales promotions or packaging, to support the examples you have listed. You may also visit the websites of relevant companies to gather more specific information on these campaigns.
   - Find three examples of deceptive or borderline marketing campaigns that appear to use their social concern as a means of selling rather than showing a true commitment to the communal good. How are you able to tell which activities are genuine and which are not?
   - What remedies, if any, would you recommend for this problem?

References

1. Quentin Anderson, Inside track: 'In defence of the NSPCC', Viewpoint: 'The furore over the charity's allocation of funds rests on a misunderstanding of its long-term goals', *Financial Times* (14 December 2000), p. 19; Tom Braithwaite, National news: 'Websites that fail children face action', *Financial Times* (8 September 2006); 'Charity donors in a chorus of protest at NSPCC wasters', *Daily Express* (13 April 2007); NSPCC's website: www.nspcc.org.uk.

Web resources

For additional classic case studies and Internet exercises, visit **www. pearsoned.co.uk/ kotler**

2. See Richard Tomkins, 'Smoke signals out as cigarette adverts meet their match', *Financial Times* (9 February 2003), p. 3; Deborah L. Vence, 'Match game', *Marketing News* (11 November 2002), pp. 1, 11–12; Neil Buckley, 'Philip Morris case brings threat of fresh tobacco suits', *Financial Times* (24 March 2003), p. 30; Gordon Fairclough, 'Study slams Philip Morris ads telling teens not to smoke – how a market researcher who dedicated years to cigarette sales came to create antismoking ads', *Wall Street Journal* (29 May 2002), p. B1.

3. 'DFS profit warning highlights threadbare furniture market', *Investors' Chronicle* (6 February 2004); Carlos Grande, 'Advertising up in effort to win shoppers', *Financial Times* (13 January 2007).

4. Excerpts from Theodore Levitt, 'The morality(?) of advertising', *Harvard Business Review* (July–August 1970), pp. 84–92; Ben Abrahams, 'The ASA: older and wiser', *Marketing* (10 July 2000), p. 3.

5. Lane Jennings, 'Hype, spin, puffery, and lies: Should we be scared?', *The Futurist* (January–February 2004), pp. 16–17. For recent examples of deceptive advertising, see 'Mobile providers sued by New York City', *Telecomworldwire* (22 July 2005), p. 1; Chad Bray, 'Federated to pay civil penalty', *Wall Street Journal* (15 March 2006), p. B3; and 'Pfizer sues P&G over Crest ads', *Wall Street Journal* (6 March 2006), p. 1.

6. See the 1987 film *The Tin Men* starring Richard Dreyfuss and Danny DeVito for some great examples of high-pressure selling, and the eventual downfalls.

7. Andrew Bounds, 'Lucrative holiday property rip-offs targeted by EU' and 'Offer of home in sun just pie in the sky for UK couple', *Financial Times* (8 June 2007), p. 8.

8. 'McDonald's to cut "Super Size" option', *Advertising Age* (8 March 2004), p. 13; Dave Carpenter, 'Hold the fries, take a walk', *The News & Observer* (16 April 2004), p. D1; Michael V. Copeland, 'Ronald gets back in shape', *Business 2.0* (January/February 2005), pp. 46–7; David P. Callet and Cheryl A. Falvey, 'Is restaurant food the new tobacco?', *Restaurant Hospitality* (May 2005), pp. 94–6; Kate McArthur, 'BK offers fat to the land', *Advertising Age* (4 April 2005), pp. 1, 60.

9. Eric Schlosser, *Fast Food Nation: The dark side of the all-American meal* (Harper Perennial, 2006); Greg Critser, *Fat Land: How Americans became the fattest people in the world* (Penguin Books, 2004); Tobias Buck and Jenny Wiggins, 'EU pushes voluntary code to tackle obesity', *Financial Times* (31 May 2007), p. 8; Beuc press release PR 013/2007, www.beuc.eu.

10. Tobias Buck, 'Brussels gets teeth into food groups' "misleading" claims', *Financial Times* (1/2 February 2003), p. 7.

11. N. Craig Smith, Robert J. Thomas and John A. Quelch, 'A strategic approach to managing product recalls', *Harvard Business Review* (September–October 1996), pp. 102–12; 'When quality control breaks down', *The European* (6–12 November 1997), p. 29; Vanessa Valkin, 'Court overturns Ford/Firestone class-action', FT.com (2 May 2002); James Mackintosh and Richard Milne, 'Electronic bugs cause recall of 1.3m cars by Mercedes', *Financial Times* (1 April 2005); James Mackintosh, 'Jaguar recalls luxury car over gears fault', *Financial Times* (17 April 2004); 'Timeline: Recent safety recalls in Japan', FT.com (25 August 2006).

12. For the little tin lamp tale, see http://www.exxonmobilchemical.com.cn/China-English/LCW/About_ExxonMobil/Our_History_in_China.asp; Mark Fagan, 'Commodity driven market', *Lawrence Journal-World* (4 May 2005), p. 1. Also see Clint Swett, 'High prices on printer cartridges feeds marketing for alternative industry', *Knight Ridder Tribune Business News* (15 February 2006), p. 1; John Gapper, 'A bid to reprint the pricing rule book', *The Economist* (21 May 2007).

13. For more discussion, see Denver D'Rozario and Jerome D. Williams, 'Retail redlining: definition, theory, typology, and measurement', *Journal of Macromarketing* (December 2005), p. 175; Jeremy Warner, 'Tragedy of Post Office closures', *The Independent* (18 May 2007).

14. See Brian Grow and Pallavi Gogoi, 'A new way to squeeze the weak?', *Business Week* (28 January 2002), p. 92; Marc Lifsher, 'Allstate settles over use of credit scores', *Los Angeles Times* (2 March 2004), p. C1; Judith Burns, 'Study finds links in credit scores, insurance claims', *Wall Street Journal* (28 February 2005), p. D3; Erik Eckholm, 'Black and Hispanic home buyers pay higher interest on mortgages, study finds', *New York Times* (1 June 2006), p. A22.

15. Jane Croft, 'Banks target poor as loan sharks face crackdown', *Financial Times* (25 November 2004); 'Tesco plans to spend PLN600mn on new store openings in Poland in 2007', *Business Wire* (18 May 2007); 'Tesco PLC, one of the most ubiquitous retail names in Britain, said Wednesday it is to open up to 25 "Tesco Express" convenience stores in the Tokyo area this year', *Kyodo News Service* (18 April 2007).

16. Information from 'Shop 'til they drop?', *Christian Science Monitor* (1 December 2003), p. 8; Gregg Easterbrook, 'The real truth about MONEY', *Time* (17 January 2005), pp. 32–5; Bradley Johnson, 'Day in the life: How consumers divvy up all the time they have', *Advertising Age* (2 May 2005); Rich Miller, 'Too much money', *Business Week* (11 July 2005), pp. 59–66; 'Bankers encourage "consumer generation" to save', *Texas Banking* (March 2006), pp. 25–6; Ralph Atkins and Andrew Bounds, 'EU needs careful nurturing to flourish', *Financial Times* (4 June 2007), p. 4; 'The future of Europe', *Financial Times Special Report* (4 June 2007).

17. Paul Metzner, *Crescendo of the Virtuoso: Spectacle, skill, and self-promotion in Paris during the age of revolution* (Berkeley: University of California Press, 1998); Bronislaw Malinowski, *Argonauts of the Western Pacific* (London: Routledge, 1922).

18. See Michael Cabanatuan, 'Toll lanes could help drivers buy time', *San Francisco Chronicle* (28 December 2004), accessed at www.sfgate.com; 'London mayor increases traffic toll, angers drivers, retailers' (3 July 2005), accessed at www.bloomberg.com; Dan Sturges, Gregg Moscoe and Cliff Henke, 'Innovations at work: Transit and the changing urban landscapes', *Mass Transit* (July/August 2006), pp. 34–8; for London's latest ploys, see http://www.cclondon.com/.

19. 'Marketing under fire', *Marketing Management* (July/August 2004), p. 5. Also see 'Media: The public wants a permanent break from ad bombardment', *Marketing Week* (1 December 2005), p. 27.

20. Gail Kemp, 'Commercial break: Should kids' TV ads be banned?', *Marketing Business* (September 1999), pp. 16–18; John Clare, 'Marketing's "material girls" aged only three', *Daily Telegraph* (23 November 1999), p. 9; Martin Lindstrom and Patricia B. Seybold, *Brandchild* (Kogan Page, 2003); see also Jonathan Hall, 'Children and the money machine', *Financial Times FT Creative Business* (18 March 2003), p. 6.

21. Paul Betts, 'Germany cannot afford EADS dogfight with France', *Financial Times* (17 May 2007); Demetri Sevastopulo, Stephanie Kirchgaessner and James Boxell, 'US scrutiny on BAE increases over halting of Saudi probe', *Financial Times* (8 May 2007); Michael Peel, Jimmy Burns and James Boxell, 'Swiss look at BAE's Saudi sales', *Financial Times* (15 May 2007); 'US scrutiny on BAE increases over halting of Saudi probe', *AFX Europe (Focus)* (8 May 2007); Michael Peel, 'UK role in arms trade puts PM's reputation at stake', *Financial Times* (31 May 2007), p. 2.

22. Greg Winter, 'Hershey is put on the auction block', *New York Times* (26 July 2002), p. 5; Adam Jones, 'Danone to place emphasis on acquisitions', FT.com (2 August 2006); 'France's Danone to buy 49 percent of Denmark's Aqua d'Or for undisclosed sum', *AP Worldstream* (19 September 2006); Haig Simonian, 'Nestlé buys Gerber for $5.5bn', FT.com (11 April 2007).

23. Oliver Wihofszki, 'Daimler wird Chrysler gunstig los', *Financial Times Deutschland* (15 May 2007).

24. R.A.F. Casert, 'Europe threatens new Microsoft fines', *AP Online* (1 March 2007).

25. For more discussion, see Jeremiah McWilliams, 'Big-box retailer takes issue with small documentary', *Knight Ridder Tribune Business News* (15 November 2005), p. 1; Nicole Kauffman, 'Movie paints a dark picture of Wal-Mart's impact on communities', *Knight Ridder Tribune Business News* (19 January 2006), p. 1; John Reid Blackwell, 'Documentarian defends Wal-Mart', *Knight Ridder Tribune Business News* (12 May 2006), p. 1; 'The global merger boom: The beat goes on', *The Economist* (10 May 2007).

26. For more details, see Paul N. Bloom and Stephen A. Greyser, 'The maturing of consumerism', *Harvard Business Review* (November–December 1981), pp. 130–9; Douglas A. Harbrecht, 'The second coming of Ralph Nader', *Business Week* (6 March 1989), p. 28; George S. Day and David A. Aaker, 'A guide to consumerism', *Marketing Management* (Spring 1997), pp. 44–8; Benet Middleton, 'Consumerism: a pragmatic ideology', *Consumer Policy Review* (November/December 1998), pp. 213–7; Colin Brown, 'Consumer activism in Europe', *Consumer Policy Review*, **8**, 6 (1998), pp. 209–12.

27. 'Slavery: Breaking the chains', *The Economist* (22 February 2007); Jonathan Birchall, 'Nike to strengthen effort to combat worker abuse', *Financial Times* (31 May 2007), p. 9.

28. Sylvie Laforet and John Saunders, 'Managing brand portfolios: How strategies have changed', *Journal of Advertising Research*, **45**, 3 (September 2005), pp. 314–27.

29. Peter M. Senge, Goran Carstedt and Patrick L. Porter, 'Innovating our way to the next industrial revolution', *MIT Sloan Management Review* (Winter 2001), pp. 24–38; information from 'BP Launches World's Greenest Service Station', BP press release, 25 April 2002.

30. See 'Sustainability Key to UPS Environmental Initiatives', UPS press release, accessed at www.pressroom.ups.com, July 2006; http://www.ricoh.co.uk/environment/index.cfm, May 2007; John Reed, 'Diesel could outpace hybrids in US', *Financial Times* (27 May 2007); speech by Sir Terry Leahy given to invited stakeholders at a joint 'Forum for the Future' and Tesco event in London on 18 January 2007.

31. Information from 'Xerox Equipment Remanufacture and Parts Reuse', accessed at www.xerox.com, August 2006; speech by Sir Terry Leahy given to invited stakeholders at a joint 'Forum for the Future' and Tesco event in London on 18 January 2007.

32. Adapted from information found in Joseph Tarnowski, 'Green monster', *Progressive Grocer* (1 April 2006), pp. 20–6.

33. Adapted from 'The Top 3 in 2005', *The Global 100 Most Sustainable Corporations in the World*, accessed at http://www.global100.org, July 2005. See also 'Alcoa named one of the most sustainable corporations in the world for second straight year', 27 January 2006, accessed at www.alcoa.com. For further information on Alcoa's sustainability programme, see Alcoa's Sustainability Report at www.alcoa.com.

34. 'Cleaning up the act: Charging for household waste is a good idea', *The Economist* (31 August 2007).

35. Robert K. Merton, 'The unanticipated consequences of purposive social action', *American Sociological Review*, **1**, 6 (December 1936), pp. 894–904; Edward Tenner, *Why Things Bite Back: Technology and the revenge of unintended consequences* (Vantage Books, 1997); Jared Diamond, *Collapse: How societies choose to fail or survive* (London: Penguin, 2005); Doug Cameron, 'Cargill chief in warning over biofuels boom', *Financial Times* (30 May 2007); Robert Mathews, 'Unforeseen consequences', *Financial Times* (24 May 2007), p. 16.

36. Robert Mathews, 'Unforeseen consequences', *Financial Times* (24 May 2007), p. 16; 'Viagra and jet lag: Mile-high hamsters', *The Economist* (24 May 2007).

37. Carlos Grande, 'Ethical consumption makes mark on branding', *Financial Times* (20 February 2007).

38. Information and quotes from Andy Milligan, 'Samsung points the way for Asian firms in global brand race', *Media* (8 August 2003), p. 8; Gerry Khermouch, 'The best global brands', *Business Week* (5 August 2002), p. 92; Leslie P. Norton, 'Value brand', *Barron's* (22 September 2003), p. 19; 'Cult brands', *BusinessWeek Online* (2 August 2004) accessed at www.businessweek.com; Bill Breen, 'The Seoul of design', *Fast Company* (December 2005), pp. 91–8; and Samsung Annual Reports and other information accessed at www.samsung.com, September 2006.

39. Information from Mike Hoffman, 'Ben Cohen: Ben & Jerry's Homemade, established in 1978', *Inc.* (30 April 2001), p. 68; and Ben & Jerry's website at www.benjerrys.com, September 2006.

40. Quotes and other information from Thea Singer, 'Can business still save the world?', *Inc.* (30 April 2001), pp. 58–71; and www.honesttea.com, September 2006. Also see Elizabeth Fuhrman, 'Honest Tea Inc.: Social and environmental sinceri-tea', *Beverage Industry* (April 2005), p. 44.

41. Joseph Webber, '3M's big cleanup', *Business Week* (5 June 2000), pp. 96–8. Also see Kara Sissell, '3M defends timing of Scotchgard phaseout', *Chemical Week* (11 April 2001), p. 33; Peck Hwee Sim, 'Ausimont targets former Scotchgard markets', *Chemical Week* (7 August 2002), p. 32; Jennifer Lee, 'E.P.A. orders companies to examine effect of chemicals', *New York Times* (15 April 2003), p. F2; and Kara Sissell, 'Swedish officials propose global ban on PFOS', *Chemical Week* (22 June 2005), p. 35.

42. See 'Transparency International Bribe Payers Index' and 'Transparency International Corruption Perception Index', accessed at www.transparency.org, August 2006; Minxin Pei, 'The dark side of China's rise', *Foreign Policy* (March/April 2006), pp. 32–40; 'Everybody's doing it', *Middle East* (April 2006), pp. 20–1; and Transparency International's web page at www.transparency.org.

43. See Social Accountability International's web page at www.sa-intl.org.

44. See Samuel A. DiPiazza, 'Ethics in action', *Executive Excellence* (January 2002), pp. 15–16, 'It's all down to personal values', accessed online at www.pwcglobal.com, August 2003, and 'Code of conduct: The way we do business', accessed at www.pwcglobal.com/gx/eng/ins-sol/spec-int/ethics/index.html, June 2006.

45. For details see http://www.fordpinto.com/blowup.htm.

46. Richard Kluger, *Ashes to Ashes: America's hundred-year cigarette war, the public health and the unabashed triumph of Philip Morris* (Vintage Books, 1997); Stanton A. Glantz, John Slade, Lisa A. Bero, Peter Hanauer and Deborah E. Barnes (eds), *The Cigarette Papers* (Berkeley: University of California Press, 1998); Peter Pringle, *Cornered: Tobacco companies at the bar of justice* (Henry Holt, 1998); Allan Brandt, *Cigarette Century: The rise, fall and deadly persistence of the product that defined America* (Basic Books, 2007); also see the star-studded Walt Disney film *The Insider* (2000) – it is not animation.

47. Andrew Ward, 'McDonald's selects oil to avoid trans fat risk', *Financial Times* (30 January 2007); Andrew Clark, 'McDonald's health drive delivers fatter profits', *The Guardian* (21 April 2007).

48. Tessa R. Salazar, 'Is the bull bar just a lot of bull?', *Philippine Daily Inquirer* (30 October 2003); 'America's favourite mode of transport is under attack', *The Economist* (16 January 2003).

49. Lloyd observed that when pastureland is in commons, so available to all, cattle-owners have a short-term interest in increasing the size of their herds. Left unchecked, the size of the herds on the commons will soon exceed their capacity and so be doomed by overgrazing. Garrett Hardin popularised and extended the term in his essay *The Tragedy of the Commons* (Science, 1968). For an example, see Tricia Holly Davis, 'Overfishing causes havoc in the global food chain', *The Times* Focus Report, World Environment Day (5 June 2007), p. 4; and 'Still waters: The global fish crisis', *National Geographic* (April 2007), pp. 32–99.

50. 'Branson to launch eco-friendly train', *Sky News* (7 June 2007); 'Cleaning up', Special report on business and climate change, *The Economist* (2 June 2007), pp. 3–4; 'Fairfield v the valley', Special report on business and climate change, *The Economist* (2 June 2007), pp. 14–18; 'Sunlit uplands', Special report on business and climate change, *The Economist* (2 June 2007), pp. 20–4.

51. 'The drive for low emissions', Special report on business and climate change, *The Economist* (2 June 2007), pp. 32–4.

52. Oliver Tickell, 'Rich countries set to make poor pay', *The Times* Focus Report, World Environment Day (5 June 2007), p. 11; 'The final cut', Special report on business and climate change, *The Economist* (2 June 2007), pp. 34–6; Joshi Venugopal, 'Drug imports: The free-rider paradox', *Express Pharma Pulse*, 11, 9 (2005), p. 8.

53. 'Irrational incandescence', Special report on business and climate change, *The Economist* (2 June 2007), p. 12; 'The drive for low emissions', Special report on business and climate change, *The Economist* (2 June 2007), pp. 32–4; www.greencarcongress.com/2006/05/fuel_consumptio.html.

Company case 2 Nestlé: singled out again and again

During the first few months, the mother's milk will always be the most natural nutriment, and every mother able to do so, should herself suckle her children.

Henri Nestlé, 1869

Nothing is a substitute for or equivalent or superior to breastmilk.

Nestlé warning, 2007

The corporate affairs department at Nestlé UK's headquarters were bracing themselves for another burst of adverse publicity. At the forthcoming General Synod of the Church of England a motion would call for a continued ban on Nescafé by the Church. They also wanted the Church Commissioners to disinvest their £1.1m (€1.6m) in Nestlé. The Church's much publicised boycott of Nescafé first occurred, amid much ridicule, in 1991, as a protest against the use of breast milk substitutes in Third World countries. In the aftermath of the 1991 vote, Nescafé claimed that its sales increased, although many churchgoers said they stopped using the brand-leading coffee. The new protest would be one of many the company had faced from Baby Food Action (BFA) protesters over decades although, according to Nestlé, the protesters' complaints had no foundation.

Nestlé SA, whose headquarters are in Vevey, Switzerland, is the world's largest food company, with annual sales of CHF 98.5bn (€60bn) and with a net profit of CHF 9bn (€5.4bn). It employs around 260,000 people in factories or operations in almost every country in the world. Henri Nestlé invented manufactured baby food 'to save a child's life' and the company have been suppliers ever since. Then, in the late 1970s and early 1980s, Nestlé came under heavy fire from activists who charged the company with encouraging Third World mothers to give up breast feeding and use a company-prepared formula. In 1974 the British charity War on Want published a pamphlet, *The Baby Killer*, that criticised Unigate and Nestlé's ill-advised marketing efforts in Africa. While War on Want criticised the entire infant formula industry, the German-based Third World Action Group issued a 'translation' of the original pamphlet

retitled *Nestlé Kills Babies*, which singled out the company for 'unethical and immoral behaviour'. The pamphlets generated much publicity. Enraged at the protest, Nestlé sued the activists for defamation. The two-year case kept media attention on the issue. 'We won the legal case, but it was a public-relations disaster', commented a Nestlé executive.

In 1977, two American social-interest groups, the Interfaith Center on Corporate Responsibility and the Infant Formula Action Coalition (INFACT), spearheaded a worldwide boycott against Nestlé. The campaign continued despite the fact that many organisations rejected the boycott. The US United Methodist Church concluded that the activists were guilty of 'substantial and sometimes gross misrepresentation', of 'inflammatory rhetoric', and of using 'wildly exaggerated figures'. The boycott was called off in 1984 when the activists accepted that the company was complying with an infant formula marketing code adopted by the World Health Organization (WHO). Since then, church, university, local government and other action groups periodically rediscover the controversy and create publicity by calling for a boycott.

'Every day 4,000 babies die from unsafe bottle feeding', explain BMA.

The main accusation now is that Nestlé's use of promotions persuaded hundreds of thousands of poverty-stricken, poorly educated mothers that formula feeding was better for their children. 'Every day 4,000 babies die from unsafe bottle feeding', explain BMA. They continue, 'Donations of infant formula can do more harm than good.' Their concern is the donation of free or low-cost supplies of infant formula to maternity wards and hospitals in developing countries. Formula feeding is usually an unwise practice in such countries because of poor living conditions and habits; people cannot or do not clean bottles properly and often mix formula with impure water. Income level does not permit many families to buy sufficient quantities of formula. The protesters hit out at industry practices generally but keep Nestlé as their prime target:

- Promotional baby booklets ignoring or de-emphasising breast feeding.

- Misleading advertising encouraging mothers to bottle-feed their babies and showing breast feeding to be old-fashioned and inconvenient.
- Gifts and samples inducing mothers to bottle-feed their infants.
- Posters and pamphlets in hospitals.
- Endorsements of bottle-feeding by milk nurses.
- Formula so expensive that poor customers dilute to non-nutritious levels.

A WHO code eliminates all promotional efforts, requiring companies to serve primarily as passive 'order takers'. It prohibits advertising, samples and direct contact with consumers. Contacts with professionals (such as doctors) occur only if professionals seek such contact. Manufacturers can package products with some form of visual corporate identity, but they cannot picture babies. The WHO code effectively allows almost no marketing. However, the code contains only *recommended* guidelines. They become *mandatory* only if individual governments adopt national codes through their own regulatory mechanisms.

WHO allows the donation of free or low-cost supplies of infant formulas for infants who cannot be breast-fed. However, the International Association of Infant Food Manufacturers (IFM) is working with WHO and UNICEF to secure country-by-country agreements with countries to end free and low-cost supplies.

Nestlé itself has a policy on low-cost supplies in developing countries, as follows:

- Where there is government agreement, Nestlé will strictly apply the terms of that agreement.
- Where there is no agreement Nestlé, in cooperation with others, will be active in trying to secure early government action.
- Where other companies break an agreement, Nestlé will work with IFM and governments to stop the breach.
- Nestlé will take disciplinary measures against any Nestlé personnel or distributors who deliberately violate Nestlé policy.

Given the repeated public relations problems that Nestlé faces, why does it not take unilateral action in ending free supplies? Since the Third World infant formula market is so small compared with Nestlé's worldwide interests, why bother with it?

Part of the answer is in Henri Nestlé's desire 'to save a child's life'. The European Commission's directive on baby food concludes that infant formula is 'the only processed foodstuff that wholly satisfies the nutritional requirements of infants' first four to six months of life.' In addition, a recent study by the American Dietetic Association concluded that 'on average, babies of 6 to 8 months who are fed with human milk receive less than 50% of the Recommended Daily Allowance (RDA) for iron and zinc, and less than 50% of the Adequate Intake (AI) for manganese, fluoride, vitamin D, vitamin B6, niacin, vitamin E, magnesium, phosphorus, biotin and thiamine.'

Another consideration is that the campaigns by North European activists have little impact on Nestlé sales, especially among poor people – a market that both Nestlé and Unilever are developing.

Few mothers in countries with very high infant mortality rates use anything other than breast milk. However, Kenya is probably typical of what happens when mothers do supplement breast milk with something else:

- 33 per cent use uji, a local food made from maize;
- 33 per cent use cow's milk;
- 28 per cent use water;
- 14 per cent use glucose;
- 11 per cent use milk powder, of which some is infant formula;
- 3 per cent use tea.

A study in the Ivory Coast shows the sort of problems that arise when Nestlé withdraws unilaterally. Other companies replaced the supplies to the affluent private nurseries, but supplies for mothers in need collapsed. As a result the main hospital was not able to 'afford to buy enough to feed abandoned babies or those whose mothers are ill'.

Questions

1. Was and is Nestlé's and the other IFM members' marketing of infant formula 'unethical and immoral'?
2. Is it the case that ethical standards should be the responsibility of organisations such as WHO and UNESCO, and that the sole responsibility of firms is to work within the bounds set?
3. Is Nestlé just unlucky or did its actions precipitate its being singled out by activists? Is the activists' focus on Nestlé unjust and itself dangerous? What accounts for Nestlé's continuing in the infant formula market despite the protests?
4. Did Nestlé benefit from confronting the activists directly in court and winning? Should firms ever confront activists directly? What other forms of action are available to the

company? Should firms withdraw from legitimate markets because of the justified or unjustified actions of pressure groups?

5. The WHO code is a recommendation to government. Is it Nestlé's responsibility to operate according to the national legislation of any given country, or to follow WHO's recommendations to that country? Do international bodies setting international standards, such as WHO and UNICEF, have a moral responsibility to make those standards clearly understood by all parties and to demand action by national governments to enact them?

6. How should Nestlé respond to the threats from the General Synod? Since Nestlé claimed sales increased after the Nescafé boycott in 1991, should it just ignore the problem?

SOURCES: John Sparks, 'The Nestlé controversy – anatomy of a boycott', Public Policy Education Fund, Inc. (June 1981); European Commission, Commission Directive on Infant Formula and Follow-on Formula, 91/321/EEC; UNICEF, *The State of the World's Children* (1992); RBL, *Survey of Baby Feeding in Kenya* (1992); Nestlé, *Nestlé and Baby Milk* (1994); Andrew Brown, 'Synod votes to end Nestlé boycott after passionate debate', *The Times* (12 July 1994); World Health Assembly Resolution 54.2 'Infant and young child nutrition' (2001); Jonathan Wheatley and Jenny Wiggins, 'The Americas: Little by little Nestlé aims to woo Brazil's poor', *Financial Times* (20 February 2007); Joanna Moorhead, 'Milking it: It was in 1977 that campaigners first called for a boycott of Nestlé because of its aggressive marketing of formula milk in the developing world. Thirty years on, have Nestlé and the other baby-milk firms cleaned up their act?', *The Guardian* (15 May 2007); Hilary Parsons, 'Response: We're not trying to undermine the baby-milk code: Nestlé is committed to the health of mothers and infants in the developing world', *The Guardian* (22 May 2007); Nestle.com (June 2007), competing websites babymilk.nestle.com (June 2007) and babymilkaction.org (June 2007).

> In action, be primitive: in foresight, a strategist.
>
> RENÉ CHAR

Strategic marketing

Mini Contents List

- Prelude case – Poor little rich brands
- Introduction
- Strategic planning
- The strategic plan
- Real Marketing 3.1 – Albumart.com: But will we make money?
- Real Marketing 3.2 – KISS (Keep It Simple Stupid)
- Marketing relationships
- The marketing plan
- Marketing organisation
- Company case 3 – Starbucks

◄ SOURCE: The Advertising Archives.

'So much for the ten-year plan
You're just another company man'

Therapy, 'Ten-year plan', on: 'So Much for the Ten-Year Plan' (2000)

Previewing the concepts

In the first chapter, we explored the marketing process by which companies create value for consumers in order to capture value in return, and in the second chapter we discussed the relationship of marketing to society in general. In this chapter we go deeper into the marketing process – designing customer-driven marketing strategies and constructing marketing programmes and plans. To begin, we look at the organisation's overall strategic planning. Next, we discuss how marketers, guided by the strategic plan, work closely with others inside and outside the firm to serve customers. We then examine marketing strategy and planning – how marketers choose target markets, position their market offerings, develop a marketing mix and manage their marketing programmes. Finally, we look at the important step of measuring and managing return on marketing investment.

After reading this chapter, you should be able to:

1. Explain company-wide strategic planning and its four steps.
2. Discuss how to design business portfolios and develop growth strategies.
3. Explain marketing's role in strategic planning and how marketing works with its partners to create and deliver customer value.
4. Describe the elements of a customer-driven marketing strategy and mix, and the forces that influence it.
5. List the marketing management functions, including the elements of a marketing plan, and discuss the importance of measurement.
6. Manage return on marketing investment.

We start by looking at a market that is booming as the super-rich in the West get richer and the new rich grow rapidly in large developing economies. Whereas the consumption of poor people across the globe is local and variable, the same luxury brands attract the super-rich globally, and it is a market where Europe is particularly strong. We start with a visit to the exclusive Costa Smeralda.

Prelude case Poor little rich brands

'We prefer the Blue Circle Café to the Sotto Vento,' exclaims Sten, the son of a Norwegian millionaire. The Sotto Vento is on the exclusive Costa Smeralda, and is Sardinia's most famous disco but, says Sten, 'is already being invaded by "the Rolex crowd".'

Sten has a point. According to Sten, those who want to show off such belongings go to Antibes or St Tropez. Costa Smeralda is different. The likes of Heidi Klum, Julia Roberts, Tom Cruise and Nicole Kidman go there so as not to be seen. They wear Gucci, Prada or Versace not to display their success but because that is what their local store sells. Whereas luxury brands bestow glamour to ordinary mortals, the super-rich who holiday at Costa Smeralda bestow glamour to the luxury brands. While most people never aspire to owning a pair of €2,000 Gucci crocodile skin loafers, some do.

Costa Smeralda retains its exclusivity by staying small, being well guarded and being accessible only by helicopter or cabin cruiser. Do not expect any glitzy bright lights – the town does not even boast street lights. However, recently life has not been so easy for the luxury brands that adorn its visitors. Many of the luxury-brand makers were founded in the 1950s by mainly Italian entrepreneur designers who are now ageing and whose families lack the design and management skills to run an increasingly competitive business.

The 'new idea' for luxury-goods makers is to control the whole value chain, from manufacture to distribution, retailing and marketing. This comes expensive where advertising costs approach 35 per cent of sales and the rental of the prime retail site they need can cost up to €10,000 per square metre. Covering such costs requires the sales volume and working capital that many of the family firms lack. According to Cedric Magnelia, of Credit Suisse First Boston, gaining sales by brand extensions into such obvious areas as perfumes has been 'done to death'. There also seems little further to gain from the 'old idea' of designers creating stunning but hugely loss-making *haute couture* while money was made from licensees selling perfumes, handbags and scarves. Down-market associations easily taint luxury brands. Yves St Laurent, TAG Heuer and Porsche all tried stretching their product ranges down-market. They all increased sales, tarnished their luxury brand names and retreated back up-market.

The formation of luxury conglomerates has become part of the 'new idea'. These offer negotiating power in obtaining retail space, skills in areas where brands could be extended, access to capital and managerial skills. Two of the biggest of these are French group LVMH (Moët Hennessy Louis Vuitton S.A), which owns Louis Vuitton, Christian Dior, Givenchy and many others, and Swiss Richemont, whose brands include Cartier, Dunhill and Piaget. The recognition of the conglomerate strategy has led to a feeding frenzy as Gucci consumes Italian shoemaker Sergio Rossi, and LVMH and Prada jointly share out Fendi with its famous Baguette handbag.

LVMH has snatched up a clutch of neglected classic luxury watch brands that are flourishing once again, such as TAG Heuer (which began as Heuer in 1860), Zenith (1865) and Chaumet (1780). Zenith is the biggest gem in the LVMH luxury watch bejewelled crown, while the most profit-making sales are generated by TAG Heuer.

Laurent Paichot, of the Federation of Swiss Watch Makers, thinks being bought by a conglomerate is the only alternative for many small watchmakers: 'Due to globalisation everything is expensive – especially advertising.' He continues, 'Bigger companies have the economic power to really push the product and consumers will buy from a brand they know well.'

However, in this industry, synergy is hard to find. Morgan Stanley Dean Witter's Claire Kent says that 'cost savings in a takeover in this industry are spurious'. How can synergy be achieved in a market where the appeal is the idiosyncratic way products are designed, made and marketed? Hermès boasts that it takes them longer to make their Kelly bags than it takes BMW to assemble a car! Even where cost savings are easy and logical to find, they can endanger brands. Richemont is eager to clarify that Mont Blanc factories do not make Cartier pens.

LVMH's broad range and strength in the Japanese market have helped it weather the economic storm better than many of its competitors. Its performance contrasts with that of Gucci whose sales are heavily down because of merchandising errors and excessive time turning round Yves St Laurent, a struggling acquisition.

A few luxury-goods makers, such as Rolex, Mondaine Watch and Prada, are holding out against the force of the 'new idea'. Mondaine intends to remain a speciality watchmaker while Rolex is adamant that it will remain independent, although it seems unlikely that Sten will be wearing one.[1]

Questions

1. What makes a luxury good or service desirable?
2. Is the economic drive for scale inconsistent with consumers' desires in the €60bn luxury-goods industry?
3. Does Sten's sneering at 'the Rolex crowd' suggest that Rolex is failing in its desire to remain an independent luxury-goods maker?

Introduction

Just like the luxury-goods makers in the prelude case, all companies need strategies to meet changing markets. TAG Heuer lost its way when stretching downmarket to increase sales volume but, financed as part of the LVMH empire, it has regained its position as the leading maker of luxury sports chronometers.

> LVMH are secretive but Jean-Christophe Babin, their chief executive, says sales run at between 500,000 and 1m units a year and that the brand has recently enjoyed 'high double digit growth'. That gives TAG Heuer an estimated 5 per cent market share – 'not bad for a single luxury watch brand,' notes Mr Babin. Bertrand Arnault, LVMH's chairman, claims TAG Heuer has become one of the group's 'star brands': 'We generate a lot of profit and a lot of cash for the group.'[2]

No one strategy is best for all companies. Each company must find the way that makes most sense, given its situation, opportunities, objectives and resources. Marketing plays an important role in strategic planning. It provides information and other inputs to help prepare the strategic plan. Strategic planning is also the first stage of marketing planning and defines marketing's role in the organisation. The strategic plan guides marketing, which must work with other departments in the organisation to achieve strategic objectives.

Here we look at the three stages of strategic market planning: first, the strategic plan and its implications for marketing; second, the marketing process; and third, ways of putting the plan into action.

Strategic planning

Overview of planning

Many companies operate without formal plans. In new companies, managers are sometimes too busy for planning. In small companies, managers may think that only large corporations need planning. In mature companies, many managers argue that they have done well without formal planning, so it cannot be very important. They may resist taking the time to prepare a written plan. They may argue that the marketplace changes too fast for a plan to be useful – that it would end up collecting dust.[3]

Failing to plan means planning to fail. Moreover, formal planning yields benefits for all types of company, large and small, new and mature. It encourages systematic thinking. It forces the company to sharpen its objectives and policies, leads to better coordination of company efforts, and provides clearer performance standards for control. The argument that planning is less useful in a fast-changing environment makes little sense. The opposite is true: sound planning helps the company to anticipate and respond quickly to environmental changes, and to prepare better for sudden developments. Such planning could have helped Carrefour, Europe's largest retailer, avoid their share price collapse after they were first dismissive of the impact of the Internet on their business and then announced a vague, €1 billion e-commerce strategy.[4]

 Failing to plan means planning to fail.

Companies usually prepare annual plans, long-range plans and strategic plans:

- The **annual plan** is a short-term plan that describes the current situation, company objectives, the strategy for the year, the action programme, budgets and controls. For an oil company, such as BP, this is about maintaining profitability and supplies through the continuing troubles in Middle East crises and other oil-producing nations, and maintaining its reputation after safety problems in the US and the North Sea.[5]

- The **long-range plan** describes the primary factors and forces affecting the organisation during the next several years. It includes the long-term objectives, the main marketing strategies used to attain them and the resources required. This long-range plan is reviewed and updated each year so that the company always has a current long-range plan. The company's annual and long-range plans deal with current businesses and how to keep them going. For BP the long-range plan looks at future oil supplies, strategies for increasingly important BRIC (Brazil, Russia, India and China) markets, and the market impact of global warming.

- The **strategic plan** involves adapting the firm to take advantage of opportunities in its constantly changing environment. It is the process of developing and maintaining a strategic fit between the organisation's goals and capabilities and its changing marketing opportunities. BP's use of its initials to represent Beyond Petroleum reflects that company's strategic view of its future, in which environmental issues are important and the era of the internal combustion engine declines.[6]

Strategic planning sets the stage for the marketing plan. It starts with its overall purpose and mission. These guide the formation of measurable corporate objectives. A corporate audit then gathers information on the company, its competitors, its market and the general environment in which the firm competes. A SWOT analysis gives a summary of the strengths and weaknesses of the company together with the opportunities and threats it faces. Next, headquarters decides what portfolio of businesses and products is best for the company and how much support to give each one. This helps to provide the strategic objectives that guide the company's various activities. Then each business and product unit develops detailed marketing and other functional plans to support the company-wide plan. Thus marketing planning occurs at the business-unit, product and market levels. It supports company strategic planning with more detailed planning for specific marketing opportunities. For instance Nestlé, the world's largest food manufacturer, develops an overall strategic plan at its headquarters in Vevey, Switzerland. Below that, each strategic group, such as confectionery, develops subordinate strategic plans. These feed into the strategic plan's national operations. At each level, marketing and other functional plans will exist. At the final level, brand plans cover the marketing of brands such as KitKat, Nescafé and Friskies Felix in national markets.

The planning process

Putting plans into action involves four stages: analysis, planning, implementation and control. Figure 3.1 shows the relationship between these functions, which are common to strategic planning, marketing planning or the planning for any other function.

- *Analysis*. Planning begins with a complete analysis of the company's situation. The company must analyse its environment to find attractive opportunities and to avoid environmental threats. It must analyse company strengths and weaknesses, as well as current and possible marketing actions, to determine which opportunities it can best pursue. Analysis feeds information and other inputs to each of the other stages.

- *Planning*. Through strategic planning, the company decides what it wants to do with each business unit. Marketing planning involves deciding marketing strategies that will help the

Annual plan—A short-term plan that describes the company's current situation, its objectives, the strategy, action programme and budgets for the year ahead, and controls.

Long-range plan—A plan that describes the principal factors and forces affecting the organisation during the next several years, including long-term objectives, the chief marketing strategies used to attain them and the resources required.

Strategic plan—A plan that describes how a firm will adapt to take advantage of opportunities in its constantly changing environment, thereby maintaining a strategic fit between the firm's goals and capabilities and its changing market opportunities.

Figure 3.1 Market analysis, planning, implementation and control

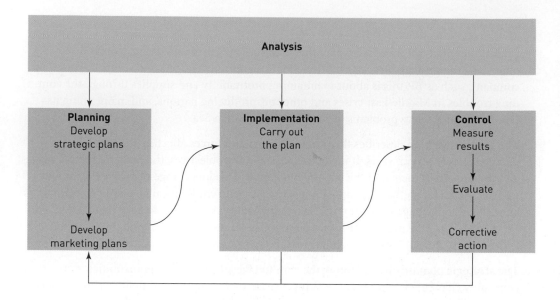

company attain its overall strategic objectives. Marketing, product or brand plans are at the centre of this.

- *Implementation.* Implementation turns strategic plans into actions that will achieve the company's objectives. People in the organisation who work with others, both inside and outside the company, implement marketing plans.

- *Control.* Control consists of measuring and evaluating the results of plans and activities, and taking corrective action to make sure objectives are being achieved. Analysis provides information and evaluations needed for all the other activities.

The strategic plan

The strategic plan contains several components: the mission, the strategic objectives, the strategic audit, SWOT analysis, portfolio analysis, objectives and strategies. All of these feed from and feed into marketing plans.

The mission

A mission states the purpose of a company. Firms often start with a clear mission held within the mind of their founder. Then, over time, the mission fades as the company acquires new products and markets. A mission may be clear, but forgotten by some managers. Other problems can occur when the mission may remain clear but no longer fits the environment. The Girl Guides would certainly not recruit successfully in today's environment with its former mission: 'to prepare young girls for motherhood and wifely duties'. The luxury-goods firms in the prelude case are struggling with their mission.

When an organisation is drifting, the management must renew its search for purpose. It must ask, What business are we in? What do consumers value? What are we in business for? What sort of business are we? What makes us special? These simple-sounding questions are among the most difficult that the company will ever have to answer. Successful companies continuously raise these questions and answer them. Asking such basic questions is a sign of strength, not uncertainty.

> ❝ Asking basic questions is a sign of strength, not uncertainty. ❞

search.ebay.com/hula skirts /ranch land /laptops
/portable video games /hedge trimmers /swimming trunks
/mystery novels /golf shoes /digital cameras
/baseball tickets /video cellphones /sprinklers
/all-terrain tires /flip-flops /sun hats
/dome tents /digital sports watches /lawnmowers
/stain removers /horseshoe sets /artificial turf

you can get it on eBay.

Many organisations develop formal mission statements that answer these questions. A **mission statement** is a statement of the organisation's purpose – what it wants to accomplish in the larger environment. A clear mission statement acts as an 'invisible hand' that guides people in the organisation, so that they can work independently and yet collectively towards overall organisational goals.

Traditionally, companies have defined their business in product terms ('we manufacture furniture'), or in technological terms ('we are a chemical-processing firm'). But mission statements should be *market-oriented*. Table 3.1 gives a series of company statements that show dimensions of marketing orientation.

Mission statement—A statement of the organisation's purpose – what it wants to accomplish in the wider environment.

What business are we in?

Asking this question helps. Market definitions of a business are better than product or technological definitions. Products and technologies eventually become outdated, but basic market needs may last for ever. A market-oriented mission statement defines the business based on satisfying basic customer needs. Thus Rolls-Royce aero engines is in the power business, not the aero-engine business. Visa's business is not credit cards, but allowing customers to 'enjoy life's potential'. Creative 3M does more than just make adhesives, scientific equipment and healthcare products; it solves people's problems with its 'ability to apply our technologies – often in combination – to an endless array of customer needs.'

Who are our customers?

This is a probing question. Who are the customers of Rolls-Royce's new Trent 1000 aero-engine? At one level it is the airframers, like Boeing and Airbus. With Trent becoming the launch engines

Table 3.1 Market-oriented business definitions

Company	Product-oriented definition	Market-oriented definition
Royal Dutch Shell	'We extract, refine and sell oil.'	'We refine and deliver products to our customers in a profitable and sustainable way.'
Nestlé	'The world's leading nutrition, health and wellness company.'	'As the world's leading nutrition, health and wellness company, we are committed to increasing the nutritional value of our products while offering better taste and more pleasure.'
EDF	'An integrated energetic utility, (that) manages all aspects of the electricity business.'	'Consolidating a competitive base in France [through] . . . the customer portfolio: loyalty and enhancement . . . Increasing revenue per customer, launching new brands and reducing sales costs are core priorities of our strategy.'
Unilever	'Owner of 400 brands spanning 14 categories of home, personal care and foods products.'	'. . . to add vitality to life. We meet everyday needs for nutrition, hygiene and personal care with brands that help people feel good, look good and get more out of life.'
Nokia	'The world leader in mobility, driving the transformation and growth of the converging internet and communications industries.'	'. . . a world where everyone can be connected . . . We focus on providing consumers with very human technology – technology that is intuitive, a joy to use, and beautiful.'

on the new Airbus A350, Rolls-Royce saved development costs and received orders worth $15.1bn (€11bn) at the 2007 Paris Airshow. Is it the airline or leasing companies that eventually buy the engines? They will certainly have to sell to them as well. Is it the pilot, the service crew or even the passenger? Unlike the competition, Rolls-Royce has a brand name that is synonymous with prestige and luxury.[7]

What are we in business for?

This is a hard question for non-profit-making organisations. Do universities exist to educate students or to train them for industry? Is the pursuit of knowledge by the faculty the main reason for their existence? If so, is good research of economic value or is pure research better?

What sort of business are we?

This question guides the strategy and structure of organisations. Companies aiming at *cost leadership* seek efficiency. Firms like Aldi run simple, efficient organisations with careful cost control. These contrast with *differentiators*, like Apple, who aim to make profits by inventing products,

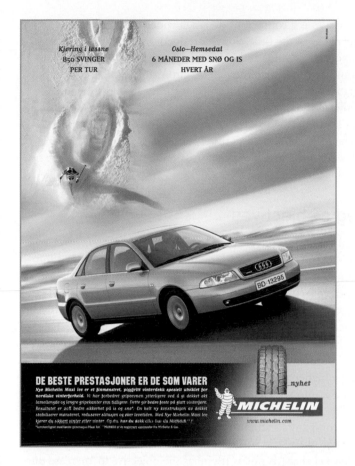

Setting company objectives and goals. Michelin defines its mission as 'service to people and their transportation', rather than reducing its purpose to the mere production of tyres. This mission leads to specific business and marketing objectives.
SOURCE: Michelin and Hjemmet Mortensen AS.

such as the iPhone, whose uniqueness gives a competitive edge. *Focused* companies concentrate upon being the best at serving a well-defined target market. They succeed by tailoring their products or services to customers they know well. Coutts & Co., a subsidiary of The Royal Bank of Scotland, does this by providing 'personal banking' to the very wealthy. Michael Porter describes a fourth option that occurs if firms do not define how they are to do business: *stuck in the middle*.[8]

Management should avoid making its mission too narrow or too broad. A lead-pencil manufacturer that says it is in the communication equipment business is stating its mission too broadly. A mission should be:

- *Realistic*. SAS is an excellent airline, but it would be deluding itself if its mission were to become the world's largest airline.

- *Specific*. It should fit the company and no other. Many mission statements exist for public-relations purposes, so lack specific, workable guidelines. The statement 'We want to become the leading company in this industry by producing the highest-quality products with the best service at the lowest prices' sounds good, but it is full of generalities and contradictions. Such motherhood statements will not help the company make tough decisions.

- *Based on distinctive competencies*. Bang & Olufsen has the technology to build micro-computers, but an entry into that market would not take advantage of its core competencies in style, hi-fi and exclusive distribution.

- *Motivating*. It should give people something to believe in. It should get a 'Yeah!', not a yawn or a 'Yuck!'. A company's mission should not say 'making more sales or profits' – profits are only a reward for undertaking a useful activity. A company's employees need to feel that their work is significant and that it contributes to people's lives. Contrast the mission of Greenpeace, 'to ensure the ability of the Earth to nurture life in all its diversity', with the strategy of ABB, '[to] offer more value for customers while building a linear organization'.

Visions guide the best missions. A vision is a contagious dream, a widely communicated statement or slogan that captures the needs of the time. Sony's president, Akio Morita, wanted everyone to have access to 'personal portable sound', and his company created the Walkman. Richard Branson thought 'flying should be fun', so he founded Virgin Airlines. Julian Richer has become a business guru after making his Richer Sounds hi-fi dealer the 'friendliest, cheapest, busiest', most profitable and productive in the industry.

The company's mission statement should provide a vision and direction for the company for the next 10–20 years. It should not change every few years in response to each new turn in the environment. Still, a company must redefine its mission if that mission has lost credibility or no longer defines an optimal course for the company.[9]

From mission to strategic objectives

The company's mission needs to be turned into strategic objectives to guide management. Each manager should have objectives and be responsible for reaching them. For example, one of the business units of Norway's Yara International is its fertiliser business unit. The fertiliser division does not say that its mission is to produce fertiliser, but 'to supply plant nutrition. That is why agronomists assist the sales organisation to identify and supply the plant nutrition solutions that help growers to grow their produce according to needs and demands of the food market.' This mission leads to a hierarchy of objectives, including business objectives and marketing objectives. The mission of increasing agricultural productivity leads to the company's business objective of researching new fertilisers that promise higher yields. Unfortunately, research is expensive and requires improved profits to plough back into research programmes. So improving profits becomes another key business objective. Profits are improved by increasing sales or reducing costs. Sales increase by improving the company's share of the domestic market, or by entering new foreign markets, or both. These goals then become the company's current marketing objectives. The objective to 'increase our market share' is not as useful as the objective to 'increase our market share to 15 per cent in two years'. The mission states the philosophy and direction of a company, whereas the strategic objectives are measurable goals.

Strategic audit

'Knowledge is power': so stated Francis Bacon, the sixteenth-century philosopher, while according to the ancient Chinese strategist Sun Zi, 'The leader who does not want to buy information is inconsiderate and can never win.' The strategic audit covers the gathering of this vital information. It is the intelligence used to build the detailed objectives and strategy of a business. It has two parts: the external audit and the internal audit.

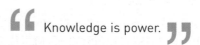

Knowledge is power.

External audit—A detailed examination of the markets, competition, business and economic environment in which the organisation operates.

The **external audit** or marketing environment audit examines the macroenvironment and task environment of a company. EuroDisney's early troubles are partly explained by an excessive faith in company strengths and too little attention being paid to the macroenvironment. French labour costs make the park much more expensive than in America, Europe's high travel costs add to guests' total bill, and the northern European climate takes the edge off all-year-round operations. EuroDisney contrasts with the success of Center Parcs, whose Dutch-invented resort hotels offer northern Europeans indoor health and leisure facilities that they can enjoy all year round.

Internal audit—An evaluation of the firm's entire value chain.

The **internal audit** examines all aspects of the company. It covers the whole *value chain* described by Michael Porter.[10] It includes the primary activities that follow the flow of goods or services through the organisation: inbound logistics, operations, outbound logistics, sales and marketing, and after-sales services. In addition, it extends to the support activities on which the primary activities depend: procurement, technology development, human resource management and the infrastructure of the firm. These go beyond traditional marketing activities, but marketing strategy depends on all of them. A key to the Italian company Benetton's international success is a system that allows it to change styles and colours rapidly. Unlike traditional mass-clothing manufacturers, which have to order fabrics in colours and patterns over a year ahead of seasons, Benetton's design and manufacturing technology allows it to change within a season.

Reading financial statements is basic to understanding the state of a company and seeing how it is developing. The operating statement and the balance sheet are the two main financial statements used. The **balance sheet** shows the assets, liabilities and net worth of a company at a given time. The **operating statement** (also called **profit-and-loss statement** or **income statement**) is the more important of the two for marketing information. It shows company sales, cost of goods sold, and expenses during a specified time period. By comparing the operating statement from one time period to the next, the firm can spot favourable or unfavourable trends and take appropriate action. Real Marketing 3.1 describes these statements in more detail and explains their construction.

SWOT analysis

SWOT analysis draws the critical strengths, weaknesses, opportunities and threats (SWOT) from the strategic audit. The audit contains a wealth of data of differing importance and reliability. SWOT analysis distils these data to show the critical items from the internal and external audits. The number of items is small for forceful communications, and they show where a business should focus its attention.

Opportunities and threats

Managers need to identify the main threats and opportunities that their company faces. The purpose of the analysis is to make the manager anticipate important developments that can have an impact on the firm. A pet food division of a multinational company could list the following.

Opportunities

- *Economic climate.* Because of improved economic conditions, pet ownership is increasing in almost all segments of the population.
- *Demographic changes.* (1) Increasing single parenthood, dual-income families and ageing will increase the trend towards convenient pet foods (from wet to dry); and (2) the ageing population will grow and increasingly keep pets as company.
- *Market.* The pet food market will follow the human market in the concern for healthy eating, pet obesity and pre-prepared luxury foods.
- *Technology.* New forms of pet food that are low in fat and calories, yet highly nutritious and tasty, will soon emerge. These products will appeal strongly to many of today's pet food buyers, whose health concerns extend to their pets.

Threats

- *Competitive activity.* A large competitor has just announced that it will introduce a new premium pet food line, backed by a huge advertising and sales promotion blitz.
- *Channel pressure.* Industry analysts predict that supermarket chain buyers will face more than 10,000 new grocery product introductions next year. The buyers accept only 38 per cent of these new products and give each one only five months to prove itself.
- *Demographic changes.* Increasing single parenthood and dual-income families will encourage the trends towards (1) pets that need little care (cats rather than dogs), and (2) smaller pets that eat less.

Balance sheet—A financial statement that shows assets, liabilities and net worth of a company at a given time.

Operating statement (profit-and-loss statement or income statement)—A financial statement that shows company sales, cost of goods sold and expenses during a given period of time.

SWOT analysis—A distillation of the findings of the internal and external audits which draws attention to the critical organisational strengths and weaknesses and the opportunities and threats facing the company.

3.1 real marketing

Albumart.com: But will we make money?

Exhibit 3.1 shows the 2007 operating statement for Albumart.com, a start-up that has avoided the big bucks and bust of Boo.com and others. They market specialised picture frames designed to display 'album art'. They enable people to make a wall decoration by slotting an old favourite vinyl album or CD cover directly into the frame. This statement is for a retailer; the operating statement for a manufacturer would be somewhat different. Specifically, the section on purchases within the 'Cost of goods sold' area would be replaced by 'Cost of goods manufactured'.

Exhibit 3.1 Operating statement for Albumart.com for year ending 31 December 2007 (€)

Gross sales			325,000
less: Sales returns and allowances			25,000
Net sales			300,000
Cost of goods sold			
Beginning inventory, 1 January 2007, at cost		60,000	
Purchases	150,000		
plus: Freight-in	10,000		
Net cost of delivered purchases		160,000	
Cost of goods available for sale		220,000	
less: Ending inventory, 31 December 2007, at cost		45,000	
Total cost of goods sold			175,000
Gross margin			125,000
Expenses			
Selling expenses		50,000	
Administrative expenses		30,000	
General expenses		20,000	
Total expenses			100,000
Net profit			25,000

The outline of the operating statement follows a logical series of steps to arrive at the firm's €25,000 net profit figure:

Net sales	€300,000
Cost of goods sold	−€175,000
Gross margin	€125,000
Expenses	−€100,000
Net profit	€25,000

The first part details the amount that Albumart.com received for the goods sold during the year. The sales figures consist of three items: gross sales, returns or allowances, and net sales. *Gross sales* is the total amount charged to customers during the year for merchandise purchased from Albumart.com. Some customers returned merchandise. If the customer gets a full refund or full credit on another purchase, we call this a return. Other customers may decide to keep the item if Albumart.com will reduce the price. This is called an allowance. By subtracting returns and allowances from gross sales:

Gross sales	€325,000
Returns and allowances	−€25,000
Net sales	€300,000

The second part of the operating statement calculates the amount of sales revenue that Albumart.com retains after paying the costs of the merchandise. We start with the inventory in the store at the beginning of 2007. During the year, Albumart.com aim to buy €150,000 worth of frames. Albumart.com also has to pay an additional €10,000 to get the products delivered, giving the firm a net cost of €160,000. Adding the beginning inventory, the cost of goods available for sale amounted to €220,000. The €45,000 ending inventory on 31 December 2007 is then subtracted to come up with the €175,000 *cost of goods sold*. The difference between what Albumart.com paid for the merchandise (€175,000) and what it sold it for (€300,000) is called the *gross margin* (€125,000).

In order to show the profit Albumart.com 'cleared' at the end of the year, we must subtract from the gross margin the expenses incurred while doing business. *Selling expenses* included two employees, advertising in music magazines and the cost of mailing the merchandise. Selling expenses totalled €50,000 for the year. *Administrative expenses* included the salary for an office manager, office supplies such as stationery and business cards, and miscellaneous expenses including an administrative audit conducted by an outside consultant. Administrative expenses totalled €30,000 in 2007. Finally, the *general expenses* of rent, utilities, insurance and depreciation came to €20,000. Total expenses were therefore €100,000 for the year. By subtracting expenses (€100,000) from the gross margin (€125,000), we arrive at the *net profit* of €25,000 for Albumart.com during 2007. Not a lot, but not a loss.

- *Politics*. EU legislation will force manufacturers to disclose the content of their pet food. This will adversely affect the attractiveness of some ingredients like kangaroo and horse meat.

Not all threats call for the same attention or concern – the manager should assess the likelihood of each threat and the potential damage each could cause. The manager should then focus on the most probable and harmful threats and prepare plans in advance to meet them.

Opportunities occur when an environmental trend plays to a company's strength. The manager should assess each opportunity according to its potential attractiveness and the company's probability of success. Companies can rarely find ideal opportunities that exactly fit their objectives and resources. The development of opportunities involves risks. When evaluating opportunities, the manager must decide whether the expected returns justify these risks. A trend or development can be a threat or an opportunity, depending on a company's strengths. The growth of Internet retailing was an opportunity for catalogue retailer Argos whose low-cost warehouse-like stores lent themselves to Internet selling. In contrast, the high cost of operating conventional stores made Internet shopping a great threat to many bricks-and-mortar retailers.[11]

Strengths and weaknesses

The strengths and weaknesses in the SWOT analysis do not list all features of a company, but only those relating to **critical success factors**. A list that is too long betrays a lack of focus and an inability to discriminate what is important. The strengths or weaknesses are *relative*, not absolute. It is nice to be good at something, but it can be a weakness if the competition is stronger. Mercedes is good at making reliable luxury cars with low depreciation, but this stopped being a strength when Honda's Acura and Toyota's Lexus beat Mercedes on all three fronts in the American market. The Japanese products were not cheap, but they were styled for the American market and came with all the extras that buyers of German luxury cars had to pay for. Finally, the strengths should be *based on fact*. In buying Safeway, an underperforming super-market chain, once-successful Morrisons massively increased their number of stores, but in this case was size a strength? Morrisons had no experience of absorbing businesses, particularly large unsuccessful ones.[12] A failure to understand true strengths can be dangerous. A well-known aircraft manufacturer for years promoted the quality of its after-sales service. Only after another company acquired it did it find out that its reputation was the worst in the industry.

A major pet food manufacturer could pitch the following strengths and weaknesses against the opportunities and threats.

Strengths

- Market leader in the dry cat food market.
- Access to the group's leading world position in food technology.
- Market leader in luxury pet foods.
- The group's excellent worldwide grocery distribution.
- Pet food market leader in several big markets, including France, Italy, Spain and South America.

Weaknesses

- Number three in the wet pet food market.
- Excessive product range with several low-volume brands.
- Most brand names are little known, and are cluttered following acquisitions.
- Relatively low advertising and promotions budget.
- Product range needs many manufacturing skills.
- Poor store presence in several large markets: Germany, UK, USA and Canada.
- Overall poor profit performance.

The pet food company shows how some parts of the SWOT balance. The strengths in dry and luxury pet foods match demographic trends, so this looks like an opportunity for growth. Access to food technology should also help the company face changing consumer tastes and legislation. The weaknesses suggest a need for more focus. Dropping some uneconomic lines in the mass wet pet food market, simplifying the brand structure and concentrating on fewer manufacturing processes could release resources for developing the dry and luxury markets. By using its access to worldwide grocery distribution, the company could become profitable and focused.

Critical success factors—The strengths and weaknesses that most critically affect an organisation's success. These are measured relative to competition.

New Look. New Mood. New Times.

New: *Meisterstück Sport*
Chronograph Stainless Steel
Automatic with Rubber Strap
and Security Clasp

Meisterstück Solitaire
Stainless Steel
Doué Ballpoint Pen

THE ART OF WRITING YOUR LIFE
Writing Instruments · Watches · Leather · Jewellery · Eyewear

Montblanc Boutiques. 60/61 Burlington Arcade. 10/11 Royal Exchange. Canada Place, Canary Wharf.
Harrods, Knightsbridge. Selfridges, Oxford Street. Call 020 7663 4830 for further details and national stockists.

Mont Blanc competes in the exquisite accessories market, capitalising on its strength as a maker of exclusive pens, to add watches, men's fragrances and other products to its range.
SOURCE: Mont Blanc and The Advertising Archives.

The business portfolio

The **business portfolio** is the collection of businesses and products that make up the company. It is a link between the overall strategy of a company and those of its parts. The best business portfolio is the one that fits the company's strengths and weaknesses to opportunities in the environment. The company must (1) analyse its *current* business portfolio and decide which businesses should receive more, less or no investment, and (2) develop growth strategies for adding *new* products or businesses to the portfolio.

Analysing the current business portfolio

Portfolio analysis helps managers evaluate the businesses making up the company. The company will want to put strong resources into its more profitable businesses and phase down or drop its weaker ones. *Financial Times*-owned publishers Dorling Kindersley needed 'remedial surgery' to allow them to concentrate on their core business of illustrated books. In doing so they scaled back activities such as CD-ROM publishing, video production and a door-to-door sales network.[13]

Management's first step is to identify the key businesses making up the company. These are strategic business units. A **strategic business unit (SBU)** is a unit of the company that has a separate mission and objectives, and which can be planned independently from other company businesses. An SBU can be a company division, a product line within a division, or sometimes just a single product or brand.

The next step in business portfolio analysis calls for management to assess the attractiveness of its various SBUs and decide how much support each deserves. In some companies, this occurs informally. Management looks at the company's collection of businesses or products and uses judgement to decide how much each SBU should contribute and receive. Other companies use formal portfolio-planning methods.

Business portfolio—The collection of businesses and products that make up the company.

Portfolio analysis—A tool by which management identifies and evaluates the various businesses that make up the company.

Strategic business unit (SBU)—A unit of the company that has a separate mission and objectives and that can be planned independently from other company businesses. An SBU can be a company division, a product line within a division, or sometimes just a single product or brand.

http://www.breitlingforbentley.com/en/ explains this long-term brand alliance between two makes of prestigious products who share a winged logo and an image of high performance.

SOURCE: Breitling.

The purpose of strategic planning is to find ways in which the company can best use its strengths to take advantage of attractive opportunities in the environment. So most standard portfolio-analysis methods evaluate SBUs on two important dimensions: the attractiveness of the SBU's market or industry, and the strength of the SBU's position in that market or industry. The best-known portfolio-planning methods are from the Boston Consulting Group, a leading management consulting firm, and by General Electric and Shell.

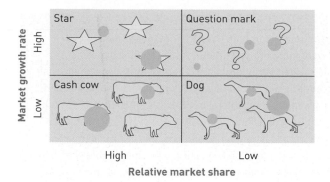

Figure 3.2 The BCG
growth–share matrix

The Boston Consulting Group box

Using the Boston Consulting Group (BCG) approach, a company classifies all its SBUs according to the *growth–share matrix* shown in Figure 3.2. On the vertical axis, *market growth rate* provides a measure of market attractiveness. On the horizontal axis, *relative market share* serves as a measure of company strength in the market. By dividing the growth–share matrix as indicated, four types of SBU can be distinguished:

1. **Stars.** Stars are high-growth, high-share businesses or products. They often need heavy investment to finance their rapid growth. Eventually their growth will slow down, and they will turn into cash cows.

2. **Cash cows.** Cash cows are low-growth, high-share businesses or products. These established and successful SBUs need less investment to hold their market share. Thus they produce cash that the company uses to pay its bills and to support other SBUs that need investment.

3. **Question marks.** Question marks are low-share business units in high-growth markets. They require cash to hold their share, let alone increase it. Management has to think hard about question marks – which ones they should build into stars and which ones they should phase out.

4. **Dogs.** Dogs are low-growth, low-share businesses and products. They may generate enough cash to maintain themselves, but do not promise to be large sources of cash.

The 10 circles in the growth–share matrix represent a company's 10 current SBUs. The company has two stars, two cash cows, three question marks and three dogs. The areas of the circles are proportional to the SBUs' sales value. This company is in fair shape, although not in good shape. It wants to invest in the more promising question marks to make them stars, and to maintain the stars so that they will become cash cows as their markets mature. Fortunately, it has two good-sized cash cows whose income helps finance the company's question marks, stars and dogs. The company should take some decisive action concerning its dogs and its question marks. The picture would be worse if the company had no stars, or had too many dogs, or had only one weak cash cow.

Once it has classified its SBUs, the company must determine what role each will play in the future. There are four alternative strategies for each SBU. The company can invest more in the business unit to *build* its share. It can invest just enough to *hold* the SBU's share at the current level. It can *harvest* the SBU, milking its short-term cash flow regardless of the long-term effect. Finally, the company can *divest* the SBU by selling it or phasing it out and using the resources elsewhere.

As time passes, SBUs change their positions in the growth–share matrix. Each SBU has a life cycle. Many SBUs start out as question marks and move into the star category if they succeed. They later become cash cows as market growth falls, then finally die off or turn into dogs towards the end of their life cycle. The company needs to add new products and units continuously, so that some of them will become stars and, eventually, cash cows that will help finance other SBUs.

Stars—High-growth, high-share businesses or products that often require heavy investment to finance their rapid growth.

Cash cows—Low-growth, high-share businesses or products; established and successful units that generate cash that the company uses to pay its bills and support other business units that need investment.

Question marks—Low-share business units in high-growth markets that require a lot of cash in order to hold their share or become stars.

Dogs—Low-growth, low-share businesses and products that may generate enough cash to maintain themselves, but do not promise to be large sources of cash.

Sony BMG, the world's second-largest music company, has a dangerously unbalanced portfolio since both Sony and BMG were forced to sell off their music publishing arms following anti-trust intervention in their merger. For a long time recorded music was their 'cash cow', and their major source of income, but this market has been hit by Internet downloads and by price pressures as more sales take place in grocery outlets. In contrast, the growth part of the music business is in live music and publishing. Publishing opens up many avenues to generate business, from owning songs through their broadcast on music stations, use in TV or films, and specialist recordings that are less generally available. Also by gaining publishing rights with new performers they can get some share in live music performances. Unfortunately, because of the enforced sell-off, Sony BMG are the only one of the five music majors without a big stage in publishing. So Sony BMG has a fading recorded music 'cash cow' and a publishing 'question mark'. They are now fighting hard to claw their way back into publishing and live music. But, so is everyone else in the industry.[14]

The General Electric grid

General Electric introduced a comprehensive portfolio planning tool called a *strategic business-planning grid* (see Figure 3.3). It is similar to Shell's *directional policy matrix*. Like the BCG approach, it uses a matrix with two dimensions – one representing industry attractiveness (the vertical axis) and one representing company strength in the industry (the horizontal axis). The best businesses are those located in highly attractive industries where the company has high business strength.

The GE approach considers many factors besides market growth rate as part of *industry attractiveness*. It uses an industry attractiveness index made up of market size, market growth rate, industry profit margin, amount of competition, seasonality and cycle of demand, and industry cost structure. Each of these factors is rated and combined in an index of industry attractiveness. For our purposes, an industry's attractiveness is high, medium or low. As an example, the Dutch chemical giant Akzo Nobel has identified speciality chemicals, coatings and pharmaceuticals as attractive. Its less attractive bulk chemical and fibre businesses are being sold.

For *business strength*, the GE approach again uses an index rather than a simple measure of relative market share. The business strength index includes factors such as the company's relative market share, price competitiveness, product quality, customer and market knowledge, sales effectiveness and geographic advantages. These factors are rated and combined in an index of business strengths described as strong, average or weak.

The grid has three zones. The green cells at the upper left include the strong SBUs in which the company should invest and grow. The amber diagonal cells contain SBUs that are medium in

Figure 3.3 GE's strategic business-planning grid

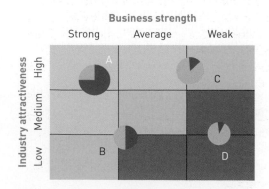

overall attractiveness. The company should maintain its level of investment in these SBUs. The three red cells at the lower right indicate SBUs that are low in overall attractiveness. The company should give serious thought to harvesting or divesting these SBUs.

The circles represent four company SBUs; the areas of the circles are proportional to the relative sizes of the industries in which these SBUs compete. The pie slices within the circles represent each SBU's market share. Thus circle A represents a company SBU with a 75 per cent market share in a good-sized, highly attractive industry in which the company has strong business strength. Circle B represents an SBU that has a 50 per cent market share, but the industry is not very attractive. Circles C and D represent two other company SBUs in industries where the company has small market shares and not much business strength. Altogether, the company should build A, maintain B and make some hard decisions on what to do with C and D.

> " One of the aims of portfolio analysis is to direct firms away from investing in markets that look attractive, but where they have no strength. "

Management would also plot the projected positions of the SBUs with and without changes in strategies. By comparing current and projected business grids, management can identify the primary strategic issues and opportunities it faces. One of the aims of portfolio analysis is to direct firms away from investing in markets that look attractive, but where they have no strength:

In their rush away from the declining steel market, four of Japan's 'famous five' big steel makers (Nippon, NKK, Kawasaki, Sumitomo and Kobe) diversified into the microchip business. They had the misplaced belief that chips would be to them in the future what steel had been in the 1950s and that they had to be part of it. The market was attractive but it did not fit their strengths. None have made money from chips. The misadventure also distracted them from attending to their core business.

The 'famous five's' failure contrasts with Eramet, a focused French company that is the world's biggest producer of ferro-nickel and high-speed steels. They owe their number one position to their decision to invest their profits in a 'second leg' that would be a logical industrial and geographical diversification for them. They bought French Commentryene and Swedish Kloster Speedsteel. They quickly integrated them and, according to Yves Rambert, their chairman and chief executive, 'found that the French and the Swedes can work together'.[15]

Problems with matrix approaches

The BCG, GE, Shell and other formal methods revolutionised strategic planning. However, such approaches have limitations. They can be difficult, time consuming and costly to implement. Management may find it difficult to define SBUs and measure market share and growth. In addition, these approaches focus on classifying *current* businesses, but provide little advice for *future* planning. Management must still rely on its judgement to set the business objectives for each SBU, to determine what resources to give to each and to work out which new businesses to add.

Formal planning approaches can also lead the company to place too much emphasis on market-share growth or growth through entry into attractive new markets. Using these approaches, many companies plunged into unrelated and new high-growth businesses that they did not know how to manage – with very bad results. At the same time, these companies were often too quick to abandon, sell or milk to death their healthy, mature businesses. As a result, many companies that diversified in the past are now narrowing their focus and getting back to the industries that they know best (see Real Marketing 3.2).

3.2 real marketing

KISS (Keep It Simple Stupid)

When times are good, many businesses catch expansion fever. 'Big is beautiful' and everyone wanted to get bigger and grow faster by broadening their business portfolios. Companies like Vivendi and Warner Bros. neglected their stodgy core businesses to acquire glamorous businesses in more attractive industries. It did not seem to matter that many of the acquired businesses fitted poorly with old ones, or that they operated in markets unfamiliar to company management.

Many firms exploded into conglomerates, sometimes containing hundreds of unrelated products and businesses. Extreme cases involved French banks and Japanese electronics companies buying Hollywood film studios. Managing these 'smörgåsbord' portfolios proved difficult. Eventually managers realised that it was tough to run businesses they knew little about. Many newly acquired businesses were also bogged down under added layers of corporate management and administrative costs. Meanwhile, the profitable core businesses withered from lack of investment and management attention.

Encumbered with the burden of their scattergun diversification, acquisition fever gave way to a new philosophy of keeping things simple: 'narrowing the focus', 'sticking to your knitting', 'the urge to purge'. They all mean narrowing the company's market focus and returning to the idea of serving one or a few core industries that the firm knows. Companies are shedding businesses that do not fit their narrowed focus and rebuilding by concentrating resources on other businesses that do. Examples are Royal Dutch/Shell's sale of their coal division, Lucas selling swathes of peripheral and underperforming activities to refocus on its core of automotive, aerospace and electronic components, and Norske Hydro ASA selling off miscellaneous businesses, such as fertilisers, to build on its core in oil and energy. The result is a smaller but more focused company: a stronger firm serving fewer markets, but serving them much better.

When Cor Boonstra joined Philips, as their first outsider to become President, he was horrified at what he found. Philips was the world's number one in lighting, number two in television tubes and number eight in semiconductors, but had lots of other activities bleeding cash and managerial time. Its lighting and tubes were under pressure from manufacturers from South Korea and Taiwan, but the ability to compete was being swamped by numerous unconnected and loss-making businesses. Boonstra also inherited a 'hopelessly bureaucratic' business with layers and layers of management between factory and consumer. His strategy was to take the company back to its core strengths in 'high-volume consumer electronics'. Marketing

...3.2

expenditure in the core businesses was to increase while the strategy was to 'close, fix or sell' the 'bleeders'. Among the non-core businesses sold are Polygram, a music and film business, a chain of video stores and loss-making Grundig. In his first two years Boonstra sold off 40 businesses, losing 28,000 workers but bringing in €8bn to invest in the core. The company shrunk from 120 businesses in 11 divisions to a less bloated eight divisions with 80 businesses, but many more factories have to go. However, all is not gloom. While becoming a less complex company, Philips is gaining market share in its major markets and profits are growing.

Philips is now facing a dilemma that concentration forces on many businesses. Should it sell the very business on which it was founded? Reckitt & Colman did that when they sold Colman's mustard. Lighting is profitable and a strong business but it is far from Philips' chosen future in consumer electronics. Breaking up is hard to do, too.

SOURCES: *The Economist*, 'Vivendi Universal: messier's mess' (8 June 2002), pp. 69–71; *The Economist*, 'Media conglomerates: tangled web' (25 May 2002), pp. 81–3; *The Economist*, 'Rising above the sludge' (15 April 2003), pp. 77–9; *The Economist*, 'Revving up for a demolition derby: Is the giant financial conglomerate a thing of the past – or is it the future?' (22 March 2007); Tony Jackson, 'Breaking up is sometimes hard to do, fortunately', *Financial Times* (11 June 2007); N. Sedaka and H. Greenfield, 'Breaking up is hard to do', 1962.

Despite these and other problems, and although many companies have dropped formal matrix methods in favour of customised approaches better suited to their situations, most companies remain firmly committed to strategic planning.

Such analysis is no cure-all for finding the best strategy. Conversely, it can help management to understand the company's overall situation, to see how each business or product contributes, to assign resources to its businesses, and to orient the company for future success. When used properly, strategic planning is just one important aspect of overall strategic management, a way of thinking about how to manage a business.[16]

Take, for example, The Walt Disney Company. Most people think of Disney as theme parks and wholesome family entertainment. But in the mid-1980s, Disney set up a powerful, centralised strategic planning group to guide the company's direction and growth. Over the next two decades, the strategic planning group turned The Walt Disney Company into a huge but diverse collection of media and entertainment businesses including five holiday resorts, 11 theme parks, two water parks, 39 hotels, eight film studios, six record labels, 11 cable television networks, and one terrestrial television network. The newly transformed company proved hard to manage and performed unevenly with film flops – *Dark Water* and *The Brothers Grimm* – that damaged the company's overall performace. Taking its eye off its core business, it even lost money on its run of traditional animated children's films in the late 1990s: *Pocahontas*, *The Hunchback of Notre Dame*, *Hercules*, *Mulan*, *Tarzan*. Recently, Disney's new chief executive disbanded the centralised strategic planning unit, decentralising its functions to divisional managers.

Figure 3.4 Product/market expansion grid

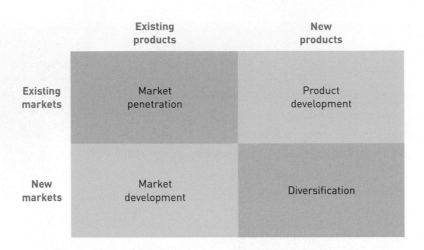

Developing growth strategies

The **product/market expansion grid**,[17] shown in Figure 3.4, is a useful device for identifying growth opportunities. This shows four routes to growth: market development, new markets, new products and diversification. We use the grid to explain how Mercedes Cars, the car division of Daimler Benz, hoped to return to profits after its €1bn loss in mid-1990.

Market penetration

Market penetration is a strategy for company growth by increasing sales of current products to current market segments without changing the product. The new C-class (medium-sized family saloon) and E-class (executive saloon) helped Mercedes-Benz increase its sales by 23 per cent, besides costing less to produce. Sales were up 40 per cent in western Europe (excluding Germany), 34 per cent in the United States and 30 per cent in Japan. In Germany, the 38 per cent growth gave a 2 per cent rise in market share.

Product development

Product development is a strategy for company growth by offering modified new products to current market segments. With its A-class small family saloon and Smart Car, Mercedes entered the small car market, while the relaunch of the Maybach brought the company back into the super-luxury price bracket. Mercedes luxury-end cars continue to prosper, although the Smart car range is being pruned and it is likely that the A-series, much loved by older consumers, will be dropped to allow the company to attract entry-level Mercedes owners with more sporty offerings.

It was hoped that the formation of DaimlerChrysler would give the combined company a chance to develop lower-priced brands worldwide through products like the Chrysler Neon and Voyager. However, there were soon worries that the build quality and association with such downmarket products is tarnishing Mercedes' reputation for safety and quality. Additionally, executing the merger between the two companies with such strong but different cultures has proved as difficult as could be expected. After making a huge loss, Mercedes sold most of its shares in Chrysler for $1.35bn (€1bn) to Ceribus, a private equity company, but in exchange had to contribute $2bn to support the new venture.

Market development

Market development is a strategy for company growth by identifying and developing new market segments for current company products. The global reputation and quality of Mercedes have made their cars highly attractive in the developing world and the BRIC countries have proved a

Product/market expansion grid—
A portfolio-planning tool for identifying company growth opportunities through market penetration, market development, new product development or diversification.

Market penetration—
A strategy for company growth by increasing sales of current products to current market segments without changing the product.

Product development—
A strategy for company growth by offering modified new products to current market segments.

Market development—
A strategy for company growth by identifying and developing new market segments for current company products.

mod. GA 479/s   www.giorgioarmani.com

GIORGIO GA ARMANI

Armani has grown from its flagship **Giorgio Armani** range using its diffusion line **Armani Collezioni** (around 20% less expensive). Beneath them were added more affordable **Emporio Armani**, casual **Armani Jeans**, everyday **Armani Exchange** and **Armani Junior** for kids.
SOURCE: The Advertising Archives.

huge opportunity for market development – particularly China and India whose economies and wealthy middle-class are growing even faster than the double-digit growth of the economy.

Diversification

Diversification was an option taken by Daimler Benz, the parent company of Mercedes cars. After rapidly moving into aerospace, its DASA defence subsidiary is now merged into the Franco-German EADS (European Aeronautic Defence and Space Company). The company is also selling loss-making subsidiaries, such as rail equipment maker Adtranz.[18]

Diversification—A strategy for company growth through starting up or acquiring businesses outside the company's current products and markets.

Bic started as a maker of disposable pens and its logo still shows Mr Ballpoint. The company then diversified with the world's first disposable razors and now more exotic razors for women as well as 'real' men!
SOURCE: The Advertising Archives.

Downsizing—Reducing the business portfolio by eliminating products of business units that are not profitable or that no longer fit the company's overall strategy.

Like many companies, Mercedes is growing stronger by getting smaller, shedding unsuccessful activities and those that are not its core business. Companies must develop not only strategies for *growing* their business portfolios but also strategies for **downsizing** them. There are many reasons why a firm might want to abandon products or markets. The market environment might change, making some of the company's products or markets less profitable. The firm may have grown too fast or entered areas where it lacks experience. This can occur when a firm enters too many foreign markets without the proper research or when a company introduces new products that do not offer superior customer value. Finally, some products or business units simply age and die.

Companies spend vast amounts of money and time launching new brands, leveraging existing ones and acquiring rivals. They create line extensions and brand extensions, not to mention channel extensions and sub-brands, to cater to the growing number of niche segments in every market. Surprisingly, most businesses do not examine their brand portfolios from time to time to check if they might be selling too many brands, identify weak ones and kill unprofitable ones. They tend to ignore loss-making brands rather than merge them with healthy brands, sell them off or drop them. Consequently, most portfolios have become jammed with loss-making and marginally profitable brands. Moreover, the surprising truth is that most brands don't make money for companies. Many corporations generate less than 80 to 90 per cent of their profits from fewer than 20 per cent of the brands they sell, while they lose money or barely break even on many of the other brands in their portfolios.[19]

When a firm finds brands or businesses that are unprofitable or that no longer fit its overall strategy, it must carefully prune, harvest or divest them. Weak businesses usually require a disproportionate amount of management attention. Managers should focus on promising growth opportunities, not fritter away energy trying to salvage fading ones.

> Managers should focus on promising growth opportunities, not fritter away energy trying to salvage fading ones.

Marketing relationships

The company's strategic plan establishes what kinds of businesses the company will operate in and its objectives for each. Then, within each business unit, more detailed planning takes place. The major functional departments in each unit – marketing, finance, accounting, purchasing, operations, information systems, human resources and others – must work together to accomplish strategic objectives.

Marketing plays a key role in the company's strategic planning in several ways. First, marketing provides a guiding *philosophy* – the marketing concept – which suggests that company strategy should revolve around building profitable relationships with important consumer groups. Second, marketing provides *inputs* to strategic planners by helping to identify attractive market opportunities and by assessing the firm's potential to take advantage of them. Finally, within individual business units, marketing designs *strategies* for reaching the unit's objectives. Once the unit's objectives are set, marketing's task is to help carry them out profitably.

Partnering with customers

Customer value and satisfaction are important ingredients in the marketer's formula for success. However, as we noted in Chapter 1, marketers alone cannot produce superior value for customers. Although it plays a leading role, marketing can be only a partner in attracting, keeping and growing customers. In addition to *customer relationship management*, marketers must also practise *partner relationship management*. They must work closely with partners in other company departments to form an effective *value chain* that serves the customer. Moreover, they must partner effectively with other companies in the marketing system to form a competitively superior *value-delivery network*. We now take a closer look at the concepts of a company value chain and value-delivery network.

Partnering with other company departments

Value chain—The series of departments that carry out value-creating activities to design, produce, market, deliver and support a firm's products.

Each company department can be thought of as a link in the company's **value chain**.[20] That is, each department carries out value-creating activities to design, produce, market, deliver and support the firm's products. The firm's success depends not only on how well each department performs its work but also on how well the activities of various departments are coordinated.

For example, Tesco's 'core purpose is *to create value for customers to earn their lifetime loyalty.*' Tesco's marketers play an important role. They learn what customers need and stock the stores' shelves with the desired products at competitively low prices. They prepare advertising and merchandising programmes and assist shoppers with customer service. Through these and other activities, Tesco's marketers help deliver value to customers.

However, the marketing department needs help from the company's other departments. Tesco's ability to offer the right products at good prices depends on the purchasing department's skill in developing the needed suppliers and buying from them at reasonable cost. Tesco's information technology department must provide fast and accurate information about which products are selling in each store. And its operations people must provide effective, low-cost merchandise handling.

A company's value chain is only as strong as its weakest link. Success depends on how well each department performs its work of adding customer value and on how well the activities of various departments are coordinated. At Tesco, if purchasing cannot wring the prices and quality from suppliers, or if operations cannot distribute merchandise cost-effectively, then marketing cannot deliver on its value promise.

Ideally, then, a company's different functions should work in harmony to produce value for consumers. But, in practice, departmental relations are full of conflicts and misunderstandings. The marketing department takes the consumer's point of view. But when marketing tries to develop customer satisfaction, it can cause other departments to do a poorer job *in their terms*. Marketing department actions can increase purchasing costs, disrupt production schedules, increase inventories and create budget headaches. Thus, the other departments may resist the marketing department's efforts.

Yet marketers must find ways to get all departments to 'think consumer' and to develop a smoothly functioning value chain. Marketing managers need to work closely with managers of other functions to develop a system of functional plans under which the different departments can work together to accomplish the company's overall strategic objectives. The idea is to maximise the customer experience across the organisation and its various customer touch points.

Jack Welch, General Electric's highly regarded former CEO, told his employees: 'Companies can't give job security. Only customers can!' He emphasized that all General Electric people, regardless of their department, have an impact on customer satisfaction and retention. His message: 'If you are not thinking customer, you are not thinking.'[21]

Partnering with others in the marketing system

In its quest to create customer value, the firm needs to look beyond its own value chain and into the value chains of its suppliers, distributors and, ultimately, its customers. Consider McDonald's, whose nearly 32,000 restaurants worldwide serve more than 50 million customers daily, capturing a more than 40 per cent share of the burger market.[22] People do not swarm to McDonald's only because they love the chain's hamburgers. In fact, consumers typically rank McDonald's behind Burger King and Wendy's in taste. Consumers flock to the McDonald's *system*, not just to its food products. Throughout the world, McDonald's finely-tuned system delivers a high standard of what the company calls QSCV – quality, service, cleanliness and value. McDonald's is effective only to the extent that it successfully partners with its franchisees, suppliers and others to jointly deliver exceptionally high customer value.

More companies today are partnering with the other members of the supply chain to improve the performance of the customer **value-delivery network**. For example, Toyota knows the importance of building close relationships with its suppliers. In fact, it even includes the phrase 'achieve supplier satisfaction' in its mission statement.

Value-delivery network— The network made up of the company, suppliers, distributors and ultimately customers who 'partner' with each other to improve the performance of the entire system.

Achieving satisfying supplier relationships has been a cornerstone of Toyota's stunning success. Toyota knows that competitors often alienate their suppliers through self-serving, heavy-handed dealings. '[Motor manufacturers] set annual cost-reduction targets [for the parts they buy],' says one supplier. 'To realize those targets, they'll do anything. [They've unleashed] a reign of terror, and it gets worse every year.' Says another, '[Ford] seems to send its people to "hate school" so that they learn how to hate suppliers.' By contrast, in survey after survey, auto suppliers rate Toyota as their most preferred customer. Rather than bullying suppliers, Toyota partners with them and helps them to meet its very high expectations. It learns about their businesses, conducts joint improvement activities, helps train their employees, gives daily performance feedback, and actively seeks out supplier concerns. Says one delighted Toyota supplier, 'Toyota helped us dramatically improve our production system. We started by making one component, and as we improved, [Toyota] rewarded us with orders for more components. Toyota is our best customer.'

Such high supplier satisfaction means that Toyota can rely on suppliers to help it improve its own quality, reduce costs and develop new products quickly. For example, when Toyota recently launched a programme to reduce prices by 30 per cent on 170 parts that it would buy for its next generation of cars, suppliers didn't complain. Instead, they pitched in, trusting that Toyota would help them achieve the targeted reductions, in turn making them more competitive and profitable in the future. In all, creating satisfied suppliers helps Toyota to produce lower-cost, higher-quality cars, which in turn results in more satisfied customers.[23]

Increasingly in today's marketplace, competition no longer takes place between individual competitors. Rather, it takes place between the entire value-delivery networks created by these competitors. Thus, Toyota's performance against competitors depends on the quality of Toyota's overall value-delivery network versus those of its competitors. Even if Toyota makes the best cars, it might lose in the marketplace if other dealer networks provide more customer-satisfying sales and service.

The marketing plan

Within an organisation's strategic plan are marketing plans for each business, product or brand. A series of separate plans is necessary because even within a well-focused company product classes can face hugely different circumstances.

> In Europe's long hot summer of 2006 Nestlé gave out profit warnings because the high temperature reduced people's consumption of some processed food while the popularity of the Atkins diet hit diet and slimming lines. Meanwhile, ice cream and mineral water sales skyrocketed. Elsewhere, the usually hot and humid north-east coast of the US hardly had a day without rain and clouds. The year 2007 looks like another shocker for Nestlé. May was the hottest on record in many European countries followed by June, the wettest on record in most of northern Europe. Meanwhile, parts of southern Europe suffered droughts and an extraordinary heatwave.

How do marketing plans embrace this uncertainty? What does a marketing plan look like? Our discussion focuses on product or brand plans that are a development of the general planning process in Figure 3.1. A product or brand plan should have an executive summary, the current marketing situation, threats and opportunities, objectives and issues, marketing strategies, action programmes, budgets and controls (see Table 3.2).

Table 3.2 Contents of a marketing plan

Section	Purpose
Executive summary	Presents a quick overview of the plan for quick management review.
Current marketing situation	The marketing audit that presents background data on the market, product, competition and distribution.
SWOT analysis	Identifies the company's main *strengths* and *weaknesses* and the main *opportunities* and *threats* facing the product.
Objectives and issues	Defines the company's objectives in the areas of sales, market share and profits, and the issues that will affect these objectives.
Marketing strategy	Presents the broad marketing approach that will be used to achieve the plan's objectives.
Marketing implementation	Specifies *what* will be done, *who* will do it, *when* it will be done and *what* it will cost.
Budgets	A projected profit-and-loss statement that forecasts the expected financial outcomes from the plan.
Controls	Indicates how the progress of the plan will be monitored.

Executive summary

The marketing plan should open with a short summary of the main goals and recommendations in the plan. Here is a short example:

> The 2008 Marketing Plan outlines an approach to attaining a significant increase in company sales and profits over the preceding year. The sales target is €24m – a planned 20 per cent sales gain. We think this increase is attainable because of the improved economic, competitive and distribution picture. The target operating margin is €2.5m, a 25 per cent increase over last year. To achieve these goals, the sales promotion budget will be €500,000, or 2 per cent of projected sales. The advertising budget will be €720,000, or 3 per cent of projected sales . . . [more details follow]

The executive summary helps top management to find the plan's central points quickly. A table of contents should follow the executive summary.

Marketing audit

The **marketing audit** is a systematic and periodic examination of a company's environment, objectives, strategies and activities to determine problem areas and opportunities. The first main section of the plan describes the target market and the company's position in it (Table 3.3 gives the questions asked). It should start with the strategic imperatives: the pertinent objectives, policies and elements of strategy passed down from broader plans. In the **current marketing situation** section, the planner provides information about the market, product performance, competition and distribution. It includes a *market description* that defines the market, including chief market segments. The planner shows market size, in total and by segment, for several past years, and then reviews customer needs together with factors in the marketing environment that may affect customer purchasing. Next, the *product review* shows sales, prices and gross margins of the principal products in the product line. A section on *competition* identifies big competitors and their individual strategies for product quality, pricing, distribution and promotion. It also shows the market shares held by the company and each competitor. Finally, a section on *distribution* describes recent sales trends and developments in the primary distribution channels.

Managing the marketing function would be hard enough if the marketer had to deal only with the controllable marketing-mix variables. Reality is harder. The company is in a complex marketing environment consisting of uncontrollable forces to which the company must adapt. The *environment* produces both threats and opportunities. The company must carefully analyse its environment so that it can avoid the threats and take advantage of the opportunities.

The company's marketing environment includes forces close to the company that affect its ability to serve its consumers, such as other company *departments*, *channel members*, *suppliers*, *competitors* and other *publics*. It also includes broader *demographic* and *economic* forces, *political* and *legal* forces, *technological* and *ecological* forces, and *social* and *cultural* forces. The company must consider all of these forces when developing and positioning its offer to the target market.

SWOT analysis

The SWOT analysis section draws from the market audit. It is a brief list of the critical success factors in the market, and rates strengths and weaknesses against the competition. The SWOT analysis should include costs and other non-marketing variables. The outstanding opportunities and threats should be given. If plans depend upon assumptions about the market, the economy or the competition, they need to be explicit.

Marketing audit—A comprehensive, systematic, independent and periodic examination of a company's environment, objectives, strategies and activities to determine problem areas and opportunities, and to recommend a plan of action to improve the company's marketing performance.

Current marketing situation—The section of a marketing plan that describes the target market and the company's position in it.

Table 3.3 Marketing audit questions

Marketing environment audit

The macroenvironment

1. *Demographic.* What primary demographic trends pose threats and opportunities for this company?

2. *Economic.* What developments in income, prices, savings and credit will impact on the company?

3. *Natural.* What is the outlook for costs and availability of natural resources and energy? Is the company environmentally responsible?

4. *Technology.* What technological changes are occurring? What is the company's position on technology?

5. *Political.* What current and proposed laws will affect company strategy?

6. *Cultural.* What is the public's attitude towards business and the company's products? What changes in consumer lifestyles might have an impact?

The task environment

1. *Markets.* What is happening to market size, growth, geographic distribution and profits? What are the large market segments?

2. *Customers.* How do customers rate the company on product quality, service and price? How do they make their buying decisions?

3. *Competitors.* Who are the chief competitors? What are their strategies, market shares, and strengths and weaknesses?

4. *Channels.* What main channels does the company use to distribute products to customers? How are they performing?

5. *Suppliers.* What trends are affecting suppliers? What is the outlook for the availability of key production resources?

6. *Publics.* What key publics provide problems or opportunities? How should the company deal with these publics?

Marketing strategy audit

1. *Mission.* Is the mission clearly defined and market-oriented?

2. *Objectives.* Has the company set clear objectives to guide marketing planning and performance? Do these objectives fit with the company's opportunities and strengths?

3. *Strategy.* Does the company have a sound marketing strategy for achieving its objectives?

4. *Budgets.* Has the company budgeted sufficient resources to segments, products, territories and marketing-mix elements?

Marketing organisation audit

1. *Formal structure.* Does the chief marketing officer have adequate authority over activities affecting customer satisfaction? Are activities optimally structured along functional, product, market and territory lines?

2. *Functional efficiency.* Do marketing, sales and other staff communicate effectively? Are the staff well trained, supervised, motivated and evaluated?

3. *Interface efficiency.* Do staff work well across functions: marketing with manufacturing, R&D, buying, personnel, etc.?

Table 3.3 (continued)

Marketing systems audit

1. *Marketing information system.* Is the marketing intelligence system providing accurate and timely information about developments? Are decision makers using marketing research effectively?

2. *Planning system.* Does the company prepare annual, long-term and strategic plans? Are they used?

3. *Marketing control system.* Are annual plan objectives being achieved? Does management periodically analyse the sales and profitability of products, markets, territories and channels?

4. *New-product development.* Is the company well organised to gather, generate and screen new-product ideas? Does it carry out adequate product and market testing? Has the company succeeded with new products?

Productivity audit

1. *Profitability analysis.* How profitable are the company's different products, markets, territories and channels? Should the company enter, expand or withdraw from any business segments? What would be the consequences?

2. *Cost-effectiveness analysis.* Do any activities have excessive costs? How can costs be reduced?

Marketing function audit

1. *Products.* Has the company developed sound product-line objectives? Should some products be phased out? Should some new products be added? Would some products benefit from quality, style or feature changes?

2. *Price.* What are the company's pricing objectives, policies, strategies and procedures? Are the company's prices in line with customers' perceived value? Are price promotions used properly?

3. *Distribution.* What are the distribution objectives and strategies? Does the company have adequate market coverage and service? Should existing channels be changed or new ones added?

4. *Advertising, sales promotion and publicity.* What are the company's promotion objectives? How is the budget determined? Is it sufficient? Are advertising messages and media well developed and received? Does the company have well-developed sales promotion and public relations programmes?

5. *Sales force.* What are the company's sales force objectives? Is the sales force large enough? Is it properly organised? Is it well trained, supervised and motivated? How is the sales force rated relative to those of competitors?

Objectives and issues

Having studied the strengths, weaknesses, opportunities and threats, the company sets objectives and considers issues that will affect them. The objectives are goals that the company would like to attain during the plan's term. For example, the manager might want to achieve a 15 per cent market share, a 20 per cent pre-tax profit on sales and a 25 per cent pre-tax profit on investment. If current market share is only 10 per cent, the question needs answering: Where are the extra sales to come from? From the competition, by increasing usage rate, by adding, and so on?

Marketing strategy

In this section of the marketing plan, the manager outlines the broad marketing strategy or 'game plan' for attaining the objectives. **Marketing strategy** is the marketing logic by which the company hopes to create this customer value and achieve these profitable relationships. The company decides which customers it will serve (segmentation and targeting) and how (differentiation and positioning). It identifies the total market, then divides it into smaller segments, selects the most promising segments, and focuses on serving and satisfying customers in these segments.

Customer-driven marketing strategy

As we emphasised throughout Chapter 1, to succeed in today's competitive marketplace, companies need to be customer centred. They must win customers from competitors, then keep and grow them by delivering greater value. But before it can satisfy consumers, a company must first understand their needs and wants. Thus, sound marketing requires a careful customer analysis.

Companies know that they cannot profitably serve all consumers in a given market – at least not all consumers in the same way. There are too many different kinds of consumers with too many different kinds of needs. And most companies are in a position to serve some segments better than others. Thus, each company must divide up the total market, choose the best segments, and design strategies for profitably serving chosen segments. This process involves *market segmentation, target marketing, differentiation* and *market positioning*. We introduce these here before they are considered in greater depth in Chapter 9.

Market segmentation

The market consists of many types of customers, products and needs. The marketer has to determine which segments offer the best opportunities. Consumers can be grouped and served in various ways based on geographic, demographic, psychographic and behavioural factors. The process of dividing a market into distinct groups of buyers who have different needs, characteristics or behaviour who might require separate products or marketing programmes is called **market segmentation**.

 It is impossible to make one [product] that is the first choice of consumers in all segments.

Every market has segments, but not all ways of segmenting a market are equally useful. For example, Tylenol would gain little by distinguishing between low-income and high-income pain reliever users if both respond the same way to marketing efforts. A **market segment** consists of consumers who respond in a similar way to a given set of marketing efforts. In the consumer electronics market, for example, the music systems bought by hi-fi buffs will consist of a series of expensive separates often of different brands – pre-amplifier, amplifier, tuner, speakers, etc., all linked together with the best of cables and installed in a room with balanced acoustic properties. Other consumers in the same income bracket may purchase a compact integrated music system, like the Bose Wave, or an inMotion to play their iPod or use iTunes on their laptop. Consumers who care mainly about price and operating economy make up another segment. It is impossible to make one music system that is the first choice of consumers in all segments. Companies are wise to focus their efforts on meeting the distinct needs of individual market segments.

Market targeting

After a company has defined market segments, it can enter one or many of these segments. **Market targeting** involves evaluating each market segment's attractiveness and selecting one or more segments to enter. A company should target segments in which it can profitably generate the greatest customer value and sustain it over time.

A company with limited resources might decide to serve only one or a few special segments or 'market niches'. Such 'nichers' specialise in serving customer segments that major competitors overlook or ignore. For example, Ferrari sells only 3,500 of its very high-performance cars each year, but at very high prices – from a modest €284,272 for its Ferrari Superamerica to a cool €1.5m for the dozen or so Ferrari FXX sports racing cars, which can be driven only on racing tracks. Most nichers are not so exotic. Benecol created a niche in the margarine market for those wanting to reduce their cholesterol level, and has since extended its range to include yogurts and cheese spreads.

Alternatively, a company might choose to serve several related segments – perhaps those with different kinds of customers but with the same basic product. Lego does this by starting with Duplo for small children and extending to Lego Factory whose trains website features enthusiasts well out of their nappies.[24] Alternatively a large company might decide to offer a complete range of products to serve all market segments.

Most companies enter a new market by serving a single segment, and if this proves successful, they add segments. Large companies may eventually seek more complete market coverage. They ape General Motors' assertion that it makes a car for every 'person, purse, and personality'. But, as GM has found, pleasing everyone is hard. What is more, in 2007 Toyota raced past GM in worldwide car sales with a strategy based on far fewer models, far fewer brands and far fewer factories than GM.[25]

Market differentiation and positioning

After a company has decided which market segments to enter, it must decide how it will differentiate its market offering for each targeted segment and what positions it wants to occupy in those segments. A product's *position* is the place the product occupies relative to competitors in consumers' minds. Marketers want to develop unique market positions for their products. If a product is perceived to be exactly like others on the market, consumers would have no reason to buy it.

Positioning is arranging for a product to occupy a clear, distinctive and desirable place relative to competing products in the minds of target consumers. As one positioning expert puts it, positioning is 'how you differentiate your product or company – why a shopper will pay a little more for your brand'.[26] Thus, marketers plan positions that distinguish their products from competing brands and give them the greatest advantage in their target markets.

BMW makes 'the ultimate driving machine'; Ford is 'built for the road ahead'; and Kia promises 'the power to surprise'. MasterCard gives you 'priceless experiences'; and whether it is an everyday moment or the moment of a lifetime, 'life takes Visa'. easyHotel offers 'a safe, clean room for the night at the best possible price' while at Caesar's Palace in Las Vegas, you can 'live famously'. Such deceptively simple statements form the backbone of a product's marketing strategy.

In positioning its product, the company first identifies possible customer value differences that provide competitive advantages upon which to build the position. The company can offer greater customer value either by charging lower prices than competitors do or by offering more benefits to justify higher prices. But if the company *promises* greater value, it must then *deliver* that greater value. Thus, effective positioning begins with **differentiation** – actually differentiating the company's market offering so that it gives consumers more value. Once the company has chosen a desired position, it must take strong steps to deliver and communicate that position to target consumers. The company's entire marketing programme should support the chosen positioning strategy.

Positioning—Arranging for a product to occupy a clear, distinctive and desirable place relative to competing products in the minds of target consumers.

Differentiation—Differentiating the market offering to create superior customer value.

Marketing mix

After deciding on its overall marketing strategy, the company is ready to begin planning the details of the marketing mix, one of the major concepts in modern marketing. The marketing mix is the set of controllable, tactical marketing tools that the firm blends to produce the response it wants in the target market. The marketing mix consists of everything the firm can do to influence the demand for its product and is covered in Chapters 11 to 20. The many possibilities can be collected into four groups of variables known as the 'four Ps': *product, price, place* and *promotion*. Figure 1.8 showed the marketing tools under each *P*.

Product means the goods-and-services combination the company offers to the target market. Thus, a Mini consists of nuts and bolts, spark plugs, pistons, headlights and thousands of other parts. BMW offers several basic Mini models ranging from the Mini One to the open-top Mini Cooper S Sidewalk but, in addition, numerous options allow people to build their own Mini. The car also comes fully serviced and with a comprehensive warranty that is as much a part of the product as the brand's name and its heritage.

Price is the amount of money customers have to pay to obtain the product. BMW calculates suggested retail prices that its dealers might charge for each Mini. But dealers rarely charge the full sticker price. Instead, they negotiate the price with each customer, offering discounts, trade-in allowances, special packages and credit terms. These actions adjust prices for the current competitive situation and bring them into line with the buyer's perception of the car's value.

Place includes company activities that make the product available to target consumers. BMW partners with a large body of independently owned dealerships that sell the company's many different models. The Mini, however, often has its own dealerships or marked-off area and branded part of a dealer's facility. BMW carefully selects and supports them strongly. The dealers keep an inventory of Minis, demonstrate them to potential buyers, negotiate prices, close sales, and service the cars after the sale.

Promotion means activities that communicate the merits of the product and persuade target customers to buy it. BMW spends almost €400m each year on advertising, more than €300 per vehicle, to tell consumers about the company and its many products.[27] Dealership salespeople assist potential buyers and persuade them that a Mini is the best car for them. BMW and its dealers offer special promotions – sales, cash rebates, low financing rates – as added purchase incentives.

An effective marketing programme blends all of the marketing mix elements into an integrated marketing programme designed to achieve the company's marketing objectives by delivering value to consumers. The marketing mix is the company's tactical toolkit for establishing strong positioning in target markets.

Some critics think that the four Ps may omit or underemphasise certain important activities. For example, they ask, 'Where are services?' Just because they don't start with a *P* doesn't justify omitting them. The answer is that services, such as banking, airline and retailing services, are products too. We might call them *service products*. 'Where is packaging?' the critics might ask. Marketers would answer that they include packaging as just one of many product decisions. All said, as Figure 1.8 suggests, many marketing activities that might appear to be left out of the marketing mix are subsumed under one of the four Ps. The issue is not whether there should be four, six or ten Ps so much as what framework is most helpful in designing integrated marketing programmes.

Marketing implementation

Marketing implementation—The process that turns marketing strategies and plans into marketing actions in order to accomplish strategic marketing objectives.

Planning good strategies is only a start towards successful marketing. A brilliant marketing strategy counts for little if the company fails to implement it properly. **Marketing implementation** is the process that turns marketing *plans* into marketing *actions* in order to accomplish strategic marketing objectives. Whereas marketing planning addresses the *what* and *why* of marketing activities, implementation addresses the *who, where, when* and *how*.

Many managers think that 'doing things right' (implementation) is as important as, or even more important than, 'doing the right things' (strategy). The fact is that both are critical to success, and companies can gain competitive advantages through effective implementation. One firm can have essentially the same strategy as another, yet win in the marketplace through faster or better execution. Still, implementation is difficult – it is often easier to think up good marketing strategies than it is to carry them out. 'Despite the enormous time and energy that goes into strategy development, . . . companies on average deliver only 63 per cent of the financial performance their strategies promise,' declares a marketing consultant. 'To close the strategy-to-performance gap, [companies need] better planning *and* execution.'[28]

> " 'Doing things right' (implementation) is as important as . . . 'doing the right things' (strategy). "

In an increasingly connected world, people at all levels of the marketing system must work together to implement marketing strategies and plans. InBev, the world's leading brewer by volume, must have marketing implementation programmes for its brands in the many markets. Describing itself as the 'world's local brewer', with a leading position in virtually every country in which it has a presence, it has many 'local' brands to plan for: the group's existing European flagship Stella Artois, Beck's (Germany's leading export beer), Skol (the world's third leading lager), Leffe (number one in Brazil) and so on. Marketing managers make decisions about target segments, branding, packaging, pricing, promoting and distributing in each market for each brand. They talk with engineering about product design, with manufacturing about production and inventory levels, and with finance about funding and cash flows. They also connect with outside people, such as advertising agencies, to plan ad campaigns, and with the news media to obtain publicity support. This can include many people and organisations. Stella Artois alone has Lowes London as its global agency, Universal McCann in France for media, Carlson Marketing Group covering direct marketing and interactive customer relationship management. The sales force urges bars, restaurants and other retailers to promote InBev products, carry ample stocks, provide ample shelf space or bar space, and use the company's display material.

Successful marketing implementation depends on how well the company blends its people, organisational structure, decision and reward systems and company culture into a cohesive action programme that supports its strategies. At all levels, the company must be staffed by people who have the needed skills, motivation and personal characteristics. The company's formal organisation structure plays an important role in implementing marketing strategy; so do its decision and reward systems. For example, if a company's compensation system rewards managers for short-run profit results, they will have little incentive to work towards long-run market-building objectives.

Finally, to be successfully implemented, the firm's marketing strategies must fit with its company culture, the system of values and beliefs shared by people in the organisation. A study of successful companies found that they have almost cult-like cultures built around strong, market-oriented missions. At companies such as Dell, Nordstrom and P&G, 'employees share such a strong vision that they know in their hearts what's right for their company.'[29]

Marketing budgets

Marketing managers must ensure that their marketing expenditure is well spent. In the past, many marketers spent freely on big, expensive marketing programmes, often without thinking carefully about the financial returns on their spending. They believed that marketing produces intangible outcomes, which do not lend themselves readily to measures of productivity or return. That is changing:

> For years, corporate marketers have walked into budget meetings like neighbourhood junkies. They couldn't always justify how well they spent past handouts or what difference it all made. They just wanted more money – for flashy TV ads, for big-ticket events, for, you know, getting out the message and building up the brand. But those heady days of blind budget increases are fast being replaced with a new mantra: measurement and accountability. Armed with reams of data, increasingly sophisticated tools, and growing evidence that the old tricks simply don't work, there's hardly a marketing executive today who isn't demanding a more scientific approach to help defend marketing strategies in front of the chief financial officer. Marketers want to know the actual return on investment (ROI) of each dollar, euro or pound spent. They want to know it often, not just annually. . . . Companies in every sector of business have become obsessed with honing the science of measuring marketing performance. 'Marketers have been pretty unaccountable for many years,' notes one expert. 'Now they are under big pressure to estimate their impact.'[30]

" Marketers have been pretty unaccountable for many years, now they are under big pressure to estimate their impact. "

In response, marketers are developing better measures of *return on marketing investment*. **Return on marketing investment** (or **marketing ROI**) is the net return from a marketing investment divided by the costs of the marketing investment. It measures the profits generated by investments in marketing activities.

It's true that marketing returns can be difficult to measure. In measuring *financial* ROI, both the *R* and the *I* are uniformly measured in monetary terms. But there is as yet no consistent definition of *marketing* ROI. 'It's tough to measure, more so than for other business expenses,' says one analyst. 'You can imagine buying a piece of equipment, . . . and then measuring the productivity gains that result from the purchase,' he says. 'But in marketing, benefits like advertising impact aren't easily put into dollar returns. It takes a leap of faith to come up with a number.'[31]

A company can assess return on marketing in terms of standard marketing performance measures, such as brand awareness, sales or market share. Campbell's Soup uses sales and share data to evaluate specific advertising campaigns. For example, in the US, analysis revealed that its recent Soup at Hand advertising campaign, which depicted real-life scenarios of consumers using the portable soup, nearly doubled both the product's trial rate and repeat use rate after the first year. The Soup at Hand campaign received a Gold Effie, an advertising industry award based on marketing effectiveness.[32]

Many companies are assembling such measures into *marketing dashboards* – meaningful sets of marketing performance metrics in a single display used to monitor strategic marketing performance. Just as automobile dashboards present drivers with details on how their cars are performing, the marketing dashboard gives marketers the detailed measures they need to assess and adjust their marketing strategies.[33]

Increasingly, however, beyond standard performance measures, marketers are using customer-centred measures of marketing impact, such as customer acquisition, customer retention and customer lifetime value. Figure 3.5 views marketing expenditures as investments that produce returns in the form of more profitable customer relationships.[34] Marketing investments result in

Return on marketing investment (or marketing ROI)—The net return from a marketing investment divided by the costs of the marketing investment.

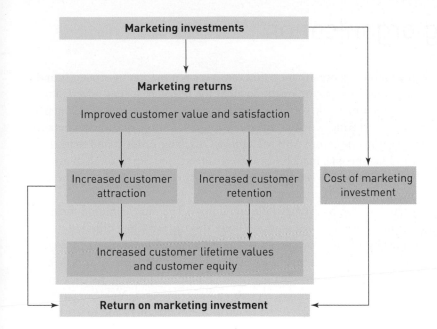

Figure 3.5 Return on marketing

SOURCE: Adapted from Roland T. Rust, Katherine N. Lemon and Valerie A. Zeithamal, 'Return on marketing: Using consumer equity to focus marketing strategy', *Journal of Marketing* (January 2004), p. 112. Reprinted with permission from the American Marketing Association.

improved customer value and satisfaction, which in turn increases customer attraction and retention. This increases individual customer lifetime values and the firm's overall customer equity. Increased customer equity, in relation to the cost of the marketing investments, determines return on marketing investment.

Regardless of how it's defined or measured, the return on marketing investment concept is here to stay. 'Marketing ROI is at the heart of every business,' exclaims one marketing executive. They have added another P to the marketing mix – 'for *profit and loss* or *performance*. We absolutely have to . . . quantify the impact of marketing on the business. You can't improve what you can't measure.'[35] We return to examining financial performance in Chapter 14, on pricing.

Marketing controls

So many surprises occur during the implementation of marketing plans that marketing departments must practise constant marketing control. **Marketing control** involves evaluating the results of marketing strategies and plans and taking corrective action to ensure that objectives are attained. Marketing control involves four steps. Management first sets specific marketing goals. It then measures its performance in the marketplace and evaluates the causes of any differences between expected and actual performance. Finally, management takes corrective action to close the gaps between its goals and its performance. This may require changing the action programmes or even changing the goals.

Operating control involves checking ongoing performance against the annual plan and taking corrective action when necessary. Its purpose is to ensure that the company achieves the sales, profits and other goals set out in its annual plan. It also involves determining the profitability of different products, territories, markets and channels.

Strategic control involves looking at whether the company's basic strategies are well matched to its opportunities. Marketing strategies and programmes can quickly become outdated, and each company should periodically reassess its overall approach to the marketplace. The marketing audit, at the beginning of the marketing planning process, is also a means of marketing control.[36]

KEY CONCEPT
www.pearson.co.uk/kotler

Marketing control—The process of measuring and evaluating the results of marketing strategies and plans, and taking corrective action to ensure that marketing objectives are attained.

Marketing organisation

The company must design a marketing organisation that can carry out marketing strategies and plans. If the company is very small, one person might do all of the research, selling, advertising, customer service and other marketing work. As the company expands, a marketing department emerges to plan and carry out marketing activities. In large companies, this department contains many specialists. Thus, large companies, from ABB to Zardoya Otis, have product and market managers, sales managers and salespeople, market researchers, advertising experts, and many other specialists. To head up such large marketing organisations, many companies have now created a *chief marketing officer* (or CMO) position.

Modern marketing departments can be arranged in several ways. The most common form of marketing organisation is the *functional organisation.* Under this organisation, different marketing activities are headed by a functional specialist – a sales manager, advertising manager, marketing research manager, customer service manager or new-product manager. A company that sells across the country or internationally often uses a *geographic organisation.* Its sales and marketing people are assigned to specific countries, regions and districts. Geographic organisation allows salespeople to settle into a territory, to get to know their customers and to work with a minimum of travel time and cost.

Companies with many very different products or brands often create a *product management organisation.* Using this approach, a product manager develops and implements a complete strategy and marketing programme for a specific product or brand. Product management first appeared at Procter & Gamble in 1929. A new company soap, Camay, was not doing well, and a young P&G executive was assigned to give his exclusive attention to developing and promoting this product. He was successful, and the company soon added other product managers.[37] Since then, many firms, especially consumer products companies, have set up product management organisations.

For companies that sell one product line to many different types of markets and customers that have different needs and preferences, a *market* or *customer management organisation* might be best. A market management organisation is similar to the product management organisation. Market managers are responsible for developing marketing strategies and plans for their specific markets or customers. This system's main advantage is that the company is organised around the needs of specific customer segments.

Large companies that produce many different products flowing into many different geographic and customer markets usually employ some *combination* of the functional, geographic, product and market organisation forms. This ensures that each function, product and market receives its share of management attention. However, it can also add costly layers of management and reduce organisational flexibility. Still, the benefits of organisational specialisation usually outweigh the drawbacks.

Marketing organisation has become an increasingly important issue in recent years. As we discussed in Chapter 1, many companies are finding that today's marketing environment calls for less focus on products, brands and territories and more focus on customers and customer relationships. More and more companies are shifting their brand management focus towards *customer management* – moving away from managing just product or brand profitability and towards managing customer profitability and customer equity. And many companies now organise their marketing operations around major customers. For example, international beverage companies such as Diageo, InBev, SABMiller and Heineken have large teams in each country or region of the world, set up to serve large retailers such as Tesco, Metro or Ahold, hotel chains such as Intercontinental Group, football clubs, bars, etc.

Reviewing the concepts

In Chapter 1, we defined *marketing* and outlined the steps in the marketing process. In Chapter 2 we looked at the social context of marketing. In this chapter, we examined company-wide strategic planning and marketing's role in the organisation. Then, we looked more deeply into marketing strategy and the marketing mix, and reviewed the major marketing management functions. So you've now had a pretty good overview of the fundamentals of modern marketing. In future chapters, we'll expand on these fundamentals.

1. Explain company-wide strategic planning and its four steps

Strategic planning sets the stage for the rest of the company's planning. Marketing contributes to strategic planning, and the overall plan defines marketing's role in the company. Although formal planning offers a variety of benefits to companies, not all companies use it or use it well.

Strategic planning involves developing a strategy for long-run survival and growth. It consists of four steps: defining the company's mission, setting objectives and goals, designing a business portfolio, and developing functional plans. *Defining a clear company mission* begins with drafting a formal mission statement, which should be market oriented, realistic, specific, motivating, and consistent with the market environment. The mission is then transformed into detailed *supporting goals and objectives* to guide the entire company. Based on those goals and objectives, headquarters designs a *business portfolio*, deciding which businesses and products should receive more or fewer resources. In turn, each business and product unit must develop *detailed marketing plans* in line with the company-wide plan.

2. Discuss how to design business portfolios and develop strategies for growth and downsizing

Guided by the company's mission statement and objectives, management plans its *business portfolio*, or the collection of businesses and products that make up the company. The firm wants to produce a business portfolio that best fits its strengths and weaknesses to opportunities in the environment. To do this, it must analyse and adjust its *current* business portfolio and develop growth and downsizing strategies for adjusting the *future* portfolio. The company might use a formal portfolio-planning method. But many companies are now designing more customised portfolio-planning approaches that better suit their unique situations. The *product/market expansion grid* suggests four possible growth paths: market penetration, market development, product development and diversification.

3. Assess marketing's role in strategic planning and explain how marketers partner with others inside and outside the firm to build profitable customer relationships

Under the strategic plan, the major functional departments – marketing, finance, accounting, purchasing, operations, information systems, human resources and

others – must work together to accomplish strategic objectives. Marketing plays a key role in the company's strategic planning by providing a *marketing-concept philosophy* and *inputs* regarding attractive market opportunities. Within individual business units, marketing designs *strategies* for reaching the unit's objectives and helps to carry them out profitably.

Marketers alone cannot produce superior value for customers. A company's success depends on how well each department performs its customer value-adding activities and how well the departments work together to serve the customer. Thus, marketers must practise *partner relationship management*. They must work closely with partners in other company departments to form an effective *value chain* that serves the customer. And they must partner effectively with other companies in the marketing system to form a competitively superior *value-delivery network*.

4. Describe the elements of a customer-driven marketing strategy and mix, and the forces that influence it

Consumer value and relationships are at the centre of marketing strategy and programmes. Through market segmentation, market targeting, differentiation and positioning, the company divides the total market into smaller segments, selects segments it can best serve, and decides how it wants to bring value to target consumers. It then designs an *integrated marketing mix* to produce the response it wants in the target market. The marketing mix consists of product, price, place and promotion decisions.

5. List the marketing management functions, including the elements of a marketing plan, and discuss the importance of measuring and managing return on marketing

To find the best strategy and mix and to put them into action, the company engages in marketing analysis, planning, implementation and control. The main components of a *marketing plan* are the executive summary, current marketing situation, threats and opportunities, objectives and issues, marketing strategies, action programmes, budgets and controls. To plan good strategies is often easier than to carry them out. To be successful, companies must also be effective at *implementation* – turning marketing strategies into marketing actions.

Much of the responsibility for implementation goes to the company's marketing department. Marketing departments can be organised in one or a combination of ways: *functional marketing organisation*, *geographic organisation*, *product management organisation*, or *market management organisation*. In this age of customer relationships, more and more companies are now changing their organisational focus from product or territory management to customer relationship management. Marketing organisations carry out *marketing control*, both operating control and strategic control. They use *marketing audits* to determine marketing opportunities and problems and to recommend short-run and long-run actions to improve overall marketing performance.

Marketing managers must ensure that their marketing budgets are being well spent. Today's marketers face growing pressures to show that they are adding value in line with their costs. In response, marketers are developing better measures of *return on marketing investment.* Increasingly, they are using customer-centred measures of marketing impact as a key input into their strategic decision making.

Discussing the concepts

1. What are the benefits of a long-range plan? Does it have any role when forces, such as e-commerce, are changing markets so rapidly?

2. Many companies undertake a marketing audit to identify the firm's strengths and weaknesses relative to competitors, and in relation to the opportunities and threats in the external environment. Why is it important that such an analysis should address relative, not absolute, company strengths and weaknesses?

3. A tour operator has its own charter airline that is also used by other tour operators. The subsidiary is smaller and less profitable than are the competing charter airlines. Its growth rate has been below the industry average during the past five years. Into what cell of the BCG growth–share matrix does this strategic business unit fall? What should the parent company do with this SBU?

4. A camera retailer finds that sales in its main product line – digital cameras – are declining. The market is mature and prices are falling. What growth strategies might the firm pursue for this product line? How might the strategic-focus tool help managers examine the growth opportunities for this line? How might a strategic marketing plan have enabled the company to foresee and plan for the decline they now face?

5. The General Electric strategic business-planning grid gives a broad overview that can be helpful in strategic decision making. For what types of decision would this grid be helpful? For what types of strategic decision would it be less useful?

6. Delays in the launch of Sony's PlayStation 3 means they lost their market lead to less expensive but innovative Nintendo Wii that has attracted many young girls to the market. Discuss how Sony could segment, position and target their PlayStation 3 to regain some of their lost market share.

Applying the concepts

1. Think of a product or service that has presented you with difficulties in recent weeks (such as late delivery or hard to locate products), then:
   - Use the Web to identify Internet-enhanced suppliers of that product or service.
   - Evaluate the strengths and weaknesses of Web providers in their ability to overcome the problem you faced.
   - Suggest alternative ways in which the Internet could be used to overcome the product or service failure you faced.

2. Take a product or service organisation you are familiar with.
   - List the key external environmental opportunities or threats that face the organisation.
   - What do you think are the organisation's main strengths and weaknesses?
   - Suggest ways in which the organisation might respond to the external forces.
   - Recommend a possible marketing strategy which will ensure that the organisation matches its internal capabilities with external opportunities.

Web resources

For additional classic case studies and Internet exercises, visit **www. pearsoned.co.uk/ kotler**

References

1. Victoria McCubbine, 'Predators stalk the gnomes', *Eurobusiness* (May 2000), pp. 29–30; 'Families out of fashion', *The Economist* (4 March 2000), p. 92; 'The cashmere revolutionary', *The Economist* (15 July 2000), p. 94; LEX column, 'Luxury goods', *Financial Times* (15 July 2003); Lydia Gard, Travel, Italy: 'Costa effective: The Costa Smeralda is a millionaires' playground, but Lydia Gard shows you where to stay in style for under £50 a night', *The Guardian* (25 June 2005); 'Does your timepiece tick the right boxes?', *The Express* (14 June 2007); Simon de Burton, FT Report – Watches and jewellery: 'Restoration of the Sleeping Beauties', *Financial Times* (8 June 2007); 'A revolution in style and innovation, TAG Heuer's Grand Carrera series raises the bar for luxury sport watches', *PR Newswire* (27 June 2007).

2. Haig Simonian, TAG Heuer CEO interview: 'This is what we're made of', *Financial Times* (8 June 2007).

3. Malcolm MacDonald, 'Ten barriers to marketing planning', *Journal of Marketing Management*, **5**, 1 (1989), pp. 1–18; Sean Ennis, 'Marketing planning in the smaller evolving firm: empirical evidence and reflections', *Irish Marketing Review*, **11**, 2 (1998), pp. 49–61.

4. Susanna Voyle, 'Carrefour fails to satisfy its investors' appetites', *Financial Times* (5 April 2000), p. 34; 'Carrefour ferme 16 magasins de sa filiale GB en Belgique', *Le Monde* (23 June 2007).

5. Tamsin Brown, 'BP hires safety czar as failure list grows', *Daily Mail* (9 May 2007); Kristen Hays, 'It's all about safety, new BP chief says', *Houston Chronicle* (15 June 2007).

6. BP's website gives a very comprehensive rolling update of the company's long-range plans and current performance: www.bp.com.

7. James Boxwell, 'Rolls-Royce lifted by air show orders', *Financial Times* (3 July 2007).

8. Michael E. Porter, *Competitive Advantage: Creating and sustaining competitive performance* (New York: Free Press, 1985); Nicholas J. O'Shaughnessy, 'Michael Porter's competitive advantage revisited', *Management Decision*, **34**, 6 (1996), pp. 12–20.

9. For more on mission statements, see 'Crafting mission statements', *Association Management* (January 2004), p. 23; Frank Buytendijk, 'Five keys to building a high-performance organization', *Business Performance Management Magazine* (February 2006), pp. 24–9; and Joseph Peyrefitte and Forest R. David, 'A content analysis of mission statements of United States firms in four industries', *International Journal of Management* (June 2006), pp. 296–301.

10. Michael Porter popularised his view of value chains through his book *Competitive Advantage: Creating and sustaining competitive performance* (New York: Free Press, 1985); also see Jim Webb and Chas Gile, 'Reversing the value chain', *Journal of Business Strategy* (March–April 2001), pp. 13–17.

11. Maija Palmer, National news: 'Internet shopping tops £100bn', *Financial Times* (18 May 2007); 'Argos joy as internet sales surge by 37 percent', *Evening Standard* (12 January 2006).

12. Geoffrey Owen, Inside track: 'What did Morrisons get right and Safeway wrong?', *Financial Times* (11 April 2003); Lydia Adetunji, 'Morrisons reports first ever full-year loss', *FT.com* (23 March 2006).

13. Tim Burt, 'A rock and roll reinvention in the bookshops', *Financial Times* (21 October 2002), p. 16; Bob Sherwood, Inside track, law & business: 'Prospects for the smart and specific', *Financial Times* (13 January 2003).

14. John Chaffin, 'Warner cutting jobs as it looks to digital future', *Financial Times* (9 May 2007), p. 28; Arndt Ohler and Matthias Lambrecht, 'Sony BMG eyes return to music publishing', *FT Deutschland* (14 May 2007), p. 25.

15. 'Mitsubishi Heavy Industries', *The Economist* (23 October 1999), pp. 119–20; 'Just possibly, something to sing about', *The Economist* (18 March 2000), pp. 97–9; 'Eromet in the black', *Le Monde* (29 March 2003); Thibault Madelin, 'Le groupe Eramet veut défendre son independence', *Les Echos* (19 April 2007); 'Eramet confiant pour le premier semestre', *Les Echos* (4 May 2007).

16. Based in part on information found at www.bcg.com/this_is_BCG/mission/growth_share_matrix.html, December 2006. For more on strategic planning, see Anthony Lavia, 'Strategic planning in times of turmoil', *Business Communications Review* (March 2004), pp. 56–60; Rita Gunther McGrath and Ian C. MacMillan, 'Market busting', *Harvard Business Review* (March 2005), pp. 80–9; and Lloyd C. Harris and Emmanuel Ogbonna, 'Initiating strategic planning', *Journal of Business Research* (January 2006), pp. 100–11.

17. H. Igor Ansoff, 'Strategies for diversification', *Harvard Business Review* (September–October 1957).

18. Haig Simonian, 'Bombardier lined up to buy Adtranz', *Financial Times* (20 July 2000), p. 29; 'The DaimlerChrysler emulsion', *The Economist* (29 July 2000), pp. 81–2; 'DaimlerChrysler: revolting', *The Economist* (2 December 2000), p. 102; 'Daimler und Mitsubishi beenden Smart-Produktion', *Frankfurter Allgemeine Zeitung* (1 July 2006); Richard Milner, 'Daimler backs out of Chrysler', *Financial Times* (15 May 2007), p. 1; 'Dis-assembly: If Daimler ditches Chrysler, whither Detroit?', *The Economist* (15 February 2007); 'Daimler lasst möglicherweise die Mercedes-A-Klasse auslaufen', *Die Welt* (2 July 2007).

19. Nirmalya Kumar, 'Kill a brand, keep a customer', *Harvard Business Review* (December 2003), pp. 87–95. For a more in-depth approach to brand portfolio management, see Sam Hill, Richard Ettenson and Dane Tyson, 'Achieving the ideal brand portfolio', *MIT Sloan Management Review* (Winter 2005), pp. 85–90.

20. Michael E. Porter, *Competitive Advantage: Creating and sustaining superior performance* (New York: Free Press, 1985); Michel E. Porter, 'What is strategy?', *Harvard Business Review* (November–December 1996), pp. 61–78. Also see Kim B. Clark *et al.*, *Harvard Business School on Managing the Value Chain* (Boston, MA: Harvard Business School Press, 2000); 'Buyer value and the value chain', *Business Owner* (September–October 2003), p. 1; and 'The Value Chain', accessed at www.quickmba.com/strategy/value-chain/, July 2006.

21. Philip Kotler, *Kotler on Marketing* (New York: Free Press, 1999), pp. 20–2; Marianne Seiler, 'Transformation trek', *Marketing Management* (January–February 2006), pp. 32–9.

22. McDonald's 2006 Fact Sheet, accessed at www.mcdonalds.com/corp/invest/pub/2006_fact_sheet.html, May 2006; 'McDonald's fetes 50th birthday, opens anniversary restaurant', *Knight Ridder Tribune Business News* (15 April 2005), p. 1; 'McDonald's Corporation', *Hoover's Company Records* (15 June 2006), p. 10974.

23. Quotes and other information from Jeffery K. Liker and Thomas Y. Choi, 'Building deep supplier relationships', *Harvard Business Review* (December 2004), pp. 104–13; Lindsey Chappell, 'Toyota aims to satisfy its suppliers', *Automotive News* (21 February 2005), p. 10; www.toyotasupplier.com, July 2006; John Reed, 'Toyota battles to keep its squeaky-clean image', *Financial Times* (2 July 2007), p. 23.

24. http://factory.lego.com/trains/

25. 'Ken Thomas, CEO: General Motors will "fight hard for every sale" after Toyota passes GM for 1st time', *AP Worldstream* (25 April 2007); 'Report: Toyota passed General Motors in 2006 global sales', *AP Worldstream* (12 June 2007).

26. Jack Trout, 'Branding can't exist without positioning', *Advertising Age* (14 March 2005), p. 28.

27. Adbrand figures: http://www.adbrands.net/members/de/bmw_de_p.htm

28. Michael C. Mankins, 'Turning great strategy into great performance', *Harvard Business Review* (July–August 2005), pp. 65–72.

29. Brian Dumaine, 'Why great companies last', *Fortune* (16 January 1995), p. 129. Also see James C. Collins and Jerry I. Porras, *Built to Last: Successful habits of visionary companies* (New York: HarperBusiness, 1995); Jeffrey S. Klein, 'Corporate cultures: Why values matter', *Folio* (December 2004), p. 23; Norm Brodsky, 'Defining – and enforcing – your company's culture might be your most important job', *Inc.* (April 2006), pp. 61–2; Graham Yemm, 'Does your culture support or sabotage your strategy?', *Management Services* (Spring 2006), pp. 34–7.

30. Adapted from Diane Brady, 'Making marketing measure up', *Business Week* (13 December 2004), pp. 112–13, with information from 'Kotler readies world for one-on-one', *Point* (June 2005), p. 3.

31. Mark McMaster, 'ROI: More vital than ever', *Sales & Marketing Management* (January 2002), pp. 51–2. Also see Paul Hyde, Ed Landry and Andrew Tipping, 'Are CMOs irrelevant?', Association of National Advertisers/Booz, Allen, Hamilton white paper, p. 4, accessed at www.ana.net/mrc/ANABoozwhitepaper, June 2005; Rob Duboff, 'Resisting gravity', *Marketing Management* (May–June 2006), pp. 37–9; and Gordon A. Wyner, 'Beyond ROI', *Marketing Management* (May-June 2006), pp. 8–9.

32. Matthew Creamer, 'Shops push affinity, referrals over sales', *Advertising Age* (20 June 2005), p. S4.

33. For more discussion, see Michael Karuss, 'Marketing dashboards drive better decisions', *Marketing News* (1 October 2005), p. 7; Richard Karpinski, 'Making the most of a marketing dashboard', *B to B* (13 March 2006), p. 18; and Bruce H. Clark, Andrew V. Abela and Tim Ambler, 'Behind the wheel', *Marketing Management* (May–June 2006), pp. 19–23.

34. For a full discussion of this model and details on customer-centred measures of return on marketing investment, see Roland T. Rust, Katherine N. Lemon and Valerie A. Zeithaml, 'Return on marketing: Using customer equity to focus marketing strategy', *Journal of Marketing* (January 2004), pp. 109–27; Roland T. Rust, Katherine N. Lemon and Das Narayandas, *Customer Equity Management* (Upper Saddle River, NJ: Prentice Hall, 2005); and Allison Enright, 'Serve them right', *Marketing News* (1 May 2006), pp. 21–2.

35. Deborah L. Vence, 'Return on investment', *Marketing News* (15 October 2005), pp. 13–14.

36. For details, see Philip Kotler and Kevin Lane Keller, *Marketing Management*, 12th edn (Upper Saddle River, NJ: Prentice Hall, 2006), pp. 719–25. Also see Neil A. Morgan, Bruce H. Clark and Rich Gooner, 'Marketing productivity, marketing audits, and systems for marketing performance assessment: Integrating multiple perspectives', *Journal of Marketing* (May 2002), pp. 363–75.

37. For more on brand and product management, see Kevin Lane Keller, *Strategic Brand Management*, 2nd edn (Upper Saddle River, NJ: Prentice Hall, 2003).

Company case 3 Starbucks

'Sex & Drugs & Rock & Roll is all my body needs,' sang Ian Dury and the Blockheads, but the real roots of rock'n'roll were in 1950s coffee bars. It was in a coffee bar next to diminutive Sun Studios in Memphis, Tennessee, that Sam Phillips negotiated the deals with Elvis Presley, Jerry Lee Lewis, Johnny Cash and Howlin' Wolf that gave African-American music to the world. It was also in the 2 I's coffee bar in Soho, London, that white Europeans, including Cliff Richard, Hank Marvin, Tommy Steele and Mickey Most, aped white Americans' aping of the music of America's Deep South.

Time moved on and the coffee bar culture declined – except in Italy, where it began. After the excitement of the British invasion, started in Liverpool, and punk with its roots in New York and London, rock music was in need of one of its periodic revolutions. This time Seattle would raise the torch.

In Seattle and elsewhere, the alienated teenagers of Generation X did not relate to the studio-enhanced, beautifully preened purveyors of corporate rock that dominated the airwaves. The fast food joints where they could eat or the downtown bars were not for them.

In mid-1980s Seattle, something was brewing. While travelling in Italy, the popularity of Milan's espresso coffee bars impressed Howard Schultz. At the time, he was director of retail operations and marketing of Starbucks, a provider of coffee to fine restaurants. He concluded that Generation X needed the coffee bar culture – slow down, 'smell the coffee' and enjoy life a little more. From little beans big things grew. The result was Starbucks, the coffee house chain that started the trend of once again enjoying coffee to its fullest. Starbucks doesn't sell just coffee, it sells *The Starbucks Experience*. As one Starbucks executive puts it, 'We're not in the business of filling bellies, we're in the business of filling souls.'

Meanwhile, in a trailer park just outside Seattle, Kurt Cobain teamed up with Chris Noveselic to form Nirvana. Kurt Cobain's answer was not to slow down. With a psyche and passion too big for one body, he expressed the pain of a generation. While Howard Schultz wanted to calm things down, Kurt Cobain's grunge filled a musical gulf that captured the emptiness felt by Generation X.

From little beans big things grew

Kurt Cobain fulfilled his rock'n'roll destiny and ended his pain by dying young. Generation X continued refilling their souls at Starbucks. Starbucks is now a powerhouse premium brand in a category in which only cheaper commodity products once existed. As the brand has perked, Starbucks' sales and profits have risen like steam off a mug of hot java. Some 44 million customers visit the company's 13,000 coffee shops in 39 countries each week. Guided by their mission (Exhibit 3.2), Starbucks' sales and earnings have more than tripled over the last five years alone.

Starbucks' success, however, has drawn a full litter of copycats, including direct competitors such as Caribou Coffee, Costa Coffee and Coffee Republic. These days it seems that everyone is peddling its own brand of premium coffee. To maintain its phenomenal growth in an increasingly overcaffeinated marketplace, Starbucks has brewed up an ambitious, multipronged growth strategy:

- *More store growth.* Almost 85 per cent of Starbucks' sales comes from its stores. So, not surprisingly, Starbucks is opening new stores at a breakneck pace. Ten years ago, Starbucks had just 1,000 stores in total – fewer than it built in 2006 alone. Although in some countries it seems that there are not many places left without a Starbucks, there's still plenty of room to expand. In 2006, Germany had only 67 branches in 21 cities. By the end of 2007 Starbucks aims to have 100. In Hamburg alone it aims to have 30 within five years. By then it will be like London where no-one in the city centre is more than 5 minutes from a Starbucks.

  Beyond opening new shops, Starbucks is expanding each store's food offerings, testing everything from Krispy Kreme doughnuts and Fresh Fields gourmet sandwiches to Greek pasta salads and assorted snacks. By offering a beefed-up menu, the company hopes to increase the average customer sales ticket while also boosting lunch and dinner traffic. To counter reduced sales in warm weather, Starbucks sells Frappuccinos and other iced products.

- *New retail channels.* The vast majority of coffee is bought in stores and sipped at home. To capture this demand,

Starbucks is also pushing into supermarket aisles. However, rather than going head-to-head with giants such as Nestlé (Nescafé) and Kraft (Maxwell House, Sanka), Starbucks struck a co-branding deal with Kraft. Under this deal, Starbucks will continue to roast and package its coffee while Kraft will market and distribute it. Both companies benefit: Starbucks gains quick entry into 25,000 supermarkets, supported by the marketing muscle of 3,500 Kraft salespeople, while Kraft tops off its coffee line with the best-known premium brand and gains quick entry into the fast-growing premium coffee segment.

Beyond supermarkets, Starbucks has forged an impressive set of new ways to bring its brand to market. Some examples: Marriott operates Starbucks kiosks in more than 60 airports, and several airlines serve Starbucks coffee to their passengers. Westin and Sheraton hotels offer packets of Starbucks coffee in their rooms. And Starbucks has a deal to operate coffee shops within Waterstones' bookshop. Starbucks also sells gourmet coffee, tea, gifts and related goods through business and consumer catalogues. And its website, Starbucks.com, has become a kind of 'lifestyle portal' on which it sells coffee, tea, coffeemaking equipment, compact discs, gifts and collectibles.

- *New products and store concepts.* Starbucks has part-nered with several firms to extend its brand into new categories. For example, it joined with PepsiCo to stamp the Starbucks brand on bottled Frappuccino drinks and a new DoubleShot espresso drink. Starbucks ice cream, marketed in a joint venture with Breyer's, is now a leading brand of coffee ice cream. Starbucks is also examining new store concepts. It's testing Café Starbucks, a European-style family bistro with a menu featuring everything from huckleberry pancakes to oven-roasted seared sirloin and Mediterranean chicken breast on focaccia. The company is also testing Circadia – a kind of bohemian coffeehouse with tattered rugs, high-speed Internet access, and live music as well as coffee specialities.

Bringing music and coffee together once again, Starbucks now sells the music it plays in its stores. It is not cutting-edge music but the Ray Charles compilation, *Genius Loves Company,* sold 5.5m copies through the coffee shops. Seeing Starbucks as a glimmer of hope for a troubled recording industry, several artists have approached the company to get access to their 4.4m weekly visitors. In response Starbucks Entertainment

has started its own record label and has signed ex-Beatle Sir Paul McCartney. Starbucks Entertainment aims to grow even faster than its parent company, releasing three new albums, including Sir Paul's, in 2007 and eight in 2008.

Integrating the company's increased concern for the environment with its lust for new business, Starbucks Entertainment is promoting *Arctic Tale*, a film co-scripted by Al Gore's daughter Kristin. Narrated by hip-hop's Queen Latifah, the tale about Nunu, a polar bear cub, and Seela, a baby walrus, the film has tracks by Shins and Ben Harper that will be played in the store. 'This is not about trying to drive more coffee business. We want to build awareness about the issue of climate change', claimed a Starbucks spokesperson.

- *International growth.* Starbucks wants to go even more global. In 1996, the company had only 11 coffeehouses outside North America. By 2007, the number had grown in 39 international markets, including more than 1,000 in Asia and 500 in the UK alone. Starbucks aims to open thousands of stores in the fast-growth BRIC (Brazil, Russia, India and China) and is already firmly established in South America. With the BRIC countries in mind, in 2006 Starbucks increased the number of stores it aims to have worldwide from 30,000 to 40,000.

Too much caffeine?

Although Starbucks' growth strategy so far has met with great success, some analysts express strong concerns. The company's share price has dropped from 45 (just over $2 earnings for each $100 of shares owned) to 35 times earnings (just under $3 earnings on $100 stock owned). This means that shareholders are still viewing the company as growth stock but not as much as they were – they expect to make their money from the company and share price growing rather than the profits. What's wrong with Starbucks' rapid expansion? Some critics worry that the company may be overex-tending the Starbucks brand name and 16.5 per cent profit margin: 'People pay up to $3.15 for a caffe latte because it's supposed to be a premium product,' asserts one such critic. 'When you see the Starbucks name on what an airline is pouring, you wonder.' Others fear that, by pursuing such a broad-based growth strategy, Starbucks will stretch its resources too thin or lose its focus.

Some even see similarities between Starbucks and a young McDonald's, which rode the humble hamburger to such incredible success. 'The similar focus on one product, the overseas opportunities, the rapid emergence as the dominant player in a new niche,' says Goldman Sachs analyst Steve Kent, 'this all applies to Starbucks, too.' Starbucks is certainly picking up some of McDonald's problems.

- Activists have Starbucks in their sights. In China Starbucks could be banished from Beijing's fabled Forbidden City amid complaints that the presence of the coffee shop in the former imperial palace constitutes an 'affront to Chinese culture'. The outlet near the rear of the Palace Museum might be removed following online protests sparked by a patriotic polemic published by a popular television anchor man, Rui Chenggang, on his personal blog. Many of China's 123m 'netizens' are sensitive to any perceived insult to their nation.
- In Ireland, where Starbucks is still in the early stages of product development, the company has been attacked by anti-globalisation activists for 'cluster bombing' where the chain opens several stores to establish its market dominance and squeeze out smaller players.
- In 2006 Oxfam entered the fray, working to raise awareness of Ethiopians' efforts to gain control over their fine coffee brands. According to Oxfam, 'In a modern economy, companies must bring their business models in line with the demands of good corporate citizenship, which goes beyond traditional philanthropic approaches to dealing with poverty.' After a lengthy public wrangle, Starbucks honoured its commitments to Ethiopian coffee farmers by becoming one of the first in the industry to join the innovative Ethiopian trademarking initiative.
- On the health front, Starbucks' big doses of coffee are also under attack. Taken in large amounts, caffeine can lead to 'caffeinism': a 'caffeine dependency' with a wide range of physical and mental conditions including nervousness, irritability, anxiety, tremulousness, muscle twitching, insomnia, headaches, respiratory alkalosis and heart palpitations. Furthermore, high usage over time can lead to peptic ulcers, erosive oesophagitis, and gastro-oesophageal reflux disease.
- Starbucks is facing increasing competition from rival coffee chains and fast-food companies. Other fast-food chains are expanding into the breakfast market that Starbucks dominates and offering similar but less expensive food. The Scottish-owned chain Costa Coffee is fighting Starbucks store by store in Ireland and has already overtaken Starbucks' coverage in the UK.
- Even worse, influential US *Consumer Report* magazine recently rated Dunkin' Donuts and McDonald's premium coffee better than Starbucks in terms of both taste and value – a piece of news picked up gleefully by the media across the world.
- To cap it all, a leaked memo to senior executives from Starbucks' founder and Chairman Howard Schultz warned that the world's largest coffee chain is 'watering down' its brand by opening too many 'sterile, cookie cutter' stores that lack soul and authenticity. Entitled 'the commoditization of the Starbucks experience,' Mr Schultz said 'We have had to make a series of decisions that, in retrospect, have led to the watering down of the Starbucks experience, and what some might call the commoditization of our brand.' He said steps to make the company more efficient, such as the introduction of automatic espresso machines, had robbed stores of character. He continued, 'We desperately need to look into the mirror and realize it's time to get back to the core and make the changes necessary to evoke the heritage, the tradition, and the passion that we all have for the true Starbucks experience . . . one of the results has been stores that no longer have the soul of the past and reflect a chain of stores versus the warm feeling of a neighborhood store. Some people even call our stores sterile [and] cookie cutter.'

Questions

1. What has suddenly made people across the world willing to pay three to four times more for a cup of coffee than they used to?
2. Is Starbucks another McDonald's? How similar and different are the two companies?
3. Evaluate the strengths, weaknesses, opportunities and threats of Starbucks. How are the trends of health concerns, the ageing population and anti-globalisation likely to affect the continued growth of the company?
4. Classify Starbucks using the BCG growth–share matrix. What are the implications of its position?
5. Thinking about the future, where do you anticipate Starbucks migrating to on the BCG matrix as the company matures? What strategy would you recommend in the light of Starbucks' future position?
6. To what extent is Starbucks' strategy adhering to its mission?

SOURCES: Jonathan Brown, 'Sex and drugs and rock'n'roll: Out of the darkness', *The Independent* (12 October 2006); Nelson D. Schwartz, 'Still perking after all these years', *Fortune* (24 May 1999), pp. 203–10; Janice Matsumoto, 'More than mocha – Café Starbucks', *Restaurants and Institutions* (1 October 1998), p. 21; Kelly Barron, 'The cappuccino conundrum', *Forbes* (22 February 1999), pp. 54–5; Stephane Fitch, 'Latte grande, extra froth', *Forbes* (19 March 2001), p. 58; Lauren Foster, Companies international: 'Starbucks plans 40,000 stores around the world', *Financial Times* (6 October 2006); Gerhard Hegmann in Munich and Birgit Dengel: Companies international: 'Starbucks looks to step up openings in Germany', *Financial Times* (5 September 2006); *Business Wire*, 'Oxfam celebrates win–win outcome for Ethiopian coffee farmers and Starbucks' (20 June 2007); *The Guardian*, 'Celebrities take on global warming' (4 July 2007); *Irish Times*, 'Coffee titans square up for turf war in Dublin' (4 July 2007); Andrew Ward, 'Sir Paul signs Starbucks record deal', *FT.com* (21 March 2007); Mure Dickie, World news: 'Starbucks faces banishment from Forbidden City', *Financial Times* (19 January 2007); Andrew Ward, 'Starbucks chairman warns of "watering down" brand', *FT.com* (23 February 2007); http://www.rockabillyhall.com/SunStudios1.html#History.

> Let the great world spin for ever
> down the ringing grooves of change.
>
> ALFRED LORD TENNYSON

Markets

Chapter 4 The marketing environment ● **Chapter 5** Consumer markets ● **Chapter 6** Business-to-business marketing ● **Chapter 7** Marketing research

PART TWO OF *PRINCIPLES OF MARKETING* examines markets. The marketing setting has undergone dramatic change in the past decade. Technological advances, globalisation, changing values, lifestyles and demographics have compelled marketers to rethink their marketing strategies and processes. In Part Two, we address how marketing is affected by changes in the market environment, changes in consumer and business-to-business markets and how these can be analysed, and finally market research – how to gather and use information about markets.

Chapter 4 looks at the marketing environment in two parts: the *microenvironment* that is specific to an organisation's operation, such as suppliers and competitors; and the *macroenvironment* of wider forces that shape society, such as the natural and political environment.

Chapter 5 explores ways of understanding consumer markets: individuals and households who buy goods and services for final consumption. The many ways of doing this give insights that can help in the design of marketing research and guide marketing decision making.

Chapter 6 looks at the business-to-business markets that account for most of the world's transactions. Although consumer marketing is the most visible, the majority of marketing is to other organisations. These include suppliers selling to retailers that sell on to final consumers, and sellers of capital equipment – such as trucks, raw materials, components or business services.

As Gunther Grass recognised, 'Information networks straddle the world. Nothing remains concealed. But the sheer volume of information dissolves the information. We are unable to take it all in.' **Chapter 7** shows how *marketing research* and marketing information systems help sift through this information, gather further information, and process and present results to support marketing decision making.

Video Case Marketing Birmingham

Birmingham, Britain's second city, has had to transform itself in recent years. The city grew during the Industrial Revolution becoming a powerhouse known as 'the workshop of the world' and the 'city of a thousand trades'. With the decline of manufacturing, the city has had to transform itself into a centre for commercial and consumer

Neil Rami
Managing Director

services. Birmingham has many assets, such as being Europe's youngest city – based on the average age of its residents, a multicultural population and a maker of things as diverse as Cadbury's chocolate, Jaguar cars and more than half of Britain's jewellery. It also boasts that the it has more canals than Venice and more acres of parks than any other city in the world. Birmingham is also the home of heavy metal music (Led Zeppelin, Judas Priest, Black Sabbath/Ozzy Osbourne, etc,) and Tolkien (Gandalf, hobbits, orcs, etc.).

Birmingham's 'thousand' trades means those marketing the city have a lot to talk about, but its diversity also makes the city complex to market. Gain some idea about the city from the its own website (www.birmingham.gov.uk), Visit Birmingham guide (www.birmingham.gov.uk), Cadbury World (www.cadburyworld.co.uk), the Balti Triangle (www.birmingham.gov.uk/balti.bcc), Jewellery Quarter (the-quarter.com) or surf the city's canals (www.canaljunction.com/canal/birmingham_navigations.htm).

After viewing the video, you may address the following questions:

1. Does the marketing of cities, such as Birmingham, Lyon or Munich, differ to that of goods and services?
2. Why is market research important? How does it help marketing decision-makers in their efforts to (a) build and sustain a brand's image and positioning; (b) develop effective marketing and communications campaigns; and (c) to determine marketing effectiveness?
3. Why must an organisation measure the economic and non-economic impacts of its marketing activities and identify ways in which new web-based technologies enable marketers to evaluate the returns on their firm's marketing spend?

The first rule of business: Find out what the man you are dealing with wants, and give it to him.

WARREN TATE

The marketing environment

Mini Contents List

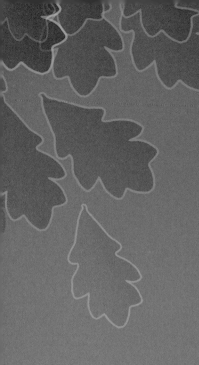

Yes, 'n' how many times can a man turn his head,
Pretending he just doesn't see?

Bob Dylan, 'Blowin' in the Wind', on 'The Freewheelin' Bob Dylan', Columbia:
B0001M0KDO, 1963

Previewing the concepts

In Part 1 (Chapters 1, 2 and 3), we addressed the basic concepts of marketing, its place in society, and the steps in the marketing process for building profitable relationships with targeted customers. In Part 2, we look deeper into the first step of the marketing process – understanding the markets, customer needs and customer wants. In this chapter, you will discover that marketing does not operate in a vacuum but rather in a complex and changing environment.

After reading this chapter, you should be able to:

1. Describe the environmental forces that affect a company's ability to serve its customers.
2. Explain how changes in the demographic and economic environments affect marketing decisions.
3. Identify the major trends in the firm's natural and technological environments.
4. Explain the key changes in the political and cultural environments.
5. Discuss how companies can react to the marketing environment.

At one time a major preoccupation of most people was getting enough food to eat. That is still true in disadvantaged parts of the world but not in wealthy countries. Humans evolved to crave for types of food that we needed to survive, including salt, sugar and fats. Now these are all within easy reach, such natural cravings are too easily fulfilled, and a major concern in societies with plenty is over-consumption of foodstuffs that endanger health. 'You are what you eat'[1] – and marketing has been implicated in damaging people's health. This is just one part of the changing face of the marketing environment. We start here by looking at 'big food'.

Prelude case Big food has a lot on its plate

I will always remember the first time I tried to buy a packet of crisps – or potato chips, if you prefer – in a New York supermarket. In vain, I searched for the single-portion packets which a European may find familiar: all I could see on the shelves were rows and rows of what appeared to be party-sized bags. Then suddenly, I noticed the slogan on Frito-Lay's Ruffles. 'Get your own bag!', it screamed, and I realised with amazement and some awe that, in the land of plenty, these enormous bags were intended for a party of one!

The Frito-Lay's website gives the crisps' calorie content as 160 calories to the ounce (28 g). On that basis, an 8 oz get-your-own bag would contain 1,280 calories, more than half the 2,500 RDA (Recommended Daily Allowance) average of calories for men and close to 65 per cent of the 2,000 RDA for women. And that is without 120 calories for a soft drink or 180 calories for a can of lager.

> Fat, salt and sugar have been the building blocks of success for most of the world's big brand owners.

Fat, salt and sugar have been the building blocks of success for most of the world's big brand owners. It is not surprising that Unilever plans cuts in its sales targets. As food companies go, Unilever is better than most: a lot of its products are reasonably nutritious and some, such as its cholesterol-busting spreads, can improve people's health. But even Unilever has been caught up in the sudden panic over obesity. Their simultaneous acquisition of SlimFast Foods, the slimming company, and Ben & Jerry's Homemade, the fattening ice-cream company, looked like a clever each-way bet. However, as people have become fatter and more desperate for a miracle remedy, Atkins has replaced SlimFast as the diet of choice, while Ben & Jerry's high-fat, premium ice-creams have begun to look gross.

Still, things could be worse. Coca-Cola, PepsiCo, McDonald's, Burger King, Cadbury Schweppes, Mars, Hershey – all are founded on products now blamed for causing obesity; and most of the rest – Kraft Foods, Nestlé, HJ Heinz, Kellogg, General Mills, Campbell Soup – make an unhealthily large contribution to the output of fatty, salty or sugary foods that are accused of contributing to the problem.

Perhaps the food industry's enthusiasm for fattening products mattered less when people's limited means restricted their ability to gorge on them. Evolutionary theory suggests we are programmed to overeat because, through most of human history, food was scarce and over-consumption was an insurance policy against lean times. So, as disposable incomes have risen, it has been hard for us to resist the temptation to binge on the food companies' heavily marketed output.

An odd result from international studies of food intake and income shows a contrast between poor and wealthy countries. In poor countries, rich people are healthier than their less well-off residents because they can afford nutritious food. In wealthy countries, people with high incomes are also healthier than those on low incomes. In this case it is because wealthy people have a healthier diet than people on low incomes who have a much higher protein intake.

Despite all the media coverage and political posturing over obesity, a recent National Opinion Poll (NOP) survey found that relatively few respondents regularly buy reduced-fat food, with the exception of dairy products. The regular purchase of all types of diet and low-fat foods has actually fallen since 2000.

Some people attempt to limit their calorie intake by choosing natural foods wisely. However, demand for convenience is such that the market for processed, reduced-fat, reduced-sugar products and calorie-counted food is large. Such foods appeal to people opting for a healthy alternative and also to slimmers, who may be tempted to buy products they may previously have considered out-of-bounds. According to McVitie's, owned by United Biscuits, this latter category has significantly contributed to increased sales of its 'Go Ahead!' brand.

Weight Watchers and Nestlé's Lean Cuisine brands are other leading brands benefiting from consumer desire for processed healthy food. Supermarket own-label brands have moved upmarket to challenge the leading brands. 'Be Good to Yourself', a low-fat range promoted as indulgent as well as healthy, is Sainsbury's biggest in-store brand. Other own-brand healthy options include 'Count on Us' from Marks & Spencer and the newly introduced 'Perfectly Balanced' range from Waitrose.

So, what happens now? Even among anti-obesity campaigners, few would advocate measures as illiberal as banning undesirable food products or taxing them out of existence, though doubtless we could think of some prime candidates (Velveeta? Spam? fish and chips?).

On the other hand, the industry seems unlikely to get away with the idea that people should simply take more exercise. Even large amounts of physical activity burn off relatively few calories: you would have to do three hours' downhill skiing or spend more than five hours on the golf course to burn off an 8 oz bag of Ruffles.

Obviously, fattening food is not tobacco: consumed in reasonable quantities, it can be a harmless treat. But given our sudden awareness of the growing human and social costs of obesity, manufacturers of the most obviously unhealthy foods and drinks are now where the tobacco industry was roughly 40 years ago, when studies on both sides of the Atlantic finally established the link between cigarette smoking and cancer.

Those studies did not, of course, lead to a ban on cigarette sales, but they did mark the beginning of the tobacco industry's demonisation. Public health campaigns began warning people of the dangers of smoking, increasing restrictions were placed on manufacturers' ability to advertise, tough new labelling laws were introduced and anti-smoking organisations sprang up to lobby for tobacco controls. Smoking went into decline and eventually, of course, the litigation began.

We should not get too carried away with the parallels: there have not yet been any claims that passive eating is dangerous, and Michael Bloomberg, New York's mayor, has not yet banned people from consuming fatty foods in the city's bars. Even so, some of the similarities are uncanny. Just as the tobacco industry responded to the health scares by introducing 'light' versions of its top brands, for example, the food industry is producing low-fat, low-sugar or low-salt versions of nearly all its best-known products.

In this context, it is worth noting that light cigarettes are now discredited and Philip Morris is in the process of appealing against a $10bn judgement that it deceived Illinois smokers into believing the cigarettes were safer than regular ones. Food companies seem to be leaving themselves open to similar claims, for example by offering reduced-fat or low-fat products that contain nearly as many calories as the regular version.

For food companies, the good news is that, even after 40 years of tobacco's demonisation, people still smoke and the tobacco industry is still making profits. On that basis, even the food industry's most fattening companies can look forward to a secure future, though they may have to forget about growth, and certainly about being much loved.[2]

Questions

1. Is the food industry executive correct in claiming: 'The food industry is nothing like the tobacco industry. Stop smoking and you will live longer; stop eating and you will die sooner.'

2. For decades people have known the impact of an unhealthy diet and what constitutes healthy eating, yet people continue to eat their way to ill health. Since this is not a new problem, what accounts for the sudden upsurge in public and political concern for obesity? Identify the actors and forces in the environment that may work for or against the food industry, showing how these may shape marketing opportunities, pose threats and influence companies' ability to serve target customers well.

3. Why is the focus on the food giants rather than the startlingly unhealthy English fried breakfast, French breakfast of croissant and caffeine-ridden coffee, or continental breakfast of egg, cheese and bread? How should the major food companies, such as Nestlé, McDonald's and Cadbury Schweppes, respond to this surge of concern?

Introduction

As the prelude case shows, companies today have to be alert and responsive to the interests and concerns of various actors in their marketing environment, not just its immediate customers. Other *actors* in this environment – suppliers, intermediaries, customers, competitors, publics and others – may work with or against the company. Major environmental *forces* – demographic, economic, natural, technological, political and cultural – shape marketing opportunities, pose threats and influence companies' ability to serve customers and develop lasting relationships with them. To understand marketing, and to develop and implement effective marketing strategies, you must first understand the environmental context in which marketing operates. Today's marketers must be adept at managing relationships with customers and external partners. However, to do this effectively, marketers must understand the major environmental factors that surround all these relationships.

A company's **marketing environment** consists of the actors and forces outside marketing that affect marketing management's ability to develop and maintain successful relationships with its target customers. Successful companies know the vital importance of constantly watching and adapting to the changing environment. The marketing environment offers both opportunities and threats. Too many other companies, unfortunately, fail to think of change as opportunity. They ignore or resist critical changes until it is almost too late. Their strategies, structures, systems and culture grow increasingly out of date. Corporations, such as once mighty airlines Ansett, Sabena, TWA and Swissair – 'the flying bank'[3] – have faced crises because they ignored environmental changes for too long. There are lessons here too for the food giants facing rising public and political concerns for obesity, as intimated in the prelude case, as well as environmental pressures facing the aviation, automotive and oil industries.

The environment continues to change rapidly, and both consumers and marketers wonder what the future will bring. More than any other group in the company, marketers must be the trend trackers and opportunity seekers. Although every manager in an organisation needs to observe the outside environment, marketers have two special aptitudes. They have disciplined methods – marketing intelligence and marketing research – for collecting information about the marketing environment. They also normally spend more time in the customer and competitor environment. By carefully and systematically studying the environment, marketers can revise and adapt marketing strategies to meet new marketplace challenges and opportunities.

> Too many other companies . . . fail to think of change as opportunity. They ignore or resist critical changes until it is almost too late.

The marketing environment consists of a microenvironment and a macroenvironment. The **microenvironment** consists of the actors close to the company that affect its ability to serve its customers – the company, suppliers, marketing intermediaries, customer markets, competitors and publics. The **macroenvironment** consists of the larger societal forces that affect the microenvironment – demographic, economic, natural, technological, political and cultural forces. We look first at the company's microenvironment.

The company's microenvironment

Marketing management's job is to build relationships with customers by creating customer value and satisfaction. However, marketing managers cannot do this alone. Figure 4.1 shows the major actors in the marketer's microenvironment. Marketing success will require building relationships

Marketing environment— The actors and forces outside marketing that affect marketing management's ability to develop and maintain successful relationships with its target customers.

Microenvironment— The actors close to the company that affect its ability to serve its customers – the company, suppliers, marketing intermediaries, customer markets, competitors and publics.

Macroenvironment— The larger societal forces that affect the whole microenvironment – demographic, economic, natural, technological, political and cultural forces.

Figure 4.1 Principal actors in the company's microenvironment

Figure 4.2 The company's internal environment

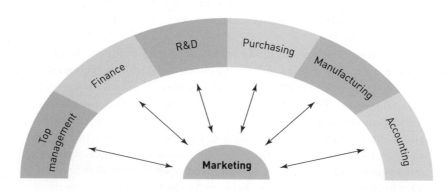

with other company departments, suppliers, marketing intermediaries, customers, competitors and various publics, which combine to make up the company's value delivery network.

The company

In designing marketing plans, marketing management should take other company groups into account – groups such as top management, finance, research and development (R&D), purchasing, manufacturing and accounting. All these interrelated groups form the internal environment (see Figure 4.2). Top management sets the company's mission, objectives, broad strategies and policies. Marketing managers make decisions within the strategies and plans made by top management. As we discussed in Chapter 3, marketing managers must work closely with other company departments, which have an impact on the marketing department's plans and actions. For example, Finance is concerned with finding and allocating funds to implement the marketing plan. The R&D department focuses on designing safe and attractive products. Purchasing worries about getting supplies and materials, whereas Operations is responsible for producing the desired quality and quantity of products. Accounting has to measure revenues and costs to help Marketing know how well it is achieving its objectives. Under the marketing concept, all of these functions must 'think customer' and should work in harmony to provide superior customer value and satisfaction.

> **"** All . . . functions must 'think customer' and should work in harmony to provide superior customer value and satisfaction. **"**

Suppliers

Suppliers—Firms and individuals that provide the resources needed by the company and its competitors to produce goods and services.

Suppliers are an important link in the company's overall customer value delivery system. They provide the resources needed by the company to produce its goods and services. Supplier developments can seriously affect marketing. Marketing managers must watch supply availability – supply shortages or delays, labour strikes and other events can cost sales in the short run and damage customer satisfaction in the long run. Marketing managers also monitor the price trends of their key inputs. Rising supply costs may force price increases that can harm the company's sales volume. Increasingly, today's marketers are treating their suppliers as partners in creating and delivering customer value.

Similarly, the success of Airbus depends on it working with a huge number of global suppliers that it needs even to design the aircraft. Chief among these are aero engine manufacturers GE and Rolls Royce and BAe, who design and build the wings, but there are thousands of others. Airbus services its customers regularly to find out how well its own suppliers are doing. This is very important since AOGs (Aircraft On Ground) cost airlines a fortune and inconvenience an airline's own customers. Its supplier recognition programme recognised the contribution suppliers make. KID Systeme, Diehl Avionik Systeme and AOA-LGG all received recent 'Exceptional Customer Support Performance' award, while awards for 'Outstanding Customer Support Performance' went to Parker, Vibro-Meter, Technofan, Goodrich Fuel and Utility Systems, Smiths Aerospace and Aircruisers.[4]

Marketing intermediaries

Marketing intermediaries are firms that help the company to promote, sell and distribute its goods to final buyers. They include *resellers, physical distribution firms, marketing services agencies* and *financial intermediaries*. **Resellers** are distribution channel firms that help the company find customers or make sales to them. These include wholesalers and retailers who buy and resell merchandise. Selecting and partnering with resellers is not easy.

No longer do consumer packaged goods manufacturers such as Nestlé, Unilever and Danone have many small, independent resellers from which to choose. They now face large and growing reseller organisations such as Tesco and Carrefour. Manufacturers court their retailers intensively. The meeting rooms in Superdrug's head office are far from dull. Each has had a makeover provided by leading suppliers, such as Hugo Boss. According to their CEO, Euan Sutherland, once the supplier finds out the opportunity, they compete to perform the makeovers, the boardroom being a particularly attractive opportunity.

Physical distribution firms help the company to stock and move goods from their points of origin to their destinations. Working with warehouse and transportation firms, a company must determine the best ways to store and ship goods, balancing factors such as cost, delivery, speed and safety. An unexpected consequence of Internet marketing is the huge increase in the number of vehicles delivering goods to homes. When suppliers never see a customer, the quality of their service is measured more by the proficiency of a van driver than a firm's own employees.

Marketing services agencies are the marketing research firms, advertising agencies, media firms and marketing consultancies that help the company target and promote its products to the right markets. When the company decides to use one of these agencies, it must choose carefully

---

Marketing intermediaries—Firms that help the company to promote, sell and distribute its goods to final buyers; they include physical distribution firms, marketing service agencies and financial intermediaries.

Resellers—The individuals and organisations that buy goods and services to resell at a profit.

Physical distribution firms—Warehouse, transportation and other firms that help a company to stock and move goods from their points of origin to their destinations.

Marketing services agencies—Marketing research firms, advertising agencies, media firms, marketing consulting firms and other service providers that help a company to target and promote its products to the right markets.

because the firms vary in creativity, quality, service and price. The company has to review the performance of these firms regularly and consider replacing those that no longer perform well.

Financial intermediaries include banks, credit companies, insurance companies and other businesses that help finance transactions or insure against the risks associated with the buying and selling of goods. Most firms and customers depend on financial intermediaries to finance their transactions. The company's marketing performance can be seriously affected by rising credit costs and limited credit. In many cases the retailers, manufacturers or services, such as package holiday providers, make more money from selling loans, extended warranties or insurance cover than they do on the products or services themselves.

Like suppliers, marketing intermediaries form an important component of the company's overall value delivery system. In its quest to create satisfying customer relationships, the company must do more than just optimise its own performance. It must partner effectively with suppliers and marketing intermediaries to optimise the performance of the entire system.

Thus, today's marketers recognise the importance of working with their intermediaries as partners rather than simply as channels through which they sell their products.

> When Coca-Cola signs on as the exclusive beverage provider for a fast-food chain, such as Subway, it provides much more than just soft drinks. It also pledges powerful marketing support. Coke assigns cross-functional teams dedicated to understanding the finer points of each retail partner's business. It conducts a staggering amount of research on beverage consumers and shares these insights with its partners. It analyses the demographics and helps partners to determine which Coke brands are preferred in their areas. Coca-Cola has even studied the design of menu boards to better understand which layouts, fonts, letter sizes, colours and visuals induce consumers to order more food and drink. Such intense partnering efforts have made Coca-Cola a runaway leader in the soft drink market.[5]

Customers

The company must study its customer markets closely. Figure 4.3 shows six types of customer market. *Consumer markets* consist of individuals and households that buy goods and services for personal consumption. *Business markets* buy goods and services for further processing or for use in their production process, whereas *reseller markets* buy goods and services to resell at a profit. *Institutional markets* are made up of schools, hospitals, nursing homes, prisons and other institutions that provide goods and services to people in their care. *Government markets* are made up of government agencies that buy goods and services in order to produce public services or transfer the goods and services to others who need them. Finally, *international markets* consist of buyers

Figure 4.3 Types of customer market

Financial intermediaries—Banks, credit companies, insurance companies and other businesses that help finance transactions or insure against the risks associated with the buying and selling of goods.

in other countries, including consumers, producers, resellers and governments. Each market type has special characteristics that call for careful study by the seller. At any point in time, the firm may deal with one or more customer markets: for example, as a consumer packaged goods manufacturer, Unilever has to communicate brand benefits to consumers as well as maintaining a dialogue with retailers that stock and resell its branded products.

Competitors

The marketing concept states that, to be successful, a company must provide greater customer value and satisfaction than its competitors do. Thus, marketers must do more than simply adapt to the needs of target consumers. They must also gain strategic advantage by positioning their offerings strongly against competitors' offerings in the minds of consumers.

No single competitive marketing strategy is best for all companies. Each firm should consider its own size and industry position compared to those of its competitors. Large firms with dominant positions in an industry can use certain strategies that smaller firms cannot afford. But being large is not enough. There are winning strategies for large firms, but there are also losing ones. And small firms can develop strategies that give them better rates of return than large firms enjoy. We will look more closely at competitor analysis and competitive marketing strategies in Chapter 10.

Publics

The company's marketing environment also includes various publics. A **public** is any group that has an actual or potential interest in or impact on an organisation's ability to achieve its objectives. Figure 4.4 shows seven types of public:

1. *Financial publics.* Financial publics influence the company's ability to obtain funds. Banks, investment houses and stockholders are the principal financial publics. A huge amount of the CEO's time in a public company is spent courting financial institutions. That is one reason why company headquarters congregate round the world's financial centres.

2. *Media publics.* Media publics include newspapers, magazines and radio and television stations that carry news, features and editorial opinion.

3. *Government publics.* Management must take government developments into account. Marketers must often consult the company's lawyers on issues of product safety, truth in advertising and other matters.

4. *Citizen action publics.* A company's marketing decisions may be questioned by consumer organisations, environmental groups, minority groups and other pressure groups. Its public relations department can help it stay in touch with consumer and citizen groups.

5. *Local publics.* Every company has local publics, such as neighbourhood residents and community organisations. Large companies usually appoint a community-relations officer to deal with the community, attend meetings, answer questions and contribute to worthwhile causes.

Public—Any group that has an actual or potential interest in or impact on an organisation's ability to achieve its objectives.

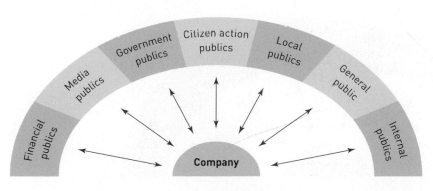

Figure 4.4 Types of public

Across all its sites McDonald's sees itself as a local business that invests in the local economy and young people. For example, in the Netherlands, 355,000 children have participated in the Ronald Sport and Activity Programme developed in collaboration with the Dutch Olympic Committee and National Federation of Sports.

6. *General public.* A company needs to be concerned about the general public's attitude towards its products and activities. The public's image of the company affects its buying. Thus, many large corporations invest huge sums of money to promote and build a healthy corporate image.

7. *Internal publics.* These include the company's workers, managers, volunteers and the board of directors. Large companies use newsletters and other means to inform and motivate their internal publics. When employees feel good about their company, this positive attitude spills over to external publics.

A company can prepare marketing plans for these publics as well as for its customer markets. Suppose the company wants a specific response from a particular public, such as goodwill, favourable word-of-mouth, or donations of time or money. The company would have to design an offer to this public that is attractive enough to produce the desired response.

We have looked at the firm's immediate or microenvironment. Next we examine the larger macroenvironment.

" A company can prepare marketing plans for these publics as well as for its customer markets. "

The company's macroenvironment

The company and all the other actors operate in a larger macroenvironment of forces that shape opportunities and pose threats to the company. Figure 4.5 shows the six major forces in the company's macroenvironment. In the remaining sections of this chapter, we examine these forces and show how they affect marketing plans.

Figure 4.5 Influential forces in the company's macroenvironment

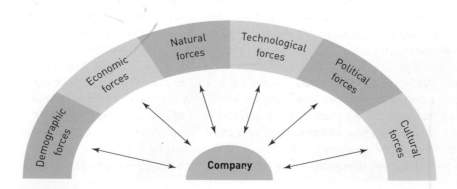

Demographic environment

Demography is the study of human populations in terms of size, density, location, age, gender, race, occupation and other statistics. The demographic environment is of major interest to marketers because it involves people, and people make up markets. Thus, marketers closely track demographic trends and developments in their markets at home and abroad. They monitor shifts in geographic population, changing age and family structures, educational characteristics and population diversity, both at home and abroad.

Here, we discuss the major demographic trends that have implications for marketing: population growth, changing age and household structure, pressures for migration and increasing diversity of the population.

Demography—The study of human populations in terms of size, density, location, age, sex, race, occupation and other statistics.

Population growth trends

Today, the total population of the 27 member states of the European Union (EU), occupying most of western Europe and parts of central and eastern Europe, is 494 million people. However, in the EU, many countries are expecting a decline in population over the coming decades, though this could be offset with new countries joining the EU over the next 20 years.[6]

Worldwide, the population is growing at an explosive rate. It now exceeds 6.5 billion people and will grow annually at a rate of 1.2 per cent, increasing to about 8.1 billion by 2030.[7] Notably, six countries are expected to account for half that increase: India for 21 per cent; China for 12 per cent; Pakistan for 5 per cent; Bangladesh, Nigeria and the US for 4 per cent each. India's population increases by more in a week than the EU's in a year!

While population over such an extended period is inherently unpredictable, one report[7] suggests that, by 2050, there would be 5.2 billion Asians, up from 3.8 billion today. There would be 1.8 billion Africans, up from 851 million today. There would be 768 million Latin Americans, up from 543 million today. There would be 448 million North Americans, up from 326 million today. But there would be only 632 million Europeans, *down* from 726 million today. Within Asia, however, there will be a noteworthy transformation: Japan's population will decline to as little as 110 million. The world's giant will be India, with a population of 1.5 billion, 17.2 per cent of the world's total, ahead even of China's 1.4 billion. Hence, although forecasts suggest that the global population is increasing, in reality the growth rate is uneven across the world. The world's large and highly diverse population poses both opportunities and challenges.

A growing population means growing human needs to satisfy, offering marketers an indication of demand for certain goods and services. Depending on the purchasing power of a nation's population, it may also mean growing market opportunities. Changes in the world's demographic environment have major implications for business. For example, consider China. More than a quarter of a century ago, to curb its skyrocketing population, the Chinese government passed regulations limiting families to one child each. As a result, Chinese children – known as 'little emperors and empresses' – are being showered with attention and luxuries under what's known as the 'six-pocket syndrome'. As many as six adults – two parents and four doting grandparents – may be indulging the whims of each 'only child'. Parents in the average Beijing household now spend about 40 per cent of their income on their cherished only child. Among other things, this trend has created huge market opportunities for children's educational products.

In China's increasingly competitive society, parents these days are keen to give their child an early edge. That is creating opportunities for companies peddling educational offerings aimed at kids. This trend has encouraged toy companies such as Denmark's Lego Group, Japan's Bandai Company (known for its Mighty Morphin Power Rangers) and America's Mattel to enter the Chinese market. Other companies, such as Disney, have moved full speed into educational products. Magic English, a Disney package that includes workbooks, flash cards and 26 videodiscs, has been phenomenally successful. Disney has also launched interactive educational CD-ROMs featuring the likes of Winnie the Pooh and *101 Dalmations'* Cruella DeVille. Lego and Disney are not alone in catering to the lucrative Chinese kiddies' market. Time Warner is testing the waters in Shanghai with an interactive language course called English Time. The 200-lesson, 40-CD set takes as long as four years for a child to complete. Time Warner is expecting strong sales, despite the 25,000 Chinese yuan (about €2,500) price, more than a year's salary for many Chinese parents.[8]

Interestingly, the one-child policy is creating another major Chinese demographic development – a rapidly ageing population. In what some deem a potential 'demographic earth-quake', by 2024 an estimated 58 per cent of the Chinese population will be over age 40. And because of the one-child policy, close to 75 per cent of all Chinese households will be childless, either because they chose to have no children or because their only child has left the nest. The result is an ageing society that will need to be more self-reliant, which in turn will cause a large growth in service markets such as senior education, leisure clubs and nursing homes.[9]

Changing age structure of the population

Baby boomers— Consumers born between 1946 and 1964.

The most noticeable demographic trend in Europe and other developed countries is the changing age structure of the population. The post-World War II 'baby boom' produced the **baby boomers**, born between 1946 and 1964. The boomers have presented a moving target, creating new markets as they grew from infancy to their pre-adolescent, teenage, young-adult and now middle-age to mature years. Baby boomers cut across all walks of life. But marketers typically have paid the most attention to the smaller upper crust of the boomer generation – its more educated, mobile and wealthy segments. These segments have gone by many names. In the 1980s, they were called 'yuppies' (young urban professionals), 'yummies' (young upwardly mobile mommies), and 'dinkies' (from DINKY, dual-income, no kids yet). In the 1990s, however, yuppies and dinkies gave way to a new breed, with names such as DEWKs (dual-earners with kids) and SLORPIES (slightly older urban professionals).

The oldest boomers are entering their sixties; the youngest are in their early forties. The maturing boomers are rethinking the purpose and value of their work, responsibilities and relationships. As they reach their peak earning and spending years, the boomers constitute a lucrative market for new housing and home remodelling, financial services, travel and entertainment, eating out, health and fitness products and just about everything else. They are approaching life with a new stability and reasonableness in the way they live, think, eat and spend. As they continue to age, they will create a large and important senior citizen market.

The baby boom was followed by a 'birth dearth' creating another generation of people born between 1965 and 1976. Author Douglas Copeland calls them *Generation X* because they lie in the shadow of the boomers and lack obvious distinguishing characteristics. Others call them the 'baby busters' or the 'generation caught in the middle' (between the larger baby boomers and later Generation Ys).

GenXers—Consumers born between 1965 and 1976.

The Generation Xers are defined as much by their shared experiences as by their age. Whereas the boomers created a sexual revolution, the **GenXers** have lived in the age of AIDS. Increasing parental divorce rates and higher employment for their mothers made them the first generation of latchkey kids. Having grown up during times of recession and corporate downsizing, they developed a more cautious economic outlook. They care about the environment and respond favourably to socially responsible companies. Although they seek success, they are less materialistic; they prize experience, not acquisition. They are cautious romantics who want a better quality of life and are more interested in job satisfaction than in sacrificing personal happiness and growth for promotion. For many of the GenXers that are parents, family comes first, career second.[10]

> " GenXers are a more sceptical bunch, cynical of frivolous marketing pitches that promise easy success. "

As a result, the GenXers are a more sceptical bunch, cynical of frivolous marketing pitches that promise easy success. Their cynicism makes them more savvy shoppers, and their financial pressures make them more value conscious. They like lower prices and a more functional look. The GenXers respond to honesty in advertising. They like irreverence and sass and ads that mock the traditional advertising approach.

Both the baby boomers and the GenXers will one day be passing the reins to Generation Y, also called the *echo boomers* or 'Millennials'. Born between 1977 and 1994, and ranging from teens to twenties, the echo boomer generation created a large and growing teen and young adult market. Generation Y oldsters who have graduated from higher education are moving up in their careers. Like the trailing edge of the Generation Xers ahead of them, one distinguishing characteristic of Generation Y is their utter fluency and comfort with computer, digital and Internet technology. Generation Y represents an attractive target for marketers. However, reaching this message-saturated segment effectively requires creative marketing approaches.

Generation Y are the first truly digital and networked generation, first through mobile phones and email but now through social networks, such as MySpace, YouTube and more upmarket Facebook. They share a childhood of Harry Potter, The Simpsons and South Park, with an obsession with celebrities – people who are famous because they are famous – and instant celebrity through reality TV, Pop Idol and the likes. The challenge for marketers is the fragmentation of the generation. There is no longer the music of the generation as many tribes commune with distinctive lifestyles, dress codes and associated music. Within Generation Y are *Hipsters*, who often explicitly reject whatever is seen as mainstream or corporate in nature. They contrast with *Chavs*, whose fashions are derived from American Hip-Hop (African-American) and Guido (Italian-American) fashions and stereotypes such as bling (gold jewellery) and designer clothing combined with elements of working-class street fashion. There are also *Emos*, whose subculture derives from hardcore punk, and post-punk *Goths* with their tendency towards a lugubrious, mystical sound and outlook. Once these subcultures were local, but now social networks and electronic communications make them large but dispersed markets that are ideally served by Internet retailers, such as Subculture Wear, or retro-look Balcony Shirts for Emos and Kathmandu for Goths.[11]

Do marketers have to create separate products and marketing programmes for each generation? Some experts warn that marketers have to be careful about turning off one generation each time they craft a product or message that appeals effectively to another. This occurred in the UK when wealthy, middle-aged, rural Burberry wearers became alienated when young, low-income, urban Chavs took to wearing the brand's distinctive check.[12] Others caution

Figure 4.6 Europe's ageing population: forecast growth in the 65+ age group to 2020

SOURCE: World Bank, *The European Marketing Pocket Book 2007*, World Advertising Research Center (www.warc.com).

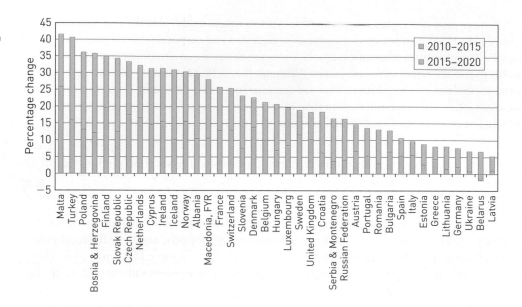

that each generation spans decades of time and many socioeconomic levels, so they do not constitute meaningful target markets. As such, marketers should form more precise age-specific segments within each group. More important, defining consumers by their birth date may be less effective than segmenting them by their lifestyle or life stage. We will examine in greater detail the bases for segmenting consumer markets in Chapter 9.

Across developed countries, the changing age structure reflects a population that is getting older, with the share of young people falling and that of the elderly rising (see Figure 4.6).

As the baby boomers, born between 1946 and 1964, move towards retirement, a smaller generation will take their place. The dependency ratio – the number of elderly and retired people compared with working-age adults – will rise everywhere in the developed economies, although more spectacularly in some countries than in others. According to forecasts based on United Nations data, this ratio will soar from 30 pensioners for every 100 working-age adults today to 70 by 2040, although there will be big disparities across the world. In Britain, for example, the dependency ratio will increase from 27 per cent to 45 per cent over the next 30 years – less than the increase in Italy or Germany. Europe, as a whole, and Japan are ageing faster than the US. In the US, the figure will be only 47, but in Japan, Italy, Spain and much of eastern Europe, it will be more than 100. Furthermore, this demographic change is not confined to advanced countries. In Latin America and most of Asia, the share of over-60s is set to double between now and 2030, to 14 per cent. In China, it will increase from less than 10 per cent in 2000 to around 22 per cent by 2030.[13]

The rapid ageing of Europe and other developed countries has been influenced by two trends. The first is the declining birth rate. The year 2006 marked the first time in modern peacetime history when more people died in Europe than were born: the 2006 EU birth rate was 10 births per 1,000 population, while the death rate was 10.1 per 1,000 people.[14] Figure 4.7(a) illustrates the downward trend in the number of babies born per woman (also called the fertility rate). Except in the US, with a fertility rate of just over 2.0, which is close to the minimum replacement

include cosmetics, fashion, music, clubs, restaurants and holidays. Whole communities thrive in the wake of gay innovativeness. For example:

> First, lesbians and gay men looking for inexpensive homes in places where they feel comfortable often turn to forgotten, run-down parts of town. Their movement creates a magnetic effect, drawing artists, performers and other creative types, many of them heterosexual. This group then attracts less hip, but more affluent young people excited by the prospect of an up-and-coming community. Developers, as well as property investors, see an opportunity and upgrade their housing stocks, pushing the areas to even more well-heeled and upmarket residents.
>
> Sophisticated speciality shops descend to capture both the benefit of population growth as well as the cash of long-time homosexual residents, many of whom are unencumbered by the financial responsibilities of offspring and therefore flush with disposable income. The retail fare on offer is then transformed from one run-down grocery to a cornucopia of boutiques, art galleries, delis and designer furniture stores. Because most gays, and their unmarried heterosexual followers, aren't rushing home to read *Winnie the Pooh* to the kids after work or staying in to put them to bed, seedy pubs are replaced by coffee shops, nice restaurants, cocktail bars and clubs.[27]

As the world grows more diverse, successful marketers will continue to diversify their marketing programmes to take advantage of opportunities in fast-growing segments.

Economic environment

Markets require buying power as well as people. The **economic environment** consists of factors that affect consumer purchasing power and spending patterns. Nations vary greatly in their levels and distribution of income. Some countries have *subsistence economies* – they consume most of their own agricultural and industrial output, hence offer few market opportunities. At the other extreme are *industrial economies*, which constitute rich markets for different kinds of goods. Marketers must pay close attention to major trends and consumer spending patterns both across and within their world markets.

Economic environment— Factors that affect consumer buying power and spending patterns.

European Union enlargement and integration

The European Union was established in 1993 by the Treaty on European Union (The Maastricht Treaty) and is the successor to the six-member European Economic Community founded in 1957: Belgium, France, Italy, Luxembourg, West Germany and the Netherlands. This became the European 15 of western states after Denmark, the UK and Ireland (1973), Greece (1981), Portugal and Spain (1986), Austria, Finland and Sweden (1995) joined the EU. By 2007 the EU had expanded to a family of 27 member states with Cyprus, the Czech Republic, Estonia, Hungary, Latvia, Lithuania, Malta, Poland, Slovakia and Slovenia (2004) and Bulgaria and Romania (2007) joining. EU enlargement and integration has been an evolving process, with five enlargements completed over the past five decades, the largest occurring on 1 May 2004 when 10 countries joined, and the most recent on 1 January 2007, when Romania and Bulgaria joined. The EU is now the largest economy in the world, with an estimated Gross Domestic Product (GDP) of €11.6 trillion in 2006 accounting for 35 per cent of world GDP; the USA has a GDP of $13.2 trillion (€9.8 trillion). The EU is also the world's largest exporter and the second largest importer. Although the OECD projects that in 2007 the Eurozone's GDP growth of 2.7 per cent will be higher than the US's 2.1 per cent, few expect the competitive edge to be maintained and America's GDP per capita is still 15 per cent higher than the EU's.

" The EU is now the largest economy in the world . . . the world's largest exporter and the second largest importer. "

A goal of European unification is the achievement of greater economic integration among member states. Of great importance to marketers is the progress towards a single market, with common policies on product regulation, and freedom of movement of all three factors of production (land, capital and labour) and of enterprise. The aim is that movement of capital, labour, goods and services between the EU member states will be as easy as within them.

The single market has implications for marketers and consumers. Efficient firms can benefit from economies of scale, increased competitiveness, lower costs, profitability and the ability to compete globally. An indication of global competitiveness is the EU being the home of 172 companies of the *Fortune Global 500* companies. Consumers benefit by the competition engendering cheaper products and services, more efficient providers, increased choice and business innovation. However, a competitive environment makes the existence of state or private monopolies more difficult. It also means that inefficient companies will lose market share and may disappear as independent entities.

Transition to a single market can have short-term negative impacts on some sectors of a national economy due to increased competition. Enterprises that previously enjoyed national market protection and national subsidy struggle to survive against their more efficient peers, even for its home markets. The EU is a trading superpower with a comparatively open economy; its single market accounts for almost a fifth of world trade in goods and a quarter in services. Half of all foreign direct investment flows into and out of the region. Yet agriculture is heavily protected, and quality standards and anti-dumping rules can be exploited to keep out competition.

The European Central Bank fears that Europe will revert towards economic protectionism amid fears that jobs are being lost to lower-cost overseas countries. Anti-competitive examples abound. France leads 'Club Med' countries that invoke anti-dumping rules to protect manufacturing and agricultural industries. Recently, Italy has managed to block the merger of Spain's Abertis with the Italian Autostrade, which would have created a pan-European infrastructure group, by a procedure described as 'moving the goalposts in the middle of a merger'.

'Historically, European economic integration has progressed when the EU has liberalised externally; and it has slowed down when the EU has gone into protectionist mode,' wrote Razeen Sally, director of the European Centre for International Political Economy. He continued: 'A Europe open to the world is a "big Europe" open within, with freer markets, competition-supporting regulation and lighter government. A protectionist Europe is a "small Europe" of big government, creeping, centralised regulation and throttled domestic markets.' Not all politicians believe in this call for a 'big Europe'. Prior to the June 2007 EU summit to discuss a renewed treaty, a grammatical change infuriated many who are committed to a competitive Europe. One of the EU's main objectives was 'to have an internal market where competition is free and undistorted'. The full stop moved so that the objective read 'to have an internal market'. Will the removal of 'free and undistorted' competition put a full stop to the EU's global competitiveness? Former competition commissioner Mario Monti sees it 'as a small sign of the EU disintegrating as a whole'.[28]

The year 1999 saw a move towards stronger economic and monetary union through implementation of the single currency, the euro. Today, 13, mainly old, EU nations have joined the single-currency or 'euro-zone': Belgium, Germany, Greece, Spain, France, Ireland, Italy, Luxembourg, the

Netherlands, Austria, Portugal, Slovenia and Finland. Denmark and the UK negotiated an 'opt-out' Protocol to the EU Treaty, granting them the option of joining the euro area or not. Both countries have nevertheless to fulfil the convergence criteria set out in the Maastricht Treaty. Having a common currency reduces the cost of trading in the EU since it removes the cost of buying and selling currency, and it also reduces the risk to firms selling goods within the euro-zone, since there is no shift in exchange rates that might change the profitability of deals.

The other member states of the European Union which are not in the euro-zone (Bulgaria, the Czech Republic, Estonia, Cyprus, Latvia, Lithuania, Hungary, Malta, Poland, Romania, Slovakia and Sweden) will join it once they have fulfilled the necessary conditions.[29]

The EU enlargement and integration process is by no means completed. Currently, accession negotiations are underway with several states, including Croatia, the Republic of Macedonia and Turkey. In order to join, the candidate state has to meet the economic and political conditions that basically require a secular, democratic government, rule of law, human rights and corresponding freedoms and institutions. States should also have the capacity to cope with market forces within the Union. Croatia is expected to join around 2010, followed by the Republic of Macedonia in 2012 and Turkey in 2015. Others waiting in the wings – Albania, Bosnia and Herzegovina, Montenegro and Serbia – hope to agree accession treaties by 2015.[30]

Economies within the EU are converging but the accession of each new group of member states tends to increase economic disparities across the European Union. Even corrected for purchasing power, there is a 12-fold difference between the richest parts of Europe – Frankfurt, Paris and London – with an average income over €65,000 Purchasing Power Parity per capita, and the poorest – Romania's Nord-Est and Bulgaria's Severozapaden, with income barely over €5,000 PPP.

Differences between member states are also significant. GDP per capita is often 10–25 per cent higher than the EU average in the 'older' western member states, but is only one-third to two-thirds of the EU average in most eastern member states. With such huge differences in income it is not surprising that there is population migration across the EU. The influx of labour is helping many sectors in the wealthy EU countries to compete more effectively. The European Commission recognises these benefits and is trying to ease the barriers to movement that many countries have imposed unilaterally.[31]

Income distribution and changes in purchasing power

Global upheavals in technology and communications in the last decade brought about a shift in the balance of economic power from the West (mainly North American and western European nations) towards the rapidly expanding economies of Asia and the Pacific Rim. Up until the Asian economic and financial crisis in 1997, many of the Asian 'tiger' economies, notably South Korea, Taiwan, Thailand, Malaysia, Indonesia and Singapore, were enjoying annual growth rates in excess of 7 per cent, compared to the 2–3 per cent found in western Europe and the USA. Official statistics have adjusted downwards the annual growth rates of these economies, in the first decade of the 2000s. However, rapid economic recovery in Singapore, Taiwan and South Korea means purchasing power income per head will exceed that of the US and western Europe.

In view of the rising importance of overseas markets as a source of growth for many western businesses, the uncertain economic climate in the Asian economies has important implications for international marketers. They must determine how changing incomes affect purchasing power and how they translate into marketing threats and opportunities for the firm.

Where consumer purchasing power is reduced, as in countries experiencing economic collapse or in an economic recession, financially squeezed consumers adjust to their changing financial situations and spend more carefully. They seek greater value in the products and services they buy. For example, 'thrift shops' have been booming in Japan, whose economy has been in recession. *Value marketing* becomes the watchword for many marketers. Rather than offering high quality at a high price, or lesser quality at very low prices, marketers have to look for ways to

Volkswagen targets people with disabilities who want to travel. It offers a Mobility Access Programme and has even modified its catchy 'Drivers Wanted' tag line to appeal to motorists with disabilities: 'All Drivers Wanted'.

SOURCE: Volkswagen.

offer the more financially cautious buyers greater value – just the right combination of product quality and good service at a fair price.

Marketers should also pay attention to *income distribution* as well as average income. Consumers with the greatest purchasing power are likely to belong to the higher socioeconomic groups, whose rising incomes mean that their spending patterns are less susceptible to economic downturns than those of lower-income groups. The *upper* economic strata of a society become primary targets for expensive luxury goods. The comfortable, *middle* income groups are more careful about their spending, but can usually afford the good life some of the time. The *lower* strata will stick close to the basics of food, clothing and shelter needs. In some countries, an *underclass* exists – people permanently living on state welfare and/or below the poverty line – who have little purchasing power, often struggling to make even the most basic purchases.

At a world level the last three decades have seen many people lifted out of poverty by their country's economic growth, first of all in south-east Asia, then more recently in China and India. However, over the past three decades in the West, the rich have grown richer, the middle class has shrunk, and the poor have remained poor.

The World Institute for Development Economics Research (WIDER) in Helsinki attempts to measure how personal wealth (including financial assets, property, consumer durables and even livestock) was distributed around the world. They found that those with more than the median of €1,613 (measured by official exchange rates) in 2000 belonged to the wealthier half of the human race. It took over 200 times more wealth than the median, €384,381, to be in the 'far from exclusive club' of 37 million adults who make up the wealthiest 1 per cent. The top 1 per cent is dominated by the Americans, Japanese and Europeans. China now occupies the middle ground, Africa the bottom. Wealth is shared less equitably than income, with 2 per cent of the world's adults having half the wealth. Many people in poor countries have next to nothing; but a lot of people in rich countries have even less than that. The Nordic countries thrive with little personal wealth but are entitled to a generous state pension that removes the need to save. Swedes have a collective net worth of less than zero and Finland has wealth per head less than South Korea.[32]

This distribution of income has created a tiered market. Many companies – such as Selfridges, Metz & Co and Le Bon Marché Rive Gauche stores – aggressively target the affluent. Other retailers – such as Lidl and Aldi stores – target those with more modest means. In fact, discounters are now the fastest growing retailers. Still other companies tailor their marketing offers across a range of markets, from the affluent to the less affluent. For example, Levi Strauss currently markets several different jeans lines. The Signature line of low-priced Levi's are found on the shelves of low-end retailers such as Wal-Mart. Levi's moderately priced Red Tab line sells at mid-priced department stores, such as El Corte Inglés or Åhléns. Boutique lines, such as Levi's [Capital E] and Warhol Factory X Levi's, sell in the Levi's Store and at high-end retailers such as Nordstrom, Galeries Lafayette and De Bijenkorf. You can buy Levi 501 jeans at any of three different price levels, although the actual prices vary hugely across Europe and the world. The Red Tab 501s sell for around €25, the Levi's [Capital E] for about €75, and the Warhol Factory X Levi's for €200 or more.[33]

Changes in the business environment are leading the rapid growth in the number of very wealthy people with a liquid investable wealth of over $1m (€0.74m). Consultants Merrill Lynch and Capgemini expected to see their combined wealth jump from around $33 trillion in 2005 to $44.6 trillion by 2010. Real Marketing 4.1 examines how to market to this super-wealthy community.

Changing consumer spending patterns

Generally, the total expenditures made by households tend to vary for essential categories of goods and services, with food, housing and transportation often using up most household income. However, consumers at different income levels have different spending patterns. Some of these differences were noted over a century ago by Ernst Engel, who studied how people shifted their spending as their income rose. He found that as family income rises, the percentage spent on food declines, the percentage spent on housing remains constant (except for such utilities as gas, electricity and public services, which decrease), and both the percentage spent on other categories and that devoted to savings increase. **Engel's laws** have generally been supported by later studies.

Changes in major economic variables such as income, cost of living, interest rates and saving and borrowing patterns have a large impact on the marketplace. Companies watch these variables by using economic forecasting. Businesses do not have to be wiped out by an economic downturn or caught short in a boom. With adequate warning, they can take advantage of changes in the economic environment.

Natural environment

The **natural environment** involves the natural resources that are needed as inputs by marketers or that are affected by marketing activities. Environmental concerns have grown steadily during the past three decades. Protection of the natural environment will remain a crucial worldwide issue facing business and the public. In many cities around the world, air and water pollution have reached dangerous levels. World concern continues to mount about global warming, and many environmentalists fear that, soon, we will be buried in our own rubbish.

Marketers should be aware of several trends in the natural environment.

Growing shortages of raw materials

Air and water may seem to be infinite resources, but some groups see long-run dangers. Air pollution chokes many of the world's large cities and water shortages are already a big problem in some parts of the world, Australia being a notable example. Renewable resources, such as forests and food, also have to be used wisely. Non-renewable resources such as oil, coal and various

Engel's laws—Differences noted over a century ago by Ernst Engel in how people shift their spending across food, housing, transportation, healthcare and other goods and services categories as family income rises.

Natural environment— Natural resources that are needed as inputs by marketers or that are affected by marketing activities.

real marketing

Marketing to those who have it all

Forget the rich; the new growth market is the super-rich. The world has more and more super-rich: the most recent data show that the top 1 per cent of taxpayers are pulling away from the rest, and the incomes of the top 0.1 per cent are growing even faster than that. Figures from London's tax authorities show the super-wealth profiles are changing. Between 1990 and 2005, Londoners' median income rose from £10,600 (€15,700) to £16,400, a rise of only 54 per cent. In 1990 an income of £57,000 ranked an earner among the top 1 per cent; now the admission price to the inner circle is up 105 per cent, to £117,000. But it is the incomes of the top 0.1 per cent that have grown most strikingly. While income tax records show that 19,000 had an annual income in excess of £500,000 in 2003–04, HM Revenue and Customs' estimates show that this has shot up to 30,000 in 2006–07.

The reason for this stretching of top-level incomes is scalable businesses, such as finance, where investing $10bn needs little more effort than investing $10m, and the most talented can reap a disproportionate share of the total rewards. Other developments that have powered this flood of super-wealth are globalisation, where business leadership can reap advantage for leaders in many markets, and the Internet. Barely 3 per cent of the super-rich are media huggers, like the Beckhams, Madonna and Paris Hilton. It is not old money either. The vast majority of the new super-rich made their own money and are still young enough to enjoy it. They are also working out how to spend it, and business is scampering to keep pace with the demands of the 'platinum pound'.

Businessknowledgesource.com suggest five keys to marketing to the very wealthy.

1. They are just like us. They like and do what we like. As 1930s banker and keen gardener Lionel Nathan de Rothschild tried to explain to the City Horticultural Society: 'No garden, however small, should contain less than two hectares (4.94 acres) of rough woodland.' Like many other people, Lionel liked gardening, just the scale is different. They have got highbrow and lowbrow tastes just like the poor and middle classes. Hip-hop is just as popular for the rich as it is for the poor. And opera music has admirers among the poor as well as the rich in their boxes at the Grand Opera. Just because Paris Hilton *can* afford to buy Leonardo da Vince's notebook, known as the Leicester Codex, does not mean she wants to – Bill Gates did.

2. The super-rich are not one culture. There is no way of targeting all the very wealthy. Marketing effort has to appeal specifically to subcultures within that general culture. You are dealing with multiple cultures. The very wealthy come from all sorts of backgrounds, a wide array of races and cultures. Some are recluses, like the late Paul Getty, while, after making his millions, Alan Sugar's joy is being a TV celebrity in 'The Apprentice'. The wealthiest people in Britain are the Indian Lakshmi Mittal and family and the Russian Roman Abramovich. As Mittal and Abramovich illustrate, many of the very wealthy now come from developing economies. Although average income is low, India has more billionaires than any other country: 36, with a total wealth of $142bn. HSBC is now extending its highly successful Private Banking operation to China where there are already an esti-mated 320,000 people with financial assets over $1m.

3. The very wealthy can indulge their tastes. As Lionel Nathan de Rothschild illus-trated, like many people, he enjoys gardening but at a different level. The rich may have the same tastes as those who are not rich but they can afford to buy different stuff: boats, mansions, fancy cars, large diamonds and designer clothes. Most people like this stuff but only because they can buy it. The rich have a lavish lifestyle, but a marketing plan aimed at the rich needs to span the whole range from mainstream tastes to lavish tastes. A case could be the marketing plan for a €4bn a year mega-yacht market. The top 10 companies in the industry compete among 5,000 owners of €150m yachts that boast one or more helipads, pools, submarines and cinemas and have an annual running cost of €50m.

4. To sell to the rich you have to be familiar with how they live, the places they go and the places they live in – to think like they do. Few selling to the very rich will ever live as they do, but successful marketers must sleep and breathe it as if they were. People who can operate in that rarefied atmosphere command a premium. The wealth market is creating jobs. The wealth management firm Fleming, Family and Partners has appropriate roots in the family of Ian Fleming, the author of the James Bond novels. They offer concierge services to their clients with a minimum investable wealth of £10m (€15m). The service goes beyond investing their client's wealth and could include getting access to exclusive clubs or sports events, or even private schools for their client's children. The new money has also awakened the market for butlers. According to Jane Urquhart, principal of the Greycoat Academy which trains butlers, the demand for 'good butlers' is soaring. Today a 'good butler' does not just serve drinks. She explains: 'He will also cook the food, organise your personal wardrobe, drive you around, take care of your diary and, of course, be the soul of discretion.'

5. Promote where the very wealthy are likely to view – magazines, television programmes, shops, events, etc. There are magazines devoted to buying yachts, to running country estates and to expensive hobbies such as horse racing. Magazines about exotic cars are bought mainly by people who can only dream but also by people who own a fleet. You might be selling something that is inexpensive, but it will not sell unless it is where the customer buys.

Don't assume that the fact that they have money automatically means they want to spend it in an irresponsible way. Remember, most of today's very wealthy know the value of money because they had to earn it.

SOURCES: Amy Yee, 'Wealthy lap up luxury goods', *Financial Times* (30 May 2007); Jane Croft, 'HSBC to target wealthy Chinese', *Financial Times* (19 June 2007); Adrian Michaels, 'Travel: Teething problems aside', *FT Weekend* (7 April 2007); Bob Sherwood, 'Super-rich transform the legal landscape', *Financial Times* (21 June 2007); Bob Sherwood, 'Offering concierge services will help keep that bond with wealthy clients', *Financial Times* (9 June 2007); Bob Sherwood, Companies International: 'Personal concierges grow in popularity', *Financial Times* (21 June 2007); 'The rich: Different but not dangerous', *Financial Times* (23 June 2007); James Brewer, 'Wealthy world of mega-yachts', *Lloyds Journal* (21 June 2007); Robert Verkaik, 'As Britain's rich get richer, supply of butlers dries up', *The Independent* (30 May 2007); *Sunday Times Rich List*, http://business.timesonline.co.uk/tol/business/specials/rich_list/rich_list_search/

minerals pose a serious problem. At one time renewable resources looked a comfortable option to ever depleting non-renewables, but no more. Unless there is a huge agricultural revolution, there is not enough land to generate the biofuels necessary to replace more than a fraction of oil currently used. Firms making products that require these scarce resources face large cost increases, even if the materials do remain available. They may not find it easy to pass these costs on to the consumer. Carbon trading has given European energy consumers an incentive to cut consumption but such incentives are rare globally. However, firms engaged in research and development and in exploration can help by developing new sources and materials.[34]

Increased cost of energy

One non-renewable resource – oil – has created the most serious problem for future economic growth. The large industrial economies of the world depend heavily on oil. Despite high energy prices, global demand continues to rise, with growth being led by China and the vibrant emerging economies. Until economical energy substitutes can be developed, oil will continue to dominate the world political and economic picture. Moreover, recent events, such as the interruption of gas deliveries to Ukraine, affecting European supplies, and Russia's halting of oil exports through Belarus to Europe in January 2007, have added to concerns about high energy prices and security of supply.

Energy prices vary by as much as 100 per cent between EU member states. The EU's dependence on imported energy is expected to rise from 50 per cent of total consumption today to 65 per cent in 2030.[35] High oil prices have fuelled greater interest in alternative energy technologies and energy efficiency. Many companies are searching for practical ways to harness solar, nuclear, wind and other forms of energy. Others are directing their research and development efforts to produce high energy-efficient technologies to meet customers' needs.

Demand for alternatives to petrol-powered vehicles has resurrected interest in the electric car. Until recently, electrified transportation, typically associated with the golf-cart and milk floats, has been slow, odd-looking and severely constrained by short battery life. The €75,000 Tesla Roadster aims to alter that perception. Set up by Martin Egerhard, Tesla Motors is a joint venture, financed by Elon Musk, the founder of PayPal, and Larry Page and Sergey Brin, the co-founders of Google. Built by Lotus in England, Tesla promises to be a vehicle like no other, a sporty electric car that confounds expectations about enviro-friendly driving. The all-electric, two-seater was unveiled in the summer of 2006 in California. It has all the traditional attributes of a sports car – a sleek, stylish body, leather interior and low, voluptuous lines, complete with Blaupunkt CD player and dash-mounted speakers. It accelerates from nought to 100 km (60 miles) per hour in just four seconds – faster than a Ferrari Spider. The difference is guilt-free fun! The battery can be recharged from an ordinary 240 volt socket in three hours, gives a range of 250 miles and has a life of at least 100,000 miles, after which it can be recycled. The manufacturer claims that Tesla costs just one cent per mile in electricity to run, and boasts twice the fuel efficiency of hybrid cars such as the Toyota Prius. Antagonists challenge these claims of greenery, stating that electric vehicles draw their power from electricity grids that are coal-fired, hence producing greenhouse gases in any case. Tesla, however, aims to offer optional home solar-photoelectric systems to power the car without drawing from electricity grids.

The bad news is that for now the car is sold only in the US, with distribution limited to a few cities. Tesla sold its first 100 cars even before they had been made! There is one problem, though. The silence of the electric motor is too alien. There is no grunt and growl of a ferocious motor. A Tesla engineer promised to change all that – soon to be introduced is software programmed to give a variety of engine roars, just like ring tones on mobile phones![36]

Increased pollution and climate change

Another environmental trend is increased pollution. Industry has been largely blamed for damaging the quality of the natural environment. Consider the disposal of chemical and nuclear wastes, the dangerous mercury levels in the ocean, the quantity of chemical pollutants in the soil and food supply, and the littering of the environment with non-biodegradable bottles, plastics and other packaging materials. In the EU, member states face tough regulations on waste disposal, which require governments to reduce the amount of biodegradable rubbish sent to landfill sites to 75 per cent of their 1995 levels by 2010, and to 35 per cent by 2020. The aim is to encourage more recycling and to dispose of industrial and domestic waste using ecologically friendly means.[37]

Too often, companies complain about the cost of complying with 'anti-pollution' regulations or implementing environmentally cleaner technologies. On the other hand, more alert managers are responding to public concerns by producing ecologically sensitive goods, using recyclable or biodegradable packaging, or adopting improved pollution controls and energy-efficient operations.

> By the end of this century, global temperatures are expected to increase by 3 degrees Centigrade . . . causing the glaciers to melt faster, leading to heavier river flows and flooding.

In addition, carbon dioxide (CO_2)-induced climate change is moving up the agenda. According to a report by the Intergovernmental Panel on Climate Change, the global warming of the past 50 years can be attributed to the industrial pumping out of greenhouse gases, primarily carbon dioxide emissions from using fossil fuels, and that further warming is unavoidable. By the end of this century, global temperatures are expected to increase by 3 degrees centigrade. Warming temperatures are causing the glaciers to melt faster, leading to heavier river flows and flooding. And, when the glaciers get smaller, the amount available for melting will reduce, resulting in water shortages.[38] On the one hand, freak storms, extreme rainfalls and severe droughts, like other extreme weather events such as Hurricane Katrina, cannot be attributed directly to global warming. On the other hand, meteorologists say that they show dramatically some of its expected effects as the globe warms. According to scientists and their prediction models, droughts and floods will become more frequent, causing a substantial increase in hazards in many regions in the world.[39] The Kyoto protocol on climate change attempts to set international targets for governments to reduce emissions and to adopt energy efficiency measures to address the problems associated with climate change. Some businesses have caught on to the economic opportunities that soaring fossil fuel costs and public concern over climate change offer.

For example, there has never been a better time to be a 'green entrepreneur'. Businesses are booming across the renewable energy sector and investment in environmental technology companies is increasing. Consequently, clean technologies, including alternative energy technologies, has become one of the fastest growing categories in the venture capital market. In Europe, venture capital investment in renewable energy and clean technology exceeded €500m in 2005. This figure is expected to rise in the years ahead. As Joachim Faber, chief executive of Allianz Global Investment, says, returns on green investments are rising, making renewable energy, in particular, one of the most attractive areas for institutional investors.[40] The trend has benefited young or start-up 'green technology' companies seeking capital for research and development, to launch their products or to enter new markets. For example, Solar Century, a London-based company that makes solar panels, started as a serious business in 2000. It was founded by Jeremy Leggett, who was driven by a conviction that turning sunlight into electricity was a promising solution to growing concern about climate change. In addition to government subsidies into renewable energy, he successfully raised over £7m (€11m) of funding from several investors over the past years. The company has more than quadrupled its turnover from £2.4m in 2003–04 to £13m in 2005–06. But what really motivated Mr Leggett extends beyond the thrill that an entrepreneur experiences. 'Global warming got me into this. It was a sense of mission. It is difficult to talk about without sounding pretentious, but that's how it happened,' says Mr Leggett.[41]

Government intervention in natural resource management

Another trend is increased government intervention in natural resource management. The governments of different countries vary in their concern and efforts to promote a clean environment. Some, like the German government, vigorously pursue environmental quality. Others, especially many poorer nations, do little about it, largely because they lack the needed funds or political will. Even the richer nations lack the vast funds and political accord needed to mount a worldwide environmental effort. The general hope is that companies around the world will accept more social responsibility, and that less expensive devices can be found to control and reduce pollution.

In most countries, industry has been pressured rather than persuaded to 'go green'. Environment protection agencies of one sort or another have been created to enforce pollution standards and to conduct pollution research. Environmental legislation has toughened up in recent years and will continue to do so in the foreseeable future. For example, in the EU, new CO_2 capping laws and schemes such as the European Emissions Trading Scheme (ETS) for CO_2 are used to help curb CO_2 emissions. The European ETS, set up in 2005, covers five industries and some 13,000 factories, deemed to be particularly dirty. Firms are given tradeable allowances covering their existing emissions. Firms wanting to exceed those limits have to buy allowances from other firms, or to buy permits from UN-approved 'clean' developing-country companies, operating under the Clean Development Mechanism, established by the Kyoto treaty. The aim is to reward industries that can reduce their CO_2 output. However, there is still much controversy regarding the viability and effectiveness of these interventions.

In the drive to cut carbon dioxide (CO_2) emissions from motor vehicles by a quarter over the next five years, the European Commission has proposed legislation that will require all manufacturers selling cars in the EU to lower average CO_2 emissions of new cars to below 120 grams per kilometre by 2012, down from an average level of 186 g/km in 1995 and 163 g/km in 2004. The industry will have to ensure that car engines emit no more than 130 g/km, with the remaining cut achieved through improving tyre and air-conditioning efficiency and greater biofuel use. Although environmental groups, such as Greenpeace, welcome the adoption of European emissions law, the proposals have sparked fierce criticism from the car industry. Manufacturers of premium cars, like BMW and Mercedes, are likely to be worst hit, their luxury and sports cars being further from meeting the 120 g/km target. Car companies argue they are mostly operating on razor-thin (1–3 per cent) margins. Development costs, estimated at between €600 and €3,000 per car, to meet these ambitious targets will run into the billions. Many producers say they will be forced to shift production abroad and become less competitive. Some, like Sergio Marchionne, Fiat's chief executive, fear the loss of some 12 million jobs, threatening the core of Europe's manufacturing base. Moreover, according to ACEA, which groups all the big manufacturers in Europe, including those based outside the EU, the industry had invested in developing greener cars only to see many of them rejected by European consumers. Consumers are not interested in buying fuel-efficient cars. They look for comfort and safety. Meanwhile, European car makers already face growing tax sanctions levied by member states on high-CO_2 cars. In the UK, car owners have to pay double the excise duty on high-emission vehicles.

However, car makers will not be alone in bearing the brunt of EU CO_2 laws. Airlines are also coming under rapid fire. Flying one fully-laden 550-seater A380 is, in energy terms, equivalent to a 14-kilometre queue of traffic on the road. In 20 years, Airbus estimates there will be 1,500 such planes. By then, the super-jumbos alone would be pumping out as much CO_2 as 5 million cars. Although still a relatively small source of CO_2 emissions, aviation's share is growing as more and more people are taking to the skies, thanks also to low-cost carriers, which are expanding fast on short-haul routes. There is strong evidence that emissions from jet engines, including the contrails (streaks of cloud) they dump in the sky, are especially damaging. Proposals are underway to make airlines part of the 'cap and trade' system. Each carrier departing from Europe would be given a CO_2 allowance. Airlines can buy additional quotas, from a low-polluting company, hence there is no net addition to global-warming gases. The problem, however, lies in the difficulty of enforcement, especially with airlines from America, which does not recognise the Kyoto protocol.

The International Air Transport Association (IATA) argues that the need to pay for environmental costs would pose further risks to world airlines' financial performance. The net loss of the world's airlines in the early half of this decade amounted to almost €33bn: carriers have been hit by terrorism, war, recession, SARS (the respiratory disease) and soaring oil prices.[42]

Global warming is not something automakers, airlines or any other industry can ignore for ever. True, polluters should shoulder the burden they impose on our planet. For consumers, it may be time to think twice before they drive or fly!

❝ A healthy ecology and a healthy economy. **❞**

Concern for the natural environment spawned the so-called green movement. Today, enlightened companies go beyond what government regulations dictate. They are developing *environmentally sustainable* strategies and practices in an effort to create a world economy that the planet can support indefinitely. They are responding to consumer demands with more environmentally responsible products. For example, General Electric is using its 'ecomagination' to create products for a better world – cleaner aircraft engines, cleaner locomotives, cleaner fuel technologies. Companies are looking to do more than just good deeds. More and more, they are recognising the link between a healthy ecology and a healthy economy. They are learning that environmentally responsible actions can also be good business.

Technological environment

Technological environment—Forces that create new technologies, creating new product and market opportunities.

The **technological environment** is perhaps the most dramatic force now shaping our destiny. Technology has released such wonders as antibiotics, robotic surgery, miniaturised electronics, laptop computers and the Internet. It has also released such horrors as nuclear missiles, chemical weapons and assault rifles. It has released such mixed blessings as cars, television and credit cards.

Our attitude towards technology depends on whether we are more impressed with its wonders or its blunders. For example, what would you think about having tiny little transmitters implanted in all of the products you buy that would allow tracking products from their point of production through use and disposal? On the one hand, it would provide many advantages to both buyers and sellers. On the other hand, it could be a bit scary. Either way, it's already happening:[43]

Technological environment: technology is perhaps the most dramatic force shaping the environment. Here, a herder makes a call on his mobile phone.

SOURCE: Joseph Van OS, Getty Images, Inc./Image bank.

Envision a world in which every product contains a tiny transmitter, loaded with information. As you stroll through the supermarket aisles, shelf sensors detect your selections and beam ads to your shopping cart screen, offering special deals on related products. As your cart fills, scanners detect that you might be buying for a dinner party; the screen suggests a wine to go with the meal you've planned. When you leave the store, exit scanners total up your purchases and automatically charge them to your credit card. At home, readers track what goes into and out of your pantry, updating your shopping list when stocks run low. For Sunday dinner, you pop a turkey into your 'smart oven', which follows instructions from an embedded chip and cooks the bird to perfection.

Seems far-fetched? Not really. In fact, it will soon be a reality, thanks to tiny radio-frequency identification (RFID) transmitters – or 'smart chips' – that can be embedded in the products you buy.

Many large firms are adding fuel to the RFID fire. For example, since March 2004, German retail giant Metro AG, the world's fifth largest retailer, has been introducing RFID in stages along its supply chain. So far, 25 of its distribution centres use the technology on the wooden pallets which carry the goods and on individual cases of products. More than 40 suppliers now attach RFID tags to their pallets. Metro views RFID technology as a way to manage the huge flow of merchandise into and out of stores more effectively, while at the same time reducing inventory losses and labour costs. Gerd Wolfram, managing director of MGI Metro Group Information Technology, says: 'We firmly believe that we'll be able to lower our operating costs with this technology and also provide our customers with a richer shopping experience.'

Metro has been testing RFID in a live retail setting at the Extra supermarket in Rheinberg, near Düsseldorf, as part of its Future Store Initiative. One concept being tested at the store is the 'smart-shelf', which automatically informs staff to replenish merchandise. RFID tags are attached to packages of Gillette razor blades, Philadelphia cream cheese containers and plastic bottles of shampoo from Procter & Gamble. As customers pick up the tagged products, signals are transmitted via a wireless network to the merchandise management system, which tracks the number in stock and issues alerts to clerks carrying PDAs.

Metro is also carrying out development work on RFID at its RFID Innovation Centre in nearby Neuss, where it is testing more than 40 applications, most of which are focused on logistics, warehousing and retail operations though a few also involve consumers. For instance, the 'smart fridge' identifies products and informs household members when expiry dates are approaching.

In Neuss, around 20 technology partners, including IT industry heavyweights IBM, Intel and SAP, are collaborating with Metro. EPCglobal, which has been leading the drive to establish a global RFID standard, has established its European performance test centre within the German centre.

The company's ultimate aim is to deploy RFID at all levels, including the individual item, at all of its 2,300 locations. But that day is years away, concedes Gerd Wolfram. 'We will see RFID increasingly replace bar codes for certain products but the technology won't be used to identify all products for a good 15 years,' he says, citing high unit prices for the tags as one of the main reasons. Unit prices, Wolfram notes, will need to fall to make RFID a viable alternative to a conventional bar code.

The technological environment changes rapidly. Marketers should be aware of the following trends in technology.

Fast pace of technological change

Think of all of today's common products that were not available 100 years ago, or even 30 years ago. Louis Pasteur and Charles Darwin did not know about automobiles, aeroplanes, radios or the electric light. Henry Ford did not know about television, aerosol cans, automatic dishwashers, air conditioners, antibiotics or computers. Glenn Miller did not know about photocopiers, synthetic detergents, tape recorders, birth control pills or earth satellites. John Lennon did not know about personal computers, smart phones, iPods or the Internet. The list is unending!

New technologies create new markets and opportunities. However, every new technology replaces an older technology. Transistors hurt the vacuum-tube industry, photocopiers killed the carbon-paper business, compact discs hurt vinyl records, and digital photography hurt the film business. When old industries fought or ignored new technologies, their business declined. Thus, marketers should watch the technological environment closely. Companies that do not keep up will soon find their products outdated.

But keeping pace with technological change is becoming more challenging for firms today. *Technology life cycles* are getting shorter. Take the typewriter. The first-generation modern mechanical typewriter dominated the market for 25 years. Subsequent generations had shorter lives – 15 years for electromechanical models, seven years for electronic versions and five years for first-generation microprocessor-based ones. And today, the average life span of some computer software products, for example, is now well under one year.

Firms must track technological trends and determine whether or not these changes will affect their products' continued ability to satisfy customers' needs. For example, children's growing obsession with MP3s, playstations and mobile phones have presented challenges to traditional toymakers such as Lego. The Danish company saw sales plummeting over the years, and by 2004 reported its biggest loss in its 73-year history.

Technologies arising in unrelated industries can also affect the firm's fortunes. The mechanical watch industry was overtaken by manufacturers of electronic components seeking new applications and growth opportunities for their quartz technology. In the 1980s, Sony built a successful, global business in products that use analogue technology, such as cathode-ray tube TVs and Walkman audio players. But the world has moved on to flat-panel liquid crystal display (LCD) and plasma TVs and silicon audio devices that use hard disc drives and memory cards. Sony's slowness in adapting to the digital age, along with the rapid decline for analogue products in the past decade, greatly impacted the performance of the company's consumer electronics division, which sustained operating losses in the first half of this decade. In TVs, where Sony used to have a loyal following, based on attractive design, brand power and its Trinitron technology, rival Sharp, capitalising on strong demand for LCD televisions, has replaced it as the brand of choice. In portable audio players, it trails Apple with a 16 per cent share compared with nearly 40 per cent for Apple's iPod.[44] Thus, businesses must assiduously monitor their technological environment to avoid missing new product and market opportunities.

Increased regulation

As products and technology become more complex, the public needs to know that these are safe. Thus, government agencies investigate and ban potentially unsafe products. Also, statutory and industry regulatory bodies exist to set safety standards for consumer products and penalise companies that fail to meet them. New technologies also may raise public concern about security and privacy.[45]

For example, the growing use of RFID technology, on anything from pharmaceutical products and pre-pay travel cards to passports and identity card systems, has caused a fair amount of controversy and prompted campaigns by privacy groups, street demonstrations in Europe, and even conspiracy theories a-plenty. The EU's information society commissioner,

Viviane Reding, has initiated a public debate about the security and privacy issues surrounding RFID. Such consultations over how the technology might be used and how data provided by the tags might be protected will help the European Commission in its review of the EU's e-privacy regulations. 'We need to ask what information RFID systems gather, how long that data will be kept and who will have access to it,' said Ms Reding. Consumer and privacy groups have expressed concern that RFID tags could be used to build up huge databases of individuals' shopping, leisure and travel habits, which could be exploited by unscrupulous businesses and also become a target for cybercriminals. European Commission officials are likely to be looking for evidence that the IT industry is taking such privacy and security considerations into account. Companies that are actively involved in RFID, including Philips, IBM and Accenture, are already working on privacy and security enhancement measures for RFID. Meanwhile, retailers, including Marks & Spencer in the UK and Metro in Germany, have also gone to some lengths to reassure consumers about RFID, for example by clearly labelling products that carry tags. Regulations may result in much higher research costs and in longer times between new-product ideas and their introduction. Marketers should be aware of these regulations when seeking and developing new products. They need to understand how new technologies can serve customer and human needs. By working closely with R&D people they can also encourage more market-oriented research. They must also be alert to the possible negative aspects of any breakthroughs or their potential abuse.

Political environment

Marketing decisions are strongly affected by developments in the political environment. The **political environment** consists of laws, government agencies and pressure groups that influence and limit various organisations and individuals in a given society.

Legislation regulating business

Even the most liberal advocates of free market economies agree that the system works best with at least some regulation. Well-conceived regulation can encourage competition and ensure fair markets for goods and services. Thus governments develop *public policy* to guide commerce – sets of laws and regulations that limit business for the good of society as a whole. Almost every marketing activity is subject to a wide range of laws and regulations.

Legislation affecting business around the world has increased steadily over the years. The European Commission has been active in establishing a new framework of laws covering competitive behaviour, fair trade practices, environmental protection, product standards, product liability and commercial transactions for the nations of the European Union. There are many more legal areas of concern to marketers, ranging from comparative advertising, pricing claims and data protection, to the marketing of unhealthy food and advertising to children. In particular, several countries have passed strong consumerism legislation. For example, Norway bans several forms of sales promotion – trading stamps, contests, premiums – as being inappropriate or unfair ways of promoting products. Thailand requires food processors selling national brands to also market low-price brands, so that low-income consumers can find economy brands on the shelves. In India, food companies must obtain special approval to launch brands that duplicate those already existing on the market, such as additional cola drinks or new brands of rice.

Understanding the public policy implications of a particular marketing activity is not a simple matter. First, there are many laws created at different levels: for example, in the EU, business operators are subject to European Commission, individual member state and specific local regulations. Also, member states vary in the extent to which they comply with EU legislation. Some

Political environment— Laws, government agencies and pressure groups that influence and limit various organisations and individuals in a given society.

may even exceed EU directives. For example, UK regulations on part-time work go further than EU rules, imposing higher costs on small businesses and deterring them from taking on new staff in order to meet growth targets. Similarly, in the UK financial services sector, businesses have to abide by the much more stringent rules set out by the Financial Services Authority which regulates all businesses in the industry.[46]

Second, the regulations are constantly changing – what was allowed last year may now be prohibited, and what was prohibited may now be allowed. Marketers are facing a climate of increasingly restrictive legislation. For example, in the UK alone, 21 new Acts, regulations or amendments affecting marketers were passed in 2005, with another 10 Bills being put before Parliament in 2006.[47] The European Commission is also constantly seeking to tighten or improve regulations. For example, the 'Better Regulation' project plans to repeal or rewrite over 200 pieces of legislation between 2005 and 2008. In the EU, deregulation and ongoing moves towards harmonisation are expected to take time, creating a state of flux, which challenges and confuses both domestic and international marketers. Not only do marketers face confusion over the number of laws, regulations and codes they have to know about, but increasingly they even need to be familiar with laws passed elsewhere in the world. For example, globally, new laws have been passed by the US, which affect marketers working via the Internet. One of these laws forbids US and overseas commercial companies from collecting personal data about 'minors', that is, children under the age of 13, irrespective of whether the data is being used for commercial purposes.

On one hand, companies complain about regulations and the need to bear the costs of compliance. It is estimated that EU firms spend €600bn a year on administration to comply with EU regulations. On the other, firms also agree that money is well spent if compliance builds trust among customers and the public at large.

For example, an ambitious piece of EU regulation concerns the Registration, Evaluation, Authorisation and Restriction of Chemicals (REACH). It will require companies to register their use of 30,000 chemicals, including 1,500 substances linked to reproductive diseases and cancers. Firms also have to present plans for finding substitutes for hazardous chemicals. According to the European Chemical Industry Council, REACH replaces 40 different directives with one broad-band legislation, making chemical registration faster and less cumbersome. Retailers also think the new rules will be better than the old ones and the costs on business are a price worth paying if it builds people's trust in chemicals and the returns to society are sustainable. The benefits to health were put at €50bn over the next 30 years, while the costs were estimated at €2.8bn to €5.2bn over the next 11 years.[48]

Business legislation has been enacted for a number of reasons. The first is to *protect companies* from each other. Although business executives may praise competition, they sometimes try to neutralise it when it threatens them. So, laws are passed to define and prevent unfair competition. Individual EU nations enforce these laws through their own competition offices or antitrust/monopolies and mergers commissions. In addition, businesses operating in the EU are expected to comply with, and can be fined for flouting, European Commission competition (or antitrust) legislation. For example, Microsoft was fined a record €497m in March 2004 when found guilty of abusing its dominant position in the market for computer operating systems, and another €280.5m in July 2006 for failing to comply with an EU antitrust ruling.[49]

The second purpose of government regulation is to *protect consumers* from unfair and unsavoury business practices. Some firms, if left alone, would make shoddy products, invade consumer privacy, tell lies in their advertising and deceive consumers through their packaging and pricing. Unfair business practices have been defined and are enforced by various agencies.

For example, the EU Directive on Privacy and Electronic Communications aims to crack down on 'spam' by giving government agencies the power to prosecute firms that send unsolicited e-mails. A host of directives exist ranging from rules on advertising and national TV broadcast production quotas, to the protection of children.[50]

Consumer protection laws also exist to ensure that suppliers offer consumers a fair deal:

In 2006, France's Senate and National Assembly passed a new law to open up the legal digital music downloading market. With some 80 per cent share of the legal music download market, Apple dominates the sector, through its iPod music players and iTunes online music store. However, Apple's proprietary system, Fairplay, is designed to work with iPods, but cannot be played on rival technology companies' devices. The law is supposed to allow customers to play music downloaded from iTunes on any one of iPod's rivals, be it a Samsung MP3 or Microsoft's Zune. In 2007, Apple was dealt a further blow when Norway's consumer ombudsman ruled that iTunes is illegal and breaks its consumer protection laws. iTunes was told to make its code available to other technology companies so as to abide by Norwegian law. It will be taken to court and fined, and the operation will be closed down if the company fails to comply. Sweden and Finland, along with the Federation of German Consumer Organisations, have backed Norway's stance, urging pan-European consumer groups to consider and present a unified position on iTunes' legality.[51]

The third purpose of government regulation is to *protect the interests of society* against unrestrained business behaviour. Profitable business activity does not always create a better quality of life. Regulation arises to ensure that firms take responsibility for the social costs of their production or products. For example, food companies face increasing pressure to address government and consumer concerns about obesity and to take more seriously the financial risks created by products that may have an adverse effect on public health. Food companies are therefore urged to cut back on junk food advertising to children and to develop healthier products. However, many are using the Internet and new media to interact with consumers, posing new challenges to regulators.

Food companies are using the Internet more and more to deepen children's exposure to marketing messages through online games and commercials, blurring the lines between advertising and entertainment. Governments are trying to crack down on the marketing of sugary and salty snacks to children to curtail rising levels of childhood obesity. However, regulators have no authority to call for changes to corporate websites, because information provided by companies on their own websites is considered 'editorial' rather than 'advertising'.

According to the non-profit Kaiser Foundation, which claims to have undertaken the first comprehensive study of online advertising to children, many of the top food brands that target kids through television advertising also used branded websites. The brand-related information contained on websites was more extensive than the information contained in a traditional 30-second television advertisement. Some websites 'recruited' children as marketers, using them to promote branded messages to their friends. 'Online advertising's reach is not as broad as that of television but it is much deeper,' said Vicky Rideout, vice-president and director of Kaiser's programme for the study of entertainment media and health. Many of the websites included 'advergames' – games in which a company's product is featured – ranging from one to more than 60 games per site. Sites also used viral marketing, which encourages children to contact their peers about a specific product, and gave children online access to television advertisements.

Governments in the US and Europe have been trying to restrict children's access to junk foods by banning them in school vending machines, and restricting the number of junk food advertisements on television. However, rapid advances in technology mean that companies are able to use other marketing methods. A recent study by UK consumer group Which? found that some food companies were encouraging children to text codes using mobile phones to enter competitions. In the US, the advertising industry is developing more detailed voluntary guidelines for online marketing to children.

Meanwhile, pressure is growing for tougher regulation, in Britain and across Europe. According to business leaders and investors, very few companies seem to have thought through the potential impact on their businesses of emerging consumer health trends, nor to have considered fully how they might capitalise on this market shift, while creating positive social impact. Companies are urged to use research and development budgets to develop healthier products, review ingredients in their products, develop clear policies on labelling, and regulate their advertising to children on new media such as the Internet. If food companies ignore these calls, they might suffer lower sales, lose consumers' trust and be hit by heavier regulation.[52]

New laws and their enforcement are likely to continue or increase. Marketers must therefore work hard to keep up with changes in regulations and their interpretations. They must watch these developments when planning their products and marketing programmes. They also need to know about the major laws protecting competition, consumers and society. Importantly, they need to understand these laws at the local, country, regional and international levels.

 New laws and their enforcement are likely to continue or increase.

Increased emphasis on ethics and socially responsible actions

Written regulations cannot possibly cover all potential marketing abuses, and existing laws are often difficult to enforce. However, beyond written laws and regulations, business is also governed by social codes and rules of professional ethics. Next, we will address the increasing interest in business ethics and social responsibility and the rising popularity of cause-related marketing.

Enlightened companies encourage their managers to look beyond what the regulatory system allows and simply to 'do the right thing'. These socially responsible firms actively seek out ways to protect the long-run interests of their consumers and the environment.

The recent rash of business scandals and increased concerns about the environment have created fresh interest in the issues of ethics and social responsibility. Almost every aspect of marketing involves such issues. Unfortunately, because these issues usually involve conflicting interests, well-meaning people can disagree honestly about the right course of action in a given situation. Thus many industrial and professional trade associations have suggested codes of ethics, and more companies are now developing policies and guidelines to deal with complex social responsibility issues.

The boom in Internet marketing has created a new set of social and ethical issues. Critics' worries about online privacy issues are the primary concern. There has been an explosion in the amount of personal digital data available. Users themselves supply some of it. They voluntarily place highly private information on social networking sites such as YouTube and MySpace or on genealogy sites, which are easily searched by anyone with a PC.

However, much of the information is systematically developed by businesses seeking to learn more about their customers, often without consumers realising that they are under the microscope. Legitimate businesses plant cookies on consumers' PCs and collect, analyse and share digital information from every mouse click consumers make at their websites. Critics are concerned that companies may now know *too* much, and that some companies might use digital data to take unfair advantage of consumers. Although most companies fully disclose their Internet privacy policies, and most work to use data to benefit their customers, abuses do occur. As a result, consumer advocates and policymakers are taking action to protect consumer privacy. In Chapter 2, we discussed a broad range of societal marketing issues in depth, and throughout the text we address, where relevant, the main public policy, social responsibility and environmental issues surrounding major marketing decisions.

To exercise their social responsibility and build more positive images, many companies are now linking themselves to worthwhile causes. These days, every product or service supplier seems to be tied to some cause.

> Buy a woolly jumper from Marks & Spencer and be assured of their commitment to animal welfare: M&S has a strict anti-fur policy and exercises a complete ban on the use of endangered species. Purchase Nescafé's Fairtrade coffee and guarantee a better deal for Third World coffee producers. Recycle an old mobile phone with Tesco, and the supermarket donates £5 (€7.5), or return a printer cartridge and they will donate £1, to Wizz-Kidz, a charity for disabled children, and be offered a chance to win a Toyota Prius.

Cause-related marketing has become a primary form of corporate giving. It lets companies 'do well by doing good' by linking purchases of the company's products or services with fund-raising for worthwhile causes or charitable organisations. Companies now sponsor dozens of cause-related marketing campaigns each year. Many are backed by large budgets and a full complement of marketing activities.

Companies are increasingly seeking to improve their positive impact on society. Here, Marks & Spencer's award-winning Children's Promise campaign reinforces the company's commitment to supporting the local community.
SOURCE: Marks & Spencer.

Cause-related marketing has stirred some controversy. Critics worry that cause-related marketing is more a strategy for selling than a strategy for giving – that 'cause-related' marketing is really 'cause-exploitative' marketing. Thus, companies using cause-related marketing might find themselves walking a fine line between increased sales and an improved image, and facing charges of exploitation. Real Marketing 4.2 shows how companies are cashing in on environmental awareness.

However, if handled well, cause-related marketing can greatly benefit both the company and the cause. The company gains an effective marketing tool while building a more positive public image. The charitable organisation or cause gains greater visibility and important new sources of funding.

Cultural environment

Cultural environment—Institutions and other forces that affect society's basic values, perceptions, preferences and behaviours.

The **cultural environment** is made up of institutions and other forces that affect society's basic values, perceptions, preferences and behaviours. People grow up in a particular society that shapes their basic beliefs and values. They absorb a world-view that defines their relationships with others. The following cultural characteristics can affect marketing decision making.

Persistence of cultural values

People in a given society hold many beliefs and values. Their core beliefs and values have a high degree of persistence. For example, many of us believe in working, getting married, giving to charity and being honest. These beliefs shape more specific attitudes and behaviours found in everyday life. *Core* beliefs and values are passed on from parents to children and are reinforced by schools, religious groups, businesses and governments.

Secondary beliefs and values are more open to change. Believing in marriage is a core belief; believing that people should get married early in life is a secondary belief. Marketers have some chance of changing secondary values, but little chance of changing core values. For example, family-planning marketers could argue more effectively that people should get married later than that they should not get married at all.

Shifts in secondary cultural values

Although core values are fairly persistent, cultural swings do take place. Consider the impact of popular music groups, movie personalities and other celebrities on young people's hair styling, clothing and sexual norms. Marketers want to predict cultural shifts in order to spot new opportunities or threats. Such information helps marketers cater to trends with appropriate products and communication appeals.

The major cultural values of a society are expressed in people's views of themselves and others, as well as in their views of organisations, society, nature and the universe.

People's views of themselves

People vary in their emphasis on serving themselves versus serving others. Some people seek personal pleasure, wanting fun, change and escape. Others seek self-realisation through religion, recreation or the avid pursuit of careers or other life goals. People use products, brands and services as a means of self-expression and buy products and services that match their views of themselves.

In the 1990s, personal ambition and materialism increased dramatically, with significant marketing implications. In a 'me-society', people buy their 'dream cars' and take their 'dream vacations'. They tend to spend to the limit on self-indulgent goods and services. Today, people appear to be adopting more conservative behaviours and ambitions. They are more cautious in their spending patterns and more value-driven in their purchases. In the 2000s, materialism,

real marketing 4.2

Cashing in on environmental awareness

It is now a decade since Unilever stopped providing refill pouches for its washing liquid owing to lack of demand. But it seems that consumers' forgotten environmental conscience is reawakening. Ecover, a private company based in Belgium that makes ecological washing and cleaning products, says sales are growing at the rate of 20 per cent per year in the UK, its biggest market, reaching £35m (€52m) in 2005. The company is building a new factory in France to keep up with demand.

A string of household names – including General Electric, Wal-Mart and Unilever – have been lining up to show off their green credentials in an effort to woo customers, at least at the high end of the market. 'This is becoming a lifestyle choice,' says Stephen Parker, managing director of Cred, an environmental consultancy. 'We are a consumer-driven society, and consumption is often a more reliable way of seeing what society wants than politics these days.'

The Institute of Grocery Distribution reports that sales of 'ethical' products are increasing by 7.5 per cent a year, compared with 4.2 per cent for conventional products. General Electric, the US conglomerate, became the biggest company to 'go green' last year, when chief executive Jeff Immelt announced a new push into providing goods that minimise damage to the environment. Mr Immelt insisted there were profits to be made in the market for goods from wind turbines to energy-saving lightbulbs. The results have been clear at GE, which announced in May that revenues from products and services under its Ecomagination brand – for environmental products – had risen from $6.2bn (€4.9bn) in 2004 to $10.1bn in 2005.

One of the more recent converts to the 'green' consumer's cause has been Wal-Mart, the US retail group better known for protests against its employment practices than its environmental concern. Lee Scott, chief executive, has pledged to invest $500m (€372m) in 'sustainability' projects and to reduce by 30 per cent the energy used in the company's stores, reduce solid waste by a quarter and double the fuel efficiency of the company's vehicle fleet within 10 years.

These companies are driven not just by the desire to cash in on increasing environmental awareness among customers. There is a practical incentive for companies to act, independently of what consumers think. Rising fuel bills mean that reduced energy use will save companies money, with the attendant bonus of cutting greenhouse gas emissions associated with the burning of fossil fuels. Companies are also keen to pre-empt any strengthening of environmental regulations, particularly moves to curb greenhouse gas emissions.

...4.2

The UK government, for instance, is considering a proposal to extend carbon dioxide emissions trading to retailers and other businesses. US states led by California are forging ahead with plans to limit emissions and bypass the federal government's reluctance to take precautionary measures against climate change. Against this backdrop, companies warn that customers will make ecologically friendly choices only if they believe they will get the same results from products as they do at present.

A case in point is P&G's 'Cool Clean' campaigns in western Europe for its laundry detergent, Ariel, which tell consumers they should lower the temperature at which they wash clothes to save energy. 'Consumers want better products that deliver a better experience. Sustainability has to be an additional benefit,' said Gianni Ciserani, managing director of P&G UK & Ireland. 'Whenever sustainable products come with trade-off on performance, we win some [consumers] but we lose others.'

Companies have another reason to beware. A previous wave of green consumerism in the 1970s fizzled out, as consumers lost interest. Just as Unilever stopped providing refill pouches 10 years ago, today's 'green' wave could also break if consumers lose interest or the economy falters.

SOURCE: Based on Fiona Harvey and Jenny Wiggins, International news: 'Companies cash in on environment awareness', *Financial Times* (14 September 2006).

---

flashy spending and self-indulgence have been replaced by more sensible spending, saving, family concerns and helping others. This suggests a bright future for products and services that serve basic needs and provide real value rather than those relying on glitz and hype.

The Yankelovich Monitor identifies several consumer segments whose purchases are motivated by self-views. Here are two examples:[53]

At capacity individuals. Tending to fall in the Gen X generation, these individuals are defined by their focus on family above all else – especially their kids! As such, shopping decisions are based on products that the whole family will love; that are also the best deal out there. With multiple demands on their time, they also seek out the quickest and most convenient ways to get information and to make purchases. For them, it's all about saving time on daily responsibilities so they can spend more quality hours with their kids.

Driven individuals. Also tending to fall in the Gen X generation, these individuals are characterised by their desire for success in all realms of life – from their family to their job to their social life. They look to establish themselves as the best and brightest; therefore factors such as exclusivity, innovation, and variety influence their shopping decisions. Additionally, they look for the most up-to-date sources of information to keep them at the head of the pack, and thus regularly rely on the Internet as a tool to stay in the know.

Marketers can target their products and services based on such self-views. For example, MasterCard targets Adventurers who might want to use their credits cards to quickly set up the experience of a lifetime. It tells these consumers, 'There are some things in life that money can't buy. For everything else, there's MasterCard.'

Even young entrepreneurs view themselves differently. Having lost the hard-nosed greed that typified the 1980s, most see themselves as 'respectable business people'. Young entrepreneurs are a mixed bunch but are more likely to identify with inspirational creators of businesses, such as Richard Branson, founder of Virgin, or 'hippies with calculators' like the founders of the smoothie-drink business Innocent Drinks.[54]

People's views of others

In past decades, observers have noted several shifts in people's attitudes towards others. Recently, for example, some trend trackers have seen a new wave of 'cocooning', in which people are going out less with others and staying home more to enjoy the creature comforts of home and hearth.

Sports events and concerts are luring smaller crowds these days. Promoters blame everything from unseasonable weather to higher petrol prices for the lousy attendance numbers. . . . But industry watchers also believe shifting consumer behavior is at work: Call it Cocooning in the Digital Age. With DVD players in most homes, broadband connections proliferating, scores of new video game titles being released each year, and hundreds of satellite and cable channels, consumers can be endlessly entertained right in their own living room – or home theatre. Add in the high costs and bother of going out, and more and more people are trading the bleachers for the couch.

Effective smoking bans in public places across Europe and crackdowns upon drink driving are inducing people to entertain at home. Pub beer sales plummeted 7 per cent in the year following Scotland introducing a smoking ban in pubs, and in Ireland music promoters predict a decline in new rock acts as smokers avoid the small venues where they start their career. To an increasing number of cocooners, 'Staying in is the new night out.'[55]

This trend suggests a greater demand for home improvement and entertainment products. 'As the . . . "nesting" or "cocooning" trend continues, with people choosing to stay home and entertain more often, the trend of upgrading outdoor living spaces has [grown rapidly],' says a home industry analyst. People are adding bigger patios with fancy gas barbecues, outdoor jacuzzis, outdoor heaters and other amenities that make the old house 'home, sweet home' for family and friends.[56]

Allied to the cocooners are the mollycoddlers who experts think are damaging the mental and physical health of their children by overprotecting them from the dreadful outdoors.

'In most highly developed countries,' says Susan Goltsman, a principal of urban design company Moore Iacofano Goltsman, 'children are not allowed to roam and range the way they did when I was younger. Every species requires this range behaviour, where you go further and further from the supervision of the parent. That doesn't happen much any more. Kids are programmed from the time they wake up in the morning to the time they go to bed. They're in classes or after-school programmes; there aren't the vacant lots where they can go and build a fort or have their own space. These no longer exist in most urban areas or people feel it's too unsafe for their children to be somewhere unsupervised. This has changed the quality of childhood.'

The Royal Society for the Prevention of Accidents (RoSPA) concurs. It is widely agreed that children need to taste broccoli, yet the taste of freedom, even more important for their well-being, is increasingly being denied them because of fears of predatory paedophiles, unstable trees, speeding vans or a host of other perceived dangers. Such dangers, statistically, are negligible. All sensible parents know that. On the other hand, paedophiles do strike, rotten branches do give way, speeding vans do mount pavements. Peter Cornall, RoSPA's head of leisure safety, has declared that 'when children spend time in the great outdoors, getting muddy, getting wet, getting stung by nettles, they learn important lessons – what hurts, what is slippery, what you can trip over from.' Mild accidents sustained outdoors, Mr Cornall asserts, are much more wholesome than accidents sustained in front of a computer screen. 'We need to ask whether it is better for a child to break a wrist falling out of a tree, or to get a repetitive-strain wrist injury at a young age from using a computer or a video games console.'

The new mollycoddling can damage children's health, adds Susan Goltsman. 'Obesity, asthma and attention deficit disorder are all environmentally related. Kids are not moving and exploring, using their bodies the way they're meant to be used – out in the world. This might sound silly but we're eating less dirt than before. When you don't eat dirt, your immune system doesn't make the kind of antibodies to protect yourself from the diseases we're seeing. So the sanitisation of the world is hurting children in insidious ways. Getting dirty, being part of nature, develops healthy human beings.'[57]

People's views of organisations

People vary in their attitudes towards corporations, government agencies, trade unions, universities and other organisations. By and large, people are willing to work for big organisations and expect them, in turn, to carry out society's work.

The late 1980s saw a sharp decrease in confidence in, and loyalty towards, business and political organisations and institutions. In the workplace, there has been an overall decline in organisational loyalty. During the 1990s, waves of company downsizings bred cynicism and distrust. And in this decade, corporate scandals at once-admired companies like Enron and WorldCom in the US, and Lernout & Hauspie and Ahold in Europe,[58] record-breaking profits for big oil companies during a period of all-time high prices at the pump and other questionable activities have resulted in a further loss of confidence in big business. Many people today see work not as a source of satisfaction, but as a necessary chore to earn money to enjoy non-work hours. This trend suggests that organisations need to find new ways to win consumer and employee confidence. They need to review their communications to make sure their messages are honest. Also, they need to review their various activities to make sure that they are coming across as 'good corporate citizens'. Although more companies are linking themselves to worthwhile causes, civil-society advocates increasingly accuse them of merely paying lip-service to corporate social responsibility; when commercial interests and social welfare collide, profits come first. Corporate citizenship is intended to be more about how companies conduct themselves with respect to their employees, consumers and broader society, than about donations and charitable giving. Thus, firms must work hard to assure the wider public that their corporate social responsibility is not profit motive masquerading as altruism.

People's views of society

People vary in their attitudes towards their society – from patriots who defend it, to reformers who want to change it, and malcontents who want to leave it. People's orientation to their society influences their consumption patterns, levels of savings and attitudes towards the marketplace.

In the emerging economies of eastern and central Europe, the Indian subcontinent and East Asia, consumers aspire to achieve the high living standards and lifestyles of people in the more advanced western countries. The display of conspicuous consumption and fondness for expensive western brands – the common label for achievement and westernisation – are highly acceptable behaviour. For the well-off, national patriotism, for example, is not an issue, since locally made goods are often viewed as inferior or less desirable than foreign imported brands. Consumers' predisposition towards western brands suggests a greater demand for goods marketed by companies of western origin, hence creating new marketing opportunities for these firms.

By contrast, in the western developed countries, the last two decades saw an increase in consumer patriotism. European consumers voice the view that sticking to locally produced goods would save and protect jobs, although their wallets, purses and voices do not sing in unison since consumption everywhere is increasingly non-national. Between 1983 and 2005, world merchandise exports increased from €1,366bn to €7,564bn, with the EU's share growing from 30.4 to 39.4 per cent of the total. Much of the fear is from competition whose share of world trade has kept very much in step with Europe's growing from 19.1 per cent of the total in 1983 to 27.4 per cent in 2005. American patriotism has been increasing gradually for the past two decades. A recent global survey on 'national pride' found that Americans ranked number-one among the 34 democracies polled while their share of world trade has shrunk from 16.8 to 14.5 per cent.[59]

People's views of nature

People vary in their attitudes towards the natural world. Some feel ruled by it, others feel in harmony with it and still others seek to master it. A long-term trend has been people's growing mastery over nature through technology and the belief that nature is bountiful. More recently, however, people have recognised that nature is finite and fragile – that it can be destroyed or spoiled by human activities.

Love of things natural has created a new 'lifestyle of health and sustainability' market – consumers seek out everything from natural, organic and nutritional products to fuel-efficient cars and alternative medicine. Business has responded by offering more products and services catering to such interests. For example, globally, the market for fortified and functional food and drinks – products that claim to give some specific health benefit – is one of the fastest growing sectors in the food industry, with sales rising 20 per cent between 2002 and 2004 to almost €65bn, according to market research company Euromonitor International. In the UK, where one in ten people buy products that claim to reduce cholesterol, such as Unilever's Flora Pro-activ brand, total Flora spread sales rose 8 per cent over 2005 to £179m (€266m). The fastest growing soft drinks were brands such as Actimel, a dairy drink, and Volvic, a bottled water, both owned by Danone, with sales growth of 26 per cent and 18 per cent respectively between 2005 and 2006.[60]

More customers are, however, demanding a holistic approach to feeling well. The wellness boom or health consumerism is becoming big business as firms pile into the wellness lifestyle market category. This broad new category consolidates a lot of sub-categories, including spas, traditional medicine and alternative medicine, behavioural therapy, spirituality, fitness, nutrition and beauty.

> **"** Wellness . . . is becoming big business as firms pile into the wellness lifestyle market. **"**

Already, the new world of wellness is becoming fiercely competitive.

Sir Richard Branson's Virgin group operates Virgin Life Care kiosks in which people can earn spendable HealthMiles. Insurers such as WellPoint and Britain's PruHealth are rewarding people who take part in health-improvement programmes with lower premiums or bigger deductibles. All the major grocery retailers are selling organic food, and even Coca-Cola is launching a wellness drink, Envigna, which claims to help consumers lose weight!

For the super-rich, there is Canyon Ranch, the premium health-spa brand of choice. Opened in 1979 by Mel Zuckerman and his exercise-fanatic wife Enid, it is America's first total vacation/fitness resort, offering $1000 (€745) per night retreats. In 2007, in Miami Beach, it opened the first of many upmarket housing estates built around a spa, called Canyon Ranch Living. Together with the Cleveland Clinic, one of the world's leading private providers of traditional medicine, it is launching an 'executive health' product combining diagnosis, treatment and, above all, prevention. It also has plans to produce food and skin-care products, a range of clothes and healthy-living educational materials.

Other firms are piling in – and doing well by helping people feel good! Revolution, a firm set up in 2005 by Steve Case, co-founder of AOL, the Internet firm, operates Miraval-Life In Balance, a rival to Canyon Ranch. Mr Case hopes to turn Miraval into the 'Nike brand of wellness', expanding from its spas, which offer 130 different experiences from yoga to organic cuisine. New initiatives include Miraval Living residential estates – one opens soon in Manhattan – skin-care lotions and food. Revolution also owns Lime.com, a wellness broadcaster, and Exclusive Resorts, on the grounds that luxury holidays are good for you. In addition, Mr Case is rolling out Revolution Health, a consumer healthcare business that will offer online health information, insurance policies and new forms of healthcare, including walk-in treatment and screening in shops such as retail outlets. Mr Case reckons that one of the roots of today's healthcare crisis is that prevention and care are not suitably joined up. A growing number of employers now promote wellness at work, both to cut costs and to reduce stress and health-related absenteeism, says Jon Denoris of Catalyst Health, a gym business in London. He has been helping the British arm of Harley Davidson, a motorbike-maker, to develop a wellness programme for its workers.

The desire to reduce healthcare costs is one force behind the rise of the wellness industry; the other is the growing demand from consumers for things that make them feel healthier. Surveys find that three out of four adults now feel that their lives are 'out of balance'.

One difficulty for wellness firms will be acquiring the expertise to operate in several different areas of the market. Another will be to maintain credibility in (and for) an industry that combines serious science with snake oil. One problem – or is it an opportunity? – in selling wellness products to consumers is that some of the things they demand may be faddish or nonsensical. Easy fixes, such as new-age therapies, may appeal to them more than harder but proven ways to improve health. And there is much debate about the health benefits of vitamin supplements, organic food and alternative medicines, let alone different forms of spirituality.[61]

People's views of the universe

Finally, people vary in their beliefs about the origin of the universe and their place in it. While the practice of religion remains strong in many parts of the world, religious conviction and practice have been dropping off gradually through the years. The annual British Social Attitudes Survey suggests that the number of people who say they are religious has changed markedly: in 1964, nearly three-quarters of British residents said they belonged to a religion and attended services, whereas by 2005, only three in ten did.[62]

However, some futurists have noted an emerging renewal of interest in religion, perhaps as part of a broader search for a new inner purpose. People have been moving away from materialism and dog-eat-dog ambition to seek more permanent values – family, community, earth, faith – and a more certain grasp of right and wrong. Some are increasingly looking to religion – Christianity, Judaism, Hinduism, Islam and others – as a source of comfort in a chaotic world. This trend reflects a 'new spiritualism' which affects consumers in everything, from the television shows they watch and the books they read, to the products and services they buy. 'Since consumers don't park their beliefs and values on the bench outside the marketplace,' adds one expert, 'they are bringing this awareness to the brands they buy. Tapping into this heightened sensitivity presents a unique marketing opportunity for brands.'[63]

However, in many overseas markets where western companies seek to expand, such as India, China and south-east Asia, society's value systems place great importance on economic achievement and material possession. The values of these 'enthusiastic materialists' are also shared by the developing markets of Europe, such as Turkey, and some Latin American countries.

Responding to the marketing environment

Many companies view the marketing environment as an 'uncontrollable' element to which they must adapt. They passively accept the marketing environment and do not try to change it. They analyse the environmental forces and design strategies that will help the company avoid the threats and take advantage of the opportunities the environment provides.

Other companies take a proactive stance towards the marketing environment. Rather than simply watching and reacting, these firms take aggressive actions to affect the publics and forces in their marketing environment. Such companies hire lobbyists to influence legislation affecting their industries and stage media events to gain favourable press coverage. They run 'advertorials' (ads expressing editorial points of view) to shape public opinion. They press lawsuits and file complaints with regulators to keep competitors in line. They also form contractual agreements to better control their distribution channels.

By taking action, companies can often overcome seemingly uncontrollable business environmental constraints. For example:

> Cathay Pacific Airlines . . . determined that many travellers were avoiding Hong Kong because of lengthy delays at immigration. Rather than assuming that this was a problem they could not solve, Cathay's senior staff asked the Hong Kong government how to avoid these immigration delays. After lengthy discussions, the airline agreed to make an annual grant-in-aid to the government to hire more immigration inspectors – but these reinforcements would service primarily the Cathay Pacific gates. The reduced waiting period increased customer value and thus strengthened [Cathay's competitive advantage].[64]

Marketing management cannot always control environmental forces. In many cases, it must settle for simply watching and reacting to the environment. For example, a company would have little success in trying to influence geographic population shifts, the economic environment or important cultural values. But whenever possible, smart marketing managers will take a *proactive* rather than *reactive* approach to the marketing environment.

WHERE YOU DEMAND WE SUPPLY.

Behind Sam Singh, captain of a Shell G Class carrier, sit 135,000 cubic metres of liquefied natural gas (LNG).

On deck, it's a balmy 25 degrees. In the insulated LNG containers, it's minus 160°C.

Sam's carrier is just one of our specialised fleet that carries over nine million tonnes of LNG around the world every year.

They bridge the gap between places like Brunei, Oman and Nigeria, with an abundance of natural gas, and markets with a rapidly rising demand like Asia, the Americas and Europe.

We have been investing in our LNG operations for over forty years. Now these efforts are paying off handsomely.

Within ten years, the number of our LNG plants will have doubled. So too will the number of countries we supply.

Why? Because by 2025 gas, the cleanest fossil fuel, could well have overtaken oil as the world's predominant source of energy.

Developing and connecting the gas markets of the world is an increasingly crucial business in which no one matches our expertise and commitment.

And if people like Sam have anything to do with it, no one ever will.

To find out more about our Gas & Power business visit www.shell.com

Businesses face great pressure to balance economic progress with social responsibility. Here, the multinational company Shell articulates the need for striking a balance between the need to protect people's way of life and the environment and to provide sustainable, affordable energy.
SOURCE: Shell International.
Agency: J. Walter Thompson.

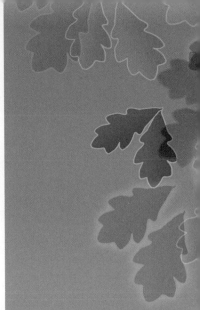

Reviewing the concepts

Companies must constantly watch and adapt to the *marketing environment* in order to seek opportunities and ward off threats. The marketing environment comprises all the actors and forces that affect the company's ability to transact business and to serve the needs of its target market effectively.

1. Describe the environmental forces that affect the company's ability to serve its customers

The company's marketing environment can be divided into the microenvironment and the macroenvironment. The *microenvironment* consists of other actors close to the company that combine to form the company's value delivery network or that affect its ability to serve its customers. It includes the company's *internal environment* – its departments and management levels – as it influences marketing decision making. *Marketing channel firms* – the firm's suppliers and marketing intermediaries, including resellers, physical distribution firms, financial intermediaries and marketing services agencies – cooperate to create customer value. Another set of forces include five types of customer *markets*: the consumer, producer, reseller, government and international markets. *Competitors* vie with the company in an effort to serve customers better. Finally, various *publics* – financial, media, government, citizen action, local, general and internal publics – have an actual or potential interest in, or impact on, the organisation's ability to meet its objectives.

The *macroenvironment* consists of larger societal forces that affect the entire microenvironment. The six forces making up the company's macroenvironment include demographic, economic, natural, technological, political and cultural forces. These forces shape opportunities and pose threats to the company.

2. Explain how changes in the demographic and economic environments affect marketing decisions

We addressed how changes in the demographic and economic environments affect marketing decisions. Today's *demographic environment* shows a changing age structure, shifting family profiles, international migration and increasing diversity. The *economic environment* includes factors that influence buying power and spending patterns. The trends are towards greater consumer concern for value. Financially squeezed consumers are also seeking just the right combination of good quality and service at a fair right price.

3. Identify the major trends in the firm's natural and technological environments

We identified the major trends in the firm's natural and technological environments. The *natural environment* shows these major trends: shortages of certain raw materials, higher pollution levels and more government intervention in natural resource management. The *technological environment* reveals rapid technological change, high R&D budgets and increased government regulation. Companies that fail to keep up with technological change will miss out on new product and marketing opportunities.

4. Explain the key changes in the political and cultural environments

Key changes are also observed in the political and cultural environments. The *political environment* consists of laws, agencies and groups that influence or limit marketing actions. The political environment has undergone three changes that affect marketing actions: increasing legislation regulating business, the rising importance of public interest groups, and increased emphasis on ethics and socially responsible actions. The *cultural environment* is made up of institutions and forces that affect a society's values, perceptions, preferences and behaviours. Although core values and beliefs held by society are fairly persistent, secondary cultural values are more open to change. Cultural values are reflected in peoples' views of themselves and others, as well as of organisations, society, nature and the universe. Some recent shifts in secondary cultural values include trends towards digital 'cocooning', less trust of institutions, greater appreciation for nature, a new spiritualism and realism and the search for more meaningful and enduring values.

5. Discuss how companies can react to the marketing environment

Companies can passively accept the marketing environment as an uncontrollable element to which they must adapt, avoiding threats and taking advantage of opportunities as they arise. Or, they can take a *proactive stance*, working to change the environment rather than simply reacting to it. Whenever possible, companies should try to be proactive rather than reactive.

Discussing the concepts

1. What can a mobile phones marketer do to take a more proactive approach to the changes in the company's marketing environment? Discuss specific forces, including macroenvironmental and microenvironmental forces. Identify the major market environmental trends that are likely to create opportunities and ones that will present threats to this company in the decade ahead.

2. What leading demographic factors must Internet service providers consider when marketing their products? Explain why each factor is so important to these providers.

3. Pressure groups, lobbyists and public interest groups play an important role in defending society's interests. Select one such group you are familiar with and describe its cause. How might goods or services providers targeted by the group respond to the demands or pressures imposed by the group?

4. Customers are becoming more concerned about the natural environment. Assume you are the marketing manager for a motor vehicle manufacturer. Your job is to reposition a sports utility vehicle (SUV) model that was once identified as a 'fuel guzzler'. The model now comes with a super-efficient, non-polluting hybrid engine. Which of the seven types of public discussed in this chapter would have the greatest impact on your plans for the more fuel-efficient model?

5. Is it a certainty that a company will lose out on new opportunities if it does not keep up with new technology? Explain. Can you think of an industry segment where technology may not play an important role?

Applying the concepts

1. Go to websites of your choice or ones that you are familiar with devoted to marketing music and movie downloads and mobile phone ring tones. These services have gained popularity in many countries across the globe. Which demographic group(s) is (are) most likely to adopt these products? What environmental forces have affected the growth of these products? Do you think that service providers have developed effective responses to meet the increasing demand for these products? Why? Why not?

2. Many well-known cause-related marketing campaigns are launched by companies with substantial resources. Using examples, discuss how smaller companies with more limited resources might implement successful cause-related marketing efforts. How can such organisations help charities with which they partner while successfully promoting their own products and services?

Web resources

For additional classic case studies and Internet exercises, visit **www. pearsoned.co.uk/ kotler**

References

1. Gillian McKeith, *You Are What You Eat* (London: Michael Joseph, 2004).

2. Richard Tomkins, 'Big food has a lot on its plate', *Financial Times* (12 February 2004); weightlossresources. co.uk; CMSinfo, 'Diet and fat free foods: a UK market briefing', Market Assessment Publications (1 November 2006), p. 73; 'Growth and its consequences: The perils of prosperity: Can you be too rich?', *The Economist* (27 April 2006).

3. See wikipedia.org/wiki/List_of_notable_business_failures for an ever-growing list of big business failures.

4. See airbus.com/store/mm_repository/pdf/att00007992/media_object_file_FAST38_Customer_Support. pdf. Diamondair also explains the economic consequences of AOG in its website diamondair.com/ aircraft/business_case.php#, and Smiths Aerospace has web pages devoted to helping out their customers and their customers' customers: smiths-aerospace.com/Products—/Customer-Services/ Service-Offerings/Aircraft-on-Ground/

5. See Sarah Lorge, 'The Coke advantage', *Sales & Marketing Management* (December 1998), p. 17; Chad Terhune, 'Coke wins a 10-year contract from Subway, ousting PepsiCo', *Wall Street Journal* (28 November 2003), p. B3; and 'The best in foodservice just got better', *Beverage Industry* (September 2004), pp. 15–16.

6. Sarah Laitner, 'EU urges action on falling population', *Financial Times* (18 March 2005); Quentin Peel, 'Indigestion', *Financial Times* (11 June 2007), p. 9.

7. See www.un.org/esa/population/unpop. Also see World POPClock, US Census Bureau, accessed online at www.census.gov, February 2007.

8. Adapted from Frederik Balfour, 'Educating the "Little Emperors": There's a big market for products that help China's coddled kids get ahead', *Business Week* (10 November 2003), p. 22. Also see Clay Chandler, 'Little emperors', *Fortune* (4 October 2004), pp. 138–50; and 'Hothousing little tykes', *Beijing Review* (5 May 2005), accessed at www.bjreview.com.cn/En-2005/05-18-e/china-5.htm.

9. See 'China's golden oldies', *The Economist* (26 February 2005), p. 74. Also see 'China economy: How do you prepare for the retirement of 1.3bn people?', *EIU ViewsWire* (27 March 2006).

10. Scott Schroder and Warren Zeller, 'Get to know Gen X and its segments', *Multichannel News* (21 March 2005), p. 55.

11. Gregg Bennett and Tony Lachowitz, 'Marketing to lifestyles: Action sports and Generation Y', *Sports Marketing Quarterly*, 13, 4 (2004), pp. 239–43. Copyright © 2004 Fitness Information Technology, Inc. Reproduced with permission in the format textbook via the Copyright Clearance Center. 'New Xbox 360 to be featured in college campus tour', *PR Newswire* (21 March 2006); William Strauss and Neil Howe, *Millennials Rising* (Vintage Books, 2000).

12. Samantha McCaughren, 'Burberry not impressed with its "chav" status', *Irish Independent* (14 April 2005).

13. Nicholas Timmins, 'Ageing populations pose challenges', Special Report: 'The world in 2005', *Financial Times* (26 January 2005), p. 2; 'Ageing population. Must try harder', *The Economist* (26 November 2005), p. 34; Stefan Wagstyl, 'An endangered species: fewer births make old Europe fear for its future', *Financial Times* (11 June 2004), p. 17; European Commission, *Demographic Statistics*, in addition to UN Population Division and OECD are further sources of information on population statistics and projections.

14. Details on the demographics of the European Union, accessed at http://en.wikipedia.org/wiki/Demographics_of_the_European_union, March 2007.

15. Katrin Bennhold, 'Europe faces labor shortages as population ages', *International Herald Tribune* (25 January 2007), accessed at www.iht.com/bin/, March 2007.

16. Stefan Wagstyl, 'An endangered species: fewer births make old Europe fear for its future', *Financial Times* (11 June 2004), p. 17; 'A survey of the 20th century. On the yellow brick road', *The Economist* (11 September 1999), p. 6; 'Too many or too few', *The Economist* (25 September 1999), p. 19; 'Like herrings in a barrel', *The Economist* (31 December 1999), pp. 13–14.

17. 'Out of Africa', *The Economist* (14 June 2003), p. 32; Martin Wolf, 'Demography: people, plagues and prosperity: five trends that promise to transform the world's population within 50 years', *Financial Times* (27 February 2003), p. 17.

18. Simon Briscoe, 'Women with degrees "more likely to reject motherhood"', *Financial Times* (25 April 2003), p. 4; Paul Bettes, 'Ageing Europe faces up to need for pension reform', *Financial Times* (28 August 2003), p. 18; 'Krybbe to grave', in 'Dancing to a new tune: a survey of the Nordic region', *The Economist* (14 June 2003), pp. 10–13; 'Turning boomers into boomerangs', *The Economist* (18 February 2006), pp. 75–7.

19. 'The grey market. Hey, big-spender', *The Economist* (3 December 2005), pp. 79–80.

20. Dan Roberts, 'The ageing business: Companies and marketers wrestle with adapting their products to older consumers' demands', *Financial Times* (20 January 2004), p. 19.

21. Data on household composition accessed online at http://europa.eu.int/comm/eurostat/Public/datashop/; also, information on changing US household composition accessed online at www.census.gov/population/projections/nation/hh-fam/.

22. *Eurostat Yearbook 2006–07* available for download at epp.eurostat.ec.europa.eu.

23. Scheherazade Daneshku and George Parker, 'Hostile UK fails to see benefits of migration', *Financial Times* (19 February 2007), p. 1; Ralph Atkins, 'Europeans' low expectations of eurozone prove widespread', *Financial Times* (29 January 2007), p. 8.

24. Sarah Laitner, 'EU urges action on falling population', *Financial Times* (18 March 2005); 'Migration' and 'Immigration and emigration', in 'Demographics of the European Union', accessed at http://en.wikipedia.org/wiki/Demographics_of_the_European_Union (March 2007), pp. 2–3; Stefan Wagstyl, 'Migration. An important test of tolerance', *Financial Times*, Special Report: The World in 2007 (24 January 2007), p. 8; 'Europe's huddled masses', *The Economist* (20 January 2007), pp. 45–6; Andrew Taylor and Miranda Green, 'Influx heats up immigration debate', *Financial Times* (23 August 2006), p. 2; Jean Eaglesham and Scheherazade Daneshkhu, 'Number of immigrants soars past forecasts', *Financial Times* (11 November 2004), p. 3. See also Philippe Legrain, *Immigrants: Your country needs them* (Little, Brown, 2007).

25. Information accessed at www.rivendellmarketing.com/ngng/ngng_profiles_set.html, June 2005; Deborah L. Vence, 'Younger GLBT market spells opportunities', *Marketing News* (1 April 2006), pp. 17, 19; Stuart Elliott, 'Hey, gay spender, marketers spending time with you', *New York Times* (26 June 2006), p. C8; www.planetoutinc.com/sales/market.html, July 2006; Laura Wood, 'Is this image of the gay consumer as a high-spending, frequent travelling goldmine reality?', *Business Wire* (21 May 2007).

26. See John Fetto and Todd Wasserman, 'IBM targets gay business owners', *Adweek* (6 October 2003), p. 8; and information from www-03.ibm.com/employment/us/diverse/awards.shtml#glbt, July 2006. The Las Vegas example is adapted from information found in Chris Jones, 'Come out, come out', *Las Vegas Review Journal* (5 March 2006), p. 1E.

27. Catherine Moye, FT Weekend – House & home: 'Thank goodness, the gays are here', *Financial Times* (4 September 2004).

28. Ralph Atkins and Andrew Bounds, FT Report – The future of Europe: 'EU needs careful nurturing to flourish', FT.com; 'European competition policy needs urgent reform', *Financial Times* (4 June 2007); 'Fit at 50?', *The Economist* (15 March 2007); George Parker, Tobias Buck and Bertrand Benoit, 'Key clause

dropped from draft EU treaty', FT.com (21 June 2007), p. 1; Tobias Buck, 'Dismay over competition threat', *Financial Times* (22 June 2007), p. 6.

29. For updates on the Euro area, visit http://ec.europa.eu/economy_finance/euro/our_currency_en.htm

30. For a more detailed discussion and analysis of EU enlargement, see http://en.wikipedia.org/wiki/ Enlargement_of_the-European_Union; 'When east meets west' in 'A survey of the EU enlargement', *The Economist* (22 November 2003); also see Stefan Wagstyl, 'Opening the door: As Europe prepares to end the divisions of the past, the disputes of the present cast a shadow', *Financial Times* (2 January 2004).

31. Scheherazade Daneshkhu, 'Financial services aided by European migration', *Financial Times* (27 March 2007); Sarah Laitner and Bertrand Benoit, 'Brussels wants fewer rules on migration', *Financial Times* (14 June 2007); Hamish McRae, 'Resentment, racism and the reality of mass migration in a globalised economy', *The Independent* (19 April 2006).

32. Bradley Johnson, 'Recession's long gone, but America's average income isn't budging', *Advertising Age* (17 April 2006), p. 22; 'The wealth of nations: Winner takes (almost) all', *The Economist* (7 December 2006).

33. 'How Levi Strauss rekindled the allure of Brand America', *World Trade* (March 2005), p. 28; Levi Strauss press releases, accessed at www.levistrauss.com (27 May 2006), and their website at www.levis.com, July 2006.

34. Leslie Crawford, FT Report – Spain: 'Industries get hot under the collar', *Financial Times* (21 June 2007); Sheila McNulty, FT Report – Energy: 'Afraid of backing the wrong horse', *Financial Times* (19 June 2007), p. 3; Peter Williams, 'Farmers told to prepare for loss of irrigation water', *AAP News – Australasia* (20 June 2007).

35. 'A sparky new policy', *The Economist* (13 January 2007), p. 61.

36. 'Gentlemen, start your engines', *The Economist* (21 January 2006), pp. 81–2; James Mackintosh, 'Cost cuts are the key to success of the Prius', *Financial Times* (16 June 2005), p. 28; 'Driven by oil price', *The Economist* (28 April 2004), p. 54; 'Not so shocking', *The Economist* (29 July 2006), p. 81; Dan Glaister, 'Batteries included', *The Guardian* (22 August 2006), pp. 6–9.

37. 'Up in smoke', *The Economist* (13 January 2007), pp. 30–1.

38. Oliver Morton, 'Cool it', in 'The World in 2007', *The Economist* (2007), p. 156.

39. Fiona Harvey, 'Cold comfort as the globe warms', Special Report – Business & Water, *Financial Times* (21 March 2007), p. 14.

40. Fiona Harvey, 'A good time to be a green entrepreneur', *Financial Times* (22 February 2006), p. 13.

41. Fiona Harvey, *op cit.*; 'One man's move into the sunlight', *Financial Times* (22 February 2006), p. 13.

42. John Reed, 'EU's CO$_2$ rules put carmakers at risk', *Financial Times* (21 March 2007), p. 27; Tobias Buck and Andrew Bounds, 'Top-end carmakers to bear brunt of drive to cut carbon dioxide emissions', *Financial Times* (8 February 2007), p. 5; Special Report – Aircraft emissions: 'The sky's the limit', *The Economist* (10 June 2006), pp. 81–3.

43. John Blau, 'RFID – the price must be right', *Financial Times* (30 May 2006), accessed at www.ft.com, March 2007; Jack Neff, 'P&G products to wear wire', *Advertising Age* (15 December 2004), pp. 1, 32; 'Gartner says worldwide RFID spending to surpass $3 billion in 2010', *BusinessWire* (13 December 2005); and information accessed online at www.autoidlabs.org, August 2006.

44. 'Screen test: Stringer's strategy will signal to what extent Sony can stay in the game', *Financial Times* (21 September 2007), p. 17.

45. Stephen Pritchard, 'Why the EU is worried about RFID', *Financial Times* (30 May 2006), accessed at www.ft.com, March 2007; Ken Munro, 'Broadcast your details with an RFID passport', *Financial Times* (28 February 2007), p. 8.

46. John Willman, 'Small business hit by over-use of EU rules', *Financial Times* (7 September 2006), p. 3.

47. CIM Insights Team, cited in *The Chartered Institute of Marketing. Hot Marketing*, Issue 9 (January 2006), p. 3; further details accessed at www.cimtraining.com, March 2007.

48. 'Red tape in Europe. Regulatory over-reach?', *The Economist* (9 December 2006), p. 78; 'Regulating chemicals. No thanks, we're Europeans', *The Economist* (26 November 2005), p. 79.

49. Tobias Buck, 'Microsoft fined for flouting EU ruling', *Financial Times* (13 July 2006), p. 17; Tobias Buck, 'Microsoft faces new antitrust complaint', *Financial Times* (23 February 2006), p. 1; Daniel Dombey, 'Brussels spells out future for Microsoft', *Financial Times* (26 March 2004), p. 25.

50. 'EU rules aim to outlaw spam', *Marketing Business* (May 2003), p. 6; for more information on the new EU directive on consumer privacy and electronic communications, visit www.informationcommissioner. gov.uk.

51. David Ibison and Emiko Terazono, 'Norway declares Apple's iTunes illegal', *Financial Times* (25 January 2007), p. 26; Economic Focus. 'Apples are not the only fruit', *The Economist* (8 July 2006), p. 80; 'Online music. Your fix or mine?', *The Economist* (11 March 2006), p. 72.

52. 'Junk food. A little less of what you fancy', *The Economist* (6 January 2007), p. 27; Jenny Wiggins, 'Food companies urged to weigh up risks', *Financial Times* (21 July 2006), p. 3; Lauren Foster and Jenny Wiggins, 'Children targeted online by food sector', *Financial Times* (20 July 2006), p. 10.

53. Adapted from descriptions found at www.yankelovich.com/products/lists.aspx, August 2006; http://www. europeansocialsurvey.org/

54. Jonathan Guthrie, 'Enterprise enters the social mainstream', *Financial Times* (22 June 2007), p. 4, based on a report from the London School of Economics in conjunction with Shell Livewire, a youth enterprise body.

55. Adapted from Ronald Grover, 'Trading the bleachers for the couch', *BusinessWeek* (22 August 2005), p. 32; 'Bands may be hit by smoking ban', *BBC News 24* (29 March 2004, news.bbc.co.uk/1/hi/ entertainment/music/3579849.stm); 'Staying in is "the new night out"', *Edinburgh Evening News* (14 May 2005); Susie Mesure, 'Smoking ban will burn a hole in beer sales, pubs warned', *Independent on Sunday* (17 June 2007).

56. 'Decked out', *Inside* (Spring 2006), pp. 76–7.

57. Simon Busch, 'A stimulating tool to help children grow', *Financial Times* (20 April 2007); Brian Viner, 'What better training for life than to climb trees?', *The Independent* (14 June 2007).

58. Robert Howell, 'How accounting executives looked the wrong way', FT Summer School Day 7: Finance, Part I, *Financial Times* (13 August 2002), p. 11.

59. Laura Feldmann, 'After 9/11 highs, America's back to good ol' patriotism', *Christian Science Monitor* (5 July 2006), p. 1; 'America's fear of China: China is a far-from-cuddly beast; but bashing it is a bad idea', *The Economist* (17 May 2007); World Trade Organization, International Trade Statistics 2006, www.wto.org.

60. Jenny Wiggins, 'Brussels to vote on healthy-food laws', *Financial Times* (16 May 2006), p. 3.

61. 'Health consumerism. The wellness boom', *The Economist* (6 January 2007), pp. 51–2; Jenny Wiggins, 'Brussels to vote on healthy-food laws', *Financial Times* (16 May 2006), p. 3.

62. 'British identity. Waning', *The Economist* (27 January 2007), pp. 28–30.

63. Quotes from Myra Stark, 'Celestial season', *Brandweek* (16 November 1998), pp. 25–6; Becky Ebankamp, 'The young and righteous', *Brandweek* (5 April 2004), p. 18.

64. Howard E. Butz Jr and Leonard D. Goodstein, 'Measuring customer value: gaining strategic advantage', *Organizational Dynamics* (Winter 1996), pp. 66–7.

Company case 4 Toyota Prius: green or geek machine?

There are many reasons why people may want a revolutionary car. Some enthusiasts enthuse about scientific and technological advances and want the latest gizmos. Others rebel against fuel price increases. Finally, people are 'concerned about the environment'.

Hoping that all of the above was true, and looking to grab a technological advantage over other car manufacturers, in 2000 Toyota introduced Prius, their first hybrid car. Prius means 'to go before', so is a name that may be very prophetic. The Prius and the Honda Insight are the first in a wave of hybrid family cars coming out ahead of similar vehicles from GM, Ford and DaimlerChrysler.

At first glance, the Prius seems to have a lot going for it. It combines a 1.5 litre, four-cylinder petrol engine and a 33-kilowatt electric motor. It comfortably seats five, if the three in the back aren't too tall or too big, and has $0.34 m^3$ of luggage space. The electric motor starts the car and operates at low speeds, using a nickel metal-hydride battery. At higher speeds, the Prius automatically switches to the internal combustion engine. Under normal motorway driving conditions, it should get 28 km per litre.

The downside is that the Prius is no muscle car. Also, it is priced about €4,000 more than the Toyota Echo, although they are nearly the same car. European manufacturers also estimate that hybrids cost between €3,300 and €5,800 more to make than a conventional car, therefore giving Toyota little margin. Of course, getting twice as many kilometres per litre of petrol will help to offset the price differential. Assuming the range and a typical 2007 price of €1/litre, the Prius owner would have to buy 4,000 litres of petrol, enough fuel for 112,000 km, which could take years. Of course, if prices were to rise drastically, that could change. But even if fuel prices doubled, you'd have to drive more than 50,000 km to make up the initial price difference.

The picture gets even gloomier when you realise that no one is going to get the estimated fuel consumption anyway. The Environmental Protection Agency (EPA) has admitted that its testing procedure overstates petrol mileage by as much as 15 per cent. It tests cars on a chassis dynamometer, where the driven wheels turn freely on a set of rotating drums – far from normal driving conditions. In addition, hybrids use regenerative braking to recharge their batteries, with the result that braking during the EPA driving cycle is feeding more energy back into the system, boosting estimated petrol mileage.

Although this offers a fuel saving, the overall cost of ownership looks less attractive. Compared with the conventionally powered Toyota Avensis 1.8 T3-S, the Prius looks poor value. Although the Prius saves on fuel, its overall running cost comes out higher than that of the equivalent Avensis. The reason is its 25 per cent higher service or contract hire cost.

Are consumers ready for hybrids?

On the brighter side, Toyota and its competitors believe that costs will decrease once production of hybrids begins to yield economies of scale. The benefits of scale would not stop with the producer. For example, a major part of the cost of the car is the nickel metal-hydride batteries. A company such as Panasonic could reduce the cost of producing batteries through research and development, if the market merited such an investment, and could further reduce the price of batteries through its own economies of scale.

However, realising that cost reductions are some way off and that fuel savings aren't going to be the key to convincing people to purchase the Prius, car manufacturers have asked for tax incentives to stimulate purchase of clean-fuel and high-mileage cars. Several governments are providing incentives to people to buy hybrid cars. The US government offers $2,000 (€1,500) federal income-reduction and the UK government offers reduced car tax on initial purchase. Electric car drivers can also avoid London's £8 (€11) per day Congestion Charge.

Are consumers ready for hybrids? Do improved gas mileage and emissions standards affect their buying decision? A glance at car sales in the last 10 years would suggest not. The biggest sales growth was in gas-guzzling 4 × 4s. After all, we rarely saw Range Rovers 10 years ago; now they're a fairly common sight. People, it seems, think it's a good idea for their neighbours to drive 'green machines' but not themselves.

Actually, when the Prius was introduced, it flew out of dealers' showrooms. Between July and October 2000, Toyota sold 2,610 Priuses and had difficulty keeping up with demand. By the end of October 2000, the cars were waitlisted until January 2001. The Prius is still hard to buy. By 2007 a million had been sold worldwide but the waiting list had grown to 18 months. Of course, much of that sales success is attributable to Toyota's clever marketing. Toyota began educating consumers about the Prius. The company established a website to distribute information and also sent e-brochures to 40,000 likely buyers just before the introduction. Within two weeks, Toyota sold 1,800 cars based on the e-mail message alone.

In all, Toyota spent €15m on promoting the Prius. There were print ads in magazines, television advertising and the Internet. Ads running before the actual introduction used the tag line 'A car that sometimes runs on gas power and sometimes runs on electric power, from a company that always runs on brain power'. These ads helped to position Toyota as an 'environmentally concerned' company and more subtly stressed the technology aspect of the car. After introduction, the ads appealed more to emotion, with tag lines such as 'When it sees red, it charges' – a reference to the car's recharging at traffic lights. The headline captured the consumer's attention through ambiguity. Only through focusing on the ad could the consumer learn why the headline was accurate. Again, the appeal is based on the technology of the car. Finally, Toyota took advantage of Earth Day to send out green seed cards shaped like Toyota's logo to prospective buyers, wrapped some Priuses in green, and gave away cars at Earth Day events.

Of course, €15m is just a drop in the ocean compared to Toyota's annual marketing budget of €200m, but Toyota was satisfied with the effectiveness of the campaign, given the 'newness' of the car and the need to explain its technology. Much of this success can also be attributed to the narrow targeting of the ads. The company expected the first hybrid car buyers to be 'techies' and early adopters (people who are highly likely to buy something new). They were right. Many Prius owners are immersed in the technology. They flood chatrooms with discussion of the car. The Priusenvy.com website urges owners to 'Kick some gas'.

Owners immediately began tinkering with the car's computer system. One owner was able to add cruise control (an option not offered by Toyota) by wiring in a few switches in the car's computer system. The founder of Priusenvy.com worked out how to use the car's dashboard display screen to show files from his laptop, play video games, and look at rear-view images from a video camera pointed out of the back of the car. One Austrian consumer installed a sniffer – a device on the car's computer network that monitors electronic messages. With the sniffer, he will be able to hook up add-ons such as a MiniDisc Player, an MP3 player, a laptop computer and a TV tuner. In the past, owners using mechanical skills customised cars with paint, lowered bodies and souped-up engines. In the future, customisation may rely on being computer savvy.

Hollywood has also fallen for the Prius. It might not have an Italian designer label, but on Sunset Strip, green is the new black. It seems that being seen to be environmentally responsible is now cool – the list of celebrity owners of the Prius includes Cameron Diaz, Leonardo DiCaprio and Jim Carrey. Even Arnold Schwarzenegger has one to park alongside his gigantic Hummer.

Even though the Internet is a major part of the Prius launch, Toyota does not sell the car from its website. Buyers go to prius.toyota.com online to pick a colour and decide whether they want a CD player and floor mats – the only options available from Toyota. After that, the dealers get involved, but it takes specially trained salespeople to explain and promote the Prius. Consequently, only 75 per cent of Toyota dealers handle the car. Many of them are not happy about the need to train salespeople. And why should they be? Margins are higher on gas-guzzlers, which are also easier to sell.

Given dealer reluctance and consumer resistance, why have Toyota and Honda spent so much on their hybrids? While part of the answer is government regulations, a bigger part of the answer is competition. Toyota have gained a technological initiative in the hybrid market and, even more importantly, have captured people's imagination. They are early winners in the public relations war. Environmentally conscious companies, such as IKEA, are switching their entire UK fleets to hybrids in a move, if successful, to roll out across the world.

European manufacturers are frustrated by the attention that politicians and the media bestow upon hybrids. Citroën compare their CZ, C1 and C3 cars with the Toyota and Honda Civic IMA hybrid. While the CZ, C1 and C3 all have marginally higher CO_2 emissions only slightly worse (108, 109 and 110 g/km respectively) than the 104 g/km of the Prius, all three cars have better fuel consumption (68.9, 68.9 and 67.3 mpg respectively) than the 65.7 mpg of the Prius. Compared with all of these, the Honda's 116 g/km and 57.3 mpg look very poor. What France has achieved with lean cars Germany is doing with technology. German advanced technology machines walked away with the top three places in the Green Car Awards at the 2007 New York motor show. First went to the Mercedes E320 Bluetec that covers 1,125 km on a tank of diesel. Runners-up were BMW's Hydrogen 7 and Volkswagen's Polo Blue Motion.

Hybrid motor cars may not be all they have been cracked up to be, but high petrol prices are driving rising demand for greener cars. Indeed, high fuel price is a boost for the Prius. Toyota is still market leader in the segment and expected to sell over 400,000 hybrids in 2006 alone.

Other car makers are racing to catch up. Ironically, most of the effort is going into making gas-guzzlers guzzle a little less. Ford has launched the world's first hybrid sports utility vehicle, while Mercedes and General Motors have rolled out giant hybrid pick-up trucks. Others are touting alternatives to petrol-driven engines. Ford's Focus FFV (flexible fuel vehicle) was launched in 2005. In Sweden, 40 per cent of all Fords sold are already FFVs. Vauxhall/Opel also offers FFV Corsa, Astra and Zafira models that can run on LPG (liquid petroleum gas) made from butane and propane and, at the flick of a button, on petrol as well.

Questions

1. What microenvironmental factors affect the introduction and sales of the Toyota Prius? How well has Toyota dealt with these factors?

2. Outline the major macroenvironmental factors – demographic, economic, natural, technological, political and cultural – that have affected the introduction and sales of the Toyota Prius. How has Toyota dealt with each of these factors?

3. Evaluate Toyota's marketing strategy so far. What has Toyota done well? How might it improve its strategy?

4. In your opinion, what are the advantages of Toyota's early entry into the hybrid market? What are the disadvantages? Have Toyota jumped too early into an expensive technology that has had its day?

SOURCES: Jeffrey Ball, 'Hybrid gas–electric car owners can get income-tax deductions', *Wall Street Journal* (22 May 2002), p. D8; Karl Greenberg, 'A wildflower grows in Torrance as Toyota gets environmentally aware', *Brandweek* (20 May 2002), p. 42; John McElroy, 'A long time coming', *Ward's Auto World* (July 2001), p. 21; Margot Roosevelt, 'Hybrid power', *Time* (11 December 2000), pp. 94–5; 'Toyota prices', *What Car? Road Test Directory* (February/ March 2004), p. 113; *What Car Buyer Guide* (March 2004), p. 253; James Mackintosh and Richard Milne, 'Hybrid makers learn to fuse green credentials with profit', *Financial Times* (20 September 2005), p. 20; John Griffiths, 'Carmakers fume at hybrids' advantage', *Financial Times* (7 October 2007), p. 3; David O'Grady, 'This year's green machines', *Independent* (18 July 2006), p. 15; John Reed and Richard Milne, 'An embattled industry tries to engineer itself out of a hole', *Financial Times* (27 April 2007), p. 11; John Reed, 'Ikea switches UK car fleet to hybrids', *Financial Times* (11 June 2007), p. 24.

No one grows Ketchup like Heinz.

What do I want? Everything! When do I want it? Now!

GRAFFITI

Consumer markets

Mini Contents List

Like a true nature's child
We were born, born to be wild

Steppenwolf, 'Born to be wild', MCA Music, 1968

Previewing the concepts

In the previous chapter, you studied the marketing environment: the *microenvironment* that is specific to an organisation's operation, such as suppliers and competitors; and the *macroenvironment* of wider forces that shape society, such as the natural and political environments.

In this and the next chapter, we'll continue with a closer look at the most important element of the marketplace – customers. The aim of marketing is to affect how customers think about and behave towards the organisation and its market offerings. To influence the *whats*, *whens* and *hows* of buying behaviour, marketers must first understand the *whys*. In this chapter, we look at buying influences and processes of the *final consumer*. In the next chapter, we'll study the buyer behaviour of *business customers*. You will see that under- standing buyer behaviour is an essential but very difficult task. In the final chapter of Part 2, we look at ways of gathering and organising market information, a process that is guided by an understanding of buyer behaviour.

After reading this chapter, you should be able to:

1. Define the consumer market and construct a simple model of consumer buyer behaviour.
2. Tell how culture, subculture and social class influence consumer buying behaviour.
3. Describe how consumers' personal characteristics and primary psychological factors affect their buying decisions.
4. List and understand the major types of buying decision behaviour and the stages in the buyer decision process.
5. Discuss how consumer decision making varies with the type of buying decision.

To get a better sense of the importance of understanding consumer behaviour, let's look first at Harley-Davidson, top-selling cult motorcycles. Who rides these big Harley 'Hogs'? What moves them to tattoo their bodies with the Harley emblem, abandon home and hearth for the open road, and flock to Harley rallies by the hundreds of thousands across the world? *You* might be surprised, but Harley-Davidson knows.

Prelude case Harley-Davidson Motorfietsen – Tijd om te rijden

Travel to the historic fortified town of Breda, in the south of The Netherlands, expecting a quiet walk through its many pedestrian squares and streets on the wrong day and you would be in for a shock. It is the town's Harley-Davidson day when the narrow streets and cafés are taken over by 6,000 big, gnarling, sparking Harleys with their leather and denim-clad rough and tough-looking owners. Noisy and not a little intimidating!

Supposedly the biggest one-day Harley event in Europe, the Breda day is one of many across the world: from the mother of them all, the annual Daytona Beach Bike Week attended by 500,000 people, to the European Bike Week in Faak, Austria, and the New Zealand National H.O.G., Auckland.

Few brands engender the intense loyalty of Harley-Davidson owners. Harley buyers have granite-like devotion to the brand. 'You don't see people tattooing Yamaha on their bodies,' observes the publisher of *Iron*, an industry publication. And according to another industry insider, 'For a lot of people, it's not that they want a motorcycle; it's that they want a Harley – the brand is that strong.' 'I'd rather push a Harley than drive a Honda,' proclaimed a T-shirt of a committed Harley owner in Breda.

Riding such intense emotions, Harley-Davidson has cruised to the top of the heavyweight motorcycle market. For several years running, sales have outstripped supply, with customer waiting lists of up to two years for popular models and street prices running well above suggested list prices. During just the past five years, Harley sales have increased more than 50 per cent, and earnings have jumped more than 75 per cent. By 2006, the company had experienced 20 straight years of record sales and income growth.

Harley-Davidson's marketers spend a great deal of time thinking about customers and their buying behaviour. They want to know who their customers are, what they think and how they feel, and why they buy a Harley Fat Boy Softtail rather than a Yamaha or a Kawasaki or a big Honda American Classic. What is it that makes Harley buyers so fiercely loyal? These are difficult questions; even Harley owners themselves don't know exactly what motivates their buying. But Harley management puts top priority on understanding customers and what makes them tick.

Who rides a Harley? You might be surprised. It's no longer the Hell's Angels crowd – the burly, black-leather-jacketed rebels and biker chicks who once made up Harley's core clientele. Motorcycles are attracting a new breed of riders – older, more affluent and better educated. Harley now appeals more to 'rubbies' (rich urban bikers) than to rebels. 'While the outlaw bad-boy biker image is what we might typically associate with Harley riders,' says an analyst, 'they're just as likely to be CEOs or investment bankers.' The average Harley customer is a 46-year-old husband with a median household income of €60,000. Also, more than 10 per cent of Harley purchases today are made by women, often as part of a 'his and hers' pairing.

Harley-Davidson makes good bikes, and to keep up with its shifting market, the company has upgraded its showrooms and sales approaches. But Harley customers are buying a lot more than just a quality bike and a smooth sales pitch. To gain a better understanding of customers' deeper motivations,

Harley-Davidson conducted focus groups in which it invited bikers to make cut-and-paste collages of pictures that expressed their feelings about Harley-Davidsons. (Can't you just see a bunch of hard-core bikers doing this?) It then mailed out 16,000 surveys containing a typical battery of psychological, sociological and demographic questions as well as subjective questions such as 'Is Harley more typified by a brown bear or a lion?'

The research revealed seven core customer types: adventure-loving traditionalists, sensitive pragmatists, stylish status-seekers, laid-back campers, classy capitalists, cool-headed loners, and cocky misfits. However, all owners appreciated their Harleys for the same basic reasons. 'It didn't matter if you were the guy who swept the floors of the factory or if you were the CEO at that factory, the attraction to Harley was very similar,' says a Harley executive. 'Independence, freedom and power were the universal Harley appeals.' 'It's much more than a machine,' says the analyst. 'It is part of their own self-expression and lifestyle.' Another analyst suggests that owning a Harley makes you 'the toughest, baddest guy on the block. Never mind that [you're] a dentist or an accountant. You [feel] wicked astride all that power.' Your Harley renews your spirits and announces your independence. As the Harley website's home page announces, 'Thumbing the starter of a Harley-Davidson does a lot more than fire the engine. It fires the imagination.' Adds a Harley dealer: 'We sell a dream here.' The classic look, the throaty sound, the very idea of a Harley – all contribute to its mystique. Owning this 'dream' makes you a part of something bigger, a member of the Harley family.

Such strong emotions and motivations are captured in a classic Harley-Davidson advertisement. The ad shows a close-up of an arm, the bicep adorned with a Harley-Davidson tattoo. The headline asks, 'When was the last time you felt this strongly about anything?' The ad copy outlines the problem and suggests a solution: 'Wake up in the morning and life picks up where it left off. . . . What once seemed exciting has now become part of the numbing routine. It all begins to feel the same. Except when you've got a Harley-Davidson. Something strikes a nerve. The heartfelt thunder rises up, refusing to become part of the background. Suddenly things are different; clearer; more real. As they should have been all along. Riding a Harley changes you from within. The effect is permanent. Maybe it's time you started feeling this strongly. Things are different on a Harley.'[1]

Questions

1. Most products and personalities come and go but others, like the Harley-Davidson, James Dean, the VW Beetle, John Lennon, Victorinox penknives, Che Guevara, Doc Martin boots, Marilyn Monroe, etc., achieve long-lasting cult status. Why do you think this occurs?

2. Harley-Davidson makes motorcycles. What do Harley-Davidson owners buy?

3. How do you think the buying process for buying a Harley-Davidson differs from buying other €20,000 products?

Introduction

The Harley-Davidson example shows that many different factors affect consumer buyer behaviour. Since the human mind contains as many interacting neurones as there are leaves in the Amazon jungle, it is not surprising that buying behaviour is not simple. Complicated it is, but understanding buyer behaviour is central to marketing management. Just as marketing ends with consumption, so marketing management must begin with understanding customers.

> Just as marketing ends with consumption, so marketing management must begin with understanding customers.

Consumer buying behaviour—The buying behaviour of final consumers – individuals and households who buy goods and services for personal consumption.

Consumer market—All the individuals and households who buy or acquire goods and services for personal consumption.

This chapter explores the dynamics of consumer behaviour and the consumer market. **Consumer buying behaviour** refers to the buying behaviour of final consumers – individuals and households who buy goods and services for personal consumption. All of these final consumers combined make up the **consumer market**. The world consumer market will consist of about 7 billion people by 2010, but the billion people living in North America, Western Europe and Japan still make up 70 per cent of the world's spending power, although a few of the new rich in the BRIC countries are now joining these super-consumers.[2] Even within these wealthy consumer markets, consumers vary tremendously in age, income, education level and tastes. They also buy an incredible variety of goods and services. How these diverse consumers make their choices among various products embraces a fascinating array of factors.

Models of consumer behaviour

> . . . *what* and *where* and *when* and *why* and *how* and *who*.

In earlier times, marketers could understand consumers well through the daily experience of selling to them. But as firms and markets have grown in size, many marketing decision makers are physically, demographically or socially remote from their customers and so must now turn to consumer research. They spend more money than ever to study consumers, trying to learn more about consumer behaviour. Author and poet Rudyard Kipling wrote:

I have six honest serving men
They taught me all I knew
Their names were what and where and when
And why and how and who

These six questions remain an excellent guide to analysing consumer behaviour: *What* do consumers buy? *Where* do they buy? *When* do they buy? *Why* do they buy? *How* do they buy? *Who* buys?[3]
Marketers must figure out what is in the buyer's 'black box'.[4]

'For companies with billions . . . on the line, the buying decision is the most crucial part of their enterprise,' states one consumer behaviour analyst. 'Yet no one really knows how the human brain makes that choice.' Often, consumers themselves don't know exactly what influences their purchases. 'Buying decisions are made at an unconscious level,' says the analyst, 'and . . . consumers don't generally give very reliable answers if you simply ask them, "Why did you buy this?"'[5]

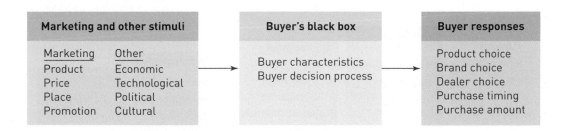

Figure 5.1 Stimulus–response model of buyer behaviour

The central question for marketers is: How do consumers respond to various marketing efforts the company might use? The starting point is the stimulus–response model of buyer behaviour shown in Figure 5.1. This figure shows that marketing and other stimuli enter the consumer's 'black box' and produce certain responses.

> For a long time what went on inside the black box of a human's brain was a complete mystery but researchers are now using functional magnetic resolution imaging (fMRI) to look inside the brain as it works. **Neuromarketing**, the use of neuro-technology to improve marketing decision making, helps us understand how people search the web, respond to brands, ads or scan supermarket shelves . . . One realisation from this research is that the brain activity for an action seems to begin about half a second before a person consciously decides to take an action. This suggests that we are not so much consciously 'making' a decision so much as becoming aware that a decision has been made. So far the discoveries from this research have not changed how we market, but the technology to aid neuromarketing is advancing fast.[6]

Neuromarketing—the use of neuro-technology to improve marketing decision making.

Marketing stimuli consist of the Four Ps: product, price, place and promotion. Other stimuli include major forces and events in the buyer's environment: economic, technological, political and cultural. All these inputs enter the buyer's black box, where they are turned into a set of observable buyer responses: product choice, brand choice, dealer choice, purchase timing and purchase amount.

The marketer wants to understand how the stimuli are changed into responses inside the consumer's black box, which has two parts. First, the buyer's characteristics influence how he or she perceives and reacts to the stimuli. Second, the buyer's decision process itself affects the buyer's behaviour. We look first at buyer characteristics as they affect buyer behaviour and then discuss the buyer decision process.

Characteristics affecting consumer behaviour

Consumer purchases are influenced strongly by cultural, social, personal and psychological characteristics, as shown in Figure 5.2. For the most part, marketers cannot control such factors, but they must take them into account. We illustrate these characteristics for the case of a hypothetical customer, Anna Flores. Anna is a married graduate who works as a brand manager in a leading consumer packaged-goods company. She wants to buy a digital camera to take on holiday. Many characteristics in her background will affect the way she evaluates cameras and chooses a brand.

Figure 5.2 Factors influencing consumer behaviour

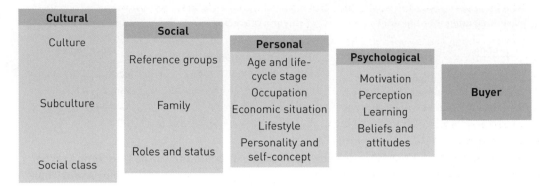

Cultural factors

Cultural factors exert the broadest and deepest influence on consumer behaviour. The marketer needs to understand the role played by the buyer's culture, subculture and social class.

Culture

Culture—The set of basic values, perceptions, wants and behaviours learned by a member of society from family and other important institutions.

Culture is the most basic cause of a person's wants and behaviour. Human behaviour is largely learned. Growing up in a society, a child learns basic values, perceptions, wants and behaviours from the family and other important institutions. Like most people in the Western world, in her childhood Anna observed and learned values about achievement and success, activity and involvement, efficiency and practicality, progress, material comfort, individualism, freedom, humanitarianism, youthfulness, and fitness and health. Sometimes we take these values for granted, but they are not cultural universals.

A trade delegation trying to market in Taiwan found this out the hard way. Seeking more foreign trade, they arrived in Taiwan bearing gifts of green caps. Unfortunately, the trip was a month before Taiwan elections, and green was the colour of the political opposition party. Even worse, according to Taiwan culture, a man wears green to signify that his wife has been unfaithful. The head of the delegation noted: 'I don't know whatever happened to those green hats, but the trip gave us an understanding of the extreme differences in our cultures.'[7]

Marketers are always trying to spot *cultural shifts* in order to imagine new products that might be wanted. For example, the cultural shift towards greater concern about health and fitness has created a huge industry for exercise equipment and clothing, lower-calorie and more natural foods, and health and fitness services.

> Danone is radically changing the foods portfolio to match increased concern for healthy living. Currently number two in the global biscuit industry, it is selling its interests in this low growth (high girth) sector to Kraft so that it can focus on the more dynamic, and healthy, drinks and dairy divisions. The acquisition of Dutch nutritional business Royal Numico NV following quickly after dumping biscuits.[8]

Further analysis of this cultural shift shows the complexity of consumer behaviour and how it varies internationally. The 13 per cent of America's population who go to the gym make it the most fitness-conscious nation, although 30 per cent of them are obese and 50 per cent overweight. In contrast, 7 per cent of the less obese British go to the gym while, in much slimmer France and Italy, only 4 per cent of the people take regular vigorous exercise.

The increased desire for leisure time has resulted in more demand for convenience products and services, such as microwave ovens and fast food. Consumers the world over are increasingly concerned about healthy eating. They are also tiring of the shopping and chopping needed to prepare family meals. According to market researchers Taylor Nelson Sofres, over the last 20 years the average time spent preparing a meal has dropped from one hour to 20 minutes. While many consumers express concern about food additives and genetically modified products, one of the fastest-growing markets is for functional foods that scientifically benefit health. For example, Flora Pro.activ is a margarine-like spread that is expensive but 'can dramatically reduce cholesterol to help maintain a healthy heart'.

Besides spending less time preparing food, eating is becoming less of a special event and more a casual activity undertaken while doing something else, such as meeting friends in an informal restaurant or watching TV. Makers of traditional crockery, such as Royal Doulton and Waterford Wedgwood, are shedding workers as they try to adjust to new consumers who no longer buy formal family dinner services but instead buy odd mugs and plates. Doing well out of the trend are craft potters, such as Moorcroft, who make expensive giftable pots, and Alchemy, who make inexpensive items for the catering trade.[9]

Subculture

Each culture contains smaller **subcultures** or groups of people with shared value systems based on common life experiences and situations. Subcultures include nationalities, religions, racial groups and geographic regions. Many subcultures make up important market segments and marketers often design products and marketing programmes tailored to their needs.

Subculture A group of people with shared value systems based on common life experiences and situations.

Islam is the world's fastest growing religion with millions of Muslims living in Europe – 1.3 million in Britain, 3.2 million in Germany and 4.2 million in France. The EU Muslim population is now greater than that of many EU countries, yet some European countries are still struggling over how and whether Muslim students and teachers should wear the headscarves that their beliefs prescribe. Meanwhile HSBC is set to offer Islamic financial products to this growing population. These differ from conventional financial products since they must follow three *sharia* rules:

1. Have no involvement with sinful industries, such as gambling, alcohol or pig meat.
2. A strict ban on *rib* – loosely translated as interest.
3. Avoid *gharar* – excessive risk taking and uncertainty.

Obeying these rules, for products that provide the same benefits as insurance, mortgages or hedge funds, demands creative solutions. For example, instead of providing a loan for a car, *sharia* rules are followed by a supplier of finance buying a car on a customer's behalf and selling it to the customer at a profit. The customer then pays for the car over a fixed period without paying any interest.[10]

The unification of Europe is creating subcultures across Europe. While young people are migrating from southern Europe and the new accession states to find well-paid work, older people from northern Europe are moving south to retire in the sun. Whole swathes of the Algarve in Portugal, and Spain's Costa del Sol, Majorca and the Canary Isles, are North European enclaves, while people moving from Poland have made Polish food one of the fastest growing parts of the grocery trade in some countries.[11]

Mature consumers are becoming an increasingly important market. Europe is old. By 2010 the EU's 81.7m people who are 65 years of age or older will make up 17.6 per cent of the EU's total population. This compares with 12 per cent in the US in 2010 and 10 per cent of the EU-25's population in 1960. By 2050, the EU-25's over-65 population is projected to grow to 134.5m, 29.9 per cent of people. Spain, with half its population older than 55 by 2050, will be the oldest country in the world, followed closely by Italy and Austria, with median ages projected to be 54.

Mature consumers are better off financially than are younger consumer groups. Because mature consumers have more time and money, they are an ideal market for exotic travel, restaurants, high-tech home entertainment products, leisure goods and services, designer furniture and fashions, financial services and healthcare services. Rock festivals are so being taken over by ageing rockers that Michael Eavis, who runs the Glastonbury Festival, is so concerned that he intends to try to recapture the youth market and appeal less to oldies in coming years. He could start by not headlining with The Who singing 'My Generation'.[12]

Their desire to look as young as they feel also makes more-mature consumers good candidates for cosmetics and personal care products, health foods, fitness products and other items that combat the effects of ageing. The best strategy is to appeal to their active, multi-dimensional lives. For example, Kellogg aired a TV spot for All-Bran cereal in which individuals ranging in age from 53 to 81 were featured playing ice hockey, water skiing, running hurdles and playing baseball, all to the tune of the Troggs singing 'Wild Thing'. And an Aetna commercial portrays a senior citizen who, after retiring from a career as a lawyer, fulfils a lifelong dream of becoming an archaeologist.

Like all other people, Anna Flores' buying behaviour will be influenced by her subculture identification. It will affect her food preferences, clothing choices, recreation activities and career goals. Subcultures attach different meanings to picture taking and this could affect both Anna's interest in cameras and the brand she buys.

Social class

Social classes—Relatively permanent and ordered divisions in a society whose members share similar values, interests and behaviours.

Almost every society has some form of social class structure. **Social classes** are society's relatively permanent and ordered divisions whose members share similar values, interests and behaviours. The registrar-general's six social classes have been widely used since the turn of the twentieth century, although all big countries have their own system. The UK Office of National Statistics uses the National Statistics Socio-Economic Classification (NS-SEC) to reflect the social changes of the last century (see Table 5.1). The scheme divides people according to their position in the

Table 5.1 National statistics – socioeconomic classification

Classification	Membership
1	Higher managerial and professional occupations
1.1	Employers and managers in large organisations (senior private and public sector employees)
1.2	Higher professionals (partners in law firms, etc.)
2	Lower managerial and professional occupations (middle managers and professionally qualified people)
3	Intermediate occupations (secretaries, policemen, etc.)
4	Small employers and sole traders
5	Lower supervisory, craft and related occupations (skilled manual workers)
6	Semi-routine occupations (shop assistants, etc.)
7	Routine occupations (semi-skilled or unskilled manual workers)

SOURCE: Office of National Statistics (ONS) Socioeconomic classification. Crown copyright material is reproduced with the permission of the Controller of HMSO under terms of the click-use licence.

labour market. Those at the bottom make a short-term exchange of cash for labour, while those at the top have long-term contracts and are rewarded by the prospect of career advancement and perks as well as a salary. Although not derived using income, the scale is a good predictor of both income and health, except for the self-employed Class 4 who are as healthy, but not as wealthy, as Classes 1 and 2. Currently the European Commission Task Force is working towards a standard set of variables for measuring socioeconomic analysis across Europe, although the data available still varies very much from country to country. In their Final Report the Task Force recommends 16 core social variables (Table 5.2). These show the changing nature of Europe, in particular the need to identify country of birth, citizenship and residence, and to recognise both legal and *de facto* marital status.[13]

Not only do class systems differ in various parts of the world: the relative sizes of the classes vary with the relative prosperity of countries. The 'diamond'-shaped classification (few people at the top and bottom with most in the middle) is typical of developed countries, although the Japanese and Scandinavian scales are flatter. In less developed countries, such as in Latin America and Africa, the structure is 'pyramid'-shaped with a concentration of poor people at the base. As countries develop, their class structure moves towards the diamond shape, although there is evidence that the gap between the richest and poorest in the English-speaking countries is now widening.

Some class systems have a greater influence on buying behaviour than others. In most western countries 'lower' classes may exhibit upward mobility, showing buying behaviour similar to that of the 'upper' classes. But in other cultures, where a caste system gives people a distinctive role, buying behaviour is more firmly linked to social class. Upper classes in almost all societies are often more similar to each other than they are to the rest of their own society. When selecting products and services, including food, clothing, household items and personal care products, they make choices that are less culture-bound than those of the lower classes. This tendency accounts for the strength of global luxury brands such as Burberry, Tag Heuer and Mont Blanc. Generally, the lower social classes are more culture-bound, although young people of all classes are less so and account for the global youth brands like adidas, Coca-Cola and Swatch.

Demographic information	**Sex** Age in completed years Country of birth Country of citizenship at time of data collection Legal marital status *De facto* marital status (consensual union) Household composition
Geographic information	Country of residence Region of residence Degree of urbanisation
Socioeconomic information	Self-declared labour status Status in employment Occupation in employment Economic sector employment Highest level of education completed Net monthly income of the household

Table 5.2 European core social variables

SOURCE: European Commission, *Task Force on Core Social Variables: Final Report*, (Brussels: Eurostat, 2007). Copyright © European Communities, 2007.

Anna Flores' occupation puts her in NS-SEC group 2 (lower managerial and professional occupations) although she has set her sights on achieving a 'higher managerial occupation'. Coming from a higher social background, her family and friends probably own expensive cameras and she might have dabbled in photography.

Social factors

A consumer's behaviour is also influenced by social factors, such as the consumer's small groups, family, and social roles and status. Because these social factors can strongly affect consumer responses, companies must take them into account when designing their marketing strategies.

Groups

Groups influence a person's behaviour. Groups that have a direct influence and to which a person belongs are called **membership groups**. Some are *primary groups* with whom there is regular but informal interaction – such as family, friends, neighbours and fellow workers. Children are particularly prone to these social pressures that account for the playground fads that permeate the school year and account for the annual convergence on a particular Christmas toy, such as Beyblades, Doctor Who Cyber Man Voice Changer Helmet and Nintendo Wii.[14] Some are *secondary groups*, which are more formal and have less regular interaction. These include organisations like religious groups, professional associations and trade unions.

Reference groups are groups that serve as direct (face-to-face) or indirect points of comparison or reference in forming a person's attitudes or behaviour. Reference groups to which they do not belong often influence people. For example, an **aspirational group** is one to which the individual wishes to belong, as when a teenage football fan follows David Beckham or a young girl idolises Amy Macdonald. They identify with them, although there is no face-to-face contact. Today's parents may be relieved that the modern pop 'heroes' are more agreeable than the rebels, acid freaks and punks that they followed.[15]

Marketers try to identify the reference groups of their target markets. Reference groups influence a person in at least three ways. They expose the person to new behaviours and lifestyles. They influence the person's attitudes and self-concept because he or she wants to 'fit in'. They also create pressures to conform that may affect the person's product and brand choices.

Membership groups— Groups that have a direct influence on a person's behaviour and to which a person belongs.

Reference groups— Groups that have a direct (face-to-face) or indirect influence on the person's attitudes or behaviour.

Aspirational group—A group to which an individual wishes to belong.

Michael Bragg of Thomas Pink explains: 'Men's designers have to dress CEOs of companies. Our sample [new] product goes to the CEO of the target companies because young corporate guys are always going to look up to the senior guys. Everyone says it is all casual, but in the business community it is not.' As one top banker explained, 'The most senior people drive influence. You emulate what you think is successful.' He found his tailor, Bhambi Custom Tailors – dresser of James Bonds – after 'admiring a suit on someone much more senior than me, a partner.'[16]

Opinion leaders—People within a reference group who, because of special skills, knowledge, personality or other characteristics, exert influence on others.

> Whether selling to kids or CEOs, [marketers] . . . must figure out how to reach opinion leaders.

Whether selling to kids or CEOs, manufacturers of products or services subjected to strong group influence must figure out how to reach **opinion leaders** – people within a reference group who, because of special skills, knowledge, personality or other characteristics, exert influence on others. Many marketers try to identify opinion leaders for their products and direct marketing efforts towards them. For example, the hottest trends in teenage music, language and fashion often start in major cities, then quickly spread to more mainstream youth in the suburbs. Thus, clothing companies that hope to appeal to fashion-conscious youth often make a concerted effort to monitor urban opinion leaders' style and behaviour. In other cases, marketers may use *buzz marketing* by enlisting or even creating opinion leaders to spread the word about their brands.

Frequent the right cafés . . . this summer, and you're likely to encounter a gang of sleek, impossibly attractive Vespa scooter riders who seem genuinely interested in getting to know you over an iced latte. Compliment them on their retro Vespa scooters glinting on the kerbside, and they'll happily pull out a pad and scribble down an address and phone number – not theirs, but that of the local 'boutique' where you can buy your own Vespa, just as (they'll confide) the rap artist Sisqo and the movie queen Sandra Bullock recently did. And that's when the truth hits you: this isn't any spontaneous encounter. Those scooter-riding models are on the Vespa payroll, and they've been hired to generate some favourable word of mouth for the recently reissued cult bikes. Welcome to the world of buzz marketing. Similar buzz marketers are now taking to the streets, cafés, nightclubs and the Internet, in record numbers. Their goal is to seek out the trendsetters in each community and subtly push them into talking up their brand to their friends and admirers.[17]

The importance of group influence varies across products and brands, but it tends to be strongest for conspicuous purchases, like a Vespa scooter. A product or brand can be conspicuous for one of two reasons. First, it may be noticeable because the buyer is one of the few people who own it – luxuries, such as a vintage Wurlitzer juke box or a Breitling Chronomat GT sports watch, are more conspicuous than necessities because fewer people own the luxuries. Second, a product such as Red Bull or Perrier can be conspicuous because the buyer consumes it in public where others can see it. Figure 5.3 shows how group influence might affect product and brand choices for four types of product – public luxuries, private luxuries, public necessities and private necessities.

In the past few years, a new type of social interaction has exploded onto the scene – online **social networking** – carried out over Internet media ranging from blogs to social networking sites such as MySpace.com and Facebook.com. This new form of high-tech buzz has big implications for marketers.

Social networking—Social interaction carried out over Internet media.

Group influence on brand choice

	Strong	Weak
Strong (Group influence on product choice)	Public Luxuries — Golf clubs, Snow skis, Yachts	Private Luxuries — TV video games, Waste disposal, Icemakers
Weak	Public Necessities — Wristwatches, Cars, Dress clothes	Private Necessities — Mattresses, Floor lamps, Refrigerators

Figure 5.3 Extent of group influence on product and brand choice
SOURCE: Adapted from William O. Bearden and Michael J. Etzel, 'Reference group influence on product and brand purchase decisions', *Journal of Consumer Research* (September 1982), p. 185, University of Chicago Press. Copyright © 1982, JCR, Inc.

Personal connections – forged through words, pictures, video and audio posted just for the [heck] of it – are the life of the new Web, bringing together the estimated 60 million bloggers, [an unbelievable] 72 million MySpace.com users, and millions more on single-use social networks where people share one category of stuff, like Flickr (photos), Del.icio.us (links), Digg (news stories), Wikipedia (encyclopaedia articles) and YouTube (video). . . . It's hard to overstate the coming impact of these new network technologies on business: they hatch trends and build immense waves of interest in specific products. They serve [up] giant, targeted audiences to advertisers. They edge out old media with the loving labour of amateurs. They effortlessly provide hyper-detailed data to marketers. If your customers are satisfied, networks can help build fanatical loyalty; if not, they'll amplify every complaint until you do something about it. [The new social networking technologies] provide an authentic, peer-to-peer channel of communication that is far more credible than any corporate flackery.[18]

Marketers are working to harness the power of these new social networks to promote their products and build closer customer relationships. For example, when Volkswagen set up a MySpace site for Helga, the German-accented, dominatrix-type blonde who appears in its controversial Volkswagen GTI ads, tens of thousands of fans signed up as 'friends'.[19] And companies regularly post ads or custom videos on video-sharing sites such as YouTube.

adidas recently reintroduced its adicolor shoe, a customisable white-on-white trainer with a set of seven colour markers. It signed up seven top creative directors to develop innovative videos designed especially for downloading to iPods and other handhelds. The directors were given complete creative control to interpret their assigned colour as they saw fit. 'The directors that we chose we feel have a good deal of underground street cred,' says an adidas marketing executive. The project was not tied specifically to the product. Rather, the directors were asked to 'celebrate colour, customization and personal expression'. The diverse set of short films was then released, one film a week, via e-mail and sites such as YouTube. The films drew more than 2.1 million viewers within three weeks, 20 million within the first two months, and the numbers were growing exponentially with each new release.[20]

Marketers need to be careful when tapping into online social networking. Ultimately, the users control the content, and online network marketing attempts can backfire.

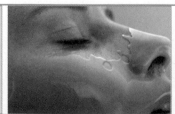

Social networking: adidas harnessed the power of social networks to reintroduce its customisable adicolor shoe. It developed innovative downloadable videos that celebrate colour and personal expression – here in pink – and then released them through e-mail and social networking sites like YouTube.

SOURCE: adidas.

General Motors tried to ignite a social network in order to promote one of their sports utility vehicles. Chevrolet's Web contest asked people to create their own ads for its Chevy Tahoe. The invitation excited masses of attention. Says one observer, 'the entries that got passed around, blogged about, and eventually covered in the mainstream media were all about the SUV's abysmal gas mileage and melting polar ice caps.' One user-generated ad proclaimed, 'Like this snowy wilderness? Better get your fill of it now. Then say hello to global warming.'[21]

Family

Family members can strongly influence buyer behaviour. We can distinguish between two families in the buyer's life. The buyer's parents make up the *family of orientation*. Parents provide a person with an orientation towards religion, politics and economics, and a sense of personal ambition, self-worth and love. Even if the buyer no longer interacts very much with his or her parents, the latter can still significantly influence the buyer's behaviour. In countries where parents continue to live with their children, their influence can be crucial.

Procter & Gamble came a cropper in the European market after their €40m launch of their new Charmin toilet roll. The company found the product's wet strength was wrong and it blocked European drains. Not because of the design of European toilets but because of a mode of consumer behaviour that must be learned in the family – how they use the toilet paper. Europeans fold their toilet paper while Americans scrunch it. 'This leads to different dynamics in the product,' says P&G; 'folding paper means you need more strength.' But even Europeans are not consistent. The British pay more than twice as much as Americans, French and Germans for their toilet rolls. Why? According to Kimberly-Clark the British demand a Rolls-Royce of toilet papers with a softer, more luxurious texture, more sheets per roll, 2 mm wider and 14 mm longer per sheet than in other countries. The island race is also sensitive to colour, choosing from ranges that include warm pink, breeze blue and meadow green. The reason for this is their desire that the colour of the tissue matches their bathrooms.[22]

The *family of procreation* – the buyer's spouse and children – has a more direct influence on everyday buying behaviour. This family is the most important consumer buying organisation in society and it has been researched extensively. Marketers are interested in the roles and relative influence of the husband, wife and children on the purchase of a large variety of products and services.

Husband–wife involvement varies widely by product category and by stage in the buying process. Buying roles change with evolving consumer lifestyles. Almost everywhere in the world, the wife is traditionally the main purchasing agent for the family, especially in the areas of food, household products and clothing. But with over 60 per cent of women holding jobs outside the home in developed countries and the willingness of some husbands to do more of the family's purchasing, all this is changing. The vast majority of increased car sales in Western Europe are by women for women, hence the market for high-value small cars.

 The wife is traditionally the main purchasing agent for the family. 🙴

Are 'metrosexual' males in decline? Advertising agency Euro RSCG Worldwide identified this group of straight men, typified by David Beckham, who enjoy such things as shopping and beauty products and who drive the market for male personal care, grooming and cosmetic products. Was the tipping point man's man Zinedine Zidane head-butting preening, sarong-sporting David Beckham in the World Cup? Manly men are elbowing the metrosexual aside in films, books and advertising. The hottest new literary genre is 'fatire', the mail equivalent of 'chicklit': examples include *Real Men Don't Apologise* and *I Hope They Sell Beer in Hell*. Advertising agencies are reconnecting to male customers after finding that campaigns did not portray their everyday lives and attitudes. Ad industry magazine *Campaign* assessed the industry as portraying men as 'castrated dweeps'. The response is campaigns like that for Coke Zero that are full of laddish swagger.[23]

Children may also have a strong influence on family buying decisions. The EU-25's 76 million children who are 14 and under wield an estimated €18bn in disposable income. They also influence an additional €100bn that their families spend on them in areas such as food, clothing, entertainment and personal care items. For example, one recent study found that kids significantly influence family decisions about where they take vacations, what food they eat and what cars and mobile phones they buy. As one fraught mother explains:

'When my children come shopping with me, it is a constant battle,' she says. 'My youngest son Johnny heads straight for the chocolate biscuits and asks why we can't have them. I've explained to the eldest two that they can't have too much of certain foods but he's too young to understand. When I put my foot down, he declares that everyone else is allowed to have it and I'm being unfair. I don't want to be seen as the enemy but I also don't want to let my children eat junk.'

To marshal this 'pester power', marketers of cars, restaurants, mobile phones and travel destinations are now placing ads on networks such as Cartoon Network and CBBC. Nickelodeon recently signed multimillion-euro advertising deals with Kia. Meanwhile consumer groups and nutritionists encourage parents to use their trip to the supermarket 'to educate your children, not fight with them.'[24]

In the case of expensive products and services, partners often make joint decisions. Anna Flores' husband may play an *influencer role* in her camera-buying decision. He may have an opinion about her buying a camera and about the kind of camera to buy. At the same time, she will be the primary decider, purchaser and user.

Consumers' buying roles

Group members can influence purchases in many ways. For example, men normally choose their own newspaper and women choose their own tights. For other products, however, the **decision-making unit (DMU)** is more complicated with people playing one or more roles:

- **Initiator**. The person who first suggests or thinks of the idea of buying a particular product or service. This could be a parent or friend who would like to see a visual record of Anna's holiday.
- **Influencer**. A person whose view or advice influences the buying decision, perhaps a friend who is a camera enthusiast or a salesperson.

Decision-making unit (DMU)—All the individuals who participate in, and influence, the consumer buying-decision process.

Initiator—The person who first suggests or thinks of the idea of buying a particular product or service.

Influencer—A person whose view or advice influences buying decisions.

- **Decider**. The person who ultimately makes a buying decision or any part of it – whether to buy, what to buy, how to buy or where to buy.
- **Buyer**. The person who makes an actual purchase. Once the buying decision is made, someone else could make the purchase for the decider.
- **User**. The person who consumes or uses a product or service. Once bought, other members of Anna's family could use her camera.

90% of cats wish that they could do the shopping.

Because 90% of cats prefer Whiskas pouches to tins every mealtime.

In our biggest ever taste test, of cat owners feeding pouches or tins, 90% of the 173,219 owners who responded expressed their cat's preference for Whiskas pouches to tins. ©Pedigree Masterfoods 2001. ®Whiskas is a Registered Trademark.

Decider—The person who ultimately makes a buying decision or any part of it – whether to buy, what to buy, how to buy, or where to buy.

Buyer—The person who makes an actual purchase.

User—The person who consumes or uses a product or service.

For Whiskas, like most household purchases, the buyer is not the consumer.
SOURCE: The Advertising Archives.

Roles and status

A person belongs to many groups – family, clubs, organisations. The person's position in each group can be defined in terms of both *role* and *status*. With her parents, Anna Flores plays the role of daughter; in her family, she plays the role of wife; in her company, she plays the role of brand manager. A **role** consists of the activities that people are expected to perform according to the persons around them. Each of Anna's roles will influence some of her buying behaviour.

Each role carries a **status** reflecting the general esteem given to it by society. People often choose products that show their status in society. For example, the role of brand manager has more status in our society than the role of daughter. As a brand manager, Anna will buy the kind of clothing that reflects her role and status.

Personal factors

A buyer's decisions are also influenced by personal characteristics such as the buyer's age and life-cycle stage, occupation, economic situation, lifestyle, and personality and self-concept.

Age and life-cycle stage

People change the goods and services they buy over their lifetimes. Tastes in food, clothes, furniture and recreation are often age related. Buying is also shaped by the **family life-cycle** – the

Role—The activities a person is expected to perform according to the people around him or her.

Status—The general esteem given to a role by society.

Family life-cycle—The stages through which families might pass as they mature over time.

All consumers do not see products in the same way. For some people shoes are to protect their feet and keep them warm. For others, shoes are a passion and they collect many pairs.

SOURCE: The Advertising Archives.

Young	Middle-aged	Older
Single	Single	Older married
Married without children	Married without children	Older unmarried
Married with children	Married with children	
Infant children	Young children	
Young children	Adolescent children	
Adolescent children	Married without dependent children	
Divorced with children	Divorced without children	
	Divorced with children	
	Young children	
	Adolescent children	
	Divorced without dependent children	

Table 5.3 Family life-cycle stages

SOURCES: Adapted from Patrick E. Murphy and William A. Staples, 'A modernised family life cycle', *Journal of Consumer Research* (June 1979), p. 16, University of Chicago Press; © Journal of Consumer Research, Inc., 1979. See also Janet Wagner and Sherman Hanna, 'The effectiveness of family life cycle variables in consumer expenditure research', *Journal of Consumer Research* (December 1983), pp. 281–91.

stages through which families might pass as they mature over time. Table 5.3 lists the stages of the family life-cycle. Although based on the transient love and marriage model of life, marketers often define their target markets in terms of life-cycle stage and develop appropriate products and marketing plans for each stage. For example, Mark Warner offers family-oriented skiing and water sports holidays with an emphasis on kids' clubs, and 'no kids' holidays for couples wanting to escape from them.

RBC Royal Bank has identified five life-stage segments. The *youth* segment includes customers youngers than 18. *Getting Started* consists of customers aged 18 to 35 who are going through first experiences, such as graduation, first credit card, first car, first loan, marriage, and first child. *Builders,* customers aged 35 to 50, are in their peak earning years. As they build careers and family, they tend to borrow more than they invest. *Accumulators,* aged 50 to 60, worry about saving for retirement and investing wisely. Finally, *Preservers,* customers over 60, want to maximise their retirement income to maintain a desired lifestyle. RBC markets different services to the different segments. For example, with *Builders,* who face many expenses, it emphasises loans and debt-load management services.[25]

Although life-cycle stages remain the same, shifting lifestyles are causing the decline of some products and growth in others. One product that has almost disappeared in recent years is the baby pram, the one-time status symbol of all mums. Besides there being fewer families with children, many mothers now work, so have less time for strolling the pram, and are more likely to travel by car than on foot.

As society changes, marketers may have to learn how to serve completely new life-cycle segments. For much of its life, families with 'young children' and 'adolescent children' were the main market for Stanley Gibbons, the world's leading postage stamp specialist. In these exciting times stamp collecting appeals to fewer children but it remains the passion of wealthy collectors with time and money on their hands. Many of these are wealthy 'young singles' or 'young married' people, such as tennis player Maria Sharapova and singer Sophie Ellis-Bexter.[26]

The Japanese call them 'parasite singles', a generation that chooses to linger in their parents' home, rent free, rather than get a steady job and start their own life. Many also become 'freeters' – those who drift from job to job rather than settling down to conventional employment. The same pattern is occurring in western countries where staying with mum is more attractive than being a mum. In most countries men linger at home much longer than women, with Italian men being the world champion lingerers. This shift in life-cycle behaviour is causing a huge shift in demand from home building to single lifestyle consumption.[27]

Psychological life-cycle stages have also been identified. Adults experience certain passages or transformations as they go through life. Thus Anna Flores may move from being a satisfied brand manager and wife to being an unsatisfied person searching for a new way to fulfil herself. In fact, such a change may have stimulated her strong interest in photography. The main stimuli to people taking photographs are holidays, ceremonies marking the progression through the life-cycle (weddings, graduations and so on) and having children to take photographs of. Marketers must pay attention to the changing buying interests that might be associated with these adult passages.

Occupation

A person's occupation affects the goods and services bought. Blue-collar workers tend to buy more work clothes, whereas office workers buy more smart clothes. Marketers try to identify the occupational groups that have an above-average interest in their products and services. A company can even specialise in making products needed by a given occupational group. Thus computer software companies will design different products for brand managers, accountants, engineers, lawyers and doctors.

Economic circumstances

Some marketers target consumers who have lots of money and resources, charging prices to match. For example, Rolex positions its luxury watches as 'a tribute to elegance, an object of passion, a symbol for all time'. Other marketers target consumers with more modest means. Timex makes more affordable watches that 'take a licking and keep on ticking'.

A person's economic situation will affect product choice. Anna Flores can consider buying a professional €5,000 Nikon D1 digital camera if she has enough enthusiasm, disposable income, savings or borrowing power. Marketers of income-sensitive goods closely watch trends in personal income, savings and interest rates. If economic indicators point to a recession, marketers can take steps to redesign, reposition and reprice their products.

Lifestyle—A person's pattern of living as expressed in his or her activities, interests and opinions.

Psychographics—The technique of measuring lifestyles and developing lifestyle classifications; it involves measuring the chief AIO dimensions (activities, interests, opinions).

Lifestyle

People coming from the same subculture, social class and occupation may have quite different lifestyles. **Lifestyle** is a person's pattern of living as expressed in his or her activities, interests and opinions. Lifestyle captures something more than the person's social class or personality. It profiles a person's whole pattern of acting and interacting in the world. The technique of measuring lifestyles is known as **psychographics**. It involves measuring the primary dimensions shown in Table 5.4. The first three are known as the *AIO dimensions* (activities, interests, opinions). Several research firms have developed lifestyle classifications. The most widely used is the SRI *Values and Lifestyles (VALS)* typology. The original VALS typology classifies consumers into nine lifestyle groups according to whether they were inner directed (for example, 'experientials'), outer directed ('achievers', 'belongers'), or need driven ('survivors'). Using this VALS classification, a bank found

Table 5.4 Lifestyle dimensions

Activities	Interests	Opinions	Demographics
Work	Family	Themselves	Age
Hobbies	Home	Social issues	Education
Social events	Job	Politics	Income
Holidays	Community	Business	Occupation
Entertainment	Recreation	Economics	Family size
Club membership	Fashion	Education	Dwelling
Community	Food	Products	Geography
Shopping	Media	Future	City or town size
Sports	Achievements	Culture	Stage in life cycle

SOURCE: Adapted from Joseph T. Plummer, 'The concept and application of lifestyle segmentation', *Journal of Marketing* (January 1974), p. 34. Reproduced with permission from the American Marketing Association.

that the businessmen they were targeting consisted mainly of 'achievers' who were strongly competitive individualists. The bank designed highly successful ads showing men taking part in solo sports such as sailing, jogging and water skiing.

Everyday-Life Research by SINUS GmbH, a German company, identifies 'social milieus' covering France, Germany, Italy and the UK. This study describes the structure of society with five social classes and value orientations:[28]

- Basic orientation: traditional – *to preserve*
- Basic orientation: materialist – *to have*
- Changing values: hedonism – *to indulge*
- Changing values: postmaterialism – *to be*
- Changing values: postmodernism – *to have, to be and to indulge.*

It distinguishes two types of value: traditional values, emphasising hard work, thrift, religion, honesty, good manners and obedience; and material values concerned with possession and a need for security. From these, SINUS developed a typology of social milieus (see Table 5.5): groups of people who share a common set of values and beliefs about work, private relationships, leisure activities and aesthetics, and a common perception of future plans, wishes and dreams. The size and exact nature of these milieus vary between the countries studied, but there are broad international comparisons.

Knowing the social milieu of a person can provide information about his or her everyday life, such as work likes and dislikes, which helps in product development and advertising. The study finds that the upmarket segments share a similar structure in all four countries, and it identifies trend-setting milieus in each country, containing heavy consumers with comparable attitudinal and sociodemographic characteristics. Important values shared by all these consumers include tolerance, open-mindedness, an outward-looking approach, career and success, education and culture, a high standard of living, hedonistic luxury consumption, individualism and Europe.

Personality and self-concept

Each person's distinct personality influences his or her buying behaviour. **Personality** refers to the unique psychological characteristics that lead to relatively consistent and lasting responses to one's own environment. Personality is usually described in terms of traits such as self-confidence, dominance, sociability, autonomy, defensiveness, adaptability and aggressiveness. Personality can

Personality—A person's distinguishing psychological characteristics that lead to relatively consistent and lasting responses to his or her own environment.

Table 5.5 Typology of social milieus

Milieu	Germany	France	Italy	UK	Description
Upper conservative	Konservatives-gehobenes	Les Héritiers	Neoconservatori	Upper class	Traditional upper-middle-class conservatives
Traditional mainstream	Floresburgerliches	Les conservateurs installés	Piccola borghesia	Traditional middle class	*Petit bourgeois* group mainly oriented to preserving the status quo
Traditional working class	Traditionsloses Arbeitermilieu	Les laborieux traditionnels	Cultura operaia	Traditional working class	Traditional blue-collar workers
Modern mainstream	Aufstiegsorientiertes	Les nouveaux ambitieux	Rampanti, plus cristadi	Social climbers, plus progressive working class	Social climber and achievement-oriented white- and blue-collar workers
Trendsetter	Technokratisch-liberales	Les managers moderns	Borghesia illuminata	Progressive middle class	Technocratic-liberals with a postmaterial orientation
Avant-garde	Hedonistisches	Les post-modernistes	Edonisti	'Thatcher's children'	Mainly young pleasure seekers
Sociocritical	Alternatives	Les néo-moralistes	Critica sociale	Socially centred	Pursuing an alternative lifestyle
Under-privileged	Traditionsloses Arbeitermilieu	Les oubliés, plus les rebelles	Sotto-proletariato urbano	Poor	Uprooted blue-collar workers and destitute

be useful in analysing consumer behaviour for certain product or brand choices. For example, coffee makers have discovered that heavy coffee drinkers tend to be high on sociability. Thus Nescafé ads show people together over a cup of coffee.

The idea is that brands also have personalities, and that consumers are likely to choose brands with personalities that match their own. A *brand personality* is the specific mix of human traits that may be attributed to a particular brand. Researchers have identified five brand personality traits:[29]

1. Sincerity (down-to-earth, honest, wholesome and cheerful)

2. Excitement (daring, spirited, imaginative and up-to-date)

3. Competence (reliable, intelligent and successful)

4. Sophistication (upper class and charming)

5. Ruggedness (outdoorsy and tough)

They have found that a number of well-known brands tend to be strongly associated with one particular trait: Land Rover with 'ruggedness', the BBC with 'competence', Virgin with 'sincerity' and BMW with 'excitement'. Hence, these brands will attract persons who are high on the same personality traits.

Self-concept (or self-image)—The complex mental picture that people have of themselves.

Many marketers use a concept related to personality – a person's **self-concept** (also called **self-image**). The basic self-concept premise is that people's possessions contribute to and reflect their identities: that is, 'we are what we have'. Thus, in order to understand consumer behaviour, the marketer must first understand the relationship between consumer self-concept and possessions.

Apple applies this concept in a recent set of ads that characterise two people as computers – one person plays the part of an Apple Mac and the other plays a PC. 'Hello, I'm a Mac,' says the person on the right, who's younger and dressed in jeans. 'And I'm a PC,' says the nerd on the left, who's wearing dweeby glasses and a jacket and tie. The two men discuss the relative advantages of Macs versus PCs, with the Mac coming out on top. The ads present the Mac brand personality as young, modern and relaxed. The PC is portrayed as buttoned down, corporate and a bit dorky. The message? If you see yourself as young and with it, you need a Mac.[30]

Anna Flores may see herself as outgoing, fun and active. Therefore, she will favour a camera that projects the same qualities. In that case the super-compact and stylish Canon Digital Ixus could attract her. 'Everybody smile and say "aaahhhh". The smallest, cutest digicam we've ever fallen for' (*Stuff* magazine, September 2000).

Really, it is not that simple. What if Anna's *actual self-concept* (how she views herself) differs from her *ideal self-concept* (how she would like to view herself) and from her *others' self-concept* (how she thinks others sees her)? Which self will she try to satisfy when she buys a camera? Because this is unclear, self-concept theory has met with mixed success in predicting consumer responses to brand images.

Psychological factors

A person's buying choices are further influenced by four important psychological factors: motivation, perception, learning, and beliefs and attitudes.

Motivation

We know that Anna Flores became interested in buying a camera. Why? What is she *really* seeking? What *needs* is she trying to satisfy?

 A need becomes a *motive* when it is aroused to a sufficient level of intensity.

A person has many needs at any given time. Some are *biological*, arising from states of tension such as hunger, thirst or discomfort. Others are *psychological*, arising from the need for recognition, esteem or belonging. Most of these needs will not be strong enough to motivate the person to act at a given point in time. A need becomes a *motive* when it is aroused to a sufficient level of intensity. A **motive** (or **drive**) is a need that is sufficiently pressing to direct the person to seek satisfaction. Psychologists have developed theories of human motivation. Two of the most popular – the theories of Sigmund Freud and Abraham Maslow – have quite different meanings for consumer analysis and marketing.

Motive (or drive)—A need that is sufficiently pressing to direct the person to seek satisfaction of the need.

Freud's theory of motivation

Sigmund Freud assumed that people are largely unconscious about the real psychological forces shaping their behaviour. He saw the person as growing up and repressing many urges. These urges are never eliminated or under perfect control; they emerge in dreams, in slips of the tongue, in neurotic and obsessive behaviour, or ultimately in psychoses.

> People are largely unconscious about the real psychological forces shaping their behaviour.

Freud's theory suggests that a person's buying decisions are affected by subconscious motives that even the buyer may not fully understand. Thus, an ageing baby boomer who buys a sporty BMW 330Ci convertible might explain that he simply likes the feel of the wind in his thinning hair. At a deeper level, he may be trying to impress others with his success. At a still deeper level, he may be buying the car to feel young and independent again.

If Anna Flores wants to purchase an expensive camera, she may describe her motive as wanting a hobby or career. At a deeper level, she may be purchasing the camera to impress others with her creative talent. At a still deeper level, she may be buying the camera to feel young and independent again.

Motivation researchers collect in-depth information from small samples of consumers to uncover the deeper motives for their product choices. They use non-directive depth interviews and various 'projective techniques' to throw the ego off guard – techniques such as word association, sentence completion, picture interpretation and role playing. These are discussed extensively in Chapter 7.

Maslow's theory of motivation

Abraham Maslow sought to explain why people are driven by particular needs at particular times.[31] Why does one person spend much time and energy on personal safety and another on gaining the esteem of others? Maslow's answer is that human needs are arranged in a hierarchy, from the most pressing to the least pressing. Maslow's hierarchy of needs is shown in Figure 5.4. In order of importance, they are (1) *physiological* needs, (2) *safety* needs, (3) *social* needs, (4) *esteem* needs, (5) *cognitive* needs, (6) *aesthetic* needs and (7) *self-actualisation* needs. A person tries to satisfy the most important need first. When that important need is satisfied, it will stop being a motivator and the person will then try to satisfy the next most important need. For

Figure 5.4 Maslow's hierarchy of needs

SOURCE: Adapted from Abraham H. Maslow, *Motivation and Personality*, 2nd edn, 1970 (Prentice Hall, Inc.).

example, a starving man (need 1) will not take an interest in the latest happenings in the art world (need 6), or in how he is seen or esteemed by others (need 3 or 4), or even in whether he is breathing clean air (need 2). But as each important need is satisfied, the next most important need will come into play:

The wine market shows how the different levels of the need hierarchy can be at play at the same time. Buyers of premium wines are seeking self-esteem and self-actualisation. They may achieve this by showing their knowledge by buying 1986 Château Ausone from a specialist wine merchant. Wine buying makes many other people anxious, particularly if it is a gift. They buy the product to fill a social need but are unable to gauge quality. To be safe they buy from a reputable store or a brand legitimised by advertising (such as Le Piat d'Or).

Maslow's hierarchy is not universal for all cultures. As the heroes of Hollywood movies amply show, Anglo-Saxon culture values self-actualisation and individuality above all else, but that is not universally so. In Japan and German-speaking countries, people are most highly motivated by a need for order (aesthetic needs) and belonging (esteem needs), while in France, Spain, Portugal and other Latin and Asian countries, people are most motivated by the need for security and belonging.

What light does Maslow's theory throw on Anna Flores' interest in buying a camera? We can guess that Anna has satisfied her physiological, safety and social needs; they do not motivate her interest in cameras. Her camera interest might come from an aesthetic need and esteem needs.

Motivation: An ageing baby boomer who buys a sporty convertible might explain that he simply likes to feel the wind in his thinning hair. At a deeper level, he may be buying the car to feel young and independent again.
SOURCE: Michelle Pedone/ Photonica Getty Images.

Or it might come from a need for self-actualisation or cognition – she might want to be a creative person and express herself through photography or explore her potential.

Perception

A motivated person is ready to act. How the person acts is influenced by his or her perception of the situation. Two people with the same motivation and in the same situation may act quite differently because they perceive the situation differently. Anna Flores might consider a fast-talking camera salesperson loud and false. Another camera buyer might consider the same salesperson intelligent and helpful.

Why do people perceive the same situation differently? All of us learn by the flow of information through our five senses: sight, hearing, smell, touch and taste. However, each of us receives, organises and interprets this sensory information in an individual way. Thus **perception** is the process by which people select, organise and interpret information to form a meaningful picture of the world. People can form different perceptions of the same stimulus because of three perceptual processes: selective attention, selective distortion and selective retention.

> ❝ People are exposed to an estimated 3,000 to 5,000 ad messages every day. ❞

Selective attention

People are exposed to a great amount of stimuli every day. For example, on average, people are exposed to an estimated 3,000 to 5,000 ad messages every day.[32] It is impossible for a person to pay attention to all these stimuli. **Selective attention** – the tendency for people to screen out most of the information to which they are exposed – means that marketers have to work especially hard to attract the consumer's attention.

Selective distortion

Even noted stimuli do not always come across in the intended way. Each person fits incoming information into an existing mindset. **Selective distortion** describes the tendency of people to adapt information to personal meanings. Anna Flores may hear the salesperson mention some good and bad points about a competing camera brand. Because she already has a strong leaning towards Fuji, Kodak or Sony, she is likely to distort those points in order to conclude that one camera is better than the others. People tend to interpret information in a way that will support what they already believe. Selective distortion means that marketers must try to understand

Perception—The process by which people select, organise and interpret information to form a meaningful picture of the world.

Selective attention—The tendency of people to screen out most of the information to which they are exposed.

Selective distortion—The tendency of people to adapt information to personal meanings.

Selective perception: It's impossible for people to pay attention to the thousands of ads they're exposed to every day, so they screen most of them out.

SOURCE: Justin Sullivan/Getty Images News/Getty Images.

258

the mindsets of consumers and how these will affect interpretations of advertising and sales information:

> Is the €160bn a year people spend on beauty products not wasted but a sensible investment? Evidence shows that people respond positively to people who are attractive. In sales jobs researchers in the UK found the pay penalty for being unattractive is 15 per cent for men and 11 per cent for women. Even being told a person is attractive or not influences people's judgement. In a recent Norwegian study, university students awarded a 20 per cent lighter sentence if they were told criminals were 'handsome' or 'pretty'.[33]

Selective retention

People will also forget much of what they learn. They tend to retain information that supports their attitudes and beliefs. Because of **selective retention**, Anna is likely to remember good points made about the Fuji and forget good points made about competing cameras. She may remember Fuji's good points because she 'rehearses' them more whenever she thinks about choosing a camera.

Because of selective exposure, distortion and retention, marketers have to work hard to get their messages through. This fact explains why marketers use so much drama and repetition in sending messages to their market.

Interestingly, although most marketers worry about whether their offers will be perceived at all, some consumers worry that they will be affected by marketing messages without even knowing it – through *subliminal advertising*.

Selective retention—The tendency of people to retain only part of the information to which they are exposed, usually information that supports their attitudes or beliefs.

> In 1957, a researcher announced that he had flashed the phrases 'Eat popcorn' and 'Drink Coca-Cola' on a screen in a New Jersey movie theatre every five seconds for 1/300th of a second. He reported that although viewers did not consciously recognise these messages, they absorbed them subconsciously and bought 58 per cent more popcorn and 18 per cent more Coke. Suddenly advertisers, popular media and consumer-protection groups became intensely interested in subliminal perception. People voiced fears of being brainwashed, and some places declared the practice illegal. Although the researcher later admitted to making up the data, the issue has not died. Some consumers still fear that they are being manipulated by subliminal messages.

Numerous studies by psychologists and consumer researchers have found little or no link between subliminal messages and consumer behaviour. It appears that subliminal advertising simply doesn't have the power attributed to it by its critics. Most advertisers scoff at the notion of an industry conspiracy to manipulate consumers through 'invisible' messages. Says one industry insider: '[Some consumers believe we are] wizards who can manipulate them at will. Ha! Snort! Oh my sides! As we know, just between us, most of [us] have difficulty getting a 2 per cent increase in sales with the help of €50 million in media and extremely liminal images of sex, money, power and other [motivators] of human emotion. The very idea of [us] as puppeteers, cruelly pulling the strings of consumer marionettes, is almost too much to bear.'[34]

Learning

Learning—Changes in an individual's behaviour arising from experience.

When people act, they learn. **Learning** describes changes in an individual's behaviour arising from experience. Learning theorists say that most human behaviour is learned. Learning occurs through the interplay of *drives, stimuli, cues, responses* and *reinforcement.*

We saw that Anna Flores has a drive for self-actualisation. A *drive* is a strong internal stimulus that calls for action. Her drive becomes a motive when it is directed towards a particular *stimulus object* – in this case, a camera. Anna's response to the idea of buying a camera is conditioned by the surrounding cues. *Cues* are minor stimuli that determine when, where and how the person responds. Seeing cameras in a shop window, hearing a special sale price, and her husband's support are all cues that can influence Anna's *response* to her interest in buying a camera.

Suppose Anna buys the Canon Ixus. If the experience is rewarding, she will probably use the camera more and more. Her response to cameras will be *reinforced.* Then the next time she shops for a camera, binoculars or some similar product, the probability is greater that she will buy a Canon product. We say that she *generalises* her response to similar stimuli.

The reverse of generalisation is *discrimination.* When Anna examines binoculars made by Olympus, she sees that they are lighter and more compact than Nikon's binoculars. Discrimination means that she has learned to recognise differences in sets of products and can adjust her response accordingly.

The practical significance of learning theory for marketers is that they can build up demand for a product by associating it with strong drives, using motivating cues and providing positive reinforcement. A new company can enter the market by appealing to the same drives that competitors appeal to and by providing similar cues, because buyers are more likely to transfer loyalty to similar brands than to dissimilar ones (generalisation). Or a new company may design its brand to appeal to a different set of drives and offer strong cue inducements to switch brands (discrimination).

Beliefs and attitudes

Belief—A descriptive thought that a person holds about something.

Through doing and learning, people acquire their beliefs and attitudes. These, in turn, influence their buying behaviour. A **belief** is a descriptive thought that a person has about something. Anna Flores may believe that a Fuji camera takes great pictures, stands up well under hard use and is good value. These beliefs may be based on real knowledge, opinion or faith, and may or may not carry an emotional charge. For example, Anna Flores' belief that a Fuji camera is heavy may or may not matter to her decision.

Marketers are interested in the beliefs that people formulate about specific products and services, because these beliefs make up product and brand images that affect buying behaviour. If some of the beliefs are wrong and prevent purchase, the marketer will want to launch a campaign to correct them.

Attitude—A person's consistently favourable or unfavourable evaluations, feelings and tendencies towards an object or idea.

People have attitudes regarding religion, politics, clothes, music, food and almost everything else. An **attitude** describes a person's relatively consistent evaluations, feelings and tendencies towards an object or idea. Attitudes put people into a frame of mind of liking or disliking things, of moving towards or away from them. Thus Anna Flores may hold such attitudes as 'Buy the best', 'The Japanese make the best products in the world' and 'Creativity and self-expression are among the most important things in life'. If so, the Canon camera would fit well into Anna's existing attitudes.

> " A company should usually try to fit its products into existing attitudes rather than try to change attitudes. "

Attitudes are difficult to change. A person's attitudes fit into a pattern and to change one attitude may require difficult adjustments in many others. Thus a company should usually try to fit its products into existing attitudes rather than try to change attitudes. Of course, there are exceptions in which the great cost of trying to change attitudes may pay off. For example:

> In the late 1950s, Honda entered the motorcycle market facing a major decision. It could either sell its motorcycles to the small but already established motorcycle market or it could try to increase the size of this market by attracting new types of consumer to its little Honda 50cc bikes. Increasing the size of the market would be more difficult and expensive because many people had negative attitudes towards motorcycles. They associated motorcycles with black leather jackets, switchblades and outlaws. Despite these adverse attitudes, Honda took the second course of action. It launched a major campaign to position motorcycles as good clean fun. Its theme, 'You meet the nicest people on a Honda', worked well and many people adopted a new attitude towards motorcycles. From this toehold in the market for small motorcycles Honda grew to be the main force in the world motorcycle industry and a major player in cars.
>
> In the 1990s, however, Honda faces a similar problem. With the ageing of the baby boomers, the market has once again shifted towards only hard-core motorcycling enthusiasts. So Honda has again set out to change consumer attitudes. Its 'Come Ride With Us' campaign aims to re-establish the wholesomeness of motorcycling and to position it as fun and exciting for everyone.[35]

Consumer decision process

The consumer's choice results from the complex interplay of cultural, social, personal and psychological factors. Although the marketer cannot influence many of these factors, they can be useful in identifying interested buyers and in shaping products and appeals to serve their needs better. Marketers have to be extremely careful in analysing consumer behaviour. Consumers often turn down what appears to be a winning offer. Polaroid found this out when it lost millions on its Polarvision instant home movie system, Ford when it launched the Edsel, RCA on its SelectaVision, Philips on its LaserVision video-disc player and TiVo personal video machines, and Bristol Aviation with its trio of the Brabazon, Britannia and Concorde airliners. So far we have looked at the cultural, social, personal and psychological influences that affect buyers. Now we look at how consumers make buying decisions: first, the types of decision that consumers face; then the main steps in the buyer decision process; and finally, the processes by which consumers learn about and buy new products.

Types of buying decision behaviour

Consumer decision making varies with the type of buying decision. Consumer buying behaviour differs greatly for a tube of toothpaste, a tennis racket, an expensive camera and a new car. More complex decisions usually involve more buying participants and more buyer deliberation. Figure 5.5 shows types of consumer buying behaviour based on the degree of involvement and the extent of the differences among brands.

Figure 5.5 Four types of buying behaviour

SOURCE: Adapted from Henry Assael, *Consumer Behaviour and Marketing Action*, 6th edn, p. 67 (Boston, MA: Kent Publishing Company, 1988).

	High involvement	Low involvement
Significant differences between brands	Complex buying behaviour	Variety-seeking buying behaviour
Few differences between brands	Dissonance-reducing buying behaviour	Habitual buying behaviour

Complex buying behaviour

Complex buying behaviour—Consumer buying behaviour in situations characterised by high consumer involvement in a purchase and significant perceived differences among brands.

Consumers undertake **complex buying behaviour** when they are highly involved in a purchase and perceive significant differences among brands, or when the product is expensive, risky, purchased infrequently and highly self-expressive. Typically, the consumer has much to learn

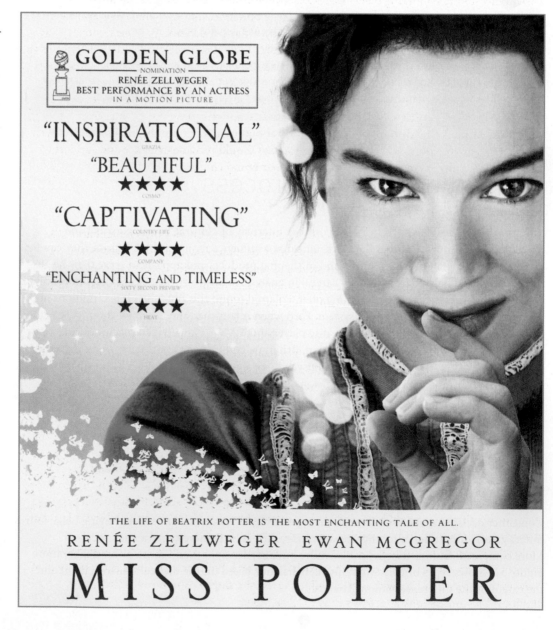

The endorsement by professional opinion leaders (film critics) is critical to attracting consumers to experience products, such as music and movies. One reason why top film stars are paid so much is that their being in a movie is itself an endorsement that increases sales and profits.

SOURCE: Ronald Grant Archive.

about the product category. For example, a PC buyer may not know what attributes to consider. Many product features carry no real meaning to the great majority of potential purchasers: an 'AMD Turion 64 X2 Dual-Core Mobile Technology TL-56w', '15.4 inch WXGA', 'NVIDIA Quatro fx 1500 graphic' or even a '1 GB (2 × 512 MB) PC2-5300 DDR2 (667 MHz) Up to 32 GB'.

This buyer will pass through a learning process, first developing beliefs about the product, then developing attitudes, and then making a thoughtful purchase choice. Marketers of high-involvement products must understand the information-gathering and evaluation behaviour of high-involvement consumers. They need to help buyers learn about product-class attributes and their relative importance and about what the company's brand offers on the important attributes. Marketers need to differentiate their brand's features, perhaps by describing the brand's benefits using print media with long copy. They must motivate store salespeople and the buyer's acquaintances to influence the final brand choice.

Dissonance-reducing buying behaviour

Dissonance-reducing buying behaviour occurs when consumers are highly involved with an expensive, infrequent or risky purchase, but see little difference among brands. For example, consumers buying floor covering may face a high-involvement decision because floor covering is expensive and self-expressive. Yet buyers may consider most floor coverings in a given price range to be the same. In this case, because perceived brand differences are not large, buyers may shop around to learn what is available, but buy relatively quickly. They may respond primarily to a good price or to purchase convenience. After the purchase, consumers might experience post-purchase dissonance (after-sales discomfort) when they notice certain disadvantages of the purchased carpet brand or hear favourable things about brands not purchased. To counter such dissonance, the marketer's after-sale communications should provide evidence and support to help consumers feel good both before and after their brand choices.

Dissonance-reducing buying behaviour— Consumer buying behaviour in situations characterised by high involvement but few perceived differences among brands.

Habitual buying behaviour

Habitual buying behaviour occurs under conditions of low consumer involvement and little significant brand difference. For example, take salt. Consumers have little involvement in this product category – they simply go to the store and reach for a brand. If they keep reaching for the same brand, it is out of habit rather than strong brand loyalty. Consumers appear to have low involvement with most low-cost, frequently purchased products.

Consumers do not search extensively for information about the brands, evaluate brand characteristics and make weighty decisions about which brands to buy. Instead, they passively receive information as they watch television or read magazines. Ad repetition creates *brand familiarity* rather than *brand conviction*. Consumers do not form strong attitudes towards a brand; they select the brand because it is familiar and may not evaluate the choice even after purchase.

Because buyers are not highly committed to any brands, marketers of low-involvement products with few brand differences often use price and sales promotions to stimulate product trial. Gaining distribution and attention at the point of sale is critical. In advertising for a low-involvement product, ad copy should stress only a few key points. Visual symbols and imagery are important because they can be remembered easily and associated with the brand. Ad campaigns should include high repetition of short-duration messages. Television is usually more effective than print media because it is a low-involvement medium suitable for passive learning. Advertising planning should be based on classical conditioning theory, in which buyers learn to identify a certain product by a symbol repeatedly attached to it.

Products can be linked to some involving personal situation. While many expensive watches promote their looks, celebrity or sports associations, Patek Philippe of Geneva show pictures of a 'new man' sleeping, sitting with a male child, and use the slogan: 'You never actually own a Patek Philippe. You merely look after it for the *next* generation.'

Habitual buying behaviour—Consumer buying behaviour in situations characterised by low consumer involvement and few significant perceived brand differences.

PATEK PHILIPPE
GENEVE
Begin your own tradition.

You never
actually own a Patek Philippe.
You merely
look after it for the *next* generation.

Gondolo
by Patek Philippe

Patek Philippe of Geneva departs from the usual approach to selling luxury watches by appealing to self-esteem, aesthetic needs or self-actualisation communicated by an association with sport, technology or exquisite design. This 'new man' ad taps into much more basic social and safety needs.

SOURCE: Patek Philippe, *Agency*: Geneva/Leagas Delaney, *Photographer*: Peggy Sirota (represented by E. M. Managed).

Variety-seeking buying behaviour

Variety-seeking buying behaviour—Consumer buying behaviour in situations characterised by low consumer involvement, but significant perceived brand differences.

Consumers undertake **variety-seeking buying behaviour** in situations characterised by low consumer involvement, but significant perceived brand differences. In such cases, consumers often do a lot of brand switching. For example, when purchasing confectionery, a consumer may hold some beliefs, choose an item without much evaluation, then evaluate that brand during consumption. But the next time, the consumer might pick another brand out of boredom or simply to try something different. Brand switching occurs for the sake of variety rather than because of dissatisfaction. Confectionery makers know this and compete to have their products in the 'golden arc' from where a person stands to make a purchase and as far as a person can reach.

In such product categories, the marketing strategy may differ for the market leader and minor brands. The market leader will try to encourage habitual buying behaviour by dominating shelf space, avoiding out-of-stock conditions and running frequent reminder advertising. Challenger firms will encourage variety seeking by offering lower prices, deals, coupons, free samples and advertising that presents reasons for trying something new.

The buyer decision process

Most large companies research consumer buying decisions in great detail to answer questions about what consumers buy, where they buy, how and how much they buy, when they buy and why they buy. Marketers can study consumer purchases to find answers to questions about what they buy, where and how much. But learning about the *whys* of consumer buying behaviour and the buying decision process is not so easy – the answers are often locked within the consumer's head.

> **"** The answers are often locked within the consumer's head. **"**

We will examine the stages that buyers pass through to reach a buying decision. We will use the model in Figure 5.6, which shows the consumer as passing through five stages: *need recognition, information search, evaluation of alternatives, purchase decision* and *postpurchase behaviour*. Clearly the buying process starts long before actual purchase and continues long after. This encourages the marketer to focus on the entire buying process rather than just the purchase decision.

This model implies that consumers pass through all five stages with every purchase. But in more routine purchases, consumers often skip or reverse some of these stages. A woman buying her regular brand of toothpaste would recognise the need and go right to the purchase decision, skipping information search and evaluation. However, we use the model in Figure 5.7 because it shows all the considerations that arise when a consumer faces a new and complex purchase situation.

To illustrate this model, we return to Anna Flores and try to understand how she became interested in buying a camera and the stages she went through to make the final choice.

Need recognition

The buying process starts with **need recognition** – the buyer recognising a problem or need. The buyer senses a difference between his or her *actual* state and some *desired* state. The need can be triggered by *internal stimuli* when one of the person's normal needs – hunger, thirst, sex – rises to a level high enough to become a drive. From previous experience, the person has learnt how to cope with this drive and is motivated towards objects that he or she knows will satisfy it.

Need recognition—The first stage of the buyer decision process in which the consumer recognises a problem or need.

Figure 5.6 Buyer decision process

Figure 5.7 Steps between evaluation of alternatives and a purchase decision

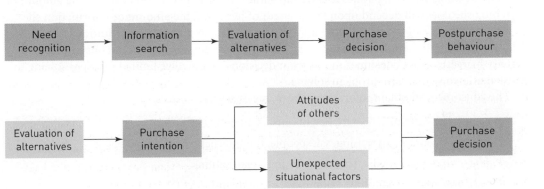

Need recognition can be triggered by advertising. This inventive ad from The LEGO Company invites consumers to think about where the first little block might lead – 'imagine . . .'
SOURCE: Copyright © 2008 The *LEGO* Group. Reproduced with permission.

A need can also be triggered by *external stimuli*. Anna passes a bakery and the smell of freshly baked bread stimulates her hunger; she admires a neighbour's new car; or she watches a television commercial for a Caribbean holiday. At this stage, the marketer needs to determine the factors and situations that usually trigger consumer need recognition. The marketer should research consumers to find out what kinds of need or problem arise, what brought them about and how they led the consumer to this particular product. Anna might answer that she felt she needed a camera after friends showed her the photographs they took on holiday. By gathering such information, the marketer can identify the stimuli that most often trigger interest in the product and can develop marketing programmes that involve these stimuli.

Compared with other animals, human beings are most conscious of visual stimulus. However, psychologists and marketers are beginning to recognise that smell is an important stimulus that often operates unconsciously. Real Marketing 5.1 examines this frontier where marketing is working hand-in-hand with science.

Information search

An aroused consumer may or may not search for more information. If the consumer's drive is strong and a satisfying product is near at hand, the consumer is likely to buy it then. If not, the consumer may simply store the need in memory or undertake an **information search** related to the need.

At one level, the consumer may simply enter *heightened attention*. Here Anna becomes more receptive to information about cameras. She pays attention to camera ads, cameras used by friends and camera conversations. Or Anna may go into *active information search*, in which she looks for reading material, phones friends and gathers information in other ways. The amount of searching she does will depend upon the strength of her drive, the amount of information she starts with, the ease of obtaining more information, the value she places on additional information and the satisfaction she gets from searching. Normally the amount of consumer search activity increases as the consumer moves from decisions that involve limited problem solving to those that involve extensive problem solving.

The consumer can obtain information from any of several sources:

Information search—The stage of the buyer decision process in which the consumer is aroused to search for more information; the consumer may simply have heightened attention or may go into active information search.

- *Personal sources:* family, friends, neighbours, acquaintances
- *Commercial sources:* advertising, salespeople, the Internet, packaging, displays
- *Public sources:* mass media, consumer-rating organisations
- *Experiential sources:* handling, examining, using the product.

real marketing 5.1

Pong: marketing's final frontier

Rolls-Royce Cars hit the headlines when it was revealed that they had developed an essence of new car spray to use on their luxurious upholstery after they found out their cars did not smell new enough. Other sellers use similar tricks. 'Next time you are indulging in a bit of retail therapy, close your eyes, inhale, listen and touch,' says Simon Harrop, director and founder of the Brand Sense Agency. He continues, 'Eighty-three per cent of marketing is focused on eyes alone . . . [but] if your senses are suitably impressed, chances are the product has been branded by a marketing strategy that appeals to all the senses – and not just sight alone, as traditional advertising does.'

There are few people selling houses who have not recognised the trick of percolating coffee when the house is viewed and few stores that have not used the attractive smell of fresh bread. Philosophers from Aristotle to Kant have ranked base smell below the noble senses of seeing, hearing and touching. Yet fragrances are one of the pillars of luxury marketing, with exclusive brands adored by the initiated.

Freud proposes an answer. Smell, he says, is a base sense but one that people have evolved to reject intellectually because of its power. Walking on two legs has taken 1,000 different types of smell receptors in our nose away from the centres of odour that obsess four-legged creatures. With taste, smell was one of the first senses to evolve – it is how amoebas find food.

Old it may be, but neglected it is not. One thousand of our genes relate to our smell receptors in the nose while only three genes control colour vision. Our smell receptors are also well connected. From the nose they first go to the limbic system – a part of the brain that drives mood, sexual urges and fear. Signals then travel to the hippocampus, which controls memories. Only then do the signals travel to the frontal lobes of the brain involved in conscious thought. Your 1,000 smell receptors are always working busily but subliminally.

One example of this subliminal effect is a range of 'odourless' steroids produced by men and women. These directly affect mood. While the masculine version cheers up women, the female version irritates men. Unfortunately, the smell of teenage men also makes people angry. Such a clash of pongs could account for some Saturday night rumbles.

There is more. A granny smell, taken from the armpits of menopausal women, makes people happy, while a mummy smell, taken from new mums, can cure depression. Smell also influences perception. Men's regard for how attractive a women smells when they have not seen her corresponds strongly to their perception of a women's visual attractiveness.

...5.1

Research shows how evolutionary logic drives people's response to smell. Although women have a stronger sense of smell than men, they are not good at identifying physically attractive guys by smell alone. They are attracted instead to the smell of men whose immune system least overlaps with their own. Mating with such partners, they are most likely to sire healthy offspring. This handy sensitivity increases when women are ovulating. Unfortunately this ability is messed up by taking contraceptive pills.

Science is helping remove a smell that no-one finds attractive, body odour (BO). This is caused by Corynebacteria (Coryn), a group of some of the 7,000 bacteria that inhabit all skin. All the bacteria live off the skin's natural fat-laden secretion but, unfortunately for some people, they attract Coryn which is a messy eater that leaves half-digested waste. Quest International, one of the world's largest fragrance houses, is working on long-active deodorants that attack Coryn rather than clogging up the sweat glands like most of the €1.5bn worth of deodorants do.

The understanding of the science of odour is moving out of the realm of the alchemy of exotic fragrances. Aromatic engineering is a rapidly growing business based on pumping designer smells into offices and stores to make customers feel happier and spend more money. Researchers have found a link between certain genes and the smells that people find attractive. People with HLA-A1 tend to dislike ambergris and musk while those with HLA-A2 like them. This genetic foundation for fragrances explains why perfumes still use the same ingredients as in biblical times. There is also growing evidence that humans have a pheromonal nasal organ, a sensor that picks up the pheromones that drive animals sex crazy!

SOURCES: Jerome Burne, 'Why smell gets up your nose', *Financial Times* (8 April 2000), p. 11; Nick Foulkes, 'Have you seen this bottle?', *How to Spend It, Financial Times* (8 April 2000), pp. 31–2; 'Making sense of scents', *The Economist* (13 March 1999), p. 137; 'The sweet smell of success', *The Economist* (25 March 2000), p. 118; 'Cor, you don't half smell', *The Economist* (27 January 2001), p. 114; Martin Lindstrom, *BRAND Sense* (London: Kogan Page, 2006); also see The Brand Sense Agency, www.brandsense.com.

The relative influence of these information sources varies with the product and the buyer. Generally, the consumer receives the most information about a product from commercial sources – those controlled by the marketer. The most effective sources, however, tend to be personal. Personal sources appear to be even more important in influencing the purchase of services. Commercial sources normally *inform* the buyer, but personal sources *legitimise* or *evaluate* products for the buyer. For example, doctors normally learn of new drugs from commercial sources, but turn to other doctors for evaluative information.

As more information is obtained, the consumer's awareness and knowledge of the available brands and features increases. In her information search, Anna learned about the many camera brands available. The information also helped her drop certain brands from consideration. A company must design its marketing mix to make prospects aware of and knowledgeable about its brand. If it fails to do this, the company has lost its opportunity to sell to the customer. The company must also learn which other brands customers consider so that it knows its competition and can plan its own appeals.

The marketer should identify consumers' sources of information and the importance of each source. Consumers should be asked how they first heard about the brand, what information they received and the importance they place on different information sources.

Evaluation of alternatives

We have seen how the consumer uses information to arrive at a set of final brand choices. How does the consumer choose among the alternative brands? The marketer needs to know about **alternative evaluation** – that is, how the consumer processes information to arrive at brand choices. Unfortunately, consumers do not use a simple and single evaluation process in all buying situations. Instead, several evaluation processes are at work.

Certain basic concepts help explain consumer evaluation processes. First, we assume that each consumer is trying to satisfy some need and is looking for certain *benefits* that can be acquired by buying a product or service. Further, each consumer sees a product as a bundle of *product attributes* with varying capacities for delivering these benefits and satisfying the need. For cameras, product attributes might include picture quality, ease of use, camera size, price and other features. Consumers will vary as to which of these attributes they consider relevant and will pay the most attention to those attributes connected with their needs.

Second, the consumer will attach different *degrees of importance* to each attribute. A distinction can be drawn between the importance of an attribute and its salience. *Salient attributes* are those that come to a consumer's mind when he or she is asked to think of a product's characteristics. But these are not necessarily the most important attributes to the consumer. Some of them may be salient because the consumer has just seen an advertisement mentioning them or has had a problem with them, making these attributes 'top-of-the-mind'. There may also be other attributes that the consumer forgot, but whose importance would be recognised if they were mentioned. Marketers should be more concerned with attribute importance than attribute salience.

Third, the consumer is likely to develop a set of *brand beliefs* about where each brand stands on each attribute. The set of beliefs held about a particular brand is known as the **brand image**. The consumer's beliefs may vary from true attributes based on his or her experience to the effects of selective perception, selective distortion and selective retention.

Fourth, the consumer is assumed to have a *utility function* for each attribute. The utility function shows how the consumer expects total product satisfaction to vary with different levels of different attributes. For example, Anna may expect her satisfaction from a digital camera to increase with better picture quality, to peak with a medium-weight camera as opposed to a very light or very heavy one and to be a compact. If we combine the attribute levels at which her utilities are highest, they make up Anna's ideal camera. The camera would also be her preferred camera if it were available and affordable.

Fifth, the consumer arrives at attitudes towards the different brands through some *evaluation procedure*. Consumers have been found to use one or more of several evaluation procedures, depending on the consumer and the buying decision.

In Anna's camera-buying situation, suppose she has narrowed her choice set to four cameras: FujiFilm FinePix F30, Canon Digital Ixus 750, Sony Cyber-shot DSC-W5 and the Nikon Coolpix P2. In addition, let us say she is interested primarily in four attributes – picture quality, ease of use, camera size and price. Table 5.6 shows how she believes each brand rates on each attribute.[36] Anna believes the Fuji will give her picture quality of 9 on a 10-point scale; is quite easy to use, 7; produces pictures of good image quality, 8; and is reasonably priced, 8. Similarly, she has beliefs about how the other cameras rate on these attributes. The marketer would like to be able to predict which camera Anna will buy.

Clearly, if one camera rated best on all the attributes, we could predict that Anna would choose it. But the brands vary in appeal. Some buyers will base their buying decision on only one

Alternative evaluation— The stage of the buyer decision process in which the consumer uses information to evaluate alternative brands in the choice set.

Brand image— The set of beliefs that consumers hold about a particular brand.

Table 5.6 A consumer's brand beliefs about cameras

Camera	Attribute			
	Picture quality	Ease of use	Facilities	Price
Fuji	9	7	8	8
Canon	8	8	6	8
Sony	8	8	6	7
Nikon	7	8	6	8

attribute and their choices are easy to predict. If Anna wants low price above everything, she should avoid the Sony, whereas if she wants the camera that is easiest to use, she could buy any other than the Fuji.

Most buyers consider several attributes, but assign different importance to each. If we knew the importance weights that Anna assigns to the four attributes, we could predict her camera choice more reliably. Suppose Anna assigns 40 per cent of the importance to the camera's picture quality, 30 per cent to ease of use, 20 per cent to its size and 10 per cent to its price. To find Anna's perceived value for each camera, we can multiply her importance weights by her beliefs about each camera. This gives us the following perceived values:

Fuji $= 0.4(9) + 0.3(7) + 0.2(8) + 0.1(8) = 8.1$

Canon $= 0.4(8) + 0.3(8) + 0.2(6) + 0.1(8) = 7.6$

Sony $= 0.4(8) + 0.3(8) + 0.2(6) + 0.1(7) = 7.5$

Nikon $= 0.4(7) + 0.3(8) + 0.2(6) + 0.1(8) = 6.9$

We would predict that Anna favours the Fuji.

This model is called the *expectancy value model* of consumer choice.[37] This is one of several possible models describing how consumers go about evaluating alternatives. Consumers might evaluate a set of alternatives in other ways. For example, Anna might decide that she should consider only cameras that satisfy a set of minimum attribute levels. She might decide that a camera must have a TV connector. This is called the *conjunctive model* of consumer choice. Or she might decide that she would settle for a camera that had a picture quality greater than 8 *or* ease of use greater than 7. This is called the *disjunctive model* of consumer choice.

How consumers go about evaluating purchase alternatives depends on the individual consumer and the specific buying situation. In some cases, consumers use careful calculations and logical thinking. At other times, the same consumers do little or no evaluating; instead they buy on impulse and rely on intuition. Sometimes consumers make buying decisions on their own; sometimes they turn to friends, consumer guides or salespeople for buying advice.

Marketers should study buyers to find out how they actually evaluate brand alternatives. If they know what evaluative processes go on, marketers can take steps to influence the buyer's decision. Suppose Anna is now inclined to buy a Fuji because of its picture quality. What strategies might another camera maker, say Canon, use to influence people like Anna? There are several. Canon could modify its camera to produce a version that has fewer features, but is lighter and cheaper. It could try to change buyers' beliefs about how its camera rates on key attributes, especially if consumers currently underestimate the camera's qualities. It could try to change buyers' beliefs about Fuji and other competitors. Finally, it could try to change the list of attributes that buyers consider or the importance attached to these attributes. For example, it might advertise that to be really useful a camera needs to be small and easy to use. What is the point in having a super-accurate camera if it takes too long to set up and is too awkward to carry around?

Purchase decision

In the evaluation stage, the consumer ranks brands and forms purchase intentions. Generally, the consumer's **purchase decision** will be to buy the most preferred brand, but two factors, shown in Figure 5.7, can come between the purchase *intention* and the purchase *decision*. The first factor is the *attitudes of others*. For example, if Anna Flores' husband feels strongly that Anna should buy the lowest-priced camera, then the chance of Anna buying a more expensive camera is reduced. Alternatively, his love of gadgets may attract him to the Fuji. How much another person's attitudes will affect Anna's choices depends both on the strength of the other person's attitudes towards her buying decision and on Anna's motivation to comply with that person's wishes.

Purchase intention is also influenced by *unexpected situational factors*. The consumer may form a purchase intention based on factors such as expected family income, expected price and expected benefits from the product. When the consumer is about to act, unexpected situational factors may arise to change the purchase intention. Anna may lose her job, some other purchase may become more urgent, or a friend may report being disappointed in her preferred camera. Thus preferences and even purchase intentions do not always result in actual purchase choice. They may direct purchase behaviour, but may not fully determine the outcome.

> **"** Preferences and even purchase intentions do not always result in actual purchase choice. **"**

A consumer's decision to change, postpone or avoid a purchase decision is influenced heavily by *perceived risk*. Many purchases involve some risk taking. Anxiety results when consumers cannot be certain about the purchase outcome. The amount of perceived risk varies with the amount of money at stake, the amount of purchase uncertainty and the amount of consumer self-confidence. A consumer takes certain actions to reduce risk, such as avoiding purchase decisions, gathering more information and looking for national brand names and products with warranties. The marketer must understand the factors that provoke feelings of risk in consumers and must provide information and support that will reduce the perceived risk.

Postpurchase behaviour

The marketer's job does not end when the product is bought. After purchasing the product, the consumer will be satisfied or dissatisfied and will engage in **postpurchase behaviour** of interest to the marketer. What determines whether the buyer is satisfied or dissatisfied with a purchase? The answer lies in the relationship between the *consumer's expectations* and the product's *perceived performance*. If the product falls short of expectations, the consumer is disappointed; if it meets expectations, the consumer is satisfied; if it exceeds expectations, the consumer is delighted.

The larger the gap between expectations and performance, the greater the consumer's dissatisfaction. This suggests that sellers should promise only what their brands can deliver so that buyers are satisfied. Some sellers might even understate product performance levels to boost later consumer satisfaction. Motoring organisations regularly give pessimistic quotes about how long they will take to reach a customer whose car breaks down. If they say they will be 30 minutes and get there in 20, the customer is impressed. If, however, they get there in 20 minutes after promising 10, the customer is not so happy.

Almost all major purchases result in **cognitive dissonance**, or discomfort caused by postpurchase conflict. After the purchase, consumers are satisfied with the benefits of the chosen brand and are glad to avoid the drawbacks of the brands not bought. However, every purchase involves compromise. Consumers feel uneasy about acquiring the drawbacks of the chosen brand and about losing the benefits of the brands not purchased. Thus, consumers feel at least some postpurchase dissonance for every purchase.[38]

Purchase decision—The stage of the buyer decision process in which the consumer actually buys the product.

Postpurchase behaviour—The stage of the buyer decision process in which consumers take further action after purchase based on their satisfaction or dissatisfaction.

Cognitive dissonance—Buyer discomfort caused by postpurchase conflict.

Why is it so important to satisfy the customer? Customer satisfaction is a key to building profitable relationships with consumers – to keeping and growing consumers and reaping their customer lifetime value. Satisfied customers buy a product again, talk favourably to others about the product, pay less attention to competing brands and advertising, and buy other products from the company. Many marketers go beyond merely *meeting* the expectations of customers – they aim to *delight* the customer.

Dissatisfied consumers respond differently. Bad word of mouth often travels farther and faster than good word of mouth. It can quickly damage consumer attitudes about a company and its products. But companies cannot simply rely on dissatisfied customers to volunteer their complaints when they are dissatisfied. Most unhappy customers never tell the company about their problem. Therefore, a company should measure customer satisfaction regularly. It should set up systems that *encourage* customers to complain. In this way, the company can learn how well it is doing and how it can improve. But what should companies do about dissatisfied customers? At a minimum, most companies offer free or local-rate contact numbers and websites to handle complaints and enquiries.

> " Bad word of mouth often travels farther and faster than good word of mouth. "

By studying the overall buyer decision, marketers may be able to find ways to help consumers move through it. For example, if consumers are not buying a new product because they do not perceive a need for it, marketing might launch advertising messages that trigger the need and show how the product solves customers' problems. If customers know about the product but are not buying because they hold unfavourable attitudes towards it, the marketer must find ways either to change the product or to change consumer perceptions.

The buyer decision process for new products

We have looked at the stages that buyers go through in trying to satisfy a need. Buyers may pass quickly or slowly through these stages and some of the stages may even be reversed. Much depends on the nature of the buyer, the product and the buying situation.

We now look at how buyers approach the purchase of new products. A **new product** is a good, service or idea that is perceived by some potential customers as new. It may have been around for a while, but our interest is in how consumers learn about products for the first time and make decisions on whether to adopt them. We define the **adoption process** as 'the mental process through which an individual passes from first learning about an innovation to final adoption', and **adoption** as the decision by an individual to become a regular user of the product.[39]

Stages in the adoption process

Consumers go through five stages in the process of adopting a new product:

1. *Awareness.* The consumer becomes aware of the new product, but lacks information about it.
2. *Interest.* The consumer seeks information about the new product.
3. *Evaluation.* The consumer considers whether trying the new product makes sense.
4. *Trial.* The consumer tries the new product on a small scale to improve his or her estimate of its value.
5. *Adoption.* The consumer decides to make full and regular use of the new product.

New product—A good, service or idea that is perceived by some potential customers as new.

Adoption process—The mental process through which an individual passes from first hearing about an innovation to final adoption.

Adoption—The decision by an individual to become a regular user of the product.

This model suggests that the new-product marketer should think about how to help consumers move through these stages. Denon, a leading manufacturer of home cinema equipment, may discover that many consumers in the interest stage do not move to the trial stage because of uncertainty and the large investment. If these same consumers would be willing to use a sound system on a trial basis for a small fee, the manufacturer should consider offering a trial-use plan with an option to buy.

Individual differences in innovativeness

People differ greatly in their readiness to try new products. In each product area, there are 'consumption pioneers' and early adopters. Other individuals adopt new products much later. This has led to a classification of people into the adopter categories shown in Figure 5.8.

After a slow start, an increasing number of people adopt the new product. The number of adopters reaches a peak and then drops off as fewer non-adopters remain. Innovators are defined as the first 2.5 per cent of the buyers to adopt a new idea (those beyond two standard deviations from mean adoption time); the early adopters are the next 13.5 per cent (between one and two standard deviations), and so forth.

The five adopter groups have differing values. *Innovators* are adventurous: they try new ideas at some risk. *Early adopters* are guided by respect: they are opinion leaders in their community and adopt new ideas early but carefully. The *early majority* is deliberate: although they are rarely leaders, they adopt new ideas before the average person. The *late majority* is sceptical: they adopt an innovation only after most people have tried it. Finally, *laggards* are tradition-bound: they are suspicious of changes and adopt the innovation only when it has become something of a tradition itself.

This adopter classification suggests that an innovating firm should research the characteristics of innovators and early adopters and should direct marketing efforts to them. For example, home computer innovators have been found to be middle-aged and higher in income and education than non-innovators and they tend to be opinion leaders. They also tend to be more rational, more introverted and less social. In general, innovators tend to be relatively younger, better educated and higher in income than later adopters and non-adopters. They are more receptive to unfamiliar things, rely more on their own values and judgement, and are more willing to take risks. They are less brand loyal and more likely to take advantage of special promotions such as discounts, coupons and samples.

Manufacturers of products and brands subject to strong group influence must find out how to reach the opinion leaders in the relevant reference groups. Earlier in this chapter we referred to opinion leaders – people within a reference group who, because of special skills, knowledge, personality or other characteristics, exert influence on others. Opinion leaders are found in all strata of society and one person may be an opinion leader in certain product areas and an

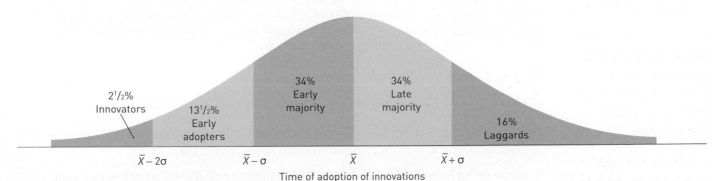

Figure 5.8 Adopter categorisation on the basis of relative time of adoption of innovations

SOURCE: From Everett M. Rogers, *Diffusion of Innovations*, 4th edn. (New York: The Free Press). Copyright © 1962, 1971, 1983 by The Free Press. Copyright © 1995 by Everett M. Rogers. Reprinted with the permission of The Free Press, a Division of Simon & Schuster Adult Publishing Group.

opinion follower in others. Marketers try to identify the personal characteristics of opinion leaders for the products, determine what media they use and direct messages at them. This often occurs in the music industry, where clubs and radio DJs are influential. In other cases, advertisements can simulate opinion leadership, showing informal discussions between people and thereby reducing the need for consumers to seek advice from others.

If Anna Flores buys a camera, both the product and the brand will be visible to others whom she respects. Her decision to buy the camera and her brand choice may therefore be influenced strongly by opinion leaders, such as friends who belong to a photography club.

Influence of product characteristics on rate of adoption

The characteristics of the new product affect its rate of adoption. Some products catch on almost overnight (iPod or FaceBook), whereas others take a long time to gain acceptance (HDTV). Five characteristics are especially important in influencing an innovation's rate of adoption. For example, consider the characteristics of HDTV in relation to the rate of adoption:

- *Relative advantage:* the degree to which the innovation appears superior to existing products. The greater the perceived relative advantage of using HDTV – say, in picture quality and ease of viewing – the sooner HDTVs will be adopted.

- *Compatibility:* the degree to which the innovation fits the values and experiences of potential consumers. HDTV, for example, is highly compatible with the lifestyles found in upper middle-class homes. However, it is not yet completely compatible with the programming and broadcasting systems currently available to consumers.

- *Complexity:* the degree to which the innovation is difficult to understand or use. HDTVs are not very complex and, therefore, once more programming is available and prices come down, will take less time to penetrate homes than more complex innovations.

- *Divisibility:* the degree to which the innovation may be tried on a limited basis. HDTVs are still relatively expensive. This will slow the rate of adoption.

- *Communicability:* the degree to which the results of using the innovation can be observed or described to others. Because HDTV lends itself to demonstration and description, its use will spread faster among consumers.

Other characteristics influence the rate of adoption, such as initial and ongoing costs, risk and uncertainty, and social approval. The new-product marketer has to research all these factors when developing the new product and its marketing programme.

To marketers, changing consumer behaviour towards sustainable consumption is the same as asking consumers to adopt a new product. The benefits from sustainable consumption are sometimes subtle and often mean consumers making a sacrifice to benefit the world. But even where there are clear benefits to the consumer as well as the environment, changing behaviour is hard. Real Marketing 5.2 looks at ways of encouraging sustainable consumer behaviour as some barriers are being faced in moving in that direction.

Consumer behaviour across international borders

Understanding consumer behaviour is difficult enough for companies marketing in a single country. For companies operating in many countries, however, understanding and serving the needs of consumers is daunting. Although consumers in different countries may have some things in common, their values, attitudes and behaviours often vary greatly. International

real marketing 5.2

Sustainable consumption: Green Sham's Law

Gresham's Law states that 'bad [defaced] money drives out the good'. We need a variation on this for sustainable consumption: Green Sham's Law – 'simplistic ideas drive out good ideas'.

Sometimes marketing to consumers is like bringing up children or training dogs. All the science and forces are there, but one little lapse and it all goes wrong. Dogs and kids learn what is right as well as what is wrong. Changing consumers 'for the better' is hard, even when the 'better' is better for them.

Take the influence of reference groups on obesity. Internet screens, programmes, magazines and official literature can be full of perfect examples of how to look and eat, but obesity is 'socially contagious'. The way we behave and what is acceptable depends on our friends. If a person you consider a friend becomes obese, your own chance of becoming obese goes up 57 per cent. That is higher than the influence of the immediate family. Among siblings the chance increases by only 40 per cent and between spouses 37 per cent. Basically, consumers' thinking goes, 'It is OK if everyone around me is doing it, be it over-eating, over-drinking, buying a 4×4 or going organic.'

The United Nations task force on sustainable tourism identifies five ways to 'change people for the better': education and information, promotion, economic market-based instruments (price), legal measures, and self-regulation. Let us look at each option and see how hard it is.

Education and information

Remember, the most influential group of people are our own friends, so it is hard to directly influence behaviour. Like any innovation, people are being asked to go through the stages of the adoption process and overcome the same hurdles as for any new product. Unfortunately there are so many messages being pumped out about sustainability that people are confused. However, one simple idea has got through that appears to benefit consumers directly: organic food. It sounds healthier, the concept of pesticides is easy to understand and lots of people have a commercial interest in promoting organics. Unfortunately the 'sustainable' credentials of organic food are questionable. Organic farming is not necessarily sustainable, reports Britain's environmental protection agency, DEFRA (the Department of Environment, Farming and Rural Affairs), in a new study conducted by the Manchester Business School. The report on 'The Environmental Impact of Food Production and Consumption' concluded that the environmental benefits of organic food production are not clear, noting that

...5.2

locally-sourced rather than globally-sourced products are not necessarily more energy efficient and that reduced use of fertilisers requires more, not less, land for agriculture, increasing pressure on natural forests and ecosystems.

Two simple cases support DEFRA's conclusions.

- French environmental campaigner Jean-Marc Jancovici has concluded that switching to organic farming is not simple. He estimates organic farming generates 30 per cent less emissions but, unfortunately, yields 50 per cent less food than conventional farming. If we want it, we have to reclaim more land or eat less, especially if we also want sustainable fuel for our cars. The other answer to gaining better yields with fewer chemicals and lower carbon footprint is genetically modified crops, but in Europe we do not like those.
- Shortly after a furore about flowers being flown in from Africa for Valentine's Day, someone did the sums. Environmentally sensitive retailer Sainsbury's concluded that the carbon footprint of local, hot-house grown flowers was 4.5 times greater than that of Fairtrade flowers flown in from Kenya.

Promotion

Innovations have more chance of succeeding if people are pushing them. Giving people a subsidy to insulate their homes better is effective because contractors or energy suppliers have an incentive to do the work. In the UK, energy suppliers such as npower or e.on's Powergen receive direct government grants for doing the work, so are keen to sell. Left to their own devices, many consumers would burn away money on heating bills rather than spend upfront.

Market-based instruments

Switching from traditional incandescent light bulbs to energy efficient, long lasting compact fluorescent light bulbs is a real win–win, saving customers money by their having to buy far fewer light bulbs and cutting their energy costs by 75 per cent, but as Philips lament, 70 per cent of the light bulbs sold are still of the incandescent type. One reason why consumers do not switch is that in Europe compact fluorescent light bulbs still cost a lot more than incandescent bulbs.

Strangely, one reason for the higher price is an EU 'anti-dumping duty' imposed on fluorescent bulbs from China that adds 66 per cent to their price. Osram, a Siemens subsidiary, wants to keep the 'anti-dumping' duty to protect its workers, although European market leader Philips, and two other competitors, want to remove it since they already manufacture in China. The World Wide Fund for Nature and other campaigners are fighting with the majority of the lighting industry to get the 'anti-dumping' duty removed, saying 'the working conditions in China are reasonable and the environmental concerns are paramount.' However, Günter Verheugen, the EU industry commissioner, questions the cut in duty, arguing that protecting European jobs is crucial.

Legal measures

Peter Mandelson, the EU's trade commissioner, hopes that in a few years consumers will have no option but to use fluorescent light bulbs, since he is pushing for incandescent bulbs to be banned across the whole of the EU within a few years. The success of government is well illustrated in the US where the average fuel consumption of cars in environmentally conscious California, which has imposed tight emission laws, is half that of cars in the unregulated mid-west.

Self-regulation

So concerned are some retailers, such as the Co-op, that they are refusing to stock incandescent bulbs and others, such as Tesco, are heavily promoting and heavily discounting fluorescent bulbs. In global markets self-regulation is difficult but, like the Co-op, companies can lead governments and adopt environmentally sustainable strategies. Examples are Sony's consumer electronics which have exceptionally low power consumption on standby, and BMW's pioneering of the recycling of their cars.

SOURCES: Christina Kamp, 'Tourism segment: Influencing consumer behaviour to promote sustainable tourism development', UN CSD NGO Steering Committee (http://csgndo.igs.org/tourism/tourdial_cons.htm), accessed 30 July 2007; *Manchester Evening News,* 'Is organic food better?' (4 May 2005); Kath Stathers, 'Can retail therapy really save the environment?', *Design Council Magazine* (2) (Summer 2007), pp. 12–17; *Financial Times,* 'Science briefing: Friends make you fat, says study' (27 July 2007), p. 7; Andrew Bounds and Sara Laitner, 'Cheaper Chinese bulbs give EU green light', *Financial Times* (27 July 2007), p. 5.

marketers must understand such differences and adjust their products and marketing programmes accordingly.

> " For companies operating in many countries . . . understanding and serving the needs of consumers is daunting. "

Sometimes the differences are obvious. For example, in the UK, where most people eat cereal regularly for breakfast, Kellogg focuses its marketing on persuading consumers to select a Kellogg's brand rather than a competitor's brand. In France, however, where most people prefer croissants and coffee or no breakfast at all, Kellogg's advertising simply attempts to convince people that they should eat cereal for breakfast. Its packaging includes step-by-step instructions on how to prepare cereal. In India, where many consumers eat heavy, fried breakfasts and 22 per cent of consumers

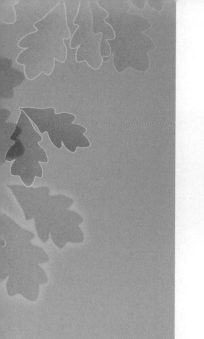

skip the meal altogether, Kellogg's advertising attempts to convince buyers to switch to a lighter, more nutritious breakfast diet.

Often, differences across international markets are subtler. They may result from physical differences in consumers and their environments. For example, Remington makes smaller electric shavers to fit the smaller hands of Japanese consumers, and battery-powered shavers for the British market, where some bathrooms have no electrical outlets. Other differences result from varying customs. Consider the following examples:

- Shaking your head from side to side means 'no' in most countries but 'yes' in Bulgaria and Sri Lanka.
- In South America, southern Europe and many Arab countries, touching another person is a sign of warmth and friendship. In the Orient, it is considered an invasion of privacy.
- In Norway or Malaysia, it's rude to leave something on your plate when eating; in Egypt, it's rude *not* to leave something on your plate.
- A door-to-door salesperson might find it tough going in Italy, where it is improper for a man to call on a woman if she is home alone.

Failing to understand such differences in customs and behaviours from one country to another can spell disaster for a marketer's international products and programmes.

Marketers must decide on the degree to which they will adapt their products and marketing programmes to meet the unique cultures and needs of consumers in various markets. On the one hand, they want to standardise their offerings in order to simplify operations and take advantage of cost economies. On the other hand, adapting marketing efforts within each country results in products and programmes that better satisfy the needs of local consumers. The question of whether to adapt or standardise the marketing mix across international markets has created a lively debate in recent years.

Reviewing the concepts

The world consumer market consists of more than 6.5 *billion* people. Consumers around the world vary greatly in age, income, education level and tastes. Understanding how these differences affect *consumer buying behaviour* is one of the biggest challenges marketers face.

1. Define the consumer market and construct a simple model of consumer buyer behaviour

The *consumer market* consists of all the individuals and households who buy or acquire goods and services for personal consumption. The simplest model of consumer buyer behaviour is the stimulus–response model. According to this model, marketing stimuli (the four Ps) and other major forces (economic, technological, political, cultural) enter the consumer's 'black box' and produce certain responses. Once in the black box, these inputs produce observable buyer responses, such as product choice, brand choice, purchase timing and purchase amount.

2. Name the four major factors that influence consumer buyer behaviour

Consumer buyer behaviour is influenced by four key sets of buyer characteristics: cultural, social, personal and psychological. Although many of these factors cannot be influenced by the marketer, they can be useful in identifying interested buyers and in shaping products and appeals to serve consumer needs better. *Culture* is the most basic determinant of a person's wants and behaviour. It includes the basic values, perceptions, preferences and behaviours that a person learns from family and other important institutions. *Subcultures* are 'cultures within cultures' that have distinct values and lifestyles and can be based on anything from age to ethnicity. People with different cultural and subcultural characteristics have different product and brand preferences. As a result, marketers may want to focus their marketing programmes on the special needs of certain groups.

Social factors also influence a buyer's behaviour. A person's *reference groups* – family, friends, social organisations, professional associations – strongly affect product and brand choices. The buyer's age, life-cycle stage, occupation, economic circumstances, lifestyle, personality and other *personal characteristics* influence his or her buying decisions. Consumer *lifestyles* – the whole pattern of acting and interacting in the world – are also an important influence on purchase decisions. Finally, consumer buying behaviour is influenced by four major *psychological factors* – motivation, perception, learning, and beliefs and attitudes. Each of these factors provides a different perspective for understanding the workings of the buyer's black box.

3. List and define the major types of buying decision behaviour and stages in the buyer decision process

Buying behaviour may vary greatly across different types of products and buying decisions. Consumers undertake *complex buying behaviour* when they are highly involved in a purchase and perceive significant differences among brands. *Dissonance-reducing behaviour* occurs when consumers are highly involved but see little difference among brands. *Habitual buying behaviour* occurs under conditions of low involvement and little significant brand difference. In situations characterised by low involvement but significant perceived brand differences, consumers engage in *variety-seeking buying behaviour.*

When making a purchase, the buyer goes through a decision process consisting of *need recognition, information search, evaluation of alternatives, purchase decision* and *postpurchase behaviour.* The marketer's job is to understand the buyer's behaviour at each stage and the influences that are operating. During *need recognition*, the consumer recognises a problem or need that could be satisfied by a product or service in the market. Once the need is recognised, the consumer is aroused to seek more information and moves into the *information search* stage. With information in hand, the consumer proceeds to *alternative evaluation,* during which the information is used to evaluate brands in the choice set. From there, the consumer makes a *purchase decision* and actually buys the product. In the final stage of the buyer decision process, *postpurchase behaviour*, the consumer takes action based on satisfaction or dissatisfaction.

4. Describe the adoption and diffusion process for new products

The product adoption process is comprised of five stages: awareness, interest, evaluation, trial and adoption. Initially, the consumer must become aware of the new product. *Awareness* leads to *interest*, and the consumer seeks information about the new product. Once information has been gathered, the consumer enters the *evaluation* stage and considers buying the new product. Next, in the *trial* stage, the consumer tries the product on a small scale to improve his or her estimate of its value. If the consumer is satisfied with the product, he or she enters the *adoption* stage, deciding to use the new product fully and regularly.

With regard to diffusion of new products, consumers respond at different rates, depending on the consumer's characteristics and the product's characteristics. Consumers may be innovators, early adopters, early majority, late majority or laggards. *Innovators* are willing to try risky new ideas; *early adopters* – often community opinion leaders – accept new ideas early but carefully; the *early majority* – rarely leaders – decide deliberately to try new ideas, doing so before the average person does; the *late majority* try an innovation only after a majority of people have adopted it; whereas *laggards* adopt an innovation only after it has become a tradition itself. Manufacturers try to bring their new products to the attention of potential early adopters, especially those who are opinion leaders.

Discussing the concepts

1. Thinking about the purchase of a hi-fi system, indicate the extent to which cultural, social, personal and psychological factors affect how a buyer evaluates hi-fi products and chooses a brand.

2. Describe and contrast any differences in the buying behaviour of consumers for the following products: a music download, a notebook computer, a pair of trainers and a breakfast cereal.

3. Why might a detailed understanding of the model of the consumer buying decision process help marketers develop more effective marketing strategies to capture and retain customers? How universal is the model? How useful is it?

4. In designing the advertising for a soft drink, which would you find more helpful: information about consumer demographics or about consumer lifestyles? Give examples of how you would use each type of information.

5. Take, for example, a new method of contraception, which is being 'sold' to young males. It is a controversial, albeit innovative concept. Your firm is the pioneer in launching this device. What are the main factors your firm must research when developing a marketing programme for this product?

6. It has been said that consumers' buying behaviour is shaped more by perception than by reality. Do you agree with this comment? Why or why not?

Applying the concepts

1. Different types of product can fulfil different functional and psychological needs.
   - List five luxury products or services that are very interesting or important to you. Some possibilities are cars, clothing, sports equipment, cosmetics or club membership. List five other necessities that you use which have little interest for you, such as pens, laundry detergent or bank accounts.
   - Make a list of words that describe how you feel about each of the products/services listed. Are there differences between the types of word you used for luxuries and necessities? What does this tell you about the different psychological needs these products fulfil?

2. Different groups may have different types of effect on consumers.
   - Consider an item you bought which is typical of what your peers (a key reference group) buy, such as a compact disc, a mountain bike or a brand of trainer. Were you conscious

that your friends owned something similar when you made the purchase? Did this make you want the item more or less? Why or why not?

● Now, think of brands that you currently use which your parents also use. Examples may include soap, shaving cream or margarine. Did you think through these purchases as carefully as those influenced by your peers or were these purchases simply the result of following old habits?

3. SRI Consulting, through the Business Intelligence Centre online, features the Values and Lifestyles Program (VALS). Visit SRI at www.sric-bi.com/VALS/presurvey.shtml to the VALS questionnaire.

● Take the survey to determine your type and then read all about your type. Why or why not does it describe you well?

● What four products have high indexes for your type? Do you buy these products?

● Compare the nine Japan-VALS segments with the US VALS. How similar are they, and are they likely to explain the European consumer?

● Other than product design, how can marketers use information from Japan-VALS?

Web resources

For additional classic case studies and Internet exercises, visit **www.pearsoned.co.uk/kotler**

References

1. See 'Breda's Harley-Davidson Day' on Webshots.com at http://community.webshots.com/album/176101205WpZFdM. Quotes and other information from Greg Schneider, 'Rebels with disposable income; aging baby boomers line up to buy high-end versions of youthful indulgences', *The Washington Post* (27 April 2003), p. F1; Ted Bolton, 'Tattooed call letters: The ultimate test of brand loyalty', accessed online at www.boltonresearch.com, April 2003; Jay Palmer, 'Vroom at the top', *Barron's* (29 March 2004), pp. 17–18; Chris Woodyard, 'Motorcycle sales rev up to top 1 million', *USA Today* (20 January 2005); Marc Gerstein, 'The road ahead for Harley', *Reuters* (13 April 2006); and the Harley-Davidson website at www.Harley-Davidson.com, July 2006.

2. See www.un.org/esa/population/unpop and www.census.gov/main/www/popclock for continuously updated projections of the world's population; Adrian Michaels, 'China's taste for luxury bears risks', *Financial Times* (5 June 2007), p. 28.

3. Rudyard Kipling, from 'The Elephant's Child' in *Just So Stories* (1902), a quote still widely used to guide business consulting; for example, see Creative Advantage (http://www.creativeadvantage.com/consulting.htm) and Michael Heath Consulting (http://www.mhconsult.com/talkingbusiness_0404.html).

4. Several models of the consumer buying process have been developed by marketing scholars. For a summary, see Leon G. Schiffman and Leslie Lazar Kanuk, *Consumer Behaviour*, 9th edn (Englewood Cliffs, NJ: Prentice Hall, 2006), Ch. 20.

5. Jim Edwards, 'Why buy?', *Brandweek* (5 October 2005), pp. 21–4.

6. Alan Mitchell, 'Advertising turns to science to get inside consumers' heads', *Financial Times* (5 January 2007), p. 10.

7. For this and other examples, see Philip R. Cateora, *International Marketing*, 8th edn (Homewood, IL: Irwin, 1993), Ch. 4; and Warren J. Keegan, Bodo Schlegelmilch and Barbara Stoettinger, *Global Marketing Management: A European perspective* (Pearson, 2000).

8. Adam Jones and James Politi, 'Kraft in talks to buy Danone biscuits', *Financial Times* (2 July 2007), p. 26; Emma Vandore, 'Danone defends Numico bid price against analysts' criticism', *AP Worldstream* (10 July 2007).

9. Brian J. Ford, *The Future of Eating* (Thames & Hudson, 2000); 'Blech', *The Economist* (15 January 2000), p. 87; 'Cooking: ready, steady, eat', *The Economist* (8 June 2002), p. 28; 'Fat or fit', *The Economist, The World in 2002* (2001); 'More industrial decline: the china syndrome', *The Economist* (25 August 2001), p. 33; 'Franchise sector turnover up five-fold in last decade', *Irish Independent* (19 July 2007).

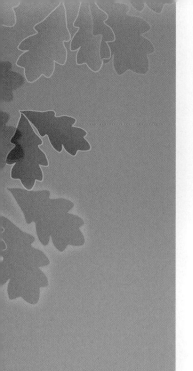

10. 'Islam in France', *The Economist* (25 October 2003), pp. 41–2; 'Europe's Muslims' and 'Muslims in Western Europe', *The Economist* (8 August 2002); 'In the name of the law', *The Guardian* (14 June 2007); 'Standard Chartered Bank launches Islamic banking brand', *Asia Pulse* (18 June 2007).

11. 'Emigration: Over there', *The Economist* (13 December 2006); Graham Hiscott, 'The Polish food wars', *The Express* (19 July 2007).

12. Information from *Eurostat Yearbook 2006–2007*; 'Whatever happened to the counterculture?', *The Economist* (24 June 2004); Steve Hemsley, 'Never too old (or rich) to rock'n'roll', *Financial Times* (26 April 2007); Harry Dunphy, 'Study finds that Eastern Europe, former Soviet republics aging fastest of world countries', *AP Worldstream* (20 June 2007).

13. Details of NS-SEC and the European initiatives can be found at www.statistics.gov.uk; Eurostat, 'Methodologies and Working Papers, Task Force on Core Social Variables: Final Report', 2007 edition (http://epp.eurostat.ec.europa.eu/cache/ITY_OFFPUB/KS-RA-07-006/EN/KS-RA-07-006-EN.PDF).

14. Richard Tomkins, 'The folly of treating children as consumers', *Financial Times* (28 November 2002), p. 23; for top toys since the 1960s see http://www.toyretailersassociation.co.uk/toty/toty65.htm.

15. For a look at the cultural twists and turns over generations, see Peter Everett, *You'll Never Want to be 16 Again* (London: BBC Publications, 1994) or Bevis Hillier, *The Style of the Century* (London: Herbert, 1993); Jon Savage, *Teenage: The creation of youth culture* (Viking Books, 2007).

16. Syl Tang, 'The tipping point', *FT Business of Fashion* (Spring/Summer 2006), pp. 12–13.

17. Michael Witte, 'Buzz-z-z marketing', *Business Week* (30 July 2001), pp. 50–6.

18. Anya Kamenetz, 'The network unbound', *Fast Company* (June 2006), pp. 69–73.

19. Saul Hansell, 'For MySpace, making friends was easy. Big profit is tougher', *New York Times* (23 April 2006), p. 3.1.

20. Quote and information from 'Colored vision adidas unleashes seven-film mobile media', *Boards* (May 2006), p. 15.

21. Quote from Anya Kamenetz, 'The network unbound', *Fast Company* (June 2006), p. 73. Also see Julie Bosman, 'Chevy tries a write-your-own-ad approach', *New York Times* (4 April 2006), p. C1; S. Alexander Haslam, Nyla R. Branscombe and Sebastian Bachmann, 'Why consumers rebel: Social identity and the etiology of adverse reactions to service failure', in S. Alexander Haslam, Daan Van Knippenberg, Michael J. Platow and Naomi Ellemers, *Social Identity at Work* (Hove: Psychology Press, 2003), pp. 293–309.

22. Sheila Jones, 'Procter & Gamble's bottom line is challenged', *Financial Times* (11 May 2000), p. 1; 'Going soft', *The Economist* (4 March 2000), p. 34; Helen Cook, 'Tissue of lies: Supermarket loses toilet paper battle', *The Mirror* (14 January 2004).

23. 'Real men get waxed', *The Economist* (3 July 2003); James Harkin, 'The return of the real men', *FT Magazine* (16/17 September 2007), pp. 22–5.

24. Kevin Downey, 'What children teach their parents', *Broadcasting & Cable* (13 March 2006), p. 26; Debbi Marco, 'How to shop without a strop', *The Express* (24 July 2007).

25. Alice Dragoon, 'How to do customer segmentation right', *CIO* (1 October 2005), p. 1.

26. Lucy Killgren, 'Passion for the new celebrity stamping-ground', *Financial Times* (19 June 2007), p. 23.

27. Stephanie Armour, 'Slowdown moves more adult kids back home', *USA Today* (24 April 2001), p. 1B; Mariko Sanchanta, 'Youth snubs life as salaryman and seeks its dream', *Financial Times* (30 September 2002), p. VI; 'Consensus and contraction', Special Survey – What Ails Japan?: *The Economist* (20 April 2002), pp. 8–10; Michiyo Nakamoto, FT Report – Japan: 'Big effort to recruit the old, the youthful and the women', *Financial Times* (6 November 2006).

28. See 'Sinus Social Milieus' at www.sociovision.com/sociovision/page?rep1=SM&rep2=Group&nom=princ-sm-uk.

29. Jennifer Aaker, 'Dimensions of measuring brand personality', *Journal of Marketing Research* (August 1997), pp. 347–56. Also see Jennifer Aaker, 'The malleable self: The role of self expression in persuasion', *Journal of Marketing Research* (May 1999), pp. 45–57; Audrey Azoulay and Jean-Noel Kapferer, 'Do brand personality scales really measure brand personality?', *Journal of Brand Management* (November 2003), p. 143; Priscilla Chan, John Saunders, Gail Taylor and Anne Souchon, 'Brand personality perception – Region or country specific?', *European Advances in Consumer Research*, **6** (2003), pp. 300–7.

30. Seth Stevenson, 'Ad report card: Mac attack' (19 June 2006), accessed at www.slate.com/id/2143810.

31. Abraham H. Maslow, *Motivation and Personality*, 2nd edn (New York: Harper & Row, 1970), pp. 80–106; E. Wooldridge, 'Time to stand Maslow's hierarchy on its head?', *People Management*, **1**, 25 (1995), pp. 17–19; for examples see Richard Tomkins, 'Luxury for all', *Financial Times* (17 July 2003).

32. Charles Pappas, 'Ad nauseam', *Advertising Age* (10 July 2000), pp. 16–18. See also Mark Ritson, 'Marketers need to find a way to control the contagion of clutter', *Marketing* (6 March 2003), p. 16; and David H. Freedman, 'The future of advertising is here', *Inc.* (August 2005), pp. 70–8.

33. 'The right to be beautiful', *The Economist* (24 May 2003), p. 9; Joanna Pitman, *On Blondes* (Bloomsbury: London, 2003).

34. Bob Garfield, '"Subliminal" seduction and other urban myths', *Advertising Age* (18 September 2000), pp. 4, 105. Also see 'We have ways of making you think', *Marketing Week* (25 September 2003), p. 14; Si Cantwell, 'Common sense; scrutiny helps catch catchy ads', *Wilmington Star-News* (1 April 2004), p. 1B; and Allison Motluk, 'Subliminal advertising may work after all' (28 April 2006), accessed at www.newscientist.com.

35. John Kay, 'Driving through the spin on Honda's big success', *Financial Times* (16 November 2004); Chris Grier, 'Motorcyclists' age, affluence trending upward – and so are accidents', *BestWire* (24 July 2007).

36. The ratings are based on those given in 'Product test: compact cameras' from the Consumers' Association magazine *Which?* (20 July 2007) on www.which.net.

37. This was developed by Martin Fishbein: see Martin Fishbein and Icek Ajzen, *Belief, Attitude, Intention, and Behaviour* (Reading, MA: Addison-Wesley, 1975).

38. See Leon Festinger, *A Theory of Cognitive Dissonance* (Stanford, CA: Stanford University Press, 1957); Leon Schiffman and Leslie Lazar Kanuk, *Consumer Behavior*, 9th edn (Upper Saddle River, NJ: Prentice Hall, 2006), pp. 219–20; Patti Williams and Jennifer L. Aaker, 'Can mixed emotions peacefully coexist?', *Journal of Consumer Research*, **28**, 4 (March 2002), pp. 636–49; Adam Ferrier, 'Young are not marketing savvy; they're suckers', *B&T Weekly* (22 October 2004), p. 13; and Martin O'Neill and Adrian Palmer, 'Cognitive dissonance and the stability of service quality perceptions', *Journal of Services Marketing*, **18**, 6 (2004), pp. 433–49.

39. The following discussion draws heavily from Everett M. Rogers, *Diffusion of Innovations*, 3rd edn (New York: Free Press, 1983). Also see Hubert Gatignon and Thomas S. Robertson, 'A propositional inventory for new diffusion research', *Journal of Consumer Research* (March 1985), pp. 849–67; Everett M. Rogers, *Diffusion of Innovations*, 4th edn (New York: Free Press, 1995); Marnik G. Dekiple, Philip M. Parker and Milos Sarvary, 'Global diffusion of technological innovations: a coupled-hazard approach', *Journal of Marketing Research* (February 2000), pp. 47–59; Peter J. Danaher, Bruce G. S. Hardie and William P. Putsis, 'Marketing-mix variables and the diffusion of successive generations of a technological innovation', *Journal of Marketing Research* (November 2001), pp. 501–14; Eun-Ju Lee, Jinkook Lee and David W. Schumann, 'The influence of communication source and mode on consumer adoption of technological innovations', *Journal of Consumer Affairs* (Summer 2002), pp. 1–27; G. Antonides, H.B. Amesz and I.C. Hulscher, 'Adoption of payment systems in ten countries – a case study of diffusion of innovations', *European Journal of Marketing*, **33**, 11/12 (1999), pp. 1123–35.

Company case 5 Shoot the dog: bye-bye Aibo

Dogs are great friends and lovely to have around but it is hard to argue with writer Justin Hankins' view that 'On the whole, pets are useless, unreliable, messy and expensive.' That is why the Boston Consulting Group's matrix in Chapter 3 tells us to shoot the expensive and unproductive 'dogs'. Large household domestic pets are environmentally unfriendly too. Beside fouling streets and barking, they consume more protein than many people in the world have to live on. What a great idea to replace 'the squelching, oozing yuckiness of the natural world' with 'the sleek, silvery shimmer' of a robo-dog like K-9, of Dr Who fame, suggests Mr Hankins. What is more, a robo-dog is much more environmentally friendly.

Sony has spent billions of yen developing the world's first robo-dog. Their Aibo ERS-7c dog has more tricks up its 32-megapixel memory stick than David Blaine. This is no simple animal or machine. Even the name has many possible meanings. Perhaps it stands for 'artificial intelligence robot'. Perhaps it refers to Aibo's camera eyes, which make it an 'eye bot', or maybe it's just Japanese for companion or pal.

What can you do with Aibo? Well, you can play with it. Aibo has a favourite toy, a pink ball, which it will chase down, pick up in its mouth, and return to you just like any real dog does if it is in the mood. If you praise Aibo, its tail wags, its eyes light up green, and it plays a happy melody. It can learn whatever name it is given and even skips across to its recharge station when its batteries run low. It's not exactly like a real dog – it is far less messy and cannot jump onto your favourite chair or eat it – but close in the sense that Aibo responds visibly to your love and affection.

Aibo can respond to praise and can learn. When you praise Aibo's behaviours, they become stronger and are more likely to be repeated. When scolded, Aibo is sometimes sad and plays a doleful melody. Other times, it responds to scolding by getting agitated and playing an angry melody while its eyes turn red. Although Aibo's responses may be different from a real dog's responses, they do represent the same emotions. Like a real dog, Aibo lets you know that it wants to play by jumping around. In addition to anger, sadness and playfulness, Aibo can show joy (eyes turn green and it plays a happy melody), surprise (eyes light up and it plays a surprised melody and gives a start), discontent (its eyes turn angry red and it moves away), and fear (when it encounters a big hole or rolls onto its back and can't get up, it plays a scared melody).

Voice commands such as 'stay', 'sit' or 'heel' wouldn't work with early Aibos because the puppy had no voice-response mechanism. Instead you gave it commands through a sound controller. Aibo responds only to perfect tones, so the sound controller contains combinations of present commands in perfect tones. Now, third-generation Aibo learns its owner's voice but it can still simply ignore you. When it is in a happy mood, it will perform tricks. Like most temperamental pets, Aibo will play or do tricks only if you're good to it.

When it's time to quit playing, you press the off or the pause button and Aibo lies down and goes to sleep. When not active, Aibo stays in its station, which serves as a battery charger. The robotic puppy comes with two lithium batteries so that one can be charged while the other is in use. A full charge lasts through about 1.5 hours of action.

Aibo comes in three colours (grey, metallic black and silver grey), has stereo microphones for ears, can recognise colours and shapes, and emits a variety of bleeps and chirps. A sensor in its head can distinguish between an amiable pat and a reproachful slap. You can set Aibo to Performance Mode, in which it does tricks, or to Game Mode, in which you control its movements. By making Aibo run and kick, you can even play robot soccer.

Ready to buy an Aibo? You won't find one for sale in any store. When launched it sold on the Internet at www.world.sony.com/robot/get/meet/html for a pricey 250,000 yen (€1,500) – twice the price of an 8-week-old pedigree puppy. Is anyone willing to pay such a stiff price? When launched in June 1999 Sony offered 5,000 Aibos in Japan and the US and all sold out in only 20 minutes. A second batch of 10,000 in November 1999 received more than 130,000 orders. Facing this greater than anticipated demand, Sony drew lots and selected winners in Japan, the United States and Europe. There appear to be lots of robot-dog's best friends out there!

One of the appealing features of Aibo is its open architecture. Based on experiences with its PlayStation video-game business, Sony decided not to develop everything in-house. Instead, it has invited other developers to create new programs for Aibo. This has resulted in the rapid development of additional memory sticks (programs) that allow you to teach Aibo new tricks or movements.

To test consumer reaction before offering them for sale, Sony demonstrated Aibos at several trade shows. Uniform reaction to the pet was 'That is so cute!' One enthusiastic consumer commented 'I love little robots. For me, it would be great. I'm single and I don't have time to keep a dog.' Another said, 'This is the coolest thing I've seen all day.' Numerous journalists privileged enough to play with Aibos found them to be lots of fun – even if they can't do anything useful.

Although Aibo isn't likely to fetch your newspaper, bring you your shoes, or scare away burglars, this little puppy had much promise from a marketing point of view. Sony hoped to create a whole new industry of entertainment robots, an industry that Sony management believe could be larger than the personal computer market. The new Aibo-like entertainment robots have broader appeal. More importantly, they may make people more comfortable with the idea of interacting with humanoid-like machines. Once that happens, robots could become nurses, maids or bodyguards. They might even become partners who will play with and talk to us. There's more than a little bit of *Star Wars*' R2D2 in all this. Back in the eighties, however, R2D2 and his companions seemed a long way off. Now, Aibo and other animal-bots appear to be bringing us into that *Star Wars* world much sooner than we thought.

To many animal lovers Aibo is a sad imitation of the real thing. However, like many products, Aibo found a market that it was not designed for. It has long been understood that dogs are important companions for older couples or singles living alone. But expensive, demanding, unreliable, messy dogs can be more than some people can handle. Not so Aibo. Increasingly, many Aibos are companions for older people. In that role Aibo could have some of the Saint Bernard's life-saving ability about him. Aibo can't run off and get help if Gran's in trouble, but it can be called and it can transmit help messages.

Aibo, with so many fans and so much potential, is no more. Aibo may be cute but Sir Howard Stringer, Sony's new boss, has killed off Aibo along with Qrio, a humanoid robot that can walk on two legs. Video killed this robo star! Aibo is not a band, a film or part of a video entertainment platform that the troubled Japanese multinational is now focusing on to generate cash and profits.

Never mind, where Aibo first trotted, others follow. South Korean company DasaTech, who cannot believe their luck with Aibo's demise, is stepping into the gap with a new robot hound. Their Genibo stands 30 centimetres tall, weighs 1.5 kilograms and understands 100 commands such as 'sit', 'roll over' and 'wag tail'. With a camera in its snout, Genibo can navigate around obstacles by itself and act as a watchdog. Where Aibo was cute, Genibo is useful *and* cute, says DasaTech.

Not so Pleo, a dinosaur robot that is the work of Furby co-creator Caleb Chung and a team of biologists, animators, robotics experts and programmers. 'Pleo is the first of a range of "designer life forms" that will be able to evolve and interact with one another,' says Ugobe, the San Francisco Bay company that has created Pleo. This could lead to a new kind of gameplay between light sabre-wielding robots on the tabletop rather than on the computer screen. Designer Mark Tilden explains: 'When we saw how fluid the prototype was, we knew we'd have to give this bot a nasty personality, and the sensors and smarts to hold his own. Of course we had to give him a personality flaw as well.' Pleo is not for lonely grannies or for people looking for a pet substitute.

'Sony set the standard for robotics in the consumer market with Aibo and they should have kept it because the market for robots is very strong,' says Bob Christopher, Ugobe's chief executive. Component costs are getting lower and Ugobe's sophisticated software and artificial intelligence allow Pleo to 'walk fluidly and balance itself and not just walk like a tin man, while at the same time being able to make emotive gestures.' Pleo took its first public strides at the Demo 2006 in Arizona and went on sale to the public in autumn 2006 for €146 – a tenth of the price of the Aibo. Will Pleo win where Aibo failed?

Questions

1. How might personal factors differ in the purchase of Aibo, Genibo or Pleo?

2. What cultural and social-class factors might affect the decision to buy a robo-pet?

3. How might reference groups affect a consumer's interest in robot pets or robots in general?

4. What motives or needs is an individual likely to be satisfying in purchasing a pet robot?

5. Why do you think Sony chose to sell Aibos only over the Internet? How might this affect a consumer's buying decision process? Was this a wise decision?

6. Aibo was a market innovation that pioneered the robo-pet market, it progressed Sony's understanding of robot technology and achieved huge media attention, but Sony could not continue to market Aibo at such a high price. Why should Ugobe do better?

SOURCES: Neil Gross and Irene Kunii, 'Man's best friend – and no scooper needed', *Business Week* (20 July 1998), p. 531; Irene Kunii, 'This cute little pet is a robot', *Business Week* (24 May 1999), pp. 56–7; Peter Landers, 'At last, a dog that barks, wags its tail, and never has to go out', *Wall Street Journal* (12 May 1999), p. B1; Ginny Parker, 'In Japan, robots are not just for factories anymore', *Greensboro News and Record* (2 November 1999), pp. B6 and B7; 'Robots', *The Economist* (5 June 1999), p. 78; Richard Shaffer, 'Can't anyone make a decent robot?', *Fortune* (19 July 1999), pp. 120–1; A. A. Milne, *Winnie the Pooh Collection* (Greenford, Middlesex: Aura, 1998); Justin Hankins, 'When Rover's a robot', *The Guardian* (30 November 2002); J. Mark Lytle, 'Mrs Tanaka with her robot teddy bear', *The Guardian* (11 September 2003); Charlotte Ricca-Smith, 'Gadgets', *The Independent* (24 September 2003); *Turkish Daily News*, 'Roll over, Aibo: Meet South Korea's new robot canine' (29 April 2006); Nicolas Asfouri, 'Why did Sony kill off its Aibo robot dog?', *The Guardian* (2 February 2006); Chris Nuttall, Companies international: 'Smooth dinosaur senses way forward for robots', *Financial Times* (6 February 2006); Sorrel Downer, 'Dear Santa . . .', *Financial Times* (2 December 2006), p. W2; Chris Nuttall, 'Complex evolution of a playful beast', *Financial Times* (11 July 2007).

MALARIA

IT ONLY TAKES ONE BITE

Planning your next great adventure? Remember, you are not immune from malaria. Kidney failure, seizures, coma and even death do happen. So before you jet off, visit your GP or Practice Nurse for advice on the best malaria protection for you and your fellow travellers.

Visit www.malariahotspots.co.uk
and then your GP or Practice Nurse

MAL/FPA/06/25064/1

March 2006

> Remember, the client's indecision is final.

KEN HORNSBY

Business-to-business marketing

Mini Contents List

◄ SOURCE: The Advertising Archives.

I got a sixty-nine Chevy with a 396
Fuelie heads and a Hurst on the floor

From Bruce Springsteen, 'Racing in the Street'
on 'Darkness on the Edge of Town', Columbia B00008Z5G8, 1978

Previewing the concepts

In the previous chapter, you studied *final consumer* buying behaviour and factors that influence it. In this chapter, we'll do the same for *business customers* – those that buy goods and services for use in producing their own products and services or for resale to others.

After reading this chapter, you should be able to:

1. Define the business market and explain how business markets differ from consumer markets.
2. Identify the major factors that influence business buyer behaviour.
3. List and define the steps in the business buying decision process.
4. Compare institutional and government markets and explain how institutional and government buyers make their buying decisions.

Any consumer product, such as Bruce Springsteen's 1969 Chevrolet, comes with lots of bits and pieces made by other people, be they the Fuelie fuel injection system, Hurst gearbox, Dunlop tyres, Bosch electronics, Girling shock absorbers, and much more. Some of these are bought by consumers but most are business-to-business (B2B) products sold by suppliers to car manufacturers.

The same is true of executive jets, a complex product made of thousands of components from around the world. In this case the B2B transactions supporting building the aircraft most often become another B2B sale when an airline, leasing company, government or multinational buys the jet as an investment. We start examining B2B marketing by looking at the rapidly growing Busjet market.

Prelude case Concorde is dead – the booming Busjet market

With timeshare you can own as much of an executive jet as you want.

SOURCE: NetJets Management.

Sales of executive jets have reached record levels, driven by strong economic growth, rising profits, the soaring bonuses of high earners and the sheer awfulness of regular air travel. Deliveries of private jets worldwide rose 18 per cent to 885 in 2006 with buyers of the most sought-after jets forced to wait a couple of years for delivery.

Right until its end, Concorde caught the eye. A supersonic jet loved by celebrities and the super-rich, Concorde outclassed both in being a super-celebrity and super-expensive. Following its final flight into Heathrow in October 2003, we can now only say 'once we had Concorde'. As the huddle of 100 enthusiasts and media people left Concorde's last flight, not everyone had tears in their eyes.

For the week following, the business media was awash with articles about business jets and Busjet timeshare. As a NetJets advertorial gloated: 'The days of Concorde may be over, but for those still seeking the luxury of fast-track air travel, there is another option . . .'

In truth, Concorde's main customers were not celebrities but regular transatlantic travellers for whom time was money. Air France's most frequent Concorde flyer was Pascal La Borge, a medical meeting planner who logged over 400 trips. For such people executive jets were often the quicker choice because they can use smaller airports close to city centres, fly on demand and offer less airport hassle. Now the Atlantic was theirs.

'The jet set' used to refer to the rich and famous who could afford the cost of early jet travel. Now almost everybody flies. Busjet travel retains that exclusive status that 'the jet set' once had as the transport of super-celebrities like Mika Häkkinen, Bill Gates and Bono, but not for long. Busjet travel is becoming the norm. Sales of Busjets, from the 'entry level' €4m Cessna

CJ1 to the €41m Airbus A319 corporate jetliner, are booming, with order books full three years ahead.

Once looked upon as an executive indulgence, the Busjets have become a logical capital investment:

- Busjet travel is down in cost. Typical running cost of the medium-sized, 8–19-seat Dassault Falcon 900EX jet is €1,500 per flying hour based on 1,000 hours per year utilisation. With four passengers the cost is less than €400 each, about the same as a business class fare. Eight people flying brings the cost to that of economy fares; with 16 seats occupied, it comes down to bucket-shop prices.

- Busjets make better use of a firm's most valuable and perishable resource – executive time. As Richard Gaona of Airbus says: 'It's not the speed of the individual aircraft that counts, but the speed at which you can get to where the business is ahead of the competition.'

- This is becoming increasingly true as flying is becoming more common and the sheer volume of traffic, as well as increased security, make scheduled flying time consuming and irksome.

- Security of passengers and information exist on a Busjet in a way that it does not in a first-class lounge or cabin. A Busjet is a mobile boardroom as well as a mobile office.

- At the top end of the range is a VIP version of Airbus's A380 superjumbo and the less spacious Boeing 787 VIP, based on Boeing's hugely successful new 787 Dreamliner. These flying hotels enable the likes of Boeing's Phil Condit to take in New York, Paris, Moscow, Beijing and Tokyo in four days out of his office.

Recognising organisations that can afford to own and operate a business jet is easy. The difficulty is in reaching key decision makers for jet purchases, understanding their motivations and decision processes, analysing what is important to them, and designing marketing approaches.

There are *rational* and *subjective* factors. A company buying a Busjet will evaluate the aircraft on quality and performance, prices, operating costs and service. However, having a superior product is not enough: marketers must also consider *human factors* that affect choice. According to Gulfstream, a leading American supplier of business jets: 'The purchase process may be initiated by the chief executive officer (CEO), a board member wishing to increase efficiency or security, the company's chief pilot, or through vendor efforts like advertising or a sales visit. The CEO will be central in deciding whether to buy the jet, but he or she will be heavily influenced by the company's pilot, financial officer and perhaps by the board itself.'

Each party in the buying process has subtle roles and needs. The salesperson who tries to impress both the CEO with depreciation schedules and the chief pilot with runway statistics will almost certainly not sell a plane if he or she overlooks the psychological and emotional components of the buying decision. 'For the chief executive,' observes one salesperson, 'you need all the numbers for support, but if you can't find the kid inside the CEO and excite him or her with the raw beauty of the new plane, you'll never sell the equipment. If you sell the excitement, you sell the jet.'

The chief pilot often has veto power over purchase decisions and may be able to stop the purchase of a certain brand of jet by simply expressing a negative opinion. In this sense, the pilot not only influences the decision but also serves as a 'gatekeeper'. Though the corporate legal staff will handle the purchase agreement and the purchasing department will acquire the jet, they usually have little to say about whether, or how, the plane is obtained and which type to select. The users of the jet – management of the buying company, important customers and others – may have an indirect role in choosing the equipment.

The involvement of many people in the purchase decision creates a group dynamic that the selling company must factor into its sales planning. Who makes up the buying group? How will the parties interact? Who will dominate and who will submit? What priorities do the individuals have?

Where is the market going? The answer is bigger, faster, cheaper and at your local showroom near you. Honda Motor has begun marketing a small business jet in an effort to gain a foothold in the lucrative and fast-growing market. The HondaJet, sold at a starting price of 435m yen (€2.7m), seats five to six passengers and will go into production in 2010. The company plans to make 70 jets a year. Even more revolutionary are very light jets that aim to pioneer a new business model for executive flying. Eclipse Aviation recently delivered its first Eclipse 500 aircraft, which is equipped with four passenger seats and priced a little over €1m – a third of the price of previous bottom-of-the-range jets.

The largest is the VIP Airbus A380. The fastest is the Bombardier Global Express (Gex) BD-700 business jet, capable of carrying eight passengers non-stop from Brussels to Buenos Aires. Cruising close to the speed of sound, it knocks an hour off shorter routes like Berlin–Los Angeles. The next stop? Gulfstream and Dassault are considering an SSBJ (Supersonic Busjet). If a €40m-plus Busjet is selling, why not a €55m SSBJ?[1]

Questions

1. What do you think are the reasons for businesses buying executive jets?

2. Is it correct to say that, unlike people in consumer markets, business buyers are rational?

3. Who are the critical people to influence when selling Busjets?

Introduction

In some ways, selling business jets to business buyers is like selling kitchen appliances to families. Busjet makers ask the same questions as consumer marketers: Who are the buyers and what are their needs? How do buyers make their buying decisions and what factors influence these decisions? What marketing programme will be most effective? Nevertheless, the answers to these questions are usually different in the case of the business buyer. Thus, the jet makers face many of the same challenges as consumer marketers – and some additional ones.

In one way or another, most large companies sell to other organisations. Companies such as ABB De La Rue (cash making and management), Norsk Hydro, Akzo Nobel (chemicals) and Arbed (steel) sell *most* of their products to other businesses. Even large consumer-products companies, which make products used by final consumers, must first sell their products to other businesses. For example, Allied Domecq makes many consumer products – La Ina sherry, Presidente brandy, Tetley tea and others. To sell these products to consumers, Allied Domecq must first sell them to wholesalers and retailers that serve the consumer market. Allied Domecq also sells food ingredients directly to other businesses through its Margetts Food and DCA Food Industries subsidiaries.

Business buyer behaviour refers to the buying behaviour of the organisations that buy goods and services for use in the production of other products and services that are sold, rented or supplied to others. It also includes the behaviour of retailing and wholesaling firms that acquire goods to resell or rent them to others at a profit. In the **business buying process**, business buyers determine which products and services their organisations need to purchase, and then find, evaluate and choose among alternative suppliers and brands. *Business-to-business (B2B) marketers* must do their best to understand business markets and business buyer behaviour. Then, like businesses that sell to final buyers, they must build profitable relationships with business customers by creating superior customer value.

Business markets

A **business market** comprises all the organisations that buy goods and services to use in the production of other products and services, or for the purpose of reselling or renting them to others at a profit. The business market is *huge*. In fact, business markets involve far more money and items than do consumer markets. For example, think about the large number of business transactions involved in the production and sale of a single set of Dunlop tyres. Various suppliers sell Dunlop the rubber, steel, equipment and other goods that it needs to produce the tyres. Dunlop then sells the finished tyres to retailers, who in turn sell them to consumers. Thus, many sets of *business* purchases were made for only one set of *consumer* purchases. In addition, Dunlop sells tyres as original equipment to manufacturers who install them on new vehicles, and as replacement tyres to companies that maintain their own fleets of company cars, trucks, buses or other vehicles.

> Business markets involve far more money and items than do consumer markets.

In some ways, business markets are similar to consumer markets. Both involve people who assume buying roles and make purchase decisions to satisfy needs. However, business markets differ in many ways from consumer markets. The main differences, shown in Table 6.1, are in *market structure and demand*, the *nature of the buying unit* and the *types of decisions and the decision process* involved.

Business buying process—The decision-making process by which business buyers establish the need for purchased products and services, and identify, evaluate and choose among alternative brands and suppliers.

Business market—All the organisations that buy goods and services to use in the production of other products and services, or for the purpose of reselling or renting them to others at a profit.

Table 6.1 Characteristics of business markets

Marketing structure and demand
Business markets contain *fewer but larger buyers*.
Business customers are *more geographically concentrated*.
Business buyer demand is *derived* from final consumer demand.
Demand in many business markets is *more inelastic* – not affected as much in the short run by price changes.
Demand in business markets *fluctuates more*, and more quickly.

Nature of the buying unit
Business purchases involve *more buyers*.
Business buying involves a *more professional purchasing effort*.

Types of decisions and the decision process
Business buyers usually face *more complex buying decisions*.
The business buying process is *more formalised*.
In business buying, buyers and sellers work closely together and build long-term *relationships*.

Market structure and demand

The business marketer normally deals with *far fewer but far larger buyers* than the consumer marketer does. Even in large business markets, a few buyers often account for most of the purchasing. For example, when Dunlop sells replacement tyres to final consumers, its potential market includes the owners of the millions of cars currently around the world. But Dunlop's fate in the business market depends on getting orders from one of only a handful of large automakers. Similarly, Bosch sells its power tools and outdoor equipment to tens of millions of consumers worldwide. However, it must sell these products through huge retail customers – B&Q, Castorama, Asda, Wal-Mart, etc. – which combined account for a huge proportion of their sales.

Fortunes can depend upon even fewer customers when governments are buyers:

> The contract of this decade is for the JSF (Joint Strike Fighter) to equip the USAF, US Navy, US Marines, Royal Air Force and Royal Navy. Won by Lockheed Martin, in collaboration with BAe Systems, Pratt & Whitney and Rolls-Royce, the initial contract is for 14 flying development aircraft at $US18.9bn (€13.8bn) and the final contract will be for approaching 500 planes. While Lockheed Martin celebrates their victory, Boeing is wounded by the failure of their X-32.[4].[2]

Derived demand—
Business demand that ultimately comes (derives) from the demand for consumer goods.

Business markets are also more *geographically concentrated*: international financial services in London, petrochemicals and synthetic fibres around Rotterdam and Amsterdam, and luxury goods in Paris. Further, business demand is **derived demand** – it ultimately derives from the demand for consumer goods. Stork Fokker is selling Glare (GLAss fibre REinforced aluminium) to Airbus for their super jumbo A380 whose demand is forecast because the consumers' demand for air travel is growing and so airlines want more capacity. If consumer demand for air travel drops, so will the demand for the A380, Glare, the Rolls-Royce Trent 900 engine and all the other products used to make the aircraft.[3]

At the other end of the technological spectrum is the huge increase in demand for light vans and delivery van operatives that has followed the boom in Internet shopping. Besides the huge growth in demand, there is also a need for vans that can stand up to the stop–start of household delivery and for electric vehicles that are less intrusive in residential areas.

The dependence on derived demand encourages B2B marketers to sometimes promote their products directly to final consumers to increase business demand. For example, the Gore-Tex name is familiar to participants in outdoor pursuits but it is the result of a B2B sale where clothing manufacturers buy Gore-Tex waterproof-breathable fabric to make outdoor clothing, shoes, etc. The fabric's reputation is such that Berghaus or North Face products boasting

When golf wear has LYCRA®, you get the fit and the swing.
(If the tag doesn't say "has it", it doesn't have it.)

You either have it or you don't.

INVISTA® sells fibre to the people who sell fabrics, to the people who sell garments, to the retailers who sell them to consumers. Advertising LYCRA® to consumers pulls the fibre through the chain.
SOURCE: INVISTA, McCann Erikson.

Gore-Tex retail at twice the price of products made from other fabrics. Similarly, INVISTA promotes DuPont Teflon directly to final consumers as a key branded ingredient in stain-repellent and wrinkle-free fabrics and leathers. You see Teflon Fabric Protector tags on Nautica and Tommy Hilfiger clothes and on home furnishing brands such as Kravet, manufacturer of Laura Ashley wall coverings and fabrics.[4] By making Teflon familiar and attractive to final buyers, INVISTA also makes the products containing it more attractive.

Inelastic demand—Total demand for a product that is not much affected by price changes, especially in the short run.

Many business markets have **inelastic demand**; that is, total demand for many business products is not affected much by price changes, especially in the short run. A drop in the price of leather will not cause shoe manufacturers to buy much more leather unless it results in lower shoe prices that, in turn, will increase consumer demand for shoes. This insensitivity to price and the huge rising demand in emerging economies has caused oil and commodity prices to surge in recent years. The prices of both oil and metals have roughly tripled since 2002. The price increase has been good for commodity producers, most of which are developing economies, but has had an insignificant impact upon increasing world demand.

Finally, business markets have more *fluctuating demand*. The demand for many business goods and services tends to change more – and more quickly – than the demand for consumer goods and services does. A small percentage increase in consumer demand can cause large increases in business demand. Sometimes a rise of only 10 per cent in consumer demand can cause as much as a 200 per cent rise in business demand during the next period. Similarly, a small decrease in consumer demand can cause business demand to collapse. Previous commodity booms, like the one mentioned above, have always been followed by slumps. The shift in developed countries' output, from metal-bashing industries to services, will curb demand, as will technological advances that provide substitutes – such as fibre optics instead of copper wire – while improved methods of mineral extraction will increase supply.[5]

 A small percentage increase in consumer demand can cause large increases in business demand.

Nature of the buying unit

Compared with consumer purchases, a business purchase usually involves *more decision participants* and a *more professional purchasing effort*. Often, business buying is done by trained purchasing agents who spend their working lives learning how to buy better. The more complex the purchase, the more likely it is that several people will participate in the decision-making process. Buying committees made up of technical experts and top management are common in the buying of major goods.

Beyond this, many companies are now upgrading their purchasing functions to 'supply management' or 'supplier development' functions. B2B marketers now face a new breed of higher-level, better-trained supply managers. These supply managers sometimes seem to know more about the supplier company than it knows about itself. Therefore, business marketers must have well-trained marketers and salespeople to deal with these well-trained buyers.

Types of decisions and the decision process

Business buyers usually face *more complex* buying decisions than do consumer buyers. Purchases often involve large sums of money, complex technical and economic considerations, and interactions among many people at many levels of the buyer's organisation. Because the purchases are more complex, business buyers may take longer to make their decisions. The business buying process also tends to be *more formalised* than the consumer buying process. Large business purchases usually call for detailed product specifications, written purchase orders, careful supplier searches and formal approval.

Finally, in the business buying process, the buyer and seller are often much *more dependent* on each other. Consumer marketers are often at a distance from their customers. In contrast, B2B marketers may roll up their sleeves and work closely with their customers during all stages of the buying process – from helping customers define problems, to finding solutions, to supporting after-sales operation. They often customise their offerings to individual customer needs. In the short run, sales go to suppliers who meet buyers' immediate product and service needs. In the long run, however, business-to-business marketers keep a customer's sales by meeting current needs *and* by partnering with customers to help them solve their problems.

In recent years, relationships between customers and suppliers have been changing from downright adversarial to close and chummy. In fact, many customer companies are now practising *supplier development*, systematically developing networks of supplier-partners to ensure an appropriate and dependable supply of products and materials that they will use in making their own products or resell to others. For example, Caterpillar no longer calls its buyers 'purchasing agents' – they are managers of 'purchasing and supplier development'. IKEA doesn't just buy from its suppliers; it involves them deeply in the process of delivering a stylish and affordable lifestyle to IKEA's customers (see Real Marketing 6.1).

Business buyer behaviour

At the most basic level, marketers want to know how business buyers will respond to various marketing stimuli. Figure 6.1 shows a model of business buyer behaviour where marketing and other stimuli affect the buying organisation and produce certain buyer responses. As with consumer buying, the marketing stimuli for business buying consist of the Four Ps: product, price, place and promotion. Other stimuli include major forces in the environment: economic, technological, political, cultural and competitive. These stimuli enter the organisation and are turned into buyer responses: product or service choice; supplier choice; order quantities; and delivery, service and payment terms. In order to design good marketing mix strategies, the marketer must understand what happens within the organisation to turn stimuli into purchase responses.[6]

Within the organisation, buying activity consists of two major parts: the buying centre, made up of all the people involved in the buying decision, and the buying decision process. The model shows that the buying centre and the buying decision process are influenced by internal organisational, interpersonal and individual factors as well as by external environmental factors.

The model in Figure 6.1 suggests four questions about business buyer behaviour: What buying decisions do business buyers make? Who participates in the buying process? What are the major influences on buyers? How do business buyers make their buying decisions?

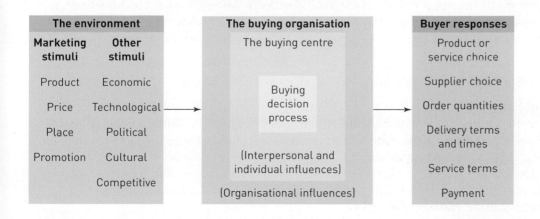

Figure 6.1 A model of business buyer behaviour

6.1 real marketing

IKEA: working with suppliers to customers clamouring for more

Giant Swedish furniture retailer IKEA doesn't just buy from its suppliers, it involves them deeply in the process of delivering a stylish and affordable lifestyle to IKEA's customers worldwide – here in Saudi Arabia.

SOURCE: Hans-Jürgen Burkard/Bilderberg.

IKEA, the world's largest furniture retailer, is the quintessential global cult brand. Last year, more than 410 million shoppers flocked to the Scandinavian retailer's 236 huge stores in 34 countries, generating more than $18bn in sales. Most of the shoppers are loyal IKEA customers – many are avid apostles. From Beijing to Brooklyn, all are drawn to the IKEA lifestyle, one built around trendy but simple and practical furniture at affordable prices.

More than any other company in the world, IKEA has become a curator of people's lifestyles, if not their lives. At a time when consumers face so many choices for everything they buy, IKEA provides a one-stop sanctuary for coolness. IKEA is far more than a furniture merchant. It sells a lifestyle that customers around the world embrace as a signal that they've arrived, that they have good taste and recognise value. 'If it wasn't for IKEA,' writes British design magazine *Icon*, 'most people would have no access to affordable contemporary design.'

As the world's Ambassador of Kul (Swedish for fun), IKEA is growing fast. Sales leapt 31 per cent between 2005 and 2007. IKEA plans to open 19 new megastores this year, including outlets in Western China and Japan. In the US, it plans to expand from its current 28 stores to more than 50 stores by 2013. The biggest obstacle to growth is not opening new stores and attracting customers. Rather, it's finding enough of the right kinds of suppliers to help design and produce the vast quantities of goods that those customers will carry out of its stores.

IKEA currently relies on about 1,800 suppliers in more than 50 countries to stock its shelves. If the giant retailer continues at its current rate of growth, it will need to double its supply network by 2010. 'We can't increase by more than 20 stores a year because supply is the bottleneck,' says IKEA's country manager for Russia. Creating stylish, durable furniture at low prices is no easy proposition. It calls for a resolute focus on design and an obsession for low costs. IKEA knows that it can't go it alone. Instead, it must develop close partnerships with suppliers around the globe who can help it develop simple new designs and keep costs down. Here's how the company describes its approach, and the importance of suppliers:

> We can't do it alone. . . . First we do our part. Our designers work with manufacturers to find smart ways to make furniture using existing production processes. Then our buyers look all over the world for good suppliers with the most suitable raw materials. Next, we buy in bulk – on a global scale – so that we can get the best deals, and you, the customers, get the lowest price.
>
> Then you do your part. Using the IKEA catalogue and visiting the store, you choose the furniture yourself and pick it up at the self-serve warehouse. Because most items are packed flat, you can get them home easily, and assemble them yourself. This means we don't charge you for things you can easily do on your own. So together we save money – for a better everyday life.
>
> SOURCE: Inter IKEA Systems B.V. 2008.

At IKEA, design is important. But no matter how good the design, a product won't find its way to the showroom unless it's also affordable. IKEA goes to the ends of the earth to find supply partners who can help it to create just the right product at just the right price. According to *BusinessWeek*, IKEA 'once contracted with ski makers – experts in bent wood – to manufacture its Poang armchairs, and it has tapped makers of supermarket trolleys to turn out durable sofas.'

The design process for a new IKEA product can take up to three years. IKEA's designers start with a basic customer value proposition. Then, they work closely with

...6.1

key suppliers to bring that proposition to market. Consider IKEA's Olle chair, developed in the late 1990s. Based on customer feedback, designer Evamaria Ronnegard set out to create a sturdy, durable kitchen chair that would fit into any décor, priced at €38. Once her initial design was completed and approved, IKEA's 45 trading offices searched the world and matched the Olle with a Chinese supplier, based on both design and cost efficiencies. Together, Ronnegard and the Chinese supplier refined the design to improve the chair's function and reduce its costs. For example, the supplier modified the back leg angle to prevent the chair from tipping easily. This also reduced the thickness of the seat without compromising the chair's strength, reducing both costs and shipping weight.

However, when she learned that the supplier planned to use traditional wood joinery methods to attach the chair back to the seat, Ronnegard intervened. That would require that the chair be shipped in a costly L-shape, which by itself would inflate the chair's retail price to €38. Ronnegard convinced the supplier to go with metal bolts instead. The back-and-forth design process worked well. IKEA introduced its still-popular Olle chair at the €38 target price. (Through continued design and manufacturing refinements, IKEA and its supplier have now reduced the price to just €21.)

Throughout the design and manufacturing process, Ronnegard was impressed by the depth of the supplier partnership. 'My job really hit home when I got a call from the supplier in China, who had a question about some aspect of the chair,' she recalls. 'There he was, halfway around the world, and he was calling me about my chair.' Now, Ronnegard is often on-site in China or India or Vietnam, working face to face with suppliers as they help to refine her designs.

Another benefit of close collaboration with suppliers is that they can often help IKEA to customise its designs to make them sell better in local markets. In China, for example, at the suggestion of a local supplier, IKEA stocked 250,000 plastic place mats commemorating the Year of the Rooster. The place mats sold out in only three weeks. Thus, before IKEA can sell the volumes of products its customer covet, it must first find suppliers who can help it design and make all those products. IKEA doesn't just rely on spot suppliers who might be available when needed. Instead, it has systematically developed a robust network of supplier-partners that reliably provide the more than 10,000 items it stocks. And more than just buying from suppliers, IKEA involves them deeply in the process of designing and making stylish but affordable products to keep IKEA's customers coming back. Working together, IKEA and its suppliers have kept fans like Jen Segrest clamouring for more:

At least once a year, Jen Segrest, a 36-year-old freelance Web designer, and her husband travel 10 hours round-trip from their home in Middletown, Ohio, to the IKEA in Schaumburg, Illinois, near Chicago. 'Every piece of furniture in my living room is IKEA – except for an end table, which I hate. And next time I go to IKEA I'll replace it,' says Segrest. To lure the retailer to Ohio, Segrest has even started a blog called OH! IKEA. The banner on the home page calls for IKEA to open a store in Ohio, since the local Target discount store does not fulfil their need.

SOURCES: Extracts, quotes and other information from Kerry Capell, 'How the Swedish retailer became a global cult brand', *BusinessWeek* (14 November 2005), p. 103; Shari Kulha, 'Behind the scenes at IKEA', *The Guardian* (29 September 2005), p. 8; Greta Guest, 'Inside IKEA's formula for global success', *Detroit Free Press* (3 June 2006); and 'Our vision: A better everyday life', accessed at www.ikea.com, December 2006.

Major types of buying situations

There are three major types of buying situations.[7] At one extreme is the *straight rebuy*, which is a fairly routine decision. At the other extreme is the *new task*, which may call for thorough research. In the middle is the *modified rebuy*, which requires some research.

In a **straight rebuy**, the buyer reorders something without any modifications. It is usually handled on a routine basis by the purchasing department. Based on past buying satisfaction, the buyer simply chooses from the various suppliers on its list. 'In' suppliers try to maintain product and service quality. They often propose automatic reordering systems so that the purchasing agent will save reordering time. 'Out' suppliers try to find new ways to add value or exploit dissatisfaction so that the buyer will consider them.

In a **modified rebuy**, the buyer wants to modify product specifications, prices, terms or suppliers. The modified rebuy usually involves more decision participants than does the straight rebuy. The 'in' suppliers may become nervous and feel pressured to put their best foot forward to protect an account. 'Out' suppliers may see the modified rebuy situation as an opportunity to make a better offer and gain new business.

A company buying a product or service for the first time faces a **new-task** situation. In such cases, the greater the cost or risk, the larger the number of decision participants and the greater their efforts to collect information will be. The new-task situation is the marketer's greatest opportunity and challenge. The marketer not only tries to reach as many key buying influences as possible but also provides help and information.

The buyer makes the fewest decisions in the straight rebuy and the most in the new-task decision. In the new-task situation, the buyer must decide on product specifications, suppliers, price limits, payment terms, order quantities, delivery times and service terms. The order of these decisions varies with each situation, and different decision participants influence each choice.

Many business buyers prefer to buy a packaged solution to a problem from a single seller. Instead of buying and putting all the components together, the buyer may ask sellers to supply

Straight rebuy—A business buying situation in which the buyer routinely reorders something without any modifications.

Modified rebuy—A business buying situation in which the buyer wants to modify product specifications, prices, terms or suppliers.

New task—A business buying situation in which the buyer purchases a product or service for the first time.

Systems selling—Selling a packaged solution to a problem, without all the separate decisions involved.

the components *and* assemble the package or system. The sale often goes to the firm that provides the most complete system meeting the customer's needs. Thus, **systems selling** is often a key business marketing strategy for winning and holding accounts.

> For example, Intershop is an outstandingly successful company, based in the former East Germany. It is world market leader in software design and licensing for more than 20,000 companies who sell over the Internet and more than 300 enterprise customers around the world, including HP, BMW, Motorola, ABB, Electronic Arts, Volkswagen, Ericsson, Sonera, Hyundai, Home Shopping Europe, Siemens and many more. To these companies, Intershop offers a full-service e-commerce, in addition to all aspects of online retailing, including fulfilment.[8]

> " Systems selling is often a key business marketing strategy for winning and holding accounts. "

Sellers increasingly have recognised that buyers like this method and have adopted systems selling as a marketing tool. Systems selling is a two-step process. First, the supplier sells a group of interlocking products. For example, the supplier sells not only glue, but also applicators and dryers. Second, the supplier sells a system of production, inventory control, distribution and other services to meet the buyer's need for a smooth-running operation.

> The Indonesian government requested bids to build a cement factory near Jakarta. An American firm's proposal included choosing the site, designing the cement factory, hiring the construction crews, assembling the materials and equipment, and turning the finished factory over to the Indonesian government. A Japanese firm's proposal included all of these services, plus hiring and training workers to run the factory, exporting the cement through their trading companies, and using the cement to build some needed roads and new office buildings in Jakarta. Although the Japanese firm's proposal cost more, it won the contract. Clearly, the Japanese viewed the problem not as just building a cement factory (the narrow view of systems selling) but of running it in a way that would contribute to the country's economy. They took the broadest view of the customer's needs. This is true systems selling.[9]

Buying centre—All the individuals and units that play a role in the business purchase decision-making process.

Users—Members of the organisation who will use the product or service; users often initiate the buying proposal and help define product specifications.

Participants in the business buying process

Who does the buying of all the huge quantities of goods and services needed by business organisations? The decision-making unit of a buying organisation is called its **buying centre**: all the individuals and units that play a role in the business purchase decision-making process. This group includes the actual users of the product or service, those who make the buying decision, those who influence the buying decision, those who do the actual buying, and those who control buying information.

The buying centre includes all members of the organisation who play any of five roles in the purchase decision process.[10]

- **Users** are members of the organisation who will use the product or service. In many cases, users initiate the buying proposal and help define product specifications.

- **Influencers** often help define specifications and also provide information for evaluating alternatives. Technical personnel are particularly important influencers.

- **Buyers** have formal authority to select the supplier and arrange terms of purchase. Buyers may help shape product specifications, but their major role is in selecting vendors and negotiating. In more complex purchases, buyers might include high-level officers participating in the negotiations.

- **Deciders** have formal or informal power to select or approve the final suppliers. In routine buying, the buyers are often the deciders, or at least the approvers.

- **Gatekeepers** control the flow of information to others. For example, purchasing agents often have authority to prevent salespersons from seeing users or deciders. Other gatekeepers include technical personnel and personal secretaries.

The buying centre is not a fixed and formally identified unit within the buying organisation. It is a set of buying roles assumed by different people for different purchases. Within the organisation, the size and make-up of the buying centre will vary for different products and for different buying situations. For some routine purchases, one person – say a purchasing agent – may assume all the buying centre roles and serve as the only person involved in the buying decision. For more complex purchases, the buying centre may include 20 or 30 people from different levels and departments in the organisation.

The buying centre concept presents a major marketing challenge. The business marketer must learn who participates in the decision, each participant's relative influence, and what evaluation criteria each decision participant uses. For example, the medical products and services group of Rentokil Initial sells disposable surgical gowns to hospitals. It identifies the hospital personnel involved in this buying decision as the head of purchasing, the operating room administrator and the surgeons. Each participant plays a different role. The head of purchasing analyses whether the hospital should buy disposable gowns or reusable gowns. If analysis favours disposable gowns, then the operating room administrator compares competing products and prices and makes a choice. This administrator considers the gown's absorbency, antiseptic quality, design and cost and normally buys the brand that meets requirements at the lowest cost. Finally, surgeons affect the decision later by reporting their satisfaction or dissatisfaction with the brand.

Influencer—A person whose views or advice carry some weight in making a final buying decision.

Buyer—The person who makes an actual purchase.

Deciders—People in the organisation's buying centre who have formal or informal powers to select or approve the final suppliers.

Gatekeepers—People in the organisation's buying centre who control the flow of information to others.

Club World. More beds, more places, more often. BRITISH AIRWAYS

Business-class flying is a classic case where the user (the flyer) is not the buyer, decider or gatekeeper. This could be a secretary, a personal assistant or a professional buyer.

SOURCE: British Airways/M&C Saatchi, *Photographer*: Gary Simpson.

The buying centre usually includes some obvious participants who are involved formally in the buying decision. For example, following from the prelude case, the decision to buy a business jet will probably involve the company's CEO, chief pilot, a purchasing agent, some legal staff, a member of top management, and others formally charged with the buying decision. It may also involve less obvious, informal participants, some of whom may actually make or strongly affect the buying decision. Sometimes, even the people in the buying centre are not aware of all the buying participants. For example, the decision about which corporate jet to buy may actually be made by a board member who has an interest in flying and who knows a lot about aeroplanes. This board member may work behind the scenes to sway the decision. Many business buying decisions result from the complex interactions of ever-changing buying centre participants.

Major influences on business buyers

Business buyers are subject to many influences when they make their buying decisions. Some marketers assume that the major influences are economic. They think buyers will favour the supplier who offers the lowest price or the best product or the most service. They concentrate on offering strong economic benefits to buyers. However, business buyers actually respond to both economic and personal factors. Far from being cold, calculating and impersonal, business buyers are human and social as well. They react to both reason and emotion.

> " Far from being cold, calculating and impersonal, business buyers are human and social as well. "

Today, most B2B marketers recognise that emotion plays an important role in business buying decisions. For example, you might expect that an advertisement promoting large trucks to corporate fleet buyers would stress objective technical, performance and economic factors. However, one ad for Volvo heavy-duty trucks shows two drivers arm-wrestling and claims, 'It solves all your fleet problems. Except who gets to drive.' It turns out that, in the face of an industry-wide driver shortage, the type of truck a fleet provides can help it to attract qualified drivers. The Volvo ad stresses the raw beauty of the truck and its comfort and roominess, features that make it more appealing to drivers. The ad concludes that Volvo trucks are 'built to make fleets more profitable and drivers a lot more possessive.'[11]

When suppliers' offers are very similar, business buyers have little basis for strictly rational choice. Because they can meet organisational goals with any supplier, buyers can allow personal factors to play a larger role in their decisions. However, when competing products differ greatly, business buyers are more accountable for their choice and tend to pay more attention to economic factors. Figure 6.2 lists various groups of influences on business buyers – environmental, organisational, interpersonal and individual.[12]

Environmental factors

Business buyers are heavily influenced by factors in the current and expected *economic environment*, such as the level of primary demand, the economic outlook and the cost of money. Another environmental factor is shortages in key materials. Many companies now are more willing to buy and hold larger inventories of scarce materials to ensure adequate supply. Business buyers also are affected by technological, political and competitive developments in the environment. Finally, culture and customs can strongly influence business buyer reactions to the marketer's behaviour and strategies, especially in the international marketing environment. The business buyer must watch these factors, determine how they will affect the buyer, and try to turn these challenges into opportunities.

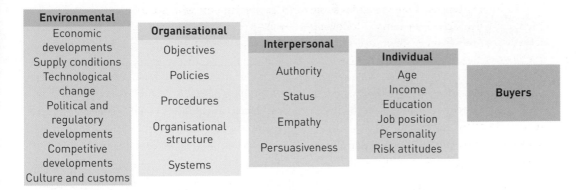

Figure 6.2 Major influences on business buyer behaviour

Organisational factors

Each buying organisation has its own objectives, policies, procedures, structure and systems, and the business marketer must understand these factors well. Questions such as these arise: How many people are involved in the buying decision? Who are they? What are their evaluative criteria? What are the company's policies and limits on its buyers?

Interpersonal factors

The buying centre usually includes many participants who influence each other, so *interpersonal factors* also influence the business buying process. However, it is often difficult to assess such interpersonal factors and group dynamics. Buying centre participants do not wear tags that label them as 'key decision maker' or 'not influential'. Nor do buying centre participants with the highest rank always have the most influence. Participants may influence the buying decision because they control rewards and punishments, are well liked, have special expertise, or have a special relationship with other important participants. Interpersonal factors are often very subtle. Whenever possible, business marketers must try to understand these factors and design strategies that take them into account.

Individual factors

Each participant in the business buying decision process brings in personal motives, perceptions and preferences. These individual factors are affected by personal characteristics such as age, income, education, professional identification, personality and attitudes towards risk. Also, buyers have different buying styles. Some may be technical types who make in-depth analyses of competitive proposals before choosing a supplier. Other buyers may be intuitive negotiators who are adept at pitting the sellers against one another for the best deal.

The business buying process

The business buying process is the decision-making process by which business buyers establish the need for purchased products and services, and identify, evaluate and choose among alternative brands and suppliers. Figure 6.3 lists the eight stages of the business buying process.[13] Buyers who face a new-task buying situation usually go through all stages of the buying process. Buyers making modified or straight rebuys may skip some of the stages. We will examine these steps for the typical new-task buying situation.

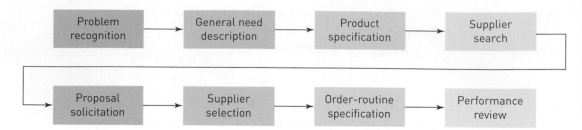

Figure 6.3 Stages of the business buying process

Problem recognition

Problem recognition—The first stage of the business buying process in which someone in the company recognises a problem or need that can be met by acquiring a good or a service.

The buying process begins when someone in the company recognises a problem or need that can be met by acquiring a specific product or service. **Problem recognition** can result from internal or external stimuli. Internally, the company may decide to launch a new product that requires new production equipment and materials. Or a machine may break down and need new parts. Perhaps a purchasing manager is unhappy with a current supplier's product quality, service or prices. Externally, the buyer may get some new ideas at a trade show, see an ad, or receive a call from a salesperson who offers a better product or a lower price. In fact, in their advertising, business marketers often alert customers to potential problems and then show how their products provide solutions.

General need description—The stage in the business buying process in which the company describes the general characteristics and quantity of a needed item.

Midas is a new company marketing a web-based software system that helps companies manage motoring fuel bills and related costs. Most businesses do not realise there is potential for savings in this area, so Midas uses public relations. They first have to make managers aware of the problem, then show how they can help solve it. They begin with the problem: 'The rising costs of oil in today's world mean that motor fuel is every bit as precious as gold. Yet you cannot manage what you do not measure.' Then give the solution: 'MIDAS – The New Innovative Way to Manage Your Company's Motor Fuel Bill.' The promotion worked to such an extent that the new business had difficulty delivering their new products to businesses, such as car hire firms with huge fleets. And won the Energy Savings Trust's Fleet Hero Award 2006.[14]

General need description

Product specification—The stage of the business buying process in which the buying organisation decides on and specifies the best technical product characteristics for a needed item.

Value analysis—An approach to cost reduction in which components are studied carefully to determine whether they can be redesigned, standardised or made by less costly methods of production.

Having recognised a need, the buyer next prepares a **general need description** that describes the characteristics and quantity of the needed item. For standard items, this process presents few problems. For complex items, however, the buyer may have to work with others – engineers, users, consultants – to define the item. The team may want to rank the importance of reliability, durability, price and other attributes desired in the item. In this phase, the alert business marketer can help the buyers define their needs and provide information about the value of different product characteristics.

Product specification

The buying organisation next develops the item's technical **product specifications**, often with the help of a value analysis engineering team. **Value analysis** is an approach to cost reduction in which components are studied carefully to determine if they can be redesigned, standardised or made by less costly methods of production. The team decides on the best product characteristics and specifies them accordingly. Sellers, too, can use value analysis as a tool to help secure a new account. By showing buyers a better way to make an object, outside sellers can turn straight rebuy situations into new-task situations that give them a chance to obtain new business.

Supplier search

The buyer now conducts a **supplier search** to find the best vendors. The buyer can compile a small list of qualified suppliers by reviewing trade directories, doing computer searches, or phoning other companies for recommendations. Today, more and more companies are turning to the Internet to find suppliers. For marketers, this has levelled the playing field – the Internet gives smaller suppliers many of the same advantages as larger competitors.

The newer the buying task, and the more complex and costly the item, the greater the amount of time the buyer will spend searching for suppliers. The supplier's task is to get listed in major directories and build a good reputation in the marketplace. Salespeople should watch for companies in the process of searching for suppliers and make certain that their firm is considered.

Supplier search—The stage of the business buying process in which the buyer tries to find the best vendors.

Proposal solicitation

In the **proposal solicitation** stage of the business buying process, the buyer invites qualified suppliers to submit proposals. In response, some suppliers will send only a catalogue or a salesperson. However, when the item is complex or expensive, the buyer will usually require detailed written proposals or formal presentations from each potential supplier.

Business marketers must be skilled in researching, writing and presenting proposals in response to buyer proposal solicitations. Proposals should be marketing documents, not just technical documents. Presentations should inspire confidence and should make the marketer's company stand out from the competition.

Proposal solicitation— The stage of the business buying process in which the buyer invites qualified suppliers to submit proposals.

Supplier selection

The members of the buying centre now review the proposals and select a supplier or suppliers. During **supplier selection**, the buying centre often will draw up a list of the desired supplier attributes and their relative importance. In one survey, purchasing executives listed the following attributes as most important in influencing the relationship between supplier and customer: quality products and services, on-time delivery, ethical corporate behaviour, honest communication and competitive prices. Other important factors include repair and servicing capabilities, technical aid and advice, geographic location, performance history and reputation. The members of the buying centre will rate suppliers against these attributes and identify the best suppliers.

Buyers may attempt to negotiate with preferred suppliers for better prices and terms before making the final selections. In the end, they may select a single supplier or a few suppliers. Many buyers prefer multiple sources of supplies to avoid being totally dependent on one supplier and to allow comparisons of prices and performance of several suppliers over time. Today's supplier development managers want to develop a full network of supplier-partners that can help the company bring more value to its customers.

Supplier selection—The stage of the business buying process in which the buyer reviews proposals and selects a supplier or suppliers.

Order-routine specification

The buyer now prepares an **order-routine specification**. It includes the final order with the chosen supplier or suppliers and lists items such as technical specifications, quantity needed, expected time of delivery, return policies and warranties. In the case of maintenance, repair and operating items, buyers may use blanket contracts rather than periodic purchase orders. A blanket contract creates a long-term relationship in which the supplier promises to resupply the buyer as needed at agreed prices for a set time period.

Many large buyers now practice *vendor-managed inventory*, in which they turn over ordering and inventory responsibilities to their suppliers. Under such systems, buyers share sales and

Order-routine specification—The stage of the business buying process in which the buyer writes the final order with the chosen supplier(s), listing the technical specifications, quantity needed, expected time of delivery, return policies and warranties.

inventory information directly with key suppliers. The suppliers then monitor inventories and replenish stock automatically as needed.

Performance review

In this stage, the buyer reviews supplier performance. The buyer may contact users and ask them to rate their satisfaction. The **performance review** may lead the buyer to continue, modify or drop the arrangement. The seller's job is to monitor the same factors used by the buyer to make sure that the seller is giving the expected satisfaction.

The eight-stage buying-process model provides a simple view of the business buying as it might occur in a new-task buying situation. The actual process is usually much more complex. In the

Intel lost market share when they backed off their 'Intel inside' campaign. It is now fighting back using the Intel name to sell its new processors.
SOURCE: The Advertising Archives.

modified rebuy or straight rebuy situation, some of these stages would be compressed or bypassed. Each organisation buys in its own way, and each buying situation has unique requirements.

Different buying centre participants may be involved at different stages of the process. Although certain buying-process steps usually do occur, buyers do not always follow them in the same order, and they may add other steps. Often, buyers will repeat certain stages of the process. Finally, a customer relationship might involve many different types of purchases going on at a given time, all in different stages of the buying process. The seller must manage the total customer relationship, not just individual purchases.

E-procurement: buying on the Internet

During the past few years, advances in information technology have changed the face of the B2B marketing process. Online purchasing, often called *e-procurement*, has grown rapidly.

Companies can do e-procurement in any of several ways. They can set up their own *company buying sites*. For example, General Electric operates a company trading site on which it posts its buying needs and invites bids, negotiates terms and places orders. Or the company can create *extranet links* with key suppliers. For instance, they can create direct procurement accounts with suppliers like Dell or Office World through which company buyers can purchase equipment, materials and supplies.

B2B marketers can help customers who wish to purchase online by creating well designed, easy-to-use websites. For example, *BtoB* magazine regularly rates Hewlett-Packard's B2B website among the very best.

The HP site consists of some 1,900 site areas and 2.5 million pages. It integrates an enormous amount of product and company information, putting it within only a few mouse clicks of the customers' computer. IT buying decision makers can enter the site, click directly into their customer segment – large enterprise business; small or medium business; or government, health or educational institution – and quickly find product overviews, detailed technical information and purchasing solutions. The site lets customers create customised catalogues for frequently purchased products, set up automatic approval routing for orders and conduct end-to-end transaction processing. To build deeper, more personalised online relationships with customers, HP.com features flash demos that show how to use the site, e-newsletters, live chats with sales reps, online classes and real-time customer support. The site has really paid off. Roughly 55 per cent of the company's total sales now come from the website.[15]

E-procurement gives buyers access to new suppliers, lowers purchasing costs and hastens order processing and delivery. In turn, business marketers can connect with customers online to share marketing information, sell products and services, provide customer support services and maintain ongoing customer relationships.

So far, most of the products bought online are MRO materials – maintenance, repair and operations. For instance, Hewlett-Packard spends 95 per cent of its €10bn MRO budget via e-procurement. And last year Delta Air Lines purchased €4.5bn worth of fuel online. Even an aquarium uses e-procurement to buy everything from exotic fish to feeding supplies, recently spending over €4bn online for architectural services and supplies to help construct a new exhibit 'Animal Planet Australia: Wild Extremes'.[16]

The amount of money spent on these types of MRO materials pales in comparison to the amount spent for items such as aeroplane parts, computer systems and steel tubing. Yet, MRO materials make up 80 per cent of all business orders and the transaction costs for order processing are high. Thus, companies have much to gain by streamlining the MRO buying process on the Web.

Business-to-business e-procurement yields many benefits. First, it shaves transaction costs and results in more efficient purchasing for both buyers and suppliers. A Web-powered purchasing programme eliminates the paperwork associated with traditional requisition and ordering procedures. One recent study found that e-procurement cuts down requisition-to-order costs by an average of 58 per cent.[17]

E-procurement reduces the time between order and delivery. Time savings are particularly dramatic for companies with many overseas suppliers. Adaptec, a leading supplier of computer storage, used an extranet to tie all of its Taiwanese chip suppliers together in a kind of virtual family. Now messages from Adaptec flow in seconds from its headquarters to its Asian partners, and Adaptec has reduced the time between the order and delivery of its chips from as long as 16 weeks to just 55 days – the same turnaround time for companies that build their own chips.

Finally, beyond the cost and time savings, e-procurement frees purchasing people to focus on more-strategic issues. For many purchasing professionals, going online means reducing drudgery and paperwork and spending more time managing inventory and working creatively with suppliers. 'That is the key,' says the HP executive. 'You can now focus people on value-added activities. Procurement professionals can now find different sources and work with suppliers to reduce costs and to develop new products.'[18]

The rapidly expanding use of e-purchasing, however, also presents some problems. For example, at the same time that the Web makes it possible for suppliers and customers to share business data and even collaborate on product design, it can also erode decades-old customer-supplier relationships. Many firms are using the Web to search for better suppliers.

E-purchasing can also create potential security disasters. Although e-mail and home banking transactions can be protected through basic encryption, the secure environment that businesses need to carry out confidential interactions is often still lacking. Companies are spending millions for research on defensive strategies to keep hackers at bay. Cisco Systems, for example, specifies the types of routers, firewalls and security procedures that its partners must use to safeguard extranet connections. In fact, the company goes even further – it sends its own security engineers to examine a partner's defences and holds the partner liable for any security breach that originates from its computer.

Not all companies or government agencies are happy with e-procurement. The European Commission and the American Federal Trade Commission are worried that e-procurement reduces competition by tying together buyers and suppliers through expensive IT systems. In contrast, Toyota and Honda are reluctant to participate in the open auctions: 'Our parts are not purchased through a bidding process. We buy them by building a relationship with our suppliers over time.' Like Cisco Systems, they are also concerned about security: 'The other companies are our rivals, and we are competing on parts.' The concerns are not only Japanese. VW do not want to be a junior partner in the site: 'GM is all about driving cost down, whereas Volkswagen sees an advantage in improving response times and increasing its responsiveness to customers.'[19]

Institutional and government markets

So far, our discussion of organisational buying has focused largely on the buying behaviour of business buyers. Much of this discussion also applies to the buying practices of institutional and government organisations. However, these two non-business markets have additional characteristics and needs. In this final section, we address the special features of institutional and government markets.

Institutional markets

The **institutional market** consists of schools, hospitals, nursing homes, prisons and other institutions that provide goods and services to people in their care. Institutions differ from one another in their sponsors and in their objectives. For example, in the United Kingdom, BUPA hospitals are operated for profit and are predominantly used by people with private medical insurance. National Health Service trust hospitals provide healthcare as part of the welfare state, while charities, such as the Terrence Higgins Trust and many small hospices, run centres for the terminally ill.

Low budgets and captive users characterise many institutional markets. For example, many campus-based students have little choice but to eat whatever food the university supplies. A catering organisation decides on the quality of food to buy for students. The buying objective is not profit because the food is provided as a part of a total service package. Nor is strict cost minimisation the goal – students receiving poor-quality food will complain to others and damage the college's reputation. Thus, the university purchasing agent must search for institutional food vendors whose quality meets or exceeds a certain minimum standard and whose prices are low.

 Low budgets and captive users characterise many institutional markets.

Many marketers have divisions to meet the special characteristics and needs of institutional buyers. For example, Heinz produces, packages and prices its ketchup and other condiments, canned soups, frozen desserts, pickles and other products differently to better serve the requirements of hospitals, colleges and other institutional markets. Nearly 20 per cent of the company's sales come from its Foodservice division, which includes institutional customers.[20]

Institutional market— Schools, hospitals, nursing homes, prisons and other institutions that provide goods and services to people in their care.

Government markets

The **government market** offers large opportunities for many companies. Government buying and business buying are similar in many ways. However, there are also differences that must be understood by companies wishing to sell products and services to governments. To succeed in the government market, sellers must locate key decision makers, identify the factors that affect buyer behaviour and understand the buying decision process.

Government organisations typically require suppliers to submit bids, and normally they award the contract to the lowest bidder. In some cases, the government unit will make allowance for the supplier's superior quality or reputation for completing contracts on time. Governments will also buy on a negotiated contract basis, primarily in the case of complex projects involving major R&D costs and risks, and in cases where there is little competition.

Government organisations tend to favour domestic suppliers over foreign suppliers. A major complaint of multinationals operating in Europe is that each country shows favouritism towards its nationals in spite of superior offers that are made by foreign firms. The European Commission is gradually removing this bias. Similarly European multinationals complain of the US government being biased towards its national suppliers, or states where there is political influence. This orientation partly explains why BAe Systems has expanded its interests in America so that it can participate in the huge US defence market.[21]

Like consumer and business buyers, government buyers are affected by environmental, organisational, interpersonal and individual factors. One unique thing about government buying is that it is carefully watched by outside publics, ranging from parliaments to private groups interested in how the government spends taxpayers' money. Because their spending decisions are subject to public review, government organisations require considerable paperwork from suppliers, who often complain about excessive paperwork, bureaucracy, regulations, decision-making delays and frequent shifts in procurement personnel. Ways of dealing with governments vary greatly from country to country, and knowledge of local practices – some dubious – is critical to achieving sales successes (see Real Marketing 6.2).

Government market— Governmental units – national and local – that purchase or rent goods and services for carrying out the main functions of government.

6.2 real marketing

Political graft: wheeze or sleaze?

A Swedish cabinet minister resigned after it was disclosed that she had bought a small toy using an official credit card. Meanwhile in Paris new Members of the European Parliament were invited to an 'official' briefing on the many perks attached to their new status. The subject excited Jean-François Hory. From his place in the front row he turned in his seat, fixed a knowing eye on his new colleagues and addressed them in the manner of an old hand talking down to university freshmen: 'One thing you need to know about travel allowances – they'll want to know your address. If you have one or more second homes, make sure you list the one furthest from Brussels.' Obviously, a return flight from Marseilles to Brussels is worth more than the tram fare from Loos-lès-Lille to Brussels.

Political corruption used to be a thing other countries did, but no more. In the United States, United Kingdom, France, Spain, Italy, Japan and elsewhere, accusations of political corruption involving businesses have shaken the countries' leaders. The problem runs deep. In 1999, Paul van Buitenen's 'whistle blowing' precipitated the resignation of all of the EU's commissioners. Eurofraud costs EU taxpayers billions of euros per year. VAT fraud alone is estimated to be €250bn annually. Sometimes the fiddles are minor, like exaggerating expense claims on Eurojaunts, but often they are not. Antonio Quatraro leapt to his death from a Brussels window. He was a European Commission official responsible for authorising subsidies. A fraud was discovered where he allegedly received backhanders for rigging the auction of Greek-grown tobacco to benefit Italian traders. The oil industry appears particularly dirty and close to governments. The same day saw the extending of an investigation into corruption at Yukos, Russia's largest company, and staff at the centre of France's Elf Company jailed and fined for the diversion of €300m for personal enrichment.

All governments have codes of practice but they are not consistent. There are also different traditions about obeying rules. In Britain, a Treasury minister had to fight for his political life and was eventually jailed following accusations that a controversial Arab businessperson had paid for a weekend that the minister had had at the Paris Ritz Hotel. The bill was less than €600 and in most other European countries he would not have had to declare such a gift. Meanwhile, Edith Cresson, the former French Prime Minister, had difficulty seeing why she should go when she was at the centre of the storm that ended in the resignation of all the European commissioners.

In Japan, the attitude towards political corruption is changing slowly. Kiichi Miyazawa resigned as finance minister after being caught up in the Recruit scandal. Recruit, an employment agency, had secretly given large tranches of its own shares to politicians, including cabinet ministers, in exchange for political favours. Nevertheless, two years later Mr Miyazawa was sufficiently 'rehabilitated' to become

Prime Minister. This follows the 'traditional' pattern for Japanese politicians caught taking bribes or *o-shoku*, 'defiling one's job'. *O-shoku* carries no moral overtones about wrongdoing; it just means that through carelessness the publicity has dishonoured the politician's honoured position. The usual line of defence in the Diet is that the politicians knew nothing, since their aides took the money. In that way the politician does not lose face, junior aides are not worth prosecuting and everyone is happy.

Transparency International[22] regularly publishes a Corruption Perception Index that focuses on the misuse of public office for private gain. Exhibit 6.1 shows a ranking of the EU and some of the rest with their scores on the index. Scandinavian countries have good reason to be proud of the standards their public servants uphold, but the variation elsewhere in Europe is marked.

Exhibit 6.1 Transparency International's Corruption Perception Index – EU and some of the rest

Country (EU countries in bold)	World ranking (1st is least corrupt, Haiti is the worst)	Index
Finland	1=	9.6
Iceland	1=	9.6
New Zealand	1=	9.6
Denmark	4	9.5
Singapore	5	9.4
Sweden	6	9.2
Switzerland	7	9.1
Norway	8	8.8
Australia	9=	8.7
Netherlands	9=	8.7
Austria	11=	8.6
Luxembourg	11=	8.6
UK	11=	8.6
Germany	16	8.0
Japan	17	7.6
France	18=	7.4
Ireland	18=	7.4
Belgium	20=	7.3
US	20=	7.3
Spain	23	6.8
Estonia	24	6.7
Portugal	26	6.6
Malta	28=	6.4
Slovenia	28=	6.4
Cyprus	37	5.6
Hungary	41	5.2
Italy	45	4.9
Czech Republic	48=	4.8
Lithuania	48=	4.8
		(Continued)

...6.2

Exhibit 6.1 (Continued)

Country (EU countries in bold)	World ranking (1st is least corrupt, Haiti is the worst)	Index
Latvia	49=	4.7
Slovakia	49=	4.7
Greece	54	4.4
Bulgaria	57	4.0
Poland	61	3.7
Romania	84	3.1
Russia	121	2.5
Haiti	163	1.8

SOURCE: Transparency International (TI) (www.transparency.org/policy_research/surveys_indices/cpi/2007).

The scale of corruption that has destroyed the careers of many European politicians is small beer compared with the 'dash' that lubricates trade in most of the developing world. Bribery and corruption matter for more moral reasons. It is increasingly acknowledged that it is bad for business. It can add to costs, generate bad publicity and, some argue, even damage the credibility of international financial markets, driving up risk premiums. The execution in Beijing of Zheng Xiaoyu, former director of China's State Food and Drug Administration, for bribe taking and dereliction of duty shows how seriously the matter is being taken in one developing economy.

This murky area is dangerous for marketers as well as Chinese officials. Fortunately some help is at hand from Bribeline, an Internet hotline aimed at building a picture of international bribery and how companies can prevent it. Within a month of its launch in July 2007, the service has received more than 1,000 reports relating to bribes in almost 100 countries. The sums involved range from less than €15 to more than €350,000.

The hotline, to which the World Bank will link from its website, is the start of a long and potentially valuable process but when selling to governments, marketers face a great dilemma. Should they follow St Ambrose's advice to St Augustine: 'When you are at Rome live in the Roman style; when you are elsewhere live as they live elsewhere'? Or should they behave like a saint?

SOURCES: The leading quotation is from 'An open letter to those unnerved by the little judges', by MEP Thierry Jean-Pierre; other sources are *The Economist* (29 January 2000), pp. 49–55; 'The honeycomb of corruption', *The Economist: China Survey* (8 April 2000), pp. 10–12; Paul van Buitenen, 'Corruption at the heart of Europe', *The Times* (14 March 2000), pp. 10–11; *The Economist*, 'Corporate ethics: big oils dirty secrets' (10 May 2003), pp. 61–2; Ankady Ostrovsky, 'Fresh Yukos probe targets oil production site in Siberia' and Robert Graham, 'French court jails Elf officials for corruption', both in *Financial Times* (13 November 2003), p. 12; Hugh Williamson, 'US seen as getting more corrupt, says watchdog', *Financial Times* (7 November 2006), p. 10; Gillian Tett and Kerin Hope, 'Bearing gifts: Investment banks risk reputation in Europe's murkier markets', *Financial Times* (1 June 2007), p. 15; Michael Peel, 'The net's new catch-all for corruption', *Financial Times* (31 July 2007), p. 12. For the Corruption Perception Index and an analysis of the impact of corruption on economic performance, visit transparency.org and report bribes on bribeline.com.

Non-economic criteria also play a great role in government buying. Government buyers are asked to favour depressed business firms and areas, small business firms, and business firms that avoid race, sex or age discrimination. Politicians will fight to have large contracts awarded to firms in their area or for their constituency to be the site of big construction projects. EuroDisney is an extreme case, as was Japan's 800bn yen (€6bn) G8 summit meeting in remote Kyushu-Okinawa. Sellers need to keep these factors in mind when seeking government business.

> " Non-economic criteria also play a great role in government buying. "

How do government buyers make their buying decisions?

Government buying practices often seem complex and frustrating to suppliers, who have voiced many complaints about government purchasing procedures. These include too much paperwork and bureaucracy, needless regulations, emphasis on low bid prices, decision-making delays, frequent shifts in buying personnel and too many policy changes. Yet, despite such obstacles, selling to the government can often be mastered. The government is generally helpful in providing information about its buying needs and procedures, and is often as eager to attract new suppliers as the suppliers are to find customers. Public sector buyers in Europe are required to follow the *Official Journal of the European Communities* (usually referred to as OJEC). This specifies that when seeking suppliers for a contract over threshold value it is illegal to advertise in national journals and values must be set in euros. The aim is to open the competition for public sector purchases across members of the European Union. OJEC also provides a Common Procurement Vocabulary and provides standards for 'social awareness' and 'green' procurement. The European Commission prosecutes buyers who do not comply with OJEC. Contracts awarded illegally can be nullified and damages awarded.

More companies now have separate marketing departments for government marketing efforts. Companies want to coordinate bids and prepare them more scientifically, to propose projects to meet government needs rather than just respond to government requests, to gather competitive intelligence, and to prepare stronger communications to describe the company's competence.

When the mighty US Fleet edged its way up the Gulf during the Iraq war, five little plastic boats led it. The little Hunt Class MCMVs (Mine Counter-Measure Vessels) were in a league of their own at the dangerous job of clearing a path for the main fleet. They were made by VT, a small British shipbuilding and support services group that is a master at selling to governments around the world. While the world's leading defence contractors seek alliances and mergers to meet the 'peace dividend's' reduced demand, VT has an order book worth £600 million (€900 million) and 14 vessels under construction, 95 per cent of them for export. Part of its strength is VT's dominance in the niche for glass-reinforced plastic (GRP) mine hunters, corvettes and patrol craft. Just the sort of ships that small navies want.

VT's strength extends beyond the vessels. With its vessels it offers a maritime training and support service where it has pioneered computer-based learning. Many clients come from the Middle East and travel with their families, so VT has built an Arabic school for 70 pupils next to the maritime training centre. It now does training for other firms selling to the Middle East, so strengthening its position in the region.

VT also provides services for air forces and navies. Revenues from its US business, VT Griffin, which runs 30 naval, army and air force bases, rose by a third in the first six months of the year. It now plans to quadruple the size of its US operations to capitalise on the huge growth in American defence spending.[23]

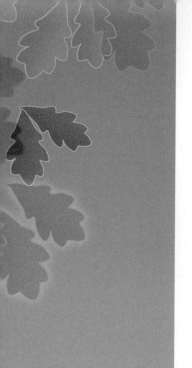

For a number of reasons, many companies that sell to the government are not as marketing oriented as VT. Total government spending is determined by elected officials rather than by any marketing effort to develop this market. Government buying has emphasised price, making suppliers invest their effort in technology to bring costs down. When the product's characteristics are specified carefully, product differentiation is not a marketing factor. Nor do advertising or personal selling matter much in winning bids on an open-bid basis.

Reviewing the concepts

Business markets and consumer markets are alike in some key ways. For example, both include people in buying roles who make purchase decisions to satisfy needs. But business markets also differ in many ways from consumer markets. For one thing, the business market is *enormous*, far larger than the consumer market.

1. Define the business market and explain how business markets differ from consumer markets

The *business market* comprises all organisations that buy goods and services for use in the production of other products and services or for the purpose of reselling or renting them to others at a profit. As compared to consumer markets, business markets usually have fewer, larger buyers who are more geographically concentrated. Business demand is derived demand, and the business buying decision usually involves more, and more professional, buyers.

2. Identify the major factors that influence business buyer behaviour

Business buyers make decisions that vary with the three types of *buying situations*: *straight rebuys*, *modified rebuys* and *new tasks*. The decision-making unit of a buying organisation – the *buying centre* – can consist of many different persons playing many different roles. The business marketer needs to know the following: Who are the major buying centre participants? In what decisions do they exercise influence and to what degree? What evaluation criteria does each decision participant use? The business marketer also needs to understand the major environmental, organisational, interpersonal and individual influences on the buying process.

3. List and define the steps in the business buying decision process

The *business buying decision process* itself can be quite involved, with eight basic stages: problem recognition, general need description, product specification, supplier search, proposal solicitation, supplier selection, order-routine specification and performance review. Buyers who face a new-task buying situation usually go through all stages of the buying process. Buyers making modified or straight rebuys may skip some of the stages. Companies must manage the overall customer relationship, which often includes many different buying decisions in various stages of the buying decision process.

Recent advances in information technology have given birth to 'e-procurement', by which business buyers are purchasing all kinds of products and services online. The Internet gives business buyers access to new suppliers, lowers purchasing costs and hastens order processing and delivery. However, e-procurement can also erode customer–supplier relationships and create potential security problems. Still, business marketers are increasingly connecting with customers online to share marketing information, sell products and services, provide customer support services and maintain ongoing customer relationships.

4. Compare the institutional and government markets and explain how institutional and government buyers make their buying decisions

The *institutional market* comprises schools, hospitals, prisons and other institutions that provide goods and services to people in their care. These markets are characterised by low budgets and captive patrons. The *government market*, which is vast, consists of government units that purchase or rent goods and services for carrying out the main functions of government.

Government buyers purchase products and services for defence, education, public welfare and other public needs. Government buying practices are highly specialised and specified, with open bidding or negotiated contracts characterising most of the buying. Government buyers operate under the watchful eye of Parliament and many private watchdog groups. Hence, they tend to require more forms and signatures, and to respond more slowly and deliberately when placing orders.

Discussing the concepts

1. How do the market structure and demand of the business markets for Michelin tyres sold to car makers differ from those selling Michelin tyres to final consumers?

2. Discuss several ways in which a straight rebuy differs from a new-task situation.

3. In a buying centre purchasing process, which buying centre participant – buyer, decider, gatekeeper, influencer or user – is most likely to make each of the following statements?

   - 'This bonding agent had better be good, because I have to put this product together.'
   - 'I specified this bonding agent on another job, and it worked for them.'
   - 'Without an appointment, no sales rep gets in to see Mr Johnson.'
   - 'Okay, it's a deal – we'll buy it.'
   - 'I'll place the order first thing tomorrow.'

4. Outline the major influences on business buyers. Why is it important for the business-to-business buyer to understand these major influences?

5. How does the business buying process differ from the consumer buying process?

6. Suppose that you own a small printing firm and have the opportunity to bid on a government contract that could bring a considerable amount of new business to your company. List three advantages and three disadvantages of working in a contract situation with the government.

Applying the concepts

1. Take your college or university as an example of a business customer for books and other educational materials. Imagine that you are a representative from a publisher who intends to establish sales to the college or university. How might you use the model of business buyer behaviour to help you develop a strategy for marketing effectively to this customer? How

Web resources

For additional classic case studies and Internet exercises, visit **www. pearsoned.co.uk/ kotler**

useful is the model? What (if any) are the limitations? Are there different levels of customers in this situation (e.g. the library as a buying centre; course team members who agree on the textbooks to recommend for student adoption and library stocks; the individual tutor who chooses recommended textbooks and requests the library to stock; or the college or university bookshop)? How might you deal with these different levels of customer?

2. Make a list of the key factors that a local government institution or agency might consider when deciding to purchase new coffee-making machines for users in its offices. Remembering how government buyers make their buying decisions, suggest a scenario that you, as a potential supplier, would use to sell to this institutional buyer.

References

1. Oliver Sutton, 'Buzjet business still buzzing', *Interavia* (September 1999), pp. 30–3; Richard Lofthouse, 'Business jet is business sense', *Interavia* (September 1999), pp. 121–4 and 'If you need to know the price . . .', *Interavia* (September 1999), pp. 127–30; 'Bombadier catches up with itself', *Interavia* (September 1999), pp. 147–8; 'When security is the issue', *Interavia* (September 1999), p. 154; *EuroBusiness* (August 2000); Bill Sweetman, 'Quiet supersonics in sight', *Interavia* (November 2001), pp. 19–20; Kevin Done, 'Business jets "hold key to supersonic travel" ', *Financial Times* (28 July 2000), p. 8; Special Report, 'Corporate aviation', *Financial Times* (7 May 2003), pp. I–IV; 'Concorde Special', *The Independent* (21 October 2003); Ann Treneman, 'The part-time jet set', *The Times Magazine* (8 November 2003), pp. 48–52; Mariko Sanchanta, Companies International: 'Honda begins selling business jets', *Financial Times* (19 October 2006); 'Boeing business jets sales momentum continues with seven new orders', *M2 Presswire* (21 May 2007); Kevin Done, Companies International: 'Demand for business jets increases to record level', *Financial Times* (13 February 2007).

2. Bill Sweetman, 'Lift fan carries Lockheed Martin to JSF victory', *Interavia* (November 2002), pp. 9–10; Demetri Sevastopuloin, The Americas: 'US agrees Joint Strike Fighter deal with Britain', *Financial Times* (13 December 2006).

3. James Boxell, 'Rolls-Royce gets lift from air show orders', *Financial Times* (4 July 2007), p. 20; Andy Slater, 'Virtual world boosts vans', *Financial Times* (9 May 2007), p. 3.

4. See Kate Macarthur, 'Teflon togs get $40 million ad push', *Advertising Age* (8 April 2002), p. 3; 'Neat pants for sloppy people', *Consumer Reports: Publisher's Edition Including Supplemental Guides* (May 2003), p. 10; 'Sales makes the wearables world go round', *Wearables Business* (24 April 2004), p. 22; Rosamaria Mancini, *HFN* (16 May 2005), p. 17; and www.teflon.invista.com, accessed September 2006.

5. 'More of everything: Does the world have enough resources to meet the growing needs of the emerging economies?', *The Economist* (14 September 2006).

6. For more discussion of business markets and business buyer behaviour, see Das Narayandas, 'Building loyalty in business markets', *Harvard Business Review* (September 2005), pp. 131–9; and James C. Anderson, James A. Narus and Wouter van Rossum, 'Customer value propositions in business markets', *Harvard Business Review* (March 2006), pp. 91–9.

7. Patrick J. Robinson, Charles W. Faris and Yoram Wind, *Industrial Buying Behavior and Creative Marketing* (Boston, MA: Allyn & Bacon, 1967). Also see James C. Anderson and James A. Narus, *Business Market Management: Understanding, creating and delivering value*, 2nd edn (Upper Saddle River, NJ: Prentice Hall, 2004), Ch. 3; and Philip Kotler and Kevin Lane Keller, *Marketing Management*, 12th edn (Upper Saddle River, NJ: Prentice Hall, 2006), Ch. 7.

8. Cait Murphy, 'Will the future belong to Germany?', *Fortune* (2 August 2000), pp. 63–70; 'Intershop muss "schnell Gewinn zeigen" ', *Borsen-Zeitung* (5 April 2007).

9. See Philip Kotler and Kevin Lane Keller, *Marketing Management*, 12th edn (Upper Saddle River, NJ: Prentice Hall, 2006), pp. 213–14.

10. See Frederick E. Webster Jr. and Yoram Wind, *Organizational Buying Behavior* (Upper Saddle River, NJ: Prentice Hall, 1972), pp. 78–80. Also see James C. Anderson and James A. Narus, *Business Market*

Management: Understanding, creating and delivering value, 2nd edn (Upper Saddle River, NJ: Prentice Hall, 2004), Ch. 3.

11. For more discussion, see Stefan Wuyts and Inge Geyskens, 'The formation of buyer–seller relationships: Detailed contract drafting and close partner selection', *Harvard Business Review* (October 2005), pp. 103–17; and Robert McGarvey, 'The buyer's emotional side', *Selling Power* (April 2006), pp. 35–6.

12. See Frederick E. Webster, Jr. and Yoram Wind, *Organizational Buying Behavior* (Upper Saddle River, NJ: Prentice Hall, 1972), pp. 33–7.

13. Patrick J. Robinson, Charles W. Faris and Yoram Wind, *Industrial Buying Behavior and Creative Marketing* (Boston, MA: Allyn & Bacon, 1967), p. 14.

14. See their product at www.midas-fms.com and www.energysavingtrust.org.uk/fleet/fleetheroawards/

15. For this and other examples, see Kate Maddox, '#1 Hewlett-Packard Co.: www.hp.com', *BtoB* (11 August 2003), p. 1; 'Great Web Sites', www.hp.com; *BtoB Online* (13 September 2004); and '10 Great Web Sites', *BtoB Online* (12 September 2005), all accessed at www.btobonline.com.

16. Karen Prema, 'National aquarium reels in savings with online buying', www.purchasing.com, accessed 2 March 2006; Karen Prema, 'SRM + e-auctions: Tools in the toolbox', *Purchasing* (6 April 2006), pp. 46–7; Susan Avery, 'At HP, indirect procurement takes more of a leadership role', www.purchasing.com, accessed 25 May 2006.

17. Demir Barlas, 'E-procurement: Steady value', www.line56.com, accessed 4 January 2005.

18. Michael A. Verespej, 'E-procurement explosion', *Industry Week* (March 2002), pp. 25–8.

19. Alexander Harney, 'Toyota set to join online trade exchange' and 'Up close but impersonal', *Financial Times* (10 March 2000), p. 33; 'A market for monopoly', *The Economist* (17 June 2000), pp. 85–6; Stuart Derrick, 'Market forces', *e.business* (July 2000), pp. 15–16.

20. H.J. Heinz Company Annual Report 2006, p. 20; accessed at http://heinz.com/2006annualreport/2006HeinzAR.pdf

21. Stephanie Kirchgaessner, 'US approves BAE takeover of Armor Holdings', FT.com (21 June 2007); 'Tank deals signal BAE resilience', *The Express* (24 July 2007); Tracey Boles, 'BAE Systems races Northrup for lucrative anti-missile deal', *The Express on Sunday* (29 July 2007).

22. Transparency International (TI) (www.transparency.org) is the global civil society organisation leading the fight against corruption. Through more then 90 chapters worldwide and an international secretariat in Berlin, Germany, TI raises awareness of the damaging effects of corruption and works with partners in government, business and civil society to develop and implement effective measures to tackle it.

23. Michael Harrison, 'VT aims for $500m sales in surging US defence sector', *The Independent* (12 November 2003); Tom Griggs, 'T Group steps out into Civvy Street', *Financial Times* (16 July 2007).

Company case 6 Biofoam: just peanuts?

Like diamonds, polystyrene peanuts are forever – their volume is growing at a rate of at least 20 million kg annually. Since their introduction in 1970, they have become one of the most popular forms of packaging material. They are lightweight, inexpensive and resilient. They conform to any shape, protect superbly, resist shifting in transit, leave no dusty residue on the goods they protect and are indestructible. That is the problem. Nearly every one of those peanuts used since 1970 is still with us – blowing in the wind or taking up space in a landfill. Worse yet, they will be with us for another 500 years. They are wonderful but not environmentally sound.

The small firm Biofoam thinks it has solved this problem and helps businesses and governments meet their environmental targets. It sells a peanut made from grain sorghum, a grain now used for animal feed. To make these sorghum peanuts, the company strips the grain of its nutritional value, presses it into pellets, and conveys it through a giant popper. The process creates a product that looks like tan cheese doodles, not so surprising given that the inventors started out to make a snack food. Nevertheless, no one wanted to eat these objects, so the inventors had to find other uses for them. According to Ed Alfke, Biofoam's CEO, the sorghum peanuts do just as good a job as the best foam peanuts and they do not cost any more. Moreover, they hold no electrostatic charge, so they will not cling to nylons or other synthetic fibres (such as your carpet or clothes). Better yet, they are 'absolutely, frighteningly natural', says Tom Schmiegel, a veteran of the plastics industry.

To dispose of a Biofoam peanut, you can: (a) put it in your waste bin, (b) throw it on your front lawn as bird food, (c) compost it, (d) put it in your dog's or cat's bowl, (e) set it out with salsa at your next party, or (f) wash it down your drain. The peanut dissolves in water and has some – although limited – nutritional value. Alfke bought into the company because of its environmentally positive stance. He is convinced that green companies will profit from a global regulatory climate that is increasingly hostile to polluters. 'The writing is on the wall for companies that are not environmentally friendly,' he says.

Biofoam initially targeted retailers who wanted to send an environmentally friendly message, helped along by the inclusion of a Biofoam pamphlet explaining the advantages of the Biofoam peanut. It targeted the heaviest users of Styrofoam peanuts who consume up to 20 truckloads of loose fill a *day*. To date, Biofoam has signed two major accounts – the Fuller Brush Company and computer reseller MicroAge.

Eventually, Biofoam will have to expand beyond environmentally sensitive firms into a broader market. To convince potential users to use Biofoam peanuts, Alfke has come up with a seemingly no-brainer option: to be environmentally responsible without having to pay more or sacrifice convenience. He is willing to install machines on the customer's premises to produce peanuts in-house – an arrangement that would give Biofoam rent-free production sites. He will even provide an employee to operate the machinery. Although this strategy might sound unusual, it has been used by other companies such as Xerox to sell copiers and Tetra Pak to sell juice boxes and milk cartons.

The in-house arrangement has benefits for the customer as well as for Biofoam. Users receive immediate, reliable, just-in-time delivery combined with on-site service and a five-year price guarantee with no intermediaries involved. With Biofoam on-site, users never run out of packaging, and they avoid the expense of stockpiling materials. Lower production costs make Biofoam's product price competitive with that of polystyrene. For Biofoam, the arrangement provides a rent-free network of regional manufacturing facilities and an intimacy with each customer. Because the host company will only consume about one-third of the output, Biofoam plans to sell the excess to smaller firms in the host's area.

However, this in-house production arrangement has disadvantages. From the host's perspective, the machinery takes up 140 m² of floor space that could be used to produce something else. Furthermore, some of the output of that 140 m² goes to other firms, benefiting Biofoam but doing nothing for the host. Furthermore, the host has a non-employee working in its plant. The peanut-making machinery is also intrusive. It consists of three machines – an extruder, a conditioning chamber and a deduster – joined by ducts and conveyor belts. The machines make lots of noise (like a giant air conditioner), making conversation in the vicinity impossible. The process creates a smell, rather like the inside of an old barn, and produces heat, a potential problem. Thus, on closer inspection, the in-house arrangement is not entirely desirable. Without this arrangement, however, costs rise considerably. If it had to ship the peanuts to users, Biofoam would have to raise the price 10 to 20 per cent.

Biofoam's competition, the polystyrene loose-fill industry, is a fragmented patchwork of diverse companies. It includes oil companies, chemical producers, fill manufacturers and regional distributors – all of which would suffer from Biofoam's success. One aggressive newcomer is EarthShell that make their packaging out of environmentally friendly natural limestone and potato starch. The industry is much more rough-and-tumble than CEO Alfke anticipated. So far, Biofoam has a microscopic market share. The company's 2000 sales totalled only €3m – not much in an industry with potential sales of €200 to €600m a year. Nevertheless, the €3m represented a five-fold increase over the previous year. Alfke now projects sales of €90m with 30 per cent pre-tax profits. These projections include sales of products other than sorghum peanuts. Alfke plans to add injectible Biofoam and stiff Biofoam packaging materials. Other promising applications have been suggested, such as using Biofoam to absorb oil spills or in medicinal applications, but Alfke does not want to talk about those. For now, 'It's important that we try to stay focused,' he claims.

Can Alfke reach his ambitious goals? Many industry observers say no. Early going was tough for the firm. Environmental claims, say these observers, do not have impact. 'That was something we worried about three years ago,' said a purchasing agent. Biofoam's sales representatives found the market less environmentally concerned. Others, however, are more optimistic. The global warming debate is now as hard to ignore as a pile of everlasting polystyrene peanuts.

Nancy Pfund, general partner of Hambrecht and Quist's Environmental Technology Fund, thinks that many firms are getting interested in environmentally friendly packaging. She notes that companies have 'internalised a lot of environmental procedures without making a lot of noise about it. You also have younger people who grew up learning about the environment in school now entering the consumer market. That's a very strong trend.' Such consumers will demand more responsible packaging.

Are companies that use Biofoam happy with it? Well, some yes, some no. On the positive side is MicroAge Computer. According to Mark Iaquinto, facilities manager, MicroAge had been searching for an acceptable alternative to polystyrene. Now that it has found Biofoam, he is convinced it can stop searching. On the negative side, Norbert Schneider, president of Fuller Brush Company, has concerns about the way the product crumbles in boxes filled with sharp-pointed brushes. Alfke says that Biofoam is working on a solution, but if it does not find one soon, Fuller Brush may change packaging suppliers.

Other firms have entered the market with biodegradable, water-soluble foams. Made from corn-starch-based thermoplastics, the products can be rinsed down the drain after use. They can be used in loose-fill packaging applications or moulded in place into shaped packaging. They compare favourably with traditional packaging materials for cost and performance.

So, facing a stiffly competitive industry, new competitors and a softening of environmental concerns, Biofoam will find the going hard. However, none of this dents Alfke's enthusiasm. Alfke was a multimillionaire before age 40. 'I've seen a lot of deals,' he claims, 'and I've never, *ever* seen a deal as good as this one.' As an experienced businessman, no doubt he *has* seen a lot of deals. He really believes in this one, but is he right?

Questions

1. Outline Biofoam's current marketing strategy.
2. Which elements of the marketing mix are most important for Biofoam to focus on?
3. What is the nature of demand in the loose-fill packaging industry? What factors shape that demand?
4. If you were a buyer of packaging materials, would you agree to Biofoam's offer of machines inside your plant? If not, how could Biofoam overcome your objections?
5. What environmental and organisational factors are likely to affect the loose-fill packaging industry? How will these factors affect Biofoam?
6. Is Alfke right? Is this a good deal? Would you have bought into the firm? Why or why not?

SOURCES: http://www.polystyrene.org/environment/environment. html; Robert D. Leaversuch, 'Water-soluble foams offer cost-effective protection', *Modern Plastics* (April 1997), pp. 32–5; 'Latest trends in . . . protective packaging', *Modern Materials Handling* (October 2002); Venessa Houlder, 'EU packaging measures: meeting the challenge', FT.com site, 26 May 2003; 'New equipment order increases manufacturing capacity for EarthShell products', *Business Wire* (31 December 2002); Peter Marsh, Inside track enterprise: 'Future blighted by a cash famine', *Financial Times* (20 March 2003); http://www.earthshell.com/; http://www.greenmonde.com/FAQs/ Starch.html.

you do
good
coffee

you do
good.

When you drink NESCAFÉ
PARTNERS' BLEND Fairtrade
certified coffee, you enjoy
an exceptionally smooth,
rich coffee. And, better still,
you help the people who grow
your coffee, their families
and their communities with
every cup. Learn more at
growmorethancoffee.co.uk

FAIRTRADE

Guarantees
a **better deal**
for Third World
Producers

Look for the FAIRTRADE
Mark on products.
www.fairtrade.org.uk

it's
all
about you NESCAFÉ

Research is cheap if you want to stay in business, expensive if you don't.

ANON

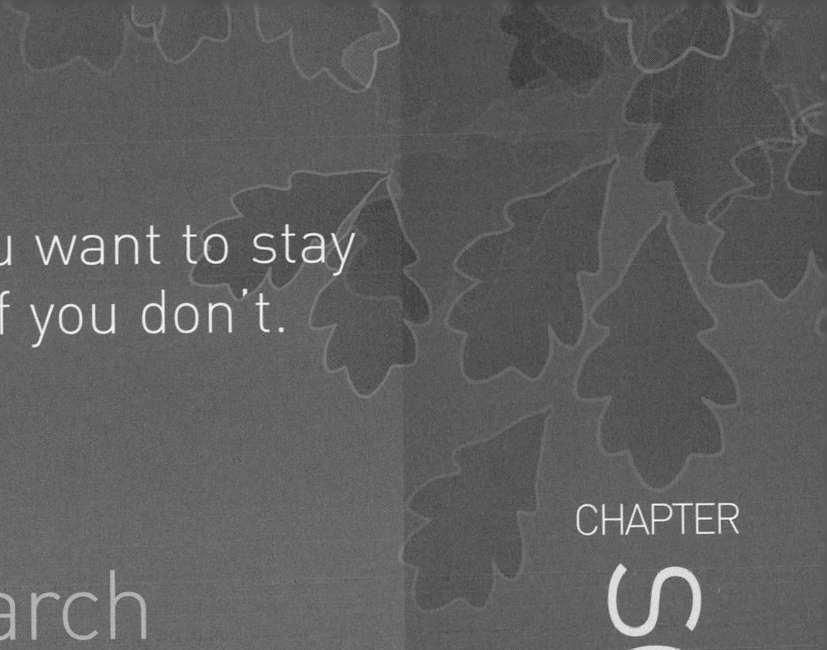

Marketing research

Mini Contents List

CHAPTER

seven

◄ SOURCE: The Advertising Archives.

'Do You Know the Future?'

The Primms, Destabilize, B00007E7GJ, 2002

Previewing the concepts

Successful marketing is likened to developing products and services that do not currently exist for customers who do not know they want them. It is about needing to know the future and marketing research can help us do just that. In the previous chapter, you learned about the complex and changing marketing environment. In this chapter, we'll continue our exploration of how marketers go about understanding the marketplace and consumers. We'll look at how to develop and manage information about important marketplace elements – about customers, competitors, products and marketing programmes. We will examine marketing information systems designed to give managers the right information, in the right form, at the right time to help them make better marketing decisions. We'll also take a close look at the marketing research process and at some special marketing research considerations. To succeed in today's marketplace, companies must know how to manage mountains of marketing information effectively.

After reading this chapter, you should be able to:

1. Explain the importance of information to the company and its understanding of the marketplace.
2. Define the marketing information system and discuss its parts.
3. Outline the steps in the marketing research process.
4. Explain how companies analyse and distribute marketing information.
5. Discuss the special issues some marketing researchers face, including public policy and ethics issues.

We'll start the chapter with a case about HIV/AIDS in Africa – one of the most intractable problems facing humankind. In the developed world the HIV/AIDS epidemic is close to being under control through education and the use of drugs that extend people's lives after they have become HIV+. Not so in the poorest continent in the world where working populations are being decimated, millions of children are orphaned and populations are declining as the sexually transmitted disease rips through society. There is hope, but it is as much about changing attitudes as distributing drugs. That is where market research is essential. In marketing terms, there is no point in running a campaign if you do not know what you are campaigning against.

Prelude case Market researching HIV/AIDS in Africa: a little achieves the unimaginable

The World Health Organization (WHO) explains it clearly. 'The human immunodeficiency virus (HIV) is a retrovirus that infects cells of the human immune system, destroying or impairing their function. In the early stages of infection, the person has no symptoms. However, as the infection progresses, the immune system becomes weaker, and the person becomes more susceptible to so-called opportunistic infections.

The most advanced stage of HIV infection is acquired immunodeficiency syndrome (AIDS). It can take 10–15 years for an HIV-infected person to develop AIDS; antiretroviral drugs can slow down the process even further.

HIV is transmitted through unprotected sexual intercourse (anal or vaginal), transfusion of contaminated blood, sharing of contaminated needles, and between a mother and her infant during pregnancy, childbirth and breastfeeding.'

In developed countries the number of deaths from HIV/AIDS is declining, although it is the western world's fastest-growing serious health condition. For example today, there are 70,000 people living with HIV/AIDS in the UK. Those most affected are gay men and African people living in the UK and diagnosed here, but probably infected in sub-Saharan Africa. A third of those living with the virus do not yet know they have it. These are the people most likely to pass it on to others.

But the situation in western countries pales into insignificance compared with the situation in sub-Saharan Africa. While WHO estimates that there are fewer than two million people with HIV/AIDS in the whole of North America, Europe and Central Asia, in sub-Saharan Africa the figure is 32 million and growing. Many of the sufferers are innocents. Mother-to-child infections have grown tenfold. The region now has 40 million HIV/AIDS orphans who, according to UNICEF, are 'putty in the hands of warlords'. In worst-hit Botswana, Namibia, Swaziland and Zimbabwe, between 20 and 25 per cent of the sexually active population are infected. A 15-year-old boy in Botswana has an 80 per cent chance of dying of HIV/AIDS.

South Africa's isolation once protected it from the epidemic, but no more. It now has more HIV/AIDS sufferers than any other country in the world and up to a third of sexually active males are HIV-positive. In 1996 the life expectancy in South Africa was over 60 years. HIV/AIDS is likely to bring it down to less than 40 years by 2010. Worse is yet to come. HIV/AIDS is hitting the most economically active members of the population. Without HIV/AIDS, Botswana's population of 40–49-year-olds would have been 300,000 in 2020. With HIV/AIDS it is expected to slump to fewer than 60,000!

Can the catastrophe be stopped? There is hope for drug donations from rich countries and the International AIDS Vaccine Initiative gives some hope. But among the gloom there are some successes. Senegal has remained largely HIV/AIDS free as a result of vigorous and unambiguous education programmes.

UNAIDS, the United Nations agency charged with fighting the disease, says the gap between Africa's needs and the donations of rich countries to help fight the disease is rising, but some local research is helping the meagre donations stretch further. Researchers in Tanzania found that spending on diseases did not relate to the disabilities and deaths they cause or the efficacy of treatment. Based on these findings, the inadequate health budget is now spent more effectively.

Uganda is close to the epicentre, but has turned the tide on HIV/AIDS. President Museveni acted on the threat as soon as he came to power. Uganda is a poor country but the President commissioned a series of inexpensive surveys (about €25,000 each) into the sexual behaviour of the population. These and other studies uncovered important reasons why HIV/AIDS is spreading:

- Sex is fun and an inexpensive recreation.
- Condoms make it less so: 'Would you eat a sweet with a wrapper on it?'
- Some men snip the ends of condoms they are about to use.
- The discussion of sex is often taboo.
- Myths abound: regular infusions of sperm make women grow beautiful and men can get rid of HIV infection by passing it on to a virgin.
- Wives who ask their husbands to use a condom are in danger of being beaten up.
- Drinking local beers is another form of inexpensive entertainment but the inebriated are prone to unsafe sex.

As Bill Gates, the world's largest donor to Africa's HIV/AIDS prevention programmes, explains, getting people to take preventive action is difficult, since 90 per cent of the HIV/AIDS sufferers in Africa do not know they have the disease. There is also considerable resistance to compulsory screening in the countries worst affected.

Realising the scale of the problem and the shortage of funds, the President of Uganda freed dozens of non-government organisations (NGOs) to educate people about unsafe sex. The NGOs used material and approaches that many other African countries found unacceptable, but within a five-year period the HIV-infected women in urban antenatal clinics fell from 30 to 15 per cent.

Increasingly sophisticated research helps target HIV/AIDS programmes. Unlike in the West, young women are the main HIV/AIDS sufferers in Africa. The WHO estimates that 4.5 per cent of South African males aged between 15 and 24 have HIV/AIDS but 14.8 per cent of women. Dr Anthony Fauci, director of the National Institute of Allergy and Infectious Diseases, warns that new infections were still hugely outpacing treatment. 'For every one person that you put in therapy, six get infected. So we're losing that game, the numbers game.' The good news is that male circumcision can cut the risk of infection by 60 per cent among men. But women are eight times more likely than men to contract HIV during unprotected sex and of more than 600,000 new infections in children each year, 90 per cent are from mother-to-child.

The toll of the HIV/AIDS epidemic in South Africa continues to mount. The number of HIV/AIDS-related deaths among the adult population increased from about 9 per cent in 1995–96 to about 40 per cent now, according to Professor Carel van Aardt of the Bureau of Market Research of the University of South Africa.

Documentary-style marketing gives marketers fresh insights into South African consumers and an understanding of critical social trends affecting HIV/AIDS. The *NOW project*, which uses video to capture the everyday reality of real people, was carried out by the Consumer Insight Agency. It is the first in-depth, qualitative review of sociographic and psychographic trends in South Africa and breaks new ground in penetrating beneath the surface of what makes South Africans tick. 'This research challenges the usual segmentation studies common in the marketing world,' says Wendy Cochrane, Director of the agency. 'Conventional studies tend to focus narrowly on demographics (race, earning power, etc.) and quantitatively derived psychographic statements. But often when marketers are briefed to "bring a segment alive" they're impossible to find. Humans are not stereotypes, and refuse to stay in boxes!' Cochrane says that the new study is a more meaningful way of making sense of the dynamic landscape. 'A powerful tool that is grounded in reality, it's the first "big picture" view of South African society where everyone from the richest "Polished Diamond" to the "Township Mama" is laid bare.'

Other studies have shown the dramatic effect of intervening where groups are prone to HIV/AIDS. The charity Camfed International believes educating girls is 'the quickest route to alleviating poverty in Africa'. It cites support for the importance of girls' education from economists such as Amartya Sen, Jeffrey Sachs and Lawrence Summers. It says the research shows that, for each additional year of education after elementary school, an African woman's income rises 15 per cent, her vulnerability to HIV/AIDS decreases sharply and her family tends to be smaller and healthier.

In Zambia, Camfed rescued 18-year-old orphaned Penelope from working as a prostitute close to the school she now attends. 'A lot of people are dying of this disease,' she explains. 'If I didn't start school, I would have died.'[1]

Questions

1. What research would you commission to gather an understanding of the behaviour leading to the spread of HIV/AIDS?
2. Is it safe to rely on 'inexpensive research' to guide campaigns as critical as those against HIV/AIDS?
3. What are the dangers and benefits of freeing a range of NGOs, such as Camfed, to drive for a social good rather than a single, well-coordinated campaign?

Introduction

In order to tackle any business or social problem, companies need information at almost every turn. As the HIV/AIDS in Africa case highlights, marketing programmes need solid information on consumer needs and wants. Even then, attitudes and behaviour are hard to change. Companies also need an abundance of information on competitors, resellers and other actors and forces in the marketplace.

With the recent explosion of information technologies, companies can now generate information in great quantities. Tesco has made a strategic advantage of that data:

> But Tesco's biggest innovation has been in the way it collects and uses customer data from its loyalty programme. Many retailers use clubs to provide nothing more sophisticated than a discount to customers as they pay for their goods. That is nothing more than paying customers to shop with you.
>
> Tesco use their database to provide insights into how customers see the company. When it revealed that families were not buying nappies or other baby supplies in their weekly shop, further research showed they were instead paying some 20 per cent more to buy these items at nearby Boots pharmacies because they trusted the Boots brand when it came to looking after their babies. So Tesco began a baby club, offering advice on pregnancy and mothering. Within two years almost four of every ten expectant parents in Britain were members and the firm had seized almost a quarter of the mother and baby market, according to 'Scoring Points', a book on the Clubcard scheme.[2]
>
> SOURCE: The Economist Newspaper Limited, London (21 June 2007).

Despite this data glut, marketers frequently complain that they lack enough information of the right kind. They don't need *more* information, they need *better* information. And they need to make better *use* of the information they already have. A former CEO at Unilever once said that if Unilever only knew what it knows, it would double its profits.[3] The meaning is clear: many companies sit on rich information but fail to manage and use it well. Companies must design effective marketing information systems that give managers the right information, in the right form, at the right time to help them make better marketing decisions.

 Marketers . . . don't need *more* information, they need *better* information.

A **marketing information system (MIS)** consists of people, equipment and procedures to gather, sort, analyse, evaluate and distribute needed, timely and accurate information to marketing decision makers. Figure 7.1 shows that the MIS begins and ends with information users – marketing managers, internal and external partners and others who need marketing information. First, it interacts with these information users to *assess information needs*. Next, it *develops needed information* from internal company databases, marketing intelligence activities and marketing research. Then it helps users to analyse information to put it in the right form for making marketing decisions and managing customer relationships. Finally, the MIS *distributes* the marketing information and helps managers *use* it in their decision making.

Marketing information system (MIS)—People, equipment and procedures to gather, sort, analyse, evaluate and distribute needed, timely and accurate information to marketing decision makers.

Figure 7.1 The marketing information system

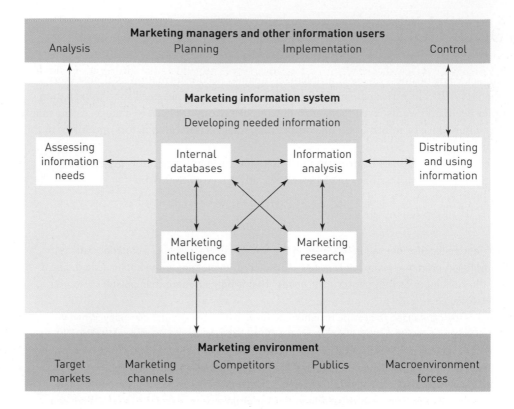

Assessing marketing information needs

The marketing information system primarily serves the company's marketing and other managers. However, it may also provide information to external partners, such as suppliers, resellers or marketing services agencies. For example, Tesco gives key suppliers access to information on customer buying patterns and inventory levels, and Dell creates tailored Premium Pages for large customers, giving them access to product design, order status and product support and service information. In designing an information system, the company must consider the needs of all of these users.

A good marketing information system balances the information users would *like* to have against what they really *need* and what it is *feasible* to offer. The company begins by interviewing managers to find out what information they would like. Some managers will ask for whatever information they can get without thinking carefully about what they really need. Too much information can be as harmful as too little. Other managers may omit things they ought to know, or they may not know to ask for some types of information they should have. For example, managers might need to know about a new product that a competitor plans to introduce during the coming year. Because they do not know about the new product, they do not think to ask about it. The MIS must monitor the marketing environment in order to provide decision makers with information they should have to make key marketing decisions.

Sometimes the company cannot provide the needed information, either because it is not available or because of MIS limitations. For example, a brand manager might want to know how competitors will change their advertising budgets next year and how these changes will affect industry market shares. The information on planned budgets probably is not available. Even if it is, the company's MIS may not be advanced enough to forecast resulting changes in market shares.

Finally, the costs of obtaining, processing, storing and delivering information can mount quickly. The company must decide whether the benefits of having additional information are worth the costs of providing it, and both value and cost are often hard to assess. By itself, information has no worth; its value comes from its *use*. In many cases, additional information will do little to change or improve a manager's decision, or the costs of the information may exceed the returns from the improved decision. Marketers should not assume that additional information will always be worth obtaining. Rather, they should weigh carefully the costs of getting more information against the benefits resulting from it.

Developing marketing information

Marketers can obtain the needed information from *internal data, marketing intelligence* and *marketing research*.

Internal data

Many companies build extensive **internal databases**, electronic collections of consumer and market information obtained from data sources within the company network. Marketing managers can readily access and work with information in the database to identify marketing opportunities and problems, plan programmes and evaluate performance.

Internal databases— Information sources that exist within the company.

Information in the database can come from many sources. The accounting department prepares financial statements and keeps detailed records of sales, costs and cash flows. Operations reports on production schedules, shipments and inventories. The marketing department furnishes information on customer transactions, demographics, psychographics and buying behaviour. The customer service department keeps records of customer satisfaction or service problems. The sales force reports on reseller reactions and competitor activities, and marketing channel partners provide data on point-of-sale transactions. Harnessing such information can provide powerful competitive advantage.

Here is an example of how one company uses its internal database to make better marketing decisions:

Pizza Hut, part of Yum! Brands, claims to have the largest fast-food customer database in the world. The database contains detailed customer information data on 40 million households, gleaned from phone orders, online orders and point-of-sale transactions at its more than 12,600 restaurants. The company can slice and dice the data by favourite toppings, what you ordered last, and whether you buy a salad with your cheese and pepperoni pizza. Pizza Hut also tracks in real time what commercials people are watching and responding to. It then uses all this data to enhance customer relationships. For example, it can target coupon offers to specific households based on past buying behaviours and preferences.[4]

Internal databases can usually be accessed more quickly and cheaply than other information sources, but they also present some problems. Because internal information was often collected for other purposes, it may be incomplete or in the wrong form for making marketing decisions. For example, sales and cost data used by the accounting department for preparing financial statements must be adapted for use in evaluating the value of specific customer segment, sales force or channel performance. Data also ages quickly; keeping the database current requires a major effort. In addition, a large company produces mountains of information, which must be well integrated and readily accessible so that managers can find it easily and use it effectively. Managing that much data requires highly sophisticated equipment and techniques.

Marketing intelligence

Marketing intelligence— Everyday information about developments in the marketing environment that helps managers prepare and adjust marketing plans.

Marketing intelligence is the systematic collection and analysis of publicly available information about competitors and developments in the marketplace. The goal of marketing intelligence is to improve strategic decision making, assess and track competitors' actions, and provide early warning of opportunities and threats.

Competitor intelligence gathering has grown dramatically as more and more companies are now busily snooping on their competitors. Techniques range from quizzing the company's own employees and benchmarking competitors' products to researching the Internet, lurking around industry trade shows, and even rooting through rivals' waste bins.

Competitor intelligence— Information gathered that informs on what the competition is doing or is about to do.

> **More and more companies are now busily snooping on their competitors.**

Much intelligence can be collected from people inside the company – executives, engineers and scientists, purchasing agents and the sales force. The company can also obtain important intelligence information from suppliers, resellers and key customers. Or it can get good information by observing competitors and monitoring their published information. It can buy and analyse competitors' products, monitor their sales, check for new patents and examine various

The New Beetle Cabriolet.

A corporate row broke out between General Motors and Volkswagen after VW recruited GM's operations guru and several of his staff.
SOURCE: The Advertising Archives.

types of physical evidence. For example, one company regularly checks out competitors' car parks – full might indicate plenty of work and prosperity; half-full might suggest hard times.

Some companies have even rifled their competitors' garbage, which is legally considered abandoned property once it leaves the premises. In one elaborate garbage-snatching incident, AirCanada was recently caught rifling through the wheelie bins of WestJet, Canada's second largest airline, in efforts to find evidence that WestJet was illegally tapping into Air Canada's computers.[5] In 'hair care wars', Procter & Gamble admitted to 'bin diving' at Unilever's headquarters. 'P&G got its mitts on just about every iota of info there was to be had about Unilever's [hair-care] brands,' notes an analyst. However, when news of the questionable tactics reached top P&G managers, they were shocked. They immediately stopped the project and voluntarily set up negotiations with Unilever to right whatever competitive wrongs had been done. Although P&G claims it broke no laws, the company reported that the bin raids 'violated our strict guidelines regarding our business policies.'[6]

Competitors often reveal intelligence information through their annual reports, business publications, trade show exhibits, press releases, advertisements and Web pages. The Internet is proving to be a vast new source of competitor-supplied information. Using Internet search engines, marketers can search specific competitor names, events or trends and see what turns up. Moreover, most companies now place volumes of information on their websites, providing details to attract customers, partners, suppliers, investors or franchisees. This can provide a wealth of useful information about competitors' strategies, markets, new products, facilities and other happenings.

Marketing intelligence: Procter & Gamble admitted to 'dumpster diving' at rival Unilever's Helene Curtis headquarters. When P&G's top management learned of the questionable practice, it stopped the project, voluntarily informed Unilever, and set up talks to right whatever competitive wrongs had been done.
SOURCE: Andy Reynolds/Stone/Getty Images.

Something as simple as a competitor's job postings can be very revealing.

For example, a few years ago, while poking around on Google's company website, Microsoft's Bill Gates came across a help-wanted page describing all of the jobs available at Google. To his surprise, he noted that Google was looking for engineers with backgrounds that had nothing to do with its Web-search business but everything to do with Microsoft's core software businesses. Forewarned that Google might be preparing to become more than just a search engine company, Gates e-mailed a handful of Microsoft executives, saying, in effect, 'We have to watch these guys. It looks like they are building something to compete with us.' Notes a marketing intelligence consultant, companies 'are often surprised that there's so much out there to know. They're busy with their day-to-day operations and they don't realize how much information can be obtained with a few strategic keystrokes.'[7]

Intelligence seekers can also pore through any of thousands of online databases. Some are free. For example, up-to-date business information is available on newspapers' searchable websites, such as *The Times* (Timesonline.co.uk), *Financial Times Deutschland* (ftd.de) and *Le Monde* (lemonde.fr), stock exchanges (londonstockexchange.com or euronext.com) or the Patent Office and Trademark database that reveals patents competitors have filed. And for a fee, companies can subscribe to any of the more than 3,000 online databases and information search services such as *Financial Times*, *The Economist*, Dialog, DataStar, LexisNexis, Dow Jones, ProQuest and Dun & Bradstreet's Online Access.

The intelligence game goes both ways. Facing determined marketing intelligence efforts by competitors, most companies are now taking steps to protect their own information. For example, Unilever conducts widespread competitive intelligence training. Employees are taught

Protection against snooping competitors: the increasing importance of security on the Internet has led to the creation of companies like Infineon, which promotes its concerns about the issue and offers solutions 'to make the Internet and IT communications a more secure place'.
SOURCE: Infineon, *Agency*: J. Walter Thompson.

not just how to collect intelligence information but also how to protect company information from competitors. According to a former Unilever staffer, 'We were even warned that spies from competitors could be posing as drivers at the minicab company we used.' Unilever even performs random checks on internal security. Says the former staffer, 'At one [internal marketing] conference, we were set up when an actor was employed to infiltrate the group. The idea was to see who spoke to him, how much they told him, and how long it took to realize that no one knew him. He ended up being there for a long time.'[8]

The growing use of marketing intelligence raises a number of ethical issues. Although most of the preceding techniques are legal, and some are considered to be shrewdly competitive, some may involve questionable ethics. Clearly, companies should take advantage of publicly available information. However, they should not stoop to snoop. With all the legitimate intelligence sources now available, a company does not need to break the law or accepted codes of ethics to get good intelligence.

Getting information by observing competitors or analysing products

Companies can get to know competitors better by buying their products or examining other physical evidence. An increasingly important form of competitive intelligence is benchmarking – taking apart competitors' products and imitating or improving upon their best features.

> Benchmarking has helped JCB keep ahead in earthmoving equipment. The company takes apart its international competitors' products, dissecting and examining them in detail. JCB also probed the manufacturing operations, the types of machine tools used, their speeds, manning levels, labour costs, quality control and testing procedures, and raw material. It built up a profile of all its main competitors' operations and performance ratios against which to benchmark. In this way, the company knew the extent to which competitors could vary their prices, what their strengths and weaknesses were, and how JCB could exploit these data to its advantage.

Getting information from people who do business with competitors

Key customers can keep the company informed about competitors and their products:

> Gillette told a large account the date on which it planned to begin selling its new Good News disposable razor. The distributor promptly called Bic and told it about the impending product launch. Bic put on a crash programme and was able to start selling its razor shortly after Gillette did.

Intelligence can also be gathered by infiltrating customers' business operations:

> Companies may provide their engineers free of charge to customers . . . The close, cooperative relationship that the engineers on loan cultivate with the customers' design staff often enables them to learn what new products competitors are pitching.

Getting information from recruits and competitors' employees

Companies can obtain intelligence through job interviews or from conversations with competitors' employees. Approaches sometimes recommended include:

- When interviewing people for jobs, pay special attention to those who have worked for competitors, even temporarily.
- Send engineers to conferences and trade shows to question competitors' technical people.
- Advertise and hold interviews for jobs that don't exist in order to entice competitors' employees to spill the beans.
- Telephone competitors' employees and ask direct and indirect questions. 'The rule of thumb', says Jonathan Lax, founder of TMA, 'is to target employees a level below where you think you should start, because that person often knows just as much as his or her senior, and they are not as frequently asked or wary.' Secretaries, receptionists and switchboard operators regularly give away information inadvertently.

Why is Europe different?

European firms lag behind their Japanese and American competitors in gathering competitive intelligence. In Japanese companies it is a long-established practice, for, as Mitsui's corporate motto says: 'Information is the life blood of the company.'

> " Information is the life blood of the company. "

Niame Fine, founder of Protec Data, believes there are differences between US and European companies. Language and cultural blocks limit cross-border intelligence gathering. Approaching competitors' employees is a subtle business and people are often put on their guard if approached by someone from a different country. She also says Europeans have greater loyalty than their job-hopping American counterparts.

Although most of these techniques are legal and some are considered to be shrewdly competitive, many involve questionable ethics. The company should take advantage of publicly available information, but avoid practices that might be considered illegal or unethical. A company does not have to break the law or accepted codes of ethics to get good intelligence. So far, many European businesses 'do as they would be done by' and linger at the ethical end of the spectrum of competitive intelligence. However, the European picture is not uniform. Paul Carratu, of Carratu International, put France and Italy alongside the US in their use of industrial espionage. One very high-profile British boss stands accused of sleuthing:

Bob Ayling, ex-chief executive of British Airways, approached easyJet's founder, Stelios Haji-Ioannou, to ask whether he could visit. Ayling claimed to be fascinated by how the Greek entrepreneur had made the budget airline formula work. Haji-Ioannou not only agreed, but allegedly showed Ayling his business plan. A year later, British Airways announced the launch of Go. 'A carbon copy of easyJet', says easyGroup's director of corporate affairs. 'Same planes, same direct ticket sales, same use of a secondary airport, and same idea to sell on-board refreshments. They succeeded in stealing our business model – it was a highly effective spying job.'[9]

Marketing research

In addition to information about competitor and marketplace happenings, marketers often need formal studies of specific situations. For example, Carlsberg wants to know what appeals will be most effective in its European Cup advertising, or Philips wants to know how many and what kinds of people will buy its next-generation HDTVs (High Definition Televisions). In such situations, marketing intelligence will not provide the detailed information needed. Managers will need marketing research.

Marketing research is the systematic design, collection, analysis and reporting of data relevant to a specific marketing situation facing an organisation. Companies use marketing research in a wide variety of situations. For example, marketing research can help marketers understand customer satisfaction and purchase behaviour. It can help them to assess market potential and market share or to measure the effectiveness of pricing, product, distribution and promotion activities.

Some large companies have their own research departments that work with marketing managers on marketing research projects. This is how P&G, Kraft, Nestlé and many other corporate giants handle marketing research. In addition, these companies – like their smaller counterparts – frequently hire outside research specialists to consult with management on specific marketing problems and conduct marketing research studies. Sometimes firms simply purchase data collected by outside firms to aid in their decision making.

The marketing research process has four steps (see Figure 7.2): defining the problem and research objectives, developing the research plan, implementing the research plan, and interpreting and reporting the findings.

Defining the problem and research objectives

Marketing managers and researchers must work closely together to define the problem and agree on research objectives. The manager best understands the decision for which information is needed; the researcher best understands marketing research and how to obtain the information. Defining the problem and research objectives is often the hardest step in the research process. The manager may know that something is wrong, without knowing the specific causes.

After the problem has been defined carefully, the manager and researcher must set the research objectives. A marketing research project might have one of three types of objectives. The objective of **exploratory research** is to gather preliminary information that will help define the problem and suggest hypotheses. The objective of **descriptive research** is to describe things, such as the market potential for a product or the demographics and attitudes of consumers who buy the product. The objective of **causal research** is to test hypotheses about cause-and-effect relationships. For example, in the UK universities recently had to investigate whether the increase in university tuition fees, from about £1,000 (€1,500) to about £3,000, would change the demand for higher education and so the scale of university provision. It did not. Managers often start with such exploratory research and later follow with descriptive or causal research.

The statement of the problem and research objectives guides the entire research process. The manager and researcher should put the statement in writing to be certain that they agree on the purpose and expected results of the research.

Marketing research—The function that links the consumer, customer and public to the marketer through information that is used to identify and define marketing opportunities and problems, to generate, refine and evaluate marketing actions, to monitor marketing performance, and to improve understanding of the marketing process.

Exploratory research—Marketing research to gather preliminary information that will help to better define problems and suggest hypotheses.

Descriptive research—Marketing research to better describe marketing problems, situations or markets, such as the market potential for a product or the demographics and attitudes of consumers.

Causal research—Marketing research to test hypotheses about cause-and-effect relationships.

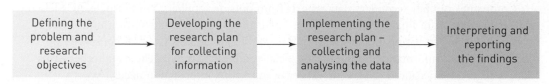

Defining the problem and research objectives → Developing the research plan for collecting information → Implementing the research plan – collecting and analysing the data → Interpreting and reporting the findings

Figure 7.2 The marketing research process

Developing the research plan

Once the research problems and objectives have been defined, researchers must determine the exact information needed, develop a plan for gathering it efficiently, and present the plan to management. The research plan outlines sources of existing data and spells out the specific research approaches, contact methods, sampling plans and instruments that researchers will use to gather new data.

Research objectives must be translated into specific information needs. For example, after having purchased Knorr as part of Bestfoods, Unilever decides to conduct research on how consumers would react to the introduction of new heat-and-go microwavable cups for its soups. Such packaging has been successful for Campbell's soups in the US – including its Soup at Hand line of hand-held, shippable soups and its Chunky and Select soup line in microwavable bowls, dubbed 'M'm! M'm! Good! To Go!'. Could it work with 'Let's make Knorr' in Europe? The containers would cost more but would allow consumers to heat their Knorr soup in a microwave oven and to eat them without using dishes. This research might call for the following specific information:

- The demographic, economic and lifestyle characteristics of current Knorr soup users. (Busy working couples might find the convenience of the new packaging worth the price; families with children might want to pay less and wash the bowls.)
- Consumer-usage patterns for Knorr soup and related products: how much they eat, where and when. (The new packaging might be ideal for adults eating lunch on the go, but less convenient for parents feeding lunch to several children.)
- Retailer reactions to the new packaging. (Failure to get retailer support could hurt sales of the new package.)
- Forecasts of sales of both new and current packages. (Will the new packaging create new sales or simply take sales from the current packaging? Will the package increase Knorr's profits?)

Knorr's managers will need these and many other types of information to decide whether to introduce the new packaging.

The research plan should be presented in a *written proposal*. A written proposal is especially important when the research project is large and complex or when an outside firm carries it out. The proposal should cover the management problems addressed and the research objectives, the information to be obtained, and the way the results will help management decision making. The proposal also should include research costs.

To meet the manager's information needs, the research plan can call for gathering secondary data, primary data or both. **Secondary data** consist of information that already exists somewhere, having been collected for another purpose. **Primary data** consist of information collected for the specific purpose at hand.

Secondary data—
Information that already
exists somewhere, having
been collected for another
purpose.

Primary data—
Information collected for
the specific purpose
at hand.

Gathering secondary data

Researchers usually start by gathering secondary data. The company's internal database provides a good starting point. However, the company can also tap a wide assortment of external information sources, including commercial data services and government sources.

Companies can buy secondary data reports from outside suppliers. For example, ACNielsen sells buyer data from a panel of 125,000 households in two dozen countries, with measures of trial and repeat purchasing, brand loyalty and buyer demographics. The *Monitor* service by Yankelovich sells information on important social and lifestyle trends. These and other firms supply high-quality data to suit a wide variety of marketing information needs.[10]

Using commercial **online databases**, marketing researchers can conduct their own searches of secondary data sources. General database services such as ProQuest and LexisNexis put an incredible wealth of information at the keyboards of marketing decision makers. Beyond commercial websites offering information for a fee, almost every industry association, government agency, business publication and news medium offers free information to those tenacious enough to find their websites. There are so many websites offering data that finding the right ones can become an almost overwhelming task.

Secondary data can usually be obtained more quickly and at a lower cost than primary data. Also, secondary sources can sometimes provide data an individual company cannot collect on its own – information that either is not directly available or would be too expensive to collect. For example, it would be too expensive for Knorr to conduct a continuing retail store audit to find out about the market shares, prices and displays of competitors' brands. But it can buy the scanner service from Information Resources, Inc., which provides this information based on scanner and other data from supermarkets in markets that are used by 95 per cent of the world's leading makers of grocery products.

Secondary data can also present problems. The needed information may not exist – researchers can rarely obtain all the data they need from secondary sources. For example, Knorr will not find existing information about consumer reactions to new packaging that it has not yet placed on the market. Even when data can be found, they might not be very usable. The researcher must evaluate secondary information carefully to make certain it is *relevant* (fits research project needs), *accurate* (reliably collected and reported), *current* (up-to-date enough for current decisions) and *impartial* (objectively collected and reported).

Online databases— Computerised collections of information available from online commercial sources or via the Internet.

Primary data collection

Secondary data provide a good starting point for research and often help to define research problems and objectives. In most cases, however, the company must also collect primary data. Just as researchers must carefully evaluate the quality of secondary information, they also must take great care when collecting primary data. They need to make sure that it will be relevant, accurate, current and unbiased. Table 7.1 shows that designing a plan for primary data collection calls for a number of decisions on *research approaches*, *contact methods*, *sampling plan* and *research instruments*.

Research approaches

Research approaches for gathering primary data include observation, surveys and experiments. Here, we discuss each one in turn.

Observational research involves gathering primary data by observing relevant people, actions and situations. For example, a bank might evaluate possible new branch locations by checking traffic patterns, neighbourhood conditions and the location of competing branches.

Researchers often observe consumer behaviour to glean insights they cannot obtain by simply asking customers questions. For instance, Fisher-Price, part of Mettal, has an observation laboratory in which it can observe the reactions of tots to new toys. The Fisher-Price Play Lab is a sunny, toy-strewn space where lucky kids get to test Fisher-Price prototypes, under the watchful

Observational research— The gathering of primary data by observing relevant people, actions and situations.

Table 7.1 Planning primary data collection

Research approaches	Contact methods	Sampling plan	Research instruments
Observation	Mail	Sampling unit	Questionnaire
Survey	Telephone	Sample size	Mechanical instruments
Experiment	Personal	Sampling procedure	
	Online		

eyes of designers who hope to learn what will get kids worked up into a new-toy frenzy. Kimberly-Clark invented a way to observe behaviour through the eyes of consumers:[11]

> " Researchers often observe consumer behaviour to glean insights they cannot obtain by simply asking customers questions. "

Kimberly-Clark, makers of Kleenex, saw sales of its Huggies baby wipes slip just as the company was preparing to launch a line of Huggies baby lotions and bath products. When traditional research didn't yield any compelling insights, K-C's marketers decided they could get more useful feedback just from watching customers' daily lives. They came up with camera-equipped 'glasses' to be worn by consumers at home, so that researchers could see what they saw. It didn't take long to spot the problems – and the opportunities. Although women in focus groups talked about changing babies at a nappy table, the truth was they changed them on beds, on floors and on top of washing machines in awkward positions. The researchers could see they were struggling with wipe containers and lotions requiring two hands. So the company redesigned the wipe package with a push-button one-handed dispenser and designed lotion and shampoo bottles that can be grabbed and dispensed easily with one hand.

Observational research can obtain information that people are unwilling or unable to provide. In some cases, observation may be the only way to obtain the needed information. In contrast, some things simply cannot be observed, such as feelings, attitudes and motives, or private behaviour. Long-term or infrequent behaviour is also difficult to observe. Because of these limitations, researchers often use observation along with other data collection methods.

A wide range of companies now use **ethnographic research**. Ethnographic research involves sending trained observers to watch and interact with consumers in their 'natural habitat'. Consider a problem faced by Marriott Hotels, an 'Upper Upscale' provider of well-appointed hotels with full, high-quality amenities including spacious rooms and bathrooms at high room rates. They are usually located in prime city-centre locations in major cities or in resorts and attract predominantly business customers, often with a high proportion of international guests.[12]

Ethnographic research— A form of observational research that involves sending trained observers to watch and interact with consumers in their 'natural habitat'.

Marriott hired the Munich Office of design firm IDEO to help it take a fresh look at business travel and to rethink the hotel experience for an increasingly important customer: the young, tech-savvy road warrior. Rather than doing the usual customer surveys or focus group research, IDEO dispatched a team of consultants, including a designer, an anthropologist, a writer and an architect, on a six-week trip to mingle with customers and get an up-close and personal view of them. Covering 12 cities, the group hung out in hotel lobbies, cafés and bars and asked guests to record what they were doing hour by hour.

By 'living with the natives', they learned that hotels are not generally good at serving small groups of business travellers. Hotel lobbies tend to be dark and better suited to killing time than conducting casual business. Marriott lacked places where guests could comfortably combine work with pleasure outside their rooms. One IDEO consultant recalls watching a female business traveller drinking wine in the lobby while trying not to spill it on papers spread out on a desk. 'There are very few hotel services that address [such] problems,' he says. The result: Marriott is reinventing the lobbies of its Marriott and Renaissance Hotels, creating a 'social zone', with small tables, brighter lights and wireless Web access that is better suited to meetings. Another area will allow solo travellers to work or unwind in larger, quiet, semi-private spaces where they won't have to worry about spilling coffee on their laptops or papers.

> 'Closely observing people where they live and work . . . allows companies to zero in on their customers' unarticulated desires.'

Ethnographic research often yields the kinds of details that just don't emerge from traditional research questionnaires or focus groups. 'The beauty of ethnography', says a research expert, 'is that it provides a richer understanding of consumers than does traditional research. Yes, companies are still using focus groups, surveys and demographic data to glean insights into the consumer's mind. But closely observing people where they live and work . . . allows companies to zero in on their customers' unarticulated desires.'[13]

Survey research, the most widely used method for primary data collection, is the approach best suited for gathering *descriptive* information. A company that wants to know about people's knowledge, attitudes, preferences or buying behaviour can often find out by asking them directly.

Survey research—The gathering of primary data by asking people questions about their knowledge, attitudes, preferences and buying behaviour.

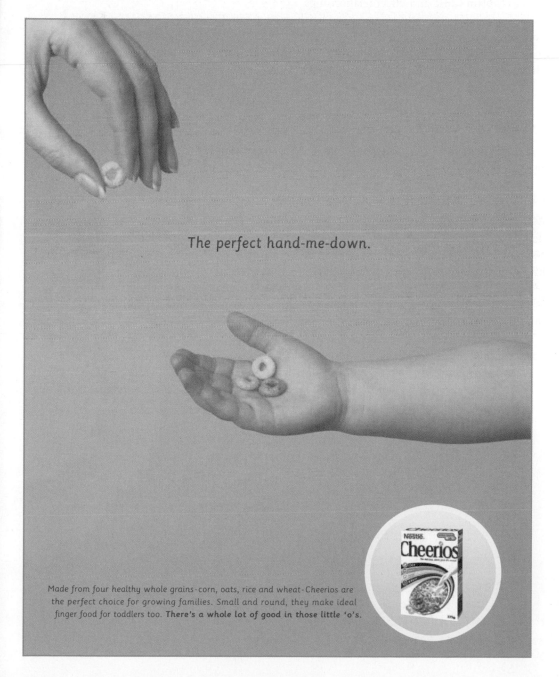

The perfect hand-me-down.

Made from four healthy whole grains-corn, oats, rice and wheat-Cheerios are the perfect choice for growing families. Small and round, they make ideal finger food for toddlers too. **There's a whole lot of good in those little 'o's.**

Observing how young children eat enables Nestlé to run a campaign that suggest an alternative serving method to that illustrated on the pack.
SOURCE: Cereal Partners, UK/Courtesy Société des Produits Nestlé S.A., trademark owners.

The major advantage of survey research is its flexibility – it can be used to obtain many different kinds of information in many different situations. However, survey research also presents some problems. Sometimes people are unable to answer survey questions because they cannot remember or have never thought about what they do and why. People may be unwilling to respond to unknown interviewers or about things they consider private. Respondents may answer survey questions even when they do not know the answer in order to appear smarter or more informed, or they may try to help the interviewer by giving pleasing answers. Finally, busy people may not take the time, or they might resent the intrusion into their privacy.

Whereas observation is best suited for exploratory research and surveys for descriptive research, **experimental research** is best suited for gathering *causal* information. Experiments involve selecting matched groups of subjects, giving them different treatments, controlling unrelated factors, and checking for differences in group responses. Thus, experimental research tries to explain cause-and-effect relationships.

For example, before adding a new sandwich to its menu, Baguette du Monde might use experiments to test the effects on sales of two different prices it might charge. It could introduce the new sandwich at one price in one outlet and at another price in another outlet. If the outlets are similar, and if all other marketing efforts for the sandwich are the same, then differences in sales in the two outlets could be related to the price charged.

Experimental research— The gathering of primary data by selecting matched groups of subjects, giving them different treatments, controlling related factors and checking for differences in group responses.

Contact methods

Information can be collected by mail, telephone, personal interview or online. Table 7.2 shows the strengths and weaknesses of each of these contact methods.

Mail, telephone and personal interviewing

Mail questionnaires can be used to collect large amounts of information at a low cost per respondent. Respondents may give more honest answers to more personal questions on a mail questionnaire than to an unknown interviewer in person or over the phone. Also, no interviewer is involved to bias the respondent's answers.

However, mail questionnaires are not very flexible – all respondents answer the same questions in a fixed order. Mail surveys usually take longer to complete, and the response rate – the number of people returning completed questionnaires – is often very low. Finally, the researcher often has little control over the mail questionnaire sample. Even with a good mailing list, it is hard to control *who* at the mailing address fills out the questionnaire.

Telephone interviewing is one of the best methods for gathering information quickly, and it provides greater flexibility than mail questionnaires. Interviewers can explain difficult questions

Table 7.2 Strengths and weaknesses of contact methods

	Mail	Telephone	Personal	Online
Flexibility	Poor	Good	Excellent	Good
Quantity of data that can be collected	Good	Fair	Excellent	Good
Control of interviewer effects	Excellent	Fair	Poor	Fair
Control of sample	Fair	Excellent	Good	Excellent
Speed of data collection	Poor	Excellent	Good	Excellent
Response rate	Fair	Good	Good	Good
Cost	Good	Fair	Poor	Excellent

SOURCE: Donald S. Tull and Del I. Hawkins, *Marketing Research: Measurement and Method*, 7th ed. (New York: Macmillan Publishing Company, 1993). Adapted with permission of the authors.

and, depending on the answers they receive, skip some questions or probe on others. Response rates tend to be higher than with mail questionnaires, and interviewers can ask to speak to respondents with the desired characteristics or even by name.

However, with telephone interviewing, the cost per respondent is higher than with mail questionnaires. Also, people may not want to discuss personal questions with an interviewer. The method introduces interviewer bias – the way interviewers talk, how they ask questions and other differences may affect respondents' answers. Finally, different interviewers may interpret and record responses differently, and under time pressures some interviewers might even cheat by recording answers without asking questions.

Personal interviewing takes two forms – individual and group interviewing. *Individual interviewing* involves talking with people in their homes or offices, on the street or in shopping centres. Such interviewing is flexible. Trained interviewers can guide interviews, explain difficult questions and explore issues as the situation requires. They can show subjects actual products, advertisements or packages and observe reactions and behaviour. However, individual personal interviews may cost three to four times as much as telephone interviews.

Group interviewing consists of inviting six to ten people to meet with a trained moderator to talk about a product, service or organisation. Participants normally are paid a small sum for attending. The moderator encourages free and easy discussion, hoping that group interactions will bring out actual feelings and thoughts. At the same time, the moderator 'focuses' the discussion – hence the name **focus group** interviewing.

Researchers and marketers watch the focus group discussions from behind one-way glass and comments are recorded in writing or on video for later study. Today, focus group researchers can even use videoconferencing and Internet technology to connect marketers in distant locations with live focus group action. Using cameras and two-way sound systems, marketing executives in a far-off boardroom can look in and listen, using remote controls to zoom in on faces and pan the focus group at will.

Focus group interviewing has become one of the major marketing research tools for gaining insights into consumer thoughts and feelings. However, focus group studies present some challenges. They usually employ small samples to keep time and costs down, and it may be hard to generalise from the results. Moreover, consumers in focus groups are not always open and honest in front of other people. 'There's peer pressure in focus groups that gets in the way of finding the truth about real behaviour and intentions,' says one marketing executive.[14]

Thus, although focus groups are still widely used, many researchers are tinkering with focus group design. For example, Cammie Dunaway, chief marketing officer at Yahoo!, prefers 'immersion groups' – four or five people with whom Yahoo!'s product designers talk informally, without a focus group moderator present. That way, rather than just seeing videos of consumers reacting to a moderator, Yahoo!'s staff can work directly with select customers to design new products and programmes. 'The outcome is richer if [consumers] feel included in our process, not just observed,' says Dunaway.[14]

Still other researchers are changing the environments in which they conduct focus groups. To help consumers relax and to elicit more authentic responses, they use settings that are more comfortable and more relevant to the products being researched. For example, they might conduct focus groups for cooking products in a kitchen setting, or focus groups for home furnishings in a living room setting. One research firm offers facilities that look just like anything from a living room or play room to a bar or even a courtroom.

Focus groups are one form of exploratory research that seeks to uncover new or hidden features of markets. They can help solve problems, such as a school which discovered that the major anxiety of parents was not educational achievement, but parents' dogs fouling the pavement outside the school when they stopped to have a chat after dropping off little Jimmie each morning. Or they can create market opportunities from understanding motives. As Real Marketing 7.1 shows, such research can often appear zany but many marketers find it invaluable.

Focus group—A small sample of typical consumers under the direction of a group leader who elicits their reaction to a stimulus such as an ad or product concept.

7.1

real marketing

'Touchy-feely' research into consumer motivations

The term *motivation research* refers to qualitative research designed to probe consumers' hidden, subconscious motivations. Because consumers often don't know or can't describe just why they act as they do, motivation researchers use a variety of projective techniques to uncover underlying emotions and attitudes. The techniques range from sentence completion, word association and inkblot or cartoon interpretation tests, to having consumers describe typical brand users or form daydreams and fantasies about brands or buying situations. Some of these techniques verge on the bizarre. One writer offers the following tongue-in-cheek summary of a motivation research session:

> Good morning, ladies and gentlemen. We've called you here today for a little consumer research. Now, lie down on the couch, toss your inhibitions out the window and let's try a little free association. First, think about brands as if they were your *friends* . . . think of your shampoo as an animal. Go on, don't be shy. Would it be a panda or a lion? A snake or a woolly worm? . . . Draw a picture of a typical cake-mix user. Would she wear an apron or a negligée? A business suit or a can-can dress?

Such projective techniques sometimes seem stupid, and some marketers dismiss such motivation research as mumbo jumbo. But many marketers routinely use such touchy-feely approaches to dig deeply into consumer psyches and develop better marketing strategies.

Many companies employ teams of psychologists, anthropologists and other social scientists to carry out motivation research. One ad agency routinely conducts one-on-one, therapy-like interviews to delve into the inner workings of consumers. Another company asks consumers to describe their favourite brands as animals or cars (say, VW versus Citroën) in order to assess the prestige associated with various brands. Still others rely on hypnosis, dream therapy or soft lights and mood music to plumb the murky depths of consumer psyches.

In an effort to understand the teenage consumer market better, ad agency BSB Worldwide recorded teenagers' rooms in 25 countries. It found surprising similarities across countries and cultures:

From the steamy playgrounds of Los Angeles to the stately boulevards of Singapore, kids show amazing similarities in taste, language and attitude. . . . From the gear and posters on display, it's hard to tell whether the rooms are in Los Angeles, Mexico City or Tokyo. Basketballs sit alongside soccer balls. Closets overflow with staples from an international, unisex uniform: Levi's or Diesel jeans and Convers or adidas trainers.

Although there are global similarities, some places are ahead of others. For generations America's west coast was the source of many new ideas, from mountain bikes to surfing the waves. Now it is surfing the net and marketers are looking east, not west.

South Korea's web-crazy, TV-shunning teenagers, and the local businesses chasing them, are at the leading edge of web and mobile technology. These innovators are the focus of western businesses trying to understand future trends. Procter & Gamble has a global marketing officer observing Asian broadband hotspots, such as Seoul's PC Bang. Some of the innovations observed, such as online discos where people tap out their dance steps on their keyboard, maybe may not transfer to the West but others will. Diageo's mobile phone service for Guinness drinkers is based on a Japanese idea. It allows users to locate the nearest bar selling the drink and give Diageo feedback on how well the bar served the brew.

Motivation researchers have reached some interesting and sometimes odd conclusions about what may be in the buyer's mind regarding certain purchases. For example, one classic study concluded that consumers resist prunes because they are wrinkled-looking and remind people of sickness and old age. Despite its sometimes unusual conclusions, motivation research remains a useful tool for marketers seeking a deeper understanding of consumer behaviour. However, these approaches do present some problems. They use small samples, and researchers' interpretations of results are often highly subjective, sometimes leading to rather exotic explanations of otherwise ordinary buying behaviour. Others believe strongly that these approaches can provide interesting nuggets of insight into the relationships between consumers and the brands they buy. To marketers who use them, motivation research techniques provide a flexible and varied means of gaining insights into deeply held and often mysterious motivations behind consumer buying behaviour.

SOURCES: Shawn Tully, 'Teens: The most global market of all', *Fortune* (6 May 1994), pp. 90–7; Tobi Elkin, 'Product pampering', *Brandweek* (16 June 1997), pp. 38–40; Leon G. Schiffman and Leslie L. Kanuk, *Consumer Behaviour*, 9th ed. (Upper Saddle River, NJ: Prentice Hall, 2007), Chapter 4; Carlos Grande, 'They've got the whole wide world in their laptops', *Financial Times* (24 July 2007), p. 16.

Online marketing research

Online marketing research—Internet-based research using online surveys, panels, experiments, focus groups, etc.

Advances in communication technologies have resulted in a number of high-technology contact methods. The latest technology to hit marketing research is the Internet. Increasingly, marketing researchers are collecting primary data through **online marketing research**—*Internet surveys, online panels, experiments* and *online focus groups*. In fact, by 2006, companies were spending an estimated 30 per cent of their marketing research budget online, making it the largest single data collection methodology.[15]

> Online marketing research . . . the largest single data collection methodology.

Online research can take many forms. A company can include a questionnaire on its website and offer incentives for completing it, or it can use e-mail, Web links or Web pop-ups to invite people to answer questions and possibly win a prize. The company can sponsor a chatroom and introduce questions from time to time or conduct live discussions or online focus groups. A company can learn about the behaviour of online customers by following their clickstreams as they visit the website and move to other sites. A company can experiment with different prices, use different headlines or offer different product features on different websites or at different times to learn the relative effectiveness of its offerings. It can float 'trial balloons' to quickly test new product concepts.

Web research offers some real advantages over traditional surveys and focus groups. The most obvious advantages are speed and low costs. Online focus groups require some advance scheduling, but results are practically instantaneous.[16]

Looking for better methods of predicting consumer acceptance to potential new products, Pepsi recently turned to Invoke Solutions, an online consumer research company, which maintained several instant-message-style online panels of 80 to 100 people. Using the panels, Pepsi delved into attitudes among GenXers towards drinking mineral water. In just a few hours, the beverage marketer was able to gather and process detailed feedback from hundreds of consumers. At first, Pepsi marketers were puzzled that the group liked the idea of high levels of mineral content in water. But after further exchanges with the online panel, Pepsi beverage scientists on the scene decided against higher mineral levels; that would require adding sugar, which consumers didn't want, to make the taste acceptable. Using the online panels, 'conclusions that could take three to four months to sort out through regular focus groups . . . got settled in a few hours,' says an Invoke executive.

Internet research is also relatively low in cost. Participants can dial in for a focus group from anywhere in the world, eliminating travel, accommodation and facility costs. For surveys, the Internet eliminates most of the postage, phone, labour and printing costs associated with other approaches. As a result, an Internet survey may be only 10 to 20 per cent as expensive as mail, telephone or personal surveys. Moreover, sample size has little influence on costs. Once the questionnaire is set up, there's little difference in cost between 10 and 10,000 respondents on the Web.

Online surveys and focus groups are also excellent for reaching the hard-to-reach – the often-elusive teen, single, affluent and well-educated audiences. It's also good for reaching working mothers and other people who lead busy lives. They respond to it in their own space and at their own convenience. The Internet also works well for bringing together people from different parts of the country, especially those in higher-income groups who can't spare the time to travel to a central site.

Using the Internet to conduct marketing research does have some drawbacks. For one, restricted Internet access can make it difficult to get a broad cross-section of respondents. However, with Internet household penetration now at 60 per cent in most developed countries, this is less of a problem. Another major problem is controlling who's in the sample. Without seeing respondents, it's difficult to know who they really are.

Even when you reach the right respondents, online surveys and focus groups can lack the dynamics of more personal approaches. The online world is devoid of the eye contact, body language and direct personal interactions found in traditional focus group research. And the Internet format – running, typed commentary severely limiting emotional reaction – greatly restricts respondent expressiveness. Although the impersonal nature of the Internet may shield people from excessive peer pressure, it also prevents people from interacting with each other and getting excited about a concept.

To overcome such sample and response problems, many online research firms use opt-in communities and respondent panels. For example, online research firm Greenfield Online provides access to 12 million opt-in panel members in more than 40 countries. Advances in technology – such as the integration of animation, streaming audio and video, and virtual environments – also help to overcome online research dynamics limitations.

Perhaps the most explosive issue facing online researchers concerns consumer privacy. Some fear that unethical researchers will use the e-mail addresses and confidential responses gathered through surveys to sell products after the research is completed. They are concerned about the use of electronic agents (such as Spambots or Trojans) that collect personal information without the respondents' consent. Failure to address such privacy issues could result in angry, less cooperative consumers and increased government intervention. Despite these concerns, most industry insiders predict healthy growth for online marketing research.[17]

Sampling plan

Marketing researchers usually draw conclusions about large groups of consumers by studying a small sample of the total consumer population. A **sample** is a segment of the population selected for marketing research to represent the population as a whole. Ideally, the sample should be representative so that the researcher can make accurate estimates of the thoughts and behaviours of the larger population.

Sample—A segment of the population selected for market research to represent the population as a whole.

 Marketing researchers usually draw conclusions about large groups of consumers by studying a small sample of the total consumer population.

Designing the sample requires three decisions. First, *who* is to be surveyed (what *sampling unit*)? The answer to this question is not always obvious. For example, to study the decision-making process for buying a family car, should the researcher interview the husband, wife, other family members, dealership salespeople, or all of these? The researcher must determine what information is needed and who is most likely to have it.

Second, *how many* people should be surveyed (what *sample size*)? Large samples give more reliable results than small samples. However, larger samples usually cost more, and it is not necessary to sample the entire target market or even a large proportion to get reliable results. If well chosen, samples of less than 1 per cent of a population can often give good reliability.

Third, *how* should the people in the sample be *chosen* (what *sampling procedure*)? Table 7.3 describes different kinds of samples. Using *probability samples*, each population member has a known chance of being included in the sample, and researchers can calculate confidence limits for sampling error. But when probability sampling costs too much or takes too much time, marketing researchers often take *non-probability samples*, even though their sampling error cannot be measured. These varied ways of drawing samples have different costs and time

Table 7.3 Types of samples

Probability sample	
Simple random sample	Every member of the population has a known and equal chance of selection.
Stratified random sample	The population is divided into mutually exclusive groups (such as age groups), and random samples are drawn from each group.
Cluster (area) sample	The population is divided into mutually exclusive groups (such as blocks), and the researcher draws a sample of the groups to interview.
Non-probability sample	
Convenience sample	The researcher selects the easiest population members from which to obtain information.
Judgement sample	The researcher uses his or her judgement to select population members who are good prospects for accurate information.
Quota sample	The researcher finds and interviews a prescribed number of people in each of several categories.

limitations as well as different accuracy and statistical properties. Which method is best depends on the needs of the research project.

Research instruments

In collecting primary data, marketing researchers have a choice of two main research instruments – the *questionnaire* and *mechanical devices*. The *questionnaire* is by far the most common instrument, whether administered in person, by phone or online.

Questionnaires are very flexible – there are many ways to ask questions. *Closed-end questions* include all the possible answers, and subjects make choices among them. Examples include multiple-choice questions and scale questions. *Open-end questions* allow respondents to answer in their own words. In a survey of airline users, Southwest might simply ask, 'What is your opinion of Ryanair?' Or it might ask people to complete a sentence: 'When I choose an airline, the most important consideration is . . . .' These and other kinds of open-end questions often reveal more than closed-end questions because respondents are not limited in their answers. Open-end questions are especially useful in exploratory research, when the researcher is trying to find out *what* people think but not measuring *how many* people think in a certain way. Closed-end questions, on the other hand, provide answers that are easier to interpret and tabulate.

Researchers should also use care in the *wording* and *ordering* of questions. They should use simple, direct, unbiased wording. Questions should be arranged in a logical order. The first question should create interest if possible, and difficult or personal questions should be asked last so that respondents do not become defensive. A carelessly prepared questionnaire usually contains many errors (see Table 7.4).

Although questionnaires are the most common research instrument, researchers also use *mechanical instruments* to monitor consumer behaviour. Nielsen Media Research attaches *people meters* to television sets in selected homes to record who watches which programmes. Retailers use *checkout scanners* to record shoppers' purchases.

Other mechanical devices measure subjects' physical responses. For example, advertisers use eye cameras to study viewers' eye movements while watching ads – at what points their eyes focus first and how long they linger on any given ad component. BlueEyes human recognition technology goes even further.

Table 7.4 A 'questionable questionnaire'

Suppose that a summer camp director has prepared the following questionnaire to use in interviewing the parents of prospective campers. How would you assess each question?

1. What is your income to the nearest hundred euros?
   People do not usually know their income to the nearest hundred euros, nor do they want to reveal their income that closely. Moreover, a researcher should never open a questionnaire with such a personal question.

2. Are you a strong or weak supporter of overnight summer camping for your children?
   What do 'strong' and 'weak' mean?

3. Do your children behave themselves well at a summer camp? Yes ☐ No ☐
   'Behave' is a relative term. Furthermore, are 'yes' and 'no' the best response options for this question? Besides, will people answer this honestly and objectively? Why ask the question in the first place?

4. How many camps mailed or e-mailed information to you last year? This year?
   Who can remember this?

5. What are the most salient and determinant attributes in your evaluation of summer camps?
   What are salient and determinant attributes? Don't use big words on me!

6. Do you think it is right to deprive your child of the opportunity to grow into a mature person through the experience of summer camping?
   A loaded question. Given the bias, how can any parent answer yes?

BlueEyes uses sensing technology to identify and interpret user reactions. The technology was originally created to help users to interact more easily with a computer, for example an 'emotion mouse' that will figure out computer users' emotional states by measuring pulse, temperature, movement and galvanic skin response. Another BlueEyes technology records and interprets human facial reactions by tracking pupil, eyebrow and mouth movement. BlueEyes offers a host of potential marketing uses. Retailers are already using the technology to study customers and their responses. And in the not-too-distant future, more than just measuring customers' physical reactions, marketers will be able to respond to them as well. An example: creating marketing machines that 'know how you feel'. Sensing through an emotion mouse that a Web shopper is frustrated, an Internet marketer offers a different screen display. An elderly man squints at a bank's ATM screen and the font size doubles almost instantly. A woman at a shopping centre kiosk smiles at a travel ad, prompting the device to print out a travel discount coupon. Several users at another kiosk frown at a risqué ad, leading a store to pull it. In the future, ordinary household devices – such as televisions, refrigerators and ovens – may be able to do their jobs when we look at them and speak to them.[18]

Implementing the research plan

The researcher next puts the marketing research plan into action. This involves collecting, processing and analysing the information. Data collection can be carried out by the company's marketing research staff or by outside firms. The data collection phase of the marketing research process is generally the most expensive and the most subject to error. Researchers should watch

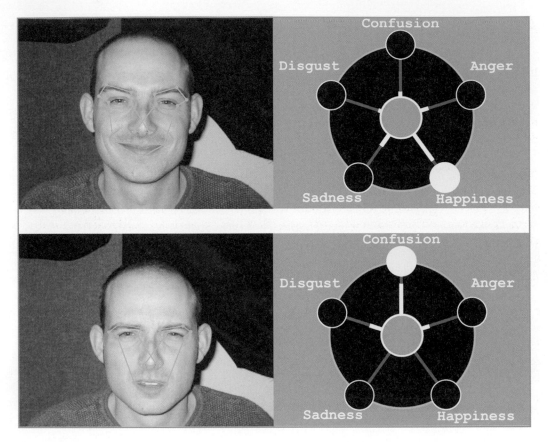

Mechanical measures of consumer response: New technologies can record and interpret human facial reactions. In the not-too-distant future, marketers may be using machines that 'know how you feel' to not just gauge customers' physical reactions, but to respond to them as well.

SOURCE: Douglas A. Fidaleo.

closely to make sure that the plan is implemented correctly. They must guard against problems with contacting respondents, with respondents who refuse to cooperate or who give biased answers, and with interviewers who make mistakes or take shortcuts.

Researchers must also process and analyse the collected data to isolate important information and findings. They need to check data for accuracy and completeness and code it for analysis. The researchers then tabulate the results and compute statistical measures.

Interpreting and reporting the findings

The market researcher must now interpret the findings, draw conclusions and report them to management. The researcher should not try to overwhelm managers with numbers and fancy statistical techniques. Rather, the researcher should present important findings that are useful in the major decisions faced by management.

However, interpretation should not be left only to the researchers. They are often experts in research design and statistics, but the marketing manager knows more about the problem and the decisions that must be made. The best research means little if the manager blindly accepts faulty interpretations from the researcher. Similarly, managers may be biased – they might tend to accept research results that show what they expected and to reject those that they did not expect or hope for. In many cases, findings can be interpreted in different ways, and discussions between researchers and managers will help point to the best interpretations. Thus, managers and researchers must work together closely when interpreting research results, and both must share responsibility for the research process and resulting decisions.

Analysing marketing information

Information gathered in internal databases and through marketing intelligence and marketing research usually requires more analysis. Managers may need help applying the information to their marketing decisions. This help may include advanced statistical analysis to learn more about the relationships within a set of data. Such analysis allows managers to go beyond means and standard deviations in the data and to answer questions about markets, marketing activities and outcomes.

Information analysis might also involve a collection of analytical models that will help marketers make better decisions. Each model represents some real system, process or outcome. These models can help answer the questions of *what if* and *which is best*. Marketing scientists have developed numerous models to help marketing managers make better marketing mix decisions, design sales territories and sales call plans, select sites for retail outlets, develop optimal advertising mixes and forecast new-product sales.

One picture is worth ten thousand words.

Advertisers and newspaper editors have long known that 'One picture is worth ten thousand words', a phrase used to promote the use of images in advertisements that appeared on the sides of trams in the 1920s. This is also true of visual information where well-presented graphics and summary statistics can clinch an argument. Swedish Professor Hans Rosling is a surprising new business guru whose software Trendalyzer conveys complex information beautifully and with great clarity. He follows a great tradition of carefully crafted visual presentation that can communicate very effectively.[19]

Distributing and using marketing information

Marketing information has no value until it is used to make better marketing decisions. Thus, the marketing information system must make the information readily available to the managers and others who make marketing decisions or deal with customers. In some cases, this means providing managers with regular performance reports, intelligence updates and reports on the results of research studies.

But marketing managers may also need non-routine information for special situations and on-the-spot decisions. For example, a sales manager having trouble with a large customer may want a summary of the account's sales and profitability over the past year, or a retail store manager who has run out of a best-selling product may want to know the current inventory levels in the chain's other stores. Increasingly, therefore, information distribution involves entering information into databases and making it available in a timely, user-friendly way.

Many firms use a company *intranet* to facilitate this process. The intranet provides ready access to research information, stored reports, shared work documents, contact information for employees and other stakeholders, and more. For example, iGo, a catalogue and Web retailer, integrates incoming customer service calls with up-to-date database information about customers' Web purchases and e-mail inquiries. By accessing this information on the intranet while speaking with the customer, iGo's service representatives can get a well-rounded picture of each customer's purchasing history and previous contacts with the company.

In addition, companies are increasingly allowing key customers and value-network members to access account, product and other data on demand through *extranets*. Suppliers, customers, resellers and other selected network members may access a company's extranet to update their

Okapis have some real identity issues.

They can't be sure who they're attracting or why.
But you can. With proven customer intelligence software from SAS.

www.sas.com/okapis

§sas. | THE POWER TO KNOW.

SAS customer intelligence software helps companies to keep a profitable, loyal customer base by leveraging customer information and developing targeted, personalised responses to customer needs.

SOURCE: Copyright © 2007 SAS Institute, Inc. All rights reserved. Reproduced with permission of SAS Institute, Inc., Cary, North Carolina, USA.

accounts, arrange purchases and check orders against inventories to improve customer service. For example, one insurance firm allows its 200 independent agents access to a Web-based database of claim information covering one million customers. This allows the agents to avoid high-risk customers and to compare claim data with their own customer databases.[20]

Thanks to modern technology, today's marketing managers can gain direct access to the information system at any time and from virtually any location. They can tap into the system while working at a home office, from a hotel room, or from the local Starbucks through a wireless network – indeed from any location where they can turn on a laptop and link up. Such systems allow managers to get the information they need directly and quickly and to tailor it to their own needs. From just about anywhere, they can obtain information from company or outside databases, analyse it using statistical software, prepare reports and presentations, and communicate directly with others in the network.

Other marketing information considerations

This section discusses marketing information in two special contexts: marketing research in small businesses and non-profit organisations, and international marketing research. Finally, we look at public policy and ethics issues in marketing research.

Marketing research in small businesses and non-profit organisations

Just like larger firms, small organisations need market information. Start-up businesses need information about their industries, competitors and potential customers, and reactions to new market offers. Existing small businesses must track changes in customer needs and wants, reactions to new products, and changes in the competitive environment.

Managers of small businesses and non-profit organisations often think that marketing research can be done only by experts in large companies with big research budgets. True, large-scale research studies are beyond the budgets of most small businesses. However, many of the marketing research techniques discussed in this chapter can also be used by smaller organisations in a less formal manner and at little or no expense. Managers of small businesses and non-profit organisations can obtain good marketing information simply by *observing* things around them. For example, retailers can evaluate new locations by observing vehicle and pedestrian traffic. They can monitor competitor advertising by collecting ads from local media. They can evaluate their customer mix by recording how many and what kinds of customers shop in the store at different times. In addition, many small business managers routinely visit their rivals and socialise with competitors to gain insights.

Managers can conduct informal *surveys* using small convenience samples. The director of an art museum can learn what patrons think about new exhibits by conducting informal focus groups – inviting small groups to lunch and having discussions on topics of interest. Retail salespeople can talk with customers visiting the store; hospital officials can interview patients. Restaurant managers might make random phone calls during slack hours to interview consumers about where they eat out and what they think of various restaurants in the area.

Managers also can conduct their own simple *experiments*. For example, by changing the themes in regular fund-raising mailings and watching the results, a non-profit manager can find out much about which marketing strategies work best. By varying newspaper advertisements, a store manager can learn the effects of things such as ad size and position, price coupons and media used.

Small organisations can obtain most of the secondary data available to large businesses. In addition, many associations, local media, chambers of commerce and government agencies provide special help to small organisations. The business sections at local libraries can also be a good source of information. Local newspapers often provide information on local shoppers and their buying patterns. Finally, small businesses can collect a considerable amount of information at very little cost on the Internet. They can scour competitor and customer websites and use Internet search engines to research specific companies and issues.

In summary, secondary data collection, observation, surveys and experiments can all be used effectively by small organisations with small budgets. Although these informal research methods are less complex and less costly, they still must be conducted carefully. Managers must think carefully about the objectives of the research, formulate questions in advance, recognise the biases introduced by smaller samples and less skilled researchers, and conduct the research systematically.[21]

International marketing research

International marketing researchers follow the same steps as domestic researchers, from defining the research problem and developing a research plan to interpreting and reporting the results. However, these researchers often face more and different problems. Whereas domestic researchers deal with fairly homogeneous markets within a single country, international researchers deal with diverse markets in many different countries. These markets often vary greatly in their levels of economic development, cultures and customs, and buying patterns.

In many foreign markets, the international researcher may have a difficult time finding good secondary data. Whereas in large developed economies marketing researchers can obtain reliable secondary data from dozens of domestic research services, many countries have almost no research services at all. Some of the largest international research services do operate in many countries. For example, ACNielsen Corporation (owned by VNU NV, the world's largest marketing research company) has offices in more than 100 countries, and 67 per cent of the revenues of the world's 25 largest marketing research firms come from outside their home countries.[22] However, most research firms operate in only a relative handful of countries. Thus, even when secondary information is available, it must usually be obtained from many different sources on a country-by-country basis, making the information difficult to combine or compare.

Because of the scarcity of good secondary data, international researchers must often collect their own primary data. Here again, researchers can face problems not found domestically. For example, they may find it difficult simply to develop good samples. Researchers in large developed economies can use current telephone directories, census data and any of several sources of socioeconomic data to construct samples. However, such information is largely lacking in many countries.

Once the sample is drawn, in developed economies researchers can usually reach most respondents easily by telephone, by mail, on the Internet or in person. Reaching respondents is often not so easy in other parts of the world. In contrast, researchers in Mexico cannot rely on telephone, Internet and mail data collection – most data collection is door to door and concentrated in three or four of the largest cities. In some countries, few people have phones or personal computers. For example, whereas there are 90 mobile phone subscriptions per 100 people and 58 PCs per 100 households in the EU-25, there are only 35 phone subscriptions and five PCs per 100 in Mexico. In Ghana, the numbers drop to two phone subscriptions and 0.3 PCs per 1,000 people. In some countries, the postal system is notoriously unreliable. In Brazil, for instance, an estimated 30 per cent of the mail is never delivered. In many developing countries, poor roads and transportation systems make certain areas hard to reach, making personal interviews difficult and expensive.[23]

Cultural differences from country to country cause additional problems for international researchers. Language is the most obvious obstacle. For example, questionnaires must be prepared in one language and then translated into the languages of each country researched. Responses must then be back-translated into the original language for analysis and interpretation. This adds to research costs and increases the risks of error.

Translating a questionnaire from one language to another is anything but easy. Many idioms, phrases and statements mean different things in different cultures. For example, a Danish executive noted, 'Check this out by having a different translator put back into English what you've translated from English. You'll get the shock of your life. I remember [an example in which] "out of sight, out of mind" had become "invisible things are insane".'[24]

Consumers in different countries also vary in their attitudes towards marketing research. People in one country may be very willing to respond; in other countries, non-response can be a major problem. Customs in some countries may prohibit people from talking with strangers. In certain cultures, research questions are often considered too personal. For example, in many Latin American countries, people may feel embarrassed to talk with researchers about their choices of shampoo, deodorant or other personal care products. Similarly, in most Muslim countries, mixed-gender focus groups are taboo, as is videotaping female-only focus groups.

Even when respondents are *willing* to respond, they may not be *able* to because of high functional illiteracy rates. And middle-class people in developing countries often make false claims in order to appear well-off. For example, in a study of tea consumption in India, over 70 per cent of middle-income respondents claimed that they used one of several national brands. However, the researchers had good reason to doubt these results – more than 60 per cent of the tea sold in India is unbranded generic tea.

Despite these problems, the recent growth of international marketing has resulted in a rapid increase in the use of international marketing research. Global companies have little choice but to conduct such research. Although the costs and problems associated with international research may be high, the costs of not doing it – in terms of missed opportunities and mistakes – might be even higher. Once recognised, many of the problems associated with international marketing research can be overcome or avoided.

Public policy and ethics in marketing research

Most marketing research benefits both the sponsoring company and its consumers. Through marketing research, companies learn more about consumers' needs, resulting in more satisfying products and services and stronger customer relationships. However, the misuse of marketing research can also harm or annoy consumers. Two major public policy and ethics issues in marketing research are intrusions on consumer privacy and the misuse of research findings.

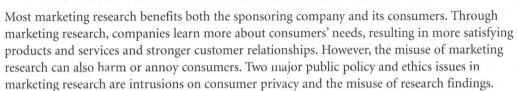

> **"** The misuse of marketing research can also harm or annoy consumers. **"**

Intrusions on consumer privacy

Many consumers feel positively about marketing research and believe that it serves a useful purpose. Some actually enjoy being interviewed and giving their opinions. However, others strongly resent or even mistrust marketing research. A few consumers fear that researchers might use sophisticated techniques to probe our deepest feelings or peek over our shoulders and then use this knowledge to manipulate our buying (see Real Marketing 7.2). Or they worry that marketers are building huge databases full of personal information about customers. For example, consider a company called Acxiom who operate in several European counties:

> Never heard of Acxiom? Chances are it's heard of you. Once upon a time a local shopkeeper knew that you had, say, three children, an old Citroën, a passion for golf and Pringle sweaters. Today Acxiom is that store clerk. It's the world's largest processor of consumer data, collecting and massaging more than a billion records a day. Acxiom's database, on up to 96 per cent of households where it operates, gives marketers a so-called real-time, 360-degree view of their customers. How? Acxiom provides a 13-digit code for every person, 'so we can identify you wherever you go', says the company's demographics guru. Each person is placed into one of 70 lifestyle clusters, ranging from 'Rolling Stones' and 'Single City Strugglers' to 'Timeless Elders'. Acxiom's catalogue offers businesses hundreds of lists, including a 'pre-movers file', updated daily, of people preparing to change residence, as well as lists of people sorted by the frequency with which they use credit cards, the size of their homes, and their interest in the 'strange and unusual'. Its customers include top credit-card issuers, top retail banks, top retailers and top car makers. Acxiom may even know things about you that you don't know yourself.[25]

There is growing concern about the 'surveillance society' where confidential personal data gleaned from sources as diverse as driving licences, medical records and store loyalty cards is now often shared without people's knowledge.

7.2 real marketing

Video mining

By stepping into a Gap store Laura Munro became a research statistic. Above her, a device resembling a smoke detector, mounted on the ceiling and equipped with a hidden camera, took a picture of her head and shoulders. The image was fed to a computer and shipped to a database, where ShopperTrak, a consumer research firm, keeps count of shoppers using cameras placed in stores and shopping centres.

ShopperTrak is the leader in an emerging market research field called 'video mining'. Video miners use advanced computer software to sort through video images, plucking data of interest to marketers, without a human ever seeing the video. ShopperTrak says it doesn't take pictures of faces. The company worries that shoppers would perceive that as an invasion of privacy. But nearly all of its videotaping is done without the knowledge of the people being taped. 'I didn't even know there was a camera up there', says Ms Munro, who popped into the shopping centre on her way home from work to find a gift for her 12-year-old daughter.

Using such video information, ShopperTrak calculates and sells many valuable titbits of data. For example, by comparing the number of people taped entering the store with the number of transactions, it arrives at a so-called 'conversion rate' – the percentage of shoppers that buys versus the percentage that only browses. At a broader level, by combining video data gleaned from retail clients and shopping centres with consumer spending data obtained from credit-card companies and banks, ShopperTrak can estimate sales and store traffic figures for the entire retail industry. Gap and other retail clients pay ShopperTrak for the store-level data.

ShopperTrak sells the broader industry data to economists, bankers and retailers. More and more companies are now employing video miners to help them spy on their customers. Video-tracking cameras, with lenses as small as a coin, can provide data on everything from the density of shopping traffic in an aisle to the reactions of a

Serving customers better or invading their privacy? Video miners use advanced computer software to sort through video images, plucking data of interest to marketers. Smile, you're being video mined!

SOURCE: Greg Kahn/Kahn Research.

shopper gazing at the latest plasma TV set. The cash register is a popular spot for cameras. But cameras can also be found in banks, fast-food outlets and hotel lobbies (but not guest rooms).

Many companies now use video mining along with other traditional methods to help gain more rapid, accurate and complete insights. For example, Kahn Research Group recently used video mining along with sales analysis and in-store behavioural tracking to determine what was and was not working to increase sales at Subway fast-food restaurants. Kahn's researchers hid golf-ball-sized cameras in several Subway restaurants to track customers' eye movements during the order process. Video analysis revealed that before and while sandwiches were being assembled, customers focused on the 'sandwich artists' rather than on the menu board or promotional displays. In particular, drinks and side-orders received little customer notice, and the researchers suggested that Subway move them to a point where consumers would view them after making the major sandwich decision but before reaching the cash register. The research also revealed that promotions dangling from the ceiling were often ignored – Subway now uses 'table tents' to remind customers to buy a snack for later.

Video mining software is fast – taking only hours to complete image interpretation tasks that might have taken weeks for humans to do. For example, Kahn's computers took only a couple of days to sift through 192 hours of tape on some 1,200 shoppers. Had Kahn tried to personally interview that many people, the process would have taken much longer, and the presence of the researchers might have annoyed shoppers and affected the results. 'Nobody knew they were being recorded,' says Greg Kahn of Kahn Research Group, 'and our work didn't interfere with the store environment.' Moreover, had people known they were being taped,' he says, 'I know many of the shoppers would have stuck their hands in front of the camera lens and refused to be recorded.'

Video mining proponents say their research cameras are less invasive than security cameras, because their subjects aren't scrutinised as closely as security suspects. The images are studied only by the software and not by people, they say, and the videos are destroyed when the research is done. And marketers use the information to give their customers improved products and better service. 'A driving force behind this technology is the fact that businesses want to be better prepared to serve their customers,' says one marketing professor.

Still, the eavesdropping potential of video mining can be unnerving. For example, Video Mining, another shopper-monitoring firm, set up cameras in two McDonald's restaurants to find out which customer types would find a new salad item most appealing. The research was done without consumers' knowledge. By measuring the shapes of people's faces, Video Mining's sensors were able to provide a breakdown

...7.2

of each salad buyers' race, gender and age. The videos also revealed the length of time these customers spent waiting in line or looking at the menu before ordering. Looking ahead, the technology already exists for matching a photo with an individual's identity.

Historically, retailers with customer databases built from the use of loyalty cards, store credit cards and other in-house programmes could link a transaction at a cash register with the face of a shopper appearing on the videotape. Smile, you're being video mined! So, although video mining offers much promise for marketers and researchers, it also raises important privacy issues. People have pretty much learned to live with millions of security cameras videotaping them in airports, government buildings, offices, schools, shops, busy intersections and elsewhere. But few consumers are aware that they are being filmed for market research. Security is one thing, but the public is not likely to be as tolerant of secret market research using videotape.

Marketers appear to recognise this fact. ShopperTrak discloses its clients – the list includes, among others, Gap, Swatch, Christie's, Swarovski, HBOS, and London's Victoria & Albert Museum and the Science Museum. However, several other research companies that videotape shoppers say they sign agreements with clients in which they pledge not to disclose their names. Their clients want the taping to be secret, worrying that shoppers would feel alienated or complain of privacy invasion if they knew.

They're probably right to worry. Katherine Albrecht, founder and director of Caspian, a consumer-advocacy group, says consumers have 'no idea such things as video tracking are going on,' and they should be informed. When she tells them about such activities, she says the response she often hears is, 'Isn't this illegal, like stalking? Shouldn't there be a law against it?' Robert Bulmash, a consumer privacy advocate, says that being in a retailer's store doesn't give a retailer 'the right to treat me like a guinea pig.' He says he wonders about assurances that images are destroyed, because there isn't any way to verify such claims. The pictures 'could be saved somewhere in that vast digital universe and some day come back to haunt us,' he says.

SOURCE: Portions adapted from Joseph Pereira, 'Spying on the sales floor: "Video miners" use cameras hidden in stores to analyze who shops, what they like', *Wall Street Journal* (21 December 2004), p. B1. Other information from Kelly Sitch, '"Mining" software studies shoppers', *The Digital Collegian* (11 January 2005), accessed at www.collegian.psu.edu/archive/2005/01/01-11-05tdc/01-11-05dscihealth-01.asp; Kahn Research Group (www.webehavior.com), July 2006; AFX Europe (Focus), 'Retailers off to strong shopping season' (27 November 2006), www.videomining.com (July 2006) and ShopperTrak at www.shoppertrak.co.uk/ (g15fbo45rhdz2yqiuq0rt455)/index.aspx# (August 2007).

The debate heated up when Google applied for patents, proudly announcing it had plans to compile psychological profiles of millions of Web users by covertly monitoring the way they play online games. The company thinks it can glean information about an individual's preferences and personality type by tracking his or her online behaviour, which could then be sold to advertisers. Details such as whether a person is more likely to be aggressive, hostile or dishonest could be obtained and stored for future use. Ad agency owner and marketing guru, Lord Saatchi, commented: 'The world's great consumer goods companies are agog at how Google's systematic, logical computation can lead the advertiser into an earthly paradise of universal enlightenment – where all the problems of selling and marketing are solved by the same method: the method of data . . . they are understandably mesmerised by the possibility that the wastage involved in the $600bn spent annually on advertising can be eliminated at the touch of a button.'

Commenting on Google, Sue Charman of the online campaign Open Rights Group said: 'I can understand why they are interested in this, but I would be deeply disturbed by a company holding a psychological profile. Whenever you have large amounts of information it becomes attractive to people – we've already seen the American federal government going to court over data from companies including Google.'

Data-sharing can be useful, but the 'surveillance society' is emerging before there is time for a public debate on developments. There is a low level of understanding among the public about who collects what information. Michael Parker, of the NO2ID (NO to IDentity cards) campaign, comments that there is an 'alarming secrecy' surrounding the use of some personal information, particularly that held by companies and with whom they share it. Others are worried about the quality of data held: the figures might accurately track spending patterns but are slow to update demographic data, such as when people marry or have children, according to Keith Dugmore of the consultancy Demographic Decisions.[26]

> « Systematic, logical computation can lead the advertiser into an earthly paradise of universal enlightenment. »

Other consumers may have been taken in by previous 'research surveys' that actually turned out to be attempts to sell them something. This unethical sales practice is far more common than market research proper, so it is rightly condemned by bodies representing professional marketers. As a result of this malpractice consumers often confuse legitimate marketing research studies with telemarketing efforts and say 'no' before the interviewer can even begin. Most, however, simply resent the intrusion. They dislike mail, telephone or Web surveys that are too long or too personal or that interrupt them at inconvenient times.

Increasing consumer resentment has become a major problem for the research industry. One recent survey found that 70 per cent of people say that companies have too much of consumers' personal information, and 76 per cent feel that their privacy has been compromised if a company uses the collected personal information to sell them products. These concerns have led to lower survey response rates in recent years.[27]

Other studies found that 59 per cent of consumers had refused to give information to a company because they thought it was not really needed or too personal, up from 42 per cent five years earlier, and 71 per cent of consumers believe that protecting information is more of a concern now than it was a few years ago. 'Some shoppers are unnerved by the idea of giving up any information at all,' says an analyst. When asked for something as seemingly harmless as a postcode, 'one woman told me she always gives the postcode for Guam, and another said she never surrenders any information, not even a postcode, because "I don't get paid to help them with market research".'[28]

The research industry is considering several options for responding to this problem. One example is the Council for Marketing and Opinion Research's 'Your Opinion Counts' and

'Respondent Bill of Rights' initiatives to educate consumers about the benefits of marketing research and to distinguish it from telephone selling and database building. The industry also has considered adopting broad standards, perhaps based on the International Chamber of Commerce's 'International Code of Marketing and Social Research Practice'. This code outlines researchers' responsibilities to respondents and to the general public. For example, it says that researchers should make their names and addresses available to participants. It also bans companies from representing activities such as database compilation or sales and promotional pitches as research.[29]

Most major companies – including IBM, CitiGroup and Microsoft – have now appointed a 'chief privacy officer (CPO)', whose job is to safeguard the privacy of consumers who do business with the company. The chief privacy officer for Microsoft says that his job is to come up with data policies for the company to follow, make certain that every programme the company creates enhances customer privacy, and inform and educate company employees about privacy issues and concerns. Similarly, IBM's CPO claims that her job requires 'multidisciplinary thinking and attitude'. She needs to get all company departments, from technology, legal and accounting to marketing and communications, working together to safeguard customer privacy.[30]

American Express, which deals with a considerable volume of consumer information, has long taken privacy issues seriously. The company developed a set of formal privacy principles in 1991, and in 1998 it became one of the first companies to post privacy policies on its website. Its online Internet privacy statement tells customers in clear terms what information American Express collects and how it uses it, how it safeguards the information, and how it uses the information to market to its customers (with instructions on how to opt out).[31]

In the end, if researchers provide value in exchange for information, customers will gladly provide it. For example, Amazon.com's customers do not mind if the firm builds a database of products they buy in order to provide future product recommendations. This saves time and provides value. Similarly, users of the comparative price shopping site Bizrate gladly complete surveys rating online seller sites and products because they can view the overall ratings of others when making purchase decisions. The best approach is for researchers to ask only for the information they need, to use it responsibly to provide customer value, and to avoid sharing information without the customer's permission.

> If researchers provide value in exchange for information, customers will gladly provide it.

Misuse of research findings

Research studies can be powerful persuasion tools; companies often use study results as claims in their advertising and promotion. Today, however, many research studies appear to be little more than vehicles for pitching the sponsor's products. In fact, in some cases, the research surveys appear to have been designed just to produce the intended effect. Few advertisers openly rig their research designs or blatantly misrepresent the findings; most abuses tend to be subtle 'stretches'. Consider the following examples:[32]

A study by Chrysler contends that consumers overwhelmingly prefer Chrysler to Toyota after test-driving both. However, the study included just 100 people in each of two tests. More importantly, none of the people surveyed owned a Japanese car, so they could be biased against Japanese cars.

A Black Flag survey asked: 'A cockroach disc . . . poisons a cockroach slowly. The dying roach returns to the nest and after it dies is eaten by other cockroaches. In turn these cockroaches become poisoned and die. How effective do you think this type of product would be in killing roaches?' Not surprisingly, 79 per cent said effective.

A poll sponsored by the disposable nappy industry asked: 'It is estimated that disposable nappies account for less than 2 per cent of the waste in landfills. In contrast, drink containers, junk mail and garden waste are estimated to account for about 21 per cent of the waste in landfills. Given this, in your opinion, would it be fair to ban disposable nappies?' Again, not surprisingly, 84 per cent said no.

Thus, subtle manipulations of the study's sample or the choice or wording of questions can greatly affect the conclusions reached.

In other cases, so-called independent research studies are actually paid for by companies with an interest in the outcome. Small changes in study assumptions or in how results are interpreted can subtly affect the direction of the results. For example, at least four widely quoted studies compare the environmental effects of using disposable nappies to those of using towelling nappies. The two studies sponsored by the towelling nappy makers conclude that towelling nappies are more environmentally friendly. Not surprisingly, the other two studies, sponsored by the disposable nappy industry, conclude just the opposite. Yet both appear to be correct *given* the underlying assumptions used.

Recognising that surveys can be abused, several associations – including the American Marketing Association, the Marketing Research Association, the Market Research Society and the International Chamber of Commerce (ICC) together with ESOMAR (the European Society for Opinion and Marketing Research) – have developed codes of research ethics and standards of conduct. For example, the ICC/ESOMAR 'International Code of Marketing and Social Research Practice' outlines researchers' responsibilities to respondents, including confidentiality, privacy and avoidance of harassment. It also outlines major responsibilities in reporting results to clients and the public.[33] In the end, however, unethical or inappropriate actions cannot simply be regulated away. Each company must accept responsibility for policing the conduct and reporting of its own marketing research to protect consumers' best interests and its own.

Reviewing the concepts

In today's complex and rapidly changing marketplace, marketing managers need more and better information to make effective and timely decisions. This greater need for information has been matched by the explosion of information technologies for supplying information. Using today's new technologies, companies can now obtain great quantities of information, sometimes even too much. Yet marketers often complain that they lack enough of the *right* kind of information or have an excess of the *wrong* kind. In response, many companies are now studying their managers' information needs and designing information systems to help managers develop and manage market and customer information.

1. Explain the importance of information to the company and its understanding of the marketplace

The marketing process starts with a complete understanding of the marketplace and consumer needs and wants. Thus, the company needs sound information in order to produce superior value and satisfaction for customers. The company also requires information on competitors, resellers and other actors and forces in the marketplace. Increasingly, marketers are viewing information not only as an input for making better decisions but also as an important strategic asset and marketing tool.

2. Define the marketing information system and discuss its parts

The *marketing information system (MIS)* consists of people, equipment and procedures to gather, sort, analyse, evaluate and distribute needed, timely and accurate information to marketing decision makers. A well-designed information system begins and ends with users.

The MIS first *assesses information needs*. The marketing information system primarily serves the company's marketing and other managers, but it may also provide information to external partners. Then, the MIS *develops information* from internal databases, marketing intelligence activities and marketing research. *Internal databases* provide information on the company's own operations and departments. Such data can be obtained quickly and cheaply but often need to be adapted for marketing decisions. *Marketing intelligence* activities supply everyday information about developments in the external marketing environment. *Market research* consists of collecting information relevant to a specific marketing problem faced by the company. Lastly, the MIS *distributes information* gathered from these sources to the right managers in the right form and at the right time.

3. Outline the steps in the marketing research process

The first step in the marketing research process involves *defining the problem and setting the research objectives,* which may be exploratory, descriptive or causal research. The second step consists of *developing a research plan* for collecting data from primary and secondary sources. The third step calls for *implementing the marketing research plan* by gathering, processing and analysing the information. The fourth step consists of *interpreting and reporting the findings.* Additional information analysis helps marketing managers apply the information and provides them with sophisticated statistical procedures and models from which to develop more rigorous findings.

Both *internal* and *external* secondary data sources often provide information more quickly and at a lower cost than primary data sources, and they can sometimes yield information that a company cannot collect by itself. However, needed information might not exist in secondary sources. Researchers must also evaluate secondary information to ensure that it is *relevant, accurate, current* and *impartial.* Primary research must also be evaluated for these features. Each primary data collection method – *observational, survey* and *experimental* – has its own advantages and disadvantages. Each of the various primary research contact methods – mail, telephone, personal interview and online – also has its own advantages and drawbacks. Similarly, each contact method has its pluses and minuses.

4. Explain how companies analyse and distribute marketing information

Information gathered in internal databases and through marketing intelligence and marketing research usually requires more analysis. This may include advanced statistical analysis or the application of analytical models that will help marketers make better decisions. To analyse individual customer data, many companies have now acquired or developed special software and analysis techniques – called *customer relationship management (CRM)* – that integrate, analyse and apply the mountains of individual customer data contained in their databases.

Marketing information has no value until it is used to make better marketing decisions. Thus, the marketing information system must make the information available to the managers and others who make marketing decisions or deal with customers. In some cases, this means providing regular reports and updates; in other cases it means making non-routine information available for special situations and on-the-spot decisions. Many firms use company intranets and extranets to facilitate this process. Thanks to modern technology, today's marketing managers can gain direct access to the information system at any time and from virtually any location.

5. Discuss the special issues some marketing researchers face, including public policy and ethics issues

Some marketers face special marketing research situations, such as those conducting research in small business, non-profit or international situations. Marketing research can be conducted effectively by small businesses and non-profit organisations with limited budgets. International marketing researchers follow the same steps as domestic researchers but often face more and different problems. All organisations need to respond responsibly to major public policy and ethical issues surrounding marketing research, including issues of intrusions on consumer privacy and misuse of research findings.

Discussing the concepts

1. Figure 7.1 describes four marketing information system activities for developing information. In groups of four, determine how these activities would apply to Reebok developing the information it needs to market a new running shoe.

2. Assume that you are a regional marketing manager for a mobile phone company. List at least three different sources of internal data and discuss how these data would help you create mobile phone services that provide greater customer value and satisfaction.

3. Marketing research over the Internet has increased significantly in the past decade. Outline the strengths and weaknesses of marketing research conducted online.

4. How does your college use an intranet to help its students access data?

5. Small businesses and non-profit organisations often lack the resources to conduct extensive market research. Assume that you are the director of fundraising for a small non-profit organisation that focuses on a social issue. List three ways, using limited resources, in which you could gather information about your primary donor group.

6. Low-income pupils taking free meals in the UK declined 20 per cent after TV chef Jamie Oliver condemned school meals as being unhealthy and dull. The government banned French fries, pizza, fish fingers, sweet desserts, biscuits and soft drinks, providing healthy main courses and fruit instead. Now 20 per cent of the poorest kids were buying unhealthy food rather than having the free school meals, and teachers had lots of fruit to take home at the end of each day. What research should be done to guide decisions about providing healthy meals that the poorest kids will eat?

Applying the concepts

1. Imagine you are an owner of a small children's retail clothing shop that specialises in up-market girls' fashions from sizes 2 to 6. You have found a potential clothing line but you are unsure whether the line will generate the sales needed to be profitable. Which type of research methodology (exploratory, descriptive or causal) is best suited to solve your research objective? Why?

2. Many consumer rights advocates argue that research data can be manipulated to support any conclusion. Assume you are attending a meeting where a research project for a new product in a new market is being presented. List five questions that you would ask to test the interpretation and objectivity of the findings being presented.

Web resources

For additional classic case studies and internet exercises, visit **www. pearsoned.co.uk/ kotler**

3. Visit zoomerang.com or another free online Web survey site. Using the tools at the site, design a short five-question survey on the dining services for your business school. Send the survey to six friends and look at the results. What did you think of the online survey method?

References

1. 'A turning point for AIDS?', *The Economist* (15 July 2000), pp. 117–19; 'Business and AIDS', *The Economist* (10 February 2001), p. 95; 'AIDS: forty million orphans', *The Economist* (30 November 2002), p. 56; 'For 80 cents more', *The Economist* (17 August 2002), pp. 19–22; 'AIDS: money, money, money', *The Economist* (28 June 2003), p. 117; Andrew Jack, 'Gates urges more HIV prevention as priority in Aids fight', *Financial Times* (15 August 2006); Michael Peel, 'A matter of life and death', *Financial Times* (2 December 2006), p. 3; Nick Partridge, 'It's 25 years and counting: Despite great advances in the treatment of Aids since Terrence Higgins died, ignorance still threatens to escalate the epidemic', *The Guardian* (4 July 2007); Rupert Cornwell, 'World is "failing to halt spread of HIV/Aids"', *The Independent* (24 July 2007); 'Authorities release HIV/AIDS surveillance report for 2006', *BBC Monitoring Service*, Botswana (1 August 2007). For WHO reports on HIV/AIDS, see www.who.int/topics/hiv_infections/en/ and the interactive Now Project web pages at www.nowproject.co.za.

2. 'Tesco: fresh, but far from easy', *The Economist* (21 June 2007).

3. See Philip Kotler, *Marketing Insights from A to Z* (Hoboken, NJ: John Wiley & Sons, 2003), pp. 80–2.

4. Jennifer Brown, 'Pizza Hut delivers hot results using data warehousing', *Computing Canada* (17 October 2003), p. 24; 'Pizza Hut, Inc.', *Hoover's Company Records* (15 May 2006), p. 89521; http://www.adbrands.net/us/yum_us.htm, accessed 3 August 2007.

5. Tracey Tyler, 'WestJet accuses rival of trap in spy case', *Toronto Star* (14 February 2006), p. D1.

6. Andy Serwer, 'P&G's covert operation', *Fortune* (17 September 2001), pp. 42–4. Also see Andrew Crane, 'In the company of spies: When competitive intelligence gathering becomes industrial espionage', *Business Horizons* (May–June 2005), pp. 233–40; and Kate MacKenzie, 'Employees may be opening door to criminals', *Financial Times* (31 May 2006), p. 4.

7. Fred Vogelstein and Peter Lewis, 'Search and destroy', *Fortune* (2 May 2005).

8. James Curtis, 'Behind enemy lines', *Marketing* (24 May 2001), pp. 28–9. Also see Brian Caufield 'Know your enemy', *Business 2.0* (June 2004), p. 89; Michael Fielding, 'Damage control: Firms must plan for counterintelligence', *Marketing News* (15 September 2004), pp. 19–20; and Bill DeGenaro, 'A case for business counterintelligence', *Competitive Intelligence Magazine* (September–October 2005), pp. 12–16.

9. James Curtis, 'Behind enemy lines', *Marketing* (24 May 2001), pp. 28–9.

10. For more on research firms that supply marketing information, see Jack Honomichl, 'Honomichl 50', special section, *Marketing News* (15 June 2006), pp. H1–H67. Other information from www.infores.com, www.smrb.com, www.nielsen.com and http://www.yankelovich.com/products/monitor.aspx, August 2006.

11. Adapted from an example in David Kiley, 'Shoot the focus group', *BusinessWeek* (14 November 2005), pp. 120–1.

12. Adapted from an example in Spencer E. Ante, 'The science of desire', *BusinessWeek* (5 June 2006), pp. 99–106; also see 'Marriott closes 2006 selected best-in-class by readers of *Business Traveler* and *Executive Travel* magazines', *PR Newswire* (2 January 2007); and Adbrands (www.adbrands.net/sectors/sector_travel.htm), 3 August 2007.

13. Spencer E. Ante, 'The science of desire', *BusinessWeek* (5 June 2006), p. 100.

14. David Kiley, 'Shoot the focus group', *BusinessWeek* (14 November 2005), p. 120.

15. 'Online research: The time has come', Greenfield Online white paper, accessed at www.greenfieldcentral.com/rcwhitepapers.htm, June 2006.

16. Adapted from an example in David Kiley, 'Shoot the focus group', *BusinessWeek* (14 November 2005), pp. 120–1.

17. For more on Internet privacy, see James R. Hagerty and Dennis K. Berman, 'Caught in the Net: New battleground over web privacy', *Wall Street Journal* (27 August 2004), p. A1; Alan R. Peslak, 'Internet

privacy policies', *Information Resources Management Journal* (January–March 2005), pp. 29–41; and Larry Dobrow, 'Privacy issues loom for marketers', *Advertising Age* (13 March 2006), p. S6.

18. See Gary H. Anthes, 'Smile, you're on Candid Computer', *Computerworld* (3 December 2001), p. 50; Claire Tristram, 'Behind BlueEyes', *Technology Review* (May 2001), p. 32; and 'Creating computers that know how you feel', accessed at www.almaden.ibm.com/cs/BlueEyes/index.html, July 2006.

19. Fred R. Barnard in the advertising trade journal *Printers' Ink*, 8 December 1921, shows an ad entitled 'One Look is Worth a Thousand Words'. Another ad by Barnard appears in the 10 March 1927 issue where 'One Picture is Worth Ten Thousand Words' is quoted as a Chinese proverb. Barnard later said it was 'a Chinese proverb, so that people would take it seriously'. Soon after, the 'proverb' would become popularly attributed to Confucius and Napoleon Bonaparte. Simon Briscoe talks of Trendalyser in 'The hidden beauty of number', *Financial Times* (17 July 2007), p. 14. Also see Edward R. Tufte, *The Visual Display of Quantitative Information* (Cheshire, CT: Graphics Press, 2001) and *Beautiful Evidence* (Cheshire, CT: Graphics Press, 2006).

20. See Darell K. Rigby and Vijay Vishwanath, 'Localization: The revolution in consumer markets', *Harvard Business Review* (April 2006), pp. 82–92.

21. For some good advice on conducting market research in a small business, see 'Marketing Research' . . . 'Basics 101', US Small Business Administration, accessed at www.sba.gov/starting_business/ marketing/research.html, August 2006; and 'Researching your market', US Small Business Administration, accessed at www.sba.gov/library/pubs/mt-8.doc, August 2006. Also information and networking opportunities from Smallbusiness | Europe at www.smallbusinesseurope.org/en/, August 2007, or the European Small Business Alliance at www.esba-europe.org/, August 2007.

22. Jack Honomichl, 'Acquisitions up, growth rate varies', *Marketing News* (15 August 2005), pp. H3–H4; Jack Honomichl, 'Honomichl 50', special section, *Marketing News* (15 June 2006), pp. H1–H67; and the AC Nielsen International Research website, accessed at www2.acnielsen.com/company/where.php, July 2006.

23. Phone, PC and other country media statistics are from www.nationmaster.com, July 2006. For a wealth of free downloadable statistics, see http://epp.eurostat.ec.europa.eu/portal/page?_pageid= 2693,61100649,2693_62309135&_dad=portal&_schema=PORTAL. They include 'EU integration seen through statistics' and the pocketbook 'Key figures on Europe', August 2007.

24. Subhash C. Jain, *International Marketing Management*, 3rd edn (Boston, MA: PWS-Kent, 1990), p. 338. Also see Debra L. Vence, 'Leave it to the experts', *Marketing News* (28 April 2003), p. 37; Gary Kaplan, 'Global research needs local coordination', *Marketing News* (15 May 2005), p. 43; and C. Samuel Craig and Susan P. Douglas, 'International research frame needs reworking', *Marketing News* (15 February 2006), pp. 33–4.

25. Adapted from Richard Behar, 'Never heard of Acxiom? Chances are it's heard of you', *Fortune* (23 February 2004), pp. 140–8, with information from www.acxiom.com, July 2006, and www.acxiom.co. uk/QuickLinks/AcxiomWorldwide/index.html, August 2007.

26. Lord Maurice Saatchi, 'Google data or human nature?', *Financial Times* (30 May 2007), p. 13; Simon Briscoe and Michael Peel, 'Errors weaken trust in data-sharing', *Financial Times* (6 August 2007), p. 3; Michael Peel, '"Surveillance society" warning on data sharing', *Financial Times* (6 August 2007), p. 1; David Adam and Bobbie Johnson, 'Google takes to analysis', *The Guardian* (1 June 2007).

27. See 'Too much information?', *Marketing Management* (January–February 2004), p. 4.

28. Margaret Webb Pressler, 'Too personal to tell?', *The Washington Post* (18 April 2004), p. F.05; 'E-mail privacy statistics', accessed at www.relemail.com/statistics.html, June 2006.

29. 'ICC/ESOMAR International Code of Marketing and Social Research Practice', accessed at www.iccwbo. org/home/menu_advert_marketing.asp, July 2006. Also see 'Respondent Bill of Rights', accessed at www.cmor.org/rc/tools.cfm?topic=4, July 2006.

30. Jaikumar Vijayan, 'Disclosure laws driving data privacy efforts, says IBM exec', *Computerworld* (8 May 2006), p. 26.

31. Information accessed at www10.americanexpress.com/sif/cda/page/0,1641,14271,00.asp, July 2006.

32. Cynthia Crossen, 'Studies galore support products and positions, but are they reliable?', *Wall Street Journal* (14 November 1991), pp. A1, A9. Also see Allan J. Kimmel, 'Deception in marketing research and practice: An introduction', *Psychology and Marketing* (July 2001), pp. 657–61; and Alvin C. Burns and Ronald F. Bush, *Marketing Research* (Upper Saddle River, NJ: Prentice Hall, 2005), pp. 63–75.

33. Drawn from www.esomar.org/uploads/pdf/ESOMAR_Codes&Guidelines_ICCCode.pdf.

Company case 7 Enterprise Rent-A-Car: measuring service quality

Surveying customers

Eric Widel steered his titanium silver BMW Series 3 Coupé into the drive, put the gear into neutral, the hand brake on and got out. Checking his mail as he did every day when he returned home, among the deluge of junk mail he noticed a letter from Enterprise Rent-A-Car. He wondered, why should Enterprise be writing?

The wreck on the highway

Then he remembered. Earlier that month, Eric had been involved in a car crash. As he was driving to work one rainy morning, another car had been unable to stop and had ploughed into his car as he waited at some traffic lights. Thankfully, neither he nor the other driver was hurt, but both cars had sustained considerable damage. His car was undriveable. Eric used his mobile to call the police, and while he was waiting for the officers to come, he had called his car insurance agent. The agent assured Eric that his policy included coverage to pay for car rental while he was having his car repaired. He told Eric to have the car towed to a nearby garage and gave him the telephone number for the Enterprise Rent-A-Car in his area. The agent noted that his company recommended using Enterprise for replacement rentals and that Eric's policy would cover up to €50 per day of the rental fee.

Once Eric had checked his car in at the body shop and made the necessary arrangements, he telephoned the Enterprise office. Within 10 minutes, an Enterprise employee had driven to the repair shop and picked him up. They drove back to the Enterprise office, where Eric completed the paperwork and rented a black Mercedes 220 CDi Elegance.

He drove the rental car for 12 days before the repair shop completed work on his car. 'I don't know why Enterprise would be writing to me,' Eric thought. 'The insurance company paid the €50 per day, and I paid the extra because the Mercedes cost more than that. I wonder what the problem could be?'

Tracking satisfaction

Eric opened the Enterprise letter to find that it was a survey to determine how satisfied he was with his rental. The survey itself was only one page long and consisted of 13 questions (see Exhibit 7.1).

Enterprise's executives believed that the company had become the world's largest rent-a-car company because of its laser-like focus on customer satisfaction and because of its concentration on serving the replacement market. It aimed to serve customers like Eric who were involved in crashes and suddenly found themselves without a car. While the better-known companies like Hertz and Avis battled for business in the cut-throat airport market, Enterprise quietly built its business by cultivating insurance agents and body-shop managers as referral agents so that when one of their clients or customers needed a replacement vehicle, they would recommend Enterprise.

Although such replacement rentals accounted for about 80 per cent of the company's business, it also served the discretionary market (leisure/holiday rentals) and the business market (renting cars to businesses for their short-term needs). It had also begun to provide on-site and off-site service at some airports.

Throughout its history, Enterprise had followed founder Jack Taylor's advice. Taylor believed that if the company took care of its customers and employees first, profits would follow. So the company was careful to track customer satisfaction.

About one in 20 randomly selected customers received a letter like Eric's. An independent company mailed the letter and a postage-paid return envelope to the selected customers. Customers who completed the survey used the envelope to return it to the independent company. That company compiled the results and provided them to Enterprise.

Continuous improvement

Meanwhile, back at Enterprise's headquarters, the company's top managers were interested in taking the

Exhibit 7.1 Service Quality survey

Please mark the box that best reflects your response to each question.

	Completely Satisfied	Somewhat Satisfied	Neither Satisfied Nor Dissatisfied	Somewhat Dissatisfied	Completely Dissatisfied
1. Overall, how satisfied were you with your recent car rental from Enterprise?	☐	☐	☐	☐	☐

2. What, if anything, could Enterprise have done better? *(Please be specific)* _____
_____
_____

3a. Did you experience any problems during the rental process? Yes ☐ No ☐

3b. If you mentioned any problems to Enterprise, did they resolve them to your satisfaction? Yes ☐ No ☐ Did not mention ☐

	Excellent	Good	Fair	Poor	N/A
4. If you personally called Enterprise to reserve a vehicle, how would you rate the telephone reservation process?	☐	☐	☐	☐	☐

	Both at start and end of rental	Just at start of rental	Just at end of rental	Neither time
5. Did you go to the Enterprise office. . . .	☐	☐	☐	☐

	Both at start and end of rental	Just at start of rental	Just at end of rental	Neither time
6. Did an Enterprise employee give you a ride to help with your transportation needs. . . .	☐	☐	☐	☐

7. After you arrived at the Enterprise office, how long did it take you to:

	Less than 5 minutes	5–10 minutes	11–15 minutes	16–20 minutes	21–30 minutes	More than 30 minutes	N/A
• pick up your rental car?	☐	☐	☐	☐	☐	☐	☐
• return your rental car?	☐	☐	☐	☐	☐	☐	☐

8. How would you rate the . . .

	Excellent	Good	Fair	Poor	N/A
• timeliness with which you were either picked up at the start of the rental or dropped off afterwards?	☐	☐	☐	☐	☐
• timeliness with which the rental car was either brought to your location and left with you or picked up from your location afterwards?	☐	☐	☐	☐	☐
• Enterprise employee who handled your paperwork . . . at the START of the rental?	☐	☐	☐	☐	☐
at the END of the rental?	☐	☐	☐	☐	☐
• mechanical condition of the car?	☐	☐	☐	☐	☐
• cleanliness of the car interior/exterior?	☐	☐	☐	☐	☐

	Yes	No	N/A
9. If you asked for a specific type or size of vehicle, was Enterprise able to meet your needs?	☐	☐	☐

	Car repairs due to accident	All other car repairs/ maintenance	Car was stolen	Business	Leisure/ vacation	Some other reason
10. For what reason did you rent this car?	☐	☐	☐	☐	☐	☐

	Definitely will call	Probably will call	Might or might not call	Probably will not call	Definitely will not call
11. The next time you need to pick up a rental car in the city or area in which you live, how likely are you to call Enterprise?	☐	☐	☐	☐	☐

	Once – this was first time	2 times	3–5 times	6–10 times	11 or more times
12. Approximately how many times in total have you rented from Enterprise (including this rental)?	☐	☐	☐	☐	☐

	0 times	1 time	2 times	3–5 times	6–10 times	11 or more times
13. Considering *all rental companies*, approximately how many times *within the past year* have you rented a car in the city or area in which you live (including this rental)?	☐	☐	☐	☐	☐	☐

next steps in their customer satisfaction programme. Enterprise had used the percentage of customers who were completely satisfied to develop its Enterprise Service Quality index (ESQi). It used the survey results to calculate an overall average ESQi score for the company and a score for each individual branch. The company's branch managers believed in and supported the process. However, top management believed that to really 'walk the talk' on customer satisfaction, it needed to make the ESQi a key factor in the promotion process. The company wanted to take the ESQi for the branch or branches that a manager supervised into consideration when it evaluated that manager for a promotion. Top management believed that such a process would ensure that its managers and all its employees would focus on satisfying Enterprise's customers.

However, the top managers realised they had two problems in taking the next step.

- First, they wanted a better survey response rate. Although the company got a 25 per cent response rate, which was good for this type of survey, it was concerned that it might still be missing important information.

- Second, it could take up to two months to get results back, and Enterprise believed it needed a process that would get the customer satisfaction information more quickly, at least on a monthly basis, so its branch managers could identify and take action on customer service problems quickly and efficiently.

Enterprise's managers wondered how they could improve the customer-satisfaction-tracking process.

Questions

1. Analyse Enterprise's Service Quality survey. What information is it trying to gather? What are its research objectives?

2. What decisions has Enterprise made with regard to primary data collection – research approach, contact methods, sampling plan and research instruments?

3. In addition to or instead of the mail survey, what other means could Enterprise use to gather customer satisfaction information?

4. What specific recommendations would you make to Enterprise to improve the response rate and the timeliness of feedback from the process?

SOURCE: Officials at Enterprise Rent-A-Car contributed to and supported development of this case.

> The meek shall inherit the earth, but they'll not increase market share.
>
> WILLIAM G. MCGOWAN

PART three

Core strategy

Chapter 8 Relationship marketing ● **Chapter 9** Segmentation and positioning ● **Chapter 10** Competitive strategy

PART THREE OF *PRINCIPLES OF MARKETING* covers core strategy, the centre of the marketing process.

A Levi's ad once claimed that 'quality never goes out of style'. That has become a byword for much of modern marketing, as marketers try to escape from making single transactions with customers to establishing relationships that both enjoy. **Chapter 8** examines how customer satisfaction, quality, value and service contribute to relationship marketing.

Within core strategy, marketing knowledge is made into the strategies that guide marketing action. Businesses mostly succeed by concentrating on a group of customers they can serve better than anyone else. **Chapter 9** explains how markets can be broken down into customer segments and how to choose the ones to target. It then looks at ways to address the target segments by creating mental associations that attract customers to the product or services.

Increasingly, it is not enough for marketers to look at customers; they must also look at what their competitors are doing and respond to them. **Chapter 10** shows that success in marketing does not mean direct confrontation with competitors. It is often best to find new ways to please customers that build upon a business's unique strengths.

Video Case Acme Whistles Ltd.

Acme Whistles is a great little company. It's a small manufacturing company, employing about 50 people, and a world market leader in its niche. You may not have heard of the company but you will certainly have heard its products. Acme is the world's leading supplier of referee's whistles, police whistles, dog whistles, whistles for the armed forces, for the emergency services, general bird warbler for classical musicians, silver Titanic whistles, whistles to call up the Lockness Monster, duck calls for hunters, Samba whistles for Rio's Mardi Gras, diamond studded silent dog whistles and much more!

Simon Topman
Managing Director

In this video, Simon Topman, the company's charismatic owner and CEO, explains the origins of the company, how the company markets globally and how it competes effectively against imitators from low cost economies.

To learn more about the company, visit Acme's prize winning website at www.acmewhistles.co.uk or a specialist whistles shop website, such as www.whistleworld.co.uk.

After viewing the video, you may address the following questions:

1. How does a manufacturer of relatively low-tech products, such as whistles, compete effectively against numerous low-cost, copycat competitors?
2. How might the marketing mix vary for products developed for consumer and industrial customers? Suggest how the company might market products such as police whistles, whistles used by sports referees or diamond-studded dog whistles?
3. What role does the Internet play in helping a small business reach global markets?

> **WARNING – Customers are perishable.**
>
> NOTICE FOR STAFF IN A FAST FOOD RESTAURANT

Relationship marketing

Mini Contents List

'(I Can't Get No) Satisfaction'

'You Can't Always Get What You Want'

The Rolling Stones, 'Forty Licks', Umtv B0007XMKUS

Previewing the concepts

'The customer experience used to end at the cash register. Today, that's where it begins,' quotes Woody Diggs, leader of the global customer relationship management practice for the consultancy Accenture.[1] Mass production and globalisation have made the developed world a land of plenty. Yet in that same land high labour costs mean service is expensive to provide. More often than not, customers trying to fulfil their wants are left wanting. Keeping customers satisfied gets harder as their expectations rise. Equally, today's companies face tough competition from around the world. Often customer relationships are the way to get an edge in a market. In previous chapters, we argued that to succeed in today's fiercely competitive markets, companies have to move from a *product and selling philosophy* to a *customer and marketing philosophy*. This chapter looks in more detail at how companies can win at being better at *meeting and satisfying consumer and customer needs*.

After reading this chapter, you should be able to:

1. Define *customer value* and discuss its importance in creating and measuring customer satisfaction.
2. Discuss the concepts of *value chains* and *value delivery systems* and explain how companies go about producing and delivering customer value.
3. Define quality and explain the importance of total quality marketing in building profitable relationships with customers.
4. Explain the importance of retaining current customers as well as attracting new ones.
5. Understand the role and operation of customer relationship management.

As the prelude case shows, even the world's leading companies have difficulty in providing the excellent product and service quality that customers demand.

Prelude case 'The most important part of a car is the distributor'

I read this car dealer's poster advertising slogan with some understanding. The copy played on the word distributor: (a) a car dealer, and (b) an electrical component that is the usual cause of old cars not starting on a wet morning. It also resonates with a recent expensive and time-consuming experience buying a luxury car.

Knowing exactly the car I wanted, I entered the city centre Mercedes dealership in a frame of mind reminiscent of Samuel Johnson's observation on second marriage: 'the triumph of hope over experience'. My last visit, three years ago, ended after an exasperating encounter with the dealer's financial advisor. I asked him the best way of financing a car for a self-employed, top rate of tax payer who was registered for Value Added Tax and drove 16,000 miles (25,600 km) per year. The result of the question was a confusion of down payments, balloon payments, etc. I tried putting the question simply to the financial advisor: 'What option gives me the lowest cost of ownership of an E230 Estate?'.

Financial advisor: 'We do not do it that way. You will have to ask your accountant.'

I left, asked my accountant, did the sums and leased a car from another dealer 50 minutes' drive from where I work.

I had two reasons to believe the city centre dealer would be better this time. I had just bought a second-hand Yaris from Pentagon Toyota and the whole transaction had been quick, efficient and friendly. In addition, Mercedes had just purchased the city centre dealership so now the dealers and their splendid cars would be one.

In summer 2003 I re-entered the city centre dealers, wanting to buy an E270 CDi Estate for cash. The reviews of the new E270 CDi were fantastic – *What Car?* rated it as 'Best Executive Car of the Year'. The Consumer Association's *Which?* surprisingly showed Mercedes plummeting two categories from among Japanese cars rated the 'Best' in reliability to an 'Average' rating. However, other reports mentioned that with the new E-class, Mercedes looked to be overcoming their quality problems.

The dealer's salesman explained to me that since the £1,950 (€3,237) 'Cockpit Management and Navigation Display (COMMAND APS)' used a DVD, I would not be able to play a CD while using the satellite navigation system. I commented that this sounded like a daft 'design feature' for something so expensive, but opted for a 'CD changer in the central console' (another £350) so I could drive and jive. For an agreed price of £36,000, delivery would be on Friday 24 October. The date was after the old Mercedes' lease expired but the Yaris could fill the gap. So far so good, but not for long.

1. Getting rid of the old car was not easy. The contract with DaimlerChrysler Services (DCS) expired on 12 October and the correspondence mentioned they would pick up the car on that day. I rang the Services company to find out when on Sunday the car would be picked up:

DCS: 'We do not pick up cars on Sunday; a driver will be coming on Monday.'

'But I will not be at home on Monday, it is a working day and I already have appointments made. Can they pick it up from work?'

DCS: 'We have no way of contacting the driver now. If you are not at home when the driver arrives on Monday you will have to pay an extra charge.'

'But the contract expires on the 12th.'

DCS: 'We did contact you to arrange the pickup last week.'

'You may have tried but I was in New Zealand and I know nothing about it.'

DCS: 'We will try to contact the driver on Monday but he may have left by the time our office opens.'

After leaving faxes, emails and answerphone messages, I eventually contacted the driver and arranged the Monday pickup at work.

2. Dropping into the city centre dealer on the way in, I went to the sales desk to ask about having a Tracker (a system that tracks stolen cars) fitted to the new car, since a review I had read said the E-series estate would initially be very popular with professional thieves. There was no-one on the sales floor. Snooping round, I found an office where several smartly dressed men stood chatting. One turned to help me: 'Can I help? You will probably want the Service Department. That is the other entrance.'

'No, I'm trying to buy a car. I need to specify a Tracker and check my car's delivery date.'

In a small open office up some stairs a sales clerk asked: 'Which Tracker do you want: Retrieve, Monitor or Horizon?'

After some discussion and being told that the top of the range Horizon was really only appropriate for expensive cars, such as a Ferrari, I opted for the Retrieve system for a one-off payment of about £300.

3. The car was ready on Monday 27 October rather than the 24th. Only three days later than promised, but it did mean that, lacking the larger car, I would have to drive to my daughter's college on both 28 October and 2 November since we could not fit her bike, grandparents and the rest of the family in another car that we would have to use, instead of the E-series estate.

4. On Monday 27th the car arrived at home and I paid an extra £299 for the Tracker. It was odd that it was not included on the bill for the car, but I assumed the Tracker was from a different company.

While checking over the car with me, the delivery driver showed me the DVD player for the navigator in the luggage compartment. 'Hang on, since the DVD player is in the luggage compartment, does that mean I could play CDs using the normal CD slot while navigating?'

Delivery driver: 'Yes, no problem. And the extra six-disc changer means you will be able to choose between seven CDs.'

'Woops: there goes £350. Never mind, the way the changer flips open does look cool.'

Later that day, at the city centre dealer's Spares Department I buy a set of £130 carrier-bars for the roof of the estate and an £82 bicycle rack. It seems a lot to transport a bike that only cost £100 several years ago but we will probably use it many times in the car's life. I would have to pick them up the next day because they were not in stock.

5. The next Saturday, trying to fix a £40 bike to the £200 rack, I had difficulty following the instructions. With the bike on the roof of the car, I could not 'Insert the anti-theft device (12) and lock the lock of the frame holder (11).' With arms above my head, I could not feel anything like a lock although there was a cable corresponding to 'the anti-theft device'. After taking down bike, bike rack and all, I found there was no lock. 'What awful quality control to leave out the lock', I thought. I was wrong. Still, I did get the bike to my daughter's college but made secure with an old bicycle lock rather than 'the lock of the frame holder'.

6. Next Monday, back to the city centre dealer. 'This bike rack's got no lock.'

Spares man: 'It should not have one.'

'But the instructions say here "lock the lock of the frame holder".'

The spares man said: 'See here – this note in the manual "Locks for locking the bicycle carrier are not included and must be ordered separately."'

'Why didn't you tell me when I bought the rack? The system is incomplete without a lock.'

Spares man: 'It is not standard.'

'Can I have a lock then?'

Spares man: 'We don't have them in stock but we can order them for you. Do you want two or four?'

'I've only got one bicycle rack; can I have one?'

Spares man: 'I am sorry but we only sell them in packs and they are £2.70 each, £5.40 for a pack of two.'

Two days later, I get a call to say I can pick up my locks.

7. In December 2003 the legislation changed to make it illegal to use a hand-held mobile phone while driving. I did not like using mobile phones while driving but since the car had numerous buttons with pictures of telephones on, I decided to have one fitted. Among the E-class accessories is listed a 'Mercedes-Benz

hands free system' for £182 or £210 depending on whether the car was with or without 'VDA pre-wiring'. I rang the Service Department of the city centre dealer.

'How much would it cost to fit a mobile phone?'

Service Department: 'Have you got a SatNav System fitted?'

'Yes.'

Service Department: 'I'll ring our Spares Department to check. . . . They say about £1,200 all included.'

'£1,200! What is the £200 system listed in the Accessories Guide?'

Service Department: 'I don't know about that. You had better talk to Spares.'

Spares Department: 'It will be between £1,000 and £1,200 depending upon the wiring needed. You need to bring your car in so we can check.'

'I think I'll wait until after Christmas at that price. Thanks.'

8. I receive a letter from Tracker saying they need a Direct Debit mandate since I opted to pay for my Tracker Network Subscription by annual payment. I rang Tracker.

'When I bought the car I was asked for a one-off payment and paid about £299 when the car was delivered.'

Tracker agent: 'Will you check your pink Tracker Order Installation Form to see what network subscription option is ticked and can you give me your TVU Serial Number?'

'There is no box ticked.'

Tracker agent: 'Oh, they are always doing that. They think we know if they leave it blank. You need to contact your dealer.'

Dealer reception: 'Tracker? I'll put you through to Customer Services.'

Customer Services: 'You'll need to speak to Sales. . . . I am sorry there is no one free now. I have left a message with our used car salesman.'

'I don't want to buy a second-hand car but I am getting to understand why I want to sell this one.'

Customer Services: 'He is busy at the moment but he will get back to you in 15 minutes. What is your telephone number?'

Two days later, I am still awaiting his call. The car is great, but the dealer . . .

Questions

1. What do you understand by the slogan 'The most important part of a car is the distributor' and is such a distinction justified when the manufacturer owns the dealership?

2. How are retailers able to survive when providing the levels of customer service described when selling such expensive luxury products? Who is at fault?

3. At what points in the sales and service interaction could the individual contact, the dealer or Mercedes intervene to improve customer satisfaction?

SOURCES: Adapted from www.whatcar.com (March 2003) and sub.which.net (October 2007).

Introduction

As the prelude case shows, even when the product is great, satisfying customers is not easy. People have come to accept that their consumption experience has become largely adversarial. Customers have got used to having products and services that deliver, so they object when companies fail to deliver the service they promise or fail to achieve what customers anticipate. Much of the frustration experienced by customers is a new *production orientation* that has occurred as firms try to cut costs by de-skilling or automating the customer interface. Few customers have avoided the frustration of having to press a series of digits to ensure their call is directed to the appropriate person, spending minutes listening to awful music while being told 'your call is important to us', then getting through to be told another number to ring.[2] The failure of many companies to give customers what they want is creating new opportunities for effective marketers. Recognising a widening gap between customers' expectations and service, NatWest Bank, a subsidiary of Royal Bank of Scotland, has hired an extra 6,000 staff so that its customers will no longer have to deal with answering machines and HSBC have linked senior executive pay to customer satisfaction.[3]

> **"** People have come to accept that their consumption experience has become largely adversarial. **"**

For much of history, there was little need for such concerns for customer relationships or satisfaction. In sellers' markets – characterised by shortages and near-monopolies – companies

Triumph's sophisticated website gives customers a chance to view their range and ask questions on fabric care, fit and much else. It also comes with desktop wallpaper and screen savers that may be attractive to the gender not represented in this 'entertainment'.

SOURCE: Triumph International Ltd. (www.triumph.com).

did not make special efforts to please customers. By contrast, in buyers' markets customers can choose from a wide array of goods and services. In these markets, if sellers fail to deliver acceptable product and service quality, they will quickly lose customers to competitors. In addition, what is acceptable today may not be acceptable to tomorrow's ever more demanding consumers. Consumers are becoming more educated and demanding, and their quality expectations have been raised by the practices of superior manufacturers and retailers. The decline of many traditional western industries in recent years – cars, cameras, shipping, machine tools, consumer electronics – offers dramatic evidence that firms offering only average quality lose their consumer franchises when attacked by superior competitors.[4]

Satisfying customer needs

Customer-centred company—A company that focuses on customer developments in designing its marketing strategies and on delivering superior value to its target customers.

To succeed or simply to survive, companies need a new philosophy. To win in today's marketplace, companies must be **customer-centred** – they must deliver superior value to their target customers. They must become adept in *building customer relationships*, not just *building products*. They must be skilful in *market engineering*, not just *product engineering*.

Too often, marketing is ignored in the boardroom of companies with the view that the job of obtaining customers is the job of the marketing or sales department. A survey conducted by the Chartered Institute of Marketing found that only 20 per cent of companies in the FTSE 100 had someone with a marketing background on their Board of Directors.[5]

Contrast this with the view of Sir John Browne, one time CEO of BP:

'We have more than 10 million interactions with customers every day; and more than 100,000 staff in 100 countries. Every action and every activity is an act of marketing.'

Like BP, winning companies have come to realise that marketing cannot do this job alone. Although marketing plays a leading role, it is only a partner in attracting and keeping customers. The world's best marketing department cannot successfully sell poorly made products that fail to meet consumer needs. The marketing department can be effective only in companies in which all departments and employees have teamed up to form a competitively superior *customer value-delivery system*.

This chapter discusses the philosophy of customer-value-creating marketing and the customer-focused firm. It addresses several important questions: What is customer value and customer satisfaction? How do leading companies organise to create and deliver high value and satisfaction? How can companies keep current customers as well as get new ones? How can companies practise total quality marketing?

Defining customer value and satisfaction

Forty years ago, Peter Drucker observed that a company's first task is 'to create customers'. However, creating customers can be a difficult task. Today's customers face a vast array of product and brand choices, prices and suppliers. The company must answer a key question: How do customers make their choices?

The answer is that customers choose the marketing offer that gives them the most value. Customers are value-maximisers, within the bounds of search costs and limited knowledge, mobility and income. They form expectations of value and act upon them. Then they compare the actual value they receive in consuming the product to the value expected, and this affects their satisfaction and repurchase behaviour. We will now examine the concepts of customer value and customer satisfaction more carefully.

Customer value

Consumers buy from the firm that they believe offers the highest **customer delivered value** – the difference between *total customer value* and *total customer cost* (see Figure 8.1). For example, suppose that a farmer wants to buy a tractor. He can buy the equipment from either his usual supplier, Massey-Ferguson, or a cheaper east European product. The salespeople for the two companies carefully describe their respective offers to the farmer.

The farmer evaluates the two competing tractors and judges that Massey-Ferguson's tractor provides higher reliability, durability and performance. He also decides that Massey-Ferguson has better accompanying service – delivery, training and maintenance – and views Massey-Ferguson personnel as more knowledgeable and responsive. Finally, the farmer places higher value on Massey-Ferguson's reputation. He adds all the values from these four sources – *product, services, personnel* and *image* – and decides that Massey-Ferguson offers more **total customer value** than does the east European tractor.

Does the farmer buy the Massey-Ferguson tractor? Not necessarily. He will also examine the **total customer cost** of buying the Massey-Ferguson tractor versus the east European tractor product. First, he will compare the prices he must pay for each of the competitors' products. The Massey-Ferguson tractor costs a lot more than the east European tractor does, so the higher price might offset the higher total customer value. Moreover, total customer cost consists of more than just monetary costs. As Adam Smith observed more than two centuries ago: 'The real price of anything is the toil and trouble of acquiring it.' Total customer cost also includes the buyer's anticipated time, energy and psychic costs. The farmer will evaluate these costs along with monetary costs to form a complete estimate of his costs.

The farmer compares total customer value to total customer cost and determines the total delivered value associated with Massey-Ferguson's tractor. In the same way, he assesses the total delivered value for the east European tractor. The farmer then will buy from the competitor that offers the highest delivered value.

How can Massey-Ferguson use this concept of buyer decision making to help it succeed in selling its tractor to this buyer? Massey-Ferguson can improve its offer in three ways. First, it can increase total customer value by improving product, services, personnel or image benefits. Second, it can reduce the buyer's non-monetary costs by lessening the buyer's time, energy and psychic costs. Third, it can reduce the buyer's monetary costs by lowering its price, providing easier terms of sale or, in the longer term, lowering its tractor's operating or maintenance costs.

Suppose Massey-Ferguson carries out a *customer value assessment* and concludes that buyers see Massey-Ferguson's offer as worth €20,000. Further suppose that it costs Massey-Ferguson

Customer delivered value—The difference between total customer value and total customer cost of a marketing offer – 'profit' to the customer.

Total customer value—The total of the entire product, services, personnel and image values that a buyer receives from a marketing offer.

Total customer cost—The total of all the monetary, time, energy and psychic costs associated with a marketing offer.

	Total customer value	(Product, services, personnel and image values)
minus	Total customer cost	(Monetary, time, energy and psychic costs)
equals	Customer delivered value	('Profit' to the consumer)

Figure 8.1 Customer delivered value

€14,000 to produce the tractor. This means that Massey-Ferguson's offer potentially generates €6,000 (€20,000 – €14,000) of *total added value*. Massey-Ferguson needs to price its tractor between €14,000 and €20,000. If it charges less than €14,000, it won't cover its costs. If it charges more than €20,000, the price will exceed the total customer value. The price Massey-Ferguson charges will determine how much of the total added value will be delivered to the buyer and how much will flow to Massey-Ferguson. For example, if Massey-Ferguson charges €16,000, it will grant €4,000 of total added value to the customer and keep €2,000 for itself as profit. If Massey-Ferguson charges €19,000, it will grant only €1,000 of total added value to the customer and keep €5,000 for itself as profit. Naturally, the lower Massey-Ferguson's price, the higher the delivered value of its offer will be and, therefore, the higher the customer's incentive to purchase from Massey-Ferguson. Delivered value should be viewed as 'profit to the customer'. Given that Massey-Ferguson wants to win the sale, it must offer more delivered value than the east European tractor does.

Some marketers might rightly argue that this concept of how buyers choose among product alternatives is too rational. They might cite examples in which buyers did not choose the offer with an objectively measured highest delivered value. Consider the following situation:

> The Massey-Ferguson salesperson convinces the farmer that, considering the benefits relative to the purchase price, Massey-Ferguson's tractor offers a higher delivered value. The salesperson also points out that the east European tractor uses more fuel and requires more frequent repairs. Still, the farmer decides to buy the east European tractor.

How can we explain this appearance of non-value-maximising behaviour? There are many possible explanations. For example, perhaps the farmer has a long-term friendship with the east European tractor salesperson. Or the farmer might have a policy of buying at the lowest price. Or perhaps the farmer is short of cash, and therefore chooses the cheaper east European tractor, even though the Massey-Ferguson machine will perform better and be less expensive to operate in the long run.

Clearly, buyers operate under various constraints and sometimes make choices that give more weight to their personal benefit than to company benefit. However, the customer delivered value framework applies to many situations and yields rich insights. The framework suggests that sellers must first assess the total customer value and total customer cost associated with their own and competing marketing offers to determine how their own offers measure up in terms of customer delivered value. If a seller finds that competitors deliver greater value, it has two alternatives. It can try to increase customer value by strengthening or augmenting the product, services, personnel or image benefits of the offer. Or it can decrease total customer cost by reducing its price, simplifying the ordering and delivery process, or absorbing some buyer risk by offering a warranty.[5]

Customer satisfaction

Consumers form judgements about the value of marketing offers and make their buying decisions based upon these judgements. *Customer satisfaction* with a purchase depends upon the product's performance relative to a buyer's expectations. A customer might experience various degrees of satisfaction. If the product's performance falls short of expectations, the customer is dissatisfied. If performance matches expectations, the customer is satisfied. If performance exceeds expectations, the customer is highly satisfied or delighted.

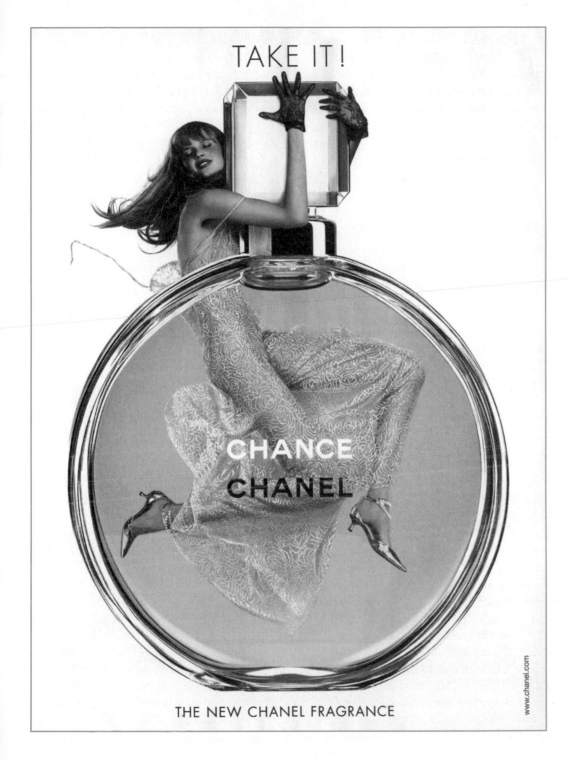

TAKE IT!

CHANCE
CHANEL

THE NEW CHANEL FRAGRANCE

www.chanel.com

'A decidedly young scent' that attracts young people to the Chanel range. 'It is . . . for those who dare to dream. Waves of freshness collide with floral notes and merge with sensual, sweet and spicy elements. It's your chance . . . TAKE IT!'. Once they have taken it, many people stick to the same range of fragrances throughout their lives.
SOURCE: The Advertising Archives.

But how do buyers form their expectations? Expectations are based on the customer's past buying experiences, the opinions of friends and associates, and marketer and competitor information and promises. Marketers must be careful to set the right level of expectations. If they set expectations too low, they may satisfy those who buy, but fail to attract enough buyers. In contrast, if they raise expectations too high, buyers are likely to be disappointed. For example, Holiday Inn ran a campaign a few years ago called 'No Surprises', which promised consistently trouble-free accommodation and service. However, Holiday Inn guests still encountered a host of problems and the expectations created by the campaign only made customers more dissatisfied. Holiday Inn had to withdraw the campaign.

> " There is no better advertisement than a satisfied customer and nothing worse than a dissatisfied one. "

Still, some of today's most successful companies are raising expectations – and delivering performance to match. These companies embrace *total customer satisfaction*. For example, Honda claims, 'One reason our customers are so satisfied is that we aren't' or, as Chris Veitch, customer service manager of Richer Sounds says, 'There is no better advertisement than a satisfied customer and nothing worse than a dissatisfied one.' These companies aim high because they know that customers who are *only* satisfied will still find it easy to switch suppliers when a better offer comes along. In one consumer packaged-goods category, 44 per cent of consumers reporting satisfaction later switched brands. In contrast, customers who are *highly satisfied* are much less ready to switch. Independent *Which?* Car Awards recognise the commitment of Lexus to excellence of its whole operation:

> In 2007 *Which?* recognised Lexus as a clear winner for customer satisfaction with its dealerships for both sales and servicing as it had done so for the previous five years. 'Parent company Toyota's build quality shines through in all Lexus models, placing the brand among the best there is for model reliability. And for owner satisfaction, Lexus tops every category it's in. Overall, 87 per cent of Lexus owners would recommend their car to a friend.'[6]

Such *customer delight* creates an emotional affinity for a product or service, beyond just a rational preference, and this creates high customer loyalty.

Today's winning companies track their customers' expectations, perceived company performance and customer satisfaction. They track this for their competitors as well. Consider the following:

> A company was pleased that it continued to find that 80 per cent of its customers said they were satisfied with its new product. However, the product seemed to sell poorly on store shelves next to the leading competitor's product. Company researchers soon learned that the competitor's product attained a 90 per cent customer satisfaction score. Company management was further dismayed when it learned that this competitor was aiming for a 95 per cent satisfaction score.[7]

There are two reasons why historical rates of customer satisfaction do not serve in the long run. As the example shows, once-acceptable levels of customer satisfaction may be overtaken by competitors. This is occurring in the car market where Japanese manufacturers are setting new standards of quality and service. The quality of European cars is better than ever before but does not come close to those of pace-setting Toyota and Honda. At the same time, customers learn from the new levels of quality available in the marketplace and so expect higher standards than before. Unwary companies therefore face 'backward creep' in which their once-acceptable standards fall behind those of the competition and the customers' increased expectations.[8]

For customer-centred companies, customer satisfaction is both a goal and an essential factor in company success. Companies that achieve high customer satisfaction ratings make sure that their target market knows it. These companies realise that highly satisfied customers produce several benefits for the company. They are less price sensitive and they remain customers for a longer period. They buy additional products over time as the company introduces related products or improvements. And they talk favourably to others about the company and its products.

Although the customer-centred firm seeks to deliver high customer satisfaction relative to competitors, it does not attempt to *maximise* customer satisfaction. A company can always increase customer satisfaction by lowering its price or increasing its services, but this may result in lower profits. In addition to customers, the company has many stakeholders, including employees, dealers, suppliers and stockholders. Spending more to increase customer satisfaction might divert funds from increasing the satisfaction of these other 'partners'. Thus the purpose of marketing is to generate customer value profitably. Ultimately, the company must deliver a high level of customer satisfaction, while at the same time delivering at least acceptable levels of satisfaction to the firm's other stakeholders. This requires a very delicate balance: the marketer must continue to generate more customer value and satisfaction, but not 'give away the house'. Many of the world's most successful companies build their strategies on customer satisfaction, but as Real Marketing 8.1 shows, you do not have to be big to succeed.

Tracking customer satisfaction

Successful organisations are aggressive in tracking both customer satisfaction and dissatisfaction. Several methods are used.

Complaint and suggestion systems

A customer-centred organisation makes it easy for customers to make suggestions or complaints. Hospitals place suggestion boxes in the corridors, supply comment cards to existing patients and employ patient advocates to solicit grievances. Some customer-centred companies may set up free customer hotlines to make it easy for customers to enquire, suggest or complain. Virgin Trains immediately hand out customer complaint forms as soon as there is any reason for passengers to complain, such as a train being delayed.

Successful companies try very hard. All visitors to Richer Sounds shops get a card showing the shop's team and saying: 'We're listening.' It's a Freepost letter addressed to Julian Richer, the owner of the chain. Inside it reads:

Thank you for your support and making us the UK's most successful hi-fi retailer. In order to maintain No. 1 position, we need to know where we've gone wrong. Suggestions or comments regarding customer service, however small, are gratefully received. Every one has Mr Richer's personal attention . . . Please, please, please let us know, as we really do care!

Customer satisfaction surveys

Complaint and suggestion systems may not give the company a full picture of customer satisfaction. One out of every four purchases results in consumer dissatisfaction, but fewer than 5 per cent of dissatisfied customers complain. Rather than complain, most customers simply switch suppliers. As a result, the company needlessly loses customers.

Responsive companies take direct measures of customer satisfaction by conducting regular surveys. They send questionnaires or make telephone calls to a sample of recent customers to find out how they feel about various aspects of the company's performance.

8.1 real marketing

Cold turkey has got me on the run

'Oh dear! Am I in trouble now.' It was a week before Christmas as the recalcitrant academic trudged up and down Castle Street trying to buy a goose for Christmas dinner. Long before Charles Dickens' time, when Scrooge sent 'the prize Turkey . . . the big one' to Bob Cratchit's house, goose was the traditional English Christmas fare. Introduced to Europe from America in the sixteenth century, turkey had displaced goose in all of Castle Street's butchers. Sick of having cold turkey salad, turkey sandwiches and that dreadful turkey curry for days after Christmas, the academic's family had decided to have goose 'for a change'. His job was to get one, but he had left it too late.

Butcher after butcher came out with the worn-out lines: 'You should have ordered one weeks ago', 'We can't get them anywhere' or 'There's no call for them these days.' Even 'A goose? They're so greasy. How about a nice fat turkey? It'll last you for days.' SCREAM!

Defeated, he slumped into his car to drive home. It was dark and on the way through a village he saw the lights of a small shop he had not noticed before – a small independent butcher, well stocked, brightly lit and full of customers. 'Funny', he thought, 'there aren't many of those these days. Still, let's have one last try.'

On joining the festive throng inside, he noticed a sign on the wall. It read:

The Ten Commandments of good business

1. The customer is the most important person in my business.
2. The customer is not dependent on us; we are dependent on him.
3. A customer is not an interruption of our work; he is the purpose of it.
4. A customer does us a favour when he calls; we are not doing him a favour by serving him.
5. The customer is part of our business, not an outsider.
6. The customer is not a cold statistic; he is a flesh and blood human being with feelings and emotions like ours.
7. The customer is not someone to argue or match wits with.
8. The customer brings us his wants; it is our job to fill those wants.
9. The customer is deserving of the most courteous and attentive treatment we can give him.
10. The customer is the lifeblood of this, and every other, business.

'Merry Christmas, what can I do for you?', asked the butcher.

'Have you a goose?', the academic asked timidly.

'I haven't got any in, but I'll get one for you. What size do you want?'

...8.1

Later on, at a local inn, the talk turned to food. 'Have you come across that great butcher in the next village?'

'Great butcher? Come off it. A butcher's a butcher's a butcher!'

'Not this one, he will do anything for you. Nice guy, too.'

Lesson: You do not have to be big to be great.

SOURCES: Charles Dickens, *A Christmas Carol* (London: Hazell, Watson & Viney, 1843); John Lennon, *Cold Turkey* (London: Apple, 1969); Bill Bryson, *Made in America* (London: Black Swan, 1998).

Magazines and consumers' associations often conduct independent surveys. These are invaluable since companies can easily be deluded by their own results.

Bozell Worldwide's Quality Poll gives a league table and shows how biased local perceptions can be. Gallup conducted a study that asked 20,000 people in 20 countries to rate the quality of manufactured goods from 12 countries. All countries rated themselves higher than other people did. The French put French goods on top, while the Japanese gave themselves twice the rating (76 per cent) that the full sample did (38.5). All other countries were optimistic too: Germans gave themselves 49 per cent against the full sample's 36 per cent and the United Kingdom 39 per cent against 22 per cent.

Ghost shopping

This involves researchers posing as buyers. These 'ghost shoppers' can even present specific problems in order to test whether the company's personnel handle difficult situations well. For example, ghost shoppers can complain about a restaurant's food to see how the restaurant handles this complaint. Research International's Mystery Shopper surveys can measure many dimensions of customer performance. By telephoning it can measure a firm's telephone technique: how many rings it takes to answer, the sort of voice and tone and, if transferred, how many leaps it took before being correctly connected.

Managers themselves should leave their offices from time to time and experience first-hand the treatment they receive as 'customers'. As an alternative, managers can phone their companies with different questions and complaints to see how the call is handled.

Lost customer analysis

Companies should contact customers who have stopped buying or who have switched to a competitor, to learn why this happened. Not only should the company conduct such *exit interviews*, it should also monitor the *customer loss rate*. A rising loss rate indicates that the company is failing to satisfy its customers.[7]

Universities and colleges usually compete by putting on new or improved courses or attracting excellent teachers, but one college's lost customer survey found major reasons for prospective students deciding to study elsewhere that were far from academic. Many prospective students and parents who visited mentioned the unsatisfactory state of the toilets in the Students' Guild and Main Hall. Others mentioned the state of the décor in some of the student halls of residence. Fixing the toilets was easy but an analysis of the halls of residences will take years to fix as all the old residences are demolished and replaced with the quality of accommodation that students and their parents now expect.

Delivering customer value and satisfaction

Customer value and satisfaction are important ingredients in the marketer's formula for success. But what does it take to produce and deliver customer value? To answer this, we will examine the concepts of a *value chain* and *value delivery system*.

Value chain

Value chain—A major tool for identifying ways to create more customer value.

Michael Porter proposed the **value chain** as the main tool for identifying ways to create more customer value (see Figure 8.2).[9] Every firm consists of a collection of activities performed to design, produce, market, deliver and support the firm's products. The value chain breaks the firm into nine value-creating activities in an effort to understand the behaviour of costs in the specific business and the potential sources of competitive differentiation. The nine value-creating activities include five primary activities and four support activities.

The primary activities involve the sequence of bringing materials into the business (inbound logistics), operating on them (operations), sending them out (outbound logistics), marketing them (marketing and sales) and servicing them (service). For a long time, firms have focused on the product as the primary means of adding value, but customer satisfaction also depends upon the other stages of the value chain. The support activities occur within each of these primary activities. For example, procurement involves obtaining the various inputs for each primary activity – only the purchasing department does a fraction of procurement. Technology development and human resource management also occur in all departments. The firm's infrastructure covers the overhead of general management, planning, finance, accounting and legal and government affairs borne by all the primary and support activities.

Figure 8.2 The generic value chain

SOURCE: From M.E. Porter, *Competitive Advantage: Creating and Sustaining Superior Performance* (New York: The Free Press, 1998). Reprinted with the permission of The Free Press, a Division of Simon & Schuster Adult Publishing Group.

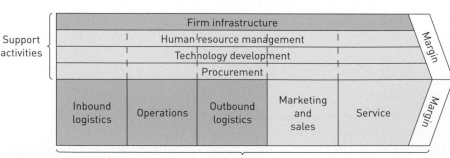

Under the value-chain concept, the firm should examine its costs and performance in each value-creating activity to look for improvements. It should also estimate its competitors' costs and performances as benchmarks. To the extent that the firm can perform certain activities better than its competitors, it can achieve a competitive advantage.

The firm's success depends not only on how well each department performs its work, but also on how well the activities of various departments are coordinated. Too often, individual departments maximise their own interests rather than those of the whole company and the customer. For example, a credit department might attempt to reduce bad debts by taking a long time to check the credit of prospective customers; meanwhile, salespeople get frustrated and customers wait. A distribution department might decide to save money by shipping goods by rail; again the customer waits. In each case, individual departments have erected walls that impede the delivery of quality customer service.

To overcome this problem, companies should place more emphasis on the smooth management of *core business processes,* most of which involve inputs and cooperation from many functional departments. These core business processes include the following:

- *Product development process.* All the activities involved in identifying, researching and developing new products with speed, high quality and reasonable cost.

- *Inventory management process.* All the activities involved in developing and managing the right inventory levels of raw materials, semi-finished materials and finished goods, so that adequate supplies are available while the costs of high overstocks are avoided.

- *Order-to-payment process.* All the activities involved in receiving orders, approving them, shipping the goods on time and collecting payment.

- *Customer service process.* All the activities involved in making it easy for customers to reach the right parties within the company to obtain service, answers and resolutions of problems.

Successful companies develop superior capabilities in managing these and other core processes. In turn, mastering core business processes gives these companies a substantial competitive edge.

Many Internet companies have fallen at the final, *customer service,* stage of the value chain. The fear of a faceless company is real among customers, especially in France and Italy, yet a recent survey found that only one-fifth of websites had human contact available through them. Across Europe only a minority of Internet users are willing to make a purchase without some personal contact, even from a well-known company. This reliance on a single, impersonal link with customers is said to account for the slow uptake of Internet shopping in some parts of Europe.

Companies are overcoming this barrier through 'click to chat' or 'click to talk' where a customer needing assistance clicks on an on-screen button to either begin a text messaging session or invite a direct telephone call from a trained operator with expert product knowledge. There are good reasons why more and more companies are moving to this way of adding value. Home Depot found the percentage of customers who make a purchase after using online chat support is about three times higher than the rate for those who are not given the option. Similarly, a live-chat intervention managed to salvage about 30 per cent of sales that customers were abandoning for various reasons after starting the check-out process.[10]

In its search for competitive advantage, the firm needs to look beyond its own value chain, into the value chains of its suppliers, distributors and, ultimately, customers. More companies

Customer value delivery system—The system made up of the value chains of the company and its suppliers, distributors and ultimately customers, who work together to deliver value to customers.

today are 'partnering' with the other members of the supply chain to improve the performance of the **customer value delivery system**. For example:

> Online Music Recognition and Searching (OMRS) is a new service that will help record stores find what people want. Many customers enter stores with a snippet of a tune in their mind and depend upon the store's staff to recognise a few lyrics or a half-remembered tune. Unfortunately, few people in record stores have the archivist's memory of the enthusiasts running the record store in Nick Hornby's *Hi-Fidelity*. OMRS overcomes the problem. Customers can hum a part of a tune that is mathematically analysed and compared with a database of recordings. The result: the customer gets the music they want, the record store makes the sale and OMRS gets a reward for their services.[11]

As companies struggle to become more competitive, they are turning, ironically, to greater cooperation. Companies used to view their suppliers and distributors as cost centres and, in some cases, as adversaries. Today, however, they are selecting partners carefully and working out mutually profitable strategies. Increasingly in today's marketplace, competition no longer takes place between individual competitors. Rather, it takes place between the entire value delivery systems created by these competitors.

Therefore, marketing can no longer be thought of as only a selling department. That view of marketing would give it responsibility only for formulating a promotion-oriented marketing mix, without much to say about product features, costs and other important elements. Under the new view, marketing is responsible for *designing and managing a superior value delivery system to reach target customer segments*. Today's marketing managers must think not only about selling today's products, but also about how to stimulate the development of improved products, how to work actively with other departments in managing core business processes and how to build better external partnerships.

Total quality management

Quality—The totality of features and characteristics of a product or service that bear on its ability to satisfy stated or implied needs.

Six Sigma—A set of practices to systematically improve processes by eliminating defects.

Defects—Non-conformity of a product or service to its specifications.

Customer satisfaction and company profitability are linked closely to product and service quality delivered through the whole value chain. Higher levels of quality result in greater customer satisfaction, while at the same time supporting higher prices and often lower costs. Therefore, *quality improvement programmes* normally increase profitability. The Profit Impact of Marketing Strategies studies show similarly high correlation between relative product quality and profitability for Europe and the US (see Figure 8.3).

The task of improving product and service quality should be a company's top priority. Most customers will no longer tolerate poor or average quality. Companies today have no choice but to adopt total quality management if they want to stay in the race, let alone be profitable. **Quality** has been variously defined as 'fitness for use', 'conformance to requirements' and 'freedom from variation'. The American Society for Quality Control defines quality as the totality of features and characteristics of a product or service that bear on its ability to satisfy stated or implied needs. This is a customer-centred definition of quality. It suggests that a company has 'delivered quality' whenever its product and service meets or exceeds customers' needs, requirements and expectations. **Six Sigma** is a name most closely associated with the practice of quality management. Originally developed by Motorola, Six Sigma is a set of practices to systematically improve processes by eliminating **defects** – non-conformity of a product or service to its specifications.[12]

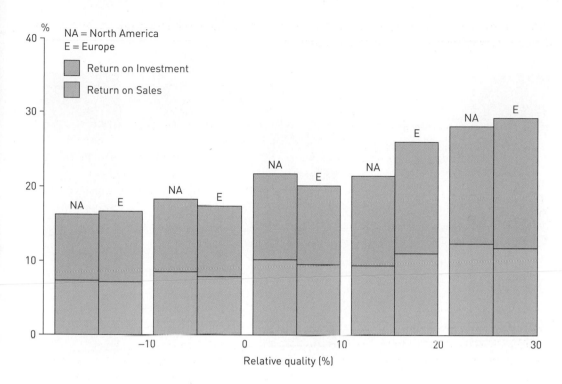

Figure 8.3 Relative quality boosts rate of return

SOURCE: Bob Luchs, 'Quality as a strategic weapon: measuring relative quality, value and market differentiation', *European Business Journal*, **2**, 4 (1990), p. 39.

" Companies today have no choice but to adopt total quality management if they want to stay in the race. "

It is important to distinguish between performance quality and conformance quality. *Performance quality* refers to the *level* at which a product performs its functions. Compare Smart Car and Lexus, Toyota's luxury brand. A Lexus provides higher performance quality than a Smart Car: it has a smoother ride, handles better and lasts longer. It is more expensive and sells to a market with higher means and requirements. *Conformance quality* refers to *freedom* from defects and the *consistency* with which a product delivers a specified level of performance. Both Lexus and Smart have exceptional reliability records and could offer equivalent conformance quality to their respective markets, since each consistently delivers what its market expects. A €100,000 car that meets all of its requirements is a quality car; so is a €10,000 car that meets all of its requirements. However, if the Lexus handles badly or if the Smart Car gives poor fuel efficiency, then both cars fail to deliver quality, and customer satisfaction suffers accordingly.

In the European Foundation for Quality Management's excellence model (Figure 8.4) marketing shares the responsibility for striving for the highest quality of a company, product or service. Marketing's commitment to the whole process needs to be particularly strong because of the central role of customer satisfaction to both marketing and **total quality management (TQM)**. Within a quality-centred company, marketing management has two types of responsibility. First, marketing management participates in formulating the *strategies and policies* that direct *resources* and strive for quality excellence. Secondly, marketing has to deliver marketing quality alongside product quality. It must perform each marketing activity to consistently high standards: marketing research, sales training, advertising, customer services and others. Much damage can be done to customer satisfaction with an excellent product if it is oversold or is 'supported' by advertising that builds unrealistic expectations.

Within quality programmes, marketing has several roles. Firstly, it has responsibility for correctly identifying customers' needs and wants, and for communicating them correctly to aid product design and to schedule production. Secondly, marketing has to ensure that customers' orders are filled correctly and on time, and must check to see that customers receive proper

Total quality management (TQM)—Programmes designed to constantly improve the quality of products, services and marketing processes.

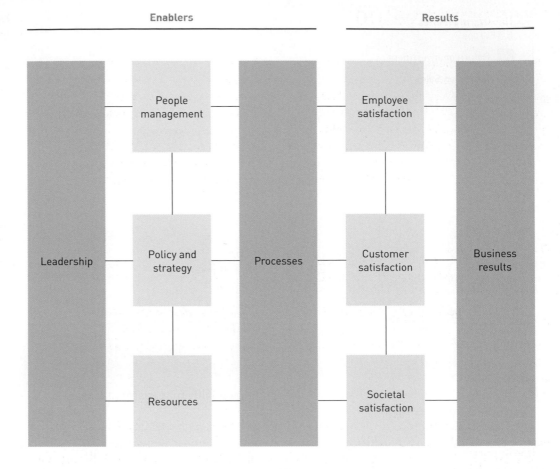

Figure 8.4 The European Foundation for Quality Management's model of business excellence

instruction, training and technical assistance in the use of their product. Thirdly, marketers must stay in touch with customers after the sale, to make sure that they remain satisfied. Finally, marketers must gather and convey customers' ideas for product and service improvement back to the company.

TQM has played an important role in educating businesses that quality is more than products and services being well produced, but is about what marketing has been saying all the time: *customer satisfaction*. At the same time, TQM extends marketing's view to realise that the acquisition, retention and satisfaction of good employees is central to the acquisition, retention and satisfaction of customers.

> If you have a complaint on a Swedish operator's Stena Ferry, employees are allowed to spend up to €1,500 to solve the problem for you – without having to obtain management approval. Stena credits this 'satisfaction strategy' developed on one of its crossings with boosting its market share. It has now been extended to all Stena routes.[13]

Total quality is the key to creating customer value and satisfaction. Total quality is everyone's job, just as marketing is everyone's job. Marketers must spend time and effort not only to improve external marketing, but also to improve internal marketing. Marketers must be the customer's watchdog or guardian, complaining loudly for the customer when the product or the service is not right. Marketers must constantly uphold the standard of 'giving the customer the best solution'.

Customer value

There is no limit to how much a company could spend to improve quality, or in other marketing efforts, to obtain and retain customers. This raises the critical question: how much is a customer worth? Companies are increasingly realising that the answer is a great deal. Internet companies are willing to pay a high price for prospective customers because they hope to turn them into *profitable customers*. We define a **profitable customer** as a person, household or company whose revenues over time exceed, by an acceptable amount, the company's costs of attracting, selling and servicing that customer. Note that the definition emphasises lifetime revenues and costs, not profit from a single transaction. Here are some dramatic illustrations of customer lifetime value:

Profitable customer— A person, household or company whose revenues over time exceed, by an acceptable amount, the company's costs of attracting, selling and servicing that customer.

> Tom Peters, noted author of several books on managerial excellence, runs a business that spends $1,500 a month on Federal Express service. His company spends this amount 12 months a year and expects to remain in business for at least another 10 years. Therefore, he expects to spend more than $180,000 on future Federal Express service. If Federal Express makes a 10 per cent profit margin, Peters' lifetime business will contribute $18,000 to Federal Express's profits. Federal Express risks all of this profit if Peters receives poor service from a Federal Express driver or if a competitor offers better service.

Few companies actively measure individual customer value and profitability. For example, banks claim that this is hard to do because customers use different banking services and transactions are logged in different departments. However, banks that have managed to link customer transactions and measure customer profitability have been appalled by how many unprofitable customers they find. Some banks report losing money on over 45 per cent of their retail customers. It is not surprising that many banks now charge fees for services that they once supplied free.

Customer retention

In the past, many companies took their customers for granted. Customers often did not have many alternative suppliers, or the other suppliers were just as poor in quality and service, or the market was growing so fast that the company did not worry about fully satisfying its customers. A company could lose 100 customers a week, but gain another 100 customers and consider its sales to be satisfactory. Such a company, operating on a 'leaky bucket' theory of business, believes that there will always be enough customers to replace the defecting ones. However, this high *customer churn* involves higher costs than if a company retained all 100 customers and acquired no new ones.

Companies must pay close attention to their customer defection rate and undertake steps to reduce it. First, the company must define and measure its retention rate. For a magazine, it would be the renewal rate; for a consumer packaged-goods firm, it would be the repurchase rate. Next, the company must identify the causes of customer defection and determine which of these can be reduced or eliminated. Not much can be done about customers who leave the region or about business customers who go out of business. But much can be done about customers who leave because of shoddy products, poor service or prices that are too high. The company needs to prepare a frequency distribution showing the percentage of customers who defect for different reasons.

A satisfaction study can show how a company has been misplacing its effort.

> A satisfaction benchmarking study for a restaurant showed that customers rated highly the restaurant's *décor* and the *size of the portions* served. However, the customers did not rate these two criteria as important. In contrast customers thought that the *quality of food* and *cleanliness of toilets* were very important but dimensions on which the restaurant performed poorly. On other dimensions that the customers thought important, the restaurant did fine: *overall cleanliness*, *speed of service* and *helpfulness of staff*. The benchmarking study clearly showed how the restaurant could improve customer satisfaction and, maybe, cut costs by reducing portions.

It is well known in service industries, where de-skilled McJobs abound, that employee satisfaction and retention precede customer satisfaction and retention. The relationship is also strong in rapid growth industries where the poaching of staff drives up wages and in many markets where making sales depends on the continuity of long-term relationships with key accounts. The SAS Institute, the world's largest software company, sees a close relationship between its performance and labour turnover. Its employee-oriented management keeps annual labour turnover at 4 per cent compared with an industry average of 20 per cent. SAS's methods go beyond the €65,000 of M&Ms it doles out to its 7,500 employees each year. The company keeps working hours down, has free healthcare on 'campus', plus gyms, tennis courts, theatres and other benefits. Employees sing the praises of the company and keep customers well satisfied – 98 per cent of them renew their licences on SAS software each year![14]

Customers incur switching costs when they change suppliers. Switching costs are beyond the purchase price and include learning how to use a new product or service, the time selecting a new supplier and the difficulty of operating the new product alongside products already owned. This 'self-incompatibility' or 'weak lock-in' is very common and faced by many consumers when they switch banks, Internet service providers, Microsoft versions, from vinyl or cassette to CDs, or from VCR to DVD. Despite the cost, customers do switch when a better offer comes along. There is little evidence of any 'strong lock-in' where incompatibility gives a leading company a lasting advantage. Having the best product or service is more important than being the first to market, or having a large customer base. Customers accept 'self-incompatibility' and switch when better offers come along.[15]

> " There is little evidence of any 'strong lock-in' where incompatibility gives a leading company a lasting advantage. "

Customer defections— The loss of customers to alternative suppliers of a similar or the same service.

By reducing **customer defections** by only 5 per cent, companies can improve profits by anywhere from 25 to 100 per cent. Unfortunately, classic marketing theory and practice centre on the art of attracting new customers rather than retaining existing ones. The emphasis has been on creating *transactions* rather than *relationships*. Discussion has focused on *pre-sale activity* and *sale activity* rather than on *post-sale activity*. Today, however, more companies recognise the importance of retaining current customers by forming relationships with them. The streaming of customer defections, or churn, is particularly important in new businesses, such as cable and satellite TV services and mobile phones where the income of a business depends on a continuous stream of earnings and where new subscribers are 'bought' with free mobile phones or set-top boxes.[16]

High churn is a fact of life for online gambling companies. In the industry high-spending advertising and the use of third-party affiliates on fixed fees gets new gamblers to sign up, but most potential gamblers visit sites once, never to return. PartyGaming.com has a modest ambition to enhance 'stickability' – it hopes that through bonuses, tournaments and loyalty schemes it can entice back at least one in every four people who visit its sites. But these incentives are secondary to the strength of the company's core product – an exciting variety of tournaments, bigger cash prizes and, in turn, more customers.[17]

New technology is giving companies opportunities to stop some churn by keeping their products up to date using software updates. Real Marketing 8.2 introduces these M2M (machine to machine) communications which mean that products or services morph to provide more or better service long after a product is purchased.

Relationship marketing

Relationship marketing involves creating, maintaining and enhancing strong relationships with customers and other stakeholders. Increasingly, marketing is moving away from a focus on individual transactions and towards a focus on building value-laden relationships and marketing networks. Relationship marketing is oriented more towards the long term. The goal is to deliver long-term value to customers and the measure of success is long-term customer satisfaction. Relationship marketing requires that all of the company's departments work together with marketing as a team to serve the customer. It involves building relationships at many levels – economic, social, technical and legal – resulting in high customer loyalty.

> **Relationship marketing—** The process of creating, maintaining and enhancing strong, value-laden relationships with customers and other stakeholders.

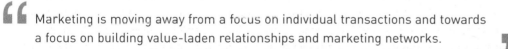

" Marketing is moving away from a focus on individual transactions and towards a focus on building value-laden relationships and marketing networks. "

We can distinguish five different levels or relationships that can be formed with customers who have purchased a company's product, such as a car or a piece of equipment:

- *Basic.* The company salesperson sells the product, but does not follow up in any way.
- *Reactive.* The salesperson sells the product and encourages the customer to call whenever he or she has any questions or problems.
- *Accountable.* The salesperson phones the customer a short time after the sale to check whether the product is meeting the customer's expectations. The salesperson also solicits from the customer any product improvement suggestions and any specific disappointments. This information helps the company continuously to improve its offering.
- *Proactive.* The salesperson or others in the company phone the customer from time to time with suggestions about improved product use or helpful new products.
- *Partnership.* The company works continuously with the customer and with other customers to discover ways to deliver better value.

8.2

real marketing

M2M marketing and morphing products

Once there was a time when, once owned, products stayed as they were. That is no more. Internet users will be used to the 'updates available' message, and their system even may be updated automatically in the case of antivirus software. Every so often, users of iTunes find out that there is a new version available that not only changes iTunes but sometimes reprogrammes the iPod. This is the beginning of the world of M2M (machine to machine) marketing.

When products were mainly mechanical, or even hard-wired electronics, their relative performance started declining as soon as they were bought. Faster than products were wearing out, new and improved variants were arriving and competitors were inventing new wheezes. This is not necessarily planned obsolescence but is a result of the inevitable march of technology, or of companies responding to environmental change. For example, Mercedes is not known for cosmetic facelifts to its products, but compare a new diesel-powered Mercedes with one produced only a few years ago and the new model is not only more responsive to the accelerator but also more fuel efficient. The reason? Diesel engine technology has improved – a new engine is in use. Hard luck for the 2005 Mercedes owner – to get the new engine they would have to buy a new car. But that is not true for the whole 2005 Mercedes. The SatNav system is electronic, so can change. Slip in a new CD and the car knows the whereabouts of new motorways or changed traffic systems all across the country or even the continent.

M2M is crucial in subscription-based services, such as mobile phones, cable or satellite TV channels, where new services may induce a subscriber to switch to obtain the latest service.

A father was incensed when he found his kids switching channels while his inappropriately named Personal Video Recorder (PVR) was downloading a film he wanted to watch. He had missed the end of two Inspector Morse episodes that way, and he was not sure he understood them without the last few minutes. Unfazed by their dad's tirade, the children responded, 'Don't worry, you can record *two* things at once now, and still watch another channel.' Sky+ had used M2M communications to update the machine, beaming down signals late at night to make the set-top box what it was not.

M2M has enabled Sky+ to respond to environmental and competitive changes. Faced with the criticism that most households are spewing out greenhouse gases

...8.2

because they keep electronic kit on standby, Sky+ has 'learned' to *automatically* go onto standby *if you do not use the box between 11 pm and 4 am.*

With new competitors entering the market with video-on-demand using TV, PC or mobile phones, users of Sky+ and Sky HD TV set-top boxes can change them to accept Sky Anytime – 'a new way to enjoy Sky TV . . . choose from a selection of top movies or TV entertainment . . . and watch them when you want.' The extra cost? Nothing.

Threatened with the prospect of people switching from BlackBerry to Palm, Microsoft, Apple or other suppliers if the company loses an upcoming court case that could stop their handsets getting access to the Internet, Research in Motions (RIM), makers of the BlackBerry, have developed a 'multi-mode edition' software that gets round the patents and that RIM could activate remotely in the event of an injunction. Using M2M technology, RIM has overcome the potentially disastrous consequences of a ruling by a judge in Richmond, Virginia.

It does not stop there. Upmarket washing machines now come with update facilities in case new detergents that work at lower temperatures or new fabrics that need a different treatment are launched during their expected lifetime.

SOURCES: Adapted from Chris Nuttallin, 'RIM software update ready ahead of hearing', *Financial Times* (10 February 2006); *Belfast Telegraph*, 'Software update blamed for Skype disruption' (20 August 2007); http://anytime.sky.com (20 August 2007).

Figure 8.5 shows that a company's relationship marketing strategy will depend on how many customers it has and their profitability. For example, companies with many low-margin customers will practise *basic* marketing. Thus Heineken will not phone all of its drinkers to express its appreciation for their business. At best, Heineken will be reactive by setting up a customer information service. At the other extreme, in markets with few customers and high margins, most sellers will move towards partnership marketing. In exploring the opportunities for the very large A380 commercial transport aircraft, Airbus Industries will work closely with the aero-engine manufacturers as well as with Lufthansa, Air France, Emirates and Singapore Airlines, who have shown interest in buying the aircraft. What specific marketing tools can a company use to develop stronger customer bonding and satisfaction? It can offer any of three customer value-building approaches:

- *Financial benefits* to the customer relationship. For example, airlines offer frequent-flyer programmes, hotels give room upgrades to their frequent guests, and supermarkets give patronage refunds. Although these reward programmes and other financial incentives build customer preference, they can be easily imitated by competitors and thus may fail to differentiate the company's offer permanently.

- *Social benefits* as well as financial benefits. Here company personnel work to increase their social bonds with customers by learning individual customers' needs and wants, and then individualising and personalising their products and services.

Figure 8.5 Relationship levels as a function of profit margin and number of customers

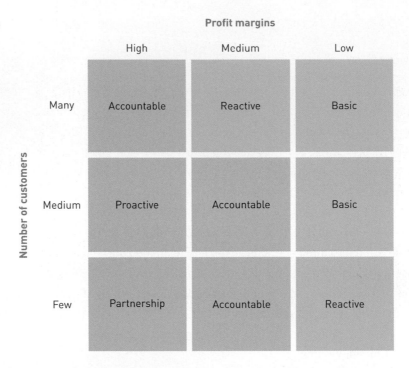

- *Structural ties* as well as financial and social benefits. For example, a business marketer might supply customers with special equipment or computer linkages that help them manage their orders, payroll or inventory. For example, Six Sigma provides access to free software to its users.

The main steps in establishing a relationship-marketing programme in a company are as follows.

- *Identify the key customers meriting relationship management.* Choose the largest or best customers and designate them for relationship management. Other customers can be added that show exceptional growth or pioneer new industry developments.

- *Assign a skilled relationship manager to each key customer.* The salesperson currently servicing the customer should receive training in relationship management or be replaced by someone more skilled in relationship management. The relationship manager should have characteristics that match or appeal to the customer.

- *Develop a clear job description for relationship managers.* Describe their reporting relationships, objectives, responsibilities and evaluation criteria. Make the relationship manager the focal point for all dealings with and about the client. Give each relationship manager only one or a few relationships to manage.

- *Have each relationship manager develop annual and long-range customer relationship plans.* These plans should state objectives, strategies, specific actions and required resources.

- *Appoint an overall manager to supervise the relationship managers.* This person will develop job descriptions, evaluation criteria and resource support to increase relationship manager effectiveness.

Volvo's Oncore and Care programmes recognise that the company has multiple relationships with its customers and ensure systematic approaches and consistent treatment across them:[18]

	Corporate clients	Drivers (corporate clients' employees)	Dealers
Volvo	Relationships govern Volvo's inclusion on entitlement list (the make of employee's company cars)	Volvo maintains a direct marketing relationship with all drivers of its cars	Volvo works hard with all its dealer network to maintain and improve its standards
Dealers	Local dealers usually deliver and service the cars	Dealers are the front line of meeting the drivers' expectations	
Drivers	Agreements reached affect which models are available to clients' employees		

When it has properly implemented relationship management, the organisation begins to focus on managing its customers as well as its products. At the same time, although many companies are moving strongly towards relationship marketing, it is not effective in all situations. Not all relationships are profitable or wanted, as James Murdoch, chief executive of BSkyB, explains:

> The company has been weeding its customer base of unprofitable subscribers who merely chased its cheapest deals. 'It's customers who have been going from offer to offer and when one expires and they call up and say "What can you give me?" and we say "You can have broadband and telephony" and they say "No, I just want a deal on TV", we say "We just don't do that any more".'[19]

Selective relationship management

Few firms today still practise true mass marketing – selling in a standardised way to any customer who comes along. Like James Murdoch of BSkyB, most marketers realise that they do not want relationships with every customer. Instead, companies are now targeting fewer, more profitable customers. Called *selective relationship management*, many companies now use customer profitability analysis to weed out losing customers and to target winning ones for pampering. Once they identify profitable customers, firms can create attractive offers and special handling to capture these customers and earn their loyalty.

Relating with more carefully selected customers

But what should the company do with unprofitable customers? If it can't turn them into profitable ones, it may even want to 'fire' customers who are too unreasonable or who cost more to serve than they are worth. For example, banks now routinely assess customer profitability based on such factors as an account's average balances, account activity, services usage, branch visits and other variables. For most banks, profitable customers with large balances are pampered with premium services, whereas unprofitable, low-balance ones get the cold shoulder.

ING Direct, a subsidiary of ING in Amsterdam, selects accounts differently. It seeks relationships with customers who don't need or want expensive pampering while firing those who do.[20] With a limited range of products including savings accounts, certificates of deposits (CDs) and home equity loans, the bank keeps things basic. Yet its profits soared more than 200 per cent just last year. ING's secret? Selective relationship management. The bank tempts low-maintenance customers with high interest rates. Then, to offset that kindness, the bank does 75 per cent of its transactions online and offers bare-bones service. ING routinely dismisses overly demanding customers. By firing clients who are too time consuming, the company has driven its cost per account to 30% of the industry average. CEO Arkadi Kuhlmann explains: 'We need to keep expenses down, which doesn't work when customers want a lot of [hand-holding]. If the average customer phone call costs us €7 and the average account revenue is €16 per month, all it takes is 100,000 misbehaving customers for costs to go through the roof. So when a customer calls too many times or wants too many exceptions to the rule, our sales associate can basically say: Look, this doesn't fit you. You need to go back to your community bank and get the kind of contact you're comfortable with . . . . It's all about finding customers who are comfortable with a self-serve business; we try to get you in and out fast. While this makes for some unhappy customers, [those are the] ones you want out the door anyway.'

Relating for the long term

Just as companies are being more selective about which customers they choose to serve, they are serving chosen customers in a deeper, more lasting way. Today's companies are going beyond designing strategies to *attract* new customers and create *transactions* with them. They are using customer relationship management to *retain* current customers and build profitable, long-term *relationships* with them. The new view is that marketing is the science and art of finding, retaining *and* growing profitable customers.

Why the new emphasis on retaining and growing customers? In the past, growing markets and an upbeat economy meant a plentiful supply of new customers. However, companies today face some new marketing realities. Changing demographics, more sophisticated competitors, and overcapacity in many industries mean that there are fewer customers to go around. Many companies are now fighting for shares of flat or fading markets.

As a result, the costs of attracting new consumers are rising. In fact, on average, it can cost 5 to 10 times as much to attract a new customer as it does to keep a current customer satisfied. For example, one recent study found that it costs a financial services institution €200 to acquire a new customer but only a little over €40 to keep one. Given these new realities, companies now go all out to keep profitable customers.[21]

> On average, it can cost 5 to 10 times as much to attract a new customer as it does to keep a current customer satisfied.

Relating directly

Beyond connecting more deeply with their customers, many companies are also connecting more *directly*. In fact, direct marketing is booming. Consumers can now buy virtually any product without going to a store – by telephone, mail-order catalogues, kiosks and online. Business purchasing agents routinely shop on the Web for items ranging from standard office supplies to high-priced, high-tech computer equipment.

Some companies, such as Dell, Direct Line Insurance and Amazon, sell *only* via direct channels. Others are 'bricks and clicks', using direct connections to supplement their other communications and distribution channels. For example, Sony sells PlayStation consoles and game cartridges through retailers, supported by a huge mass-media advertising budget. However, Sony also uses its www.PlayStation.com website to build relationships with game players of all ages. The site offers information about the latest games, news about events and promotions, game guides and support, and even online forums in which game players can swap tips and stories. Yet others, including Dixon's, are quitting the High Street to concentrate on becoming an online discount electrical store.

Some marketers have hailed direct marketing as the 'marketing model of the next century'. They envision a day when all buying and selling will involve direct connections between companies and their customers. Whatever the future, the proportion of direct sales continues to increase. With many high value items, such as holidays, hotels, car rentals, financial services and flights, becoming predominantly direct sales, it will be little time before close on half of trade is direct. We will take a closer look at the world of direct marketing in Chapter 18.

Customer relationship management

Companies are awash with information about their customers. Smart companies capture information at every possible customer *touch point*. These touch points include customer purchases, sales force contacts, service and support calls, website visits, satisfaction surveys, credit and payment interactions, market research studies – every contact between the customer and the company.

The trouble is that this information is usually scattered widely across the organisation. It is buried deep in the separate databases, plans and records of many different company functions and departments. To overcome such problems, many companies use customer relationship management (CRM) to manage detailed information about individual customers and carefully manage customer touch points. In recent years, there has been an explosion in the number of companies using CRM. One research firm found that 97 per cent of businesses plan to boost spending on CRM technology within the next two years.[22]

CRM is implemented through the use of sophisticated software and analytical tools that integrate customer information from all sources, analyse it in depth, and apply the results to build stronger customer relationships. CRM integrates everything that a company's sales, service and marketing teams know about individual customers to provide a 360-degree view of the customer relationship. It pulls together, analyses and provides easy access to customer information from all of the various touch points. Companies use CRM analysis to assess the value of individual customers, identify the best ones to target, and customise the company's products and interactions to each customer.

CRM analysts develop data warehouses and use sophisticated data mining techniques to unearth the riches hidden in customer data. A data warehouse is a company-wide electronic storehouse of customer information – a centralised database of finely detailed customer data that needs to be sifted through for gems. The purpose of a data warehouse is not to gather information – many companies have already amassed endless stores of information about their customers. Rather, the purpose is to allow managers to integrate the information the company already has. Then, once the data warehouse brings the data together for analysis, the company uses high-powered data mining techniques to sift through the mounds of data and dig out interesting relationships and findings about customers.

Customers are an investment.
Maximize your return.

PeopleSoft Customer Relationship Management lets you capitalize on every customer interaction across your enterprise.

Only PeopleSoft CRM is fast to implement, easy to use, and delivers smart business processes for managing your customer relationships. It integrates real-time information across your organization to help determine the most profitable ways to manage customers. Simply, PeopleSoft CRM turns every point of customer contact into a profit opportunity. Learn more by visiting us at www.peoplesoft.com/realtime or call 1-888-773-8277.

PeopleSoft® | **Customer Relationship Management**

© 2003 PeopleSoft, Inc. PeopleSoft is a registered trademark of PeopleSoft, Inc.

CRM is big business with many companies, such as PeopleSoft, offering to help 'capitalise on every customer interaction across your enterprise'.
SOURCE: People Soft UK & Ireland.

Companies can gain many benefits from customer relationship management. By understanding customers better, they can provide higher levels of customer service and develop deeper customer relationships. They can use CRM to pinpoint high-value customers, target them more effectively, cross-sell the company's products, and create offers tailored to specific customer requirements. Consider the following example:

Ping, the golf equipment manufacturer, has used CRM successfully for about two years. Its data warehouse contains customer-specific data about every golf club it has manufactured and sold for the past 15 years. The database, which includes grip size and special assembly instructions, helps Ping design and build golf clubs specifically for each of its customers and allows for easy replacement. If a golfer needs a new nine iron, for example, he can call in the serial number and Ping will ship an exact club to him within two days of receiving the order – a process that used to take two to three weeks. . . . This faster processing of data has given Ping a competitive edge in a market saturated with new products. 'We've been up; the golf market has been down,' says Steve Bostwick, Ping's marketing manager. Bostwick estimates the golf market to be down about 15 per cent, but he says Ping has experienced double-digit growth.[23]

CRM benefits do not come without cost or risk, not only in collecting the original customer data but also in maintaining and mining it. Worldwide, companies will spend an estimated €25bn to €50bn this year on CRM software alone from companies such as PeopleSoft, Siebel Systems, SAP, Oracle and SPSS. Yet more than half of all CRM efforts fail to meet their objectives. The most common cause of CRM failures is that companies mistakenly view CRM only as a technology and software solution. But technology alone cannot build profitable customer relationships. 'CRM is not a technology solution – you can't achieve . . . improved customer relationships by simply slapping in some software,' says a CRM expert. Instead, CRM is just one part of an effective overall *customer relationship strategy*. 'Focus on the R,' advises the expert. 'Remember, a relationship is what CRM is all about.'[24]

When it works, the benefits of CRM can far outweigh the costs and risks. Based on regular polls of its customers, Siebel Systems claims that customers using its CRM software report an average 16 per cent increase in revenues and 21 per cent increase in customer loyalty and staff efficiency. 'No question that companies are getting tremendous value out of this,' says a CRM consultant. 'Companies [are] looking for ways to bring disparate sources of customer information together, then get it to all the customer touch points.' The powerful new CRM techniques can unearth 'a wealth of information to target that customer, to hit their hot button.'[25]

When to use relationship marketing

Relationship marketing is not effective in all situations, although CRM systems are reducing the value threshold at which it becomes appropriate. Transaction marketing, which focuses on one sales transaction at a time, is more appropriate than relationship marketing for customers who have short time horizons and can switch from one supplier to another with little effort or investment. This situation often occurs in 'commodity' markets, such as steel, where various suppliers offer largely undifferentiated products. A customer buying steel can buy from any of several steel suppliers and choose the one offering the best terms on a purchase-by-purchase basis. The fact that one steel supplier works at developing a longer-term relationship with a buyer does not automatically earn it the next sale; its price and other terms still have to be competitive. Global e-procurement systems, like the motor industry's Covisint and aerospace's Exostar, where buyers flag their requirements on the Internet, are tightening profit margins and breaking down close relationships between buyers and suppliers. For example, by using Internet auctions and exchanges BAe Systems decreased its purchasing bill by 5 per cent and its number of suppliers from 14,000 to 2,000.[26]

In contrast, relationship marketing can pay off handsomely with customers that have long time horizons and high switching costs, such as buyers of office automation systems. It can also be part of an e-procurement system, such as Covisint, that will involve suppliers in new product development. When buying complex systems, buyers usually research competing suppliers carefully and choose one from whom they can expect state-of-the-art technology and good long-term service. Both the customer and the supplier invest a lot of money and time in building the relationship. The customer would find it costly and risky to switch to another supplier and the

Figure 8.6 Comparing customer relationship revenues with relationship costs

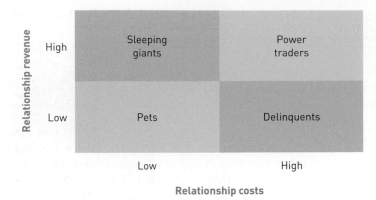

seller would find that losing this customer would be a considerable loss. Thus each seeks to develop a solid long-term working relationship with the other. It is with such customers that relationship marketing has the greatest pay-off.

In these situations, the 'in-supplier' and 'out-supplier' face very different challenges. The in-supplier tries to make switching difficult for the customer. It develops product systems that are incompatible with those of competing suppliers and installs its own ordering systems which simplify inventory management and delivery. It works to become the customer's indispensable partner. Out-suppliers, in contrast, try to make it easy and less costly to switch suppliers. They design product systems that are compatible with the customer's system, that are easy to install and learn, that save the customer a lot of money, and that promise to improve through time.

The appropriateness of transaction versus relationship marketing depends on the type of industry and the wishes of the particular customer. Some customers value a high-service supplier and will stay with that supplier for a long time. Other customers want to cut their costs and will switch suppliers readily to obtain lower costs.

Thus relationship marketing is not the best approach in all situations. For it to be worthwhile, relationship revenue needs to exceed relationship costs. Figure 8.6 suggests that some customers are very profitable *sleeping giants*, which generate significant revenue and are profitable but relatively undemanding. Much of the relationship marketing activity is taken up by the *power traders*, which provide significant revenue but are demanding. These are as profitable as the *pets*, which provide little revenue but have appropriately small relationship costs. Transaction marketing is probably adequate for these. The most difficult group is the *delinquents*, which provide little revenue but are demanding. What can a company do about these? One option is to shift the *delinquent* customers to products that are likely to be less difficult to operate or less complicated. Prepaid mobile phone services do this by providing contracts to less well-off customers who prepay for the phone's use. Banks' high charges on unnegotiated overdrafts are a way of doing this. If these actions cause the unprofitable customer to defect, so be it. In fact, the company might benefit by *encouraging* these unprofitable customers to switch to competition.

Partner relationship management

When it comes to creating customer value and building strong customer relationships, today's marketers know that they can't go it alone. They must work closely with a variety of marketing partners. In addition to being good at *customer relationship management*, marketers must also be good at partner relationship management. Major changes are occurring in how marketers partner with others inside and outside the company to jointly bring more value to customers. Through partner relationships, corporations can increase their profitability by changing the competitive environment. Governments realise this and therefore block deals that give companies

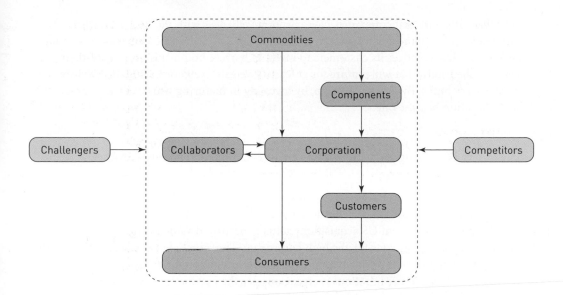

Figure 8.7 The 8 Cs competitive domain

too much marketing power. One case is the blocking of the proposed merger of American Airlines and British Airways, since the link would give them too much power at London's Heathrow airport.

The 8 Cs framework (Figure 8.7) shows how corporations can increase their marketing power through relationships. They can have links with the following:

- *Competitors.* This automatically increases a company's strength in the market and its buying power. Acquisitions and mergers between one-time competitors are always occurring as firms try to grow to face global competition. The names of many leading companies reflect past mergers: DaimlerChrysler, Vivendi Universal and GSK (GlaxoSmithKline) and Lloyds TSB (Trustee Savings Bank).

- *Challengers.* It is common for established companies to grow by acquiring small companies that challenge existing products or bring exciting new ideas. Hence the purchase of new-age products, such as Snapple or Ben & Jerry's ice-cream, by food giants, and Google's acquisition of YouTube and MySpace by News Corporation.[27]

- *Collaborators.* These can be outside the industry but add some marketing strength to an alliance. One such link-up is between McDonald's, Coca-Cola and Disney; another is between Sony and Ericsson Mobile Communications to provide mobile multimedia devices and phones.

- *Commodities.* Oil companies own major brands but most of their stock market valuation is based upon their oil reserves. When Royal Dutch/Shell revised their estimated reserves downward their share price immediately fell.

- *Components.* Many car companies own companies that supply them. Many firms have pulled away from the risk of too much vertical integration that compounds the risk of any downturn in sales. Once GM used to own the rubber plantations as a source of raw materials for the tyres they put on their automobiles. An increasing number of global companies, such as Nike, own the brand and little else. Their strength is in design and marketing where most value is added, and not in low value-added activities, such as manufacturing.

- *Customers.* Just as oil companies own their raw material supplier, the refiners also own the petrol stations that sell their branded fuel to consumers. Some luxury goods makers both own their stores and design, market and manufacture their products to keep control of the goods and their customers' experience.

● *Consumers.* It is rare that companies have corporate alliances with the final consumer, although there are some creative exceptions. Bruichladdich, an independent maker of Islay single malt whisky, entices its customers to invest in barrels, hogsheads or butts of their newly distilled spirit that will mature for at least 10 years (£2,295 or €3,400 for 500 litres in a fresh sherry butt!). By this mechanism, by investing in maturing whisky, the customer and the corporation become one.[28]

> ❝ Making an acquisition is easier than making it work. ❞

Big mergers grab headlines but making an acquisition is easier than making it work. Besides raising the wrath of regulatory bodies, most mergers fail. The Boston Consulting Group estimates that 64 per cent of recent US acquisitions actually destroyed value for the acquirer's shareholders. There are several reasons for the high failure rate. These include technical issues, like the difficulty of blending the joint company's information technology, but the major problem is the clash of cultures when two organisations merge. Consider the inevitable contrast between Vivendi's base in French utilities and Universal, their Hollywood film studio. This proves a particular problem with cross-border mergers, such as with Daimler and Chrysler, although the clash can be between industrial sectors, as with Time Warner and AOL. The broad problem is that the excitement of mergers and acquisitions often distracts managers from running their existing businesses and that there are few top managers with the skills or interest to manage the merger to success.

Reviewing the concepts

Today's customers face a growing range of choices in the products and services they can buy. They base their choices on their perceptions of *quality*, *value* and *service*. Companies need to understand the determinants of *customer value* and *satisfaction*. *Customer delivered value* is the difference between *total customer value* and *total customer cost*. Customers will normally choose the offer that maximises their delivered value.

1. Define *customer value* and discuss its importance in creating and measuring customer satisfaction

Customer value is the difference between total customer value and total customer cost of a marketing offer – 'profit' to the customer. It is important to marketers because customers value-maximise, within the bounds of search costs and limited knowledge, mobility and income. Consumers form judgements about the value of marketing offers and make their buying decisions based upon these expectations based on the customer's past buying experiences, the opinions of friends and associates, and marketer and competitor information and promises.

Customer satisfaction with a purchase depends upon the product's performance relative to those expectations. If a purchase meets or exceeds expectations, customers are more likely to rebuy and communicate favourably about the product. Today's winning companies continually track their customers' expectations, perceived company performance and customer satisfaction, since any decline will influence future sales and profits.

2. Discuss the concepts of *value chains* and *value delivery systems* and explain how companies go about producing and delivering customer value

The value chain breaks the firm into nine value-creating activities in an effort to understand the behaviour of costs in the specific business and the potential sources of competitive differentiation. The nine value-creating activities include five primary activities and four support activities. Customer satisfaction also depends upon all parts of the value chain. Customer value can be added through the primary activities: inbound logistics, manufacturing or processing operations, outbound logistics, marketing and sales, or after-sales service. All of the primary activities can be helped to provide customer value through the support activities: procurement, technology development, human resource management or the firm's infrastructure.

3. Define *quality* and explain the importance of total quality marketing in building profitable relationships with customers

Quality is the totality of features and characteristics of a product or service that bear on its ability to satisfy stated or implied needs. Performance quality refers to the *level* at which a product performs its functions, while conformance quality refers to freedom from defects and the *consistency* with which a product delivers a specified level of performance. Since most customers no longer tolerate poor or average quality, companies have to adopt total quality management if they want to survive or thrive. Total quality is the key to creating the customer value and satisfaction that is the bedrock of achieving a customer's favourable attitude towards a product or service and their willingness to form a profitable relationship with a company.

4. Explain the importance of retaining current customers as well as attracting new ones

Classic marketing theory and practice centre on the art of attracting new customers rather than retaining existing ones. However, the cost of attracting new customers is much higher than the expenditure that is necessary to prevent existing customers defecting. A customer lifetime value is the amount by which revenues from a given customer over time will exceed the company's costs of attracting, selling and servicing that customer. Although each transaction may be small, the lifetime value of a customer is a good indicator of the true value of an existing customer.

5. Understand the role and operation of customer relationship marketing and CRM

Customer relationship marketing provides the key to retaining customers and involves building financial and social benefits as well as structural ties to customers. Customer relationship marketing systems integrate strategy, IT and relationship marketing to deliver value to customers and treat them individually. Companies must decide the level at which they want to build relationships with different market segments and individual customers, from such levels as basic, reactive, accountable and proactive to full partnership.

Customer relationship management (CRM) systems consists of software and analytical tools that integrate customer information from all sources, analyse it in depth, and apply the results to build stronger customer relationships. CRM systems integrate everything that a company's sales, service and marketing teams know about individual customers to provide a 360-degree view of the customer relationship. Companies use CRM analysis to assess the value of individual customers, identify the best ones to target, and customise the company's products and interactions to each customer.

Discussing the concepts

1. Describe a situation in which you became a 'lost customer'. Did you drop the purchase because of poor product quality, poor service quality or both? What should the firm do to 'recapture' lost customers?

2. Recall a purchase experience in which the sales assistant or some other representative of an organisation went beyond the normal effort and 'gave his/her all' to produce the utmost in service quality. What impact did the noticeable effort have on the purchase outcome?

3. Total quality management is an important approach to providing customer satisfaction and company profits. How might total quality be managed for the following product and service offerings: (a) a packaged food product; (b) a restaurant meal; (c) a public utility (such as power supply or garbage collection); (d) a family holiday; (e) a university education?

4. Recall incidents when you have purchased, or tried to purchase, similar items through the Internet, direct marketing call centres or bricks-and-mortar stores. How does the meaning of service quality differ across the three channels and how did they compare in operation?

5. Thinking of the operation of a not-for-profit organisation, such as a charity, propose some ways in which relationship marketing could help them collect money from donors.

Applying the concepts

1. Write a letter of complaint to a firm about one of its products or services. What was the firm's response? Did you receive a refund or replacement product, a response letter or no reply at all? How does the type of response affect your attitude towards the company?

2. Determine two or three relatively obscure subjects on which you could need to purchase a book, for example house prices, the history of puppetry or Portuguese cooking. Then visit several Web book retailers, either bricks-and-clicks or clicks only, and compare the quality of their electronic service and the mechanisms they use to build relationships (sites could include amazon.com, amazon.co.uk, bol.com, waterstones.com). Compare the best with a search at a local bricks-and-mortar bookstore.

Web resources

For additional classic case studies and Internet exercises, visit **www. pearsoned.co.uk/ kotler**

References

1. Alan Cane, 'IT nears its limits on customer satisfaction', FT.com (13 June 2007).

2. Shoshana Zuboff and James Maxim's influential book *The Support Economy: Why corporations are failing individuals and the next episode of capitalism* (London: Allen Lane, 2003) is reviewed in 'Face value: Giving people what they want', *The Economist* (10 May 2003), p. 70.

3. This and other examples of how banks have rediscovered being nice to customers are in 'Banking: Love me', *The Economist* (23 February 2002), p. 34, and Peter Thal Larsen, 'HSBC to link bonuses to customer satisfaction', *Financial Times* (15 June 2007).

4. Alastair Jamieson, 'We can't get no satisfaction – so why not complain more?', *The Scotsman* (20 August 2007).

5. 'Hard-edged marketing', Agenda Paper on The Chartered Institute of Marketing's website www.cim.co.uk (2003); Emiko Terazono, 'Always on the outside looking in', FT.com (4 August 2003).

6. www.which.net.

7. Armand V. Feigenbaum, 'A challenge creeping up', *Financial Times* (10 January 2001), p. 14.

8. Anya Sostek, 'Customer satisfaction goes flat; report shows e-business numbers slip', *Pittsburgh Post-Gazette* (14 August 2007).

9. Michael E. Porter, *Competitive Advantage: Creating and sustaining superior performance* (New York: Free Press, 1985) and 'What is strategy?', *Harvard Business Review* (November–December 1996), pp. 61–78. Also see David Walters, 'Implementing value strategy through the value chain', *Management Decision*, **38**, 3 (2000), pp. 160–78; Kim B. Clark *et al.*, *Harvard Business School on Managing the Value Chain* (Boston, MA: Harvard Business School Press, 2000); 'Buyer value and the value chain', *Business Owner* (September–October 2003), p. 1; and 'The value chain', accessed at www.quickmba.com/strategy/value-chain/, July 2006.

10. Jonathan Birchall, 'One click gets you in touch with an expert', *Financial Times* (20 March 2007).

11. The enthusiasts in Nick Hornby's book *Hi-Fidelity* (London: Indigo, 1995) and film *Hi-Fidelity* (2000), besides having great knowledge of music, also provide examples of atrocious customer service. Also see 'Music-recognition software: om tiddly om pom', *The Economist* (19 October 2002), p. 107; and the OMRS website www.omras2.com/cgi-sys/cgiwrap/musicstr/view/Main/WebHome.

12. John Maxey, David Rowlands, Michael L. George and Malcolm Upton, *The Lean Six Sigma Pocket Toolbook: A quick reference guide to 70 tools for improving quality and speed* (New York: McGraw-Hill, 2005). For a published application, see 'Adventures in Six Sigma: How the problem-solving technique helped Xerox', *Financial Times* (23 September 2005).

13. Tom Lester, 'The cost of not caring for your customers', *Financial Times* (30 January 2006). Also see A.-L. Ackfeldt and V.W. Wong, 'The antecedents of prosocial service behaviours: An empirical investigation', *Services Industries Journal*, **26**, 7 (2006), pp. 727–45.

14. Chartered Institute of Marketing, 'Customer retention', in *Marketing Means Business* (Moor Hall, Cookham, Berks: Chartered Institute of Marketing, 1999), pp. 84–8; Fiona Harvey, 'Of chocolates and profit sharing', *Financial Times* (26 July 2000), p. 13; 'Workers of the world, stop moaning', *The Guardian* (16 August 2000); Malcolm McDonald, 'Up close and personal', *Marketing Business* (September 1998), pp. 52–5.

15. Stan Liebowitz, *Rethinking the Network Economy* (AMACOM, 2002); 'Economic focus: first will be last', *The Economist* (28 September 2002), p. 101.

16. Stephanie Kirchgaessner and Louisa Hearn, 'Telewest suffers from customer defections', FT.com, 31 July 2003; Richard Wray, 'Sky keeps churning in its search for 10 million bigger spenders: Defections limit net growth to 183,000 customers, Murdoch says', *The Guardian* (1 February 2007); Matt Moore, 'Deutsche Telekom's 2nd quarter profit falls 40 percent as fixed-line exodus continues', *AP Worldstream* (9 August 2007).

17. Roger Blitz, '"Stickability" ambition to combat high churn levels', *Financial Times* (3 May 2007).

18. Peter Bartram, 'Engineering for growth', *Marketing Business* (February 2000), pp. 24–7.

19. Richard Wray, 'Virgin Media will be no threat', *The Guardian* (1 February 2007).

20. Adapted from information found in Elizabeth Esfahani, 'How to get tough with bad customers', *Business 2.0* (October 2004), p. 52. Also see Amey Stone, 'Bare bones, plump profits', *Business Week* (14 March 2005), p. 88; and Steve Bergsman, 'The Orange Mortgage', *Mortgage Banking* (June 2006), pp. 48–53.

21. See Phillip E. Pfeifer, 'The optimal ratio of acquisition and retention costs', *Journal of Targeting* (February 2005), pp. 179–88; and Bruce Clapp, 'Common misconceptions about retention programs', *Bank Marketing* (May 2006), p. 50.

22. Kate Maddox, 'CRM to outpace other IT spending', *BtoB* (11 March 2002), pp. 2, 33.

23. For these and other examples, see Leslie Berger, 'Business intelligence: insights from the data pile', *New York Times* (13 January 2002), p. A9, and Geoffrey James, 'Profit motive', *Selling Power* (March 2002), pp. 68–73, or specify your own customised club on www.pingeurope.com.

24. Darrell K. Rigby, 'Avoid the four perils of CRM', *Harvard Business Review* (February 2002), pp. 101–9; Michael Krauss, 'At many firms, technology obscures CRM', *Marketing News* (18 March 2002), p. 5.

25. Robert McLuhan, 'How to reap the benefits of CRM', *Marketing* (24 May 2001), p. 35; S. Sellar, 'Dust off that data', *Sales and Marketing Management*, **151**, 5 (1999), p. 72; Eric Almquist, Carla Heaton and Nick Hall, 'Making CRM make money', *Marketing Management* (May–June 2002), pp. 16–21; Geoff Martin, *Financial Times* (4 July 2001); Malcolm McDonald, 'On the right track', *Marketing Business* (April 2000), pp. 28–9; 'I want a relationship', *Marketing Business* (*e-business*: 2000), pp. vi–vii; Alan Cane, 'IT near its limits in satisfying customers', *Financial Times* (13 June 2007).

26. Kim Benjamin, 'BA's on-line flight path', *e-business* (June 2000), pp. 55–60; Nikki Tait, 'Racing down the electronic highway', *Financial Times: e-procurement* (Winter 2000), pp. 18–19; Geoff Nairn, 'Launching a strike against military costs', *Financial Times: e-procurement* (Winter 2000), pp. 20–1.

27. LEX column: 'Taking on YouTube', *Financial Times* (23 March 2007).

28. See www.bruichladdich.com, www.islaywhiskysociety.com/bruichladdich/index.html, visit the Isle of Islay, or best of all have one mixed half-and-half with pure Scottish water.

Company case 8 Abel & Cole – the Greener Grocer

'We are really enjoying this new treat and delighting in treating ourselves so well, with the help of your company,' gushes one of Abel & Cole's delighted new customers. Another enthuses, 'Congratulations on a wonderful service – I look forward to being a customer for many years and to doing a little bit to help change the face of food shopping . . .' The company comments, 'We get emails like this every day and they make us very happy!'

'Top of the feelgood food chain'

What have Abel & Cole done to create such missionary zeal among their customers? After all, almost all Abel & Cole do is the online sales of fresh fruit and vegetables – primary products often traded as commodities with no identity attached to them. What is more (or less), with Abel & Cole you cannot even get what you want when you want it. Abel & Cole deliver the 'commodities' in mixed boxes of local produce that is in season. That is, you only get apples, strawberries and new potatoes when they are being harvested. For example, order their Season Salad Box on 23 August for £9 (about €13) and you get basil, beetroot, carrots, celery, green batavia lettuce, tomatoes and white onions. A week later and the salad served will have to change because you get alfalfa, carrots, cos lettuce, fennel, spinach, tomatoes and white onions. Fortunately, Abel & Cole's website contains recipes to tell you what to do with your alfalfa, mung sprouts or anything else you might get.

However, Abel & Cole sell much more than just fruit and veg – you can choose from over 800 other things, including local meat, fish, bread, cheeses, wine, beer, pies and much more. And they listen to customers: 'You can customise your Abel & Cole box – just tell us any things you dislike; we'll keep a note of them. If they're planned for the box, we'll give you something else instead.'

As *The Guardian*'s Janice Turner explains: 'I never used to care about the lives my vegetables led before they arrived in my fridge. But that was before I ordered a box of organic produce from Abel & Cole, and pored over its newsletter detailing the happy origins of my carrots and courgettes. One's vegetables say a lot about a person these days: not so long ago, dinner-party chic was about exotic, obscurely "sourced" ingredients: only Italian flour and pancetta would do for the River Café cookbook classes. But today the buzz-words are local, seasonal, ethically farmed and, above all, organic. And not supermarket organic either, swathed in nasty plastic. If you want to be at the very top of the feel-good food chain, you will have plonked on your doorstep, in a recyclable cardboard box, a bunch of nubbly pears and muddy potatoes and a few other unasked-for items you don't even know how to cook.'

She continues: 'Sure enough, there is a pile-up of fennel in my fridge and last week we had a batch of very weather-beaten pears – 'they grow like this on the tree . . . the brown areas just add texture,' prattles the newsletter. But Andy, my driver, is very friendly (although I can't comment on his legs), the potatoes are delicious, it saves me a fourth weekly visit to Sainsbury's and, in our control-freak age, it is child-ishly pleasing sometimes just to receive a surprise. Besides, in the hierarchy of food consumption, I like to think I am near the top. Just below the ultimate urban-cool foodies with their allotments and chickens, and the staff to do all the work.'

A principled retailer

Abel & Cole's principles explain the company's outstanding growth and relationship with its adoring customers.

1. Bring our customers superb food and drink

'We seek out small producers who take great pride in their work. All our food is certified organic or from a sustainable source, such as our wild sea fish. We offer variety and reflect the seasons through the different produce appearing in our boxes.' The foundation of Abel & Cole's customer relationships is the company's relationship to its suppliers. 'We invest in suppliers,' explains Keith Abel, one of the company's founders. By offering long-term contracts with prices that recognise the additional costs of farming organically, the company gave farmers the confidence to convert to organic farming. That gave them access to suppliers who are 'more passionate in their commitment' than the latecomers who are converting to organic at the behest of supermarkets.

2. Offer a friendly and efficient service

'We want to make your life easier – our online ordering system means you can do your weekly shop in less than 10 minutes, and delivery is free! Set up regular orders, exclude anything you don't like from your box and let us know your holiday dates so that we automatically skip deliveries. Everything we sell can be delivered on a regular basis, from weekly to eight-weekly. We love to hear from you by phone or email. We have the UK's best customer service (it's official – we won the National Customer Service Award 2006 and 2007!). Find out what it's like – give us a ring!'

'Eighty per cent of our customers are out when we deliver,' says Abel. 'We leave boxes on their doorstep.' If it gets stolen they replace it, no questions asked. Abel & Cole trust their customers and their customers trust them.

The company even has a bunch of keys given to them by the owners so that drivers can leave boxes inside.

'Older customers love the service,' says Ella Heeks, the company's managing director. 'It reminds them of the grocer's boy coming round on his bicycle.' This old-fashioned gentility underlies Abel & Cole, a return to a type of shopping which builds relationships and connections – between customer and delivery man, cook and farmer.

Good service comes from great committed people, not from paying incentives to people who are going through the motions. Happy staff make happy customers. Abel & Cole say 'we have amusing people working here . . . We take pride in being cheerful . . . Suits are for funerals, not work . . . It's important to have as much fun at work as you do outside work.'

3. Buy British whenever possible – and no air freight, ever!

'Our rule is to buy British whenever possible. We have a network of more than 60 independent producers, and all our meat, fish, dairy and bread are always British. We buy as much British fruit and veg as the seasons provide. At the peak of the British harvest, that means almost everything is British. When British farms aren't harvesting, we go abroad. Our principles remain the same: we work directly with them, treat them fairly and stay as close to the UK as possible. The same goes for things you can't get from Britain, for example olive oil, wine and bananas (Fair Trade of course!). We never air freight produce – it generates approximately 30 times more carbon dioxide than sea freight – totally crazy!'

The firm has a policy of never air-freighting anything or shipping produce from the other side of the globe when the same crop is grown in Europe. Seventy per cent of produce in the company's boxes is sourced from British growers. By comparison, 76 per cent of organic fruit and vegetables sold in supermarkets comes from abroad – and it has typically clocked up tens of thousands of food miles. When the ethical farming group Sustain analysed a sample basket of 26 imported organic items, it found they had travelled a distance equivalent to six times round the equator (240,000 km). 'Such a journey releases as much polluting carbon dioxide into the atmosphere as a four-bedroom household cooking meals for eight months.'

4. Give a fair deal to farmers (and fishermen, bakers, cheesemakers . . .)

'We believe that working closely with our producers benefits everyone – they get more security, and more time to focus on the food. And we get to eat it! We plan crops and agree fair prices in advance with our growers. We help smaller producers supply us, for example by providing loans or asking them to grow new varieties that you'll want to eat.'

Unlike many supermarket chains, Abel & Cole do not try to whittle down their suppliers' profits. It pays growers a fair price and does not try to cut them down to a low percentage while enjoying a much higher margin itself.

5. Take care of the environment

'We've designed our whole business to be good for the environment – that's why we're called the greener grocer. In practice, this means:

- looking after nature . . . only selling organic . . . giving loans and support to organic farmers . . . finding sustainable options for things where there are no organic standards, like wild fish;
- using less energy . . . focusing on seasonal foods . . . keeping food miles down . . . collecting from our farms . . . delivering to you on fixed days;
- keeping waste down . . . sending you minimum packaging . . . collecting it for reuse . . . reusable crates from our farms . . . giving away leftovers . . . composting leftover leftovers . . . recycling everything else;
- keeping pollution down by . . . using green electricity . . . putting biodiesel in our vans . . . never air freighting . . . experimenting with alternative fuels.'

The vegetable boxes are collected from doorsteps and reused, all the veg comes in brown paper rather than supermarket plastic punnets, and the van routes are planned to minimise fuel consumption.

Shipping, the import method preferred by Abel & Cole, generates 50 times less carbon dioxide than air freight and six times less than transport by road. Each kiwi fruit the company ships by sea from New Zealand would consume its own weight in aviation fuel if it were transported by air. For every calorie of iceberg lettuce flown in from Los Angeles to Europe, 127 calories of fuel are burned. According to Sustain, locally-grown spring onions bought through a box scheme generate 300 times less carbon dioxide than a bunch flown in from Mexico and bought from a supermarket on a shopping trip by car. When buying food conventionally rather than through a box scheme, the average family emits eight tonnes of carbon dioxide a year just from the production, processing, packaging and distribution of their food, compared with 4.4 tonnes from their car. Abel & Cole's whole operation is impeccably green: if waste is cut by a certain margin, some employees can receive a bonus, which was once achieved simply when someone thought to reuse the bags bananas come in as bin-liners.

6. Look after our staff

'We are placed at number 14 in Britain's best places to work. Our staff gets free fruit and veg, pensions, a bike scheme and the best summer picnics in the world. More importantly, their rights are respected, they get fair pay, good management, and first pick of all new vacancies. We've promoted so many people into new, challenging roles that we've got a full-time trainer to support them. You should probably come and work here yourself!'

People who 'worked all hours' in the company's early days often outgrew their capabilities. The company tries to be supportive or find them other jobs, but as a last resort it sought to make leaving easy. Explained Abel, 'You say something like "take a nice long holiday and I'll write a great reference, because you are brilliant at running a team of eight, but 48 is too many for you". Attracting enthusiastic foodies and greenies was not enough to making the company work. Attracting experienced professionals from big companies has been critical to Abel & Cole's growth.

7. Insist on the highest standards of animal welfare
'All of our meat, eggs and farmed fish are organic. Organic represents the highest standard animal welfare. Organically-reared animals must be free range and have access to pasture or rangeland for most of their lives. There is an emphasis on preventing illnesses by responsible management rather than waiting until they strike, and pastures must be tested regularly to prevent the build-up of disease. The routine use of antibiotics is prohibited, and animals are allowed to mature naturally so they do not suffer the health problems associated with accelerated growth. The breeds used in organic farming tend to be naturally slower to mature than those used in conventional farming, giving better quality of meat.'

8. Give back to the community
- 'The Farmer's Choice is our non-profit scheme and it raises over £4,000 a week for schools, at the same time as getting the kids eating organic fruit and veg' (www.abel-cole.co.uk/default.aspx?tab=AboutUs&menu1=13).
- 'We also donate organic food to Naomi House Children's Hospice in Andover' (http://www.naomihouse.org.uk).
- 'Every Christmas, we help charities to lay on Christmas dinners with the best organic turkeys in Britain. This year, we helped Kids' Company (http://www.kidsco.org.uk) and The Passage (http://www.passage.org.uk) – a day centre for the homeless.'
- 'Any bruised produce that doesn't make it into your boxes is given to the gorillas, tortoises and monkeys at Longleat Safari Park.'

A green heart and 'balls of steel'

Like Body Shop and Café Direct, Abel & Cole classes itself as a social enterprise, which seeks to maximise social as well as financial returns. As they grow, like other businesses they need access to capital, but many that have listed on public markets have found themselves under pressure to maximise profits at the expense of their social purpose. Getting Abel & Cole to its present profitable state was not easy. Keith Abel knows how hard it is to start a business and raise capital for growth – especially if a company has objectives beyond making money. He says, 'Anyone setting up a business is going to have to accept

that it's going to take five years to get it off the ground and ten to work. Also, there's still no seed capital around – if you want to start you need balls of steel.'

What of the future and the competition from regular supermarkets who eye Abel & Cole's green credentials and growth? Is consuming Abel & Cole's organic and green groceries a passing fad of the chattering classes? Abel & Cole's Beatrice Rose quickly dispels the idea. 'It isn't just a fashion thing. We try not to be too worthy; we aim to provide a convenient way of shopping which is more ethical.' Keith Abel's response to competition has been to restate his commitment to ethical policies that put principle before the short-term convenience of customers. 'People come into organics via the supermarkets. Then they get interested in the broader picture about the businesses that they are buying from,' he says. 'The message is getting through that intensive farming produces crap food. That you can buy a chicken for £1.99 but you might as well eat dog shit. People from all walks of life are realising you have to spend a bit more to get better food and that organic isn't just healthier, but also tastes bloody brilliant.'

Questions

1. What relationships are key to Abel & Cole's success?
2. Are the relationships sustainable as the company continues to grow?
3. What accounts for the customers' delight with Abel & Cole, whose core product is expensive groceries delivered in predetermined quantities when most people are out?
4. Is Abel's intention to 'restate his commitment to ethical policies' sufficient to compete against powerful retailers, such as Tesco and Wal-Mart?

SOURCES: Andrew Purvis, 'Look, no worms . . .', *The Observer* (16 January 2005); Kate Burt, 'Vegetarians, be proud of what you eat', *The Guardian* (3 August 2005); Janice Turner, 'Perfect delivery', *The Guardian* (30 May 2005); Keith Abel, 'Your business: business wisdom', *Financial Times* (7 January 2006); Mike Scott, 'CAF looks at social cap market', *Financial Times* (4 December 2006); *Financial Times*, 'Greener than thou is the motto' (23 November 2006); Alicia Clegg, 'Strong shoots from green roots', *Financial Times* (23 November 2006); Bill Law, 'Online retailing bandwagon picks up speed', *Belfast Telegraph* (4 June 2007).

PHONE, CAMERA, EMAIL, GAMES, MUSIC...
MY BLACKBERRY HAS EVERYTHING.
A BIT LIKE MY HEALTH CLUBS, ACTUALLY.

Duncan Bannatyne. BlackBerry® User
and Shrewd Spotter of Opportunities.

See how BlackBerry can support, inspire and
surprise you. Go to **blackberrypeople.co.uk**

::: **BlackBerry**.

I don't know the key to success but the key to failure is trying to please everyone.

BILL CROSBY

Segmentation and positioning

Mini Contents List

- Prelude case – Classic Car Club
- Introduction
- Market segmentation
- Market targeting
- Differentiation and positioning
- Real Marketing 9.1 – The place is the thing
- Real Marketing 9.2 – Staples: on the button
- Company case 9 – Coffee-Mate

◄ SOURCE: The Advertising Archives.

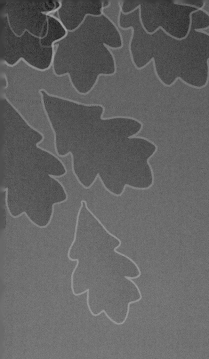

'Men are all the same' (Coups de roulis, operetta 'Les Hommes Sont Biens Tous les Mêmes')

Composed by André Messager, on 'C'est ça la vie, c'est ça l'amour': French Operetta Arias, performed by Birmingham Symphony Orchestra with Susan Graham, conducted by Yves Abel, Erato: B00005UW0Z, 2002

Previewing the concepts

So far, you've learned what marketing is and about the importance of understanding consumers and the marketplace environment. With that as background, you're now ready to delve deeper into marketing strategy and tactics. This chapter looks further into key customer-driven marketing strategy decisions – how to divide up markets into meaningful customer groups (*segmentation*), choose which customer groups to serve (*targeting*), create market offerings that best serve targeted customers (*differentiation*) and position the offerings in the minds of consumers (*positioning*). The chapters that follow explore the tactical marketing tools – the Four Ps – by which marketers bring these strategies to life.

After reading this chapter, you should be able to:

1. Define the four major steps in designing a customer-driven marketing strategy: market segmentation, market targeting, differentiation and positioning.
2. List and discuss the major bases for segmenting consumer and business markets.
3. Explain how companies identify attractive market segments and choose a market targeting strategy.
4. Discuss how companies position their products for maximum competitive advantage in the marketplace.

As an opening example of segmentation, targeting, differentiation and positioning at work, we start by looking at the Classic Car Club, a fast-growing car hire company with a difference. Started by enthusiasts, it has dreams to sell and is a format that is attracting enthused customers and 'me-too' start-ups that are copying the idea.

Prelude case Classic Car Club

On Friday night, after a longer and harder week than usual, Gordon drove out of the staff car park onto the bypass in his trusty old diesel estate. It was not the time for speeding. The traffic was heavy, the night was closing in and soothing Classic FM was on the radio.

All was relaxing until a lad in a white van swerved and pushed into the lane two cars up front while gesticulating in a manner consistent with his FCUK sticker in his rear window. A line of drivers' minds were dragged from the FM-induced mood as they slammed on brakes.

The traffic flow restarted and Brahms calmed.

Within minutes, the diesel estate pulled into the garage between a Bentley Mulsanne S and a Porsche 911 Carrera Tiptronic. Rob walked across. 'You're wanting the Ferrari Testosterone, yes?' After a brief familiarisation and swapping of keys, Gordon left the family diesel and delicately eased the Ferrari out of the garage. The 300 bhp engine behind the driver's seat sounded so Ferrari. The car so light; the engine so eager. A light touch on the accelerator and the car exploded forwards. The machine was eager to go but better to ease into the car's huge potential rather than playing on a busy road.

Classic FM did not fit the enthusiasm and burr of the Ferrari and no radio stations ever played anything remotely appropriate

'For decision makers only'

The First and Largest Prestige and Performance Car Club in the World

P1 offers its members the ultimate way to enjoy up to 6,000 miles driving a £5m garage of the world's finest and fastest cars, without the costs of ownership. Now in its seventh year P1 has branches in the South and North of England each providing access to amongst others the Ferrari F430, Ford GT, Porsche 997 Turbo and Aston Martin V8 Vantage. Recent arrivals include the Ferrari 599 GTB, Lamborghini Gallardo Spyder and Bentley Continental GTC. Forward orders joining the fleet this year include the Aston Martin V8 Vantage Roadster, Porsche 997 GT3 RS, Audi R8 and Maserati Granturismo.

For membership call P1 South: 01372 374400, P1 North: 01606 737954 or visit www.p1international.com

A car hire company that sells its very distinctive range of cars to a very distinctive niche market segment.

SOURCE: P1 International Limited 2007.

at this time on Friday night. An old Bruce Springsteen album was in the CD player. It kicked off with *Born to Run* – 'Chrome wheeled, fuel injected and steppin' out over the line' – a rising song to blast in the weekend. Life could not get much better than this, but it did.

Out of the city and on to country lanes, there, at the side of the road, was the lad with his white van. This time he was not gesticulating at other road users but at his motor that was not running. Gordon smiled and waved, as Springsteen burst into 'Thunder Road', and let the prancing horse free.

This is not a fairy tale. On Monday morning the Ferrari turned back into a diesel estate and another week of work began. But next Friday it was to be a family car with a difference – a Maserati 3200 GT which he would pick up on a trip to Copenhagen. And in a month's time, a Corvette Z06 from the New York branch.

The cars are part of the stable of the Classic Car Club, a membership organisation that hires out cars to drool over. For about €3,000 a year, members hire cars based on a points system that varies with time of year, weekend or weekday and make of car. The price includes everything but fuel. Some of the cars are true classics, such as the Triumph TR6, Daimler V8, E-type and Mark II Jaguars. Others, including a Porsche Boxter, TVR and Aston Martin, are more modern but still interesting to drive. All for averaging under €100 per driving day – less than a normal car hire and certainly for a lot less than owning a classic car. As the *Independent on Sunday* commented, 'I've scratched my head long and hard to find a catch: there isn't one.'

Whatever the dream that the Classic Car Club offers to its members, the club has its owners scratching their heads too. According to Rob, the branch manager, we are basically a specialised car hire company. While Enterprise is a guardian angel when people have a car crash, we are the devil who fulfils people's dreams.

Unfortunately, most members want to hire the same exotic open-topped cars on sunny weekends in summer. Many times the stock of cars is all out while on other occasions most rest in the garage. Downtime can also be a problem. These cars are real classics and some are ageing. Breakdowns can and do occur and take cars off the road for weeks. There are also the speeding fines incurred by members who do not realise they can exceed the speed limit from a standing start in seconds in a car that is designed to attract attention.[1]

Questions

1. What allows a small business, like the Classic Car Club, to succeed against huge global players in the car hire business, and is it a business concept that could work elsewhere in the world?

2. Being a small company looking for a membership that is a very small fraction of the total population, how should the club promote itself and what is its target market?

3. How could the club increase its income and even the load on its cars by appealing to additional market segments or segmenting its own customer base?

Introduction

Companies recognise that they cannot appeal to all buyers in the marketplace or at least not to all buyers in the same way. Buyers are too numerous, too widely scattered and too varied in their needs and buying practices. Moreover, the companies themselves vary widely in their abilities to serve different segments of the market. Instead, like the Classic Car Club, a company must identify the parts of the market that it can serve best and most profitably. It must design customer-driven marketing strategies that build the *right* relationships with the *right* customers.

Thus, most companies have moved away from mass marketing and towards **target marketing** – identifying market segments, selecting one or more of them, and developing products and marketing programmes tailored to each. Instead of scattering their marketing efforts (the 'shotgun' approach), firms are focusing on the buyers who have greater interest in the values they create best (the 'rifle' approach).

Figure 9.1 shows the four major steps in designing a customer-driven marketing strategy. In the first two steps, the company selects the customers that it will serve. Market segmentation involves dividing a market into distinct groups of buyers with different needs, characteristics or behaviours, who might require separate products or marketing mixes. The company identifies different ways to segment the market and develops profiles of the resulting market segments. **Targeting** consists of evaluating each market segment's attractiveness and selecting one or more market segments to enter.

In the final two steps, the company decides on a value proposition – on how it will create value for target customers. Differentiation involves actually differentiating the firm's market offering to create superior customer value. **Positioning** consists of arranging for a market offering to occupy a clear, distinctive and desirable place relative to competing products in the minds of target consumers. We discuss each of these steps in turn.

Target marketing—Directing a company's marketing effort towards serving one or more groups of customers sharing common needs or characteristics.

Targeting—The process of evaluating each market segment's attractiveness and selecting one or more segments to enter.

Positioning—Arranging for a product to occupy a clear, distinctive and desirable place relative to competing products in the minds of target consumers.

Market segmentation

Markets consist of buyers, and buyers differ in one or more ways. They may differ in their wants, resources, locations, buying attitudes and buying practices. Through market segmentation, companies divide large, heterogeneous markets into smaller segments that can be reached more efficiently and effectively with products and services that match their unique needs. In this section, we discuss four important segmentation topics: segmenting consumer markets, segmenting business markets, segmenting international markets and requirements for effective segmentation.

Figure 9.1 Steps in market segmentation, targeting and positioning

Calvin Klein represents several layers of segmentation: youth, gender, wealth and a lifestyle interest in fashion. The brand name keys into the young market using text messaging shorthand.
SOURCE: The Advertising Archives.

Segmenting consumer markets

There is no single way to segment a market. A marketer has to try different segmentation variables, alone and in combination, to find the best way to view the market structure. Table 9.1 outlines the major variables that might be used in segmenting consumer markets. Here we look at the major *geographic*, *demographic*, *psychographic* and *behavioural* variables.

 There is no single way to segment a market.

Geographic segmentation

Geographic segmentation calls for dividing the market into different geographical units such as nations, regions, states, counties, cities or even neighbourhoods. A company may decide to operate in one or a few geographical areas, or to operate in all areas but pay attention to geographical differences in needs and wants.

Many companies today are localising their products, advertising, promotion and sales efforts to fit the needs of individual regions, cities and even neighbourhoods. For example, one consumer products company sent additional cases of its low-calorie snack foods to stores in neighbourhoods near WeightWatchers clinics. Coca-Cola developed four ready-to-drink canned coffees for the Japanese market, each targeted to a specific part of the country. Curry Pringles crisps are sold in England and Funky Soy Sauce Pringles in Asia.[2]

Other companies are seeking to cultivate as-yet untapped geographical territory. For example, having become the leading supermarket chain and finding it difficult to buy land for further Tesco supermarkets, the company has developed other formats to serve different communities; going down in size, these are:

- *Tesco Metro*, like the first in London's Covent Garden, are mostly located in city centres and in the high streets of small towns.

Geographic segmentation—Dividing the market into different geographical units such as nations, regions, states, counties, cities or neighbourhoods.

Table 9.1 Market segmentation variables for consumer markets

Variable	Typical breakdowns
Geographic	
Region	These can vary in scale from, say, Europe, through groupings of countries (Scandinavia), nations (Finland), to regions within countries (Lapland).
Country size	Giant (USA), large (Germany, Spain), medium (The Netherlands, Australia) or small (Malta, Lithuania).
City size	Under 5,000; 5,000–20,000; 20,000–50,000; 50,000–100,000; 100,000–250,000; 250,000–500,000; 500,000–1,000,000; 1,000,000–4,000,000; 4,000,000 and over.
Density	Urban, suburban, rural.
Climate	Tropical, sub-tropical, temperate, etc.
Demographic	
Age	Under 6, 6–11, 12–19, 20–34, 35–49, 50–64, 65+.
Gender	Male, female.
Family size	1–2, 3–4, 5+.
Family life cycle	Young, single; young, married, no children; young, married, youngest child under 6; young, married, youngest child 6 or over; older, married with children; older, married, no children under 18; older, single; other.
Income	Under €10,000; 10,000–15,000; 15,000–20,000; 20,000–30,000; 30,000–50,000; 50,000–75,000; 75,000–100,000; 100,000 and over.
Occupation	Professional and technical; managers, officials and proprietors; clerical, sales; craftsmen, foremen; operatives; farmers; retired; students; homemakers; unemployed.
Education	Grade school or less; some high school; high school graduate; university; postgraduate; professional.
Religion	Catholic, Protestant, Jewish, Islamic, etc.
Race	White, Black, Polynesian, Chinese, etc.
Nationality	American, British, German, Scandinavian, Latin American, Middle Eastern, Japanese, etc.
Psychographic	
Social class	Lower lowers, upper lowers, working class, middle class, upper middles, lower uppers, upper uppers.
Lifestyle	Achievers, believers, strivers.
Personality	Compulsive, gregarious, authoritarian, ambitious.
Behavioural	
Purchase occasion	Regular occasion, special occasion.
Benefits sought	Quality, service, economy.
User status	Non-user, ex-user, potential user, first-time user, regular user.
Usage rate	Light user, medium user, heavy user.
Loyalty status	None, medium, strong, absolute.
Readiness state	Unaware, aware, informed, interested, desirous, intending to buy.
Attitude towards product	Enthusiastic, positive, indifferent, negative, hostile.

- *Tesco Express* are neighbourhood convenience stores that stock mainly food with an emphasis on higher-margin products and everyday essentials.
- *One Stop* are very small stores that do not carry the Tesco name.

Some stores are even more specialised, such as Tesco Calais that specialises in bulk selling of alcohol to people from the UK returning from holidays in continental Europe or who have crossed the English Channel for the day on a 'booze cruise'.

Demographic segmentation

Demographic segmentation divides the market into groups based on variables such as age, gender, family size, family life cycle, income, occupation, education, religion, race, generation and nationality. An example is Saga that started marketing holidays to pensioners but whose services now include insurance, financial services, books, DVDs, CDs and even SAGAzone, an online community.[3] Demographic factors are the most popular bases for segmenting customer groups. One reason is that consumer needs, wants and usage rates often vary closely with demographic variables. Another is that demographic variables are easier to measure than most other types of variables. Even when market segments are first defined using other bases, such as benefits sought or behaviour, their demographic characteristics must be known in order to assess the size of the target market and to reach it efficiently.

Age and life-cycle stage

Consumer needs and wants change with age. Some companies use **life-cycle segmentation** (or **age segmentation**), offering different products or using different marketing approaches for different age and life-cycle groups. For example, for kids, Procter & Gamble sells Crest Spinbrushes featuring favourite children's characters. For adults, it sells more serious models, promising 'a dentist-clean feeling twice a day'. And Nintendo, long known for its youth-oriented video games, has launched a sub-brand, Touch Generations, which targets ageing baby boomers. Touch Generations offers video games such as 'Brain training: how old is your brain?', designed

Demographic segmentation—Dividing the market into groups based on demographic variables such as age, gender, family size, family life cycle, income, occupation, education, religion, race, generation and nationality.

Life-cycle segmentation (or age segmentation)—Offering products or marketing approaches that recognise the consumer's changing needs at different stages of their life.

YOU CAN'T GET THEM OLD UNTIL YOU GET THEM NEW.

HUNDREDS OF BORING LECTURES. A SUMMER FRAMING HOUSES. A FIGHT AT A REPLACE-MENTS CONCERT. 5 FAKE ID'S. BACKPACKING IN THE COHUTTAS. HELL WEEK. A STRING OF DEADBEAT ROOMMATES. ONE DULL POCKETKNIFE.

Lifestyle segmentation: Duck Head targets a casual student lifestyle, claiming 'You can't get them old until you get them new.'

SOURCE: Duck Head Apparel Co.

to 'exercise the noggin' and keep the mind young. The aim is to 'lure in older non-gamers by offering skill-building – or at least less violent, less fantasy-based – titles that might appeal to [older consumers] more than . . . *Grand Theft Auto*.'

Marketers must be careful to guard against stereotypes when using age or life-cycle segmentation. For example, although some 70-year-olds require wheelchairs, others play tennis. Similarly, whereas some 40-year-old couples are sending their children off to college, others are just beginning new families or have decided never to have children at all. Thus, age is often a poor predictor of a person's life cycle, health, work or family status, needs and buying power. Companies marketing to mature consumers usually employ positive images and appeals. For example, ads for Olay's ProVital – designed to improve the elasticity and appearance of the 'maturing skin' of women over 50 – feature attractive older spokeswomen and uplifting messages.

Gender

Gender segmentation—Dividing a market into different groups based on gender.

Gender segmentation has long been used in clothing, cosmetics, toiletries and magazines. For example, L'Oréal offers Men's Expert skincare products and a VIVE For Men grooming line. Ads proclaim, 'Now L'Oréal Paris brings its grooming technology and expertise to men . . . because you're worth it too.' Nike has recently stepped up its efforts to capture the women's sportswear market. It wasn't until 2000 that Nike made women's shoes using moulds made from women's feet, rather than simply using a small man's foot mould. Since then, however, Nike has changed its approach to women. It has overhauled its women's clothing line – called Nikewomen – to create better fitting, more colourful, more fashionable workout clothes for women. Its revamped nikewomen.com website features these products, along with workout trend highlights. And Nike has been opening Nikewomen stores in several major cities.[4]

> Soon you will be popping either pink or blue drugs. Globally, even young children are expected to act differently towards pain. Girls can weep but boys are expected to be stoic. Research has now shown that the genders do feel pain differently and react differently to pain-relieving drugs. For a long time the male-dominated armed forces issued morphine to help people in severe pain. Morphine works for men, but women in pain respond better to nalbuphine, a drug that is not so effective on men.[5]

Income

Income segmentation—Dividing a market into different income groups.

Income segmentation has long been used by the marketers of products and services such as automobiles, clothing, cosmetics, financial services and travel. Many companies target affluent consumers with luxury goods and convenience services. Europe's epicentres of luxury goods include such places as the Via della Spiga and Piazza Duomo in Milan, and avenue Montaigne and rue du Faubourg-St-Honoré in Paris – the homes of *haute couture*.

Credit-card companies offer super-premium credit cards dripping with perks, such as Visa's Signature Card, MasterCard's World Card and AmEx's super-elite Centurion card. The hard-to-acquire black Centurion card is issued by invitation only, to customers who spend more than €100,000 a year on other AmEx cards and meet other not-so-clear requirements. Then, the select few who do receive the card pay about €2,000 annual fee for the privilege of carrying it.

However, not all companies that use income segmentation target the affluent. For example, many retailers – such as Aldi, Lidl, Matalan and Poundstretcher with its slogan 'Shop Smart, Live Well' – successfully target low- and middle-income groups. The core market for such stores is families with incomes under €20,000. According to marketing mythology, when Family Dollar real-estate experts scout locations for new stores, they look for lower-middle-class neighbourhoods where people wear less expensive shoes and drive old cars that drip a lot of oil.

With their low-income strategies, they have forced the major retailers to fight back with low-priced lines, such as Tesco Value lines that are aimed at low-income families, using simple packaging to keep the retail cost as low as possible.[6]

Psychographic segmentation

Psychographic segmentation divides buyers into different groups based on social class, lifestyle or personality characteristics. People in the same demographic group can have very different psychographic make-ups.

> People in the same demographic group can have very different psychographic make-ups.

In Chapter 5, we discussed how the products people buy reflect their *lifestyles*. As a result, marketers often segment their markets by consumer lifestyles and base their marketing strategies on lifestyle appeals. For example, AmEx promises 'a card that fits your life'. Its 'My life. My card.' campaign provides glimpses into the lifestyles of famous people with whom consumers might want to identify, including Robert DeNiro and Kate Winslet.

Marketers have also used *personality* variables to segment markets. For example, marketing for Honda motor scooters *appears* to be aimed at fashionable twenty-somethings but it is *actually* aimed at a much broader personality group. One old ad, for example, showed a delighted child bouncing up and down on his bed while the announcer says, 'You've been trying to get there all your life.' The ad reminded viewers of the euphoric feelings they got when they broke away from authority and did things their parents told them not to do. Thus, Honda is appealing to the rebellious, independent kid in all of us. In fact, 22 per cent of scooter riders are retired. Competitor Vespa sells more than a quarter of its scooters to the over-50s. 'The older buyers are buying them for kicks,' says one senior. 'They never had the opportunity to do this as kids.'[7]

Behavioural segmentation

Behavioural segmentation divides buyers into groups based on their knowledge, attitudes, uses or responses to a product. Many marketers believe that behavioural variables are the best starting point for building market segments.

Occasions

Buyers can be grouped according to occasions when they get the idea to buy, make their purchase or use the purchased item. **Occasion segmentation** can help firms build up product usage. Here are two examples.

Rohan Travel Unlimited is more than a clothing company; it is 'the original travel clothing company'. The company's hi-tech clothes are made for adventuring outdoors. They explain, 'our clothing has been worn everywhere, fraternising in Indian trains, birding on the Norfolk coast, grafting in the Antarctic (and the Arctic), behind the lens on safari, on business on Vancouver, labouring in Yorkshire cowsheds, stripping under the car and drifting in the Amazon.' For Rohan, travel is a . . . 'state of mind which is about looking forward, outward, learning, applying, enjoying the world. And this state of mind shapes our thinking, our priorities, our uniqueness, our direction and our design. For Rohan, travel is a metaphor for how we live – a place where durability, thoughtful design, easy practicality and simplicity are values which make life richer and more rewarding.' In reality, Rohan clothes are as likely to be warn travelling to the

Psychographic segmentation—Dividing a market into different groups based on social class, lifestyle or personality characteristics.

Behavioural segmentation—Dividing a market into groups based on consumer knowledge, attitude, use or response to a product.

Occasion segmentation—Dividing the market into groups according to occasions when buyers get the idea to buy, actually make their purchase or use the purchased item.

supermarket as exploring the source of the Nile, but Rohan's focus gives a small company a clear target and design criteria.[8]

The turkey farmer Bernard Matthews fought the seasonality in the turkey market. In some European countries the American bird was as synonymous with Christmas as Santa Claus. He had a problem. In most families, Christmas dinner was the only meal big enough to justify buying such a big bird. His answer was to repackage the meat as turkey steaks, sausages and burgers, and promote them for year-round use. His reformulated turkey is so successful that he is now reformulating New Zealand lamb.

After Eight is a confectionary aimed at clearly defined usage situation: together with other people, relaxing and late.
SOURCE: The Advertising Archives.

User status

Markets can be segmented into non-users, ex-users, potential users, first-time users and regular users of a product. For example, blood banks cannot rely only on regular donors. They must also recruit new first-time donors and remind ex-donors – each will require different marketing appeals. The UK's national Blood Transfusion Service went even further, targeting people with appeals based on a person's blood group:

- People with O− blood group can only accept blood from O− donors. In addition, your blood is 'so good' that anyone else can use it, so it is very useful to have around.
- AB− is the rarest blood of all so you are one of very few donors . . .

Included in the potential user group are consumers facing life-stage changes – such as newly-weds and new parents – who can be turned into heavy users. For example, P&G acquires the names of parents-to-be and showers them with product samples and ads for its Pampers and other baby products in order to capture a share of their future purchases. It invites them to visit Pampers.com and join MyPampers.com, giving them access to expert parenting advice, Parent Pages e-mail newsletters, coupons and special offers.

Usage rate

Some markets also segment into light, medium and heavy user groups. Heavy users are often a small percentage of the market, but account for a high percentage of total buying. For example, the owner of a pub in a mining town knew that 41 per cent of the adult population of the village buy beer. However, the heavy users accounted for 87 per cent of the beer consumed – almost seven times as much as the light users. Clearly, the owner would prefer to attract heavy users to his pub rather than light users.

HMV subsidiary Fopp pursues a business model that seeks to exploit the fact that customers buying videos, music and books are usually browsers, a logic also followed by Fnac in France and by Borders. Where Fopp differs from these larger chains, however, is its focus on one type of heavy user: the 'Fifty Quid Bloke' (£50 man). This refers to upper social class (A and B1) males, aged between 25 and 45 with money to burn. Traditional retail philosophy has it that this is a hard group to reach, but Fopp manages to persuade the Fifty Quid Bloke to part with £38 (€56) on an average visit when average expenditure in rival retailers is much lower.[9]

Loyalty status

A market can also be segmented by consumer loyalty. Consumers can be loyal to brands (Tide) and companies (Mercedes). Buyers can be divided into groups according to their degree of loyalty. Some consumers are completely loyal – they buy one brand all the time. For example, Apple has a small but almost cult-like following of loyal users:[10]

It's the 'Cult of the Mac', and it's populated by 'macolytes'. Urbandictionary.com defines a macolyte as 'One who is fanatically devoted to Apple products, especially the Macintosh computer. Also know as a Mac Zealot.' (Sample usage: 'He's a macolyte; don't even *think* of mentioning Microsoft within earshot.') How about Anna Zisa, a graphic designer from Milan who doesn't really like tattoos but stencilled an Apple tat on her bum. 'It just felt like the most me thing to have,' says Zisa. 'I like computers. The apple looks good and sexy. All the comments I have heard have been positive, even from Linux and Windows users.' And then there's Taylor Barcroft, who has spent the past 11 years travelling the country in an RV on a mission to be the Mac cult's ultimate 'multimedia historical videographer'. He goes to every Macworld Expo, huge trade shows centred on the Mac, as well as all kinds of other tech shows – and videos anything and everything Apple. He's accumulated more than 3,000 hours of videos. And he's never been paid a dime to do any of this, living off an inheritance. Barcroft owns 17 Macs. Such fanatically loyal users helped keep Apple afloat during the lean years, to survive as the sole major PC maker outside Microsoft's clutches, and now to be at the forefront of Apple's burgeoning iPod–iTunes empire.

Others consumers are somewhat loyal – they are loyal to two or three brands of a given product or favour one brand while sometimes buying others. Still other buyers show no loyalty to any brand. Either they want something different each time they buy, or they buy whatever's on sale.

A company can learn a lot by analysing loyalty patterns in its market. It should start by studying its own loyal customers. For example, by studying 'macolytes', Apple can better pinpoint its target market and develop marketing appeals. By studying its less loyal buyers, the company can detect which brands are most competitive with its own. By looking at customers who are shifting away from its brand, the company can learn about its marketing weaknesses.

Using multiple segmentation bases

Marketers rarely limit their segmentation analysis to only one or a few variables. Rather, they are increasingly using multiple segmentation bases in an effort to identify smaller, better-defined target groups. Thus, a bank may not only identify a group of wealthy retired adults but also, within that group, distinguish several segments based on their current income, assets, savings and risk preferences, housing and lifestyles.

Geodemographics—The study of the relationship between geographical location and demographics.

One good example of multivariable segmentation is **geodemographics**, an increasingly used segmentation method. Originally developed by the CACI Market Analysis Group as ACORN (A Classification Of Residential Neighbourhoods), it uses 40 variables from population census data to group residential areas. Geodemographics is developing fast. ACORN has been joined by PIN (Pinpoint Identified Neighbourhoods), Mosaic and Super Profile. Linking them to consumer panel databases is increasing the power of basic geodemographic databases. CCN Marketing has since extended this process to cover the EU using its EuroMOSAIC (Table 9.2).

Such segmentation provides a powerful tool for marketers of all kinds. It can help companies to identify and better understand key customer segments, target them more efficiently, and tailor market offerings and messages to their specific needs.

Segmenting business markets

Consumer and business marketers use many of the same variables to segment their markets. Business buyers can be segmented geographically, demographically (industry, company size), or by benefits sought, user status, usage rate and loyalty status. Yet business marketers also use some

Segment, segment, segment! Dark and Lovely cuts the market several ways to find their niche: race, age, gender and lifestyle (organics).
SOURCE: The Advertising Archives.

additional variables which, as Table 9.3 shows, include business customer *demographics* (industry, company size), *operating characteristics, buying approaches, situational factors* and *personal characteristics*.

The table lists important questions that business marketers should ask in determining which customers they want to serve. By going after segments instead of the whole market, companies have a much better chance to deliver value to consumers and to receive maximum rewards for close attention to consumer needs. Almost every company serves at least some business markets. For example, we've mentioned AmEx as the 'My life. My card.' company that offers

Table 9.2 CCN EuroMOSAIC households across Europe (per cent)

Category	Name	B	D	IRL	I	NL	N	E	S	GB
E01	Elite suburbs	8	16	6	4	5	18	1	8	12
E02	Service (sector) communities	22	20	29	12	14	7	17	18	16
E03	Luxury flats	9	7	2	5	8	8	7	3	5
E04	Low-income inner city	5	9	10	8	11	10	1	8	9
E05	High-rise social housing	–	3	–	8	11	4	1	7	5
E06	Industrial communities	12	13	5	19	14	10	18	12	19
E07	Dynamic families	17	8	10	13	14	15	5	9	14
E08	Lower-income families	9	4	12	8	6	7	7	7	8
E09	Rural/agricultural	14	14	21	17	13	17	23	19	6
E10	Vacation/retirement	4	6	4	5	4	3	19	9	6

credit cards to end-consumers. But AmEx also targets businesses in three segments – merchants, corporations and small businesses. It has developed distinct marketing programmes for each segment.

> By going after segments instead of the whole market, companies have a much better chance to deliver value to consumers.

In the merchants' segment, AmEx focuses on convincing new merchants to accept the card and on managing relationships with those that already do. For larger corporate customers, the company offers a corporate card programme, which includes extensive employee expense and travel management services. It also offers this segment a wide range of asset management, retirement planning and financial education services. Finally, for small business customers, AmEx has created the OPEN: Small Business Network, 'the one place that's all about small business'. Small business cardholders can access the network for everything from account and expense management software to expert small-business management advice and connecting with other small business owners to share ideas and get recommendations.[11]

Observing business buyer behaviour can uncover business market opportunities in the same way as anthropological studies of consumers.

Yotel questions the conventional wisdom that travelling executives need a luxury hotel near an airport. Yotel offers small, low-cost 'cabins' only seven square metres in size for a standard tariff of about £50 a night. However, they are sited in the airport terminal and allow travellers who require simply a night's sleep and a shower to save money and stay close to departure gates. The rooms are small but a lot larger that the space that any first-class passenger gets on a long-haul flight. What is more, Yotel expects to rent the same rooms out to several customers per day – each of whom will drop in for a few hours to sleep before or between flights.[12]

Table 9.3 Primary segmentation variables for business markets

Demographics

- *Industry.* Which industries that buy this product should we focus on?

- *Company size.* What size companies should we focus on?

- *Location.* What geographical areas should we focus on?

Operating variables

- *Technology.* What customer technologies should we focus on?

- *User/non-user status.* Should we focus on heavy, medium or light users, or non-users?

- *Customer capabilities.* Should we focus on customers needing many services or few services?

Purchasing approaches

- *Purchasing function organisations.* Should we focus on companies with highly centralised or decentralised purchasing organisations?

- *Power structure.* Should we focus on companies that are engineering dominated, financially dominated or marketing dominated?

- *Nature of existing relationships.* Should we focus on companies with which we already have strong relationships or simply go after the most desirable companies?

- *General purchase policies.* Should we focus on companies that prefer leasing? Service contracts? Systems purchases? Sealed bidding?

- *Purchasing criteria.* Should we focus on companies that are seeking quality? Service? Price?

Situational factors

- *Urgency.* Should we focus on companies that need quick delivery or service?

- *Specific application.* Should we focus on certain applications of our product rather than all applications?

- *Size of order.* Should we focus on large or small orders?

Personal characteristics

- *Buyer–seller similarity.* Should we focus on companies whose people and values are similar to ours?

- *Attitudes towards risk.* Should we focus on risk-taking or risk-avoiding customers?

- *Loyalty.* Should we focus on companies that show high loyalty to their suppliers?

SOURCES: Adapted from Thomas V. Bonoma and Benson P. Shapiro, *Segmenting the Industrial Market* (Lexington, MA: Lexington Books, 1983); see also John Berrigan and Carl Finkbeiner, *Segmentation Marketing: New methods for capturing business* (New York: Harper Business, 1992).

Segmenting international markets

Few companies have either the resources or the will to operate in all, or even most, of the countries that dot the globe. Although some large companies, such as Royal Dutch Shell or Sony, sell products in more than 200 countries, most international firms focus on a smaller set. Operating in many countries presents new challenges. Different countries, even those that are close together, can vary greatly in their economic, cultural and political make-up. Thus, just as they do within their domestic markets, international firms need to group their world markets into segments with distinct buying needs and behaviours.

Companies can segment international markets using one or a combination of several variables. They can segment by *geographical location*, grouping countries by regions such as Western Europe, the Pacific Rim, the Middle East or Africa. Geographical segmentation assumes that nations close to one another will have many common traits and behaviours. Although this is often the case, there are many exceptions. For example, although the US and Canada have much in common, both differ culturally and economically from neighbouring Mexico. Even within a region, consumers can differ widely. For example, some marketers lump all Central and South American countries together. However, the Dominican Republic is no more like Brazil than Italy is like Sweden. Many Central and South Americans don't even speak Spanish, including 140 million Portuguese-speaking Brazilians and the millions in other countries who speak a variety of Indian dialects.

World markets can also be segmented on the basis of *economic factors*. For example, countries might be grouped by population income levels or by their overall level of economic development. A country's economic structure shapes its population's product and service needs and, therefore, the marketing opportunities it offers. Countries can be segmented by *political and legal factors* such as the type and stability of government, receptivity to foreign firms, monetary regulations and the amount of bureaucracy. Such factors can play a crucial role in a company's choice of which countries to enter and how. *Cultural factors* can also be used, grouping markets according to common languages, religions, values and attitudes, customs and behavioural patterns.

Segmenting international markets based on geographic, economic, political, cultural and other factors assumes that segments should consist of clusters of countries. However, many companies use a different approach called **intermarket segmentation**. They form segments of consumers who have similar needs and buying behaviour even though they are located in different countries. For example, Mercedes and Rolex target the world's well-to-do, regardless of their country. And Swedish furniture giant IKEA targets the aspiring global middle class – it sells good-quality furniture that ordinary people worldwide can afford.

MTV targets the world's teenagers. The world's 1.2 billion teenagers have a lot in common: they study, shop and sleep. They are exposed to many of the same major issues: love, crime, homelessness, the environment, lack of 'enough' money, and working parents. In many ways, they have more in common with each other than with their parents. 'Last year I was in 17 different countries,' says one expert, 'and it's pretty difficult to find anything that is different, other than language, among a teenager in Japan, a teenager in the UK, and a teenager in China.' Says another, 'Global teenagers in Buenos Aires, Beijing and Bangalore swing to the beat of MTV' although the playlist in each country is distinctly different. MTV bridges the gap between cultures, appealing to what teens around the world have in common. Sony, adidas, Nokia and many other firms also actively target global teens. For example, adidas's 'Impossible Is Nothing' theme appeals to teens the world over.[13]

Requirements for effective segmentation

Clearly, there are many ways to segment a market, but not all segmentations are effective. For example, buyers of table salt could be divided into blond and brunette customers. But hair colour obviously does not affect the purchase of salt. Furthermore, if all salt buyers bought the same amount of salt each month, believed that all salt is the same, and wanted to pay the same price, the company would not benefit from segmenting this market.

To be useful, market segments must be:

- *Measurable*. The size, buying power and profiles of the segments need measuring. **Measurability** is the degree to which the size, purchasing power and profits of a market

Intermarket segmentation—Forming segments of consumers who have similar needs and buying behaviour even though they are from different countries.

Measurability—The degree to which the size, purchasing power and profits of a market segment can be measured.

segment can be measured. Certain segmentation variables are difficult to measure. For example, there are about 40 million left-handed people in Europe – almost equalling the entire population of Poland – yet few firms target them. The crucial problem may be that the segment is hard to identify and measure.

In contrast, the one-time repressed gay market is becoming increasingly important. Some companies, such as Massow Financial Services or the travel agents Sensations and D Tours, are specialising in the gay market. Others, such as the British Tourist Authority, KLM, the Royal Shakespeare Company and Absolut Vodka, have products and campaigns tailored to the community. Estimates put the gay market at between 6 and 20 per cent of the population and Mintel's Pat Neviani-Aston admits that reliable estimates are few because of people's residual unwillingness to reveal their true sexuality.

- *Accessible.* The market segments can be effectively reached and served. Suppose a fragrance company finds that heavy users of its brand are single men and women who stay out late and socialise a lot. Unless this group lives or shops at certain places and is exposed to certain media, its members will be difficult to reach.

- *Substantial.* The market segments are large or profitable enough to serve. A segment should be the largest possible homogeneous group worth pursuing with a tailored marketing programme. It would not pay, for example, for a car maker to develop cars especially for people whose height is greater than two metres. However, where fixed costs are lower, such markets can be served by the likes of High and Mighty who retail clothes for 'big or tall men'.

- *Differentiable.* The segments are conceptually distinguishable and respond differently to different marketing mix elements and programmes. If married and unmarried women respond similarly to a sale of perfume, they do not constitute separate segments.

- *Actionable.* Effective programmes can be designed for attracting and serving the segments. For example, although one small regional airline identified seven market segments, their staff was too small to develop separate marketing programmes for each segment.

Market targeting

Market segmentation reveals the firm's market segment opportunities. The firm now has to evaluate the various segments and decide how many and which segments it can serve best. We now look at how companies evaluate and select target segments.

Evaluating market segments

In evaluating different market segments, a firm must look at three factors: segment size and growth, segment structural attractiveness, and company objectives and resources. The company must first collect and analyse data on current segment sales, growth rates and expected profitability for various segments. It will be interested in segments that have the right size and growth characteristics. But 'right size and growth' is a relative matter. The largest, fastest-growing segments are not always the most attractive ones for every company. Smaller companies may lack the skills and resources needed to serve the larger segments, or they may find these segments too competitive. Such companies may target segments that are smaller and less attractive, in an absolute sense, but that are potentially more profitable for them.

> The largest, fastest-growing segments are not always the most attractive ones for every company.

The company also needs to examine major structural factors that affect long-run segment attractiveness.[14] For example, a segment is less attractive if it already contains many strong and aggressive *competitors*. The existence of many actual or potential *substitute products* may limit prices and the profits that can be earned in a segment. The relative *power of buyers* also affects segment attractiveness. Buyers with strong bargaining power relative to sellers will try to force prices down, demand more services and set competitors against one another – all at the expense of seller profitability. Finally, a segment may be less attractive if it contains *powerful suppliers* who can control prices or reduce the quality or quantity of ordered goods and services.

Even if a segment has the right size and growth and is structurally attractive, the company must consider its own objectives and resources. Some attractive segments can be dismissed quickly because they do not mesh with the company's long-run objectives, or the company may lack the skills and resources needed to succeed in an attractive segment. The company should enter only segments in which it can offer superior value and gain advantages over competitors.

Selecting target market segments

After evaluating different segments, the company must now decide which and how many segments it will target. A **target market** consists of a set of buyers who share common needs or characteristics that the company decides to serve.

Because buyers have unique needs and wants, a seller could potentially view each buyer as a separate target market. Ideally, then, a seller might design a separate marketing programme for each buyer. However, although some companies do attempt to serve buyers individually, most face larger numbers of smaller buyers and do not find individual targeting worthwhile. Instead, they look for broader segments of buyers. More generally, market targeting can be carried out at several different levels. Figure 9.2 shows that companies can target very broadly (undifferentiated marketing), very narrowly (micromarketing) or somewhere in between (differentiated or concentrated marketing).

Undifferentiated marketing

Using an **undifferentiated marketing** (or **mass-marketing**) strategy, a firm might decide to ignore market segment differences and target the whole market with one offer. This mass-marketing strategy focuses on what is *common* in the needs of consumers rather than on what is *different*. The company designs a product and a marketing programme that will appeal to the largest number of buyers.

As noted earlier in the chapter, most modern marketers have strong doubts about this strategy. Difficulties arise in developing a product or brand that will satisfy all consumers. Moreover, mass marketers often have trouble competing with more-focused firms that do a better job of satisfying the needs of specific segments and niches.

Differentiated marketing

Using a **differentiated marketing** (or **segmented marketing**) strategy, a firm decides to target several market segments and designs separate offers for each. All regular airlines use

---

Target market—A set of buyers sharing common needs or characteristics that the company decides to serve.

Undifferentiated marketing (or mass-marketing)—A market-coverage strategy in which a firm decides to ignore market segment differences and go after the whole market with one offer.

Differentiated marketing (or segmented marketing)—A market-coverage strategy in which a firm decides to target several market segments and designs separate offers for each.

Figure 9.2 Target marketing strategies

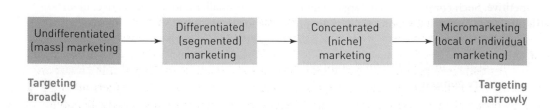

Targeting broadly → Targeting narrowly

Undifferentiated (mass) marketing → Differentiated (segmented) marketing → Concentrated (niche) marketing → Micromarketing (local or individual marketing)

The diversity of Europe's population is creating new segments to be targeted. Cosmetics change to fit different complexions, as does the celebrity endorsement.
SOURCE: The Advertising Archives.

differentiated marketing to squeeze as much revenue as they can out of their flights. British Airways has slotted in an extra layer in its highly segmented long-range flights where some seats sell for more than 10 times the cost of others: World Traveller, World Traveller Plus with larger seats and some privileges, Club World (business class) and First. The airline's focus on cultivating the higher-paying segments gives it a return on equity twice that of any other large European airline.[15] Gap now has four different retail formats – Gap, Banana Republic,

Old Navy, and its most recent addition, Forth & Towne – to serve the varied needs of different fashion segments. And Estée Lauder offers hundreds of different products aimed at carefully defined segments:

Second only to L'Oréal, Estée Lauder, a world-leading marketer of prestige beauty and cosmetics products, is an expert in creating differentiated brands that serve the tastes of different market segments. Many of the top-ten best-selling prestige perfumes and make-up brands belong to Estée Lauder. There's the original Estée Lauder brand, with its gold and blue packaging, which appeals to older, 50+ baby boomers. Then there's Clinique, the company's most popular brand, perfect for the middle-aged mum with no time to waste and for younger women attracted to its classic free gift offers. For young, fashion-forward consumers, there's M.A.C., which provides make-up for clients like Pamela Anderson and Marilyn Manson. For the young and trendy, there's the Stila line, containing lots of shimmer and uniquely packaged in clever containers. And, for the New Age type, there's upscale Aveda, with its salon, make-up and lifestyle products, based on the art and science of earthy origins and pure flower and plant essences, celebrating the connection between Mother Nature and human nature.[16]

By offering product and marketing variations to segments, companies hope for higher sales and a stronger position within each market segment. Developing a stronger position within several segments creates more total sales than undifferentiated marketing across all segments. Estée Lauder's combined brands give it a much greater market share than any single brand could.

P&G markets numerous different brands of detergent, which compete with each other on supermarket shelves. The detergent portfolio is led by Tide, the group's second biggest brand overall, with annual sales in excess of $3bn. It is supported by number 2 brand Ariel, itself a $2bn product. Supporting these twin giants is a collection of other laundry products including detergents Bold, Cheer, Gain, Dreft, Era and Ivory Snow. Regional products include Daz in the UK and Dash in France and Germany. Together these multiple brands capture four times the market share of nearest rival Unilever.

Similarly, Unilever's difference in the tough laundry detergent market is supported by multiple brands. It is the number one detergent marketer in developing and emerging markets and among the leaders in several European countries. There are three main detergent families.

- Omo is the biggest, with global sales of around €2bn. It is the market leader in several countries including Brazil, Indonesia, Morocco, South Africa and Thailand. The product is also known in some markets under different names, for example Persil in the UK and Sunil in Germany, although all go under the 'Dirt is Good' banner.
- Surf, Unilever's number two family, is positioned as a value-for-money product. Local variants include Drive in Latin America and Skip in France.
- Radiant, the third brand, is sold mainly in developing markets, with a focus on whiteness at low prices. It is also distributed under the names Brilhante (in Latin America) and Rin (in India).

However, in the laundry detergent market Unilever is losing ground to P&G's onslaught.

But differentiated marketing also increases the costs of doing business. A firm usually finds it more expensive to develop and produce, say, 10 units of 10 different products than 100 units of one product. Developing separate marketing plans for the separate segments requires extra marketing research, forecasting, sales analysis, promotion planning and channel management, and trying to reach different market segments with different advertising increases promotion costs. Thus, the company must weigh increased sales against increased costs when deciding on a differentiated marketing strategy.

Concentrated marketing

A third market-coverage strategy, **concentrated marketing** (or **niche marketing**), is especially appealing when company resources are limited. Instead of going after a small share of a large market, the firm goes after a large share of one or a few smaller segments or niches. For example, Tetra Pak dominates the world's aseptic liquid food packaging, Tetra (no connection!) sells 80 per cent of the world's tropical fish food, and Steiner Optical captures 80 per cent of the world's military binoculars market.

Concentrated marketing (or niche marketing)—A market-coverage strategy in which a firm goes after a large share of one or a few submarkets.

Through concentrated marketing, the firm achieves a strong market position because of its greater knowledge of consumer needs in the niches it serves and the special reputation it acquires. It can market more *effectively* by fine-tuning its products, prices and programmes to the needs of carefully defined segments. It can also market more *efficiently*, targeting its products or services, channels and communications programmes towards only those consumers that it can serve best and most profitably.

Whereas segments are fairly large and normally attract several competitors, niches are smaller and may attract only one or a few competitors. Niching offers smaller companies an opportunity to compete by focusing their limited resources on serving niches that may be unimportant to or overlooked by larger competitors. Mills & Boon, which has grown to be one of the world's most successful publishers, targets its inexpensive romantic novels at women in search of romance. The company has researched and knows its market:

- Having the word 'wedding' in a book title guarantees higher sales.
- The heroine is often plain, not gorgeous, to promote reader identification: 'no oil painting in the way of looks'; kind and polite and pleasant and unobtrusive. And best of all, homely.
- The best settings for the story are a hospital or an aircraft (lots of chance for life or death action); doctors and pilots are the best heroes.
- The novels always end happily.

Like Mills & Boon, through concentrated marketing, a firm can achieve a strong market position in the segments (or niches) it serves because of its greater knowledge of the segments and its special reputation. It also enjoys many operating economies because of specialisation in production, distribution and promotion. A firm can earn a high rate of return on its investment from well-chosen segments. Mills & Boon are at last stepping out from middle-age romance into 'chick lit'. According to Gemma Clutterbuck, senior product manager at Red Dress Ink, 'The early chick lit books were loose and frothy, but we are moving it forward.'[17]

> " The low cost of setting up shop on the Internet makes it even more profitable to serve seemingly minuscule niches. "

Today, the low cost of setting up shop on the Internet makes it even more profitable to serve seemingly minuscule niches. Small businesses, in particular, are realising riches from serving small niches on the Web. Here is a 'Webpreneur' who achieved astonishing results:

> Sixty-three-year-old British artist Jacquie Lawson taught herself to use a computer only a few years ago. Last year, her online business had sales of over £2m (€3m). What does she sell? Online cards. Lawson occupies a coveted niche in the electronic world: a profitable, subscription-based website (**www.jacquielawson.com**) where she sells her highly stylised e-cards without a bit of advertising. While the giants – Hallmark and American Greetings – offer hundreds of e-cards for every occasion, Lawson offers only about 50 in total, the majority of which she intricately designed herself. Revenue comes solely from members – 81 per cent from the US – who pay £4 a year. Last year, membership climbed from 300,000 to 500,000 and the membership renewal rate is close to 70 per cent. Last December, Lawson's website attracted 22.7 million visitors, more than double that of closest rival **AmericanGreetings.com**. Lawson's success with a business model that has stumped many media giants speaks to both the Internet's egalitarian nature and her own stubborn belief that doing it her way is the right way.[18]

Concentrated marketing can be highly profitable. At the same time, it involves higher-than-normal risks. Companies that rely on one or a few segments for all of their business will suffer greatly if the segment turns sour, or larger competitors may decide to enter the same segment with greater resources. For these reasons, many companies prefer to diversify in several market segments.

Micromarketing

Micromarketing—A form of target marketing in which companies tailor their marketing programmes to the needs and wants of narrowly defined geographic, demographic, psychographic or behavioural segments.

Differentiated and concentrated marketers tailor their offers and marketing programmes to meet the needs of various market segments and niches. At the same time, however, they do not customise their offers to each individual customer. **Micromarketing** is the practice of tailoring products and marketing programmes to suit the tastes of specific individuals and locations. Rather than seeing a customer in every individual, micromarketers see the individual in every customer. Micromarketing includes *local marketing* and *individual marketing*.

Local marketing

Local marketing— Marketing that involves tailoring brands and promotions to the needs and wants of local customer groups.

Local marketing involves tailoring brands and promotions to the needs and wants of local customer groups – cities, neighbourhoods and even specific stores. Marks & Spencer is the UK's largest clothing retailer with 760 stores in more than 30 countries and 520 stores in the UK alone as of March 2007. It also sells high-quality food. 'Marks and Sparks' is a British institution as much as a shop, so it is surprising that the retailer loved by so many does not offer its customers all the same range of goods. With such wide national coverage, each store is tailored to fit the local market. The merchandise in the Bridge Street branch of Shakespeare's Stratford-upon-Avon is tailored to the wealthy local market and the town's huge tourist industry. The Solihull branch is tailored for the wealthy local business community who may shop elsewhere for their fine clothes but treasure the store's food hall. Meanwhile, the Tamworth branch is customised to serve a large working community with lower income.

Local marketing has some drawbacks. It can drive up manufacturing and marketing costs by reducing economies of scale. It can also create logistics problems as companies try to meet the varied requirements of different regional and local markets. Further, a brand's overall image might be diluted if the product and message vary too much in different localities.

Still, as companies face increasingly fragmented markets, and as new supporting technologies develop, the advantages of local marketing often outweigh the drawbacks. Local marketing helps a company to market more effectively in the face of pronounced regional and local differences in demographics and lifestyles. It also meets the needs of the company's first-line customers – retailers – who prefer more fine-tuned product assortments for their neighbourhoods.

Individual marketing

In the extreme, micromarketing becomes **individual marketing** – tailoring products and marketing programmes to the needs and preferences of individual customers. Individual marketing has also been labelled *one-to-one marketing*, *mass customisation* and *markets-of-one marketing*.

The widespread use of mass marketing has obscured the fact that for centuries consumers were served as individuals: the tailor custom-made the suit, the cobbler designed shoes for the individual, the cabinet-maker made furniture to order. Today, however, new technologies are permitting many companies to return to customised marketing. More powerful computers, detailed databases, robotic production and flexible manufacturing, and interactive communication media such as e-mail and the Internet – all have combined to foster 'mass customisation'. *Mass customisation* is the process through which firms interact one-to-one with masses of customers to design products and services tailor-made to individual needs.[19]

Visitors to Nike's NikeID website can personalise their trainers by choosing from hundreds of colours and putting an embroidered word or phrase on the tongue. Companies selling all kinds of products – from computers, confectionery, clothing and golf clubs to fire engines – are customising their offerings to the needs of individual buyers. Consider this example:

> LEGO recently launched LEGO Factory, a website (LEGOFactory.com) where LEGO fans can 'design their own ultimate LEGO model, show it off, and bring it to life'. Using LEGO's free, downloadable Digital Designer software, customers can create any structure they can imagine. Then, if they decide to actually build their creation, the software, which keeps track of which pieces are required, sends the order to LEGO. There, employees put all the pieces into a box, along with instructions, and ship it off. Customers can even design their own boxes. The software also lets proud users share their creations with others in the LEGO community, one of the traditional building blocks of the company's customer loyalty. The LEGO Factory Gallery features winning designs and lets users browse and order the inspired designs of others.[20]

Consumer goods marketers are not the only ones going one-to-one. Business-to-business marketers are also finding new ways to customise their offerings. For example, John Deere manufactures seeding equipment that can be configured in more than two million versions to individual customer specifications. The seeders are produced one at a time, in any sequence, on a single production line.

One-to-one marketing has made relationships with customers more important than ever.

Unlike mass production, which eliminates the need for human interaction, one-to-one marketing has made relationships with customers more important than ever. Just as mass production was the marketing principle of the last century, mass customisation is becoming a marketing principle for the twenty-first century. The world appears to be coming full circle – from the good old days when customers were treated as individuals, to mass marketing when nobody knew your name, and back again.

Individual marketing—
Tailoring products and marketing programmes to the needs and preferences of individual customers.

Individual marketing: At the LEGO Factory website, fans can design their own ultimate LEGO model, show it off and bring it to life.

SOURCE: Copyright © 2008 The *LEGO* Group. Used with permission.

The move towards individual marketing mirrors the trend in consumer *self-marketing*. Increasingly, individual customers are taking more responsibility for determining which products and brands to buy. Consider two business buyers with two different purchasing styles. The first sees several salespeople, each trying to persuade him to buy his or her product. The second sees no salespeople but rather logs on to the Internet. She searches for information on available products; interacts electronically with various suppliers, users and product analysts; and then makes up her own mind about the best offer. The second purchasing agent has taken more responsibility for the buying process, and the marketer has had less influence over her buying decision.

As the trend towards more interactive dialogue and less advertising monologue continues, self-marketing will grow in importance. As more buyers look up consumer reports, join Internet product-discussion forums, and place orders by phone or online, marketers will have to influence the buying process in new ways. They will need to involve customers more in all phases of the product development and buying processes, increasing opportunities for buyers to practise self-marketing.

Choosing a targeting strategy

Companies need to consider many factors when choosing a market targeting strategy. Which strategy is best depends on *company resources*. When the firm's resources are limited, concentrated marketing makes the most sense. The best strategy also depends on the degree of *product variability*. Undifferentiated marketing is more suited for uniform products such as grapefruit or steel. Products that can vary in design, such as cameras and automobiles, are more suited to differentiation or concentration. The *product's life-cycle stage* also must be considered. When a firm introduces a new product, it may be practical to launch only one version, and undifferentiated marketing or concentrated marketing may make the most sense. In the mature stage of the product life cycle, however, differentiated marketing begins to make more sense.

Another factor is *market variability*. If most buyers have the same tastes, buy the same amounts and react the same way to marketing efforts, undifferentiated marketing is appropriate. Finally, *competitors' marketing strategies* are important. When competitors use differentiated or concentrated marketing, undifferentiated marketing can be suicidal. Conversely, when competitors use undifferentiated marketing, a firm can gain an advantage by using differentiated or concentrated marketing.

Socially responsible target marketing

Smart targeting helps companies to be more efficient and effective by focusing on the segments that they can satisfy best and most profitably. Targeting also benefits consumers – companies reach specific groups of consumers with offers carefully tailored to satisfy their needs. However, target marketing sometimes generates controversy and concern. The biggest issues usually involve the targeting of vulnerable or disadvantaged consumers with controversial or potentially harmful products.

> ❝ Target marketing sometimes generates controversy and concern. ❞

For example, over the years, the cereal industry has been heavily criticised for its marketing efforts directed towards children, for example in the breakfast cereal market. Critics worry that premium offers and high-powered advertising appeals presented through the mouths of lovable animated characters will overwhelm children's defences. The marketers of toys and other children's products have been similarly battered, often with good justification.[21]

Other problems arise when the marketing of adult products spills over into the kid segment – intentionally or unintentionally. For example, the tobacco and beer companies are accused of targeting under-age smokers and drinkers. Some critics have even called for a complete ban on advertising to children.

A coalition of charities is demanding baby milk be treated like tobacco and subjected to a total advertising ban. The National Childbirth Trust, Save The Children and UNICEF say the current partial ban is not enough, and parents have been left confused. They want the ban on infant milk adverts to include 'follow-on' milks for older babies. At present, companies are not allowed to advertise formula milk for babies less than six months old but they are allowed to promote so-called follow-on milks, a range for children aged between six months and two years.

The charities accuse baby milk companies of using their follow-on milks to promote their products for younger infants by giving them the same name and logo so as to make them 'virtually indistinguishable'. Buxom glamour model Jordan fanned the flames of this debate when her picture appeared in a glossy magazine giving a brand of infant formula to her five-week-old daughter, Princess Tiaamii, with an advert for the company on the next page.[22]

The meteoric growth of the Internet and other carefully targeted direct media has raised fresh concerns about potential targeting abuses. The Internet allows increasing refinement of audiences and, in turn, more precise targeting. This might help makers of questionable products or deceptive advertisers to more readily victimise the most vulnerable audiences. Unscrupulous marketers can now send tailor-made deceptive messages directly to the computers of millions of unsuspecting consumers.[23]

Not all attempts to target children, minorities or other special segments draw such criticism. In fact, most provide benefits to targeted consumers. For example, Colgate makes a large selection of toothbrushes and toothpaste flavours and packages for children – from Colgate Barbie, Blues Clues and SpongeBob SquarePants Sparkling Bubble Fruit toothpastes to Colgate LEGO BIONICLE and Bratz character toothbrushes. Such products help make tooth brushing more fun and get children to brush longer and more often. Bratz dolls are appropriately targeted at minority consumers: Jade has unspecified Asian heritage, tan-skinned Fianna is said to be of Brazilian descent, Kumi Japanese, Kiana a Native American, and dolls of unspecified origin but a variety of tones.

Thus, in target marketing, the issue is not really *who* is targeted but rather *how* and for *what*. Controversies arise when marketers attempt to profit at the expense of targeted segments – when they unfairly target vulnerable segments or target them with questionable products or tactics. Socially responsible marketing calls for segmentation and targeting that serve not just the interests of the company but also the interests of those targeted.

Differentiation and positioning

Product's position—The way the product is defined by consumers on important attributes – the place the product occupies in consumers' minds relative to competing products.

Beyond deciding which segments of the market it will target, the company must decide on a *value proposition* – on how it will create differentiated value for targeted segments and what positions it wants to occupy in those segments. A **product's position** is the way the product is *defined by consumers* on important attributes – the place the product occupies in consumers' minds relative to competing products. 'Products are created in the factory, but brands are created in the mind,' says a positioning expert.[24]

In the automobile market, the Toyota Yaris and Honda Fit are positioned on economy, Mercedes and Cadillac on luxury, and Porsche and BMW on performance. Volvo positions powerfully on safety, and Toyota positions its fuel-efficient, hybrid Prius as a high-tech solution to the energy shortage: 'How far will you go to save the planet?', it asks. Audi is marketed as having superior German technology: 'Vorsprung durch Technik'. Real Marketing 9.1 contains more examples of how physical locations are used to position brands.

Porsche positions powerfully on performance and the sense of freedom it generates – pure emotion.
SOURCE: Reprinted by permission of Porsche cars North America, Inc.

real marketing 9.1

The place is the thing

Towns have long used famous characters to position the locations and give them a theme. Often these have some historical association, having been born, lived or died there. Some of Europe's more conspicuous cases are Mozart's Salzburg, Wagner's Bayreuth and Shakespeare's Stratford-upon-Avon. Other towns have positioned themselves with mythical or literary characters, such as Ashby-de-la-Zouch's Ivanhoe (who fought the Black Knight at Ashby Castle) or Nottingham's claimed Robin Hood (whose enemy, the Sheriff of Nottingham, supposedly lived there). The City of Nottingham was upset when Doncaster opened Robin Hood Airport, which is close to Sherwood Forest where Robin Hood, his Merry Men or indeed mythical Yorkshire bandit Robert Hod, fictitiously resided. Doncaster had an interesting choice in naming the airport, since Sir Walter Scott started his novel *Ivanhoe*, which also includes Robin Hood, in Doncaster.

Besides using people to position places, places position portfolios of products. Belgian InBer is Europe's largest brewer. It retains its hold on the European market by trading on the geographical heritage of its products. The company certainly has plenty of heritages to trade on. First trading in Belgium as Den Hoorn in 1366, it changed its name to Artois 400 years later. Stella Artois remains Belgium's favoured tipple; elsewhere it is marketed as being 'reassuringly expensive'. Another one of InBer's brands, Bass, can probably lay claim to the best product placement of all time, having a prominent position in Manet's *A Bar at the Folies Bergère*. Other beers it promotes are Boddingtons, 'the cream of Manchester', Newcastle Brown and Caffrey's Irish beer.

Whitbread, once owner of many of InBer's drinks, positions its restaurant chains geographically. Their Pizza Hut and TGI Friday's are both positioned as American, although the Hut is for families and TGI is for twenty-somethings. Café Rouge is French, Costa Coffee Italian, Brewers Fayre 'Olde Englande' and Beefeaters British and carnivore.

The source is traditionally important to water, as two of Nestlé Waters' current brands illustrate. Source Perrier is quintessentially French but is a product invented and originally owned and marketed by Sir St John Harmsworth, an English aristocrat who bought a spa containing the spring where the water originates. Sir St John marketed the product at a time when Frenchness was admired by the middle classes. It was first advertised as the 'champagne of mineral water'. However, the brand is not all French – the shape of Perrier's green bottles is based on the Indian clubs he used for exercising.

▶

...9.1

Ashbourne Water comes from a spring on land owned by Nestlé in Ashbourne, Derbyshire, a county in the north of England long associated with the fresh streams and open country of the Peak District National Park. However, in a burst of honesty the bottled label betrayed the location of Nestlé's UK head office in Croydon, an industrial town south of London!

With manufacturers increasingly chasing low wages, there are signs that the 'Made in . . .' label may help keep some jobs in high-wage economies. Consumers shun Prada bags that are not made in Italy, Louis Vuitton from outside France and non-Swiss Cartier. The resistance may stretch beyond luxury goods as local consumers react against the disloyalty of firms. Dyson vacuum cleaner sales dropped sharply in Europe when the firm broadcast that it was switching manufacture from Europe to Malaysia.

SOURCES: Michelin Green Guides to Austria, Germany and Great Britain; Alison Smith, 'Whitbread to shake up restaurants', *Financial Times* (1 November 2000), p. 27; Dan Bilefsky, 'Interbrew offer set to raise €3.3bn', *Financial Times* (9 November 2000), p. 33; Mike Levy, 'Marketing Cinderellas', *Marketing Business* (July/August 2000), pp. 26–7; Fred Kapner, 'The last sector where Made in Europe matters', *Financial Times* (4 December 2003), p. 16; Peter Marsh, 'Dust is settling on the Dyson clean-up', *Financial Times* (12 December 2003), p. 12; Frank Richard Prassel, *The Great American Bandit* (University of Oklahoma Press, 1993); *A Gest of Robyn Hode*, in R.B. Dobso and J. Taylor, *Rymes of Robin Hood* (London: Heinemann, 1976); Sir Walter Scott, *Ivanhoe*, 1819.

Consumers are overloaded with information about products and services. They cannot re-evaluate products every time they make a buying decision. To simplify the buying process, consumers organise products, services and companies into categories and 'position' them in their minds. A product's position is the complex set of perceptions, impressions and feelings that consumers have for the product compared with competing products.

 Consumers are overloaded with information about products and services.

Consumers position products with or without the help of marketers. But marketers do not want to leave their products' positions to chance. They must *plan* positions that will give their products the greatest advantage in selected target markets, and they must design marketing mixes to create these planned positions.

Positioning maps

In planning their differentiation and positioning strategies, marketers often prepare *perceptual positioning maps*, which show consumer perceptions of their brands versus competing products on important buying dimensions. Figure 9.3 shows a positioning map for the large luxury sports utility vehicle market.[25] The position of each circle on the map indicates the brand's perceived positioning on two dimensions – price and orientation (luxury versus performance). The size of each circle indicates the brand's relative market share. Thus, customers view the market-leading Cadillac Escalade as a moderately priced large luxury SUV with a balance of luxury and performance.

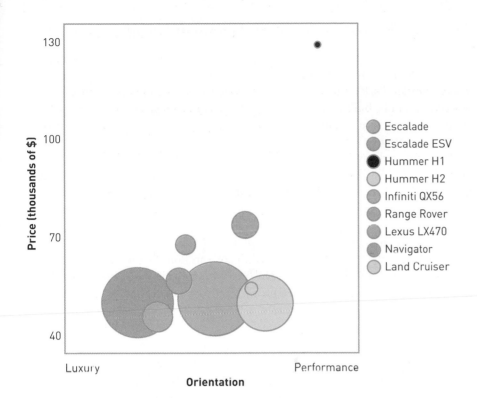

Figure 9.3 Positioning map: large luxury SUVs

The original Hummer H1 is positioned as a very high-performance SUV with a price tag to match. Hummer targets the current H1 Alpha towards a small segment of well-off rugged individualists. According to the H1 website, 'The H1 was built around one central philosophy: function – the most functional off-road vehicle ever made available to the civilian market. The H1 Alpha not only sets you apart, but truly sets you free.'

By contrast, although also oriented towards performance, the Hummer H2 is positioned as a more luxury-oriented and more reasonably priced luxury SUV. The H2 is targeted towards a larger segment of urban and suburban professionals. 'In a world where SUVs have begun to look like their owners, complete with love handles and mushy seats, the H2 proves that there is still one out there that can drop and give you 20,' says the H2 website. The H2 'strikes a perfect balance between interior comfort, on-the-road capability, and off-road capability.'

Choosing a differentiation and positioning strategy

Some firms find it easy to choose a differentiation and positioning strategy. For example, a firm well known for quality in certain segments will go for this position in a new segment if there are enough buyers seeking quality. But in many cases, two or more firms will go after the same position. Then, each will have to find other ways to set itself apart. Each firm must differentiate its offer by building a unique bundle of benefits that appeals to a substantial group within the segment.

The differentiation and positioning task consists of three steps: identifying a set of possible customer value differences that provide competitive advantages upon which to build a position, choosing the right competitive advantages, and selecting an overall positioning strategy. The company must then effectively communicate and deliver the chosen position to the market.

Identifying possible value differences and competitive advantages

To build profitable relationships with target customers, marketers must understand customer needs better than competitors do and deliver more customer value. To the extent that a company can differentiate and position itself as providing superior value, it gains **competitive advantage**.

Competitive advantage— An advantage over competitors gained by offering consumers greater value, either through lower prices or by providing more benefits that justify higher prices.

But solid positions cannot be built on empty promises. If a company positions its product as *offering* the best quality and service, it must actually differentiate the product so that it *delivers* the promised quality and service. Companies must do much more than simply shout out their positions in ad slogans and taglines. They must first *live* the slogan. For example, when Staples' research revealed that it should differentiate itself on the basis of 'an easier shopping experience', the office supply retailer held back its 'Staples: That was easy' marketing campaign for more than a year. First, it remade its stores to actually deliver the promised positioning (see Real Marketing 9.2).

To find points of differentiation, marketers must think through the customer's entire experience with the company's product or service. An alert company can find ways to differentiate itself at every customer contact point. In what specific ways can a company differentiate itself or its market offer? It can differentiate along the lines of *product, services, channels, people* or *image.*

Product differentiation takes place along a continuum. At one extreme we find physical products that allow little variation: chicken, steel, aspirin. Yet even here some meaningful differentiation is possible. For example, Nutro supplies its dry pet foods only through specialist pet supply or animal feed stores and is recommended by vets and dog breeders. Nutro claims pets prefer Nutro Choice which, because it is more concentrated than competitors' products, causes their animals to evacuate smaller, firmer stools. At the other extreme are products that can be highly differentiated, such as automobiles, clothing and furniture. Such products can be differentiated on features, performance, or style and design. Thus, Volvo provides new and better safety features; Miele designs its dishwasher to run more quietly; Bose positions its music systems on their striking design and sound characteristics; Bang and Olufsen as being modern and stylish. Similarly, companies can differentiate their products on such attributes as consistency, durability, reliability or repairability.

Beyond differentiating its physical product, a firm can also differentiate the services that accompany the product. Some companies gain *services differentiation* through speedy, convenient or careful delivery. In addition to differentiating its physical product, the firm can also differentiate the services that accompany the product. Some companies gain competitive advantage through speedy, reliable or careful *delivery*. Harrods, the luxury retailer, delivers to its customers using replica vintage vans – a service particularly popular at Christmas. At the other end of the scale, Domino's Pizza promises delivery in less than 30 minutes or reduces the price.

Emirates Airlines aim to make their journeys a relaxing experience for their First and Business Class passengers from start to finish. To do this they offer 'a complimentary personal airport transfer in a chauffeur-driven luxury car – from home or hotel to the airport, and then again on arrival, to your ultimate destination.' The cars are usually gleaming new silver-grey Mercedes. In contrast, fun-loving Virgin Atlantic offers passengers a chance to celebrate on board, and Thomson offers passengers in-flight competitions with prizes.

Speed of service is a competitive advantage used by many firms. Fast food is now common in the world's high streets and shopping centres, along with services like one-hour photo processing and Vision Express's one-hour service for spectacles. These services provide a direct benefit to customers by giving rapid gratification and allowing services to be completed within one shopping trip. Speed also helps sell more expensive goods. Abbey, a subsidiary of Grupo Santander, found that its success in providing large mortgages depended upon how fast it could confirm that it would give a person a home loan. It responded by allowing local managers to make loan decisions rather than processing applications centrally. In the car market Toyota's two-day policy means that it can supply a well-equipped Lexus within two days, while many other luxury car makers expect prospects to wait months for custom-built cars.

real marketing 9.2

Staples: on the button

These days, Staples really is riding the easy button. But only five years ago, things weren't so easy for the office supply superstore – or for its customers. The ratio of customer complaints to compliments was running an awful eight to one at Staples stores. The company's slogan – 'Yeah, we've got that' – had become a joke. Customers grumbled that items were often out of stock and said the sales staff was unwilling to help.

easy

Now there's an easy button for your business.

It's called Staples.

Wouldn't it be nice if daily tasks around the office got a little easier? When you shop Staples, it will be as easy as – well – pressing a button. Visit us at **staples.com/easy** to find out what our Easy Button℠ can do for you today.

 **STAPLES**

that was easy

The 'Staples: That was easy' marketing campaign has played a major role in repositioning Staples. But marketing promises count for little if not backed by the reality of the customer experience.

SOURCE: Staples The Office Superstore, LLC.

...9.2

After many focus groups and interviews, Shira Goodman, Staples' executive VP for marketing, concluded: 'Customers wanted an easier shopping experience.' That simple statement has resulted in one of the most successful marketing campaigns in recent history, built around the now familiar 'Staples: That was easy' tagline. But Staples' turnaround took a lot more than simply assailing customers with a new slogan. Before it could promise customers a simplified shopping experience, Staples had to actually deliver one. First, it had to fulfil the slogan.

When it launched in 1986, Staples was one of the very first office supply superstores. However, by the mid-1990s, the marketplace was full of specialist and general retailers offering office supplies, and a raft of other online sellers. Due to the increased competition, Staples' sales fell for the first time in 2001.

Market research conducted by Staples in-house team revealed that although shoppers expected Staples and its competitors to always have stock, price was not important. Customers in nearly all cases wanted an effortless shopping experience. They requested well-informed staff who could take the hassle out of shopping.

The 'Staples: That was easy' slogan was the brilliant outcome of that research. The tagline, however, remained a secret until Staples could update the look of its stores. The retailer slimmed down its inventory, shedding about 800 products including items such as Britney Spears backpacks, which were unattractive to the corporate world. Instead of being stored above customers' heads, office chairs were displayed on the shop floor so customers could sit on them. Clearer signage and re-trained staff helped direct shoppers to the right parts of the stores. Staples launched a printer cartridge promise in response to finding out that ink availability was a big concern for their customers. Lastly, their messages were tightened up, with a long letter mailed to potential customers simplified to two sentences.

Only when all of the customer-experience pieces were in place did Staples begin communicating its new positioning to customers. It was nearly a year before the stores were up to standard, Goodman says, but 'once we felt that the experience was significantly easier, we changed the tagline.' The company hired a new ad agency, McCann-Erickson Worldwide. McCann copywriters and art directors brainstormed the idea of 'easy'. As the creative session dragged on, the group's director said she wished she could just push a button and have a great ad appear, as she was hungry and wanted to got to lunch – thus the Easy Button was born. 'It took an amorphous concept and made it tangible,' Goodman says. The Easy Button was soon featured in a series of successful TV adverts, the first of which appeared in January 2005. In one spot, an emperor pushes the button to produce a huge wall to repel invaders; another has an office worker pressing the button to make printer cartridges fall from the sky.

On the web, Staples created a downloadable Easy Button toolbar, which transferred shoppers directly to Staples.com, and billboards suggested to commuters that an Easy Button would be helpful in heavy traffic.

Soon customers were asking is they could buy real Easy Buttons, so Staples began selling 7-cm red plastic buttons that when pushed said 'That was easy'. Staples donates more than €500,000 in button profits to charity each year, and sold its millionth button in 2006. The Easy Button was marketed as a stress ball, and before long home movies starring the button appeared on YouTube. The Easy Button is bigger than its category', says a McCann executive creative director.

The repositioning campaign was a success. The five-year rebranding odyssey has helped make €11.8 billion Staples the runaway leader in office retail. In addition to the success of the buttons, customer recall of Staples advertising has doubled to 70 per cent, compared with the industry average of 43 per cent. In 2006, Staples' profits were up 18 per cent while those of the competition slumped. According to Goodman, Staples now receives twice as many compliments as complaints at its stores. No doubt about it, the 'Staples: That was easy' marketing campaign has played a major role in repositioning Staples. Beyond pulling customers to the company's stores and website, the Easy Button is now part of American popular culture. But marketing promises count for little if not backed by the reality of the customer experience. Goodman attributes Staples' recent success more to the easy-does-it push within stores than to the 'That was easy' catchphrase and campaign. 'What has happened at the store has done more to drive the Staples brand than all the marketing in the world,' she says.

SOURCES: Adapted from portions of Michael Myser, 'Marketing made easy', *Business 2.0* (June 2006), pp. 43–4, and Lisa Tarter, 'Staples launches customer reviews from PowerReviews to help make shopping easier for small businesses and consumers alike', *Business Wire* (24 July 2007).

Installation can also differentiate one company from another. IBM, for example, is known for its quality installation service for its servers. It delivers all pieces of purchased equipment to the site at one time, rather than sending individual components to sit and wait for others to arrive. And when asked to move IBM equipment and install it in another location, IBM often moves competitors' equipment as well. Dixon's online retailers know how bad it can be buying online and then awaiting delivery. Their response is allowing buyers to choose a delivery slot when they order and the offer of installing new products and taking away the old one. If they find an earlier delivery slot they will even ring up to ask if you would really mind if they delivered a few days early. Companies can further distinguish themselves through their *repair services*. Many a car buyer would gladly pay a little more and travel a little further to buy a car from a dealer that provides top-notch repair service.

Firms that practise *channel differentiation* gain competitive advantage through the way they design their channel's coverage, expertise and performance. Amazon, Dell and the Direct.Line Group set themselves apart with their smooth-functioning direct channels.

Companies can gain a strong competitive advantage through *people differentiation* – hiring and training better people than their competitors do. Singapore Airlines enjoys an excellent reputation largely because of the grace of its flight attendants. People differentiation requires that a company select its customer-contact people carefully and train them well. For example, Disney trains its theme park people thoroughly to ensure that they are competent, courteous and friendly – from the hotel check-in agents, to the monorail drivers, to the ride attendants, to the people who sweep Main Street USA. Each employee is carefully trained to understand customers and to 'make people happy'.

Even when competing offers look the same, buyers may perceive a difference based on company or brand images. Thus companies work to establish *images* that differentiate them from competitors. A company or brand image should convey a singular and distinctive message that communicates the product's main benefits and positioning. Developing a strong and distinctive image calls for creativity and hard work. A company cannot implant an image in the public's mind overnight using only a few advertisements. If 'IBM means service', this image must be supported by everything the company says and does.

Symbols can provide strong company or brand recognition and image differentiation. Companies design signs and logos that provide instant recognition. They associate themselves with objects or characters that symbolise quality or other attributes, such as the Mercedes star, the Johnnie Walker character, the Michelin man or the Lacoste crocodile. The company might build a brand around some famous person. The perfume Passion is associated with Elizabeth Taylor and Longines watches with an image of Audrey Hepburn from *Breakfast at Tiffany's*. Some companies even become associated with colours, such as Kodak (yellow), Benson & Hedges (gold) or Ferrari (red).

The chosen symbols must be communicated through advertising that conveys the company or brand's personality. The ads attempt to establish a story line, a mood, a performance level – something distinctive about the company or brand. The atmosphere of the physical space in which the organisation produces or delivers its products and services can be another powerful image generator, as with TGI Friday's restaurants for American memorabilia and Scruffy Murphy's Pubs with Irish memorabilia. Thus a bank that wants to distinguish itself as the 'friendly bank' must choose the right building and interior design – layout, colours, materials and furnishings – to reflect these qualities, a far cry from the majestic edifices that many banks have inherited.

A company can also create an image through the types of event it sponsors. Perrier, the bottled water company, became known by laying out exercise tracks and sponsoring health sports events. Other organisations have identified themselves closely with cultural events, such as orchestral performances and art exhibits. Still other organisations support popular causes. For example, Heinz gives money to hospitals and Quaker gives food to the homeless.

Choosing the right competitive advantages

Suppose a company is fortunate enough to discover several potential differentiations that provide competitive advantages. It now must choose the ones on which it will build its positioning strategy. It must decide *how many* differences to promote and *which ones*.

How many differences to promote

Many marketers think that companies should aggressively promote only one benefit to the target market. Ad man Rosser Reeves, for example, said a company should develop a *unique selling proposition* (USP) for each brand and stick to it. Each brand should pick an attribute and tout itself as 'number one' on that attribute. Buyers tend to remember number one better, especially in this over-communicated society. Thus, Crest toothpaste consistently promotes its anti-cavity protection, and sophisticated John Lewis department stores have been 'Never knowingly undersold' since 1925.

Other marketers think that companies should position themselves on more than one differentiator. This may be necessary if two or more firms are claiming to be best on the same attribute. Today, in a time when the mass market is fragmenting into many small segments, companies are trying to broaden their positioning strategies to appeal to more segments. For example, Unilever introduced the first three-in-one bar soap – Lever 2000 – offering cleansing, deodorising *and* moisturising benefits. Clearly, many buyers want all three benefits. The challenge was to convince them that one brand can deliver all three. Judging from Lever 2000's outstanding success, Unilever easily met the challenge. However, as companies increase the number of claims for their brands, they risk disbelief and a loss of clear positioning.

Which differences to promote

Not all brand differences are meaningful or worthwhile; not every difference makes a good differentiator. Each difference has the potential to create company costs as well as customer benefits. A difference is worth establishing to the extent that it satisfies the following criteria:

- *Important.* The difference delivers a highly valued benefit to target buyers.
- *Distinctive.* Competitors do not offer the difference, or the company can offer it in a more distinctive way.
- *Superior.* The difference is superior to other ways in which customers might obtain the same benefit.
- *Communicable.* The difference is communicable and visible to buyers.
- *Pre-emptive.* Competitors cannot easily copy the difference.
- *Affordable.* Buyers can afford to pay for the difference.
- *Profitable.* The company can introduce the difference profitably.

❝ Not all brand differences are meaningful or worthwhile. ❞

Many companies have introduced differentiations that failed one or more of these tests. When the Westin Stamford Hotel in Singapore once advertised that it is the world's tallest hotel, it was a distinction that was not important to most tourists – in fact, it turned many off. Polaroid's Polarvision, which produced instantly developed home movies, also bombed. Although Polarvision was distinctive and even pre-emptive, it was inferior to another way of capturing motion, namely camcorders. Thus, choosing competitive advantages upon which to position a product or service can be difficult, yet such choices may be crucial to success.

Selecting an overall positioning strategy

The full positioning of a brand is called the brand's **value proposition** – the full mix of benefits upon which the brand is differentiated and positioned. It is the answer to the customer's question 'Why should I buy your brand?' Volvo's value proposition hinges on safety but also includes reliability, roominess and styling, all for a price that is higher than average but seems fair for this mix of benefits.

Figure 9.4 shows possible value propositions upon which a company might position its products. In the figure, the five green cells represent winning value propositions – differentiation and positioning that give the company competitive advantage. The blue cells, however, represent losing value propositions. The centre cell represents at best a marginal proposition. In the following

Value positioning—A range of positioning alternatives based on the value an offering delivers and its price.

Figure 9.4 Possible value propositions

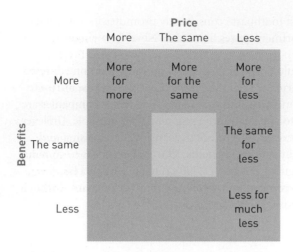

sections, we discuss the five winning value propositions upon which companies can position their products: more for more, more for the same, the same for less, less for much less, and more for less.

More for more

'More-for-more' positioning involves providing the most upscale product or service and charging a higher price to cover the higher costs. Mont Blanc writing instruments, Mercedes cars, Loewe TVs, Miele and Dualit Kitchen appliances – each claims superior quality, craftsmanship, durability, performance or style and charges a price to match. Not only is the market offering high in quality, it also gives prestige to the buyer. It symbolises status and a loftier lifestyle. Often, the price difference exceeds the actual increment in quality.

Sellers offering 'only the best' can be found in every product and service category, from hotels, restaurants, food and fashion to cars and household appliances. Consumers are sometimes surprised, even delighted, when a new competitor enters a category with an unusually high-priced brand. Starbucks coffee entered as a very expensive brand in a largely commodity category. Dyson came in as a premium vacuum cleaner with a price to match, touting 'No clogged bags, no clogged filters, and no loss of suction means only one thing. It's a Dyson.'

In general, companies should be on the lookout for opportunities to introduce a 'more-for-more' brand in any underdeveloped product or service category. Yet 'more-for-more' brands can be vulnerable. They often invite imitators who claim the same quality but at a lower price. Luxury goods that sell well during good times may be at risk during economic downturns when buyers become more cautious in their spending.

'More for much more' is growing with new wealth. An off-the-rack Armani men's suit at €1,200 is certainly more for more, but you can pay between €3,000 and €15,000 to have the same suit made to measure. Across at Chanel a delicate ladies' tweed suit is priced at €3,000 but, if you want that extra bit of embroidered detail, the price jumps to over €5,000.[26]

More for the same

Companies can attack a competitor's more-for-more positioning by introducing a brand offering comparable quality but at a lower price. For example, in the US Toyota introduced its Lexus line with a 'more-for-the-same' value proposition versus Mercedes and BMW. Its first ad headline read: 'Perhaps the first time in history that trading a $72,000 (€52,000) car for a $36,000 car could be considered trading up.' It communicated the high quality of its new Lexus through rave reviews in car magazines and through a widely distributed videotape showing side-by-side comparisons of Lexus and Mercedes automobiles. It published surveys showing that Lexus dealers were providing customers with better sales and service experiences than were Mercedes dealerships. Many Mercedes owners switched to Lexus, and the Lexus repurchase rate has been 60 per cent, twice the industry average.

The same for less

Offering 'the same for less' can be a powerful value proposition – everyone likes a good deal. For example, Dell offers equivalent quality computers at a lower 'price for performance'. Price fighters, such as Tesco, run a 'PRICE CH£CK': 'We shop around so you don't have to . . . Every week we check over 10,000 prices in Asda, Sainsbury's and Morrison's stores to guarantee you low prices every day.' 'Category killers' are typically 'big box' (very large out-of-town) retailers who don't claim to offer different or better products. Instead, they offer many of the same brands as department stores and speciality stores but at deep discounts based on superior purchasing power and lower-cost operations. Examples are Home Depot, Praktiker and B&Q Warehouse in the home improvement and do-it-yourself sector. Other companies develop imitative but lower-priced brands in an effort to lure customers away from the market leader. For example, AMD makes less expensive versions of Intel's market-leading microprocessor chips.

Less for much less

A market almost always exists for products that offer less and therefore cost less. Few people need, want or can afford 'the very best' in everything they buy. In many cases, consumers will gladly settle for less than optimal performance or give up some of the bells and whistles in exchange for a lower price. For example, many travellers seeking accommodation prefer not to pay for what they consider unnecessary extras, such as a pool, an attached restaurant, or mints on the pillow. The whole of the easyGroup is based on this price-slashing model: easyJet, easyCar, easyHotel, easyCruise . . .

'Less-for-much-less' positioning involves meeting consumers' lower performance or quality requirements at a much lower price. For example, the easyHotel concept is based on the same no-frills service of other Easy brands, offering double or twin rooms per night in London for as little as £30 (€45) in a space of about 6 square metres, and making services such as cleaning and television optional extras. The rooms are in three sizes: small, very small and tiny. Only three of London's easyHotel rooms have windows, a privilege for which guests pay a premium. There is no room service, minibar, porter, wardrobe or restaurant. Sounds too good to be true? Sounds too awful to be bearable? As one easyFan raved: 'I would have travelled anywhere in the country to spend a night at the new hotel. I'm not here because I want to stay in London but because of the hotel. I'm a big fan of the easy products.'[27]

More for less

Of course, the winning value proposition would be to offer 'more for less'. Many companies claim to do this. And, in the short run, some companies can actually achieve such lofty positions. For example, Richer Sounds, a hi-fi, home cinema and flat-screen TV specialist, is a bricks-and-clicks retailer. The aim is to give more for less, and have fun while doing so, says founder Julian Richer:

'We're one of the few retailers on the planet where you can enjoy the lowest possible prices in real stores without having to take your chance on the web. Our website, like any other website, can only help you so much; that's why we have stores across the country that also save you the cost of delivery! There's nothing like seeing your purchase in the flesh, having the chance to compare it to the numerous other hot deals on our shelves and take it home today! . . . Our buyers are the sharpest in the business, enabling us to offer the lowest possible prices.'[28]

Yet in the long run, companies will find it very difficult to sustain such best-of-both positioning. Offering more usually costs more, making it difficult to deliver on the 'for-less' promise. Companies that try to deliver both may lose out to more focused competitors. Facing competition from purely Internet retailers selling a broad range of electrical goods, Richer Sounds has to fight to hold its market position by keeping costs down and service quality high.

All said, each brand must adopt a positioning strategy designed to serve the needs and wants of its target markets. 'More for more' will draw one target market, 'less for much less' will draw another, and so on. Thus, in any market, there is usually room for many different companies, each successfully occupying different positions. The important thing is that each company must develop its own winning positioning strategy, one that makes it special to its target consumers.

Developing a positioning statement

Positioning statement—
A statement that summarises company or brand positioning. It takes this form: *To* (target segment and need) *our* (brand) *is* (concept) *that* (point of difference).

Company and brand positioning should be summed up in a **positioning statement**. The statement should follow the form: *To (target segment and need) our (brand) is (concept) that (point of difference).*[29] For example: 'To *busy, mobile professionals who need to always be in the loop, BlackBerry* is *a wireless connectivity solution* that *allows you to stay connected to data, people and resources while on the go, easily and reliably – more so than competing technologies.*' Sometimes a positioning statement is more detailed:

> To young, active soft-drink consumers who have little time for sleep, Mountain Dew is the soft drink that gives you more energy than any other brand because it has the highest level of caffeine. With Mountain Dew, you can stay alert and keep going even when you haven't been able to get a good night's sleep.

Note that the positioning first states the product's membership in a category (Mountain Dew is a soft drink) and then shows its point of difference from other members of the category (has more caffeine). Placing a brand in a specific category suggests similarities that it might share with other products in the category. But the case for the brand's superiority is made on its points of difference.

Sometimes marketers put a brand in a surprisingly different category before indicating the points of difference. DiGiorno is a frozen pizza whose crust rises when the pizza is heated. But instead of putting it in the frozen pizza category, the marketers positioned it in the delivered pizza category. Their ad shows party guests asking which pizza delivery service the host used. But, says the host, 'It's not delivery, its DiGiorno!' This helped highlight DiGiorno's fresh quality and superior taste over the normal frozen pizza.

Communicating and delivering the chosen position

Once it has chosen a position, the company must take strong steps to deliver and communicate the desired position to target consumers. All the company's marketing mix efforts must support the positioning strategy.

Positioning the company calls for concrete action, not just talk. If the company decides to build a position on better quality and service, it must first *deliver* that position. Designing the marketing mix – product, price, place and promotion – involves working out the tactical details of the positioning strategy. Thus, a firm that seizes on a more-for-more position knows that it must produce high-quality products, charge a high price, distribute through high-quality dealers and advertise in high-quality media. It must hire and train more service people, find retailers who have a good reputation for service, and develop sales and advertising messages that broadcast its superior service. This is the only way to build a consistent and believable more-for-more position.

> " Positioning the company calls for concrete action, not just talk. "

Companies often find it easier to come up with a good positioning strategy than to implement it. Establishing a position or changing one usually takes a long time. In contrast, positions that have taken years to build can quickly be lost. Once a company has built the desired position, it must take care to maintain the position through consistent performance and communication. It must closely monitor and adapt the position over time to match changes in consumer needs and competitors' strategies. However, the company should avoid abrupt changes that might confuse consumers. Instead, a product's position should evolve gradually as it adapts to the ever-changing marketing environment.

Reviewing the concepts

In this chapter, you've learned about the major elements of a customer-driven marketing strategy: segmentation, targeting, differentiation and positioning. Marketers know that they cannot appeal to all buyers in their markets, or at least not to all buyers in the same way. Buyers are too numerous, too widely scattered and too varied in their needs and buying practices. Therefore, most companies today practise *target marketing* – identifying market segments, selecting one or more of them, and developing products and marketing mixes tailored to each.

1. Define the major steps in designing a customer-driven marketing strategy

The major steps are market segmentation, targeting, differentiation and positioning. Customer-driven marketing strategy begins with selecting which customers to serve and deciding on a value proposition that best serves the targeted customers. It consists of four steps. *Market segmentation* is the act of dividing a market into distinct groups of buyers with different needs, characteristics or behaviours who might require separate products or marketing mixes. Once the groups have been identified, *market targeting* evaluates each market segment's attractiveness and selects one or more segments to serve. Market targeting consists of designing strategies to build the *right relationships* with the *right customers*. *Differentiation* involves actually differentiating the market offering to create superior customer value. *Positioning* consists of positioning the market offering in the minds of target customers.

2. List and discuss the major bases for segmenting consumer and business markets

There is no single way to segment a market. Therefore, the marketer tries different variables to see which give the best segmentation opportunities. For consumer marketing, the major

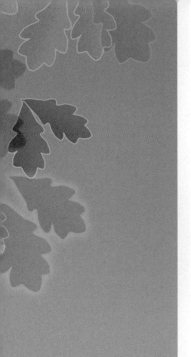

segmentation variables are geographic, demographic, psychographic and behavioural. In *geographic segmentation*, the market is divided into different geographical units such as nations, regions, states, counties, cities or neighbourhoods. In *demographic segmentation*, the market is divided into groups based on demographic variables, including age, gender, family size, family life cycle, income, occupation, education, religion, race, generation and nationality. In *psychographic segmentation*, the market is divided into different groups based on social class, lifestyle or personality characteristics. In *behavioural segmentation*, the market is divided into groups based on consumers' knowledge, attitudes, uses or responses to a product.

Business marketers use many of the same variables to segment their markets. But business markets also can be segmented by business consumer *demographics* (industry, company size), *operating characteristics*, *purchasing approaches*, *situational factors* and *personal characteristics*. The effectiveness of segmentation analysis depends on finding segments that are *measurable*, *accessible*, *substantial*, *differentiable* and *actionable*.

3. Explain how companies identify attractive market segments and choose a market targeting strategy

To target the best market segments, the company first evaluates each segment's size and growth characteristics, structural attractiveness and compatibility with company objectives and resources. It then chooses one of four market targeting strategies – ranging from very broad to very narrow targeting. The seller can ignore segment differences and target broadly using *undifferentiated* (or *mass*) *marketing.* This involves mass producing, mass distributing and mass promoting about the same product in about the same way to all consumers. Or the seller can adopt *differentiated marketing* – developing different market offers for several segments. *Concentrated marketing* (or *niche marketing*) involves focusing on only one or a few market segments. Finally, *micromarketing* is the practice of tailoring products and marketing programmes to suit the tastes of specific individuals and locations. Micromarketing includes *local marketing* and *individual marketing*. Which targeting strategy is best depends on company resources, product variability, product life-cycle stage, market variability and competitive marketing strategies.

4. Discuss how companies differentiate and position their products for maximum competitive advantage in the marketplace

Once a company has decided which segments to enter, it must decide on its *differentiation and positioning strategy.* The differentiation and positioning task consists of identifying a set of possible differentiations that create competitive advantage, choosing advantages upon which to build a position, choosing the right competitive advantages, and selecting an overall positioning strategy. The brand's full positioning is called its *value proposition* – the full mix of benefits upon which the brand is positioned. In general, companies can choose from one of five winning value propositions upon which to position their products: more for more, more for the same, the same for less, less for much less, or more for less. Company and brand positioning are summarised in positioning statements that state the target segment and need, the positioning concept and specific points of difference. The company must then effectively communicate and deliver the chosen position to the market.

Discussing the concepts

1. What are the benefits of mass marketing versus market segmentation for a business? Discuss in relation to examples of product and service providers.

2. The European Union, with its member states, is now viewed as an attractive and distinctive geographic market segment. Do you agree with this view? To what extent can businesses market in the same way to different consumers in member states? What does this imply about market segmentation?

3. Financial services providers are looking to segment their markets in the face of greater competition and ever more demanding customers. Would segmentation work for financial services? Show how financial services providers might go about segmenting their markets and implementing selected targeting strategies.

4. Famous personalities are often used in advertising products. Think of examples you know and work out what values the personality brings to the brand.

5. Britain is a laggard in terms of sustainable domestic waste disposal. When the government reduced 'black bin' (general refuse collection) from weekly to every second week, and 'chipping bins' so that people are charged for the volume of their general waste disposal, there was uproar. How could segmentation help with the adoption of these environmentally friendly ideas?

Applying the concepts

1. By looking at advertising and at products themselves, we can often see how marketers are attempting to position their products and what target market they hope to reach.

   - Define the positioning of and target markets for Coca-Cola, Pepsi Cola, Red Bull, Tango and Mountain Dew.
   - Define the positionings of and target markets for KitKat, Lion Bar, Snickers, Aero, Mars Bars and Twix.
   - Do you think that the soft drinks and confectionery industries achieve distinctive positioning and target markets? Are some more clearly defined than others?

2. A successful family-owned convenience store in Measham (postcode DE12 7GF) has a chance to purchase a second store in nearby Appleby Magna (postcode DE12 7AQ). Visit www.upmystreet.com to view the ACORN geodemographics of the two locations and suggest how the convenience store's merchandise and promotions should be adjusted to meet the needs of Appleby Magna.

Web resources

For additional classic case studies and Internet exercises, visit **www. pearsoned.co.uk/ kotler**

References

1. See www.classiccarclub.co.uk or manhattan.classiccarclub.com; Nick Hornby, 'Thunder Road', in *31 Songs* (London: Penguin, 2003); Helium Report, *Classic Car Club of Manhattan's Carbon Fiber Collection Adds Modern Exotics* (28 February 2007); 'The divo: Inside', *Time Out New York* (8–14 June 2006); Bruce Springsteen, *Born to Run*, CBS 69170, 1975.

2. For these and other examples, see Darell K. Rigby and Vijay Vishwanath, 'Localization: The revolution in consumer markets', *Harvard Business Review* (April 2006), pp. 82–92.

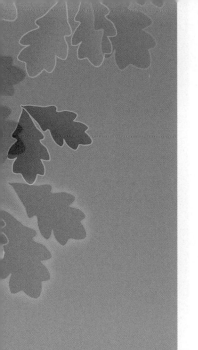

3. Stacy-Marie Ishmael, 'The Saga story', *Financial Times* (26 June 2007); Cleve West, 'Far pavilions', *The Independent* (4 August 2007).

4. See Fara Warner, 'Nike changes strategy on women's apparel', *New York Times* (16 May 2005), accessed at www.nytimes.com; and Thomas J. Ryan, 'Just do it for women', *SGB* (March 2006), pp. 25–6.

5. 'Pain perception: Sex and drugs', *The Economist* (23 July 2005), pp. 73–4.

6. Robert Berner, 'Out-discounting the discounter', *Business Week* (10 May 2004), pp. 78–79; 'The almighty dollar store', *Wall Street Journal: The Classroom Edition* (March 2005), accessed at www.wsjclassroomedition.com/archive/05mar/econ_dollarstore.htm; Debbie Howell, 'Dollar', *DSN Retailing Today* (21 November 2005), pp. 11–12; Bernadette Casey, 'Retailers better learn the real value of a dollar', *DSN Retailing Today* (13 March 2006), p. 6; Andrew Johnson, 'Discount brands retailer has £2.3m target for float', *The Express* (6 August 2007); Laura Wood, 'By 2012, the top ten global discount retailer markets are expected to account for US$13.84tr in total retail sales', *Business Wire* (7 August 2007).

7. See Maureen Wallenfang, 'Appleton, Wis.-area dealers see increase in moped sales', *Knight Ridder Tribune Business News* (15 August 2004), p. 1; Louise Lee, 'Love those boomers', *BusinessWeek* (24 October 2005), pp. 94–100; and Honda's website at www.powersports.honda.com/scooters/, July 2006.

8. Extracted from Rohan's vision on http://www.rohan.co.uk/info/OurVision_1.aspx, 11 August 2007. Also see Gemma Bowes, Escape: Travel wardrobe: The verdict: 'Chic or freak? Rohan boasts its travel wear can cope with any situation. Gemma Bowes takes up the challenge on a trip to Italy', *The Observer* (3 April 2005).

9. Danuta Kean, Business life: 'Deep inside the mind of the bloke', *Financial Times* (15 May 2007); David Prosser, 'CD's demise very much exaggerated', *The Independent* (1 August 2007).

10. Portions adapted from Alan T. Saracevic, 'Author plumbs bottomless depth of Mac worship', accessed at www.sfgate.com, 12 December 2004. Definition from http://www.urbandictionary.com/define.php?term=Macolyte&r=d, August 2006.

11. Information from http://home.americanexpress.com/home/mt_personal.shtml, August 2006.

12. Jonathan Guthrie, 'Capsule hotel to open at Gatwick', *Financial Times* (21 June 2007), p. 5; Sally Shalam, Travel: Weekend: Home: 'Yotel, Gatwick airport', *The Guardian* (30 June 2007).

13. See Arundhati Parmar, 'Global youth united', *Marketing News* (28 October 2002), pp. 1, 49; '"Impossible is nothing" adidas launches new global brand advertising campaign', accessed at www.adidas.com, 5 February 2004; 'Teen spirit', *Global Cosmetic Industry* (March 2004), p. 23; Johnnie L. Roberts, 'World tour', *Newsweek* (6 June 2005), pp. 34–6; and the MTV Worldwide website, www.mtv.com/mtvinternational.

14. See Michael Porter, *Competitive Advantage* (New York: Free Press, 1985), pp. 4–8, 234–6. For more recent discussions, see Stanley Slater and Eric Olson, 'A fresh look at industry and market analysis', *Business Horizons* (January–February 2002), pp. 15–22; Kenneth Sawka and Bill Fiora, 'The four analytical techniques every analyst must know: 2. Porter's Five Forces analysis', *Competitive Intelligence Magazine* (May–June 2003), p. 57; and Philip Kotler and Kevin Lane Keller, *Marketing Management*, 12th edn (Upper Saddle River, NJ: Prentice Hall, 2006), pp. 342–3.

15. 'British Airways and Iberia: Paella in the sky', *The Economist* (18 April 2007), pp. 34–5.

16. Nina Munk, 'Why women find Lauder mesmerizing', *Fortune* (25 May 1998), pp. 97–106; Christine Bittar, 'New faces, same name', *Brandweek* (11 March 2002), pp. 28–34; Robin Givhan, 'Estée Lauder, sending a message in a bottle', *The Washington Post* (26 April 2004), p. C.01; and information accessed at www.elcompanies.com, www.stila.com and www.macmakeup.com, July 2006.

17. Joseph McAleer, 'A saga of romance, big business and unrequited lust', *The Times* (29 October 1999), pp. 37–8; John Walsh and Jojo Moyes, 'Swoon! Mills & Boon make eyes at male readers', *The Independent* (28 September 2000), p. 1; Ashling O'Connor, 'Mills & Boon develops a passion for "chick lit"', *Financial Times* (12 April 2002); Fiona Macleod, 'True love is still a classic winner', *The Scotsman* (10 August 2007).

18. Gwendolyn Bounds, 'How an artist fell into a profitable online card business', *Wall Street Journal* (21 December 2004), p. B1; David Smith, 'UK's cottage industry beats US internet giants', *The Observer* (12 February 2006), accessed at http://oberserver.guardian.co.uk.

19. For a good discussion of mass customisation and relationship building, see Don Peppers and Martha Rogers, *Managing Customer Relationships: A strategic framework* (Hoboken, NJ: John Wiley & Sons, 2004), Ch. 10.

20. Example adapted from Michael Prospero, 'Lego's new building blocks', *Fast Company* (October 2005), p. 35, with information from http://factory.lego.com/, August 2006.

21. See Susan Linn, *Consuming Kids: The hostile takeover of childhood* (New York: The New Press, 2004); Suzy Bashford, 'Time to take more responsibility?', *Marketing* (11 May 2005), pp. 32–6; Sonia Reyes, 'Kraft Foods cited for misleading kids', accessed at www.brandweek.com, 4 August 2005; and William MacLeod, 'Does advertising make us fat? No!', *Brandweek* (20 February 2006), p. 19.

22. 'Baby milk ads "should be banned"', BBC News, 6 August 2007, http://news.bbc.co.uk/1/hi/health/6933188.stm; 'Ban on baby milk adverts?', BBC Radio 1, 6 August 2007, www.bbc.co.uk/radio1/news/newsbeat/070807_breast_feeding.shtml.

23. See 'FBI Internet Crime Complaint Center releases stats', *States News Service* (6 April 2006).

24. Jack Trout, 'Branding can't exist without positioning', *Advertising Age* (14 March 2005), p. 28.

25. Adapted from a positioning map prepared by students Brian May, Josh Payne, Meredith Schakel and Bryana Sterns, University of North Carolina, April 2003. SUV sales data furnished by WardsAuto.com, June 2006. Price data from www.edmunds.com, June 2006.

26. Syl Tang, Business of fashion: 'The hand-made's tale', *Financial Times* (2 March 2007); Venessa Friedman, 'There are other ways to get attention', *Financial Times* (23/24 September 2006), p. W3.

27. Danielle Demetriou, 'A compact orange cell for £20. It must be easyHotel', *The Independent* (3 August 2005).

28. richersounds.com, 12 August 2007; Andrew Penman and Michael Greenwood, 'Sorted and the city: Julian Richer', *The Mirror* (28 November 2003); Michael Dempsey, 'A sound business strategy', FT.com (15 June 2004).

29. See Bobby J. Calder and Steven J. Reagan, 'Brand design', in Dawn Iacobucci (ed.), *Kellogg on Marketing* (New York: John Wiley & Sons, 2001), p. 61. The Mountain Dew example is from Alice M. Tybout and Brian Sternthal, 'Brand positioning', in Iacobucci, op. cit., p. 54.

Company case 9 Coffee-Mate

Greg, category manager for coffee creamers, was evaluating his ad agency's proposal for Coffee-Mate (Exhibit 9.1). The £25m (€37m) a year coffee creamer market was small with a household penetration of only 18 per cent. Despite the growth of private labels to take 37 per cent of the market, Coffee-Mate's £1.5m advertising budget had enabled it to hold a 55 per cent market share and squeeze both private label and other brands (Complement, Kenco and Compleat). However, budgets were being squeezed, so unless the advertising campaign could show some sales gain, there was a danger that the category could be milked to provide income to invest in food products with more growth potential.

Competition in the coffee creamer market

The coffee creamer market is distinct from the declining £43m instant dry milk market (Marvel, St Ivel Five Pints and Pint Size). Dried or powdered milk had been associated with slimming (e.g. Marvel adopted this positioning). Dried or powdered milk is not a direct substitute for coffee creamers because of its poor mixing qualities. It is used as a whitener in tea or coffee only in 'emergencies' when the household has run out of milk.

The coffee creamer market is undergoing a change in parallel with consumers' developing tastes for skimmed and semi-skimmed milk in their coffee. Milk is the most popular whitener for coffee. Although cream is thought to be the best whitener, consumers perceive cream as reserved, ritualistic and appropriate for special occasions but not for daily use.

Powdered or dried milk is a distress product; creamers are regarded as an indulgence, although non-users did not see creamers as anything like a substitute for cream and were generally suspicious of the product.

Coffee-Mate is a blend of dried glucose and vegetable fat, but cannot be legally defined as non-dairy,

Exhibit 9.1 Proposed TV ad to boost sales

Vision	Sound
Jane and John, an affluent thirty-something couple, are entertaining two other similar couples.	Soft soul music playing throughout.
They are ending their meal by drinking coffee out of fine china cups and eating After Eights.	
Jane looks, alarmed, at John. John glances at the empty cream jug.	John (to one of the other guests): 'Do you want another cup?'
	Guest 1: 'Yes, please.'
	Guest 2: 'Me, too! With cream!'
Jane rushes into kitchen and frantically looks for cream (there is none) and milk (all gone).	Jane (thinking quickly): 'I'll make it!'
Jane pauses, smiles, then gets out the Coffee-Mate. Jane pours the coffee and adds the Coffee-Mate.	
Jane returns with coffee. Guest sips the coffee containing Coffee-Mate.	Guest 1: 'Lovely, even better than the last one!'
	Guest 2: 'Yes, how do you do it?'
John smiles quizzically (and admiringly) at Jane. Jane leans back in her chair, smiling knowingly.	Voice: 'Coffee-Mate, never be without it!'

since it also contains milk derivatives. Recent improvements to the product include the relaunch of Coffee-Mate 100 g and 200 g in straight-sided glass jars with paper labels, and a 'Nidoll-contoured' jar with shrink-wrapped label. Packs of 500 g and 1 kg are available in cartons with an inner bag. When Coffee-Mate Lite, a low-fat alternative to Coffee-Mate, was introduced, cannibalisation of volume was minimal. The volume generated by Lite is a key feature in the development of the brand, which has experienced a 10 per cent growth in sales volume in the first three years following Lite's launch.

The Coffee-Mate consumer

The average Coffee-Mate consumer buys 1.5 kg annually. There is no *strong* demographic bias among coffee creamer buyers although there is a slight skew towards 45–64-year-olds, two-person households and households without children. Heavy buyers of Coffee-Mate have a slight bias towards lower social class, aged 45+, 2–3-person households with children. Coffee-Mate Lite users have a slight bias towards 45–64-year-olds, full-time working housewives and households without children.

AGB Superpanel data suggest that buyers of Coffee-Mate use all brands and types of coffee. The creamer market has a low interest level since it is not a weekly shopping item. Reasons given for lapsed usage were similar to non-users (Exhibit 9.2).

Exhibit 9.3 Consumption by income group (per person/week)

Weekly income (£)	Weekly expenditure (£)
645+	0.25
475–644	0.19
250–474	0.20
125–249	0.18
0–124	0.17
125+ (no earners)	0.32
0–125 (no earners)	0.19
Old-age pensioners	0.34

SOURCE: National Food Survey, pub. MAFF. Crown copyright material is reproduced under the terms of the click-use licence with the permission of the Controller of HMSO.

Because Coffee-Mate and Coffee-Mate Lite are 'consumed' with coffee, popularity and demand will also be affected by the annual coffee consumption, which is static at a low 3 kg per head in the UK (about 1.5 cups per day). The figure for Italy, France and Germany is 5 kg, and 11–13 kg in the Benelux region and Scandinavia. The National Food Survey suggests that the higher a household's income, the more it spends on coffee (Exhibit 9.3). Childless households are the most intense coffee drinkers (Exhibit 9.4).

Dried milk

The image of powdered milk is as a distress product where the *brand* is *bought*, but the *product* is

Exhibit 9.2 Reasons for lapsing and rejection (number of respondents)

Spontaneous response	Lapsing	Rejection
Don't drink coffee	11	22
Drink black coffee	5	6
Prefer milk	50	33
Prefer skimmed milk	5	3
Don't like them	10	18
Leaves coffee too hot	2	1
No need to use them	5	5
Don't think to buy them	1	4
Doesn't mix	4	1
Prefer pure things	4	3
Fattening	2	2
Too rich/creamy	1	2
Other	5	3
Don't know	4	9

Exhibit 9.4 Consumption by household size (per person/week)

Adults in household	Children in household	Weekly expenditure (£)
1	0	0.27
1	1+	0.15
2	0	0.25
2	1	0.18
2	2	0.15
2	3	0.15
2	4+	0.11
3	0	0.23
3+	1–2	0.16
3+	3+	0.12
4+	0	0.25

SOURCE: National Food Survey, pub. MAFF. Crown copyright material is reproduced under the terms of the click-use licence with the permission of the Controller of HMSO.

tolerated: 'You tend to buy powdered milk thinking that you will need it when you run out, and occasionally you do.' 'Powdered milk is useful if you run out of real milk. You can make it up and use it just like the real thing, but it doesn't taste too good. You have to be a bit desperate to want to use it.'

Other negatives attach to dry milk. Respondents considered it to be inconvenient to prepare. Frequently its performance is seen as disappointing: it is 'lumpy', resulting in 'bits' floating on the top of their coffee. The product also tends to 'congeal' when spooned into tea or coffee. When made up and poured, the product's poor taste qualities are apparent: 'We have had it in our Cornflakes when we've run out, but quite honestly, it tastes so disgusting that in the future I don't think I'd bother.' 'It's all right for baking, but if you want to use it like real milk, it's not really advisable.'

Whiteners/coffee creamers

Coffee creamers have a more polarised image across users and non-users. *Loyal* or *confirmed creamer users* regard creamer as almost a treat. These hedonistic and indulgent properties are sometimes enhanced by the brand (e.g. Coffee-Mate) being perceived as having relaxing or comforting benefits: 'Creamers are a little bit of an indulgence. They make coffee taste so much better. They add something to it which improves the taste.' 'First thing in the morning I tend to have coffee with semi-skimmed milk, but towards 11 o'clock I want something which is more relaxing, more substantial, so I have coffee with Coffee-Mate. It seems to be comforting.'

Creamers' taste is a motivating force behind usage. Loyal users appreciate the thicker, creamier taste. Creamers are considered to supplement the taste of coffee, to complement and improve its flavour. For Coffee-Mate, the perceptions are extremely positive. Users enjoy its sweet delivery, stating that they need not add sugar to it. Fans feel that it does produce a creamy cup of coffee whether or not it is added to instant or freshly brewed 'real' coffee: 'Coffee without Coffee-Mate, just made with milk, tastes like it's got something missing.' 'Coffee-Mate kind of lifts the flavour. It makes a richer, better-tasting cup of coffee, whether it be an instant or a real one.'

Non-users' perceptions of coffee creamers are tainted by their negative attitudes towards dried milk. Creamers are something you have put by for an emergency: 'If someone gave me a cup of coffee with creamer in it, I would think they were doing it because they had run out of milk. I wouldn't have thought it was because they like the taste of it. Surely nobody could like the taste.'

Thus, in marked contrast to the users, non-users describe creamers as changing the taste of coffee, masking its pure taste rather than enhancing it. They also criticised its high sugar content, which the consumers feel delivers a flavour that is unacceptably sweet. They perceive it to be a poor alternative to cream: 'You can always tell when someone's used creamers, it just tastes powdery. It doesn't taste like cream, it has a taste all of its own.' 'Whiteners taste nothing like cream. They taste powdery. You always know when they're there.'

Lapsed users still see creamers as a bit of an indulgence and a treat. However, they feel an element of guilt in using the product: 'I like coffee creamers – I like the taste. But I stopped using them because I felt I was putting on too much weight and I needed to cut down. I just think there is too much in there, it's just glucose syrup and vegetable fat.' 'My husband had to go on a low-cholesterol diet and I figured that there was just too much fat in the coffee creamers. We've become accustomed now to drinking it black, or with very little skimmed milk.'

Health concerns are having an impact upon milk consumption. This change has been prompted by consumers' concern over health in general, and their level of fat intake in particular. Some consumers found it difficult to wean themselves and their families off milk, initially, and then semi-skimmed milk, in favour of the fully skimmed variety. However, many are persistent in adopting an overall preventative health maintenance regime as well as controlling their weight. So, while a few retained the notion that a cup of real coffee made with cream was the ideal, many others considered their ideal to be coffee drunk with just a dash of milk or black. Coffee-Mate is in danger of being redundant since it is perceived to be too close to cream in its taste and texture while its creamy association is increasingly deemed unhealthy. Coffee-Mate Lite may redeem the situation by offering the same benefits of creamy and rich taste without causing injury to health and weight.

Consumer analyses

TGI User Surveys covering instant/ground coffee and powdered milk/coffee creamer markets yielded five potential consumer groups for Coffee-Mate.

'Sharon and Tracy' – experimentalists (sample proportion: 15.4 per cent)

They like to enjoy themselves and try new things. They enjoy spending money happily and seem to be very materialistic and status conscious. They go out frequently and are uninterested in political or environmental issues. Although they are heavy users of instant coffee, they are low-level users of ground coffee. They claim to use Nescafé granules and Maxwell House powder most often. They are below-average users of the category and average users of Coffee-Mate, but heavy users of cream.

They are younger (15–44 years) with a mid- to down-market bias (C2D) and children. They are of middle income (£15,000 up to £30,000), but live in state-owned property, in underprivileged areas.

They read many 'low brow' newspapers and the 'mums' magazines such as Bella, Chat and Woman. They are heavy users of commercial terrestrial TV, breakfast programmes and satellite TV and are heavy listeners to pop radio channels. They cannot resist buying magazines and read papers for entertainment rather than for news.

They spend average to high amounts on the main grocery shop. They love shopping for anything, be it food, clothes, kitchen gadgets or whatever. They like to keep up with fashion and believe they are stylish, and feel it is important to try to keep looking young. They will try anything new. They will respond to seeing new things in advertising or in the store.

They are very gregarious and socialise often (heavy users of pubs, wine bars and restaurants). They like to enjoy life and not worry about the future. They holiday abroad (eat, drink and lie in the sun) and like to treat themselves. They tend to spend money without thinking, spend more with their credit card and are no good at saving their money. They feel that it is important for people to think they are doing well. They buy cars for their looks and believe that brands are better than own labels.

They are not really using Coffee-Mate as much as one would have expected.

'Eileen and Mary' – cost constrained, older, conservative (23.6 per cent)

Very price aware, they budget when shopping and look for lowest prices. They are very traditional in their habits (don't like foreign food or foreign holidays). They worry about food ('food is not safe nowadays'), feel safe using products recommended by experts and think fast food is junk. They think it is worth paying more for organic fruit and vegetables and environmentally friendly products, but don't do much about it, perhaps because they can't afford to.

They are light users of instant coffee, using Maxwell House brands most often. They are average users of dried milk but are not really users of Coffee-Mate and never use cream. They are older (55+) and down-market (C2DE). They are not working or are retired in one- or two-person households; hence fewer of this type have children at home. They live in multi-ethnic areas, council areas and underprivileged areas on a low household income (£5,000–11,000).

They read the tabloid press and Bella and Chat. They are also heavy users of terrestrial commercial ITV and listen to commercial pop radio stations.

Their expenditure on grocery shopping is low and they tend to shop daily at small grocers. They enjoy shopping, but always look for the lowest prices, decide what they want before they go shopping and budget for every penny. They frequently enter competitions, find saving difficult, save for items they want and like to pay cash.

They are very conservative. They like routine, dislike untidiness, would buy British if they could, have a roast on Sundays and prefer brands to own label. They believe job security is more important than money, would rather have a boring job than no job, and prefer to do rather than take responsibility. Due to both their age and financial constraints, they socialise rarely. Most of this group never entertain friends to a meal, never go to a pub, a wine bar or a restaurant.

'Sarah and Anna' – affluent, young foodies (24.4 per cent)

Unencumbered by children and well off, they love both travelling and food (many claim to be vegetarian). They do not have to budget and can afford to treat themselves to perfume and foreign holidays, preferably more than once a year. They are not interested in additional channels on satellite TV and tend to be light users of all media.

They are heavy users of coffee and ground coffee. They buy decaffeinated, Gold Blend, Alta Rica and Cap Colombie. They are above-average users of creamers, claim to buy Coffee-Mate and Marvel most often, and also use cream.

Aged 35–54, predominantly ABC1, they earn above-average incomes and work full time. They live in areas of affluent minorities, young married suburbs and metro singles, in one- or two-person households.

They read quality newspapers, are light users of commercial radio but they do listen to the radio (usually the BBC) in the car.

They have a high expenditure on their main grocery shop (£71+) but shop infrequently at a large grocery supermarket. They really enjoy cooking and food, read recipes in magazines and like to try out new foods. Their tastes will be varied as they also enjoy travelling abroad on holiday, where they avoid the package trips and like to do as much as possible.

They entertain frequently and invite friends for meals. They also use pubs and wine bars, though not as much as 'Sharon and Tracy', and they are heavy users of restaurants.

They are health conscious (well, they can afford to be) and claim to include fibre in their diet, eat wholemeal bread, have less fat in their diet and eat fewer sweets and cakes. They are prepared to pay more for food without additives and for environmentally friendly products. They also exercise.

They can afford to treat themselves and prefer to buy one good thing rather than many cheap ones. They also like to keep up with technology and want to stand out from the crowd. In their fortunate position they enjoy life and don't worry about the future.

They claim never to buy any product tested on animals, use recycling banks and disapprove of aerosols more than the population at large. They make use of credit cards, especially for business, like to be well insured and consult professional advisers.

'Dawn and Lisa' – cost constrained, young families (13.9 per cent)

This group is severely constrained by their low incomes. But unlike the previous group, they are often young, working part-time or are unemployed or students. They are also not remotely concerned about health or the environment. Many left school at 15 or 16.

They are heavy users of instant coffee but do not use ground coffee. They buy Nescafé granules and Maxwell House powder. They are below-average users of creamers and never use cream.

This group is biased towards the 15–34 age group and is down-market (C2DE) with low incomes (£5,000–11,000). They tend to live in state housing in fading industrial areas. They have young families and there is a slightly greater bias to larger families than in other groups.

They read the tabloid press, *Bella* and *Chat*, and they are heavy viewers of commercial terrestrial and satellite TV, and heavy listeners to independent radio.

Their expenditure on the main grocery shop is low and they shop daily or once a week at discount grocery stores. They always look for the lowest price, watch what they spend, budget for every penny and look out for special offers. They want to save but find it difficult.

As a result of their difficult financial circumstances, they rarely use wine bars, pubs or restaurants. They claim to enjoy going to the pub, but cannot afford to these days. Similarly, when they can afford a holiday, they prefer to do so in the UK.

They have little time or money to worry about the environment or health issues, and claim that health food is bought by fanatics. They believe that frozen food is as nutritious as fresh foods. They tend to buy own label, presumably because it is cheaper rather than because they believe own-label goods are better than branded goods.

'Dorothy and Amy' – affluent (22.7 per cent)

This group does not have to be price conscious. They are older, sometimes retired or working part-time, and are well off. Often they own their house outright. They are, however, fairly traditional. They are not interested in travelling abroad, they are not health conscious and they are not media aware.

They are the people most likely to be buying Coffee-Mate. They buy instant coffee to the same degree as the rest of the population and are light users of ground coffee. But they use creamers as well as cream.

Dorothy and Amy are older (55+) and are up-market (AB and C1). They still have a reasonable household income despite being retired (£25,000+) and their children have left home. They are clearly a group who have disposable income and are not worried about budgeting. They are to be found in affluent minorities, older suburbs and young married suburbs.

They are readers of quality press, light viewers of ITV and never listen to commercial radio. They are not media aware, claiming to watch little TV and not to notice posters, and do not expect ads to entertain.

Their expenditure on the main grocery shop is above average. They do not enjoy shopping as much as other groups, are not price conscious but are prudent with money (consider themselves good at saving). They do not want to try new things, are not keen to keep up with the latest fashion and are not concerned with their appearance. They buy foreign goods if possible, will pay extra for quality goods, but are not really indulgent.

This is a group whose attitudes tend to lag. They get a great deal of pleasure from gardening and others often ask their advice on the matter. As a group they are happy with their standard of living. They do not often go to pubs, wine bars or restaurants, but they do have people home for meals.

Questions

1. What are the main benefits of Coffee-Mate and what is limiting its sales?
2. Should Coffee-Mate be mass marketed, aimed at one segment or aimed at multiple segments?
3. Evaluate the segments from TGI's user survey for target attractiveness and their fit to Coffee-Mate's strengths. Which of the segments would you target and why?
4. Evaluate the proposed ad for the target market and benefits promoted. Will the ad help propel Coffee-Mate's further growth? Create an alternative ad for your chosen target market.
5. How would the promotion of Coffee-Mate change with the benefits promoted and the competition targeted?
6. Defend your choice of famous personalities who could be used to help position Coffee-Mate in each different segment.

SOURCES: Company sources.

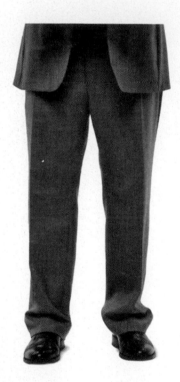

I run
Microsoft
Office

So do I

See the latest episodes of PC and Mac
apple.com/uk

I don't meet competition, I crush it.

CHARLES REVSON

Competitive strategy

Mini Contents List

- Prelude case – PS3 blues and X-box 360° turn as wee Wii wins
- Introduction
- Competitor analysis
- Competitive strategies
- Real Marketing 10.1   Marketing where the money is: customer coddling
- Real Marketing 10.2 – Tesco: playing in the big guys' back yard
- Balancing customer and competitor orientations
- Company case 10 – Bose: competing by being truly different

'Lovers, Not Fighters'

Milky Wimpshake, Fortuna Pop B00006398U, 2005

Previewing the concepts

In previous chapters, you explored the basics of markets, buyer behaviour and the value of targeting market segments. You have learned that the aim of marketing is to create value *for* customers in order to capture value *from* consumers in return. Good marketing companies win, keep and grow customers by understanding customer needs, designing customer-driven marketing strategies, constructing value-delivering marketing programmes, and building customer and marketing partner relationships. But marketers are not alone in the marketplace. Other companies are competing for a share of customers' minds, customers' money and the market.

In this chapter, we pull all of the marketing basics together. Understanding customers is an important first step in developing profitable customer relationships, but it is not enough. To gain competitive advantage, companies must use this understanding to design market offers that deliver more value than the offers of *competitors* seeking to win the same customers. In this chapter, we look first at competitor analysis, the process companies use to identify and analyse competitors. Then, we examine competitive marketing strategies by which companies position themselves against competitors to gain the greatest possible competitive advantage.

After reading this chapter, you should be able to:

1. Discuss the need to understand competitors as well as customers through competitor analysis.
2. Explain the fundamentals of competitive marketing strategies based on creating value for customers.
3. Illustrate the need for balancing customer and competitor orientations in becoming a truly market-centred organisation.

We first examine the computer games machine market, a market where the competition is as bloody as *Mortal Kombat* or *Grand Theft Auto: San Andreas*. As you read about the games machine market, ask yourself: What is it like in the run-up to the Christmas season when you are responsible for launching a new games machine against the mighty competitors? The machine will have taken millions to develop and will win or lose depending on sales over the few weeks running up to Christmas. In 2006, mighty Sony got it wrong.

Prelude case PS3 blues and X-box 360° turn as wee Wii wins

In the games machine market life is even more challenging than *Tomb Raider*, more aggressive than *Grand Theft Auto* and more brutal than *Resident Evil*. In the early 1980s, no home could be without a video game console and a dozen cartridges. By 1983 Atari, Mattel and a dozen other companies offered some version of a video game system and industry sales topped €3.6bn worldwide. Then, by 1985, home video game sales had plummeted to €100m. Game consoles gathered dust, and cartridges, originally priced as high as €40 each, sold for €5. Industry leader Atari was hardest hit. Atari sacked 4,500 employees and sold the subsidiary at a fraction of its 1983 worth. Industry experts blamed the death of the industry on the fickle consumer. Video games, they said, were a passing fad.

However, Nintendo, a 100-year-old toy company from Kyoto, Japan, did not agree. In late 1985, on top of the ruins of the video game business, the company introduced its Nintendo Entertainment System (NES). A year later, Nintendo had sold over 1m NES units. By 1991 Nintendo and its licensees had annual sales of $4bn in a now revitalised €5bn video game industry. Nintendo had 80 per cent share of the world market. Forty per cent of Japanese households and about 20 per cent of US and EU households had a NES.

How did Nintendo do it? First, it recognised that video game customers were not so much fickle as bored. The company sent researchers to visit video arcades to find out why alienated home video game fans still spent hours happily pumping arcade machines. The researchers found that Nintendo's *Donkey Kong* and similar games were still mainstays of the arcades, even though home versions were failing. The reason? The arcade games offered better quality, full animation and challenging plots. Home video games, on the other hand, offered only crude quality and simple plots. Despite their exotic names and intro-ductory hype, each new home game was boringly identical to all the others, featuring slow characters that moved through ugly animated scenes to the beat of monotonous, synthesised tones. Kids had outgrown the first-generation home video games.

Nintendo saw the fall of the video game industry as an opportunity. It set out to differentiate itself by offering superior quality – by giving home video games customers a full measure of quality entertainment value for their money. Nintendo designed a basic game system that sold for about €100 yet boasted near arcade-quality graphics. Equally important, it developed innovative and high-quality *Game Packs* to accompany the system. New games constantly appear and mature titles are weeded out to keep the selection fresh and interesting. The games contain consistently high-quality graphics, and game plots vary and challenge the user. Colourful, cartoon-like characters move fluidly about cleverly animated screens. The most popular games involved sword-and-sorcery conflicts, or the series of *Super Mario* fantasy worlds, where young heroes battle to save endangered princesses or fight the evil ruler, *Wart*, for peace in the *World of Dreams*.

By differentiating itself through superior products and service, and by building strong relationships with its customers, Nintendo built a seemingly invincible quality position in the video game market. But it soon came under attack. New competitors such as Sony and Sega exploited the opportunities created as Nintendo junkies became bored and sought the next new video thrill. Sony beat Nintendo at its own game – product superiority – when it hit the market with its PlayStation machine, an advanced new system that offered even richer graphics, more lifelike sound and more complex plots. Nintendo countered with the Nintendo 64 and a fresh blast of promotion, but the competition has intensified and, while Nintendo were being discounted, the PlayStation was the Christmas hit toy of 1997.

Meanwhile the computer games world is attacked for being 'violent, destructive, xenophobic, racist and sexist'. Sega Europe has also been attacked for marketing gruesome games such as *Mortal Kombat* and *Murder Death Kill*. The industry has been criticised for cultivating a generation of 'Video Kids' for whom 30 seconds without scoring is boring; moral zombies hooked on worlds where the rules are shot or be shot, consume or be consumed, fight or lose. In Japan, where many of the games come from, consumers are more broad-minded than in most western countries. Nintendo needs to extend its customer range beyond the terminally fickle teenage males. Sega spon-sored road shows with teen magazines, and put girls in its TV ads after complaints from schoolchildren on its 'advisory board' about sexism in advertising. Sega Europe created a new toy division to target 'housewives with children, instead of 14-year-old boys'. The first product was Pico, an electronic learning aid for kids that has taken a 'significant' share of the Japanese high-tech toys market. The €9m European launch included TV, press and posters with a full below-the-line campaign. Next came an 'electronic learning aid that thinks it's a toy' for three-to seven-year-olds. At the older end of the market more cere-bral 'stealth games' are taking hold in Japan. *Metal Gear Solid* and *Theft* reward silence, concealment and strategy more than bang and blast. Is this new thrust making gaming more civilised? No way.

While Nintendo and Sega chased the new markets, Sony's PlayStation blasted the 1997 Christmas market with the 'arcade feel' of *Ridge Racer* and *Crash Bindicoot* and 'scary, tension building' *Doom*. It is the kids who drive the games market and

Exhibit 10.1 Peak sales of games consoles

Peak sales year	Format	Games consoles	Peak annual sales
1982	Atari	Atari	10 m
1989	8-bit	NES, Master System	11 m
1993	16-bit	Megadrive/Genesis, SNES, 300	14 m
1997	32/64-bit	PlayStation, N64, Saturn	32 m
2003	128-bit	PS2, X-box, Nintendo Game Cube, Dreamcast	45 m
2006	256-bit[a]	PS3, X-box 360, Nintendo Wii	34 m[b]

[a]The new processors use new technology so the 256-bit description does not really apply. The PS3 has a 'cell processor' which boasts 35 times the power of the PS2.
[b]Estimate based on cumulative sales to mid-2007 of PS3, X-box 360 and Wii.

what they want is power and the latest cult machine. Three years after PlayStation blasted the competition, their €450 PlayStation 2 (PS2) was aimed to do the same again for Christmas 2000. With Internet access, CD and DVD playability, the PS2's 128-bit microprocessor had twice the power of then-current PCs. So powerful was the PS2's processor that its export had to be specially licensed by the Japanese government since it had the performance necessary to guide a cruise missile.

However, Sony did not have it all their own way. Sega launched their Dreamcast a year before PS2 but sales were lacklustre and the machine and its games were soon discounted. The market also attracted the mighty Microsoft whose X-box appeared in late 2001. Unlike other games machines, the X-box is intended for use in a living room using the family TV and operating Microsoft's PC products. Nintendo, too, is fighting back with their Game Cube.

The battle between Sony, Microsoft and Nintendo pushed world games console sales to new heights in 2003 (Exhibit 10.1) but worldwide sales for 2006 were forecast to be less than 10 million. But that forecast did not stop an even bigger investment for even better machines to gladden the hearts of game players. The latest round began in 2005 with Microsoft's X-box 360. Then, in 2006 Nintendo's Wii appeared while Sony launched the PlayStation 3 (PS3). With the battle started, Microsoft, Sony and Nintendo all claim to be on top.

Microsoft boasts that it has sold the most consoles: 10m X-box 360s since its launch. The 360 is popular in America and Europe, but is doing badly in Japan. The head start means that the 360 has the best line-up of games, an important reason for choosing a console. Microsoft's online service, Xbox Live, is also impressive, offering game and video downloads and allowing gamers to play together online.

Nintendo boasts that its new console has taken off the fastest, having sold nearly 6m units. The low-cost Wii is proving so popular that it is still hard to come by months after its launch, and is generating by far the most buzz. In part this is because the Wii's motion-sensitive controller means even non-gamers can quickly start playing tennis, golf or bowling.

Nintendo argues that it has expanded the market to non-gamers who were put off by the complexity of modern games. Sceptics argue that the Wii's novelty will wear off, that the Wii lacks the 'high-definition' graphics of its rivals and has only rudimentary online features.

Sony's claim to leadership is based on its PS2 sales; the PS2 actually outsold both the X-box 360 and the Wii in America during December 2006. Its maker insists that the PS3's relatively modest sales – 2m units since November – are the result of supply shortages, though anecdotal evidence suggests that PS3s are far easier to find than Wiis. Despite the PS3's high price – $499 (€368) and $599 (€442) in America, and €499 and €599 in Europe – Sony had to slash jobs as it posted record losses. Concerned that the high price was putting buyers off, or prompting them to wait for price cuts, it cut price by 20 per cent in Japan and $100 in the US.

Yoichi Wada, chief executive of Square Enix, one of Japan's leading game developers, thinks Microsoft and Sony have got it wrong. 'Powerful next-generation consoles such as Microsoft's X-box and Sony's PlayStation 3 are mismatched to the gaming environment,' he says, 'and handheld game devices are set to dominate sales.' He explains, 'the demographics of gamers have undergone a sea change in the past few years . . . There is a new breed of gamers in the market – we have to make games for all kinds of people.'[1]

Questions

1. Have Microsoft and Sony gone too far in creating more advanced and powerful machines when the market wanted entertainment?
2. What are the key ingredients for success in the computer games market?
3. Using information from the case, and your own knowledge, compare the competitive strengths and weaknesses of the competitors in the computer game machine market. Who do you think will be the long-term winners and why?

Introduction

Today's companies face their toughest competition ever. In previous chapters, we argued that to succeed in today's fiercely competitive marketplace, companies will have to move from a product-and-selling philosophy to a customer-and-marketing philosophy. As John Chambers, CEO of Cisco Systems, put it: 'Make your customer the centre of your culture.'

This chapter spells out in more detail how companies can outperform competitors in order to win, keep and grow customers. To win in today's marketplace, companies must become adept not just in *managing products*, but in *managing customer relationships* in the face of determined competition. Understanding customers is crucial, but it's not enough. Building profitable customer relationships and gaining **competitive advantage** requires delivering *more* value and satisfaction to target consumers than do *competitors*.

In this chapter, we examine *competitive marketing strategies* – how companies analyse their competitors and develop successful, value-based strategies for building and maintaining profitable customer relationships. The first step is **competitor analysis**, the process of identifying, assessing and selecting key competitors. The second step is developing **competitive marketing strategies** that strongly position the company against competitors and give it the greatest possible competitive advantage.

Competitor analysis

To plan effective marketing strategies, the company needs to find out all it can about its competitors. It must constantly compare its marketing strategies, products, prices, channels and promotion with those of close competitors. In this way the company can find areas of potential competitive advantage and disadvantage. As shown in Figure 10.1, competitor analysis involves first identifying and assessing competitors and then selecting which competitors to attack or avoid.

> " Competitor analysis involves . . . selecting which competitors to attack or avoid. "

Identifying competitors

Normally, it would seem a simple matter for a company to identify its competitors. Boeing knows that Airbus is its strongest competitor; and Nokia knows that it competes with Motorola.[2] At the most obvious level, a company can define its *product category competition* as other companies offering a similar product and services to the same customers at similar prices. Thus Volvo might see Mercedes as a foremost competitor, but not Rolls-Royce cars or Reliant (makers of the three-wheeled cars that Mr Bean bullies).

In competing for people's money, however, companies actually face a much wider range of competitors. More broadly, the company can define its *product competition* as all firms making the same product or class of products. Volvo could see itself as competing against all other car manufacturers. Even more broadly, competitors might include all companies making products

Competitive advantage—
An advantage over competitors gained by offering consumers greater value, either through lower prices or by providing more benefits that justify higher prices.

Competitor analysis—The process of identifying key competitors; assessing their objectives, strategies, strengths and weaknesses, and reaction patterns; and selecting which competitors to attack or avoid.

Competitive marketing strategies—Strategies that strongly position the company against competitors and that give the company the strongest possible strategic advantage.

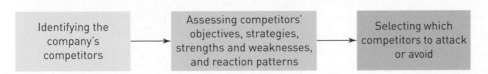

Figure 10.1 Steps in analysing competitors

that supply the same service. Here Volvo would see itself competing against not only other car manufacturers, but also the makers of trucks, motorcycles or even bicycles. Finally and still more broadly, competitors might include all companies that compete for the same consumer's money. Here Volvo would see itself competing with companies that sell major consumer durables, foreign holidays, new homes or extensive home repairs or alterations.

Companies must avoid 'competitor myopia'. A company is more likely to be 'buried' by its latent competitors than its current ones. For example, it wasn't other printed publishers that forced *Encyclopedia Britannica* to radically review its business after 240 years; it was first CD- and DVD-based reference works, such as Encarta, and then the Internet, including Wikipedia. For decades, Kodak held a comfortable lead in the photographic film business. It saw only Fuji as its major competitor in this market. However, in recent years, Kodak's major new competition has come not from Fuji and other film producers, but from Sony, Canon and other digital camera makers, and from a host of digital image developers and online image-sharing services.

Because of its myopic focus on film, Kodak was late to enter the digital imaging market. It paid a heavy price. With digital cameras now outselling film cameras, and with film sales plummeting 20 per cent every year, Kodak has faced major sales and profit setbacks, massive lay-offs, and a 74 per cent drop in its stock over the past five years. Kodak is now changing its focus to digital imaging, but the transformation will be difficult. The company has to 'figure out not just how to convince consumers to buy its [digital] cameras and home printers but also how to become known as the most convenient and affordable way to process those images,' says an industry analyst. 'That means home and store printing as well as sending images over the Internet and . . . [mobile] phones.'[3]

Companies can identify their competitors from the *industry* point of view. They might see themselves as being in the oil industry, the pharmaceutical industry or the beverage industry. A company must understand the competitive patterns in its industry if it hopes to be an effective 'player' in that industry. Companies can also identify competitors from a *market* point of view. Here they define competitors as companies that are trying to satisfy the same customer need or build relationships with the same customer group.

From an industry point of view, Diageo might see its competition to Johnnie Walker as Pernod-Ricard's Ballantine's, Grant's, the Erdington Group's Famous Grouse, and other brands of blended scotch whisky. From a market point of view, however, the customer really wants an after-dinner drink. This need can be satisfied by a more expensive single malt whisky, such as Cardhu, a North American whisky, a cognac or a liqueur. Similarly, Crayola crayons might define its competitors as other makers of crayons and children's drawing supplies, but from a market point of view, it would include all firms making recreational products for children.

In general, the market concept of competition opens the company's eyes to a broader set of actual and potential competitors. One approach is to profile the company's direct and indirect competitors by mapping the steps buyers take in obtaining and using the product. Figure 10.2 illustrates a *competitor map* of Eastman Kodak in the digital imaging business.[4] In the centre is a list of consumer activities: buying a camera, taking photos, creating digital photo albums, printing photos and others. The first outer ring lists Kodak's main competitors with respect to each consumer activity: Canon and Sony for buying a camera, Flickr for sharing and printing photos, and so on. The second outer ring lists indirect competitors – Apple, Motorola, Ricoh and others – who may become direct competitors. This type of analysis highlights both the competitive opportunities and the challenges a company faces.

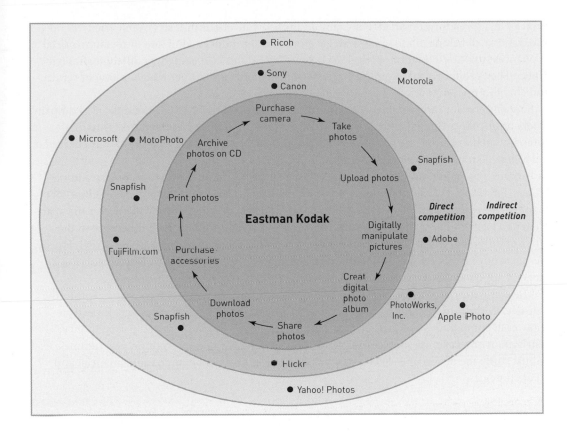

Figure 10.2 Competitor map
for Eastman Kodak

SOURCE: Adapted from Jeffrey
F. Rayport and Bernard J.
Jaworski, *e-Commerce* (New
York: McGraw-Hill, 2001),
p. 53. Copyright © 2001 The
McGraw-Hill Companies, Inc.

Assessing competitors

Having identified the main competitors, marketing management now asks: What are competitors' objectives – what does each seek in the marketplace? What is each competitor's strategy? What are the various competitors' strengths and weaknesses, and how will each react to actions the company might take?

Determining competitors' objectives

Each competitor has a mix of objectives. The company wants to know the relative importance that a competitor places on current profitability, market share growth, cash flow, technological leadership, service leadership and other goals. Knowing a competitor's mix of objectives reveals whether the competitor is satisfied with its current situation and how it might react to different competitive actions. For example, a company that pursues low-cost leadership will react much more strongly to a competitor's cost-reducing manufacturing breakthrough than to the same competitor's advertising increase.

A company also must monitor its competitors' objectives for various segments. If the company finds that a competitor has discovered a new segment, this might be an opportunity. If it finds that competitors plan new moves into segments now served by the company, it will be forewarned and, hopefully, forearmed.

Identifying competitors' strategies

The more that one firm's strategy resembles another firm's strategy, the more the two firms compete. In most industries, the competitors can be sorted into groups that pursue different strategies. A **strategic group** is a group of firms in an industry following the same or a similar

Strategic group—A group
of firms in an industry
following the same or a
similar strategy.

strategy in a given target market. For example, in the white goods industry, AEG, Tricity Bendix and Zanussi all belong to the same strategic group. Each produces a full line of medium-priced appliances supported by good service. In contrast, Miele and LG belong to a different strategic group. They produce a narrower line of higher-quality appliances, offer a higher level of service and charge a premium price.

Some important insights emerge from identifying strategic groups. For example, if a company enters one of the groups, the members of that group become its key competitors. Thus, if a company such as Dyson entered the second group, against Miele and LG, it could only succeed if it developed strategic advantages over these competitors.

Although competition is most intense within a strategic group, there is also rivalry among groups. First, some of the strategic groups may appeal to overlapping customer segments. For example, no matter what their strategy, all major appliance manufacturers will go after the apartment and homebuilders segment. Second, the customers may not see much difference in the offers of different groups – they may see little difference in quality between LG and AEG. Finally, members of one strategic group might expand into new strategy segments. Thus, Bosch has a range of appliances that compete with both the premium and medium-priced ranges.

The company needs to look at all of the dimensions that identify strategic groups within the industry. It must understand how each competitor delivers value to its customers. It needs to know each competitor's product quality, features and mix; customer services; pricing policy; distribution coverage; sales force strategy; and advertising and sales promotion programmes. And it must study the details of each competitor's R&D, manufacturing, purchasing, financial and other strategies.

Assessing competitors' strengths and weaknesses

Marketers need to assess each competitor's strengths and weaknesses carefully in order to answer the critical question: What *can* our competitors do? As a first step, companies can gather data on each competitor's goals, strategies and performance over the past few years. Admittedly, some of this information will be hard to obtain. For example, business-to-business marketers find it hard to estimate competitors' market shares because they do not have the same syndicated data services that are available to consumer packaged-goods companies.

Companies normally learn about their competitors' strengths and weaknesses through secondary data, personal experience and word of mouth. They can also conduct primary marketing research with customers, suppliers and dealers. Or they can **benchmark** themselves against other firms, comparing the company's products and processes to those of competitors or leading firms in other industries to find ways to improve quality and performance. Benchmarking has become a powerful tool for increasing a company's competitiveness.

Benchmarking—The process of comparing the company's products and processes to those of competitors or leading firms in other industries to find ways to improve quality and performance.

Estimating competitors' reactions

Next, the company wants to know: What *will* our competitors do? A competitor's objectives, strategies, strengths and weaknesses go a long way towards explaining its likely actions. They also suggest its likely reactions to company moves such as price cuts, promotion increases or new-product introductions. In addition, each competitor has a certain philosophy of doing business, a certain internal culture and guiding beliefs. Marketing managers need a deep understanding of a given competitor's mentality if they want to anticipate how the competitor will act or react.

Each competitor reacts differently. Some do not react quickly or strongly to a competitor's move. They may feel their customers are loyal; they may be slow in noticing the move; they may lack the funds to react. Some competitors react only to certain types of moves and not to others. Other competitors react swiftly and strongly to any action. Thus, as Unilever knows, P&G does not let a new detergent come easily into the market. Many firms avoid direct competition with P&G and look for easier prey, knowing that P&G will react fiercely if challenged.

In some industries, competitors live in relative harmony; in others, they fight constantly. Knowing how major competitors react gives the company clues on how best to attack competitors or how best to defend the company's current positions. The major European airlines behaved in this way for a long time until price-busting Ryanair and easyJet came along.

Selecting competitors to attack and avoid

A company has already largely selected its major competitors through prior decisions on customer targets, distribution channels and marketing-mix strategy. Management must now decide which competitors to compete against most vigorously.

Strong or weak competitors

The company can focus on one of several classes of competitors. Most companies prefer to compete against *weak competitors*. This requires fewer resources and less time. But in the process, the firm may gain little. You could argue that the firm also should compete with *strong competitors* in order to sharpen its abilities. Moreover, even strong competitors have some weaknesses, and succeeding against them often provides greater returns.

Most companies prefer to compete against *weak competitors*.

A useful tool for assessing competitor strengths and weaknesses is **customer value analysis**. The aim of customer value analysis is to determine the benefits that target customers value and how customers rate the relative value of various competitors' offers. In conducting a customer value analysis, the company first identifies the major attributes that customers value and the importance customers place on these attributes. Next, it assesses the company's and competitors' performance on the valued attributes.

The key to gaining competitive advantage is to take each customer segment and examine how the company's offer compares to that of its major competitor. If the company's offer delivers greater value by exceeding the competitor's offer on all important attributes, the company can charge a higher price and earn higher profits, or it can charge the same price and gain more market share. But if the company is seen as performing at a lower level than its major competitor on some important attributes, it must invest in strengthening those attributes or finding other important attributes where it can build a lead on the competitor.

Customer value analysis—Analysis conducted to determine what benefits target customers value and how they rate the relative value of various competitors' offers.

Close or distant competitors

Most companies will compete with *close competitors* – those that resemble them most – rather than *distant competitors*. Thus, adidas competes more against Nike than against Converse or Clarks. Land Rover competes with Jeep and Hummer rather than against Porsche or Lexus.

At the same time, the company may want to avoid trying to 'destroy' a close competitor. For example, in the late 1970s, Bausch & Lomb moved aggressively against other soft lens manufacturers with great success. However, this forced weak competitors to sell out to larger firms such as Johnson & Johnson. As a result, Bausch & Lomb now faces much larger competitors – and it suffered the consequences. Johnson & Johnson acquired Vistakon, a small nicher. Backed by Johnson & Johnson's deep pockets, however, the small but nimble Vistakon developed and introduced its innovative Acuvue disposable lenses. With Vistakon leading the way, Johnson & Johnson is now the world's contact lens maker while Bausch & Lomb lags in fourth place.[5] In this case, success in hurting a close rival brought in tougher competitors.

'Good' or 'bad' competitors

A company really needs and benefits from competitors. The existence of competitors results in several strategic benefits. Competitors may help increase total demand. They may share the costs of market and product development and help to legitimise new technologies. They may serve less-attractive segments or lead to more product differentiation. Finally, they lower the anti-trust risk and improve bargaining power versus labour or regulators. For example, by aggressively pricing its computer chips, Intel, which supplies the processors for four out of every five computers, could make things even more difficult for smaller rival AMD. However, even though AMD may be chipping away at its microprocessor market share, Intel may want to be careful about trying to knock AMD completely out. If for no other reason than to keep the regulators at bay, Intel needs AMD and other rivals to stick around.[6]

> " A company really needs and benefits from competitors. "

However, a company may not view all of its competitors as beneficial. An industry often contains *'good' competitors* and *'bad' competitors*.[7] Good competitors play by the rules of the industry. Bad competitors, in contrast, break the rules. They try to buy share rather than earn it, take large risks, and play by their own rules. For example, Yahoo! Music Unlimited sees Napster, Rhapsody, AOL Music, Sony Connect and most other digital music download services as good competitors. They share a common platform, so that music bought from any of these competitors can be played on almost any playback device. However, governments, consumer groups and competitors see Apple's iTunes Music Store as a bad competitor, one that plays by its own rules at the expense of the industry as a whole.

With the iPod, Apple created a closed system with mass appeal. Apple came late to the MP3 player market but its iconic iPod range now dominates the market. In 2003 Apple cut a deal with the Big Five record companies that locked up its device. The music companies wanted to sell songs on iTunes, but they were afraid of Internet piracy. So Apple promised to wrap their songs in its FairPlay software – the only copy-protection software that is iPod-compatible. Other digital music services such as eMusic and Napster have since reached similar deals with the big record labels. But Apple refused to license FairPlay to them. So those companies turned to Microsoft for copy protection. That satisfied fearful music companies, but it means none of the songs sold by those services can be played on the wildly popular iPod. And music downloaded from iTunes will play *only* on an iPod, making it difficult for other MP3 players that support the Microsoft format to get a toehold. The situation has been a disaster for Apple's competitors. iTunes holds a commanding lead over its rivals, selling more than 75 per cent of all digital music. It recently sold its billionth song.

Several governments are taking a stronger stance against iTunes than against music piracy. In Europe, Norway leads the way. Their powerful ombudsman set a deadline of 1 October 2007 for Apple to make its codes available to other technology companies so that it abides by Norwegian law. If it fails to do so, it will be taken to court, fined and eventually closed down. The European Commission is standing back, but The Netherlands, Germany and France are following Norway's lead. In a move that Apple dubbed 'state-sponsored piracy', the French parliament has recently passed a law that would force 'interoperability' on media groups. It challenges Apple to make songs taken from its iTunes online music store playable on competitors to its own iPod music player. Besides upsetting Apple, the legislation is triggering a fierce protest from industry. Francisco Mingorance, European director of policy at the Business Software Alliance, is concerned with a part of the law that threatens software publishers with fines if their products are used for piracy. He said legitimate software could suffer.[8]

The implication is that 'good' companies would like to shape an industry that consists of only well-behaved competitors. A company might be smart to support good competitors, aiming its attacks at bad competitors. Thus, Yahoo! Music Unlimited, Napster and other digital music competitors will no doubt support one another in trying to break Apple's stranglehold on the market.

Designing a competitive intelligence system

We have described the main types of information that companies need about their competitors. This information must be collected, interpreted, distributed and used. The cost in money and time of gathering competitive intelligence is high, and the company must design its competitive intelligence system in a cost-effective way.

The competitive intelligence system first identifies the vital types of competitive information and the best sources of this information. Then, the system continuously collects information from the field (sales force, channels, suppliers, market research firms, trade associations, websites) and from published data (government publications, speeches, articles). Next the system checks the information for validity and reliability, interprets it and organises it in an appropriate way. Finally, it sends key information to relevant decision makers and responds to enquiries from managers about competitors.

With this system, company managers will receive timely information about competitors in the form of phone calls, e-mails, bulletins, newsletters and reports. In addition, managers can connect with the system when they need an interpretation of a competitor's sudden move, or when they want to know a competitor's weaknesses and strengths, or when they need to know how a competitor will respond to a planned company move.

Smaller companies that cannot afford to set up formal competitive intelligence offices can assign specific executives to watch specific competitors. Thus, a manager who used to work for a competitor might follow that competitor closely; he or she would be the 'in-house expert' on that competitor. Any manager needing to know the thinking of a given competitor could contact the assigned in-house expert.

Competitive strategies

Having identified and evaluated its major competitors, the company must now design broad competitive marketing strategies by which it can gain competitive advantage through superior customer value. But what broad marketing strategies might the company use? Which ones are best for a particular company, or for the company's different divisions and products?

Approaches to marketing strategy

No one strategy is best for all companies. Each company must determine what makes the most sense given its position in the industry and its objectives, opportunities and resources. Even within a company, different strategies may be required for different businesses or products. Johnson & Johnson uses one marketing strategy for its leading brands in stable consumer markets – such as Tylenol, or Johnson's baby products – and unsurprisingly a different marketing strategy for its high-tech healthcare businesses and products – such as Monocryl surgical sutures or NeuFlex finger joint implants.

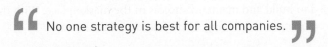

" No one strategy is best for all companies. "

Companies also differ in how they approach the strategy-planning process. Many large firms develop formal competitive marketing strategies and implement them religiously. However, other companies develop strategy in a less formal and orderly fashion. Some companies, such as Virgin Atlantic Airways and BMW's Mini unit, succeed by breaking many of the 'rules' of marketing strategy. Such companies don't operate large marketing departments, conduct expensive marketing research, spell out elaborate competitive strategies and spend huge sums on advertising. Instead, they sketch out strategies 'on the fly', stretch their limited resources, live close to their customers, and create more satisfying solutions to customer needs. They form buyer's clubs, use buzz marketing and focus on winning customer loyalty. Not all marketing strategies must follow in the footsteps of marketing giants and those that do not are sometimes very successful.

Approaches to marketing strategy and practice often pass through three stages: entrepreneurial marketing, formulated marketing and 'intrepreneurial' marketing.[9]

- *Entrepreneurial marketing.* Most companies are started by individuals who live by their wits. They visualise an opportunity, construct flexible strategies on the backs of envelopes, and knock on every door to gain attention. Simon Topman, owner and CEO of Acme, even calls himself 'Simon the Whistle', since it 'gives me a chance to have a joke with the gatekeepers I organise and get to the top people'. One of Simon's tales provides an example of entrepreneurial marketing in action.

After eventually agreeing to be dragged to see *Titanic* only two years after its release, towards the end of the film he was entranced. Not by Leonardo DiCaprio fighting bravely to save his love, nor by Kate Winslet in her clinging white dress. What he noticed was between her lips: an Acme Thunderer whistle. What a product placement – although he did not put it there. Within days he had the Titanic Whistle on the market and sold 15,000 in the first week and still selling 4,000 a week. 'We have almost sold a bigger weight in whistles than the *Titanic*,' he enthuses.[10]

- *Formulated marketing.* As small companies achieve success, they inevitably move towards more formulated marketing. They develop formal marketing strategies and adhere to them closely. Stonyfield Farm was once entrepreneurially marketed by its founder. Now 85 per cent owned by Groupe Danone, the subsidiary now has a formal marketing department that carries out market research and plans strategy. Although Stonyfield may remain less formal in its strategy than the P&Gs of the marketing world, it employs many of the tools used in these more developed marketing companies.

- *'Intrepreneurial' marketing.* Many large and mature companies get stuck in formulated marketing. A little down the road from Audi's Ingolstadt headquarters in Bavaria is Audi Electronics Venture, a wholly owned subsidiary designed to exploit new technology, such as sensors that can 'see' the road ahead to distinguish between cars and pedestrians, and brace the vehicle accordingly. The luxury carmaker's electronics centre is designed to catch any glitches before production starts. Audi Electronics Venture is to develop radical new applications.[11]

The bottom line is that there are many approaches to developing effective competitive marketing strategy. There will be a constant tension between the formulated side of marketing and the creative side. It is easier to learn the formulated side of marketing, which has occupied most of our attention in this book. But we have also seen how marketing creativity and passion in the strategies of many of the companies we've studied – whether small or large, new or mature – have helped to build and maintain success in the marketplace. With this in mind, we now look at broad competitive marketing strategies companies can use.

Basic competitive strategies

Almost three decades ago, Michael Porter suggested four basic competitive positioning strategies that companies can follow – three winning strategies and one losing one.[12] The three winning strategies include:

- *Overall cost leadership.* Here the company works hard to achieve the lowest production and distribution costs. Low costs let it price lower than its competitors and win a large market share. IKEA, Toyota and easyGroup are leading practitioners of this strategy.

- *Differentiation.* Here the company concentrates on creating a highly differentiated product line and marketing programme so that it comes across as the class leader in the industry. Most customers would prefer to own this brand if its price is not too high. JCB and Land Rover follow this strategy for heavy construction equipment and off-road vehicles, respectively.

- *Focus.* Here the company focuses its effort on serving a few market segments well rather than going after the whole market. For example, new luxury hotel chain Solis's target customer is aged 40–55, an ageing baby boomer who might be on the road as much as 100 days of the year.

> Glassmaker AFG Industries focuses on users of tempered and coloured glass. It makes 70 per cent of the glass for microwave oven doors and 75 per cent of the glass for shower doors and patio tabletops. Similarly, Hohner owns a stunning 85 per cent of the harmonica market.[13]

Companies that pursue a clear strategy – one of the above – are likely to perform well. The firm that carries out that strategy best will make the most profits. Firms that do not pursue a clear strategy – *middle-of-the-roaders* – do the worst. Marks & Spencer and Holiday Inn encountered difficult times because they did not stand out as the lowest in cost, highest in perceived value, or best in serving some market segment. Middle-of-the-roaders try to be good on all strategic counts, but end up being not very good at anything.

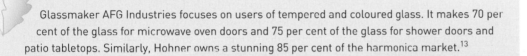

Middle-of-the-roaders do the worst.

More recently, two marketing consultants, Michael Treacy and Fred Wiersema, offered new classifications of competitive marketing strategies.[14] They suggest that companies gain leadership positions by delivering superior value to their customers. Companies can pursue any of three strategies – called *value disciplines* – for delivering superior customer value. These are:

- *Operational excellence.* The company provides superior value by leading its industry in price and convenience. It works to reduce costs and to create a lean and efficient value-delivery system. It serves customers who want reliable, good-quality products or services, but who want them cheaply and easily. Examples include Amazon.com, IKEA, Dell and Tesco.

- *Customer intimacy.* The company provides superior value by precisely segmenting its markets and tailoring its products or services to match exactly the needs of targeted customers. It specialises in satisfying unique customer needs through a close relationship with and intimate knowledge of the customer. It builds detailed customer databases for segmenting and targeting, and empowers its marketing people to respond quickly to customer needs. Customer-intimate companies serve customers who are willing to pay a premium to get precisely what they want. They will do almost anything to build long-term customer loyalty and to capture customer lifetime value. Examples include Coutts private banking, British Airways, Lexus, Laithwaite online wine sellers – 'from the vineyard to your door' – and several credit card companies (see Real Marketing 10.1).

- *Product leadership.* The company provides superior value by offering a continuous stream of leading-edge products or services. It aims to make its own and competing products obsolete. Product leaders are open to new ideas, relentlessly pursue new solutions, and work to get new products to market quickly. They serve customers who want state-of-the-art products and services, regardless of the costs in terms of price or inconvenience. Examples include Nokia, Apple and Sony.

Some companies successfully pursue more than one value discipline at the same time. For example, FedEx excels at both operational excellence and customer intimacy. However, such companies are rare – few firms can be the best at more than one of these disciplines. By trying to be *good at all* of the value disciplines, a company usually ends up being *best at none*.

Treacy and Wiersema found that leading companies focus on and excel at a single value discipline, while meeting industry standards on the other two. Such companies design their entire value delivery network to single-mindedly support the chosen discipline. For example, easyJet knows that customer intimacy and product leadership are important. Compared with other discounters, it offers very good customer service and an excellent product assortment. Still, it purposely offers less customer service and less product depth than do regular airlines, which pursue customer intimacy. Instead, easyJet focuses obsessively on operational excellence – on reducing costs and streamlining its order-to-delivery process in order to make it convenient for customers to buy just the right products at the lowest prices.

By the same token, Laithwaite wants to be efficient and to employ the latest technologies. But what really sets the wine retailers apart is its customer advisors and the consistent quality of the wine they recommend. At a different level the Ritz-Carlton chain of luxury hotels creates custom-designed experiences to coddle its customers:

Check into any Ritz-Carlton hotel around the world, and you'll be amazed at how well the hotel's employees anticipate your slightest need. Without ever asking, they seem to know that you want a non-smoking room with a king-size bed, a non-allergenic pillow, and breakfast with decaffeinated coffee in your room. How does Ritz-Carlton work this magic? At the heart of the system is a huge customer database, which contains information gathered through the observations of hotel employees. Each day, hotel staff – from those at the front desk to those in maintenance and housekeeping – discreetly record the unique habits, likes and dislikes of each guest on small 'guest preference pads'. These observations are then transferred to a corporate-wide 'guest preference database'. Every morning, a 'guest historian' at each hotel reviews the files of all new arrivals who have previously stayed at a Ritz-Carlton and prepares a list of suggested extra touches that might delight each guest. Guests have responded strongly to such personalised service. Since inaugurating the guest-history system, Ritz-Carlton has boosted guest retention by 23 per cent. An amazing 95 per cent of departing guests report that their stay has been a truly memorable experience.

Classifying competitive strategies as value disciplines is appealing. It defines marketing strategy in terms of the single-minded pursuit of delivering superior value to customers. Each value discipline defines a specific way to build lasting customer relationships.

real marketing 10.1

Marketing where the money is: customer coddling

Some companies go to extremes to coddle big spenders. From carmakers like Lexus and BMW to hotels like Ritz-Carlton and FourSeasons, companies give their well-heeled customers exactly what they need – and even more.

For example, concierge services are no longer the sole province of five-star hotels and fancy credit cards. They are starting to show up at airlines, retailers and even electronic-goods makers. Sony Electronics, for instance, offers a service for its wealthiest customers, called Cierge, that provides a free personal shopper and early access to new gadgets, as well as 'white-glove' help with the installation. Then there's British Airways' 'At Your Service' programme – available to a hand-picked few of the airline's gold-level élite customers. There's almost nothing that the service won't do for members – tracking down hard-to-get Wimbledon tickets, for example, or running errands around town, sitting in a member's home to wait for the plumber or cable guy, or even planning your wedding, right down to the cake.

But when it comes to stalking the well-to-do, perhaps nowhere is the competition greater than in the credit-card industry. To rise above the credit-card clutter and to attract high-end card holders, the major credit-card companies have created a new top tier of superpremium cards – Visa's Signature card, MasterCard's World card and American Express's super-élite Centurion card. Affluent customers are extremely profitable. While premium cards represent only 1.5 per cent of the consumer credit cards issued by Visa, MasterCard and American Express, they account for 20 per cent of the spending. And well-to-do cardholders tend to default a lot less, too.

The World MasterCard programme targets what it calls the 'mass affluent' and reaches 15 million wealthy households. Visa's Signature card zeros in on 'new affluent' households, those with incomes exceeding €100,000. Its seven million card-holders account for 3 per cent of Visa's consumer credit cards but 18 per cent of Visa sales. Both cards feature a pack of special privileges. For its Signature card, Visa advertises, 'The good life isn't only in your reach – it's in your wallet.' In addition to the basics, such as no preset spending limit and 24-hour concierge services, Visa promises 'upgrades, perks and discounts' at major airlines, restaurants and hotels, and special treatment at partners like the Ritz-Carlton, men's fashion designer Ermenegildo Zegna and watchmaker Audemars Piguet.

But when it comes to premium cards, the American Express Centurion card is the 'élite of the élite' for luxury card carriers. This mysterious, much-coveted black credit card is issued by invitation only, to customers who spend more than €110,000 a year

on other AmEx cards and meet other not-so-clear requirements. Then, the select few who do receive the card pay a €2,000 annual fee just for the privilege of carrying it. But the Centurion card comes dripping with perks and prestige. The elusive plastic, with its elegant matte finish, is coveted by big spenders. 'A black card is plastic bling-bling,' says an industry observer, 'a way for celebrities, athletes and major business people to express their status.'

Wearing a T-shirt and jeans, Peter H. Shankman doesn't look like a high flier, but American Express knows better. After he was snubbed by salesmen at a Giorgio Armani boutique, the 31-year-old publicist saw 'an unbelievable attitude reversal' at the cash register when he whipped out his black AmEx Centurion card. In June, a Radio Shack cashier refused the card, thinking it was a fake. 'Trust me,' he said. 'Run the card. I could buy a Learjet with this thing.'

An exaggeration, perhaps. But AmEx's little black card is decidedly the 'It' card for big spenders. Some would-be customers go to absurd lengths to get what they see as a must-have status symbol. Hopefuls have written poems to plead their cases. Others say they'll pay the fee but swear not to use the card – they want it just for show. 'Every week I get phone calls or letters, often from prominent people, asking me for the card,' says AmEx's head of consumer cards, Alfred Kelly. Who? He won't say. In fact, AmEx deliberately builds an air of mystery around the sleek card, keeping hush-hush such details as the number of cards in circulation.

Analysts say AmEx earns back many times what it spends on perks for black-card customers in both marketing buzz and fees. Basic services on the Centurion card include a personal travel counsellor and concierge, available 24/7. Beyond that, almost anything goes. Feel like shopping at Bergdorf Goodman to buy the latest in French fashion at midnight? No problem. Travelling abroad in first class? Take a pal – the extra ticket is free. The royal treatment often requires elaborate planning. One AmEx concierge arranged a bachelor party for 25, which involved a four-day trip that included 11 penthouse suites, travel by private jet, and a meet-and-greet with an owner of a sports team. The tab was more than €200,000.

How did Shankman earn his card? All the travel and entertainment charges he racks up hosting his clients prompted AmEx to send it to him. It arrived in December, along with a 43-page manual. Recently, Shankman sought reservations for Spice Market, an often-overbooked restaurant, to impress a friend. He called his concierge. 'Half an hour later it was done,' says Shankman. Membership does have its privi-leges. When American Express seeks new Centurion cardholders, it does so discreetly. Recently, when it wanted to expand the élite list in Europe without attracting the ineligible, it mailed invitations to the top 1 per cent of its platinum card holders. The mailing contained a card embedded in a glass paperweight with an invitation to meet personally with American Express's European president.

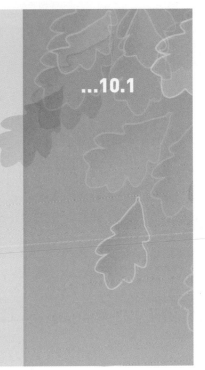

...10.1

So, how many people actually have a Centurion card? 'About the same number of people who can afford a Mercedes Maybach,' says Desiree Fish, a spokeswoman for American Express. The best guess is that only about 5,000 people worldwide have a Centurion card in their back pocket. But wow, how they spend when they take it out.

SOURCES: American Express example adapted from Mara Der Hovanesian, 'This black card gives you carte blanche', *Business Week* (9 August 2004), p. 54. Quotes and other information from David Carr, 'No name, but plenty of bling-bling for show', *New York Times* (13 September 2004), p. C11; Eleena de Lisser, 'How to get an airline to wait for your plumber – in battle for biggest spenders, British Airways, Sony roll out hotel-style "concierge" service', *Wall Street Journal* (2 July 2002), p. D1; James Tenser, 'Cards play their luxury hand right', *Advertising Age* (13 September 2004), pp. S13–S14; Frederick H. Lowe, 'Cards for the rich: They're different, indeed', *Credit Card Management* (February 2005), pp. 18–22; Eric Dash, 'New spots for the credit card companies show fierce competition for the high-end consumer', *New York Times* (11 May 2005), p. C0, 'The 10 best DM campaigns', *Campaign* (16 December 2005), p. 38; Emma Cowing, 'How to bag a billionaire', *The Scotsman* (17 March 2006); Stephen McGinty, 'A lesson for the super-rich on splashing out the mega-bucks – Rokos's basement diving pool sets the pace', *The Scotsman* (9 August 2007).

Competitive positions

Firms competing in a given target market, at any point in time, differ in their objectives and resources. Some firms are large, others small. Some have many resources, others are strapped for funds. Some are mature and established, others new and fresh. Some strive for rapid market share growth, others for long-term profits. And the firms occupy different competitive positions in the target market.

We now examine competitive strategies based on the roles firms play in the target market – leader, challenger, follower or nicher. Suppose that an industry contains the firms shown in Figure 10.3. Forty per cent of the market is in the hands of the **market leader**, the firm with the largest market share. Another 30 per cent is in the hands of **market challengers**, runner-up firms that are fighting hard to increase their market share. Another 20 per cent is in the hands of **market followers**, other runner-up firms that want to hold their share without rocking the boat. The remaining 10 per cent is in the hands of **market nichers**, firms that serve small segments not being pursued by other firms. A number of European companies are global leaders in terms of their market value: BASF (chemicals), Vinci (construction and minerals), EDF (electricity), Siemens (electrical and electrical equipment), e.on (gas, water and multi-utilities), BHP Billiton (mining) and L'Oréal (personal goods). In food, Europe has the world's top four companies who are, in order, Nestlé, Unilever, Danone and Cadbury Schweppes. However, since many of Europe's leading companies are still emerging from their national base, at a global level many of its top companies are market challengers or followers (see Table 10.1).

Table 10.2 shows specific marketing strategies that are available to market leaders, challengers, followers and nichers.[15] Remember, however, that these classifications often do not apply to a whole company, but only to its position in a specific industry. Large companies such as GSK,

Market leader—The firm in an industry with the largest market share; it usually leads other firms in price changes, new product introductions, distribution coverage and promotion spending.

Market challenger—A runner-up firm in an industry that is fighting hard to increase its market share.

Market follower—A runner-up firm in an industry that wants to hold its share without rocking the boat.

Market leader	Market challengers	Market followers	Market nichers
40%	30%	20%	10%

Figure 10.3 Hypothetical market structure

Table 10.1 European leaders' world ranking

Sector	World leader	Market value ($bn)	European leader	Market value ($bn)	World ranking
Aerospace	Boeing (US)	70	BAE Systems	25	5
Beverages	Coca-Cola (US)	111	Diageo	60	3
General merchandisers	Wal-Mart (US)	194	Tesco	77	3
Motors	Toyota (Japan)	231	DaimlerChrysler	87	2
Petroleum	Exxon Mobil (US)	430	Royal Dutch/Shell	214	2
Pharmaceuticals and Biotechnology	Pfizer (US)	179	GSK	157	3
Telecommunications	AT&T (US)	246	Vodafone	140	3
Banking	Citigroup (US)	253	HSBC	202	3

SOURCE: *FT Global 500* (2007). Copyright © 2007 Financial Times Limited.

Table 10.2 Strategies for market leaders, challengers, followers and nichers

Leader	Expand total market, protect market share, expand market share
Challenger	Full frontal attack, indirect attack
Follower	Follow closely, follow at a distance
Nicher	Target by customer, market, quality-price, service; multiple niching

Market nicher—A firm in an industry that serves small segments that the other firms overlook or ignore.

Nestlé, Unilever, L'Oréal or Diageo might be leaders in some markets and nichers in others. For example, P&G leads in many segments, such as laundry detergents and shampoo, but it challenges Unilever in the hand soaps and Kimberly-Clark in facial tissues. Such companies often use different strategies for different business units or products, depending on the competitive situations of each.

Market leader strategies

Most industries contain an acknowledged market leader. The leader has the largest market share and usually leads the other firms in price changes, new-product introductions, distribution coverage and promotion spending. The leader may or may not be admired or respected, but other firms concede its dominance. Competitors focus on the leader as a company to challenge, imitate or avoid. A market leader's life is not easy. It must maintain a constant watch. Other firms keep challenging its strengths or trying to take advantage of its weaknesses. The market leader can easily miss a turn in the market and plunge into second or third place. A product innovation may come along and hurt the leader (as when Apple developed the iPod and took the market lead from Sony's portable audio devices). The leader might grow arrogant or complacent and misjudge the competition (as when Sainsbury's lost its lead to Tesco in the UK, Sears to Wal-Mart in the US, and GM to Toyota globally). Or the leader might look old-fashioned against new and peppier rivals (as when Levi's lost serious ground to more current or stylish brands like Gap, FCUK, DKNY or Benetton).

> " A market leader's life is not easy. "

To remain number one, leading firms can take any of three actions. First, they can find ways to expand total demand. Second, they can protect their current market share through good defensive and offensive actions. Third, they can try to expand their market share further, even if market size remains constant.

Expanding the total demand

The leading firm normally gains the most when the total market expands. If the world purchase more hybrid automobiles, Toyota stands to gain the most because it sells the world's largest share of hybrids. However, if the move is towards diesel, VW, Mercedes, Renault and Citroën stand to win.

Market leaders can expand the market by developing new users, new uses and more usage of its products. They usually can find *new users* in many places. For example, L'Oréal might find new fragrance users in its current markets by convincing men who do not use fragrances (often

Trading with the market leader has its advantages.

Greater liquidity, in the first place. Eurex is the market leader in European fixed income derivatives with futures and options on the Euro Bund, Euro Bobl and Euro Schatz. Our extensive product range provides you with the right hedging and trading tools to optimize your investments. Small wonder the world's most heavily traded fixed income futures are listed and traded at Eurex. Think big. Think Eurex. www.eurexchange.com

what can we do for you? EX eurex

Size isn't everything but Eurex's market leadership gives it the liquidity and extensive product range that gives it a competitive advantage.

SOURCE: Eurex. *Photographer*: Karin Hieronymi.

masquerading as aftershave) to try them. Or it might expand into new geographic segments, perhaps by selling its fragrances in other countries.

Marketers can expand markets by discovering and promoting *new uses* for the product. For example, WD40, a penetrating oil traditionally used to loosen rusty nuts and screws, is now the world's number one multi-purpose problem solver. It cleans, protects, penetrates, lubricates and displaces moisture like no other product on earth. Having left the garage, its fans have found it can loosen stuck Lego bricks, remove lipstick from fabric and prevent slugs climbing up plant pots! Its website lists 2,000 uses and still counting.[16]

Finally, market leaders can encourage *more usage* by convincing people to use the product more often or to use more per occasion. For generations the makers of Worcester Sauce (condiment), Marmite (spread) and Bovril (beverage) have urged people to use their product in a vast range of menus rather than just in the single main use.

Protecting market share

While trying to expand total market size, the leading firm must also protect its current business against competitors' attacks. P&G must constantly guard against Unilever; Mercedes against Lexus in the luxury car market; British Airways against Virgin Atlantic out of London; and McDonald's against Burger King.

What can the market leader do to protect its position? First, it must prevent or fix weaknesses that provide opportunities for competitors. It must always fulfil its value promise. Its prices must remain consistent with the value that customers see in the brand. It must work tirelessly to keep strong relationships with valued customers. The leader should 'plug holes' so that competitors do not jump in.

But the best defence is a good offence, and the best response is *continuous innovation*. The leader refuses to be content with the way things are and leads the industry in new products, customer services, distribution effectiveness and cost-cutting. It keeps increasing its competitive effectiveness and value to customers. And when attacked by challengers, the market leader reacts decisively. For example, consider Nestlé's defence of their leading position in the instant coffee market.

With more than 3,000 cups consumed every second, Nescafé is the world's leading coffee brand with a global share of about 56 per cent and market leadership in virtually every major market. It was not always that way. Nestlé gained its dominant position as a result of the global spread of Nescafé so that coffee finally eclipsed tea as the world's favourite hot drink. Nestlé captured market share of the coffee thanks to Gold Blend's coffee granules that 'locks more flavour in' and a highly successful long-running series of romantic soap-opera style TV ads starring actors Tony Head and Sharon Maugham.

Nescafé fights a continuous defence against Kraft's portfolio of brands that include Maxwell House, Kenco, Hag, Splendid and Jacobs. One part of the strategy is defence in breadth, with a range of variants for all tastes: Nescafé Original, Blend 37, Gold Blend (Taster's Choice in the US), Alta Rica, Cap Colombie or Kenjara, decaffeinated and half-caffeinated versions, and café-inspired products such as Espresso, Cappucino, Latte and Mocha. Nescafé also launched iced ready-to-drink Nescafé Ice and Nescafé Xpress in Asia in the early 1990s and have since rolled them out globally. Where there are local variations, dedicated brands, such as Dallmayr in Germany, fill the gap. New variants are Nespresso, a super-premium coffeemaker brand, less pricy Nescafé Dolce Gusto, and Nescafé Energo, containing additional vitamins and minerals.

Nestlé's latest defence was not against Kraft but a new sort of competitor. Oxfam accused Nescafé of making excessive profits from coffee brands and, at the same time, the company facing inroads into some markets with Fairtrade products. In response, Nestlé became the first big coffee marketer to introduce a fair trade brand: Partners' Blend, made of coffee beans from Ethiopia and El Salvador.

Nescafé defends its strong leading position in the instant coffee market by having numerous instance coffees, like Expresso, that surround the Nescafé core brand.
SOURCE: The Advertising Archives.

Expanding market share

Market leaders can also grow by increasing their market shares further. In many markets, small market share increases mean very large sales increases. For example, globally we consume 50 billion beverage servings each day. A 0.1 per cent increase in market share in the drinks people consume means 18 billion servings a year.[17]

Studies have shown that, on average, profitability rises with increasing market share. Because of these findings, many companies have sought expanded market shares to improve profitability.

Beiersdorf, makers of Nivea, defend its position as the world's number one personal care brand by developing brands products that relate to the original Nivea skin cream.
SOURCE: The Advertising Archives.

General Electric, for example, declared that it wants to be at least number one or two in each of its markets or else get out – 'Be one or two in all we do'. GE shed its computer, air-conditioning, small appliances and television businesses because it could not achieve top-dog position in these industries.

> " Be one or two in all we do. "

However, some studies have found that many industries contain one or a few highly profitable large firms, several profitable and more focused firms, and a large number of medium-sized firms with poorer profit performance. It appears that profitability increases as a business gains share relative to competitors in its *served market*. For example, BMW holds only a small share of the total car market, but it earns high profits because it is the leading brand in the luxury-performance car segment. And it has achieved this high share in its served market because it does other things right, such as producing high-quality products with a great image that are exciting to drive.

Companies must not think, however, that gaining increased market share will automatically improve profitability. Much depends on their strategy for gaining increased share. There are many high-share companies with low profitability and many low-share companies with high profitability. The cost of buying higher market share may far exceed the returns. Higher shares tend to produce higher profits only when unit costs fall with increased market share, or when the company offers a superior-quality product and charges a premium price that more than covers the cost of offering higher quality.

Market challenger strategies

Firms that are second, third or lower in an industry are sometimes quite large, such as Mercedes, Royal Dutch Shell, BP, GSK and Airbus. These runner-up firms can adopt one of two competitive strategies: they can challenge the leader and other competitors in an aggressive bid for more market share (market challengers), or they can play along with competitors and not rock the boat (market followers).

A market challenger must first define which competitors to challenge and its strategic objective. The challenger can attack the market leader, a high-risk but potentially high-gain strategy. Its goal might be to take over market leadership. Or the challenger's objective may simply be to wrest more market share. Although it might seem that the market leader has the most going for it, challengers often have what some strategists call a 'second-mover advantage'. The challenger observes what has made the leader successful and improves upon it. Consider Ryanair, a real challenger in the European airline industry:

Ryanair started without the high costs and traditional practices of Europe's national airlines operating out of expensive airport hubs and sales networks. The company slashed selling costs by selling directly to consumers, providing a no-frills service and amazingly low fares. Their simple provision helps them turn the aircraft round quickly and so achieve high utilisation on short-haul flights. Ryanair's strength continues to be its combination of cost control and pricing flexibility, achieved by flying to under-utilised regional airports that keep prices down because they want to attract the visitors that Ryanair can provide. Ryanair is ahead of its rivals on cost even before it takes off. Airport and ground-handling charges cost Ryanair £4.90, out of an average fare of £33. That contrasts with low-cost rival easyJet which pays airport service charges of £10.75 per passenger to fly from slightly grander airports. Where Ryanair led, others follow. Perennial challenger Virgin is taking Ryanair's business model to fly US domestic flights as Virgin Blue.[18]

Alternatively, the challenger can avoid the leader and instead challenge firms its own size, or smaller local and regional firms. These smaller firms may be underfinanced and not serving their customers well. Several of the major beer companies grew to their present size not by challenging large competitors, but by gobbling up small local or regional competitors. If the company goes after a small local company, its objective may be to put that company out of business. The important point remains: the challenger must choose its opponents carefully and have a clearly defined and attainable objective.

How can the market challenger best attack the chosen competitor and achieve its strategic objectives? It may launch a *full frontal attack*, matching the competitor's product, advertising,

Virgin is one of the world's leading airlines but still plays the part of the challenger. Like this ad, much of its advertising is attackingly comparative.

SOURCE: Virgin Atlantic.

price and distribution efforts. It attacks the competitor's strengths rather than its weaknesses. The outcome depends on who has the greater strength and endurance. If the market challenger has fewer resources than the competitor, a frontal attack makes little sense. For example,

The runner-up razor manufacturer in Brazil attacked Gillette, the market leader. The attacker was asked if it offered the consumer a better razor. 'No,' was the reply. 'A lower price?' 'No.' 'A clever advertising campaign?' 'No.' 'Better allowances to the trade?' 'No.' 'Then how do you expect to take share away from Gillette?' 'Sheer determination,' was the reply. Needless to say, the offensive failed. Even great size and strength may not be enough to challenge a firmly entrenched, resourceful competitor successfully.

Rather than challenging head-on, the challenger can make an *indirect attack* on the competitor's weaknesses or on gaps in the competitor's market coverage. Tesco aims to do this in the US market where it is challenging mighty Wal-Mart in its home market. Real Marketing 10.2 highlights this David taking the battle into Goliath's camp.

Market follower strategies

Not all runner-up companies want to challenge the market leader. Challenges are never taken lightly by the leader. If the challenger's lure is lower prices, improved service or additional product features, the leader can quickly match these to defuse the attack. The leader probably has more staying power in an all-out battle for customers. After years of unsuccessfully challenging P&G in the US laundry detergent market, Unilever recently decided to throw in the towel and become a follower instead. P&G captures 55 and 75 per cent shares of the liquid and powder detergent markets, respectively, versus Unilever's 17 and 7 per cent shares. P&G has out-muscled competitors on every front. For example, it batters competitors with a relentless stream of new and improved products. Recently, P&G spent more than $50m (€38m) introducing one new product alone, Tide with Downy. In response to the onslaught, Unilever has cut prices and promotion on its detergents to focus on profit rather than market share.[19]

A follower can gain many advantages. The market leader often bears the huge expenses of developing new products and markets, expanding distribution and educating the market. By contrast, as with challengers, the market follower can learn from the leader's experience. It can copy or improve on the leader's products and programmes, usually with much less investment. Although the follower will probably not overtake the leader, it can often be as profitable.

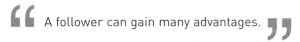 A follower can gain many advantages.

Following is not the same as being passive or a carbon copy of the leader. A market follower must know how to hold current customers and win a fair share of new ones. It must find the right balance between following closely enough to win customers from the market leader but following at enough of a distance to avoid retaliation. Each follower tries to bring distinctive advantages to its target market – location, services, financing. The follower is often a major target of attack by challengers. Therefore, the market follower must keep its manufacturing costs and prices low or its product quality and services high. It must also enter new markets as they open up.

Market nicher strategies

Almost every industry includes firms that specialise in serving market niches. Instead of pursuing the whole market, or even large segments, these firms target sub-segments. Lars Olrik, chief executive of Keronite, knows that money can still come out of 'clever technology' and niching. His company recently opened a new plant to provide anti-corrosion coatings for metal parts made from aluminium and magnesium. The parts are used in industries such as automotive and engineering. He reckons sales from the plant should double in the next few years. He envisages opening other factories to establish the process, which he says has few rivals around the world, in countries such as the US and China.[20]

Why is niching profitable? The main reason is that the market nicher like Keronite ends up knowing the target customer group so well that it meets their needs better than other firms that casually sell to that niche. As a result, the nicher can charge a substantial mark-up over costs because of the added value. Whereas the mass marketer achieves high volume, the nicher achieves high margins.

10.2 real marketing

Tesco: playing in the big guys' back yard

Sir Terry Leahy, Tesco's CEO, is setting up shop in America, home of mighty Wal-Mart. 'Clearly it's high risk,' he accepts. 'But we've carefully balanced the risk. If it fails it's embarrassing. It might show up in my career. It'll cost an amount of money that's easily affordable – call it £1 billion (€1.5bn) if you like. If it succeeds then it's transformational.'

Highly focused retailers, like IKEA and Body Shop, have succeeded. But establishing a foothold in America's already populated retail market against established competition has proved as difficult as establishing the early settlements on America's shores. A few early settlers survived to take the country from the Native Americans but few retailers have made much impression in the world's largest market. Sainsbury's, Marks & Spencer and Carrefour are among the many European retailers that have tried their luck in America and come off worse.

It is not just going west that is difficult. Mighty Wal-Mart, with almost twice the sales of Carrefour and Tesco combined, has had trouble exporting their low-priced philosophy to Europe. In Germany it gave up after it underestimated the importance of trade links with suppliers and the strength of Germany's own discounters. In the UK, after Wal-Mart acquired Asda, they lost market share and dropped to third place after Sainsbury and Tesco – even while Sainsbury and Morrison supermarkets were suffering difficulties themselves. Worldwide, few retailers have successfully broken into the grocery market of a developed country. Unlike the world of clothing, where a global culture has created global brands, such as Zara, Gap and H&M, the globalisation of food retailing is limited by food tastes, and shopping habits differ hugely from country to country. Now relatively small Tesco is taking the battle to Wal-Mart in a rare attack on a market leader.

Tesco has already identified 100 sites to begin its $500m (€370m) a year campaign. The company plans to pepper some of America's fastest-growing states, opening three of its Fresh & Easy local grocery stores a week. By American retailing standards, not a big splash but a mere ripple.

So far Tesco has been furtive, having spent years gathering detailed information on every aspect of American life – poking around in America's kitchen cupboards, watching them cook and following them as they shopped. Tesco's past success has come partly from its excellent use of customer data, and the locations of its early stores seem part of a plan to gain local knowledge. In downtown Phoenix, Fresh & Easy will be in the poorest parts of town; in neighbouring Chandler it will be building its stores within reach of the city's richest inhabitants.

Change what the Americans eat

Tesco is not just entering a market, it is setting out to change the way Americans shop and eat. Fresh & Easy will sell a range of preservative-free 'ready-meals' that, so far, hardly exist in large parts of America. 'American supermarkets have not been innovative with prepared foods,' says Harvard Business School's Rajiv Lal. 'You can't eat them more than three days in the week without eating the same stuff.' Why? Taking Wal-Mart's lead, American supermarkets competed mainly by taking costs out of their supply chains. They also have cheap labour available and large distances to contend with. That encouraged supermarkets to concentrate on food which has a long shelf-life because it has been dried, canned, frozen or otherwise preserved, or which is prepared from raw ingredients on site.

In contrast, Britain's expensive labour and crowded island have encouraged retailers to seek economies from centralised food preparation. They make a wide and varied range of meals that can last for a few days and cater for Britain's rich ethnic mix: Indian curries, Chinese noodles, vegetarian organic foods, and much more – stuff that most Americans have never even heard of, never mind eaten. Tesco stores are also more sophisticated because they have to rely on regular, frequent deliveries and the ability to switch from selling sandwiches at lunchtime to selling ready-meals and cooled wines in the evening. Tesco aims to bring that sophistication to their American stores.

Tesco also surmises that, with worries about obesity, there is more interest in healthy eating. Demand for organic products is already soaring. Upmarket Whole Foods Market with its dramatic merchandising has already revolutionised the way fresh produce is sold in America.

Change how the Americans shop

Will Americans be as willing to park their cars to grab a Fresh & Easy ready-meal? American grocery stores are splitting into those that sell luxury goods, such as Whole Foods Market, and those that sell cheap ones, such as Wal-Mart. Both of these sectors are growing. Retailers catering to the mid-market, such as Safeway, are being squeezed.

Tesco aims to make the middle way work by attracting shoppers from all the main social groups. Fresh & Easy's mid-sized outlets will be a tenth of the size of an average Wal-Mart, although three times the size of a typical 7-Eleven convenience store. Why that size? Tesco thinks that people in too much of a rush to stop at a large supermarket will drop in at their smaller stores that are closer to home and which,

because they carry fewer products, will be easier to navigate. The numerous 7-Eleven stores are such tiny outlets that their range is limited. Fresh & Easy will be the first chain in America to combine convenience with quality.

'When you look at Americans, they shop more frequently than British people and they have to shop around many more retailers, because no one retailer gives them what they want,' says Sir Terry. 'The opportunity [for us] is that they will shop less often if they get more of what they want in one place.'

Healthy and green but not easy

Besides following the trend towards healthy eating and organic foods, Tesco is also reacting to environmentalism by presenting itself as both healthy and green. In environmentally conscious California, Tesco's distribution centre will have the largest solar-panel roof in the state. Its stores will use low-energy lighting and its refrigerated trucks are designed to be energy efficient.

Have Tesco got it right? If they have, the local competition will follow. Wal-Mart is already responding to the way Whole Foods Market is marketing fresh food, and Ralph's grocery chain recently opened a new Fresh Fare store in California. Retaliatory action could also come from America's numerous fast-food chains.

David Lannon, president of the North Atlantic Region for Whole Foods Market, says 'Tesco is better than the major supermarkets in the US. They're cleverer and more efficiently run.' Some, however, worry that their success elsewhere in the world may have coloured Tesco's view of the ready-meals it is proposing to sell in America. Tesco has had notable success in adapting its expertise to serve underdeveloped markets: South Korea, Thailand, Hungary and Poland, to name just a few. Sir Terry also has experience in clearing up the wreckage after the company's failed venture into the French market.

Have Tesco got it right this time? Fresh & Easy is a £1bn risk. If it works, it will change the ways Americans eat and shop, and to work it has to do just that. 'If it succeeds then it's transformational' and Sir Terry will also earn £11.5m in Tesco shares as a bonus tied to the venture.

SOURCES: Elizabeth Rigby and Henry Tricks, 'Tesco faces an international expansion challenge', *Financial Times* (3 June 2005), p. 24; Elizabeth Rigby, 'Struggling to discover long-term growth in an increasingly cutthroat retail market', *Financial Times* (13 June 2005), p. 23; *The Economist*, 'Tesco: Fresh, but far from easy' (21 June 2007); Jonathan Birchall, 'Tesco goes green in US', *FT.com site* (13 February 2007); Jonathan Birchall, 'Tesco aims to fill "grocery gap"', *Financial Times* (28 June 2007); Elizabeth Rigby, 'Leahy set for £11m windfall on US success', *Financial Times* (30 May 2007), p. 17.

Fisherman's Friend's unique packaging, advertising and function help it hold its market niche.
SOURCE: Lofthouse of Fleetwood Ltd.

Nichers try to find one or more market niches that are safe and profitable. An ideal market niche is big enough to be profitable and has growth potential. It is one that the firm can serve effectively. Perhaps most importantly, the niche is of little interest to major competitors. And the firm can build the skills and customer goodwill to defend itself against a major competitor as the niche grows and becomes more attractive. Here's an example of a profitable nicher.

Logitech has become a €1bn global success story by focusing on human interface devices – computer mice, game controllers, keyboards, PC video cameras and others. It makes every variation of computer mouse imaginable. Over the years, Logitech has flooded the world with more than 500 million computer mice of all varieties, mice for left- and right-handed people, wireless mice, travel mice, mini mice, mice shaped like real mice for children, and 3-D mice that let the user appear to move behind screen objects. Breeding mice has been so successful that Logitech dominates the world mouse market, with giant Microsoft as its runner-up. Niching has been very good for Logitech. Its sales and profits have more than doubled in just the past six years.[21]

The key idea in niching is specialisation. A market nicher can specialise along any of several market, customer, product or marketing mix lines. For example, it can specialise in serving one type of *end user*, as when a law firm specialises in the criminal, civil or business law markets.

The nicher can specialise in serving a given *customer-size* group. Many nichers specialise in serving small and mid-size customers who are neglected by the majors.

> " The key idea in niching is specialisation. "

Some nichers focus on one or a few *specific customers*, selling their entire output to a single sector, such as the major oil companies. Still other nichers specialise by *geographic market*, selling only in a certain locality, region or area of the world. An example is Countax:

Countax survives as a small manufacturer of upmarket small ride-on lawnmowers in the UK, a country obsessed with sports on well-manicured lawns: cricket, lawn tennis, crown green bowling and croquet. While Americans want yard tractors and most other countries just want to cut the grass, the British want striped lawns on a par with the quads in Oxbridge colleges. Countax mowers create the pristine lawns that the wealthy locals with a £1m (€1.5m) house with 1–2 acres (0.4–0.8 hectares) of lawn want.

Quality-price nichers operate at the low or high end of the market. Finally, *service nichers* offer services not available from other firms. For example, lastminute.com provides online facilities to book anything from Kaiser Chiefs concerts to Caribbean cruises, and it does not have to be last-minute either. The company aims to be 'the number one European e-commerce lifestyle player by delighting our customers with great-value inspiration and solutions'.

Multiple niching— Adopting a strategy of having several independent offerings that appeal to several different sub-segments of customers.

Niching carries some major risks. For example, the market niche may dry up, or it might grow to the point that it attracts larger competitors. Land Rover's Range Rover pioneered the luxury SUV market, but so attractive was it that every carmaker from Cadillac to Porsche, from Hummer to Lexus, joined in. That is why many companies practise **multiple niching**. By developing two or more niches, a company increases its chances for survival. Even some large firms prefer a multiple niche strategy to serving the total market. For example:

Alberto Culver is a €2.6bn company that has used a multiple niching strategy to grow profitably without incurring the wrath of a market leader. The company, known mainly for its Alberto VO5 hair products, has focused its marketing muscle on acquiring a stable of smaller niche brands. It niches in hair, skin and personal care products (Alberto VO5, St Ives, Motions, Just for Me, Pro-Line, TRESemme, and Consort men's hair products), beauty supplies retailing (Sally Beauty Supply stores), seasonings and sweeteners (Molly McButter, Mrs Dash, SugarTwin, Baker's Joy) and home products (static-cling fighter Static Guard). Most of its brands are number one in their niches. Alberto Culver's CEO explains the company's philosophy this way: 'We know who we are and, perhaps more importantly, we know who we are not. We know that if we try to out-Procter Procter, we will fall flat on our face.'[22]

Balancing customer and competitor orientations

Whether a company is a market leader, challenger, follower or nicher, it must watch its competitors closely and find the competitive marketing strategy that positions it most effectively. And it must continually adapt its strategies to the fast-changing competitive environment. This question now arises: Can the company spend *too* much time and energy tracking competitors, damaging its customer orientation? The answer is yes! A company can become so competitor centred that it loses its even more important focus on maintaining profitable customer relationships.

A **competitor-centred company** is one that spends most of its time tracking competitors' moves and market shares and trying to find strategies to counter them. This approach has some pluses and minuses. On the positive side, the company develops a fighter orientation, watches for weaknesses in its own position, and searches out competitors' weaknesses. On the negative side, the company becomes too reactive. Rather than carrying out its own customer relationship strategy, it bases its own moves on competitors' moves. As a result, it may end up simply matching or extending industry practices rather than seeking innovative new ways to create more value for customers.

A **customer-centred company**, by contrast, focuses more on customer developments in designing its strategies. Clearly, the customer-centred company is in a better position to identify new opportunities and set long-run strategies that make sense. By watching customer needs evolve, it can decide what customer groups and what emerging needs are the most important to serve. Then it can concentrate its resources on delivering superior value to target customers. In practice, today's companies must be **market-centred companies**, watching both their customers and their competitors. But they must not let competitor watching blind them to customer focusing.

Figure 10.4 shows that companies have moved through four orientations over the years. In the first stage, they were product oriented, paying little attention to either customers or competitors. In the second stage, they became customer oriented and started to pay attention to customers. In the third stage, when they started to pay attention to competitors, they became competitor oriented. Today, companies need to be market oriented, paying balanced attention to both customers and competitors. Rather than simply watching competitors and trying to beat them on current ways of doing business, they need to watch customers and find innovative ways to build profitable customer relationships by delivering more value than competitors do. As noted previously, marketing begins with a good understanding of consumers and the marketplace.

Competitor-centred company—A company whose moves are mainly based on competitors' actions and reactions; it spends most of its time tracking competitors' moves and market shares and trying to find strategies to counter them.

Customer-centred company—A company that focuses on customer developments in designing its marketing strategies and on delivering superior value to its target customers.

Market-centred company—A company that pays balanced attention to both customers and competitors in designing its marketing strategies.

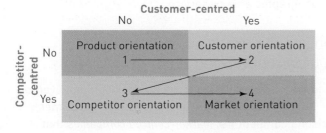

Figure 10.4 Evolving company orientations

Reviewing the concepts

Today's companies face their toughest competition ever. Understanding customers is an important first step in developing strong customer relationships, but it's not enough. To gain competitive advantage, companies must use this understanding to design market offers that deliver more value than the offers of *competitors* seeking to win over the same customers. This chapter examines how firms analyse their competitors and design effective competitive marketing strategies.

1. Discuss the need to understand competitors as well as customers through competitor analysis

In order to prepare an effective marketing strategy, a company must consider its competitors as well as its customers. Building profitable customer relationships requires satisfying target consumer needs *better than competitors do*. A company must continuously analyse competitors and develop *competitive marketing strategies* that position it effectively against competitors and give it the strongest possible *competitive advantage*.

Competitor analysis first involves identifying the company's major competitors, using both an industry-based and a market-based analysis. The company then gathers information on competitors' objectives, strategies, strengths and weaknesses, and reaction patterns. With this information in hand, it can select competitors to attack or avoid. Competitive intelligence must be collected, interpreted and distributed continuously. Company marketing managers should be able to obtain full and reliable information about any competitor affecting their decisions.

2. Explain the fundamentals of competitive marketing strategies based on creating value for customers

Which *competitive marketing strategy* makes the most sense depends on the company's industry, and on whether it is a market leader, challenger, follower or nicher. A *market leader* has to mount strategies to expand the total market, protect market share and expand market share. A *market challenger* is a firm that tries aggressively to expand its market share by attacking the leader, other runner-up companies or smaller firms in the industry. The challenger can select from a variety of direct or indirect attack strategies.

A *market follower* is a runner-up firm that chooses not to rock the boat, usually from fear that it stands to lose more than it might gain. But the follower is not without a strategy and seeks to use its particular skills to gain market growth. Some followers enjoy a higher rate of return than the leaders in their industry. A *market nicher* is a smaller firm that is unlikely to attract the attention of larger firms. Market nichers often become specialists in some end use, customer size, specific customer, geographic area or service.

3. Illustrate the need for balancing customer and competitor orientations in becoming a truly market-centred organisation

A competitive orientation is important in today's markets, but companies should not overdo their focus on competitors. Companies are more likely to be hurt by emerging consumer needs and new competitors than by existing competitors. *Market-centred companies* that balance consumer and competitor considerations are practising a true market orientation.

Discussing the concepts

1. Discount retailer Lidl is attempting to identify its competitors but wants to avoid competitor myopia. Name some of its potential competitors from both an industry and a market point of view.

2. Why is it important to understand competitors' objectives?

3. What is the difference between entrepreneurial, formulated and 'intrepreneurial' marketing? What are the advantages and disadvantages of each?

4. Apply Treacy and Wiersema's value disciplines to online search engines. Identify a company that competes according to each discipline.

5. What are the advantages and disadvantages of a market-nicher competitive strategy?

6. Why is it important for a company to maintain a balance between customer and competitor orientations?

Applying the concepts

1. Form a small group and conduct a customer-value analysis for five local restaurants. Who are the strong and weak competitors? For the strong competitors, what are their vulnerabilities?

2. Lufthansa is Europe's largest airline yet is less profitable than its smaller rivals BA and Ryanair. Explore the competitive alternatives open to Lufthansa in the reformulated and increasingly competitive airline industry.

3. Tiffany & Co. is a high-profile firm in the luxury retail jewellery market. Visit www.tiffany.com/about/Timeline.aspx and review the Tiffany historical timeline for important events. What is Tiffany & Co.'s dominant marketing strategy?

Web resources

For additional classic case studies and Internet exercises, visit www.pearsoned.co.uk/kotler

References

1. *The Economist* (8 May 1999), pp. 122–3; 'Game wars', *The Economist* (22 April 2000), p. 72; Louise Kehoe, 'Microsoft to take on video game leaders', *Financial Times* (10 March 2000), p. 25; Oliver Edwards, 'X-box is no dog', *EuroBusiness* (May 2000), pp. 35–6; Satham Sanghera, 'Sega moves to increase share of UK market', *Financial Times* (13 October 2000), p. 3; Bryon Acohido, 'Microsoft bets on Xbox, but some skeptical', *USA Today* (24 April 2001), p. 6B; 'Video games: console wars', *The Economist* (22 June 2002), pp. 71–2; Michiyo Nakamoto, 'Time for former champ to lift its game', *Financial Times* (29 August 2003), p. 25; 'Loading . . . please wait: The transition to the next generation of consoles is proving tricky, as usual', *The Economist* (23 February 2006); 'Console wars: All three combatants claim victory', *The Economist* (22 March 2007); Richard Waters, 'Microsoft forced to raise ante in games wars', *Financial Times* (8 August 2007); Mariko Sanchanta, 'Sony to cut jobs to prop up PS3', *Financial Times* (8 June 2007), p. 28.

2. Christopher Brown-Humes, Robert Budden and Andrew Gowers, 'Nokia is the great telecom survivor. But the amount of 3G technology means this is no time for complacency', *Financial Times* (18 November 2002), p. 21; 'Going, Boeing', *The Economist* (19 April 2003), pp. 44–5.

3. Leon Lazaroff, 'Kodak big picture focusing on image change', *Knight Ridder Tribune Business News* (26 January 2006). Also see Brad Stone, 'What's Kodak's strategy?', *Newsweek* (16 January 2006), p. 25.

4. Adapted from Jeffrey F. Rayport and Bernard J. Jaworski, *e-Commerce* (New York: McGraw-Hill, 2001), p. 53.

5. Johanna Bennett, 'Turn around, bright eyes', *Barron's* (16 May 2005), p. 48.

6. Edward F. Moltzen, 'Intel, AMD go at it again', *CRN* (29 March 2004), p. 80; Jon Birger, 'Second-mover advantage', *Fortune* (20 March 2006), pp. 20–1; 'Advanced micro devices', *Hoover's Company Records*

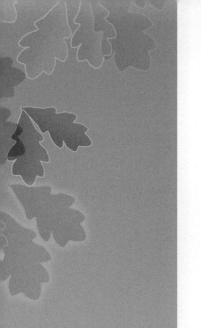

(15 May 2006), p. 10037; Chris Nuttall, 'Intel eats away at AMD's share of chips', *Financial Times* (3 May 2007), p. 25.

7. See Michael Porter, *Competitive Advantage: Creating and sustaining superior performance* (New York: Free Press, 1998), Ch. 6.

8. Devin Leonard, 'The player', *Fortune* (20 March 2006), p. 54; Tom Braithwaite, 'France approves égalité for Apple's iTunes', *Financial Times* (12 May 2006); David Ibison and Emiko Terazono, 'Norway declares Apple's iTunes illegal', *Financial Times* (25 January 2007); Victor Keegan, 'Now it's operators v handset makers', *The Guardian* (16 August 2007).

9. See Philip Kotler and Kevin Lane Keller, *Marketing Management*, 12th edn (Upper Saddle River, NJ: Prentice Hall, 2006), pp. 13–14; Sam Hill and Glenn Rifkin, *Radical Marketing* (New York: HarperBusiness, 1999); Gerry Khermouch, 'Keeping the froth on Sam Adams', *Business Week* (1 September 2003), p. 54; and information accessed at www.bostonbeer.com, August 2006.

10. See T. John Foster, 'Whistle wizards' (Birmingham: Acme Whistles, 2002), and the company's acclaimed website, www.acmewhistles.co.uk.

11. Richard Milne, 'Drive to escape the mass market', *Financial Times* (18 August 2005), p. 9.

12. Michael E. Porter, *Competitive Strategy: Techniques for analyzing industries and competitors* (New York: Free Press, 1980), Ch. 2, and 'What is strategy?', *Harvard Business Review* (November–December 1996), pp. 61–78. Also see Richard Allen *et al.*, 'A comparison of competitive strategies in Japan and the United States', *S.A.M. Advanced Management Journal* (Winter 2006), pp. 24–36.

13. Philip Kotler and Kevin Lane Keller, *Marketing Management*, 12th edn (Upper Saddle River, NJ: Prentice Hall, 2006), p. 243; Amy Yee, 'On a new lap of luxury market', *Financial Times* (20–21 August 2005), p. 9.

14. See Michael Treacy and Fred Wiersema, 'Customer intimacy and other value disciplines', *Harvard Business Review* (January–February 1993), pp. 84–93; Michael Treacy and Fred Wiersema, *The Discipline of Market Leaders: Choose your customers, narrow your focus, dominate your market* (New York: Perseus Press, 1997); Fred Wiersema, *Customer Intimacy: Pick your partners, shape your culture, win together* (Santa Monica, CA: Knowledge Exchange, 1998); and Fred Wiersema, *Double-Digit Growth: How great companies achieve it – no matter what* (New York: Portfolio, 2003).

15. For more discussion, see Philip Kotler and Kevin Lane Keller, *Marketing Management*, 12th edn (Upper Saddle River, NJ: Prentice Hall, 2006), Ch. 11.

16. http://www.wd40.com/pdfs/WD-40_2000UsesList.pdf

17. Adbrands, The Coca-Cola Company Profile, www.adbrands.net/members/us/cocacola_us_p.htm, 17 August 2007.

18. Daniel Dombey, Kevin Done, Andrea Felsted and Nicolas Madelain, 'No-frills operators have transformed the market but their business model may be harder to sustain if costs start to rise', *Financial Times* (12 December 2002); Dan Roberts, 'Threat to Ryanair's business model', *Financial Times* (28 August 2003); LEX column: 'Ryanair', *Financial Times* (6 February 2007); LEX column: 'Virgin's US take-off', *Financial Times* (8 August 2007).

19. Jack Neff, 'Unilever cedes laundry war', *Advertising Age* (27 May 2002), pp. 1, 47; Veronica MacDonald, 'Soaps and detergents: Going the world over to clean', *Chemical Week* (26 January 2005), pp. 21–3; Jack Neff, 'Unilever 3.0: CEO not afraid to copy from P&G', *Advertising Age* (23 October 2005), p. 8; Kerri Walsh, 'Brand extensions clean up', *Chemical Week* (1 February 2006), pp. 24–8.

20. Peter Marsh, 'Light amid the manufacturing gloom', *Financial Times* (3 June 2005).

21. 'Logitech aims at convergence for new growth', *Wall Street Journal* (16 June 2004), p. 1; Logitech Annual Report, www.logitech.com, 1 April 2006; 'Logitech International S.A.', *Hoover's Company Records* (1 June 2006), p. 42459.

22. Jim Kirk, 'Company finds itself, finds success: Alberto-Culver adopts strategy of knowing its strengths and promoting small brands, rather than tackling giants', *Chicago Tribune* (22 January 1998), Business Section, p. 1; 'Alberto-Culver Company', *Hoover's Company Records* (1 June 2006), p. 10048; www.alberto.com, July 2006.

Company case 10 Bose: competing by being truly different

Forrester Research's 2006 survey of consumer electronics and personal computer companies drew the conclusion that the 'trust in consumer technology companies is eroding'. Why is consumer trust important? Forrester's Ted Schadler answered: 'Trust is a powerful way to measure a brand's value and its ability to command a premium price or drive consumers into a higher-profit direct channel. A decline in trust causes brand erosion and price-driven purchase decisions, which in turn correlates with low market growth.'

But despite the decline in trust for most technology companies, Forrester made another surprising finding. Consumer trust in Bose was riding high. In fact, Bose far outscored all other companies in Forrester's survey. Not bad, considering that it was the first time the company had been included. Forrester pointed out that these results were no fluke, noting that Bose has 10 million regular users but more than 17 million consumers who aspire to use the brand (compared to 7 million for next-highest Apple). These high levels of consumer trust result from philosophies that have guided Bose for more than 40 years. Most companies today focus heavily on building revenue, profits and stock price. They try to outdo the competition by differentiating product lines with features and attributes that other companies do not have. Although Bose pays attention to such factors, its true differentiation derives from the company's unique corporate philosophy.

The Bose philosophy

You can't understand Bose the company without taking a look at Bose the man: Amar Bose, the company's founder and still its CEO. In the 1950s, while working on his third degree in electrical engineering, he combined it with his strong interest in music. When he purchased his first hi-fi system – a model that he believed had the best specifications – he was very disappointed in the system's ability to reproduce realistic sound. So he set out to find his own solution. Thus began a stream of research that would ultimately lead to the founding of his company in 1964. From those early days, Amar Bose worked around certain core principles that have guided the philosophy of the company.

In conducting his first research on speakers and sound, he did something that has since been repeated time and time again at Bose. He ignored existing technologies and started entirely from scratch. Bose president Bob Maresca provides insights on the company today that date back to Amar Bose's original philosophy: 'We are not in it strictly to make money,' he says. 'Dr Bose is extremely eclectic in his research interests. The business is almost a secondary consideration.' For this reason, Amar Bose ploughs all of the privately held company's profits back into research. This practice reflects his avid love of research and his belief that it will produce the highest-quality products. But he also does this because he can. Bose has been quoted many times saying, 'if I worked for another company, I would have been fired a long time ago,' pointing to the fact that publicly held companies have long lists of constraints that don't apply to his privately held company. That is why Bose has always vowed that he will never take the company public. 'Going public for me would have been the equivalent of losing the company. My real interest is research – that's the excitement – and I wouldn't have been able to do long-term projects with shareholders breathing down my neck.'

This commitment to research and development has led to the high level of trust that Bose customers have for the company. It also explains their almost cult-like loyalty. Customers know that the company cares more about their best interests – about making the best product – than about maximising profits. But for a company not driven by the bottom line, Bose does just fine. Although performance figures are tightly held, analysts estimate that between 2004 and 2006, the company's revenues increased more than 38 per cent. According to market information firm NPD Group, Bose leads the market in home speakers with a 12.6 per cent share. Not only were home speakers the company's original product line, but they remain one of its largest and most profitable endeavours.

Groundbreaking products

The company that started so humbly now has a breadth of product lines beyond its core home audio line.

Additional lines target a variety of applications that have captured Amar Bose's creative attention over the years, including military, automotive, homebuilding/remodelling, aviation, test equipment, and professional and commercial sound systems. The following are just a few of the products that illustrate the innovative breakthroughs produced by the company.

Speakers

Bose's first product, introduced in 1965, was a speaker. Expecting to sell thousands of speakers that first year, Bose made 60 but sold only 40. The original Bose speaker evolved into the 901 Direct/Reflecting speaker system launched in 1968. The speaker was so technologically advanced that the company still sells it today. The system was designed around the concept that live sound reaches the human ear via direct as well as reflected channels (off walls, ceilings and other objects). The configuration of the speakers was completely unorthodox. They were shaped like an eighth of a sphere and mounted facing into a room's corner. The speakers had no woofers or tweeters and were very small compared to the high-end speakers of the day. The design came much closer to the essence and emotional impact of live music than anything else on the market and won immediate industry acclaim. However, Bose had a hard time convincing customers of the merits of these innovative speakers. At a time when woofers, tweeters and size were everything, the 901 series flopped.

In 1968, a retail salesman explained to Amar Bose why the speakers weren't selling: 'Look, I love your speaker but I cannot sell it because it makes me lose all my credibility as a salesman. I can't explain to anyone why the 901 doesn't have any woofers or tweeters. A man came in and saw the small size, and he started looking in the drawers for the speaker cabinets. I walked over to him, and he said, "Where are you hiding the woofer?" I said to him, "There is no woofer." So he said, "You're a liar," and he walked out.'

Bose eventually worked through the challenges of communicating the virtues of the 901 series to customers through innovative display and demonstration tactics. The product became so successful that Amar Bose now credits the 901 series for building the company. The list of major speaker innovations at Bose is a long one. In 1975, the company introduced concert-like sound in the bookshelf-size 301 Direct/Reflecting speaker system. Fourteen years of research led to the 1984 development of acoustic waveguide speaker

technology, a technology found today in the award-winning Wave radio, Wave music system and Acoustic Wave music system. In 1986, the company again changed conventional thinking about the relationship between speaker size and sound. The Acoustimass system enabled palm-size speakers to produce audio-quality equivalent to that of high-end systems many times their size. The technological basis of the Acoustimass system is still in use in Bose products today.

Headphones

Bob Maresca recalls that, 'Bose invested tens of millions over 19 years developing headset technology before making a profit. Now, headsets are a major part of the business.' Initially, Bose focused on noise reduction technologies to make headphones for pilots that would block out the high level of noise interference from planes. Bose headphones combined both passive and active noise reduction methods. Passive methods involve physically blocking out noise with sound-deadening insulation. Active methods are much more complex, involving circuitry that samples ambient noise and then cancels it out by creating sound waves opposite to the 'noise' waves. Bose quickly discovered that airline passengers could benefit as much as pilots from its headphone technology. Today, Bose sells its QuietComfort and Triport headphone lines for use in a variety of consumer applications.

Automotive suspensions

Another major innovation at Bose has yet to be introduced. The company has been conducting research since 1980 on a product outside its known areas of expertise: automotive suspensions. Amar Bose's interest in suspensions dates back to the 1950s when he bought both a Citroën DS-19C and a Pontiac Bonneville, each riding on unconventional air suspension systems. Since that time, he's been obsessed with the engineering challenge of achieving good cornering capabilities without sacrificing a smooth ride.

Bose is now on the verge of introducing a suspension that it believes will accomplish this feat better than any system to date. The basics of the system include an electromagnetic motor installed at each wheel. Based on inputs from road-sensing monitors, the motor can retract and extend almost instantaneously. If there is a bump in the road, the suspension reacts by 'jumping' over it. If there is a pothole, the suspension allows the wheel to extend downward, but then retracts it quickly enough that the pothole is not felt. In addition to these comfort-producing capabilities, the wheel motors are strong enough to prevent the car from rolling and pitching during an aggressive manoeuvre. The suspension system has been designed so that it can be bolted right onto the chassis of current production cars, thus minimising both time and expense for manufacturers. Initially, the cost of the system will put it in the class of luxury automobiles. Currently, Bose is demonstrating the system only to a handful of companies, with the intention of partnering with one manufacturer before rolling it out to others.

Eventually, Bose anticipates that wider adoption and higher volume will bring the price down to the point where the suspension could be found in all but the least expensive cars. At an age when most people have long ago retired, 76-year-old Amar Bose works every day, either at the company's headquarters or at his home. 'He's got more energy than an 18-year-old,' says Maresca. 'Every one of the naysayers only strengthens his resolve.' This work ethic illustrates the passion of the man who has shaped one of today's most innovative and yet most trusted companies. His philosophies have produced Bose's long list of groundbreaking innovations.

Even now, as the company prepares to enter the world of automotive suspensions, it continues to achieve success by following another one of Dr Bose's basic philosophies: 'The potential size of the market? We really have no idea. We just know that we have a technology that's so different and so much better that many people will want it.'

Questions

1. Based on the business philosophies of Amar Bose, how do you think Bose goes about analysing its competition?

2. Which of the text's three approaches to marketing strategy best describes Bose's approach?

3. Using the Michael Porter and Treacy and Wiersema frameworks presented in the text, which basic competitive marketing strategies does Bose pursue?

4. What is Bose's competitive position in its industry? Do its marketing strategies match this position?

5. In your opinion, is Bose a customer-centred company?

6. What do you think will happen when Amar Bose leaves the company?

SOURCES: Brian Dumaine, 'Amar Bose', *Fortune Small Business* (1 September 2004), accessed online at www.money.cnn.com/magazines/fsb/; Olga Kharif, 'Selling sound: Bose knows', *Business Week Online* (15 May 2006), accessed online at www.businessweek.com; Mark Jewell, 'Bose tries to shake up auto industry', *Associated Press* (27 November 2005); 'Bose introduces new QuietComfort 3 Acoustic Noise-Canceling Headphones', *Business Wire* (8 June 2006); 'Forrester Research reveals the most trusted consumer technology brands', press release accessed online at www.forrester.com; also see 'About Bose', accessed online at www.bose.com, (June 2006); Paul Taylor, 'Earbuds that let your music bloom', *FT Weekend – Shopping* (10 March 2007); *Which? Report*, 'Home-cinema' (10 August 2007) on www.which.net.

Video Case Voluntary Service Overseas

Vicky Starnes
Interim Head of Marketing

Voluntary Service Overseas (VSO) is the largest independent (non-governmental) volunteer-sending organisation in the world. The international development charity has a distinct way of helping people in less developed countries. It contributes by sending experienced volunteers to live and work as equals alongside local partners. These professionals usually volunteer their services and work on a subsistence level income to teach or, increasingly, teaching teachers how to teach. The organisation's marketing budget is minimal yet it has three main marketing tasks: to persuade people in developing counties to accept their service; to attract skilled volunteers to donate one or more years to the charity; and to raise money.

More about the charity can be found on their websites in The Netherlands (www.vso.nl), Ireland (www.vso.ie) or the UK (www.vso.uk). You can also read stories from volunteers on the charities blogsite (www.vso-stories.net) or visit their fundraising pages (www.justgiving.com/vsofundraising).

After viewing the video, you may address the following questions:

1. How does the marketing of services differ from that of physical goods?
2. What are the particular marketing challenges facing not-for-profit organisations such as VSO?
3. How does a non-profit service organisation like VSO resolve the conflict between the level of marketing spend and public concerns for donations being spent on excessive marketing rather than on the causes the charity is set up to serve?

> A hamburger by any other name costs twice as much.

EVAN ESAR (MODERN MARKETER)

PART four

Product

IN PART FOUR OF *PRINCIPLES OF MARKETING* we look at the first component in the marketing mix – the product. Designing good products that customers want to buy is a challenging task. Customers do not buy mere products. They seek product benefits and are often willing to pay more for a brand that genuinely solves their problems. **Chapter 11** explores how marketers can satisfy customer needs by adding value to the basic product; it also shows the complexity arising in product, branding and packaging decisions, and how various forces in the environment pose tough challenges for marketers.

Markets do not stand still. Companies must adapt their current offerings or create new ones in response to changing customer needs, or to take advantage of new marketing and technological opportunities. **Chapter 12** looks at how to develop and commercialise new products. Importantly, after launch, marketing managers must carefully manage the new product over its lifetime to get the best return from their new-product effort.

While Chapters 11 and 12 deal with products, **Chapter 13** looks more specifically at intangible products or services. It examines the unique characteristics of services and how organisations adapt their approach when marketing them.

mini bottle
big refreshment

Coca-Cola 250ml

Enjoy Coke® MINIS

Mini moments of
great Coke® taste.

the Coke side of life™

> What's in a name? That which we call a rose by any other name would smell as sweet.

WILLIAM SHAKESPEARE

Product and branding strategy

Mini Contents List

◄ SOURCE: The Advertising Archives.

'. . . ain't nothin' but a campaign
freedom ain't nothin' but a brand name'

From 'Kkkampain' by Promoe on 'The Long Distance Runner', Burning Heart, B0001FT29Y

Previewing the concepts

In this chapter, we will define the term 'product' and then look at major classifications of products. Then we will discuss the important decisions that marketers make regarding individual products, product lines and product mixes. Next, we move from decisions about individual products to the critically important issue of how marketers build and manage their brands. Finally, we address socially responsible product decisions and some complex considerations in international product decisions.

After reading this chapter, you should be able to:

1. Define the term *product* including the core, actual and augmented product.
2. Explain the main classifications of products.
3. Describe the decisions companies make regarding their individual products, product lines and product mixes.
4. Discuss branding strategy – the decisions that companies make in building and managing their brands.
5. Discuss additional branding issues with respect to socially responsible brand decisions and international marketing.

Charles Revson, the founder of Revlon, recognised that: 'In the factory we make cosmetics. In the store we sell hope.' If that is the case, there is a lot of hope pinned on L'Oréal, the global leader in cosmetics with a portfolio that contains many of the world's biggest hair and beauty products, including Garnier, Maybelline and Lancôme.

Prelude case L'Oréal: are you worth it?

L'Oréal sells cosmetics and toiletries to consumers around the world. One market that has certainly been booming lately is that for hair care products. Brands such as Elvive, Lancôme, Helena Rubenstein and Kérastase, part of the L'Oréal stable, are capitalising on this trend. In one sense, L'Oréal's hair care products – shampoo, conditioners, styling agents – are no more than careful mixtures of chemicals with different smells and colours. But L'Oréal knows that when it sells shampoos and conditioners, it sells much more than a bottle of coloured or fragrant soapy fluids – it sells what the fluids can do for the women who use them.

Many hair care products are promoted using alluring chat-up lines: 'Your hair is instantly shinier, stronger, healthier, and getting better and better and . . . .' Who would believe that shampoos and conditioners that are designed to rinse away can have any lasting benefits? But women do not see shampoos and conditioners that way. Many things beyond the ingredients add to a shampoo's allure. While hair is dead, it is organic, so will respond to some care and attention. Many consumers believe that their favourite shampoo does more than wash away the grit in their hair; it makes them feel good about themselves.

> L'Oréal sells much more than a bottle of coloured or fragrant soapy fluids – it sells what the fluids can do for the women who use them.

Thanks to recent scientific breakthroughs, many hair care products can make a difference. The L'Oréal laboratories in Paris, employing 2,500 employees, dedicate over €270m a year to R&D. This investment pays. For example, Kérastase, part of the L'Oréal group, developed Ceramide F – a synthetic copy of naturally occurring hair ceramides – which reconstructs the hair's internal structure. Sounds far fetched? But consumers say it works. Kérastase Forcintense revitalises hair that is severely damaged through colouring, overstyling or perming. Other L'Oréal product innovations include colour and conditioning agents – Majirel, Majirouge and Majiblond – for treating fading hair colours due to washing or sunlight, and special formulations – Majimèches – for blondes. All these functional benefits enable L'Oréal to promote the brand's superior performance benefits to consumers.

The wash-in, wash-out nature of hair care suggests that product performance alone may be sufficient to satisfy users. Hairstylist Sam McKnight says that it is an emotionally charged marketplace: a bad hair day means an unhappy woman. There is also a limit to what all the scientific breakthroughs in hair care can do for how a woman feels when she has had a hair wash. McKnight argues that scents and colours must be chosen carefully to match women's desires, moods and lifestyles. His new range of products eschew science and concentrate on the smell. Called 'Sexy', they are expensive, exclusive and smell like no other shampoo has ever smelled before.

Additionally, hair care brands have done well because of the advertising spends that have gone in to promote shampooing as a pleasurable pastime rather than an activity akin to doing a load of washing. L'Oréal and rival firms know just how important this is. Brands such as Elvive, Pantene (by Procter & Gamble) and Organics (by Elida/Lever Fabergé) have advertising spends that will make a girl's hair curl. L'Oréal's leading brand Elvive also tries to capture the essence of pleasure using advertisements that sound tempting: 'Because I'm worth it', says L'Oréal.

Companies also have to play on the shampoo's name, an important product attribute. Names such as Sexy, Dream Hair Sensational and Frizz-Ease suggest that the shampoos and conditioners will do something more than just wash your hair. L'Oréal must also package its hair care products carefully. To consumers, the bottle and package are the most tangible symbols of the product's image. Bottles must feel comfortable, be easy to handle and help to differentiate the product from other brands on the shelf.

So when a woman buys hair shampoos and conditioners, she buys much, much more than simply soapy fluids. The product's image, its promises, its feel, its name and package, even the company that makes it, all become a part of the *total product*.

Hope in a bottle or just so much hype? The answer: it's up to each of us to decide whether we're worth it.[1]

Questions

1. Distinguish between the core, tangible and augmented product that L'Oréal sells.
2. A hair care product's name is a central product attribute. What are the key branding decisions that L'Oréal's marketing managers have to make?
3. L'Oréal markets its hair care products worldwide. What major considerations does the firm face in determining global product decisions?

Introduction

The product is usually the first and most basic marketing consideration. We start with a seemingly simple question: What is a product? As the preview case shows, toiletries and cosmetics are more than just toiletries and cosmetics when L'Oréal sells them. Well, what is water? That's right, water. As it turns out, to a FIJI Water customer, water is more than just a liquid you draw out of the tap to wash down a sandwich or to quench your thirst after a workout. FIJI Water is 'The nature of water'. Danone's Evian mineral water is 'the natural source of youth'.

What is a product?

Product—Anything that can be offered to a market for attention, acquisition, use or consumption that might satisfy a want or need. It includes physical objects, services, persons, places, organisations and ideas.

Services—Activities, benefits or satisfactions offered for sale that are essentially intangible and do not result in the ownership of anything.

We define a **product** as anything that is offered to a market for attention, acquisition, use or consumption that might satisfy a want or need. Products include more than just tangible goods. Broadly defined, products include physical objects, services, persons, places, organisations, ideas or mixes of these entities. Throughout this text, we use the term *product* broadly to include any or all of these entities. Thus, a pair of adidas trainers, a Volvo truck, a Nokia mobile phone and a cup of cappuccino at Costa Coffee are products. But so are a Club Med vacation, online investment services and medical advice from your family doctor.

Services are products that consist of activities, benefits or satisfactions that are offered for sale that are essentially intangible and do not result in the ownership of anything. Examples are banking, hotel, hairdressing, airline, retail, tax-preparation and home repair services. Because of the importance of services in the world economy, we will look at services marketing in greater detail in Chapter 13.

Products, services and experiences

Product is a key element in the overall *market offering*. Marketing mix planning begins with formulating an offering that brings value to target customers. This offering becomes the basis upon which the company builds profitable relationships with customers.

A company's market offering often includes both tangible goods and services. Each component can be a minor or a major part of the total offer. At one extreme, the offer may consist of a *pure tangible good*, such as soap, toothpaste or salt – no services accompany the product. At the other extreme are *pure services*, for which the offer consists primarily of a service. Examples include a doctor's consultation or financial services. Between these two extremes, however, many goods-and-services combinations are possible. We will examine in greater detail the concept of the tangible–intangible continuum for goods and services in Chapter 13.

Today, as products and services become more commoditised, many companies are moving to a new level in creating value for their customers. To differentiate their offers, beyond simply making products and delivering services, they are creating and managing customer *experiences* with their products or company.

Experiences have always been important in the entertainment industry – Disney has long manufactured memories through its movies and theme parks. Today, however, all kinds of firms are recasting their traditional goods and services to create experiences. For example, car manufacturers like Mercedes-Benz do more than just make and sell high-end cars. They take additional steps to create special experiences for consumers.[2]

To extend its reach Mercedes-Benz has opened Mercedes-Benz World at Brooklands, a state-of-the-art complex and the company's biggest brand experience centre, sited next to the historic Brooklands racetrack and museum in Surrey, England. Inside the architecturally stunning and futuristic building, visitors are treated to a replica of Karl Benz's ground-breaking three-wheeled Patent Motor Wagen, alongside every model currently available in the UK, from Smart to Maybach and Mercedes-Benz SLR McLaren. Other features include iconic classic Mercedes, a host of interactive exhibits, a stylish restaurant, café, boutique and comprehensive conference centre, events and hospitality facilities. Other major attractions are the handling circuits and an off-road motor circuit on which visitors can experience the full range of Mercedes-Benz cars. According to the Head of Mercedes Car Group, 'The opening of our new brand centre in the UK marks another important milestone in our history, and enables our customers to appreciate just what it is that makes our brands and products so very special.' And, of course, before, during and after all these experiences, shopping does go on – and the purchases become memorabilia for the experiences visitors have. In a sense, the attraction is much more than a visitor centre – it's a place where imaginations soar, from the boutiques to special events, from the café to the handling circuits and beyond.

Companies that market experiences realise that customers are really buying much more than just products and services. They are buying what those offers will *do* for them.

> Customers are really buying much more than just products and services. They are buying what those offers will *do* for them.

Levels of product

Product planners need to think about the product on three levels. Each level adds more customer value. The most basic level is the **core product**, which addresses the question: *What is the buyer really buying?* As Figure 11.1 illustrates, the core product stands at the centre of the total product. It consists of the core, problem-solving benefits that consumers seek. A woman buying lipstick buys more than lip colour – remember what Charles Revson said, 'In the factory, we make cosmetics; in the store we sell hope.' Theodore Levitt has pointed out that buyers 'do not buy

Core product—The core problem-solving services or benefits that consumers are really buying when they obtain a product.

Figure 11.1 Three levels of product

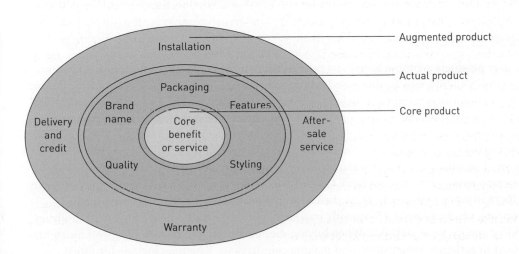

quarter-inch drills; they buy quarter-inch holes'. Thus when designing products, marketers must first define the core of *benefits* that the product will provide to consumers.

At the second level, product planners must turn the core benefit into an **actual product**. They need to develop as many as five characteristics: a *quality level*, product and service *features*, *styling*, a *brand name* and *packaging*. For example, the BlackBerry is an actual product. Its name, parts, styling, features, packaging and other attributes have all been combined carefully to deliver the core benefit of staying connected.

Finally, the product planner must build an **augmented product** around the core and actual product by offering additional customer services and benefits. BlackBerry must offer more than just a communications device. It must provide consumers with a complete solution to mobile connectivity problems. Thus, when consumers buy a BlackBerry, the company and its dealers also might give buyers a warranty on parts and workmanship, instructions on how to use the device, quick repair services when needed, and a freephone number and website to use if they have problems or questions. To the consumer, all of these augmentations become an important part of the total product.

Therefore, a product is more than a simple set of tangible features. Consumers tend to see products as complex *bundles of benefits* that satisfy their needs. When developing products, marketers must first identify the *core* consumer needs that the product will satisfy. They must then design the *actual* product and finally find ways to *augment* it in order to create the bundle of benefits that will best satisfy customers.

Today, most competition takes place at the product augmentation level. Successful companies add benefits to their offers that will not only *satisfy* but also *delight* the customer. However, each augmentation costs the company money, and the marketer has to ask whether customers will pay enough to cover the extra cost. Moreover, augmented benefits soon become *expected* benefits. For example, hotel guests now expect cable television, Internet access, trays of toiletries and other amenities in their rooms. This means that competitors must search for still more features and benefits to differentiate their offers and deliver the most satisfying customer experience.

Product classifications

Products can be classified according to their durability and tangibility. **Non-durable products** are goods that are normally consumed quickly and used on one or a few usage occasions, such as beer, soap and food products. **Durable products** are products used over an extended period of time and normally survive for many years. Examples are refrigerators, cars and furniture.

Marketers have also divided products and services into two broad classes based on the types of customer that use them – consumer products and industrial products. Broadly defined, products also include other marketable entities such as experiences, organisations, persons, places and ideas.

Consumer products

Consumer products are those bought by final consumers for personal consumption. Marketers usually classify these goods further based on *consumer shopping habits* – how consumers go about buying them. Consumer products include *convenience products, shopping products, speciality products* and *unsought products*. These products differ in the way consumers buy them and therefore in how they are marketed (see Table 11.1).

Convenience products are consumer goods and services that the consumer usually buys frequently, immediately and with a minimum of comparison and buying effort. Examples are soap, sweets, newspapers and fast food. Convenience goods are usually low priced, and marketers place them in many locations to make them readily available when customers need them.

Shopping products are less frequently purchased goods that customers compare carefully on suitability, quality, price and style. When buying shopping products, consumers spend much time and effort in gathering information and making comparisons. Examples include furniture,

Actual product—A product's parts, quality level, features, design, brand name, packaging and other attributes that combine to deliver core product benefits.

Augmented product—Additional consumer services and benefits built around the core and actual products.

Non-durable product—A consumer product that is normally consumed in one or a few uses.

Durable product—A consumer product that is usually used over an extended period of time and that normally survives many uses.

Consumer product—A product bought by final consumers for personal consumption.

Convenience product—A consumer product that the customer usually buys frequently, immediately, and with a minimum of comparison and buying effort.

Shopping product—A consumer product that the customer, in the process of selection and purchase, characteristically compares on such bases as suitability, quality, price and style.

Table 11.1 Marketing considerations for consumer products

Marketing consideration	Type of consumer product			
	Convenience	Shopping	Speciality	Unsought
Customer buying behaviour	Frequent purchase, little planning, little comparison or shopping effort, low customer involvement	Less frequent purchase, much planning and shopping effort, comparison of brands on price, quality, style	Strong brand preference and loyalty, special purchase effort, little comparison of brands, low price sensitivity	Little product awareness or knowledge; if aware, little or even negative interest
Price	Low price	Higher price	High price	Varies
Distribution	Widespread distribution, convenient locations	Selective distribution in fewer outlets	Exclusive distribution in only one or a few outlets per market area	Varies
Promotion	Mass promotion by the producer	Advertising and personal selling by both producer and resellers	More carefully targeted promotion by both producer and resellers	Aggressive advertising and personal selling by producer and resellers
Examples	Toothpaste, magazines, laundry detergent	Major appliances, televisions, furniture, clothing	Luxury goods, such as Rolex watches or fine crystal	Life insurance, blood donations

clothing, used cars and major household appliances. Shopping products marketers usually distribute their products through fewer outlets but provide deeper sales support to help customers in their comparison efforts.

Speciality products are consumer goods with unique characteristics or brand identification for which a significant group of buyers is willing to make a special purchase effort. Examples include specific brands and types of car, high-priced home entertainment systems and photographic equipment, luxury goods, designer clothes and the services of medical or legal specialists. A jukebox, for example, is a speciality good because buyers are usually willing to travel great distances to buy one. Buyers normally do not compare speciality goods. They invest only the time needed to reach dealers carrying the wanted products.

Unsought products are consumer goods that the consumer either does not know about or knows about but does not normally think of buying. Most major new innovations are unsought until the consumer becomes aware of them through advertising. Classic examples of known but unsought goods are life insurance, home security systems, pre-planned funeral services and blood donations. By their very nature, unsought goods require a lot of advertising, personal selling and other marketing efforts.

Industrial products

Industrial products are those bought for further processing or for use in conducting a business. Thus the distinction between a consumer product and an industrial product is based on the *purpose* for which the product is purchased. If a consumer buys a lawnmower for home use, the

Speciality product—A consumer product with unique characteristics or brand identification for which a significant group of buyers is willing to make a special purchase effort.

Unsought product—A consumer product that the consumer either does not know about or knows about but does not normally think of buying.

Industrial product—A product bought by individuals and organisations for further processing or for use in conducting a business.

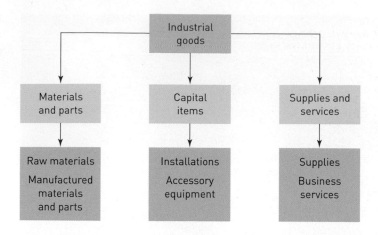

Figure 11.2 Classification of industrial goods

lawnmower is a consumer product. If the same consumer buys the same lawnmower for use in a landscaping business, the lawnmower is an industrial product.

There are three groups of industrial products: *materials and parts*, *capital items* and *supplies and services* (see Figure 11.2).

Materials and parts are industrial goods that become a part of the buyer's product, through further processing or as components. They include raw materials and manufactured materials and parts.

Raw materials consist of farm products (wheat, cotton, livestock, fruits,vegetables) and natural products (fish, timber, crude petroleum, iron ore).

Manufactured materials and parts include component materials (iron, yarn, cement, wires) and component parts (small motors, tyres, castings). Component materials are usually processed further – for example, pig iron is made into steel, and yarn is woven into cloth. Component parts enter the finished product complete with no further change in form, as when Dyson or Miele put small motors into their vacuum cleaners and Volvo and Fiat add tyres to their motor vehicles. Most manufactured materials and parts are sold directly to industrial users. Price and service are the most significant marketing factors, while branding and advertising tend to be relatively less important.

Capital items are industrial products that help in the buyers' production or operations, including installations and accessory equipment. *Installations* consist of buildings (factories, offices) and fixed equipment (generators, drill presses, large computer systems, lifts). *Accessory equipment* includes portable factory equipment and tools (hand tools, lift trucks) and office equipment (personal computers, photocopiers, desks). These products do not become part of the finished product. They have a shorter life than installations and simply aid in the production process.

Supplies and services are industrial products that do not enter the finished product at all. *Supplies* include operating supplies (lubricants, coal, paper, pencils) and repair and maintenance items (paint, nails, brooms). Supplies are the convenience goods of the industrial field because they are usually purchased with a minimum of effort or comparison. *Business services* include maintenance and repair services (window cleaning, computer repair) and business advisory services (legal, management consulting, advertising). Such services are usually supplied under contract.

Materials and parts— Industrial products that enter the manufacturer's product completely, including raw materials and manufactured materials and parts.

Capital items—Industrial goods that partly enter the finished product, including installations and accessory equipment.

Supplies and services— Industrial products that do not enter the finished product at all.

Organisations, persons, places and ideas

In addition to tangible products and services, in recent years marketers have broadened the concept of a product to include other market offerings – namely, organisations, persons, places and ideas.

> Marketers have broadened the concept of a product to include . . . organisations, persons, places and ideas.

Organisations often carry out activities to 'sell' the organisation itself. *Organisation marketing* consists of activities undertaken to create, maintain or change the attitudes and behaviour of target consumers towards an organisation. Both profit and not-for-profit organisations practise organisation marketing. Business firms sponsor public relations or *corporate image advertising* campaigns to polish their images and market themselves to various publics. For example, with the launch of Ovi, Nokia is positioning itself as an Internet company providing music downloads, games, maps and other online applications (see the Company case at the end of this chapter).[3] Similarly, not-for-profit organisations, such as churches, colleges, charities, museums and performing arts groups, market their organisations in order to raise funds and attract members or patrons.

People can also be thought of as products. *Person marketing* consists of activities undertaken to create, maintain or change attitudes or behaviour towards particular people. All kinds of people use person marketing to build their reputations. Presidents or prime ministers of nations market themselves, their parties and their policies to get needed votes and support. Entertainers and sports figures use marketing to promote their careers and improve their impact and incomes. Professionals such as doctors, lawyers, accountants and architects market themselves in order to build their reputations and increase business. Business leaders use person marketing as a strategic tool to develop their companies' fortunes as well as their own. Businesses, charities, sports teams, fine arts groups, religious groups and other organisations also use well-known personalities to help sell their products or causes. Brands such as Tag Heuer, adidas, Nike, Coca-Cola and others have invested millions of euros to link themselves with celebrities. For example, more than a dozen different companies – including Nike, Tag Heuer, NetJets, Gillette, Wheaties and Accenture – combine to pay more than $80m a year to link themselves with golf superstar Tiger Woods.[4]

The skilful use of person marketing can turn a person's name into a powerhouse brand. For example, 1930s tennis star Fred Perry's empire started with sports clothes and tennis equipment but has now transformed itself into a retro fashion brand with related indie music interests.[5] Like many top European designers, Gianni Versace made his name synonymous with style across the Versace Group, which is now headed by Donatella Versace: Gianni Versace Couture, Versace Jeans Couture, Versace Home Collection and Versace Collection. The high-end Gianni Versace Couture includes jewellery, watches, fragrances, cosmetics and home furnishings, but other interests extend to the luxurious Palazzo Versace hotel.[6]

Place marketing involves activities undertaken to create, maintain or change attitudes or behaviour towards particular places. Cities, states, regions and even entire nations compete to attract tourists, new residents, conventions and company offices and factories. Poland promotes itself as a new holiday destination with '1000 years of tradition and New European adventure', while New Zealand positions itself clearly with '100% Pure New Zealand' and New York shouts, 'I Love New York!' The Icelandic Tourist Board invites visitors to Iceland by advertising that it has 'Discoveries the Entire Year'. Icelandair, the only airline that serves the island, partners with the tourist board to sell world travellers on the wonders of Iceland – everything from geothermal spas and glacier tours to midnight golf and clubbing. Ireland is an outstanding place marketer. The Irish Development Board has attracted over 1,200 companies to locate their plants in Ireland. At the same time, the Irish Tourist Board has built a flourishing tourism business, and the Irish Export Board has created attractive markets for Irish exports.[7]

Ideas can also be marketed. In one sense, all marketing is the marketing of an idea, whether it be the general idea of owning a hybrid – electric and petrol-driven car – or the specific idea that the Lexus GS 450h is the world's first high-performance hybrid vehicle, providing exhilarating performance while keeping to category-beating low CO_2 emissions and fuel consumption.

However, we narrow our focus to the marketing of *social ideas*. This area has been called *social marketing*, which involves the use of commercial marketing concepts and tools in programmes designed to influence individuals' behaviour to improve their well-being and that of society.

Social marketing programmes include public health campaigns to reduce smoking, alcoholism, drug abuse, child abuse and overeating. An example is the successful Stop Aids campaign run by the Swiss Aids Foundation:

> The initial audience of the campaign was gay men, but as the epidemic grew it reached out to a national audience. During the campaign, condom use and attitudes towards the epidemic were continually measured. Condom use among men between the ages of 17–30 years, for example, increased from 8% to almost 50%. One *product* was the condom; another *product* was anti-discrimination and later needle exchange. The Swiss were convinced that as long as Aids was feared, risky sex would remain underground. As well as being on radio and TV, community groups organised special events and new *distribution points* opened throughout the country for condoms and for counselling.
>
> An early success of the campaign was the creation of *Hot Rubber*, its own brand of condom for gay men. Through its own distribution channels and targeted marketing, the Swiss Aids Foundation set out to make condoms readily available, to diminish the stigma and embarrassment associated with purchasing them, and to encourage consistent use. The effectiveness of the Hot Rubber brand's promotion is illustrated in its sales volume. In the first nine months of the campaign, condom sales rose from 2,000 units per month to more than 55,000, leveling off a year later at 75,000 units.[8]

Other social marketing efforts include environmental campaigns to promote wilderness protection, clean air and conservation. Still others address issues such as family planning, human rights and equal opportunity. But social marketing involves much more than just advertising – the Social Marketing Institute (SMI) encourages the use of a broad range of marketing tools. 'Social marketing goes well beyond the promotional '*P*' of the marketing mix to include every other element to achieve its social change objectives,' says the SMI's executive director. Many public marketing campaigns fail because they assign advertising the primary role and fail to develop and use all the marketing mix tools.[9]

Product decisions

Marketers make product decisions at three levels: individual product decisions, product-line decisions and product-mix decisions. We discuss each in turn.

Individual product decisions

Here, we look at decisions relating to the development and marketing of individual products, namely *product attributes*, *branding*, *packaging*, *labelling* and *product-support services*.

Product attributes

Developing a product involves defining the benefits that the product will offer. These benefits are communicated and delivered by tangible product attributes, such as *quality, features, style* and *design*. Decisions about these attributes are particularly important as they greatly affect consumer reactions to a product. We will now discuss the issues involved in each decision.

Product quality

Product quality is one of the marketer's major positioning tools. Quality has a direct impact on product performance; hence, it is closely linked to customer value and satisfaction. In the narrowest sense, quality can be defined as 'freedom from defects'. But most customer-centred companies go beyond this narrow definition. Instead, they define quality in terms of customer satisfaction. For example, Siemens defines quality this way: 'Quality is when our customers come back and our products don't.'[10] This customer-focused definition suggests that quality begins with customer needs, goes beyond customer satisfaction and ends with customer retention.

> **❝** Quality has a direct impact on product performance. **❞**

We covered 'Total quality management' (TQM) and its importance to customer relationships in Chapter 8. TQM is an approach in which all the company's people are involved in constantly improving the quality of products, services and business processes. For most top companies, customer-driven quality has become a way of doing business. Today, most companies are taking a 'return on quality' approach, viewing quality as an investment and holding quality efforts accountable for bottom-line results.[11]

Product quality has two dimensions – level and consistency. In developing a product, the marketer must first choose a quality level that will support the product's positioning in the target market. Here, product quality means performance quality – the ability of a product to perform its functions. It includes the product's overall durability, reliability, precision, ease of operation and repair and other valued attributes. Some of these attributes can be measured objectively, but, from a marketing viewpoint, quality should be measured in terms of buyers' perceptions.

Beyond quality level, high quality can also mean high levels of quality *consistency*. Here, product quality means *conformance quality* – freedom from defects and *consistency* in delivering a targeted level of performance. All companies should strive for high levels of conformance quality.

Product features

A product can be offered with varying features. A 'stripped-down' model, one without any extras, is the starting point. The company can create more features by adding higher-level models. Features are a competitive tool for differentiating the company's product from competitors' products. Being the first producer to introduce a valued new feature is one of the most effective ways to compete.

How can a company identify new features and decide which ones to add to its product? The company should periodically survey buyers who have used the product and ask these questions: How do you like the product? Which specific features of the product do you like most? Which features could we add to improve the product? How much would you pay for each feature? The answers provide the company with a rich list of feature ideas. The company can then assess each feature's *value* to customers versus its *cost* to the company. Features that customers value highly in relation to costs should be added, while those that add little value in relation to costs should be dropped.

Product style and design

Another way to add customer value is through distinctive *product style and design*. Some companies have reputations for outstanding style and design, such as Bang & Olufsen in consumer electronics and Braun in shavers and small household appliances. Some companies have integrated style and design with their corporate culture. They recognise that design is one of the most powerful competitive weapons in a company's marketing arsenal.

Consider IKEA, the Swedish home furnishing chain. Its corporate culture is 'småländsk' – thrift is a virtue, no extravagance is allowed. This identity is reflected in IKEA's thrifty (but stylish) designs and the dominance of traditional Scandinavian materials of light wood, linen and cotton textiles. Another company, the carmaker Saab, promotes a design philosophy of simplicity and purity. 'There are few excesses; they follow the principle of "form follows function", a design philosophy embraced by 20th-century architects and industrial designers which states that the shape of a building or object should be predicated on its intended purpose. We also believe in fidelity to materials – when it's plastic, we don't try to make it look like wood,' says a Saab spokesperson.[12]

Many companies, however, lack a 'design touch'. Their product designs function poorly or are dull or common looking. Some companies like Fiat Auto have learnt that design and style matters.

The Italian car company's European market share had collapsed from 10 per cent in 1990 to 6 per cent in 2003. Part of the problem is that they have alienated drivers by succeeding in making some rather ugly-looking cars: *Car* magazine has described Fiat's Multipla people-carrier as having 'bozz-eyed swamp-hog looks' and that its Dobio MPV is a 'Toytown-styled utilo-box' that is 'very big if you're desperate for space. But you'd have to be.' To reverse the falling European sales, Fiat's design director, Humberto Rodriguez, first set out to 'abolish all the strange things' they have done to these vehicles and to spearhead a new design direction for the automotive group – sleeker, family-feeling cars that may not necessarily be head-turners, like the Multipla is; but they will not leave the driver cringing with embarrassment. Leading by design, there are accolades for the company's new cars and the recovery of the company's climb back from an aesthetic and financial brink.[13]

Design is a broader concept than style. *Style* simply describes the appearance of a product. A sensational style may grab attention and produce pleasing aesthetics, but it does not necessarily make the product *perform* better. In some cases, it might even result in worse performance. For example, a chair may look great yet be extremely uncomfortable. Unlike style, *design* is more than skin deep – it goes to the very heart of a product. Good design contributes to a product's usefulness as well as to its looks.

Omega has capitalised on successful design: the iconic Speedmaster, created in 1957 and selected by NASA to be worn in space, is still going strong today.
SOURCE: Omega/SA/Photo copyright NASA.

Good design begins with a deep understanding of customer needs. More than simply creating product or service attributes, it involves shaping the customer's product-use experience. Consider the design process behind Procter & Gamble's Swiffer CarpetFlick.

P&G's innovative Swiffer home-cleaning gadget was really cleaning up. However, it only worked on hardwood, tile and linoleum floors, and some 75 per cent of floors are carpeted. P&G needed to find a way to 'Swiffer' a carpet. Award-winning and international design firm IDEO set out to help P&G design a solution. But IDEO didn't start in its labs with R&D-like scientific research. Instead, IDEO designers went into people's homes, taking photographs and asking questions about how they cleaned their carpets. There was a young mother who complained that the noise of the vacuum scared her child, but she had time to vacuum only when he was asleep. There was an older woman with a damaged knee who relied on two vacuums – a heavy one for once-a-week cleaning when she took painkillers for her knee, and one she could easily lift for spot cleaning. Most consumers found vacuum cleaners bulky, noisy and hard to use; carpet sweepers were more convenient but not very effective.

With this deep understanding of customer needs, IDEO's design team immersed itself in an intensive, ten-month development effort, attacking countless messy carpet squares – sucking, scraping, stamping, sticking and trying anything else they could come up with to clean carpet. The result was a revolutionary new carpet sweeping system, the Swiffer CarpetFlick, which flicks dirt, crumbs and other small bits off the carpet and traps them onto a disposable adhesive cartridge. The CarpetFlick design certainly looks good – it is sleek, stylish and very 'Swifferesque'. But it works even better than it looks. It is quiet, convenient and effective – just the thing for 'quick carpet clean-ups between vacuuming'.[14]

Thus, product designers should think less about product attributes and technical specifications and more about how customers will use and benefit from the product. IDEO has used this same customer-experience approach to develop award-winning designs for everything from high-tech consumer electronics products and more user-friendly software to more satisfying and functional hotel room, retail store and health clinic layouts.[15]

Just as good design can improve customer value, cut costs and create strong competitive advantage, poor design can result in lost sales and embarrassment.

When you're a bike-lock maker whose slogan is 'Tough World, Tough Locks', it doesn't get much tougher than finding out that most of the locks you've been making for the past 30 years can be picked with a Bic pen. That, sadly, is what happened to Ingersoll-Rand subsidiary Kryptonite, after bloggers began posting videos showing just how easy it was to pop open the company's ubiquitous U-shaped locks. Kryptonite reacted quickly, agreeing to exchange old locks for new Bic-proof ones. But the damage was already done. The news spread quickly through cycling chatrooms and blogs, and within weeks the company was sued for alleged product defects. The design mistake damaged Kryptonite's pocketbook as well as its reputation. Exchanging the locks cost the company an estimated $10m. In the meantime, many dealers receive no shipments of new locks, costing Kryptonite as much as an additional $6m in sales.[16]

"" Poor design can result in lost sales and embarrassment. **""**

Branding

Perhaps the most distinctive skill of professional marketers is their ability to build and manage brands. A **brand** is a name, term, sign, symbol, design or a combination of these, that identifies the maker or seller of the product or service. Consumers view a brand as an important part of a product, and branding can add value to a product. For example, consumers would perceive a bottle of Chanel perfume as a high-quality, expensive product. But the same perfume in an unmarked bottle would probably be viewed as lower in quality, even if the fragrance were identical. A brand can provide a guarantee of reliability and quality. For example, a book buyer might not entrust her credit card details with an unknown online book store, but would have little hesitation doing so when buying from Amazon.com as experience had taught her to trust the Amazon brand.

Branding has become so strong that today hardly anything goes unbranded. Salt is packaged in branded containers, common nuts and bolts are packaged with a distributor's label and automotive parts – spark plugs, tyres, filters – bear brand names that differ from those of the carmakers. Even fruits, vegetables, dairy products and poultry are branded – Sunkist oranges, Del Monte pineapples, Horizon Organic or Flora Pro-activ milk, Ocean Spray cranberry juice.

Branding helps buyers in many ways. Brand names help consumers identify products that might benefit them. Brands also say something about product quality and consistency – buyers who always buy the same brand know that they will get the same features, benefits and quality each time they buy. Brand names also increase the shopper's efficiency – imagine going into a supermarket and finding thousands of generic products.

Branding also gives the seller several advantages. The brand name becomes the basis on which a whole story can be built about a product's special qualities. For example:

Brand—A name, term, sign, symbol or design, or a combination of these that identifies the goods or services of one seller or group of sellers and differentiates them from those of competitors.

Ocean Spray is an agricultural cooperative of cranberry growers who wanted to expand the market for their crop. Cranberries have some very interesting properties that are all used in the product's manufacture: they float, they bounce if they are not ruptured, and a range of flavours and colours that can be injected into them. But the great success of the cranberry growers and the researchers that they employ is promoting the health benefit of the food, to such an extent that doctors often recommend the juice to their patients. As Ocean Spray explain: 'We all know cranberries are good for us. They are fruit, after all. And we all know fruits and veggies are good for you. In fact, it's been shown that a diet rich in fruits and vegetables may reduce the risk of some types of cancers and other chronic diseases. But cranberries aren't your average fruit. They help cleanse and purify the body. But do you know how? They contain powerful nutrients called proanthocyanidins, thankfully referred to as PACs, which research suggests help keep certain bacteria from sticking inside the body. And the PACS in cranberries are different from other fruits, which gives them more "anti-stick" potential. They also have something called antioxidants, like flavonoids and vitamin C, which helps to strengthen the immune system. In fact, cranberries have more naturally-occurring antioxidants per gram than most other common fruit.' Hardly any part of the body does not benefit by this amazing fruit and the benefits keep rolling in. Research from the University of Oulu, Finland, found that regular consumption of a cranberry juice beverage reduced the recurrence of UTIs [urinary tract infections] by about half, in women studied.[17]

SOURCE: *British Medical Journal*, June 2001, pp. 71–75. Reproduced with permission from the BMJ Publishing Group.

The seller's brand name and trademark provide legal protection for unique product features that otherwise might be copied by competitors. Branding also increases innovation by giving producers an incentive to look for new features that can be protected against imitating competitors. Thus, branding results in more product variety and choice for consumers. Also, branding helps the seller to segment markets. For example, Cadbury offers Dairy Milk, Roses and other brands, not just one general confectionery product for all consumers. General Mills can offer Cheerios, Wheaties, Chex, Total, Kix, Golden Grahams, Trix and many other cereal brands, not just one general breakfast product for all consumers.

Building and managing brands are, perhaps, the marketer's most important tasks. We will discuss branding strategy in more detail later in the chapter. Real Marketing 11.1 looks at the tricky business of inventing brand names.

Packaging

Packaging—The activities of designing and producing the container or wrapper for a product.

Packaging involves designing and producing the container or wrapper for a product. Traditionally, the primary function of the package was to hold and protect the product. In recent times, however, numerous factors have made packaging an important marketing tool. Increased competition and clutter on retail store shelves means that packages must now perform many sales tasks – from attracting attention, to describing the product, to making the sale.

Companies are realising the power of good packaging to create instant consumer recognition of the company or brand. For example, in an average supermarket, which stocks 15,000 to 17,000 items, the typical shopper passes by some 300 items per minute, and more than 60 per cent of all purchases are made on impulse. In this highly competitive environment, the package may be the seller's last chance to influence buyers. Not long ago, the package was merely the product's receptacle, and the brand message was elsewhere – usually on TV. But changes in the marketplace environment are now making the package itself an increasingly important selling medium.[18]

Poorly designed packages can cause headaches for consumers and lost sales for the company. By contrast, innovative packaging can give a company an advantage over competitors and boost sales. Sometimes even seemingly small packaging improvements can make a big difference. For example, Heinz revolutionised the 170-year-old condiments industry by inverting the good old ketchup bottle, letting customers quickly squeeze out even the last bit of ketchup. In the year following the new bottle's debut, Heinz ketchup sales grew at three times the industry rate. It started a packaging trend that quickly spread to other categories. Similarly, Nabisco learned that many customers for Chips Ahoy chocolate chip were frustrated by those hard-to-use, end-opening bags. They often transferred the biscuits into jars for easier access and to keep them fresh. Nabisco solved both problems by creating a resealable bag that opens from the top. In the following year, the new packaging achieved sales nearly double those of the old packaging. 'Companies make a lot of money by making things less annoying,' says a packaging expert.[19]

> " Poorly designed packages can cause headaches for consumers and lost sales for the company. "

In recent years, product safety has also become a major packaging concern. We have all learnt to deal with hard-to-open 'childproof' packaging. Following the rash of product tampering scares during the 1980s, most drug producers and food makers now put their products in tamper-resistant packages. In making packaging decisions, the company also must heed growing environmental concerns. More and more companies have gone 'green' by reducing their packaging and using environmentally responsible packaging materials.

real marketing 11.1

Naming brands: part science, part art, and more than a little instinct

Every company wants a name that's 'sticky' – one that stands out from the crowd, a catchy handle that will remain fresh and memorable over time. But such names are hard to find, especially because naming trends change. Some of the greatest brand names were not invented at all. Cadbury, Nestlé, Disney, Mercedes, J P Morgan, Kellogg's and Honda are all named after founders or members of their family. Other great names are uninspiring initials of words that describe a company from what it was or from part of its origin, such as BP, IBM, GE, SAP, UBS, HSBC and BMW. No longer do companies allow the decisions to be so arbitrary. Whereas the 1990s were all about idiosyncratic names (Yahoo!, Google, Fish, O_2) or trademark proof (Novartis, Aventis, Lycos, Diageo), tastes in the new millennium have changed.

Today's style is to build corporate identity around words that describe the spirit of what they actually are. The new names are all about purity, clarity and organicism. For example, names like Silk (soy milk), Carphone Warehouse (mobile phones), Blackboard (educational software), e-bookers (electronic booking agency) and Full Throttle (energy drink) are simple and make innate sense. 'There's a trend toward meaning in words. When it comes down to evocative words versus straightforward names, straightforward will win in testing every time,' says an executive from a New York branding firm.

Embracing real words over fake ones hardly comes as a surprise, of course. But why has it taken so long for this idea to catch on? In part, the wave of meaningless names during the 1990s can be traced to a spike in trademark applications that resulted from the surge in dot-com start-ups. In 1985, 64,677 applications were filed. Ten years later that number was up by 300 per cent, before peaking at 375,428 in 2000. As the pool of registered trademarks has grown, so has the challenge of finding an available name. In that context, choosing a whimsical or made-up name was a simple way to sidestep the crowd. There was also some method to this madness: a company with a new and different word can supply whatever associations it chooses and expand into any business it wants.

But the problem with all these meaningless names became clear as the number of companies using them grew. As more and more Accentures and Covisints appeared the landscape, it became harder for consumers to keep track of the differences between them. Change came after the economic boom went bust and the number of trademark applications declined. Coming up with unique names is still difficult, but the pressure to come up with something that a company can call its own has subsided.

▶

...11.1

Hence, the return to grace of real, natural-sounding names. Of course, there's really nothing all that novel about using natural-sounding brand names. Apple Computer did it more than 25 years ago, as did Kwik-Fit, a car service company that also betrays that period's love of ugly spellings. So where did low-cost airline's name JetBlue come from?

Traditionally, airlines have names that either refer to the carrier's geographic roots (Air France, British Airways, Southwest) or evoke the idea of global reach (United, or the now defunct Pan American and Trans World Airlines). But as a new airline with plans to offer budget travellers a trendy and unique way to fly, JetBlue decided to take a different approach. 'We didn't want to jump on the made-up word bandwagon,' recalls JetBlue's VP for corporate communications. 'We wanted to use a real word, but we didn't want it to sound like an airline.'

Working first with its ad agency and then with branding consultancy Landor Associates, the airline came up with early ideas such as Fresh Air, Taxi, Egg and It. But the name Blue – with its simple evocation of clear skies and tranquility – emerged a winner. After trademark lawyers pointed out that it would be impossible to protect the name Blue on its own, TrueBlue emerged. But that name was already held by a car-rental agency. Eventually, JetBlue was born. The name worked, and when JetBlue launched in 2000, so did the branding model. The new airline's success spawned a naming trend among other discount carriers, including United's Ted, Delta's Song, BMI's Baby or even Australia's Virgin Blue or executive jet flying Blue Airline.

Ted, Song and Baby? What do those words have to do with the airline industry? 'It's effective to use ordinary words out of context,' says consultant Laura Ries, co-author of *The 22 Immutable Laws of Branding*. It also works to use names 'that are suggestive of the category. These are names like Blockbuster, Amazon, Palm and easyJet. Assuming the words are simple, your brand name will be easy to say, spell and remember.' Likewise, firms are also realising that some organic names are fun to say – and that makes them easier to spread by word of mouth. In an age where everything can be found by Googling them, simple names double-up duty as easy-to-remember keywords.

That's what happened to Aliph, a start-up that recently launched its first product – a device built from military-grade technology that allows people talking on mobile phones to be heard over background noise. No one can remember Aliph, but the product's name, Jawbone, refers to both the idiomatic expression for talking and the fact that the device works by monitoring jawbone and cheek vibrations. 'We knew we would have to be different in every way – from the design of the device to our name,' says Aliph's head of product development. The name turned out to be a handy way for customers to find the product. Aliph was able to buy the jawbone.com domain, and

...11.1

now when people type 'jawbone' into Google, the company's site comes up first in the results. Indeed, the search engine might be the best indicator of how sticky a name really is.

So, it's clear that finding just the right brand name is hard work. There's certainly some science to it, and some basic rules that need to be heeded. But there's also a big dose of art, and more than a little instinct. Try it yourself. Pick a product and see if you can come up with a better name for it. How about Moonshot? Tickle? Vanilla? Treehugger? Simplicity? Sorry. Google them and you'll find that they're already taken.

SOURCES: From Alex Frankel, 'The new science of naming', *Business 2.0* (December 2004), pp. 53–5; and Bill Bryson, *Made in America* (Black Swan, 1998).

For example, Tetra Pak, a Swedish multinational, is noted for its innovative packaging that takes environmental concerns into account. Tetra Pak invented an 'aseptic' package that enables milk, fruit juice and other perishable liquid foods to be distributed without refrigeration. Not only is this packaging more environmentally responsible, it also provides economic and distribution advantages. Aseptic packaging allows dairies to distribute milk over a wider area without investing in refrigerated trucks and facilities. Supermarkets can carry Tetra Pak packaged products on ordinary shelves, allowing them to save expensive refrigerator space. Tetra Pak's motto is 'the package should save more than it cost'. Tetra Pak advertises the benefits of its packaging to consumers directly and even initiates recycling programmes to save the environment.

Labelling

Labels perform several functions and may range from simple tags attached to products to complex graphics that are part of the package. At the very least, the label *identifies* the product or brand, such as the name 'Sunkist' stamped on oranges. The label might also *grade* the product, or *describe* several things about the product – who made it, where it was made, when it was made, its contents, how it is to be used and how to use it safely. Finally, the label might *promote* the product and support its positioning.

For example, in the never-ending search for ways to stand out, the clothing industry seems to be rediscovering the promotional value of the product label.

" The clothing industry seems to be rediscovering the promotional value of the product label. "

Some clothing labels send strong messages. A 'booklet tag' hanging from a workout garment might reinforce the brand's positioning, describing in detail how the garment is used by certain high-profile athletes or what types of special materials are used in its construction. Other, brasher statements include pocket flashers and 'lenticular tags', which generate 3-D or animation effects. At the other extreme, tagless heat-transfer labels are replacing sewn-in woven labels, promising ultimate comfort. Even low-key labels are using more brilliant colours or elaborate graphics, beautifying the product and reinforcing the brand message. Rich treatments on labels add pizzazz to luxury items; futuristic tags support emerging technical, man-made fabrications; tags adorned with playful characters evoke a sense of fun for kids' garments. 'The product label is a key cog in branding strategy,' says a labelling expert. 'The look, feel, or even smell of the label – if done creatively – can complement a brand.'[20]

Along with the positives, there has been a long history of legal concerns about packaging and labels. Labels can mislead customers, fail to describe important ingredients or fail to include needed safety warnings. As a result, many countries have introduced laws to regulate labelling. Across Europe there is a great tangle of laws that the European Commission is trying to clear through the EU Directive on Packaging and Packaging Waste (94/62/EC, 2004/12/EC, Packaging Standards CEN TC261). Their aim of achieving a single market for packaged products in the European Union and for the free movement of goods in a global marketplace is frequently threatened by packaging regulations which restrict or prevent market access.[21]

Labelling has also been affected in recent times by *unit pricing* (stating the price per unit of standard measure), *open dating* (stating the expected shelf life of the product) and *nutritional labelling* (stating the nutritional values in the product). In the case of the latter, sellers are required to provide detailed nutritional information on food products. In some countries, the use of health-related terms such as *low-fat*, *light* and *high-fibre* is also regulated. As such, sellers must ensure that their labels contain all the required information and comply with national or international (e.g. US, EU) requirements.

Product-support services

Customer service is another element of product strategy. A company's offer usually includes some support services, which can be a minor or a major part of the total offer. In Chapter 13, we will discuss services as products in themselves. Here, we address **product-support services** – services that augment actual products. More and more companies are using product-support services to gain competitive advantage.

Product-support services—Services that augment actual products.

Good customer service makes sound business sense. It costs less to keep the goodwill of existing customers than it does to attract new customers or woo back lost customers. A study comparing the performance of businesses that had high and low customer ratings of service quality found that the high-service businesses managed to charge more, grow faster and make more profits.[22] Clearly, marketers need to develop effective service strategies.

Determining customers' service needs involves more than simply monitoring complaints that come in over free-phone lines or on comment cards. A company should design its product and support services to meet the needs of target customers. However, customers vary in the value they assign to different services. Some consumers want credit and financing services, fast and reliable delivery or quick installation. Others put more weight on technical information and advice, training in product use, or after-sale service and repair. The first step is to survey customers periodically to assess the value of current services and to obtain ideas for new ones.

Once the company has assessed the value of various support services to customers, it must next assess the costs of providing these services. It can then develop a package of services that will both delight customers and yield profits to the company. Customer service consultant Colin Shaw shows the insights that can be gained from secret shopping:

First to Hamleys world-famous toy shop on London's Regent Street. 'As we walked around the bears section of the toy store, Mr Shaw discussed the ways in which the company was exemplary. It understood, for instance, that emotional engagement was key to good customer service, going to great lengths to entertain customers with free demonstrations and employing engaging assistants, some of whom were out-of-work actors. Hamleys also understood, he said, how stimulation of the five senses could enhance the customer experience: everywhere you go in the store there are things to see, hear, touch, smell and taste. "A natural company if ever there was one."'

Then, a few steps on, the Regent Street branch of HSBC bank. 'Were it a person it would have slashed its wrists. The windows were filthy; the floor was littered with rubbish; the reception desk was unmanned; and when a member of staff did eventually arrive she seemed more interested in gossiping to a friend than dealing with us, potential customers. "Typical of a transactional organisation," remarked Mr Shaw.'[23]

Many companies are now using a sophisticated mix of phone, e-mail, fax, Internet and interactive voice and data technologies to provide support services that were not possible before. Consider the following examples.

Some online merchants are watching where you surf, then opening a chat window on your screen to ask – just as they would in the store – if you have questions about the goods they see you eyeing. For example, at the BT site, clicking on the Ask Emma button puts you in with a virtual assistant who can answer your questions about the service. Wander into the section for business clients and a pop-up chat box appears for a real online questions-and-answers session with a real assistant. Such pop-up chat features have increased online questions by 65 per cent. The BT broadband service help desk takes proactive chat one step further with co-browsing. This feature essentially lets chat agents take control of a customer's computer screen, opening Web pages directly on their browser to help solve their problem. In the future, 'call cams' will even let customers see an agent on their screen and talk directly through voice-over-Web capabilities.[24]

Product line decisions

Beyond decisions about individual products, product strategy also calls for building a product line. A **product line** is a group of products that are closely related because they function in a similar manner, are sold to the same customer groups, are marketed through the same types of outlet, or fall within given price ranges. For example, Nokia produces several lines of telecommunications products, Philips produces several lines of audio entertainment systems and adidas produces several lines of athletic shoes and clothings. We will examine the major product line decisions next.

Product line—A group of products that are closely related because they function in a similar manner, are sold to the same customer groups, are marketed through the same types of outlet, or fall within given price ranges.

Product line length decisions

The major product line decision involves *product line length* – the number of items in the product line. The line is too short if the manager can increase profits by adding items; the line is too long if the manager can increase profits by dropping items. Managers need to conduct a periodic *product line analysis* to assess each product item's sales and profits and to understand how each item contributes to the line's performance.

Product line length is influenced by company objectives and resources. Companies that want to be positioned as full-line companies, or to increase market share, usually carry longer lines. Companies seeking high short-term profitability generally carry shorter lines consisting of selected items. Another objective may be to allow upselling. For example, BMW seeks to move customers from its entry level 3-series models to 5- and 7-series models. Another objective might be to allow cross-selling: Hewlett-Packard sells printers as well as cartridges. Still another objective might be to travel with their customers through their life, hence Versace retail outlets range from Versace Collection and Versace Jeans Couture diffusion lines to exclusive Gianni Versace Couture.

Over time, product line managers tend to add new products. As the manager adds items, several costs rise: design and engineering costs, inventory carrying costs, manufacturing changeover costs, order-processing costs, transportation costs and promotional costs to introduce new items. Thus, the company must plan product line growth carefully. It can systematically lengthen its product line in two ways: by *line stretching* or by *line filling*. **Product line stretching** occurs when a company lengthens its product line beyond its current range. The company can stretch its line downward, upward, or both ways (see Figure 11.3).

Product line stretching— Increasing the product line by lengthening it beyond its current range.

Downward stretch

Companies located at the upper end of the market can stretch their lines downwards. A company may stretch downwards to plug a market hole that otherwise would attract a new competitor or to respond to a competitor's attack on the upper end. Or it may add low-end products because it finds faster growth taking place in the low-end segments. Mercedes stretched downwards for all these reasons. Facing a slow-growth luxury car market and attacks by Japanese car makers on its high-end positioning, Mercedes successfully introduced its C-class cars, then the A-class and finally the Smart car, though that shows signs of being one stretch too far.[25]

Upward stretch

Companies at the lower end of the market may want to stretch their product lines *upwards*. Sometimes, companies stretch upwards in order to add prestige to their current products. They may be attracted by a faster growth rate or higher margins at the higher end, or they may simply want to position themselves as full-line manufacturers. For example, Toyota launched an up-market line – Lexus – and used an entirely new name rather than its own name. Other companies have included their own names in moving up-market. In an almost parallel move to Toyota, VW acquired Bentley to top their Skoda, Seat and Audi ranges. In another sector, Gallo introduced Ernest and Julio Gallo Varietals and priced these wines at more than twice the price of its regular wines.[26]

Stretching upwards can be risky. The higher-end competitors not only are well entrenched, but also may strike back by entering the lower end of the market. Prospective customers may not believe that the newcomer can produce quality products. Finally, the company's salespeople and distributors may lack the expertise to serve the higher end of the market.

Stretching upwards can be risky.

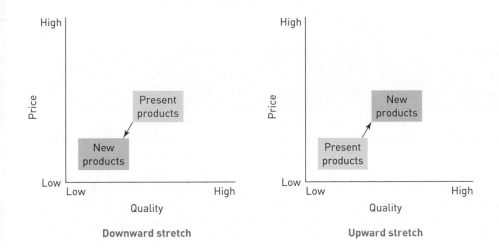

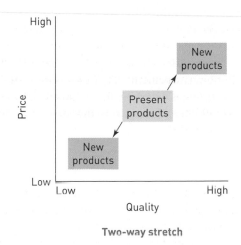

Figure 11.3 Product-line stretching decisions

Two-way stretch

Companies in the middle range of the market may decide to stretch their lines in both directions, as did Sony and Marriott:

Sony did this to hold off copycat competitors of its Walkman line of personal tape players. Sony introduced its first Walkman in the middle of the market. As imitative competitors moved in with lower-priced models, Sony stretched downwards. At the same time, in order to add lustre to its lower-priced models and to attract more affluent consumers keen to trade up to a better model, Sony stretched the Walkman line upwards. It sells more than 100 models, ranging from a plain playback-only version for €30 to a high-tech, high-quality €550 version that both plays and records. Using this two-way stretch strategy, Sony came to dominate the global personal tape player market.

Marriott did this with its hotel product line. Along with regular Marriott hotels, it added new branded hotel lines to serve both the upper and lower ends of the market. Renaissance Hotels & Resorts aims to attract and please top executives; Marriott is aimed at upper and middle managers; Courtyard by Marriott caters for salespeople and other 'road warriors'. ExecuStay provides temporary housing for those relocating or away on long-term assignments of 30 days or longer. Residence Inn provides a relaxed, residential atmosphere – a home away from home for people who travel for a living – while Fairfield Inn provides their cheapest, most basic hotels with limited facilities.[27]

The major risk with this strategy is that some travellers will trade down after finding that the lower-price hotels in the Marriott chain give them pretty much everything they want. However, Marriott would rather capture its customers who move downward than lose them to competitors.

Product line-filling decisions

Product line filling— Increasing the product line by adding more items within the present range of the line.

An alternative to product line stretching is **product line filling** – adding more items within the present range of the line. There are several reasons for product line filling: reaching for extra profits, satisfying dealers, using excess capacity, being the leading full-line company and plugging holes to keep out competitors. Thus Cadbury's Dairy Milk line includes Fruit & Nut, Whole Nut, Mint Chips, Caramel, Bubbly, Crunchie Bits, Crispies, Short Cake Biscuit, Turkish Delight and Milk Flake. However, line filling is overdone if it results in cannibalisation and customer confusion. The company should, therefore, ensure that new items are *noticeably different* from existing ones.

Product-mix decisions

Product mix (product portfolio, product assortment)— The set of all product lines and items that a particular seller offers for sale to buyers.

A company with several product lines has a product mix. A **product mix** (or **product portfolio** or **product assortment**) consists of all the product lines and items that a particular seller offers for sale. Colgate's product mix consists of four major product lines: oral care, personal care, home care and pet nutrition. Each product line consists of several sub-lines. For example, the home care line consists of dishwashing, fabric conditioning and household cleaning products. Each line and sub-line has many individual items. Altogether, Colgate's product mix includes hundreds of items.

> A company's product mix has four important dimensions: width, length, depth and consistency.

A company's product mix has four important dimensions: width, length, depth and consistency. Product mix *width* refers to the number of different product lines the company carries. For example, Unilever markets a fairly wide product mix consisting of many product lines, including paper, food, household cleaning, cosmetics and personal care products. By contrast, Colgate markets a fairly contained product mix, consisting of personal and home care products. Other companies, such as 3M, market more than 60,000 products. A typical large supermarket may stock as many as 100,000 to 120,000 items.

Product mix *length* refers to the total number of items the company carries within its product lines. Nestlé Waters is by far the world's leading mineral water company by revenues. Its best-known brands are the two mineral waters which made up the Nestlé Waters old name of Perrier Vittel. The company also has a portfolio of 70 other brands including Pellegrino, Buxton, Poland Spring, Pure Life and Aquarel.

Product mix *depth* refers to the number of versions offered of each product in the line. For example, Unilever offers different sizes and formulations (liquid, powder, tablet) of laundry detergent. Colgate toothpastes come in 11 varieties, ranging from Colgate Total, Colgate Tartar Control, Colgate 2in1 and Colgate Cavity Protection to Colgate Sensitive, Colgate Fresh Confidence, Colgate Max Fresh, Colgate Simply White, Colgate Sparkling White, Colgate Kids Toothpastes and Colgate Baking Soda & Peroxide. Then, each variety comes in its own special forms and formulations. For example, you can buy Colgate Total in regular, mint fresh stripe, whitening paste and gel, advanced fresh gel, or 2in1 liquid gel versions.[28]

Finally, the *consistency* of the product mix refers to how closely related the various product lines are in end use, production requirements, distribution channels or some other way. Unilever's packaged goods lines are consistent insofar as they are consumer products that go through the same distribution channels. The lines are less consistent insofar as they perform different functions for buyers.

These product-mix dimensions provide the handles for defining the company's product strategy. The company can increase its business in four ways:

1. It can add new product lines, widening its product mix. In this way, its new lines build on the company's reputation in its other lines.

2. The company can lengthen its existing product lines to become a more full-line company.

3. It can add more product versions of each product and thus deepen its product mix.

4. The company can pursue more product line consistency, or less, depending on whether it wants to have a strong reputation in a single field or in several fields.

Branding strategy: building strong brands

Brands are viewed as *the* major enduring asset of a company, outlasting the company's specific products and facilities. John Stewart, co-founder of Quaker Oats, once said, 'If this business were split up, I would give you the land and bricks and mortar, and I would keep the brands and trademarks, and I would fare better than you.' A former CEO of McDonald's agrees. Consider a situation where every asset the company owns, every building and every piece of equipment were destroyed in a terrible natural disaster. McDonald's CEO argues that he would be able to borrow all the money to replace these assets very quickly because of the value of the brand. The brand is more valuable than the totality of all these assets![29]

Thus, brands are powerful assets that must be carefully developed and managed. In this section, we examine the key strategies for building and managing brands.

> **"** Brands are viewed as *the* major enduring asset of a company, outlasting the company's specific products and facilities. **"**

Brand equity

Brands are more than just names and symbols. They are a key element in the company's relationships with consumers. Brands represent consumers' perceptions and feelings about a product and its performance – everything that the product or service *means* to consumers. In the final analysis, brands exist in the minds of consumers.

The real value of a strong brand is its power to capture consumer preference and loyalty. Brands vary in the amount of power and value they have in the marketplace. Some brands are largely unknown to most buyers. Other brands have a high degree of consumer *brand awareness*. Still others – such as Ferrari, Mini, The Ritz, Chanel, BBC and others – become larger-than-life icons that maintain their power in the market for years, even generations. These brands enjoy *brand preference* – buyers select them over the others – and they command a high degree of *brand loyalty*. These brands win in the marketplace not simply because they deliver unique benefits or reliable service. Rather, they succeed because they forge deep connections with customers.

Consumers sometimes bond *very* closely with specific brands. Consider the feelings of one couple about the DeWalt power tool brand:[30]

> Rick and Rose Whitaker weren't comfortable with the idea of a formal wedding with white gown and morning dress. They kept coming back to the fact that Rick, a carpenter, had a passion for power tools. Specifically, DeWalt power tools. So at the July nuptials, Rose, Rick and 50-plus guests gathered in Rick's garden wearing DeWalt's trademark yellow-and-black T-shirts. From there, they made their way to a wooden chapel that they had built with their DeWalt tools. There they exchanged power tools and cut the cake with a power saw.

Brand equity—The positive differential effect that knowing the brand name has on customer response to the product or service.

A powerful brand has high **brand equity**. Brand equity is the positive differential effect that knowing the brand name has on customer response to the product or service. Brands have higher brand equity when they have higher brand loyalty, name awareness, perceived quality, strong brand associations and other assets such as patents, trademarks and channel relationships.[31] One measure of a brand's equity is the extent to which customers are willing to pay more for the brand. One study found that 72 per cent of customers would pay a 20 per cent premium for their brand of choice relative to the closest competing brand; 40 per cent said they would pay a 50 per cent premium. Customers for some brands like Heinz are willing to pay a 100 pcr cent premium.[32]

A brand with strong brand equity is a valuable asset. Companies try to put a value on their brands. *Brand valuation* is the process of estimating the total financial value of a brand. Measuring the actual equity of a brand name is difficult. However, Interbrand's 2007 study of the world's leading brands puts Coca-Cola at the top with a value of $65bn, with the leading European brands in the top 20 being fifth-placed Nokia at $34bn, Mercedes (10th) at $24bn, BMW (13th) at $22bn and Louis Vuitton (17th) at $20bn.[33]

Because it is so hard to measure, companies usually do not list brand equity on their balance sheets. Although it is difficult to incorporate brand values in balance sheets, accounting standards compel firms to put a value on their acquired brands on their balance sheets. Accounting for brands may pose a challenge to marketers in the new millennium, but given the recent mergers and acquisition trends in Europe, assessing how much brands are worth helps management to see the link between the money spent on acquiring a brand and the value created.

Brand accounting makes sense as it gets managers to consider how they might manage the acquired brand as an asset that the company has paid for, often handsomely. For example, Mannesmann paid nearly £20bn (€30bn) for the mobile phone brand Orange only to be snatched up themselves by Vodafone for €140bn. Volkswagen snapped up Rolls-Royce Motor Cars Ltd for £479m, although their acquisition included the Bentley brand but not Rolls-Royce. BMW snapped up the Rolls-Royce car brand for £80m. Unilever paid $20.3bn (€14.9bn) for Bestfoods, the maker of Knorr soups and Hellmann's mayonnaise.

High brand equity provides a company with many competitive advantages. A powerful brand enjoys a high level of consumer brand awareness and loyalty, and the company will incur lower marketing costs relative to revenues. Because consumers expect stores to carry the brand, the company has more leverage in bargaining with retailers. The brand name also carries high credibility, making it easier to launch line and brand extensions. For example, Unilever leveraged its well-known Persil brand to introduce dishwashing detergent. A powerful brand offers the company some defence against fierce price competition.

Above all, however, a powerful brand forms the basis for building strong and profitable customer relationships. Therefore, the fundamental asset underlying brand equity is *customer equity* – the value of the consumer relationships that the brand creates. A powerful brand is important, but what it really represents is a profitable set of loyal customers. The proper focus of marketing is building customer equity – extending *loyal customer lifetime value* – with brand management serving as a major marketing tool. Says one marketing expert, 'Companies need to be thought of as portfolios of customers and not portfolios of products.'[34]

> " The fundamental asset underlying brand equity is *customer equity*. "

Building strong brands

Branding poses challenging decisions to the marketer. Figure 11.4 shows the major brand strategy decisions involving brand positioning, brand name selection, brand sponsorship and brand development. We will examine each of these in turn.

Brand positioning

Marketers need to position their brands clearly in target customers' minds. They can position brands at several levels.[35]

1. *Attributes*. At the lowest level, a company can position the brand on product attributes. For example, Mercedes suggests such attributes as 'well engineered', 'well built', 'durable', 'high prestige', 'fast', 'expensive' and 'high resale value'. The company may use one or more of these attributes in its advertising for the car. For years, Mercedes advertised 'Engineered like no other car in the world'. This provided a positioning platform for other attributes of the car. The Body Shop markets their products' natural, environmentally friendly ingredients, unique scents and special textures. However, attributes are the least desirable level for brand positioning. Competitors can easily copy attributes. More important, customers are not interested in attributes as such; they are interested in what the attributes will do for them.

2. *Benefits*. A brand can be better positioned by associating its name with a desirable *benefit*. Therefore, attributes must be translated into functional and emotional benefits. Thus, The Body Shop can go beyond product ingredients and talk about the resulting beauty benefits, such as clearer skin from its Tea Tree Oil Facial Wash and sun-kissed cheeks from its Bronzing Powder. Some successful brands positioned on benefits are Volvo (safety), Lexus (quality) and Nike (performance). Even promoting the brand on one or more of its benefits can be risky. Suppose Mercedes touts its main benefit as 'high performance'. If several competing brands emerge with as high or higher performance, or if car buyers begin placing less importance on performance as compared to other benefits, Mercedes will need the freedom to move into a new benefit positioning.

3. *Beliefs and values*. The strongest brands go beyond attribute or benefit positioning. They are positioned on strong *beliefs and values*. These brands pack an emotional wallop. Thus, The Body Shop can talk not just about environmentally friendly ingredients and skin-care benefits, but about how purchasing these products empowers its socially conscious customer to 'make up your mind, not just your face'.[36] Successful brands engage customers on a deep, emotional

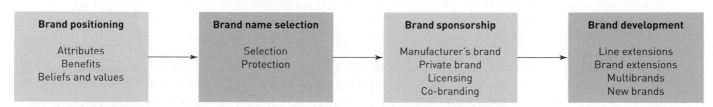

Brand positioning	Brand name selection	Brand sponsorship	Brand development
Attributes	Selection	Manufacturer's brand	Line extensions
Benefits	Protection	Private brand	Brand extensions
Beliefs and values		Licensing	Multibrands
		Co-branding	New brands

Figure 11.4 Major brand strategy decisions

Safety is a consistent feature of the Mercedes brand even though adhering to the drive for safety makes their cars more expensive than many others.

SOURCE: The Advertising Archives.

level. Brands such as Prada, Louis Vuitton, Moet & Chandon and Guinness rely less on a product's tangible attributes and more on creating surprise, passion and excitement surrounding a brand. A brand also says something about the buyers' values. Thus Mercedes buyers value high performance, safety and prestige. A brand marketer must identify the specific groups of car buyers whose values coincide with the delivered benefit package.

4. *Personality.* A brand also projects a personality. Motivation researchers sometimes ask, 'If this brand were a person, what kind of person would it be?' Consumers might visualise a Mercedes car as being a wealthy, middle-aged business executive. The brand will attract people whose actual or desired self-images match the brand's image.

All this suggests that a brand is a complex symbol. If a company treats a brand only as a name, it misses the point of branding. The challenge of branding is to develop a deep set of meanings or associations for the brand. When positioning a brand, the marketer should establish a mission for the brand and a vision of what the brand must be and do. Marketers must decide the level(s) at which they will position the brand. The most lasting and sustainable meanings of a brand are its core values and personality. They define the brand's essence. Thus Mercedes stands for 'high achievers and success'. The company must build its brand strategy around creating and protecting these values and personality. Although Mercedes has recently yielded to market pressures by introducing lower-priced models, this might prove risky. Marketing less expensive models might dilute the personality that Mercedes has built up over the decades.

In the final analysis, a brand is the company's promise to deliver a specific set of features, benefits, services and experiences consistently to the buyers. It can be thought of as a contract to the customer regarding how the product or service will deliver value and satisfaction. The brand promise must be simple and honest. easyHotel, for example, offers clean rooms and low prices but certainly not expensive furniture or large bathrooms. In contrast, Ritz-Carlton offers luxurious rooms and a truly memorable experience but does not promise low prices.

Brand name selection

A good name can add greatly to a product's success. However, finding the best brand name is a difficult task. It begins with a careful review of the product and its benefits, the target market and proposed marketing strategies. After that, naming a brand becomes part science, part art and a measure of instinct (see Real Marketing 11.1).

Desirable qualities for a brand name include the following:

1. It should suggest something about the product's benefits and qualities. Examples are Pro-activ (a cholesterol-lowering dairy product), Oasis (a refreshing fruit drink), Frisp (a light savoury snack) and TimeOut (a chocolate biscuit to go with coffee or tea breaks).

2. It should be easy to pronounce, recognise and remember. Short names help. Examples are Dove (soap), Yale (security products) and Hula Hoops (potato crisps shaped like the name). But longer ones are sometimes effective, such as 'I Can't Believe It's Not Butter' margarine or Andrew Lloyd Webber's 'Really Useful Company'.

3. The brand name should be distinctive. Examples are easyJet, Google and Virgin, or even diminutively named O_2, BP or GE.

4. It should be extendable: Amazon.com began as an online bookseller but chose a name that would allow expansion into other categories.

5. The name should translate easily (and meaningfully) into foreign languages. For example, in Chinese, Ferrari is pronounced as 'fa li li', the Chinese symbols for which mean 'magic, weapon, pull, power', which flatter the brand. But accountancy firm Price Waterhouse was reported to have been translated as 'expensive water closet'.

6. It should be capable of registration and legal protection. A brand name cannot be registered if it infringes on existing brand names. Also, brand names that are merely descriptive or suggestive may not be protectable. For example, Rolls-Royce in particular has problems with businesses that want to be the Rolls-Royce of everything from toilet paper to exclusive night clubs but it is usually able to protect its name. In contrast, and at the other end of the price spectrum, the easyGroup have difficulty in defending themselves against a host of companies calling themselves easy*anything*, and Miller failed to hold on to Lite, a name they tried to make their own.[37]

Once chosen, the brand name must be protected. Many firms try to build a brand name that will eventually become identified with the product category. Brand names such as Hoover, Kleenex, Levi's, Scotch Tape, Post-it Notes, Formica and Fiberglass have succeeded in this way. However, their

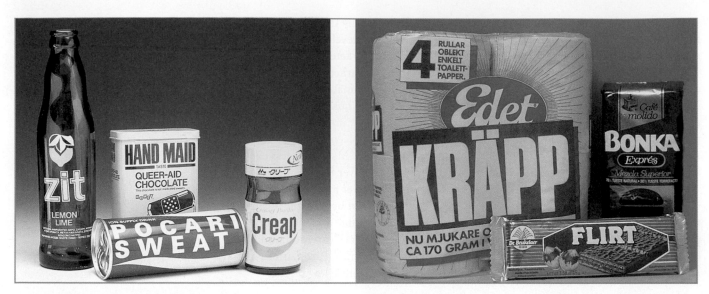

Finding a name for a product designed for worldwide markets is not easy. Companies must avoid the pitfalls inherent in injudicious product naming.

SOURCE: Interbrand.

very success may threaten the company's rights to the name. Many originally protected brand names, such as cellophane, aspirin, nylon, kerosene, linoleum, yo-yo, trampoline, escalator, thermos and shredded wheat, are now generic names that any seller can use. To protect their brands, marketers present them carefully using the registered trademark symbol, but brand protection is no easy task. For many marketers, it has posed an uphill climb. Consider the following.

> " Many originally protected brand names, such as cellophane, aspirin, nylon, kerosene, . . . , shredded wheat, are now generic names that any seller can use. "

Philips' razors, Wall's ice-cream, Pampers nappies, Wrigley's chewing-gum, Nestlé's confectionery, . . . the range of trademark cases passing before the European Court of Justice, the European Union's ultimate arbiter on trademark law, could hardly be more diverse.

Nestlé, the Swiss confectionery and food group, which makes KitKat, has trademarked the phrase 'Have a Break, Have a KitKat'. But it lost its battle to secure similar intellectual property rights over the simpler 'Have a Break' phrase. Its application to the Trade Mark Registry was turned down after objections by US-owned arch-rival Mars. The Registry said that the mark was 'devoid of any distinctive character' and therefore lacked 'inherent distinctiveness'. Nestlé, however, appealed to the High Court, pointing to consumer research suggesting that use of the mark 'Have a Break' elicited the response 'Have a KitKat' from a substantial number of snack-munchers – and also that a chocolate bar called 'Have a Break' would be supposed to come from the makers of KitKat. But Mr Justice Rimer had regarded the survey exercise as 'somewhat pointless', acknowledging that many of those questioned associated the phrase 'Have a Break' with KitKat or were reminded of the chocolate bar. He added: 'The survey demonstrated, and could demonstrate, no more than that a high proportion of the public will make the association. It did not, and could not, show that "Have a Break" had acquired a distinctiveness as a result of its use as a mark.'

In another case concerning Wrigley's Doublemint (chewing gum), a preliminary opinion narrowed the extent to which brand names with a descriptive element can be protected. Under the EU's Community Trade Mark Regulation, names made up solely of descriptions are barred from registration. Nevertheless, back in 2001 Procter & Gamble succeeded in registering the Pampers 'Baby Dry' brand. Baby Dry's success, according to Francis Jacobs, Advocate-General (A-G), was because of its 'extreme ellipsis, unusual structure, resistance to any intuitive grammatical analysis' and the fact that it was an 'invented term'. In the case of Doublemint, 'whose features are . . . very considerably less marked', while the word 'doublemint' might not appear in any dictionary, 'its creation is essentially limited to removing the space between two words which may well be used together descriptively.'

What about the trademarking of shapes? Compared to names or slogans, 'shapes' has been a thorny area for intellectual property law, partly because a shape is often marketed in association with a brand name. 'It's often difficult to prove sufficient distinctiveness for a secondary mark [such as the shape]', said Elaine Rowley, a lawyer at Marks & Clerk, a trademark specialist. A long legal tussle between Philips and Remington over electric shaver designs finally provided guidance in 2002 for 'functional shapes'. Essentially, a company cannot monopolise an engineering design by registering it as a trademark. While the famous Coke bottle has long been trademarked, other cases – such as Unilever's Viennetta ice-cream dessert – are only now working their way through the court. Unilever, who makes Viennetta, claims that the fancily decorated block of ice-cream represents a distinctive shape. But lawyers say there is still confusion over the extent to which 'aesthetic shapes' can be trademarked. What is meant by 'distinctiveness'?

In the Viennetta case, a High Court judge said he was inclined to refuse registration of the ice-cream's shape as a trademark. First, although Viennetta was widely recognised by the public, it had not been shown that Unilever had used the shape to denote trade origin or that the public depended on the shape alone to denote trade origin. 'What has not been proved is that any member of the public would rely upon the appearance alone to identify the goods. They recognise it but do not treat it as a trademark', the judge suggested. Secondly, he said the shape had not acquired a 'distinctive character' because a small but significant proportion of the public confused other fancy ice-cream desserts with Viennetta: research submitted by Unilever suggested that 15 per cent of those questioned confused other products with Viennetta.

Trademark parameters in such areas as colour and smell are even more controversial. Colour is an area that is attracting a great deal of interest. In a recent Libertel case – where the Dutch group was trying to register a shade of orange for telecoms-related goods and services – the advocate-general decided that it could not be determined how the company planned to use the colour in relation to its services and products, and found that a colour in itself – unassociated with any other element or object – could not be a trademark. It looks like very broad registrations will face an uphill task.

As for smell, a German applicant – a Mr Sieckmann – was rebuffed by the court. He had attempted to register an olfactory mark, by outlining its chemistry, depositing a sample of the scent in a container, and describing it verbally as 'balsamically fruity with a slight hint of cinnamon'. But the court said his efforts failed to meet the registration requirement that a mark's representation be 'clear, precise, self-contained, easily accessible, intelligible, durable and objective'.

Certainly, trademark battles will rage on and the European Commission's efforts to harmonise trademark standards and build up a cohesive body of case law have some way to go. Meanwhile, marketers have to be prepared for plenty of courtroom surprises![38]

Brand sponsorship

A manufacturer has four sponsorship options. The product may be launched as a **manufacturer's brand** (or **national brand**), as when Sony, Nestlé and Samsung sell their output under their own manufacturer's brand names. Or the manufacturer may sell to intermediaries that give it a **private brand** (also called a **middleman brand**, **retailer brand**, **distributor brand** or **store brand**). For example, Cott is one of the world's largest makers of soft drinks, but its name is almost unknown to consumers because it makes store-branded foods and drinks that it supplies to retailers worldwide. Although most manufacturers create their own brand names, others market **licensed brands**. For example, some clothing and fashion accessory sellers pay large fees to put the names or initials of fashion innovators such as Calvin Klein, Pierre Cardin and Gucci on their products. Finally, companies can join forces and **co-brand** a product. This is becoming prevalent in the mobile phone market where the product is also an MP3 player (Sony-Ericsson), an in-car entertainment system (Mercedes-Benz iPod) or a fashion item (Prada by LG).

Manufacturers' brands versus private brands

Manufacturers' brands have long dominated the retail scene. In recent times, however, an increasing number of retailers and wholesalers have created their own private or store brands. In many industries, these private brands are giving manufacturers' brands a real run for their money.

In the so-called *battle of the brands* between manufacturers' and private brands, retailers have many advantages. They control what products they stock, where they go on the shelf and which ones they will feature in local circulars. Private brands can be hard to establish and costly to stock and promote. However, intermediaries can often locate manufacturers with excess capacity that will produce the private label at a low cost, resulting in a higher profit margin for the reseller. Private labels also give intermediaries exclusive products that cannot be bought from competitors, resulting in higher store traffic and loyalty. Retailers price their store brands lower than comparable manufacturers' brands, thereby appealing to budget-conscious shoppers, especially in difficult economic times. For example, in the UK, the grocery retailer Tesco sells its own line of clothing, promoted under the private label George; and Sainsbury's offers its own brand of laundry detergents, called Novon, which is marketed alongside branded products produced by Procter & Gamble and Unilever. Moreover, most shoppers believe that store brands are often made by one of the larger manufacturers anyway. They're right. National brand makers such as Birds Eye, Del Monte, Kimberly-Clark and Sara Lee also make store brands.

To fend off private brands, leading brand marketers must invest in R&D to bring out new brands, new features and continuous quality improvements. They must design strong advertising programmes to maintain high awareness and preference. They must find ways to 'partner' with major distributors in a search for distribution economies and improved joint performance. An example is Fairtrade, which has persuaded some retailers to drop own labels in favour of their own. One example is the Co-operative Group in the UK:

The Co-op has switched all its own-brand coffee to the ethically sound Fairtrade label following the success of a similar move with chocolate. The retailer says the change, which guarantees a price for the beans, would return much-needed revenue to the growers and would lift the value of the Fairtrade coffee market by 15 per cent and bring £4m a year in extra sales, a figure set to grow quickly. The move could be seen as not being entirely altruistic. Fairtrade coffee is a rising star among brands, with sales rising 27 per cent in the year before the Co-op acted. Also, when the Co-op switched all its own-brand chocolate bars to Fairtrade, sales rose 21 per cent within six months.[39]

Licensing

Most manufacturers take years and spend millions to create their own brand names. However, some companies license names or symbols previously created by other manufacturers, names of well-known celebrities or characters from popular movies and books. For a fee, any of these can provide an instant and proven brand name.

Clothing and accessories sellers pay large royalties to adorn their products – from blouses to ties and linens to luggage – with the names or initials of well-known fashion innovators such as Calvin Klein, Gucci, Tommy Hilfiger or Armani.

Sellers of children's products attach an almost endless list of character names to clothing, toys, school supplies, linens, dolls, lunch boxes, cereals and other items. Licensed character names range from classics such as Winnie the Pooh, Beatrix Potter and Disney characters, Thomas the Tank Engine, and Scooby Doo to the more recent Teletubbies, Bob the Builder, Powerpuff Girls and Harry Potter characters. Currently, a number of top-selling retail toys are products based on television shows and movies, such as the Cyberman Voice Changer Helmet based on Dr Who, the Spider-Man Triple Action Web Blaster, and the continuous stream of James Bond Aston Martin toy cars.

Name and character licensing has grown rapidly in recent years. More and more for-profit and non-profit organisations are licensing their names to generate additional revenues and brand recognition. Beatrix Potter pioneered the market with merchandise appearing almost as soon as her little books, but the first big splash was the coonskin cap craze tied in with Disney's 1954 Davy Crockett film. Given a great boost by *Star Wars*, annual retail sales of licensed products grew from only €8bn in 1977 to €100bn in 1987 and more than €400bn today. Today's biggest winner is Harry Potter whose success has made J K Rowling more wealthy than the Queen of England. Licensing can be a highly profitable business for many companies. For example, Nickelodeon has developed a stable full of hugely popular characters – such as Dora the Explorer, the Rugrats, and SpongeBob SquarePants. Products sporting these characters generate more than €5bn in annual retail sales. 'When it comes to licensing its brands for consumer products, Nickelodeon has proved that it has the Midas touch,' states a brand licensing expert.[40]

Corporate brand licensing – renting a corporate trademark or logo made famous in one category and using it in a related category – has also grown in popularity. Some examples include Cosmopolitan underwear, swimwear and home furnishings; Royal Ascot ties, hats, cashmere socks and jewellery; Porsche sunglasses, Hummer fragrances, Loctite nail polish, JCB toys, and Cambridge University teddy bears, clothes and accessories.

> **Corporate brand licensing—**A form of licensing whereby a firm rents a corporate trademark or logo made famous in one product or service category and uses it in a related category.

Co-branding

Although companies have been co-branding products for many years, there has been a recent resurgence in co-branded products. Co-branding occurs when two established brand names of different companies are used on the same product or service. Examples of co-branding across companies are the Senseo coffeemaker, which carries both the Philips (appliances) and the Douwe Egberts (coffee) brands; the BeerTender in-home draught brewing system, sold by Krups (appliances) and Heineken (beer); Orbit White chewing gum co-branded with Crest toothpaste; and McDonald's Rolo milkshake. Companies also take advantage of co-branding across their product ranges. Examples of this are the Gillette M3 Power shaving equipment with Duracell (both brands owned by Procter & Gamble) and Nestlé ice-cream sandwiches and sundae co-branded with Carnation.

Co-branding partners seek to mutually enhance each other's service or product brand through close association. This offers many advantages. Because each brand dominates in a different category, the combined brands create broader consumer appeal and greater brand equity. Co-branding also allows companies to expand their existing brand into a category they might otherwise have difficulty entering alone. For example, consider the co-branding efforts of Visa and Mastercard who are invariably found co-branded with banks but also with charities, such as the Royal Society for the Protection of Birds which also co-brands with Scottish and Southern Energy PLC to supply 'green energy'. Similarly, the World Wide Fund for Nature co-brands its Visa cards with MBNA Europe Bank and electricity with Ecotricity as 'ecofriendly electricity: electric energy'.[41]

Co-branding has its limitations. Such relationships usually involve complex legal contracts and licences. Co-branding partners must carefully coordinate their advertising, sales promotion and other marketing efforts. Finally, when co-branding, each partner must trust that the other will take good care of its brand. If a company chooses the wrong partner, or the partner suffers a setback or bad publicity, the company will be tainted by the association.

Brand development

A company has four choices when it comes to developing brands (see Figure 11.5). It can introduce *line extensions*, *brand extensions*, *multibrands* or *new brands*.

Line extensions

Line extensions occur when a company extends existing brand names to new forms, colours, sizes, ingredients or flavours of an existing product category. Thus, after generations of keeping true to the original format of KitKat, Nestlé's top chocolate bar, it successfully extended the two and four finger range to KitKat Chunky in 1999. This success was soon followed by repeated extensions including KitKat Low-Carb, KitKat Minis and KitKat Ice Cream. Finding their number two bar brand Aero was losing sales, in 2006 the brand was boosted by Aero Bubbles, a new line extension designed to compete with Mars's Maltesers.

A company introduces line extensions as a low-cost, low-risk way to introduce new products, or it might want to meet consumer desires for variety, to use excess capacity or simply to command more shelf-space from resellers. However, line extensions involve some risks. An overextended brand might lose its specific meaning, falling into the 'line-extension trap'. Heavily extended brands can also cause consumer confusion or frustration. A consumer buying cereal at a supermarket might be confronted by more than 150 brands, including up to 30 different brand flavours and sizes of oatmeal. Quaker alone offers its original Quaker Oats, several flavours of Quaker instant oatmeal, and several dry cereals such as Oatmeal Squares, Toasted Oatmeal and Toasted Oatmeal-Honey Nut.

Another risk is that sales of an extension may come at the expense of other items in the line. A line extension works best when it takes sales away from competing brands, not when it 'cannibalises' the company's other items.

Brand extensions

A **brand extension** (or brand stretching) extends a current brand name to new or modified products in a new category. For example, Victorinox extended its venerable Swiss Army brand

Line extension— Extending an existing brand name to new forms, colours, sizes, ingredients or flavours of an existing product category.

Brand extension— Extending an existing brand name to new product categories.

Figure 11.5 Brand development strategies

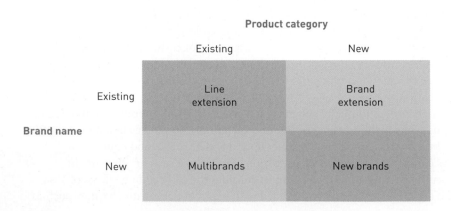

Product category

	Existing	New
Existing	Line extension	Brand extension
New	Multibrands	New brands

Brand name

from multi-tool knives to products ranging from cutlery and ballpoint pens to watches, luggage and clothing. Swatch spread from watches into telephones. And Honda stretched its company name to cover different products such as its cars, motorcycles, lawnmowers, marine engines and snowmobiles.

A brand-extension strategy offers many advantages. A well-regarded brand name helps the company enter new product categories more easily as it gives a new product instant recognition and faster acceptance. For example, Sony puts its name on most of its new electronic products, creating an instant perception of high quality for each new product. A brand extension also saves the high advertising costs usually required to build a new brand name.

Burberry, with its checks, is a classy brand across the world but when they launched entry level items, including baseball caps, its adoption by young rowdy 'chavs' in some countries alienated their upmarket customers. Burberry was even banned from some inner-city pubs!

SOURCE: The Advertising Archives.

At the same time, a brand-extension strategy involves some risk. Brand extensions such as Bic pantyhose and fragrances, Heinz pet food and Cadbury soup and synthetic meat met early deaths. The extension may confuse the image of the main brand. And if a brand extension fails, it may harm consumer attitudes towards the other products carrying the same brand name.

> " Brand extensions such as Bic pantyhose and fragrances, Heinz pet food and Cadbury soup and synthetic meat met early deaths. "

Further, a brand name may not be appropriate to a particular new product, even though it is well made and satisfying. Would you consider buying a Harley-Davidson cake-decorating kit or an Evian water-filled padded bra (both tried and failed)? A brand name may lose its special positioning in the consumer's mind through overuse. *Brand dilution* occurs when consumers no longer associate a brand with a specific product or even highly similar products. Companies that are tempted to transfer a brand name must research how well the brand's associations fit the new product.[42]

Multibrands

Multibrand strategy—A brand strategy under which a seller develops two or more brands in the same product category.

Companies often introduce additional brands in the same category. Thus, companies such as Unilever and Procter & Gamble market many different brands in each of their product categories. **Multibranding** offers a way to establish different features and appeal to different buying motives. It also allows a company to secure more reseller shelf-space. Or the company may want to protect its major brand by setting up *flanker* or *fighter brands*. Seiko uses different brand names for its higher-priced watches (Seiko Lasalle) and lower-priced watches (Pulsar) to protect the flanks of its mainstream Seiko brand. Further, companies such as Unilever, Nestlé, Masterfoods and Procter & Gamble create individual brand identities for each of their products. Unilever's line of laundry detergents – Persil/Omo, Surf, etc. – have distinct labels, with the corporate name hardly featured. Similarly, Procter & Gamble produces at least nine brands of laundry products – Ariel, Bold, etc.

These manufacturers argue that a multibrand strategy permits finer segmentation of the market, with each brand name suggesting different functions or benefits appealing to different buying motives of different customer segments.

Range branding strategy—A brand strategy whereby the firm develops separate product range names for different families of product.

Some companies develop multiple brands, not for individual products but for different families of products. For example, the Japanese electronics group Matsushita uses **range branding** – it develops separate range names for its audio-hifi product families (Technics, National, Panasonic and Quasar).

A major drawback of multibranding is that each brand might obtain only a small market share, and none may be very profitable. The company may end up spreading its resources over many brands instead of building a few brands to a highly profitable level. These companies should reduce the number of brands they sell in a given category and set up tighter screening procedures for new brands.

Corporate branding strategy—A brand strategy whereby the firm makes its company name the dominant brand identity across all of its products.

The multibranding approach contrasts with the **corporate branding** strategy. In corporate branding, the firm makes its company name the dominant brand identity across all of its products, as in the case of Mercedes-Benz, Philips and Heinz. The main advantages are economies of scale in marketing investments and wider recognition of the brand name. It also facilitates the launch of new products, especially when the corporate name is well established.

Company and individual branding strategy—A branding approach that focuses on the company name and individual brand name.

Other companies have used a **company and individual branding** approach. This focuses on both the corporate and individual brand names. Kellogg's (e.g. Cornflakes, Just Right, Raisin Bran, Rice Krispies, Coco Pops, Nutri-Grain, etc.), Nestlé (KitKat, Nescafé, Coffee-Mate, etc.) and Cadbury's (e.g. Dairy Milk, Roses, Milk Tray) are supporters of this branding strategy.

New brands

A company might believe that the power of its existing brand name is waning and a new brand name is needed. Or it may create a new brand name when it enters a new product category for which none of the company's current brand names are appropriate. Thus, Toyota established a separate family name – the Lexus – for its new luxury executive cars in order to create a distinctive identity for the latter and to position these well away from the traditional mass-market image of the 'Toyota' brand name. And Siemens' introduced a new line of upmarket, fashion mobile phones in 2003 under a new brand name – Xelibri – to create a distinctive identity for these phones.

As with multibranding, offering too many brands can result in a company spreading its resources too thinly. In some industries, such as consumer-packaged goods, consumers and retailers have become concerned that there are already too many brands, with too few differences between them. Thus, Lever Brothers, Procter & Gamble and other large consumer product marketers are now pursuing *megabrand* strategies – weeding out weaker brands and focusing their marketing dollars only on brands that can achieve the number-one or number-two market-share positions in their categories.

Managing brands

Companies must manage their brands carefully. First, the brand's positioning must be continuously communicated to consumers. Major brand marketers often spend huge amounts on advertising to create brand awareness and to build preference and loyalty. Such campaigns can help to create name recognition, brand knowledge and maybe even some brand preference. However, the fact is that brands are not maintained by advertising but by the *brand experience*. Today, customers come to know a brand through a wide range of contacts and touch points. These include advertising, but also personal experience with the brand, word of mouth, personal interactions with company people, company Web pages, telephone interactions, and many others. Any of these experiences can have a positive or negative impact on brand perceptions and feelings. The company must put as much care into managing these touch points as it does into producing its ads.

The brand's positioning will not take hold fully unless everyone in the company lives the brand. Therefore the company needs to train its people to be customer centred. Even better, the company should carry on internal brand building to help employees understand and be enthusiastic about the brand promise. Many companies go even further by training and encouraging their distributors and dealers to serve their customers well.

All of this suggests that managing a company's brand assets can no longer be left only to brand managers. Brand managers do not have enough power or scope to do all the things necessary to build and enhance their brands. Moreover, brand managers often pursue short-term results, whereas managing brands as assets calls for longer-term strategy. Thus, some companies are now setting up brand asset management teams to manage their major brands. Canada Dry and Colgate-Palmolive have appointed *brand equity managers* to maintain and protect their brands' images, associations and quality, and to prevent short-term actions by over-eager brand managers from hurting the brand.

Finally, companies need to periodically audit their brands' strengths and weaknesses.[43] They should ask: Does our brand excel at delivering benefits that consumers truly value? Is the brand properly positioned? Do all of our consumer touch points support the brand's positioning? Do the brand's managers understand what the brand means to consumers? Does the brand receive proper, sustained support? The brand audit may turn up brands that need more support, brands that need to be dropped, or brands that must be rebranded or repositioned because of changing customer preferences or new competitors.

Additional product considerations

Marketers have to address two additional considerations: social responsibility in product decisions and issues of international product marketing.

Product decisions and social responsibility

Product decisions have attracted much public attention in recent years. When making such decisions, marketers should consider carefully public policy issues and regulations involving: acquiring or dropping products, patent protection, product quality and safety, and packaging and product warranties.

Regarding the addition of new products, the government or competition authorities may prevent companies from adding products through acquisitions if the effect threatens to reduce competition. Companies dropping products must be aware of their legal obligations, written or implied, to their suppliers, dealers and customers who have a stake in the discontinued product. Socially responsible marketers should also avoid the excesses of planned obsolescence – deliberately causing products to become obsolete before they need replacement. Companies must also obey patent laws when developing new products. A company cannot make its product illegally similar to another company's established product.

In whichever country manufacturers offer their products, they must also comply with specific laws regarding product quality and safety which serve to protect consumers. For example, various Acts provide for the inspection of sanitary conditions in the meat- and poultry-processing industries. Safety legislation has been passed to regulate fabrics, chemical substances, cars, toys, drugs and poisons. Irrespective of whether laws exist to regulate companies' actions, consumers expect companies to behave ethically. If consumers have been injured by a product that has been designed defectively, they can sue manufacturers or dealers. Product liability suits can cost manufacturers millions of euros in compensation paid to victims. Faulty products also cost the company because of the need to recall and replace faulty merchandise.

Sony's battery recall problem started after Dell's widely-publicised recall of Sony batteries. At first Sony refused to say how many laptop makers were using the potentially faulty batteries, or how many of the devices had been sold. Then a battery failure occurred on an IBM ThinkPad – long the laptop of choice for travelling executives – as the machine was being carried aboard an aircraft at Los Angeles International airport. According to the US Consumer Product Safety Commission, overheating was 'causing enough smoke and sparking that a fire extinguisher was used to put it out.' The high-profile incident stimulated the Japanese electronics maker into starting a worldwide replacement programme for all its laptop batteries that meet certain specifications, regardless of who made the machines. However, Sony still held back, saying its global replacement programme would not be obligatory but that it would depend on the outcome of 'consultations' with individual computer makers. 'Sony will work with those that choose to participate,' they explained.[44]

But Sony's product recall is a small issue compared with the damage done to China, Inc. following the recall of dangerous dog food, toothpaste, children's clothes and toys 'Made in China'. Real Marketing 11.2 looks at the recall of dangerous toys and the repercussions.

real marketing 11.2

Mattel, 'Made in China' and 10,000 doll tears

Sony's problems seem minor compared to the battering of toy maker Mattel with its successive recalls of toys made in China. After global recall of 18 million Chinese-made toys caused by concerns about lead paint and magnets that could harm children, Mattel's share price fell 6 per cent in one morning's trading. The withdrawal covered some of the toy maker's most popular lines, such as Polly Pocket dolls, Doggie Day Care play sets and Barbie play sets. The group is also recalling 436,000 die-cast cars featuring the Sarge character from the Walt Disney film *Cars*. The toy was produced by Early Light Industrial, one of Mattel's contract manufacturing plants in China, which had subcontracted the painting of parts of the toy to another company.

Unsurprisingly, Mattel said it had improved procedures for testing the safety of its products. 'We have immediately implemented a strengthened three-point check system,' said Jim Walter, Mattel's senior vice-president of worldwide quality assurance. 'We've met with vendors to ensure they understand our tightened procedures and our absolute requirement of strict adherence to them.' Robert Eckert, Mattel's chairman and chief executive, said the company had 'rigorous procedures'. He added Mattel would be 'vigilant and unforgiving in enforcing quality and safety'.

These quality failures extend well beyond Mattel. The crisis in China's toy industry began in June, when New York-based RC2 recalled 1.5 million Thomas the Tank Engine products made in Guangdong because they contained lead paint. Chinese authorities have banned the factories behind the RC2 and the earlier Mattel recalls from exporting toys.

Both Lee Der and Early Light, the Chinese factories making the offending toys, had worked with Mattel for more than 15 years and have blamed subcontractors and suppliers for the use of lead-based paints. Both companies have factories in the Pearl River Delta – Lee Der in Foshan and Early Light in Dongguan. RC2's June recall of Thomas the Tank Engine and other toys involved Hansheng Wood, in Dongguan.

China has reason to be peeved about the damage it has suffered, since both Lee Der Industrial and Early Light Industrial were started by Hong Kong entrepreneurs. 'The damage caused by this year's recalls has been for China Inc's brand image. The "Made in China" label is misleading,' according to the China Toy Association; it should more accurately read: "Made in China – by Hong Kong".' About 65 per cent of the world's toys are made in Hong Kong's hinterland, the Pearl River Delta. 'These incidents have involved major importers and caused significant damage to the image and reputation of the Hong Kong toy industry,' the Federation of Hong Kong Industries admitted. But then added: 'Manufacturers have always found it difficult to comply with different product safety standards applied in the EU, the US and Japan.'

...11.2

The product recalls damaged Mattel but the impact is much greater in China. Zhang Shuhong, Lee Der's founder, committed suicide after his company was ruined by the scandal. In contrast, Francis Choi, chairman of Early Light, survives as one of Hong Kong's richest men. Chinese authorities have now banned the factories behind the RC2 and Mattel recalls from exporting toys, and inspection authorities in China's southern Guangdong province now say they are enforcing toy safety reporting standards stricter than those required by the EU's EN71 standard for toys. However, an unnamed industry executive said: 'I hope the Chinese authorities will back off a bit. My opinion is that they have overreacted.'

China's General Administration of Quality Supervision, Inspection and Quarantine (AQSIQ) has also introduced the nation's landmark recall systems for unsafe food products and toys amid efforts to improve product safety. The regulations state that producers must take the prior and major responsibilities for preventing and eliminating unsafe food and toys. The regulations also require manufacturers to stop production and sales, notify vendors and customers, and report to the quality control authorities when product defects are found.

To help quell anxiety about product quality, a group of domestic and foreign reporters had a one-day tour of testing lab and toy factories. Jetta (China) Industry Co. Ltd showed to reporters how it tested toys. 'A doll is normally tested for 10,000 times whether it can smile and cry as designed, and we have an employee specially in charge of testing this function.' Details like the doll's laughing and crying times were recorded each time it was tested.

There will be a lot more than dolls' tears after this fiasco.

SOURCES: Matthew Garrahan, 'Mattel shares tumble on another global recall of toys made in China', *Financial Times* (15 August 2007); *Financial Times*, 'Toy trouble for Hong Kong too' (5 September 2007); Tom Mitchell and Robin Kwong, 'China tightens safety reporting rules for toys', *Financial Times* (14 August 2007); *BBC Monitoring Service*, 'China unveils recall systems for unsafe food products, toys' (31 August 2007); *BBC Monitoring Service*, 'China reassures foreign media toy quality with factory tour' (4 September 2007).

For a more detailed discussion of the ethical issues concerning products and business actions towards socially responsible product marketing, see Chapter 2.

International product decisions

International marketers face special product and packaging challenges. For a start, they must decide what products to introduce in which countries, and then how much to standardise or adapt their products and services for world markets.

On the one hand, companies would like to standardise their offerings. Standardisation helps a company to develop a consistent worldwide image. It minimises the need to duplicate research and development efforts and also lowers product design, manufacturing and marketing costs of offering a large variety of products. On the other hand, consumers around the world differ

The technology can be standard but sales can be increased by customising products and promotions like the Sony Ericsson W850i Walkman phone to fit particular target markets.
SOURCE: The Advertising Archives.

widely in their cultures, attitudes and buying behaviours. Markets also vary in their economic conditions, competition, legal requirements and physical environments. Companies must usually respond to these differences by adapting their product offerings. For example, Cadbury sells kiwi-filled Cadbury Kiwi Royale in New Zealand, Frito-Lay sells Nori Seaweed Lay's potato chips for Thailand and A la Turca corn chips with poppy seeds and a dried tomato flavour for Turkey.[45]

Packaging also presents new challenges for international marketers. Packaging issues can be subtle. For example, names, labels and colours may not translate easily from one country to another. Consumers in different countries also vary in their packaging preferences. Europeans like efficient, functional, recyclable boxes with understated designs. In contrast, the Japanese often use packages as gifts. Thus in Japan, Lever Brothers packages its Lux soap in stylish gift

boxes. Packaging may even have to be tailored to meet the physical characteristics of consumers in various parts of the world. For instance, soft drinks are sold in smaller cans in Japan to fit the smaller Japanese hand better.

Companies may have to adapt their packaging to meet specific regulations regarding package design or label contents. For instance, some countries ban the use of any foreign language on labels; other countries require that labels be printed in two or more languages. Labelling laws vary greatly from country to country. Thus, although product and package standardisation can produce benefits, the international company must usually modify its offerings to the unique needs of specific international markets.

In summary, product strategy calls for a set of complex decisions on product line, product mix, branding, packaging and support service strategy. These decisions should be taken with a full understanding of customer needs and wants and competitors' strategies. Because marketers operate in increasingly complex environments, product and branding decisions cannot be made in isolation of the broader, particularly regulatory and societal, forces affecting product decisions. Market-oriented companies create value-laden offerings that satisfy customer wants through addressing the many issues surrounding product decisions and maintaining consistency with broad company objectives.

Reviewing the concepts

A *product* is more than a simple set of tangible features. The concept of a product is complex and can be viewed on three levels. The *core product* consists of the core problem-solving benefit(s) that the customer seeks when they buy a product. The *actual product* exists around the core and includes the features, styling, design, quality level, brand name and packaging. The *augmented product* is the actual product plus the various services offered with it, such as warranty, free delivery, installation and maintenance.

1. Define *product* and the major classifications of products and services

Broadly defined, a *product* is anything that can be offered to a market for attention, acquisition, use or consumption that might satisfy a want or need. Products include physical objects but also services, events, persons, places, organisations, ideas or mixes of these entities. Products fall into two broad classes based on the types of consumers that use them. *Consumer products* – those bought by final consumers – are usually classified according to consumer shopping habits (convenience products, shopping products, speciality products and unsought products). *Industrial products* – purchased for further processing or for use in conducting a business – include materials and parts, capital items and supplies and services. Other marketable entities – such as organisations, persons, places and ideas – can also be thought of as products.

2. Describe the decisions companies make regarding their individual products, product lines and product mixes

Individual product decisions involve product attributes, branding, packaging, labelling and product support services. *Product attribute* decisions involve product quality, features, and style and design. *Branding* decisions include selecting a brand name and developing a brand strategy. *Packaging* provides many key benefits, such as protection, economy, convenience and promotion. Package decisions often include designing *labels*, which identify, describe and possibly promote the product. Companies also develop *product support services* that enhance customer service and satisfaction and safeguard against competitors.

Most companies produce a product line rather than a single product. A *product line* is a group of products that are related in function, customer-purchase needs or distribution channels. *Line stretching* involves extending a line downward, upward or in both directions to occupy a gap that might otherwise by filled by a competitor. In contrast, *line filling* involves adding items within the present range of the line. All product lines and items offered to customers by a particular seller make up the *product mix*. The mix can be described by four dimensions: width, length, depth and consistency. These dimensions are the tools for developing the company's product strategy.

3. Discuss branding strategy – the decisions companies make in building and managing their brands

Some analysts see brands as *the* major enduring asset of a company. Brands are more than just names and symbols – they embody everything that the product or service *means* to consumers. *Brand equity* is the positive differential effect that knowing the brand name has on customer response to the product or service. A brand with strong brand equity is a very valuable asset.

In building brands, companies need to make decisions about brand positioning, brand name selection, brand sponsorship and brand development. The most powerful *brand positioning* builds around strong consumer beliefs and values. *Brand name selection* involves finding the best brand name based on a careful review of product benefits, the target market and proposed marketing strategies. A manufacturer has four *brand sponsorship* options: it can launch a *manufacturer's brand* (or national brand), sell to resellers who use a *private brand*, market *licensed brands* or join forces with another company to *co-brand* a product. A company also has four choices when it comes to developing brands. It can introduce *line extensions*, *brand extensions*, *multibrands* or *new brands*.

Companies must build and manage their brands carefully. The brand's positioning must be continuously communicated to consumers. However, brands are not maintained by advertising but by the *brand experience*. Customers come to know a brand through a wide range of contacts and interactions. The company must put as much care into managing these touch points as it does into producing its ads. Thus, managing a company's brand assets can no longer be left only to brand managers. Some companies are now setting up brand asset management teams to manage their major brands. Finally, companies must periodically audit their brands' strengths and weaknesses. In some cases, brands may need to be repositioned because of changing customer preferences or new competitors.

4. Address additional product issues: socially responsible product decisions and international marketing

Marketers must consider the potential impacts of their product decisions on customers, businesses and society. They must be aware of the public policy issues and regulations involving acquiring or dropping products, patent protection, product quality and safety, and product warranties. There are also special challenges facing international product marketers. International marketers must decide how much to standardise or adapt their offerings for world markets.

Discussing the concepts

1. What are the three levels at which a product may be viewed? In your answer, use product examples to show how these different levels may be applied to help product marketers define their product offering.

2. Various classes of consumer products differ in the ways that consumers buy them. Provide examples of the four types of consumer products and discuss how they differ in the way they are marketed.

3. What is a brand? Why are many people willing to pay more for branded products than for unbranded products? What does this say about the value of branding for both the buyer and seller?

4. Make a list of brands that you are familiar with. Consider the levels at which brand positioning can occur. How are the brands that you have selected positioned on these levels?

5. What are the brand sponsorship options available to a manufacturer? What are the opportunities and risks of each approach? How does a manufacturer decide which option is the most appropriate for its products?

6. What are the major ethical issues concerning products and brands? Discuss the actions that marketers should take to deal with these concerns.

Applying the concepts

1. A strong brand is often considered by managers to be their company's most important asset. Interbrand, the branding consultancy, analyses economic earnings forecasts for the world's best-known brands and translates those forecasts into brand valuations (www.interbrand.com).

    a. According to recent studies (http://bwnt.businessweek.com/brand/2006/ accessed 10 May 2007) , Coca-Cola, Microsoft, IBM, GE, Intel, Nokia, Toyota, Mercedes-Benz, BMW and Louis Vuitton are among the world's top 20 brands. Why do these brands command so much respect?

    b. What makes a strong brand? How would you measure brand equity?

    c. What does it take a brand (like Coca-Cola) to become the number one brand in the world?

    d. Identify the top ten brands in the world today (visit http://bwnt.businessweek.com/brand/). Examine the websites of these brands for indicators of brand strength. Based on your answers to question 2(b), draw a grid that evaluates each of the brands based on the characteristics you listed. Examine the information in your grid. Which company is superior based on your own evaluation?

2. Imagine that you are the marketing director of a UK-based food manufacturer. Recently, your company has added organic versions of several of its major canned food brands that will be marketed in the EU and US. As many other food manufacturers look to the organic market, they are also keeping a keen eye on emerging regulations, especially the strict standards on the use of the word 'organic'. In the US, in particular, regulations state that foods labelled as 'organic' must consist of at least 95% organically produced ingredients. Those labelled 'made with organic ingredients' must contain at least 70% organic ingredients. If a product contains less than 70% organic ingredients, the term organic cannot be used anywhere on the front of the package. In addition, operations that process organic food must be certified by one of

60 USDA-accredited certifying agents. If not, a fine of up to $10,000 (€7,400) will be levied for any seller who mislabels a product. To comply with these regulations, the company will have to invest more money in product development to incorporate a higher level of organic ingredients.

a. Do you think that the regulations for 'organic' food labelling make good sense? Why do you think there is a need for strict regulations to control 'organic labelling' on food packages?

b. To what extent do you think the average consumers will know the differences in organic label designations?

c. Recommend a brand development strategy for the organic line of products to be marketed in the US.

d. How would you differentiate the organic, from the company's traditional, line of cooking sauces?

Web resources

For additional classic case studies and Internet exercises, visit **www.pearsoned.co.uk/kotler**

References

1. Carmel Allen, How to Spend It: 'Profit and gloss', *FT Weekend* (October 2000), pp. 63–4; Birna Helgadottir, Business: 'The glamazons are here', *FT Weekend* (29 July 2000), pp. 30–3; William Hall and John Willman, 'Success without a ripple', *Financial Times* (13 March 2000), p. 14; 'How L'Oréal grew to dominate market', *Canberra Times* (9 July 2007); 'What do the "spokesmodels" say about race and L'Oréal?', *The Guardian* (2 August 2007); 'L'Oréal table sur une nouvelle année de croissance à deux chiffres du bénéfice', *Les Echos* (31 August 2007); 'L'Oréal optimiste pour 2007', *Le Figaro* (1 September 2007).

2. 'Mercedes-Benz World goes "live"', *Mercedes Magazine* (Winter 2006/07), p. 4.

3. Maija Palmer, 'Nokia's Ovi opens doors to the internet', *Financial Times* (29 August 2007).

4. See 'The Celebrity 100', *Forbes*, accessed at www.forbes.com, July 2006; and Reed Tucker, 'Tiger Woods', *Fortune* (17 October 2005), p. 142.

5. David Owen, 'Fred Perry's surprise big hit', *Financial Times* (14 November 2005); Jon Henderson and Denis Campbell, 'Style secret of Murray's mint', *The Observer* (26 February 2006); also see www.fredperry.com/index.asp.

6. 'Il gruppo Versace torna a distribuire il dividendo', *Il Sole 24 Ore* (27 July 2007).

7. For more on marketing places, see Philip Kotler, Donald Haider and Irving J. Rein, *Marketing Places* (New York: Free Press, 2002). Information on examples from Steve Dougherty, 'In a cold country, the nights are hot', *New York Times* (19 December 2004), section 5, p. 1; www.TravelTex.com, www.iloveny.state.ny.us and www.visiticeland.com, October 2006; www.polandtour.org and www.newzealand.com, August 2007.

8. Based on a Social Marketing Institute (SMI) success story at www.social-marketing.org/success/cs-stopaids.html. For other success stories, see www.social-marketing.org/success.html (August 2007).

9. See Alan R. Andreasen, Rob Gould and Karen Gutierrez, 'Social marketing has a new champion', *Marketing News* (7 February 2000), p. 38. Also see Philip Kotler, Ned Roberto and Nancy Lee, *Social Marketing: Improving the quality of life*, 2nd edn (Thousand Oaks, CA: Sage Publications, 2002); and www.social-marketing.org, August 2006.

10. Quotes and definitions from Philip Kotler, *Kotler on Marketing* (New York: Free Press, 1999), p. 17; and www.asq.org, July 2006.

11. See Roland T. Rust, Christine Moorman and Peter R. Dickson, 'Getting return on quality: Revenue expansion, cost reduction, or both?', *Journal of Marketing* (October 2002), pp. 7–24; and Roland T. Rust, Katherine N. Lemon and Valerie A. Zeithaml, 'Return on marketing: Using customer equity to focus marketing strategy', *Journal of Marketing* (January 2004), p. 109.

12. Gunilla Kines, 'A walk on the safe side', *The European Magazine* (24–30 April 1997), p. 12; Maria Werner, 'IKEA's design for thrifty, stylish living', *ibid.*, p. 15; Ivar Holm, *Ideas and Beliefs in Architecture and Industrial Design: How attitudes, orientations, and underlying assumptions shape the built environment* (Oslo School of Architecture and Design, 2006).

13. James MacKintosh, 'Fiat facelift ditches ugly cars', *Financial Times* (29 May 2003), p. 12; Paul Betts, 'Sunny prospects for the Club Med car manufacturers', *Financial Times* (26 July 2007); Richard Hammond, 'Fiat's feat', *The Mirror* (20 July 2007).

14. Sarah Lacy, 'How P&G conquered carpet', *BusinessWeek Online* (23 September 2005), accessed at www.businessweek.com/innovate/content/sep2005/id20050923_571639 and www.ideo.com/portfolio/re.asp?x=19002839, 4 September 2007.

15. For these and other examples, see Lee Gomes, 'To design away tears, SAP aims to make simpler software', *Wall Street Journal* (21 June 2006), p. B1; Lisa Chamberlain, 'Going off the beaten path for new design ideas', *New York Times* (12 March 2006); and IDEO's website at http://ideo.com/portfolio/, August 2006; also see Edwin Heathcote, 'What is the point of design?', *Financial Times* (11 February 2006), p. 1.

16. Based on Adam Horowitz *et al.*, '101 dumbest moments in business', *Business 2.0* (January–February 2005), p. 104; and Jason Norman, 'Kryptonite's PR Maven Donna Tocci can not be broken', *Bicycle Retailer and Industry News* (1 June 2005), p. 39.

17. T. Kontiokari, K. Sundqvist, M. Nuutinen, T. Pokka, M. Koskela and M. Uhari, 'Randomised trial of cranberry–lingonberry juice and *Lactobacillus* GG drink for the prevention of urinary tract infections in women', *British Medical Journal* (2001), pp. 1571–5.

18. Thomas Hine, *The Total Package: The evolution and secret meaning of boxes, bottles, cans, and tubes* (Darby, PA: Diane Publ., 2001, orig. Boston, MA: Little, Brown, 1995).

19. For these and other examples, see Susanna Hamner, 'Packaging that pays', *Business 2.0* (July 2006), pp. 68–9; and www.nabiscoworld.com/chipsahoy/.

20. Based on Thomas J. Ryan, 'Labels grow up', *Apparel* (February 2005), pp. 26–9.

21. IDS provides the information resource for the packaging industry at www.idspackaging.com/ Packaging_supplier_information_gold_2-1-2-5-europen.html.

22. Gary Cokins, 'How do you connect quality directly to profitability?', *Quality Profits* **2**, 2, pp. 1–2.

23. Sathnam Sanghera, 'Plain and simple truth about good customer service', *Financial Times* (22 June 2006); Colin Shaw, *The DNA of Customer Experience: How emotions drive value* (Basingstoke: Palgrave Macmillan, 2007).

24. Example adapted from Michelle Higgins, 'Pop-up sales clerks: Web sites try the hard sell', *Wall Street Journal* (15 April 2004), p. D.1. Also see Dawn Chmielewski, 'Software that makes tech support smarter', *Knight Ridder Tribune Business News* (25 December 2005), p. 1.

25. James Mackintosh, 'Mercedes smarts from record loss', *Financial Times* (29 April 2005); 'Smart ist Schuld: Mercedes verkauft weniger Autos', *Die Welt* (8 May 2007).

26. Dan Glaister, 'Gallo dynasty: Winemaker who brought grapes of wealth to California dies, aged 97: Founder turned a modest family brewing firm into world's largest producer', *The Guardian* (8 March 2007).

27. Information accessed online at www.marriott.com, August 2006, and www.adbrands.net/sectors/ sector_travel.htm.

28. Information about Colgate's product lines accessed at www.colgate.com/app/Colgate/US/Corp/Products. cvsp, August 2006.

29. See 'McAtlas shrugged', *Foreign Policy* (May–June 2001), pp. 26–37; and Philip Kotler and Kevin Lane Keller, *Marketing Management*, 12th edn (Upper Saddle River, NJ: Prentice Hall, 2006), pp. 290–1.

30. Al Ehrbar, 'Breakaway brands', *Fortune* (31 October 2005), pp. 153–70. Also see 'DeWalt named breakaway brand', *Snips* (January 2006), p. 66.

31. Jean Noel Kapferer, *The New Strategic Brand Management: Creating and sustaining brand equity long term*, 3rd edn (London: Kogan Page, 2004); Kevin Lane Keller, *Strategic Brand Management: Building, measuring, and managing brand equity*, 2nd edn (Academic Internet Publishers, 2006).

32. Scott Davis, *Brand Asset Management: Driving profitable growth through your brands* (San Francisco: Jossey-Bass, 2000). Also see Kusum Ailawadi, Donald R. Lehman and Scott A. Neslin, 'Revenue premium as an outcome measure of brand equity', *Journal of Marketing* (October 2003), pp. 1–17.

33. Interbrand, 'Best global brands 2007', www.interbrand.com/best_brands_2007.asp.

34. Larry Selden and Yoko S. Selden, 'Profitable customer: Key to great brands', *Point* (July–August 2006), pp. 7–9. Also see Roland T. Rust, Katherine N. Lemon and Valerie A. Zeithaml, 'Return on marketing:

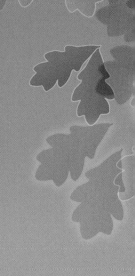

Using customer equity to focus marketing strategy', *Journal of Marketing* (January 2004), p. 109; and Connie S. Olasz, 'Marketing's role in a relationship age', *Baylor Business Review* (Spring 2006), pp. 2–7.

35. See Scott Davis, *Brand Asset Management: Driving profitable growth through your brands*, 2nd edn (San Francisco: Jossey-Bass, 2002). For more on brand positioning, see Philip Kotler and Kevin Lane Keller, *Marketing Management*, 12th edn (Upper Saddle River, NJ: Prentice Hall, 2006), Ch 10.

36. See Jacquelyn A. Ottman, Edwin R. Strattford and Cathy L. Hartman, 'Avoiding green marketing myopia', *Environment* (June 2006), pp. 22–37.

37. Stelios Haji-Ioannou, 'Confessions of a serial entrepreneur about the tough job of defending the Easy brand', *Financial Times* (7 August 2003).

38. Nikki Tait, Special Report – Intellectual Property: 'Time to test the boundaries', *Financial Times* (30 April 2003), p. II; Nikki Tait, 'Viennetta trademark case cuts no ice with judge', *Financial Times* (19 December 2002), p. 3; Nikki Tait, 'Nestlé loses battle over "Have a Break" trademark', *Financial Times* (3 December 2002), p. 4.

39. Sophy Buckley, 'Co-op to bring all own-brand coffee under Fairtrade label', *Financial Times* (13 November 2003). For an excellent scientific review of own-label marketing, see Nimalya Kumar and Jan-Benedict E. M. Steenkamp, *Private Label Strategy* (Harvard Business School Press, 2007).

40. Jay Sherman, 'Nick puts muscle behind everGirl', *TelevisionWeek* (5 January 2004), p. 3; 'Nickelodeon unveils three new toy lines based on hit properties', *PR Newswire* (10 February 2006).

41. Wendy Zellner, 'Your new banker?', *Business Week* (7 February 2005), pp. 28–31; Kathleen Day, 'Piggy banker?', *The Washington Post* (12 February 2006), p. F1.

42. For more on the use of line and brand extensions and consumer attitudes towards them, see Franziska Volckner and Henrik Sattler, 'Drivers of brand extension success', *Journal of Marketing* (April 2006), pp. 18–34; and Chris Pullig, Carolyn J. Simmons and Richard G. Netemeyer, 'Brand dilution: When do new brands hurt existing brands?', *ibid.*, pp. 52–66.

43. Kevin Lane Keller, 'The brand report card', *Harvard Business Review* (January 2000), pp. 147–57; Kevin Lane Keller, *Strategic Brand Management: Building, measuring, and managing brand equity*, 2nd edn (Academic Internet Publishers, 2006), pp. 766–7; David A. Aaker, 'Even brands need spring cleaning', *Brandweek* (8 March 2004), pp. 36–40.

44. Richard Waters, Companies and markets: 'Sony's battery woes deepen in wake of ThinkPad fire', *Financial Times* (29 September 2006), p. 1.

45. For these and other examples, see Darell K. Rigby and Vijay Vishwanath, 'Localization: The revolution in consumer markets', *Harvard Business Review* (April 2006), pp. 82–92.

Company case 11 Is it a phone? No! Is it an MP3 player? No! Is it an Internet company? Yes, it's Ovi!

Mobile operators watched cautiously when Nokia declared an important strategic shift, positioning itself as an Internet company with the announcement of an online music service intended to rival Apple's iTunes. Olli-Pekka Kallasvuo, chief executive of the Finnish handset maker, will offer details of the new worldwide service in London at a lavish event to include a concert featuring Grammy-winning musicians at the Ministry of Sound nightclub. Mr Kallasvuo explained the move: 'Phones are not enough any more. Great companies renew themselves from time to time. This is the beginning of the next new step for Nokia.' With the new brand Ovi, Nokia will run music download services (up against iTunes), games (up against Sony and Microsoft), maps (up against Google) and other online applications. Ovi – which means 'door' in Finnish – would open new market possibilities, pronounced Mr Kallasvuo.

When asked whether Nokia was deliberately copying Apple's popular design features, Anssi Vanjoki, head of Nokia's multimedia business, said: 'If there is something good in the world, that helps the user interface, we will copy it with pride.' He dismissed suggestions that the Ovi platform would receive a cold shoulder from mobile phone operators, such as Vodafone and Orange, who have been developing their own Internet services. 'There is not only one operator strategy out there. There are many operators who say we don't have the resources to develop our own services and are saying please Nokia give us a platform,' he said. If operators did not want to use Nokia's Ovi service, Nokia would continue to support them in other ways, he said.

Some analysts suggested that smaller operators, such as Bouygues of France or Wind in Italy, might prefer to use Nokia's portal rather than develop their own. 'Outside of North America and Western Europe this could be welcomed with open arms. Operators in these regions have a different business model, they just want to sell more minutes of airtime, not develop their own services,' said Ben Wood, analyst at CCS Insight.

Although sales of multimedia phones, which have functions like music players or cameras, would increase from 80 million last year to 120 million in 2007, mobile operators' own music offerings have so far failed to gain traction in the market. Most mobile music users simply 'sideload' music from their computer direct to their handset. According to data published by M: Metrics, the research company, of the approximately 36 million people who listened to music on their mobile phone from April to June 2007 in the US and Europe's five biggest markets, fewer than 14 per cent had downloaded from an operator portal.

The announcement follows news in June that Nokia was to make its services division one of the group's three core businesses – the first time it had been recognised as a separate unit. The launch will be the most substantial push Nokia has made into offering online services since it opened the Club Nokia website in 1998 when it offered games, ringtones and other content. Club Nokia kept a low profile after concerns were raised by important mobile operators such as Vodafone, which intended to launch their own music and entertainment services.

Nearly 10 years later, the era of deferring to mobile operators may be over. If mobile operators feel threatened by the music service, they may shun Nokia's new flagship music handset, the N81, which is also expected to be unveiled today [29 August 2007] as a competitor to Apple's iPhone. However, Nokia said it had had 'very positive discussions' with operators about the planned music service, and was 'confident it could reach agreement' with them. 'The N81 is not part of our current plan but we wouldn't rule out carrying it in the future,' said '3', which runs one of the UK's most successful music services.

Apple is also understood to have negotiated highly favourable terms with network operators wishing to include its iPhone handset in their portfolios, another sign of the waning power of operators. 'It has become clear that mobile operators don't have the first idea about how to create services,' says Richard Windsor, telecommunications analyst at Nomura. 'They have no user loyalty and no brand power, which is why they have had to make strong concessions to Apple'.

Nokia's music site will be based on Loudeye, the US online music company that Nokia bought for $60m (€45m) in 2006. Loudeye has a music library of about

1.6 million tracks, fewer than the 5 million held by iTunes and Napster's more than 3 million. Nokia had been experimenting with mobile music in a low-key way since autumn 2006, when it launched an Internet site called Music Recommenders.

Nokia is also likely to announce other online services. In July 2007, the mobile handset maker bought Twango, the social networking site, for an undisclosed sum. This month [August 2007] it launched – without much fanfare – a content-sharing website, Mosh, designed for mobile handset users. It has also announced a series of deals to bring new games on to its N-Gage mobile phone games service.

Nokia might not be the only handset maker to shift into services. Sony Ericsson, which sold 60 million music phones last year, has also dabbled in music services, with the launch in 2006 of M-Buzz that features new artists from the Sony BMG label. Miles Flint, chief executive of Sony Ericsson, has hinted there could be more to come.

Analysts say a broad shift into services may be necessary for mobile equipment companies as revenues from hardware sales begin to fall. Many reckon it could be difficult for handset makers to compete with more established Internet companies. But it could pay off in the long run. 'These services are not going to have a massive impact on Nokia's balance sheet this year or next – but they have an eye for the long term,' said Ben Wood, analyst at CCS Insight. 'The web will inevitably become a more important part of people's lives and they need to at least have a seat at the table.'

Questions

1. Why is Nokia making this sudden change into becoming an Internet service provider rather than a maker of mobile phones?
2. What are the dangers in making such a large shift and how do Nokia's strengths help overcome them?
3. Why might Nokia have decided to use the separate brand name Ovi rather than using a name based on Nokia?
4. Nokia has been particularly successful in providing mobile phones for the business market. Will these professional devices sit easily alongside Ovi?
5. How does Nokia's strategic shift change the competitors and products with which the company is competing and how strong is it in these markets?

SOURCES: Based on Maija Palmer, 'Nokia set to strike a fresh strategic note', *Financial Times* (29 August 2007) and Maija Palmer, 'Nokia's Ovi opens doors to the internet', *Financial Times* (29 August 2007).

LOVE
NEW
SQUEEZE ME
YEAST EXTRACT
MARMITE
CONTAINS B VITAMINS • 100% VEGETARIAN
NEW MARMITE SQUEEZY...
MARMITE
HATE

Every invention is received by a cry
of triumph which soon turns into
a cry of fear.

BERTOLT BRECHT

New-product development and product life-cycle strategies

Mini Contents List

◄ SOURCE: The Advertising Archives.

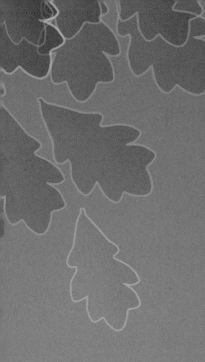

'A new broom sweeps clean, but an old broom knows every corner'

From the album 'A New Broom Sweeps Clean, But an Old Broom Knows Every Corner' by Rosine, The Orchard, B0000508LJ

Previewing the concepts

In the previous chapter, you learnt how marketers manage individual products or brands and entire product mixes. In this chapter, we will examine two additional product topics: developing new products and managing products through their life-cycles. New products are the lifeblood of an organisation. However, as the Hoki case illustrates, new-product marketing is fraught with uncertainty. The likely outcome for a new fish to eat is similar to that for rock bands, films, mobile phones or a new computer game: most fail; some are quite successful; a few become outstandingly successful. The first part of this chapter lays out a process for finding and growing successful new products. Once introduced, marketers want their products to enjoy a long and profitable life. In the second part of the chapter, you will see that products pass through several life-cycle stages and that each stage poses new challenges requiring different marketing strategies and tactics.

After reading this chapter, you should be able to:

1. Explain how companies find and develop new-product ideas.
2. List and define the steps in the new-product development process and the major considerations in managing this process.
3. Describe the stages of the product life-cycle.
4. Explain how marketing strategy changes during a product's life-cycle.

Prelude case Hoki, by any other name, tastes just as oily

A *National Geographic* magazine's special issue on 'The Global Fish Crisis' starts with a cry of despair:

> The oceans are in deep blue trouble. From the northernmost reaches of the Greenland Sea to the swirl of the Antarctic Circle, we are gutting our seas of fish. Since 1900, many species may have declined by 90 per cent, and it's getting worse. Nets are scouring reefs. Supertrawlers vacuum up shrimps. Nations flout laws.

To wealthy western customers it just means that a healthy fish diet costs a bit more, but it means hunger in poor countries where people once fished using traditional methods to feed themselves. Since 1950 the world fish catch has grown from 20 million metric tons a year to close to 100 million metric tons. We are now tucking into 6 million metric tons of tuna steaks a year compared with 0.5 metric tons in 1950. The world's oceans are a huge reservoir of protein that is just there for the taking and industrial fishing once allowed us to take more and more. But no more!

The world's fishing fleets are taking a bigger and bigger amount out of rapidly diminishing fish stocks. It is estimated that 30 per cent of world stocks are overfished. Industrial fishing has already wiped out 90 per cent of the population of swordfish, marlin and the bigger types of tuna.

It is hard to imagine how common fish once were. When whalers first discovered Nantucket, the whale population was so dense that 'you could walk from the island to the mainland over their backs' and the lobster, now a luxury food, was so inexpensive in Elizabethan times that there was a rule that apprentices could not be fed the crustacean more than twice a week.

Europe's appetite for fish appears insatiable, taking 40 per cent of the world's imported fish. The largest consumers are Spain, Portugal and Lithuania, whose people eat an average of 45 kg of sea fish a year, more than double the European average. Overfishing has already reduced the local catch of cod and hake. Prices have risen and the EU heavily subsidises local fishermen to keep them in business.

To firms like Unilever, the declining fish population causes an ethical and economic problem. Unilever sells its fish in Europe under the Birds Eye, Iglo, Findus, Frudesa and Knorr brands The company agrees with many retailers, including Tesco and Wal-Mart, who strive to sell fish from sustainable stocks. The problem is that people still want to eat the fish such as cod that have always been part of their diet. To get out of this fix the Birds Eye division came up with hoki, a white fish from New Zealand waters, an 'ocean-friendly' alternative to cod.

Market research indicated that consumers would buy the unfamiliar-sounding steaks and fish fingers if the incentives were right. Unilever's strategy was to promote the fish heavily in supermarkets and make sure it was sold at the same price as or more cheaply than cod. Birds Eye followed the market research evidence, launched hoki and failed. In marketing *Macruronus novaezelandiae*, Unilever certainly had many names to choose from since, in addition to the Maori name hoki, the fish's other names are blue grenadier, blue hake, New Zealand whiptail, whiptail and whiptail hake.

The company underestimated the public's love of cod. The company were forced to admit that consumer resistance was likely to prevent it achieving its target of sourcing all its supplies from sustainable fisheries. By the end of this year it will be closer to 60 per cent than 100 per cent. Hoki turned out to be unappealing, being slightly oilier and fishier-tasting than cod. The New Zealand connection, designed to appeal with its connotations of quality and purity, was not enough to change minds.

But other factors were also at play. Price is more important to most consumers than sustainability. Competition between the supermarkets on cod fish fingers drove down the shelf price compared with hoki. 'In some supermarkets, cod fish fingers were cheaper than the more sustainable hoki option, making a complete mockery of suggestions that cod stocks might be in danger – as did the fact that the shelves were still packed to the hilt with cod products,' says Forum for the Future, a sustainable development charity that works with about 150 companies.

It is also very difficult to convey the facts about declining fish stocks to consumers, says Jonathon Porritt, director of Forum for the Future. Globally, just 24 per cent of the world's fish stocks remain underexploited or moderately exploited, according to the United Nations Food and Agriculture Organisation. But the situation varies within species. Cod is in serious danger of being fished out completely in the North Sea, a disaster that would echo the 1980s collapse of Newfoundland's cod fishery, says the report. But cod stocks off Iceland, for example, are a lot healthier.

Hoki marketing was also hit by controversy. The Marine Stewardship Council's (MCS) certification of the hoki fishery as sustainable attracted criticism from environmental groups, concerned about fur seals and seabirds being killed as a side-effect of fishing. The New Zealand government is also worried about the sustainability of the hoki fish population. In 2007, Fisheries Minister Jim Anderton set new catch limits, including cutting the total allowable hoki catch by 10 per cent to 91,040 tonnes – with the eastern stock total allowable commercial catch increased by 5,000 tonnes and the western stock cut by 15,000 tonnes. Even so, some complain that the New Zealand government hasn't gone far enough with cuts to hoki quotas and is running scared of job losses that further cuts would necessitate.

Another problem has been the limited number of certified fisheries. So far only 12 have been certified under the MSC independent process. This has created something of a catch-22. Some processors and retailers are reluctant to embark on marketing campaigns without more certainty about supplies. In the absence of pressure from them, there are fewer incentives for the fishing industry to change tack. However, this seems set to change, with more than 20 other fisheries around the world moving towards certification, including salmon and albacore, a fish similar to tuna. Crucially the large Alaskan Bering Sea cod fishery is close to certification. 'It will mean that supermarkets can display cod with the MSC logo next to cod without it, and allow customers to notice the difference,' says Forum for the Future's *Fishing for Good* report. 'This is exactly what happens now with Fairtrade bananas: they sit right next to standard bananas and are taking proportionally more and more of the sales.'

Unilever hopes to make use of the certification of the huge Alaskan pollock fishery. The group plans to sell prepared fish dishes containing pollock in the UK and Germany. There will be some important differences from the hoki experiment. Pollock will not be marketed in big red letters as 'an excellent alternative to cod'. Indeed the name, with which English speakers may not be entirely comfortable, may not feature on the front of the packs at all, says Thomas Lingard, corporate responsibility manager at Unilever UK. Sustainability will come second to messages about taste and quality, says Mr Lingard. Market research shows that half of the small number of people in the UK who bought pollock in the past six months did so because they liked the taste – but only 12 per cent because it was not endangered. On the other hand, one in five of those who had not bought pollock did not like the look of it.

This time Unilever hopes the market research is right. Unilever aims to use its marketing strength to drive more sustainable fish consumption. 'The strong, consistent message from the powerful Birds Eye brand for the past five decades, that cod is the best eating fish, has surely contributed to consumer reliance on that fish.'[1]

Questions

1. Was Unilever's failure with hoki a case of a product poorly marketed or a product that will not sell, however marketed?
2. Although they failed with New Zealand whiptail, Unilever think they will succeed with Alaskan pollock. How has their marketing effort changed to make success more likely?
3. Is the name important to the success or failure of a new product? Would *Macruronus novaezelandiae* have more chance of success if one of its other names were used or even an invented name, as New Zealand did when it renamed China's *míhóu táo* the kiwifruit?

Introduction

As the hoki case suggests, a company must be good at developing and managing new products. It must also accept some failures, learn from them and try, try again. Every product seems to go through a life cycle – it is born, goes through several phases, and eventually dies as newer products come along that better serve consumer needs. This product life cycle presents two major challenges: first, because all products eventually decline, a firm must be good at developing new products to replace ageing ones (the challenge of *new-product development*); and second, the firm must be good at adapting its marketing strategies in the face of changing tastes, technologies and competition as products pass through life-cycle stages (the challenge of *product life-cycle strategies*). We first look at the problem of finding and developing new products and then at the problem of managing them successfully over their life cycles.

New-product development strategy

Given the rapid changes in consumer tastes, technology and competition, companies must develop a steady stream of new products and services. A firm can obtain new products in two ways. One is through *acquisition* – by buying a whole company, a patent or a licence to produce someone else's product. Many large companies have decided to acquire existing brands rather than to create new ones because of the rising costs of developing and introducing major new products. The other route to obtaining new products is through **new-product development** in the company's own research-and-development department. By new products we mean original products, product improvements, product modifications and new brands that the firm develops through its own R&D efforts. In this chapter, we focus on new-product development – how businesses create and market new products.

New-product development—The development of original products, product improvements, product modifications and new brands through the firm's own R&D efforts.

Risks and returns in new-product development

New products are important – to both customers and the marketers who serve them. Consumers like new products because they solve problems and bring variety to their lives. Companies love new products because they are a key source of growth. Yet, new-product development can be very risky. For a start, innovation is expensive. For example, pharmaceutical firms spend €400m on average to develop a new drug. A new car platform can cost nearly €750m.[2] This pales in comparison to what it costs firms like Sony to develop breakthrough consumer entertainment products – the company invested almost 200bn yen (€1.7bn) in Cell, the semiconductor for its PlayStation3.[3] And that's just the cost of developing the supercomputer-on-a-chip!

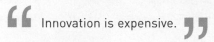
Innovation is expensive.

New-product development takes time. Although companies can dramatically shorten their development time, in many industries such as pharmaceuticals, biotechnology, aerospace and food, new-product development cycles can be as long as 10–15 years. For example, the new-product launch cycle of consumer product firms such as Gillette may be anything from two to ten years. Launch delays, and the uncertainty and unpredictability of market environments, further raise the risks of commercialisation.[4]

New products face tough odds. For example, Daimler's Smart car, which first appeared in 1998, has been consistently in the red since it was launched. By 2005, when annual losses reached €600m, the German carmaker had considered closing or selling the unit. But, in a renewed drive to bring

Smart to profitability, Daimler decided to invest a further €1bn in the division.[5] Despite a huge investment and fevered speculation that it could be even bigger than the Internet, Segway sold only 6,000 of its human transporters in the 18 months following its launch, a tiny fraction of projected sales. Segway has yet to do more than gain small footholds in niche markets, such as urban touring and police departments.[6] Other costly product failures from sophisticated companies include Omo/Persil Power (Unilever), New Coke (Coca-Cola Company), Svit 2-in-1 dry cleaning cloths (Henkel), Mars Lite (Masterfoods) and Breakfast Mates cereal-and-milk combos (Kellogg). Studies put the failure rate of new consumer goods at 90 per cent. For example, of the 30,000 new food, beverage and beauty products launched each year, an estimated 70 to 90 per cent fail within just 12 months. Moreover, failure rates for new industrial products may be as high as 30 per cent. Still another estimates new-product failures to be as high as 95 per cent.[7]

Despite the risks, firms that learn to innovate well become less vulnerable to attacks by new entrants which discover new ways of delivering added value, benefits and solutions to customers' problems.

Why do new products fail?

Why do so many new products fail? There are several reasons. Although an idea may be good, the company may overestimate market size. There just wasn't the demand for the product. For example, electronic books (e-books) promised to deliver vast amounts of reading materials in a single light-weight package – travellers did not have to haul hefty paperbacks around on vacations and business trips. Like many publishers, Random House UK made a foray into e-books at the turn of the decade. However, the product did not catch on. According to the company's interactive director, 'It wasn't for lack of thought or interest – it's just because the consumer market didn't happen.'[8]

The actual product may be poorly designed. There may be technological drawbacks. In the case of e-books, readers tend to read fiction in particular ways – curled up on a couch or sitting on a bus or train. E-books need a digital display, but readers rarely want to sit in front of a PC or carry a cumbersome laptop.

It may be a 'me too' product which is no better than products that are already established in the marketplace. Or it might be incorrectly positioned in the market, launched at the wrong

Product failures: Visiting the US New Product Showcase and Learning Center is like finding yourself in some nightmare version of a supermarket. Each product failure represents squandered dollars and hopes.

SOURCE: New Product Showcase and Learning Center. NewProductWorks.

Whatever your age,
does it have to show?

Double Serum 38

An advanced formula to combat the appearance of fine lines and wrinkles. Double Serum contains 38 key ingredients to deliver an intensive vitality boost to ageing skin. The reward is softer, smoother, firmer skin that makes you look younger and feel younger.

Extra-Firming Day Cream

Helps erase signs of fatigue and improve skin tone. This rich, instantly absorbed cream ensures maximum comfort, provides an excellent base for make-up and protects the skin from environmental harm.

Extra-Firming Night Cream

While you sleep, nourishing plant extracts moisturize and strengthen your skin. This process of renewal brings a fresher, radiant bloom to tired skin, giving you a younger-looking, more beautiful complexion.

No one understands your skin better.

Dermatologically tested, hypoallergenic, non-comedogenic.
No animal testing. Extra-Firming Day Cream
contains Clarins exclusive 'Anti-pollution' Complex.

Three ways to revitalize
and renew.

CLARINS
PARIS

Identifying market opportunities and meeting customer needs: one effect of the ageing population is the intensive effort to develop 'anti-ageing' products that stop people looking older.
SOURCE: The Advertising Archives.

time, overpriced or advertised and promoted badly. A high-level executive might push a favourite idea despite poor marketing research findings. Sometimes the costs of product development are higher than expected and sometimes competitors fight back harder than anticipated.

What influences new-product success?

Because so many new products fail, companies are anxious to learn how to improve their chances of new-product success. One way is to find out what successful new products have in common.

Several studies suggest that new-product success depends on developing a *unique superior product* that offers customers better quality, new features and higher value in use. Another key success factor is a *well-defined product concept* prior to development. The company carefully defines and assesses the target market, the product requirements and the benefits before proceeding. New products that are better than existing products at *meeting market needs* and delivering what customers really wanted invariably do well. Other success factors have also been suggested – senior management commitment, relentless commitment to innovation, smooth functioning and proficiency in executing the new-product development process.[9]

> ❝ New-product success depends on developing a unique superior product that offers customers better quality, new features and higher value in use. ❞

Successful new-product development may be an even bigger challenge in the future. New products must meet growing social and government constraints, such as consumer safety and environmental standards. The costs of finding, developing and launching new products will increase steadily due to rising manufacturing, media and distribution costs. Many companies that cannot afford the huge sums of money needed for new-product development will emphasise product modification and imitation rather than true innovation. Even when a new product is successful, rivals are so quick to copy it that the new product is destined to have only a short life.

The new-product development process

So, companies face a problem – they must develop new products, but the odds weigh heavily against success. In all, to generate successful new products, a company must understand its consumers, markets and competitors and develop products that offer superior value to customers. It must carry out strong *new-product planning* and set up a systematic *new-product development process* for finding and growing new products. Let us now take a look at the major steps in the new-product development process.

The new-product development process for finding and growing new products consists of nine main steps (see Figure 12.1).

New-product strategy

Effective product innovation is driven by a well-defined *new-product strategy*. The new-product strategy serves four purposes: first, it gives direction to the new-product team and *focuses team effort;* second, it provides a basis to *integrate* functional or departmental efforts; third, it allows tasks to be *delegated* to team members, who can be left to operate independently; and fourth, the

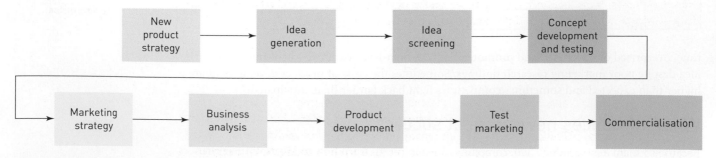

Figure 12.1 Steps in new-product development

very act of producing and getting managers to agree on a strategy requires *proactive*, not reactive, planning. A new-product strategy draws managers' attention to the reasons or *rationale* behind the firm's search for innovation opportunities, the *product/market* and *technology* to focus on, the major *goals* or *objectives* (market share, cash flow, profitability, etc.) to be achieved, and *guidelines* on the nature or level of innovativeness that will sell the new product.[10] The strategy also spells out the priority to be placed on developing really new or breakthrough products, modifying existing ones and imitating competitors' products. Given that many or most new-product ideas are likely to be unsuitable for development, senior management has to establish specific criteria for new-product idea selection. Ideas are accepted based on their ability to meet specific *strategic roles*. A new product's strategic role might be to (a) help the company maintain its industry position as an innovator, (b) defend a market-share position, (c) enter a future new market or (d) exploit the firm's special strengths or technology in a new way.

Idea generation

Idea generation – the search for new-product ideas – should be proactive and systematic rather than haphazard. A company typically has to generate many ideas in order to find a few good ones. A survey of product managers found that of 100 proposed new-product ideas, 39 begin the product development process, 17 survive the development process, eight actually reach the marketplace and only one eventually reaches its business objectives. For pharmaceuticals companies, it can take some 6,000 to 8,000 starting ideas to produce one commercial success.[11]

To obtain a flow of new-product ideas, the company can tap many sources. Major sources of new-product ideas include internal sources and external sources such as customers, competitors, distributors, suppliers and others.

> **Idea generation—The systematic search for new-product ideas.**

Internal idea sources

Using *internal sources*, the company can find new ideas through formal research and development. It can pick the brains of its executives, scientists, engineers, designers, manufacturing and salespeople. Some companies have developed successful 'intrapreneurial' programmes that encourage employees to think up and develop new product ideas. For example, 3M's well-known '15 per cent rule' allows employees to spend 15 per cent of their time 'bootlegging' – working on projects of personal interest, whether or not those projects directly benefit the company.

Samsung has even built a special centre to encourage and support new-product innovation internally – its Value Innovation Program (VIP) Centre in Suwon, South Korea. The VIP Centre is the ultimate round-the-clock idea factory in which company researchers, engineers and designers commingle to come up with new-product ideas and processes. The invitation-only centre features workrooms, dorm rooms, training rooms, a kitchen and a basement filled with games, a gym and sauna. Almost every week, the centre announces a 'world's first' or 'world's largest' innovation. Recent ideas sprouting from the VIP Centre include a 102-inch plasma HDTV and a process to reduce material costs on a multi-function printer by 30 per cent. The centre has helped Samsung, once known as the maker of cheap knock-off products, become one of the world's most innovative and profitable consumer electronics companies.[12]

External idea sources

Customers

Good new-product ideas also come from observing and listening to customers. The company can analyse customer questions and complaints to find new products that better solve consumer problems. Companies such as Philips, Sony, Toyota and many other effective innovators are known to have their design engineers talk with final consumers to get ideas for new products. Or company engineers and salespeople can meet with or work alongside customers to get suggestions and ideas.

For example, Danish toy maker LEGO did just that when it turned to its adult fans to help develop Mindstorms, a product range that lets consumers design and programme robots controlled by a 'brain' – a programmable LEGO brick. Lego created a top-secret Mindstorms User Panel involving over 100 participants for its developer programme.[13] LEGO also displayed a customer-centred approach to new product development when it invited 250 LEGO train-set enthusiasts to visit its New York office to assess new designs. 'We pooh-poohed them all,' said one LEGO fan, an Intel engineer from Portland. But the group gave LEGO lots of new ideas, and the company put them to good use. 'We literally produced what they told us to produce,' says a LEGO executive. The result was the 'Santa Fe Super Chief' set. Thanks to 'word-of-mouse' endorsements from the 250 enthusiasts, LEGO sold out the first 10,000 units in less than two weeks with no additional marketing.[14]

Customers often create new products and uses on their own, and companies can benefit by putting them on the market. For example, for years customers were spreading the word that Avon Skin-So-Soft bath oil and moisturiser was also a terrific bug repellent. Whereas some consumers were content simply to bathe in water scented with the fragrant oil, others carried it in their backpacks to mosquito-infested campsites or kept a bottle on the decks of their beach houses. Avon turned the idea into a complete line of Skin-So-Soft Bug Guard products, including Bug Guard Mosquito Repellant Moisturising Towelettes and Bug Guard Plus, a combination moisturiser, insect repellent and sunscreen.[15]

Finally, some companies even give customers the tools and resources to design their own products. Notes one expert, 'Not only is the customer king, now he is market-research head, R&D chief, and product-development manager, too.'[16] For example:

Computer games maker Electronic Arts (EA) noticed that its customers were making new content for existing games and posting it online for others to use freely. It began shipping basic game-development tools with its games, and feeding customer innovations to its designers to use in creating new games. 'The fan community has had a tremendous influence on game design,' says an EA executive, 'and the games are better as a result.'[16]

Companies must be careful not to rely too heavily on customer input when developing new products. For some products, especially highly technical ones, customers may not know what they need. Also, customers want to be surprised; they want to be delighted, to be offered something that's better than they expected or imagined could be possible – like iPods, smart phones and Tom-Tom satellite navigators. Also, customers may not always know their *future* needs and wants. If a telecommunications operator like BT had asked customers 30 years ago what new telephone service they wanted, they would not have thought of fixed-line broadband service. Similarly, if Philips Electronics had questioned consumers 40 years ago about what new audio technology they wanted, they would never have described anything like an MP3 – the idea would not have occurred to them.

This is one of the reasons why Nokia employs a team of people around the world whose job is to think 10 years ahead and dream up ideas. They have to anticipate future needs before the consumer has even become aware of them. They must also predict the innovations of their rivals, so that the company can be one step ahead. Every so often, the ideas team hold focus groups for ordinary users and ask them what they want from their phones when they are on the move. The users are offered a handful of new ideas and their reactions are videoed. The team always pay attention to the quirky suggestions because there is often a lot of truth in them. The company also consults anthropologists to help unravel consumers' reactions, and these generate leads which give the team something to build on. It was anticipating needs before they exist that brought about Nokia's revolutionary 9000 Communicator, which was, at the time, the world's first all-in-one mobile communications device – a fax, phone, digital diary, calculator and palm-top computer all rolled into one.[17]

Competitors

Beyond customers, companies can tap other external sources. For example, competitors can be a good source of new-product ideas. Companies watch competitors' ads and other communications such as new-product pre-announcements, to get clues about their new products. They can research competing competitors' products and services. For example, they can find out what customers like and dislike about competitors' products. Or they can buy competitors' new products, take them apart to see how they work, analyse their sales, and decide whether they should bring out a new product of their own.

Distributors, suppliers and others

Distributors and suppliers can also contribute many good new-product ideas. Distributors are close to the market and can pass along information about consumer problems and new-product possibilities. Suppliers can tell the company about new concepts, techniques and materials that can be used to develop new products. Other idea sources include trade magazines, shows and seminars, government agencies, new-product consultants, design firms, advertising agencies, marketing research firms, university and commercial laboratories, science parks and inventors.

Idea screening

The purpose of idea generation is to create a large number of ideas. The purpose of the succeeding stages is to *reduce* that number. The first idea-reducing stage is **idea screening** which helps spot good ideas and drop poor ones as soon as possible. Product development costs rise greatly in later stages, so the company should go ahead only with those product ideas that will turn into profitable products.

> " Many companies have well-designed systems for rating and screening new-product ideas.

Most companies require their executives to write up new-product ideas on a standard form that can be reviewed by a new-product committee. The write-up describes the product, the target market and the competition. It makes some rough estimates of market size, product price, development time and costs, manufacturing costs and rate of return. The committee then evaluates the idea against a set of general criteria. For example, at Kao Corporation, the large Japanese consumer-products company, the new-product committee asks questions such as these: Is the product truly useful to consumers and society? Is this product good for our particular company? Does it mesh well with the company's objectives and strategies? Do we have the people, skills and resources to make it succeed? Does it deliver more value to customers than competing products? Is it easy to advertise and distribute? Many companies have well-designed systems for rating and screening new-product ideas.

Concept development and testing

An attractive idea must be developed into product concepts. It is important to distinguish between a *product idea*, a *product concept* and a *product image*. A **product idea** is an idea for a possible product that the company can see itself offering to the market. A **product concept** is a detailed version of the idea stated in meaningful consumer terms. A **product image** is the way consumers perceive an actual or potential product.

Idea screening
Screening new-product ideas in order to spot good ideas and drop poor ones as soon as possible.

Product idea—An idea for a possible product that the company can see itself offering to the market.

Product concept—A detailed version of the new-product idea stated in meaningful consumer terms.

Product image—The way consumers perceive an actual or potential product.

Concept development

After more than a decade of development, Daimler begins to commercialise its experimental fuel-cell-powered electric car. This car's low-polluting fuel-cell system runs directly on hydrogen, which powers the fuel-cell with only water as a by-product. It is highly fuel efficient and gives the new car an environmental advantage over today's super-efficient petrol – electric hybrid cars.

Daimler released over 100 'F-Cell' cars around the world so that they could be tested under varying weather conditions, traffic situations and driving styles. Based on the tiny Mercedes A-class, the car accelerates quickly, reaches speeds of 90 miles per hour, and has a 280-mile driving range, giving it a huge edge over battery-powered electric cars which travel only about 80 miles before needing 3–12 hours of recharging.[18]

Daimler's next task is to develop this new product into alternative product concepts, find out how attractive each concept is to customers and choose the best one. For example, the following product concepts for the fuel-cell electric car might be created:

● *Concept 1.* A moderately priced subcompact designed as a second family car to be used around town. The car is ideal for running errands and visiting friends.

● *Concept 2.* A medium-cost sporty compact appealing to young people.

● *Concept 3.* An inexpensive subcompact 'green' car appealing to environmentally conscious people who want practical, low-polluting transportation.

● *Concept 4.* A high-end sport-utility vehicle (SUV) appealing to those who love the space SUVs provide but lament the poor petrol mileage.

Concept testing

Concept testing—Testing new-product concepts with a group of target consumers to find out whether the concepts have strong consumer appeal.

Concept testing calls for testing new-product concepts with a group of target consumers. The concepts may be presented to consumers symbolically or physically. Here, in words, is *Concept 3*:

An efficient, fun-to-drive, fuel-cell-powered electric subcompact car that seats four. This methanol-powered high-tech wonder provides practical and reliable transportation with virtually no pollution. It goes up to 85 miles per hour and, unlike battery-powered electric cars, it never needs recharging. It's priced, fully equipped, at €25,000.

Mercedes-Benz already has the largest fleet of fuel cell vehicles worldwide. In the summer of 2010, Mercedes-Benz will launch the first series-production car with a local zero-emission fuel-cell drive in the guise of the B-Class Fuel Cell.
SOURCE: Daimler AG.

1. Do you understand the concept of a fuel-cell-powered electric car?
2. Do you believe the claims about the car's performance?
3. What are the main benefits of the fuel-cell-powered electric car compared with a conventional car?
4. What are its advantages compared with a battery-powered electric car?
5. What improvements in the car's features would you suggest?
6. For what uses would you prefer a fuel-cell-powered electric car to a conventional car?
7. What would be a reasonable price to charge for the car?
8. Who would be involved in your decision to buy such a car? Who would drive it?
9. Would you buy such a car? (Definitely, probably, probably not, definitely not)

Table 12.1 Questions for fuel-cell-powered electric car concept test

For some concept tests, a word or picture description might be sufficient. However, a more concrete and physical presentation of the concept will increase the reliability of the concept test. After being exposed to the concept, consumers then may be asked to react to it by answering questions such as those in Table 12.1.

The answers will help the company decide which concept has the strongest appeal. For example, the last question asks about the consumer's intention to buy. Suppose 10 per cent of the consumers said they 'definitely' would buy and another 5 per cent said 'probably'. The company could project these figures to the full population size in this target group to estimate sales volume. Even then, the estimate is uncertain, largely because consumers do not always carry out stated intentions. Potential customers may like the idea of the new product, but may not be prepared to pay for one! It is still important to carry out product concept tests in order to assess customers' response and to identify aspects of the concept that potential buyers particularly liked or disliked. Feedback might suggest ways to refine the concept, thereby increasing its appeal to customers.

Marketing strategy development

Suppose Daimler found that Concept 3 for the fuel-cell-powered electric car tests best. The next step is to develop a **marketing strategy development**, designing an initial marketing strategy for introducing this car to the market.

The **marketing strategy statement** consists of three parts. The first part describes the target market, the planned product positioning, and the sales, market share and profit goals for the first few years. Thus:

> The target market is younger, well-educated, moderate-to-high income individuals, couples or small families seeking practical, environmentally responsible transportation. The car will be positioned as more fun to drive and less polluting than today's internal combustion engine cars or hybrid cars. It is also less restricting than battery-powered electric cars which must be recharged regularly. The company will aim to sell 100,000 cars in the first year, at a loss of not more than €15m. In the second year, the company will aim for sales of 120,000 cars and a profit of €25m.

The second part of the marketing strategy statement outlines the product's planned price, distribution and marketing budget for the first year.

Marketing strategy development—Designing an initial marketing strategy for a new product based on the product concept.

Marketing strategy statement—A statement of the planned strategy for a new product that outlines the intended target market, the planned product positioning, and the sales, market share and profit goals for the first few years.

The fuel-cell-powered electric car will be offered in three colours and will have optional air-conditioning and power-drive features. It will sell at a retail price of €20,000 – with 15 per cent off the list price to dealers. Dealers who sell more than 10 cars per month will get an additional discount of 5 per cent on each car sold that month. An advertising budget of €20m will be split 50–50 between national and local advertising. Advertising will emphasise the car's fun spirit and low emissions. During the first year, €100,000 will be spent on marketing research to find out who is buying the car and to determine their satisfaction levels.

The third part of the marketing strategy statement describes the planned long-run sales, profit goals and marketing mix strategy:

The company intends to capture a 3 per cent long-run share of the total car market and realise an after-tax return on investment of 15 per cent. To achieve this, product quality will start high and be improved over time. Price will be raised in the second and third years if competition permits. The total advertising budget will be raised each year by about 10 per cent. Marketing research will be reduced to €60,000 per year after the first year.

Business analysis

Business analysis—A review of the sales, costs and profit projections for a new product to find out whether these factors satisfy the company's objectives.

Once management has decided on its product concept and marketing strategy, it can evaluate the business attractiveness of the proposal. **Business analysis** involves a review of the sales, costs and profit projections for a new product to find out whether they satisfy the company's objectives. If they do, the product proceeds to the product development stage.

To estimate sales, the company looks at the sales history of similar products and conducts surveys of market opinion. It then estimates minimum and maximum sales to assess the range of risk. After preparing the sales forecast, management can estimate the expected costs and profits for the product, including marketing, R&D, manufacturing, accounting and finance costs. The company then uses the sales and costs figures to analyse the new product's financial attractiveness.

Product development

Product development— Developing the product concept into a physical product in order to ensure that the product idea can be turned into a workable product.

So far, for many new-product concepts, the product may have existed only as a word description, a drawing or perhaps a crude mock-up. If the product concept passes the business test, it moves into **product development**. Here, R&D or engineering develops the product concept into a physical product. The product development step, however, now calls for a large jump in investment. It will show whether the product idea can be turned into a workable product.

The R&D department will develop one or more physical versions of the product concept. R&D hopes to design a prototype that functions, is able to satisfy and excite consumers and can be produced quickly and at budgeted costs. Developing a successful prototype can take days, weeks, months or even years.

Often, products undergo rigorous tests to make sure that consumers will find value in them or that they perform safely and effectively.[19]

Behind a locked door in the basement of Louis Vuitton's elegant Paris headquarters, a mechanical arm hoists a brown-and-tan handbag a half-metre off the floor – then drops it. The bag, loaded with a 4-kg weight, will be lifted and dropped, over and over again, for four days. This is Vuitton's test laboratory, a high-tech torture chamber for its fabled luxury goods. Another piece of lab equipment bombards handbags with ultraviolet rays to test resistance to fading. Still another tests zippers by tugging them open and shutting them 5,000 times. There's even a mechanised mannequin hand, with a Vuitton charm bracelet around its wrist, being shaken vigorously to make sure none of the charms fall off.

A new product must have the required functional features and also convey the intended psychological characteristics. The fuel-cell-powered electric car, for example, should strike consumers as being well built, comfortable and safe. Management must learn what makes consumers decide that a car is well built. To some consumers, this means that the car has 'solid-sounding' doors. To others, it means that the car is able to withstand heavy impact in crash tests. Consumer tests are conducted, in which consumers test-drive the car and rate its attributes. For some products, prototyping and product development may involve both the key intermediaries that supply the product or service and the final consumer or end-user.

When designing products, the company should look beyond simply creating products that satisfy consumer needs and wants. Too often, companies design their new products without enough concern for how the designs will be produced. Companies may minimise production problems by adopting an approach towards product development called *design for manufacturability and assembly* (DFMA). Using this approach, companies work to fashion products that are *both satisfying and easy to manufacture*. This often results not only in lower costs but also in higher-quality and more reliable products.

> Look beyond simply creating products that satisfy consumer needs and wants . . . Companies work to fashion products that are *both* satisfying *and* easy to manufacture.

Test marketing

If the product passes functional and consumer tests, the next step is **test marketing**, the stage at which the product and marketing programme are introduced into more realistic market settings.

Test marketing gives the marketer experience with marketing the product before going to the great expense of full introduction. It lets the company test the product and its entire marketing programme – positioning strategy, advertising, distribution, pricing, branding and packaging and budget levels. The company also learns how consumers and dealers react to the product. The results can be used to make better sales and profit forecasts. Thus a good test market can provide a wealth of information about the potential success of the product and marketing programme.

The amount of test marketing needed varies with each new product. Test marketing costs can be high, and it takes time that may allow competitors to gain advantages. When the costs of developing and introducing the product are low or when management is already confident about the new product, the company may do little or no test marketing. In fact, test marketing by consumer-goods firms has been declining in recent years. Companies often do not test-market simple line extensions or copies of successful competitor products.

However, when introducing a new product requires a big investment, or when management is unsure of the product or marketing programme, the company may do a lot of test marketing.

Test marketing—The stage of new-product development where the product and marketing programme are tested in more realistic market settings.

Although test marketing costs can be high, they are often small when compared to the costs of making a major mistake. Still, test marketing doesn't guarantee success. For example, Procter & Gamble tested its Fit produce rinse heavily for five years. Although market tests suggested the product would be successful, P&G pulled the plug on it shortly after its introduction.[20]

When using test marketing, consumer-products companies usually choose one of three approaches – standard test markets, controlled test markets or simulated test markets.

Standard test markets

Using standard test markets, the company finds a small number of representative test cities, conducts a full marketing campaign in these cities and uses store audits, consumer and distributor surveys and other measures to gauge product performance. These results are used to forecast national sales and profits, to discover potential product problems and to fine-tune the marketing programme.

Standard market tests have some drawbacks. They can be very costly and may take a long time – some last as long as three to five years. Moreover, competitors can monitor test-market results or even interfere with them by cutting their prices in test locations, increasing their promotion or even buying up the product being tested. Finally, test markets give competitors a look at the company's new product well before it is introduced nationally. Thus, competitors may have time to develop defensive strategies and may even beat the company's product to the market.

Despite these disadvantages, standard test markets are still widely used for major market testing. However, many companies today are shifting towards quicker and cheaper controlled and simulated test marketing methods.

Controlled test markets

Several research firms keep controlled panels of stores which have agreed to carry new products for a fee. Controlled test-marketing systems such as ACNielsen's Scantrack[21] and Information Resources Inc.'s (IRI) BehaviorScan track individual behaviour from the television set to the checkout counter.

In each BehaviorScan market, IRI maintains a panel of shoppers who report all of their purchases by showing an identification card at checkout in participating stores and by using a handheld scanner at home to record purchases at non-participating stores.[22] Within test stores, IRI controls such factors as shelf placement, price and in-store promotions. IRI also measures TV viewing in each panel household and sends special commercials to panel members' television sets. Direct mail promotions can also be tested.

Controlled Test Markets: IRI's BehaviorScan system tracks individual consumer behaviour for new products from the television set to the checkout counter.

SOURCE: Peter Cade/Stone/Getty Images (left). Steve Krongard/Stone/Getty Images (right).

Detailed electronic scanner information on each consumer's purchases is fed into a central computer, where it is combined with the consumer's demographic and TV viewing information and reported daily. Thus, BehaviorScan can provide store-by-store, week-by-week reports on the sales of new products being tested. Such panel purchasing data enables in-depth diagnostics not possible with retail point-of-sale data alone, including repeat purchase analysis, buyer demographics, and earlier, more accurate sales forecasts after just 12 to 24 weeks in market. Most importantly, the system allows companies to evaluate their specific marketing efforts.

Controlled test markets usually cost less than standard test markets. Also, because retail distribution is 'forced' in the first week of the test, controlled test markets can be completed much more quickly than standard test markets. As in standard test markets, controlled test markets allow competitors to get a look at the company's new product. And some companies are concerned that the limited number of controlled test markets used by the research services may not be representative of their products' markets or target consumers. However, the research firms are experienced in projecting test market results to broader markets and can usually account for biases in the test markets used.

Simulated test markets

Companies also can test new products in a simulated shopping environment. The company or research firm shows ads and promotions for a variety of products, including the new product being tested, to a sample of consumers. It gives consumers a small amount of money and invites them to a real or laboratory store, where they may keep the money or use it to buy items. The researchers note how many consumers buy the new product and competing brands.

This simulation gives a measure of trial and the commercial's effectiveness against competing commercials. The researchers then ask consumers the reasons for their purchase or non-purchase. Some weeks later, they interview the consumer by phone to determine product attitudes, usage, satisfaction and repurchase intentions. Using sophisticated computer models, the researchers then project national sales from results of the simulated test market. Recently, some marketers have begun to use interesting new high-tech approaches to simulated test market research, such as virtual reality and the Internet.

Simulated test markets overcome some of the disadvantages of standard and controlled test markets. They usually cost much less, can be run in eight weeks and keep the new product out of competitors' view. Yet, because of their small samples and simulated shopping environments, many marketers do not think that simulated test markets are as accurate or reliable as larger, real-world tests.

Still, simulated test markets are used widely, often as 'pre-test' markets. Because they are fast and inexpensive, they can be run to assess quickly a new product or its marketing programme. If the pre-test results are strongly positive, the product might be introduced without further testing. If the results are very poor, the product might be dropped or substantially redesigned and retested. If the results are promising but indefinite, the product and marketing programme can be tested further in controlled or standard test markets.

Test marketing new business-to-business or industrial products

Business marketers use different methods for test marketing their new products, such as product-use tests, trade shows, distributor/dealer display rooms, and standard or controlled test markets.

Product-use tests

Here the business marketer selects a small group of potential customers who agree to use the new product for a limited time. The manufacturer's technical people watch how these customers use the product and learns about customer training and servicing requirements. After the test, the marketer asks the customer about purchase intent and other reactions.

Trade shows

These shows draw a large number of buyers who view new products in a few concentrated days. The manufacturer sees how buyers react to various product features and terms, and assess buyer interest and purchase intentions.

Distributor and dealer display rooms

The new industrial product may be placed next to other company products and possibly competitors' products in the showrooms. This method yields preference and pricing information in the normal selling atmosphere of the product.

Standard or controlled test markets

The company may produce a limited supply of the product which is sold to customers in a limited number of geographical areas. The new product is given full advertising, sales promotion and other marketing support. Such test markets enable the company to test the product and its marketing programme in real market situations.

Commercialisation

Commercialisation—Introducing a new product into the market.

Test marketing gives management the information needed to make a final decision about whether to launch the new product. If the company goes ahead with **commercialisation** – that is, introducing the new product into the market – it will face high costs. The company may have to build or rent a manufacturing facility. It must gear up production to meet demand, as failure to do so can leave an opening in the market for competitors to step in. In the case of a major new consumer packaged good, it may have to spend hundreds of millions of euros on advertising, sales promotion and other marketing efforts in the first year. For example, when Procter & Gamble introduced its new Fusion six-blade razor, it spent an eye-popping $1bn (€750m) on global marketing support.[23]

The company launching a new product must make four decisions.

When?

First, it must decide on introduction timing – whether the time is right to introduce the new product. If it cannibalises the sales of the company's other products, its introduction may be delayed. If the new product can be improved further, or if the economy is down, the company may wait until the time is ripe to launch it. Still another reason to delay new product launch is to minimise teething problems.

O_2, part of Spain's Telefónica group, delayed the launch of its fixed line broadband service in the UK by 6 months in order to avoid the problems many of its competitors had to endure. According to O_2 chief executive Peter Erskine, rival Warehouse Carphone angered thousands of broadband customers who were either not connected promptly or cut off completely as they switched onto Carphone's telecommunications network. In a fiercely competitive market, already dominated by early entrants including British Sky Broadcasting, BT, Virgin Media and Carphone, O_2 had to ensure it was in a position to effectively roll out more of its network, as it geared up for the launch and to avoid any teething problems.[24]

Where?

The company must decide where to launch the new product – in a single location, a region, several regions, the national market or the international market? Few companies have the confidence, capital and capacity to launch new products into full national or international distribution. They will develop a planned *market rollout* over time. In particular, small companies may enter attractive cities or regions one at a time. Larger companies may quickly introduce new products into several regions or into the entire national market.

Companies such as Apple, Nokia, Unilever, P&G and Philips with international distribution systems may introduce new products through global rollouts. Apple's iPhone first went on sale in America in June 2007, followed by the European launch in the autumn, and Asian roll-out in 2008.[25] In a swift and successful global assault – its fastest global rollout ever – P&G quickly introduced its SpinBrush low-priced, battery-powered toothbrush into 35 countries. Such rapid worldwide expansion overwhelmed rival Colgate's Actibrush brand. Within a year of its introduction, SpinBrush was outselling Actibrush by a margin of two to one.[26]

To whom?

Within the rollout markets, the company must target its distribution and promotion to customer groups who represent the best prospects. These prime prospects have been identified by the firm in earlier research and test marketing. For instance, Vertu, Nokia's 'retro-modern' mobile phone, with a sapphire face and a body available in platinum, white gold or stainless steel and sold at an astonishing €20,000, was targeted at movie stars and the super-rich kids. Generally, firms must fine-tune their targeting efforts, starting with the innovators, then looking especially for early adopters, heavy users and opinion leaders. Opinion leaders are particularly important as their endorsement of the new product has a powerful impact upon adoption by other buyers in the marketplace.

How?

The company must also develop an *action plan* for introducing the new product into the selected markets. It must spend the marketing budget on the marketing mix and various other activities.

For example, when Siemens launched its new fashion mobile phone brand, Xelibri, the main thrust of its marketing strategy was to establish credibility as a fashion brand. Xelibri hosted the opening party of the London Fashion Week to which celebrities and opinion-leading editors and journalists of the fashion press were invited to celebrate 'Xelibri's birthday party'. This, together with other selected fashion events and a comprehensive PR campaign, drew huge media attention, including the support of fashion industry influencers, while creating high brand and product awareness among fashion-savvy people globally. David LaChapelle, the celebrated fashion photographer, was assigned to create pictures to emphasise Xelibri's fashionable, provocative image, consistent with its intended brand identity. Advertising was used to sustain the high brand awareness already created by the other communication tools; TV and cinema ads reinforced Xelibri's fashion statement. Being positioned as a fashion accessory, upmarket department stores like Selfridges in the UK and Peek & Cloppenburg in Germany, that did not sell mobile phones before, were used as the primary distribution channel for this new phone line. To broaden the product's reach, traditional mobile phone retail outlets were used, but worked to specially agreed point-of-sale arrangements to support Xelibri's fashion positioning.[27]

Managing new-product development

The new-product development process shown in Figure 12.1 highlights the important activities needed to find, develop and introduce new products. However, new-product development involves more than just going through a set of steps. Companies must take a holistic approach to managing this process. Successful new-product development requires a customer-centred, team-based and systematic effort.

Customer-centred new-product development

Customer-centred new-product development— New-product development that focuses on finding new ways to solve customer problems and create more customer-satisfying experiences.

Above all else, new-product development must be customer centred. When looking for and developing new products, companies often rely too heavily on technical research in their R&D labs. But like everything else in marketing, successful new-product development begins with a thorough understanding of what consumers need and value. **Customer-centred new-product development** focuses on finding new ways to solve customer problems and create more customer-satisfying experiences.

One recent study found that the most successful new products are ones that are differentiated, solve major customer problems, and offer a compelling customer value proposition.[28] Thus, for products ranging from bathroom cleaners to jet engines, today's innovative companies are getting out of the research lab and mingling with customers in the search for new customer value. Consider the following:[29]

Although P&G is famous for its attention to data collection and market research, Jim Stengel, global marketing officer of Procter & Gamble, is a firm believer in the importance of observation. He insists his marketers should have a wider view; that they should get out of their offices and into the streets and the stores – to see things for themselves. Thus, people at all levels of P&G look for fresh ideas by tagging along with and talking to customers as they shop for and use the company's products. When one P&G team tackled the problem of *reinventing bathroom cleaning*, it started by *listening with its eyes*. The group spent many hours watching consumers clean their bathrooms. They focused on 'extreme users', ranging from a professional house cleaner who scrubbed grout with his fingernail to four single guys whose idea of cleaning the bathroom was pushing a filthy towel around the floor with a big stick. If they could make both users happy, they figured they had a home run. One big idea – a cleaning tool on a removable stick that could both reach shower walls and get into crannies – got the green light quickly. Consumers loved the prototype, patched together with repurposed plastic, foam and duct tape. Some refused to return it. The idea became P&G's highly successful Mr. Clean Magic Reach bathroom cleaning tool.

As Stengel said, 'We often find consumers can't articulate [what they want]. That's why we need to have a culture of understanding. There can't be detachment. You can't just live away from the consumer and the brand and hope to gain insights from data and reading . . . . You have to be experiential. And some of our best ideas are coming from people getting out there and experiencing and listening.'

Thus, customer-centred new-product development begins and ends with solving customer problems. As one expert asks: 'What is innovation after all, if not products and services that offer fresh thinking in a way that meets the needs of customers?'[30]

Team-based new-product development

Good new-product development also requires a total-company, cross-functional effort. Some companies organise their new-product development process into the orderly sequence of steps shown in Figure 12.1, starting with idea generation and ending with commercialisation. Under this *sequential product development* approach, one company department works individually to complete its stage of the process before passing the new product along to the next department and stage. This orderly, step-by-step process can help bring control to complex and risky projects. But it also can be dangerously slow. In fast-changing, highly competitive markets, such slow-but-sure product development can result in product failures, lost sales and profits, and crumbling market positions.

In order to get their new products to market more quickly, many companies use a **team-based new-product development** approach. Under this approach, company departments work closely together in cross-functional teams, overlapping the steps in the product development process to save time and increase effectiveness. Instead of passing the new product from department to department, the company assembles a team of people from various departments that stays with the new product from start to finish. Such teams usually include people from the marketing, finance, design, manufacturing and legal departments, and even supplier and customer companies. In the sequential process, a bottleneck at one phase can seriously slow the entire project. In the simultaneous approach, if one functional area hits snags, it works to resolve them while the team moves on.

The team-based approach does have some limitations. For example, it sometimes creates more organisational tension and confusion than the more orderly sequential approach. However, in rapidly changing industries facing increasingly shorter product life cycles, the rewards of fast and flexible product development far exceed the risks. Companies that combine both a customer-centred approach with team-based new-product development gain a big competitive edge by getting the right new products to market faster (see Real Marketing 12.1)

Team-based new-product development—An approach to developing new products in which various company departments work closely together, overlapping the steps in the product development process to save time and increase effectiveness.

Systematic new-product development

Finally, the new-product development process should be holistic and systematic rather than haphazard. Otherwise, few new ideas will surface, and many good ideas will sputter and die. To avoid these problems, a company can install an *innovation management system* to collect, review, evaluate and manage new-product ideas.

The company can appoint a respected senior person to be the company's innovation manager. It can set up Web-based idea management software and encourage all company stakeholders – employees, suppliers, distributors, dealers – to become involved in finding and developing new products. It can assign a cross-functional innovation management committee to evaluate proposed new-product ideas and help bring good ideas to market. It can create recognition programmes to reward those who contribute the best ideas.[31]

The innovation management system approach yields two favourable outcomes. First, it helps create an innovation-oriented company culture. It shows that top management supports, encourages and rewards innovation. Second, it will yield a larger number of new-product ideas, among which will be found some especially good ones. The good new ideas will be more systematically developed, producing more new-product successes. No longer will good ideas wither for the lack of a sounding board or a senior product advocate.

Thus, new-product success requires more than simply thinking up a few good ideas, turning them into products and finding customers for them. It requires a holistic approach for finding new ways to create valued customer experiences, from generating and screening new-product ideas to creating and rolling out want-satisfying products to customers.

12.1 real marketing

Electrolux: cleaning up with customer-centred, team-based new-product development

You will never meet Catherine, Anna, Maria or Monica. But the future success of Swedish home appliances maker Electrolux depends on what these four women think. Catherine, for instance, a type A career woman who is a perfectionist at home, loves the idea of simply sliding her laundry basket into a washing machine, instead of having to lift the clothes from the basket and into the washer. That product idea has been moved onto the fast-track for consideration.

So, just who are Catherine and the other women? Well, they don't actually exist. They are composites based on in-depth interviews with some 160,000 consumers from around the globe. To divine the needs of these mythical customers, 53 Electrolux employees – in teams that included designers, engineers and marketers hailing from various divisions – gathered in Stockholm one winter for a week-long brainstorming session. The Catherine team began by ripping photographs out of a pile of magazines and sticking them onto poster boards. Next to a picture of a woman wearing a sharply tailored suit, they scribbled some of Catherine's attributes: driven, busy and a bit overwhelmed.

With the help of these characters, Electrolux product developers search for the insights they need to dream up the next batch of hot products. It's a new way of doing

Customer-centered new-product development: Electrolux's new-product team starts by watching and talking with consumers to understand their problems. Here, they build a bulletin board packed with pictures and Post-its detailing consumers struggling with household cleaning chores and possible product solutions. Then the team moves to the lab to create products that solve customer problems. 'We were thinking of you when we developed this product,' says Electrolux.

SOURCE: AB Electrolux.

things for Electrolux, but then again, a lot is new at the company. When Chief Executive Hans Straberg took the helm in 2002, Electrolux – which sells products under the Electrolux, Eureka and Frigidaire brands – was the world's number-two home appliances maker behind Whirlpool. The company faced spiralling costs while its middle-market products were gradually losing out to cheaper goods from Asia and Eastern Europe. Competition in the United States, where Electrolux gets 40 per cent of its sales, was ferocious. The company's stock was treading water.

Straberg had to do something radical, especially in the area of new-product innovation. So he began breaking down barriers between departments and forcing his designers, engineers and marketers to work together to come up with new products. He also introduced an intense focus on the customer. He set out to become 'the leader in our industry in terms of systematic development of new products based on consumer insight.'

At the Stockholm brainstorming session, for example, group leader Kim Scott urges everyone 'to think of yourselves as Catherine.' The room buzzes with discussion. Ideas are refined, sketches drawn up. The group settles on three concepts: *Breeze*, a clothes steamer that also removes stains; an *Ironing Centre*, similar to a trouser-press but for shirts; and *Ease*, the washing machine that holds a laundry basket inside its drum.

Half the group races off to the machine shop to turn out a prototype for *Breeze*, while the rest stay upstairs to bang out a marketing plan. Over the next hour, designer Lennart Johansson carves and sandpapers a block of peach-coloured polyurethane until a contraption that resembles a cross between an electric screwdriver and a handheld vacuum begins to emerge. The designers in the group want the *Breeze* to be smaller, but engineer Giuseppe Frucco points out that would leave too little space for a charging station for the 1,500-watt unit.

For company veterans such as Frucco, who works at Electrolux's fabric care research and development centre in Porcia, Italy, this dynamic groupthink is a refreshing change: 'We never used to create new products together,' he says. 'The designers would come up with something and then tell us to build it.' The new way saves time and money by avoiding the technical glitches that crop up as a new design moves from the drafting table to the factory floor. The ultimate goal is to come up with new products that consumers will gladly pay a premium for: gadgets with drop-dead good looks and clever features that ordinary people can understand without having to pore through a thick users' manual. 'Consumers are prepared to pay for good design and good performance,' says CEO Straberg.

Few companies have pulled off the range of hot new offerings that Electrolux has. One clear hit is a cordless stick and hand vacuum. Available in an array of metallic hues with a rounded, ergonomic design, this is the Cinderella of vacuums. Too

...12.1

attractive to be locked up in the broom cupboard, it calls out to be displayed in your kitchen. In fewer than two years on the market, it commanded 50 per cent of the European market for stick vacs.

Electrolux is crafting such new products even while moving away from many traditional customer research tools. The company relies less heavily on focus groups and now prefers to interview people in their homes where they can be videotaped pushing a vacuum or shoving laundry into the washer. 'Consumers think they know what they want, but they often have trouble articulating it,' says Electrolux's senior vice-president for global design. 'But when we watch them, we can ask, "Why do you do that?" We can change the product and solve their problems.'

This customer-centred, team-based new-product development approach is producing results. Under the new approach, new-product launches have almost doubled in quantity, and the proportion of new-product launches that exceed anticipated unit sales is now running at 50 per cent of all introductions, up from around 25 per cent previously. As a result, Electrolux's sales, profits and share price are all up sharply.

It all boils down to understanding consumers and giving them what they need and want. According to a recent Electrolux annual report:

'Thinking of you' sums up our product offering. That is how we create value for our customers – and thereby for our shareholders. All product development and marketing starts with understanding consumer needs, expectations, dreams and motivation. That's why we contact tens of thousands of consumers throughout the world every year . . . . The first steps in product development are to ask questions, observe, discuss and analyse. So we can actually say, 'We were thinking of you when we developed this product.'

Thanks to such thinking, Electrolux has now grown to become the world's biggest household appliances company. Catherine and the other women would be pleased.

SOURCES: Adapted from Ariene Sains and Stanley Reed, 'Electrolux cleans up', *BusinessWeek* (27 February 2006), pp. 42–3; with quotes and extracts adapted from 'Products developed on the basis of consumer insight', *Acceleration . . . Electrolux Annual Report* (7 April 2006), p. 7; accessed at www.electrolux.com/node60.aspx. Additional information from Caroline Perry, 'Electrolux doubles spend with new strategy', *Marketing Week* (16 February 2006), pp. 7–9.

More than this, successful new-product development requires a whole-company commitment. As the examples of P&G and Electrolux show, in these and other companies which are among the world's most innovative – such as Apple, Google, Toyota Motor, General Electric, 3M and IKEA – the entire culture encourages, supports and rewards innovation.[32]

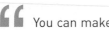

A recent *BusinessWeek* – Boston Consulting Group (BCG) annual survey of the world's most innovative companies places Apple in number one position, followed by Google, Toyota Motors, GE, Microsoft, P&G, 3M, Walt Disney, IBM and Sony. European businesses featured in the top 50 include Nokia, BMW, Virgin Group, IKEA, Daimler, BP, Royal Philips Electronics and Volkswagen. According to the report, the leaders of these companies recognise that developing breakthrough products, introducing new operational processes and implementing new business models do not happen overnight. They do not rely on quick fixes and incremental line extensions. Instead, they work hard to create an entrepreneurial culture that fosters innovation. And they build organisations capable of sustaining innovation. To do this requires investing for the long term and taking risks. But importantly, they focus on what really matters – hiring the most talented employees and providing the environment they need to thrive. As Arthur Levinson, CEO of Genentech, Inc., the world's leading biotechnology company, says, 'You can make it really complicated or really simple.'[33]

“ You can make it really complicated or really simple. **”**

We have looked at the problem of finding and developing new products. We will now examine the problem of managing them over their life cycle.

Product life-cycle strategies

After launching the new product, the management challenge lies in making sure that the product enjoys a long and healthy life. The new product is not expected to sell for ever, but the company will want to earn a decent profit to cover all the effort and risk that went into launching it. Management is aware that each product will have a life cycle, although the exact shape and length is not known in advance.

Figure 12.2 shows a typical **product life cycle (PLC)**, the course that a product's sales and profits take over its lifetime. The product life cycle has five distinct stages:

1. *Product development* begins when the company finds and develops a new-product idea. During product development, sales are zero and the company's investment costs mount.
2. *Introduction* is a period of slow sales growth as the product is being introduced in the market. Profits are non-existent in this stage because of the heavy expenses of product introduction.

Product life cycle (PLC)— The course of a product's sales and profits over its lifetime. It involves five distinct stages: product development, introduction, growth, maturity and decline.

Figure 12.2 Sales and profits over the product's life from inception to demise

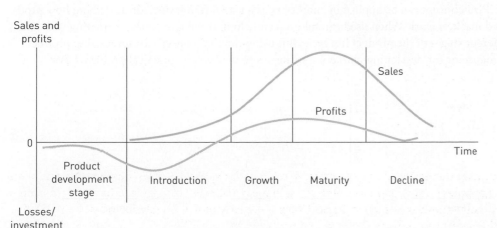

3. *Growth* is a period of rapid market acceptance and increasing profits.

4. *Maturity* is a period of slowdown in sales growth because the product has achieved acceptance by most potential buyers. Profits level off or decline because of increased marketing outlays to defend the product against competition.

5. *Decline* is the period when sales fall off and profits drop.

Not all products follow the product life cycle. Some products are introduced and die quickly; others stay in the mature stage for a long, long time. Some enter the decline stage and are then cycled back into the growth stage through strong promotion or repositioning. It seems that a well-managed brand could live forever. Such venerable brands as Johnnie Walker, Moët et Chandon, Coca-Cola, Horlicks, Gillette, Carlsberg, Beck's, Maggi, Milka, Miele, Ritz, Rolls-Royce and Tabasco, for instance, are still going strong after more than 100 years.

The PLC concept can describe a product class (petrol-engined cars), a product form (MPV) or a brand (Kia Carens, Renault Scenic). The PLC concept applies differently in each case. Product classes have the longest life cycles. The sales of many product classes stay in the mature stage for a long time. Product forms, in contrast, tend to have the standard PLC shape. Product forms such as 'cream deodorants', the 'dial telephone' and 'cassette tapes' passed through a regular history of introduction, rapid growth, maturity and decline. A specific brand can enjoy an enduring life cycle, but it can also change quickly because of changing competitive attacks and responses.

The PLC concept can also be applied to what are known as styles, fashions and fads. Their special life cycles are shown in Figure 12.3. A **style** is a basic and distinctive mode of expression. For example, styles appear in British homes (Edwardian, Victorian, Georgian), clothing (formal, casual) and art (realistic, surrealistic, abstract). Once a style is invented, it may last for generations, coming in and out of vogue. A style has a cycle showing several periods of renewed interest.

A **fashion** is a currently accepted or popular style in a given field. For example, the more formal 'business attire' look of corporate dress of the 1980s and early 1990s has now given way to the 'business casual look' of today. Fashions tend to grow slowly, remain popular for a while, then decline slowly.

Fads are temporary periods of unusually high sales driven by consumer enthusiasm and immediate product or brand popularity.[34] They tend to enter quickly, are adopted with great zeal, peak early and decline very fast. A fad may be part of an otherwise normal life cycle, as in the case of recent surges in the sales of razor scooters and yo-yos. Or the fad may comprise a brand's or product's entire life cycle, such as Pet Rocks, Rubik's Cube and Furbys.

Fads appeal to people who are looking for excitement, a way to set themselves apart or something to talk about to others. However, they do not survive for long because they normally do not satisfy a strong or lasting need or satisfy it well.

The PLC concept can be applied by marketers as a useful framework for describing how products and markets work. When used carefully, it can help in developing good marketing strategies for different stages of the product life cycle. But using the PLC concept for forecasting product performance or for developing marketing strategies presents some practical problems. For

Style—A basic and distinctive mode of expression.

Fashion—A currently accepted or popular style in a given field.

Fad—A temporary period of unusually high sales driven by consumer enthusiasm and immediate product or brand popularity.

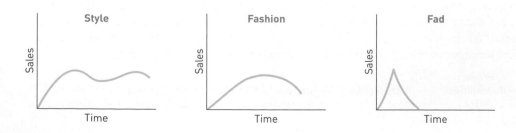

Figure 12.3 Marketers need to understand and predict style, fashion and fad

example, managers may have trouble identifying which stage of the PLC the product is in or pinpointing when the product moves into the next stage. They may also find it hard to determine the factors that affect the product's movement through the stages.

> " Using the PLC concept for forecasting product performance or developing marketing strategies presents some practical problems. "

In practice, it is difficult to forecast the sales level at each PLC stage, the length of each stage and the shape of the PLC curve. Using the PLC concept to develop marketing strategy can also be difficult because strategy is both a cause and a result of the product's life cycle. The product's current PLC position suggests the best marketing strategies, and the resulting marketing strategies affect product performance in later life-cycle stages.

Moreover, marketers should not blindly push products through the traditional stages of the product life cycle. 'As marketers instinctively embrace the old life-cycle paradigm, they needlessly consign their products to following the curve into maturity and decline,' notes one marketing professor. Instead, smart marketers often defy the 'rules' of the life cycle and position their products in unexpected ways. By doing this, 'companies can rescue products foundering in the maturity phase of their life cycles and return them to the growth phase. And they can catapult new products forward into the growth phase, leapfrogging obstacles that could slow consumers' acceptance.'[35]

> " Companies can rescue products foundering in the maturity phase . . . and return them to the growth phase. And they can catapult new products forward into the growth phase. "

We looked at the product development stage of the product life cycle in the first part of the chapter. Now let us look at strategies for each of the other life-cycle stages.

Introduction stage

The **introduction stage** starts when the new product is first launched. Introduction takes time, and sales growth is apt to be slow. Well-known products such as frozen foods, personal computers, DVDs and mobile telephones lingered for many years before they entered a stage of rapid growth.

In this stage, as compared to other stages, profits are negative or low because of the low sales and high distribution and promotion expenses. Much money is needed to attract distributors and build their inventories. Promotion spending is relatively high to inform consumers of the new product and get them to try it. Because the market is not generally ready for product refinements at this stage, the company and its few competitors produce basic versions of the product. These firms focus their selling on those buyers who are the most ready to buy. For radical product technologies, such as mobile phones, PCs and personal digital assistants, when they were first marketed, business or professional users were the earliest group of buyers to be targeted. Often, innovative technologies are aimed at niche segments rather than the mainstream market. Take smart fabrics and interactive textiles (SFITs). Before their commercial launch, Vivometrics's LifeShirt products were sold into military and emergency services markets for monitoring the heart rate of personnel in the field.

A company might adopt one of several marketing strategies for introducing a new product. It can set a high or low level for each marketing variable, such as price, promotion, distribution and

Introduction stage—The product life-cycle stage when the new product is first distributed and made available for purchase.

product quality. Considering only price and promotion, for example, management might *skim the market slowly* by launching the new product with a high price and low promotion spending. The high price helps recover as much gross profit per unit as possible, while the low promotion spending keeps marketing spending down. Such a strategy makes sense when the market size is small, when most consumers in the market know about the product and are willing to pay a high price (these consumers are typically called the 'innovators'), and when there is little immediate potential competition. If, however, most consumers in the limited market are unaware and know little about the innovation, and require educating and convincing, a high level of promotion spending is required. A high-price, high-promotion strategy also helps the firm to *skim rapidly* the price-insensitive end of the market in the early stages of the new product's launch.

On the other hand, a company might introduce its new product with a low price and heavy promotion spending (a *rapid penetration* strategy). This strategy promises to bring the fastest market penetration and the largest market share, and it makes sense when the market is large, potential buyers are price sensitive and unaware of the product, there is strong potential competition, and the company's unit manufacturing costs fall with the scale of production and accumulated manufacturing experience. A low-price but low-promotion spend (or *slow penetration* strategy) may be chosen instead if buyers are price conscious, but the firm wants to keep its launch costs down because of resource constraints.

A company, especially the *market pioneer*, must choose a launch strategy that is consistent with the intended product positioning. It should realise that the initial strategy is just the first step in a grander marketing plan for the product's entire life cycle. If the pioneer chooses its launch strategy to make a killing, it may be sacrificing long-run revenue for the sake of short-run gain. As the pioneer moves through later stages of the life cycle, it will have to continuously formulate new pricing, promotion and other marketing strategies. It has the best chance of building and retaining market leadership if it plays its cards correctly from the start.

Growth stage

Growth stage—The product life-cycle stage at which a product's sales start climbing quickly.

If the new product meets market needs or stimulates previously untapped needs, it will enter a **growth stage**, in which sales will start climbing quickly. The early adopters will continue to buy, and later buyers will start following their lead, especially if they hear favourable word-of-mouth. Attracted by the opportunities for profit, new competitors will enter the market. They will introduce new product features, improve on the pioneer's product and expand the market for the product. The increase in competitors leads to an increase in the number of distribution outlets, and sales jump just to build reseller inventories. Prices remain where they are or fall only slightly. Companies keep their promotion spending at the same or a slightly higher level. Educating the market remains a goal, but now the company must also meet the competition.

Profits increase during the growth stage, as promotion costs are spread over a large volume and as unit-manufacturing costs fall. The firm uses several strategies to sustain rapid market growth as long as possible. It improves product quality and adds new product features and models. It enters new market segments and new distribution channels. It shifts some advertising from building product awareness to building product conviction and purchase, and it lowers prices at the right time to attract more buyers.

In the growth stage, the firm faces a trade-off between high market share and high current profit. By spending a lot of money on product improvement, promotion and distribution, the company can capture a dominant position. In doing so, however, it gives up maximum current profit, which it hopes to make up in the next stage.

Maturity stage

Maturity stage—The stage in the product life cycle where sales growth slows or levels off.

At some point, a product's sales growth will slow down and the product will enter a **maturity stage**. This maturity stage normally lasts longer than the previous stages, and it poses strong

challenges to marketing management. Most products are in the maturity stage of the life cycle and, therefore, most of marketing management deals with the mature product.

The slowdown in sales growth results in many producers with many products to sell. In turn, this overcapacity leads to greater competition. Competitors begin to mark down prices, increase their advertising and sales promotions, and raise their R&D budgets to develop better versions of the product. These steps lead to a drop in profit. Some of the weaker competitors start dropping out of the industry, and the industry eventually contains only well-established competitors.

Although many products in the mature stage appear to remain unchanged for long periods, most successful ones stay alive through continually evolving to meet changing consumer needs. Product managers should do more than simply ride along with or defend their mature products – a good offence is the best defence. They should look for new ways to innovate in the market (market development) or to modify the product (product development) and the marketing mix (marketing innovation).

Market development

Here, the company modifies the market in order to increase the consumption of the current product. It may reposition the brand and aim it at new users and new market segments that are currently not served by the company. For example, Johnson & Johnson targeted the adult market with its baby powder and shampoo, and Lucozade introduced a new line of drinks aimed at younger users, not convalescents who were the original target segment for the brand. The company may also look for ways to increase product usage among present customers. Amazon.com sends permission-based e-mails to regular customers, letting them know when their favourite authors or performers publish new books or CDs.

With energy drinks, such as Red Bull or Gatorade, having a distinctly masculine appeal, Vittel+energy responded to a market opportunity to energise women.

SOURCE: The Advertising Archives.

Product development

The company might try modifying the product by changing characteristics, such as quality, features, style or packaging, to attract new users and to inspire more usage. It might improve the product's quality and performance – its durability, reliability, speed or taste. In an attempt to maintain its dominance of the world computer-games market, five years after the launch of PlayStation 1, Sony introduced PlayStation 2 (PS2), which offered a jump in performance and versatility. The PS2 incorporated two new semiconductor chips, the 'Emotion engine' 128-bit processor, and 'Graphics Synthesiser', which give far richer and more detailed graphics than the first-generation machine. Its digital video disc (DVD) player also showed recorded films, and with a software upgrade, users could plug it into digital cable networks, transforming the PlayStation into a broadband Internet-access device that can download games, films and music produced by the company's other business divisions.[36] This was followed by the launch of the PS3 in November 2006, technically an even more advanced machine powered by a 3.2 gigahertz 'Cell', a supercomputer chip, along with an in-built Blu-Ray high-definition DVD player that enables users to enjoy both shockingly real games graphics and high-definition movies.[37]

The company might improve the product's styling and attractiveness. Thus, car manufacturers restyle their cars to attract buyers who want a new look. The makers of consumer food and

Falling Star
Irony Medium aluminium

swatch+
IRONY

www.swatch.com

Once watches were either expensive or dull digitals — then along came the Swatch range that is continually changing and that many people collect — even a Swatch club with a regular stream of exclusive designs.
SOURCE: The Advertising Archives.

household products introduce new flavours, colours, ingredients or packages to revitalise consumer buying. For example, in the US, Cadbury sought to revitalise its Snapple brand, which had experienced flat sales, by introducing new tea varieties. It also entered the sports drink sector by introducing a drink called Accelerade. Or, the firm might add new features that expand the product's usefulness, safety or convenience.

Marketing mix modification

Marketers can also try to modify the marketing mix – improving sales by changing one or more marketing-mix elements. The firm can cut price to attract new users and competitors' customers. It can launch a better advertising campaign or use aggressive sales promotions – trade deals, discounts, premiums and contests. The company can also enter larger market channels, using mass merchandisers, as Dell Computers did when it pioneered telephone selling of personal computers. Finally, the company can improve sales by offering new or improved services to buyers.

Today, most British homes are supplied with gas, while those that do not burn gas are more likely to heat their homes with oil or electricity, instead of coal. However, CPL, the UK's leading solid fuel merchant and distributor, says that, despite the declining trend, there is still life in the sector. The product has changed – typically coal was delivered loose to homes in one-hundredweight sacks, but today CPL sells an increasing amount of four-kilogram bags of smokeless fuel from supermarkets and garage forecourts. The latter distribution channels are ideal for occasional users – they burn the fuel not to warm up the home, but because they like the romantic atmosphere it creates. Burning coal is increasingly a lifestyle choice for many users, according to an industry spokesperson. So, never underestimate the potential for turning around any dying commodity! Designer fuels, next.[39]

 Never underestimate the potential for turning around any dying commodity!

Decline stage

Decline stage—The product life-cycle stage at which a product's sales decline.

The sales of most product forms and brands eventually dip. This **decline stage** may be slow, as in the case of oatmeal cereal, or rapid, as in the case of cassette and VHS tapes. Sales may plunge to zero, or they may drop to a low level where they continue for many years.

Sales decline for many reasons, including technological advances, shifts in consumer tastes and increased competition. As sales and profits decline, some firms withdraw from the market. Those remaining may prune their product offerings. They may drop smaller market segments and marginal trade channels, or they may cut the promotion budget and reduce their prices further.

Carrying a weak product can be very costly to a firm, and not just in profit terms. There are many hidden costs. A weak product may take up too much of management's time. It often requires frequent price and inventory adjustments. It requires advertising and sales force attention that might be better used to make 'healthy' products more profitable or to create new ones. A product's failing reputation can cause customer concerns about the company and its other products. The biggest cost may well lie in the future. Keeping weak products delays the search for replacements, creates a lopsided product mix, hurts current profits and weakens the company's foothold on the future.

For these reasons, companies need to pay more attention to their ageing products. The firm should identify those products in the decline stage by regularly reviewing sales, market shares, costs and profit trends. Then management must decide whether to maintain, harvest for cash or drop each of these declining products.

Repackaging a product in an original way can revitalise a product category.

SOURCE: The Advertising Archives.

12.2 real marketing

FT

Smile! Leica captures the good old days

The march of technology leaves its mark on many industries. Consumers' insatiable appetite for the latest gadget often rapidly obsoletes old technologies and companies' means of delivering consumer benefits. As the saying goes, 'New technology often kills old business.'

The same may be said of the camera industry. Sales of digital cameras have overtaken those of their traditional analogue peers. In the middle of this computerised maelstrom sits Leica, the German-based camera equipment and sports optics maker.

But, to counter the digital tide in the early 2000s, Leica launched the MP, a mechanical analogue camera that relies on design and manufacturing techniques harking back to the 1950s. Jean-Jacques Viau, product marketing manager, brushed aside fears, describing the MP as 'a logical move'. He added: 'For every action, there is a contrary reaction.'

Leica occupies a small upmarket niche and aims to show that smaller operators can thrive by rejecting mainstream trends and catering for that vocal minority, more interested in precision instruments than in increasing electronic automation. As Mr Viau said: 'We could be the shelter for people who react to the changes of model every six months.' That shelter does not come cheap. The MP costs about £1,850 (€2,775) *excluding* the lens.

Unlike the more common single-lens reflex cameras – where you look directly through the lens – rangefinders such as the MP have separate viewfinder and focusing devices. Leica may have invented 35 mm photography but it does not have the rangefinder market to itself. In recent years, it has been coming to terms with competitors using former German brand names, most of which have been snapped up by the Japanese.

Cosina saw a gap in the market for a cheaper rangefinder and launched the Voigtlander Bessa range – at about a quarter of the price of a Leica. Other companies include Contax, owned by Japan's Kyocera; Konica; and Rollei, an independent German-based company. The resurgence of interest in back-to-basics cameras has been pronounced and has benefited Leica. Robert White, an independent retailer in the south of England, says: 'People are realising there's more to life than a piece of plastic. It's back to the good old days.'

For a while, Leica was bucking the mass digital trend, with discerning photographers snapping up its luxury analogue cameras. Although Leica continued to trade on its illustrious history, sales slumped as digital photography marched on. The firm nearly collapsed in 2005. Leica hopes to make a comeback with the launch of a digital version of its rangefinder camera, the M8, in late 2006. Although Leica has sold compact digital cameras since 1998, Leica fanatics have been waiting for a digital version of its M-series rangefinders. Unlike a single-lens reflex camera, where the photographer looks through the lens while composing and focusing, a rangefinder camera uses a separate viewfinder with a 'split-image' focusing system. This makes it smaller and quieter, and explains Leica's popularity among photo-journalists. The new M8 combines classic Leica craftsmanship with modern digital trimmings, such as a 10.3-megapixel sensor.

But can the new camera revive this luxury brand? Most Leicas are sold to art photographers, rich hobbyists and collectors. The new M8 will cost around €3,500 – without a lens. Leica makes other cameras too, such as its R-series single-lens reflex cameras. But, says Ralph Nebe, Leica's marketing director, 'the most important impact on us was the loss in sales of the rangefinder camera.' As a result, he says, launching a digital rangefinder is crucial. Leica is hoping that late is better than never. Having lost €30m since 2004, and undergone a series of restructurings since 1997, sales have since picked up, growing by 16 per cent in the year to April 2006. But not everyone is convinced that the company has turned the corner. In September 2006, the French luxury-goods firm, Hermès, sold its 31.5 per cent stake in Leica to ACM Projektentwicklung, an Austrian investment firm that already owned 36 per cent.

Despite the launch of the M8, photography's switch from film to digital technology could spell trouble for Leica. In the digital era, photography has become as dependent on computers as on cameras. 'The newer generation coming up are less enamoured by high-end camera manufacturers,' says Steve Hoffenberg, an analyst at Lyra Research in Massachusetts. Others, however, argue that Leica caters to a unique audience willing to pay for quality and cachet. Richard Caplan, a specialist Leica shop in London, had 25 orders for the M8 before it was even announced!

SOURCES: Adapted from 'Leica refocuses', *The Economist* (30 September 2006), p. 92. Copyright © The Economist Newspaper Limited, London (30 September 2006). Ian Chapman, 'A camera focused on luxury', *Financial Times* (31 March 2003), p. 15; see also Scott Morrison, 'Consumer photography develops speedily', *Financial Times* (12 January 2004), p. 29; and Amy Yee and Dan Roberts, 'Kodak hopes for digital boom', *Financial Times* (23 January 2004), p. 25.

Management may decide to *maintain* its brand without change in the hope that competitors will leave the industry. For example, Procter & Gamble made good profits by remaining in the declining liquid soap business as others withdrew. Alternatively, management may decide to reposition the brand in the hope of moving it back into the growth stage of the product life cycle. Or management may find new ways to revitalise the business, as in the case of Leica, the German-based camera equipment and sports optics maker which sought to buck the mass digital camera trend through targeting discerning photographers with a new line of upmarket equipment (see Real Marketing 12.2).

Management may decide to *harvest* the product, which means reducing various costs (plant and equipment, maintenance, R&D, advertising, sales force) and hoping that sales hold up. If successful, harvesting will release cash and increase the company's profits in the short run. Or management may decide to drop the product from the line. It can sell it to another firm or simply liquidate it at salvage value. For example, declining real ale sales in the UK caused dozens of regional brewers to close down, while others including the country's largest brewers, Bass and Whitbread, sold off their brewing interests to foreign groups such as the Belgian Interbrew.[40] If the company plans to find a buyer for the declining product business, it will not want to run down the product through harvesting.

Table 12.2 summarises the key characteristics of each stage of the product life cycle. The table also lists the marketing objectives and strategies for each stage.[41]

Table 12.2 Summary of product life-cycle characteristics, objectives and strategies

	Introduction	Growth	Maturity	Decline
Characteristics				
Sales	Low sales	Rapidly rising sales	Peak sales	Declining sales
Costs	High cost per customer	Average cost per customer	Low cost per customer	Low cost per customer
Profits	Negative	Rising profits	High profits	Declining profits
Customers	Innovators	Early adopters	Middle majority	Laggards
Competitors	Few	Growing number	Stable number beginning to decline	Declining number
Marketing objectives	Create product awareness and trial	Maximise market share	Maximise profit while defending market share	Reduce expenditure and milk the brand
Strategies				
Product	Offer a basic product	Offer product extensions, service, warranty	Diversify brand and models	Phase out weak items
Price	Use cost-plus	Price to penetrate market	Price to match or beat competitors	Cut price
Distribution	Build selective distribution	Build intensive distribution	Build more intensive distribution	Go selective: phase out unprofitable outlets
Advertising	Build product awareness among early adopters and dealers	Build awareness and interest in the mass market	Stress brand differences and benefits	Reduce to level needed to retain hard-core loyals
Sales promotion	Use heavy sales promotion to entice trial	Reduce to take advantage of heavy consumer demand	Increase to encourage brand switching	Reduce to minimal level

SOURCE: From P. Kotler, *Marketing Management: Analysis, Planning, Implementation, and Control*, 12th edn. (Upper Saddle River, New Jersey: Prentice Hall, 2006), p. 332. Copyright © 2003. Reprinted with permission of Pearson Education, Inc.

Reviewing the concepts

A company's current products face limited life spans and must be replaced by newer products. But new products can fail—the risks of innovation are as great as the rewards. The key to successful innovation lies in a company-wide effort, strong planning and a systematic *new-product development* process.

1. Explain how companies find and develop new-product ideas

Companies find new-product ideas from a variety of sources. Many new-product ideas stem from *internal sources*. Companies conduct formal research and development, pick the brains of their employees and brainstorm at executive meetings. Other ideas come form *external sources*. By conducting surveys and focus groups and analysing *customer* questions and complaints, companies can generate new-product ideas that will meet specific consumer needs. Companies track *competitors'* offerings and inspect new products, dismantling them, analysing their performance and deciding whether to introduce a similar or improved product. *Distributors and suppliers* are close to the market and can pass along information about consumer problems and new-product possibilities.

2. List and define the steps in the new-product development process and the major considerations in managing this process

We examined the new-product development process which covers nine stages. The process starts with determining the *new-product strategy*, which provides direction for the new-product development effort. The next stage is *idea generation*, followed by *idea screening*, which reduces the number of ideas based on the company's own criteria. Ideas that pass the screening stage continue through *product concept development*, in which a detailed version of the new-product idea is stated in meaningful consumer terms. In the next stage, *concept testing*, new-product concepts are tested with a group of target customers to determine whether the concepts have strong customer appeal. Strong concepts proceed to *marketing strategy development*, in which an initial marketing strategy for the new product is developed from the product concept. In the *business-analysis* stage, a review of the sales, costs and profit projections for a new product is conducted to determine whether the new product is likely to satisfy the company's objectives. With positive results here, the ideas become more concrete through *product development* and *test marketing*. Finally, the company goes ahead with *commercialisation* if test-market results are positive.

New-product development involves more than just going through a set of steps. Companies must take a systematic, holistic approach to managing this process. Successful new-product development requires a customer-centred, team-based, systematic effort.

3. Describe the stages of the product life cycle

Each product has a *life cycle* marked by a changing set of problems and opportunities. The sales of the typical product follow an S-shaped curve made up of five stages. The cycle begins with the *product development stage* when the company finds and develops a new-product idea. The *introduction stage* is marked by slow growth and low profits as the product is distributed to the market. If successful, the product enters a *growth stage*, which offers rapid sales growth and increasing profits. Next comes a *maturity stage* when sales growth slows down and profits stabilise. Finally, the product enters a *decline stage* in which sales and profits dwindle. The company's task during this stage is to recognise the decline and to decide whether it should maintain, harvest or drop the product.

4. Describe how marketing strategies change during the product's life cycle

In the *introduction stage*, the company must choose a launch strategy consistent with its intended product positioning. Much money is needed to attract distributors or resellers and build their inventories and to inform consumers of the new product and achieve trial. In the *growth stage*, companies continue to educate potential consumers and distributors. In addition, the company works to stay ahead of the competition and sustain rapid market growth by improving product quality, adding new product features and models, entering new market segments and distribution channels, shifting advertising from building product awareness to building product conviction and purchase, and lowering prices at the right time to attract new buyers.

In the *maturity stage*, companies continue to invest in maturing products and consider modifying the market, the product and the marketing mix. When *modifying the market*, the company seeks to increase the consumption of the current product. When *modifying the product*, the company changes some of the product's characteristics – such as quality, features or style – to attract new users or inspire more usage. When *modifying the marketing mix*, the company aims to improve sales by changing one or more of the marketing-mix elements. Once the company recognises that a product has entered the *decline stage*, management must decide whether to *maintain* the brand without change, hoping that competitors will drop out of the market; *harvest* the product, reducing costs and trying to maintain sales; or *drop* the product, selling it to another firm or liquidating it at salvage value.

Discussing the concepts

1. Why is it important for companies to stimulate the generation of new-product ideas within an organisation? Should a company draw new-product ideas from a variety of sources? What might be the most valuable sources of new-product ideas?

2. Is new-product concept testing important? How might the Internet assist marketers in their efforts to determine potential customers' attitudes and responses towards new-product ideas?

3. Under what conditions would you consider not to test-market a new product or service? Discuss using appropriate products or services that meet these no-need-to-test criteria.

4. Identify and discuss some potential problems with the product life-cycle concept. Is the concept a useful marketing-planning tool? Why or why not?

5. Which product life-cycle stage, if any, is the most important? Which stage is the riskiest? Which stage offers the greatest profit potential? At which stage do managers have to make trade-offs between high market share and high current profit? Explain using practical examples.

Applying the concepts

1. Defibrillators are medical devices commonly used by fire-fighters and paramedics to treat victims of sudden cardiac arrest with an electric charge that restarts their hearts. A high proportion of sudden cardiac arrests occur in the home, with only a small proportion of victims receiving

the life-saving electric charge. Philips is marketing a portable consumer defibrillator called the HeartStart. The device, about the size of a handheld video game, can be operated by any individual and does not require a trained medical provider. A consumer is guided by voice-activation through each step, while smart technology provides specific instructions based on feedback to the main system. You may visit http://www.heartstart.com for information on this product.

(a) How might this product have moved through the different stages of new-product development?

(b) Write a marketing strategy statement for this new product. How might the marketing strategy for HeartStart change as it moves through the product life cycle?

2. The marketing of socially responsible clothing in Europe grew some 30 per cent in 2005. Marks & Spencer (M&S) is one of the retailers in the UK embracing socially responsible fashion. In March 2006, M&S began selling fair-trade-certified T-shirts. By July 2006, the line expanded to jeans, underwear, shorts, vests and socks. The philosophy behind fair trade is to support the more than 100 million households worldwide who are involved in cotton production. The farmers, especially in poor countries, are vulnerable to low cotton prices. Moreover, a common reaction is for the farmers to use more pesticides to increase their yields, thus fuelling an environmental as well as a social issue. According to M&S's head of corporate responsibility, nearly 80 per cent of the retailer's consumers wanted to know more about how clothing products were made. M&S launched a 'look-behind-the-label' campaign, bringing its new socially responsible clothing to consumers' attention (www2.marksandspencer.com/thecompany/trustyour_mands/index.shtml). According to the company, the new products are a response to consumers' questions about how cotton is produced and their realisation of the environmental and social issues that are involved.

(a) How did M&S test-market fair-trade-certified clothing?

(b) In what stage of the product life cycle are these trade-certified clothing products?

(c) Do you think that the trend towards fair-trade-certified clothing is set to grow? Will the product life cycle curve follow the shape of a style, fashion or fad? Explain.

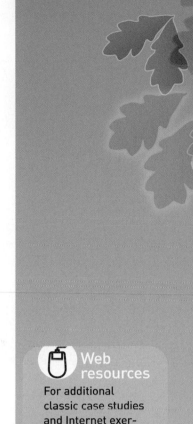

Web resources

For additional classic case studies and Internet exercises, visit **www.pearsoned.co.uk/kotler**

References

1. Alison Maitland, 'Hoki: The white sustainable fish that got away', *Financial Times* (13 July 2005); 'Fish & birds loose sustainability ranting' [*sic*], *New Zealand Times* (5 October 2007); Owen Hembry, 'Hoki cuts not enough in long term', *New Zealand Herald* (4 October 2007); 'Sharpening their harpoons', *The Economist* (26 May 2007), p. 77; 'Still waters: The global fish crisis', *National Geographic* (April 2007), pp 33–98.

2. Katrijn Gielens and Jan-Benedict E. M. Steenkamp, 'What drives new product success? An investigation across products and countries' (Cambridge, MA: Marketing Science Institute), Report 2004, No. 04-108.

3. Michiyo Nakamoto, 'Screen test: Stringer's strategy will signal to what extent Sony can stay in the game', *Financial Times* (21 September 2005), p. 17.

4. George Chryssochoidis and Veronica Wong, 'Rolling out new products across multiple markets: Reasons for delays', *Journal of Product Innovation Management*, **15**, 1 (January 1998), pp. 16–41.

5. Bernard Simon, 'Daimler hopes US may save Smart', *Financial Times* (27 March 2006), accessed online at www.ft.com, August 2007; James Mackintosh and Richard Milne, 'DaimlerChrysler looks at selling off Smart car division if turnaround fails', *Financial Times* (9 January 2006), p. 1.

6. Rick Romell, 'Moving in the right direction: Segways catch on in niche markets', *Milwaukee Journal Sentinel* (10 June 2006), p. 1D.

7. For these and other facts and examples, see Jena McGregor, 'How failure breeds success', *BusinessWeek* (10 July 2006), p. 42; and John T. Gourville, 'Eager sellers and stony buyers', *Harvard Business Review* (June 2006), pp. 98–106; see also Robert G. Cooper, 'New product success in industrial

firms', *Industrial Marketing Management*, **21** (1992), pp. 215–23; and William Bolding, Ruskin Morgan and Richard Staelin, 'Pulling the plug to stop the new product drain', *Journal of Marketing Research* (February 1997), pp. 164–76.

8. Danny Bradbury, Special Report – Digital Business: 'E-books turning over a new leaf', *Financial Times* (12 April 2006), p. 4.

9. For an excellent review, see Mitzie M. Montoya-Weiss and Roger Calantone, 'Determinants of new product performance: A review and meta-analysis', *Journal of Product Innovation Management*, **11** (1994), pp. 397–417. See also Don H. Lester, 'Critical success factors for new product development', *Research-Technology Management* (January–February 1998), pp. 36–43; Michael Song and Mark E. Parry, 'A cross-national comparative study of new product development processes: Japan and United States', *Journal of Marketing* (April 1997), pp. 1–18; Jerry Wind and Vijay Mahajan, 'Issues and opportunities in new product development', *Journal of Marketing Research* (February 1997), pp. 1–12; and Robert G. Cooper and Elko J. Kleinschmidt, *New Product: The key factors in success* (Chicago: American Marketing Association, 1990).

10. C. Merle Crawford, *New Products Management*, 4th edn (Boston, MA: Irwin, 1994), Ch. 3.

11. See Rosbeth Moss Kanter, 'Don't wait to innovate', *Sales and Marketing Management* (February 1997), pp. 22–4; Greg A. Steven and James Burley, '3,000 raw ideas equals 1 commercial success!', *Research-Technology Management* (May–June 1997), pp. 16–27.

12. Based on material from Peter Lewis, 'A perpetual crisis machine', *Fortune* (19 September 2005), pp. 58–67.

13. Lauren Foster and David Ibison, 'Spike the robot helps Lego rebuild strategy', *Financial Times* (22 June 2006), p. 26.

14. Based on quotes and information from Robert D. Hof, 'The power of us', *Business Week* (20 June 2005), pp. 74–82. See also Robert Weisman, 'Firms turn R&D on its head, looking outside for ideas', *The Boston Globe* (14 May 2006), p. E1.

15. Information accessed at www.avon.com, August 2006.

16. 'Business: The rise of the creative consumer; the future of innovation', *The Economist* (12 March 2005), p. 75.

17. Lisa Wirkkala, 'Sibelius? No, it's my mobile', *The European Magazine* (17–23 April 1997), p. 7.

18. See 'DaimlerChrysler presents California with three F-cell fuel cell vehicles', *Fuel Cell Today* (1 June 2005), accessed at www.fuelcelltoday.com; Steven Ashley, 'On the road to fuel-cell cars', *Scientific American* (1 March 2005), p. 62; and Kathy Jackson, 'Calif. leads the way in fleet fuel cell tests', *Automotive News* (5 June 2006), p. 35.

19. Example adapted from Carol Matlack, 'The Vuitton machine', *Business Week* (22 March 2004), pp. 98–102.

20. Jack Neff, 'Is testing the answer?', *Advertising Age* (9 July 2001), p. 13; Dale Buss, 'P&G's rise', *Potentials* (January 2003), pp. 26–30. For more on test marketing, see Philip Kotler and Kevin Lane Keller, *Marketing Management*, 12th edn (Upper Saddle River, NJ: Prentice Hall, 2006), pp. 653–5.

21. Information on Nielsen Scantrack from www.acnielsen.com/products/ScanTrackSelect.html.

22. Information on BehaviorScan accessed at www.infores.com/public/us/analytics/productportfolio/bscannewprodtest.htm, September 2007.

23. See Jack Neff, 'Six-blade blitz', *Advertising Age* (9 September 2005), pp. 3, 53; and William C. Symonds, 'Gillette's new edge', *BusinessWeek* (6 February 2006), p. 44.

24. Andrew Parker, 'O$_2$ delays its broadband launch again', *Financial Times* (17 May 2007), p. 20.

25. 'Drop the computer', *The Economist* (13 January 2007), p. 57.

26. See Jack Neff, 'New SpinBrush line backed by $30 million', *Advertising Age* (9 September 2002), p. 36; and Jenn Abelson, 'Firms likely to shed some products', *Knight Ridder Tribune Business News* (22 June 2005), p. 1.

27. Based on information presented in 'Xelibri: A Siemens mobile adventure', a case study written by F. Clemens, H. Hedderich and H. Sassmann (under supervision of Lutz Kaufmann), WHU, Otto Beisheim Graduate School of Management, Vallendar, Germany, 2003. The case study is distributed by ECCH Collection, England and USA (for more information, visit: http://www.ecch.cranfield.ac.uk).

28. Robert G. Cooper, 'Formula for success', *Marketing Management* (March–April 2006), pp. 19–23.

29. Adapted from information in Jennifer Reingold, 'The interpreter', *Fast Company* (June 2005), pp. 59–61; and Jonah Bloom, 'Beth has an idea', *Point* (September 2005), pp. 9–14. Quote taken from Gary Silverman, 'How can I help you?', *FT Magazine* (4/5 February 2006), pp. 16–19. Also see Larry Selden and Ian C. MacMillan, 'Manage customer-centric innovation – systematically', *Harvard Business Review* (April 2006), pp. 108–16.

30. Lawrence A. Crosby and Sheree L. Johnson, 'Customer-centric innovation', *Marketing Management* (March–April 2006), pp. 12–13.

31. See Philip Kotler, *Kotler on Marketing* (New York: Free Press, 1999), pp. 43–4; Judy Lamont, 'Idea management: Everyone's an innovator', *KM World* (November/December 2004), pp. 14–16; and J. Roland Ortt, 'Innovation management: Different approaches to cope with the same trends', *Management* (2006), pp. 296–318.

32. Jena McGregor, 'The world's most innovative companies', *Business Week Special Report* (4 May 2007), accessed online at http://www.businessweekcom/innovate/content/may2007/id20070504_051674.htm, May 2007; see also Blair Sheppard and Michael Canning, 'Innovation culture', *Leadership Excellence* (January 2006), p. 18.

33. Jena McGregor, *op. cit.*

34. This definition is based on one in Bryan Lilly and Tammy R. Nelson, 'Fads: Segmenting the fad-buyer market', *Journal of Consumer Marketing*, **20**, 3 (2003), pp. 252–65.

35. Youngme Moon, 'Break free from the product life cycle', *Harvard Business Review* (May 2005), pp. 87–94.

36. 'In their dreams', *The Economist* (26 February 2000), pp. 99–100.

37. Maija Palmer, 'Europe fans help Sony's PS3 to a record-breaking launch', *Financial Times* (29 March 2007), p. 17; Michiyo Nakamoto, 'Screen test: Stringer's strategy will signal to what extent Sony can stay in the game', *Financial Times* (21 September 2005), p. 17; Chris Nuttall, 'Console makers go for a slam dunk', *Financial Times* (17 November 2006), p. 10.

38. Jenny Wiggins, 'Cadbury set to invest in new brands', *Financial Times* (21 February 2007), p. 22.

39. Andrew Taylor, '"Designer fuel" finds new role in the home', *Financial Times* (7 March 2003), p. 25. For more information on CPL housecoal products, see www.cpldistribution.co.uk.

40. 'Battling brewers', *The Economist* (18 March 2000), pp. 89–90; 'Brewer's droop', *Business FT Weekend Magazine* (29 July 2000), pp. 34–6.

41. For a more comprehensive discussion of marketing strategies over the course of the product life cycle, see Philip Kotler and Kevin Lane Keller, *Marketing Management*, 12th edn (Upper Saddle River, NJ: Prentice Hall, 2006), pp. 321–35.

Company case 12 CEM: innovating out of decline

Peter Fishpool, Chief Executive of CEM (Christian Education Movement), a charity that develops and delivers religious education products and services in the UK, called a meeting to address the disappointing sales performance in CEM's business streams in 2006. Up until a year or so ago, income from several of its traditional offerings had grown steadily, while revenue growth for a couple had largely remained static. However, the recent sales trend raised concerns for the small charity that is reliant on earned income from its commercial products and services for survival. There is a need to review not only the future development of the business lines and the company's longer-term strategy, but, in the short to medium term, the marketing and product development strategies to revitalise CEM products and services.

Background of CEM

Birmingham (UK)-based CEM is a registered charity and a company limited by guarantee. It is not funded by the Government and depends on income earned from its business activities – primarily religious education (RE) publications and services – and the generosity of supporters, including charitable foundations, churches and individuals.

CEM provides advice, resources and opportunities for teaching and learning in schools, the church and the family group, focusing on religious education in a multi-cultural society.

CEM operates under two distinct brands. Under *RE Today*, it publishes multi-faith RE books for teachers (RE Today Publications) and distributes multi-faith subscription packages to individuals and schools (RE Today Subscriptions), as well as providing RE consultancy and in-service training to the education sector (Professional Services). Under *Christian Education*, CEM runs three streams of activity: Church Publications, Church Subscriptions, and activities under the sub-brand International Bible Reading Association (IBRA), all of which supply educational resources to the Christian community. CEM also produces various multimedia resources to compliment this range of products (Video & CD). Each of the two brands follows a distinct marketing strategy.

In recognising the need for the company to adopt a more market and customer-centred approach to managing its activities, a marketing officer was appointed in 2005. A dedicated marketing function has now been created. As part of a more market-oriented approach, new-product development (NPD) is being considered as a potential driver of CEM's future strategic development.

How CEM is organised

The Board of Trustees is responsible for the charity and meets around five times a year to review organisational developments. The Board appoints the Chairperson, Vice-Chairperson and Treasurer as the Business Planning Group to work with the Chief Executive, Peter Fishpool. In practice, Peter Fishpool is responsible for all decision-making regarding CEM strategy and resource allocation. He is the channel to the Board of Trustees and fundamentally takes the lead in most business development activity.

Peter has been CEO for over five years. Prior to taking up this position, he ran a team of 12 people as the communications secretary for the national headquarters of the Quaker organisation in Britain. He looked after fundraising and internal communications, gaining experience through raising millions of pounds from individual donations, legacies and grants. Before that, he was a youth worker and also a teacher. His management training also included some aspects of innovation and product development. When it comes to innovative activity and the development of new products and services, Peter is supportive of all staff and encourages organisation-wide participation. His entrepreneurial outlook means he is open to looking at doing new things in innovative ways.

CEM has a flat structure made up of a small team of 13 people – nine head office staff and four working from home in different locations around the UK. There is an annual turnover of about £1 million. A newly appointed treasurer is of the view that CEM is cash rich. From a commercial background, the new treasurer also feels that the organisation should be investing rather than holding onto resources for 'a rainy day'.

Staff who work on the multi-faith schools side of the organisation are sometimes anxious that their public image will be clouded by the Christian orientation of the church-side publications. CEM does not have a proactive sales team. The closest thing internally are the three 'sales' staff, who function more as a customer service operation.

Current NPD strategy

Business development strategy is not especially evident as the begetter of new projects. According to Peter Fishpool, 'CEM is not a planned economy in that sense, but much more organic.' New-product development in CEM is led by where the money is. The CEO is encouraging staff members that the organisation should now look beyond RE into the related Humanities or cross-curricular areas such as 'values' education. Staff have so far been resistant to the idea, saying that CEM specialises in RE and that it would be dangerous to dilute the brand name by exploring other areas.

Because of its size, there has never been a *dedicated* marketing or NPD function in CEM. All activity tends to be carried out at the project level, for which a new-product champion is chosen, depending on the nature of the project. Staff sometimes volunteer to take a project on, but are sometimes asked to do something by the CEO. Being allocated to a particular project in the past has sometimes resulted in poor performance. The CEO takes on personally some projects if an opportunity seems too good to miss. On the other hand, problems have occurred in the past, when members of staff have promoted schemes and helped find money to finance a particular product, but then were not in a position to properly follow these through themselves. In these cases, it has sometimes been necessary to buy in freelance staff to complete projects. Project planning is mainly short-term, as it is dependent on funding. Products tend to be developed first and then promoted in 'suitable markets'.

There is a routine process in place for regular projects which CEM has been producing for years. A mixture of well-tried and tested systems and experience means that staff usually feel confident about doing these. For example, developing old products into new frameworks and re-editing existing material is easily done. The more complex the project, the longer the development takes. Therefore, more radical innovations are often opportunistic and depend on funding and sources of additional expertise. One recently suggested project has been pushed back because it requires an understanding of CD-ROM development beyond immediate CEM capabilities.

Development may sometimes have to be postponed because of staff changes. The impact of such uncontrollable events was highlighted recently by the sudden resignation of a relatively new member of staff. Based in Leeds, she was consciously appointed for her expertise in an area in which CEM is lacking – Special Educational Needs (SEN) in RE. CEM had hoped this appointment would broaden its scope, but after six months, the adviser's position was not thriving as expected and she consequently left the organisation. A number of issues have since been identified which had previously been overlooked:

- SEN is a poorly funded area within the education sector.
- Yorkshire was already well supplied with RE advisers.
- The adviser was not comfortable with the degree of personal selling needed to establish herself in the marketplace.

As a result, CEM is now looking elsewhere for a member of staff. It has turned away from SEN and is looking in the south-east for a replacement with more general primary expertise.

Idea generation

For CEM, money can sometimes be the spark of invention. Conversations are held with people who can offer funding and ideas for a project. Ideas also stem from different departments within CEM, such as the publications team, who occasionally take 'tentative stabs' in coming up with products. Unsolicited manuscripts sometimes get presented. Most new projects stem from discussions with the advisers. They know what is required by teachers they speak to through their work and the seed of an idea gets developed through their team meetings. Peter Fishpool claims, 'CEM is not short of ideas, but short of people-power to manage the transition from having a new idea to having a new aspect of the organisation that is able to work economically.'

New products are referred to during regular staff meetings. If the project is funded externally, the source of funding often has the final say. One particular product which did not sell very well is viewed as a 'misconception in terms of the overall package'. CEM was offered the project with money attached, which Peter Fishpool felt was 'too good to refuse'. In retrospect, he thinks CEM should have been talking with the original project developers earlier on in the process, because the organisation did not have much input into the end product.

Unless substantial funding is provided, concepts are more feasible for CEM if they require few extra resources. New concepts are tested in a small way with practising teachers. When CEM has a clear idea of the likely shape of a product, there might be a meeting with teachers to review the final format.

CEM service development

As with most charities, service provision is also a large part of CEM's business. The main differences between CEM product development and service development is the customisation involved. The schools education market varies greatly at a regional level, so most CEM consultancy services are developed around specific client requirements. Staff based regionally develop their own new services which are measured in terms of days of their time. It is deemed appropriate for them to have such autonomy, as they are out there talking to the market and are able to look for new opportunities. The CEO does not control this process, which is often initiated through business contacts. As this only affects the staff member involved, it is not seen as necessary to involve HQ. However, the CEO sometimes feels anxious to make sure that staff are using up time in the most productive ways.

Peter Fishpool believes that if CEM can reach the right audience with current products, they will sell. This mirrors the general belief in CEM that dwindling awareness is the main reason behind reduction in sales. But customer needs and requirements are also changing. CEM has to respond with new and improved products and services that fit these evolving needs.

As the CEM team convenes, Peter is keen for everyone to contemplate the further development of CEM products and services and that there are important NPD-related issues to resolve.

Questions

1. Identify the key factors that influence the success of organisations such as CEM.
2. At what stage of the product life cycle are RE products and services as a category?
3. Critically evaluate CEM's current new-product development approach.
4. Recommend and justify a new product development strategy and process for the organisation.
5. Taking into account the product life-cycle concept, what should CEM do to revitalise its major business streams? Recommend specific ideas for CEM in the areas of market penetration, product development and market development.

SOURCE: This case study was developed by Jennifer Smith, Aston Business School, UK, based on CEM records, with permission.

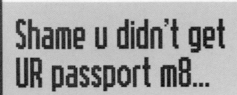

Economic competition is not war, but competition is mutual service.

EDWIN CANON

Marketing services

Mini Contents List

CHAPTER

thirteen

'Satisfaction Guaranteed (Or Take Your Love Back)'

From 'Satisfaction Guaranteed' by Harold Melvin and the Blue Notes on 'The Essential Harold Melvin and the Blue Notes', Epic/Legacy, B0002S94UW

Previewing the concepts

Services have grown dramatically in recent decades. For example, services account for around 71 per cent of gross domestic product (GDP) in the European Union, 73 per cent of Japan's GDP and 79 per cent of GDP in the US.[1] Furthermore, in the developed nations, more people are currently employed in services than in all other sectors of the economy put together. In addition, a lot of international trade no longer involves putting things into a crate and sending them abroad on ships! More and more, the global economy is dominated by services. Services are growing rapidly in the world economy, making up 37 per cent of the value of all international trade.[2] According to the World Trade Organization (WTO), global service exports are worth about 2 trillion euros in 2007. Growth in service exports has been particularly strong in sectors such as commercial services, travel and tourism, and transportation. WTO data place the EU as the largest single exporter of services ($1.104 trillion or €0.817 trillion), accounting for almost half of total global service exports, followed by Asia ($543 billion; one fifth of total), North America ($420 billion; 17 per cent) and the rest of the world.[3]

After reading this chapter, you should be able to:

1. Describe the nature and special characteristics that affect the marketing of services.
2. Identify the additional marketing considerations that services require.
3. Explain the marketing strategies for improving service differentiation, quality and productivity.
4. Describe the nature and special characteristics of non-profit marketing.

We start with looking at Stena Line, a ferry company that has to strive to keep customers happy by getting passengers to their destinations safely and on time as well as operating restaurants, bars, shops, entertainment and many other operations designed to make passengers happy and wanting to come back for more of the Stena experience.

Prelude case Stena Line: sailing out of troubled waters

ANNA ACKFELDT[*]
Aston Business School, UK

Stena Line, the Swedish international transport and travel service company, is among the world's largest organisations for ferry traffic. With a modern fleet of 35 ships, Stena Line operates a network of 18 strategically located ferry routes in Scandinavia and around the UK. In 2006, between these routes, some 12 million passengers travelled with Stena Line, while nearly 1.6 million units of freight and 2.2 million cars were carried by its fleet.

Stena Line started out in 1962 as a small local company, when it launched the Gothenburg–Fredrikshaven route, followed by the Gothenburg–Kiel route in 1967. In 1980, Stena Line merged with its local competitor, Sessanlinjen, which gave it a local ferry monopoly in Gothenburg. This merger was the start of a rapid expansion programme which was sustained over the 1980s, mainly through the organic growth of ferry routes and introduction of new services. By 1987 Stena Line had become the seventh largest service export company in Sweden. However, by the 1990s, Stena Line had to face some critical decisions regarding its future.

When Sweden became a member of the EU in 1995, one important consequence for Stena Line's operations was the abolition of the duty-free licences. On-board sales contributed approximately 45 per cent to Stena Line's profit, and the duty-free sales generated most of this profit. Mainly due to the high cost of alcohol and tobacco in the domestic market, for many passengers duty-free shopping on board was a reason to travel on short cruises on the Gothenburg–Fredrikshaven route. Competitively priced alcoholic beverages, gambling and entertainment on board and shopping in Denmark were also part of the motivation to travel with Stena Line.

It was expected that passenger numbers, revenue and profit margins would decrease when the duty-free licences were abolished. Also, the Scandinavian market was saturated and the rapid expansion and modernisation of the fleet had put pressure on the organisation's profitability and finances. Stena Line's response was to continue its geographic expansion into The Netherlands and the UK to counteract the expected losses in duty-free licences in Scandinavia. The company invested in new and larger vessels, added new routes and acquired more competitors. The coordination and restructuring of the international acquisitions, subsequent rationalisation of the Scandinavian operations, and the effects of the recession in the early 90s almost took their toll. However, Stena Line continued to battle through these hard times.

The vision of the company is to become 'The No 1 Ferry Company and always customers' first choice' (Stena AB 2006 Annual Report, p. 6). To achieve this vision, it had to offer an attractive service – a route network where every route has an optimum geographical location and enjoys market-dominance and high traffic frequency. The fleet of vessels operating the routes must be modern, well maintained and adapted to suit well-defined customer groups. A wide range of products and services catering to the needs, wants and desires of well-defined customer groups needs to be provided. The service offered should be perceived by the customers as providing value for money and service delivery staff are seen to be friendly and positive. Staff policy has to create an attractive workplace where employees are motivated to deliver high-quality service.

Over time, the level of competition has also increased. Stena Line's main competitors have traditionally been other ferry companies, but low-price airlines, the English Channel tunnel and the bridge across Öresund have become direct competitors. Haulage companies, business travellers and holidaymakers now have more choices of transportation services. The challenge for Stena Line, therefore, is to continuously strive to improve the level of efficiency and to be more efficient than competitors in all spheres of their operation. In addition, the provision of excellent service is a key success factor in this highly competitive market.

As part of the aim to provide excellent service and products, the company recognises that a market-oriented approach is required. In recent years, customer relationship management programmes, staff training and internal marketing strategies have been implemented throughout the organisation to complement the market-oriented strategy. An annual employee survey is conducted to measure employee attitudes towards their jobs and the organisation. Training and development courses are used as tools to increase the level of efficiency, knowledge and confidence of the employees. Internal marketing tools are used to communicate relevant and important information to employees.

Stena Line also recognises that individual business units should be given the autonomy to innovate and to implement their own strategies. Hence, Stena Line is a decentralised organisation with autonomous business units. Management introduced a 'satisfaction strategy', which has been extended to all Stena Line's routes. Unit managers have the authority to do what it takes to achieve planned marketing and customer satisfaction objectives, providing these are consistent with wider corporate values. Operational managers and their teams are, in turn, empowered and held accountable for their tasks and to deliver results according to set objectives. For example, if passengers have a complaint with the ferry service, employees are empowered to spend up to £1,000 (€1,440) to solve the problem without having to get management approval.

Stena Line's investments in service quality improvements, its service operations strategy and service delivery systems started to pay off in the early 2000s. Profit-wise, 2006 became the best year since the mid-1990s by almost doubling the annual results from 2005. Passenger numbers are increasing as are revenue from on-board sales activities and freight volumes. Service quality and customer satisfaction ratings have also improved continuously, as Stena Line's six yearly customer satisfaction surveys demonstrate. In 2006, 42 per cent of customers were very satisfied with the service they receive, were loyal to Stena Line and felt it provided value for money. The aim is to increase this satisfaction rating by 3 percentage units per year over the next three years. According to Alan Gordon, Stena Line's route director, who developed the staff empowerment scheme for ferry staff on the Stranraer–Belfast route, he has never had to pay out the £1,000. Before the scheme, they expected to receive four complaints for every compliment. Now, they get three compliments for every complaint!

Questions

1. What constitutes the service offering for travellers with Stena Line and is this the same for truck drivers, business travellers and holidaymakers? In your answer, identify the tangible and intangible aspects of the service and the criteria that these different customer groups might consider when selecting Stena Line over alternative modes of transport.

2. What are the main aspects of the service that distinguish it from physical products?

3. What is internal marketing and why is this practice important to Stena Line? Discuss how the company's staffing policy, internal marketing strategy and customer relations programme affect service quality, customer satisfaction and profits.

---

*Company vision as reported in Stena AB 2006 Annual Report, p. 6; the information in the case is compiled from annual reports, newspaper clippings, industry reports and other secondary data. Adapted from original case by Anna Ackfeldt with permission.

Introduction

The increase in demand for consumer and industrial services has been influenced by a number of factors. First, rising affluence has increased consumers' desire to contract out mundane tasks such as cleaning, cooking and other domestic activities, giving rise to a burgeoning convenience industry. Second, rising incomes and more leisure time have created greater demand for a whole array of leisure services and sporting activities. Third, higher consumption of sophisticated technologies in the home (e.g. home computers, multimedia entertainment equipment, security systems) has increased the need for specialist services to install and maintain them. In the case of business customers, more complex markets and technologies have triggered companies' need for the expertise and knowledge of service organisations, such as market research agencies, marketing and technical consultants. Furthermore, firms facing increasing pressure to reduce costs are buying in services rather than incurring the overheads involved in performing specialised tasks in-house. The need to remain flexible has also led to firms hiring services that provide use without ownership. Finally, an increasing number of firms are keen to focus on their core competences. They are beginning to contract out non-core activities, such as warehousing and transportation, thus stimulating the growth of specialist business service organisations. All these developments have, in turn, led to a growing interest in the special problems of marketing services.

Service industries vary greatly. In most countries, governments offer services: for example, legal, employment, healthcare, military, police, fire and postal services, schools and regulatory agencies. The private non-profit sector offers services such as museums, charities, churches, colleges, foundations and hospitals. A large number of business organisations offer services – airlines, banks, hotels, insurance companies, consulting firms, medical and legal practices, entertainment companies, advertising and market research agencies, retailers and others.

The questions posed in the Stena prelude case get us to think about the nature of the service offering. For example, there are the tangible aspects (e.g. a modern fleet, duty-free shops, restaurants) and intangible elements (entertainment value, friendliness of service staff, availability of ferry routes) of the total service experience. In this chapter, we will address the particular features of services that make service marketing different from marketing physical goods. We will examine the marketing strategies and marketing mix implications for service management. Because of their growing importance to international trade, we will address issues concerning the international marketing of services. As not-for-profit organisations also form an important element of service, we will discuss how they can benefit from applying marketing principles.

As a whole, selling services presents some special problems calling for special marketing solutions.[4] Let us now examine the nature and special characteristics of service organisations that affect the marketing of services.

Nature and characteristics of a service

KEY CONCEPT
www.pearson.co.uk/kotler

Defining services and categories of service mix

A **service** is any activity or benefit that one party can offer to another which is essentially intangible and does not result in the ownership of anything. Its production may or may not be tied to a physical product.

Service offerings include activities such as renting a hotel room, depositing money in a bank account, downloading songs from iTunes or Zunes, sending and receiving e-mails, text messaging, travelling on a ferry or an aeroplane, visiting a doctor, getting a haircut, watching a professional sport, seeing a movie at the cinema and getting advice from a solicitor. Services may

Service—Any activity or benefit that one party can offer to another which is essentially intangible and does not result in the ownership of anything.

be linked to the sale of a physical good. For example, kitchen unit purchases may involve a major element of service if professional design and installation are required. A Miele washing machine may be sold with a five-year maintenance contract, and delivery and installation services.

> There is rarely such a thing as a pure service or a pure good.

Service offerings can contain a combination of the intangible (waiter service in a restaurant) and tangible (the food that is served). As such, there is rarely such a thing as a pure service or a pure good. In trying to distinguish between goods and services, it may be more appropriate to consider the notion of a goods–service continuum, with offerings ranging from tangible-dominant to intangible-dominant[5] (see Figure 13.1).

Firms can create a differential advantage by seeking to balance the degree of tangible/intangible elements associated with their offering. Five categories of offering can be distinguished:

1. The offering consists of a *pure tangible good*, such as soap, toothpaste or salt – no services accompany the product.

2. The offering consists of a *tangible good accompanied by one or more services* – the sales of products such as home entertainment systems and cars are often dependent on the quality and availability of accompanying customer services (e.g. display rooms, delivery, repair and maintenance, installation advice and warranty fulfilment). In a sense, car manufacturers such as Mercedes and Ford are more service intensive than manufacturing intensive, with a significant proportion of their revenues linked to the financial services (e.g. leasing packages, purchase loans) offered to car-buyers. In Chapter 11, we identified these service elements as customer support services forming a part of the total offering – they facilitate and enhance the use of the core product, but are not service products in themselves.

3. Many service providers also supply physical products along with their basic service. A *hybrid offer* consists of equal parts of goods and services. Examples include restaurants that provide both food and service, custom tailors that measure and sew up garments for clients, and retailers that supply a range of manufactured goods in relation to their special role as channel intermediaries.

4. A *service with accompanying minor goods* consists of a major service along with additional services and supporting goods. For example, airline passengers primarily buy transportation service, but the trip also includes some tangibles such as food, drinks, headphones and an

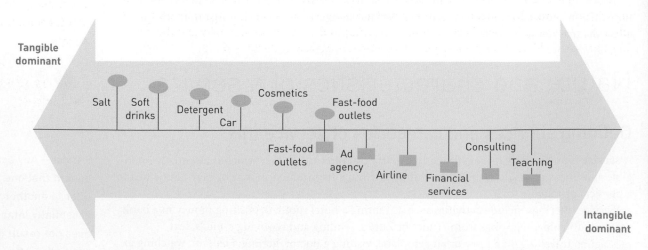

Figure 13.1 The tangible–intangible continuum for goods and services

in-flight magazine. The service also requires a capital-intensive good – an aircraft – but the primary offer is a service.

5. The offering is a *pure service*, consisting primarily of a service such as a haircut, babysitting, consulting, insurance and Internet banking services.[6]

Because the service mix varies, it is difficult to generalise about services without further distinctions. One useful distinction is the nature of ownership – that is, whether they are private (e.g. warehousing and distribution firms, banks) or public (e.g. police, state-run hospitals) sector organisations. Another is the type of market – consumer (e.g. household insurance policy provider, retailer) or industrial (e.g. computer bureau). Services can also involve high customer contact, where the service involves the customer's presence, as in the case of hairdressing and healthcare. Or there is low customer contact, as in dry cleaning and car repair, where the services are directed at objects. Services can be people-based (e.g. software design, consultancies, education) or equipment-bound (e.g. automated car washes, vending machines, automatic cash dispensers). People-based services can be further distinguished according to whether they rely on highly professional staff, such as legal advisers and medical practitioners, or unskilled labour, such as window cleaning, porters and caretakers.

The wide variety of service offerings means that service providers must address the problems specific to their particular service in order to create and maintain a competitive advantage. Despite this variety across sectors, there are a number of characteristics that are unique to services that affect the design of marketing programmes.

Service characteristics and marketing implications

A company must consider four special service characteristics when designing marketing programmes: *intangibility, inseparability, variability and perishability* (see Figure 13.2). We will look at each of these characteristics in the following sections.[7]

> " Intangibility, inseparability, variability and perishability. "

Intangibility

Service intangibility means that services cannot be readily displayed, so they cannot be seen, tasted, felt, heard or smelt in advance of purchase. You can examine the colour, features and performance of a flat-panel television before buying the product. You can test-drive cars before deciding which model to buy. In contrast, you cannot evaluate the quality of a haircut before the service is performed. A person undergoing cosmetic surgery cannot see the outcome before the purchase. Airline passengers have nothing but a ticket and the promise that they and their luggage will arrive safely at the intended destination, hopefully at the same time.

Service intangibility—A major characteristic of services – they cannot be seen, tasted, felt, heard or smelt before they are bought.

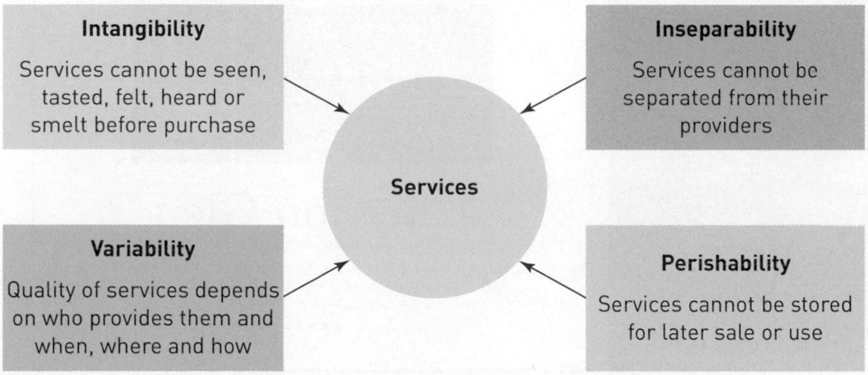

Figure 13.2 Four service characteristics

The intangibility of services makes it difficult for buyers to evaluate the service before consumption. Because service offerings lack tangible characteristics that the buyer can evaluate before purchase, uncertainty is increased. To reduce uncertainty, buyers look for 'signals' of service quality. They draw conclusions about quality from the place, people, price, equipment and communications that they can see. Therefore, the service provider's task is to make the service tangible in one or more ways and to send the right signals about quality. This is also called *evidence management* in which the service organisation presents its customers with organised, honest evidence of the benefits it offers. Whereas product marketers are challenged to add intangibles (e.g. fast delivery, extended warranty, after-sales service) to their tangible offers, service marketers try to add tangible cues suggesting high quality to their intangible offers. In other words, they practise evidence management.[8]

Consider a hotel at the luxury end of the market. It must make this positioning strategy tangible in every aspect of customer contact through a number of marketing tools. Rather than leaving that evidence to chance, it has to carefully manage a set of visual and experiential clues. The *place* or hotel's physical setting should give an appropriate sense of style, grandeur or opulence: its exterior and interior must look beautiful, chic and be designed to look more than just a place to sleep. According to one executive working for the Leading Hotels of the World group, it is increasingly important for the group's hotels to invest in creating more beautiful environments, as many of their guests look for individuality and a 'wow' factor in the places in which they choose to stay.[9] Thus, the lobby might shift from being merely a 'foyer', dominated by the reception and concierge desk, to becoming a grand sitting room, resembling more of a social space where guests can meet friends and business associates in an elegant setting. The hotel's staff (i.e. *people*) should be properly dressed, attentive and responsive, providing consistently good service so that frequent travellers are assured of a seamless service every time they visit. Other *equipment* can also influence visitors' impressions of the hotel – proper furniture in guest rooms, health and fitness or wellness centre and spa facilities. The hotel's *communication materials* should suggest smartness, elegance and luxury, with carefully chosen words and photos that communicate the hotel's positioning. For example, the hotel can create ever more chic interiors and give guests the opportunity to view photographs of rooms and public spaces on the Web before they place a booking. The hotel has to create strong brand associations or *symbols* that capture the very essence of its positioning. Because

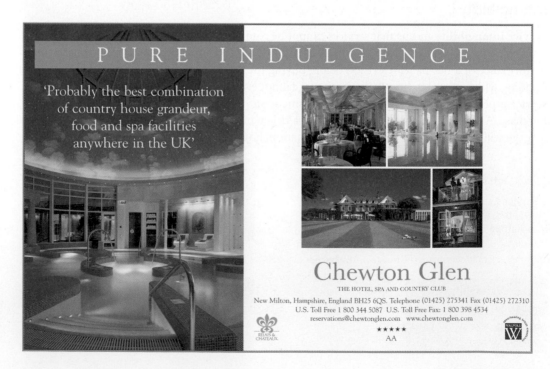

A hotel like Chewton Glen tangibilises its service offering by advertising the grandeur of its country house setting and its fine dining and spa facilities.

SOURCE: Chewton Glen.

service intangibility increases purchase risk, buyers tend to be more influenced by word-of-mouth, which gives credibility to the service, than by advertising messages paid for by the service provider. As such, the service provider's reputation is important. For example, first-time customers who lack prior exposure to the luxury hotel (or any hotel) are likely to get recommendations from friends or colleagues. The service provider should stimulate word-of-mouth communication by targeting satisfied customers who could be encouraged to recommend the hotel to peers and friends.

Inseparability

Physical goods are produced, then stored, later sold to users and, still later, consumed. In contrast, services are first sold, then produced and consumed at the same time and in the same place. **Service inseparability** means that services cannot be separated from their providers. If a service employee provides the service, then the employee becomes a part of the service. For example, a waiter is a part of the restaurant service provided and has to be present to deliver the service to the customer. Moreover, the waiter cannot deliver the service if there are no customers. Similarly, a teacher in a classroom cannot conduct the teaching session if there are no students attending class. In other words, the customers participate actively in co-producing the service product.

Because the customer is also present as the service is produced, *provider–customer interaction* is a special feature of services marketing. Both the provider and the client affect the service outcome. How a waiter serves the restaurant's clients or how a doctor treats her patient, for example, influences the client's judgement of the overall service delivered. The extent to which a teacher is able to develop a rapport with the students in the classroom will influence the quality of their learning experience. Thus, it is important for service staff to be trained to interact well with clients.

A second feature of the inseparability of services is that other customers are also present or involved. The customers in a restaurant, students in the class or passengers in a train, for example, are also present while an individual consumer is consuming the service. Their behaviour can determine the satisfaction that the service delivers to the individual customers. For example, an unruly crowd in the restaurant would spoil the atmosphere for other customers dining there and reduce satisfaction. The implication for management would be to ensure that other customers involved in the service do not interfere with each other's satisfaction.

Because of the simultaneity of service production and consumption, service providers face particular difficulty when demand rises. A goods manufacturer can make more, or mass-produce and stock up in anticipation of growth in demand. This is not possible for service operators like restaurants or a law firm. Service organisations have therefore to pay careful attention to managing growth, given the constraints. A high price is used to ration the limited supply of the preferred provider's service. Several other strategies exist for handling the problem of demand growth. First, the service provider can learn to work with larger groups, so that more customers are serviced simultaneously. For example, bigger sites or premises are used by retailers to accommodate larger numbers of customers, and a pop concert will cater for a larger audience if held in an open-air sports arena than in an enclosed concert hall. Second, the service provider can learn to work faster. Productivity can be improved by training staff to do tasks and utilise time more efficiently. Finally, a service organisation can train more service providers.

Variability

As services involve people in production and consumption, there is considerable potential for variability. **Service variability** means that the quality of services depends on who provides them, as well as when, where and how they are provided. As such, service quality is difficult to control. For example, some hotels have a reputation for providing better service than others. Within a given hotel, one registration-desk employee may be cheerful and efficient, whereas another, standing just a few feet away, may be unpleasant and slow. Even the quality of a single hotel employee's service varies according to his or her energy and frame of mind at the time of each customer encounter.

Service inseparability—A major characteristic of services – they are produced and consumed at the same time and cannot be separated from their providers, whether the providers are people or machines.

Service variability—A major characteristic of services – their quality may vary greatly depending on who provides them and when, where and how.

The ability to satisfy customers depends heavily on the behaviour of customer-facing or front-line service employees. A brilliant marketing strategy will achieve little if service employees do their job badly and deliver poor-quality service.

Service firms can take several steps towards quality control.[10] First, they should invest in recruiting the right employees and providing excellent training, regardless of whether employees are highly-skilled professionals or low-skilled workers. Front-line employees should be empowered to take actions or do what is necessary to ensure that customers are treated well and to deal with customer complaints satisfactorily. However, training in many companies often boils down to little more than pep talks. In order for training to make a real difference to employees' behaviour, companies ensure that training focuses on helping employees to develop essential skills to do their jobs well. Consider the following example:

> Denmark's ISS is one of the world's largest facility service companies, specialising in providing cleaning, property, office support, catering and security services, to customers in over 50 countries across Europe, Asia, South America and Australia. ISS trains its staff relentlessly. Take ISS's commercial cleaning service offering. This involves far more than just running a vacuum cleaner over the carpet. ISS serves big clients – factories, hospitals and offices. To do this well and profitably, employees must do their job efficiently. This means conserving time and cleaning supplies, improving quality and avoiding accidents and injuries. This is difficult enough in ordinary office buildings. At hospitals, chemical plants and factories, the equipment and skills needed can be demanding. Employees must be able to spot and deal instantly with idiosyncratic customers they come across in the job. In the first six months on the job, employees are given training in cleaning techniques, such as knowing which chemicals to use for specific stains and surfaces, and in safety. In the next six months, employees move on to applied economics – they learn to interpret clients' contracts, how profitable a contract is and how the client's profitability contributes to that of ISS's local branch. This is invaluable if the employee is promoted to team leader, which can occur after a year. Once employees become team leaders, they receive training on how to deal with customers, coach junior staff in the team and learn management techniques that will help them meet performance targets, based on both profitability and customer retention. All this training helps ISS staff to do their jobs well.

❝ Knowing how to do something well and being motivated to do it are different things. ❞

Knowing how to do something well and being motivated to do it are different things. The second step towards quality control is to motivate staff by providing employee incentives that emphasise and reward quality, such as employee-of-the-month awards or bonuses based on customer feedback.

> ISS relies on using teamwork and peer pressure to motivate employees to do their best. For example, although most of the clients can be handled by a single person, ISS groups its cleaners into two- or three-person hit-squads rather than sending one person to each site. The squad works together and travels from site to site. Although seemingly inefficient, the extra motivation more than offsets the costs.

The third step is to increase the visibility of service employees and their accountability to customers – for example, car dealerships can let customers talk directly with the mechanics working on their cars. A firm can monitor customer satisfaction regularly through suggestion and complaint systems, customer surveys and comparison shopping. When poor service is found, it is corrected.

> In the case of ISS, management views contact between ISS supervisors and its clients' site managers as crucial. If clients are dissatisfied with the service, superiors get to know about it. In order to generate more contact with customers, ISS rescheduled many of its clients so that its teams overlap for half an hour or so with office workers, making it easier for clients to voice their complaints.[11]

Fourth, service firms can increase the consistency of employee performance by substituting equipment for staff (e.g. vending machines, automatic cash dispensers), and through standardising the service-performance process throughout the organisation. This is done by developing a service blueprint that shows events and processes or job procedures in a flowchart, which alerts employees to potential fail points. The aim is to ensure activities are done properly. For example, consider the service blueprint for a company that delivers flowers. The customer's experience is limited to dialling the phone (or accessing the company's website), making choices and placing the order. Behind the scenes, the company's employee collects payment, gathers the flowers, wraps or places them in a container and arranges delivery. Any one of these tasks can be done properly or badly.

Perishability

Service perishability means that services cannot be stored for later sale or use. Some dentists and doctors charge patients for missed appointments because the service value existed only at that point and disappeared when the patient did not show up. The perishability of services is not a problem when demand is steady. However, when demand fluctuates, service firms often have difficult problems. For example, public transportation companies have to own much more equipment because of rush-hour demand than they would if demand were even throughout the day.

Service firms can use several strategies for producing a better match between demand and supply.

On the demand side, *differential pricing* – that is, charging different prices at different times – will shift some demand from peak periods to off-peak periods. Examples are cheaper early-evening movie prices, low-season holidays and reduced weekend train fares to attract more users. Airline companies offer heavily discounted 'standby' tickets to fill unbooked seats. Or *non-peak demand* can be increased, as in the case of business hotels developing mini-vacation weekends for tourists.

Complementary services can be offered during peak times to provide alternatives to waiting customers, such as cocktail lounges to sit in while waiting for a restaurant table and automatic tellers in banks. *Reservation systems* can also help manage the demand level – airlines, hotels, dentists and doctors use them regularly.

On the supply side, firms can hire *part-time employees* to serve peak demand. Schools add part-time teachers when enrolment goes up, and restaurants call in part-time waiters and waitresses to handle busy shifts. *Peak-time efficiency* can be improved by rescheduling work so that employees do only essential tasks during peak periods. Some straightforward tasks can be shifted to consumers (e.g. packing their own groceries). Or providers can develop *shared services*, as when several hospitals share an expensive piece of medical equipment. Finally, a firm can plan ahead by developing *facilities for future expansion*, as when an airline company buys more wide-bodied jumbo jets in anticipation of future growth in international air travel or a theme park

Service perishability—A major characteristic of services – they cannot be stored for later sale or use.

may buy surrounding land for later development. Service firms have to consider using any of the above strategies for achieving a better match between demand and supply.

Marketing strategies for service firms

Just like manufacturing firms, smart service businesses use marketing to position themselves or their brands more strongly in chosen target markets. Budget airlines like Ryanair and easyJet have successfully positioned themselves as no-frills, low-cost carriers. Tesco promises to do what it can to make every shopping trip that little bit better for customers, because 'Every little helps'. The supermarket strives to meet customer wants – clear aisles, product availability, good prices, no queues and great staff.[12] Credit Suisse positions itself as the bank that helps customers realise new opportunities by 'Thinking new perspectives'. These and other service firms establish their positioning through traditional marketing mix activities. However, because service firms differ from tangible products, they require additional marketing approaches.

Three additional Ps

The services company can develop superior service delivery by addressing three additional Ps of services marketing: *people*, *physical environment* and *process*. These are often referred to as the additional three Ps in services marketing.[13]

Because most services are provided by *people*, the selection, training and motivation of customer-contact or front-line employees can make a huge difference in customer satisfaction. Ideally, employees should display competence, a caring attitude, responsiveness, initiative, problem-solving ability and goodwill.

Because of the intangibility of service products, service organisations can demonstrate their service quality by developing a superior *physical environment* in which the service product is presented and delivered. Customers look to the physical environment for cues to the likely quality of a service. As we saw earlier, hotels will pay a great deal of attention to interior décor and ambience to project a superior service to target customers. Some retailers, such as Galeries Lafayette (Paris) and Harrods (London), have effectively developed the physical environment, giving a very distinctive look or style to their outlets. Hence, by managing the physical environment, service businesses can communicate the firm's customer value proposition to target customers.

Service organisations can also design a superior delivery *process*. For example, many grocery chains now offer online shopping and home delivery as a better way to shop than having to drive, park, wait in line and take groceries home. Service companies can choose among different service processes to deliver their service: restaurants can use different modes of delivery ranging from fast-food and self-service to waiter-service. Students can study for a business degree through different delivery modes (for example, on-campus, distance-learning, full-time or part-time).

The service–profit chain

In a product business, products are fairly standardised and can sit on the shelves waiting for customers. But in a service business, the customer and front-line service employee *interact* to create the service. Thus service providers must work to interact effectively with customers to create superior value during service encounters. Effective interaction, in turn, depends on the skills of front-line service employees and on the support processes backing these employees.

> Successful service companies focus their attention on *both* their customers and their *employees*.

Successful service companies focus their attention on *both* their customers and their *employees*. They understand the *service–profit chain*, which links service firms' profits with employee and customer satisfaction. This chain consists of five links:[14]

1. Internal service quality – superior employee selection and training, a quality work environment and strong support for those dealing with customers, which results in . . .

2. Satisfied and productive service employees – more satisfied, loyal and hardworking employees, which results in . . .

3. Greater service value – more effective and efficient customer value creation and service delivery, which results in . . .

4. Satisfied and loyal customers – satisfied customers who remain loyal, repeat purchase and refer other customers, which results in . . .

5. Healthy service-profits and growth – superior service firm performance.

Therefore, reaching service profits and growth goals begins with taking care of those who take care of customers. All of this suggests that, in order to achieve favourable service outcomes, service marketing requires more than just traditional external marketing but also *internal marketing* and *interactive marketing* (see Figure 13.3).

Internal marketing means that the service firm must orient and motivate its customer-contact employees and supporting service people to work as a *team* to provide customer satisfaction. It is not enough to have a marketing department doing traditional marketing while the rest of the company goes its own way. For the firm to deliver consistently high service quality, marketers must get everyone in the organisation to be customer-centred. In fact, internal marketing must *precede* external marketing. It makes little sense to advertise excellent service before the company's staff is ready, willing and able to provide it. Hence companies such as Stena Line, ISS and many others that strive to deliver superior service, seek to instil in employees a sense of pride and to motivate them by recognising and rewarding outstanding service deeds.

Interactive marketing means that perceived service quality depends heavily on the quality of the buyer–seller interaction during the service encounter. In product marketing, product quality often depends little on how the product is obtained. But in services marketing, especially in high-contact and professional services, service quality depends on the service deliverer and the quality of the delivery. Service marketers cannot assume that they will satisfy the customer simply by providing good technical service. This is because the customer judges service quality not only by its *technical quality* (e.g. the success of the surgery, the tastiness of the food served in the restaurant), but also by its *functional quality* (e.g. whether the surgeon showed concern and inspired confidence, whether the waiter was friendly and polite). Also, each interaction is a 'moment of truth' for the provider, where not just the service encounter, but also the organisation, will be decisively judged by the customer. Service marketers, therefore, have to master interactive marketing skills.[15] Thus, service businesses such as Ritz-Carlton select only 'people who care

Internal marketing— Marketing by a service firm to train and effectively motivate its customer-contact employees and all the supporting service people to work as a team to provide customer satisfaction.

Interactive marketing— Marketing by a service firm that recognises that perceived service quality depends heavily on the quality of buyer–seller interaction.

Figure 13.3 Three types of marketing in service industries

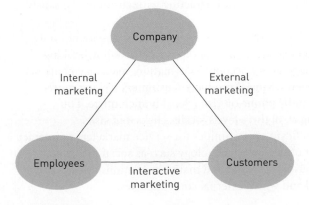

CONTINUING THE TRADITION OF
SHANGRI-LA HOSPITALITY

SHANGRI-LA
HOTELS *and* RESORTS

For reservations at Asia' s finest luxury hotels, please call London (44 20) 8747 8485,
your travel consultant, any Shangri-La or Traders hotel or book on-line at www.shangri-la.com
AUSTRALIA • MAINLAND CHINA • HONG KONG SAR • FIJI ISLANDS • INDONESIA • MALAYSIA • MYANMAR • PHILIPPINES • SINGAPORE • TAIWAN • THAILAND • UNITED ARAB EMIRATES

This Shangri-La advertisement focuses on the hotel's people (its sales force) as one of the main selling propositions.
SOURCE: Shangri-La International Hotel Management Limited/TBWA Hong Kong.

about people' and instruct them carefully in the fine art of interacting with customers to satisfy their every need.

In today's marketplace, companies must know how to deliver interactions that are not only 'high-touch' but also 'high-tech'. For example, thanks to Internet technology, online banking customers can log on to the bank's website and access account information, make payments, set up direct debits or bank transfers and buy new financial products. Customers seeking more personal interactions can contact service reps by phone or visit a local branch office. Thus, companies can master interactive marketing at all three levels – calls, clicks *and* visits.

Although Internet technology offers significant opportunities for service marketers to interact more effectively with customers, the advent of new web technology such as social media is making a huge impact on the way service businesses build and maintain relationships not only with customers, but also with their internal and wider, external constituencies.

Consider a professional services firm such as a management consultancy. Since its most important assets are its people, social media can be used to build and maintain a greater sense of community among employees and clients. For example, firms can use internal webcasts to provide information to employees. As many consultants travel and spend time at client sites, company news and information on human resource benefits could be communicated by mobile devices. Consultants can share experiences and seek advice from fellow workers on private online forums. Employees can also use a shared private wiki to collaborate on projects.

In the case of recruitment of new talent, recruiters can tap into career networks such as LinkIn and Vault to identify and reach prospective employees.

Social media such as e-communities can also help firms to strengthen and expand client relationships. For example, consultants could moderate podcast sessions where clients share experiences on hot topics such as corporate governance, innovation or global leadership. Podcasts and webinars series can be used to attract, educate, engage and influence prospects. And senior consultant blogs can be used to establish industry thought leadership. Thus, social computing technologies offer excellent opportunities to engage and influence the firm's employees, customers, prospects and partners and, in turn, to build lasting, trusted relationships.[16]

Today, as competition and costs increase, and as productivity and quality decrease, more marketing sophistication is needed. Service companies face three major marketing tasks: they want to increase their *competitive differentiation, service quality* and *productivity*. Although these activities interact, we will address each separately.

Managing differentiation

In these days of intense price competition, service marketers often complain about the difficulty of differentiating their services from those of competitors. In many countries in Europe, deregulation of major service industries – telecommunicaitons, transportation, energy, financial services – has resulted in intense price competition. To the extent that customers view the service of different providers as similar, they care less about the provider than the price. For example, customers are lured to bank online because of the advantages of 24-hour service and the tempting deals (higher savings rates or lower transaction costs) that the online banks can offer them. Similarly, budget airlines mushroomed because many fliers care more about travel cost than service.

Service differentiation therefore poses particular challenges. Service intangibility and inseparability mean that consumers rarely compare alternative service offerings in advance of purchase in the way that potential buyers of products do. Differences in the attractiveness or value of competing services are therefore not readily obvious to the potential buyer.

However, services can be differentiated. The solution to price competition is to develop a differentiated *offer, delivery* or *image*.

Offer

The offer can include *innovative features* that set one company's offer apart from competitors' offers. The service provider offers the customer not only what he or she expects – the primary service package – but also secondary service features. Some hotels offer car-rental, banking and business-centre services in their lobbies and free high-speed Internet connections in their rooms. Airlines differentiate their offers on the basis of special or unique services. Consider the following.

According to a recent ad, you can 'RELAX' when you fly business class with Qantas. Its award-winning 'Skybed' has in-built back massager and an extensive range of seat adjustments, offering outstanding comfort in every position.

If you want an experience that 'feels like cloud nine', then, as one ad says: 'there's no better way (than) to fly' Lufthansa business class – you will have your very own 'PrivateBed' that feels like home, and broadband Internet access and real-time surfing that makes 'the airplane feel like a cyber café'.

Virgin Upper Class cabin has a private area for beauty and massage treatments.

British Airways offers spa services at its Arrivals Lounge at Heathrow airport and softer in-flight beds, plumper pillows and cozier blankets. Says one ad: 'Our simple goal is to deliver the best service you could ask for, without you having to ask.'

But what do you make of this strapline? 'Be wise. Real-time BBC text news, business and sports headlines. Fly Emirates. Keep discovering.' Perhaps, this is the airline for you if you always have to 'know what's happening in the world while you're travelling around it.'

Many companies are using new technologies such as the Internet and broadband communications technology to offer innovative features that were not previously possible.

In the face of cut-price offers from competitors such as Carphone Warehouse, the British telecommunications company BT sought to grow its broadband customer base by offering customers BT Vision, an Internet protocol TV (IPTV) service. BT customers receive a personal video recorder with a Freeview digital tuner to obtain terrestrial TV programmes. The recorder enables users to access BT Vision's video-on-demand library through a fixed-line broadband connection.[17]

Unfortunately, service differentiation exposes a second problem – service innovations cannot be patented and are easily copied. Still, the service company that innovates regularly will usually gain a succession of temporary advantages over competitors. Moreover, an innovative reputation may help it keep customers who want to go with the best.

❝ Service innovations cannot be patented and are easily copied. **❞**

Delivery

The service firm can differentiate its brand by offering a better and faster service *delivery system*. The basis for differentiation depends on the nature of the service business. Some suppliers such as hotels, banks and professional service providers may focus on having more able and reliable customer-contact people. Others such as retailers, distributors and logistics companies seek to be more reliable in their on-time delivery order completeness and order-cycle time. Some are better at handling emergencies and responding quickly to customer enquiries. Still others, such as Tesco,

Wal-Mart and Metro create better information systems and adopt technologies such as the use of bar coding and radio frequency identity devices (RFID) to improve service delivery and quality.

Image

Brand image takes time to develop and cannot be copied by competitors. Although image is important to all organisations, it is particularly important to service providers because of its potential to signal tangible value to target customers. However, service intangibility and variability mean that a consistent service brand image is not easily built. Despite the difficulty, service companies can distinguish their service by creating unique and powerful images, through symbols and branding. Lloyds Bank in the UK adopted the black horse as its symbol, conveying an image of strength. Other well-known service symbols include McDonald's Golden Arches and the International Red Cross. The Ritz, British Airways and Hard Rock Café all enjoy superior brand positioning which has taken years to develop. Management consultancies such as Accenture and Booz Allen & Hamilton have also developed powerful corporate brand images. In recent ad campaigns, Accenture's promise that 'We know what it takes to be a Tiger' and Booz Allen & Hamilton's tagline, 'helping people to excel' capture the continuing mystique of consulting and the promise that the firm's professionals can offer clients a reliable substitute for individual leadership.[18] Other service providers, such as Dutch logistics company TPG and Britain's Co-operative Bank, have created distinct corporate identities through investing their skills in good causes and taking the lead in practising moral marketing (see Real Marketing 13.1).

Managing service quality

One of the major ways a service firm can differentiate itself is by delivering consistently higher quality than its competitors. Like product marketers, service providers need to set quality goals through identifying what target customers *expect* concerning service quality. Unfortunately, quality in service industries is harder to define, judge or quantify than product quality. For instance, it is harder to quantify service quality because intangibility means that physical dimensions, like performance, functional features or maintenance cost, can seldom be measured and used as benchmarks. It is harder to agree on the quality of a haircut than on the quality of a hair dryer. The inseparability of production and consumption means that service quality must be defined on the basis of both the *process* in which the service is delivered and the actual *outcome* experienced by the customer. Again, it is difficult to quantify standards or reference points against which service delivery process and performance outcomes are measured. Customer retention is, perhaps, the best measure of quality – a service firm's ability to hang on to its customers depends on how consistently it delivers value to them.

❝ Customer retention is, perhaps, the best measure of quality. **❞**

Measuring quality and exceeding customer expectations

Despite the difficulty, service organisations can measure service quality. In practice, the provider has to determine how customers of the service *perceive* quality. Studies suggest that customer assessments of service quality are the result of a comparison of what they *expect* with what they *experience*.[19] Thus, to improve quality, service marketers have to identify (a) what target customers' expectations are, (b) the key determinants of service quality (that is, the key criteria customers use to judge both the quality of their experience and the outcome of a service encounter), and (c) how customers rate the firm's service in relation to these criteria against what they expected. The key is to exceed the customer's service quality expectations.

An important study highlights the key determinants of perceived service quality. Figure 13.4 summarises these dimensions.[20] Customers' service expectations are formed from past

real marketing

Moral marketing pays: doing well by doing good

When Peter Bakker became the CEO of Dutch mail and logistics company TPG in 2001, he made a conscious decision to engage in moral activities on behalf of the company. Bakker chose to support humanitarian projects, in this case world famine. TPG embarked on a five-year partnership with the United Nations World Food Programme (WFP) which involved a sophisticated contributions programme. Instead of just donating money, TPG uses its particular skills to advise on reducing logistics costs and offers the use of its cargo aircraft for emergency relief flights. Also on offer are its experience in fund-raising and a good communications network.

But how can TPG be sure that its moral activities are adding to the value of the company, not detracting from it? Bakker believes that by investing its skills in a good cause, a company can create more value than by more conventional value-added techniques.

TPG made sales of €11.9bn in 2003. In 2004, it posted record quarterly revenues and was on track to achieve more than 10 per cent profit growth. Although the direct link with profit growth 'was not part of the plan', the company found its genuine desire to do good has been good for the company in return. An Internet survey of 2,000 staff found that 92 per cent gave the highest possible score to the question 'Do you think the partnership with WFP has created value for TPG?' Moreover, Bakker believes that the company's moral ethos inspires employee motivation and that this increased motivation leads to increased profits. 'You grow your profit in a service company by making your customers happy,' he says. 'The best way [to do this] is to make sure your people are motivated.' Fortune has ranked TPG as one of the 10 best European companies to work for. TPG is one of the biggest firms in the Netherlands. It is leading the way for companies to wear their moral dimension on their sleeve and wants other companies to work actively to deal with global crises.

In the financial services market, the Co-operative Bank in the UK has taken a lead in practising moral marketing, by identifying that it has a responsibility to the wider world and bringing political and social issues to the fore. It has ethical policy statements on human rights, social enterprise, arms trading and ecological impact. The bank commits not to invest in any companies, parent companies or countries that it considers to flout the terms of its ethical policy statements. In practice, this means 'we will not invest in any government or business which fails to uphold basic human rights within its sphere of business' or 'any business whose links to an oppressive regime are a continuing cause for concern' (www.co-operativebank.co.uk). It supports charities, co-operatives, credit unions and community finance initiatives.

The bank has rejected millions of pounds' worth of business that conflicts with its ethical policy. For example, it does not invest in currency speculation, companies involved in tobacco product manufacture and any business involved in the manufacture or transfer of armaments to oppressive regimes. The bank enables customers to have a say in where their money is invested – it pursues and amends its policies by asking its customers for their views. It takes its pledge seriously, campaigning on issues it identifies as being important to its customers, such as the Safer Chemicals campaign that it instigated early in 2004.

But, does it pay? According to the Co-operative Bank's Chief Executive, around 20 per cent of the pre-tax profit it posted in 2001 was attributable to the banks' ethical position. Its 'ethical stance' has served to differentiate the organisation from competitors, and, like TPG, it has added value for the company.

Arguably, there is nothing wrong in using ethical positioning to attract more customers. However, for it to be sustained, that moral stance must be genuine and appropriate.

SOURCES: CIM Insights Team, 16 December 2004, at www.cim.co.uk/ins/past_agendas.cfm?choice=TBL, accessed 30 May 2007; information on The Co-operative Bank at www.co-operativebank.co.uk, accessed 30 May 2007; 'Does business ethics pay?', Institute of Business Ethics, 2004; see also Alison Maitland 'Mailman with a hunger to help', *Financial Times* (11 September 2004), p. 10.

encounters and experiences, word-of-mouth and the firm's communications, such as advertising, direct mail, Internet communications, sales campaigns and so forth. In addition, there are 10 dimensions of quality that influence customers' perceived service quality. These include:

1. *Access* (is the service easy to get access to and delivered on time?)
2. *Credibility* (is the company credible and trustworthy?)
3. *Knowledge* (does the service provider really understand customers' needs?)
4. *Reliability* (how dependable and consistent is the service?)

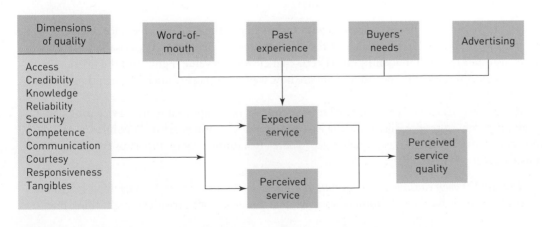

Figure 13.4 Key determinants of perceived service quality

Service differentiation: At British Airways, says this ad, 'Our goal is simple: to deliver the best service you can ask for, without you having to ask.'

5. *Security* (is the service low-risk and free from danger?)

6. *Competence* (are staff knowledgeable and in possession of the skills required to deliver good service?)

7. *Communication* (how well has the company explained its service?)

8. *Courtesy* (are staff polite, considerate and sensitive to customers?)

9. *Responsiveness* (are staff willing and quick to deliver the service?)

10. *Tangibles* (do the appearance of staff, the physical environment and other tangible representations of the service reflect high quality?).

The first five dimensions are concerned with the quality of the *outcome* of service provided, while the last five are related to the quality of the delivery *process*. The service organisation can undertake customer research to identify the criteria that customers value highly and the firm's performance in these criteria and to compare how well it meets customers' expectations compared to competitors.

If perceived service exceeds *expected service*, customers are apt to use the service provider again. If *perceived service* falls below the *expected service*, customers are disappointed. Any mismatch between the two is a 'quality gap'. There are a number of quality gaps that cause unsuccessful service delivery:

1. *The gap between consumer expectations and management perception.* Management might not correctly perceive what customers want. Mobile phone service providers might think that

customers want sophisticated technology, but users may be more attracted to low price and simplicity.

2. *The gap between management perception and service quality specification.* Management might correctly perceive customers' wants but not set a performance standard. The restaurant manager may tell staff to deliver a 'fast' service to customers but does not specify this in minutes.

3. *The gap between service quality specification and service delivery.* Personnel might be poorly trained or are incapable or unwilling to meet the set standard. Or they may be working to conflicting standards, such as taking time to listen to customers and serving them quickly.

4. *The gap between service delivery and external communications.* The service provider's advertising and presentations by its sales representatives influence customers' expectations. A hotel brochure emphasises its wide range of guest services and beautiful bedrooms, but the guest arrives to find that the room he's been given is plain and tacky looking, while the very service he expects to use – the gym – is closed for maintenance until further notice. Here, external communications have distorted the customer's expectations.

5. *The gap between perceived service and expected service.* Customers may misperceive service quality. For example, the helpful clothing store attendant may follow the customer round the store, pointing to the 'new arrivals', while constantly asking the customer if she could assist him in choosing an item. The customer basically expects to be left to make up his own mind. Although the store assistant is trying to show care, the customer will interpret this level of attention as a source of annoyance and irritation.

The service quality manager's goal is therefore to narrow the quality gap, taking into account that what is being measured is perceived quality, which is always a judgement by the customer. Hence, what the customer thinks is reality, is reality; quality is whatever the customer says it is.

Implementing service quality management

The firm's understanding of customers' needs and the ability to provide consistent and dependable service are achieved through internal marketing and continual investment in employee quality and performance. The reputation and credibility of the service provider and customers' perceived risk are interrelated. If consumers trust the service provider, they expect the service to be free from danger, which reduces perceived risk in using the service. Credibility can be improved through effective communication of service quality in the firms' advertising, and through endorsements by satisfied customers. Access can be improved by having multi-site locations and extending distribution, including on- and off-line channels. Waiting times can be reduced through synchronising supply and demand and/or addressing staff productivity problems.

Various studies have shown that well-managed service organisations share a number of common practices. These are summarised below.

1. *Customer obsession.* Top service companies are '*customer obsessed*'. They have a clear sense of their target customers and their needs. They have developed a distinctive strategy for satisfying customer needs that wins enduring customer loyalty.

2. *Top management commitment.* The best service organisations persistently show *top management commitment to quality*. Management at companies such as ISS, Marks & Spencer, American Express and McDonald's look not only at financial performance, but also at service performance. They nurture a quality culture that encourages and rewards personnel for good service delivery.

3. *High service quality standards.* The best service firms *set high service quality standards*. Swissair, for example, aims to have 96 per cent or more of its passengers rate its service as good or superior; otherwise, it takes action. The standards must be set *appropriately* high. A 98 per cent

accuracy standard may sound good, but using this standard, 64,000 Federal Express packages would be lost each day, 10 words would be misspelt on each page, 400,000 prescriptions would be misfilled daily, and drinking water would be unsafe eight days a year. Top service companies do not settle for merely good service; they aim for 100 per cent defect-free service.[21]

4. *Self-service technologies (SSTS)*. Service businesses use SSTS to improve service quality.[22] Self-checkout at hotels, self-check-in at the airport, self-ticket purchasing and self-customisation of product purchases on the Internet are just a few examples of how many person-to-person interactions are being replaced by self-service technologies. In domestic and international air travel, an increasing number of airlines are introducing mobile ticketing and check-in services. For example, frequent flyers with Finnair can check-in using SMS (text messaging) on their mobile phones. Japan Airlines' 'Touch and Go' system allows Integrated Circuit (IC) cardholders to board domestic flights without a physical ticket or boarding pass. Customers whose mobile phones have an RF (radio frequency) chip can collect their boarding pass from a self-service kiosk at the airport. Smart companies, however, ensure that they enable customers to contact the company when they need more information than the SST provides. For example, online travel and hotel reservation websites often include a telephone number for customers to call/click on should they wish to speak with a service representative.

5. *Monitoring systems*. Top service firms monitor service performance. They *watch service performance closely* – both their own and that of competitors. They communicate their concerns about service quality to employees and provide performance feedback. They use methods such as comparison shopping, customer surveys, suggestion schemes and customer complaint programmes. At Nationwide, the British building society, directors regularly meet 100 or more customers in evening sessions and comments are recorded and analysed. Careful monitoring of service delivery performance reveals where services can be improved and how they might best be sold to customers.

6. *Good service recovery*. Customers like to see things right first time. Unlike product manufacturers, which can adjust their machinery and inputs until everything is perfect, service quality will always vary, depending on the interactions between employees and customers. Problems will inevitably occur. Mistakes are a critical part of every service. As hard as they try, even the best service companies will have an occasional late delivery, burnt steak, or grumpy employee. When things go wrong, customer complaints are an opportunity for companies to remedy poor service. *Good service recovery* can turn angry customers into loyal ones. In fact, good recovery can win more customer purchasing and loyalty than when things had gone well in the first place. When companies are responsive and deal with poor service promptly and effectively, they can win back customer confidence and loyalty. Therefore companies should take steps to not only provide good service every time, but also to recover from service mistakes when they do occur.[23]

The first step is to *empower* front-line service employees – that is, to give them the authority, responsibility and incentives they need to recognise, care about and tend to customer needs. As the Stena Line case suggests, well-trained employees are given the authority to do whatever it takes, on the spot, to keep customers happy. Similarly, ISS employees have 'a license to act' and are expected to do so.[24] Such empowered employees can therefore act quickly and effectively to keep service problems from resulting in lost customers.

Companies also establish effective *complaint procedures* to capture opportunities to recover from service mistakes. Studies of customer dissatisfaction show that customers are dissatisfied with their purchase about 25 per cent of the time but only about 5 per cent complain. The rest either feel that complaining is not worth the effort or do not know how or to whom to complain.[25] Because only a small minority of dissatisfied customers ever complain, the firm should proactively attract complaints from disenchanted customers. Channels of communication should be kept open to enable customers to easily offer feedback. Today, customers themselves use different channels of complaint, ranging from a personal visit to the store, the telephone or letter, to e-mail and company websites. Or they may turn to social media such as blogs, e-communities and online social networks to publicise their unhappy service encounters which may damage the service provider's reputation. Companies should therefore have policies, systems and procedures to offer a high level of customer service and care in service-recovery situations. Consider the following:

> In the spring of 2007, Tesco sought to avert a public relations disaster caused by the sale of contaminated petrol. The contaminated fuel was thought to have damaged the oxygen sensor in vehicle exhausts. Tesco ran full-page advertisements in several national newspapers promising customers that it would pay for any damage to their cars caused by faulty fuel. 'If petrol bought at Tesco has damaged your car, we'd like to say how sorry we are. More to the point, we'd like to promise to pay for the repairs,' it said. Although the compensation costs ran into millions of pounds, Tesco was committed to appeasing their customers. 'Our relationship is with our customers and that is what comes first and then obviously there will be discussions further down the line [about] what the source of the problem was,' said the company.[26]

Importantly, service-obsessed organisations *develop a non-threatening culture* – staff are not penalised for unintentional 'mistakes'. Instead, they are encouraged to analyse, resolve and learn from complaints. In addition to practising a 'no-blame policy', staff are rewarded for creating service-recovery opportunities.

7. *Satisfying employees and customers.* Well-managed service companies *satisfy employees as well as customers.* They believe that good employee relations will result in good customer relations. Management clearly defines and communicates service level targets to ensure employees are knowledgeable of the service goals they must achieve and to manage customer expectations from their interaction with the service provider. Consistent with an internal marketing orientation, management seeks to create an environment of employee support, rewarding good performance and engendering positive employee job satisfaction.

> For example, ISS policy on corporate sustainability stresses proper working conditions, good working relations and utilisation of human resources. Total quality management is firmly upheld – staff are trained so that they can do their jobs well and derive satisfaction from them. Management also believes that all employees must be treated with respect and fairness. Happy and satisfied customers yield happy employees.

Managing productivity

With their costs rising rapidly, service firms are under great pressure to increase service productivity. The problem is particularly acute where the service is labour intensive. Productivity can be improved in several ways.

1. Service providers can train current employees better or hire new ones who will work harder or more skilfully.

2. They can increase the quantity of their service by giving up some quality (e.g. doctors having to handle more patients by giving less time to each).

3. The provider can 'industrialise the service' by adding equipment and standardising production, as in McDonald's assembly-line approach to fast-food retailing. Commercial dishwashing,

jumbo jets and multiple-unit cinemas (i.e. cineplexes and megaplexes) all represent the use of technological advances to increase service output.

4. Service providers can also increase productivity by designing more effective services. How-to-quit-smoking clinics and health-and-fitness recommendations may reduce the need for expensive medical services later on. To improve throughput, some National Health Service providers in the UK have introduced a system of patient support whereby a doctor would phone a patient to ascertain whether a clinic appointment is necessary before issuing a prescription for medicines, which can be collected later by the patient.

5. Providers can also give customers incentives to substitute their own labour for the company labour. Examples include self-service food outlets and petrol stations, automatic car-washes and pay-and-display facilities in car parks, all of which reduce the need to employ service attendants.

6. Service providers can harness the power of technology. Although we often think of technology's power to save time and costs in manufacturing companies, it also has great – and often untapped – potential to make service workers more productive. As we saw earlier, technologies ranging from well-designed, user-friendly websites, new information appliances and smartcards and other self-service technologies can be used to give customers access to better service and make service workers more productive. For example, websites have become the most important shop window for many airlines. Recognising that an increasing number of passengers are booking tickets online, British Airways (BA) revamped its website in the mid-2000s, making it more user-friendly. 'BA.com' has transformed the way the company sells its tickets and the way it stays in touch with its customers. The ability to check-in and choose your seat online, as well as the facility to print your own boarding card at home, has proved very popular. Recognising that many frequent flyers also prefer the convenience of a 'one-stop' travel shop, BA.com has also added services such as booking hire cars, hotels and guided tours at destinations. BA is not alone in exploiting the Web. According to the International Air Transport Association, with all airlines switching to e-ticketing by 2007, the industry saves around \$3bn (approximately €2.2bn) a year.[27]

> " Some productivity steps help standardise quality, increasing customer satisfaction. But other productivity steps lead to too much standardisation. "

However, companies must avoid pushing productivity so hard that they reduce perceived quality. Some productivity steps help standardise quality, increasing customer satisfaction. But other productivity steps lead to too much standardisation and can rob consumers of a customised service. Attempts to industrialise a service or to cut costs by using technology to replace employees can make a service company more efficient in the short run. But they can also reduce its longer-run ability to innovate, maintain service quality and flexibility, or respond to consumer needs and desires.[28] In attempting to improve service productivity, companies must be mindful of how they create and deliver customer value. In short, they should be careful not to take the 'service' out of services.

We have addressed strategies for handling the marketing problems that service organisations face. Next, we will examine the special challenges facing non-profit organisations.

Marketing in non-profit organisations

The non-profit, third or social sector, as it is variously known, is a large and growing sector. These organisations seek to achieve objectives other than primarily economic ones such as market share and profit. The sector includes providers of services such as education (schools, universities), healthcare (hospitals, clinics) and public services (local authorities) and organisations that support, promote or engage in specific causes such as provision of emergency relief operations (International Red Cross), alleviating hunger (Oxfam), supporting children in need (NCH, the children's charity) and the protection of animals and birds (Royal Society for the Prevention of Cruelty to Animals, Royal Society for the Protection of Birds).

Internationally, the non-profit sector is as important in developed countries such as The Netherlands, Ireland, Belgium, the UK, Scandinavia and the US, as it is in eastern and central Europe and other parts of the developing world. For example, we are well aware of the work that non-profit organisations are doing in the developing countries, particularly to combat the spread of HIV/Aids. A study of the economies of 26 countries shows that the sector accounts for over $1.2 trillion in expenditures worldwide, employs over 30 million full-time workers and is taking on staff at more than twice the rate of the economy as a whole.[29] Moreover, most non-profit organisations operate in the services sector and account for a large proportion of all service provision in most European countries, hence why we discuss non-profit marketing in this chapter.

Marketing in profit-making firms often involves influencing customer behaviour. For example, adidas uses marketing to influence consumers to buy its brand of sportswear and accessories rather than those made by rival producers. Retailers rely on marketing to influence customers to shop at their store instead of competitor outlets. Service providers like banks and hotels seek to influence customers to use their service and, through internal marketing, ensure that front-line employees deliver exceptional customer service.

Managers in non-profit organisations also need to apply marketing in order to influence behaviour – e.g., influencing volunteers to come forward, donors to give money, service beneficiaries (or clients) to seek help, staff to be 'client-friendly' and so forth. For example, in recent years, Oxfam has sought to reposition its high-street charity store image in response to the growing trend towards ethical shopping (see Real Marketing 13.2). The charity also seeks to respond to and satisfy customer needs. For example, customers can register their details with staff and tell them what kind of clothes they would like. Items are then selected from donations and put to one side for the buyer to try on. In one store (in Lincoln) where the free, personal shopping service was first introduced, it raised £1,775 in its first month.[30]

However, marketers face particular challenges when doing marketing in the non-profit environment. Next, let's examine the non-profit environment and some of the important characteristics of non-profit marketing that distinguish it from marketing in for-profit organisations.[31]

The non-profit environment

A major change in the last twenty years has been the growth of *social marketing* characterised by an increasing trend towards the application of private sector marketing to improve social welfare.[32] In many countries, both the government and for-profit sectors have a growing interest in 'social enterprise'. For example, many government agencies play a major role in social welfare provision and have missions similar to non-profit organisations. In addition, profit-oriented corporations are increasingly engaging in the social sector through cause-related marketing, venture philanthropy and volunteer programmes. For example, Deutsche Post World Net, the leading logistics group worldwide, which transports around 5 per cent of total world trade, is aware of the strain businesses like theirs put on the environment. Along with other global organisations, it works in partnership with the United Nations Global Compact to address the challenges of carbon emissions and to develop sustainable logistics.

There also has been growing emphasis on the international expansion of non-profit marketing. Increasingly, non-profits recognise the importance of international markets with many working with local and international non-profit agencies to carry out the work of providing or sustaining various social programmes (e.g., WWF and environmental quality protection and beautification, Greenpeace's environmental campaigns and Goodwill Industries International's vocational rehabilitation programmes). In recent years, more and more non-profit organisations rely on partnerships with profit-oriented organisations for support. For example,

real marketing

Oxfam: sustainable fashion

The first Oxfam Shop opened nearly 60 years ago in Oxford, raising funds by selling donated items to new owners. Today, Oxfam has a network of nearly 750 charity stores across Britain, selling second-hand cast-offs or surplus new items, ranging from books and designer clothes to trinkets and tea-pots. High street shop sales are worth some £80m a year, yielding about £25m profit, which is spent on its anti-poverty programmes worldwide.

In recent years, ethically conscious fashion has grown in importance, with companies such as Marks & Spencer, New Look, Sainsbury's supermarkets and other stores experimenting with organic clothing ranges. Sales of Fairtrade cotton soared by more than 3,000 per cent in 2006. Oxfam was one of the pioneers of ethical shopping ever since opening its first shop, but it is now trying to make up for lost ground.

Oxfam's director of trading David McCullough said: 'We were one of the people who pioneered the principles of fair trading shopping 40 years ago but we have forgotten to tell people how central we are to the whole ethical debate. When we sell products, the money doesn't go to the shareholders of the company, it goes to fight poverty.' All the charity's clothes come from donations. About 15 per cent of products are bought from west Africa, India, Bangladesh and other countries where the charity operates. But, as McCullough said, 'There is a disconnect at the moment between the public perception of Oxfam shops and the reality and people who strongly support the Oxfam cause and shopping in our stores.'

Oxfam wants to change its image as a seller of cast-offs to poor students and middle-aged rummagers, and to target the booming market of wealthy consumers who have a conscience about how products are made. To help reposition Oxfam's store image, Jane Shepherdson, a long-standing supporter of Oxfam and once fashion retail store Topshop brand director, took on an advisory role at the charity. She'd work unpaid for Oxfam, turning some of its charity clothes stores into a fashion chain for ethically conscious shoppers. Shepherdson has also been highly critical about the trend on the high street to sell ever-cheaper clothes bought from the developing world. She argued that consumers were finding it 'a bit boring' to open their wardrobes and find them full of 'cheap rubbish'. She warned that if clothes were too cheap, 'someone, somewhere down the line is paying'.

Instead, her aim is to offer an 'ethical clothes' range that pays heed to the working conditions in which they are produced and to 'green' factors. One initiative is the use of organic cotton: 'It is also about sustainable fashion – if you buy from Oxfam you are recycling. That message gets lost sometimes.'

...13.2

In its drive to extend its reach to well-off consumers with a conscience, Oxfam also launched Britain's first online charity shop in September 2007. The shop, www.oxfam.org.uk/shop, will initially sell donated items – including clothes, books, music, household goods and collectors' items such as stamps and coins – offering shoppers the chance to buy one-off and reused items. They will be sold at fixed prices in the same way as second-hand items at Oxfam's high street stores. In the latest move in ethical retailing, Oxfam's online shop will also sell more than 100 new fairtrade goods, including jewellery, gifts, chocolate and coffee – and its alternative gift range Oxfam Unwrapped.

Oxfam director Barbara Stocking said: 'At a time when how we buy is at the forefront of people's minds, Oxfam's online shop gives people a real way to buy more ethically. This is the *one website* where customers will know that all their purchases will directly support Oxfam working with people in poverty across the world.'

Specialist online volunteers select and upload the items for sale, which are sold at fixed prices, and will add new items to the site every day. One hundred and twenty thousand donated items will be on sale online by spring 2008. Vintage and vinyl will meet classical and cool as the likes of Armani, Diesel and Frank Usher feature in an eclectic range of clothing – joining a signed *Thomas the Tank Engine* annual, a first edition of *The Importance of Being Earnest,* a Roxy Music record, and a 1960s jack-in-a-box.

With online sales expected to make up at least 17 per cent of the UK's retail market by the end of 2007, Oxfam hopes to tap into the growing trend and raise more funds for its work by obtaining the best price for its items. Selling donated items online has already shown its potential: in the last financial year, Oxfam raised £300,000 by selling on eBay and Abe Books.

Oxfam shop manager Jill Whittingham, from Nantwich in Cheshire, said: 'By taking part in this, we can showcase a range of our goods to customers throughout the UK as opposed to only our local area and we expect to increase the amount we raise as a result. This can only be good news as it will mean we can provide more funds for Oxfam's lifechanging work.'

SOURCES: Adapted and based on Jenny Davey, 'Oxfam stores get touch of Topshop', *Sunday Times* (24 June 2007), p. 3. Copyright © Jenny Davey. NI Syndication Limited, 24 June 2007; Rebecca Smithers, 'Oxfam launches online charity shop', *Society Guardian* (14 September 2007), accessed online at http://society.guardian.co.uk. Copyright Guardian News and Media Ltd 2007; more information on the charity available at www.oxfam.org.uk.

more and more non-profit organisations and profit-oriented firms are jointly undertaking cause-related marketing. Companies benefit because they improve their profits while improving their public image as well as employee morale. As we have indicated earlier in this chapter as well as in Chapters 1, 2 and 4, many corporations are embracing cause-related marketing in response to growing public criticisms of socially irresponsible corporate practices.

However, liaisons of this nature have also raised concerns about the ethics of both the profit-oriented firms and the non-profits that participate in these ventures. They also challenge non-profit marketers about the appropriateness of using powerful marketing techniques to influence behaviours relating to highly sensitive and volatile issues such as Aids, child abuse, abortion and so forth.[33] Hence, to do well, non-profit marketers have to take on board these concerns when applying marketing concepts and tools to achieve the organisation's objectives. They also need to consider the characteristics of non-profit marketing that distinguish it from those of profit-oriented marketing organisations.

When Aids first appeared the publicity changed sexual habits. Now it is no longer newsworthy, Britain's National Health Service saves people's lives and saves the nation money by encouraging people to take care.

SOURCE: The Advertising Archives.

Characteristics of non-profit marketing

Although non-profit marketing employs commercial marketing concepts, it is not the same as, and arguably is much harder than, profit-oriented marketing. Let's address some of the important differences.

Influencing non-existent or negative demand vs satisfying customer needs

Non-profit marketers often have to influence non-existent or negative demand. Sometimes the attitudes and behaviours that a non-profit organisation is trying to influence may be entirely new to the target audience (for example, to adopt a healthy diet). Households need to learn what a healthy diet entails, in the first instance, hence behaviour-change marketing has to focus on educating target audiences about food nutrition, selection, preparation, and so on. Non-profit marketers may also be promoting a behaviour that the target market finds distasteful or that requires them to make sacrifices. For example, exercising regularly is not anticipated by those who have never done it. Chain-smokers and heavy drinkers are unlikely to quit the habit willingly. Because it causes personal discomfort, people may not be inclined to conserve energy by turning down the heating in their house. Drivers feel personally inconvenienced if they have to obey speed regulations and slow down. The challenge for the social marketer in these cases is less about satisfying customers' needs but more to educate them about issues and ideas and to increase social awareness, which will, in turn, change their behaviour.

 Non-profit marketers often have to influence non-existent or negative demand.

Multiple publics

Non-profit organisations typically serve several groups or publics. Two broad groups are *donors* (individuals who support the interest of the organisation, government, companies, trusts) and *clients* (target audiences or recipients of the service, beneficiaries). For example, a community hospital may be part-funded by a trust and private sponsors and part-funded by users or clients of the hospital facilities. The hospital administrators have to satisfy the needs or expectations of both donor and client groups. Marketing programmes have to be developed to build and maintain multiple relationships.

The need to satisfy various target groups also creates particular challenges for non-profit institutions, which can lead to conflicting objectives and difficulties in gauging success. For example, a university may set objectives for research quality, student intake, quality of teaching and the range of courses on offer. It may be very successful at increasing the courses offered and marketing its courses, resulting in an increase in student numbers. However, more students may reduce the quality of the students' learning experience because of the larger class sizes. They may also negatively impact the university's research quality as the time available for lecturers to conduct research and publish declines. As a consequence, the expectations of students and the service deliverer are not fully met. In fact, the service is made worse.

Intense public scrutiny

Although all organisations are expected to behave in an ethical and responsible manner, non-profit organisations have a higher standard to meet, because typically they have special obligations to the community or society at large. For example, a local authority responsible for delivering essential public services, a charity that works in the interest of abused children or one that aims to protect endangered wildlife, are challenged to meet their community's social service or value-expressive needs. But they also tend to receive special rights, privileges or financial support from government and contributions of time from volunteers or money from benefactors to enable them to achieve the organisation's ends. Non-profits do not merely advance their supporters' interests, they also use society's resources (for example, donations) and goodwill to meet society's needs. When the goal is to improve the target audience or wider society's welfare, non-profits will attract formal or informal scrutiny by the government, the funding body or the general public. And, in the case of publicly-funded agencies, it is only natural for taxpayers to be interested in how their money is being spent. Hence, when developing a marketing programme, they must exercise greater care and attention to its aims and how these are attained. More intense public scrutiny makes risk-taking more difficult in non-profit marketing and increases the importance of public relations in the marketing mix.

Investing in good causes: This campaign aimed at Asian females aims to raise awareness about the importance of education and to make sure all girls get a quality education.
SOURCE: Save the Children.

Marketing strategies for non-profit organisations

One of the central tenets of this book is that organisations that adopt a marketing mindset – that is, put the customer at the heart of everything they do – will be more successful in creating and sustaining customer value and relationships than those that fail to adopt this philosophy. Good marketing starts with determining the target audience to be served and then designing and delivering the offering that will satisfy their needs or expectations better than competitors' products. This approach is as relevant to companies like Tesco and Unilever seeking to maintain a strong market position in a competitive environment as it is for churches, museums and charities seeking to attract congregations, visitors and donors respectively and to maintain demand for their service offerings. Both groups of organisations have to work hard to create and maintain mutually beneficial exchanges between individuals (e.g., customers, congregations, visitors, donors) and the organisation. Thus, the marketing principles relevant to profit-oriented firms are also applicable to their non-profit counterparts. Targeting, positioning, differentiation and marketing-mix (product/service, price, delivery, communications) decisions have to be made by both for-profit and non-profit organisations. Next, we address these decisions, taking into account the unique features of non-profit organisations.

Segmentation, targeting and positioning

As mentioned above, non-profits have to serve multiple publics. Although they can be broadly divided into two segments – donors and clients (or customers) – sub-segments of individuals and organisations have to be identified. Segmentation bases used could be general (e.g., demographics, personality, psychographics, values) or behavioural (e.g., beliefs, past behaviour, decision-making unit role or stage in decision process). Having identified and profiled potential segments, they must select target groups.

For example, an anti-smoking campaign might aim at those who smoke heavily and are highly resistant to quitting the habit, as opposed to light smokers. The government agency must decide whether to use its limited budget to target, say, a smaller group of heavy users or the larger group of light users who might be more easily persuaded to stop smoking. In some non-profit situations, such as fundraising, campaigns have to be customised for corporations, foundations and major donors or individuals. An opera may segment its clients into 'subscribers' (couples who are regular opera-goers), 'frequent attenders' (young, lower income, often attending with a friend) and 'infrequent attenders' (not regular opera fans but attracted by a well-known opera or featured star). Each segment will require a separate marketing strategy to increase attendance and customer loyalty. However, going for every segment can be expensive and impractical for many non-profit organisations. The organisation has to consider how to target the selected segments. There are four broad strategic choices:

1. *Undifferentiated marketing.* The organisation goes after the whole market with one offer instead of differentiating the needs of consumers. Examples include a school that uses one approach to teach pupils with different learning capabilities; a church that runs one religious service for a congregation of 6- to 80-year-olds, and a blood donation agency that uses the same campaign to reach different donor groups sensitive to social and physiological risks (e.g., being labelled a 'coward' by others, infections) and psychological fears (e.g., fear of needles).

2. *Differentiated marketing.* The organisation goes for multiple segments, developing a different offering (product, communications campaign) for each targeted segment. A family planning agency might offer different levels of support and advice to clients who seek relief and health assurances for pregnancy prevention and want immediate solutions, as opposed to 'infertiles' who are trying to conceive. Although differentiated marketing achieves higher customer responsiveness, it can lead to higher production, research, communications, media and staff

training costs. Organisations could offset the higher costs of differentiation by reducing the number of target segments.

3. *Concentrated marketing.* Instead of spreading its resources thinly, the organisation devotes its marketing effort to only one or two segments. It can develop deeper customer and market knowledge, while achieving operating economies through adopting a focused strategy. For example, an environmental agency may decide to focus only on the problem of water pollution.

4. *Mass customisation.* The non-profit organisation customises the offering to each individual that it serves in a chosen segment. Examples are commonly found in behaviour-change programmes such as rehabilitation centres for drug-abusers, and smoking and alcohol abuse clinics.

If the non-profit organisation uses a concentrated or differentiated strategy, it has to evaluate the best one(s) to serve based on segment attractiveness, its requirements for success, meeting the organisation's objectives and the organisation's strengths and weaknesses. Finally, when matching segment opportunities to the organisation's (typically limited) resources, managers should focus on segments in which it has a differential advantage.

Non-profit organisations are not immune to competition. Potential donors may choose to give money to one charity instead of another, give time instead of money to the chosen charity, or not to give anything at all. Seldom does a week go by without some charity writing, calling or knocking on one's door asking for a donation to their worthy cause. How often have you said, 'Oh dear, not *another* charity asking me for money!'

Politicians run campaigns to secure your votes. But you may bin their direct mail or are out when they make their door-to-door visits. Universities have to compete to attract the *best* students. And patients may choose to use the National Health Service provider or go private.

Social-awareness campaign managers may think that they are not in competition. They're wrong. If the objective is to influence (even alter) behaviour, such as 'don't drink and drive', 'eat healthily' or 'cruelty to children must stop', the intended 'targets' either may not pay attention to their communications and/or are highly resistant to change.

In the *mind* of the target donor or client, there are choices – alternative solutions. Hence, non-profit marketers have to work hard to create awareness of, and to position and differentiate, their offerings. This means finding out where their offerings lie in the target audience's *mind* and the associations the target has with it. Marketing campaigns such as the NSPCC's 'Cruelty to children must stop. FULL STOP' campaign created strong awareness of the scale of child abuse in our society and the urgency to '*stop it happening altogether*'.[34] But why should someone give money or time to the NSPCC over another children's charity? To be successful, the organisation has to differentiate itself in the eyes of the target audience. It has to demonstrate that involvement in or donations to the organisation will achieve the target audience's own needs and wants, as well as provide better value in meeting those needs. Superior positioning can also be achieved through building or differentiating the organisation's brand. For example, the 'Oxfam' brand is a short-hand for 'poverty fighter' and 'famine relief'.

Thus, non-profit organisations can apply fundamental marketing principles in order to create customer value and long-lasting relationships. They should develop a marketing strategy aimed at influencing target audiences and eliciting desirable responses or influencing customer behaviour. This can be achieved by segmenting the market, developing a positioning strategy and building or differentiating their brand or brands. Next, they must develop and implement the marketing mix.

Developing the marketing mix

The service product characteristics (e.g., intangeability, perishability, etc.) covered earlier in this chapter also apply to non-profits. Non-profit organisations are constantly in search of financial support. Although they obtain funds from other sources (government, corporate and non-corporate foundations, individuals, sales of services, membership fees/subscriptions and so forth), fund-raising is essential to their survival. Next, we will address the implications of fund-raising pressures for non-profit marketing.

The fund-raiser must understand potential donors' needs and wants and then demonstrate how giving to the non-profit organisation will meet those needs and wants. There are a number of implications for communications strategy. In cause-related and event marketing, which are frequently employed by non-profit organisations, messages must clearly and convincingly convey to target audiences the organisation's mission and the worthiness of the cause, and the controls that are in place to ensure the funds will not be wasted on unnecessary bureaucracy, for example a track record of success and availability of trained staff. Advertising and non-personal communications through paid media and under clear sponsorship have to be planned and coordinated like any other element of the marketing mix. Marketers, however, should be especially alert to ethical issues. Communications must aim to create positive attitudes towards fund-raising events and to increase donors' trust and confidence in the organisation and its cause.

Personal communications are often essential in fund-raising and volunteer recruitment, as they are in issue-awareness and public-education campaigns, where changes in behaviour (e.g., quit smoking, don't drink and drive) are sought. Thus, personnel selection and training and internal marketing to personal communicators are key to success. Non-profit organisations should also pay special attention to the role of public relations in generating positive word-of-mouth and creating a buzz around fund-raising events. PR also maintains and enhances the organisation's public image. As mentioned earlier, it has gained prominence because of the sector's propensity to face more intense public scrutiny. Non-profit organisations' PR specialists can also influence target audience behaviour by acting as public advocates, conducting education or issue-awareness programmes, working with and enlisting the help of the media, lobbying and creating events to promote the organisation's cause.

Pricing decisions for non-profit services may not follow the principles that apply to for-profit firms. In the latter, the aim is to achieve target profitability by setting price at a level to cover costs, with the ceiling price being determined by what the customer is prepared (or not prepared) to pay (Chapter 14 will address pricing issues). Non-profit organisations like a community swimming pool and sports centre may be subsidised by taxpayers and may price low to encourage local residents to use the facilities. Other non-profits, like state-funded schools, provide their services free. Non-profits are therefore unlikely to use price to signal value (e.g., a premium price reflecting superior quality), or as a basis of competitive advantage. Instead, they rely on other elements of the marketing mix such as service delivery quality and differentiation, brand positioning and customer relationship building skills to achieve competitive success.

Reviewing the concepts

Marketing has been broadened in recent years to cover services. As we move towards a *world service economy*, marketers need to know more about marketing services.

1. Describe the nature and special characteristics that affect the marketing of services

Services are products that consist of activities, benefits or satisfactions offered for sale that are essentially intangible. Services are characterised by four key characteristics. First, services are *intangible* – they cannot be seen, tasted, felt, heard or smelt. Services are *inseparable* from their service providers. Services are *variable* because their quality depends on the service provider as well as the environment surrounding the service delivery. Services are also *perishable*. As a result they cannot be stored, built up or back-ordered.

2. Identify the additional marketing considerations that services require

Each characteristic poses particular problems and requires certain marketing approaches. Marketers work to find ways to make the service more tangible; to increase the productivity of providers who are inseparable from their products; to standardise the quality in the face of variability; and to improve demand shifts and supply capacities in the face of service perishability. In addition to the four Ps marketing approach, service organisations have to manage three additional Ps: *people, physical evidence* and *processes*.

Successful service companies focus attention on *both* customers and employees. They understand the *service–profit chain*, which links service firm profits with employee and customer satisfaction. Services marketing strategy calls not only for external marketing, but also for *internal marketing* to motivate employees, and for *interactive marketing* to create service delivery skills among service providers.

3. Explain the marketing strategies for improving service differentiation, quality and productivity

To succeed, service marketers have to excel in creating *competitive differentiation* and in managing service *quality* and *service productivity*. Service organisations can develop differentiated offerings, delivery or image.

Service quality is tested at each service encounter. Service businesses must manage service quality in order to meet or exceed customer expectations. To maintain high service quality, managers have to determine *service quality dimensions* and identify *customers' expectations of service quality*. The gaps that exist between customers' expectations of service quality and the service quality experienced determine customer satisfaction. Well-managed service organisations also share common practices which enable them to attain high customer satisfaction: *customer obsession, top management commitment, high quality standards*, use of *self-service technologies*, thorough *systems for monitoring service performance* and *customer complaints* (*good service recovery*) and *satisfying employees as well as customers*.

With their costs rising rapidly, service firms face great pressure to increase service productivity by *hiring and fostering more skilful workers through better selection and training, making quantity–quality trade-offs, 'industrialising' the service, creating more effective services, substituting customer labour for service providers' labour* and *using technology to save time and money*.

4. Describe the nature and special characteristics of non-profit marketing.

The non-profit sector is a large and growing sector. The non-profit environment is characterised by the increasing trend towards *social marketing* – the application of private sector marketing to improve social welfare. There also has been growing emphasis on the international expansion of non-profit marketing. More and more non-profit organisations are also looking to profit-oriented firms to undertake cause-related marketing.

Non-profit organisations must generate income in order to fund their activities and to survive, but their purpose is to achieve objectives other than economic ones like market share and profit. Like for-profit marketers, managers in non-profit organisations also need to apply marketing in order to influence target market behaviour such as encouraging volunteers to come forward, donors to give money, service beneficiaries (or clients) to seek help, staff to be 'client-friendly' and so forth. However, marketers face particular challenges when doing marketing in the non-profit environment.

Although non-profit marketing employs commercial marketing concepts, it is not the same as, and arguably is much harder than, profit-oriented marketing. Some important differences in non-profit marketing include the need to influence non-existent or negative demand vs satisfying customer needs; serving of multiple publics including two broad groups – *donors* and *clients* (target audiences or recipients of the service, beneficiaries); and the facing of more intense public scrutiny.

The marketing principles of segmentation, targeting, positioning and differentiation, and the development of a marketing mix, which are relevant to profit-oriented firms are also applicable to non-profit organisations. However, these decisions must take into account the unique features of non-profit organisations. In particular, non-profit organisations have to pay special attention to cause-related and event marketing and to tailor communications programmes to increase the effectiveness of their fund-raising activities. Pricing decisions for non-profit services may not follow the principles that apply to for-profit firms. Instead, non-profit organisations rely on other elements of the marketing mix such as service delivery quality and differentiation, brand positioning and customer relationship building skills to achieve competitive success.

Discussing the concepts

1. Some service marketers maintain that service marketing is different from product marketing and requires different skills. Some product marketers disagree, arguing that 'good marketing is good marketing'. What is your position on this debate? Discuss, using examples to illustrate whether product and services are fundamentally different or highly related.

2. Consider the following: (a) banking and financial service provider; (b) mobile phone service operator; (c) employment agency; (d) restaurant. Explain how the activities of these organisations meet the four special characteristics of a service. In your answer, show how these characteristics impact the organisation's marketing approach.

3. What are internal and interactive marketing? Give examples of how service firms or organisations might use these concepts to enhance their service–profit chain.

4. Think about your own experiences of bad service encounters. Did the firms concerned have easy channels for customers to register complaints? Why is it important for firms to have established procedures for capturing customer complaints? Explain.

5. To what extent does marketing in a non-profit organisation differ from that in a profit-oriented service business? Discuss, using relevant practical examples.

Applying the concepts

1. The core service in the airline industry is transportation. The 'problem-solving' benefit for the customer is travel from one place to another. The popularity of low-budget, no-frills airlines suggests that many customers are more concerned about travel cost than good service. It would seem that low price is the single most important differentiation factor. How have traditional airlines such as KLM, British Airways, Air France and others responded to the threat posed by their low-cost rivals? Consider the appropriateness of the three key tasks – increasing competitive differentiation, high service quality and productivity – for developing a sustainable differential advantage in the airline industry.

Web resources

For additional classic case studies and Internet exercises, visit **www. pearsoned.co.uk/ kotler**

2. Think about your experience of a recent service encounter (e.g., buying a meal from a fast-food outlet, making a purchase of DVDs from an online store, going to the movies, a dental check-up, etc.). Based on the quality dimensions indicated in Figure 13.4, evaluate the service quality provided. To do this, score each criterion from 1 to 10, according to its importance (that is, value) to you. Then, score each criterion from 1 to 10, based on your perception of how well the service was provided. Analyse the scores. What do they tell you about the service you expected and perceived? What are the marketing implications for the service provider? Explain.

References

1. Data from CIA, *The World Factbook*, 2007, accessed at http://www.cia.gov/cia//publications/factbook/economy, June 2007.

2. See World Trade Organization, *International Trade Statistics 2005*, p. 23, accessed at www.wto.org, August 2006.

3. Jean-Louis Renaud, 'World trade in services', *EDC Economics* (July 2006), accessed at www.edc.ca/english/, June 2007.

4. Ronald Henkoff, 'Service is everybody's business', *Fortune* (27 June 1994), pp. 48–60; Adrian Palmer and Catherine Cole, *Services Marketing: Principles and practice* (Upper Saddle River, NJ: Prentice Hall, 1995), pp. 56–60; Valerie Zeithaml and Mary Jo Bitner, *Services Marketing* (New York: McGraw-Hill, 1996), pp. 8–9; Michael van Biema and Bruce Greenwald, 'Managing our way to higher service-sector productivity', *Harvard Business Review* (July–August 1997), pp. 87–95.

5. G. Lynn Shostack, 'Breaking free from product marketing', *Journal of Marketing*, **41** (April 1997), pp. 73–80.

6. For more on definitions and classifications of services, see Christopher H. Lovelock and Jochen Wirtz, *Services Marketing: People, technology, strategy*, 6th edn (Upper Saddle River, NJ: Prentice Hall, 2007).

7. See Leonard L. Berry, 'Services marketing is different', *Business* (May–June 1980), pp. 24–30; Karl Albrecht, *At America's Service* (Homewood, IL: Dow-Jones-Irwin, 1988); William H. Davidow and Bro Uttal, *Total Customer Service: The ultimate weapon* (New York: Harper & Row, 1989).

8. See Leonard Berry and Neeli Bendapudi, 'Clueing in customers', *Harvard Business Review* (February 2003), pp. 100–6; and Theodore Levitt, 'Marketing intangible products and product intangibles', *Harvard Business Review* (May–June 1981), pp. 94–102.

9. Jeff Mills, 'Seeking a sense of place', Special Report – Business Travel: *Financial Times* (15 March 2005), p. 3.

10. For more discussion, see James L. Heskett, 'Lessons in the service sector', *Harvard Business Review* (March–April 1987), pp. 122–4; E. Gummesson, *Quality Management in Service Organisations* (New York: International Service Quality Association, St John's University, 1993).

11. Information on ISS Group from www.issworld.com, accessed June 2007; 'Service with a smile', *The Economist* (25 April 1998), pp. 85–6.

12. Tesco's core purpose and values and 'Every little helps' strategy from www.tescocorporate.com, accessed June 2007.

13. B.H. Booms and M.J. Bitner, 'Marketing strategies and organisational structures for service firms', in J. Donnelly and W.R. Gearoge (eds), *Marketing of Services* (Chicago: American Marketing Association, 1981), pp. 47–51.

14. See James L. Heskett, W. Earl Sasser, Jr. and Leonard A. Schlesinger, *The Service Profit Chain: How leading companies link profit and growth to loyalty, satisfaction, and value* (New York: Free Press, 1997) and *The Value Profit Chain: Treat employees like customers and customers like employees* (New York: Free Press, 2003); 'Recovering from service failure', *Strategic Direction* (June 2006), pp. 37–40; and Eugene W. Anderson and Vikas Mittal, 'Strengthening the satisfaction–profit chain', *Journal of Service Research* (November 2000), pp. 107–20.

15. Christian Gronroos, 'A service quality model and its marketing implications', *European Journal of Marketing*, **18**, 4 (1984), pp. 36–44, and 'Internal marketing – theory and practice', in T.M. Bloch, G.D. Upah and V.A. Zeithaml (eds), *Services Marketing in a Changing Environment* (American Marketing

Association, 1985); see also Neeru Malhotra and A. Mukherjee, 'Analysing the commitment–service quality relationship: a comparative study of retail banking call centres and branches', *Journal of Marketing Management* **19** (2003), pp. 941–71.

16. Based on Cinny Little, 'Social revolution', *The Marketer* (November 2006), pp. 10–12.

17. Andrew Parker, 'BT to launch new TV service', *Financial Times* (28 November 2006), p. 18.

18. Christopher McKenna, 'Image is everything', Special Report – Business Consulting: *Financial Times* (20 November 2006), p. 2; see also Christopher McKenna, *The World's Newest Profession: Management consulting in the twentieth century* (Cambridge University Press, 2006).

19. C. Gronroos, *Service Management and Marketing: Customer management in service competition* (Chichester: Wiley, 2007), pp. 76–7; see also A. Parasuraman, Valerie A. Zeithaml and Leonard L. Berry, 'A conceptual model of service quality and its implications for future research', *Journal of Marketing*, **49** (Fall 1985), pp. 41–50; Zeithaml, Berry and Parasuraman, *Delivering Service Quality: Balancing customer perceptions and expectations* (New York: Free Press, 1990); Parasuraman, Zeithaml and Berry, 'Reassessment of expectations as a comparison standard in measuring service quality: Implications for further research', *Journal of Marketing*, **58** (January 1994), pp. 111–24.

20. Michael K. Brady and J. Joseph Crorin, Jr, 'Some new thoughts on conceptualizing perceived service quality', *Journal of Marketing*, **65** (July 2001), pp. 34–49; A. Parasuraman, Valerie A. Zeithaml and Leonard L. Berry, 'A conceptual model of service quality and its implications for future research', *Journal of Marketing*, **49** (Fall 1985), pp. 41–50; Berry and Parasuraman, *Marketing Services: Competing through quality* (New York: Free Press, 1991), p. 16.

21. James L. Heskett, W. Earl Sasser, Jr and Christopher W.L. Hart, *Service Breakthroughs* (New York: Free Press, 1990).

22. Mary Jo Bitner, 'Self-service technologies: What do customers expect?', *Marketing Management* (Spring 2001), pp. 10–11; Matthew L. Meuter, Amy L. Ostrom, Robert J. Roundtree and Mary Jo Bitner, 'Self-service technologies: Understanding customer-satisfaction with technology based service encounters', *Journal of Marketing*, **64** (July 2000), pp. 50–64.

23. Stephen W. Brown, 'Practicing best-in-class service recovery', *Marketing Management* (Summer 2000), pp. 8–9; James G. Maxham III, 'Service recovery's influence on consumer satisfaction, positive word-of-mouth, and purchase intentions', *Journal of Business Research* (October 2001), p. 11; David E. Bowen, 'Internal service recovery: developing a new construct', *Measuring Business Excellence* (2002), p. 47.

24. Information from 'ISS corporate values', www.issworld.com, accessed June 2007.

25. Leonard L. Berry and A. Parasuraman, *Marketing Services: Competing through quality* (New York: Free Press, 1991); Stephen W. Brown and Murali Chandrashekaran, 'Customer evaluations of service complaint experiences: Implications for relationship marketing', *Journal of Marketing* (April 1998), pp. 60–76.

26. Elizabeth Rigby and Chris Bryant, 'Supermarket chains offer to pay for car repairs', *Financial Times* (7 March 2007), p. 4.

27. 'Special report. The travel industry', *The Economist* (1 October 2005).

28. See Leonard A. Schlesinger and James L. Heskett, 'The service-driven service company', *Harvard Business Review* (September–October 1991), pp. 72–81; and Michael van Biema and Bruce Greenwald, 'Managing our way to higher service-sector productivity', *Harvard Business Review* (July–August 1997), pp. 87–95.

29. Lester M. Salamon and Wojciech Sokolowski, 'Volunteering in cross-national perspective: Evidence from 26 countries', Working Paper, The Johns Hopkins Comparative Nonprofit Sector Project, 2001; Lester M. Salamon and Associates, *Global Civil Society At-a-Glance*, Institute for Policy Studies, Center for Civil Society Studies (CCSS), Johns Hopkins University, 2001; for more information about the work undertaken by the CCSS, see http://www.jhu.edu/~cnp.

30. 'Charity offers personal shopping' (4 January 2007), accessed at www.news.bbc.co.uk/1/hi/england/lincolnshire/6231001.stm.

31. See Alan R. Andreasen and Philip Kotler, *Strategic Marketing for Nonprofit Organizations*, 6th edn (Upper Saddle River, NJ: Prentice Hall, 2003).

32. Simon Caulkin, 'How the not-for-profit sector became big business', *The Observer* (12 February 2006), accessed at www.observer.com, August 2007.

33. Miklós Marschall, 'The nonprofit sector in a centrally planned economy', in Helmut K. Anheiser and Wolfgang Seibel (eds), *The Third Sector: Comparative studies of nonprofit organizations* (Berlin: Walter de Gruyter, 1990), pp. 277–91.

34. For more information visit www.nspcc.org.uk.

Company case 13 The Ritz

The Ritz is not just a hotel, it is style, sophistication, wealth, all mixed with fun and gaiety. Since Irving Berlin wrote 'Putting on the Ritz' legions of artists, from Ella Fitzgerald to Judy Garland, have taken up the refrain. Whole albums are still dedicated to the theme that rose in the 1920s but from London to Boston, from Bali to Bahrain, the Ritz retains its glitter. One of the latest places to savour is the Ritz-Carlton Berlin on the central Potsdamer Platz – offering a special introductory price per room of only €165! The hotel chain achieved this repeated success by continuing to try hard at catering for the needs of the most demanding customers of all – the rich.

The Ritz is now part of the Ritz-Carlton chain of luxury hotels that caters to the top 5 per cent of corporate and leisure travellers. The company's 'Credo' sets lofty customer service goals: 'The Ritz-Carlton Hotel is a place where the genuine care and comfort of our guests is our highest mission. We pledge to provide the finest personal service and facilities for our guests who will always enjoy a warm, relaxed yet refined ambience. The Ritz-Carlton experience enlivens the senses, instils well-being, and fulfils even the unexpressed wishes and needs of our guests.' The company's Web page concludes: 'Here a calm settles over you. The world, so recently at your door, is now at your feet.'

The Credo is more than just words on paper – Ritz-Carlton delivers on its promises. In surveys of departing guests, some 95 per cent report that they've had a truly memorable experience. In fact, at Ritz-Carlton, exceptional service encounters have become almost commonplace. Take the experiences of Nancy and Harvey Heffner of Manhattan, who stayed at the Ritz-Carlton Naples, in Naples, Florida (recently rated the best hotel in the United States, fourth best in the world, by *Travel & Leisure* magazine). As reported in the *New York Times*:

> 'The hotel is elegant and beautiful', Mrs Heffner said, 'but more important is the beauty expressed by the staff. They can't do enough to please you.' When the couple's son became sick last year in Naples, the hotel staff brought him hot tea with honey at all hours of the night, she said. When

> Mr Heffner had to fly home on business for a day and his return flight was delayed, a driver for the hotel waited in the lobby most of the night.

Such personal, high-quality service has also made the Ritz-Carlton a favourite among conventioneers. 'They not only treat us like kings when we hold our top-level meetings in their hotels, but we just never get any complaints', comments one convention planner. 'Perhaps the biggest challenge a planner faces when recommending the Ritz-Carlton at Half Moon Bay to the boss, board and attendees is convincing them that meeting there truly is work', says another. 'The . . . first-rate catering and service-oriented convention services staff [and] the Ritz-Carlton's ambience and beauty – the elegant, Grand Dame-style lodge, nestled on a bluff between two championship golf courses overlooking the Pacific Ocean – makes a day's work there seem anything but.'

In 1992, Ritz-Carlton became the first hotel company to win the Malcolm Baldrige National Quality Award. Since its incorporation in 1983, the company has received virtually every major award that the hospitality industry bestows. More importantly, service quality has resulted in high customer retention: more than 90 per cent of Ritz-Carlton customers return. And despite its hefty room rates, the chain enjoys a 70 per cent occupancy rate, almost nine points above the industry average.

Most of the responsibility for keeping guests satisfied falls to Ritz-Carlton's customer-contact employees. Thus, the hotel chain takes great care in selecting its personnel. 'We want only people who care about people', notes the company's vice president of quality. Once selected, employees are given intensive training in the art of coddling customers. New employees attend a two-day orientation, in which top management drums into them the '20 Ritz-Carlton Basics'. Basic number one: 'The Credo will be known, owned, and energized by all employees.'

Employees are taught to do everything they can to never to lose a guest. 'There's no negotiating at Ritz-Carlton when it comes to solving customer problems', says the quality executive. Staff learn that *anyone* who receives a customer complaint *owns* that complaint until it's resolved (Ritz-Carlton Basic number 8). They are trained to drop whatever they're doing to help a customer – no matter what they're doing or what their department. Ritz-Carlton employees are empowered to handle problems on the spot, without consulting higher-ups. Each employee can spend up to €2,000 to redress a guest grievance, and each is allowed to break from his or her routine for as long as needed to make a guest happy. 'We master customer satisfaction at the individual level', adds the executive. 'This is our most sensitive listening post . . . our early warning system.' Thus, while competitors are still reading guest comment cards to learn about customer problems, Ritz-Carlton has already resolved them.

> Staff learn that *anyone* who receives a customer complaint *owns* that complaint until it's resolved.

Ritz-Carlton instils a sense of pride in its employees. 'You serve', they are told, 'but you are not servants.' The company motto states, 'We are ladies and gentlemen serving ladies and gentlemen'. Employees understand their role in Ritz-Carlton's success. 'We might not be able to afford a hotel like this,' says employee Tammy Patton, 'but we can make it so people who can afford it will want to keep coming here.'

And so they do. When it comes to customer satisfaction, no detail is too small. Customer-contact people are taught to greet guests warmly and sincerely, using guest names when possible. They learn to use the proper language with guests – phrases such as *good morning, certainly, I'll be happy to, welcome back*, and *my pleasure*, never *Hi* or *How's it going?* The Ritz-Carlton Basics urge employees to escort guests to another area of the hotel rather than pointing out directions, to answer the phone within three rings and with a 'smile', and to take pride and care in their personal appearance. As the general manager of the Ritz-Carlton Naples puts it, 'When you invite guests to your house, you want everything to be perfect.'

Ritz-Carlton recognises and rewards employees who perform feats of outstanding service. Under its 5-Star Awards programme, outstanding performers are nominated by peers and managers, and winners receive plaques at dinners celebrating their achievements. For on-the-spot recognition, managers award Gold Standard Coupons, redeemable for items in the gift shop and free weekend stays at the hotel. Ritz-Carlton further rewards and motivates its employees with events such as Super Sports Day, an employee talent show, luncheons celebrating employee anniversaries, a family picnic, and special themes in employee dining rooms. As a result, Ritz-Carlton's employees appear to be just as satisfied as its customers are. Employee turnover is less than 30 per cent a year, compared with 45 per cent at other luxury hotels.

Ritz-Carlton's success is based on a simple philosophy: to take care of customers, you must first take care of those who take care of customers. Satisfied employees deliver high service value, which then creates satisfied customers. Satisfied customers, in turn, create sales and profits for the company.

Questions

1. Most people see a Ritz-Carlton hotel as a swanky building on a prime site, such as London's Piccadilly, but is the structure the essence of the hotel chain's success?

2. What accounts for the Ritz-Carlton's continued success?

3. Even the Ritz does not charge €2,000 to stay, so how can the company justify allowing employees to spend 'up to €2,000 to redress a guest grievance'?

4. What are the key determinants of the service quality perceived by the Ritz-Carlton's customers?

5. To serve its globe-hopping customers the hotel chain has to provide the same level of service 'from London to Boston, from Bali to Bahrain'. What are the barriers to offering services that are 'the same' or of 'the same quality' within so many cultures? How can such uniform service quality be achieved?

SOURCES: Quotes and other information from Duff McDonald, 'Roll out the blue carpet', *Business 2.0* (May 2004); Edwin McDowell, 'Ritz-Carlton's keys to good service', *New York Times* (31 March 1993), p. D1; 'The Ritz-Carlton, Half Moon Bay', *Successful Meetings* (November 2001), p. 40; *Wall Street Journal* (20 June 2002), p. D1; N.V. Henderson, 'Ritz-Carlton Las Vegas captures AAA Five Diamond Award within months of opening', *Business Wire* (17 November 2003); *Wall Street Journal*, 'Ritz-Carlton tops Four Seasons' (27 August 2003); *AP Worldstream*, 'New Ritz-Carlton opens on Berlin's central Potsdamer Platz' (11 January 2004); 'Putting on the Ritz: Capital sings Irving Berlin', *Capital* (1992); www.ritzcarlton.com (February 2004); Bruce Serlen, 'Ritz Carlton retains hold on corporate deluxe buyers,' *Business Travel News* (7 February 2005); Peter Sanders, 'Takin' off the Ritz – a tad', *Wall Street Journal* (23 June 2006), p. B1; Jo Johnson, 'Global traveller: Places to go, things to see, food to eat', *Financial Times* (17 September, 2007); and www.ritzcarlton.com (October 2007).

Video Case Saint Paul's Cathedral

Saint Paul's Cathedral is an iconic brand that is viewed differently by its different publics. It is the Cathedral of the City of London – London's financial district – and one of the wealthiest corners of the world. It is also a historic monument of great emotional significance. Burnt down and rebuilt after the first fire of London in 1666 it survived the second great fire during the

Lucy Winkett
Residentary Canon

Blitz in 1940 (see the Cathedral's timeline at www.stpauls.co.uk). To 700,000 visitors a year, the Cathedral a tourist attraction with a glorious interior and a dome that provides a great view of London. You can take a virtual tour by visiting www.sphericalimages.com/stpauls/virtual_tour.htm. To many, St. Paul's is the venue of widely-viewed events, such as the marriage of Prince Charles and Lady Diana Spencer. It also houses one of the world's leading musical foundations, the Cathedral Choir, and one of Britain's best schools where the choristers and other fee paying children are educated. The Cathedral's wealth and breadth of riches make it a huge asset, but a very complicated brand.

Although a hugely important national monument as a Cathedral of the Church of England, St. Paul's receives insignificant state funding and has to survive from the collection at religious services and other money it can generate from its numerous and varied stakeholders.

After viewing the video, you may address the following questions:

1. To what extent is Saint Paul's marketing operation different to that faced by the commercial operations that surround it?
2. The Cathedral wants to get short-stay tourists to London to make Saint Paul's one of the three attractions that they typically go to during their visit. Attendance at the Cathedral's four daily services is free, but most visitors are tourists who pay an entrance fee and additional charges for entering other parts of the Cathedral, such as the dome. To what extent do you think price influences the number of visitors the Cathedral attracts relative to the other elements of the marketing mix?
3. The Cathedral's marketing manager says the aim is to maximise the number of visitors. Given the complexity of the product, suggest alternative targets the marketing department could set itself other than sales transactions? How could the concept of long-run customer value change the relationship between the cathedral and those who use it?

Price: value plus a reasonable sum for the wear and tear of conscience in demanding it

AMBROSE PIERCE

Price

PART five

Chapter 14 Pricing

IN PART FIVE OF *PRINCIPLES OF MARKETING* we cover an element of the marketing mix that is both easy and expensive to manipulate – price.

According to one pricing expert, pricing lets a company 'get paid for the value it creates for customers.'[1] If effective product development, promotion and distribution sow the seeds of business success, effective pricing is the harvest. Firms successful at creating customer value with the other marketing mix activities must still capture some of this value in the prices they earn. Yet, despite its importance, many firms do not handle pricing well. Often, firms rely on price cutting to attract customers quickly. This is a poor route to long-term market success, because giving a 10 per cent price cut to a customer can mean taking a 50 per cent cut in profits. The industrialist Philip Armour explained that businesses often resort to price-cutting: 'Anybody can cut prices, but it takes brains to make a better article.'

In this chapter, we will firstly examine the internal and external factors that influence pricing decisions and general pricing approaches. Then, we will dig into pricing strategies – new-product pricing, product mix pricing, price adjustment and price reaction strategies.

Buy sheep, sell deer.

ANON

Pricing

Mini Contents List

- Prelude case – The Oresund Bridge: over or under, down and out, again and again
- What is price?
- Factors to consider when setting prices
- Real Marketing 14.1 – Economic Value Added
- New-product pricing strategies
- Product-mix pricing strategies
- Price-adjustment strategies
- Real Marketing 14.2 – Pricing around the world
- Price changes
- Company case 14 – BMI Baby, Buzz, ValuJet, easyJet: easy come, easy go

◀ SOURCE: Surf/bbh.

'You're really just a jerk,
On my way, you know I Won't Pay Your Price.'

From Mötorhead, '(I Won't) Pay Your Price', on 'Overkill', Sanctuary Records,
B0008BPK2HA

Previewing the concepts

Companies today face a fierce and fast-changing pricing environment. Increasing customer price consciousness has put many companies in a 'pricing vice'. Many companies bemoan the fact that they have virtually no pricing power. They are not able to raise prices, and often, the pressure to slash them continues unabated. It seems that almost every company, from cars and chemicals to travel and telecommunications, is slashing prices, and that is hurting their profits.

Yet, cutting prices is often not the best answer. Reducing prices unnecessarily can lead to lost profits and damaging price wars. It can signal to customers that the price is more important than the customer value that the brand delivers. Instead, companies should sell value, not price. They should persuade customers that paying a higher price for the company's brand is justified by the greater value they gain. Most customers will gladly pay a fair price in exchange for real value. The challenge is to find the price that will let the company make a fair profit by getting paid for the customer value it creates.

In this chapter, we examine the process of setting prices and the development of pricing strategies and programmes. First, we define price. Next, we look at the factors marketers must consider when setting prices and examine general pricing approaches. We then address pricing strategies available to marketers: new-product pricing strategies for products in the introductory stage of the product life-cycle, product-mix pricing strategies, price adjustments that account for customer differences and changing situations, and strategies for initiating and responding to price changes.

After reading this chapter, you should be able to:

1. Discuss the role of pricing and why it is important to understand customer value perceptions when setting prices.
2. Discuss the importance of company and product costs in setting prices.
3. Identify and define the other important internal and external factors affecting a firm's pricing decisions.
4. Describe the major strategies for pricing new products.
5. Explain how companies determine a set of prices that maximise the profits from the total product mix.
6. Discuss how companies adjust prices which take into account different customer and market situations.
7. Discuss the key issues relating to initiating and responding to price changes.

Pricing products is easy when it is viewed in isolation, but like all elements of the marketing mix, price does not exist in isolation. It is linked to raw material prices and labour, to customers' perception of a product, to its distribution and, as the Oresund Bridge case shows, to what people are willing to pay and the value of the product to potential customers.

Prelude case The Oresund Bridge: over or under, down and out, again and again

The Oresund Bridge (Øresundsbron) is a combined two-track rail and four-lane road bridge across the Oresund strait between Denmark and Sweden. This time it was supposed to be different, but it was not. Governments have no problem commissioning grand projects that go under or over the sea, but they do have problems in keeping costs down and getting people to use the facility. Within a year of being opened it looked like the Øresundsbron, which links Copenhagen to Malmö, was going the way of similar attempts to join up bits of land.

There is a pattern in the joining of conspicuous bits of land:

1. The idea is so obvious that people start thinking about joining them long before the technology is available. Some designs for an 'Øresundsbron' date from 1886, and even earlier than that Napoleon planned to attack Britain using a tunnel under the English Channel.
2. Governments take over the prestige project which then suffers cost overruns.
3. Too few people use the facility to cover its cost.
4. Some form of regular subsidy is sought.

The poor management structure during the construction of the Channel Tunnel linking England and France resulted in a two-year delay and a cost that reached €11bn compared with the originally estimated €4.7bn. Forecasts of the level of traffic using the tunnel were too optimistic, resulting in financial problems for Eurotunnel, the Channel Tunnel's operator. London & Continental, the consortium awarded the contract to build and operate the high-speed railway between London and the Channel Tunnel, was also in trouble, the number of passengers between London, Paris and Brussels being 50 per cent below forecasts. Eurotunnel is now seeking wide-ranging changes to the way the tunnel is funded to overcome 'fundamental structural problems in the cross-channel rail industry'. Basically, not enough people use the tunnel. Cross-channel travel is up but advanced ferries and luxurious ferries are biting increasingly into the market and people are increasingly using low-cost easyJet and Ryanair. A particular change in the market is the number of passengers who fly and then hire a car rather than shipping their own.

Embarrassing as they are, the Channel Tunnel's problems were minor compared with Japan's recent bridge building. The Akashi Kaikyo Bridge is the longest suspension bridge in the world. It crosses the Akashi Straits, connecting the city of Kobe to Awaji Island, and cost 800 billion yen (€8.5bn). However, spectacular as it is to behold, locals and Japanese taxpayers

wonder what it is for. Authorities claimed that some 37,000 cars would use the bridge each day, although only 100–200 a day ever used the ferry between Kobe and Awaji Island. The bridge was to bring all manner of economic opportunities to the residents of Awaji and the equally impoverished island of Shikoku. Although a great aesthetic and engineering success, people still do not want to go to Awaji. After an initial burst of enthusiasm, daily use remains little above the numbers who used the ferry.

Shortly after opening, it looked like the Oresund bridge-cum-tunnel was going the same way as its predecessors. Not only was its use far below forecast but also it looked like its use could go even lower. Novo Nordisk, a Danish drug firm that moved its HQ to Malmö to take advantage of the 'bridge effect', urged its Danish staff to limit their trips to Malmö by working more from home. Swedish furniture chain IKEA went even further and banned its employees from using the bridge on company business. They are told to make the crossing using the ferry. The ferry is a lot slower than the bridge but also a lot less expensive.

The Danish and Swedish governments initiated the Øresundsbron project in 1991. The aim was to build a fixed link across the Oresund Region, which comprises Zeeland, Lolland-Falster and Bornholm, on the Danish side, as well as Scania and Sweden. The construction of this bridge was to provide stronger and more intense cooperation regarding the economy, education, research and culture between the two nations, as well as constituting the link to the European mainland for Sweden. In July 2000, the €1.5bn bridge-cum-tunnel opened to traffic. The investment was to be recouped from the thousands of cars crossing the bridge every day. The link is changing local life. More Swedes are visiting the cafés and galleries of Copenhagen, although Malmö does not seem so attractive to the Danes for a day trip.

Economic reality is proving to be well short of expectations. Peaking at 20,000 crossings a day soon after opening, traffic fell to 6,000. Seventy-five per cent more people cross the straits than did before the construction but numbers are way below target. An advertising campaign aims to attract more people to use the bridge but price seems to be the problem. With many fewer cars than expected crossing the bridge, the Danish and Swedish governments have to find a route to a better possible return on investment, by changing their pricing strategy.

There are currently two types of fares, depending on whether drivers pay at the toll station or whether they sign an agreement which offers discounts for frequent travellers.

Exhibit 14.1 Oresund Bridge: typical pricing (€)

Vehicle type	Length	Basic price	4-trip card	10-trip card	Business rate 7,501–10,000 trips (per trip)
Motorcycle	–	17	34	104	–
Private vehicle	Up to 6 m	32	64	192	12.10
Private vehicle	6 m to 9 m	64	128	192	26.89
Lorry	9 m to 12 m	82.80	–	–	38.31

Motorists who cross the bridge only a few times a year will pay 'the cash price', while those who use the bridge regularly will be in a position to benefit considerably from a subscription agreement (Exhibit 14.1). The Danish tax minister is proposing a tax deduction for people to commute across the bridge, in order to encourage greater use.

At last, after many lean years traffic is rising. The year 2005/06 saw a rapid increase in the volume of traffic on the bridge, although the Øresundsbro Konsortiet (Oresund Bridge Consortium) still racked up a €73m loss on the year. The traffic gain is not from the business expected, being due mainly to Danes buying homes in Sweden and commuting to their work in Denmark. The price of housing in Malmö is much lower than in Copenhagen. Also, although a single car ride across the bridge costs €32, price discounts of up to 75 per cent are now available for regular users. A train journey costs even less at €10. In 2004 almost 17 million people travelled over the bridge, 10.6 million in cars and 6.2 million by train.

The recovery is maybe encouraging the government to span the last bit of water that divides major EU countries: a tunnel or bridge across the 33 km of the North Channel between County Down or County Antrim, in Northern Ireland, and the Mull of Galloway, near Stranraer, in Scotland. But why stop there – how about joining Cyprus to Greece or Turkey?[2]

Questions

1. Why do you think the forecasts for national or international prestige projects, including the Anglo-French Concorde, Britain's Millennium Dome, the Channel Tunnel and Øresundsbron, are so far off target? Is price *the* problem?

2. Why is the Øresundsbro Konsortiet still losing money despite the increase in traffic?

3. Since it looks as though these prestige projects will never recover their costs, never mind produce a financial return on investment, what criteria should be used in evaluating pricing alternatives?

4. From the consumer perpective, why is using the Øresundsbron more attractive now than when it first opened? Is similar new demand likely to help the Channel Tunnel or the Akashi Kaikyo Bridge?

5. Suggest an alternative pricing schedule for the Øresundsbron, giving the reasons for your pricing decision.

What is price?

In the narrowest sense, **price** is the amount of money charged for a product or service. More broadly, price is the sum of all the values that consumers exchange for the benefits of having or using a product or service. Historically, price has been the major factor affecting buyer choice. In recent decades, non-price factors have gained importance. However, price still remains one of the most important elements determining a firm's market share and profitability.

Price is the only element in the marketing mix that produces revenue; all other elements represent costs. Price is also one of the most flexible marketing mix elements. Unlike product features and channel commitments, price can be changed quickly. At the same time, pricing is the number one problem facing many marketers. Yet, many companies do not handle pricing well. One frequent problem is that companies are too quick to cut prices in order to gain a sale rather than convincing buyers that their product's greater value is worth a higher price. Other common mistakes include pricing that is too cost-oriented rather than customer-value oriented and pricing that does not take the rest of the marketing mix into account. Some managers view pricing as a big headache, preferring instead to focus on the other marketing mix elements. However, smart managers treat pricing as a key strategic tool for creating and capturing customer value. They recognise that prices have a direct impact on the firm's bottom line. More importantly, as a part of a company's overall value proposition, price plays a key role in creating customer value and building customer relationships.

Price—The amount of money charged for a product or service, or the sum of the values that consumers exchange for the benefits of having or using the product or service.

Factors to consider when setting prices

The price the company charges will fall somewhere between one that is too high to produce any demand and one that is too low to produce a profit. Figure 14.1 summarises the major considerations in setting price. Customer perceptions of the product's value set the ceiling for prices. If customers perceive that the price is greater than the product's value, they will not buy the product. Product costs set the floor for prices. If the company prices the product below its costs, company profits will suffer. In setting its price between these two extremes, the company must consider a number of other internal and external factors, including its overall marketing strategy and mix, the nature of the market and demand, and competitors' strategies and prices.

Customer perceptions of value

In the end, the customer will decide whether a product's price is right. Pricing decisions, like other marketing mix decisions, must start with customer value. When customers buy a product, they exchange something of value (the price) in order to get something of value (the benefits of having or using the product). Effective, customer-oriented pricing involves understanding how

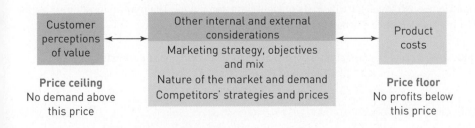

Figure 14.1 Considerations in setting price

Figure 14.2 Cost-based versus value-based pricing

SOURCE: From T. T. Nagle and R. K. Holden, *The Strategy and Tactics of Pricing*, 3rd edn. (Upper Saddle River, New Jersey: Prentice Hall, 1995). Copyright © 1995. Reprinted with permission of Pearson Education, Inc.

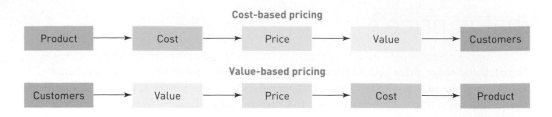

much value consumers place on the benefits they receive from the product and setting a price that captures this value.

> " In the end, the customer will decide whether a product's price is right. "

Value-based pricing

Value-based pricing— Setting price based on buyers' perceptions of product values rather than on cost.

Good pricing begins with a complete understanding of the value that a product or service creates for customers. **Value-based pricing** uses buyers' perceptions of value, not the seller's cost, as the key to pricing. Value-based pricing means that the marketer cannot design a product and marketing programme and then set the price. Price is considered along with the other marketing-mix variables *before* the marketing programme is set.

Figure 14.2 compares cost-based pricing with value-based pricing. Cost-based pricing is product driven. The company designs what it considers to be a good product, adds up the costs of making the product and sets a price that covers costs plus a target profit. Marketing must then convince buyers that the product's value at that price justifies its purchase. If the price turns out to be too high, the company must settle for lower mark-ups or lower sales, both resulting in disappointing profits.

Value-based pricing reverses this process. The company sets its target price based on customer perceptions of the product value. The targeted value and price then drive decisions about product design and what costs can be incurred. As a result, pricing begins with analysing consumer needs and value perceptions and a price is set to match consumers' perceived value.

It's important to remember that 'good value' is not the same as 'low price'.

Consider light bulb manufacturer Thorn selling its 10W 2D energy-saving electric light bulbs to a hotel manager. The SL18 costs far more to make than a conventional 60-watt tungsten light bulb, so a higher price has to be justified. Value pricing helps by looking at the hotel manager's total cost of ownership rather than the price of electric light bulbs. The life-cycle costs of the manager using a tungsten bulb for the 1,000 hours that they last includes the price of the bulb (60c), the labour cost of replacing it (50c) and electricity (€4.80). The life-cycle cost of the tungsten bulb is therefore €5.90. The Thorn 10W 2D bulb uses a sixth of the electricity of a conventional bulb and lasts eight times longer. Its life-cycle cost must therefore be compared with the cost of owning eight tungsten bulbs: 8 × €5.90 = €47.20. To work out the value of the Thorn bulb, its cost of ownership is also considered: changing the bulb 50c and electricity €6.40 (one-sixth the electricity costs of eight tungsten bulbs). The maximum value-based price of the Thorn bulb to the hotel manager is therefore:

Maximum value-based price = competitor's cost of ownership − own operating costs
= €47.20 − (€6.40 + 50c)
= €40.30

Using this evidence, Thorn can argue that it is worth the hotel manager paying a lot more than 60c to buy the energy-saving bulb. It is unrealistic to think that the manager would pay the full €40.30, but based on these figures, the actual price of €10.00 for the Thorn energy-saving bulb looks very reasonable. At first sight it seems hard to justify replacing a 60c tungsten bulb with a €10.00 energy-saving one, but value-based pricing shows the hotel manager is saving €30.00 by doing so. The value-based pricing using life-cycle costs can be used to justify paying a premium price on products, from low-energy light bulbs to airliners.[3]

A company using value-based pricing must find out what value buyers assign to different competitive offers. However, companies often find it hard to measure the value customers will attach to their products or services. For example, calculating the cost of ingredients in a meal at a fancy restaurant is relatively easy. But assigning a value to other satisfactions such as taste, environment, relaxation, conversation and status is very hard. Moreover, these values will vary both for different consumers and in different situations.

Still, consumers will use these perceived values to evaluate a product's price, so the company must work to measure them. Sometimes consumers are asked how much they would pay for a basic product and for each benefit added to the offer. Or a company might conduct experiments to test the perceived value of different product offers. If the seller charges more than the buyers' perceived value, the company's sales will suffer. If the seller charges less, its products sell very well, but they produce less revenue than they would if they were priced at the level of perceived-value.

Thus, marketers must try to understand the consumer's reasons for buying the product and set the price according to consumer perceptions of the product's value. Because consumers vary in the values they assign to different product features, marketers often vary their pricing strategies for different segments. They offer different sets of product features at different prices. For example, Toshiba offers under-€200 compact, 15-inch TVs for consumers who want basic sets, and €1200 42-inch HD-ready digital LCD TV models loaded with picture enhancement features for consumers who want the latest technology.

We now examine two types of value-based pricing: *good-value pricing* and *value-added pricing*.

Good-value pricing

During the past decade, marketers have noted a fundamental shift in consumer attitudes towards price and quality. Many companies are bringing their pricing approaches into line with changing economic conditions and consumer price perceptions. More and more, marketers have adopted **good-value pricing** strategies – offering just the right combination of quality and good service at a fair price.

In many cases, this has involved the introduction of less expensive versions of established brand-name products. Armani offers the less-expensive, more casual Armani Exchange fashion line. Holiday Inn offers cheaper rates for rooms in Holiday Inn Express budget hotels. In other cases, such as IKEA and Wal-Mart, good-value pricing has involved redesigning existing brands to offer more quality for a given price or the same quality for less.

An important type of value pricing at the retail level is *everyday low pricing (EDLP)*. EDLP involves charging a constant, everyday low price with few or no temporary price discounts. In contrast, *high–low pricing* involves charging higher prices on an everyday basis but running frequent promotions to lower prices temporarily on selected items.

The king of EDLP is Wal-Mart, which practically defined the concept. Except for a few sale items every month, Wal-Mart promises everyday low prices on everything it sells. These constant prices eliminate week-to-week price uncertainty. However, to offer everyday low prices, a company must first have everyday low costs, in order to make money at the lower prices that it charges for the products that it sells.

Good-value pricing—
Offering just the right combination of quality and good service at a fair price.

Value-added pricing

In many business-to-business marketing situations, the pricing challenge is to build and maintain the company's *pricing power* – its power to escape price competition and to justify higher prices and margins without losing market share. To retain pricing power, a firm must retain or build the value of its market offer. This is especially true for suppliers of commodity products, which are characterised by little differentiation and intense price competition. If companies rely on price to capture and retain business, they reduce whatever they're selling to a commodity and run the risk of losing customer loyalty.

To increase their pricing power, many companies adopt *value-added* strategies. Rather than cutting prices to match competitors, they attach value-added services to differentiate their offers and thus support higher prices.

In the computer business, suppliers such as HP and IBM continued to sell through retail outlets rather than adopting the 'direct-only' business model pioneered by number one rival Dell. By not working through physical stores, the cost benefits this brought to the supply chain enabled Dell to outsell competitors who were unable to match it on price. However, in 2005, HP's market share increased by over a percentage point, while Dell's market share shrank slightly, the first time ever since it became one of the major PC vendors a decade ago. Dell says that the problem is that it dropped prices too much. According to the company's chief executive, Dell needs to 'reinvigorate growth' by investing in customer support and improving quality. Another factor hurting Dell is that growth in the PC business is coming from the consumer market and emerging countries rather than the corporate market, which accounts for some 85 per cent of Dell's sales. Dell's lack of retail presence has put it at a disadvantage to rivals. Consumers tend to want to see and touch computers before buying them. They also want to be able to return the equipment easily if it breaks. Sales in markets outside the US often rely on the advice of sales staff. The absence of physical stores has also stymied efforts to expand beyond PCs, which represent more than 60 per cent of Dell's sales, into consumer electronics products such as televisions and home entertainment systems. Moreover, large corporations are increasingly purchasing computers as part of a package of services from vendors such as consultancies who can provide added-value in the way of delivering total solutions and to address specific business problems. Not surprisingly, with its established sales channel, large and well-regarded services division and efficient supply chain, rival HP is now better placed in the battle for sales for higher-margin, value-adding computer servers. By wringing out costs and driving prices down, Dell thrived on the basis of its low price, good value strategy. However, success may not last too long. Challenged by value-adding suppliers, in a cut-throat market, Dell's low-price, good-value pricing strategy is proving to be unsustainable.[4]

SOURCE: Copyright © The Economist Newspaper Limited, London (13 May 2006).

Company and product costs

Whereas customer-value perceptions set the price ceiling, costs set the floor for the price that the company can charge. **Cost-based pricing** involves setting prices based on the costs of producing, distributing and selling the product plus a fair rate of return for the company's effort and risk. A company's costs may be an important element in its pricing strategy. Many companies, such as Ryanair, Toyota and Wal-Mart, work to become the 'low-cost producers' in their industries. Companies with lower costs can set lower prices that result in greater sales and profits.

Types of cost

A company's costs take two forms, fixed and variable. **Fixed costs** (also known as overheads) are costs that do not vary with production or sales level. For example, a company must pay each

Cost-based pricing— Setting prices based on the costs of producing, distributing and selling the product plus a fair rate of return for effort and risk.

Fixed costs—Costs that do not vary with production or sales level.

month's bills for rent, heat, interest and executive salaries, whatever the company's output. If an airline has to fly a sector with few passengers on board, it may save on the costs accounted for by cabin crew and passenger service, but all other costs, including flight crew, fuel and maintenance, are fixed.

Variable costs vary directly with the level of production. Each personal computer produced by the manufacturer involves a cost of computer chips, wires, plastic, packaging and other inputs. These costs tend to be the same for each unit produced, their total varying with the number of units produced.

Total costs are the sum of the fixed and variable costs for any given level of production. Management wants to charge a price that will at least cover the total production costs at a given level of production. The company must watch its costs carefully. If it costs the company more than competitors to produce and sell its product, the company will have to charge a higher price or make less profit, putting it at a competitive disadvantage.

Variable costs—Costs that vary directly with the level of production.

Total costs—The sum of the fixed and variable costs for any given level of production.

Costs at different levels of production

To price wisely, management needs to know how its costs vary with different levels of production. For example, suppose the Irish radio manufacturer Roberts has built a factory to produce 1,000 luxury travel clocks per day. Figure 14.3(a) shows the typical short-run average cost curve (SRAC). It shows that the cost per clock is high if Roberts' factory produces only a few per day. But as production moves up to 1,000 clocks per day, average cost falls because fixed costs are spread over more units, with each one bearing a smaller fixed cost. Roberts can try to produce more than 1,000 clocks per day, but average costs will increase because the plant becomes inefficient. Workers wait for machines, the machines break down more often and workers get in each other's way.

> ❝ To price wisely, management needs to know how its costs vary. ❞

If Roberts believed it could sell 2,000 clocks a day, it should consider building a larger plant. The plant would use more efficient machinery and work arrangements. Also, the unit cost of producing 2,000 units per day would be lower than the unit cost of producing 1,000 units per day, as shown in the long-run average cost (LRAC) curve (Figure 14.3(b)). In fact, a 3,000-capacity plant would be even more efficient, according to Figure 14.3(b). But a 4,000 daily production plant would be less efficient because of increasing diseconomies of scale – too many workers to manage, paperwork slows things down and so on. Figure 14.3(b) shows that a 3,000 daily production plant is the best size to build if demand is strong enough to support this level of production.

Costs as a function of production experience

Suppose Roberts runs a plant that produces 3,000 clocks per day. As Roberts gains experience in producing clocks, it learns how to do it better. Workers learn short-cuts and become more familiar with their equipment. With practice, the work becomes better organised and Roberts

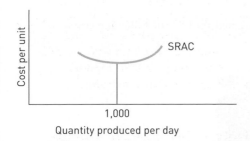

(a) Cost behaviour in a fixed-size plant

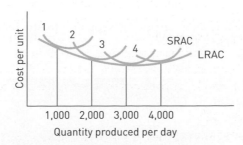

(b) Cost behaviour over different-sized plants

Figure 14.3 Cost per unit at different levels of production

Figure 14.4 Cost per unit as a function of accumulated production: the experience curve

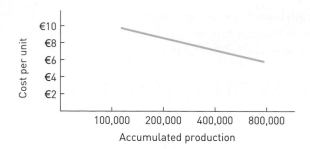

finds better equipment and production processes. With higher volume, Roberts becomes more efficient and gains economies of scale. As a result, average cost tends to fall with accumulated production experience. This is shown in Figure 14.4.[5] Thus the average cost of producing the first 100,000 clocks is €10 per clock. When the company has produced the first 200,000 clocks, the average cost has fallen to €9. After its accumulated production experience doubles again to 400,000, the average cost is €7. This drop in the average cost with accumulated production experience is called the **experience curve** (or **learning curve**).

If a downward-sloping experience curve exists, this is highly significant for the company. Not only will the company's unit production cost fall; it will fall faster if the company makes and sells more during a given time period. But the market has to stand ready to buy the higher output. To take advantage of the experience curve, Roberts must get a large market share early in the product's life-cycle. This suggests the following pricing strategy. Roberts should price its clocks low; its sales will then increase and its costs will decrease through gaining more experience, and then it can lower its prices further.

Some companies have built successful strategies around the experience curve. For example, Bausch & Lomb consolidated its position in the soft contact lens market by using computerised lens design and steadily expanding its one Soflens plant. As a result, its market share climbed steadily to 65 per cent. However, a single-minded focus on reducing costs and exploiting the experience curve will not always work. Experience-curve pricing carries some major risks. The aggressive pricing might give the product a cheap image. The strategy also assumes that competitors are weak and not willing to retaliate by meeting the company's price cuts. Finally, while the company is building volume under one technology, a competitor may find a lower-cost technology that lets it start at lower prices than the market leader, who still operates on the old experience curve.

Cost-based pricing

Experience curve (or learning curve)—The drop in the average per-unit production cost that comes with accumulated production experience.

The simplest pricing method is **cost-plus pricing** – adding a standard mark-up to the cost of the product. Construction companies, for example, submit job bids by estimating the total project cost and adding a standard mark-up for profit. Lawyers, accountants and other professionals typically price by adding a standard mark-up to their costs. Some sellers tell their customers they will charge cost plus a specified **mark-up**: for example, aerospace companies price this way to the government.

Cost-plus pricing—Adding a standard mark-up to the cost of the product.

Mark-up/mark-down—The difference between selling price and cost as a percentage of selling price or cost.

To illustrate *mark-up* pricing, suppose a toaster manufacturer had the following costs and expected sales:

Variable cost	€10
Fixed cost	€300,000
Expected unit sales	50,000

Then the manufacturer's cost per toaster is given by:

$$\text{Unit cost} = \text{Variable cost} + \frac{\text{Fixed costs}}{\text{Unit sales}} = €10 + \frac{€300,000}{50,000} = €16$$

Now suppose the manufacturer wants to earn a 20 per cent mark-up on sales. The manufacturer's mark-up price is given by:

$$\text{Mark-up price} = \frac{\text{Unit cost}}{1.0 - \text{Desired return on sales}} = \frac{€16}{1.0 - 0.2} = €20$$

The manufacturer would charge dealers €20 a toaster and make a profit of €4 per unit. The dealers, in turn, will mark up the toaster. If dealers want to earn 50 per cent on sales price, they will mark up the toaster to €40 (€20 + 50 per cent of €40). This number is equivalent to a *mark-up on cost* of 100 per cent (€20/€20).

Does using standard mark-ups to set prices make logical sense? Generally, no. Any pricing method that ignores demand and competitors' prices is not likely to lead to the best price. Suppose the toaster manufacturer charged €20 but sold only 30,000 toasters instead of 50,000. Then the unit cost would have been higher, since the fixed costs are spread over fewer units and the realised percentage mark-up on sales would have been lower. Mark-up pricing works only if that price actually brings in the expected level of sales.

Brio, the Swedish toy maker and distributor, has seen a major drop in both profits and sales for its toys in recent years. While the Brio brand symbolises a high-quality toy, robust enough to become a family heirloom to be passed down from brother to sister and to the next generation, parents see Brio toys as being far too expensive. Besides, these days, parents can buy basic toy products of the same quality from supermarket chains and furniture retailers like IKEA, who are churning out their own private-label toys at a fraction the price Brio charges. Brio realised that in its quest to fulfil its vision of 'the good toy', the company had ignored the question of whether parents could afford to buy it. The company had placed too much emphasis on the value (premium) of the toys and not enough on their cost![6]

Still, mark-up pricing remains popular for a number of reasons. First, sellers are more certain about costs than about demand. By tying the price to cost, sellers simplify pricing – they do not have to make frequent adjustments as demand changes. Second, when all firms in the industry use this pricing method, prices tend to be similar and price competition is thus minimised. Third, many people feel that cost-plus pricing is fairer to both buyers and sellers. Sellers earn a fair return on their investment, but do not take advantage of buyers when demand increases.

Break-even analysis and target profit pricing

Another cost-oriented pricing approach is **break-even pricing** or a variation called **target profit pricing**. The firm tries to determine the price at which it will break even or make the target profit it is seeking. Target pricing uses the concept of a *break-even chart*, which shows the total cost and total revenue expected at different sales volume levels. Figure 14.5 shows a break-even chart for the toaster manufacturer discussed here. Fixed costs are €300,000 regardless of sales volume. Variable costs are added to fixed costs to form total costs, which rise with volume. The total revenue curve starts at zero and rises with each unit sold. The slope of the total revenue curve reflects the price of €20 per unit.

Break-even pricing— Setting price to break even on the costs of making and marketing a product.

Target profit pricing— Setting price to make a target profit.

Figure 14.5 Break-even chart for determining target price

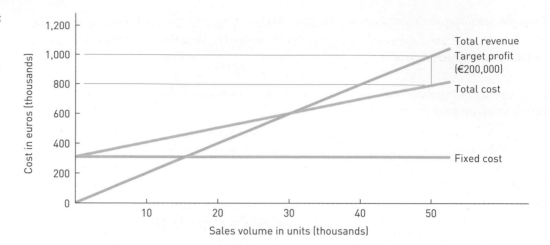

The total revenue and total cost curves cross at 30,000 units. This is the *break-even volume*. At €20, the company must sell at least 30,000 units to break even: that is, for total revenue to cover total cost. Break-even volume can be calculated using the following formula:

$$\text{Break-even volume} = \frac{\text{Fixed cost}}{\text{Price} - \text{Variable cost}} = \frac{€300,000}{€20 - €10} = 30,000$$

If the company wants to make a target profit, it must sell more than 30,000 units at €20 each. Suppose the toaster manufacturer has invested €1,000,000 in the business and wants to set a price to earn a 20 per cent return or €200,000. In that case, it must sell at least 50,000 units at €20 each. If the company charges a higher price, it will not need to sell as many toasters to achieve its target return. But the market may not buy even this lower volume at the higher price. Much depends on the price elasticity and competitors' prices.

The manufacturer should consider different prices and estimate break-even volumes, probable demand and profits for each. This is done in Table 14.1. The table shows that as price increases, break-even volume drops (column 2). But as price increases, demand for the toasters also falls off (column 3). At the €14 price, because the manufacturer clears only €4 per toaster (€14 less €10 in variable costs), it must sell a very high volume to break even. Even though the low price attracts many buyers, demand still falls below the high break-even point and the manufacturer loses money. At the other extreme, with a €22 price, the manufacturer clears €12 per toaster and must sell only 25,000 units to break even. But at this high price, consumers buy too few toasters and profits are negative. The table shows that a price of €18 yields the highest profits. Note that none

Table 14.1 Break-even volume and profits at different prices

(1) Price (€)	(2) Unit demand needed to break even (000)	(3) Expected unit demand at given price (000)	(4) Total revenues = (1) × (3) (€000)	(5) Total cost[a] (€000)	(6) Profit = (4) − (5) (€000)
14	75	71	994	1,010	−16
16	50	67	1,072	970	102
18	37.5	60	1,080	900	180
20	30	42	840	720	120
22	25	23	506	530	−24

[a]Assumes a fixed cost of €300,000 and a constant unit variable cost of €10.

of the prices produces the manufacturer's target profit of €200,000. To achieve this target return, the manufacturer will have to search for ways to lower fixed or variable costs, thus lowering the break-even volume.

For example, Airbus Industries based their forecasts for their superjumbo A3XX on the superior break-even that it will offer airlines who buy it. Although much larger than its major competitor, the Boeing B747-400, the A3XX operating cost means that it breaks even at a fraction of its total capacity.[7]

Aircraft	Boeing 747-400	Airbus A3XX
Passenger capacity	413	555
Break-even: passengers	290	323
Profitable seats: beyond break-even	123	232
Break-even: percentage of capacity	70%	58%

Other internal and external considerations affecting pricing decisions

Customer perceptions of value set the upper limit for prices, and costs set the lower limit. However, in setting prices within these limits, the company must consider a number of other internal and external factors. Internal factors affecting pricing include the company's overall marketing strategy, objectives and marketing mix, as well as other organisational considerations. External factors include the nature of the market and demand, competitors' strategies and prices and other environmental factors.

> Customer perceptions of value set the upper limit for prices, and costs set the lower limit.

Overall marketing strategy, objectives and mix

Price is only one element of the company's broader marketing strategy. Thus, before setting price, the company must decide on its overall marketing strategy for the product or service. If the company has selected its target market and positioning carefully, then its marketing-mix strategy, including price, will be fairly straightforward. For example, when Toyota decided to produce its Lexus cars to compete with European luxury cars in the higher-income segment, this required charging a high price consistent with the brand's up-market positioning. In contrast, when it introduced its Yaris model – 'the car that you can afford to drive is finally the car you actually want to drive' – this positioning required charging a low price. Thus pricing strategy is largely determined by decisions on market positioning.

At the same time, the company may seek to achieve additional objectives. General pricing objectives might include *survival, current profit maximisation, market-share leadership* or *product-quality leadership.*

Companies set *survival* as their fundamental objective if they are troubled by too much capacity, heavy competition or changing consumer wants. To keep a factory going, a company may set a low price through periods of low demand, hoping to increase prices when demand recovers. In this case, profits are less important than survival. As long as their prices cover variable costs and some fixed costs, they can stay in business. However, survival is only a short-term objective. In the long run, the firm must learn how to add value or face extinction.

Many companies use *current profit maximisation* as their pricing goal. Here, they emphasise current financial results rather than long-run performance. They estimate what demand and costs will be at different prices and choose the price that will produce the maximum current profit, cash flow or return on investment.

Other companies want to obtain *market-share leadership*. They believe that the company with the largest market share will enjoy the lowest costs and highest long-run profit. To become the market-share leader, these firms set prices as low as possible. For example, in the battle for market-share leadership of digital TV transmission, the British satellite television company BSkyB priced its TV set-top converters below cost, almost giving them away 'free' although they cost over €500 each to produce. The strategy amounted to a subsidy of some €1bn. The assumption was that, in the short term, market share gains would lead to long-term profitability based on future income flows generated by customer subscription charges for access to BSkyB's channels.

A company might decide that it wants to achieve *product-quality leadership*. This normally calls for charging a high price to cover such quality and the high cost of R&D. For example, Jaguar's limited edition XJ220 sold for £400,000 (€600,000) each, but had wealthy customers queuing to buy one.

A company might also use price to attain other more specific objectives. It can set prices to attract new customers or to profitably retain existing ones. It may set prices low to prevent competition from entering the market or set prices at competitors' levels to stabilise the market. It can price to keep the loyalty and support of resellers or to avoid government intervention. Prices can be reduced temporarily to create excitement for a brand. Or, one product may be priced to help the sales of other products in the company's line. Thus, pricing may play an important role in helping to accomplish the company's objectives at many levels.

Non-profit and public organisations may adopt a number of other pricing objectives. A university aims for *partial cost recovery*, knowing that it must rely on private funds or endowments and public grants to cover the remaining costs. A non-profit hospital may aim for *full cost recovery* in its pricing. A non-profit theatre company may price its productions to fill the maximum number of theatre seats. A social service agency may set a *social price* geared to the varying income situations of different clients.

Price is only one of the marketing-mix tools that a company uses to achieve its marketing objectives. Price decisions must be coordinated with product design, distribution and promotion decisions to form a consistent and effective marketing programme. Decisions made for other marketing-mix variables may affect pricing decisions. For example, producers using many resellers that are expected to support and promote their products may have to build larger reseller margins into their prices. The decision to position the product on high-performance quality will mean that the seller must charge a higher price to cover higher costs.

Companies often make their pricing decisions first and then base other marketing-mix decisions on the prices that they want to charge. Here, price is a crucial product-positioning factor that defines the product's market, competition and design. The intended price determines what product features can be offered and what production costs can be incurred.

Target costing—A technique to support pricing decisions, which starts with deciding a target cost for a new product and works back to designing the product.

Many firms support such price-positioning strategies with a technique called **target costing**, a potent strategic weapon. Target costing reverses the usual process of first designing a new product, determining its cost and then asking 'Can we sell it for that?' Instead, it starts with an ideal selling price based on customer-value considerations and then targets costs that will ensure that the price is met:

> When starting up, Swatch surveyed the market and identified an unserved segment of watch buyers who wanted 'a low-cost fashion accessory that also keeps time'. Armed with this information about market needs, Swatch set out to give consumers the watch they wanted at a price they were willing to pay, and it managed the new product's costs accordingly. Like most watch buyers, targeted consumers were concerned about precision, reliability and durability. However, they were also concerned about fashion and affordability. To keep costs down, Swatch designed fashionable simpler watches that contained fewer parts and that were constructed from high-tech but less expensive materials. It then developed a revolutionary automated process for mass-producing the new watches and exercised strict cost controls throughout the manufacturing process. By managing costs carefully, Swatch was able to create a watch that offered just the right blend of fashion and function at a price consumers were willing to pay. As a result of its initial major success, consumers have placed increasing value on Swatch products, allowing the company to introduce successively higher-priced designs.[8]

Other companies de-emphasise price and use other marketing-mix tools to create *non-price* positions. Often, the best strategy is not to charge the lowest price, but rather to differentiate the marketing offer to make it worth a higher price.

> For example, London's City Airport and the airlines that fly from there do not compete on price. Instead they offer the retailing, speed of processing and convenience wanted by frequent-flying executives. Surveys show that City Airport's regular users prefer using the aircraft's own stairs and braving the English weather rather than wait, hunched under luggage racks while air bridges are connected.[9]

Some marketers even *feature* high prices as part of their positioning. For example, Porsche proudly advertises its Boxster roadster as 'Happiness. As purchased with money.' And Steinway offers 'the finest pianos in the world', with a price to match. Steinway's grand pianos can cost as much as €130,000.

Thus the marketer must consider the total marketing mix when setting prices. If the product is positioned on non-price factors, then decisions about quality, promotion and distribution will strongly affect price. If price is a crucial positioning factor, then price will strongly affect decisions made about the other marketing-mix elements. Even so, marketers should remember that buyers rarely buy on price alone. Instead, they seek product and service offerings that give them the best value in terms of benefits received for the price paid.

Organisational considerations

Management must decide who within the organisation should set prices. Companies handle pricing in a variety of ways. In small companies, prices are often set by top management rather

Bosch products are more expensive than white goods made by other manufacturers. They justify the higher price based on product performance, reliability and a longer useful life.

SOURCE: The Advertising Archives.

than by the marketing or sales departments. In large companies, pricing is typically handled by divisional or product line managers. In industrial markets, salespeople may be allowed to negotiate with customers within certain price ranges. Even so, top management sets the pricing objectives and policies, and it often approves the prices proposed by lower-level management or salespeople.

In industries in which pricing is a key factor (airlines, aerospace, steel, oil companies), companies will often have pricing departments to set the best prices or help others in setting them. These departments report to the marketing department or top management. Others who have an influence on pricing include sales managers, production managers, finance managers and accountants.

A Steinway piano costs a lot, but buyers aren't looking for bargains. When it comes to a Steinway, price is nothing, the Steinway experience is everything.
SOURCE: Steinway & Sons.

As mentioned earlier, pricing decisions are affected by additional external factors such as the nature of the market and demand, competition and other environmental elements.

The market and demand

While costs set the lower limit of prices, the market and demand set the upper limit. As noted earlier, good pricing starts with an understanding how customers' perceptions of value affect the prices they are willing to pay. Both consumer and industrial buyers balance the price of a product or service against the benefits of owning it. Thus, before setting prices, the marketer must understand the relationship between price and demand for its product. In this section, we take a deeper look at the price–demand relationship and how it varies for different types of markets. We then discuss methods for analysing the price–demand relationship.

Pricing in different types of market

The seller's pricing freedom varies with different types of market. Economists recognise four types of market, each presenting a different pricing challenge: *pure competition, monopolistic competition, oligopolistic competition* and *pure monopolistic competition.*

Under **pure competition**, the market consists of many buyers and sellers trading in a uniform commodity such as wheat, copper or financial securities. No single buyer or seller has much effect on the going market price. A seller cannot charge more than the going price because buyers can obtain as much as they need at the going price. Nor would sellers charge less than the market price because they can sell all they want at this price. If price and profits rise, new sellers can easily enter the market. In a purely competitive market, marketing research, product development, pricing, advertising and sales promotion play little or no role. Thus sellers in these markets do not spend much time on marketing strategy.

Pure competition—A market in which many buyers and sellers trade in a uniform commodity – no single buyer or seller has much effect on the going market price.

651

Monopolistic competition—A market in which many buyers and sellers trade over a range of prices rather than a single market price.

Under **monopolistic competition**, the market consists of many buyers and sellers that trade over a range of prices rather than a single market price. A range of prices occurs because sellers can differentiate their offers to buyers. Either the physical product can be varied in quality, features or style or the accompanying services can be varied. Each company can create a quasi-monopoly for its products because buyers see differences in sellers' products and will pay different prices for them. Sellers try to develop differentiated offers for different customer segments and, in addition to price, freely use branding, advertising and personal selling to set their offers apart. For example, Apple's iPod is differentiated from dozens of other brands of MP3 players through strong branding and advertising, reducing the impact of price. Because there are many competitors in such markets, each firm is less affected by competitors' pricing strategies than in oligopolistic markets.

Oligopolistic competition—A market in which there are a few sellers that are highly sensitive to each other's pricing and marketing strategies.

Under **oligopolistic competition**, the market consists of a few sellers that are highly sensitive to each other's pricing and marketing strategies. The product can be uniform (steel, aluminium) or non-uniform (cars, computers). There are few sellers because it is difficult for new sellers to enter the market. Each seller is alert to competitors' strategies and moves. If a steel company slashes its price by 10 per cent, buyers will quickly switch to this supplier. The other steel makers must respond by lowering their prices or increasing their services. An oligopolist is never sure that it will gain anything permanent through a price cut. In contrast, if an oligopolist raises its price, its competitors might not follow this lead. The oligopolist would then have to retract its price increase or risk losing customers to competitors.

Pure monopoly—A market in which there is a single seller – it may be a government monopoly, a private regulated monopoly or a private non-regulated monopoly.

In a **pure monopoly**, the market consists of one seller. The seller may be a government monopoly (a postal service), a private regulated monopoly (a power company) or a private non-regulated monopoly (Microsoft Windows). Pricing is handled differently in each case. A government monopoly can pursue a variety of pricing objectives: set price below cost because the product is important to buyers who cannot afford to pay full cost; set price either to cover costs or to produce good revenue; or set price quite high to slow down consumption or to protect an inefficient supplier.

In a regulated monopoly, the government permits the company to set rates that yield a 'fair return', which enables the company to maintain and expand its operations as needed. Non-regulated monopolies are free to price at what the market will bear. However, they do not always charge the full price for a number of reasons: a desire not to attract competition, a desire to penetrate the market faster with a low price, or a fear of government regulation.

Analysing the price–demand relationship

Each price the company might charge leads to a different level of demand. The relation between the price charged and the resulting demand level is shown in the demand curve in Figure 14.6(a). The demand curve shows the number of units that the market will buy in a given time period at different prices that might be charged. In the normal case, demand and price are inversely related: that is, the higher the price, the lower the demand. Thus the company would sell less if it raised its price from P_1 to P_2. In short, consumers with limited budgets will probably buy less of something if its price is too high.

Figure 14.6 Inelastic and elastic demand

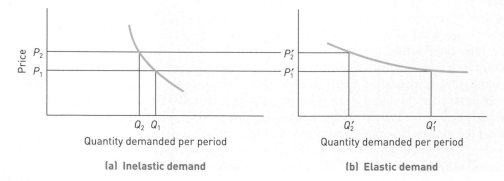

(a) Inelastic demand

(b) Elastic demand

In the case of prestige goods, the demand curve sometimes slopes upward. Consumers think that higher prices mean more quality.

> **"** Consumers think that higher prices mean more quality. **"**

Gibson Guitar Corporation once toyed with the idea of lowering its prices to compete more effectively with Japanese rivals such as Yamaha and Ibanez. To its surprise, Gibson found that its instruments didn't sell as well at lower prices. 'We had an inverse [price–demand relationship]', noted Gibson's chief executive. 'The more we charged, the more product we sold.' At a time when other guitar manufacturers have chosen to build their instruments more quickly, cheaply and in greater numbers, Gibson still promises guitars that 'are made one-at-a-time, by hand. No shortcuts. No substitutions.' It turns out that low prices simply aren't consistent with 'Gibson's century-old tradition of creating investment-quality instruments that represent the highest standards of imaginative design and masterful craftsmanship.'[10]

Still, if the company charges too high a price, the level of demand will be lower.

Most companies try to measure their demand curves by estimating demand at different prices. The type of market makes a difference. In a monopoly, the demand curve shows the total market demand resulting from different prices. If the company faces competition, its demand at different prices will depend on whether competitors' prices stay constant or change with the company's own prices.

Price elasticity of demand

Marketers also need to know **price elasticity** – how responsive demand will be to a change in price. Consider the two demand curves in Figure 14.6. In Figure 14.6(a) above, a price increase from P_1 to P_2 leads to a relatively small drop in demand from Q_1 to Q_2. In Figure 14.6(b), however, a similar price increase leads to a large drop in demand from Q'_1 to Q'_2. If demand hardly changes with a small change in price, we say the demand is *inelastic*. If demand changes greatly, we say the demand is *elastic*. The price elasticity of demand is given by the following formula:

Price elasticity—A measure of the sensitivity of demand to changes in price.

$$\text{Price elasticity of demand} = \frac{\%\ \text{change in quantity demanded}}{\%\ \text{change in price}}$$

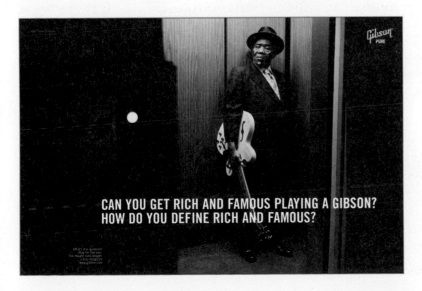

The demand curve sometimes slopes upward: Gibson was surprised to learn that its high-quality instruments didn't sell as well at lower prices.

Suppose demand falls by 10 per cent when a seller raises its price by 2 per cent. Price elasticity of demand is therefore –5 (the minus sign confirms the inverse relation between price and demand) and demand is elastic. If demand falls by 2 per cent with a 2 per cent increase in price, then elasticity is –1. In this case, the seller's total revenue stays the same: that is, the seller sells fewer items, but at a higher price that preserves the same total revenue. If demand falls by 1 per cent when the price is increased by 2 per cent, then elasticity is $-\frac{1}{2}$ and demand is inelastic. The less elastic the demand, the more it pays for the seller to raise the price.

What determines the price elasticity of demand? Buyers are less price sensitive when the product they are buying is unique or when it is high in quality, prestige or exclusiveness. They are also less price sensitive when substitute products are hard to find or when they cannot easily compare the quality of substitutes. Finally, buyers are less price sensitive when the total expenditure for a product is low relative to their income or when another party shares the cost.[11]

If demand is elastic rather than inelastic, sellers will consider lowering their price. A lower price will produce more total revenue. This practice makes sense as long as the extra costs of producing and selling more do not exceed the extra revenue. At the same time, most firms want to avoid pricing that turns their products into commodities. In recent years, forces such as deregulation and the instant price comparisons afforded by the Internet and other technologies have increased consumer price sensitivity, turning products ranging from telephones and computers to new automobiles into commodities in consumers' eyes.

Marketers need to work harder than ever to differentiate their offerings when a dozen competitors are selling virtually the same product at a comparable or lower price. More than ever, companies need to understand the price sensitivity of their customers and prospects and the trade-offs people are willing to make between price and product characteristics.

Price influence on profits

Increasing *sales volume* in items sold is the driving force behind much marketing activity. There are good reasons for this: increased sales show success and a growing company, increased market share shows competitive success and, if sales do not match production, capacity will be underused or customers disappointed.

Unfortunately, when price is used to increase sales volume, *sales value* – the proceeds from sales – may reduce. *Sales value* and *sales volume* do not always move hand in hand. A company that increases sales by 5 per cent by cutting prices by 10 per cent increases sales volume but reduces sales value, as the example in Table 14.2 shows.

Table 14.2 How discounts influence sales and profits

Action	Regular price	10% discount	Percentage change
Sales			
Price (€)	1.00	0.90	
Sales volume	100	105	
Sales value (€)	100.00	94.50	(5.5)
Cost of goods sold			
Unit cost (€)	0.50	0.50	
Sales (units)	100	105	
Cost (€)	50.00	52.50	5.0
Gross profit	50.00	42.00	(16.0)
Other trading expenses	40.00	40.00	0.0
Net profit	10.00	2.00	(80.0)
Return on sales (%)	10.0	2.1	

Gross profit is the difference between net proceeds from sales and the cost of goods sold. The costs are the variable costs incurred each time a product is made. They typically include raw materials, labour, energy and so on. The interplay between gross profit and price is dramatic. The popular idea of 'everyday low prices' increases sales volumes and value, but not always by enough to cover lost margins. The example in Table 14.2 shows that a 10 per cent price cut has much more impact on *gross profits* than do sales.

Net profit is the surplus remaining after all costs have been taken. The gross profit shows the contribution made to the company by each unit sold, but neglects many other trading expenditures incurred such as fixed costs (building rates and staff) and strategic investments (e.g., research and development). Interest paid on debts is sometimes excluded because it depends on the capital structure of the company. The fixed cost means that *net profit* is more volatile than *gross profit* (see Table 14.2). This sensitivity encourages companies to convert some of their fixed costs into variable ones: for example, hiring trucks rather than buying them.

Net profit—The difference between the income from goods sold and all expenses incurred.

Return on sales (or *margin*) measures the ratio of profit to sales:

$$\text{Return on sales} = \frac{\text{Net profit}}{\text{Sales}}$$

This is useful in comparing businesses over time. During a four-year period a company may find both sales and net profit increasing, but are profits keeping pace with sales? In Table 14.2 the 10 per cent price promotion gives an increase in sales volume, but a big reduction in return on sales. The interplay between price, sales, profits and investment makes these and other ratios central to marketing decision making and control. Real Marketing 14.1 introduces *Economic Value Added* (EVA), a measure that has become increasingly important in recent years.

Competitors' strategies and prices

Another external factor affecting the company's pricing decisions is competitors' costs, prices and market offerings. Consumers will base their judgements of a product's value on the prices that competitors charge for similar products. A consumer who is thinking about buying a Canon digital camera will evaluate Canon's price and value against the prices and value of comparable products made by Nikon, Minolta, Kodak, Sony and others.

In addition, the company's pricing strategy may affect the nature of the competition it faces. If Canon follows a high-price, high-margin strategy, it may attract competition. A low-price, low-margin strategy, however, may stop competitors or drive them out of the market. Canon needs to benchmark its costs and value against competitors' costs and value to learn whether it is operating at a cost (value) advantage or disadvantage. It can then use these benchmarks as a starting point for its own pricing.

In assessing competitors' pricing strategies, the company should ask several questions. First, how does the company's market offering compare with competitors' offerings in terms of customer value? If consumers perceive that the company's product or service provides greater value, the company can charge a higher price. If consumers perceive less value relative to competing products, the company must either charge a lower price or change customer perceptions to justify a higher price.

Next, how strong are current competitors and what are their current pricing strategies? If the company faces a host of smaller competitors charging high prices relative to the value they deliver, it might charge lower prices to drive weaker competitors out of the market. If the market is dominated by larger, low-price competitors, the company may decide to target unserved market niches with value-added products at higher prices. For example, your local independent bookstore isn't likely to win a price war against online sellers like Amazon. It would be wiser to add special customer services and personal touches that justify higher prices and margins.

Finally, the company should ask, How does the competitive landscape influence customer price sensitivity?[12] For example, customers will be more price sensitive if they see few differences

14.1 real marketing

Economic Value Added

Return on capital employed (ROCE)

Some companies, such as grocery chains, have low returns on sales but are profitable. They achieve this because the critical measure is return on capital employed (ROCE). This is the product of return on sales (ROS) and the speed at which assets are turned over (the activity ratio):

$$\text{ROCE} = \text{ROS} \times \text{Activity} = \frac{\text{NP}}{\text{Sales}} \times \frac{\text{Sales}}{\text{Assets}}$$

By turning over its assets four times each year, a supermarket can achieve a 20 per cent return on capital employed although its return on sales is only 5 per cent, while an exclusive clothes shop has very high margins but turns its assets over slowly.

$$\text{Supermarket ROCE} = \frac{5}{100} \times \frac{100}{25} = 20 \text{ per cent}$$

$$\text{Clothes shop ROCE} = \frac{40}{100} \times \frac{100}{300} = 13.3 \text{ per cent}$$

These are powerful ratios that can define how a company can do business. Aldi, the German discount grocery chain, succeeds with margins half those of many grocers. Its margins are very low (2–3 per cent), but it keeps its return on capital employed high by high stock turnover and keeping its other assets low.

There are two benefits from increasing asset turnover: improved return on capital employed, and reduced fixed costs. The firm that hires trucks rather than buying them reduces its fixed costs and, therefore, its sensitivity to volume changes. Also, by reducing its assets it increases its activity ratio and return on capital employed. Increased asset turnover is one of the direct benefits of just-in-time (JIT) and lean manufacturing. JIT cuts down the assets tied up in stock and improves quality, while lean manufacturing reduces investment in plant.

Capital cost covered (C³)

Assets cost money and return on capital costs takes that into account. It is a powerful tool because it combines three critical business ratios:

$$C^3 = \text{ROS} \times \text{Activity} \times \text{Capital efficiency}$$
$$= \frac{\text{NP}}{\text{Sales}} \times \frac{\text{Sales}}{\text{Assets}} \times \frac{\text{Assets}}{\text{Cost of capital}}$$

The cost of capital is the average cost of debt and shareholder equity. For a supermarket the figure is 10 per cent per year. With assets of €25 million, the cost of capital is €25m $\times$ 0.10 = €2.5m, giving:

$$C^3 = \frac{5}{100} \times \frac{100}{25} \times \frac{25}{2.5} = \frac{NP}{CC} = 2.0$$

In other words, the net profit is double the capital cost – the company is healthy. This ratio is more discriminating than the familiar distinction between profit and loss. If the capital cost covered is below zero, a firm is making a loss. A capital cost covered above zero indicates a profit. However, capital cost covered between zero and 1 shows that a firm is in profit but not adding value – its profit does not cover its cost of capital.

Economic Value Added (EVA)

EVA makes a direct comparison between the cost of capital and net profits. It is a simple idea that has hugely increased the value of companies using it. Many leading companies see EVA as a way of examining the value of their investments and strategy. The supermarket's EVA is:

EVA – Net profit – Cost of capital = 5 – 2.5 = €2.5m

Profit, economic value added and capital cost covered are related concepts: profit shows how a company's trading is going, EVA shows a company's wealth creation in monetary terms, while capital cost covered gives the rate of wealth creation.

Category	C^3	EVA	NP	Economic state
I	>1	>0	>0	A profitable company which is adding economic value
II	0–1	<0	>0	A company whose profits do not cover the cost of capital
III	<0	<0	<0	A loss-making company

The supermarket is a clear category I company. This contrasts with the clothes store whose capital, at 16.25 per cent, is more expensive because the clothes market is cyclical and fashion-dependent. Assets of €300m give a capital cost of €48.75m.

	C^3	EVA (€m)	NP (€m)	Category
Supermarket	2.0	2.5	5	I
Clothes store	0.8	(9.5)	40	II

Many of the *dot bombs* (dot-com companies that went bust) never strayed beyond being category III companies, never making any net profits (NP < 0) after having a high advertising spend with low margins and sales volume.

between competing products. They will buy whichever product costs the least. The more information customers have about competing products and prices before buying, the more price sensitive they will be. Easy product comparisons help customers to assess the value of different options and to decide what prices they are willing to pay. Finally, customers will be more price sensitive if they can switch easily from one product alternative to another.

What principle should guide decisions about what price to charge relative to those of competitors? The answer is simple in concept but often difficult in practice: no matter what price you charge – high, low or in between – be certain to give customers superior value for that price.

Other external factors

When setting prices, the company must also consider other factors in its external environment. *Economic conditions* can have a strong impact on the firm's pricing strategies. Economic factors such as boom or recession, inflation and interest rates affect pricing decisions because they affect both consumer perceptions of the product's price and value and the costs of producing a product. Other factors such as *demographic* and *technological* trends and *ecological environmental* pressures can also affect prices due to their influence on product supply and demand. Consider the recent increases in food prices in some countries in Europe.

According to Peter Brabeck, chairman of Nestlé, the world's largest food company, food prices are set for a period of 'significant and long-lasting' inflation. The rises in food prices reflect not only short-term factors but also long-term and structural changes in supply and demand. Brabeck cited population growth, rising demand from 'the phenomena of India and China' and the use of food products by biofuel producers as causes of pressure in international food markets. 'They will have a long-lasting impact on food prices,' Brabeck told the *Financial Times* during a visit to China.

No doubt, concern is intensifying among economists and European food producers that demand for agricultural commodities will remain strong because of higher incomes in emerging markets. These improved incomes lead people to consume more dairy products and meat. And the growth of the biofuel industry has led to increasing demand for cereals, oilseeds and vegetable oils. Corn prices have risen 68 per cent, while barley and wheat prices are up 53 and 50 per cent respectively, over 2006–07. Sugar, milk and cocoa prices have also soared, resulting in the biggest increase in retail food prices in three decades in some countries. Reports from international organisations forecast food price rises of between 20 and 50 per cent over the next decade. In the short term, food producers are having success in passing some of the increases on to the consumer. Warburton's, the UK's leading bread brand, and Premier Foods, owner of the Hovis bread brand, have increased the price of bread in 2007. SABMiller, owner of Peroni and Pilsner Urquell brands, have put up beer prices to counter higher costs for brewing materials such as malt, barley and hops. Nestlé and Procter & Gamble have both raised prices of their coffee brands to combat higher raw coffee prices. But analysts warn that sales cannot be sustained and that food companies will not be able to pass all of their higher costs on to consumers indefinitely.

However, some analysts believe the long-term risk of higher food prices is exaggerated. On the one hand, the pressure on food manufacturers will pass as biofuel producers develop technologies that require less raw material or use non-edible parts of food. On the other hand, some food manufacturers are exploring ways to change the ingredients they use. For example, about 4 per cent of Unilever's sales are exposed to edible oils such as sunflower, palm, rapeseed and soyabean. According to Jan Westrate, director of Unilever's food research operations, the company is '. . . looking at how [it] can further reduce use of edible oils while retaining the same quality.'[13]

The company must also consider the impact its prices will have on other parties in its environment. How will *resellers* react to various prices? The company should set prices that give resellers a fair profit, encourage their support and help them to sell the product effectively.

The *government* is another important external influence on pricing decisions. Finally, *social concerns* may have to be taken into account. In setting prices, a company's short-term sales, market share and profit goals may have to be tempered by broader societal considerations.

We've now seen that pricing decisions are subject to an incredibly complex set of customer, company, competitive and environmental forces. To make things even more complex, companies seldom set a single price. Rather, they adopt a pricing structure covering different items in their line. This pricing structure changes over time as products move through their life cycles. The company adjusts product prices to reflect changes in costs and demand, and to account for variations in buyers and situations. As the competitive environment changes, the company considers when to initiate price changes and when to respond to them. Let us now examine the major pricing strategies available to marketers.[14]

New-product pricing strategies

Pricing strategies usually change as the product passes through its life cycle. The introductory stage is especially challenging. Companies bringing out an innovative product face the challenge of setting prices for the first time. They can choose between two strategies: *market-skimming pricing* and *market-penetration pricing*.

Market-skimming pricing

Many companies that invent new products initially set high prices to 'skim' revenues layer by layer from the market, a strategy called **market-skimming pricing**. Sony frequently uses this strategy. When Sony introduced the world's first high-definition television (HDTV) to the Japanese market in 1990, the high-tech sets cost about €35,000. These televisions were purchased only by customers who could afford to pay a high price for the new technology. Sony rapidly reduced the price over the next several years to attract new buyers. By 1993 a 28-inch HDTV cost a Japanese buyer just over €4,800. In 2001, a Japanese consumer could buy a 40-inch HDTV for about €1,600, a price that many more customers could afford. An entry-level HDTV set now sells for less than €600 in the major European and US markets, and prices continue to fall. In this way, Sony skimmed the maximum amount of revenue from the various segments of the market.[15]

Market skimming makes sense only under certain conditions. First, the product's quality and image must support its higher price. Second, buyers are not price-sensitive and a sufficient number of them must want the product at that price. Third, the costs of producing a smaller volume cannot be so high that they cancel the advantage of charging more. Finally, competitors should not be able to enter the market easily and undercut the high price.

Market-skimming pricing—Setting a high price for a new product to skim maximum revenues layer by layer from the segments willing to pay the high price; the company makes fewer but more profitable sales.

Market-penetration pricing

Rather than setting a high initial price to skim off small but profitable market segments, some companies use **market-penetration pricing**. They set a low initial price in order to *penetrate* the market quickly and deeply – to attract a large number of buyers quickly and win a large market share. The high sales volume results in falling costs, allowing the company to cut its price even further. For example, Dell used penetration pricing to sell high-quality computer products

Market-penetration pricing—Setting a low price for a new product in order to attract large numbers of buyers and a large market share.

Mutually inclusive.

SONY
BRAVIA.

BRAVIA. LCD TV. THE WORLD'S FIRST TELEVISION
FOR MEN AND WOMEN. It's true, men and women can
actually agree on a television. Specifically, the only one that
can deliver both performance and style in Sony Full HD no
matter what you choose to watch. So while men and women
may like different features of the BRAVIA, there's
one thing they both like: The world's most powerful
HD experience. Find out more at sony.com/HDTV

Full HD
1080

like.no.other

Market-skimming pricing: Sony priced it's early HDTVs high, then reduced prices gradually over the years to attract new buyers.

through lower-cost direct channels. Its sales soared when IBM, Compaq, Apple and other competitors selling through retail stores could not match its prices.

Several conditions favour setting a low price. First, the market must be highly price-sensitive, so that a low price produces more market growth. Second, production and distribution costs must fall as sales volume increases. Finally, the low price must help keep out the competition and the penetration pricer must maintain its low-price position – otherwise the price advantage may be only temporary. For example, Dell faced difficult times when IBM and Compaq established their own direct distribution channels. However, through its dedication to low production and distribution costs, Dell retained its price advantage and established itself as the industry's number-one PC maker.

Product-mix pricing strategies

The strategy for setting a product's price often has to be changed when the product is part of a product mix. In this case, the firm looks for a set of prices that maximises the profits on the total product mix. Pricing is difficult because the various products have related demand and costs, and face different degrees of competition. Five *product-mix pricing* situations are summarised in Table 14.3.

Product line pricing	Optional-product pricing	Captive-product pricing	By-product pricing	Product-bundle pricing
Setting price steps between product line items	Pricing optional or accessory products sold with the main product	Pricing products that must be used with the main product	Pricing low-value by-products to get rid of them	Pricing bundles of products sold together

Table 14.3 Product-mix pricing strategies

Product line pricing

Companies usually develop product lines rather than single products. In **product line pricing**, management must decide on the price steps to set between the various products in a line.

The price steps should take into account cost differences between the products in the line, customer evaluations of their different features and competitors' prices. In many industries, sellers use well-established *price points* for the products in their line. Thus, men's clothing stores might carry men's suits at three price levels: €200, €400 and €600. The customer will probably associate low-, average- and high-quality suits with the three price points. Even if the three prices are raised a little, men normally will buy suits at their own preferred price points. The seller's task is to establish perceived quality differences that support the price differences. If the price difference between two successive products is small, buyers will usually buy the more advanced product. This will increase company profits if the cost difference is smaller than the price difference. If the price difference is large, however, customers will generally buy the less advanced products.

Product line pricing—Setting the price steps between various products in a product line based on cost differences between the products, customer evaluations of different features and competitors' prices.

Optional-product pricing

Many companies use **optional-product pricing** – offering to sell optional or accessory products along with their main product. For example, a Toyota Yaris customer may choose to add satellite navigation, a CD autochanger or alloy wheels. And an iPod buyer can also choose from a bewildering array of accessories, everything from travel chargers and FM transmitters to external speakers and armband carrying cases.

Pricing these options is a sticky problem. For example, car companies have to decide which items to include in the base price and which to offer as options. Mercedes Benz and BMW's basic cars once came famously under-equipped. Typically the customer has to pay extra for a CD player (prices vary), electric windows (€350), sun roof (€900) and security system (€550). The basic model is stripped of so many comforts and conveniences that most buyers reject it. They pay for extras or buy a better-equipped version. More recently, however, European and US car makers have followed the example of the Japanese competitors and included in the basic price many useful items previously sold only as options. Most advertised prices today represent well-equipped cars.

Optional-product pricing—The pricing of optional or accessory products along with a main product.

Captive-product pricing

Companies that make products that must be used along with a main product are using **captive-product pricing**. Examples of captive products are razor blade cartridges, printer cartridges and video games. Producers of the main products (razors, printers and video game consoles) often price them low and set high mark-ups on the supplies. Thus Gillette sells low-priced razors, but makes money on the replacement blades. HP makes very low margins on its printers but very

Captive-product pricing—Setting a price for products that must be used along with a main product, such as blades for a razor and film for a camera.

high margins on printer cartridges and other supplies. Sony and other video games makers sell game consoles at low prices and obtain the majority of their profits from the video games.

In the case of services, this strategy is called **two-part pricing**. The price of the service is broken into a *fixed fee* plus a *variable usage rate*. Thus a telephone company charges a monthly rate – the fixed fee – plus charges for calls beyond some minimum number – the variable usage rate. Amusement parks charge admission plus additional fees for food and other park features. Theatres charge admission and then generate additional revenues from concessions. And mobile phone companies charge a flat rate for a basic calling plan, then charge for minutes over what the plan allows. The service firm must decide how much to charge for the basic service and how much for the variable usage. The fixed amount should be low enough to induce usage of the service; profit can be made on the variable fees.

By-product pricing

In producing processed meats, petroleum and agricultural products, chemicals and other products, there are often **by-products**. If the by-products have no value and if getting rid of them is costly, this will affect the pricing of the main product. Using **by-product pricing**, the manufacturer will seek a market for these by-products and should accept any price that covers more than the cost of storing and delivering them. By-products can even turn out to be profitable. For example, the paper maker MeadWestvaco has turned what was once considered chemical waste into profit-making products.

MeadWestvaco created a separate company, Asphalt Innovations, which creates useful chemicals entirely from the by-products of MeadWestvaco's wood-processing activities. In fact, Asphalt Innovations has grown to become the world's biggest supplier of specialty chemicals for the paving industry. Using the salvaged chemicals, paving companies can pave roads at a lower temperature, create longer-lasting roads, and more easily recycle road materials when roads need to be replaced. What's more, salvaging the by-product chemicals eliminates the costs and environmental hazards once associated with disposing of them.[16]

Product-bundle pricing

Using **product-bundle pricing**, sellers often combine several of their products and offer the bundle at a reduced price. For example, hotels may sell specially priced packages that include room, meals and tickets to entertainment events. Fast-food restaurants bundle a burger, fries and a soft drink at a value-meal or combo price. Telecommunications companies bundle land and mobile phone services and high-speed Internet connections at a low combined price. Price bundling can promote the sales of products consumers might not otherwise buy, but the combined price must be low enough to get them to buy the bundle.[17]

Price-adjustment strategies

Companies usually adjust their basic prices to account for various customer differences and changing situations. Table 14.4 summarises seven price-adjustment strategies: *discount and allowance pricing, segmented pricing, psychological pricing, promotional pricing, geographical pricing, dynamic pricing* and *international pricing*.

Two-part pricing—A strategy for pricing services in which price is broken into a fixed fee plus a variable usage rate.

By-products—Items produced as a result of the main factory process, such as waste and reject items.

By-product pricing—Setting a price for by-products in order to make the main product's price more competitive.

Product-bundle pricing—Combining several products and offering the bundle at a reduced price.

Table 14.4 Price adjustment strategies

Discount and allowance pricing	Segmented pricing	Psychological pricing	Promotional pricing	Geographical pricing	Dynamic pricing	International pricing
Reducing prices to reward customer responses such as paying early or promoting the product	Adjusting prices to allow for differences in customers, products and locations	Adjusting prices for psychological effect	Temporarily reducing prices to increase short-run sales	Adjusting prices to account for the geographical location of customers	Adjusting prices continually to meet the characteristics and needs of individual customers and situations	Adjusting prices in international markets

Discount and allowance pricing

Most companies adjust their basic price to reward customers for certain responses, such as early payment of bills, volume purchases and off-season buying. These price adjustments – called *discounts* and *allowances* – can take many forms.

The many forms of discounts include a **cash discount** which is a price reduction to buyers who pay their bills promptly. A typical example is '2/10, net 30', which means that although payment is due within 30 days, the buyer can deduct 2 per cent if the bill is paid within 10 days. Such discounts are customary in many industries and help to improve the sellers' cash situation and reduce bad debts and credit-collection costs.

A **quantity discount** is a price reduction to buyers who buy large volumes. A typical example is Pilot Hi-Tecpoint Rollerball pens from Staples Office Supplies at £3.99 (€5.58) for a pack of three, £7.49 (€10.48) for six and £12.68 (€17.75) for 12. Wine merchants often give '12 for the price of 11' and Costco and Makro, the trade warehouses, automatically give discounts on any product bought in bulk. Such discounts provide an incentive to the customer to buy more from one given seller, rather than from many different sources. Price does not always decrease with the quantity purchased. More often than realised, people pay a **quantity premium**, a surcharge paid by buyers who purchase high volumes of a product.

A **trade discount** (also called a **functional discount**) is offered by the seller to trade channel members that perform certain functions, such as selling, storing and record keeping. Manufacturers may offer different functional discounts to different trade channels because of the varying services they perform, but manufacturers must offer the same functional discounts within each trade channel.

A **seasonal discount** is a price discount to buyers who buy merchandise or services out of season. For example, lawn and garden equipment manufacturers will offer seasonal discounts to retailers during the autumn and winter to encourage early ordering in anticipation of the heavy spring and summer selling seasons. Hotels, motels and airlines will offer seasonal discounts in their slower selling periods. Seasonal discounts allow the seller to keep production steady or stabilise capacity utilisation during the entire year.

Allowances are another type of reduction from the list price. For example, **trade-in allowances** are price reductions given for turning in an old item when buying a new one. Trade-in allowances are most common in the car industry, but are also given for other durable goods.

Cash discount—A price reduction to buyers who pay their bills promptly.

Quantity discount—A price reduction to buyers who buy large volumes.

Quantity premium—A surcharge paid by buyers who purchase high volumes of a product.

Trade discount (or functional discount)—A price reduction offered by the seller to trade channel members that perform certain functions, such as selling, storing and record keeping.

Seasonal discount—A price reduction to buyers who buy merchandise or services out of season.

Trade-in allowance—A price reduction given for turning in an old item when buying a new one.

Promotional allowance—
A payment or price reduction to reward dealers for participating in advertising and sales-support programmes.

Segmented pricing—
Selling a product or service at two or more prices that allows for differences in customers, products and locations, rather than based on differences in costs.

Promotional allowances are payments or price reductions to reward dealers for participating in advertising and sales-support programmes.

Segmented pricing

Companies will often adjust their basic prices to allow for differences in customers, products and locations. In **segmented pricing**, the company sells a product or service at two or more prices, even though the difference in prices is not based on differences in costs. Segmented pricing takes several forms:

1. *Customer-segment pricing.* Different customers pay different prices for the same product or service. Museums, for example, will charge a lower admission price for young people, the unwaged, students and senior citizens. Many teenagers in Britain and elsewhere in Europe pay for their mobile phone services on a pre-paid basis, which is more expensive than the tariff for a monthly contract.

2. *Product-form pricing.* Different versions of the product are priced differently, but not according to differences in their costs. For instance, a 1-litre bottle of Evian mineral water may cost €1.50 at your local supermarket. But a 50 ml aerosol can of Evian Brumisateur Mineral Water Spray sells for a recommended retail price of €5.49 at beauty boutiques and spas. The water is all from the same source in the French Alps, and the aerosol packaging costs little more than the plastic bottles. Yet you pay about 15 cents per 100 ml for one form and €10.98 per 100 ml for the other.

Product-form pricing: Evian water in a 1-litre bottle might cost you 15 cents per 100 ml at your local supermarket, whereas the same water might run €10 per 100 ml when sold in 50 ml aerosol cans as Evian Brumisateur Mineral Water Spray moisturizer.

SOURCE: Photo by Jim Whitmer.

3. *Location pricing.* A company charges different prices for locations, even though the cost of offering each location is the same. For instance, theatres vary their seat prices because of audience preferences for certain locations, and UK universities charge higher tuition fees for non-EU students.

4. *Time pricing.* Prices vary by the season, the month, the day and even the hour. Some public utilities vary their prices to commercial users by time of day and weekend versus weekday. Telephone companies offer lower 'off-peak' charges, electricity costs less at night and resorts give seasonal discounts.

For segmented pricing to be an effective strategy, certain conditions must exist. The market must be segmentable and the segments must show different degrees of demand. Members of the segment paying the lower price should not be able to turn round and resell the product to the segment paying the higher price. Competitors should not be able to undersell the firm in the segment being charged the higher price. Nor should the costs of segmenting and watching the market exceed the extra revenue obtained from the price difference. Most importantly, segmented prices should reflect real differences in customers' perceived value. Otherwise, in the long run, the practice will lead to customer resentment and ill will.

Psychological pricing

Price says something about the product. For example, many consumers use price to judge quality. A €120 bottle of perfume may contain only €5 worth of scent, but some people are willing to pay the €120 because this price indicates something special.

In using **psychological pricing**, sellers consider the psychology of prices and not simply the economics. For example, consumers usually perceive higher-priced products as having higher quality. When they can judge the quality of a product by examining it or by calling on past experience with it, they use price less to judge quality. But when they cannot judge quality because they lack the information or skill, price becomes an important quality signal.

> " When [customers] cannot judge quality . . . price becomes an important quality signal. "

Psychological pricing is particularly apparent in airport duty-free shops where people buy expensive items in unfamiliar categories. In such outlets, exquisite malt whiskies are often sold inexpensively but inexperienced buyers are attracted by grandly packaged and overpriced blended whiskies.

Another aspect of psychological pricing is **reference prices** – prices that buyers carry in their minds and refer to when looking at a given product. The reference price might be formed by noting current prices, remembering past prices or assessing the buying situation. Sellers can influence or use these consumers' reference prices when setting price. For example, a company could display its product next to more expensive ones in order to imply that it belongs in the same class. Department stores often sell women's clothing in separate departments differentiated by price: clothing found in the more expensive department is assumed to be of better quality. Companies also can influence consumers' reference prices by stating high manufacturer's suggested prices, by indicating that the product was originally priced much higher or by pointing to a competitor's higher price.

Even small differences in price can suggest product differences. Consider a stereo priced at €300 compared to one priced at €299.99. The actual price difference is only 1 cent, but the psychological difference can be much greater. For example, some consumers will see the €299.99 as a price in the €200 range rather than the €300 range. The €299.99 is more likely to be seen as a bargain price, whereas the €300 price suggests more quality. Complicated numbers, such as

Psychological pricing—A pricing approach that considers the psychology of prices and not simply the economics; the price is used to say something about the product.

Reference prices—Prices that buyers carry in their minds and refer to when they look at a given product.

€247.41, also look less appealing than rounded ones, such as €250. Some psychologists argue that each digit has symbolic and visual qualities that should be considered in pricing. Thus, 8 is round and even and creates a soothing effect, whereas 7 is angular and creates a jarring effect.[18]

Promotional pricing

Promotional pricing— Temporarily pricing products below the list price, and sometimes even below cost, to increase short-run sales.

With **promotional pricing**, companies will temporarily price their products below list price and sometimes even below cost to create buying excitement. Promotional pricing takes several forms. Supermarkets and department stores will price a few products as *loss leaders* to attract customers to the store in the hope that they will buy other items at normal mark-ups. Sellers will also use *special-event pricing* in certain seasons to draw more customers. Thus furniture and home furnishings are promotionally priced every January to attract weary Christmas shoppers back into the stores.

Manufacturers will sometimes offer *cash rebates* to consumers who buy the product from dealers within a specified time; the manufacturer sends the rebate directly to the customer. Rebates have recently been popular with carmakers and producers of durable goods and small appliances.

Some manufacturers offer *low-interest financing*, *longer warranties* or *free maintenance* to reduce the consumer's 'price'. This practice has recently become a favourite of the car industry. The seller may simply offer *discounts* from normal prices to increase sales and reduce stocks. However, promotional pricing can have adverse effects. If used too frequently and copied by competitors, price promotions can create 'deal-prone' customers who wait until brands go on sale before buying them. Equally, constantly reduced prices can erode a brand's value in the eyes of customers. Marketers sometimes use price promotions as a quick fix instead of sweating through the difficult process of developing effective longer-term strategies for building their brands.

In fact, one observer notes that price promotions can be downright addicting to both the company and the customer:

> 'Price promotions are the brand equivalent of heroin: easy to get into but hard to get out of. Once the brand and its customers are addicted to the short-term high of a price cut it is hard to wean them away to real brand building . . . . But continue and the brand dies by 1000 cuts.'[19]

The frequent use of promotional pricing can also lead to industry price wars. Such price wars usually play into the hands of only one or a few competitors – those with the most efficient operations. For example, until recently, the computer industry avoided price wars. Computer companies, including IBM, Hewlett-Packard and Gateway, showed strong profits as their new technologies were snapped up by eager consumers. When the market cooled, however, many competitors began to unload PCs at discounted prices. In response, Dell, the industry's undisputed low-cost leader, started a brutal price war that only it could win. The result was nothing short of a rout. IBM has since sold off its PC unit to Lenovo, and Gateway struggles with razor-thin profit margins. Dell emerged atop the worldwide PC industry.[20]

The point is that promotional pricing can be an effective means of generating sales in certain circumstances but can be damaging if taken as a steady diet.

Geographical pricing

A company must also decide how to price its products to customers located in different parts of the country or the world. Should the company risk losing the business of more distant customers by charging them higher prices to cover the higher shipping costs? Or should the company charge all customers the same prices regardless of location? We will look at five **geographical pricing** strategies for the following hypothetical situation:

> Tromsø a.s. is a Norwegian paper products company selling to customers all over Europe. The cost of freight is high and affects the companies from whom customers buy their paper. Tromsø wants to establish a geographical pricing policy. It is trying to determine how to price a Nkr1,000 order to three specific customers: Customer A (Oslo), Customer B (Amsterdam) and Customer C (Barcelona).

One option is for Tromsø to ask each customer to pay the shipping cost from the factory to the customer's location. All three customers would pay the same factory price of Nkr1,000 (€806), with Customer A paying, say, Nkr100 for shipping; Customer B, Nkr150; and Customer C, Nkr250. Called **FOB-origin pricing**, this practice means that the goods are placed *free on board* (hence, *FOB*) a carrier. At that point the title and responsibility pass to the customer, who pays the freight from the factory to the destination.

Because each customer picks up its own cost, supporters of FOB pricing feel that this is the fairest way to assess freight charges. The disadvantage, however, is that Tromsø will be a high-cost firm to distant customers. If Tromsø's main competitor happens to be in Spain, this competitor will no doubt outsell Tromsø in Spain. In fact, the competitor would outsell Tromsø in most of southern Europe, whereas Tromsø would dominate the north.

Uniform delivered pricing is the exact opposite of FOB pricing. Here, the company charges the same price plus freight to all customers, regardless of their location. The freight charge is set at the average freight cost. Suppose this is Nkr150. Uniform delivered pricing therefore results in a higher charge to the Oslo customer (who pays Nkr150 freight instead of Nkr100) and a lower charge to the Barcelona customer (who pays Nkr150 instead of Nkr250). On the one hand, the Oslo customer would prefer to buy paper from another local paper company that uses FOB-origin pricing. On the other hand, Tromsø has a better chance of winning over the Spanish customer. Another advantage of uniform delivered pricing is that it is fairly easy to administer.

Zone pricing falls between FOB-origin pricing and uniform delivered pricing. The company sets up two or more zones. All customers within a given zone pay a single total price; the more distant the zone, the higher the price. For example, Tromsø might set up a Scandinavian zone and charge Nkr100 freight to all customers in this zone, a northern European zone in which it charges Nkr150 and a southern European zone in which it charges Nkr250. In this way, the customers within a given price zone receive no price advantage from the company. For example, customers in Oslo and Copenhagen pay the same total price to Tromsø. The complaint, however, is that the Oslo customer is paying part of the Copenhagen customer's freight cost. In addition, even though they may be within a few miles of each other, a customer just barely on the south side of the line dividing north and south pays much more than one that is just barely on the north side of the line.

Using **basing-point pricing**, the seller selects a given city as a 'basing point' and charges all customers the freight cost from that city to the customer location, regardless of the city from which the goods are actually shipped. For example, Tromsø might set Oslo as the basing point and charge all customers Nkr100 plus the freight from Oslo to their locations. This means that a Copenhagen customer pays the freight cost from Oslo to Copenhagen, even though the goods may be shipped from Tromsø. Using a basing-point location other than the factory raises the total price for customers near the factory and lowers the total price for customers far from the factory.

Geographical pricing— Setting prices for customers located in different parts of the country or world.

FOB-origin pricing— A geographic pricing strategy in which goods are placed free on board a carrier; the customer pays the freight from the factory to the destination.

Uniform delivered pricing— A geographic pricing strategy in which the company charges the same price plus freight to all customers, regardless of their location.

Zone pricing— A geographic pricing strategy in which the company sets up two or more zones. All customers within a zone pay the same total price; the more distant the zone, the higher the price.

Basing-point pricing— A geographic pricing strategy in which the seller designates some city as a basing point and charges all customers the freight cost from that city to the customer location, regardless of the city from which the goods are actually shipped.

If all sellers used the same basing-point city, delivered prices would be the same for all customers and price competition would be eliminated. Industries such as sugar, cement, steel and cars used basing-point pricing for years, but this method has become less popular today. Some companies set up multiple basing points to create more flexibility, quoting freight charges from the basing-point city nearest to the customer.

Finally, the seller that is anxious to do business with a certain customer or geographical area might use **freight-absorption pricing**. Using this strategy, the seller absorbs all or part of the actual freight charges in order to get the desired business. The seller reasons that if it gets more business, its average costs will fall and more than compensate for its extra freight cost. Freight-absorption pricing is used for market penetration and to hold on to increasingly competitive markets.

Freight-absorption pricing—A geographic pricing strategy in which the company absorbs all or part of the actual freight charges in order to get the desired business.

Dynamic pricing

Throughout most of history, prices were set by negotiation between buyers and sellers. *Fixed price* policies – setting one price for all buyers – is a relatively modern idea that arose with the development of large-scale retailing at the end of the nineteenth century. Today, most prices are set this way. However, some companies are now reversing the fixed-pricing trend. They are using **dynamic pricing** – adjusting prices continually to meet the characteristics and needs of individual customers and situations.

For example, consider how the Internet has affected pricing. From the mostly fixed-pricing practices of the past century, the Web seems now to be taking us back – into a new age of fluid pricing. Prices can change from hour to hour and from customer to customer. 'Potentially, [the Internet] could push aside sticker prices and usher in an era of dynamic pricing,' says one writer, 'in which a wide range of goods would be priced according to what the market will bear – instantly, constantly.'[21]

Dynamic pricing—Charging different prices depending on individual customers and situations.

Dynamic pricing offers many advantages for marketers. It enables sellers to *target offers to specific customers*. For example, Internet sellers such as Amazon can mine their databases to gauge a specific shopper's desires, measure his or her means, instantaneously tailor products to fit that shopper's behaviour, and price products accordingly. Dynamic pricing also allows online sellers to *adjust prices according to changes in demand or costs*. Sellers can offer promotions on slow-moving and unsold items or nudge prices upwards on hot-selling goods. For example, Lastminute.com, the opportunistic dotcom, helps the leisure sector sell unbooked hotel rooms and unsold entertainment tickets and to fill flights close to their sell-by date. Insurance companies such as More Than, part of the Royal & Sun Alliance group, can change prices 'on the fly' to reflect changes in supply and demand or to balance the mix of high- and low-risk customers.

Buyers also benefit from the Web and dynamic pricing. A wealth of *shopping bots* – such as Shopica.com, DealTime.com, BizRate.com, ShopGenie.com, shopzilla.com, Yahoo! Shopping, PriceGrabber.com, insure-supermarket.com, mysimon.com and others – *offer instant product and price comparisons* from thousands of vendors. For instance, PriceGrabber.com lets shoppers browse by category or search for specific products and brands. It then searches the Web and reports back links to sellers, recommending merchants and the best prices along with customer reviews. In addition to simply finding the best product and the vendor with the best price for that product, customers armed with price information may *negotiate lower prices*.

Buyers can also *negotiate prices at online auction sites and exchanges*. Suddenly the centuries-old art of haggling is back in vogue. Want to sell that antique pickle jar that's been collecting dust for generations? Post it on eBay, the world's biggest online flea market. Want to name your own price for a hotel room or rental car? Visit Priceline.com or another reverse auction site. Want to bid on a ticket to a Coldplay show? Check out Ticketmaster.com, which now offers an online auction service for concert tickets.

Dynamic pricing can also be controversial. Most customers would find it galling to learn that the person in the next seat on that flight from Schiphol to Malpensa paid 20 per cent less just because he or she happened to call at the right time or buy through the right sales channel.

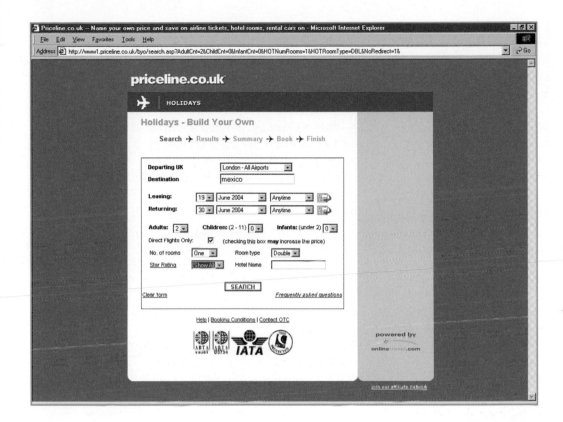

Build your own holidays and save a fortune. More and more travellers are doing just that by using online services like Priceline.

SOURCE: www.priceline.com.

Amazon learned this some years ago when it experimented with lowering prices to new customers in order to woo their business. When regular customers learned through Internet chatter that they were paying generally higher prices than first-timers, they protested loudly. An embarrassed Amazon.com halted the experiments.

Dynamic pricing can also be controversial.

Moreover, critics have raised concerns that variable or dynamic pricing may do a disservice to unsuspecting consumers and question the ethics of some practices. For example, in the case of motor insurance, the insurer seeks to balance the mix of low- and high-risk drivers as well as sales and prices over a trading period, which could be as short as every three months, a week or even a day. As a result, the price of premiums depends on where the consumer's request for a quote comes in the cycle. Whether consumers get their timing right is pure chance. Furthermore, consumers may have to spend a lot of their precious time searching the Internet and entering personal details on forms so they can be offered a price. They may also not realise that the price they are quoted often comes down to whether they are the type of motorist the insurer wants to do business with. In the end, those firms that adopt ethical pricing policies and build trust with prospective customers will gain in the long run.

Dynamic pricing makes sense in many contexts – it adjusts prices according to market forces, and it often works to the benefit of the customer. But marketers need to be careful not to use dynamic pricing to take advantage of customer groups, damaging important customer relationships.

International pricing

Companies that market their products internationally must decide what prices to charge in the different countries in which they operate. In some cases, a company can set a uniform worldwide

real marketing

Pricing around the world

Around the world, popular culture and brands are increasingly transnational. People in Thailand wear Levi's and eat at McDonald's while the British and Americans drive Toyotas and Israelis drink Bordeaux. Yet, despite the fact that the world is consuming in more identical patterns than ever before, one of the ways in which nations remain distinct is in how high or low prices are in their local markets.

So, why are the same products priced differently around Europe, the US and the world? Why does an 8-gigabyte iPod Nano cost $242 (€175) on Amazon.com in the US but €199.90 on Germany's Amazon.de and £106.72 (€155) on Britain's Amazon.co.uk? These are virtually identical products aimed at exactly the same audience, but one costs almost 30 per cent more than another. Why does Vodafone Germany charge €42.50 (£29.25) per month for up to 5 gigabytes' worth of mobile broadband services, compared to £45 (€65.38) for 1 gigabyte per month in the UK? This means a German laptop user pays only £0.0058 per megabyte, whereas a UK user is charged £0.045 per megabyte, i.e., almost eight times more for essentially the same service.

That Argentinean wine costs more in New York than Buenos Aires should come as no surprise. It has longer to travel and more associated costs in getting it to market. The same applies to oil and car parts. In general, the closer the product is to its source, the less it will cost. But that rationale does not apply all the time. Consider Apple's iPod again. It is made in China or Taiwan for US and British markets. The costs associated with bringing it to market in either country are relatively similar. So why does one cost so much more?

Several factors affect pricing of various consumer goods around the world.

First, *tariffs* (or lack thereof) can affect the price. In certain countries, such as the US and Britain, high taxes on tobacco sales result in a doubling and even tripling of the cost. In other countries, such as China, prices are fixed to hold the cost down for many products. As a spokesman for Philip Morris International wrote: 'As with many consumer goods, the prices for cigarettes vary from one country to another. This reflects varying levels of consumer purchasing power in individual countries, as well as in the case of cigarettes, varying levels of tobacco excise taxation. In fact, in most countries tobacco excise taxes are the major contributor to the retail selling price.'

But it's not just taxes that account for cross-border price differentials. Another reason is *currency valuation*. When the US dollar is weak compared with many other currencies, it buys less. That is one reason why the iPod Nano may seem

Price is only one element of the company's broader marketing strategy. If the company has selected its *target market* and *positioning*, its marketing mix strategy, including price, will be fairly straightforward. Some companies position their products on price and then tailor other marketing mix decisions to the prices they really want to charge. Other companies de-emphasise price and use other marketing mix tools to create non-price positions.

Common pricing *objectives* might include *survival*, *current profit maximisation*, *market-share leadership* or *customer retention and relationship building*. Pricing decisions must also be coordinated with product design, distribution and promotion decisions to form a consistent and effective marketing programme. Finally, in order to coordinate pricing goals and decisions, management must decide who within the *organisation* is responsible for price. Top management usually sets pricing policies, but some pricing authority may be delegated to lower-level managers, including salespeople, production, finance and accounting managers.

Other *external* pricing considerations include the *nature of the market and demand*, *competitors' prices and offers*, and *environmental factors* such as the economy, reseller needs and government actions. The seller's pricing freedom varies with different types of market. Ultimately, the consumer decides whether the company has set the right price. The customer weighs the price against the perceived values of using the product – if the price exceeds the sum of the values, consumers will not buy the product. So, the company must understand concepts such as *demand curves* (the price–demand relationship) and *price elasticity* (consumer sensitivity to prices). The more *inelastic* the demand, the higher the company can set its price. Consumers also compare a product's price to the prices of *competitors'* products. A company therefore must learn the customer value and prices of competitors' offers.

5. Describe the major strategies for pricing new products

Pricing is a dynamic process. Companies design a *pricing structure* that covers all their products. They change this structure over time and adjust it to account for different customers and situations. Pricing strategies usually change as a product passes through its life cycle. In pricing innovative new products, the company can use *market-skimming pricing* by initially setting high prices to 'skim' the maximum amount of revenue from various segments of the market, or it can use *market-penetrating pricing* by setting a low initial price to penetrate the market deeply and win a large market share.

6. Explain how companies find a set of prices that maximises the profits from the total product mix

When the product is part of a product mix, the firm searches for a set of prices that will maximise the profits from the total mix. In *product line pricing*, the company decides on price steps for the entire set of products it offers. In addition, the company must set prices for *optional products* (optional or accessory products included with the main product), *captive products* (products that are required for use of the main product), *by-products* (waste or residual products produced when making the main product), and *product bundles* (combinations of products at a reduced price).

7. Discuss how companies adjust their prices to take into account different types of customers and situations

Companies apply a variety of *price adjustment strategies* to account for differences in consumer segments and situations. In *discount and allowance pricing*, the company establishes cash, quantity, functional or seasonal discounts, or varying types of allowances.

A second strategy is *segmented pricing*, where the company sells a product at two or more prices to accommodate different customers, product forms, locations or times. Sometimes companies consider more than economics in their pricing decisions, using *psychological pricing* to better communicate a product's intended position. In *promotional pricing*, a company offers discounts or temporarily sells a product below list price as a special event, sometimes even selling below cost as a *loss leader*. Another approach is *geographical pricing*, whereby the company decides how to price to distant customers, choosing from such alternatives as FOB pricing, uniform-delivered pricing, zone pricing, basing-point pricing and freight-absorption pricing. Finally, *international pricing* means that the company adjusts its price to meet different conditions and expectations in different world markets.

8. Discuss the key issues related to initiating and responding to price changes

When a firm initiates a *price change*, it must consider customers' and competitors' reactions. It must also anticipate the probable reactions of suppliers, intermediaries and government. There are different implications to *initiating price cuts* and *initiating price increases*. Buyer reactions to price changes are influenced by the meaning customers see in the price change. Competitors' reactions flow from a set reaction policy or a fresh analysis of each situation.

The company that faces a price change initiated by a competitor must try to understand the competitor's intent as well as the likely duration and impact of the change. When facing a competitor's price change, the company might sit tight, reduce its own price, raise perceived quality, improve quality and raise price, or launch a fighting brand.

Discussing the concepts

1. Many companies do not handle pricing well. The chapter points out that companies often focus too much on cost, rather than the value the product offering creates. What are the differences between cost-based and value-based pricing? Why is it important for marketers to take into account customer value perceptions when setting prices?

2. Pricing decisions are based on costs and customer perceptions of value, in addition to other internal and external factors. Discuss these other internal and external factors and how they might affect the pricing of a new Samsung MP3 player.

3. Why would BlackBerry choose market-skimming pricing rather than market-penetration pricing for a new line of smartphones? Why would Nintendo choose market-penetration rather than market-skimming pricing for its new line of Wii games console?

4. The Internet has affected pricing. For example, some companies are adopting the concept of dynamic pricing on the Internet. How is dynamic pricing used on the Internet and what are the benefits for customers and the firms that are using this price adjustment strategy?

5. Imagine that you are the manager of a consumer electronics and home entertainment department store. Formulate rules that govern (a) initiating a price cut, (b) initiating a price increase, (c) a negative reaction from buyers to a price change by your company, (d) a competitor's response to your price change, and (e) your response to a competitor's price change. In your answer, explain the assumptions underlying your proposed rules.

Applying the concepts

1. Conduct a survey of prices for computer printers offered by different companies (e.g. Hewlett-Packard, Epson, Canon, Océ, Xerox as well as retailer own-brands). If possible, visit the retail stores or go to the websites of the retail stores that sell these products to obtain price information.

   (a) Are there any identifiable patterns in the pricing of different brands and types of printers (e.g. home, office, portable, basic, advanced)? Are there differences in pricing at different locations (e.g. retail versus direct/online)?

   (b) What pricing approaches appear to be used by different companies and their retailers?

   (c) What internal and external factors are important to consider when deciding a pricing strategy in this industry?

2. Space travel for the average person once seemed probable only in science fiction stories. But on 28 April 2001, Dennis Tito, a California multi-millionaire, became the first-ever space tourist. Tito travelled on a Russian Soyuz capsule, proving that an everyday civilian can endure the trip. Tito's trip, along with advances in rocket technology, accelerated opportunities for space tourism. Virgin Group's Richard Branson has recently pioneered this area by establishing Virgin Galactic, which plans to offer a fleet of spaceships for travel into outer space. Virgin Galactic, whose headquarters will be based in New Mexico, plans to build a $200m (€148m) spaceport on a 27-square-mile area in the southern part of the state. The company is collecting refundable deposits of $20,000 (€14,800) for the first year of travel. The deposits will be applied to the full fare of $148,000 for each trip into outer space (visit www.virgingalactic. com to learn more about space tourism).

   (a) How should a company set price for a new, high-technology product or service? What new-product pricing strategy is Virgin Galactic using for its space trips? Is this pricing strategy sustainable over time?

   (b) How might the entrance of a competitor affect the pricing?

   (c) How might Virgin Galactic bundle other products or services with space travel?

Web resources

For additional classic case studies and Internet exercises, visit **www.pearsoned.co.uk/ kotler**

References

1. Thomas T. Nagle and John E. Hogan, *The Strategy and Tactics of Pricing*, 4th edn (Upper Saddle River, NJ: Prentice Hall, 2006), p. 1.

2. 'A not-so-popular Nordic bridge', *The Economist* (7 October 2000), p. 61; 'Asia: the bridge to nowhere in particular', *The Economist* (4 April 1998), p. 42; Robert Wright, 'Eurotunnel in traffic volume downturn', *Financial Times* (21 January 2004); 'Øresundsbron Konsortiet report operating result of DKK686m', *Nordic Business Report* (4 March 2003); 'Danish minister proposes tax relief for Oresund commuter', *Nordic Business Report* (6 June 2003); 'Oresund Bridge consortium reports loss of DKK543m', *Nordic Business Report* (15 March 2006); William MacNamara, 'Eurotunnel cuts losses to €32m', *Financial Times* (31 August 2007); 'Irish eye up a 21-mile bridge . . . to Scotland', *The Scotsman* (23 August 2007); www.bridgepros.com/project/Oresund%20Bridge/. For prices and traffic information, see www.oresundsbron.com.

3. Values taken from 'Energy-saving light bulbs', *Which?* (May 1993), pp. 8–10; also see 'Low energy light bulbs', *Which?* (October 1999).

4. 'For whom the Dell tolls', *The Economist* (13 May 2006), pp. 78–9.

5. Here accumulated production is drawn on a semi-log scale, so that equal distances represent the same percentage increase in output.

6. Nicholas George, 'Brio's toy trains hit the buffers', *Financial Times* (29 August 2003), p. 10.

7. Kevin Done, 'Building the superjumbo', *Financial Times* (2 November 2000), p. 21; Rebecca Hoar, 'Fight for the skies', *EuroBusiness* (May 2000), pp. 68–72.

8. See Timothy M. Laseter, 'Supply chain management: The ins and outs of target costing', *Purchasing* (12 March 1998), pp. 22–5. Also the Swatch Web page at www.swatch.com; Archie Lockamy III and Wilbur I. Smith, 'Target costing for supply chain management: Criteria and selection', *Industrial Management & Data Systems*, **100**, 5 (2000), pp. 210–18; and Melanie Wells, 'On his watch', *Forbes* (18 February 2002), pp. 93–4.

9. David Humphries, 'Niche airports for high-flyers', *How To Spend It* (London: Financial Times, 2000), pp. 8–10.

10. Joshua Rosenbaum, 'Guitar maker looks for a new key', *Wall Street Journal* (11 February 1998), p. B1; information accessed at www.gibson.com, June 2007.

11. Thomas T. Nagle and John E. Hogan, *The Strategy and Tactics of Pricing*, 4th edn (Upper Saddle River, NJ: Prentice Hall, 2006), Ch. 7.

12. See Robert J. Dolan, 'Pricing: A value-based approach', Harvard Business School Publishing, 9-500-071 (3 November 2003).

13. Jenny Wiggins, 'Breakfast toast set to become a luxury item', *Financial Times* (10 July 2007), p. 21; Geoff Dyer, 'Nestlé chief fears food price inflation', *Financial Times* (5 July 2007), accessed at www.ft.com, July 2007.

14. For comprehensive discussions of pricing strategies, see Thomas T. Nagle and John E. Hogan, *The Strategy and Tactics of Pricing*, 4th edn (Upper Saddle River, NJ: Prentice Hall, 2006).

15. See Philip Kotler and Kevin Lane Keller, *Marketing Management*, 12th edn (Upper Saddle River, NJ: Prentice Hall, 2006), p. 438; and Robert Evatt, 'Video fans tuning in to HDTV experience: Prices of high-definition television sets continue to fall', *Tulsa World* (16 July 2006), p. 1.

16. Michael Buettner, 'Charleston, S.C.-based Asphalt Innovations turns waste into helpful product', *Knight Ridder Tribune Business News* (18 October 2004), p. 1; www.meadwestvaco.com, accessed July 2006.

17. See Thomas T. Nagle and John E. Hogan, *The Strategy and Tactics of Pricing*, 4th edn (Upper Saddle River, NJ: Prentice Hall, 2006), pp. 244–7; Stefan Stremersch and Gerard J. Tellis, 'Strategic bundling of products and prices: A new synthesis for marketing', *Journal of Marketing Research* (January 2002), pp. 55–72; Chris Janiszewski and Marcus Cunha, Jr, 'The influence of price discount framing on the evaluation of a product bundle', *Journal of Marketing Research* (March 2004), pp. 534–46.

18. For more discussion, see Manoj Thomas and Vicki Morvitz, 'Penny wise and pound foolish: The double-digit effect in price cognition', *Journal of Consumer Research* (June 2005), pp. 54–64; Heyong Min Kim and Luke Kachersky, 'Dimensions of price salience: A conceptual framework for perceptions of multi-dimensional prices', *Journal of Product and Brand Management*, **15**, 2 (2006), pp. 139–47; Michel Wedel and Peter S.H. Leeflang, 'A model for the effects of psychological pricing in Gabor–Granger price studies', *Journal of Economic Psychology*, **19**, 2 (1998), pp. 237–60; Tridib Mazumdar and Purushottam Papatla, 'An investigation of reference price segments', *Journal of Marketing Research* (May 2000), pp. 246–58; Indrajit Sinha and Michael Smith, 'Consumers' perceptions of promotional framing of price', *Psychology & Marketing* (March 2000), pp. 257–71; and Tulin Erdem, Glenn Mayhew and Baohong Sun, 'Understanding reference-price shoppers: a within- and across-category analysis', *Journal of Marketing Research* (November 2001), pp. 445–57.

19. Tim Ambler, 'Kicking price promotion habit is like getting off heroin – hard', *Marketing* (27 May 1999), p. 24. Also see Robert Gray, 'Driving sales at any price?', *Marketing* (11 April 2002), p. 24; Lauren Kellere Johnson, 'Dueling pricing strategies', *MIT Sloan Management Review* (Spring 2003), pp. 10–11; and Peter R. Darke and Cindy M.Y. Chung, 'Effects of pricing and promotion on consumer perceptions: It depends of how you frame it', *Journal of Retailing*, **81**, 1 (2005), pp. 35–47.

20. See 'Dell, the conqueror', *Business Week* (24 September 2001), pp. 92–102; Andy Serwer, 'Dell does domination', *Fortune* (21 January 2002), pp. 70–5; Pui-Wing Tam, 'H-P gains applause as it cedes PC market share to Dell', *Wall Street Journal* (18 January 2005), p. C1; Andrea Orr, 'Doors closing on creaky gateway', *Daily Deal* (10 February 2006); Richard Waters, 'HP sees unexpected jump in profits for PCs computer technology', *Financial Times* (16 February 2006), p. 25; and 'The merits of a diverse portfolio', *Business Today* (2 July 2006), p. 10.

21. Robert D. Hof, 'Going, going, gone', *Business Week* (12 April 1999), pp. 30–2. Also see Philip Kotler and Kevin Lane Keller, *Marketing Management*, 12th edn (Upper Saddle River, NJ: Prentice Hall, 2006), pp. 432–3.

22. Mariko Sanchanta and Chris Nuttall, 'Sony slashes cost of PlayStation 3', *Financial Times* (10 July 2007), p. 19.

Company case 14 BMI Baby, Buzz, ValuJet, easyJet: easy come, easy go

Michael O'Leary, the ebullient chief executive of Ryanair, takes some beating. Not only has he created Europe's leading low-cost airline, but also in a market that attracts flamboyant extroverts Michael O'Leary puts Virgin's Sir Richard Branson in the shade. To announce the opening of two additional bases at Rome Ciampina and Barcelona-Girona, he turned up dressed as the Pope. His pronouncements were as exuberant as his look. He announced he had overtaken British Airways in the previous month's short-haul traffic and declared Ryanair would double in size during the next decade, overtaking Europe's existing short-haul market leaders Air France, British Airways and Lufthansa.

'We make money with falling air fares. And we make stinking piles of money with rising fares . . . . We could be a monster, it's scary,' declares Mr O'Leary. While regular airlines whined about the impact of 9 11, Ryanair's market share and cash mountain grew. 'With our business model,' he proclaimed, 'we will soon be offering to fly people across Europe for free.'

If you get it right, the low-cost formula is a route to high rewards in an airline industry better known for chronic loss makers. It has worked for 20 years for Southwest Airlines in the US, the original low-cost pioneer. By 2003, Ryanair had established itself as one of the world's most profitable airlines. It trades on a racy forward price/earnings ratio of more than 36, a level normally reserved for growth companies, not airlines.

Others follow Ryanair's business model. With easyJet, Stelios Haji-Ioannou, the son of a wealthy Greek ship-owner, is challenging Ryanair and is extending his pricing model to hire cars, with easyCar. All these low-cost operations use a dynamic pricing model that matches price and demand minute buy minute. Book an easyCar Mercedes early and most days you will get an excellent deal. However, as the booking date approaches prices can go up or down to achieve the best return. Mr Haji-Ioannou now intends to extend the idea to cinemas where prices will vary hugely to match supply and demand. On the run-up to the Oscars, he was in Hollywood to broker a deal with film companies to get the flexibility he wants.

Established airlines are responding differently to the low-cost challenge. British Airways sold their low-cost airline, Go, after years of heavy losses but in the hope of making 'a small profit' in the year of the sale. According to their new chief executive, Rod Eddington, the new team at BA decided that Go does not fit in with his vision of running a profitable (high-cost) full-service airline. There have been enough casualties along the way to show that the low-cost model is far from being a one-way bet: KLM's Buzz did not run smoothly, and in the US a fatal crash ruined highly successful ValuJet and Air Littoral was killed off.

Virgin Express, Sir Richard Branson's Brussels and Nasdaq-listed attempt at setting up a no-frills carrier, provided further proof of the pitfalls waiting for operators that fail to control their costs. Its losses are still mounting. In contrast to its fast growing rivals, it is retrenching by cutting routes and selling aircraft.

'In this business it's low-cost that wins,' says Mr O'Leary. 'Ninety-nine per cent of people want the cheapest price. They don't want awards for the in-flight magazine or the best coffee. The brand, who cares? It has to be safe, on time and cheap. It's a bus service, it's transport.'

It is not all easy flying for established low-cost airlines, either. easyJet's high aircraft utilisation rate makes it especially vulnerable to delays; it may face difficulties protecting its name and branding; the business is subject to strong seasonal variations; it may not meet its growth targets; rapid growth may be difficult to manage; it will incur significant costs acquiring additional aircraft; it is exposed to fuel price fluctuations; and there are the well-publicised problems with landing charges at Luton airport, its main hub.

Whatever the risks put forward by careful investment bankers, most aviation analysts believe that it is easyJet and Ryanair that are the likely low-cost winners. Both airlines solely operate simple fleets and keep operations simple by offering no free food. Ray Webster, easyJet chief executive, says there are important differences between easyJet and Ryanair. Whereas Dublin-based Ryanair has flourished during much of its first decade using older second-hand aircraft, easyJet has chosen to use new aircraft, believing in the cost advantages to be gained from lower maintenance needs, the ability to achieve high utilisation levels, quick turnaround times and greater reliability of service.

Ryanair has been ruthless about offering the lowest fares available, and a vital part of its strategy is to fly to secondary airports with much lower charges. It has also been expanding its network to more leisure destinations. By contrast, easyJet uses more main airports that people want to use and that attracts higher-paying business passengers as well as leisure travellers. As a result, easyJet is seeking to add greater depth to the network by using the growing fleet to increase frequencies rather than destinations. Because it started later than Ryanair, easyJet has also been able to avoid using travel agents as a key way of keeping distribution costs low.

Mr O'Leary is just as devoted a believer in the power of the Internet to cut sales and marketing costs, but says that at Ryanair these savings are still feeding through to the bottom line, whereas they have already been booked at easyJet. The Web also gives an 'amazing capacity to fill our aircraft very quickly and we can sell with very little advertising,' says Mr O'Leary, who is planning to add more routes next year to secondary airports, where the costs are low. 'There is a huge floating population in London that just wants to fly somewhere. If you make it very cheap they just go for a weekend anyway,' he says. Publicly he pours scorn on his rivals' strategies, but perhaps even Ryanair would be forced to admire the easyJet low-cost toilet strategy.

Both airlines are adding new Boeings at a rapid pace to meet forecast growth rates. In the easyJet case, they order the aircraft with one toilet removed in order to cram in one more seat. 'There are no free meals or free drinks on board. If people have to pay, they consume less. There is less waste, the cabin crew themselves can do the clean up. We don't have to stock the galleys and clean the aircraft at the airport. And people use the toilets less, so we can take one out.'

Having failed to take on the low-cost airlines at their own game, the established airlines are using their powerful political influence to hobble the new competition. Legislation forcing airlines to pay fixed penalties for delays will be particularly painful to the low-cost operators with little margin to cover fines and high utilisation that gives them less time to make up for delays.

Ryanair is particularly hit by the European Commission's upholding a complaint that they illegally received incentives granted by Belgium's Walloon government to encourage the airline to fly from Charleroi airport. Ryanair may repay €4m of concessions it received in cut-price landing fees and handling charges.

While Ryanair still reels from the Charleroi judgement, two more complaints hit the European Commission's desk, this time about two deals with French regional airports: Strasbourg and Pau. However, Ryanair are starting to win in the courts as well as the air. In May 2007, it won a local court case against Lufthansa over its deal to use Frankfurt-Hahne airport. Ryanair is certainly not scared of fighting fight after fight. It is conducting a long-running war with the Irish regulator over passenger charges at Dublin airport, complaining the charges it imposed meant Ryanair's passengers would end up paying for a new terminal that they did not use. Days later the Irish Consumers' Association came in for an ear-bashing. Mr O'Leary has also targeted BAA, the main UK airport operator, which he said should be broken up; LastMinute.com, the travel website, was accused of 'telling porkies' and he said the UK's environment minister was 'foolish' and 'hasn't a clue what he's talking about'.

Beside the passengers that flood to the airline, Ryanair has some other allies. The Assembly of European Regions has also complained that the European Commission's decision is 'a direct threat to the existence of European airports'. They explain that low-cost airlines have had 'enormous impact' on regional development, particularly tourism and small business. Giving the power back to the flag-carriers in their major airports will further concentrate activities and visitors in a few congested hubs, like Heathrow and Orly. Commenting on the failure of a fellow low-cost airline, a Ryanair spokesman said: 'The fall of Air Littoral is a direct consequence of misguided French government policy, which seeks to promote and protect the high fare airline Air France, while denying ordinary consumers choice, competition and access to low fares.' Wolfgang Kurth, chef executive of Germany's Hapag-Lloyd Express and president of the newly formed European Low Fares Airline Association (ELFAA), states their case. Low-cost airlines have 'enabled large numbers of consumers to travel at a fraction of the cost, allowed previously unprofitable airports to become viable and profitable entities, and also have benefited regional development and the growth of tourism.'

Ryanair has changed the way people fly in Europe. Its low-cost operation has many airlines beaten but the

European Commission is its big enemy now. The airline is currently smarting after the European competition commissioner blocked its €1.48bn bid to take over Aer Lingus, the Irish national carrier, saying it would lead to a monopoly that could lead to higher prices and a declining service. Michael O'Leary vows to appeal and keep on fighting. Is it really Ryanair that is the cause of keeping air fares in some parts of Europe high? Michael O'Leary thinks not. Ryanair maintained its barrage of complaints against governments and regulators, airport authorities and competitors, with a blast against the European Commission. Ryanair alleges hundreds of millions of euros of illegal state aid has subsidised state airlines and that Brussels has failed to act. The low-cost airline said it would sue the Commission for 'its repeated failure to take action on a number of state-aid complaints involving Air France-KLM, Lufthansa, Alitalia and Olympic Airways, which were submitted to the Commission over a year ago'.

Questions

1. What is stimulating the growth of budget airlines and what explains the economics behind Michael O'Leary's claim that Ryanair could soon be flying people around Europe for free?

2. What allows Europe's new budget airlines to keep their costs down and which operator has the advantage?

3. Does the Internet have a distinct role in the budget airlines' operations?

4. How does the European Commission's claim that Charleroi priced their landing fees and handling charges too low for Ryanair square with ELFAA's claim that it is low-cost airlines that have allowed regional airports to thrive profitably? How do you think the regional airports arrived at their fees and charges?

5. What is the likely impact of easyJet's style on pricing when applied to cinemas? Could a similar pricing approach apply in other circumstances when price and demand do not match, such as major sporting events, rock concerts and inner-city parking?

SOURCES: Kevin Done, 'Ryanair reveals expansion plans', *Financial Times* (5 December 2003); Kevin Done, 'Regions braced for Ryanair fallout', *Financial Times* (29 January 2004); Mary Watkins, 'Brussels outlaws Ryanair subsidy', *Financial Times* (3 February 2004); Kevin Done, 'Ryanair faces more complaints on airport subsidies', *Financial Times* (5 February 2004); Joanna Chung, 'EasyJet issues upbeat challenge to Ryanair', *Financial Times* (6 February 2004); Toby Shelley, 'Ryanair threatens to sue EU over subsidies', *Financial Times* (10 July 2007); Kevin Done, 'Aer Lingus renews attack on Ryanair as profits fall', *Financial Times* (31 August 2007); www.easyjet.com; www.ryanair.com. By pricing a car on www.easycar.com you will get a table that clearly shows how the hire charges adjust with supply and demand.

Video Case Electrolux

Hans Straberg
CEO & President

AB Electrolux is a world leader in the intensely competitive cleaning and kitchen appliances market for consumers and professional users. Its product range includes refrigerators, dishwashers, washing machines, vacuum cleaners and cookers. The company is a global market leader in many of the individual product categories in which it competes, with annual sales of €11.1 billion in 2007, making it narrowly second to American Maytag in the world.

The company is proud of its focus on innovative designs (see its website (www.electrolux.com) based on extensive consumer knowledge using the slogan 'Thinking for You'. Besides Electrolux, the company has AEG-Electrolux, Zanussi, Eureka and Frigidaire brands with which to cover its professional and consumer markets.

After viewing the video, you may address the following questions:

1. The kitchen appliance market in the developed world is saturated with everyone already having a kitchen full of appliances. How can Electrolux squeeze more revenue out of such a mature market?
2. How does Electrolux make 'Thinking of you' more than just a 'slogan' and how does it use the strapline in its marketing communications to guide the company's operations both internally and in the market place?
3. How might Electrolux develop an integrated marketing communications programme to promote its global brands across numerous nationalities and market segments across the world?

Promise, large promise, is the soul of an advertisement.

DR JOHNSON (WRITER AND LEXICOGRAPHER)

Promotion

PART SIX

IN PART SIX OF *PRINCIPLES OF MARKETING* we cover the third element of the marketing mix – promotion. We show how organisations communicate with their various target markets.

Companies must do more than just create customer value. They must also use promotion to clearly and persuasively communicate that value. Promotion is not a single tool but rather a mix of several tools. There is no one best communication tool or approach to use. Ideally, under the concept of *integrated marketing communications*, the company will carefully coordinate these promotion elements to deliver a clear, consistent and compelling message about the organisation and its products or services.

Chapter 15 introduces you to the various promotion mix tools. Here, we'll examine the rapidly changing communications environment and the need for integrated marketing communications. We then discuss the steps in developing marketing communications and the promotion budgeting process.

Chapter 16 addresses two mass-communication tools – advertising and public relations efforts. These are mainly indirect, non-personal forms of communications. We see how they can be used to communicate customer value and to achieve different types of response from consumers.

Chapter 17 examines the role of personal selling and sales promotions in creating and communicating customer value. Personal selling consists of interpersonal communications with customers and prospects to make sales and maintain customer relationships. Sales promotion consists of short-term incentives to encourage customer purchasing, reseller support and sales force efforts. While mass advertising and public relations are useful for building brand awareness and influencing consumer attitudes and preferences towards a brand, personal selling and sales promotions are aimed at building sales.

Chapter 18 addresses the role of direct marketing tools for communicating and building one-to-one relationships with target customers. Non-personal, direct marketing tools such as telephone, television, mail, catalogues, computers and new digital media have become important vehicles for communicating messages as well as interacting and doing business with customers. We will explore in greater depth how online marketing, the fastest growing form of direct marketing, and new digital technologies, are used to create customer value in the electronic marketplace.

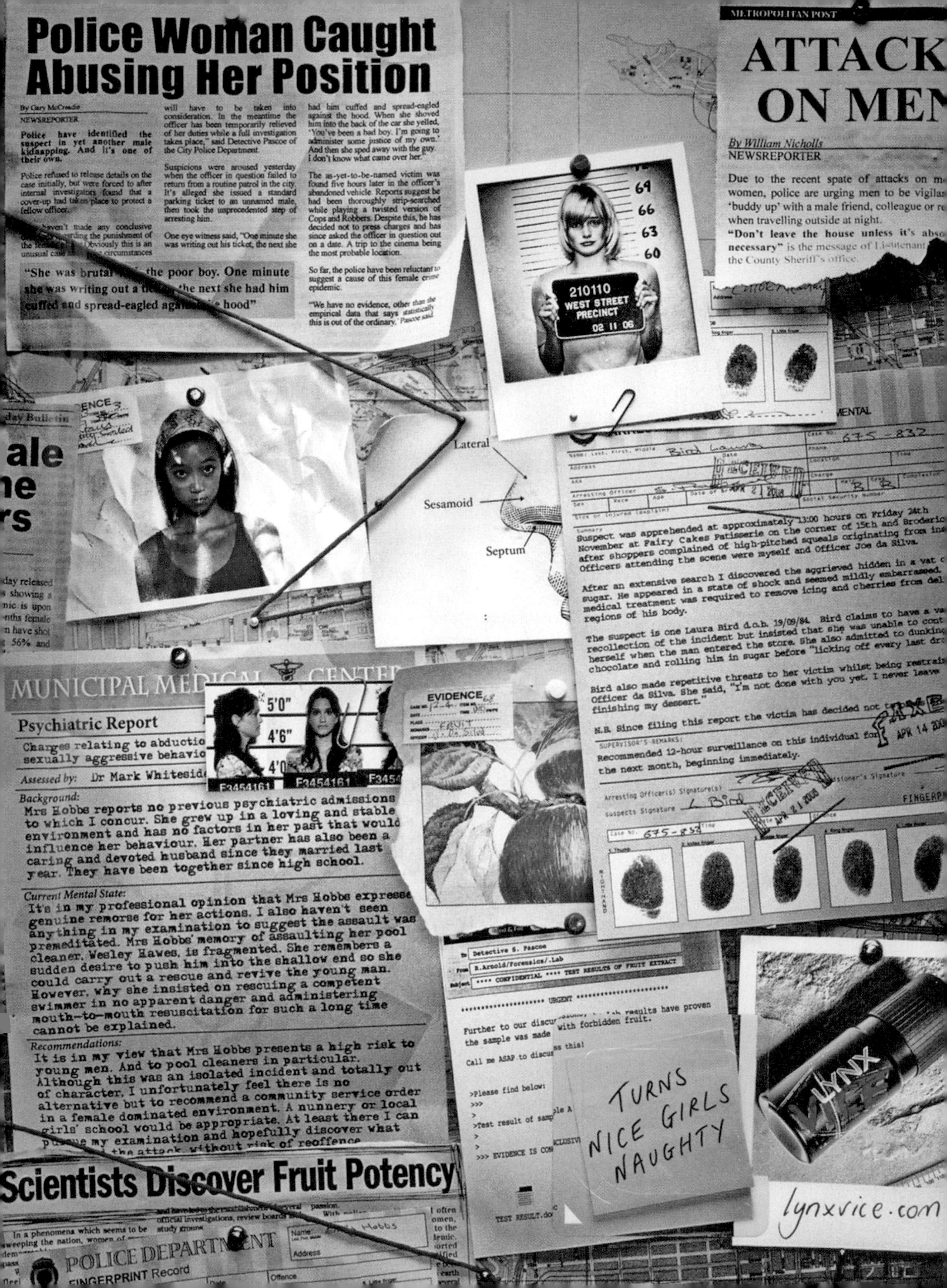

Police Woman Caught Abusing Her Position

By Gary McCreadie
NEWSREPORTER

Police have identified the suspect in yet another male kidnapping. And it's one of their own.

Police refused to release details on the case initially, but were forced to after internal investigators found that a cover-up had taken place to protect a fellow officer.

[text obscured] haven't made any conclusive [text] regarding the punishment of the female [text] Obviously this is an unusual case [text] circumstances

"She was brutal [text] the poor boy. One minute she was writing out a ticket the next she had him cuffed and spread-eagled against the hood"

will have to be taken into consideration. In the meantime the officer has been temporarily relieved of her duties while a full investigation takes place," said Detective Pascoe of the City Police Department.

Suspicions were aroused yesterday when the officer in question failed to return from a routine patrol in the city. It's alleged she issued a standard parking ticket to an unnamed male, then took the unprecedented step of arresting him.

One eye witness said, "One minute she was writing out his ticket, the next she was writing out his ticket, the next she

had him cuffed and spread-eagled against the hood. When she shoved him into the back of the car she yelled, 'You've been a bad boy. I'm going to administer some justice of my own.' And then she sped away with the guy. I don't know what came over her.

The as-yet-to-be-named victim was found five hours later in the officer's abandoned vehicle. Reports suggest he had been thoroughly strip-searched while playing a twisted version of Cops and Robbers. Despite this, he has decided not to press charges and has since asked the officer in question out on a date. A trip to the cinema being the most probable location.

So far, the police have been reluctant to suggest a cause of this female crime epidemic.

"We have no evidence, other than the empirical data that says statistically this is out of the ordinary," Pascoe said.

METROPOLITAN POST

ATTACK ON MEN

By William Nicholls
NEWSREPORTER

Due to the recent spate of attacks on m[en] women, police are urging men to be vigilant 'buddy up' with a male friend, colleague or re[lative] when travelling outside at night.

"Don't leave the house unless it's abso[lutely] necessary" is the message of Lieutenant [text] the County Sheriff's office.

210110
WEST STREET PRECINCT
02 11 06

...day Bulletin

ale he rs

[text] released [text] showing a [text]ic is upon [text]nths female [text] have shot [text] 56% and

Lateral

Sesamoid

Septum

MUNICIPAL MEDICAL CENTER

Psychiatric Report

Charges relating to abduction [and] sexually aggressive behaviour

Assessed by: Dr Mark Whiteside

Background:
Mrs Hobbs reports no previous psychiatric admissions to which I concur. She grew up in a loving and stable environment and has no factors in her past that would influence her behaviour. Her partner has also been a caring and devoted husband since they married last year. They have been together since high school.

Current Mental State:
It's in my professional opinion that Mrs Hobbs expresse[s] genuine remorse for her actions. I also haven't seen anything in my examination to suggest the assault was premeditated. Mrs Hobbs' memory of assaulting her pool cleaner, Wesley Hawes, is fragmented. She remembers a sudden desire to push him into the shallow end so she could carry out a rescue and revive the young man. However, why she insisted on rescuing a competent swimmer in no apparent danger and administering mouth-to-mouth resuscitation for such a long time cannot be explained.

Recommendations:
It is in my view that Mrs Hobbs presents a high risk to young men. And to pool cleaners in particular. Although this was an isolated incident and totally out of character. I unfortunately feel there is no alternative but to recommend a community service order in a female dominated environment. A nunnery or local girls' school would be appropriate. At least there I can [pur]sue my examination and hopefully discover what [caused] the attack without risk of reoffence

EVIDENCE 68

Name: Last, First, Middle Bird Laura
Case No. 675 - 832

RECEIVED APR 21 2008

Summary
Suspect was apprehended at approximately 13:00 hours on Friday 24th November at Fairy Cakes Patisserie on the corner of 15th and Broderick after shoppers complained of high-pitched squeals originating from ins[ide] the store. Officers attending the scene were myself and Officer Joe da Silva.

After an extensive search I discovered the aggrieved hidden in a vat o[f] sugar. He appeared in a state of shock and seemed mildly embarrassed. medical treatment was required to remove icing and cherries from del[icate] regions of his body.

The suspect is one Laura Bird d.o.b. 19/09/84. Bird claims to have a va[gue] recollection of the incident but insisted that she was unable to cont[rol] herself when the man entered the store. She also admitted to dunking chocolate and rolling him in sugar before "licking off every last dr[op]"

Bird also made repetitive threats to her victim whilst being restrain[ed by] Officer da Silva. She said, "I'm not done with you yet. I never leav[e] finishing my dessert."

N.B. Since filing this report the victim has decided not t[o] FAXED APR 14 200[8]

SUPERVISOR'S REMARKS:
Recommended 12-hour surveillance on this individual for the next month, beginning immediately.

Arresting Officer(s) Signature(s)
Suspects Signature L Bird
RECEIVED APR 21 2008

Case No. 675 - 83[2]

To: Detective S. Pascoe
From: R.Arnold/Forensics/.Lab
Subject: **** CONFIDENTIAL **** TEST RESULTS OF FRUIT EXTRACT

****************** URGENT ******************

Further to our discu[ssion] with forbidden fruit. the sample was made [text]

Call me ASAP to discu[ss] this!

>Please find below:
>>>
> >Test result of samp[le] A
>
> >>> EVIDENCE IS CO[N]CLUSIV[E]

TURNS NICE GIRLS NAUGHTY

LYNX

Scientists Discover Fruit Potency

In a phenomena which seems to be sweeping the nation, women of [text]

lynxvice.com

> Beat your gong and sell your candies.

CHINESE PROVERB

Communicating customer value: integrated marketing communications strategy

Mini Contents List

◀ SOURCE: The Advertising Archives.

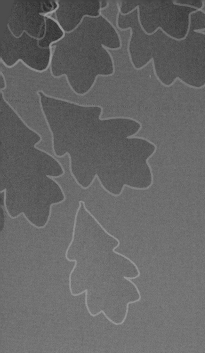

Previewing the concepts

In early chapters we have examined the environment in which marketing operates, marketing strategy and how we develop and price products. We also examined customer behaviour. Now it is time to look at how we get our message across to the customer. In this chapter we look at the totality of integrated marketing communication.

Building good customer relationships calls for more than just developing a good product, pricing it attractively and making it available to target customers. Companies must also *communicate* their value propositions to customers, and what they communicate should not be left to chance. Just as good communication is important in building and maintaining any kind of relationship, it is a critical element in a company's efforts to build profitable customer relationships.

To communicate well, companies often employ advertising agencies to develop the ads, sales promotion specialists to design sales-incentive programmes, direct-marketing specialists to develop databases and interact with customers and prospects, and public relations firms to develop corporate images. They train their salespeople to be friendly, helpful and persuasive. For most companies, the question is not *whether* to communicate, but *how much to spend* and *in what ways*. All of their communications efforts must be blended into a consistent and coordinated communications programme.

After reading this chapter, you should be able to:

1. Define the major promotion tools and discuss the factors that must be considered in shaping the overall promotion mix.
2. Discuss the process and advantages of integrated marketing communications in communicating customer value.
3. Outline the steps in developing effective marketing communications.
4. Explain the methods for setting the promotion budget and factors that affect the design of the promotion mix.

We are all familiar with hard sell, a sales encounter when the potential customer is put under a lot of pressure to buy.[1] It is a stereotypical view of selling where a salesperson aims to achieve a victory over a potential customer. It sometimes works, sometimes does not and is often associated with questionable marketing tactics. We start by looking at how BMW's super-luxury car subsidiary, Rolls-Royce Motors, uses a completely different way of relating to their customers.

Prelude case Rolls-Royce

Premium car companies often like to talk about making every customer count. When Rolls-Royce Motors does so, it is difficult to doubt its sincerity. The British super-luxury marque, owned by Germany's BMW, sells barely 800 cars a year. Retail prices for the company's Phantom cars start at £203,500 (€300,000) and models with many customised features can cost millions, making every sale made or forgone an event for the carmaker.

But Rolls-Royce's rarefied prices pose special marketing challenges. The company's target customers are people with liquid assets of at least $30m (€22m), a group Capgemini estimates numbers about 85,000 worldwide. 'Conventional car companies tend to push cars down a pipeline and expect people to buy them,' says Ian Robertson, Rolls-Royce's chairman and chief executive. 'We are dealing in a very small niche right at the pinnacle.'

Rolls-Royce, which does not report financial results independently of its German parent group, also does not disclose the size of its marketing budget, which Mr Robertson describes as 'very small'. However, the company recently spoke to the *Financial Times* about some of its techniques for marketing to the super-rich.

If conventional marketing could be compared with a shotgun approach, one company official says, Rolls-Royce's was more like a sniper rifle. 'It's really about being intelligent about how we network,' he says. While the brand does a limited amount of print advertising, people with enough money to buy a Rolls are difficult to address, Mr Robertson says, and do not respond to conventional advertisements. They also tend to have lots of people around to protect them from unwanted sales pitches, among other things. 'For these people, drinks of vintage champagne are nothing special,' he says. 'You have to capture their imagination by offering them something they can't otherwise get.'

The marque's main point of contact with existing and potential customers is through its 79 independently owned dealerships worldwide. It chooses dealers who 'live in the same world, drive the same cars, have the same yachts and aircraft' as its customers, Mr Robertson says. Its London dealership in Berkeley Square in Mayfair, owned by luxury chain H. R. Owen, organises 'wonderful lunches' and dinners for 'like-minded people' at hotels such as the Lanesborough or the Dorchester, says Rodney Turner, director of Rolls-Royce Motor Cars London. 'We're dealing with the children of parents who have had a link with our business for years,' Mr Turner says. 'We like to make them feel very special.'

People who attend Rolls-Royce's meals, he says, often transact millions of pounds' worth of business that has nothing to do with cars, but which gives the events added cachet. The dealership holds about four such events a year. 'We don't over-egg the pudding,' he says. 'If you did too many, people wouldn't want to come.'

Europe's other small top-end brands face similar challenges of making every marketing euro count. Lamborghini, owned by Volkswagen's Audi premium car group, last year sold a record 2,087 cars, which retail in the €150,000–€350,000 range. 'We have one foot in the car business and one foot in the luxury business,' says Stephan Winkelmann, the brand's president and chief executive. Lamborghini teams up with strategic partners such as the Versace fashion house, which designed the interiors of its special edition Murcielago roadster. The company also does a bit of non-paid product placement by offering its cars for films (*Mission: Impossible III*, *Batman Begins*), and splashes its brand on retail items from keyholders to baseball caps and ties.

At the recent North American International Auto Show in Detroit, Lamborghini's exhibit attracted close attention from photographers, partly thanks to two young hostesses posed next to its cars – a politically incorrect but effective practice most other carmakers these days eschew.

Rolls-Royce opts for a distinctly less flashy approach, shunning co-branding in favour of word of mouth. In New York, the brand recently hosted a dinner party at a Fifth Avenue property normally closed to the public (and which Mr Robertson declines to identify). Last year it flew in the designer of the Phantom to discuss his work over dinner at a Miami restaurant. 'Our customers like a degree of kudos. They can tell friends they had dinner with Rolls-Royce, or they met the designer of the Phantom,' says Graeme Grieve, Rolls-Royce's sales and marketing director.

Because of the carmaker's small customer base, it can also afford to stay in personal contact with its buyers. Loyalty is high among customers, especially in the US, where about 30 per cent of business comes from repeat purchasers. Last year, Mr Robertson personally signed letters to all of its 2,700 customers of the past three years, and sent out a coffee-table album to previous buyers. The book features individual testimonials from buyers such as Japanese fashion designer Nigo, now on his third Phantom. 'Before the new Phantom was launched, Rolls-Royce had the image of a car for middle-aged men,' the book quotes him saying. 'But the Phantom is unique: it has both faces – old and young.' Sheikh Jaber Al-Abdullah Al-Jaber Al-Sabah, a member of Kuwait's ruling family, extols the virtues of his extended-wheelbase Phantom. 'We had it personalised by including a number of additional bespoke details,' he says.

'I think owning a car such as the Phantom is tantamount to possessing a rare art masterpiece; it is something that will remain distinguished and valuable for all time.' The raves from figures such as Nigo may be calculated to help freshen Rolls-Royce's image as a producer of top-quality but old-fashioned cars. The company recently launched its Phantom Drophead Coupé, the first convertible since the Phantom was relaunched under BMW's ownership. Rolls-Royce says the Drophead is aimed at leading the brand 'in a more informal direction' and 'attracting new buyers to the marque'.

The focus on individual 'bespoke' features may also serve Rolls-Royce's interests, as the company earns a significant portion of its undisclosed profit from them. While Rolls-Royce's unit sales last year were essentially flat – 802, up from 796 – its revenues rose by 10 per cent, indicating the company is earning more per vehicle than previously. The brand recently sold a full-stretch Phantom to a customer in China – one of the fastest-growing markets for luxury cars – for $2.2m. Another cigar-smoking customer who did not like the standard Phantom's furnishings ordered a crystal ashtray, a refrigerator for champagne and space for two glass flutes at the door base.

In its Beverly Hills dealership, the brand sometimes caters to impulse buyers, who have been known to charge their cars on a credit card. Many Asian customers, by contrast, like to spend time thinking about what they want, ordering special features, and waiting for delivery. Like many other car companies, Rolls-Royce invites customers buying a car, or contemplating a purchase, to its plant at Goodwood in Sussex.

Unlike other car factories, the £65m, four-year-old facility is quiet, as many components are made and assembled by hand – a key selling point. Customers can watch woodworking, stitching and final assembly from an observation platform. The gestation period for a final sale can then be anywhere from two hours to years. 'In some cases, customers came to the site, disappeared for two years, and then we got a phone call,' says Mr Grieve.

Questions

1. Car companies typically use print, TV, online and other advertising as well as offering buyers rebates, discounts and other incentives to get a sale. Often, they resort to hard sell. Why does Rolls-Royce use a 'soft sell' approach to reaching target customers?
2. To what extent do you agree with the communications strategy used by the luxury car company?
3. What are the factors that must be considered when designing the firm's communications strategy? What role does the communications mix play in building and maintaining customer value?

SOURCE: Adapted from John Reed, 'Rolls works hard on its soft sell', *Financial Times* (6 February 2007), p. 10.[2]

Introduction

Building good customer relationships calls for more than just developing a good product, pricing it attractively and making it available to target customers. Companies must also *communicate* their value propositions to customers, and what they communicate should not be left to chance. Just as good communication is important in building and maintaining any kind of relationship, it is a critical element in a company's efforts to build profitable customer relationships.

To communicate well, companies often employ advertising agencies to develop the ads, sales promotion specialists to design sales-incentive programmes, direct-marketing specialists to develop databases and interact with customers and prospects, and public relations firms to develop corporate images. They train their salespeople to be friendly, helpful and persuasive. For most companies, the question is not *whether* to communicate, but *how much to spend* and *in what ways*. All of their communications efforts must be blended into a consistent and coordinated communications programme.

A company has to communicate with not only consumers, but also its intermediaries and various publics. Its intermediaries communicate with their consumers and publics. Consumers have word-of-mouth communication with each other and with other publics. Meanwhile, each group provides feedback to every other group. The company therefore has to manage a complex marketing communications system (see Figure 15.1).

In this chapter, we begin by defining the major promotion tools. Next, we explore the rapidly changing communications environment and the need for integrated marketing communications. We then discuss the factors that must be considered in shaping the overall communications mix and the steps in developing marketing communications. Finally, we explain the approaches for setting the promotion budget.

In Chapter 16, we'll look at two *mass-communication tools* – advertising and public relations. Chapter 17 examines the *sales force* and *sales promotion* as communication and promotion tools. Direct and online marketing will be explored in greater depth in Chapter 18.

The promotion mix

A company's total **promotion mix** – also called its **marketing communications mix** – consists of the specific blend of advertising, sales promotion, public relations, personal selling and direct marketing tools that the company uses to persuasively communicate customer value and build customer relationships. Let us define the five major promotion tools:[3]

> **Promotion mix (or marketing communications mix)**—The specific mix of advertising, sales promotion, public relations, personal selling and direct marketing tools that the company uses to persuasively communicate customer value and build customer relationships.

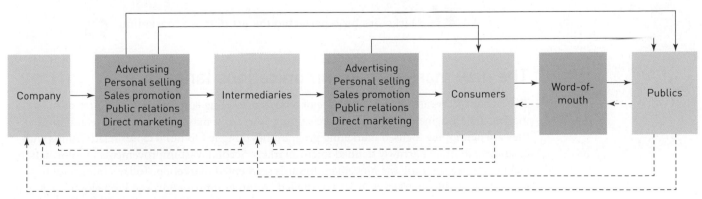

Figure 15.1 The marketing communications system

Advertising—Any paid form of non-personal presentation and promotion of ideas, goods or services by an identified sponsor.

Sales promotion—Short-term incentives to encourage purchase or sale of a product or service.

Public relations—Building good relations with the company's various publics by obtaining favourable publicity, building up a good 'corporate image', and handling or heading off unfavourable rumours, stories and events.

Personal selling—Personal presentation by the firm's sales force for the purpose of making sales and building customer relationships.

Direct marketing—Direct connections with carefully targeted individual consumers both to obtain an immediate response and to cultivate lasting customers.

- **Advertising.** Any paid form of non-personal presentation and promotion of ideas, goods or services by an identified sponsor.
- **Sales promotion.** Short-term incentives to encourage the purchase or sale of a product or service.
- **Public relations.** Building good relations with the company's various publics by obtaining favourable publicity, building up a good 'corporate image', and handling or heading off unfavourable rumours, stories and events.
- **Personal selling.** Personal presentation by the firm's sales force for the purpose of making sales and building customer relationships.
- **Direct marketing.** Direct connections with carefully targeted individual consumers both to obtain an immediate response and to cultivate lasting customers.

Each category involves specific promotional tools used to communicate with consumers. For example, advertising includes broadcast, radio, print, Internet, outdoor and other forms. Sales promotion includes discounts, coupons, point-of-purchase displays and demonstrations. Personal selling includes sales presentations, trade shows and incentive programmes. Public relations includes press releases, sponsorships, special events and Web pages. Direct marketing includes catalogues, telephone marketing, kiosks, the Internet and more.

Thanks to technological breakthroughs, people can now communicate through traditional media (newspapers, radio, telephone, television) as well as through newer types of media (mobile phones, computers). The new technologies have encouraged more companies to move from mass communication to more targeted communication and one-to-one dialogue.

At the same time, communication goes beyond these specific promotion tools. The product's design, its price, the shape and colour of its package, and the stores that sell it – *all* communicate something to buyers. Thus, although the promotion mix is the company's primary communication activity, the entire marketing mix – promotion *and* product, price and place – must be coordinated for greatest communication impact.

Integrated marketing communications

In past decades, marketers have perfected the art of mass marketing – selling highly standardised products to masses of customers. In the process, they have developed effective mass-media communications techniques to support their mass-marketing strategies. In particular, large companies routinely invest huge sums of money in TV, magazine or other mass media advertising, reaching tens of millions of customers with a single ad. Today, however, marketing managers face some new marketing communications realities.

 Marketers have perfected the art of mass marketing.

The new marketing communications landscape

Two major factors are changing the face of today's marketing communications. First, as mass markets have fragmented, marketers are shifting away from mass marketing. More and more, they are developing focused marketing programmes designed to build closer relationships with customers in more narrowly defined micro-markets. Second, vast improvements in information technology are speeding the movement towards segmented marketing. Today's information technology enables marketers to amass detailed customer information and keep closer track of customer needs.

Improved information technology has also caused striking changes in the ways in which companies and customers communicate with each other. The digital age has spawned a host of new information and communication tools – from mobile phones, iPods and the Internet to satellite and cable television systems, and personal video recorders (PVR). The new technologies give companies exciting new media tools for interacting with targeted consumers and to reach smaller customer segments with more tailored messages. They also give consumers more control over the nature and timing of messages they choose to send and receive.

The shifting marketing communications model

The shift towards segmented marketing and the explosive developments in information and communications technology have had a dramatic impact on marketing communications. Just as mass marketing once gave rise to a new generation of mass-media communications, the shift towards targeted marketing and the changing communications environment are giving birth to a new marketing communications model. Although television, magazines and other mass media remain very important, their dominance is now declining. Advertisers are now adding a broad selection of more specialised and highly targeted media to reach smaller customer segments with more personalised messages. The new media range from speciality magazines, satellite and cable television channels and video on demand (VOD) to product placements in television programmes and video games, Internet catalogues, e-mail and online audio sites such as podcasts. In all, companies are doing less *broadcasting* and more *narrowcasting*.

Given the changing communications environment, marketers must rethink the roles of various media and promotion tools in communicating customer value and building lasting customer relationships.

Consumers are also changing in the way they consume media, providing companies with greater opportunity to develop interactive consumer-generated communications (see Real Marketing 15.1). Consumers, especially younger ones, appear to be turning away from the major television networks in favour of cable or satellite TV or altogether different media. Many young people already spend more time online than they do watching TV. In some countries, major TV broadcasters already stream their channels online in an attempt to ensure they do not lose a generation of young viewers who are more accustomed to YouTube than the traditional TV. For example, in the UK, the BBC and ITV are building audiences online through their iPlayer and ITV.com services respectively.[4]

As mass media costs rise, audiences shrink, ad clutter increases and more and more viewers use video on demand and personal video recording systems to skip past disruptive television commercials, many sceptics even predict the demise of the old mass-media mainstay – the 30-second television commercial. Thus, many large advertisers are shifting their advertising budgets away from network television in favour of more targeted, cost-effective, interactive and engaging media.

Some industry insiders, however, see a more gradual shift to the new marketing communications model. They note that broadcast television and other mass media such as radio and newsprint still capture a lion's share of the promotion budgets of most major marketing firms, a fact that isn't likely to change quickly. In countries such as France, the UK and Sweden, TV advertising makes up about 31, 30 and 22 per cent respectively of total advertising spend. By contrast, the share of spending on Internet advertising in these countries is respectively 3.7, 9.8 and 8.5 per cent.[5] In the view of Yahoo!'s boss, Terry Semel, many big corporations still allocate only 2–4 per cent of their marketing budgets to the Internet, although the medium represents about 15 per cent of consumers' media consumption – and is growing.[6]

Although some may question the future of the 30-second spot, it's still very much in use today. Moreover, television offers many promotional opportunities beyond the 30-second commercial. One advertising expert advises: 'Because TV is at the forefront of many technological advances [such as PVRs and video on demand], its audience will continue to increase. So if

15.1 real marketing

For fun, fame and fortune, try do-it-yourself (DIY) advertising

In order to reach out to fashion-conscious young consumers, retailer Wal-Mart introduced an online project called 'School my way' which encouraged youths to check out the styles on the website and to express their own style. Jointly sponsored by Sony, the project aimed to trigger interactive consumer-generated advertising, using an online competition inviting school students to create their own Web pages and videos. Winners' videos would be used in TV and cinema commercials.

The rapid spread of high-speed Internet connections, together with the greater ease with which people can put their own text, audio and video content on the Web and edit it, have changed media consumption from a passive experience to an interactive one. The same factors are also contributing to increased viewing of video on the Web, including video advertising, previously available mainly on television.

'This is the most creative generation that ever lived,' according to Aaron Cohen, chief executive of Bolt.com, a user-generated content site. One of the campaigns the company has run is a competition to create a cyberspace 'virtual band', sponsored by the Wendy's hamburger chain. 'For these consumers, everything is recorded on their phones or on digital cameras. Just as watching television is entertaining for many older people, for them, putting up music and videos and being part of a group talking about this is entertaining.'

MySpace.com, the world's biggest social networking site, owned by Rupert Murdoch's News Corporation, allows registered users to create personal profiles and put up blogs, video and songs, link to other users and communicate with them. Many prominent advertisers such as Toyota and Wendy's fast-food restaurant are using the site. Hollywood is using it to create buzz about films. Many more are testing its use for creating profiles based around made-up characters promoting a product.

Reggie Bradford, chief executive of ViTrue, a company that provides marketers with the technology to create interactive advertising, predicts that interactive advertising will become increasingly popular. 'We are just scratching the surface. Instead of a small number of ad agency executives creating the best ads, millions of people will be contributing to creating the best ads. This is a huge change that will really enhance brand advertising.'

However, many advertisers remain cautious about the use of certain new media. Spending on Internet video commercials is small compared to overall spend in the rapidly growing Internet advertising sector. YouTube, the fast-growing video-watching site, which boasts over 100 million video downloads a day, does not carry much advertising, in spite of its reach. The risks of being associated with inappropriate or illegally reproduced content might damage a brand's reputation.

Indeed, companies must balance the opportunities to harness consumers' creativity with the perils of handing over control to the Internet. For example, when GM launched its new Tahoe 2007 SUV model in early 2006, the brand's new advertising-building website allowed viewers to add their own text to a selection of clips and music. This generated more than 3,000 responses attacking the company over fuel economy, global warming and its safety record. Hardly the kind of results GM was hoping to obtain from its effort to create an online community aimed at reinforcing customer loyalty and providing valuable marketing feedback.

By contrast, the online retailer Amazon.com has developed its online reviews to create user profile pages that can include photographs, e-mail addresses and lists of recommendations. These can then be linked to other selected 'Amazon friends'. It is also continuing to test 'tagging', which allows a user to create a personal set of links connecting a variety of recommended product pages under topics such as 'money' or 'amazing story'.

Tim Stock, president of scenarioDNA, a brand consultancy, argues that the Amazon site reflects a more appropriate understanding of the role that social networking can play. 'A lot of companies are still misunderstanding what social networks are,' he says. 'They're not websites . . . they're people who use the technology to connect. So you have to do something that is authentic, and offer something to make them want to use it. You are tapping in to what people do naturally.'

New Web tools and cheap technology make it easy for people to create their own material for advertising. Online blogs, pictures, videos and music can be home-made or edited versions of existing content. But they require people to do some work rather than just sit back and watch something. Why should anyone take the time and trouble to make advertisements for a company that is not their client or employer? According to one source, the reasons are:

- *'It's fun.* Contributors enjoy the creative aspects and entertainment of making their own videos or music.

- *Fifteen minutes of fame.* Many websites offer the chance to get your art, video or music shown to the world, either online or on television or even in film advertising. You no longer need to have good contacts or luck to get one of a handful of jobs at advertising agencies.

- *Prizes.* Probably the most traditional of incentives, prizes are already used in many marketing campaigns. The chance to win fashionable clothes, electronic goods or tickets to concerts or film screenings, often with exclusive access to stars, remains a popular way for companies to try to encourage participation.

...15.1

- *Money.* Advertising agencies are starting to experiment with paying people to reflect the popularity of their advertisements, using the pay-per-click model commonly used in the online advertising world. As well as giving amateurs an incentive to try to make great advertisements, this model might also encourage agency employees to do their most creative work incognito, unhampered by the need for client approval.'

SOURCE: Adapted from Aline van Duyn and Jonathan Birchall, 'Wal-Mart's amateur advertisers', *Financial Times* (21 July 2006), p. 8; 'Murdoch's space', *The Economist* (1 April 2006), p. 67. Copyright © The Economist Newspaper Limited, London (1 April 2006).

you think that TV is an ageing dinosaur, or you're a national advertiser who is thinking of moving ad spend away from TV, maybe you should think again.'[7]

    ❝ We need to reinvent the way we market to consumers. **❞**

Thus, it seems likely that the new marketing communications model will consist of a gradually shifting mix of both traditional mass media and a wide array of exciting new, more targeted, more personalised media. 'We need to reinvent the way we market to consumers,' says A.G. Lafley, chief executive of Procter & Gamble, one of Europe's leading advertisers,[8] in terms of spend. 'Mass marketing still has an important role, [but] we need new models to initially coexist with mass marketing, and eventually to succeed it.'[9]

The need for integrated marketing communications

The shift from mass marketing to targeted marketing, and the use of a richer mix of media and communication approaches, pose a problem for marketers. Customers are bombarded by commercial messages from a broad range of sources. But consumers do not distinguish between message sources the way marketers do. In the consumer's mind, messages from different media and promotional approaches blur into one – they all become part of a single message about the company. Conflicting messages from these different sources can result in confused company images, brand positions and customer relationships.

All too often, companies fail to integrate their various communications channels. The result is a hodgepodge of communications to consumers. Mass media advertisements say one thing, while a price promotion sends a different signal and a product label creates still another message. Company sales literature says something altogether different and the company's website seems out of sync with everything else.

The problem arises because these communications often come from different company sources. Advertising messages are planned and implemented by the advertising department or advertising agency. Personal selling communications are developed by sales management. Other functional specialists are responsible for public relations, sales promotion events, Internet marketing and other forms of marketing communication.

However, although these companies have separated their communications tools, customers won't. Customers may do a bit of Web-surfing to find out about companies' products or services, but this does not mean that they no longer pay attention to TV or magazine ads or take any notice of firms' sales promotion campaigns.[10]

Carefully blended mix of promotion tools

Figure 15.2 Integrated marketing communications

Today, more companies are adopting the concept of **integrated marketing communications (IMC)**. Under this concept, as illustrated in Figure 15.2, the company carefully integrates its many communications channels to deliver a clear, consistent, and compelling message about the organisation and its brands.[11]

IMC calls for recognising all contact points where the customer may encounter the company and its brands. Each *brand contact* will deliver a message, whether good, bad or indifferent. The company wants to deliver a consistent and positive message with each contact. IMC leads to a total marketing communication strategy aimed at building strong customer relationships by showing how the company and its products can help customers solve their problems.

IMC ties together all of the company's messages and images. The company's television and print advertisements have the same message, look and feel as its e-mail, online and personal selling communications. And its public relations materials project the same image as its website. Creative approaches to integrating marketing communications can make a significant impact on brand growth.

Integrated marketing communications (IMC)— The concept under which a company carefully integrates and coordinates its many communications channels to deliver a clear, consistent and compelling message about the organisation and its products.

For example, in a recent campaign to revitalise its market share, Daz (one of several laundry brands owned by P&G) harnessed the power of entertainment in an attempt to reconnect with its target audience – family households that do a lot of washing, but with a limited budget. Daz's research showed that TV drama programmes epitomised by soap operas have a strong influence on Daz buyers. In 2003, Daz launched the 'Cleaner Close' campaign, in the form of a spoof soap opera, set in a small, urban community. The campaign line was: 'Daz. The soap you can believe in.' The TV campaign was then extended to other media:

- *Print.* Print adverts and advertorials in selected magazines to create further intrigue around the storylines developed on TV.

- *Online.* A brand new Daz website (www.dazwhite.co.uk) was launched to enable consumers to interact more with the 'Cleaner Close' characters and to see episodes they had missed or to view episodes again.

- *Packages.* The reverse side of the Daz packaging featured a potted storyline of 'Cleaner Close', engaging consumers in 'laundry mode'.

- *Experiential.* A roadshow was launched to engage consumers even more – thousands of consumers across the UK were auditioned to star in an episode of 'Cleaner Close'.

- *News.* The advertiser incorporated news into the 'Cleaner Close' campaign.

The campaign was further supported by magazines, radio, outdoor and PR. Throughout the duration of the campaign, Daz relied on TV to build awareness and affinity for the stories and characters. Initial interests were further exploited by extending the campaign to other media which sustained consumer engagement. The integrated communications strategy paid off with brand share for Daz rising from 7.5 per cent before the launch of the campaign in 2002 to 9.7 per cent by June 2006.[12]

In the past, no one person was responsible for thinking through the communication roles of the various promotion tools and coordinating the promotion mix. Members in different departments often disagreed on how to split the promotion budget. The sales manager would rather hire a few more salespeople than spend a few hundred thousand euros more on a single television commercial. The public relations manager felt that he or she could do wonders with some money shifted from advertising to public relations.

IMC calls for recognising all contact points where the customer may encounter the company, its products and its brands. To help implement integrated marketing communications, some companies appoint a marketing communications director who has overall responsibility for the company's communications efforts. This helps to produce better communications consistency and greater sales impact. It places the responsibility in someone's hands – where none existed before – to unify the company's image as it is shaped by thousands of company activities.

A view of the communication process

Integrated marketing communications involves identifying the target audience and shaping a well-coordinated promotional programme to achieve the desired audience response. Too often, marketing communications focus on overcoming immediate awareness, image or preference problems in the target market. But this approach to communication is too short-sighted. Today, marketers are moving towards viewing communications as *managing the customer relationship over time*, that is, from the pre-selling and selling, to purchase and post-purchase stages.

Because customers differ, communications programmes need to be developed for specific segments, niches and even individuals. Importantly, given the new interactive communications technologies, companies must ask not only 'How can we reach our customers?' but also 'How can we find ways to let our customers reach us?'

Thus, the communication process should start with an audit of all the potential contacts target customers may have with the company and its brands. For example, someone buying a new personal video recorder may talk to others, see television commercials, read articles and advertisements in newspapers and magazines, visit various websites and try out appliances in one or more stores. The marketer needs to assess the influence that each of these communications experiences will have at different stages of the buying process. This understanding helps marketers to allocate their communication budget more effectively and efficiently.

To communicate effectively, marketers need to understand how communication works. Communication involves the nine elements shown in Figure 15.3. Two of these elements are the major parties in a communication – the *sender* and the *receiver*. Another two are the major

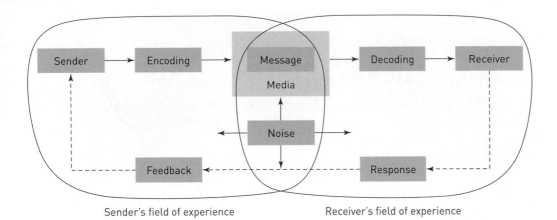

Figure 15.3 Elements in the communication process

Sender's field of experience

Receiver's field of experience

communication tools – the *message* and the *media*. Four more are primary communication functions – *encoding, decoding, response* and *feedback*. The last element is *noise* in the system. We will explain each of these elements using an ad for Ericsson mobile phones.

- *Sender.* The *party sending the message* to another party – in this case, Ericsson.
- *Encoding.* The process of *putting the intended message or thought into symbolic form* – Ericsson's advertising agency assembles words and illustrations into an advertisement that will convey the intended message.
- *Message.* The *set of words, pictures or symbols* that the sender transmits – the actual Ericsson mobile phone ad.
- *Media.* The *communication channels* through which the message moves from sender to receiver – in this case, the specific magazines that Ericsson selects.
- *Decoding.* The process by which the receiver *assigns meaning to the symbols* encoded by the sender – a consumer reads the Ericsson mobile phone ad and interprets the words and illustrations it contains.
- *Receiver.* The *party receiving the message* sent by another party – the consumer or business customer who reads the Ericsson mobile phone ad.
- *Response.* The reactions of the receiver after being exposed to the message – any of hundreds of possible responses, such as the customer is more aware of the attributes of the Ericsson mobile phone, actually buys the mobile phone advertised, or does nothing.
- *Feedback.* The part of the *receiver's response communicated back to the sender* – Ericsson's research shows that consumers like and remember the ad, or consumers write or call the company praising or criticising the ad or its products.
- *Noise.* The *unplanned static or distortion* during the communication process, which results in the receiver getting a different message from the one the sender sent – for example, the customer is distracted while reading the magazine and misses the Ericsson mobile phone ad or its key points.

For a message to be effective, the sender's encoding process must mesh with the receiver's decoding process. Thus, the best messages consist of words and other symbols that are familiar to the receiver. The more the sender's field of experience overlaps with that of the receiver, the more effective the message is likely to be. Marketing communicators may not always *share* their consumers' field of experience. For example, an advertising copywriter from one social stratum might create an ad for consumers from another stratum – say, wealthy business executives. However, to communicate effectively, the marketing communicator must understand the consumer's field of experience.

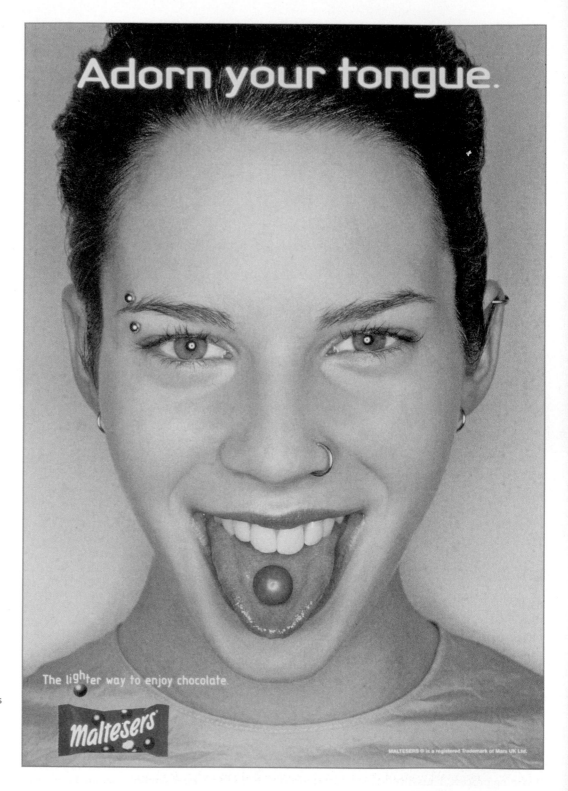

Marketers need to encode messages aimed at specific audiences. As this ad shows, confectioners know their market. Alongside ads for size 0 models, clothes, cosmetics and fragrances in fashion magazines are adverts for another indulgence product: chocolate!
SOURCE: The Advertising Archives.

This model points out the key factors in good communication. Senders need to know what audiences they want to reach and what responses they want. They must be good at encoding messages that take into account how the target audience decodes them. They must send messages through media that reach target audiences and they must develop feedback channels so that they can assess the audience's response to the message.

Steps in developing effective communication

We now examine the steps in developing an effective integrated communications and promotion programme. The marketing communicator must identify the target audience, determine the communication objectives, design a message, choose the media through which to send the message, and collect feedback to measure the promotion's results.

Identifying the target audience

A marketing communicator starts with a clear target audience in mind. The audience may be potential buyers or current users, those who make the buying decision or those who influence it. The audience may be individuals, groups, special publics or the general public. The target audience will heavily affect the communicator's decisions on *what* will be said, *how* it will be said, *when* it will be said, *where* it will be said and *who* will say it.

Determining the communication objectives

Once the target audience has been defined, the marketing communicator must decide what response is sought. Of course, in many cases, the final response is *purchase*. But a purchase results from a long consumer decision-making process. The marketing communicator needs to know where the target audience now stands and to what stage it needs to be moved. To do this, he or she must determine whether or not the customer is ready to buy.

The target audience may be in any of six **buyer-readiness stages** – the stages that consumers normally pass through on their way to making a purchase. These stages are *awareness, knowledge, liking, preference, conviction* and *purchase* (see Figure 15.4). They can be described as a *hierarchy of consumer response stages*. The purpose of marketing communication is to move the customer along these stages and ultimately to achieve final purchase.

Buyer-readiness stages—The stages that consumers normally pass through on their way to purchase, including awareness, knowledge, liking, preference, conviction and purchase.

Awareness

The marketing communicator's target market may be totally unaware of the product, know only its name or know one or a few things about it. If most of the target audience is unaware, the communicator tries to create initial awareness and brand name recognition. This process can begin with simple messages that repeat the company or product name. For example, when the Orange mobile phone service was launched in the early 1990s, it began with an extensive pre-launch, 'teaser' advertising campaign to create name familiarity. In the months leading up to the launch, ads for Orange created curiosity and awareness by emphasising the brand name, but did not reveal the service.

Knowledge

The target audience might be aware of the existence of the company, its product or brand, but not know much more. The company needs to learn how many people in its target audience have little, some or much knowledge about its offering. At launch, Orange ads created knowledge by informing potential buyers of the company's service and innovative features.

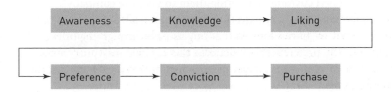

Figure 15.4 Buyer-readiness stages

Liking

Assuming target audience members *know* the product, how do they *feel* about it? Once potential buyers knew about Orange, the company's marketers sought to move them along to the next stage – to develop positive feelings about the brand. Orange wanted to make a dry, technical sector – telecommunications – as relevant to as many consumers as possible. They wanted potential consumers to feel 'warm' and develop a liking towards the mobile phone operator. Orange used emotive language, relying on words such as 'Hello', 'Listen' or 'Cry' on billboard campaigns to build an emotional brand connection with target customers. If the audience looks unfavourably on the brand, the communicator has to find out why, and then resolve the problems identified before developing a communications campaign to generate favourable feelings.

Preference

The target audience might *like* the product, but not *prefer* it to others. In this case, the communicator must try to build consumer preference by promoting the product's quality, value and other beneficial features. The communicator can check on the campaign's success by measuring the audience's preferences again after the campaign. If Orange finds that many potential customers like its service offering but prefer other mobile phone operators' brands, it will have to identify those areas where its offerings are not as good as competing deals and where they are better. It must then promote its advantages to build preference among prospective clients, while redressing its weaknesses.

Conviction

A target audience might *prefer* the product, but not develop a *conviction* about buying it. Thus some customers may prefer Orange to other mobile phone network brands, but may not be absolutely sure that it is what they should subscribe to. The communicator's job is to build conviction that the offering is the best one for the potential buyer. Orange sought to make mobile phones accessible to consumers. In the early 1990s, mobile phone service operators such as Cellnet and Vodafone were largely focused on serving corporate and home-office or business users. Orange wanted to make mobile phones a right, not a privilege for a few people. Their promotion messages were straightforward and emphasised the benefits of the product, not the technology behind it.

A combination of the promotion-mix tools should be used to create preference and conviction. Advertising can be used to build emotional brand connections and to extol the advantages the product offers over competing brands by the brand. Press releases and public relations activities could be used to stress the brand's specific features, such as its innovativeness or performance. Direct marketing tools could be used or dealer salespeople could also be encouraged to tell buyers about the product or service options, value for the price and after-sale service.

Purchase

Finally, some members of the target audience might be convinced about the product, but not quite get around to making the *purchase*. Potential buyers might decide to wait for more information or for the economy to improve. The communicator must lead these consumers to take the final step. Actions might include offering special promotional prices, rebates or premiums. Salespeople might call or write to selected customers, inviting them to visit the company's website or to visit the sales outlet for a special demonstration or product trial.

In discussing buyer readiness stages, we have assumed that buyers pass through *cognitive* (awareness, knowledge), *affective* (liking, preference, conviction), and *behavioural* (purchase) stages, in that order. This '*learn–feel–do*' sequence is appropriate when buyers have high involvement with a product category and perceive brands in the category to be highly differentiated, such as the purchase of a car. But consumers often follow other sequences. For example, they might follow a '*do–feel–learn*' sequence for high-involvement products with little perceived differentiation, such as a central heating system. Still a third sequence is the '*learn–do–feel*' sequence, where consumers have low involvement and perceive little differentiation, as is the case when they buy a product such as salt. Nevertheless, by understanding consumers' buying stages and their appropriate sequence, the marketer can do a better job of planning communications.

Of course, marketing communications alone cannot create positive feelings and purchases for the product. The product itself must provide superior value for the customer. So, for example, Orange must give customers better value than existing service providers. In fact, outstanding marketing communications can actually speed the demise of a poor product. The more quickly potential buyers learn about the poor product, the more quickly they become aware of its faults. Thus, good marketing communication calls for 'good deeds followed by good words'.

 Marketing communication calls for 'good deeds followed by good words'.

Designing a message

Having defined the desired audience response, the communicator turns to developing an effective message. Ideally, the message should get *Attention*, hold *Interest*, arouse *Desire* and obtain *Action* (a framework known as the AIDA model). In practice, few messages take the consumer all the way from awareness to purchase, but the AIDA framework suggests the desirable qualities of a good message.

In putting the message together, the marketing communicator must decide what to say (*message content*) and how to say it (*message structure and format*).

Message content

The communicator has to figure out an appeal or theme that will produce the desired response. There are three types of appeal: rational, emotional and moral. **Rational appeals** relate to the audience's self-interest. They show that the product will produce the desired benefits. Examples are messages showing a product's quality, economy, value or performance. Thus, in its ads, Mercedes informs buyers why Mercedes is the best choice: its cars are 'engineered like no other car in the world', stressing engineering design, performance and safety.

Emotional appeals attempt to stir up either positive or negative emotions that can motivate purchase. Communicators may use positive emotional appeals such as love, humour, pride, promise of success and joy. As we saw earlier, Orange used emotive language to connect with target customers. At the core of Orange's campaign was the famous slogan, 'The future's bright, the future's orange.' The emotive way Orange marketed its service enabled the company to 'talk to people on a human level. People who were scared of technology were reassured by Orange's approach,' says a spokesperson for Orange.[13]

Other examples of emotional appeals can be found:

> British Telecom's 'Make someone happy with a phone call' and 'It's good to talk' campaigns stir a bundle of strong emotions. Ad campaigns for Häagen-Dazs equate ice-cream with pleasure: one classic ad tells consumers how 'It is the *intense* flavour of the finest ingredients combined with *fresh* cream that is essentially Häagen-Dazs', and is followed by the strapline: 'Now it's on everybody's lips'.

Rational appeals— Message appeals that relate to the audience's self-interest and show that the product will produce the claimed benefits; examples are appeals of product quality, economy, value or performance.

Emotional appeals— Message appeals that attempt to stir up negative or positive emotions that will motivate purchase; examples are fear, guilt, shame, love, humour, pride and joy appeals.

A GOOD NIGHT'S
SLEEP MEANS A
GOOD DAY AHEAD

A BED THAT'S HAND MADE SPECIFICALLY FOR YOU IS AN
INVESTMENT THAT PAYS OFF EVERY MORNING OF YOUR LIFE.

SAVOIR BEDS
SINCE 1905

For a brochure telephone 020 7486 2222 www.savoirbeds.co.uk

Advertisers can use humour and appeal to consumers' sensory pleasures as seen in this ad by Savoir Beds.
SOURCE: Savoir Beds. *Agency:* Large, Smith and Walford Partnership.

Communicators can also use negative emotional appeals, such as fear, guilt and shame appeals that get people to do things they should (brush their teeth, eat more healthily, buy new tyres) or to stop doing things they shouldn't (smoke, drink and drive, eat unhealthy foods). For example, a recent British Heart Foundation anti-smoking campaign used the song 'I've got you under my skin', accompanied by images of potentially fatal blood clots, to get across its message – 'A blood clot kills a smoker every 35 minutes.' A BBC TV licensing campaign reminds students of just how important it is to buy a licence while at university. It used anti-humour to communicate the following message: 'What's black and white and full of students? Our database. Watching TV without a licence is not funny. Then again, what you might find even less amusing is that we know every unlicensed address in the country, including student accommodation. Seriously, get a TV licence.'[14]

Moral appeals are directed to the audience's sense of what is 'right' and 'proper'. They are often used to urge people to support social causes such as a cleaner environment, helping the

Moral appeals—Message appeals that are directed to the audience's sense of what is right and proper.

disadvantaged, better community relations or human rights. An example of a moral appeal is the Salvation Army headline, 'While you're trying to figure out what to get the man who has everything, don't forget the man who has nothing.'

Message structure

Marketers must also decide *how* to say it. There are three message-structure issues. The first is whether to draw a conclusion or to leave it to the audience. Research suggests that drawing a conclusion was usually more effective where the target audience is less likely to be motivated or may be incapable of arriving at the appropriate conclusion. More recent research, however, suggests that in many cases where the targets are likely to be interested in the product, the advertiser is better off asking questions to stimulate involvement and motivate customers to think about the brand, and then letting them come to their own conclusions.

The second message-structure issue is whether to present the strongest arguments first or last. Presenting them first gets strong attention, but may lead to an anticlimactic ending. The third message structure issue is whether to present a one-sided argument (mentioning only the product's strengths), or a two-sided argument (touting the product's strengths while also admitting its shortcomings). Usually, a one-sided argument is more effective in sales presentations – except when audiences are highly educated or likely to hear opposing claims or when the communicator has a negative association to overcome. In this spirit, Heinz ran the message 'Heinz Ketchup is slow good' and Listerine ran the message 'Listerine tastes bad twice a day.' In such cases, two-sided messages can enhance the advertiser's credibility and make buyers more resistant to competitor attacks.[15]

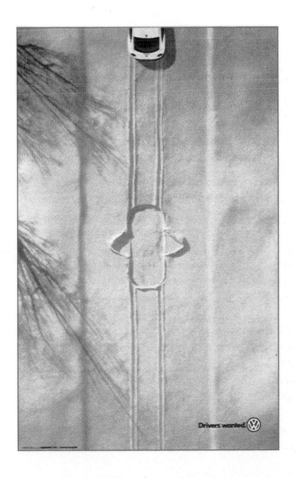

Message format: to attract attention, advertisers can use distinctive formats, novelty and eye-catching pictures, as in this award-winning Volkswagen ad.
SOURCE: Reproduced by kind permission of Volkswagen of America, Inc. and Arnold Worldwide, *Photographer*: © Steve Bronstein.

Message format

The marketing communicator also needs a strong *format* for the message. In a print ad, the communicator has to decide on the headline, copy, illustration and colour. To attract attention, advertisers can use novelty and contrast, eye-catching pictures and headlines, distinctive formats, message size and position, and colour, shape and movement. If the message is to be carried over the radio, the communicator has to choose words, sounds and voices. The 'sound' of an announcer promoting banking services should be different from one promoting an iPod.

If the message is to be transmitted on television or conveyed in person, then all these elements plus body language have to be planned. Presenters plan their facial expressions, gestures, dress, posture and even hairstyles. If the message is carried on the product or its package, the communicator has to watch texture, scent, colour, size and shape. Take colour, for example. Colour affects moods and can elicit a range of emotions from feelings of warmth, passion and love to fear, aggression and hunger. Age, gender and cultural associations also play a role in how consumers perceive colour and their reaction to a certain colour.

> Colours speak for brands. Red is associated with intense emotions, ranging from passion, love, sex, ripeness, fertility . . .

Bright, bold, bursting colours are an essential part of the marketing landscape. Colours speak for brands. Red is associated with intense emotions, ranging from passion, love, sex, ripeness, fertility, confidence and heat to urgency, strength, risk, danger, challenge and revolution. Red is the colour of choice for some of the world's most famous brands, including Coca-Cola, Toyota, Marlboro, Canon, Kellogg's, Oracle, Colgate, Shell and Smirnoff. In the case of Coca-Cola, named the top global brand by brand consultancy Interbrand, its red circle, the 'Spencerian' script, the prominent double 'C' and the famous, narrow waisted bottle, combine to make up the brand's iconography, which underlines the brand image which is instantly recognised by consumers around the world.

The simple use of colour and copy also helped to build *The Economist* magazine as a global brand. Its white-on-red billboard campaigns featuring punchy headlines such as 'f.y.i.' and 'Insider reading', with '*The Economist*' appearing small in the lower right corner of the poster, made the ads instantly recognisable, even at a distance. The colour red lent a warmth to a serious product.

Meanwhile, Virgin has used the colour red to link activities across the whole group. The company's in-house guide, *The Virgin Red Book,* which is used to help staff deal with suppliers, has as its opening statement, 'Red is the lifeblood of our look.' Virgin's brand marketing executives explain that the aim is to ensure that red is reproduced as accurately and consistently as possible across the range of materials. Virgin chose red for the launch of Virgin Atlantic in 1984, in order to differentiate itself from its main competitors, BA, British Caledonian and Pan-Am, which had predominantly blue liveries consistent with the conservative image of airlines then. 'Red is a bold way of standing out and challenging the competition,' says Ashley Stockwell of Virgin's brand marketing team.

The challenge for marketers is how to choose the correct colour for a particular brand or product. Consumers respond to colour at a behavioural level, as in the elicitation of different emotional responses. It is also a learned response, where anything from age, income and other demographics can affect people's reaction to certain colours. For example, blue is more popular with grown-up, mature people while red is more appealing to young, lively, fun people.

Cultural associations also affect how people perceive and react to certain colours. Green is the colour of the environment in Europe, considered sacred across Islam, and a lucky colour in

Ireland. A company can use blue packaging for a cold medicine in the US, but the colour is associated with coldness in China, where users are likely to look for warmth in healing products. In the West, white is for brides and black is for funerals. But, in China and much of the East, red is for brides and white is for funerals. Yellow is the colour of caution in Europe but an imperial Chinese colour denoting grandeur and mystery, while it is the colour of despair in Brazil.

Advertisers who serve global markets must choose colours that appeal to consumers on both behavioural and cultural levels. Cultural sensitivity, however, depends on the product or brand. As in the case of prominent global brands, like Coca-Cola, Virgin and others, the colour reflects the very image that comes with the brand.[16]

Even when an individual is exposed to a message, he or she may pay no attention to the message because it is either boring or irrelevant. The communicator increases the chances of the message attracting the attention of the target audience by taking into consideration the following factors:

- The message must have a practical value to the target audience because such individuals are in the market for the product (for example, it would probably not be cost-effective to advertise pension schemes to undergraduates, who are unlikely to see the relevance of such policies).
- The message must interest the target group.
- The message must communicate new information about the product or brand. Consumers pay more attention to new messages.
- The message must reinforce or help to justify the buyer's recent purchase decisions – if you have recently bought a PVR, it is likely that you will notice, or your attention will be quickly drawn to, ads for the product (a phenomenon called cognitive dissonance reduction).
- The message must be presented in such a way as to make an impact.

While advertisers' basic aim is to get their ads noticed, they must be sensitive to, and comply with, codes of practice operated by the industry watchdogs or country regulators. Messages should create maximum impact but without causing public offence and irritation.

There is a fine dividing line between attracting and irritating consumers. There are also the bad taste ads and ones using 'shock tactics' which can also do much damage. In the UK, one RSPCA (Royal Society for the Prevention of Cruelty to Animals) campaign drew attention to the plight of horses exported for consumption by using a harrowing image of a dead pony hanging from a hook. Although the advertising watchdog, the ASA, had no intention to frustrate the worthy efforts of the RSPCA, it upheld public complaints of the visual image used in the ad which was deemed misleading and grossly offensive.

In an attempt to use product placement to promote its Dove brand, the consumer-goods firm Unilever integrated its Dove body wash into the TV series 'The Apprentice'. Candidates in the series competed to design a new ad campaign for the product. However, Unilever's executives were worried when one of the teams came up with an idea which was full of sexual innuendo and a gay theme.[17]

Choosing media

The communicator must now select *channels of communication*. There are two broad types of communication channel: *personal* and *non-personal*.

Personal communication channels

Personal communication channels—Channels through which two or more people communicate directly with each other, including face to face, person to audience, on the phone, through mail or e-mail or through an Internet 'chat'.

Word-of-mouth influence—Personal communication about a product between target buyers and neighbours, friends, family members and associates.

In **personal communication channels**, two or more people communicate directly with each other. They might communicate face to face, over the telephone or mobile phone, through the mail or even through an Internet 'chat'. Personal communication channels are effective because they allow for personal addressing and feedback.

Some personal communication channels are controlled directly by the company. For example, company salespeople contact target buyers. Other personal communications about the product may reach buyers through channels not directly controlled by the company. These might include independent experts – consumer advocates, online buying guides and others – making statements to target buyers. Or they might be neighbours, friends, family members and associates talking to target buyers. This last channel, known as **word-of-mouth influence**, has considerable effect in many product areas.

Personal influence carries great weight for products that are expensive, risky or highly visible. For example, buyers of cars and major appliances often go beyond mass-media sources to seek the opinions of knowledgeable people. A recent study found that more than 90 per cent of customers trust 'recommendations from consumers', whereas trust in ads runs from a high of about 40 per cent to less than 10 per cent. It's also a major reason for Amazon's success in growing sales per customer. You have probably made an Amazon purchase based on another customer's review or the 'Customers who bought this also bought . . .' section.

> More than 90 per cent of customers trust 'recommendations from consumers', whereas trust in ads runs from a high of about 40 per cent to less than 10 per cent.

Companies can take steps to put personal communication channels to work for them. For example, they can create *opinion leaders* – people whose opinions are sought by others – by supplying influencers with the product on attractive terms or by educating them so that they can inform others. This is also called **buzz marketing** – cultivating opinion leaders and getting them to spread information about a product or service to others in their communities. Companies could work through community members such as local radio personalities, heads of local organisations or community leaders. They can also use influential people in their advertisements or develop advertising that has high 'conversation value'.

Buzz marketing—Cultivating opinion leaders and getting them to spread information about a product or service to others in their communities.

However, marketers must consider not only the benefits but also the pitfalls of selling products by word-of-mouth:[18]

When it came to promoting its new video-game console, the Wii, in America, Nintendo recruited a handful of carefully chosen suburban mothers in the hope that they would spread the word among their friends that the Wii was a gaming console the whole family could enjoy together. Nintendo thus became the latest company to use 'word-of-mouth' marketing. Nestlé, Sony and Philips have all launched similar campaigns in recent months to promote everything from bottled water to electric toothbrushes. As the power of traditional advertising declines, what was once an experimental marketing approach is becoming more popular.

After all, no form of advertising carries as much weight as an endorsement from a friend. 'Amway and Tupperware know you can blend the social and economic to business advantage,' says Walter Carl, a marketing guru at Northeastern University. The difference now, he says, is that the Internet can magnify the effect of such endorsements.

The difficulty for marketers is creating the right kind of buzz and learning to control it. Negative views spread just as quickly as positive ones, so if a product has flaws, people will soon find out. And Peter Kim of Forrester, a consultancy, points out that when Microsoft sent laptops loaded with its new Windows Vista software to influential bloggers in an effort to get them to write about it, the resulting online discussion ignored Vista and focused instead on the morality of accepting gifts and the ethics of word-of-mouth marketing. Bad buzz, in short.

BzzAgent, a controversial company based in Boston that is one of the leading exponents of word-of-mouth marketing, operates a network of volunteer 'agents' who receive free samples of products in the post. They talk to their friends about them and send back their thoughts. In return, they receive rewards through a points programme – an arrangement they are supposed to make clear. This allows a firm to create buzz around a product and to see what kind of word-of-mouth response it generates, which can be useful for subsequent product development and marketing. In April 2007, BzzAgent launched its service in Britain. Dave Balter, BzzAgent's founder, thinks word-of-mouth marketing will become a multi-billion dollar industry. No doubt he tells that to everyone he meets.

SOURCE. Copyright © The Economist Newspaper Limited, London (7 April 2007).

Non-personal communication channels

Non-personal communication channels are media that carry messages without personal contact or feedback. They include major media, atmospheres and events. Important **media** include print media (newspapers, magazines, direct mail), broadcast media (radio, television), display media (billboards, signs, posters) and online and electronic media (e-mail, websites, CDs, DVDs). **Atmospheres** are designed environments that create or reinforce the buyer's leanings towards buying a product. Thus lawyers' offices and banks are designed to communicate confidence and other factors that might be valued by their clients. **Events** are occurrences staged to communicate messages to target audiences. For example, public relations departments arrange press conferences, grand openings, shows and exhibits, public tours and other events to communicate with specific audiences.

Non-personal communication affects buyers directly. In addition, using mass media often affects buyers indirectly by causing more personal communication. Communications first flow from television, magazines and other mass media to opinion leaders and then from these opinion leaders to others. Thus opinion leaders step between the mass media and their audiences and carry messages to people who are less exposed to media. This suggests that mass communicators should aim their messages directly at opinion leaders, letting them carry the message to others. For example, pharmaceutical firms direct their new drugs promotions at the most influential doctors and medical experts first – the 'thought leaders' in the profession; if they are persuaded, their opinions have an impact upon the new product's acceptance by others in the field. Thus opinion leaders extend the influence of the mass media. Or they may alter the message or not carry the message, thus acting as gatekeepers.

> " Opinion leaders step between the mass media and their audiences. "

Selecting the message source

In either personal or non-personal communication, the message's impact on the target audience is also affected by how the audience views the communicator. The credibility and attractiveness

Non-personal communication channels—Media that carry messages without personal contact or feedback, including media, atmospheres and events.

Media—Non-personal communications channels including print media (newspapers, magazines, direct mail), broadcast media (radio, television), and display media (billboards, signs, posters).

Atmospheres—Designed environments that create or reinforce the buyer's leanings towards consumption of a product.

Events—Occurrences staged to communicate messages to target audiences; examples are news conferences and grand openings.

Message source—The company, the brand name, the salesperson of the brand, or the actor in the ad who endorses the product.

of the **message source** – the company, the brand name, the spokesperson for the brand, or the actor in the ad who endorses the product – must therefore be considered.

Messages delivered by highly credible sources are more persuasive. Thus, many food companies promote to doctors, dentists and other healthcare experts to motivate these professionals to recommend their products to patients. For example, for years, Sensodyne Toothpaste has promoted the product in dental surgeries, and ads use endorsements by dental practitioners to persuade target users to adopt the brand. But, to remain credible, the source must be perceived by the target audience as being an expert where the product is concerned, and trustworthy: that is, objective and honest in his or her opinion of the benefits claimed for the product.

Marketers also hire celebrity endorsers – well-known athletes, actors, fashion models and even cartoon characters – to deliver their brand messages. Golfer Tiger Woods speaks for Nike, Buick, Accenture and a dozen other brands. Basketball pro LeBron James vouches for Nike and Coca-Cola's Powerade and Sprite brands. And young golfer Michelle Wie lends her image to brands such as Nike and Sony.

However, there are risks involved and companies must be careful when selecting celebrities to represent their brands. Picking the wrong spokesperson can result in embarrassment and a tarnished image. McDonald's, Sprite and Nutella found this out when super-spokesperson Kobe Bryant was charged with sexual assault. H&M, Chanel and Burberry had to publicly dismiss supermodel Kate Moss after she was reportedly photographed using cocaine. And Pepsi, McDonald's, Roots and Ford faced embarrassment when gambling scandals threatened to dirty the squeaky-clean image of their spokesperson, hockey star Wayne Gretzky.

Collecting feedback

After sending the message, the communicator must research its effect on the target audience. This involves asking the target audience members whether they remember the message, how many times they saw it, what points they recall, how they felt about the message, and their past and present attitudes towards the product and company. The communicator would also like to measure behaviour resulting in the message – how many people bought a product, talked to others about it or visited the store.

Figure 15.5 shows an example of feedback measurement for two hypothetical brands. Looking at Brand A, we find that 80 per cent of the total market is aware of it, that 60 per cent of those

Figure 15.5 Feedback measurements for two brands

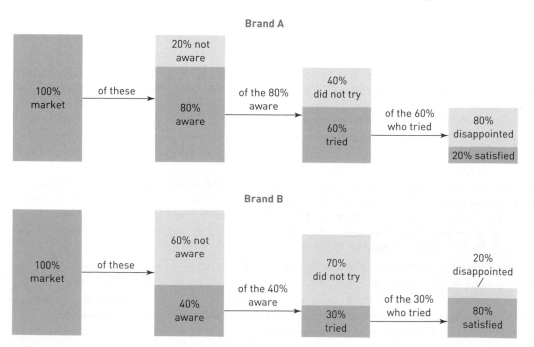

aware of it have tried it, but that only 20 per cent of those who tried it were satisfied. These results suggest that although the communication programme is creating *awareness*, the product fails to give consumers the *satisfaction* they expect. Therefore, the company should try to improve the product while staying with the successful communication programme. In contrast, only 40 per cent of the total market is aware of Brand B, only 30 per cent of those aware of Brand B have tried it, but 80 per cent of those who have tried it are satisfied. In this case, the communication programme needs to be stronger to take advantage of the brand's power to create customer satisfaction.

Setting the total promotion budget and mix

We have looked at the steps in planning and sending communications to a target audience. But how does the company decide on the total *promotion budget* and its division among the major promotional tools to create the *promotion mix*? By what process does it blend the tools to create integrated marketing communications? Let's take a look at these questions.

Setting the total promotion budget

One of the hardest marketing decisions facing a company is how much to spend on promotion. John Wanamaker, an American department store magnate, once said: 'I know that half of my advertising is wasted, but I don't know which half. I spent $2 million for advertising, and I don't know if that is half enough or twice too much.' Thus, it is not surprising that industries and companies vary widely in how much they spend on promotion. Promotion spending may be 10 to 12 per cent of sales for consumer packaged goods and less than 1 per cent for industrial machinery products. Within a given industry, both low and high spenders can be found.[19]

> 'I know that half of my advertising is wasted, but I don't know which half.'

How does a company decide on its promotion budget? There are four common methods used to set the total budget for advertising: the *affordable method*, the *percentage-of-sales method*, the *competitive-parity method* and the *objective-and-task method*.[20]

Affordable method

A common 'rule-of-thumb' used by many companies is the **affordable method**. They set the promotion budget at the level they think the company can afford. They start with total revenues, deduct operating expenses and capital outlays, and then devote some portion of the remaining funds to advertising. Small businesses often use this method, reasoning that the company cannot spend more on advertising than it has.

Unfortunately, this method of setting budgets completely ignores the effect of promotion on sales. It tends to place advertising last among spending priorities, even in situations where advertising is critical to the firm's success. It leads to an uncertain annual promotion budget, which makes long-range market planning difficult. Although the affordable method can result in overspending on advertising, it more often results in underspending.

Affordable method— Setting the promotion budget at the level management thinks the company can afford.

Percentage-of-sales method

Percentage-of-sales method—Setting the promotion budget at a certain percentage of current or forecasted sales or as a percentage of the unit sales price.

In the **percentage-of-sales method**, marketers set their promotion budget at a certain percentage of current or forecast sales. Or they budget a percentage of the unit sales price. Automotive companies usually budget a fixed percentage for promotion based on the planned car price. Fast-moving consumer goods companies usually set it at some percentage of current or anticipated sales.

The percentage-of-sales method has advantages. It is simple to use and helps managers think about the relationship between promotion spending, selling price and profit per unit. The method supposedly creates competitive stability because competing firms tend to spend about the same percentage of their sales on promotion.

However, despite these claimed advantages, the percentage-of-sales method has little to justify it. It wrongly views sales as the *cause* of promotion rather than as the *result*.[21] Although studies have found a positive correlation between promotional spending and brand strength, this relationship often turns out to be effect and cause, not cause and effect. Stronger brands with higher sales can afford the biggest ad budgets.

Thus, the percentage-of-sales budget is based on availability of funds rather than on opportunities. It may prevent the increased spending sometimes needed to turn around falling sales. It fails to consider whether a higher or lower level of spending would be more profitable. Because the budget varies with year-to-year sales, long-range planning is difficult. Finally, the method does not provide any basis for choosing a *specific* percentage, except what has been done in the past or what competitors are doing.

Competitive-parity method

Competitive-parity method—Setting the promotion budget to match competitors' outlays.

Other companies use the **competitive-parity method**, setting their promotion budgets to match competitors' outlays. They watch competitors' advertising or get industry promotion-spending estimates from publications or trade associations, and then set their budgets based on the industry average.

Two arguments support this method. First, competitors' budgets represent the collective wisdom of the industry. Second, spending what competitors spend helps prevent promotion wars. Unfortunately, neither argument is valid. There are no grounds for believing that the competition has a better idea of what a company should be spending on promotion than does the company itself. Companies differ greatly in terms of market opportunities and profit margins, and each has its own special promotion needs. Finally, there is no evidence that budgets based on competitive parity prevent promotion wars.

Objective-and-task method

Objective-and-task method—Developing the promotion budget by (1) defining specific objectives, (2) determining the tasks that must be performed to achieve these objectives, and (3) estimating the costs of performing these tasks. The sum of these costs is the proposed promotion budget.

The most logical budget-setting method is the **objective-and-task method**, whereby the company sets its promotion budget based on what it wants to accomplish with promotion. The method entails (1) defining specific promotion objectives, (2) determining the tasks needed to achieve these objectives and (3) estimating the costs of performing these tasks. The sum of these costs is the proposed promotion budget.

The objective-and-task method forces management to spell out its assumptions about the relationship between amount spent and promotion results. But it is also the most difficult method to use. Managers have to set sales and profit targets and then work back to what tasks must be performed to achieve desired goals. Often it is hard to figure out which specific tasks will achieve stated objectives. For example, suppose Philips wants 95 per cent awareness for its latest PVR player model during the six-month introductory period. What specific advertising messages and media schedules would Philips use to attain this objective? How much would these messages and media schedules cost? Philips management must consider such questions, even though they are hard to answer. The main advantage of this method is that it gets managers to define their communication objectives, how each objective will be met using selected promotion tools and the financial implications of alternative communication programmes.

Setting the overall promotion mix

The concept of integrated marketing communications suggests that it must blend the promotion tools carefully into a coordinated *promotion mix*. But how does the company determine what mix of promotion tools it will use?

Companies are always looking for ways to improve promotion by replacing one promotion tool with another that will do the same job more economically. Companies within the same industry may differ greatly in the design of their promotion mixes. For example, Hewlett-Packard relies on advertising and promotion to retailers, whereas Dell uses more direct marketing. Designing the promotion mix is even more complex when one tool must be used to promote another. Thus, when a company decides to run a sales promotion campaign, it also has to run ads to inform the public. When Lever Brothers uses consumer advertising and a sales promotion campaign to support the launch of a new laundry detergent, it also has to set aside money to promote this campaign to the resellers to win their support.

Many factors influence the marketer's choice of promotion tools. We now look at these factors.

The nature of each promotion tool

Each promotion tool has unique characteristics and costs. Marketers must understand these characteristics in selecting the promotion mix.

Advertising

The many forms of advertising make it hard to generalise about its unique qualities. However, several qualities can be noted:

- Advertising can reach masses of geographically dispersed buyers at a low cost per exposure. For example, TV advertising can reach huge audiences.

- Beyond its reach, large-scale advertising by a seller says something positive about the seller's size, popularity and success.

- Because of advertising's public nature, consumers tend to view advertised products as standard and legitimate – buyers know that purchasing the product will be understood and accepted publicly.

- Advertising enables the seller to repeat a message many times, and lets the buyer receive and compare the messages of various competitors.

- Advertising is also very expressive, allowing the company to dramatise its products through the artful use of visuals, print, sound and colour.

- On the one hand, advertising can be used to build up a long-term image for a product (such as Mercedes-Benz car ads). On the other hand, advertising can trigger quick sales (as when department stores like Debenhams and Selfridges advertise a weekend sale).

Advertising also has some shortcomings:

- Although it reaches many people quickly, advertising is impersonal and cannot be as persuasive as can company salespeople.

- Advertising can carry on only a one-way communication with the audience, and the audience does not feel that it has to pay attention or respond.

- In addition, advertising can be very costly. Although some advertising forms, such as newspaper and radio advertising, can be done on smaller budgets, other forms, such as network TV advertising, require very large budgets.

Personal selling

Personal selling is the most effective tool at certain stages of the buying process, particularly in building up buyers' preferences, convictions and actions. Compared to advertising, personal selling has several unique qualities:

- It involves personal interaction between two or more people, so each person can observe the other's needs and characteristics and make quick adjustments.

- Personal selling allows all kinds of relationships to spring up, ranging from matter-of-fact selling relationships to personal friendships. An effective salesperson keeps the customer's interests at heart in order to build a long-term relationship by solving customer problems.

- Finally, with personal selling the buyer usually feels a greater need to listen and respond, even if the response is a polite 'no thank you'.

These unique qualities come at a cost, however. A sales force requires a longer-term commitment than does advertising – advertising can be turned on and off, but sales force size is harder to change. Personal selling is also the company's most expensive promotion tool, costing companies several hundred euros on average per sales call.

Sales promotion

Sales promotion includes a wide assortment of tools – coupons, contests, price reductions, premium offers, free gifts and others – all of which have many unique qualities:

- They attract consumer attention and provide information that may lead to a purchase.

- They offer strong incentives to purchase by providing inducements or contributions that give additional value to consumers.

- Sales promotion can be used to dramatise product offers and to boost sagging sales.

- Moreover, sales promotions invite and reward quick response. Whereas advertising says 'buy our product', sales promotion offers incentives to consumers to 'buy it now'.

Although companies use sales promotion tools to create a stronger and quicker response, sales promotion effects are usually short-lived. They are often not as effective as advertising or personal selling in building long-run brand preference. To be effective, marketers must carefully plan the sales promotion campaign and offer target customers genuine value.

Public relations

Public relations (PR) offers several unique qualities. It is all those activities that the organisation does to communicate with target audiences which are not directly paid for.

- PR is very believable: news stories, features, sponsorships and events seem more real and believable to readers than ads do.

- Public relations can reach many prospects who avoid salespeople and advertisements – the message gets to the buyers as 'news' rather than as a sales-directed communication.

- Like advertising, PR can dramatise a company or product.

Marketers tend to under-use public relations or to use it as an afterthought. Yet a well-thought-out public relations campaign used with other promotion-mix elements can be very cost-effective.

 Marketers tend to under-use public relations or to use it as an afterthought. **,,**

Direct marketing

Although there are many forms of direct marketing – direct mail, telemarketing, electronic marketing, online marketing and others – they all share four distinctive characteristics:

- Direct marketing is non-public as the message is normally addressed to a specific person.
- It is immediate as messages can be prepared very quickly.
- It can be customised, so messages can be tailored to appeal to specific customers.
- It is interactive: it allows a dialogue between the communicator and the consumer, and messages can be altered depending on the consumer's response.

Thus, direct marketing is well suited to highly targeted marketing efforts and to building one-to-one customer relationships.

Promotion mix strategies

Marketers can choose from two basic promotion mix strategies – *push* promotion or *pull* promotion. Figure 15.6 contrasts the two strategies. The relative emphasis on the specific promotion tools differs for push and pull strategies. A **push strategy** involves 'pushing' the product through marketing channels to final consumers. The firm directs its marketing activities (primarily personal selling and trade promotion) towards channel members to induce them to carry the product and to promote it to final consumers.

Using a **pull strategy**, the producer directs its marketing activities (primarily advertising and consumer promotion) towards final consumers to induce them to buy the product. If the pull strategy is effective, consumers will then demand the product from channel members, who will in turn demand it from producers. Thus under a pull strategy, consumer demand 'pulls' the product through the channels.

Push strategy—A promotion strategy that calls for using the sales force and trade promotion to push the product through channels. The producer promotes the product to channel members to induce them to carry the product and to promote it to final consumers.

Pull strategy—A promotion strategy that calls for spending a lot on advertising and consumer promotion to induce final consumers to buy the product. If the strategy is effective, consumers will then demand the product from channel members, who will in turn demand it from producers.

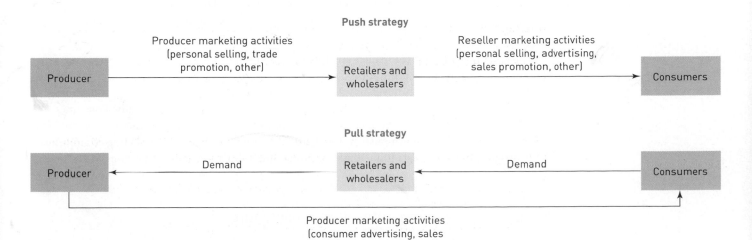

Figure 15.6 Push versus pull promotion strategy

Some small industrial-goods companies use only push strategies; some direct-marketing companies use only pull. However, most large companies use some combination of both. For example, companies such as Kraft and Unilever use mass-media advertising to pull consumers to their products and a large sales force and trade promotions to push their products through the channels.

In recent years, consumer-goods companies have been decreasing the pull portions of their promotion mixes in favour of more push. One reason for this shift towards push strategies is that mass-media campaigns have become more expensive and less effective in recent years. Companies are increasing their segmentation efforts and tailoring their marketing programmes more narrowly, making national advertising less suitable than localised retailer promotions. Moreover, in these days of brand extensions and me-too products, companies sometimes have trouble finding meaningful product differences to feature in advertising. So, they have differentiated their brands through price reductions, premium offers, coupons and other push techniques.

Another reason for the shift from pull to push has been the growing strength of retailers. Big retail chains in Europe have greater access now than ever before to product sales and profit information. They have the power to demand and get what they want from suppliers. And what they want is margin improvements – that is, more push. Mass advertising bypasses them on its way to the consumers, but push promotion benefits them directly. Consumer promotions give retailers an immediate sales boost and cash from trade allowances pads retailer profits. Thus, producers must often use push to obtain good shelf space and other support from important retailers.

However, many marketers are concerned that the reckless use of push will lead to fierce price competition and a continual spiral of price slashing and margin erosion, leaving less money to invest in the product R&D, packaging and advertising that is required to improve and maintain long-run consumer preference and loyalty. If used improperly, push promotion can mortgage the brand's future for short-term gains. Sales promotion buys short-run reseller support and consumer sales, but advertising build long-run brand equity and consumer preference. By robbing the media advertising budget to pay for more sales promotion, companies might win the battle for short-term earnings, but lose the war for long-run brand equity, consumer loyalty and market share.

One well-known marketing consultant, Jack Trout, cautions that some product categories tend to self-destruct by always being on sale. Trout offers several 'commandments of discounting', such as: 'Thou shalt not offer discounts because everyone else does', 'Thou shalt be creative with your discounting', 'Thou shalt put time limits on the deals' and 'Thou shalt stop discounts as soon as you can.'[22]

> Some product categories tend to self-destruct by always being on sale.

Thus, many consumer companies are now rethinking their promotion strategies and reversing the trend by shifting their promotion budgets back towards advertising. They realise that it is not a question of sales promotion versus advertising, or of push versus pull. Success lies in finding the best mix of the two – consistent advertising to build long-run brand value and consumer preference and sales promotion to create short-run trade support and consumer excitement. The company needs to blend both push and pull elements into an integrated marketing communications programme that meets immediate consumer and retailer needs as well as long-run strategic needs.

Factors in designing promotion mix strategies

Companies consider many factors when designing their promotion mix strategies, including the *type of product/market*, the *buyer-readiness stage* and the *product life-cycle stage*.

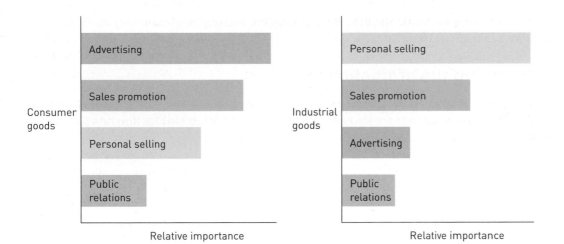

Figure 15.7 Relative importance of promotion tools in business-to-consumer versus business-to-business markets

Type of product/market

The importance of different promotional tools varies between consumer and business markets (see Figure 15.7). Business-to-consumer (B2C) companies usually 'pull' more, putting more of their funds into advertising, followed by sales promotion, personal selling and then public relations. Advertising is relatively more important in consumer markets because there are a larger number of buyers, purchases tend to be routine and emotions play a more important role in the purchase-decision process. In contrast, business-to-business (B2B) marketers tend to 'push' more, putting more of their funds into personal selling, followed by sales promotion, advertising and public relations. In general, personal selling is used more heavily with expensive and risky goods and in markets with fewer and larger sellers.

Although advertising is less important than sales calls in B2B markets, it still plays an important role. Advertising can build product awareness and knowledge, develop sales leads and reassure buyers. Similarly, personal selling can add a lot to B2C companies' marketing efforts. It is simply not the case that 'salespeople put products on shelves and advertising takes them off'. Well-trained consumer-goods salespeople can sign up more dealers to carry a particular brand, convince them to give more shelf space and urge them to use special displays and promotions.

Buyer-readiness stage

The effects of the promotional tools vary for the different buyer-readiness stages. Advertising and public relations play an important role in the awareness and knowledge stages, even more so than that played by 'cold calls' from salespeople. Customer liking, preference and conviction are more affected by personal selling, closely followed by advertising. Finally, closing the sale is mostly done with sales calls and sales promotion. Advertising and public relations are the most cost-effective at the early stages of the buyer decision process, while personal selling, given its high costs, should focus on the later stages of the customer buying process.

Product life-cycle stage

The effects of different promotion tools also vary with stages of the product life-cycle. In the introduction stage, advertising and public relations are good for producing high awareness, and sales promotion is useful in getting early trial. Personal selling efforts must be used to get the trade to carry the product. In the growth stage, advertising and public relations continue to be powerful influences, whereas sales promotion can be reduced because fewer incentives are needed. In the mature stage, sales promotion again becomes important relative to advertising. Buyers know the brands and advertising is needed only to remind them of the product. In the decline stage, advertising is kept at a reminder level, public relations is dropped and salespeople give the product only a little attention. Sales promotion, however, might continue strong in order to stimulate trade and prop up sales.

Integrating the promotion mix

Having set the promotion budget and mix, the company must now take steps to see that all of the promotion mix elements are smoothly integrated. Here is a checklist for integrating the firm's marketing communications.

- *Analyse trends – internal and external – that can affect the company's ability to do business.* Look for areas where communications can help the most. Determine the strengths and weaknesses of each communications function. Develop a combination of promotional tactics based on these strengths and weaknesses.

- *Audit the pockets of communications spending throughout the organisation.* Itemise the communications budgets and tasks and consolidate these into a single budgeting process. Reassess all communications expenditures by product, promotional tool, stage of the life cycle, and observed effect.

- *Identify all customer touch points for the company and its brands.* Work to ensure that communications at each point are consistent with the overall communications strategy and that communications efforts are occurring when, where and how *customers* want them.

- *Team up in communications planning.* Engage all communications functions in joint planning. Include customers, suppliers and other stakeholders at every stage of communications planning.

- *Create compatible themes, tones and quality across all communications media.* Make sure each element carries your unique primary messages and selling points. This consistency achieves greater impact and prevents the unnecessary duplication of work across functions.

- *Create performance measures that are shared by all communications elements.* Develop systems to evaluate the combined impact of all communications activities.

- *Appoint a director responsible for the company's persuasive communications efforts.* This move encourages efficiency by centralising planning and creating shared performance measures.[23]

KEY CONCEPT
www.pearson.co.uk/kotler

Socially responsible marketing communication

In shaping its promotion mix, a company must be aware of the large body of legal and ethical issues surrounding marketing communications. Most marketers work hard to communicate openly, truthfully and honestly with consumers and resellers. Still, abuses may occur, and public policy makers have developed a substantial body of laws and regulations to govern advertising, personal selling, sales promotion and direct marketing activities.

In an environment of increasing legislation, marketers in general have to be more knowledgeable about the many laws that impact communications practices. In the EU, there are many regulations and codes that govern advertising, sales promotions, direct marketing and selling activities. Some of these are EU directives, some are set by national governments and some by other organisations which may or may not be independent of government. In the UK, for example, the Advertising Standards Authority, a self-regulatory body with no connection with the government, was set up by the advertising industry to police the rules laid down in the advertising codes (see Real Marketing 15.2).

real marketing   15.2

We're decent, legal, honest and truthful: Who needs laws?

The launch of commercial TV brought advertising directly into people's homes and with it, a new system of advertising control. In the UK, the marketing industry is keen to be 'decent, legal, honest and truthful' to the extent that it has provided codes of practice to uphold standards in marketing practice. Who needs laws if self-regulation works? This is the ethos underpinning the workings of the Advertising Standards Authority (ASA).

In 1962, the ASA was founded, marking the introduction of the advertising industry's first codes of practice. The ASA enforces marketing rules by way of the Committee of Advertising Practice (CAP) Code which applies to TV and radio advertising, direct marketing, sales promotion and commercial messages sent by e-mail, text and some Internet advertising.

The ASA's role is to maintain standards so that consumers and business can both benefit from healthy competition on fair terms. The self-regulatory system is independent of the government and carries no force of law, and the ASA has no power to impose fines. Its weapon is the bad publicity from 'complaint upheld' findings. Ads that break the rules are required to be withdrawn without having to resort to legal bans. Media owners' participation in the system also means that the advertisers that fail to cooperate with the ASA can be denied access to advertising space, ensuring that misleading, harmful or offensive ads do not appear. Since 1988, self-regulation has been further supported by statutory powers under the Control of Misleading Advertisements Regulations.

How does it work?

Every complaint counts. Just one complaint can trigger an ASA investigation which could lead to an expensive campaign being pulled. However, a large number of complaints may not always lead to a ban. For example, a KFC Zinger Crunch Salad TV ad became the most complained about ad of all time – not for reasons of sex or nudity, but for showing call centre staff singing with their mouths full. Complainants feared the ad would encourage bad table manners. The ASA rejected the complaints on the grounds that table manners which are cultivated in children over a period of time would not be compromised by a single ad.

The ASA's decision has to be consistent, proportionate and yet responsive to consumer concerns. What ads are appropriate to display in public space in a diverse society? What types of images are acceptable for children to see? What is the

difference between bad taste and offence? Where do the boundaries of acceptability lie? When assessing complaints, the ASA always considers the target market and the context in which the ad appears. Images relevant to a product being advertised are more acceptable than gratuitous images used to attract attention. So, Wonderbra's bold approach to advertising its 'push-up plunge' bras – as manifested in the 'Hello Boys' ad campaign – was acceptable because the image was appropriate to the product being advertised, whereas other advertisers using similar imagery for unrelated products have had their ads withdrawn. An ad with sexual reference in a lads' magazine, aimed at 16–30-year-old men, will cause less offence than if it appeared in a TV listings magazine. An ad unsuitable for children may be acceptable if it appears in media where only adults will see it. For example, Vodafone fell foul of this rule when a promotional lozenge was included in a direct mailing to adults. A toddler had ripped open the brightly-coloured envelope and nearly choked on the enclosed lozenge. The ASA upheld the mother's complaint that the direct mailing was irresponsible.

Once a complaint is received, ASA staff assess the ad and, in the case of misleading claims, an adjudication is drafted for consideration by the ASA's Council, comprising people from all walks of life. Each ad is judged on its merit and in context, and against the criteria laid down in the advertising codes. Headline claims, terms and conditions, small print, pricing claims, special offers and comparisons are examples of areas covered by the advertising codes. Decisions are taken by majority vote. Failure to respond to the ASA results in an automatic 'upheld' ruling. The final ruling is published on the ASA's website (www.asa.org.uk). Ads with complaints upheld must be withdrawn or amended before they can appear again. As a last resort, the ASA can refer advertisers or broadcasters refusing to cooperate to the Office of Fair Trading of Ofcom for legal action, a course which is rarely needed.

Targeting helps but be realistic! Beware of poor or incomplete targeting. Advertisers must be realistic about who will see the ad, especially if the message could confuse, upset or distress particular audiences. When baby charity Tommy's Campaign planned a campaign featuring an ultrasound scan of a stillborn baby, it proved impossible to isolate new mothers and women who had lost a baby. The ASA upheld complaints that the campaign could cause distress to pregnant women or anyone who had lost a baby.

Documentary proof for claims before the ad appears. Misleading advertisements form over three-quarters of the complaints received by the ASA each year. Self-regulation requires advertisers to prove that the claims they make in their ads are true. Advertisers must therefore hold documentary evidence for all the claims they make before the ads appear. This evidence must be produced to support the claim if the ad is challenged and complaints are taken up by the ASA.

...15.2

Changing regulatory landscape. Marketers operate in a changing environment. Technological developments such as the Internet and new digital technologies have brought fresh challenges of adapting existing rules to accommodate new media. For example, back in the mid-2000s, the ASA's responsibilities in the area of new media were not as extensive as in other areas of advertising. E-mail was within its remit, but viral marketing and companies' claims on their own websites did not fall within the scope of the British Code of Advertising, Sales Promotion and Direct Marketing. Even so, the ASA showed it had clout. When Vivendi Universal Games created a viral promotion with an attached video clip for the PlayStation2 game *Cold Winter*, because it was distributed as an e-mail, the ASA had jurisdiction and ruled that the ad was 'likely to cause offence'. Changes in public policy such as current concerns about obesity and binge drinking are also influencing regulations on food and alcohol advertising. Changing public opinion also dictates what communications content is deemed acceptable or not.

However, one thing has stayed constant over time – the requirement for marketers to comply with advertising codes to keep advertising standards high. According to the director of communications for the ASA, research shows consistently that a vast majority of ads appearing in the UK do comply with the rules. Compliance is central to the effectiveness and reputation of a system such as the ASA and testimony that self-regulation works.

SOURCES: Adapted from Claire Forbes, 'Be careful what you promise', *The Marketer*, Issue 17 (October 2005), pp. 17–21; and Louella Miles, 'Playing the game', *The Marketer*, Issue 17 (October 2005), pp. 6–9 (www.cim.co.uk/TheMarketer); For more information about the UK's ASA, visit www.asa.org.uk.

In Chapter 4, we looked at the impact of increasing regulation and implications for marketers. Here, we discuss the issues regarding advertising, sales promotion and personal selling. Issues concerning direct marketing will be addressed in Chapter 18.

Advertising and sales promotion

By law, companies must avoid false or deceptive advertising. Advertisers must not make false claims, such as suggesting that a product cures something when it does not. They must avoid ads that have the capacity to deceive, even though no one may actually be deceived. A car cannot be advertised as getting 45 km per gallon unless it does so under typical conditions, and a diet-bread cannot be advertised as having fewer calories simply because its slices are thinner.

Sellers must avoid bait-and-switch advertising or deceptive sales promotions that attract buyers under false pretences. For example, a large retailer advertised a dishwashing machine at €250. However, when consumers tried to buy the advertised machine, the seller downplayed its features, placed faulty machines on showroom floors, understated the machine's performance and took other actions in an attempt to switch buyers to a more expensive machine. Such actions are both unethical and illegal.

A company's trade promotion activities are also closely regulated. For example, in some countries, sellers cannot favour certain customers through their use of trade promotions. They must make promotional allowances and services available to all resellers on proportionately equal terms.

Beyond simply avoiding legal pitfalls, such as deceptive or bait-and-switch advertising, companies can use advertising and other forms of promotion to encourage and promote socially responsible programmes and actions.

For example, together with its bottlers and partners, Coca-Cola is working with the United Nations and its agencies to advance community water efforts in support of the Millennium Development Goals. In its 'This is our drop' ad campaign, the company draws attention to its involvement in water access and sanitation reconstruction work in the tsunami-hit areas of Thailand, Sri Lanka, Indonesia and the Maldives. And, as founding partners in the Global Water Challenge, the company works with other corporations and humanitarian organisations to bring safe drinking water and sanitation to the communities that need it most.[24]

The earth-moving equipment manufacturer Caterpillar is one of several companies and environmental groups forming the Tropical Forest Foundation, which is working to save the great Amazon rainforest. It promotes the cause through advertising and pages on its website.[25]

The *Financial Times* worked with the charity Crisis to raise funds to help provide homeless people with the opportunities they need to start a new life. In a recent ad campaign readers and subscribers of the FT were urged to 'use your company Christmas budget to open doors for homeless people'. Sponsors were invited to donate their company's Christmas card budget to Crisis. In return, the company will get a public acknowledgemet of their gift printed in the FT and a festive e-card to make their clients aware of the ethical choice the company has made.[26]

Personal selling

A company's salespeople must follow the rules of 'fair competition'. Some countries have enacted deceptive sales acts that spell out what is not allowed. For example, salespeople may not lie to consumers or mislead them about the advantages of buying a product. To avoid bait-and-switch practices, salespeople's statements must match advertising claims.

Much personal selling involves business-to-business trade. In selling to businesses, salespeople may not offer bribes to purchasing agents or to others who can influence a sale. They may not obtain or use technical or trade secrets of competitors through bribery or industrial espionage. Finally, salespeople must not disparage competitors or competing products by suggesting things that are not true.

No doubt, the laws governing sales and marketing practices differ across countries. There is also much confusion about conflicting codes and regulations, which is further complicated by differences between legal codes – laws which companies must obey – and codes of practice, which companies voluntarily support. In addition, confusion arises about the interpretation of EU Directives, with some countries in Europe imposing stricter requirements for practices than others.

The EU directive called the Privacy and Electronic Communications Regulations (PECR) 2003 allowed EU members to decide whether or not to adopt business-to-business (B2B) opt-out as opposed to opt-in for digital marketing communications sent to employees of limited companies. Almost half of the EU members went for B2B opt-in but the UK chose B2B opt-out, or what is called 'soft opt-in'. This means that, under the 2003 Rules for digital marketing in the UK, getting 'prior opt-in' agreement from customers is not necessary before sending marketing e-mails or SMS, provided contact details were collected 'in the course of a sale or negotiations for a sale'. If, at the same time, the individual is informed that marketing e-mails or SMS might be sent to them in the future, and given an easy way to 'opt out', then provided future digital messages promote the marketer's similar products and always include an opt-out opportunity, the marketer is complying with 'soft opt-in' rules. By contrast, in the EU countries adopting stricter enforcement of this ruling, the exemption applies only where an 'actual sale has taken place', rather than where there were 'negotiations for a sale'. For example, when a UK company runs a prize promotion, sponsors can collect competition entrant data and apply the 'soft opt-in' on the basis of 'negotiation for a sale'. But, in Germany and The Netherlands, marketers can use the soft opt-in only if an actual sale had occurred.[27]

As the global marketplace shrinks and more business is conducted across borders and via the Internet, marketers must increase their knowledge of the laws and regulations governing sales and marketing communications practices in other countries. They have to be aware of how they differ across the countries in which they operate, when designing cross-border communications programmes.

Beyond understanding and abiding by these laws and regulations, companies should ensure that they communicate honestly and fairly with consumers and resellers. Although most marketers may comply with laws and follow the industry's codes of practice, many may not fulfil their legal obligations as much as they should. A minority may even wilfully ignore the law and conduct illegal practices. However, in the long run, socially responsible marketers will reap the benefits of self-restraint and keeping on the right side of the law. They will avoid the 'evolutionary war' that will develop between marketers and customers. Consider the following scenario:[28]

Technology has spawned new channels for communication messages to reach customers and new ways to invade their privacy. In response, customers have set up defences to guard against marketers' unsolicited approaches – they have anti-spam software and pop-up blockers on their PCs; they edit out the ads on personal video recorders; they screen out unwanted phone calls using telephone preference services and call minder systems. Marketers find ways round these defences such as the use of anti-anti-pop-up blockers. As the battle increases, the law intervenes to restrain marketers' advance. Marketers continue to find loopholes. In turn, the law steps in more strongly. Experts argue that something must be done. Marketers have the option of working even harder to circumvent the legal obstacles in their path or they can self-regulate more effectively in the hope that short-term restraint may lead to longer-term freedom.

Reviewing the concepts

In this chapter, we learnt how companies use integrated marketing communications (IMC) to communicate customer value. Modern marketing calls for more than just creating customer value by developing a good product, pricing it attractively and making it available to target customers. Companies also must clearly and persuasively *communicate* that value to current and prospective customers. To do this, they must blend five promotion mix tools, guided by a well-designed and implemented integrated marketing communications strategy.

1. Define the five promotion tools and discuss the factors that must be considered in shaping the overall promotion mix

A company's total *promotion mix* – also called its *marketing communications mix* – consists of the specific blend of *advertising, personal selling, sales promotion, public relations* and *direct-marketing* tools that the company uses to persuasively communicate customer value and build customer relationships. Advertising includes any paid form of non-personal presentation and promotion of ideas, goods or services by an identified sponsor. In contrast, public relations focuses on building good relations with the company's various publics by obtaining favourable unpaid publicity. Personal selling is any form of personal presentation by the firm's sales force for the purpose of making sales and building customer relation-ships. Firms use sales promotion to provide short-term incentives to encourage the purchase or sale of a product or service. Finally, firms seeking immediate response from targeted individual customers use non-personal direct-marketing tools to communicate with customers.

2. Discuss the process and advantages of integrated marketing communications in communicating customer value

Recent shifts towards targeted or one-to-one marketing, coupled with advances in informa-tion and communications technology, have had a dramatic impact on marketing communica-tions. As marketing communicators adopt richer but more fragmented media and promotion mixes to reach their diverse markets, they risk creating a communications hodgepodge for consumers. To prevent this, more companies are adopting the concept of *integrated marketing communications* (*IMC*). Guided by an overall IMC strategy, the company works out the roles that the various promotional tools will play and the extent to which each will be used. It carefully coordinates the promotional activities and the timing of when major campaigns take place. Finally, to help implement its integrated marketing strategy, the company appoints a marketing communications director who has overall responsibility for the company's communications efforts.

3. Outline the steps in developing effective marketing communications

In preparing marketing communications, the communicator's first task is to *identify the target audience* and its characteristics. Next, the communicator has to determine the *communication objectives* and define the response sought, be it *awareness, knowledge, liking, preference*, *conviction* or *purchase*. Then a *message* should be constructed with an effective content and structure. *Media* must be selected, for both personal and non-personal communication. The communicator must find highly credible sources to deliver messages. Finally, the communicator must collect *feedback* by watching how much of the market becomes aware, tries the product and is satisfied in the process.

4. Explain the methods for setting the promotion budget and factors that affect the design of the promotion mix

The company has to decide how much to spend for promotion. The most popular approaches are to spend what the company can afford, to use a percentage of sales, to base promotion on competitors' spending, or to base it on an analysis and costing of the communication objectives and tasks.

The company has to divide the *promotion budget* among the major tools to create the *promotion mix*. Companies can pursue a *push* or a *pull* promotional strategy, or a combination of the two. The best specific blend of promotion tools depends on the type of product/market, the buyer's readiness stage and the product life-cycle stage.

People at all levels of the organisation must be aware of the many legal and ethical issues surrounding marketing communications. Companies must work hard and proactively at communicating openly, honestly and agreeably with their customers and resellers.

Discussing the concepts

1. Many companies are shifting their emphasis from mass marketing to more targeted marketing, resulting in the use of a richer mixture of promotion tools, coupled with advances in information and communications technology, to communicate customer value. Discuss the reasons for this shift in marketing communications philosophy. Using practical examples, show how an integrated marketing communications strategy might enable marketers to more effectively reach target customers.

2. Outline the elements of the communications process. Why is it important for marketers to understand these elements? Your answer should also consider the implications for the promotion mix.

3. The marketing communicator can use one or more types of appeals or themes to produce a desired response from target customers.

   (a) What are these types of appeals?

   (b) Provide an example of each type of appeal – you should use real examples of advertisements found in magazines.

   (c) For each advert, explain why the communicator chose to use the particular appeal.

4. David Beckham, Tiger Woods, Lewis Hamilton and numerous other well-known sports personalities have had a huge impact on advertising and endorsements. Explain the positive and negative consequences of using celebrity figures to promote a company's products or services. What impact does the use of celebrity endorsers have on the average person?

5. Explain how a brand manager for Aquafresh toothpaste might use each of the common methods for setting total promotion budgets. What is the preferred method? Explain.

Applying the concepts

1. Find and describe examples of promotional activities that illustrate communicators' use of narrowcasting, non-traditional communications or advertising and innovative media technologies.

   (a) Make a list of these promotional activities. How effective are each of these activities in promoting a company's product or service? Illustrate using practical examples.

   (b) How might advertising in new media environments such as in-game (video game) advertising and online, real-time advertising targeted at online video gamers, offer unique opportunities for marketers to practise integrated marketing communications? How might it appeal to marketers when considering buyer-readiness stages?

   (c) What social responsibility concerns might such forms of communications raise?

2. Select a company that has been running an ad campaign for its product or service. Find relevant ads in magazines and other print media (e.g., newspapers) that contain print advertising for the brand you have selected. Where possible, get a copy of the ads from current and back issues of the magazines and the printed material you have accessed. Visit the company's website and find the online advertisements for the selected product or service brand. Now examine the traditional print and online ads closely.

   (a) How consistent are the message content, structure and format?

   (b) Which response(s) is the campaign seeking to obtain: awareness, knowledge, liking, preference, conviction or purchase?

   (c) Do you think the ad campaign is successful in achieving the desired response? Why or why not?

Web resources

For additional classic case studies and Internet exercises, visit **www. pearsoned.co.uk/ kotler**

References

1. Marc S. Blevins, *Hard Sell* (Bloomington, IN: AuthorHouse, 2005).

2. Also visit the company's website, www.rolls-roycemotorcars.com, and that of their London showroom (www.rrmc-london.com).

3. The first four of these definitions are adapted from Peter D. Bennett, *The AMA Dictionary of Marketing Terms*, 2nd edn (New York: McGraw-Hill, 1995); others are from www.marketingpower.com/live/ mg-dictionary.php?, accessed August 2006.

4. Andrew Edgecliffe-Johnson and Emiko Terazono, 'Fight for the YouTube generation', *Financial Times* (2 May 2007), p. 5.

5. Figures from 'Advertising expenditure by country & medium', *The European Marketing Pocket Book 2007*, World Advertising Research Center (WARC) in association with Nielsen Media Research, p. 35.

6. 'The online ad attack', *The Economist* (30 April 2005), p. 64.

7. Mike Shaw, 'Direct your advertising dollars away from TV at your own risk', *Advertising Age* (27 February 2006), p. 29. Also see John Consoli, '2005 spending rose 4.2 percent, says Nielsen Monitor-Plus', *MediaWeek* (15 March 2006), accessed at www.mediaweek.com; and Claire Atkinson, 'Measured network TV ad spending fell last year', *Advertising Age* (6 March 2006), accessed at www.adage.com.

8. Information on advertising expenditure of global advertisers in Europe from *The European Marketing Pocket Book 2007*, *op. cit.*, pp. 22–31.

9. Jack Neff, 'P&G chief: We need new model now', *Advertising Age* (15 November 2004), pp. 1, 53.

10. Don E. Schultz, 'New media, old problem: Keep Marcom integrated', *Marketing News* (29 March 1999), p. 11.

11. Don E. Schultz and Philip J. Kitchen, *Communication Globally: An integrated marketing approach* (New York: McGraw-Hill, 2000); Don E. Schultz and Heidi Schultz, *IMC: The next generation* (New York: McGraw-Hill, 2004); also see David Picton and Amanda Broderick, *Integrated Marketing Communications*, 3nd edn (New York: Financial Times Management, 2008).

12. Laurence Green (ed.), *Advertising Works 15. Proving the effectiveness of marketing communications* (Henley-on-Thames: Institute of Practitioners in Advertising and World Advertising Research Center, 2007), Ch. 16, pp. 249–63; David Murphy, 'The integrated approach', *Marketing Business* (May 2003), pp. 15–19.

13. Quote from Ian Sclater, 'Flushed with success', *The Marketer*, Issue 16 (September 2005), p. 27.

14. Information on British Heart Foundation anti-smoking and the BBC TV licensing ad campaigns from Laurence Green (ed.), *Advertising Works 15, op. cit.*, Chs. 9 and 15, pp. 127–44 and 243–8; for more on fear appeals, see Punam Anand Keller and Lauren Goldberg Block, 'Increasing the persuasiveness of fear appeals: The effect of arousal and elaboration', *Journal of Consumer Research* (March 1996), pp. 448–59.

15. For more on communications and consumer behaviour, see Leon G. Schiffman and Leslie Lazar Kanuk, *Consumer Behavior*, 9th edn (Upper Saddle River, NJ: Prentice Hall, 2006), Chs. 8 and 9; Alan G. Sawyer and Daniel J. Howard, 'Effects of omitting conclusions in advertisements to involved and uninvolved audiences', *Journal of Marketing Research* (November 1991), pp. 467–74; and Cornelia Pechmann, 'Predicting when two-sided ads will be more effective than one-sided ads: the role of correlational and correspondent inferences', *Journal of Marketing* (November 1992), pp. 441–53.

16. Anna Ronay, 'Paint your brand', *The Marketer*, Issue 16 (September 2005), pp. 6–9; Jamie Seaton, 'Marrying culture and colour', *op. cit.*, p.15; Ian Sclater, 'Flushed with success', *op. cit.*, pp. 25–7; information also from www.cim.co.uk/knowledgehub (Chartered Institute of Marketing) and www.colorcom.com/why_color.html (Institute for Colour Research), both accessed August 2007.

17. 'Lights, cameras, brands', *The Economist* (29 October 2005), pp. 81–2.

18. 'Building buzz', *The Economist* (7 April 2007), p. 76.

19. For more on advertising spending by company and industry, see 'Ad to sales ratios, 2005 edition', *Advertising Age* (1 March 2006), accessed at http://adage.com/datacenter/article.php?article_id=106936.

20. For more on setting promotion budgets, see W. Ronald Lane, Karen Whitehill King and J. Thomas Russell, *Kleppner's Advertising Procedure*, 16th edn (Upper Saddle River, NJ: Prentice Hall, 2005), Ch. 6; and Kissan Joseph and Vernon J. Richardson, 'Free cash flow, agency costs, and the affordability method of advertising budgeting', *Journal of Marketing* (January 2002), pp. 94–107.

21. David Allen, 'Excessive use of the mirror', *Management Accounting* (June 1996), p. 12; Laura Petrecca, '4A's will study financial returns on ad spending', *Advertising Age* (April 1997), pp. 3, 52; Dana W. Hayman and Don E. Schultz, 'How much should you spend on advertising?', *Advertising Age* (26 April 1999), p. 32.

22. Jack Trout, 'Prices: Simple guidelines to get them right', *Journal of Business Strategy* (November–December 1998), pp. 13–16.

23. Based on Matthew P. Gonring, 'Putting integrated marketing communications to work today', *Public Relations Quarterly* (Fall 1994), pp. 45–8. Also see Philip Kotler, *Marketing Management*, 12th edn (Upper Saddle River, NJ: Prentice Hall, 2006), pp. 558–61.

24. Information about Coca-Cola's joint efforts with the United Nations from www.thecoca-colacompany.com, accessed July 2007.

25. Information from www.tropicalforestfoundation.org/about.html, accessed August 2006.

26. Information from www.sendasinger.com, accessed July 2007; see also advertisement in *Financial Times Special Report. Corporate Citizenship & Philanthropy* (5 July 2007), p. 11.

27. Stephen Groom, 'You've never had it so good', *The Marketer*, Issue 17 (October 2005), pp. 10–13; information on marketing and the law from 'Professional marketing standards', The Chartered Institute of Marketing, www.cim.co.uk, accessed July 2007, and 'The long arm of the law: marketers and legislation', *Shape the Agenda* (The Chartered Institute of Marketing, 2005), accessed at www.shapetheagenda.com, July 2007.

28. Extracted from 'The evolutionary war', in 'The long arm of the law', *op. cit.*

Company case 15 Absolut Vodka: Samantha and the Hunk on the Level

PONTUS ALENROTH, ROBERT BJORNSTROM, JOAKIM ERIKSSON AND THOMAS HELGESSON*
Halstad University, Sweden

With sales in 126 markets globally, Absolut Vodka is now the third largest spirit in the world. V&S of Stockholm, Sweden, is the international brand owner and manufacturer of ABSOLUT VODKA as well as Plymouth Gin, Danzka Vodka, Level Vodka, ABSOLUT CUT and Fris Vodka. Absolut's market showing is surprising given it comes from Sweden, a country with highly restrictive licensing laws that do not allow spirits to be advertised. However, in the last two decades, Absolut has grown from being a little-known brand made in a country with no reputation in the spirits market to the world's leading premium brand of vodka.

When Lars Olsson Smith, Sweden's 'King of Vodka', introduced a new kind of 'Absolut Rent Brännvin' (Absolutely Pure Vodka) in 1879, little did he realise it would become the world's leading premium vodka a century later. In the nineteenth century the self-made spirits tycoon introduced a revolutionary rectification/continuous distillation method, which is still used in producing Absolut Vodka. The result was a clear, high-quality vodka, free from dangerous and bad-tasting by-products. As its label shows, Absolut Vodka trades on its heritage:

ABSOLUT
Country of Sweden

VODKA

This superb vodka
was distilled from grain grown
in the rich fields of Sweden.
It has been produced by the famous
old distilleries of Shus
in accordance with more than
400 years of Swedish tradition.
Vodka has been sold under the name
Absolut since 1879.

The bottle continues to be the centrepiece in campaigns like 'ABSOLUT MAGIC'. This ad reinforces the vodka's aura of exclusiveness, timelessness and sheer magic.

Absolut's website (www.absolut.com) allows every aspect of the label's claims to be explored.

Despite its long traditions, Absolut Vodka's success was late in coming. In 1979, Vin & Sprit (now called V&S), the Swedish state-owned alcohol monopoly, decided to export the vodka to the US. After objections from American authorities, the name Absolutely Pure Vodka was changed to Absolut Vodka. Consultants had surveyed the US spirits market and found 'a clearly discernible consumer trend towards "white spirits" [such as vodka, gin and white rum] as opposed to "brown spirits" [brandy, whisky and dark rum]; white spirits are seen as being purer and healthier.' V&S had no marketing or product design experience, so it employed outside teams of marketing and management experts to create a product for the newly discovered market.

The design of the bottle was recognised at an early stage as crucial to success. Absolut's Gunnar Broman had the idea when he saw some eighteenth-century medicine bottles in a Stockholm antique shop. The bottles were elegant, different, simple and very Swedish. In reality, vodka was sold as a medicine in similar bottles during the eighteenth and nineteenth centuries. Broman argued his case for more than a year until the bottle was finally approved and the manufacturing problems were overcome. The resulting Absolut bottle was very different from that of competitors. It was considered a masterpiece in glass design: a timeless shape with fine lines and the exceptionally clear glass that distinguish Absolut from other premium vodkas.

Absolut's acceptance in the US market did not come easy. When Absolut's team first presented their ideas to New York agency NW Ayer, some of the agency's staff were thrilled but most shook their heads, thinking 'who wants to drink a vodka from Sweden anyway?'. But, after many meetings, they agreed on the theme of 'Absolut Country of Sweden Vodka'. The bottle should be made of clear glass with silver text on it. They tested their idea by putting their bottles among the other big brands to see how it looked.

One of the people working with the Absolut account, Myron Poloner, fell in love with the bottle. He could sit and watch the 'medicine bottle' for hours and one night it struck him. The bottle should have no label at all. You should be able to see right through it. The vodka should be a premium vodka for well-educated people with a high income who could afford to eat out. They liked to hold parties at their home and to show off.

Attempts to sell the idea to US distributors met with the same cool reaction as the early meetings with the ad agency. 'Who has ever heard of a Swedish vodka? And it doesn't have a label. It'll disappear on the shelf. It will never sell!'

Carillon Importers Ltd, based in Manhattan, had a different view. Carillon's leader, Al Singer, accepted 'the challenge' the moment he saw the product. However, the company had only one salesman, Michel Roux, but he was to play a leading role in the success of Absolut Vodka. Singer did not want to work with a big New York

agency, preferring instead Martin Landey Arlow. Landey and Singer also wanted to change the bottle, making it taller and with a thicker bottom. One day, as a joke, one of Broman's employees put a coin on the bottle's shoulder. The Americans loved it, so his staff decided to create a seal. They tried shields, swords, guns, naked women, men's heads, etc. Broman's office was coincidentally located in Absolut's founder Lars Olsson Smith's old house. While there he thought, why not put 'The king of vodka's' head on the seal? The president of Vin & Sprit, Lars Lindmark, decided that the ABSOLUT VODKA letters should be blue for the 80 proof bottles and red for the 100 proof ones. And so the bottle changed to that we know today.

Unfortunately, Martin Landey had to stop acting for Carillon because of a conflict of interest with another, more profitable client in the spirits business. TBWA, another New York agency, heard about Carillion, contacted Singer and got the account. Geoff Hayes and Graham Turner were assigned to Absolut. One evening Hayes was sketching while watching TV. Trying to find a symbol of purity and simplicity, he made a halo. Soon his floor was covered with different ad-ideas, all with a humorous twist. The next day, he showed his ads to Turner. They changed the name for the Absolut Purity ad to Absolut Perfection. Absolut Heaven showed the bottle with wings. Fifteen minutes later they had a dozen different Absolut 'something' ads.

The Absolut, Carillon and TBWA staff loved the idea. 'All advertising should centre around the bottle, the product should not be identified with any particular lifestyle, and the approach should have a timeless yet contemporary feel to it.' Every advertisement has two features in common: the depiction of an Absolut bottle and a two- or three-word caption beginning with the word 'Absolut'. It hit the US market in 1979 and Absolut soon became the biggest-selling imported vodka brand.

The innovative way of marketing Absolut contrasted directly with that of the established brands. As David Wachsman points out, the advertising of spirits in the United States used 'one of three formats: a roomful of exceedingly happy people, a celebrity holding a glass, or old-fashioned settled family life'. Then came 'Absolut Perfection' and hundreds of different ads.

Absolut Vodka is a highly premium-priced vodka and therefore has an aura of up-market exclusiveness. Considering the target market and the early magazine ads (Absolut Perfection, etc.), a tie-up with the arts world was inevitable. The first step in this direction was taken in 1985 when the New York cult pop artist

Andy Warhol was commissioned to paint the Absolut Vodka bottle. Today Absolut cooperates with artists and designers in all the contemporary arts. 'The purity and clarity' of the product, says Göran Lundquist, the then President of The Absolut Company (now V&S Absolut Spirits), a part of the V&S Group, is a 'timeless source of inspiration' (the current President of V&S Absolut Spirits and CEO of the V&S Group is Bengt Baron). There are now over 3,000 works in the Absolut collection. All feature some aspect of the bottle or its label. Like other very successful campaigns, the marketing is so sensational that the product receives a huge amount of free media exposure. In Absolut's case this has even occurred in markets, like Sweden, that did not allow alcohol advertising.

Absolut's unconventional marketing has generated demand for its ads – the advertising agency receives thousands of requests for ad reprints. The ads have become a modern icon. Besides winning the Effie and the Kelly awards, Absolut was honoured with an induction into America's Marketing Hall of Fame. That seal of approval confirmed Absolut's success and impact on the American lifestyle, especially since the only other brands that have received such an honour are Coke and Nike. 'Absolut Art' is also achieving international recognition. Warhol's and other key US works, together with others specially commissioned from French artists Bosser and Delprat, were shown at Paris's prestigious Lavignes-Bastille Gallery. From there, the exhibition moved to London's Royal College of Art, where new works by British artists, including Peter Blake, were added. The exhibition then travelled to Berlin, Munich and Milan. Over 350 artists and fashion designers have now produced Absolut ads. Their cult status is reflected in home3.swipenet.se and www.absolutad.org, websites dedicated to Absolut art.

An ingenious bottle and creative marketing played a crucial part in the Absolut saga, but V&S's distribution partnership was also crucial to its success. However, Absolut had to bid farewell to Carillon, its original distributor, in 1995 and teamed up with Seagrams. After a long and fruitful relationship, Absolut had outgrown Carillon. In 2001, following the sale of the spirit division of Seagrams, V&S set up its New York-based American subsidiary, The Absolut Spirits Company, which is the importer of ABSOLUT in the USA. At the same time, V&S formed a new distribution setup for the US with Future Brands, a joint venture between V&S and Jim Beam Brands.

The Absolut Akademi aims to create 'a competitive edge through people': 'The goal is to build a quality culture around a quality product.' Another tool in marketing is the *Absolut Reflexions* magazine, which is distributed in all markets. Used as a PR tool, *Absolut Reflexions* spreads news of the brand, its advertising and activities to consumers all over the world.

V&S followed its Absolut's success in the US with attacks on the European, Asian and Pacific markets. Compared with the United States, the European market is slow-growing, fragmented and conservative. Europe has many leisure drinking cultures, but these vary from region to region and there are well-established traditions everywhere. Except for countries where vodka is the national drink, the European vodka market is under-developed. Vodka is drunk by only 4 per cent of consumers in Europe, compared to 21 per cent of Americans. To repeat its American success, Absolut will need clever and innovative strategies tailored specifically for each of Europe's submarkets. V&S is bullish about Absolut's chances in Europe. 'We have built up a wide experience of operating abroad and we are confident we can meet the competition', says V&S's Margareta Nyström. The company believes that wherever there is a demand for premium vodka, Absolut Vodka is the optimal choice. 'Absolut Vodka proves itself time and time again as more than just a fine vodka: it's an idea. And nothing can stop an idea whose time has come.'

After years as a challenger in the spirits market, Absolut is the leading brand that many are following. V&S are defending its position by extending its product range by acquisition and new product launches. Early 2004 saw the launch of Level Vodka in the US. V&S's Carl Horton, president and chief executive of The Absolut Spirits Company, explains: 'Level is our long-awaited entry into the vibrant super-premium vodka segment.' Level aims for a perfect balance of smoothness and character, which is achieved by a unique combination of two distillation methods: 'One taste and consumers will see it's a completely new level of vodka.'

While attacking the super-premium market with Level Vodka, V&S combined the iconic brand with the equally iconic *Sex in the City* series. In a campaign reminiscent of the impact of the early Absolut ads, in the 'Hop, Skip and a Week' episode of *Sex in the City*, Samantha Jones makes a deal for her latest lover to appear in a fictional ABSOLUT HUNK ad where he is nude but for a suggestively placed Absolut Vodka bottle. Absolut paid nothing for the 'product placement', but both *Sex in the City* and Absolut gained hugely from the publicity surrounding the 'appearance'. Fiction became reality as the ABSOLUT HUNK ad appeared all over New York City, including on a huge Times Square billboard. ABSOLUT HUNK is now the new 'it' drink in New York bars.

Modern, controversial and arty it might be, but is it marketing? Absolut's advertising is a style icon. The brand has one of the ad industry's most admired and most consistently imaginative marketing campaigns and ads themselves have become collector's items, selling for as much as €40 for a page torn out of an old glossy magazine! Despite all the accolades, it lingers as the world's number 3 premium spirits brand by volume, behind Diageo's Smirnoff vodka that has overtaken Bacardi rum as the world top selling spirit.

Is style still enough? Competition from all directions is ferocious. Some of the excitement has gone out of the market. Absolut is now mainstream rather than cult, and competition within the industry is fiercer: around 90 new vodka products were introduced into the US alone between 1999 and 2002. Smirnoff is now bolstered by the success of its Smirnoff Ice ready-to-drink, a segment that Absolut was very slow to recognise. Always pitching itself as upscale and 'premium', since 2000 a new range of 'super-premium' vodkas, such as Belvedere and Grey Goose, have attacked the market, positioning themselves above even Absolut. Grey Goose saw its sales grow to almost 2 million cases even before Bacardi moved in and purchased it. Absolut now finds itself sandwiched between two giants in the drinks industry, the all-powerful Diageo's mass-selling Smirnoff and Bacardi's premium Grey Goose. But Absolut also has a big new friend, since many of the world's leading drinks makers, Bacardi, Diageo, Pernod Ricard and Anheuser-Busch, as well as private equity firms, are salivating over the

chance to buy V&S, which has been put up for sale by the Swedish government.

Questions

1. What is the foundation of Absolut Vodka's success? Is it the vodka, the bottle, the distribution or the promotion?

2. How does Absolut's marketing build upon American trends in the late 1980s and early 1990s? Is Absolut a fashion product that will decline with the trends?

3. Do you believe that Absolut Vodka 'is an idea whose time has come' and that nothing can stop its success?

4. V&S's European campaign uses ads in the same style as those that have been so successful in the United States. Do you think the US approach will work in other regions?

5. Since Absolut Vodka is such a lifestyle product, would you recommend that V&S should extend the brand into other markets in the same way as Virgin has extended into video games, PCs, cola and vodka?

6. Absolut's successful advertising has benefited greatly from the publicity it generated. Can advertising campaigns be designed to create such media attention or is their success just good fortune?

SOURCES: Adapted from the following: Andrew Edgecliff-Johnson, 'Drinks disposal leave Seagram with hangover', *Financial Times* (20 November 2000), p. 36; John Thornhill, 'Trying to make selling spirits seriously easy', *Financial Times* (1 September 2000), p. 16; 'Drink ads box clever', *The Irish Times* (23 August 2003); 'Level Vodka to launch nationally in 2004', *Business Wire* (6 November 2003); David Ibison, 'Fortune urges state backing for V&S bid', *Financial Times* (16 August 2007); Richard Wachman, Business & Media: Opinion: 'Market forces', *The Observer* (26 August 2007); www.absolut.com.

*The authors wrote the original case 'Absolut Vodka: Absolutely Successful' on which this case is based.

It is far easier to write ten passable sonnets than to write an advertisement that will take in a few thousand of the uncritical buying public.

ALDOUS HUXLEY

Advertising and public relations

Mini Contents List

◀ SOURCE: Carlsberg, the official beer of Glastonbury.

'All that's left in any case
Is advertising space ooooohh'

Robbie Williams, 'Advertising Space', on 'Intensive Care', Chrysalis, B000B5UL7G, 2005

Previewing the concepts

In Chapter 15, we looked at overall integrated marketing communications planning. In this and the next few chapters, we'll dig more deeply into the specific marketing communications tools. In this chapter, we will explore the mass communications tools – advertising and public relations. These are also largely non-personal forms of communication and promotion. In the next chapter, we will examine personal selling and sales promotions, which play an important role in directly influencing or encouraging purchase or sale of a product.

After reading this chapter, you should be able to:

1. Define the roles of advertising and public relations in the promotion mix.
2. Describe the main decisions involved in developing an advertising programme.
3. Define the role of public relations in the promotion mix.
4. Explain how companies use public relations to communicate with and influence important publics.

We start with a situation that often faces an advertising agency – the desire of a manufacturer to revitalise a tired old product, in this case *Monopoly*, a board game that almost everyone already owns, and at a time when games are associated more with TV game shows or computer games. Board games, these days, are for the bored. Or are they for you?

Prelude case Bored? Let's play Monopoly

In 1904 Elizabeth Magie patented and sold what was to become her *Landlord's Game* with which she hoped to demonstrate the unfairness of monopolies. By the early 1930s a version of the game called Monopoly was created, using contributions from several players, and patented by Charles Darow in 1935. As counters, he used charms from a bracelet. With its odd counters, street names, park bench and jail, it was much like the version of Monopoly sold today. So far, the game that Elizabeth Magie invented to explain one of the evils of business has been played by 750 million people and is 'the most played [commercial] board game in the world.'[1]

The London version of the game was launched by Hasbro in 1935. To celebrate its 70th anniversary, Hasbro launched a new limited edition of the game – Monopoly Here & Now, depicting 21st century London. The company's overall marketing objective was to achieve a 15 per cent increase in total sales value of Monopoly by the end of 2005. This would be obtained by:

- selling all the Monopoly Here & Now limited edition stock by the end of 2005;
- increasing sales in the summer season by 30 per cent year-on-year, thus breaking the entrenched seasonality of board game sales – key sales occur in the Christmas shopping months of November and December;
- creating a 'buzz' around Monopoly;
- broadening the appeal of the brand beyond young families.

Barriers to overcome

However, Hasbro faced a number of barriers in meeting these ambitious sales growth targets. The vast majority of families already owned a set of the game. It would be difficult to persuade people to pay a premium for a game they already own. Fewer families have the time or interest in playing board games these days. The lack of category interest beyond the family target meant that the limited edition game must reach a broader audience than families.

Hasbro's market research showed that people had fond memories of playing the game, supported by consumers' narratives of playing strategy, how they sneaked extra notes from the bank when other players were not looking, and the humorous Community Chest cards. But less positive memories were also uncovered: the game is complicated, takes too long to play and is boring, especially when you're losing. When presented with the updated limited edition game, many respondents became much more enthusiastic. The new board game depicted London in the 21st century, with updated locations, modern game pieces and revised property prices. The research suggested that the key to creating marketing buzz was to centre on how London has changed, and then to get people to discover the new board game for themselves and to reignite their passion for

Monopoly by getting them to play it, rather than merely associating it with their childhood days.

These ideas provided the basis for a radical experiential communications campaign to reinvigorate Monopoly. The approach adopted by London agency DDB was to encourage people to actively engage with brand communications. For one month, the streets of London were turned into Monopoly Live, a giant, real-life game of Monopoly Here & Now. London black cabs were recruited and equipped with GPS transmitters to act as life-size playing pieces. A host of prizes were offered and anyone in the country could sign on to play via a dedicated website.

Pulling it off

Consumers were able to participate in Monopoly Live by visiting www.monopolylive.com. They could join in every day, with each game lasting 24 hours. The event lasted one month. Each player was given £15 million of virtual Monopoly money at the beginning of the game. The player spent his or her money on property and strategically placed apartments and hotels. Finally, each player selected a playing piece. The agency had recruited 18 London black taxis to act as playing pieces – three taxis each for a total of six play pieces. As the taxis went around their daily business, their movements gained or lost players' virtual money over 24 hours as their passing locations were logged by the GPS transmitters.

Prizes were awarded every day of the competition to persuade people to sign up and play in the live event. The grand prize – having the player's mortgage/rent paid for a whole year – was announced by a prize draw at the end of the event! The condition for entry was one entry to the draw for every £1 million the player made.

The integrated communications push

The conventional communications approach in the toy industry is TV advertising, as retailers need to be assured that the product will be adequately supported. In the case of Monopoly Here & Now, the advertisers took a radical approach in placing the brand experience – Monopoly Live – at the core of the campaign.

On 12 June 2005, teaser stories covered in the Sunday press were used to build up to launch day, 16 June, when the Monopoly Here & Now site went live concomitant with the game going on sale. The launch was supported by a 'win a trip to Philadelphia' prize draw promotion and a launch event and charity sale with Cherie Booth (wife of Britain's former Prime Minister Tony Blair). In the days following, press coverage from the launch event gave Monopoly Here & Now further publicity, with GMTV Kids *Toonatik* coverage and competition and a 'play

Monopoly at school' week to raise money for Monopoly's charity, Shelter, creating further appeal for the event. The week commencing 20 June 2005 saw the launch of Monopoly Live, aided by online advertising and a Yahoo! home page banner link to monopolylive.com. In addition, TV advertising (20-second executions) featured across major networks including Channel 4, Five and GMTV, and in satellite daytime and selected prime time viewing hours (e.g., 'Big Brother' eviction night). Adding to the buzz were radio advertising (30-second executions) and competitions (win a game) on local radio across the nation.

Public relations (PR) was leveraged to trigger debates around the changes to London on the Here & Now game board as reflected in the following letter to a local newspaper:

> I was amused to read that in the new version of Monopoly devised to reflect the changing face of London, they have replaced the railway stations with London City Airport and Stansted, and Bond Street has been axed for the King's Road. But what have they done about free parking? (Tom Byers, W1; *Evening Standard* letters page, January 2005)

Last, but not least, as 'playing pieces' the taxis provided an outdoor presence which brought the idea to life. Says one respondent in DDB's qualitative market research, 'The most exciting thing was seeing a Monopoly cab when I was in Soho, it made it come to life and all the more exciting.'

How it worked

Both TV and radio advertising were used to build awareness of the new game and entice people to go online and discover the new board game for themselves. According to quantitative research undertaken for Hasbro, TV advertising was the most significant driver of the core audience – mums – to the website. The online advertising was very effective at directing players through to the monopolylive.com website to play the game, delivering 240,552 visits, resulting in 43,597 registered players. PR's role in alerting people to the new board game and getting them to discuss the updates was also gauged to be a great success, with some £3.7 million worth of value created by the planned PR and word-of-mouth generated by the sheer intrigue of Monopoly Live. The participating taxi drivers also became mouthpieces for the event. Post-campaign research showed that they frequently chatted to passengers about the promotion, thus building awareness and intrigue with tourists asking to take pictures of the cab.

The event captured the imagination of 'bloggers' who were attracted to the scale of the live event and the novelty of using GPS tagging of the London cabs. Those who played Monopoly Live wrote about the game in several hundred blogs and websites during the campaign, contributing further to the online buzz as many more joined in the form of chat forum discussions. Other online media sites, such as wired.com, also picked up on the story, featuring the monopolylive.com web address on their own websites. Before long, offline or traditional media were also covering the story in detail. This ripple effect

sustained the conversation value among media and players alike, while fuelling the buzz throughout the event.

Overall, the communications campaign was a tremendous success. Over a million unique users visited the monopolylive.com site in one month. A total of 189,699 played the game an average of three times. A hardcore of (older) players played every day.

Paybacks?

With sales value of £1,525,546, Monopoly Here & Now became the best-selling family game of 2005, followed in second place by Monopoly Classic (£1,303,243). Here & Now stocks sold out just two weeks before Christmas. The campaign not only created a buzz around Monopoly in its 70th anniversary year, it also succeeded in engaging and inducing a broader audience to buy Monopoly. Overall, Monopoly sales by the end of 2005 were up 35 per cent on the previous year, double Hasbro's initial sales target. It overcame the summer seasonal slump, with sales of Monopoly board games (Classic, Simpsons, Star Wars) up 200 per cent year-on-year, which was carried through to Christmas.

The Monopoly Here & Now board game was launched in many European markets at the same time, but the Monopoly Live event was only run in the UK. The play Monopoly Live campaign generated an additional £1.5 million in sales value, compared to a total campaign cost of £600,000 including media and production. In addition, the campaign created long-lasting value to Hasbro in the following ways: modernising Monopoly in the eyes of consumers and retailers; creating a database of 156,115 opted-in consumers for Hasbro's future marketing activities; motivating Hasbro partners to provide free prizes and incentives to enhance sales promotion programmes – £30,000 in free prize funds was donated by partners and sponsors; the value of game-enhancing text messages sent by players to Hasbro – in excess of £5,000 of text revenue were generated during the campaign; and the use of the UK event as a test market for Hasbro Global marketing.

Is advertising dead? Certainly not. The success of the Monopoly Here & Now campaign shows how in today's cluttered communications environment, novel approaches to consumer engagement can make a difference![1]

Questions

1. Who are the major target audiences for Monopoly board games?

2. What are the major issues to be considered by Hasbro and its advertising agency in designing a launch campaign for Monopoly Here & Now?

3. Drawing on the key lessons to be learnt from Here & Now's launch campaign, to what extent is the idea transferable to other European markets? What are the implications for the development and execution of such a campaign in these markets?

Introduction

Companies must do more than simply create customer value. As we gather from the prelude case, firms must clearly and persuasively communicate that value to target consumers. They must inform consumers about product or service benefits and carefully position these in consumers' minds. To do this, they must skilfully use the mass-promotion tools of *advertising* and *public relations*. Advertising involves communicating the company's or brand's value proposition by using paid media to inform, persuade and remind consumers. Public relations involves building good relations with various company publics – from consumers and the general public to the media, investor, donor and government publics. As with all of the promotion mix tools, advertising and public relations must be blended into the overall integrated marketing communications programme.

Advertising

Advertising can be traced back to the very beginnings of recorded history. Archaeologists working in the countries around the Mediterranean Sea have dug up signs announcing various events and offers. The Romans painted walls to announce gladiator fights, and the Phoenicians painted pictures promoting their wares on large rocks along parade routes. During the Golden Age in Greece, town criers announced the sale of cattle, crafted items and even cosmetics. An early 'singing commercial' went as follows: 'For eyes that are shining, for cheeks like the dawn. For beauty that lasts after girlhood is gone. For prices in reason, the woman who knows will buy her cosmetics from Aesclyptos.'

Modern advertising, however, is a far cry from these early efforts. In Europe, advertisers now run up an estimated annual advertising bill of approximately €91bn, while annual spend in the US is more than $271bn (€200bn); worldwide ad spending exceeds an estimated €443bn. Procter & Gamble, the world's largest advertiser, spent more than $7.9 billion worldwide in 2006.[2]

We define **advertising** as any paid form of non-personal presentation and promotion of ideas, goods or services through mass media such as newspapers, magazines, television or radio by an identified sponsor.

Although advertising is used mostly by business firms, a wide range of not-for-profit organisations, professionals and social agencies also use advertising to promote their causes to various target publics. In the UK, for example, total ad spend in 2005 within the government and public sector was £613m (€883m), making it the eighth highest spending category. Advertising is a good way to inform and persuade, whether the purpose is to sell Nokia mobile phones worldwide or to encourage smokers to give up the habit. Advertising is used in order to stimulate a response from the target audience. The response may be perceptual in nature: for example, the consumer develops specific views or opinions about the product or brand, or these feelings are altered by the ad. The response could be behavioural: for instance, the consumer buys the product or increases the amount that he or she buys.

Advertising—Any paid form of non-personal presentation and promotion of ideas, goods or services by an identified sponsor.

Important decisions in advertising

Marketing management must make four important decisions when developing an advertising programme (see Figure 16.1): setting advertising objectives, setting the advertising budget, developing advertising strategy (message decisions and media decisions) and evaluating advertising campaigns.

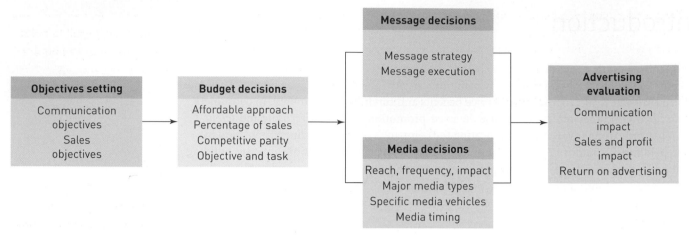

Figure 16.1 Main advertising decisions

Advertising objective—A specific communication task to be accomplished with a specific target audience during a specific period of time.

Informative advertising— Advertising used to inform consumers about a new product or feature and to build primary demand.

Setting advertising objectives

The first step is to set **advertising objective**. These objectives should be based on decisions about the target market, positioning and marketing mix, which define the job that advertising must do in the total marketing programme.

An advertising objective is a specific communication task to be accomplished with a specific target audience during a specific period of time. Advertising objectives can be classified by primary purpose – whether the aim is to inform, persuade or remind. Table 16.1 lists examples of each of these objectives.

Informative advertising is used heavily when introducing a new product category. In this case, the objective is to build primary demand. Thus producers of DVD players first informed consumers of the image quality and convenience benefits of the new product.

Table 16.1 Possible advertising objectives

Informative advertising	
• Communicating customer value	• Informing the market of a price change
• Telling the market about a new product	• Describing available services
• Explaining how the product works	• Correcting false impressions
• Suggesting new uses for a product	• Building a brand and company image
Persuasive advertising	
• Building brand preference	• Persuading customers to purchase now
• Encouraging switching to your brand	• Persuading customers to receive a sales call
• Changing customer perceptions of product attributes	• Convincing customers to tell others about the brand
Reminder advertising	
• Reminding customers that the product may be needed in the near future	• Keeping the product in customers' minds during off-seasons
• Maintaining customer relationships	• Reminding customers where to buy the product
• Maintaining top-of-mind product awareness	

Persuasive advertising becomes more important as competition increases. Here, the company's objective is to build selective demand. For example, once DVD players became established, Sony began trying to persuade consumers that *its* brand offered the best quality for their money.

Some persuasive advertising has become **comparison advertising** (sometimes called **'knocking copy'**), in which a company directly or indirectly compares its brand with one or more other brands:

> For example, in its classic comparative campaign, Avis, the car rental company, positioned itself against market-leading Hertz by claiming 'We try harder.' Virgin Atlantic's ad campaign for its Upper Class Suite reminds business-class travellers that its fully flat bed measures at least $7\frac{1}{2}$ inches longer and up to 13 inches wider than BA's Club World seat, hence making it 'the biggest boy in business class'.

There are potential dangers in using comparison advertising. As often happens with comparison advertising, both sides complain that the other's ads are misleading. All too often, such ads invite competitor responses, resulting in an advertising war that neither competitor can win.

In the EU, comparative advertising is allowed in some countries, but not in others. For example, its use is legal in the United Kingdom. In Belgium and Germany, however, the approach is regarded as a form of unfair competition. For example, a relatively harmless Carlsberg commercial with the tagline 'Probably the best lager in the world' could not be run in those countries because it implicitly identifies products offered by rivals. Similarly, Avis's 'We try harder' ad would not have been allowed in Germany because, although nobody is named, Hertz is presumed to be the only real competitor.

While there are ongoing efforts to harmonise EU rules on comparative advertising, in the meantime, advertisers in the region must be sensitive to individual country codes of practice and legislation. This style of communication will probably always exist in one form or another, as most advertising is essentially comparative – after all, the aim of the advertiser is to persuade the consumer to respond to one product offering rather than another.[3]

Reminder advertising is important for mature products as it helps to maintain customer relationships and keep consumers thinking about the product. Expensive Persil and Fairy Liquid television ads are often designed to build and maintain brand relationships rather than informing or persuading consumers to buy in the short run. Advertisers might also want to maintain customer relationships by assuring existing customers that they have made the right choice in buying the company's product. For example, car firms might use reminder advertising that depicts satisfied owners enjoying some special feature of their new car.

Advertising's goal is to move consumers through the buyer-readiness stages discussed in the previous chapter. Some reminder advertising is designed to move people to immediate action. For example, a local newspaper ad for a weekend sale encourages store visits. However, many of the other ads focus on building or strengthening long-term customer relationships. For example, a Nike television ad in which well-known athletes 'just do it' never directly asks for a sale. Instead, the goal is to somehow change the way the customers think or feel about the brand.

Setting the advertising budget

After determining its advertising objectives, the company next sets its *advertising budget* for each product. Four commonly used methods for setting promotion budgets were discussed in

Persuasive advertising—Advertising used to build selective demand for a brand by persuading consumers that it offers the best quality for their money.

Comparison advertising (or 'knocking copy')—Advertising that compares one brand directly or indirectly to one or more other brands.

Reminder advertising—Advertising used to maintain customer relationships and keep consumers thinking about a product.

Chapter 15. Here we discuss some specific factors that should be considered when setting the advertising budget:

- *Stage in the product life cycle.* A brand's advertising budget often depends on its stage in the product life cycle. New products typically need large advertising budgets to build awareness and to gain consumer trial. In contrast, mature brands usually require lower budgets as a ratio of sales.

- *Market share.* Market share also impacts the amount of advertising needed. Because building the market or taking market share from competitors requires larger advertising spending than does simply maintaining current share, low-share brands usually need more advertising spending as a percentage of sales.

- *Competition and clutter.* In a market with many competitors and high advertising clutter, a brand must be advertised more heavily to be noticed above the noise in the market.

- *Advertising frequency.* When many repetitions are needed to present the brand's message to consumers, the advertising budget must be larger.

- *Product differentiation.* Undifferentiated brands – those that closely resemble other brands in their product class (coffee, laundry detergents, chewing gum, beer, soft drinks) – may require heavy advertising to set them apart. When the product differs greatly from those of competitors, advertising can be used to point out the differences to consumers.

> " Large consumer companies use lots of image advertising without really knowing its effects. "

No matter what method is used, setting the advertising budget is no easy task. How does a company know whether it is spending the right amount? Some critics maintain that large consumer packaged-goods firms tend to overspend on advertising, while business-to-business (B2B) companies generally underspend on advertising. They claim that, on the one hand, the large consumer companies use lots of image advertising without really knowing its effects. They overspend as a form of 'insurance' against not spending enough. On the other hand, business advertisers tend to rely too heavily on their sales forces to bring in orders. They underestimate the power of company and product image in pre-selling to B2B customers. Thus they do not spend enough on advertising to build customer awareness and knowledge.

Some companies, including Procter & Gamble, Unilever and Coca-Cola, have built sophisticated statistical models to determine the relationship between promotional spending and brand sales, and to help determine the 'optimal investment' across various media. Still, because so many factors affect advertising effectiveness, some controllable and others not, measuring the results of advertising spending remains an inexact science. In most cases, managers must rely on large doses of judgement along with more quantitative analysis when setting advertising budgets.[4]

Developing advertising strategy

Advertising strategy covers two major elements: creating the advertising messages and selecting the advertising media. In the past, companies viewed media planning as secondary to the message-creation process. Many companies also developed messages and media independently. The creative department first created the advertisements, then the media department selected the best media for carrying these advertisements to the desired target audiences. Separation of the functions often caused friction between 'creatives' and media planners.

Today, however, media fragmentation, soaring media costs and more focused target marketing strategies have promoted the importance of the media planning function. In some cases, an advertising campaign might begin with a good message idea followed by the choice of appropriate media. In other cases, however, a campaign might begin with a good media opportunity,

ABSOLUT VODKA: media planners work with creatives to design ads targeted to specific media audiences. 'ABSOLUT BRAVO' appears in theatre playbills. 'ABSOLUT CHICAGO' targets the Windy City.

SOURCE: Reproduced by permission of V&S Vin & Sprit AB (publ). ABSOLUT country of Sweden logo, ABSOLUT, ABSOLUT bottle design and ABSOLUT calligraphy are trademarks owned by V&S Vin & Sprit AB, copyright © 2003 V&S Vin & Sprit AB (publ).

followed by advertisements designed to take advantage of that opportunity. Increasingly, companies are realising the benefits of planning these two important activities jointly. More and more advertisers are orchestrating a closer harmony between their messages and the media that deliver them. Media planning is no longer an after-the-fact complement to a new ad campaign. Media planners are now working more closely than ever with creatives to allow media selection to help shape the creative process, often before a single ad is written. In some cases, media people are even initiating ideas for new campaigns.

For example, Absolut Vodka long recognised the importance of tight media-creative partnerships. For more than 25 years, Absolut Vodka created a wonderful assortment of creative ads that were tightly targeted to the audiences of the media in which they appeared.

The Absolut team and its ad agency meet with a slew of magazines to set Absolut's media schedule. The team first goes through hundreds of the produced ads, which all run frequently in a copy rotation, and, if needed, the agency's creative department then creates the media-specific ads. The result is a wonderful assortment of very creative ads for Absolut, tightly targeted to audiences of the media in which they appear. For example, an 'Absolut Bravo' ad in playbills has roses adorning a clear bottle, whereas business magazines contain an 'Absolut Merger' foldout. In some cases, the creatives even developed ads for magazines not yet on the schedule, such as a clever 'Absolut Centrefold' ad for *Playboy* magazine. The ad portrayed a clear, unadorned playmate bottle ('11-inch bust, 11-inch waist, 11-inch hips'). In all, Absolut has developed more than 800 ads for the campaign that's lasted over two decades. At a time of soaring media costs and cluttered communication channels, a closer cooperation between creative and media people has paid off handsomely for Absolut. Largely as a result of its breakthrough advertising, Absolut captured a sizeable share of the global vodka market.[5]

Creating the advertising message

No matter how big the budget, advertising can succeed only if commercials gain attention and communicate well.

The changing message environment

Good advertising messages are especially important in today's costly and cluttered advertising environment. Fifty or so years ago, the average household in most developed nations received just the two or three national or network TV channels and a handful of major national newspapers and magazines. Today, the average household can receive numerous television channels and radio stations and has thousands of magazines to choose from. Add the countless radio stations, and a continuous barrage of catalogues, direct mail, Internet, e-mail, online ads and out-of-home media. Consumers are bombarded with ads at home, at work and at all points in between!

> " Advertising clutter bothers some consumers, it also causes big problems for advertisers. "

If all this advertising clutter bothers some consumers, it also causes big problems for advertisers – it is very costly. Network TV advertisers could pay tens to hundreds of thousands of euros for a single 30-second slot during a popular prime-time TV programme. Also, their ads are sandwiched in with a clutter of other commercials, announcements and network promotions in any viewing hour. Such clutter in television and other ad media has created an increasingly hostile advertising environment.

Until recently, television viewers were very much a captive audience for advertisers. Viewers had only a few channels to choose from. But today's digital wizardry has given consumers a rich new set of information and entertainment choices. With the growth in cable and satellite TV, the Internet, video-on-demand (VOD) and DVDs, today's viewers have many more options. Digital technology has also armed consumers with an arsenal of tools for choosing what they watch or don't watch. They can avoid ads by watching commercial-free channels. But many are choosing *not* to watch ads at all. With the remote-control, they mute sound during a commercial or 'zip' around the channels to see what else is on. With PVRs, viewers can also 'zap' commercials by fast-forwarding through recorded programmes. Similarly, as the number of VOD viewers increases over the next few years, they will be able to watch programming on their own time terms, with or without commercials.

Thus, advertisers can no longer force-feed the same old ad messages to captive consumers through traditional media. Just to gain, hold and sustain viewers' attention, today's advertising messages must be better planned, more imaginative, more entertaining and more rewarding to consumers, as we saw in both the Daz 'Cleaner Close' ad campaign, discussed in the previous chapter, and the 'Monopoly Here & Now' campaign featured in this chapter's prelude case. Both campaigns were exemplified by content that was interesting, useful and entertaining enough to invite consumers and to draw them in to engage in the brand. By getting it right, consumers would want to see the ads again and again. Creative strategy, therefore, plays an increasingly important role in helping advertisers break through the clutter and gain attention for their products.

Message strategy

The first step in creating effective advertising messages is to decide what general message will be communicated to consumers – to plan the *message strategy*. Generally, the purpose of advertising is to get target consumers to think about or react to the product or company in a certain way. People will respond only if they believe they will benefit from doing so. Thus, developing an effective message strategy usually begins with identifying target customer *benefits* that can be used as advertising appeals. Ideally, advertising message strategy follows directly from the company's broader positioning and customer value strategies.

Message strategy statements tend to be plain, straightforward outlines of benefits and positioning points that the advertiser wants to stress. The advertiser must develop a compelling **creative concept** – or '*big idea*' – that will bring the message strategy to life in a distinctive and memorable way. At this stage, simple message ideas become great ad campaigns. Usually, a copywriter and art director will team up to generate many creative concepts, hoping that one of these

Creative concept—The compelling 'big idea' that will bring the advertising message strategy to life in a distinctive and memorable way.

Developing an effective message strategy usually begins with identifying target customers and *benefits* that can be used as advertising appeals. Advertisers like Ford develop campaigns for each of their target markets. This campaign is not aimed at grannies.
SOURCE: The Advertising Archives.

concepts will turn out to be the big idea. The creative concept may emerge as a visualisation, a phrase or a combination of the two.[6]

Generally, the creative concept should guide the choice of specific appeals to be used in an ad campaign. Advertising appeals should have three characteristics. First, they should be *meaningful*, pointing out benefits that make the product more desirable or interesting to target customers. Second, appeals must be *believable* – consumers must believe that the product or service will deliver the promised benefits. This objective is usually difficult because many consumers doubt the truth of advertising in general.

Appeals should also be *distinctive* in terms of telling consumers how the product is different from or better than competing brands. For example, the most meaningful benefit of owning a wristwatch is that it keeps accurate time, yet few watch ads feature this benefit. Instead, based on the distinctive benefits they offer, watch advertisers might select any of a number of advertising themes. For years, Swatch has featured style, fun and fashion, whereas Rolex stresses luxury and status. Advertisers should therefore pre-test each ad to determine that it has the maximum impact, across the three dimensions of appeal.

Message execution

The advertiser now has to turn the 'big idea' into an actual ad execution that will capture the target market's attention and their interest. The impact of the message depends not only on *what* is said, but also on *how* it is said. The creative people must find the best style, tone, words and

Benetton ads are not as controversial as they used to be (see http://press.benettongroup.com/ben_en/image_gallery/campaigns/?branch_id=1109) but are creative and attractive in their use of multicultural models and bright colours.

SOURCE: The Advertising Archives.

format for executing the message. Any message can be presented in different **execution styles**, such as the following:

Execution style—The approach, style, tone, words and format used for executing an advertising message.

- *Slice of life.* This style shows one or more people using the product in a normal setting. For example, the classic Persil laundry detergent commercials show the role of the mother who knows she can rely on Persil to keep her family's washing clean, white and bright.

- *Lifestyle.* This style shows how a product fits in with a particular lifestyle. Ads for the UK outdoor clothing manufacturer Rohan Designs often show consistency between their 'technically clever clothing' and the adventurous lifestyles of their wearers. One print ad, with the mountains of North Wales as a backdrop, states, 'This is our heartland. It is our inspiration, our drawing board and our test bed. It's where our journey starts . . . . Inspired by the mountains . . . – tough enough to take on the world.'

- *Fantasy.* This style creates a fantasy around the product or its use. For instance, many ads are built around dream themes. One commercial for adidas shoes features a guy dreaming he can outrun everything wearing his adidas. It closes with the statement 'Impossible is nothing.' Gap introduced a perfume named Dream. Ads show a woman sleeping blissfully and suggest that the scent is 'the stuff that clouds are made of'.

- *Mood or image.* This style builds a mood or image around the product, such as beauty, love or serenity. No claim is made about the product except through suggestion. For example, ads for Singapore Airlines feature soft lighting and refined flight attendants pampering relaxed and happy customers. Timotei shampoo is associated with nature and simplicity – a strategy that has worked in many countries across the world.

- *Musical.* Here people or cartoon characters sing about the product or the ad is built around a song or some well-known music. The aim is to associate emotional responses to the music with the product. For example, one of the most famous ads in history was a Coca-Cola ad built around the song 'I'd like to teach the world to sing'.

- *Personality symbol.* This style creates a character that represents the product. The character might be *animated* (e.g. Shrek for Hewlett-Packard office systems, Felix the Cat for Purina's Felix cat food) or *real* (e.g. Kate Moss for Top Shop women's fashion; Gary Lineker for Walkers' Crisps; Lewis Hamilton for TAG Heuer watches).

- *Technical expertise.* This style shows the company's expertise in making the product. Thus Mercedes promotes its investment in intelligent technologies to build tomorrow's energy-efficient cars, and Volkswagen-Audi cars imply German engineering superiority with their strap line 'Vorsprung durch Technik'.

- *Scientific evidence.* This style presents survey or scientific evidence that the brand is better or better liked than one or more other brands. Danone's ads for Actimel, a probiotic yoghurt drink, assured users that the drink was not only tasty but also made them feel better. Communications drew attention to scientific evidence that Actimel works because it contains the friendly live bacteria, L.C. Imunitas, which is involved with the immune system, hence strengthening the body's natural defences against coughs and colds.

- *Testimonial evidence or endorsement.* This style features a highly believable or likeable source endorsing the product. It could be ordinary people saying how much they like a given product or a celebrity presenting the product.

> " Positive tones that evoke happiness, feelings of achievement, fun and excitement tend to be more effective. "

The advertiser must also choose a *tone* for the ad. Positive tones that evoke happiness, feelings of achievement, fun and excitement tend to be more effective than negative tones. By contrast, negative appeals that evoke fear may discourage viewers from looking at the advertisement, and

Just what the environment needs from a car. Water.

If nature had one wish, what do you think it would be? A car that doesn't produce exhaust?
We thought so too. That's why our hydrogen powered Fuel Cell vehicles only emit water.
In fact, as they've proven in recent road tests, they may well be the alternative drive systems of
the future. At DaimlerChrysler Research we're developing these intelligent technologies today.
For the automobiles of tomorrow.

To find out more about 'Energy for the Future' visit www.daimlerchrysler.com

DAIMLERCHRYSLER
Answers for questions to come.

DaimlerChrysler promotes its energy-efficient, intelligent technologies as alternative drive systems of the future.
SOURCE: Daimler AG Stuttgart, Germany.

so would be counterproductive. Some advertisers use humour to break through the commercial clutter. At the same time, companies may also want to avoid humour (or other ad appeals) that might take attention away from the message.

The advertiser must also use memorable and attention-getting *words* in the ad.

For example, rather than claiming simply that 'a BMW is a well-engineered car', BMW uses more creative and high-impact phrasing: 'The ultimate driving machine'. Instead of saying that Häagen-Dazs is 'a good tasting ice-cream', its ads say that it is 'Our passport to indulgence: passion in a touch, perfection in a cup, summer in a spoon, one perfect moment.' The World Wide Fund for Nature doesn't say, 'We need your money to help save nature.' Instead, it says 'We share the sky. We share the future. Together, we can be a force of nature.' To impress upon watch connoisseurs the value of its watches, Patek Philippe does not simply state 'Invest in a Patek Philippe.' Instead, the preciousness of its timepieces is eloquently conveyed in its 'Begin your *own* tradition' ad campaign which carries the strapline, 'You never actually own a Patek Philippe. You merely look after it for the next generation.'

Finally, *format* elements make a difference in an ad's impact as well as in its cost. A small change in ad design can make a big difference in its effect. The *illustration* is the first thing the reader notices – it must be strong enough to draw attention. Next, the *headline* must effectively motivate the right people to read the copy. Finally, the *copy* – the main block of text in the ad – must be simple but strong and convincing.

Importantly, all the elements – style, tone, words, format, copy – must effectively work together to persuasively present customer value.

Selecting advertising media

The advertiser must next decide upon the media to carry the message. The main steps in **advertising media** selection are: (1) deciding on *reach*, *frequency* and *impact*; (2) choosing among chief *media types*; (3) selecting specific *media vehicles*; and (4) deciding on *media timing*.

Deciding on reach, frequency and impact

To select media, the advertiser must decide what reach and frequency are needed to achieve advertising objectives. **Reach** is a measure of the *percentage* of people in the target market who are exposed to the ad campaign during a given period of time. For example, the advertiser might try to reach 70 per cent of the target market during the first three months of the campaign. **Frequency** is a measure of how many *times* the average person in the target market is exposed to the message. For example, the advertiser might want an average exposure frequency of three.

But advertisers want to do more than just reach a given number of consumers a specific number of times. The advertiser must also decide on the desired **media impact** – the qualitative value of a message exposure through a given medium. For example, for products that need to be demonstrated, messages on television may have more impact than messages on radio because television uses sight and sound. The same message in a national newspaper may be more believable than in a local weekly. Products for which consumers provide input on design or features might be better promoted at a website than in a direct mailing.

More generally, the advertiser wants to choose media that will *engage* consumers rather than simply reach them. The 'Monopoly Here & Now' ad campaign encouraged consumers to actively engage with the brand's communications by turning the streets of London into a giant, real-life game of Monopoly, using the taxis as playing pieces, and by using the online advertising platform to encourage people to play the 'Monopoly live' game for themselves, as opposed to merely associating it with their childhood. And the more people who played Monopoly Live, the greater the likelihood that they'd purchase the 'Here & Now' board game.

Thus, advertisers and media agencies are placing increasing importance on measuring media engagement. Although TV media engagement can be determined, such measures are harder to come by for other media. Current measurements used by advertisers include media metrics such as ratings, readership, listener-ship, click-through rates and so forth. However, engagement with a brand occurs inside the consumer's mind, not inside the advertising medium. Only when the

Advertising media—The vehicle through which advertising messages are delivered to their intended audiences.

Reach—The percentage of people in the target market exposed to an ad campaign during a given period.

Frequency—The number of times the average person in the target market is exposed to an advertising message during a given period.

Media impact—The qualitative value of an exposure through a given medium.

targeted customer truly connects and gets engaged with the brand idea, can the advertiser begin to build longer-lasting customer relationships.

Choosing among major media types

The media planner has to know the reach, frequency and impact of each of the major media types. The major media types are newspapers, television, direct mail, radio, magazines, outdoor and the Internet. As shown in Table 16.2, each medium has advantages and limitations.

How do advertisers select appropriate media from the range of media available? Media planners consider many factors when making their media choices. They want to choose media that will effectively and efficiently present the advertising message to target customers. Thus, they must consider each medium's impact, message effectiveness and cost.

The *media habits of target consumers* will affect media choice, and advertisers look for media that reach target consumers effectively. So will the *nature of the product*: for example, fashions are best advertised in colour magazines and car performance is best demonstrated on television.

Different *types of message* may require different media: for instance, a message announcing a big sale tomorrow will require radio or newspapers; a message with a lot of technical data might require magazines or direct mailings or an online ad and website. *Cost* is also an important consideration in media choice: whereas network television is expensive, newspaper or radio advertising costs much less but also reaches fewer consumers. The media planner looks at both

Table 16.2 Profiles of major media types

Medium	Advantages	Limitations
Newspapers	Flexibility; timeliness; local market coverage; broad acceptance; high believability	Short life; poor reproduction quality; small pass-along audience
Television	Good mass-market coverage; low cost per exposure; combines sight, sound and motion; appealing to the senses	High absolute cost; high clutter; fleeting exposure; less audience selectivity
Radio	Good local acceptance; high geographic and demographic selectivity; low cost	Audio presentation only; low attention (the 'half-heard' medium); fleeting exposure; fragmented audiences
Magazines	High geographic and demographic selectivity; credibility and prestige; high-quality reproduction; long life; good pass-along readership	Long ad purchase lead time; high cost; some waste circulation; no guarantee of position
Direct mail	High audience selectivity; flexibility; no ad competition within the same medium; allows personalisation	Relatively high cost per exposure; 'junk mail' image
Outdoor	Flexibility; high repeat exposure; low cost; low message competition; good positional selectivity	Little audience selectivity; creative limitations
Internet	High selectivity; low cost; immediacy; interactive capabilities	Demographically skewed audience; relatively low impact; audience controls exposure

the total cost of using a medium and the cost per 1,000 exposures – the cost of reaching 1,000 people using the medium.

The mix of media must be re-examined regularly. For a long time, television and magazines dominated in the media mixes of national advertisers, with other media often neglected. However, as discussed in the previous chapter, the media mix appears to be shifting. As mass-media costs rise, audiences shrink and exciting new digital media emerge, many advertisers are finding new ways to reach consumers. They are supplementing the traditional mass media with more specialised and highly targeted media that cost less, target more effectively and engage consumers more fully.

For example, cable television and satellite television systems are booming. Such systems allow narrow programming formats such as all sports, all news, nutrition, arts, home improvement and gardening, cooking, travel, history, finance and others that target select groups.

> " Advertisers can take advantage of . . . 'narrowcasting' to 'rifle in' on special market segments. "

Advertisers can take advantage of such 'narrowcasting' to 'rifle in' on special market segments rather than use the 'shotgun' approach offered by network broadcasting. Cable and satellite television media seem to make good sense. But, increasingly, ads are popping up in far less likely places. In their efforts to find less costly and more highly targeted ways to reach consumers, advertisers have discovered a dazzling collection of alternative media. These days, no matter where you go or what you do, you will probably run into some form of advertising, from ads you are used to in magazines and newspapers and on TV and the radio, to the not-so-subtle product placements in video games and movies. And you're likely to find ads – well, anywhere: shopping carts, shopping bags, supermarket floors, parking meters, city buses, football stadiums, railway stations, airports, taxi cabs. Ad space is being sold on DVD cases, car park tickets, golf scorecards, delivery trucks, pizza boxes, petrol pumps, ATMs and public lavatories. Even your mobile phone has been invaded by innovative marketers (see Real Marketing 16.1).

Another important trend affecting media selection is the rapid growth in the number of 'media multitaskers' – people who absorb more than one medium at a time. More and more TV viewers are simply not satisfied with 'just watching TV'. While watching TV, you also read a magazine, and with your PC parked on your lap, you log on and make a Skype call. Then, you send an SMS text message and delete a message from your mobile phone service supplier reminding you to 'make the most of new lower call rates throughout Europe'! What's more, if today's kids are any indication, media multitasking is on the rise. It's not uncommon to find a teenage boy chasing down photos of Keira Knightly on Google, IM-ing (instant messaging) several friends at once, listening to a mix of music on iTunes, and talking on a mobile phone to a friend, all the while, in the midst of the multimedia chaos, trying to complete an essay he's got open in a Word file a few layers down on his desktop.[7] Thus, media planners need to take such media interactions into account when selecting the types of media they will use.

Selecting specific media vehicles

The media planner must now choose the best **media vehicles** – that is, specific media within each general media type. For example, in The Netherlands, television vehicles include Net 5, RTL 4, 5 and 7, and Veronica. Newspaper vehicles include *De Telegraaf*, *Metro* and *Spits*. Magazines include *Kampioen*, *Allerhande* and *Linda*. Similarly, in the UK, television vehicles selected might include ITV, Five, Film Four and Eurosport. Magazines might include *Harper's Bazaar*, *FHM* and *Sky the Magazine*. Newspaper vehicles could include the *Daily Mirror*, *News of the World* and *The People*.

In most cases, there is an incredible number of choices. For radio and television, and in any one country, there are numerous stations and channels to choose from, together with hundreds, even thousands, of programme vehicles – the particular programmes or shows where the

Media vehicles—Specific media within each general media type, such as specific magazines, television shows or radio programmes.

16.1 real marketing

Mobile advertising: signing up for real-time discounts

Singapore, small and rich and where consumers compete to own the latest smart phone, is a good place to test what might work in mobile advertising. In a trial with 1,000 volunteer customers, Singapore operator M1 has launched a location-based marketing drive. Having opted in, a user walking along Orchard Road, a main shopping street in the city-state, receives messages offering discounts in stores or restaurants as they approach them. Shopkeepers, who are typically cutting 10 per cent off prices, capture customers who might otherwise have passed them by. Restaurants can offer discounts to attract early and late diners, extending their full-capacity hours. According to Neil Montefiore, chief executive of M1, mobile users, attracted by the discounts, have rushed to sign up.

In December 2006, M1 launched another innovation – an opt-in service whereby text messages are scanned for keywords, and the user is sent a 10-second advertising display. So, a text about a stockbroker would prompt an advertiser's display of share indices, or financial information. More than 6,000 M1 customers have signed up. The operator has also tested a service which allows customers to photograph barcodes on advertising billboards with their phones if they want to know more about a product or offer. The phone's browser connects to the advertiser's website.

These marketing experiments are all voluntary: M1's operating licence – like those of operators in Europe and the US – bars it from releasing personal user data or delivering advertising without the consumer's express consent. In each trial, the advertising interaction is brief. In a 200-metre walk along Orchard Road, a user might get three discount offers. 'Any more, and it can become irritating,' says Mr Montefiore. The advertising is also highly targeted and tends to build on campaigns using other media.

This is one of the ways the mobile industry is seeking to exploit the data about consumers' lifestyles and habits captured in mobile phones. Jamyn Edis, senior manager in the Digital Advertising Practice of consultants Accenture, says: 'Operators are banking on getting incremental revenue from advertising to get income up and churn down.'

But most in the industry believes mobile advertising will respond to consumer 'pull' for relevant adverts, rather than broadcast 'push' for universal advertising messages. The screen is simply too small to carry advertisements beside the content, as desktop computers do.

'Ultimately,' says Ilkka Raiskinen, senior vice-president multimedia at Nokia, the Finnish phone-maker, 'you need a real-time brokering mechanism' to place advertisements relevant to a user's interests, location and time. But the technology is not there yet. For now, operators must rely on users to select content of interest to them. Scott Beaumont, for example, runs Refresh Mobile, owner of Mobizines, which delivers specially adapted magazines such as entertainments guide *Time Out* and gossip magazine *OK!* to handsets.

A user connecting to the *Popjustice* magazine, which contains music, interviews and so on, would see an advert lasting between two and five seconds while the magazine loads. It then minimises automatically to the bottom of the screen. To view it again, the user can select a tab, and navigate further to get more information about the product.

Advertisers to date include Volvo magazines, Sony Ericsson and Accenture, seeking to recruit via technical titles. Mr Beaumont says he is seeing repeat business from advertisers. Adverts for one new phone achieved a click-through rate above 15 per cent, perhaps with the aid of novelty value. But Mr Beaumont issues a warning – advertisers must avoid sending spam-type SMS marketing messages, which is counter-productive. For mobile advertising to work, 'user experience must, must, must come first,' says Mr Beaumont.

Rob Bamforth, principal analyst at research group Quocirca, believes operators will ultimately gain, however, because they will sell more air-time, even if they have to offer discounts to get phone users to opt in to adverts. It is early days, says Steven Trews, European chief of mobile media solutions for handset maker Motorola: most smart phone owners have yet to use their operator's portal. 'Only 20 per cent have opened the browser on their mobile, and for some operators, the figure is as low as 10 per cent,' he says.

To encourage users to join the mobile Internet – and build a critical mass that will attract more advertisers – Motorola introduced Screen3 on its handsets, so that they can automatically connect to a designated portal (normally that of the operator, at zero cost) when switched on.

Adding a feature called Motocast will enable its partner, wire service Reuters, to deliver streamed news to the handset. Reuters will be able to place advertisements within the content, and adding a news service enhances consumer acceptance of the adverts.

Such advertising innovations are unlikely to deliver a quick bonanza to operators, however. TNS Media Intelligence began measuring mobile phone advertising in France. In the first four months of 2006, spending on mobile telephone advertising in the country of 60m people was just €2.4m, out of a national advertising spend over the same period of €6.5bn. But according to research firm VisionGain, from 2005, when mobile advertising revenues were $255m in Europe and the US, mobile advertising revenues are expected to reach $1bn in 2009.

Advertisers, operators, handset makers and innovators will be watching pilot schemes for ways of advertising without irritating users. Asia, with higher smart

...16.1

phone penetration, is expected to lead, with Europe following and the US, still predominantly a voice market, behind. When enough people start using the mobile Internet, says Motorola's Mr Trews: 'mobile advertising will happen in a massive way.' For the mobile and advertising industries, realising the advertising potential of smart phones without alienating users is an awesome challenge.

SOURCE: Adapted from Ross Tieman, 'Mobile marketing: Volunteers sign up for adverts', *Financial Times* (18 April 2007), p. 5.

commercial should be broadcast. Prime-time programmes are the favourites, but costs escalate with the popularity of the programme.

In the case of magazines, the media planner must look up circulation figures and the costs of different ad sizes, colour options, ad positions and frequencies for specific magazines. Each country has its own high- or general-circulation magazines (for example, radio and TV guides) which reach general audience groups. There is also a vast selection of special-interest publications that enable advertisers to reach special groups of audiences (for example, business magazines to reach business executives). The planner selects the media that will do the best job in terms of selectively reaching the target customer group. Then he or she must evaluate each magazine on factors such as credibility, status, reproduction quality, editorial focus and advertising submission deadlines. The media planner ultimately decides which vehicles give the best reach, frequency and impact for the money.

Media planners have to compute the *cost per thousand* persons reached by a vehicle. For example, if a full-page, four-colour advertisement in a monthly business *magazine* costs €220,500 and its readership is 3 million people, the cost of reaching each group of 1,000 persons is about €71. The same advertisement in a regional trade magazine may cost only €99,000 but reach only 970,000 persons, giving a cost per thousand of about €100. The media planner would rank each magazine by cost per thousand and favour those magazines with the lower cost per thousand for reaching target consumers.

The media planner must also consider the costs of producing ads for different media. Whereas newspaper ads may cost very little to produce, flashy television ads may cost millions. Media costs vary across different countries, so care must be taken not to generalise the figures.

Thus the media planner must balance media costs against several media impact factors. First, the planner should balance costs against the media vehicle's *audience quality*. For a personal digital assistant (PDA) ad, business magazines would have a high-exposure value; magazines aimed at new parents or woodwork enthusiasts would have a low-exposure value. Second, the media planner should consider *audience engagement*. Readers of fashion magazines such as *Vogue*, for example, typically pay more attention to ads than do readers of a business magazine. Third, the planner should assess the vehicle's *editorial quality*. For example, the *Financial Times* and *The Economist* are more prestigious and believable than newspapers such as *The Sun* or weeklies and celebrity magazines such as *Hello!* and *Now*.

Deciding on media timing

The advertiser must also decide how to schedule the advertising over the course of a year. Suppose sales of a product peak in December and drop in March. The firm can vary its advertising to follow the seasonal pattern, to oppose the seasonal pattern, or to be the same all year. Most firms do some seasonal advertising. Some do *only* seasonal advertising: for example, many department stores advertise – usually their seasonal sales – in specific periods in the year, such as Christmas, Easter and summer. Advertisers can also ensure greater efficiency in running their TV campaigns – in terms of the number of television impacts and their price – by shifting TV campaigns into cheaper months.

Finally, the advertiser must choose the pattern of the ads. **Continuity** means scheduling ads evenly within a given period. **Pulsing** means scheduling ads unevenly over a given time period. Thus 52 ads could be either scheduled at one per week during the year or pulsed in several bursts. The idea is to advertise heavily for a short period to build awareness that carries over to the next advertising period. Those who favour pulsing feel that it can be used to achieve the same impact as a steady schedule, but at a much lower cost. However, some media planners believe that although pulsing achieves minimal awareness, it sacrifices depth of advertising communications.

Continuity—Scheduling ads evenly within a given period.

Pulsing—Scheduling ads unevenly, in bursts, over a certain time period.

Evaluating advertising effectiveness and return on advertising investment

Advertising accountability and **return on advertising investment** have become hot issues for most companies. Increasingly, top management is asking: 'How do we know that we're spending the right amount on advertising?' and 'What return are we getting on our advertising investment?'

Advertisers should regularly evaluate two types of advertising results: the communication effects and the sales and profit effects. Measuring the *communication effects* of an ad or ad campaign tells whether the ads and media are communicating the ad message well. Individual ads can be tested before or after they are run. Before an ad is placed, the advertiser can show it to consumers, ask how they like it, and measure message recall or attitude changes resulting from it. After an ad is run, the advertiser can measure how the ad affected consumer recall or product awareness, knowledge and preference. Pre- and post-evaluations of communication effects can be made for entire advertising campaigns as well.

Return on advertising investment—The net return on advertising investment divided by the costs of the advertising investment.

> **❝** It is important for advertisers to evaluate the performance of an ad or ad campaign. **❞**

Advertisers are generally quite good at measuring the communication impacts of their ads and ad campaigns. However, financial impacts such as sales and profit effects of advertising are often much harder to measure. Questions such as 'What sales and profits are caused by an ad that increases brand awareness by 20 per cent and brand preference by 10 per cent?' are not easy to answer. Sales (or *trials*) and profits are typically affected by many factors besides advertising, such as product features, price and availability. Despite the difficulties, it is important for advertisers to evaluate the performance of an ad or ad campaign.

Figure 16.2 shows the levels of effects or consumer responses that advertisers are likely to monitor and measure with respect to advertising campaigns:

- The change in brand awareness is determined by the number of customers who were previously *unaware* of the brand and the number who *notice* the advertisement and are now *aware* of the brand, or by the difference in the number of customers who are aware that the brand exists before and after the campaign. If there has been little increase or even a decline in brand awareness, the advertiser has to determine whether the reason is the poor impact achieved by the communications campaign or that customers *forget* because of poor recall or inadequate advertising investment.

- Consumers' attitudes towards a brand can be gauged before and after a campaign. An informative ad allows consumers to *learn* more about product/brand benefits. If the message

Figure 16.2 Advertising: measuring communications and sales effectiveness

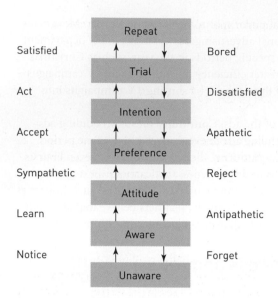

is poorly targeted or product claims are unbelievable, consumers are *antipathetic* towards the brand. They do not develop any liking for the product. Advertisers may have to redesign the copy to generate greater interest among customers or to improve message content in order to enhance the level of comprehension of brand benefits among target customers.

- Consumers who are *sympathetic* towards advertised brand benefits would manifest their favourable response in the form of stated brand preference. Similarly, before-and-after (the campaign) studies would enable changes in consumer brand preference to be determined. Reasons for brand *rejection* should be identified so that communication weaknesses can be redressed.

- An advertising campaign may be used to turn preference among customers into more definite *intention* to buy. Again, this response can be measured and changes in the level of buying intent may be determined.

- As mentioned earlier, it is usually difficult to measure the sales (and profit) effects of a campaign. One way to measure the sales and profit effects of advertising is to compare past sales and profits with past advertising expenditures. Another way is through experiments. For example, to test the effects of different advertising levels, Danone could vary the amount it spends on advertising in different market areas and measure the differences in resulting sales levels. More complex experiments could be designed to include other variables, such as differences in the ads or media used.

- If the customer is *satisfied* with the brand he or she has bought, this will lead to *repeat* purchase on another buying occasion. The extent to which advertising or a specific 'reminder' campaign affects repeat purchase is difficult to measure because of the difficulty of separating out the immediate and long-term effects of advertising. 'Before-and-after' type studies and controlled experiments can be used, nonetheless, to detect changes in purchase and usage frequency. Again, advertisers should obtain consumer feedback to increase their understanding of the impact of communications on repeat purchase. Advertising may not be blamed for non-repeat sales due to the nature of product consumption: for example, consumers get *bored* with the same product and want variety. In this case, advertising is not powerful enough to arrest that desire. Few of us would relish the thought of surviving on an uninterrupted diet of Heinz soup and Heinz baked beans all year round!

Because so many factors affect advertising effectiveness, some controllable and others not, measuring the results of advertising spending remains an inexact science. Marketers must often rely on large doses of judgement along with quantitative analysis when assessing advertising performance.

Other advertising considerations

In developing advertising strategies and programmes, the company must address two additional questions. First, how will it organise the advertising function – who will perform the advertising tasks? Second, how will the company adapt its advertising strategies and programmes to the complexities of international markets?

Organising for advertising

Different organisations handle advertising in different ways. In small and medium-sized companies, advertising might be handled by someone in the sales or marketing department. Large companies might set up advertising departments whose job it is to set the advertising budget, work with the ad agency and handle dealer displays and other advertising not done by the agency. Most companies, small or large, tend to use outside advertising agencies because they offer several advantages.

There are disadvantages in relinquishing the advertising function to an outside agency: loss of total control of the advertising process, a reduction in flexibility, conflicts arising when the agency dictates working practices, and client inability to exercise control or coordination. Despite the potential problems, however, most firms find that they benefit from employing the specialised expertise of agencies.

How does an advertising agency work? Advertising agencies were started in the mid-to-late nineteenth century by salespeople and brokers who worked for the media and received commission for selling advertising space to companies. As time passed, the salespeople began to help customers prepare their ads. Eventually they formed agencies and grew closer to the advertisers than to the media.

Today's agencies employ specialists who can often perform advertising tasks – research, creative work – better than the company's own staff. Agencies bring an outside point of view to solving a company's problems, along with years of experience from working with different clients and situations. Thus, even companies with strong advertising departments of their own use advertising agencies.

Some ad agencies are huge – Japan's Dentsu and New York-based McCann-Erickson have annual worldwide revenues of over 250bn yen (€2.7bn) and $1.9bn (€1.4bn) respectively. In recent years, many agencies have grown by gobbling up other agencies, thus creating huge agency holding companies. The largest of these agency 'megagroups', Omnicom Group, headquartered in New York, includes several large advertising, public relations and promotion agencies with combined worldwide revenues of almost $10.5bn. Following close in second place is London-based WPP Group with worldwide revenues estimated at just over £5bn (€7.4bn).[8] Most large advertising agencies have the staff and resources to handle all phases of an advertising campaign for their clients, from creating a marketing plan to developing ad campaigns and preparing, placing and evaluating ads.

Agencies usually have four departments: creative, which develops and produces ads; media, which selects media and places ads; research, which studies audience characteristics and wants; and business, which handles the agency's business activities. Each account is supervised by an account executive and people in each department are usually assigned to work on one or more accounts.

Ad agencies have traditionally been paid through commission and fees. Higher commissions are paid to the well-recognised agencies for their ability to place more advertisements in media.

However, the commission system is under fire from both advertisers and agencies. Larger advertisers are increasingly reluctant to pay more for the same services received by smaller ones simply because they place more advertising. Advertisers also argue that the commission system drives agencies away from low-cost media and short advertising campaigns. Agencies, on the other hand, reason that they should be paid more to perform extra services for an account. Importantly, the commission formula overlooks important emerging media such as the Internet and search engine advertising. As we saw in the prelude case study, unique and creative approaches to reaching consumers mean that ad agencies are having to adopt media that go beyond traditional TV and other offline advertising. As a result, agency payment methods include anything from fixed retainers or straight hourly fees for labour to incentives tied to performance of the agencies' ad campaigns.

Another trend is affecting the agency business. Many agencies have sought growth by diversifying into related marketing services. These new diversified agencies offer a one-stop shop – a complete list of integrated marketing and promotion services under one roof, including advertising, sales promotion, marketing research, public relations and direct and online marketing. Some have added marketing consulting, television production and sales training units in order to become full 'marketing partners' to their clients.

However, many agencies are finding that advertisers do not want much more from them than traditional media advertising services plus direct marketing, sales promotion and sometimes public relations. Thus, many agencies have recently limited their diversification efforts in order to focus more on traditional services or their core expertise.

International advertising decisions

We have discussed advertising decisions in general. International advertisers face many complexities not encountered by domestic advertisers. When developing advertising for international markets, a number of basic issues must be considered.

Standardisation or differentiation

The most basic issue concerns the degree to which global advertising should be adapted to the unique characteristics of various country markets. Some large advertisers have attempted to support their global brands with highly standardised worldwide advertising, with campaigns that work as well in Bangkok as they do in Budapest. For example, Coca-Cola's Sprite brand uses standardised appeals to target the world's youth. Ads for Gillette's Venus razors are almost identical worldwide, with only minor adjustments to suit the local culture. Ericsson, the Swedish telecommunications giant, spent €70m on a standardised global television campaign with the tag line 'make yourself heard.'

"Pan-European advertising . . . is complicated."

Standardisation produces many benefits, such as lower advertising costs, greater coordination of global advertising efforts and a more consistent worldwide image. However, standardisation also has drawbacks. Most importantly, it ignores the fact that country markets differ greatly in their cultures, demographics and economic conditions. Pan-European advertising, for example, is complicated because of the EU's cultural diversity as reflected in the differences in circumstances, language, traditions, music, beliefs, values and lifestyles among its 27 member nations. Even the emerging European markets such as the three Baltic countries – Estonia, Latvia and Lithuania – differ in terms of language, currencies and consumer habits. Cultural differences also exist across Asian countries – Japanese and Indonesian consumers are as unlike as the Germans and Italians.

Thus, most international advertisers 'think globally, but act locally'. They develop global advertising *strategies* that make their worldwide advertising efforts more efficient and consistent. Then they adapt their advertising *programmes* to make them more responsive to consumer needs and expectations within local markets. In many cases, even when a standard message is used, execution styles are adapted to reflect local moods and consumer expectations. For example, Coca-Cola has a pool of different commercials that can be used in or adapted to several different international markets. Some can be used with only minor changes – such as language – in several different countries. Local and regional managers decide which commercials work best for which markets.

Standardised advertising is more likely to work for capital goods or business-to-business marketing, where customer targets are more homogeneous in their needs and buy the product for the same reasons. For example, whether for a European, Asian or American construction company, the purchase of bulldozers is influenced by similar economic factors (for example, productivity, lifetime cost of running the equipment, parts delivery). By contrast, consumer-goods advertising is less amenable to cross-cultural standardisation. However, considerable similarities are found in segments, such as the world's rich to whom lifestyle goods and brands like Mont Blanc, Chanel, Cartier and LVMH appeal. Similarly, youth culture across the globe may be targeted with a common message. Brands such as Nike, Pepsi and Jeep are advertised in much the same way globally; Jeep has created a worldwide brand image of ruggedness and reliability; Nike urges Americans, Africans, Asians and Europeans alike to 'Just do it'; Nokia uses a standard appeal to target the world's youth.

Centralisation or decentralisation

Global advertisers are concerned with the degree to which advertising decision making and implementation should be centralised or decentralised. Five key factors influence the choice between centralisation and decentralisation of the responsibility for international advertising decisions and implementation:

1. *Corporate and marketing objectives.* A company whose global marketing objectives dominate over domestic objectives is likely to centralise advertising and communications decisions.

2. *Product uniformity.* The more similar the product or service marketed across different countries, the greater the feasibility of a uniform approach, which allows for centralised management of advertising.

3. *Product appeal.* Underlying the product's appeal are consumers' motivations for using or owning the product, which may differ across cultures, whatever the demographic or psychographic characteristics of consumers. Golf club membership is a status purchase in Singapore; in the United Kingdom it is a moderate leisure activity, which is little associated with exclusivity. Where underlying appeals vary significantly, decentralised decision making makes better sense.

4. *Cultural sensitivities.* Where a product's usage and appeal are culture-bound in terms of the local attitudes towards consumption, habits and preferences, as in the case of drinks and food products, more decentralisation is necessary.

5. *Legal constraints.* Individual country rules and regulations affect advertising decisions and their implementation. Decentralisation of responsibility to tap local wisdom and knowledge makes sense where strict country regulations apply. As discussed in the previous chapter, variations in codes of practice as well as the extent to which EU legislations are implemented by EU nations mean that cross-border advertisers must remain alert to subtle differences in order to avoid costly mistakes.

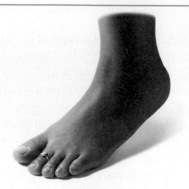

INDIA

Married

CANADA

Married

Never underestimate the importance of local knowledge.

Where a wedding ring goes is just something you grow up knowing when you're a local.

At HSBC, we have banks in more countries than anyone else. And each one is staffed by local people.

We have offices in 79 countries and territories; Europe, Asia-Pacific, the Americas, the Middle East, and Africa. Being local enables them to offer insights into financial opportunities and create service initiatives that would never occur to an outsider.

It means our customers get the kind of local knowledge and personal service that you'd expect of a local bank.

And a level of global knowledge and widely sourced expertise that you wouldn't.

The world's local bank

HSBC prides itself as 'the world's local bank' using a standardised message to reinforce its global strengths.
SOURCE: HSBC Holdings plc.
Agency: Lowe Worldwide.
Photographer: Richard Pullar.

The modes used by firms vary. Some organisations exert tight control from the centre and closely monitor changes that are made in executions to fit local culture and conditions. Some corporations give local management a degree of freedom to develop advertising within broad strategic guidelines, but with central directives on agencies and media buying groups. Yet others may give local management total autonomy over both strategy development and local implementation.

Media planning, buying and costs

International media planning is more complicated than local media planning as the media situation differs from country to country. To plan effectively, international advertisers require high-quality, reliable cross-country media and audience research data. In some countries, there is inadequate media research. Moreover, research techniques and measurement standards vary greatly across countries, making cross-country comparisons of media research data almost impossible. Unless reliable inter-country comparisons can be made, international advertisers will find it difficult to evaluate and quantify international media effectiveness. In the EU, the European Association of Advertising Agencies brings together data to help pan-European media researchers. Pan-European research projects, funded jointly by advertisers, agencies and print and TV media, have generated data that help media planners go some way towards building more effective campaigns across Europe as well as in individual territories.[9]

Prices and preference for certain media also may vary greatly across countries. One survey suggests that, in the Scandinavian countries, print media dominate as an advertising medium, with two in three consumers polled voicing positive attitudes towards print advertising; only one in five held the same opinion of TV advertising. The preference for the printed word has important implications for advertising media choice.[10] Another report suggests that at least 40 of the top 50 pan-European advertisers have consolidated their media buying into a single network in order to get cheaper prices. Nonetheless, cultural differences remain in buying preferences. For example, in Italy, the number of spots advertisers tend to buy (also called the average advertising weight) is much higher than in the rest of Europe. According to one source, cultural differences stem from what planners feel 'happy' with, rather than rational reasons, often resulting in local resistance to centralised or standardised approaches. Hence, it is difficult to standardise pan-European media strategies. If the Marketing Director at HQ were to tell her Italian operation that it is running advertising weights that are two-and-a-half times higher than those run by the firm's other European operations, she will literally have to take on the Italian marketing team.[11]

Thus, firms that advertise their products in different country markets must select the media to use based on a consideration of their target groups and the budget available and must adapt their media strategy based on the media scene and relative media cost-effectiveness in different countries.

International advertising regulations

Countries also differ in the extent to which they regulate advertising practices. Many countries have extensive systems of laws restricting how much a company can spend on advertising, the media used, the nature of advertising claims and other aspects of the advertising programme. Such restrictions often require advertisers to adapt their campaigns from country to country.

For example, alcoholic products cannot be advertised in India or in Muslim countries. Comparative ads, while acceptable and even common in the United States and Canada, are less commonly used in the EU, unacceptable in Japan, and illegal in India and Brazil. China bans sending e-mail for advertising purposes to people without their permission, and all advertising e-mail that is sent must be titled 'advertisement'.

China also has restrictive censorship rules for TV and radio advertising; for example, the words *the best* are banned, as are ads that 'violate social customs' or present women in 'improper ways'. McDonald's once avoided government sanctions there by publicly apologising for an ad that crossed cultural norms by showing a customer begging for a discount. Similarly, Coca-Cola's Indian subsidiary was forced to end a promotion that offered prizes, such as a trip to Hollywood, because it violated India's established trade practices by encouraging customers to buy in order to 'gamble'.[12]

In Europe, we have seen increasing legislation governing marketing to children and the advertising of tobacco and alcohol.

In Sweden, Norway and Denmark, TV advertising to children under 12 is banned. To play it safe, McDonald's advertises itself in Sweden as a family restaurant. Advertising to children is also restricted in Belgium, Ireland, Holland, Austria, Italy and Poland. Greece bans TV ads for toys before 10 p.m. In the UK, rising levels of obesity among young children have prompted calls for tougher controls aimed at advertising of unhealthy foods high in fat, sugar and salt. New regulations enforced on 1 April 2007 prohibit the marketing of most food and drinks to pre-school and primary children, and they will be extended to under-16s in 2008.[13] Tobacco advertising, including worldwide sponsorships of events such as Formula One, is banned. For alcohol advertising, Sweden and Finland impose strict limitations, while in France, all forms of alcohol advertising are banned. Denmark, Germany and the UK have called for stricter regulations or health warnings to be placed on packaging.

The European Commission continues to resolve the patchwork of national advertising regulations in order to bring order into the EU's multi-billion-euro advertising industry. Cross-border advertising will develop further with the growth of online interactive media and electronic commerce. However, cultural and regulatory differences mean that advertising campaigns can never be truly pan-European.

Thus although advertisers may develop standardised strategies to guide their overall advertising efforts, specific advertising programmes and executions are usually adapted to meet local cultures and customs, media characteristics and advertising regulations.

Having discussed advertising in the previous sections, let us now examine public relations.

KEY CONCEPT
www.pearson.co.uk/kotler

Public relations

Another important mass-promotion technique is **public relations (PR)**. This concerns building good relations with the company's various publics by obtaining favourable publicity, building up a good corporate image and handling or heading off unfavourable rumours, stories and events. PR has become an increasingly vital communication tool, especially as traditional forms of advertising struggle to capture consumers' attention. Public relations departments perform any or all of the following functions:

- *Press relations or press agency.* Creating and placing newsworthy information in the news media to attract attention to a person, product or service.
- *Product publicity.* Publicising specific products.
- *Public affairs.* Building and maintaining local, national and international relations.
- *Lobbying.* Building and maintaining relations with legislators and government officials to influence legislation and regulation.
- *Investor relations.* Maintaining relationships with shareholders and others in the financial community.
- *Development.* Public relations with donors or members of non-profit organisations to gain financial or volunteer support.

Public relations is used to promote products, people, places, ideas, activities, organisations and even nations. Companies use public relations to build good relations with consumers,

Public relations (PR)— Building good relations with the company's various publics by obtaining favourable publicity, building up a good corporate image, and handling or heading off unfavourable rumours, stories and events. Major PR functions include press relations, product publicity, public affairs, lobbying, investor relations and development.

investors, the media and their communities. Trade associations have used public relations to rebuild interest in declining commodities such as eggs, apples, milk and potatoes. Even nations have used public relations to attract more tourists, foreign investment and international support. Companies can use PR to manage their way out of crisis, as in the case of Johnson & Johnson's masterly use of public relations to save Tylenol from extinction after its product-tampering scare.

The role and impact of public relations

Public relations can have a strong impact on public awareness at a much lower cost than advertising can. The company does not pay for the space or time in the media. Rather, it pays for staff to develop and circulate information and to manage events. If the company develops an interesting story, it could be picked up by several different media, having the same effect as advertising that would cost millions of euros. It would have more credibility than advertising.

> " Public relations can have a strong impact on public awareness at a much lower cost than advertising can. "

Public relations results can sometimes be spectacular. Consider how IKEA used PR to create a buzz for a recent venture – the Ikea Hostel (see Real Marketing 16.2).

Despite its potential strengths, public relations is often described as a marketing stepchild because of its limited and scattered use. The public relations department is usually located at corporate headquarters. Its staff is so busy dealing with various publics – stockholders, employees, legislators, city officials – that public relations programmes to support product marketing objectives may be ignored. Moreover, marketing managers and public relations practitioners do not always talk the same language. Many PR practitioners see their job as simply communicating. In contrast, marketing managers tend to be much more interested in how advertising and public relations affect brand building, sales and profits and customer relationships.

This situation is changing, however. Although public relations still captures only a small portion of the overall marketing budgets of most firms, PR is playing an increasingly important brand-building role. For example, investment bank Veronis Suhler Stevenson, which specialises in media, predicts that PR spending will grow by 9 per cent a year in the next few years, compared to 6.7 per cent a year for overall advertising spend. The trend is confirmed by Hans Bender, Procter & Gamble's manager of external relations. In an internal study, P&G found that the return on promotion investment was often better from a PR campaign than from traditional forms of advertising. Although traditional forms of advertising and marketing would remain important for the company, Mr Bender says that the proportion of the brand's marketing budget will rise in the years ahead.[14]

> " The dominance of advertising is over . . . public relations is quietly becoming the most powerful marketing communications tool. "

However, two well-known marketing consultants go so far as to conclude that advertising doesn't build brands, PR does. In their book *The Fall of Advertising and the Rise of PR*, the consultants Al and Laura Ries proclaim that the dominance of advertising is over, and that public relations is quietly becoming the most powerful marketing communications tool.

16.2 real marketing

Bed and breakfast IKEA style

Back in the summer of 2007, Swedish furniture retailer IKEA opened its first hotel in Norway. This was no ordinary hotel. For IKEA, it's no ordinary foray into the hospitality business either. The startling event was captured in the travel pages of *The Guardian Unlimited* – read on to find out more.

Check in to the Ikea bridal suite for a flat-pack honeymoon

It brought us Swedish meatballs, Billy bookshelves and endless queues on the London North Circular on Saturday afternoons. Now Ikea is going one step further and opening the Ikea Hostel, where customers can stay overnight if they haven't finished their shopping.

Later this month, Ikea Norway will let shoppers sleep overnight in one of its two Oslo warehouses, an operation that will last a week. 'It will be like an alternative hostel,' said company spokesman Frode Ullebusl.

'There will be the regular dormitory with lots of beds stacked up together. We will also have a bridal suite, with a round bed and a hanging chandelier, and the luxury suite, where customers can enjoy breakfast in bed,' he said. Family rooms will also be available for parents and children to join into the Ikea fun. None of the guests will be charged for their stay.

Mr Ullebust said that, as far as he knew, this was Ikea's first foray into the hotel business. Every night, the 30 lucky few will be able to stack up on meatballs, Norwegian salmon and cranberry mousse, as Ikea is offering free dinner and breakfast at the usual canteen.

Whereas Brits may associate the Swedish furniture giant with screaming kids, traffic jams in the parking lot and an occasional riot when a new warehouse opens, it seems Norwegians see a trip to Ikea as the ultimate tourist attraction.

'Around 900,000 visitors come to visit Ikea during the summer holidays. It's more than one of the biggest attractions in Norway, the Holmenskollen ski jump, gets in one year,' claimed Mr Ullebust.

'We have five Ikea stores in Norway, all situated next to the four biggest cities, which are all in the south of the country. We found that people from the north of Norway include a visit to Ikea as part of their holidays,' said the spokesman. 'The Ikea Hostel will make the destination complete.'

Overnight stayers can check in to their new abodes from 10 p.m., an hour before closing time, but will have to be quick in the morning. 'The shop opens at 10 a.m. so if they are lazy, people might get woken up by shoppers testing out their mattresses,' said Mr Ullebust.

Customers will also be able to take their bedsheets home afterwards. 'It's a nice souvenir,' he added, 'We will also give them bathrobes with the Ikea Hostel logo on, and some slippers, so they won't get cold at night.'

And to top it off, Ikea fans can join a very private tour of the building. 'Ikea never sleeps. They can go on a tour of the warehouse. They will enjoy Ikea by night,' said the spokesman. In addition, four employees will be on hand to look after the Ikea lodgers.

Eager applicants . . . apply for an overnight stay, by filling in a form and saying why they want to sleep at Ikea – a question many a frazzled Saturday shopper may wonder.

Of the 1,200 people who applied to stay at the Ikea Hostel, 150 were selected. One lucky couple explained, 'We're getting married on Saturday and spent all our money on the wedding. We have nothing left for a hotel and our honeymoon, so we thought it would be fun to sleep at Ikea instead.'

One family saw the event as a novel way to round off the summer break. 'Our three kids spotted this on the internet. We were going to spend our holidays around Oslo and thought staying at Ikea would be a fun thing to do,' said the mother, Vanya Olsen. She added, 'It's cheap, it's different and we can shop before going home. I quite like that table in our room. Maybe I am going to buy one tomorrow.'

SOURCES: Gwladys Fouché, 'Norwegian queue for chance to stay at Ikea', *The Guardian* (14 July 2007), accessed online at www.guardian.co.uk, August 2007; this news story also appeared in *Guardian Unlimited* (13 July 2007), accessed online at www.guardian.co.uk/travel/jul13/travelnews.norway/, August 2007. Copyright © Guardian News and media Limited 2007.

The birth of a brand is usually accomplished with [public relations], not advertising. Our general rule is [PR] first, advertising second. [Public relations] is the nail, advertising the hammer. [PR] creates the credentials that provide the credibility for advertising. . . . Anita Roddick built The Body Shop into a major international brand with no advertising at all. Instead, she travelled the world on a relentless quest for publicity. . . . Until recently Starbucks Coffee Co. didn't spend a hill of beans on advertising, either. In 10 years, the company spent less than $10m (€8.2m) on advertising, a trivial amount for a brand that delivers annual sales of [in the billions]. Wal-Mart Stores became the world's largest retailer . . . with very little advertising. . . . In the toy field, Beanie Babies became highly successful . . . and on the Internet, Amazon.com became a powerhouse brand with virtually no advertising.[15]

Although the book created much controversy, and most marketers wouldn't agree with the 'fall of advertising', the point is a good one. Advertising and public relations should work hand in hand to build and maintain brands.

Major public relations tools

PR professionals use several tools. One essential tool is *news*. Here the goal of PR is to secure positive coverage of the firm or its product or service in the media. PR professionals find or create favourable news about the company and its products or people. Sometimes news stories occur naturally. At other times, the PR person can suggest events or activities that would create news.

Speeches also create product and company publicity. Increasingly, company executives must field questions from the media, or they could give talks at trade associations or sales meetings. These events can either build or hurt the company's image.

Another common PR tool is *special events*, ranging from news conferences, press tours, grand openings and firework displays to laser shows, hot-air balloon releases, multimedia presentations, eye-catching or star-studded spectaculars and educational programmes designed to reach and interest target publics. As we saw in Real Marketing 16.2, the 'IKEA Hostel' event, a novelty in its own right, created a buzz and excitement that added value to IKEA consumers.

Public relations people also prepare *written materials* to reach and influence their target markets. These materials include annual reports, brochures, articles and company newsletters and magazines.

Audiovisual materials, such as films, slide-and-sound programmes, DVDs and online videos are being used increasingly as communication tools.

Corporate-identity materials also help create a corporate identity that the public immediately recognises. Logos, stationery, brochures, signs, business forms, business cards, buildings, uniforms and even company cars and trucks make effective marketing tools when they are attractive, distinctive and memorable.

Finally, companies might improve public goodwill by contributing money and time to *public service activities*: campaigns to raise funds for worthy causes – for example, to fight illiteracy,

The birth of a brand is often accomplished with public relations, not advertising. For example, Beanie Babies have been highly successful with virtually no advertising.
SOURCE: The Image Works.

support the work of a charity, or assist the aged and handicapped – help to raise public recognition.

Sponsorship is any vehicle through which corporations gain public relations exposure. Corporate sponsorships have become an important promotional tool for companies looking to lift their brand image, or introduce new product lines or services. Some companies have used sponsorship as a strategic promotional tool to launch new products and services or to create long-lasting brand value. By creating new consumer experiences, companies make sponsorship 'work harder'. And by adding value to consumers, they add value to the brand. Consider the following:

London's Millennium Dome is more a 'white elephant' than a landmark building. One reason why the decision of O₂, the UK mobile phone network, to sponsor it seems controversial. Sponsorship usually makes sense when it aligns a company's brand with something consumers already find attractive.

But O₂ argues that its £6m (€9m)-a-year deal to rename the venue 'The O₂' makes marketing sense. The sponsorship involves far more than just badging the Dome with its brand. O₂ will also use its deal with Anschutz Entertainment Group to improve visitors' experience of events staged at the venue by integrating the latest mobile phone technology throughout the building, thereby showcasing its latest broadband and wi-fi services. O₂ expects the arrangements will generate extra revenue, both by encouraging existing O₂ customers to take up the extra services and by attracting new customers.

For example, O₂ customers will be able to take advantage of digital ticketing. Rather than purchase a paper ticket, they will receive a barcode on their mobile phones that will give them access to an event as well as extras such as members-only facilities, including fast-track entry, reserved parking and discounted drinks or food.

'You have to go way beyond "badging" to be credible as a sponsor nowadays,' says Ben Robinson, managing partner of Stream, a brand entertainment agency. 'Our starting point is to add value to the consumer, then use that to add value to the brand.'

Mr Robinson argues that sponsorship should no longer be seen as simply a media investment. 'By pushing sponsorship further – such as by creating new events and content associated with them – brand owners can create tangible assets able to grow in value over time rather than simply being just another media cost.'

Matthew Key, O₂'s UK chief executive, agrees: 'When we launched [the company], our shirt sponsorship deal with Arsenal was important to raise awareness of the brand, but to make the most of sponsorship nowadays – and to really stand out from the crowd – sponsorship deals must be a real partnership between parties, adding value to our customers by deepening their customer experience.'

The same thinking underpins O₂'s sponsorship of the England rugby union team by offering exclusive perks to its customers at certain matches – including a special bar manned by former England international team players.

Other brands taking bold steps to make sponsorship work harder include Audi, the carmaker. Audi has launched its own digital TV channel to drive brand awareness and create a tangible asset with long-term value. MasterCard, the financial services group, has held 'Priceless Evenings', featuring live acts such as The Corrs and Texas performing in a special event for MasterCard customers. Customers unable to attend still benefited from retail discounts on featured artists.

Sony Computer Entertainment offers yet another example of how firms can push the idea of sponsorship further. One of the company's latest sponsorships, The PlayStation Season, involved partnering with a number of different arts institutions, including the English National Opera and Sadler's Wells, to collaborate on the creation of new content. 'And it's not just about generating conventional media coverage. Built into this is a digital strategy to generate interest and dialogue through websites and blogs,' says Carl Christopher, sponsorship and events manager for Sony Computer Entertainment Europe.[16]

As we discussed in the previous chapter, marketers are now also designing *buzz marketing* campaigns to generate excitement and favourable word-of-mouth for their brands. Buzz marketing takes advantage of *social networking* processes by getting consumers themselves to spread information about a product or service to others in their communities. For example, as we saw in this chapter's opening case, the positive word-of-mouth that followed the Hasbro's Monopoly Here & Now campaign not only created a buzz around Monopoly, but also persuaded people to buy it.

A company's *website* can also be a good public relations vehicle. Consumers and members of other publics can visit the site for information and entertainment. Websites can also be ideal for handling crisis situations. Companies can set the site up with information about the crisis and the firm's responses. Staff can also comb the Internet to look for newsgroups discussing the episode and post links to the site. As more and more people look to the Internet for information, a 'web' of opportunity now unfolds for public relations.

One of the most important benefits of using company websites for public relations is a greater control of message consistency. Publicity material can be used to support sales, where appropriate. For example, since an online press release is going straight to the consumer, rather than journalists, links to sales or customer enquiries can be made and consumers' response can be attained instantaneously.

Although the Internet can be a useful medium for public relations work, it is not a substitute for journalists and their high-impact editorials. Thus, the firm's online PR efforts have to be supplemented with direct and face-to-face communications with journalists and other opinion-formers.

Major public relations decisions

As with the other promotion tools, in considering when and how to use product public relations, management should set PR objectives, choose the PR messages and vehicles, implement the PR plan and evaluate the results.

Setting public relations objectives

The *objectives* for public relations are usually defined in relation to the types of news story to be communicated, the communication objectives to be achieved (for instance, awareness creation, knowledge dissemination, generation of specific publicity for target groups) and the specific target audiences.

Choosing public relations messages and vehicles

Message themes for the public relations exercise should be consistent with the organisation's PR objectives. Sometimes the choice of PR messages and tools will be clear-cut. At other times, the organisation has to create the news rather than find it by sponsoring noteworthy events. Creating events is especially important in publicising fund-raising drives for non-profit organisations. In the past, fund-raisers have created a large set of special events, ranging from art exhibits, auctions and dinners, to marathons, walkathons and swimathons.

Implementing the public relations plan

The PR campaign must be implemented with care. For example, a *great* story is easy to place, but, unfortunately, most stories are not earth-shattering and would not get past busy editors. Media fragmentation has resulted in an explosion in the number of ways consumers seek news and entertainment. Many are turning to websites, cable TV, Internet and satellite radio and podcasts. Consequently, original news content becomes even more sought after. Thus well-written and well-produced PR will more likely get an airing. Moreover, PR professionals have to acquire a good feel for what media editors will feature in their papers, magazines or websites. Finally, to ensure their PR material is published, they should establish good relationships with media editors, viewing them as a 'market' to be satisfied.

Evaluating public relations results

Public relations results are difficult to measure because PR is used with other promotion tools and its impact is often indirect. Ideally, the company should measure the change in product awareness, knowledge and attitude resulting from the publicity campaign. If advertising and sales promotion were also increased during the PR campaign, their contribution has to be considered. Finally, sales and profit impact, if obtainable, is the best measure of public relations effort.

As with the other promotion tools, in considering when and how to use product public relations, management should set PR objectives, choose the PR messages and vehicles, implement the PR plan and evaluate the results. The firm's public relations should be blended smoothly with other promotion activities within the company's overall integrated marketing communications effort.

Reviewing the concepts

Companies must do more than deliver good products and services – they have to inform customers about product benefits and carefully position these in customers' minds. To do this, they must skilfully employ mass-promotions to target specific buyers. The three mass-promotion tools are *advertising*, *sales promotion* and *public relations*.

1. Define the role of advertising in the promotion mix

Advertising – the use of paid media by a seller to inform, persuade and remind buyers about its products or organisation – is an important promotion tool for communicating the value that marketers create for their customers. Advertising takes many forms and has many uses. Although advertising is used mostly by business firms, a wide range of non-profit organisations, professionals and social agencies also use advertising to promote their causes to various target publics.

2. Describe the major decisions involved in developing an advertising programme

Advertising decision making involves decisions about the advertising objectives, the budget, the message, the media and, finally, the evaluation of results. Advertisers should set clear target, task and timing *objectives*, whether the aim is to inform, persuade or remind buyers. Advertising's goal is to move consumers through the buyer-readiness stages discussed in the previous chapter. Some advertising is designed to move people to immediate action. However, many of the ads we see today focus on building or strengthening long-term customer relationships. The advertising *budget* can be based on sales, on competitors' spending or on the objectives and tasks of the advertising programme. The size and allocation of the budget depend on many factors.

Advertising strategy consists of two major elements: creating advertising *messages* and selecting advertising *media*. The *message decision* calls for planning a message strategy and executing it effectively. Good advertising messages are especially important in today's costly and cluttered advertising environment. Just to gain and hold attention, today's advertising messages must be better planned, more imaginative, more entertaining and more rewarding to consumers. The *media decision* involves defining reach, frequency and impact goals, choosing major media types, selecting media vehicles and deciding on media timing. Message and media decisions must be closely coordinated for maximum campaign effectiveness.

Finally, *evaluation* calls for evaluating the communication and sales effects of advertising before, during and after the advertising is placed. Advertising accountability has become a hot issue for most companies. Other important advertising issues involve *organising* for advertising and dealing with the complexities of international advertising.

Companies that advertise their products in different country markets can apply the basic principles relating to domestic advertising, but they must take into account the complexities involved in international advertising. They must address the similarities and differences in customer needs and buying behaviour, as well as cultural, socio-economic, political and regulatory environments across country markets, which will affect the decision to standardise or differentiate advertising strategies and executions.

3. Define the role of public relations in the promotion mix

Public relations – gaining favourable publicity and creating a favourable company image – is the least used of the major promotion tools, although it has great potential for building consumer awareness and preference. Public relations is used to promote products, people, places, ideas, activities, organisations and even nations. Companies use public relations to build good relations with consumers, investors, the media and their communities. Public relations can have a strong impact on public awareness at a much lower cost than advertising can, and public relations results can sometimes be spectacular. Although public relations still captures only a small portion of the overall marketing budgets of most firms, PR is playing an increasingly important brand-building role.

4. Explain how companies use public relations to communicate with their publics

Companies use public relations to communicate with their publics by setting PR objectives, choosing PR messages and vehicles, implementing the PR plan and evaluating PR results. To accomplish these goals, public relations professionals use several tools such as *news*, *speeches* and *special events*. They also prepare *written*, *audiovisual* and *corporate identity materials* and contribute money and time to *public service activities*. *Buzz marketing* is a form of public relations that gets consumers themselves to spread word-of-mouth information about the company and its brands. The Internet has also become a major public relations tool.

Discussing the concepts

1. Advertisers must develop compelling creative concepts or big ideas that will bring their message strategies to life in a distinctive way. Look at some print (e.g. magazine, press) advertisements. You could also use examples of TV or online ads. Find what you perceive to be compelling creative concepts. Evaluate the appeals and execution styles used in these ads. Discuss the extent to which the selected ads persuasively present customer value.

2. What factors make the marketer's task of setting advertising budgets difficult?

3. Companies often run advertising and public relations efforts at the same time. Can their efforts be separated? How might a company determine the effectiveness of each element in this mix?

4. Discuss the role of public relations in building a brand. Use practical examples to support your arguments.

5. Why is public relations sometimes referred to as a marketing stepchild? What could be done to correct this problem?

Applying the concepts

1. You are the marketing manager for a new line of women's personal care products sold under the Versace label – an upmarket, designer clothing brand. Propose and justify the advertising strategy for the launch of this new product line. How might you evaluate the effectiveness of the proposed advertising strategy?

Web resources

For additional classic case studies and Internet exercises, visit **www.pearsoned.co.uk/kotler**

2. Since its launch into the consumer market in 1999, Splenda (sucralose) has become a common sweetener used in more than 3,500 food products. Splenda's advertising slogan is 'made from sugar, so it tastes like sugar'. Splenda has cut into sugar's market share. But Splenda's campaign has attracted much attention from competitors, social advocacy groups and nutritional experts. According to these groups, Splenda violates 'truth in advertising' codes of some countries with its 'made from sugar' slogan. They claim that, although currently produced from a sugar molecule, Splenda is an artificial sweetener that can be produced without sugar. Moreover, the chemical name assigned to Splenda – sucralose – is misleading because it closely resembles the chemical name of sugar – sucrose. Recently, campaigns from these groups have been launched to educate the public and to expose Splenda's unethical behaviour. Some of these efforts include encouraging consumers to take action, by telling friends about the misleading claims, sending letters of complaints directly to the parent company – Johnson & Johnson – and writing letters to other authorities such as industry regulators to highlight the potentially serious consumer misunderstandings that might result from Splenda's advertising. But one thing's for sure – there are no conclusive tests regarding the long-term safety of consuming Splenda.

(a) What is the objective of Splenda's 'made from sugar, so it tastes like sugar' message and campaign? Is this slogan an effective appeal?

(b) To what extent do you think the campaigns used by opponents of Splenda will be effective?

(c) What might be the impacts on Splenda's market position? Value to consumer? Longer-term brand value?

(d) How might the company respond to these charges of misleading advertising claims? Outline a public relations programme for gaining public trust in the light of these allegations. Explain and justify your recommendations.

References

1. Based on 'Monopoly here & now', in Laurence Green (ed.), *Advertising Works 15. Proving the effectiveness of marketing communications* (Henley-on-Thames: Institute of Practioners in Advertising and World Advertising Research Center, 2007), Ch. 20, pp. 319–32; the instruction booklet comes with the 70th Anniversary Edition of Monopoly (Hasbro cites that over 750 million people have played Monopoly); Rod Kennedy, *Monopoly: The story behind the world's best-selling game* (Layton, UT: Gibbs Smith, 2004).

2. Details of European advertising expenditure based on estimates of ad spend by country and medium reported in 'Advertising expenditure by country and medium', *European Marketing Pocket Book 2007* (Henley-on-Thames: World Advertising Research Center and Nielsen Media Research, 2007), p. 35; for information on US and international advertising spending, see Lisa Sanders, 'Global ad spend to rise to 6 percent in 2006', *Advertising Age* (5 December 2005), p. 1; and '100 Leading National Advertisers', special issue of *Advertising Age* (26 June 2006).

3. See Patricia Nacimiento, 'Germany: Higher court takes new view on comparative advertising', *International Commercial Litigation* (July/August 1998), p. 47; John Shannon, 'Comparative ads call for prudence', *Marketing Week* (22 May 1999), p. 32.

4. See Andrew Ehrenberg, Neil Barnard and John Scriven, 'Justifying our advertising budgets', *Marketing & Research Today* (February 1997), pp. 38–44; Dana W. Hayman and Don E. Schultz, 'How much should you spend on advertising?', *Advertising Age* (26 April 1999), p. 32; J. Thomas Russell and W. Ronald Lane, *Kleppner's Advertising Procedure*, 15th edn (Upper Saddle River, NJ: Prentice Hall, 2002), pp. 145–9; and Kissan Joseph and Vernon J. Richardson, 'Free cash flow, agency costs, and the affordability method of advertising budgeting', *Journal of Marketing* (January 2002), pp. 94–107.

5. Lynne Roberts, 'New media choice: Absolut Vodka', *Marketing* (9 April 1998), p. 12; Eleftheria Parpis, 'TBWA: Absolut', *Adweek* (9 November 1998), p. 172; and the Q&A section at www.absolutvodka.com (March 2000).

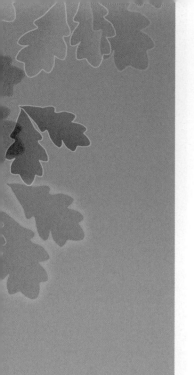

6. See also the classic text by Judith Corstjens, *Strategic Advertising: A practitioner's handbook* (Oxford: Heinemann Professional Publishing, 1990).

7. Adapted from information found in 'Multi-taskers', *Journal of Marketing Management* (May–June 2004), p. 6, and Claudia Wallis, 'The multitasking generation', *Time* (27 March 2006), accessed at www.time.com.

8. Information on advertising agency revenues from 'Advertising Age's Special Agency Report', *Advertising Age* (1 May 2006) and 'Top 25 advertising organisations worldwide', *European Marketing Pocket Book 2007, op. cit.*, p. 20.

9. Boris Kaz, 'Researching the pan-European media market', *Admap* (July–August 1996), pp. 31–2; John Shannon, 'Research boost for pan-Euro TV', *Marketing Week* (19 April 1996), p. 29.

10. John Shannon, 'TV ads struggle in Scandinavia', *Marketing Week* (20 September 1996), p. 26.

11. Alastair Ray, 'Time to sort out big local differences', *Financial Times FT Creative Business* (9 September 2003), p. 6.

12. See Alexandra Jardine and Laurel Wentz, 'It's a fat world after all', *Advertising Age* (7 March 2005), p. 3; George E. Belch and Michael A. Belch, *Advertising and Promotion* (New York: McGraw-Hill/Irwin, 2004), pp. 666–8; Jonathan Cheng, 'China demands concrete proof of ads', *Wall Street Journal* (8 July 2005), p. B1; Cris Prystay, 'India's brewers cleverly dodge alcohol-ad ban', *Wall Street Journal* (15 June 2005), p. B1; and Dean Visser, 'China puts new restrictions on cell phone, e-mail advertising', *Marketing News* (15 March 2006), p. 23.

13. Emiko Terazano, 'Ban on junk food adverts: "should be bolder"', *Financial Times* (29 March 2006), p. 5.

14. 'Do we have a story for you!', *The Economist* (21 January 2006), pp. 59–60.

15. Al Ries and Laura Ries, 'First do some publicity', *Advertising Age* (8 February 1999), p. 42; also see their book *The Fall of Advertising and the Rise of PR* (New York: HarperBusiness, 2002). For points and counterpoints and discussions of the role of public relations, see Robert E. Brown, 'Book review: The Fall of Advertising and the Rise of PR', *Public Relations Review* (March 2003), pp. 91–3; and David Robinson, 'Public relations comes of age', *Business Horizons* (May–June 2006), pp. 247–56.

16. Based on Meg Carter, 'Sponsorship branding takes on new name', *Financial Times* (13 March 2007), p. 12.

Company case 16 Ninety per cent of spend wasted!

DAVID BOWEN*

If half the money spent on advertising is wasted, at least 90 per cent of the money spent on brand sites is flushed away. Why?

The principal reason is that brand-builders have failed to realise just how different the Web is from other media. In particular, it is hopeless at soundbites. Brand-builders want to get across short messages by osmosis and association – nothing awkward like logic. The Web is just too literal and too sophisticated: it is marvellous for explaining the intricacies of the Martian landscape, or offering a choice of 2 million books, but it falls down badly when trying to sell you a bar of chocolate or a bottle of vodka.

Let us start with the vodka – ABSOLUT VODKA. Its site (www.absolut.com) epitomises this failure to get to grips with the medium. It is possibly the most elaborate brand-building site on the Web, and probably the biggest waste of money. I see a group of clever Swedes sitting around wondering if they can create a 'multimedia experience that truly conveys our brand values'. The result is a sub-daytime TV experience, with naff music, stilted voiceovers and pretty pictures trying to dress up desperately thin content. A few advertisements, cocktail recipes and some truly embarrassing features: try the 'Night out' in the ABSOLUT VANILLA section for a good cringe. This site is worthless because it is pointless. If you are going to spend a lot of money on a branding site, give it a job.

It is interesting to contrast national offerings from the same company to see what a difference this makes. Take Coca-Cola. Most of its national sites (accessible from www.coke.com) contain what has become a standard mix of TV ads, games, screensavers and the like – soft content that has hardly moved on in the last five years and reflects a depressing lack of imagination. By contrast, MyCokeMusic.com, part of the UK offering, is a branding site with a purpose. Here you can download a track or an album for less than iTunes prices, or stream a track (that is, listen to it once) for as little as 1p.

Coca-Cola sponsors the UK charts so the site fits perfectly with its image and, best of all, generates revenue.

Alternatively, look at the Guinness site (www.guinness.com). It asks on the home page where you are. Say you are in the US and you get a standard branding site, with ads (including an archive), product and company information, and a small store where you can buy a T-shirt but not a drink – all a bit ho-hum really. However, tell it you are in the UK, and you will find a site hung on the company's rugby sponsorship. Here is a sophisticated Fantasy Rugby game linked to the Six Nations tournament. I will be amazed if it is not a success.

Weetabix, the cereal company, has a site (www. weetabix.co.uk) that is sometimes useful, sometimes not. When it is supporting a cereal packet competition, it is essential. However, when there are no competitions, it is just another branding site – pleasant enough but pointless!

Guinness, Coke and Weetabix are lucky (or clever): they have seen ways of using the Web to support their overall promotional activity. But what do you do if you have no such hook? A good starting point is to follow Mars's lead with the Mars Bar. There is no Mars Bar site, but how many companies have such nerve? We have a product; therefore, we *must* have a website. OK, but make sure you get the right balance between money spent and effectiveness.

> The most common mistake is to spend a little and get nothing.

The most common mistake is to spend a little and get nothing. Hershey has a site for its KitKat (www.kitkatbar. com) that consists of one page that invites you to 'learn more about KIT KAT' (yes, they do use the wrong type set) wafer bar and directs you to a really exciting page of nutritional information. The only link in the main area is to an Ad Alert, a pop-up window warning that this website 'may be trying to sell you something'. Nestlé's KitKat site does little better. It says welcome to KITKAT.COM then, clicking on the Union Flag, gave the message 'KitKa$h – The KitKash promotion has now closed.' The once exciting www.kitkat.co.uk now just leaps to the no KitKa$h message. Not so much 'Have a break, have a KitKat' but 'Have a break, KitKat is broken'. Well, at least it is cheap – but why not go the Mars Bar route and spend the money in the pub instead?

The Americans call the Mars Bar a Milky Way, and it does have a site (www.milkyway.com). While much more elaborate than KitKat's, it is still thin: a list of ingredients, two television ads, some history, recipes and a product locator (put in your zip code and find a retailer). Some of these are marginally useful, especially if you want to turn your Milky Way into pink mousse tart, but how many people would really look on the Web for a retailer that sells a common confectionery? Or go online to watch a telly ad? I am not singling Milky Way out – it is one of thousands with a similarly dull mix.

Online games can work. They do not have to be complex to be engaging. My children and I have wasted a few happy hours playing Air Hockey at the Mini UK site (www.mini.co.uk); it is remarkably like Pong, which I used to play in the Seventies. If you do want something more sophisticated, locate – if you can – the fantasy football game at Coke UK (www.cocacola.co.uk): too clever for me. To see how the Web projects brand exclusivity apart from the e-commerce experience visit BMW's Mini Cooper site. Unfortunately you will have to own a Mini Cooper or have a friend that does because the site has sections accessible only to registered owners.

Given the plethora of such games and other diversions, these sites will flourish only if they get a loyal following – which leads me on to a site for which I have a special fondness. Acdoco is a North of England-based manufacturer of specialist cleaning products. Its site (www.acdo.co.uk) also has the 'world's longest-running

online soap', called The Laundorama. This semi-animated cartoon is very silly, and aimed firmly at students. The company sees it as a way of competing with the giants without pouring money into television ads. Does it work? Well, it has been going since April 1998: someone must think it does. At least – thank heavens – it is different.

Questions

1. How do Web-based communications differ from the other elements of the communications mix?
2. What are the websites mentioned trying to achieve?
3. Why does David Bowen draw a distinction between most of the websites he details in the case and those that explain the intricacies of the Martian landscape (http://marsrovers.nasa.gov/home/) or offer a choice of two million books (www.amazon.com)?
4. Does it matter or not if 'half the money spent on advertising is wasted' or '90 per cent of money spent on brand sites is flushed away'?
5. How can marketers evaluate the return on the money they spend upon brand sites and other advertising?

SOURCES: This case is based on David Bowen's article 'In search of a mission', *Financial Times* (5 February 2004), © David Bowen; Jonathan Birchall, FT report – Business of luxury: 'Weaving the web around exclusive brand sales', *Financial Times* (4 June 2007); *PR Newswire*, J.D. Power and Associates Reports: 'Breaking web site design standards can prove successful in establishing brand identity' (18 July 2007); and the websites mentioned, accessed on 28 August 2007.

*David Bowen works for the website effectiveness consultancy Bowen Craggs & Co. (www.bowencraggs.com).

Everyone lives by selling something.

ROBERT LOUIS STEVENSON

Personal selling and sales promotion

Mini Contents List

- Prelude case – Arla Foods – rethinking its sales force strategy and structure
- Personal selling
- Managing the sales force
- The personal selling process
- Real Marketing 17.1 – Cross-cultural selling: in search of universal values
- Sales promotion
- Real Marketing 17.2 – Sales promotions under siege: What should companies do?
- Company case 17 – Britcraft Jetprop: Whose sale is it anyhow?

◄ SOURCE: Avon Cosmetics Ltd.

'The Selling of Hope and the Death of Guilt'

Apoc on 'salesmanshipwrecked', Lab-Oratory, B000CAAPYE, 2003

Previewing the concepts

In the previous two chapters, you learned about communicating customer value through integrated marketing communications (IMC) and about two elements of the promotion mix – advertising and public relations. This chapter is about two more IMC elements – *personal selling* and *sales promotion*. Personal selling involves making direct connections with customers aimed at building customer-unique value. It is the interpersonal arm of marketing communications in which the sales force interacts with customers and prospects to build relationships and make sales. Sales promotion consists of short-term incentives to encourage customer purchasing, reseller support and sales force efforts. While mass advertising and public relations are useful for building brand awareness and influencing consumer attitudes and preferences towards a brand, personal selling and sales promotions are aimed towards eliciting action – customers' decision to buy.

As you read on, remember that although this chapter examines personal selling and sales promotions as separate tools, they must be carefully integrated with other elements of the marketing communication mix.

After reading this chapter, you should be able to:

1. Discuss the role of a company's salespeople in creating value for customers and building customer relationships.
2. Identify and explain the major sales force management steps.
3. Discuss the personal selling process, distinguishing between transaction-oriented marketing and relationship marketing.
4. Explain how sales promotion campaigns are developed and implemented.

We begin by looking at Arla Foods, a cooperative owned by European dairy farmers that besides selling perishable farm commodities, such as milk, has several leading brands of cheese and preserved milk that add value to the raw produce.

Prelude case   Arla Foods – rethinking its sales force strategy and structure

Arla Foods, Europe's second-largest dairy by turnover, is a cooperative of 10,500 Danish and Swedish farmers. It achieved its present scale after a series of mergers including MD Foods AMBA, which merged with Arla of Sweden to form Arla Foods AMBA and Arla Foods Plc in the UK. A further joint venture between Arla Foods Plc and Fronterra brought together the market-leading Lurpak and Anchor brands. Arla Foods UK grew further in 2003 through the merger with Express Dairies in the UK. The company also has sales subsidiaries in France, Germany, Greece, Italy, Poland, Norway, Sweden and the Middle East.

Arla Foods covers the entire spectrum of dairy products sold in markets across the world. Forty-five per cent of its turnover is from liquid milk products for which important markets are the UK, Sweden and Denmark. At 25 per cent of turnover, the second-largest product group is cheeses, sold primarily under strong brand names, including a full range of mould cheeses sold in world markets under the Rosenborg brand and cream cheeses sold under the Buko brand in Germany. Preserved milk products account for 14 per cent of Arla Foods' turnover, sold under the Puck name in the Middle East and under the DANO brand of packed full-fat milk powder products sold in the Middle East and Asia. In South America, these products are marketed under the Milex brand. Butter and butter spreads account for most of the remainder of Arla Foods' turnover, in which the main product is Lurpak, the Danish dairy industry's flagship brand in export markets. The largest market for Lurpak is the UK where, following the launch of Lurpak Spreadable, the brand is now the largest butter brand. Lurpak is also market leader in the Middle East.

Sold mostly unbranded, fresh milk is a truly fast-moving consumer good with enormous consequences if scheduling, production and distribution are not closely controlled. The margin of such commodity products is also extremely small with the major multiples dictating the market and constantly striving to reduce prices throughout the supply chain. As a result, first-class systems of communication, cost management and short interval control are required to manage this risk.

Europe's dairy industry is dominated by national producers. Generic products are typically marketed by product type, such as brie, feta, camembert and so forth, which are internationally known. Arla faces increasing competition not only from national and local producers, but also from international companies with a track record in product development and branding.

A number of important changes have occurred in the European market environment in the past decade. These include the withdrawal of EU subsidies to the export of dairy products to non-EU countries in 1996, the increasing concentration of food retailers in Europe and the increasing centralisation in retailers' buying decision making as well as product mix planning. Arla accounts for a third of total EU exports of feta cheese. The end of subsidies to exports to markets such as the Middle East has had a big impact on the company's profits, putting heavy pressure on the company to shift milk used for feta production to other products (such as milk powders and yellow cheeses) for EU customers.

Apart from deciding which product group(s) to emphasise, another major problem confronting Arla is how to develop a more effective sales and marketing structure to compete cost-effectively in these market situations.

In the past, the company has based its sales organisation on geographical and national considerations. Moreover, the focus of the sales force was on individual stores rather than retail chains or key accounts. With the emerging retail concentration and centralisation of buying and planning functions in customers' organisations, Arla recognises the need to respond to these pressures and to consider the options for managing the sales function, from analysing sales to managing key accounts. The time was right for dramatic action.

A key opportunity arose when one customer – a large international retailer – introduced the idea of key account management to the company. This one customer's European turnover exceeded the turnover of many of Arla's subsidiaries, making it more important than some of the company's geographic markets. Arla decided to introduce key account management in its sales and marketing organisations, starting in Denmark, where retail concentration is high and the company has a dominant market position. Essentially, three key account managers were appointed to serve specific key accounts, divided into FDB, the Danish co-operative; DS, a private retail group together with Aldi, part of a German retail group; and other retailers. The key account managers worked as a team with three trade managers (who have in-store marketing and space management expertise) in relation to the specific key accounts. The Sales Director coordinated the key account managers, while the trade managers reported to the national trade marketing manager. In this way, Arla could achieve optimisation of the sales force, while also ensuring that know-how is shared through coordination of trade marketing.

The organisational change piloted in Denmark was later introduced in Sweden, but reactions from both Arla's subsidiary and major Swedish retailers were less positive. At headquarters, Arla is contemplating what steps to take next. What should the sales force strategy and organisational structure for sales be? Should the key account management format be applied in other markets? Should the key account managers be responsible for the sales force assigned to their key account? Existing sales forces also vary in size, from 15 down to four people. Large sales forces dealing with stores with more autonomous management see to tasks such as sales, merchandising, displays, placing signs and posters and new campaigns. Smaller sales forces serve the highly centralised retailers and handle merchandising and displays. New developments must also take into account different workloads, skills and career developments for sales forces and key account managers serving different retailers and geographic markets. What will satisfy customer and employee requirements? Finally, can the new structure that is evolved be successfully applied to Arla's operations across Europe?

The need to review the sales operation is now particularly important because of sudden changes in the market. After years of being squeezed by supermarkets to sell dairy produce at very low prices, surging demand in the Far Eastern markets has coincided with low production caused by extraordinarily wet weather in northern Europe and Canada and extremely dry weather in southern Europe and Australia, forcing up the price of animal feed. Demand for dried milk, an internationally traded commodity, has doubled, thus encouraging farmers to sell on the global market rather than supplying locally. Owing to the increased demand for powdered milk from countries in the Middle East and Asia, farmers can now earn €0.44 per litre by selling into that market (up from €0.25 at the start of the year), €0.32 per litre in the liquid milk market and €0.31 in the cheese market. For now, selling is no problem; buying the raw materials is the real headache.

Questions

1. Why does Arla rely on a sales force to sell its products?
2. What are the key considerations that Arla needs to take into account in setting its sales force's objectives, strategy, structure and compensation? Identify the trade-offs involved in each of these decisions.
3. What are the key challenges facing the company in developing and implementing an organisational structure that will satisfy both customers and employees (sales force, marketing and key account managers)? Recommend and justify a strategy for Arla.

SOURCES: Based on Mogéns Bjerre, 'MD Foods AMBA: a new world of sales and marketing', in *Understanding Marketing: A European Casebook,* Celia Philips, Ad Pruyn and Marie-Paule Kestemont (eds), pp. 30–41 (Reproduced with permission, copyright © John Wiley & Sons Ltd, Chichester, UK 2000); Tom Griggs, 'Companies UK: Arla Foods to buy rest of UK arm', *Financial Times* (21 October 2006), accessed online at www.ft.com, August 2007; Dan Buglass, 'Arla Foods' rise to 25p continues milk producers' price increases', *The Scotsman* (22 August 2007); Jenny Wiggins, 'Shoppers to pay as demand rises for milk powder', *Financial Times* (28 August 2007), accessed online at www.ft.com, August 2007.

The questions in the prelude case reflect some of the critical issues that management must address when determining sales force strategy and structure. Indeed, the decisions called for are relevant not only for Arla Foods, but also for any firm that uses a sales force to help it market its goods and services.

Personal selling

'Nothing Happens Until Somebody Sells Something' is the oldest adage in sales. However great the design, however grand the plan, it is a sale that makes a dream a reality. Companies around the world use sales forces to sell products and services to business customers and final consumers. Sales forces are found in non-profit as well as profit organisations. For example, universities use recruiters to attract new students and churches use membership committees to attract new members. Hospitals and museums use fund-raisers to contact donors and raise money. In the first part of this chapter, we examine personal selling's role in the organisation, sales force management decisions and the personal selling process.

 Nothing happens until somebody sells something.

The nature of personal selling

Selling is one of the oldest professions in the world. The people who do the selling go by many names: *salespeople, sales representatives, account executives, sales consultants, sales engineers, field representatives, agents, marketing representatives* and *account development reps*, to name a few.

People hold many stereotypes of salespeople – including some unfavourable ones. 'Salesman' may bring to mind the image of Arthur Miller's pitiable Willy Loman in *Death of a Salesman* or Meredith Willson's cigar-smoking, backslapping, joke-telling Harold Hill in *The Music Man* or the super showman Barnum and 'the greatest show on earth'. These examples depict salespeople as loners, travelling their territories, trying to foist their wares on unsuspecting or unwilling buyers.

Modern salespeople are, however, a far cry from these unfortunate stereotypes. Today, most professional salespeople are well-educated, well-trained men and women who work to build and maintain long-term customer relationships. They succeed not by taking customers in but by helping them out – they listen to their customers, assess customer needs and organise the company's efforts to solve customer problems.

Consider Airbus, the aerospace company that markets commercial aircraft. It takes more than a friendly smile and a firm handshake to sell expensive aeroplanes. Selling high-tech aircraft at €100m or more per order is complex and challenging. A single big sale can run into billions of euros. Airbus salespeople head up an extensive team of company sales specialists – sales and service technicians, financial analysts, planners, engineers – all dedicated to finding ways to satisfy airline customer needs. The selling process is nerve-rackingly slow – it can take two to three years from the first sales presentation to the day the sale is announced. Sometimes top executives from both the airline and the company are brought in to close the deal. After getting the order, salespeople must stay in almost constant touch to keep track of the account's equipment needs and to make certain the customer stays satisfied. Success depends on building solid, long-term relationships with customers, based on performance and trust.

Salesperson—An individual representing a company to customers by performing one or more of the following activities: prospecting, communicating, selling, servicing, information gathering and relationship building.

The term **salesperson** covers a wide range of positions. At one extreme, a salesperson might be largely an *order taker*, such as a department store salesperson standing behind the counter. At the other extreme are the *order getters*, salespeople whose job demands *creative selling* and *relationship building* for products and services ranging from appliances, industrial equipment and aircraft to insurance, consultancy and information technology services. In this chapter, we focus on the more creative types of selling and on the process of building and managing an effective sales force.[1]

The role of the sales force

Personal selling is the interpersonal arm of the promotion mix. Advertising consists of one-way, non-personal communication with target consumer groups. In contrast, personal selling involves two-way personal communication between salespeople and individual customers – whether face to face, by telephone, through video or Web conferences or by other means. Personal selling can be more effective than advertising in more complex selling situations. Salespeople can probe customers to learn more about their problems and then adjust the marketing offer to fit the special needs of each customer and negotiate terms of sale. They can also build long-term personal relationships with key decision makers.

The role of personal selling varies from company to company. Some firms have no salespeople at all – for example, organisations that sell only online or through catalogues or through manufacturers' representatives, sales agents or brokers. In most firms, however, the sales force plays a major role. In companies that sell business products and services, such as ABB or DuPont, the company's salespeople work directly with customers. In consumer product companies, such as Nestlé, adidas and Unilever, which sell through intermediaries, final consumers rarely meet salespeople or even know about them. Still, the sales force plays an important behind-the-scenes role. It works with wholesalers and retailers to gain their support and to help them to be more effective in selling the company's products.

The sales force serves as the critical link between a company and its customers. In many cases, salespeople serve both masters – the seller and the buyer. First, they *represent the company to customers*. They find and develop new customers and communicate information about the company's products and services. They sell products by approaching customers, presenting their products, answering objections, negotiating prices and terms, and closing sales. In addition, they provide customer service and carry out market research and intelligence work.

At the same time, salespeople *represent customers to the company*, acting inside the firm as a 'champions' of customers' interests and managing buyer–seller relationships. Thus, the salesperson often acts as an '*account manager*' who manages the relationship between the seller and buyer. Salespeople relay customer concerns about company products and actions back inside to those who can handle them. They learn about customer needs and work with marketing and non-marketing people in the company to develop greater customer value. The old view was that salespeople should worry about sales and the company should worry about profit. However, the current view holds that salespeople should be concerned with more than just producing sales – they should work with others in the company to produce *customer value* and *company profit*.

As companies move towards a stronger market orientation, their sales forces are becoming more market focused and customer oriented. Today, organisations expect salespeople to look at sales data, measure market potential, gather market intelligence and develop marketing strategies and plans. They should know how to coordinate the firm's efforts towards delivering customer value and satisfaction. A market-oriented rather than a sales-oriented sales force will be more effective in the long run. Beyond winning new customers and making sales, it will help the company to create long-term, profitable relationships with customers. As such, the company's sales team can be a central force in an organisation's relationship marketing programme. Relationship marketing is discussed in greater detail in Chapter 8.

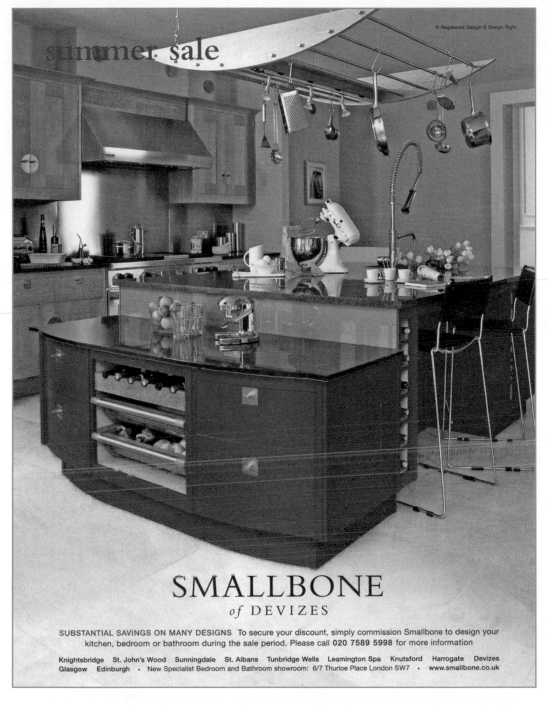

SMALLBONE
of DEVIZES

SUBSTANTIAL SAVINGS ON MANY DESIGNS To secure your discount, simply commission Smallbone to design your kitchen, bedroom or bathroom during the sale period. Please call **020 7589 5998** for more information

Knightsbridge   St. John's Wood   Sunningdale   St. Albans   Tunbridge Wells   Leamington Spa   Knutsford   Harrogate   Devizes
Glasgow   Edinburgh   •   New Specialist Bedroom and Bathroom showroom: 6/7 Thurloe Place London SW7   •   www.smallbone.co.uk

If you are having a new kitchen you may soon discover the need for personal selling and customising.
SOURCE: The Advertising Archives.

Managing the sales force

We define **sales force management** as the analysis, planning, implementation and control of sales force activities. It includes designing sales force strategy and structure and recruiting, selecting, training, compensating, supervising and evaluating the firm's salespeople. The major sales force management decisions are shown in Figure 17.1. We'll examine each of these decisions next.

Sales force management—The analysis, planning, implementation and control of sales force activities. It includes designing sales force strategy and structure and recruiting, selecting, training, supervising and evaluating the firm's salespeople.

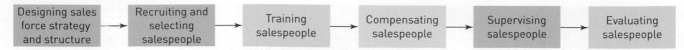

Figure 17.1 Major steps in sales force management

Designing sales force strategy and structure

Marketing managers face several sales force strategy and design questions. How should salespeople and their tasks be structured? How big should the sales force be? Should salespeople sell alone or work in teams with other people in the company? Should they sell in the field or by telephone or on the Web?

Sales force strategy

Every company competes with other firms to get orders from customers. Thus it must base its strategy on an understanding of the customer buying process. A company can use one or more of several sales approaches to contact customers. An individual salesperson can talk to a prospect or customer in person or over the phone, or make a sales presentation to a buying group. Similarly, a sales *team* (such as a company executive, a salesperson and a sales engineer) can make a sales presentation to a buying group. In *conference selling*, a salesperson brings resource people from the company to meet with one or more buyers to discuss problems and opportunities. In *seminar selling*, a company team conducts an educational seminar about state-of-the-art developments for a customer's technical people.

Often, the salesperson has to act as an account manager who arranges contacts between people in the buying and selling companies. Because salespeople need help from others in the company, selling calls for teamwork. Others who might assist salespeople include top management, especially when big sales are at stake; technical people who provide technical information to customers; customer service representatives who provide installation, maintenance and other services to customers; and office staff, such as sales analysts, order processors and secretaries.

Once the company decides on a desirable selling approach, it can use either a direct or a contractual sales force. A *direct* (or *company*) *sales force* consists of full- or part-time employees who work exclusively for the company. A *contractual sales force* consists of manufacturers' reps, sales agents or brokers who are paid a commission based on their sales.

Sales force structure

Sales force strategy influences the structure of the sales force. A company can divide up sales responsibilities along any of several lines. The decision is simple if the company sells only one product line to one industry with customers in many locations. In that case the company would use a *territorial sales force structure*. If the company sells many products to many types of customer, it might need either a *product sales force structure*, a *customer sales force structure*, or a combination of the two.

Territorial sales force structure

In the **territorial sales force structure**, each salesperson is assigned to an exclusive geographic area and sells the company's full line of products or services to all customers in that territory. This organisation clearly defines each salesperson's job and fixes accountability. It also increases the salesperson desire to build local business relationships that, in turn, improve selling effectiveness. Finally, because each salesperson travels within a small geographic area, travel expenses are relatively small.

Territorial sales force structure—A sales force organisation that assigns each salesperson to an exclusive geographic territory in which that salesperson sells the company's full line.

Product sales force structure

Salespeople must know their products, which is not an easy task if the company's products are numerous, unrelated and technically complex. This, together with the growth of product management, has led many companies to adopt a **product sales force structure**, in which the sales force sells along product lines. For example, a company such as Kodak uses different sales forces for its film products and its industrial products. The film products sales force deals with simple products that are distributed intensively, whereas the industrial products sales force deals with complex products that require technical understanding.

The product structure can lead to problems, however, if a given customer buys many of the company's products. For example, a healthcare products and services company may have several product divisions, each with a separate sales force. Using a product sales force structure might mean that several salespeople might end up calling on the same hospital on the same day. This means that they travel over the same routes and wait to see the same customer's purchasing agents. These extra costs must be weighed against the benefits of better product knowledge and attention to individual products.

Product sales force structure—A sales force organisation under which salespeople specialise in selling only a portion of the company's products or lines.

Customer sales force structure

More and more companies are using a **customer sales force structure**, whereby they organise the sales force along customer or industry lines. Separate sales forces may be set up for different industries, for serving current customers versus finding new ones, and for major accounts versus regular accounts.

Organising the sales force around customers can help a company build closer relationships with important customers. For example, giant ABB, the Swiss-based industrial equipment maker, changed from a product-based to a customer-based sales force. The new structure resulted in a stronger customer orientation and improved service to clients:

Customer sales force structure—A sales force organisation under which salespeople specialise in selling only to certain customers or industries.

David Donaldson sold boilers for ABB. After 30 years, Donaldson sure knew boilers, but he didn't know much about the broad range of other products offered by ABB's Power Plant division. Customers were frustrated because as many as a dozen ABB salespeople called on them at different times to peddle their products. Sometimes representatives even passed each other in customers' lobbies without realising that they were working for the same company. ABB's bosses decided that this was a poor way to run a sales force. So, David Donaldson and 27 other power plant salespeople began new jobs. [Donaldson] now also sells turbines, generators, and three other product lines. He handles six major accounts . . . instead of a [mixed batch] of 35. His charge is to know the customer intimately and sell him the products that help him operate productively. Says Donaldson: 'My job is to make it easy for my customer to do business with us . . . I show him where to go in ABB whenever he has a problem.' The president of ABB's power plant businesses [adds]: 'If you want to be a customer-driven company, you have to design the sales organisation around individual buyers rather than around your products.'[2]

 My job is to make it easy for my customer to do business with us.

Complex sales force structures

When a company sells a wide variety of products to many types of customer over a broad geographical area, it often combines several types of sales force structure. Salespeople can be specialised by customer and territory, by product and territory, by product and customer, or by territory, product and customer. A salesperson might then report to one or more line and staff managers. No single structure is best for all companies and situations. Each organisation should select a structure that best serves the needs of its customers and fits its overall marketing strategy.

A good sales structure can mean the difference between success and failure. Companies should periodically review their sales force organisations to be certain that they serve the needs of the company and its customers.

Sales force size

Once the company has set its structure, it is ready to consider *sales force size*. Sales forces may range in size from only a few salespeople to tens of thousands. Salespeople constitute one of the company's most productive – and most expensive – assets. Therefore, increasing their number will increase both sales and costs.

Many companies use some form of **workload approach** to set sales force size. The company first groups accounts according to size, account status or other factors related to the amount of effort required to maintain them. It then determines the number of salespeople needed to call on each class of accounts the desired number of times.

The company might reason as follows. Suppose we have 1,000 Type-A accounts each requiring 36 calls a year, and 2,000 Type-B accounts each requiring 12 calls a year. In this case, the sales force's *workload*, as defined by the number of calls it must make per year, is 60,000 calls (36,000 + 24,000). Suppose our average salesperson can make 1,000 calls a year. The company thus needs 60 salespeople (60,000/1,000).

Other sales force strategy and structure issues

Sales management also have to decide who will be involved in the selling effort and how various sales and sales support people will work together.

Outside and inside sales forces

The company may have an **outside sales force** (or **field sales force**), an **inside sales force** or both. Outside salespeople travel to call on customers, whereas inside salespeople conduct business from their offices via telephone, the Internet or visits from buyers.

Some inside salespeople provide support for the outside sales force, freeing them to spend more time selling to major accounts and finding major new prospects. For example, technical sales support people provide technical information and answers to customers' questions. Sales assistants provide administrative backup for outside salespeople. They call ahead and confirm appointments, follow up on deliveries, and answer customers' questions when outside salespeople cannot be reached.

Other inside salespeople do more than just provide support. *Telemarketers* and *Web sellers* use the phone and Internet to find new leads and qualify prospects or to sell and service accounts directly. **Telemarketing** and Web selling can be very effective, less costly ways to sell to smaller, harder-to-reach customers. Depending on the complexity of the product and customer, a telemarketer can make 20–33 decision-maker contacts a day, compared to the average of four that an outside salesperson can make. And whereas an average field sales call can cost €300 or more, a routine industrial telemarketing call costs between €7 and €30 depending on the complexity of the call.

Just as telemarketing is changing the way that many companies go to market, the Internet offers explosive potential for restructuring sales forces and conducting sales operations. More and more companies are now using the Internet to support their personal selling efforts, ranging from selling and training salespeople to conducting sales meetings and servicing accounts. Electronic negotiations are also taking root, with more and more organisations using the Web to conduct sales negotiations.

Workload approach—An approach to setting sales force size, whereby the company groups accounts into different classes according to size, account status or other factors related to the effort required to maintain them, and then determines how many salespeople are needed to call on them the desired number of times.

Outside sales force (or field sales force)—Outside salespeople who travel to call on customers in the field.

Inside sales force—Salespeople who conduct business from their offices via telephone, the Internet or visits from prospective customers.

Telemarketing—Using the telephone to sell directly to consumers.

Team selling

As products become more complex, and as customers grow larger and more demanding, a single salesperson simply can't handle all of a large customer's needs. Instead, most companies are now using **team selling** to service large, complex accounts. Sales teams can unearth problems, solutions and sales opportunities that no individual salesperson could. Such teams might include people from any area or level of the selling firm – sales, marketing, technical and support services, R&D, engineering, operations, finance and others. In team selling situations, the salesperson shifts from 'soloist' to 'orchestrator', helping to coordinate company-wide efforts to build profitable customer relationships.

In many cases, the move to team selling mirrors similar changes in customers' buying organisations. Increasingly, sales people are calling on teams of buying people. One salesperson just cannot do it all or be an expert in everything the company brings to the customer. Thus, they have strategic account teams, led by customer business managers.

Team selling—Using teams of people from sales, marketing, production, finance, technical support, and even upper management to service large, complex accounts.

> **The salesperson shifts from 'soloist' to 'orchestrator'.**

Some companies, such as IBM, Xerox, Unilever and Procter & Gamble, have used teams. Sales reps are organised into 'customer business development (CBD) teams'. Each CBD team is assigned to a major customer. Teams consist of a customer business development manager, several account executives (each responsible for a specific category of products), and specialists in marketing strategy, operations, information systems, logistics and finance. This organisation places the focus on serving the complete needs of each important customer. The idea is to grow the firm's business by working as a 'strategic partner' with its key customers or accounts, not just as a supplier. By helping the customer grow its business, the company can, in turn, grow its own.

Team selling does have some pitfalls. Selling teams can confuse and overwhelm customers who are used to working with only one salesperson. Salespeople who are used to having customers all to themselves may have trouble learning to work with and trust others on a team. Finally, difficulties in evaluating individual contributions to the team selling effort can create some sticky compensation issues.

Key account management

Continuing relationships with large customers dominate the activities of many sales organisations. For makers of fast-moving consumer goods such as Procter & Gamble, Nestlé, Unilever and Danone, the relationship is with major retailers such as Tengelmann, Carrefour, Tesco or Ahold. The importance of these retailers has changed the way marketing as a whole is being organised. *Account managers* often orchestrate the relationship with a single retailer, although some will manage several smaller retailers or a group of independent retail outlets. A major retailer will typically carry major manufacturers' brands, so the account manager's role is one of increasing the profitability of sales through the channel. In this arrangement a great deal of sales promotions effort and advertising is customised for retailers that want exclusive lines or restrict the type of promotions that are adopted. The account manager's role is to maintain regular contacts at all levels between the organisations. When the client or prospect is particularly important, key account managers are responsible for building and maintaining mutually beneficial relationships between the buying and selling teams.[3]

Recruiting and selecting salespeople

At the heart of any successful sales force operation is the recruitment and selection of good salespeople. The performance difference between an average salesperson and a top salesperson can be substantial. In a typical sales force, the top 30 per cent of the salespeople might bring 60 per cent of the sales. Thus careful salesperson selection can greatly increase overall sales force performance.

Beyond the differences in sales performance, poor selection results in costly turnover. When a salesperson quits, the costs of finding and training a new salesperson, plus the costs of lost sales, can be very high. Also, a sales force with many new people is less productive than one with a stable membership, and turnover disrupts important customer relationships.[4]

What are the traits of a good salesperson?

Selecting salespeople would not be a problem if the company knew what traits spell surefire sales success. If it knew that good salespeople were outgoing, aggressive and energetic, for example, it could simply check applicants for these characteristics. Many successful salespeople, however, are also bashful, soft-spoken and laid back.

So, what sets great salespeople apart from all the rest? In an effort to profile top sales performers, Gallup Management Consulting Group, a division of the well-known Gallup polling organisation, interviewed hundreds of thousands of salespeople. Its research suggests that the best salespeople possess four key talents: intrinsic motivation, disciplined work style, the ability to close a sale, and perhaps most important, the ability to build relationships with customers.[5]

Super salespeople are motivated from within. 'Different things drive different people – pride, happiness, money, you name it,' says one expert. 'But all great salespeople have one thing in common: an unrelenting drive to excel.' Some salespeople are driven by money, a hunger for recognition, or the satisfaction of competing and winning. Others are driven by the desire to provide service and to build relationships. The best salespeople possess some of each of these motivations.

Whatever their motivations, salespeople must also have a disciplined work style. If salespeople are not organised and focused, and if they do not work hard, they cannot meet the ever-increasing demands customers make these days. Great salespeople are tenacious about laying out detailed, organised plans, then following through in a timely, disciplined way. Says one sales trainer, 'Some people say it's all technique or luck. But luck happens to the best salespeople when they get up early, work late, stay up till two in the morning working on a proposal or keep making calls when everyone is leaving at the end of the day.'

Other skills mean little if a salesperson can't close the sale. So what makes for a great closer? For one thing, it takes unyielding persistence. 'Great closers are like great athletes,' says one sales trainer. 'They're not afraid to fail, and they don't give up until they close.' Great closers also have a high level of self-confidence and believe that they are doing the right thing.

 Great closers are like great athletes.

Perhaps most important in today's relationship-marketing environment, top salespeople are customer problem solvers and relationship builders. They instinctively understand their customers' needs. Talk to sales executives and they'll describe top performers in these terms: *empathetic, patient, caring, responsive, good listeners, honest*. Top performers can put themselves on the buyer's side of the desk and see the world through their customers' eyes. They don't want just to be liked, they want to add value for their customers.

When recruiting, companies should analyse the sales job itself and the characteristics of its most successful salespeople to identify the traits needed by a successful salesperson in their industry. Does the job require a lot of planning and paperwork? Does it call for much travel? Will the salesperson face a lot of rejections? Will the salesperson be working with high-level buyers? The successful sales candidate should be suited to these duties.

Companies spend hundreds of millions of euros to train their salespeople in the art of selling.
SOURCE: Digital Vision Limited.

Recruiting procedures and selection

After management has decided on essential talents and traits, it must *recruit* the desired candidate. The human resources department looks for applicants by getting names from current salespeople, using employment agencies and placing classified ads. Another source is to attract top salespeople from other companies. Proven salespeople need less training and can be immediately productive.

Recruiting will attract many applicants, from which the company must select the best. The selection procedure can vary from a single informal interview to lengthy testing and interviewing. Many companies give formal tests to sales applicants. Tests typically measure sales aptitude, analytical and organisational skills, personality traits and other characteristics. But test scores provide only one piece of information in a set that includes personal characteristics, references, past employment history and interviewer reactions.[6]

Training salespeople

New salespeople may spend anything from a few weeks or months to a year or more in training. The average initial training period is four months. Then, most companies provide continuous sales training via seminars, sales meetings and the Web throughout the salesperson's career.

Training programmes have several goals. First, salespeople need to know about customers and how to build relationships with them. So the training programme must teach them about different types of customers and their needs, buying motives and buying habits. Because salespeople must know how to make effective presentations and to sell effectively, they need to be trained in the basics of the selling process. Salespeople also need to know and identify with the company, its products and its competitors. So an effective training programme teaches them about the company's objectives, organisation and chief products and markets, as well as about the strategies of major competitors. Finally, salespeople need to understand field procedures and responsibilities. They learn how to divide time between active and potential accounts and how to use an expense account, prepare reports and route communications effectively.

Today, many companies are adding Web-based training to their sales training programmes to cut training costs and make training more efficient. Online training may range from simple text-based product information to Internet-based sales exercises that build sales skills to sophisticated simulations that recreate the dynamics of real-life sales calls.

Compensating salespeople

To attract salespeople, a company must have an attractive compensation plan. These plans vary greatly both by industry and by companies within the same industry. Compensation is made up of several elements – a fixed amount, a variable amount, expenses and fringe benefits. The fixed amount, usually a salary, gives the salesperson some stable income. The variable amount, which might be commissions or bonuses based on sales performance, rewards the salesperson for greater effort and success. Expense allowances, which repay salespeople for job-related expenses, let salespeople undertake needed and desirable selling efforts. Fringe benefits, such as paid vacations, sickness or accident benefits, pensions and life insurance, provide job security and satisfaction.

Management must decide what *mix* of these compensation elements makes the most sense for each sales job. Different combinations of fixed and variable compensation give rise to four basic types of compensation plans – straight salary, straight commission, salary plus bonus and salary plus commission.

The sales force compensation plan can both motivate salespeople and direct their activities. If sales management wants salespeople to emphasise new account development, it might pay a bonus for opening new accounts. Thus, the compensation plan should direct the sales force towards activities that are consistent with overall marketing objectives.

Table 17.1 shows how a company's compensation plan should reflect its overall marketing strategy. For example, if the strategy is to grow rapidly and gain market share, the compensation

Table 17.1 The relationship between overall marketing strategy and sales force compensation

	Strategic goal		
	To gain market share rapidly	**To solidify market leadership**	**To maximise profitability**
Ideal salesperson	• An independent self-starter	• A competitive problem solver	• A team player • A relationship manager
Sales focus	• Deal making • Sustained high effort	• Consultative selling	• Account penetration
Compensation role	• To capture accounts • To reward high performance	• To reward new and existing account sales	• To manage the product mix • To encourage team selling • To reward account management

SOURCE: Adapted from Sam T. Johnson, 'Sales compensation: In search of a better solution', *Compensation and Benefits Review* (November–December), pp. 53–60. Copyright © 1993 by Sage Publications, Inc. Journals. Reproduced with permission of Sage Publications, Inc. Journals in the format Textbook via Copyright Clearance Center.

plan might include a large commission component, coupled with a new-account bonus to encourage high sales performance and new-account development. In contrast, if the goal is to maximise current account profitability, the compensation plan might contain a larger base-salary component, with additional incentives for current account sales and customer satisfaction. In fact, more and more companies are moving away from high-commission plans that may drive salespeople to make short-term grabs for business. They may even ruin a customer relationship because they were pushing too hard to close a deal. Instead, companies are designing compensation plans that reward salespeople for building customer relationships and growing the long-run value of each customer.[7]

Supervising salespeople

New salespeople need more than a territory, compensation and training – they need *supervision* and *motivation*. The goal of supervision is to help salespeople 'work smart' by doing the right things in the right ways. The goal of motivation is to encourage salespeople to 'work hard' and energetically toward sales force goals. If salespeople work smart and work hard, they will realise their full potential, to their own and the company's benefit.

Directing salespeople

How much should sales management be involved in helping salespeople manage their territories? It depends on everything from the company's size to the experience of its sales force.

Developing customer targets and call norms

Companies vary in how closely they supervise their salespeople. Many help their salespeople in identifying customer targets and setting call norms. Some may also specify how much time their sales force should spend prospecting for new accounts and set other time management priorities. If left alone, many salespeople will spend most of their time with current customers, which are better-known quantities. Moreover, whereas a prospect may never deliver any business, salespeople can depend on current accounts for some business. Therefore, unless salespeople are rewarded for opening new accounts, they may avoid new-account development.

Using sales time efficiently

Companies also direct salespeople in how to use their time efficiently. One tool is the weekly, monthly or annual *call plan* that shows which customers and prospects to call on and which activities to carry out. Activities include taking part in trade shows, attending sales meetings and carrying out marketing research. Another tool is *time-and-duty analysis*. In addition to time spent selling, the salesperson spends time travelling, waiting, eating, taking breaks and doing administrative chores.

Figure 17.2 shows how salespeople spend their time. On average, active selling time accounts for only 10 per cent of total working time! If selling time could be raised from 10 per cent to 30 per cent, this would triple the time spent selling or negotiating and talking face-to-face with potential customers.[8] Companies are always looking for ways to save time – simplifying record-keeping, finding better sales call and routing plans, supplying more and better customer information, and using phones, e-mail or videoconferencing instead of travelling. Consider the changes GE made to increase its sales force's face-to-face selling time.[9]

Figure 17.2 How salespeople spend their time

SOURCE: Proudfoot Consulting. Data used with permission.

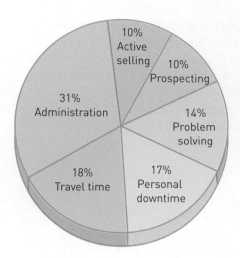

- 10% Active selling
- 10% Prospecting
- 14% Problem solving
- 17% Personal downtime
- 18% Travel time
- 31% Administration

When Jeff Immelt became General Electric's new chairman, he was dismayed to find that members of the sales team were spending far more time on deskbound administrative chores than in face-to-face meetings with customers and prospects. 'He said we needed to turn that around,' recalls Venki Rao, an IT leader in global sales and marketing at GE Power Systems, a division focused on energy systems and products. '[We need] to spend four days a week in front of the customer and one day for all the admin stuff.' GE Power's salespeople spent much of their time at their desks because they had to go to many sources for the information needed to sell multimillion-dollar turbines, turbine parts and services to energy companies worldwide. To fix the problem, GE created a new sales portal, a kind of 'one-stop shop' for just about everything they need. The sales portal connects the vast array of existing GE databases, providing everything from sales tracking and customer data to parts pricing and information on planned outages. GE also added external data, such as news feeds. 'Before, you were randomly searching for things,' says Bill Snook, a GE sales manager. Now, he says, 'I have the sales portal as my home page, and I use it as the gateway to all the applications that I have.' The sales portal has freed Snook and 2,500 other users around the globe from once time-consuming administrative tasks, greatly increasing their face time with customers.

Many firms have adopted sales force automation systems – computerised, digitised sales force operations that let salespeople work more effectively anytime, anywhere. Companies now routinely equip their salespeople with new-age technologies such as laptops, smart phones, wireless Web connections, webcams for videoconferencing and customer-contact and relationship management software. Armed with these technologies, salespeople can more effectively and efficiently profile customers and prospects, analyse and forecast sales, schedule sales calls, make presentations, prepare sales and expense reports and manage account relationships. The result is better time management, improved customer service, lower sales costs and higher sales performance.[10]

Perhaps the fastest-growing sales force technology tool is the Internet. Sales organisations around the world are now saving money and time by using a host of Web approaches to train reps, hold sales meetings and conduct live sales presentations.[11]

Sales force automation: Many sales forces have gone high tech, equipping salespeople with everything from smart phones, wireless Web connections and videoconferencing to customer-contact and relationship management software that helps them to be more effective and efficient.
SOURCE: Javier Pierini/ Photodisc/Getty Images.

For example, for the past few years, chemicals company Fisher Scientific International has been using the Internet to teach the majority of its salespeople in the privacy of their homes, cars, hotel rooms or wherever else they bring their laptops. To get updates on Fisher's pricing or refresh themselves on one of the company's highly technical products, all salespeople have to do is log on to the website and select from the lengthy index.

Training is only one of the ways sales organisations are using the Internet. Many companies are using the Web to make sales presentations and service accounts.

For example, computer and communications equipment maker NEC Corporation has adopted Web-based selling as an essential marketing tool. After launching a new server line, NEC began looking for ways to cut down on difficult and costly sales force travel. According to Dick Csaplar, marketing manager for the new server line, NEC's old sales approach – travelling to customer sites to pitch NEC products – had become unworkable. Instead, NEC adopted a new Web-based sales approach. Although the initial goal was to cut costs and keep people off aeroplanes, Web selling has now grown into an intrinsic part of NEC's sales efforts. Web selling has reduced travel time and costs. Whereas the average daily cost of salesperson travel is around €600, an hour-long Web conference costs just €60. But more importantly, Web selling lets sales reps meet with more prospective customers than ever before, creating a more efficient and effective sales organisation. Csaplar estimates that he's doing 10 customer Web conferences a week, during which he and his sales team show prospects product features and benefits. Customers love it because they get a clear understanding of NEC's technology without having to host the NEC team on-site. Web-based selling is also an effective way to interact with customers and to build customer relationships. 'By the time we're done with the webcast, the customer understands the technology, the pricing and the competition, and we understand the customer's business and needs,' he says. Without webcasts, 'we'd be lost on how to communicate with the customer without spending a lot of money,' says Csaplar. 'I don't see us ever going back to the heavy travel thing.'

The Web can also be a good channel tool for selling to hard-to-reach customers.

For example, the big pharmaceutical companies typically employ huge sales forces (often called 'detailers') to reach thousands of practising physicians. However, these reps are finding it harder than ever to get through to the busy doctors. The answer: increasingly, it's the Web. The pharmaceutical companies now regularly use product websites, e-mail marketing and videoconferencing to help reps deliver useful information to physicians on their home or office PCs. Using direct-to-doctor Web conferences, companies can make live, interactive medical presentations to any physician with a PC and Web access, saving both the customer's and the rep's time.

The Internet can also be a handy way to hold sales strategy meetings.

Consider Cisco Systems, which provides networking solutions for the Internet. Sales meetings used to take an enormous bite out of Cisco's travel budget. Now the company saves about over €1m per month by conducting many of those sessions on the Web. Whenever Cisco introduces a new product, it holds a Web meeting to update salespeople, in groups of 100 or more, on the product's marketing and sales strategy. Usually led by the product manager or a Director of Sales, the meetings typically begin with a 10-minute slide presentation that spells out the planned strategy. Then, salespeople spend the next 50 or so minutes asking questions via teleconference. The meeting's leader can direct attendees' browsers to competitors' websites or ask them to vote on certain issues by using the software's instant polling feature.

Thus, Web-based technologies can produce big organisational benefits for sales forces. They help conserve salespeople's valuable time, save travel money and give salespeople a new vehicle for selling and servicing accounts. But the technologies also have some drawbacks. For starters, they're not cheap. And such systems can intimidate low-tech salespeople or clients who are not comfortable with using the Web. Also, Web tools are susceptible to server crashes and other network difficulties, not a happy event when you're in the midst of an important sales meeting or presentation.

For these reasons, some high-tech experts recommend that sales executives use Web technologies for training, sales meetings and preliminary client sales presentations, but resort to old-fashioned, face-to-face meetings when the time draws near to close the deal.

Motivating salespeople

Beyond directing salespeople, sales managers must also motivate them. Some salespeople will do their best without any special urging from management. To them, selling may be the most fascinating job in the world. But selling can also be frustrating. Salespeople usually work alone, and they must sometimes travel away from home. They may face aggressive, competing sales-people and difficult customers. They sometimes lack the authority to do what is needed to win a sale and may thus lose large orders that they have worked hard to obtain. Therefore, salespeople often need special encouragement to do their best.

Management can boost sales force morale and performance through its organisational climate, sales quota and positive incentives.

Organisational climate

Organisational climate reflects the feeling that salespeople have about their opportunities, value and rewards for good performance. Some companies treat salespeople as if they are not very important, and performance suffers accordingly. Other companies treat their salespeople as valued contributors and allow virtually unlimited opportunity for income and promotion. Not surprisingly, these companies enjoy higher sales force performance and less turnover.

Sales quotas

Many companies motivate their salespeople by setting **sales quotas** – standards stating the amount they should sell and how sales should be divided among the company's products. Compensation is often related to how well salespeople meet their quotas.

Sales quotas—Standards set for salespeople, stating the amount they should sell and how sales should be divided among the company's products.

Positive incentives

Companies also use various positive incentives to increase sales force effort. *Sales meetings* provide social occasions, breaks from routine, chances to meet and talk with 'company brass', and opportunities to air feelings and to identify with a larger group. Companies also sponsor *sales contests* to spur the sales force to make a selling effort above what would normally be expected. Other incentives include honours, merchandise and cash awards, trips and profit-sharing plans.

Evaluating salespeople

Thus far we have described how management communicates what salespeople should be doing and how it motivates them to do it. This process requires good feedback, which means getting regular information from salespeople to evaluate their performance.

Sources of information

Management gets information about its salespeople in several ways. The most important source is the *sales report*, including weekly or monthly work plans and longer-term territory marketing plans. The work plan describes intended calls and routing, which provide management with information on the salespeople's whereabouts, and provides a basis for comparing plans and performance. The territory marketing plan outlines how new accounts will be built and sales from existing accounts increased. Salespeople also write up their completed activities on *call reports* and turn in *expense reports* for which they are partly or wholly repaid.

Additional information comes from personal observation, customers' letters and complaints, customer surveys and talks with other salespeople.

Formal evaluation of performance

Using various sales force reports and other information, sales management *formally evaluates* members of the sales force. Formal evaluation forces management to develop and communicate clear standards for judging performance. It evaluates salespeople on their ability to 'plan their work and work their plan'. It also provides salespeople with constructive feedback which helps them to improve future performance and to motivate them to perform well.

On a broader level, management should evaluate the performance of the sales force as a whole. Is the sales force accomplishing its customer relationship, sales and profit objectives? Is it working well with other areas of the marketing and company organisation? Are sales-force costs in line with outcomes? As with other marketing activities, the company wants to measure its *return on sales investment*.[12]

We have looked at the key issues concerning sales force management – designing and managing the sales force. Next we turn to the actual personal selling process.

The personal selling process

Personal selling is an ancient art that has spawned a large literature and many principles. Effective salespeople operate on more than just instinct – they are highly trained in methods of territory analysis and customer management. Effective companies take a *customer-oriented approach* to personal selling. They train salespeople to identify customer needs and to find solutions. This approach assumes that customer needs provide sales opportunities, and that customers appreciate good suggestions and will be loyal to salespeople who have their long-term interests at heart. By contrast, companies that use a *sales-oriented approach* rely on high-pressure selling techniques. They assume that customers will not buy except under pressure, that they are influenced by a slick presentation and that it does not matter even if they feel regret after signing the order.

Steps in the selling process

Selling process—The steps that the salesperson follows when selling, which include prospecting and qualifying, pre-approach, approach, presentation and demonstration, handling objections, closing and follow-up.

Prospecting—The step in the selling process in which the salesperson identifies qualified potential customers.

The **selling process** consists of several steps that the salesperson must master (see Figure 17.3). These steps focus on the goal of getting new customers and obtaining orders from them. However, many salespeople spend much of their time maintaining existing accounts and building long-term customer relationships. We will address the relationship aspect of the personal selling process in a later section.

Prospecting and qualifying

The first step in the selling process is **prospecting** – identifying qualified potential customers. Approaching the right potential customers is crucial to selling success. The salesperson must often approach many prospects to get just a few sales. Although the company supplies some leads, salespeople need skill in finding their own. The best source is referrals. Salespeople can ask current customers for referrals and cultivate other referral sources, such as suppliers, dealers, non-competing salespeople and bankers. They can also search for prospects in directories or on the Web and track down leads using the telephone and direct mail. Or they can drop in unannounced on various offices (a practice known as 'cold calling').

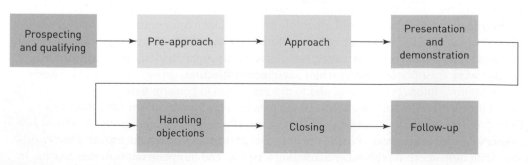

Figure 17.3 Major steps in effective selling

Salespeople need to know how to *qualify* leads: that is, how to identify the good ones and screen out the poor ones. Prospects can be qualified by looking at their financial ability, volume of business, special needs, location and possibilities for sales growth.

Pre-approach

Before calling on a prospect, the salesperson should learn as much as possible about the organisation (what it needs, who is involved in the buying) and its buyers (their characteristics and buying styles). This step is known as the **pre-approach**. The salesperson can consult standard industry and online sources, acquaintances and others to learn about the company. The salesperson should set *call objectives*, which may be to qualify the prospect, to gather information or to make an immediate sale. Another task is to decide on the best approach, which might be a personal visit, a phone call or a letter. The best timing should be considered carefully because many prospects are busiest at certain times. Finally, the salesperson should give thought to an overall sales strategy for the account.

Pre-approach—The step in the selling process in which the salesperson learns as much as possible about a prospective customer before making a sales call.

Approach

During the **approach** step, the salesperson should know how to meet and greet the buyer, and get the relationship off to a good start. This step involves the salesperson's appearance, his or her opening lines and the follow-up remarks. The opening lines should be positive to build goodwill from the beginning of the relationship. This opening might be followed by some key questions to learn more about the customer's needs, or by showing a display or sample to attract the buyer's attention and curiosity. As in all stages of the selling process, listening to the customer is crucial.

Approach—The step in the selling process in which the salesperson meets and greets the buyer to get the relationship off to a good start.

Presentation and demonstration

The **presentation** is that step in the selling process where the salesperson tells the product 'story' to the buyer, presenting customer benefits and showing how the product solves the customer's problems. The problem-solver salesperson fits better with today's marketing concept than does a hard-sell salesperson or the glad-handing extrovert. Buyers today want solutions, not smiles; results, not razzle-dazzle. They want salespeople who listen to their concerns, understand their needs and respond with the right products and services.

Presentation—The step in the selling process in which the salesperson tells the product 'story' to the buyer, highlighting customer benefits.

> Buyers today want solutions, not smiles; results, not razzle-dazzle.

This *need-satisfaction approach* calls for good listening and problem-solving skills.[13] The qualities that buyers dislike most in salespeople include being pushy, late, deceitful and unprepared or disorganised. The qualities they value most include empathy, good listening, honesty, dependability, thoroughness and follow-through. Great salespeople know how to sell, but more importantly they know how to listen and to build strong customer relationships. Says one professional, 'Salespeople must have the right answers, certainly, but they also have to learn how to ask those questions and listen.'[14]

Today, advanced presentation technologies allow for full multimedia presentations to only one or a few people. CDs and DVDs, online presentation technologies and handheld and laptop computers with presentation software have replaced the flipchart.

Handling objections

Customers almost always have objections during the presentation or when asked to place an order. The problem can be either logical or psychological, and objections are often unspoken. In **handling objections**, the salesperson should use a positive approach, seek out hidden objections,

Handling objections—The step in the selling process in which the salesperson seeks out, clarifies and overcomes customer objections to buying.

With personal selling, the customer feels a greater need to listen and respond, even if the response is a polite 'no thank you'.
SOURCE: Jon Feingersh/Stock Boston.

ask the buyer to clarify any objections, take objections as opportunities to provide more information, and turn the objections into reasons for buying. Every salesperson should be trained in the skills of handling objections.

Closing

Closing—The step in the selling process in which the salesperson asks the customer for an order.

After handling the prospect's objections, the salesperson now tries to close the sale. Some salespeople do not get around to **closing** or do not handle it well. They may lack confidence, feel guilty about asking for the order or fail to recognise the right moment to close the sale. Salespeople should know how to recognise closing signals from the buyer, including physical actions, comments and questions. For example, the customer might sit forward and nod approvingly or ask about prices and credit terms.

Salespeople can use one of several closing techniques. They can ask for the order, review points of agreement, offer to help write up the order, ask whether the buyer wants this model or that one, or note that the buyer will lose out if the order is not placed now. The salesperson may offer the buyer special reasons to close, such as a lower price or an extra quantity at no charge.

Follow-up

Follow-up—The last step in the selling process, in which the salesperson follows up after the sale to ensure customer satisfaction and repeat business.

The last step in the selling process – **follow-up** – is necessary if the salesperson wants to ensure customer satisfaction and repeat business. Right after closing, the salesperson should complete any details on delivery time, purchase terms and other matters. The salesperson should then schedule a follow-up call when the initial order is received to make sure there is proper installation, instruction and servicing. This visit would reveal any problems, assure the buyer of the salesperson's interest and reduce any buyer concerns that might have arisen since the sale.

International selling

The typical sales process can be applied in international selling. However, intercultural trade always requires special efforts in tailoring sales and negotiation approaches (see Real Marketing 17.1).

real marketing 17.1

Cross-cultural selling: in search of universal values

Face-to-face selling is the least easily controlled part of international marketing. Academics and consultants have drawn up numerous lists of 'do's and don'ts' based on examining negotiations within particular cultures. Increasingly, international marketers are turning to both culture-specific negotiation studies and general cultural research in an attempt to understand the cultural values that influence negotiation behaviour and how best to adapt their selling styles.

One popular tool is Geert Hofstede's 'five universal values' framework for defining national culture. These five aspects are as follows.

- *Time orientation.* This is a culture's sense of immediacy. Generally, Asians have longer time orientations than western cultures and tend to spend a longer time establishing a personal relationship at the start of the negotiation process. This is one reason why western business people found *karaoke* sessions rewarding when negotiating with Japanese and Korean executives! Because the relationship is the *content* of the negotiation, and the basis of the longer-term benefits derived from the deal, as opposed to the short-term aspects of the deal in progress, the 'relationship approach' will better fit Asian cultures than it would western cultures. The lesson: when selling to someone with a long-term orientation culture, expect to spend more time on forming the client relationship, rather than merely focusing on the contract.

- *Aversion to uncertainty.* The level of risk that negotiators will bear is partly a function of the level of uncertainty that they are used to in their culture. For countries where people reflect a higher tolerance of ambiguity, such as the UK and Denmark, the salesperson may spend less time probing the buyer's needs before closing the deal. In countries such as France, where people have lower tolerance of uncertainty, the French salesperson may take longer to clarify exactly what it is that the customer needs.

- *Acceptance of unequal power.* The level of inequality that people expect and accept in their jobs and lives – also called 'power distance' by Hofstede – also affects negotiation style. In high power distance cultures, subordinates would only approach high-level superiors with a problem of great importance. By contrast, in low power distance cultures, staff at a lower level in the corporate hierarchy are more accustomed to being treated like equals by their superiors, with whom they feel they can discuss matters directly. So, when negotiating with a buyer used to weighting status heavily, the seller organisation should ensure that salesperson seniority matches that of the buyer.

- *Individualism or collectivism.* This reflects the person's level of independence and degree of freedom. The US and UK are generally regarded as individualistic

societies which value freedom and independence. In collectivistic cultures, such as Japan and China, people's sense of value is derived from belonging to a group. Consequently, negotiators influenced by the latter culture may take more time and effort to reach consensus and closure.

● *Masculinity and femininity.* Achievement and possessions reflect masculine values, while the social environment and helping others tap femininity. People tend to lie along the masculinity–femininity continuum. In masculine cultures, exemplified by Austria in Hofstede's study, salespeople use an assertive style, which can be off-putting if applied in feminine cultures, such as Denmark. The latter would place more emphasis on partnership to achieve both parties' desired outcomes. Those in the middle of this continuum would value the establishment of good relationships with clients as much as hard facts and contractual details.

The five universal values offer a base for addressing cross-cultural settings in international selling and the need for adaptation of the selling approach. However, neither Hofstede nor advocates of his model suggest that successful international negotiation comes from following the old adage 'when in Rome, do as the Romans do'. Rather, the experts argue that negotiators do not negotiate with someone from their own culture in the same way that they negotiate with someone from another culture. So, knowing how Swedish people negotiate with each other seldom gives much help in predicting how they will negotiate with their Japanese counterpart. Moreover, as an increasing proportion of international executives are educated abroad or have broad overseas experience, they may adapt their cultural styles to show familiarity with their foreign negotiators' cultural values. Imagine a German salesperson adopting the French 'win–win' approach when negotiating with her French client and the French client using 'win–lose' techniques typically associated with German negotiation style. The key, therefore, lies not so much in *mimicking* the foreign client's cultural values, but in subtle *adaptation* to fit the other negotiator's style.

SOURCES: Geert Hofstede, *Culture's Consequences: Comparing values, behaviors, institutions and organizations across nations*, 2nd edn (London: Sage Publications, 2003); Anne Macquin and Dominique Rouziés, 'Selling across the culture gap', *Financial Times*, FT Mastering Global Business, Part Seven (1997), pp. 10–11; Geert Hofstede, *Cultures and Organisations: Software of the mind* (London: McGraw-Hill, 1991); Sergey Frank, 'Global negotiating', *Sales and Marketing Management* (May 1992), pp. 64–9; J.C. Morgan and J.J. Morgan, *Cracking the Japanese Market* (New York: Free Press, 1991).

Personal selling and customer relationship management

The principles of personal selling as described are *transaction oriented*, in that their aim is to help salespeople close a specific sale with a customer. But in many cases, the company is not seeking simply a sale: it has targeted a major customer that it would like to win and keep. The company would like to show the customer that it has the capabilities to serve the customer over the long haul, in a mutually profitable relationship. The sales force usually plays an important role in building and managing profitable customer relationships.

More companies today are moving away from transaction marketing, with its emphasis on making a sale. Instead, they are practising **relationship marketing**, which emphasises maintaining profitable long-term relationships with customers by creating superior customer value and satisfaction. They realise that, when operating in maturing markets and facing tougher competition, it costs a lot more to wrest new customers from competitors than to keep current ones.

Today's large customers favour suppliers who can sell and deliver a coordinated set of products and services to many locations, and who can work closely with customer teams to improve products and processes. For these customers, the first sale is only the beginning of the relationship.

Unfortunately, many companies are not set up for these relationship realities. They often sell their products through separate sales forces, each working independently to close sales. Their technical people may not be willing to lend time to educate a customer. Their engineering, design and manufacturing people may have the attitude that 'it's our job to make good products and the salesperson's to sell them to customers'. Their salespeople focus on pushing products towards customers rather than listening to customers and providing solutions.

However, the more successful companies recognise that winning and keeping accounts requires more than making good products and directing the sales force to close lots of sales. It requires listening to customers, understanding their needs and carefully coordinating the whole company's efforts to create customer value and to build lasting relationships.

Having addressed personal selling's role in creating customer value, the major sales force management steps and the personal selling process, we now examine sales promotion.

> **Relationship marketing—**
> The process of creating, maintaining and enhancing strong, value-laden relationships with customers and other stakeholders.
>
> **Sales promotion—**
> Short-term incentives to encourage purchase or sales of a product or service.

Sales promotion

Sales promotion consists of short-term incentives, in addition to the basic benefits offered by the product or service, to encourage the purchase or sale of a product or service. Whereas advertising offers reasons to buy a product or service, sales promotion offers reasons to buy *now*.

Sales promotion includes a wide variety of promotion tools designed to stimulate earlier or stronger market response. These tools are used by many organisations – manufacturers, distributors, retailers, trade associations and non-profit institutions – and may be targeted towards the consumer or final buyer, business customers, the trade or retailer and the company's sales force. **Consumer promotions** include money-off, coupons, premiums, contests and others. **Trade promotions** (or **retailer promotions**) range from special discounts, free goods and loyalty bonuses to training. **Business promotions** include many of the same tools used for consumer or trade promotions such as conventions and trade shows, as well as sales contests. **Sales force promotions** include bonuses, commissions, free gifts and competitions.

> **Consumer promotion—** Sales promotion designed to stimulate consumer purchasing, including samples, coupons, rebates, prices-off, premiums, patronage rewards, displays, and contests and sweepstakes.
>
> **Trade (or retailer) promotion—**Sales promotion designed to gain reseller support and to improve reseller selling efforts, including discounts, allowances, free goods, cooperative advertising, push money, and conventions and trade shows.

Rapid growth of sales promotion

Several factors have contributed to the rapid growth of sales promotion, particularly in consumer markets. First, inside the company, product managers face greater pressures to increase their current sales, and promotion is increasingly viewed as an effective short-run sales tool. In mature markets, manufacturers are striving to maintain market share through a balance between longer-term 'share-of-voice' gained from advertising and shorter-term incentives for the consumer. Second, externally, the company faces more competition, and competing brands are less differentiated. Increasingly, competitors are using sales promotion to help differentiate their offers. Third, advertising efficiency has declined because of rising costs, media clutter and legal restraints. Sales promotion used in conjunction with other communications, such as personal selling and direct marketing, can offer a more cost-effective route to reach target consumers. Fourth, consumers have become more deal-oriented and ever-larger retailers are demanding more deals from manufacturers. Finally, developments in information technology, the reduction

Business promotion—
Sales promotion designed to generate business leads, stimulate purchase, reward business customers and motivate the salesforce.

Sales force promotion—
Sales promotion designed to motivate the sales force and make sales force selling efforts more effective, including bonuses, contests and sales rallies.

in data storage and retrieval costs, and the increased sophistication of targeting techniques have enabled companies to implement sales promotions and to more effectively monitor and measure the performance of sales promotion campaigns.

The growing use of sales promotion has resulted in *promotion clutter*, similar to advertising clutter. Consumers are increasingly 'tuning out' promotions, weakening their ability to trigger immediate purchase. Manufacturers are now searching for ways to rise above the clutter, such as offering larger coupon values, creating more dramatic point-of-purchase displays or developing more creative sales promotion campaigns that stand out from the crowd.

In developing a sales promotion programme, a company must set sales promotion objectives and then select the best tools for accomplishing these objectives.

Setting sales promotion objectives

Sales promotion objectives vary widely. First, let's consider *consumer promotions*. Sellers may use consumer promotions to: (1) increase short-term sales; (2) build long-term market share; (3) urge consumers to try a new product; (4) lure consumers away from competitors' products; (5) encourage consumers to 'load up' on a mature product; or (6) reward loyal customers, hence enhancing long-term customer relationships.

Objectives for *trade promotions* include: (1) getting retailers to carry new items and more stock; (2) inducing them to buy ahead; and (3) persuading them to advertise the company's products and give them more shelf space.

For the *sales force*, objectives may be to: (1) get more sales force support for current or new products; or (2) stimulate salespeople to sign up new accounts.

Sales promotions are usually used together with advertising, personal selling or other promotion mix tools. Consumer promotions must usually be advertised and can add excitement and pulling power to ads. Trade and sales force promotions support the firm's personal selling process.

As with other communications objectives, sales promotion objectives should be measurable. Rather than stating that the promotion aims to increase sales, the objective should be specific about the level of increase, who the main targets are and whether increased sales are expected to come from first-time buyers or from current consumers who are loading up or bringing forward their purchase.

In general, rather than creating only short-term sales or temporary brand switching, sales promotions should help to reinforce the product's position and build long-term customer relationships. Increasingly, marketers are avoiding 'quick fix', price-led promotions in favour of **consumer relationship-building promotions** designed to build brand equity by promoting the product's positioning and reinforcing the selling message.

Examples include all the 'frequency marketing programmes', 'loyalty card schemes' and 'loyalty clubs' that have mushroomed in recent years. Most hotels, retailers and airlines now offer frequent-guest/buyer/flyer programmes offering rewards to regular customers. If properly designed, every sales promotion tool has the potential to build consumer relationships.

Consumer relationship-building promotions—
Sales promotions that promote the product's positioning and include a selling message along with the deal.

For example, cash-back credit card schemes reward users with rebates (that is, cash) based on their spending. The BA Miles Amex card encourages frequent flyers to collect miles which can be redeemed against BA flights. In addition, customers spending more than £20,000 (approximately €28,500) on this card also receive a free flight for their partner, doubling, in effect, their reward. According to Moneysaving expert.com which uses its online 'LoyaltyChecker' and 'RewardsChecker' calculators to compare the value of different reward points and credit card spend, cashback reward schemes often give a higher return than points-based loyalty credit cards because consumers can put the cash towards travel or other spending. They can also be used with other shopping loyalty cards such as Tesco's Clubcard to 'double dip', thus earning two sets of rewards. The highest-paying cashback cards typically offer close to 1 per cent of spending, or more for introductory periods or for high spenders. For example, American Express Platinum credit card pays up to 1.5 per cent cashback, while Amex and Morgan Stanley Platinum and Egg Money pay new customers triple cashback for the first three months. So, if you are a high spender, and always pay off your bill in full every month, using one of these cards could earn you hundreds of pounds (or euros) of cash back a year.

As competition intensifies, some retailers have sought to differentiate and to increase the value of their rewards. The beauty products retailer Body Shop International introduced the 'Love your body membership' in an attempt to revitalise sales in the US. The consumer pays an initial joining fee of £6 (€9), which entitles the holder to a 10 per cent discount for one year, together with a free birthday gift and other gifts, according to spending on the card. In the UK, the company introduced The Body Shop People card, which is free on application and offered the choice of savings on particular purchases or a donation of an equivalent amount to charities nominated by the group.[15]

Sales promotions have certain limitations. Sellers need to recognise that new triers at whom their promotions are targeted consist of consumers of the product category, loyal users of another brand and users who frequently switch brands. Sales promotions often attract the last group – *brand switchers* – because non-users and users of other brands do not always notice or act on a promotion. Brand switchers are looking mostly for low price or good value. Sales promotions are unlikely to turn them into loyal brand users. Moreover, when a company uses price promotion for a brand too much of the time, consumers begin to think of it as a cheap brand. Or, many consumers will buy the brand only when there is a special offer. As a result, researchers argue that sales promotion activities do not build long-term consumer preference and loyalty, as does advertising. Instead, they only boost short-term sales that are not sustained over the long run. Marketers therefore rarely use sales promotion for dominant brands because it would do little more than subsidise current users.[16]

Sales promotions often attract . . . brand switchers.

Despite the dangers, many consumer packaged-goods companies continue to use sales promotions. They maintain that sales promotions benefit manufacturers by letting them adjust to short-term fluctuations in supply and demand and differences in customer segments. Sales promotions encourage consumers to try new products instead of always staying with their current ones. They lead to more varied retail formats, such as the everyday-low-price store or the promotional-pricing store, which give consumers more choice. Finally, sales promotions lead to greater consumer awareness of prices, and consumers themselves enjoy the satisfaction of taking advantage of price specials.[17]

Major sales promotion tools

Many tools can be used to accomplish sales promotion objectives. The promotion planner selects these tools by considering the sales promotion objectives, the type of market, the competition and the cost-effectiveness of each tool. Let's look at the main consumer and trade promotion tools.

Consumer promotion tools

The main consumer promotion tools include samples, coupons, cash refunds, price packs, premiums, advertising specialities, patronage rewards, point-of-purchase displays and demonstrations, and contests, sweepstakes and games.

Samples—Offers to consumers of a trial amount of a product.

Samples are offers of a trial amount of a product. Sampling is the most effective, but most expensive, way to introduce a new product or to create excitement for an existing one. Consumer packaged-goods marketers tend to use sampling as part of their promotion strategy. Some samples are free; for others, the company charges a small amount to offset its cost. The sample might be delivered door to door, sent by mail, handed out in a store, attached to another product or featured in an ad. Sometimes, samples are combined into sample packs, which can then be used to promote other products and services.

Coupons—Certificates that give buyers a saving when they purchase a product.

Coupons are certificates that give buyers a saving when they purchase specified products. They can promote early trial of a new brand or stimulate sales of a mature brand. However, when used excessively, they result in coupon clutter and a decline in redemption rates. Thus, many major consumer goods companies are issuing fewer coupons and targeting them more carefully. They are also cultivating new outlets for distributing coupons, such as supermarket shelf dispensers, electronic point-of-sale coupon printers, e-mail and online media or even text-messaging systems. For example, text-message couponing is gaining popularity in Europe and the US as well as in Asian countries including Singapore, India and Japan.

Cash refund offers (or rebates)—Offers to refund part of the purchase price of a product to consumers who send a 'proof of purchase' to the manufacturer.

Cash refund offers (or **rebates**) are like coupons except that the price reduction occurs after the purchase rather than at the retail outlet. The consumer sends a 'proof of purchase' to the manufacturer, which then refunds part of the purchase price by mail.

Price packs—Reduced prices that are marked by the producer directly on the label or package.

Price packs or reduced prices offer consumers savings off the regular price of a product. The reduced prices are marked by the producer directly on the label or package. Price packs can be single packages sold at a reduced price (such as two for the price of one) or two related products banded together (such as a toothbrush and toothpaste). Price packs are very effective – even more so than coupons – in stimulating short-term sales.

Premiums—Goods offered either free or at low cost as an incentive to buy a product.

Premiums are goods offered either free or at low cost as an incentive to buy a product. A premium may come inside the package (in-pack) or outside the package (on-pack) or through the mail. Premiums are sometimes mailed to consumers who have sent in a proof of purchase, such as a box top. A *self-liquidating premium* is a premium sold below its normal retail price to consumers who request it. Kellogg often incorporates premiums with its cereals and related products. A recent campaign is noteworthy in its attempt to encourage families and children to stay fit and healthy by taking the 'Kellogg's Cycle10 Challenge'.

To reinforce the message that Kellogg's cereals can help individuals towards meeting the recommended daily allowance of essential vitamins and iron, Kellogg adopted the 'Wake up to Breakfast' theme in its cereal brand communications. Consistent with the 'health and wellbeing' theme, the company teamed up with Sustrans, the leading sustainable transport charity, to get users in the UK and Ireland to take the 'Kellogg's Cycle10 challenge' – cycle 10 miles or 10 km every week with the family and friends. They could join the charity's National Cycle Network, bringing them 150 or more family-friendly cycle rides whose routes could be printed off from the www.kelloggs.co.uk/cycling and www.kelloggs.ie/cycling sites. To keep track of their progress, they could claim their free Cyclometer which allows them to monitor how far and fast they have cycled. And, to add further value, consumers could also get special cycling discounts from selected local retailers.

Advertising specialities—Useful articles imprinted with an advertiser's name, given as gifts to consumers.

Advertising specialities are useful articles imprinted with an advertiser's name, logo or message that are given as gifts to consumers. Typical promotional items include pens, calendars, key rings, coffee mugs, mouse pads, T-shirts, caps and golf balls.

Patronage rewards—Cash or other awards for the regular use of a certain company's products or services.

Patronage rewards are cash or other awards offered for the regular use of a certain company's products or services. For example, airlines offer 'frequent flyer plans', awarding points for miles travelled that can be turned in for free airline trips. Hotels have adopted 'honoured guest' plans

Price-led promotions such as 'buy one get one free' are very effective in stimulating short-term sales. However, when a company uses price promotion for a brand excessively, consumers begin to think of it as a cheap brand.

SOURCE: Iceland Foods Plc. The Advertising Archives.

that award points to users of their hotels. And supermarkets and retailers issue 'reward' or 'loyalty points' which translate into money-off vouchers that can be used towards future purchases. As noted earlier, reward or loyalty schemes that offer genuine paybacks on spending can be used to build lasting consumer relationships.

Point-of-purchase (POP) promotions—Displays and demonstrations that take place at the point of purchase or sale.

Point-of-purchase (POP) promotions include displays and demonstrations that take place at the point of purchase or sale. Think of your last visit to the local supermarket. Chances are good that you were tripping over aisle displays, promotional signs or demonstrators offering free tastes of featured food products. Unfortunately, many retailers do not like to handle the hundreds of displays, signs and posters they receive from manufacturers each year. Manufacturers have responded by offering better POP materials, offering to set them up and tying them in with television, print or online messages.

Competitions, sweepstakes, lotteries and games—Promotions that offer customers the chance to win something – cash, goods or trips – by luck or extra effort.

Competitions, sweepstakes, lotteries and games give consumers the chance to win something, such as cash, trips or goods, by luck or through extra effort. A *competition* calls for consumers to submit an entry – a jingle, slogan, guess or suggestion – to be judged by a panel that will select the best entries. A *sweepstake* calls for consumers to submit their names for a draw. For a *lottery*, consumers buy tickets which enter their names into a draw. A *game* presents consumers with something, such as bingo numbers or missing letters, every time they buy, which may or may not help them win a prize. A sales contest urges dealers and sales force to increase their efforts, with prizes going to the top performers.

Sales promotions in Europe

Like advertising, sales promotion techniques also face different legal constraints across Europe. The UK has the most liberal regulatory regime for sales promotion in Europe. Countries like Poland, Hungary and the Czech Republic also have relatively liberal policies on promotions and incentives. By contrast, legal controls have been stricter in Belgium, Germany, France and, notably so, in Norway. In Belgium, for example, retailers are not allowed to offer discounts of more than 33 per cent – a rule that prevents them from running 'buy-one-get-one-free' offers. In France, Belgium, Spain, Portugal, Italy, Luxembourg, Greece and Ireland, retailers are also not allowed to entice customers into their shops by offering sales below cost – that is, selling at a loss. In Ireland, to run a prize draw by mail or SMS (mobile phone text messaging), the company needs to secure the help of a registered charity, which is paid, so that, from a legal point of view, the charity becomes the promoter of the firm's campaign. In Spain, all games of chance, including instant wins, must be registered. This involves not only a fee of about 10 per cent of the prize fund, but also multiple registrations in each of the many autonomous regions of Spain. In Italy, a permit from the Finance Ministry is required for a promotion and, where prizes are involved, the promoter must deposit with the Ministry a sum of money equivalent to the prize fund, just in case they were tempted not to award the prizes in the end!

As you can see, there are myriad different national rules and barriers to running sales promotions across the EU. On the one hand, marketers lament the fact that their industry is also assailed by wave after wave of changing EU laws. On the other, critics charge that the increased regulation is a backlash to a morally and ethically bankrupt marketing community. Yet others agree that tighter controls are welcome to ensure that consumers' interests are protected from the unsavoury practices of sharp companies. An important part of the EU Commission's efforts therefore has been to build a single market through the introduction of new rules to free up restrictive regulations, on the one hand, while preventing unfair trade practices and protecting consumers' interests on the other. For example, the EU recently passed a new Unfair Commercial Practices Directive; member states are, to a greater or lesser extent, incorporating the new legislation into national laws and codes (see Real Marketing 17.2).

> There are myriad different national rules and barriers to running sales promotions across the EU.

real marketing

17.2

Sales promotions under siege: What should companies do?

The Unfair Commercial Practices Directive comes into force in April 2008 and, in the words of the EU itself, it is hoped that 'EU consumers will be given the same protection against aggressive or misleading marketing whether they buy locally or from other Member States' markets. Businesses will benefit from having a clear set of common EU rules to follow, rather than a myriad of divergent national laws and court case rulings, as is currently the case.' Specifically it seeks to ban unfair, misleading and aggressive business practices. These include:

- False or deceptive statements relating to key product factors
- Omission of material information
- Use of coercion or undue influence
- Providing false or untruthful information.

Such activities are to be illegal if they are likely to deceive the average consumer and are likely to cause him or her to take a transactional decision, i.e. a purchase that he or she might otherwise not have taken.

The Directive also prohibits 31 other specific offences, including:

- Bait-and-switch type advertising
- Limited offers – 'Today Only'
- Adverts disguised as editorial
- Pyramid schemes.

Of major concern to marketers are restrictions on 'free offers': 'Falsely creating the impression of free offers' – for example, an ad in a mail order catalogue states that you will receive a free pair of sunglasses, when in fact this only applies to persons ordering other products from the catalogue!.

So what can companies do to avoid further legislation and impositions on marketers' creativity? The simple answer is to do the right thing – comply with the rules. They reflect all that a reasonable consumer would expect of a promoter. Here's a checklist to ensure that promoters get the basics right.

Getting the basics right

A. Terms and Conditions – Checklist. Always have one and seek expert advice before committing to print or going live. All significant decision-making information should

...17.2

be provided at the time of sale/entry:

- Closing date
- Any restriction on the number of entries or prizes that may be won
- Any requirements of proof of purchase
- Clear description of prizes and any limitations or restrictions
- Any age or other restrictions
- How and when winners will be notified and results published
- The criteria for judging entries
- Where appropriate, the ownership of copyright of entries
- Whether and how entries are returnable by the promoter
- How full rules can be obtained
- Whether any cash alternative is available
- Any permissions required – e.g., parent or employer
- Any intention to use winners in post-event publicity
- The name of the promoter and address.

B. Is the entry form sensibly designed for data input and with clear entry instructions? Ideally the consumer should be able to keep a set of terms and conditions once they send in the application form. Does it meet Data Protection requirements – with appropriate opt-ins or opt-outs, clearance from mail/phone preference lists and so forth?

C. Additional requirements for competitions

- Are the criteria for judging stated? Are they clear, practical and specific or loose and woolly?
- Has an independent and competent judge been appointed? Have you budgeted for the cost of physically dealing with all entries?
- What is the procedure for dealing with more than one correct entry – that is, is there a tie-breaker?

D. Additional requirements for prize draws

- If a purchase is implied via an on-pack promotion, have you included a statement that no purchase is necessary (NPN)? It should be as prominent as any other method of entry.
- How will the NPN be run – via regular draws or at end of promotion?
- Has it the same chance of winning in an independently supervised draw?
- What controls are there on the handling house to ensure that it is handled correctly with no 'loss' of winners or transfer of data?
- Will the draws be conducted by an independent person or body?

E. Additional requirements for Instant Wins

- Instant Wins require a lot more consideration and care – and must comply with the country's Gambling Act (in the UK, this requires a free entry route; this and the distribution and seeding of winning packs must be independently supervised).

...17.2

- How will the NPN be operated? Via a random number generator, in which case allow for risk of incremental prizes? Or by opening actual promotional packs, in which case allow for the cost of wastage?
- Have you ensured that only the correct amount of winning tokens have been produced – no more, no less?
- Have they been randomly and securely seeded into the main production run?
- Is there an independent audit statement to this effect – as required by the code?

SOURCE: Adapted from Jeremy Stern, Institute of Sales Promotion, Director of Compliance, 'Promotions under siege?', *Sales Promotion* (26 April 2007). Sales Promotion Publishing Ltd., accessed online at www.salespromo.co.uk/article/150, July 2007.

Trade promotion tools

Trade promotion can persuade retailers or wholesalers to carry a brand, give it shelf space, promote it in advertising and push it to consumers. Shelf space is so scarce these days that manufacturers often have to offer price-offs, allowances, buy-back guarantees or free goods to retailers and wholesalers to get products on the shelf and, once there, to keep them on it.

Manufacturers use several trade promotion tools. Many of the tools used for consumer promotions – contests, premiums, displays – can also be used as trade promotions. Alternatively, the manufacturer may offer a straight **discount** off the list price on each case purchased during a stated period of time (also called a *price-off*, *off-invoice* or *off-list*). The offer encourages dealers to buy in quantity or to carry a new item. Dealers can use the discount for immediate profit, for advertising or for price reductions to their customers.

Manufacturers may also offer an **allowance** (usually so much off per case) in return for the retailer's agreement to feature the manufacturer's products in some way. An *advertising allowance* compensates retailers for advertising the product. A *display allowance* compensates them for using special displays.

Manufacturers may offer *free goods*, which are extra cases of merchandise, to intermediaries who buy a certain quantity or that feature a certain flavour or size. They may offer *push incentives* – cash or gifts to dealers or their sales force to 'push' the manufacturer's goods. Manufacturers may give retailers free *speciality advertising items* that carry the company's name, such as pens, pencils, coffee mugs, calendars, paperweights, matchbooks and memo pads.

Business promotion tools

Companies spend huge sums of money each year on promotion to industrial customers. These business promotions are used to generate business leads, stimulate purchases, reward customers and motivate salespeople. Business promotion includes many of the same tools used for consumer or trade promotions. Here, we focus on two of the main business promotion tools – conventions and trade shows and sales contests.

Conventions and trade shows

Many companies and trade associations organise conventions and trade shows to promote their products. Firms selling to the industry show their products at the trade show. Vendors receive many benefits, such as opportunities to find new sales leads, contact customers, introduce new products, meet new customers, sell more to present customers and educate customers with

Discount—A straight reduction in price on purchases during a stated period of time.

Allowance—(1) Reduction in price on damaged goods. (2) Promotional money paid by manufacturers to retailers in return for an agreement to feature the manufacturer's product in some way.

Some trade shows are huge. At this year's International Consumer Electronics Show, 2,500 exhibitors attracted more than 150,000 professional visitors.
SOURCE: Consumer Electronics Association.

publications and audiovisual materials. Trade shows also help companies reach many prospects not reached through their sales forces.

Some trade shows are huge. For example, the annual International Consumer Electronics Show typically attracts over 2,500 exhibitors and more than 150,000 professional visitors. Others such as the BAUMA mining and construction equipment trade show are even more impressive. The 2006 show in Munich, Germany, boasted some 2,800 exhibitors from 47 countries who presented their latest product innovations to more than 416,000 attendees from 171 countries.[18]

Sales contests

A *sales contest* is a contest for salespeople or dealers to motivate them to increase their efforts over a given period. Sales contests motivate and recognise good company performers, who may receive trips, cash prizes or other gifts. Some companies award points for performance, which the receiver can turn in for any of a variety of prizes. Sales contests work best when they are tied to measurable and achievable sales objectives (such as finding new accounts, reviving old accounts or increasing account profitability). Employees must also believe they have an equal chance of winning. If not, they will not take up the challenge.

Developing the sales promotion programme

Beyond selecting the types of sales promotions to use, marketers must make several other decisions in designing the full sales promotion programme. First, they must decide on the *size of the incentive*. A certain minimum incentive is necessary if the promotion is to succeed; a larger incentive will produce more sales response. The marketer must ensure that the promotion genuinely offers extra value and incentives to targets. Importantly, the promotion must not mislead and the firm must be able to honour redemptions. If not, the campaign could backfire, exposing the firm to bad publicity which damages its reputation and brand image.

The marketer must also set *conditions for participation*, such as whether the promotion should be offered to everyone or only to select groups, proof of purchase or closing date of the offer (see also Real Marketing 17.2).

For example, if a company is running a prize draw in the UK, it must include terms of sales and conditions (ts&cs) to cover the firm's obligations as dictated by regulatory guidelines set by the British Code of Advertising, Sales Promotion and Direct Marketing (www.cap.org.uk). As a minimum requirement, the firm must clearly specify how consumers might participate in the promotion, a description of the prizes available and applicable closing date. The promoter must also state their full name and business address. The ts&cs also govern the promoter's relationship with each entrant and agreement on the promoter's part to operate the prize draw in accordance with the ts&cs and to award the prize as stated. Applicable disclaimers must also be made clear.

A recent sales promotion run by the budget airline Ryanair in Ireland shows why prize descriptions are important. As the lucky one-millionth customer of the airline in Ireland, Jane O'Keeffe was, according to the promotional material, entitled to free flights with Ryanair for life. When Ryanair later changed her free flight entitlement to a maximum number per year, O'Keeffe sued for breach of contract. She won and was awarded £43,098 damages.

Ts&cs can be incredibly important should things go wrong. The Mirror Group Newspapers (MGN) ran a scratchcards game with a main prize of £50,000. An administrative error resulted in more winning scratchcards distributed than planned, with 1,472 winning cards eventually declared void. One of the winners took his claim to court, with MGN being liable for a total of £100 million payout. Thanks to the small print, which allowed the promoter to declare scratchcards void in the event of an error, MGN successfully defended this claim.[19]

The marketer must then decide how to *promote and distribute the promotion* programme itself. A money-off coupon could be given out in a package, at the store, via the Internet or in an advertisement. Each distribution method involves a different level of reach and cost. Increasingly, marketers are blending several media into a total campaign concept.

The *length of the promotion* is also important. If the sales promotion period is too short, many prospects (who may not be buying during that time) will miss it. If the promotion runs too long, the deal will lose some of its 'act now' force.

The marketer also must decide on the *response mechanism*: that is, the redemption vehicle used by the customer who takes part in the promotion. Immediate reward – for example, a price reduction, or a free gift attached to the product on offer – often yields a higher response. If the incentive requires further action to be taken by the consumer – for instance, to make another purchase or to collect the required number of tokens in promotion packs and then post these off to claim a gift or free product – the redemption rate can be reduced.

Companies should prepare implementation plans for each promotion, covering lead time and sell-off time. *Lead time* is the time necessary to prepare the programme before launching it. *Sell-off time* begins with the launch and ends when the promotion ends.

Evaluation is also very important. Many companies fail to evaluate their sales promotion programmes, while others evaluate them only superficially. Yet marketers should work to measure the returns on their sales promotion investments, just as they should seek to assess the returns on other marketing activities. The most common evaluation method is to compare sales before, during and after a promotion. Suppose a company has a 6 per cent market share before the promotion, which jumps to 10 per cent during the promotion, falls to 5 per cent right after and rises to 7 per cent later on. The promotion seems to have attracted new triers and more buying from current customers. After the promotion, sales fall as consumers use up their stocks. The long-run rise to 7 per cent means that the company gained some new users. If the brand's share had returned to the old level, then the promotion would have changed only the *timing* of demand rather than the *total* demand.

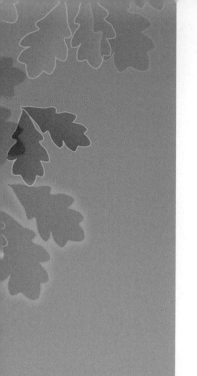

Marketers should therefore ask whether the promotion attracted new customers or more purchasing from current customers. Can we hold on to these new customers and purchases? Will the long-run customer relationship and sales gains from the promotion justify its costs?

The firm should undertake consumer *surveys* which will provide information on how many consumers recall the promotion, what they thought of it, how many took advantage of it and how it affected their buying. Sales promotions can also be evaluated through *experiments* that vary factors such as incentive value, timing, duration and distribution method.

Clearly, sales promotion plays an important role in the total promotion mix. To use it well, the marketer must define the sales promotion objectives, select the best tools, design the sales promotion programme, implement the programme and evaluate the results. Moreover, sales promotion must be coordinated carefully with other promotion mix elements within the integrated marketing communications programme.

Reviewing the concepts

This chapter investigates personal selling and sales promotion. Personal selling is the interpersonal arm of the communications mix. Sales promotion consists of short-term incentives to encourage the purchase or sale of a product or service.

1. Discuss the role of a company's salespeople in creating value for customers and building customer relationships

Most companies use salespeople, and many companies assign them an important role in the marketing mix. For companies selling business products, the firm's salespeople work directly with customers. Often, the sales force is the customer's only direct contact with the company and therefore may be viewed by customers as representing the company itself. In contrast, for consumer product companies that sell through intermediaries, consumers usually do not meet salespeople or even know about them. The sales force works behind the scenes, dealing with wholesalers and retailers to obtain their support and helping them become effective in selling the firm's products.

As an element of the promotion mix, the sales force is very effective in achieving certain marketing objectives and carrying out such activities as prospecting, communicating, selling and servicing and information gathering. But with companies becoming more market-oriented, a customer-focused sales force also works to produce both *customer satisfaction* and *company profit*. The sales force plays a key role in developing and managing profitable *customer relationships*.

2. Identify and explain the six major sales force management steps

High sales force costs necessitate an effective sales management process consisting of six steps: designing sales force strategy and structure, recruiting and selecting, training, compensating, supervising, and evaluating salespeople and sales force performance.

In designing a sales force, sales management must decide on the strategy (team, conference, seminar selling; direct or contractual sales force); what type of sales force structure will work best (territorial, product, customer, or complex structure); how large the sales force should be; who will be involved in the selling effort; and how its various sales and sales support people will work together (inside or outside sales forces and team selling).

To hold down the high costs of hiring the wrong people, salespeople must be recruited and selected carefully. In recruiting salespeople, a company may look to job duties and the characteristics of its most successful salespeople to suggest the traits it wants in its salespeople. It must then look for applicants through recommendations of current salespeople, employment agencies, classified ads and the Internet and other recruitment channels. In the selection process, the procedure can vary from a single informal interview to lengthy testing and interviewing. After the selection process is complete, training programmes familiarise new salespeople not only with the art of selling, but also with the company's history, its products and policies and the characteristics of its market and competitors.

The sales force compensation system helps to reward, motivate and direct salespeople. In addition to compensation, all salespeople need supervision, and many need continuous encouragement because they must make many decisions and face many frustrations. Periodically, the company must evaluate their performance to help them do a better job. In evaluating salespeople, the company relies on getting regular information gathered through sales reports, personal observations, customers' letters and complaints, customer surveys, and conversations with other salespeople.

3. Discuss the personal selling process, distinguishing between transaction-oriented marketing and relationship marketing

The art of selling involves a seven-step *selling process*: *prospecting and qualifying*, *preapproach*, *approach*, *presentation and demonstration*, *handling objections*, *closing* and *follow-up*. These steps help marketers close a specific sale and as such are *transaction oriented*. However, a seller's dealings with customers should be guided by the larger concept of *relationship marketing*. The company's sales force should help to orchestrate a whole-company effort to develop profitable long-term relationships with key customers based on superior customer value and satisfaction.

4. Explain how sales promotion campaigns are developed and implemented

Sales promotion campaigns call for setting sales promotions objectives (in general, sales promotions should be *consumer relationship building*); selecting tools; developing and implementing the sales promotion programme by using *consumer promotion tools* (coupons, cash refund offers, price packs, premiums, advertising specialities, patronage rewards, point-of-purchase promotions, and contests, sweepstakes and games), *trade promotion tools* (discounts, allowances, free goods push money) and *business promotion tools* (conventions, trade shows, sales contests). It also involves deciding on the size of the incentive, the conditions for participation, how to promote and distribute the promotion package and the length of the promotion. After this process is completed, the company evaluates its sales promotion results.

Discussing the concepts

1. DuPont sells thousands of industrial and consumer products worldwide. It serves industries as diverse as aerospace, agriculture and healthcare. Describe how the company can best structure its sales force.

2. The ability to build customer relationships with customers is arguably the most important of a salesperson's key talents. Do you agree? Explain.

3. Describe the steps involved in the personal selling process. Which step do you think is most difficult? Which step is the most critical to successful selling? Which step do you think is usually done best? Explain.

4. Explain why there has been rapid growth in the use of sales promotions.

5. To what extent do you think companies are using sales promotions to build and maintain customer relationships? Critically evaluate the role of sales promotion as a customer relationship building tool.

Applying the concepts

1. Salespeople are increasingly attracted to sophisticated tools to perform more cost-effectively when on the road. Many are using customer relationship management (CRM) tools such as those offered by SAP (www.sap.com) to enable them to gather customer contact information, check updated product inventories and keep track of order information. If you visit SAP online, you will find information on SAP's CRM systems, outlining features including sales planning and forecasting, territory management, account and contact management, lead and opportunity management, quotation and order management, contract management, incentive and commission management, time and travel management and sales analysis.

   (a) Identify the CRM functions that apply to sales force management and those that are more relevant to the salesperson's daily role with customers.

   (b) Show how these functions fit in with the personal selling process for a sales representative selling a new line of earth-moving equipment to an existing large customer. Which functions are critical for success?

   (c) Why might a company choose not to use sophisticated systems to support selling? Explain.

2. Suppose you are the marketing manager for a company that plans to launch a new brand of energy drink to be sold in supermarkets. What sales promotion tools might you consider? Recommend and justify a sales promotion plan for the launch.

 Web resources

For additional classic case studies and Internet exercises, visit **www. pearsoned.co.uk/ kotler**

References

1. See David Jobber and Geoff Lancaster, *Selling and Sales Management*, 7th edn (Harlow: FT/Prentice-Hall, 2007).

2. Charles Fleming and Leslie Lopez, 'The corporate challenge – no boundaries: ABB's dramatic plan is to recast its structure along global lines', *Wall Street Journal* (28 September 1998), p. R16. *Wall Street Journal* (Central Edition) by Charles Fleming and Leslie Lopez. Copyright 1998 by Dow Jones & Company, Inc. Reproduced with permission of Dow Jones & Company, Inc. in the format Textbook via Copyright Clearance Center. For further information, see www.abb.com; see also Emin Babakus, David W. Cravens, Ken Grant, Thomas N. Ingram and Raymond W. LaForge, 'Investigating the relationships among sales, management control, sales territory design, salesperson performance, and sales organisation effectiveness', *International Journal of Research in Marketing*, **13**, 2 (October 1996), pp. 345–60.

3. For more discussion of key account management, see Peter Cheverton, *Key Account Management*, 3rd edn (London: Kogan Page, 2004) and Malcolm McDonald and Diana Woodburn, *Key Account Management: The definitive guide*, 2nd edn (Oxford: Butterworth-Heinemann, 2006). For a global account management perspective, see Peter Cheverton, *Global Account Management: A complete action kit of tools and techniques for key global customers* (London: Kogan Page, 2006).

4. Thomas R. Wotruba and Pradeep K. Tyagi, 'Met expectations and turnover in direct selling', *Journal of Marketing* (July 1991), pp. 24–35; Chad Kaydo, 'Overturning turnover', *Sales & Marketing Management* (November 1997), pp. 50–60.

5. Quotes and other information in this section on super salespeople are from Geoffrey Brewer, 'Mind reading: What drives top salespeople to greatness?', *Sales & Marketing Management* (May 1994), pp. 82–8; Andy Cohen, 'The traits of great sales forces', *Sales & Marketing Management* (October 2000), pp. 67–72; Julia Chang, 'Born to sell?', *Sales & Marketing Management* (July 2003), pp. 34–8; Henry Canaday, 'Recruiting the right stuff', *Selling Power* (April 2004), pp. 94–6. Also see Tom Andel, 'How to cultivate sales talent', *Official Board Markets* (23 April 2005), pp. 14–16; and Kevin McDonald, 'Therapist, social worker or consultant?', *CRN* (December 2005–January 2006), p. 24.

6. See Robert G. Head, 'Systemizing salesperson selection', *Sales & Marketing Management* (February 1992), pp. 65–8; 'To test or not to test', *Sales & Marketing Management* (May 1994), p. 86; Elena Harris, 'Reduce recruiting risks', *Sales & Marketing Management* (May 2000), p. 18; and Erin Stout, 'Recruiting and hiring for less', *Sales & Marketing Management* (May 2002), p. 61.

7. Geoffrey Brewer, 'Brain power', *Sales & Marketing Management* (May 1997), pp. 39–48; Don Peppers and Martha Rogers, 'The money trap', *Sales & Marketing Management* (May 1997), pp. 58–60; Don Peppers and Martha Rogers, 'The price of customer service', *Sales & Marketing Management* (April 1999), pp. 20–1; Erin Stout, 'Is your pay plan on target?', *Sales & Marketing Management* (January 2002), p. 18.

8. See Henry Canaday, 'How to increase the times reps spend selling', *Selling Power* (March 2005), p. 112; George Reinfeld, '8 tips to help control the hand of time', *Printing News* (9 January 2006), p. 10; and David J. Cichelli, 'Plugging sales "time leaks"', *Sales & Marketing Management* (April 2006), p. 23.

9. See Gary H. Anthes, 'Portal powers GE sales', *Computerworld* (2 June 2003), pp. 31–2. Also see Betsy Cummings, 'Increasing face time', *Sales & Marketing Management* (January 2004), p. 12; and David J. Cichelli, 'Plugging sales "time leaks"', *Sales & Marketing Management* (April 2006), p. 23.

10. For extensive discussions of sales force automation, see the May 2005 issue of *Industrial Marketing Management*, which is devoted to the subject.

11. Rich Thomaselli, 'Pharma replacing reps', *Advertising Age* (January 2005), p. 50; Daniel Tynan, 'Next best thing to being there', *Sales & Marketing Management* (April 2004), p. 22; Rebecca Aronauer, 'Looking good', *Sales & Marketing Management* (April 2006), pp. 41–4; Eilene Zimmerman, 'Casting the net wide', *Sales & Marketing Management* (April 2002), pp. 50–6.

12. For more on return on sales investment, see Tim Lukes and Jennifer Stanley, 'Bringing science to sales', *Marketing Management* (September–October 2004), pp. 36–41.

13. Stephen B. Castleberry and C. David Shepherd, 'Effective interpersonal listening and personal selling', *Journal of Personal Selling and Sales Management* (Winter 1993), pp. 35–49; John F. Yarbrough, 'Toughing it out', *Sales & Marketing Management* (May 1996), pp. 81–4.

14. Betsy Cummings, 'Listening for deals', *Sales & Marketing Management* (August 2005), p. 8, and 'Do customers hate salespeople?', *Sales & Marketing Management* (June 2001), pp. 44–51; Rosemary P. Ramsey and Ravipreet S. Sohi, 'Listening to your customers: The impact of perceived salesperson listening behavior on relationship outcomes', *Journal of Academy of Marketing Science* (Spring 1997), pp. 127–37.

15. Steve Lodge, 'Cashback is king', *Financial Times* (6 May 2007), p. 11, and 'Following a new flight path', *op. cit.*, pp. 10–11; Alison Smith, 'Body Shop in trial of loyalty card scheme', *Financial Times* (22 January 2004), p. 20.

16. Louise O'Brien and Charles Jones, 'Do rewards really create loyalty?', *Harvard Business Review* (May–June 1995), pp. 75–82; Graham R. Dowling and Mark Uncles, 'Do customer loyalty programs really work?', *Sloan Management Review* (Summer 1997), pp. 71–82.

17. For an in-depth analysis and strategic perspective of the role of sales promotions, see Tony Yeshin, *Sales Promotion* (Andover: Thomson Learning, 2006); also see John Philip Jones, 'The double jeopardy of sales promotions', *Harvard Business Review* (September–October 1990), pp. 145–52.

18. See 'Nearly half a million attend Bauma trade show', *Pit & Quarry* (May 2004), p. 16; and 'Record breaking 2006 International CES reflects strength of computer technology industry', press release on Consumer Electronics Association website, www.cesweb.org, 8 January 2006.

19. James Pond, 'No purchase necessary, but some care and attention', *The Marketer*, Issue 29 (November 2006), p. 37.

Company case 17 Britcraft Jetprop: Whose sale is it anyhow?*

On 14 April 1997, Bob Lomas, sales administration manager at Britcraft Civil Aviation (BCA), received a telephone call from Wing Commander Weir, the air attaché for the United Kingdom in a European nation. The wing commander had found out that the national air force (NAF) of the European nation (hereafter Country) was looking for a lighter, utility/transport aircraft to replace its ageing freight/transport aircraft for intra-European operations. The air attaché thought the Britcraft Jetprop, BCA's top-selling aircraft, was a suitable candidate.

Britcraft Aviation

Britcraft Aviation is owned by Britcraft Group Ltd, a British company with global engineering interests. Before being bought by Britcraft, BCA was a differently named independent company, known for designing and producing many famous military aircraft in the past. Military and executive aircraft were sold by Britcraft Military Aviation (BMA) and Britcraft Executive Aviation (BEA), located at a different site from that of the civil division.

The Jetprop's major rival was a similar aircraft made by Fokker, a Dutch company that was Britcraft's main competitor. The Jetprop was designed as a regional airliner, particularly for developing countries. Unlike the Fokker, the Jetprop was a low-winged aircraft, with an unobstructed passenger area, which gave it aerodynamic, structural and maintenance advantages. All components used on auxiliary services were selected for proven reliability, long overhaul life and ease of provisioning, enabling the aircraft to achieve the primary design objective of low maintenance costs and high operator utilisation. The aircraft was fully fail-safe, whereby any failure due to fatigue developed sufficiently slowly for it to be detected during routine inspection before it became dangerous. The Jetprop also gave short take-off and landing (STOL) performance from semi-prepared runways. The primary design objectives remained the main selling features of the aircraft.

Sales organisation

BCA's sales organisation, which covered civil and military sales, was responsible for selling the Jetprop. A number of these sales became VIP transports for heads of state. Each year, markets were analysed and a list was made of the most likely sales prospects for the coming 12 months. Area sales managers received 'designated areas' comprising several prospective customers grouped geographically. There were exceptions due to special relationships that a salesperson had developed in the past. With time, new prospects were added to the designated areas.

Doug Watts, whose designated area included the air forces of Malaysia, Thailand, Zaïre (now the Democratic Republic of Congo) and Germany, was the area sales manager eventually responsible for the NAF prospect. Like several other area sales managers, he had joined Britcraft after a distinguished career in the UK's Royal Air Force (RAF). A few area sales managers without RAF experience had previously worked in the company's technical departments. The Sales Department had a very high status in the company, occupying a series of ground-floor offices at the front of the Jetprop factory.

The sales engineers were all technically qualified, a number having postgraduate degrees. They were responsible for providing technical support to the Sales Department and did considerable routine work associated with the sales effort. Although they were not working directly for the area sales managers, their work usually related to one part of the world, requiring frequent contact with one or two people in the Sales Department, which was located close to the Sales Engineering Department.

Ian Crawford, the marketing director of Britcraft, worked at Britcraft's HQ in London. He was responsible for marketing for the whole of Britcraft Aviation in the United Kingdom and overseas. He also managed Britcraft Aviation's regional executives – senior executives strategically based to cover all the world's markets.

The opening phase

After receiving the telephone call from Wing Commander Weir, Bob Lomas circulated news of the prospect. Doug Watts took overall responsibility for it. Although BCA had agents in the Country, these had either not heard of the NAF requirement or failed to tell the company about it. BCA therefore made direct contact with the national authorities in the Country. Following a visit to Herr Hans

Schijlter, the defence secretary, Bob Lomas sent copies of the standard Jetprop military brochure directly to the Ministry of Defence. Lieutenant Colonel Schemann, junior defence secretary, acknowledged its receipt. The next contact made was with Lieutenant General Baron von Forster, defence attaché to the Country's embassy in London, whom Bob Lomas had met at the Hanover Air Show. The general confirmed the NAF's interest in new equipment and asked for details of the Jetprop to pass on to the authorities.

On 6 July, Air Commodore Netherton informed John Upton of Britcraft that the NAF probably had a requirement for a state VIP aircraft. The retired RAF air commodore had lived in the capital of the Country for eight years, where he had been responsible for the Queen's Flight. He founded Eilluft AG, a group that dominated civil aircraft maintenance and light aircraft operations in the Country. He was an *ad hoc* agent for the prospective sale of Britcraft's fighter aircraft. As an accredited agent for BMA, he became an agent in the Country for BCA. The sales organisations of BEA, which produced the Britcraft executive jet for VIPs, and BCA were told of the sales opportunity.

In response, Geoff Lancaster, deputy sales manager of BCA, sent copies of the Jetprop brochure to Air Commodore Netherton to pass on to the prospective customer. As the air commodore was not familiar with the Jetprop, a letter enclosed with the brochures outlined some of the selling points (e.g. the size of the accommodation, low price, full galley and toilet facilities, uses short airfields, available credit terms) that he could use. The letter also mentioned that the Country's minister of defence had recently flown in a Jetprop of the Queen's Flight and was favourably impressed.

On 10 July, Air Commodore Netherton met the officer in charge of the Operations Requirements Branch of the NAF, who confirmed plans to replace several types of transport aircraft. Simultaneously, Wing Commander Weir contacted Ron Hill, the executive director of marketing for BCA, requesting the company to contact the Long Term Planning Department of the NAF directly about its requirement. Major Graff or, alternatively, Colonel Beauers and Lieutenant Colonel Horten, were suitable contacts there.

Work in Iran prevented Ron Hill from attending a meeting arranged on behalf of Doug Watts by Brian Cowley, the Jetprop sales manager. Instead, Steve Williams, his executive assistant, took his place. The discussions – between Steve Williams, Air Commodore Netherton, Major Graff (the officer in command of re-equipment evaluations) and Lieutenant Colonel Horten (the second in command of the Planning Department) – went well. They noted that the Jetprop was among the replacements considered. Fokker had, however, already demonstrated its aircraft, which many in the NAF favoured. The final requirement would be for two or three general transport aircraft plus possibly one for the paratroop training school at NAF-Graz. A Short Skyvan had already given a demonstration as a paradrop aircraft and the Canadians wanted to demonstrate their aircraft.

The Jetprop's demonstration to the NAF would be on 20 October. Major Graff asked for further evidence to support the Jetprop. The advantages of the Jetprop over the Fokker aircraft were highlighted, which were lack of bonding and spot welding, no pneumatics, fail-safe design, progressive maintenance and rough-airfield performance. During the visit they met briefly with Colonel Beauers, the officer commanding the Long Term Planning Department, whom Air Commander Netherton had known well for a number of years, but who was soon to move to NATO HQ. After the meeting the air commodore expressed the hope that, provided the presentation in October went well and the NAF wanted the aircraft, the political people would agree to the purchase. He added that the sale of the paradrop aircraft seemed likely to depend upon support from Colonel Smit, the commanding officer of NAF-Graz, while the main issue, he thought, would be the aircraft's ability to operate safely, fully loaded for a parachute-training mission, from the NAF-Graz airstrip, which was grass and only 650 metres long.

Following the visit, Ernie Wentworth, a senior sales engineer, managed the technical selling effort. Through the Sales Department customer specifications engineer, the Production Planning Department was asked for a delivery schedule and the Estimating Department was requested to cost the aircraft. Other technical departments also became involved in supplying cost and performance evaluations. The Contracts Department would finally negotiate a price for the package of aircraft, spares, guarantees, and after-sales services required.

Major Graff later requested details of the take-off and landing performance of the Jetprop at NAF-Graz. Since it was marginal, Air Commodore Netherton concluded that the only course was to convince the airfield's commanding officer to extend the runway.

Before the scheduled demonstration took place, a number of the NAF personnel – Lt Col Horten (chief of Plans and Studies), Lt Col Wabber (chief of Pilot Training), Major Bayer and Major Graff (Plans and Studies) – were invited to attend the UK's biennial Farnborough Air Show where they were entertained by Britcraft. The meeting progressed well. Nine NAF officers visited BCA for the demonstration of the Jetprop in October, including officers from NAF Planning, Plans and Studies, Avionics, Technical Section, Supply/Spares and HQ Transport.

During the visit, technical specialists looked after most of the NAF officers, while the Long Term Planning Department people discussed contractual details. Prices for the basic version and additional options – strengthened floor for cargo operations, and large freight door – were also presented. The cost of avionics, spares and other equipment that allowed the aircraft to perform a wide variety of roles would be additional.

On the whole, the demonstration and presentation went very well, although Major von Betterei, 'from whom it was difficult even to wring a smile', was evidently 'Fokker oriented'. Air Commodore Netherton and he had been able to talk separately with the senior officer present, with whom they had a 'long and useful discussion about compensation'.

The second phase

Compensation or offset is an increasingly common part of large international sales. It usually involves a provision being made for the vendor or the vendor's country to buy goods from the customer's country. The discussion with Colonel Zvinek, of NAF Planning, Plans and Studies, during the demonstration marked the first occasion when offset appeared accompanying the NAF's procurement of transport aircraft.

The BEA advised the BCA that the offset was critical. In the past, the BEA had lost to the French, who offered very high offset, in the sale of two executive jet aircraft to the NAF. Meanwhile, BMA warned BCA not to use any of the compensation it had already earmarked for a possible sale of military trainer aircraft.

Air Commodore Netherton sought clarification from Herr Maximilian, an under-secretary in the Ministry of Economic Affairs, who was responsible for advising the Country's ministerial committee on offset. Herr Maximilian said offset had recently been between 60 and 70 per cent of the value of a contract and had been completed by the delivery date of the last aircraft. He felt that ideally the work should relate directly to the major project being considered, but should not involve the manufacture of main subassemblies such as wings, airframes or engines. He concluded by saying that negotiations were the responsibility of the vendor alone, who should not increase prices as a result of the required activities.

Soon after his visit to Herr Maximilian, the NAF gave the replacement top priority with a schedule for finalising the requirement in March 1998, signing of letter of intent by mid-1998, contract and deposit payment in late 1998 and delivery and full payment in 1999.

Colonel Zvinek, who originally doubted the Jetprop, was converted since the demonstration, together with all the other important NAF officers concerned. All that was necessary was to assemble an acceptable offset.

Some time passed with little further progress being made with the sale. It became evident that Fokker was offering a very substantial offset, aided by its shareholding in Baden GmbH, which owned Nationale Flugzeugwerke AG (NFW), the Country's largest airframe manufacturer, and which already manufactured Fokker parts.

Early in 1998, Kevin Murphy, the contracts manager for BCA, sent a firm proposal to Colonel Zvinek, with the Sales Engineering Department offering new performance and weight information that showed Jetprop in a better light.

Some days later an urgent email came from Roger Woods of Britcraft, who had met Colonel Horten at a cocktail party in the capital, noting that Fokker's exceptional offset looked like losing Britcraft the deal. Air Commodore Netherton talked to Colonel Horten and then confirmed that the offset was 'not big business'. Further, Messrs Jones and Bedwell of BMA, who were in the Country at that time negotiating a large offset deal with the Ministry of Economic Affairs, found that 'offset would not really be involved on such a small order'.

In a subsequent meeting in April 1998, Major Graff informed Air Commodore Netherton that there was a feeling that the Jetprop was inferior to the Fokker on several technical grounds and the price of €13,930,000 compared unfavourably with the Fokker offer. The total cost, including the price of spares, was more than the amount budgeted. A new formal offer of €13,230,000, entailing a reduction in the number of roles the aircraft had to perform, went to the Country before the end of April.

At the Paris Air Show on 13 June, Doug Watts met Major Graff who emphasised that the offset was important, and that the NAF wanted to change the aircraft specifications and a new quotation would be necessary. Steve Williams had left Britcraft, so Geoff Lancaster took over negotiations. Wing Commander Weir was contacted who said he would probably be able to help in arranging some offset deal, but added that diplomatic circles generally felt that it was 'Britain's turn' to obtain a contract.

On 16 July Geoff Lancaster, Major Graff and Air Commodore Netherton visited Herr Maximilian at the Ministry of Economic Affairs. Four alternative offset arrangements were discussed:

1. Bought-out equipment for the Jetprop could be purchased from the Country's firms.
2. Basic aircraft could be flown to the Country to be finished and new avionics fitted by a NAF contractor.

3. Britcraft's vendors could subcontract work into the Country.
4. The Country's industry could build a future batch of Jetprops.

Herr Maximilian's response to the suggestion was not enthusiastic. He underlined his government's concern about offset being related directly to the contract or involving the NAF or the government. He quoted that, in the recent sale of two Boeing aircraft to the Country's national airline, Boeing had agreed to place €30m of work with the Country's industry in the first year and €150m over the next 10 years. The figures suggested that the offset was far more than the price of the two aircraft.

After leaving the ministry, Geoff Lancaster told Major Graff the consequence of further delay in placing a firm order. Delays would reduce the likelihood of Britcraft being able to supply at the original price. Several customers were also on the verge of signing contracts for Jetprops. Major Graff worried about the delay, but said there was little he could do. His recommendations for purchase would go on to General Petsch, which would constitute the official NAF requirements. They would then go through a sequence of decision-makers: the air force adviser, the defence secretary, Hans Schijller, who would examine the report closely but not consider offset, and the minister of defence, the Prime Minister and the minister for economic affairs, would make the final decision. Before Geoff Lancaster left the Country it was agreed to arrange for a group of NAF officers to visit Schiller Aviation, an independent airline which had recently bought some Jetprops. Air Commodore Netherton escorted the group on the visit and later reported that the airline was 'very complimentary' about the aircraft and Britcraft support.

The offset

In an attempt to arrange the necessary offset, several channels were investigated. A team of Britcraft design and production engineers investigated what work could be 'put out' to subcontractors in the Country. Negotiations with a number of companies did not come to fruition. Eventually, a company, Coles & Turf, offered to buy €45m worth of the Country's goods for a commission of 10 per cent. Britcraft felt that the commission rate requested left no room for them to make a profit on the contract, and eventually got Coles & Turf to agree to €15m of offset.

On 16 October there came a blow to the NAF deal. A Brazilian operator signed a contract with BCA for six aircraft. This meant that the NAF aircraft would be from the more expensive batch 15 rather than the original batch 14 and would cost more – €14,700,000. The NAF reluctantly accepted the price increase and signed a letter of intent in November. Roden AG agreed to accept €4,500,000 worth of specified subcontract work.

As April approached, a team at Britcraft was preparing to make a trip to the Country for final negotiations and contract signing. A day before they were due to leave, Dick Drake, the commercial director, received an email from the Country's authorities. It read:

> Department of Economic Affairs urgently expect more precision about your commitment and also a sensible increase of work for national industry. It is quite obvious that the 10 per cent offset is absolutely unsatisfactory. A reply is expected by 29 April.

A copy of the message went to Air Commodore Netherton, to which Dick Drake added:

> It is virtually certain that it will be necessary for me to reply on Friday that we regret we are unable to increase our commitment and the only other offset is that which they already know about from the aero-engine supplier. However, before replying, I would like to know whether Weir still believes it is Britain's turn.

Questions

1. Trace the stages in the buying process and how the Country's interests changed from one stage to the next. Why were the Country's interests changing and was Britcraft keeping pace with the changes?
2. How well did the strengths of the Jetprop match the needs of the NAF?
3. Identify the players in the buying centre and gauge their role and influence. How well did Britcraft manage the complexity of the buying centre and their diverse needs?
4. Discriminate between the sales roles of the people in Britcraft.
5. Did Britcraft's structure help or hinder its sales campaign? How could it be changed for the better?
6. What were Britcraft's main failings and strengths? Do you think it will win the sale or is it too out of touch with the needs of the NAF and the Country's government? What could it do at this late stage? Is it still 'Britain's turn'?

---

*This case is based on in-company records and documents. For this reason the identity of the buyer and the seller and the names of the people in the case are disguised.

MSN Messenger. It's instant mischief.

Flirt, banter, gossip or just catch up – without saying a word.
On-screen conversations that are more instant than an email
and more discreet than a phone call. Got something to say?
Then join in the fun at **msn.co.uk/messenger**

msn

msn.co.uk

Business is like riding a bicycle. Either you keep moving or you fall down.

JAMES BEASLEY SIMPSON

Direct and online marketing: building direct customer relationships

Mini Contents List

- Prelude case – Cool Diamonds: are they forever?
- Direct marketing
- Growth and benefits of direct marketing
- Customer databases and direct marketing
- Forms of direct marketing
- Real Marketing 18.1 – 'Flick to click' shoppers turn to new page
- Online marketing
- Real Marketing 18.2 – Corporate website performance: are you being served?
- Integrated direct marketing
- Company case 18 – Viagogo goes west

◄ SOURCE: The Advertising Archives.

'Diamonds are a girl's best friend.
Tiffany's! Cartier! Black Starr! Frost Gorham!'

Marilyn Monroe, 'Diamonds are a girl's best friend', from the film
'Gentlemen Prefer Blondes', 20th Century Fox Home Entertainment, 1953

Previewing the concepts

Many of the marketing and promotion tools that we've examined in previous chapters were developed in the context of *mass marketing*: targeting broad markets with standardised messages and offers distributed through intermediaries. Today, however, with the trend towards more narrowly targeted or one-to-one marketing, many companies are adopting *direct marketing*, either as a primary marketing approach or as a supplement to other approaches. Increasingly, companies are using direct marketing to reach carefully targeted customers more efficiently and to build stronger, more personal, one-to-one relationships with them.

Advances in information technology and new digital media are transforming the way direct marketing is performed by companies today. In this chapter, we will explore the role of direct marketing as an IMC element. First, we will examine the major forms of direct marketing and their role in communicating customer value in a general context. We will then examine in greater depth the role of marketing tools for making customer connections and creating customer value in online and new digital 'marketing spaces'.

After reading this chapter, you should be able to:

1. Define direct marketing and discuss its benefits to customers and companies.
2. Identify and discuss the major forms of direct marketing.
3. Explain how companies have responded to the Internet and powerful new technologies with online and digital marketing strategies.
4. Discuss how marketers go about conducting marketing in electronic market spaces to profitably deliver more value to customers.
5. Overview the public policy and ethical issues presented by direct marketing.

Wealthy customers who buy jewellery from Tiffany's, the jewellers that Marilyn Monroe sang about and Audrey Hepburn dreamed of, receive exceptional service. But not all buyers are willing or able to pay the high margins necessary to cover the cost of low-turnover high-service jewellers. We start by looking at a Belgian company that has taken this traditional market by storm by selling these evocative high-value products to consumers over the Internet – diamonds over the ether.

Prelude case Cool Diamonds: are they forever?

Turning Cool Diamonds into the largest Internet-based jewellers in Europe has been an incredible journey for the Einhorn family. The glamorous world of diamond trading is in the blood of the founder of Cool Diamonds' Michel Einhorn. But it was the spilling of blood that prompted his father, Kurt, to become a diamond trader and later inspired his son to follow him into the family business, based in Antwerp.

At the age of 12, Kurt had escaped with his mother from a train bound for Auschwitz. He was hiding among the sacks on a coal merchant's cart, when a border guard began prodding the pile with his bayonet and struck Kurt's hand. But Kurt did not move a muscle and the pair escaped over the border into Switzerland. His mother had used a diamond ring worth £5,000 (€7,500) in today's money, hidden in her hair, to bribe the coal merchant – this saved their lives.

With 300 members of his family now working in the diamond business based in Belgium, Michel Einhorn has the right credentials when it comes to selling diamond jewellery, as well as a ready supply of high-quality gems.

Based in London's Hatton Garden, Michel came up with the innovative idea of selling diamonds on the Web. Together with partner Chris O'Farrell, they formed Cool Diamonds in 1999.

E-diamonds: luxury that won't cost the earth

Diamonds are the ultimate statement of ardour and affection. Diamond jewellery makes a breathtaking gift. But they're not just a girl's best friend. Today, young trendies – from Britney Spears and Mel C to David Beckham and Denise Van Outen – are flashing their belly-button studs and ear studs.

The Internet is changing the face of diamond purchasing. By keeping abreast with the most up-to-date technology supporting the Web, and using the latest JSP-xml language, information loads twice as fast as that of their main US competitor, Bluenile, while remaining accessible to large companies using protective computer firewalls. The cooldiamonds.com site gives customers a three-dimensional view of a piece of jewellery. According to Michel, 'With just one click of the mouse, you can drag the piece from the left and to the right as it rotates before your eyes – the only thing you cannot do is touch it!' The site now attracts more than 3.1 million hits a month and sells thousands of euros' worth of beautiful designer pieces at the click of a button – without the purchaser ever having set eyes on the jewel before it drops on to their doormat. However, it is also possible for the potential customer to make an appointment to visit the Hatton Garden offices if a personal viewing is preferred.

On cooldiamonds.com, visitors can choose from an ever-expanding range of jewellery, including navel studs and toe rings as well as the more conventional bracelets, rings, earrings and pendants. All combine classic elegance with modern design. Cool Diamonds takes the mystique out of diamond buying. Customers can select a design they like and then separately specify the stone according to the four Cs: cut (shape), clarity (from flawless to severely blemished), colour (from white to dirty yellow) and carat (size). There is a fifth C – cost. If they click on 'more expensive', it will go up first by size. If it is too expensive, they can change the clarity or the colour. Customers have more choice because they can select a piece of diamond jewellery 'off-the-peg' or have Cool Diamonds created a bespoke piece just for them.

However, choice is not the only benefit that Cool Diamonds offers customers. A purchase from Cool Diamonds offers good value for money because prices are kept low as there are no expensive overheads, such as prestigious retail premises to maintain. In addition, traditional retail prices carry a huge mark-up, typically reflecting the cost of centrally located outlets, massive stocks and the long chain of middlemen (dealers, cutters, jewellery manufacturers) involved in the trade (also called the diamond pipeline). Moreover, the stock does not need to be duplicated as it is kept in one central location. As such, it can offer the public better value – about 40 per cent of high-street prices. Customers can pay with a credit card over the Internet, which is simple and secure, or they can make a purchase by telephoning Cool Diamonds direct. All diamonds are independently certified, and purchasers have a 10-day money-back guarantee if they change their mind.

Cool Diamonds bucks the trend . . .

While doom and gloom surrounds the luxury goods market, Cool Diamonds is experiencing a huge growth in hits on the site with sales to match. Within three years of setting up online, Cool Diamonds became profitable and has since added to its credibility as the leading designer diamond jewellery site by linking up with well-known names in the world of fashion.

The company is always looking for fresh talent to design for the site. When it undertook a commission from Jasper Conran, the British designer of 'modern classicism', to design stunning accessories for the site, hits on the site shot up to an incredible 853,000 a month, with increased sales. Cool Diamonds also works in partnership with the prestigious Central Saint Martin's College of Art and Design. In 2002, the Cool Diamonds Award was launched: an annual presentation aimed at rewarding the best of the up-and-coming British design talent. In 2003, the award went to 22-year-old design student Franky Wongkar of Indonesia for his 'organically' inspired design for a pair of diamond earrings. In 2004, the award focused on pendants. Winning designs are available for sale from the Cool Diamonds website. In addition, since it purchased the *Atelier* collection of haute couture diamond jewellery designed by the late Gianni Versace, the site has attracted more than 1.3 million hits a month, providing an innovative sales outlet for a superb collection of rings, bracelets, necklaces and earrings, retailing from €4,000 to €40,000.

Cool Diamonds forever

Cool Diamonds appears to be doing a good job persuading people that diamonds are forever. They have used a unique combination of skills that underpin their business rather than the millions of pounds of venture funding behind other, now failed, Internet sites. 'We are thriving', says Michel Einhorn.

Cool Diamonds grew the business naturally and has seen a steady increase in hits and sales, which have trebled over the past two years. Creative use of public relations has enabled the company to expand consumer awareness as well as fostering excellent relations with the fashion press. In the past, Cool Diamonds benefited from the positive endorsement given by the UK's Consumers' Association in its *Which*? Magazine. However, Cool Diamonds had restricted their advertising spend, relying mainly on word-of-mouth (or word-of-Web) recommendations and PR to communicate their 'sparkle' to the public. It is highly rewarding from the company's perspective to have *Vogue*, *Tatler*

and the *FT* writing features about Cool Diamonds. As the business is growing, the company has recently decided to reinvest all profits in a serious advertising campaign to drive future growth.

In a bid to replicate its success in the UK, Cool Diamonds has also opened an office in France. However, the Cool Diamonds French operation has yet to make a strong impact, with the site attracting around 150,000 hits a month. The founding partners believe that there are lessons to be learnt from the rapid decline of pan-European e-tailer Boo.com – mismanagement as well as trying to expand too quickly without taking time to build local teams. In the UK, customers seem to have developed a strong taste for diamonds, and many are happy to buy through the Internet. However, French consumers appear less than enthusiastic about buying diamond jewellery online.

In the last few years, the company has revolutionised the way in which diamonds are bought. Gone is the mystique. In its place, customers are offered an Internet site that is design-led, fast, friendly and safe, offering an unprecedented amount of choice to a worldwide client base. Meanwhile, as business in the UK booms, Michel Einhorn has to determine how best to proceed to ensure Cool Diamonds, like their stones, will be forever.

SOURCES: Based on company data provided by Cool Diamonds; materials supplied by Molly McKellar Public Relations, London; more information about the company's products available at www.cooldiamonds.com; see also Simon London. 'Don't let diamonds get you down', *Financial Times* (31 May 2000), p. 18; John-Paul Flintoff, 'Diamond geezers', *Weekend FT* (18 August 2000), pp. 18–22; David Andrews, 'A discount on screen gems', *Daily Express* (14 June 2000), p. 19; Sarah Williams, 'Diamonds are forever', *Internet Investor* (October 2000), pp. 76–7.

Cool Diamonds has revolutionised the way in which diamond jewellery can be purchased.

SOURCE: cooldiamonds.com Ltd. Molly McKellar Public Relations, London.

Questions

1. Evaluate Cool Diamonds' marketing approach to date. Identify the major factors that have influenced its success. What problems do you see with their current approach?
2. What are the major challenges facing Cool Diamonds in the future?
3. What marketing recommendations would you make to Cool Diamonds, taking into account the ways in which Cool Diamonds can attract people to visit their website and to eventually buy expensive diamond jewellery through their site?
4. Is it a good idea for Cool Diamonds to reinvest all profits in a serious advertising campaign to compound its future growth? Explain your answer. What steps might the company take to sustain planned growth in the UK and its overseas markets?

Direct marketing

Cool Diamonds along with many other companies is leading a resurgence in direct marketing as companies link directly to consumers over the Internet or through telephone selling. **Direct marketing** consists of direct communications with carefully targeted individual customers to obtain an immediate response and cultivate lasting customer relationships. Direct marketers communicate directly with customers, often on a one-to-one, interactive basis. Using detailed databases, they tailor their marketing offers and communications to the needs of narrowly defined segments or even individual buyers. Beyond brand and image building, they usually seek a direct, immediate and measurable consumer response.

Direct marketing—Direct communications with carefully targeted individual customers to both obtain an immediate response and cultivate lasting customer relationships.

The new direct-marketing model

Early direct marketers – catalogue companies, direct mailers and telemarketers – gathered customer names and sold their goods mainly through the post and by telephone. Today, fired by rapid advances in database technologies and new marketing media – especially the Internet and other electronic channels – direct marketing has undergone a dramatic transformation.

Direct marketing can take the form of direct distribution – as marketing channels that contain no intermediaries. We also include direct marketing as one element of the promotion mix – as an approach for communicating directly with customers. In actuality, direct marketing is both these things.

Most companies still use direct marketing as a supplementary channel or medium for marketing their goods. Thus, companies such as Volvo, Mercedes and Lexus market mostly through mass-media advertising and their dealer networks but also supplement these channels with direct marketing. Their direct marketing includes promotional CD or DVD materials mailed directly to prospective buyers and their Web pages that provide customers with information about various models, competitive comparisons, financing, and dealer locations. Similarly, department stores like John Lewis and Marks & Spencer, and supermarkets like Tesco and Carrefour, sell the majority of their merchandise off their store shelves but also through direct mail, telemarketing and online catalogues.

 This new *direct model* changes the way companies think about building relationships with customers.

However, for many companies today, direct marketing is more than just a supplementary channel or medium. For these companies, direct marketing – especially Internet marketing and e-commerce – constitutes a new and complete model for doing business. More than just another marketing channel or advertising medium, this new *direct model* changes the way companies think about building relationships with customers. Rather than using direct marketing and the Internet as supplemental approaches, firms employing the direct model use it as the *only* approach. Firms such as eBay, Dell, online bookseller Amazon, lingerie retailer Figleaves.com, CoShopper.com (Norwegian Internet shopping company), Direct Line (UK-based insurance company) and easyJet, the low-cost airline operator, have built their entire approach to the marketplace around direct marketing.

Growth and benefits of direct marketing

Direct marketing has become the fastest-growing form of marketing. In Europe, direct marketing is also referred to as distance-selling. Years ago, the direct marketing channel was largely dominated by mail and telephone. Today, direct marketing encompasses all forms of online communications, and marketing offers through e-mail, websites, interactive television, mobile communications and other interactive communications media. The products and services offered range from clothing, books, CDs and DVDs, to wine, financial services and airline, theatre and railway tickets.

According to the Federation of European Direct and Interactive Marketing (FEDMA), which comprises country members' direct marketing associations and over 200 direct marketing company members, annual direct marketing expenditure in Europe is now over €100bn.[1] Contrast this with a total direct marketing spend of €46bn in 2002.[2]

Direct marketing continues to become more Web-oriented, and Internet marketing is claiming a fast-growing share of direct marketing spending and sales. In recent years, sales over the Internet have increased rapidly, increasing threefold in some new EU countries since 2000. By 2004, online sales reached an average level of around 25 per cent, ranging from 7 per cent to about 50 per cent of total direct marketing sales, depending on the maturity of the Internet market in various EU countries. In some countries it is rapidly becoming the dominant channel, accounting for a high proportion of direct marketing-driven sales (e.g., Czech Republic 36 per cent, Hungary 15 per cent, Slovak Republic 12 per cent).[3]

In most of the eastern European countries, direct marketing is relatively underdeveloped for a variety of reasons, such as consumer attitudes, legal environment, taxation and income levels, differences in the level of performance of postal services and the availability of retail outlets, as well as varying levels of consumer interest and the degree of restrictive legislation. Nevertheless, because of the rapidly developing availability of access to the Internet and the relatively good performance of postal services in eastern Europe, direct-marketing sales are expected to grow in the next few years. For example, investment by UK businesses in direct marketing to Europe has grown tremendously. This trend has led to cross-border market expansion opportunities for specialist direct marketing service providers. Consider the following.[4]

The opening of the European market to competition from the UK – along with the flood of trade opportunities in the 10 [now 12] new EU member states – has attracted massive interest from UK companies. Netherlands-based DMC International, which specialises in business-to-business direct marketing, including data acquisition, data enhancement and management, and production and localisation services, recently opened a UK office to cope with the increased demand from the UK for DM services.

Jim Foster, CEO of DMC International, comments, 'Since 1993, we have observed a steady increase in demand for our services from the UK. By 2005, almost half of our clients were based in the UK. We felt we could maintain a better relationship with them by opening a UK based office.' According to Erika Rey, the UK Director of DMC International, 'DM [Direct marketing] has been used locally for a long time but many companies now want to use it to launch a product or service internationally, which can present problems in markets where they have no DM experience.' Companies are resorting to DM as their primary marketing method. Rey adds that successful direct marketing is not just a matter of buying customer data. 'Creating the best lists for the required location is a complicated and sensitive task which requires plenty of local knowledge.'

As growth in direct marketing investment continues, many direct marketing companies are now operating in the 12 new member states, with many more companies expanding to other countries such as Croatia.

Whether employed as a complete business model or as a supplement to a broader integrated marketing mix, direct marketing brings many benefits to both buyers and sellers.

Benefit to buyers

Direct marketing benefits buyers in many ways. For buyers, direct marketing is *convenient, easy* and *private*. Direct marketers never close their doors, and customers don't have to battle traffic, find parking spaces and trek through stores to find products. From the comfort of their homes or offices, they can browse catalogues or company websites at any time of the day or night. Business buyers can learn about products and services without tying up time with salespeople.

Direct marketing often gives shoppers greater product *access* and *selection*. For example, unrestrained by physical boundaries, direct marketers can offer an almost unlimited selection to consumers almost anywhere in the world. For instance, by making computers to order and selling directly, Dell can offer buyers thousands of self-designed PC configurations, many times the number offered by competitors who sell preconfigured PCs through retail stores. And just compare the huge selections offered by many Web merchants to the more meagre assortments of their bricks-and-mortar counterparts. For instance, log on to lightbulbs-direct.com, and you'll be overwhelmed with every imaginable kind of light bulb or lamp – incandescent bulbs, fluorescent bulbs, projection bulbs, germicidal bulbs, sewing machine bulbs, medical and dental bulbs – you name it. No physical store could offer handy access to such a vast selection.

Beyond a broader selection of sellers and products, online and Internet channels also give buyers access to a wealth of comparative *information*, information about companies, products and competitors, at home and around the globe. Good catalogues and websites often provide more information in more useful forms than even the most helpful retail salesperson can. For example, the Amazon.com site offers more information than most of us can digest, ranging from top-10 product lists, extensive product descriptions, and expert and user product reviews to recommendations based on customers' previous purchases.

Finally, direct marketing – especially online buying – is *interactive* and *immediate*. Customers can often interact with the sellers by phone or on the seller's website to create exactly the configuration of information, products or services they desire, then order them on the spot. Moreover, direct marketing gives customers a greater measure of control. Consumers decide which catalogues they will browse and which websites they will visit.

Benefit to sellers

For sellers, direct marketing is a powerful tool for *building customer relationships*. Using database marketing, today's marketers can target small groups or individual consumers and promote their offers through personalised communications. The one-to-one nature of direct marketing enables companies to interact with customers by mail, phone or online, learn more about their needs, and tailor products and services to specific customer tastes. In turn, customers can ask questions and volunteer feedback. For example, Nestlé's baby food division maintains a database of new parents and mails them personalised packages of gifts and advice at key stages in the baby's life. Because they reach more interested consumers at the best times, direct marketing materials receive higher readership and response.

 Direct marketing is a powerful tool for *building customer relationships*.

Direct marketing also offers sellers a *low-cost, efficient, speedy* alternative for reaching their markets. Direct marketing has grown rapidly in business-to-business marketing, partly in response to the ever-increasing costs of marketing through the sales force. When personal sales calls cost several hundred euros per contact, they should be made only when necessary and to high-potential customers and prospects. Lower-cost-per-contact media – such as telemarketing, direct mail and company websites – often prove more cost-effective. Similarly, online direct marketing results in lower costs, improved efficiencies and speedier handling of channel and logistics functions, such as order processing, inventory handling and delivery. Direct marketers such as Amazon.com or Dell also avoid the expense of maintaining a store and the related costs of rent, insurance and utilities, passing the savings along to customers.

Direct marketing can also offer greater *flexibility*. It allows marketers to make ongoing adjustments to their prices and programmes, or to make immediate and timely announcements and offers. For example, airlines, hotels and travel agencies take advantage of the flexibility and immediacy of the Web to share low-fare offers directly with customers.

Finally, direct marketing gives sellers *access to buyers* that they could not reach through other channels. Smaller firms can mail catalogues to customers outside their local markets and post customer hotline or free phone numbers to handle orders and enquiries. Internet marketing is a truly global medium that allows buyers and sellers to click from one country to another in seconds. Even small marketers find that they have ready access to global markets.

Customer databases and direct marketing

Customer database—An organised collection of comprehensive data about individual customers or prospects, including geographic, demographic, psychographic and buying behaviour data.

Effective direct marketing begins with a good customer database. A **customer database** is an organised collection of comprehensive data about individual customers or prospects, including geographic, demographic, psychographic and behavioural data. The database gives companies a snapshot of how their customers look and behave. A good customer database can be a potent relationship-building tool.

Many companies confuse a customer mailing list with a customer database. A customer mailing list is simply a set of names, addresses and telephone numbers. A customer database contains much more information. In consumer marketing, the customer database might contain a customer's demographics (age, income, family members, birthdays), psychographics (activities, interests and opinions) and buying behaviour (buying preferences and the recency, frequency and monetary value – RFM – of past purchases). In business-to-business marketing, the customer profile might contain the products and services that the customer has bought, past volumes and prices, key contacts (and their ages, birthdays, hobbies and favourite foods), competing suppliers, status of current contracts, estimated customer spending for the next few years, and assessments of competitive strengths and weaknesses in selling and servicing the account.

Companies must distinguish between *transaction-based* and *custom-built* marketing databases. Transactional databases are put in by an accounts department for the purpose of sending invoices or bills out and getting money back. By contrast, custom-built databases focus on what the firm's marketing people need to know to serve and satisfy customers profitably and better than the competition can – for example, the most cost-effective way to reach target customers, the net worth of a transaction, customers' requirements and lifetime values, lapsed customers and why they departed, why competitors are making inroads and where. Armed with the information in their databases, these companies can identify small groups of customers to receive fine-tuned marketing offers and communications.

Some of these databases are huge. For example, in the UK, the retailer Tesco has built a customer database containing 40 terabytes' worth of customer information, roughly three times the number of printed characters in the US Library of Congress. Internet portal Yahoo! records every click made by every visitor, adding some 400 billion bytes of data per day to its database – the equivalent of 800,000 books. And Wal-Mart captures data on every item, for every customer, for every store, every day. Its database contains more than 570 terabytes of data – that's 570 trillion bytes, far greater than the storage horsepower of 100,000 personal computers.[5]

Companies use their databases in many ways. They use them to locate good potential customers and to generate sales leads. They can mine their databases to learn about existing customers in detail, and then fine-tune their market offerings and communications to the special preferences and behaviours of target segments or individuals. The database can help a company make attractive offers of product replacements, upgrades or complementary products, just when customers might be ready to act. In all, a company's database can be an important tool for building stronger long-term customer relationships and deepening customer loyalty.

For example, pet food company Nestlé Purina maintains a database of cat and dog breeders who are recruited as brand ambassadors for Purina pet food. The breeders are encouraged to contact the company every time a new litter is born. The company then sends out weaning food and a free starter pack containing nutritional information and pedigree certificates with the Purina logo, to give to the new owners. Masterfoods, the market leader in pet food, also maintains an exhaustive pet database. In key European markets such as Germany, the company has the names of virtually every family that owns a cat, obtained from veterinarians registered on its Katzen-Online.de website. The company offers a free 'How to Take Care of Your Cat' booklet. Pet owners who request the booklet fill out a questionnaire, providing their cat's name, age, birthday and other information. To build a lasting relationship with the pet owner, every year the company sends a birthday card to each cat, along with a new cat food sample and money-saving coupons for Masterfoods brands.

Hence, a rich customer database allows the company to build profitable new business by locating good prospects, anticipating customer needs, cross-selling products and services and rewarding loyal customers. But many companies are sceptical about the returns on investment in databases. The recent growth in companies' customer databases has led to information overload, making it increasingly difficult to grab customers' attention.[6]

Like many other marketing tools, database marketing requires a special investment. Companies must invest in computer hardware, database software, analytical programming, communication links and skilled personnel. The database system must be user-friendly, fit for its intended purpose and available to various marketing groups, including those in product and brand management, new-product development, advertising and promotion, direct mail, telemarketing, Web marketing, field sales, order fulfilment and customer service. However, a well-managed database should lead to sales customer-relationship gains that will more than cover its costs.[7]

Loyal customers are made, not born. More and more companies are seeking to create and maintain better relationships with customers. This ad draws companies' attention to CRM software tools for communicating and managing relationships with customers.
SOURCE: SAP Global Marketing.
Agency: OgilvyOne Worldwide Ltd.

Forms of direct marketing

The major forms of direct marketing – as shown in Figure 18.1 – include personal selling, direct-mail marketing, catalogue marketing, telephone marketing, direct-response television (DRTV) marketing, kiosk marketing, new digital direct marketing and online marketing.

We examined personal selling in depth in Chapter 17. Here, we'll examine the other direct marketing forms.

Figure 18.1 Forms of direct marketing

Direct-mail marketing

Direct-mail marketing involves sending an offer, announcement, reminder or other item to a person at a particular address. Using highly selected mailing lists, direct marketers send out millions of mail pieces each year – letters, catalogues, ads, brochures, samples, CDs, DVDs and other 'salespeople with wings'. According to FEDMA, direct mail is by far the largest direct marketing medium. Direct mail is strong in countries with efficient and relatively inexpensive postal systems (e.g. the UK, Sweden) and weak where the post is slow and delivery unreliable (e.g. Spain, Italy). In Finland, it is the preferred channel for direct marketing.

Direct mail is well suited to direct, one-to-one communication. It permits high target-market selectivity, can be personalised, is flexible and allows easy measurement of results. Although direct mail costs more than mass media, such as television or magazines, per 1,000 people reached, the people who are reached are much better prospects. Direct mail has proved successful in promoting all kinds of products, from books, music, DVDs and magazine subscriptions to insurance, gift items, clothing, gourmet foods and industrial products. In one campaign launched by petroleum company Shell, a mailing to motorists who were not necessarily Shell customers produced a 50 per cent response. Incentives were a free road-map and the chance to win three months' worth of free petrol. Direct mail is also used by charities, such as UNICEF, Oxfam, NCH (the Children's Charity) and Action Aid, which rely on correspondence selling to persuade individuals to donate to their causes.

The direct-mail industry constantly seeks new methods and approaches. For example, CDs and DVDs are now among the fastest-growing direct-mail media. One study showed that including a CD or DVD in a marketing offer generates responses between 50 and 600 per cent greater than traditional direct mail.[8] New forms of delivery have also become popular, such as *fax mail, voice mail* and *e-mail*. Fax mail and voice mail are subject to the same do-not-call restrictions as telemarketing, so their use has been limited in recent years. However, e-mail is booming as a direct marketing tool. Today's e-mail messages have moved far beyond the drab

Direct-mail marketing— Direct marketing through mailings that include letters, catalogues, ads, CDs, DVDs, samples, foldouts and other 'salespeople on wings' sent to prospects on mailing lists.

text-only messages of old. The new breed of e-mail ad uses animation, interactive links, streaming video and personalised audio messages to reach out and grab attention.

> Including a CD or DVD in a marketing offer generates responses between 50 and 600 per cent greater than traditional direct mail.

E-mail and other new forms deliver direct mail at incredible speeds compared to the Post Office's 'snail mail' pace. Yet, much like mail delivered through traditional channels, they may be resented as 'junk mail' or **'spam'** if sent to people who have no interest in them. For this reason, smart marketers are targeting their direct mail carefully so as not waste their money and recipients' time. They are designing permission-based programmes, sending e-mail ads only to those who want to receive them (e-mail marketing is discussed more fully in a later section).

Catalogue marketing

Catalogue shopping once started almost as explosively as the Internet, though few of us might remember this. Cataloguers' sales pitch was remarkably similar too – no need to struggle to the store, vast choice, lower prices. Today, the growth in mail-order catalogue shopping has slowed. The European mail-order catalogue market was worth €43.5bn in 2003, and is expected to grow to about €45.5bn in 2009. According to Mintel, the retail analyst, mail catalogue sales in the UK plummeted from 53 per cent to 25 per cent of total home shopping sales as online sales overtook them, rising from 9 per cent to 32 per cent in 2004.[9] But catalogues are increasingly used by store retailers, who see them as an additional medium for cultivating sales. Most consumers enjoy receiving catalogues and will sometimes even pay to get them. Many catalogue marketers even sell their catalogues at bookstores and magazine stands. Many business-to-business marketers also rely heavily on catalogues.

Advances in technology, along with the move towards personalised one-to-one marketing, have resulted in exciting changes in **catalogue marketing**. With the stampede to the Internet, more and more catalogues are going electronic. A variety of new Web-only cataloguers have emerged, and many traditional print or mail-order catalogue firms have added Web-based catalogues to their marketing mixes. For example, click on the Shopping link at www.quelle.com, the German-owned mail order company, which operates in 15 countries across Europe, and you can flip through the latest Quelle catalogue page by page online. According to a recent publication by the market research institute Nielsen//NetRatings, Quelle, with more than 15 per cent share of the €20bn German mail-order market, was the third most accessed online trader in Germany, behind only eBay and Amazon. The share of Internet orders is always on the rise and is now more than 38 per cent of total sales orders at Quelle. Quelle expects half of the group's sales from its 40 million or so customers in Europe to come via the Net within the next five years. Likewise, other mail-order companies such as 3 Suisses and La Redoute in France, and Lands' End, have also seen an increasing proportion of sales generated online in recent years.[10]

However, although the Internet has provided a new avenue for catalogue sales, all you have to do is to check your mailbox to know that printed catalogues remain the primary medium. Research shows that print catalogues generate many of those online orders. Customers who receive print catalogues are more likely to buy online, and they spend more than customers who did not receive catalogues.[11] Moreover, many former Web-only companies (e.g. dabs.com that sells PCs, printers and a range of home and business office equipment and supplies) have created printed catalogues to expand their business.

Catalogues can also be an effective sales and relationship builder. A recent study in the US, conducted by Frank About Women, a marketing-to-women communications company, found that a majority of women who receive catalogues are actively engaged with them. Eighty-nine percent of the participants revealed that they do more than just browse through the catalogues they receive in the mail. They circle or 'tab' the items that they want, fold over the corners of pages and tear pages out. Some 69 per cent save their catalogues to look through again. More than just a buying tool, many women view catalogues as a source of entertainment and inspiration. Women claim to love perusing catalogues almost like reading a women's magazine, looking for ideas for everything from decorating to fashion to that extra-special gift. Seventy-five per cent of women surveyed agreed that they find catalogue browsing really enjoyable, fun and relaxing, with 74 per cent agreeing that they get excited when a new catalogue arrives.[12]

These sentiments echo the findings of research into UK catalogue shoppers by Experian, a data group. According to Experian, the 'humble catalogue' is thriving in the digital age as home shoppers find new pleasure in 'flicking and clicking' (see Real Marketing 18.1).

Web-based catalogues present a number of benefits compared with printed catalogues. They save on production, printing and mailing costs. Whereas print-catalogue space is limited, online catalogues can offer an almost unlimited amount of merchandise. Web catalogues also allow real-time merchandising: products and features can be added or removed as needed, and prices can be adjusted instantly to match demand. Finally, online catalogues can be spiced up with interactive entertainment and promotional features, such as games, contests and daily specials.

Along with the benefits, however, Web-based catalogues also present challenges. Whereas a print catalogue is intrusive and creates its own attention, Web catalogues are passive and must be marketed. Attracting new customers is much more difficult for a Web catalogue than for a print catalogue. Thus, even cataloguers who are sold on the Web are not likely to abandon their print catalogues.

Telephone marketing

Telephone marketing or **telemarketing** uses the telephone to sell directly to consumers and business customers. We're all familiar with telephone marketing directed towards consumers, but business-to-business marketers also use telephone marketing extensively. Marketers use *outbound* telephone marketing to generate and qualify sales leads, and sell directly to consumers and businesses. Calls may also be for research, testing, database building or appointment making, as a follow-up to a previous contact, or as part of a motivation or customer-care programme.

Inbound freephone numbers are used to receive orders from television and print ads, direct mail or catalogues. Marketers also use inbound telephone calls to receive customer enquiries and complaints.

When properly designed and targeted, telemarketing provides many benefits, including purchasing convenience and increased product and service information. At the same time, some consumers may appreciate the genuine and well-presented offers they receive by telephone. However, the explosion in unsolicited outbound telephone marketing over the years has annoyed many consumers who object to the almost daily 'junk phone calls' that pull them away from the dinner table or clog up their answering machines. Thus, many telemarketers are shifting to alternative methods for capturing new customers and sales, from direct mail and direct response TV to live-chat Web technology that prompts customers to call in. Many of these marketers are shifting their call-centre activity from making cold calls on often resentful customers to managing existing customer relationships. They are developing 'opt-in' calling systems, in which they provide useful information and offers to customers who have invited the company to contact them by phone or e-mail.

Telephone marketing (or telemarketing)—Using the telephone to sell directly to consumers.

" The explosion in unsolicited outbound telephone marketing over the years has annoyed many consumers who object to the almost daily 'junk phone calls'. "

18.1 real marketing

'Flick to click' shoppers turn to new page

Once the preserve of consumers buying cheap items on credit, the sector has swelled as high-street chains and even exclusively online retailers embrace the old world of print as a new way to drive sales. Upmarket consumers who once shunned catalogues have become hooked after the Internet lent respectability to companies such as Argos, whose 1,778-page catalogue boasts a dinosaur holding a toothbrush beneath an engagement ring in front of a dartboard next to a mobile phone!

Some 70 per cent of consumers surveyed by Experian Integrated Marketing said they had recently shopped from home, suggesting phenomenal growth in the category, driven by broadband penetration. But 80 per cent of the home shoppers said they had looked at the printed catalogue before ordering online – demonstrating a surprisingly close relationship between the two media.

More likely than Argos to be gracing coffee tables are the catalogues of John Lewis or Next – high-street stalwarts turned publishing phenomena. 'Brands realised that to stay ahead of online retailers they needed to have a 'flick to click' strategy and it's paid off,' says Mark Peacock, an analyst at Experian. 'Catalogues have a long shelf life and they are a permanent fixture in the majority of homes . . . as are computers, so consumers can flick through a catalogue on the sofa at any time and then go online to place an order quickly. It's a devastatingly simple but highly effective marketing tactic.'

There has also been an upturn in respectability and snob appeal. 'When the Internet came along it made home shopping more socially acceptable. It's not just something that poor people do,' says Alan White, chief executive of N. Brown, one of the largest players in the sector, publishing 17 catalogues, including J D Williams and Simply Be, and offering niche products such as 'wider-fitting footwear' and 'larger-size underwear'. Chief beneficiary and one cause of the move upmarket has been Boden, founded 16 years ago by Johnnie Boden, a former investment banker, and worn by fellow Old Etonian David Cameron and half the country's 'yummy mummies'. Last year it reported a 26 per cent increase in turnover to £128.5m, while pre-tax profit increased by £8.7m to £22.8m.

The company's online orders are yet to reach the levels found by Experian but have risen dramatically – from 1 per cent in 1999 to 60 per cent today: 90 per cent of those have read the catalogue first. 'The quality of the image is still better in the catalogue than it is online,' says Mark Binnington, marketing director of Boden. 'You can browse it in bed or on the kitchen table.'

The White Company targets a similar demographic with its classic-styled house-hold goods and clothing. 'Whether it's a luxury rug or a Jermyn Street shirt, these

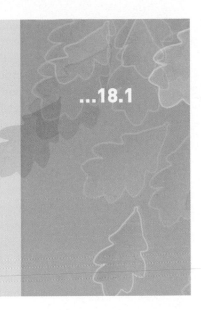

...18.1

cash-rich, time-poor consumers want to shop when they feel like it, without cutting into the precious little free time they have,' says Mr Peacock.

There are some other surprising new adopters from the world of new media: ASOS, which has prospered with a pure online fashion offering, went into old media with the launch of its own magazine. 'We suddenly realised if we could combine a customer magazine with our customer database, that would be quite a hefty magazine that acted like a catalogue,' says Nick Robertson, its chief executive.

SOURCE: Tom Braithwaite, '"Flick to click" shoppers turn to new page', *Financial Times* (9 August 2007), p. 3. Reproduced with permission from *Financial Times*.

Direct-response television marketing

Direct-response television (DRTV) marketing takes one of two major forms. The first is *direct-response television advertising*. Direct marketers air television spots, 60 or 120 seconds long, which persuasively describe a product or service and give customers a telephone number or website for ordering. Direct-response television advertising is mainly used to build brand awareness, convey brand/product information, generate sales leads and build a customer database. The main focus of DRTV marketing is in selling a single product. It is more important to gain high selling rates than to establish a long-term customer relationship.

A special form of DRTV marketing is *infomercials*. Here, TV viewers encounter longer, 15- or 30-minute advertising programmes for a single product, during which the features or virtues of a product are discussed by 'experts' before an audience.

For years, infomercials have been associated with somewhat questionable pitches for juicers and other kitchen gadgets, get-rich-quick schemes, and nifty ways to stay in shape without working very hard at it. In recent years, however, a number of large companies have begun using infomercials to sell their wares over the phone, refer customers to retailers, send out coupons and product information, or attract buyers to their websites. Organisations using DRTV marketing range from mail order (e.g. Sounds Direct), leisure (e.g. Scandinavian Seaways) and financial services (e.g. Direct Line, AA Insurance Services) to cars (e.g. GM, Land Rover, Fiat), PCs (e.g., Dell, IBM), fast-moving consumer goods (e.g. Procter & Gamble, Martini, McVitie's) and government departments (e.g. the British army, US navy). DRTV marketing has also been used by charities and fund-raising campaigners to persuade viewers to offer donations or volunteer services. Examples include the 'Live Aid' campaign that captured the imagination of millions of people across the globe, 'Children in Need' and many other international fund-raising events.

Direct response TV commercials are usually cheaper to make and the media purchase is less costly. Moreover, unlike most media campaigns, direct-response ads always include a customer hotline or freephone number, or Web address, making it easier for marketers to track phone calls and website hits generated by the ads. In a business environment where marketers are obsessed with return on investment, direct response TV advertising enables marketers to track the impact of their pitches. They can use DRTV advertising to build brand awareness while simultaneously generating leads and sales. For these reasons, DRTV advertising is growing more quickly than traditional broadcast and cable advertising.

Home-shopping channels, another form of direct-response television marketing, are TV shopping programmes broadcast on host channels or entire channels dedicated to selling goods and

Direct-response television (DRTV) marketing— The marketing of products or services via television commercials and programmes which involve a responsive element, typically the use of a freephone number that allows consumers to phone for more information or to place an order for the goods advertised.

services. The aim of TV shopping channels is to generate multiple orders and to develop a long-term customer relationship.

Programme hosts chat with viewers by phone and offer a large product mix, ranging from fitness, health and beauty, to jewellery, homewares and self-improvement offerings. The presentation of products is upbeat and a theatrical atmosphere is created, often with the help of special or celebrity guests, and up-to-date information can be given on product availability, creating further buying excitement. The viewer is asked to buy the product via the telephone number displayed or directly via the 'red button', if viewing on an interactive TV-capable set (see 'New digital direct marketing technologies' below). Examples of home-shopping channels include QVC (available in the US, Japan, Germany, UK), Consumenten (consumer channel, The Netherlands), Laphrodite TV (fashion channel, France), Top TV (Czech Republic) and other TV shopping channels such as TV Shop which operates across Europe, including Austria, Germany, the Netherlands, UK, Ireland and the Scandinavian countries.

In recent years, direct-response TV advertising is giving way to interactive TV (iTV). This new digital technology lets TV viewers interact with TV programming and advertising using their remote controls. We will address iTV in more detail in a later section (see 'New digital direct marketing technologies').

Kiosk marketing

As consumers become more and more comfortable with computer and digital technologies, many companies are placing information and ordering machines – called *kiosks* (in contrast to vending machines, which dispense actual products) – in stores, airports and other locations. Kiosks are popping up everywhere these days, from self-service hotel and airline check-in devices to in-store ordering kiosks that let you order merchandise not carried in the store.

In-store Kodak, Fuji and HP kiosks let customers transfer pictures from memory sticks, mobile phones and other digital storage devices, edit them and make high-quality colour prints. Kiosks in Hilton hotel lobbies let guests view their reservations, get room keys, view pre-arrival messages and check in and out.[13] Business marketers also use kiosks. For example, Dow Plastics places kiosks at trade shows to collect sales leads and to provide information on its 700 products. The kiosk system reads customer data from encoded registration badges and produces technical data sheets that can be printed at the kiosk or faxed or mailed to the customer.

New digital direct marketing technologies

Today, thanks to a wealth of new digital technologies, direct marketers can reach and interact with consumers just about anywhere, at anytime about almost anything. Here, we look into several exciting new digital direct marketing technologies: mobile phone marketing, podcasts and vodcasts, and interactive TV (iTV).

Mobile phone marketing

Mobile phone connections in western and eastern Europe are projected to grow from 745 million in 2006 to 908 million in 2010 (see Table 18.1), while mobile advertising revenue will increase 15 per cent, from around $225.7m in 2006 to over $259.2m by 2010. Mobile ad revenues are also predicted to grow in North America ($148.3m in 2006 increasing to $187.2m in 2010, up 26 per cent), China and India (up 74 per cent from $66.6m in 2006 to $116.2m in 2010) and Asia Pacific countries (a 16 per cent rise from $122.1m in 2006 to $142m by 2010).[14]

Many marketers view mobile phones as the next big direct marketing medium. Mobile marketers use text messaging (SMS) and multimedia messages (MMS) to reach consumers on

Region	2006	2010
North America	253.0	327.5
Latin America	293.4	402.2
Western Europe	433.4	500.2
Eastern Europe	321.1	408.0
China and India	642.4	1,085.6
Asia Pacific	362.8	478.1
Middle East/Africa	301.1	536.4
World	2,607.5	3,738.2

Table 18.1 Mobile phone connections worldwide: growth projections (millions)

SOURCE: From '2007 marketing fact book', *Marketing News* (15 July 2007), p. 28. Reprinted with permission from American Marketing Association, Ovum Ltd.

their mobile phones – one of the most personal devices people own. According to one expert, by 2010 the mobile phone will have turned into 'a remote control for life: broadband or Wi-Fi web browsing, listening to music, watching TV, navigating to the next meeting, scanning in business cards, paying for train tickets, monitoring jogging distances and calorie use, making cheap voice over internet (VoIP) calls or turning on a personal video recorder at home if they are running late.'[15] A recent survey shows that 89 per cent of major brands will be marketed via mobile phones by 2008. More than half of those brands will likely spend up to 25 per cent of their marketing budgets on mobile marketing.[16]

> ❝ Mobile phones . . . the next big direct marketing medium. ❞

Marketers of all kinds are now integrating mobile phones into their direct marketing. Mobile phone promotions include everything from ring-tone give-aways, mobile games and ad-supported content to text-in contests and chances to win prizes. As we saw in Chapter 16, mobile phones are also being used in location-based advertising and promotions whereby consumers receive messages offering discounts in stores or restaurants as they approach them.

Perhaps nowhere is mobile phone marketing more advanced than in Japan.

In Japan, life revolves around mobile phones, and marketers know it. Take Nami, a 37-year-old graphic designer in Tokyo who regularly uses her phone to send and receive e-mails on the go. Her 11-year-old daughter enjoys downloading wallpaper and animated trailers featuring Disney characters, while Nami's boyfriend relies on his phone's global positioning system to navigate Tokyo's labyrinthine streets. The family can also use mobile phones to buy a can of soft drinks from high-tech vending machines, receive e-coupons from neighbourhood stores, and even have their fortunes told. Digital coupons are taking off, as are GPS-based promotions used by retailers to target people near their stores.

Japanese direct marketers are experimenting with new ways to use the mobile devices for brand-building. Nestlé, for example, used a new technology called Quick Response (QR) codes, which can be scanned like digital barcodes. QR codes on print and outdoor ads can be read by mobile phone cameras, which redirect the user's phone to a designated mobile URL site where the user can retrieve more information. Nestlé used QR codes in a campaign to launch a canned drink called Nescafé Shake. It promoted Shake with two 15-minute short films that humorously communicated a sense of fun around the act of 'shaking' with a story about a slacker kid who winds up with a dog's wagging tail on his behind. A QR code on promotional materials led mobile phone users to a mobile site where they could download the film as well as its original music as songs or ring tones. In the first three weeks after Nestlé's 'Nonta's Tail' film debuted, 120,000 people visited the mobile site and another 550,000 watched the film on the Internet.[17]

Technologies such as mobile barcodes are not only popular in Japan, but are spreading across other countries. For example, companies such as OP3 are leading the way in developing new and exciting mobile technologies to create customer value and build customer relationships.

Most mobile marketing tends to prompt consumers to respond to an SMS or MMS message by sending a text message to a short code number. For example, when Peugeot introduced the 1007 compact car, TV and billboard advertising carried a short code that allowed people to text in to reserve a test drive at the nearest dealership. But new digital technologies are transforming the world of mobile marketing.

Outside Japan and Korea, OP3 is the market leader in what's called '2D bar codes'. Using its 'ShotCode' technology, any printed material becomes truly interactive. ShotCodes can be printed on newspapers, magazines, product packaging (e.g., a box or a tin), CD/DVD cases, business cards – yes, literally any physical medium. When a picture of the ShotCode is taken using a mobile camera phone, the mobile phone automatically makes an Internet connection with the producer or distributor of the product or the service provider, allowing the user to obtain more information on the company's products, special offers and so forth. OP3 launched a recent

Mobile phone marketing:
To launch its Nescafé Shake canned drink in Japan, Nestlé used Quick Response codes, which can be scanned like UPC codes by a cell phone, to direct consumers to marketing pitches for the new product.
SOURCE: Toru Yamanaka/AFP/ Getty Images.

campaign for Coca-Cola involving 40 million ShotCodes on 40 million Sprite bottles in Mexico. Consumers who scanned the ShotCodes could win any one of 5 million prizes, including free pizzas from Domino's Pizza, free movie rentals from Blockbusters video rental retailer, etc. In terms of response rate, the company claims that the ShotCode campaign outperformed conventional mobile phone marketing using 'old-tech' SMS text-messaging 2 to 1.

Because the user is invited to sign up personal details, advertisers benefit through building a detailed database for each customer, enabling more highly targeted customer communications. In addition to creating direct connections with consumers from print material, ShotCodes allow companies to reach customers where it matters most and to build one-on-one relationships. Meanwhile, consumers can gain instant gratification due to the capacity to instantly access information, respond and interact with providers – all within a click of the phone![18]

Thus, mobile marketing can offer an unrivalled channel for one-to-one relationship building. Smart marketers increasingly develop targeted campaigns that encourage consumers to initiate a relationship, building trust and tying them into a community. A key advantage of mobile marketing is that, unlike direct mail or e-mail, people tend to read their mobile phone messages. According to one mobile messaging service provider, about 94 per cent of text messages get read. Response rates for well-designed mobile marketing campaigns may be as high as 25 per cent, according to another industry expert. 'The key to successful [mobile] marketing is relevance,' says Ariya Priyasantha, managing director of ActiveMedia Technology, a mobile content aggregator. He adds, 'Customers get a sense of personalised communication delivered direct to their pocket, since they initiate the dialogue. Only a one-to-one phone call can beat that level of personalisation.'[19]

Podcasts and vodcasts

Podcasting and vodcasting are the latest on-the-go, on-demand technologies. The name *podcast* derives from Apple's now-everywhere iPod. With podcasting, consumers can download audio files (**podcasts**) or video files (**vodcasts**) from the Internet to an iPod or other handheld device, and then listen to or view them whenever and wherever they wish. They can search for podcast topics through sites such as iTunes or through podcast networks such as PodTrac, Podbridge or PodShow. These days, you can download podcasts or vodcasts on an exploding array of topics, everything from your favourite radio programme, a recent sit-com episode, or current sports features to the latest music video or games console commercial. Increasingly, this new medium is drawing much attention from marketers. Many are now integrating podcasts and vodcasts into their direct marketing programmes in the form of ad-supported podcasts, downloadable ads and informational features and other promotions.

Podcast—An audio file downloaded from the Internet to an Apple iPod or other handheld device.

Vodcast—A video file downloaded from the Internet to an Apple iPod or other handheld device.

For example, in the US, Volvo sponsors podcasts on Autoblog, and Absolut Vodka buys ads on PodShow programmes. Kraft Foods offers hundreds of recipes using the iPod's text function and Nestlé Purina publishes podcasts on animal training and behavioural issues.[20] Honda offered a vodcast as part of a new ad campaign for its Honda Civic. The vodcast consists of a two-minute, 'This is what a Honda feels like' ad, in which human voices replicate the sounds that passengers hear in a Honda Civic. The vodcast also includes behind-the-scenes footage of the making of the ad. According to a Honda marketing executive, this dynamic new medium 'is enabling people to experience what a Honda feels like from one of their most personal and closest touch points – their iPod.'[21]

Interactive TV (iTV)

Advertisers from a range of sectors, including cars, travel, telecommunications and financial services, are using iTV to deliver more complex messages and information to target viewers. iTV is poised to take off as a direct marketing medium as more and more households adopt satellite broadcasting systems which offer digital interactive capabilities.

Interactive TV gives marketers an opportunity to reach targeted audiences in an interactive, more involving way. Audiences are encouraged to interact with the company's ads through an impulse response format which invites them to press the 'red button' on the remote control device for more information.

Vodafone used iTV to explain the services on offer in what feels like a Vodafone 'live service'. Viewers appear to pay more attention during interactive TV commercial breaks.

MTV ran the classic arcade game Pong during the ad breaks on its channels and invited viewers to play. Players accumulated points but those who switched channels lost their scores. Advertisers who use iTV state that interactivity follows similar rules to direct-response TV. While ads aired during daytime and peak times generate more response, those shown during lower-rating programmes were also consistently successful. Some advertisers argue that pressing the red button is more effective than a telephone call to action. Yet others have found that the rate of response via interactive TV was nine times higher than via a phone number.[22]

The main uses of iTV are as a supplement to TV, including accessing linked pages providing more in-depth information about the programmes, accessing electronic programme guides, voting for contestants (e.g., who gets thrown out of the latest reality TV show), participating in quizzes, selecting alternative camera angles (e.g., watching a soccer game from cameras at either goal or midfield) and so forth. Industry experts believe that the use of iTV ads might increase sales, particularly impulse buys. However, results depend on the nature of the product and the style and placement of the advert. Just as in conventional TV advertising, there is no reason to assume that an unattractive proposition becomes more appealing simply because it is interactive.[23]

According to Forrester Research, greater standardisation of iTV costs and processes and increasing household penetration of interactive digital TV are key to increasing European interactive TV advertising revenues, which grew from €1.1bn in 2002 to almost €18bn by 2007. Industry observers also note that a major challenge for advertisers and commercial TV broadcasters providing programme-linked interactive content, is to balance iTV's capacity to build interactive brand advertising against the need to keep viewers who are watching the channel-related programme, rather than the interactive ad content. One industry observer, Bill Gash, founder of interactive consultancy Partners in Television, highlights the dilemma facing commercial TV channels such as ITV in the UK. He says, 'Seventy per cent of ITV's business is brand advertising. But ITV can't afford to lead viewers out of the broadcast stream.' 'The challenge will be to make interactive advertising appealing to brand advertisers without destabilising the existing business model.'[24]

Mobile phone marketing, podcasts and vodcasts and interactive TV offer exciting direct marketing opportunities. But marketers must be careful to use these new direct marketing approaches wisely. As with other direct marketing forms, marketers who use them risk backlash from consumers who may resent such marketing as an invasion of their privacy. Marketers must target their direct marketing offers carefully, bringing real value to customers rather than making unwanted intrusions into their lives.

Online marketing

As noted earlier, **online marketing** is the fastest-growing form of direct marketing. Recent technological advances have created a digital age. Widespread use of the Internet and other powerful new technologies are having a dramatic impact on both buyers and the marketers who serve them. In this section, we examine how marketing strategy and practice are changing to take advantage of today's Internet technologies.

Online marketing— Company efforts to market products and services and build customer relationships over the Internet.

Marketing and the Internet

Much of the world's business today is carried out over digital networks that connect people and companies. The **Internet** (the **Net**), a vast public web of computer networks, connects users of all types all around the world to each other and to an amazingly large information repository. Internet usage continues to grow steadily. Internet household penetration in the European Union countries varies as shown in Table 18.2. It is highest in Sweden, where 75.6 per cent of the country's population have access to the Internet, followed by Portugal (73.8 per cent), The Netherlands (73.3 per cent) and Denmark with a penetration rate of 69.2 per cent. There are now over 252 million Internet users in the expanded EU, representing an overall growth of 167.8 per cent between 2000 and 2007. As Table 18.2 shows, Internet usage has risen disproportionately in the new accession states, notably in Latvia, Romania, Lithuania, Bulgaria and the Czech Republic. According to Internet World Stats, the number of Web users worldwide reached nearly 972 million in early 2007, up from nearly 700 million in 2004.[25] Another source estimates that the world's online population will reach almost 1,801 million by 2010, with users in Asia Pacific totalling some 757 million, followed by 450.7 million across eastern and western Europe and 287.9 million in North America.[26]

Internet (the Net)—A vast public web of computer networks connecting users of all types all around the world to each other and to a large 'information repository'.

> **"** The Web has fundamentally changed customers' notions of convenience, speed, price, product information and service. **"**

The Internet has given marketers a whole new way to create value for customers and build customer relationships. The Web has fundamentally changed customers' notions of convenience, speed, price, product information and service. The success of early *click-only* companies – the so-called dot-coms such as Amazon.com, eBay, Expedia and others – caused existing *bricks-and-mortar* manufacturers and retailers to re-examine how they served their markets. Now, almost all of these traditional companies have set up their own online sales and communications channels, becoming *clicks-and-mortar* competitors. It's hard to find a company today that doesn't have a substantial Web presence.

Online marketing domains

The four major online marketing domains are shown in Figure 18.2. They include B2C (business to consumer), B2B (business to business), C2C (consumer to consumer) and C2B (consumer to business).

Business to consumer (B2C)

The popular press has paid the most attention to **business-to-consumer (B2C) online marketing** – selling goods and services online to final consumers. Today's consumers can buy almost anything online – from clothing, kitchen gadgets and airline tickets to computers, cars and home

Business-to-consumer (B2C) online marketing— The online selling of goods and services to final consumers.

Table 18.2 Internet usage, growth and penetration in the European Union

European Union	Internet users (000s)	Use growth 2000–2007 (%)	Penetration (% population)
Austria	4,680	121.4	56.6
Belgium	5,100	155.0	48.5
Bulgaria	2,200	411.6	28.7
Cyprus	326	171.7	33.6
Czech Republic	5,100	410	50.0
Denmark	3,763	92.9	69.2
Estonia	690	88.2	51.8
Finland	3,286	70.5	62.3
France	30,838	262.8	50.3
Germany	50,471	110.3	61.2
Greece	3,800	280.0	33.5
Hungary	3,050	326.6	30.4
Ireland	2,060	162.8	50.2
Italy	30,764	133.1	51.7
Latvia	1,030	586.7	45.2
Lithuania	1,222	443.0	35.9
Luxembourg	315	215.0	68.0
Malta	127	218.0	33.0
Netherlands	12,060	209.2	73.3
Poland	11,400	307.1	29.9
Portugal	7,783	211.3	73.8
Romania	4,940	517.5	23.4
Slovakia	2,500	284.6	46.5
Slovenia	1,090	263.3	55.5
Spain	19,765	266.8	43.9
Sweden	6,890	70.2	75.6
United Kingdom	37,600	144.2	62.3
Total European Union	252,819	167.8	51.3
Total Europe	314,792	199.5	38.8

Note: Figures last updated March 2007.

SOURCE: Internet usage in the European Union – EU 27 (www.internetworldstats.com/stats9.htm).

	Targeted to consumers	Targeted to businesses
Initiated by business	B2C (business to consumer)	B2B (business to business)
Initiated by consumer	C2C (consumer to consumer)	C2B (consumer to business)

Figure 18.2 Online marketing domains

Some products lend themselves beautifully to electronic marketing. People know what is being sold and it is important to be aware and act quickly to get the items you want.

SOURCE: The Advertising Archives.

mortgages. In the US, some 65 per cent of online users now use the Internet to shop. In 2005, US consumers spent an estimated $114bn online, and consumer Internet spending is expected to reach $144bn by 2010.[27] The number of people shopping online in Europe has also grown rapidly in recent years. Over 100 million Internet shoppers in Europe now spend an average of €1,000 each per year online. By the end of 2006, online retail sales exceeded the €100bn mark, according to a report by Forrester Research.[28] The analyst predicts European Web sales will more than double between 2006 and 2011, reaching €263bn as the number of Internet shoppers grows to 174 million. Forrester predicts the more confident online shoppers will increase their average annual online retail spend to €1,500. Two-thirds of European online shoppers are based in the UK and Germany. According to Forrester, the UK has set the pace for the rest of Europe, generating more than a third of total European online retail sales. The UK's lead is predicted to continue, with the average UK Web shopper spending €2,410 annually by 2011, up from €1,744 in 2006. Perhaps more importantly, the Internet now influences a rising proportion of total retail sales – sales transacted online plus those carried out offline but encouraged by online research.

Although high street shops are still the most important retail channel for most consumers, according to Forrester, multi-channel buying will continue to grow in the years ahead. Thus, smart marketers are employing integrated multi-channel strategies that use the Web to drive sales to other marketing channels.

As more and more people find their way onto the Web, the population of online consumers is becoming more mainstream and diverse. Over half of online shoppers in Europe are in the 25 to 44 age group. The average profile of an online shopper also differs between northern and southern Europe. While tech-savvy young consumers are still the typical Internet shoppers in countries like Spain and Italy, online shopping in northern Europe has become slightly more representative of mainstream consumers in that it has ceased to be a male-dominated domain, according to the report. According to Forrester Research, European women are now the driving force behind the sharp growth in e-shopping in Europe: a survey showed that by 2005, some 27.4 million women were buying products online compared to 17 million in 2002.[29]

Thus, the Web now offers marketers a palette of different kinds of consumers seeking different kinds of online experiences. However, Internet consumers still differ from traditional offline consumers in their approaches to buying and in their responses to marketing. In the Internet exchange process, customers initiate and control the contact. Traditional marketing targets a somewhat passive audience. In contrast, online marketing targets people who actively select which websites they will visit and what marketing information they will receive about which products and under what conditions. Thus, the new world of online marketing requires new marketing approaches.

Business to business (B2B)

Although the popular press has given the most attention to B2C websites, **business-to-business (B2B) online marketing** is also flourishing. B2B marketers use B2B websites, e-mail, online product catalogues, online trading networks, barter sites and other online resources to reach new business customers, serve current customers more effectively and obtain buying efficiencies and better prices.

Most major business-to-business marketers now offer product information, customer purchasing and customer support services online. Beyond simply selling their products and services online, companies can use the Internet to build stronger relationships with important business customers. For example, corporate buyers can visit engineering group ABB's website (www.abb.com), select detailed descriptions of ABB's products and solutions, request sales and service information and interact with staff members. Some major companies conduct almost all of their business on the Web. For example, networking equipment and software maker Cisco Systems takes more than 80 per cent of its orders over the Internet.

Business-to-business (B2B) online marketing— Using B2B websites, e-mail, online product catalogues, online trading networks, barter sites and other online resources to reach new business customers, serve current customers more effectively and obtain buying efficiencies and better prices.

check in

check out

check out

check out

check out

Check out your hotel before you check in. Expedia.co.uk has a variety of hotels to choose from whatever your budget. We provide photos, a detailed list of facilities and even a map of where you'll be staying. So whether you know where you want to stay or you're just looking for inspiration, we'll help you create and plan every aspect of your trip, just the way you want it.

Expedia.co.uk
What's your perfect trip?

The success of early *click-only* companies such as Expedia caused existing *bricks-and-mortar* manufacturers and starters to re-examine how they served their markets.

SOURCE: The Advertising Archives.

B2B exchanges are now found in a host of industries ranging from motor vehicles, aerospace and petroleum, to chemicals, food, energy, pharmaceuticals and many others. Online B2B exchanges enable buyers to gain efficiencies on many levels, from the identification of new sources of supply and negotiations, to carrying out transactions and payments and supply-chain management functions such as production line planning and collaborative product design and development. Many of these exchanges take place in **online trading networks** – online market-places in which buyers and sellers share information and complete transactions efficiently. For example, online trading networks such as Antwerp's DocCheck portal (www.antwerpes.com) bring the European healthcare market players together on the Internet. With 350,000 users and 1,200 cooperating websites, DocCheck is the largest platform in the medical products market for exchanging information, online services and e-commerce. It offers pharmaceutical companies the opportunity to set up buying groups for their sales departments or to integrate complete shops with an individual product range into their Internet operation. Others such as America's Ariba (www.ariba.com) and Commerce One (www.commerceone.com) help multinationals cut procurement costs, while China's Alibaba (www.alibaba.com) serves to build markets for China's small and medium-sized companies and foreign businesses by enabling these companies to trade with each other and linking them to global supply chains.[30]

Online trading networks—Huge online marketplaces in which B2B buyers and sellers find each other online, share information and complete transactions efficiently.

Consumer to consumer (C2C)

Much **consumer-to-consumer (C2C) online marketing** and communication occurs on the Web between interested parties over a wide range of products and subjects. In some cases, the Internet provides an excellent means by which consumers can buy or exchange goods or information directly with one another. For example, eBay, Amazon.com Auctions, Overstock.com and other auction sites offer popular marketspaces for displaying and selling almost anything, from art and antiques, coins, stamps and jewellery to computers and consumer electronics.

Consumer-to-consumer (C2C) online marketing—Online exchanges of goods and information between final consumers.

eBay's C2C online trading community of more than 181 million registered users worldwide (greater than the combined populations of France, Spain and Britain!) transacted some $40bn in trades last year. On any given day, the company's website lists more than 16 million items up for auction in more than 45,000 categories. Such C2C sites give people access to much larger audiences than the local flea market or newspaper classifieds (which, by the way, are now also going online). Interestingly, based on its huge success in the C2C market, eBay has now attracted a large number of B2C sellers, ranging from small businesses peddling their regular wares to large businesses liquidating excess inventory at auction.[31]

In other cases, C2C involves interchanges of information through Internet forums that appeal to specific special-interest groups. Such activities may be organised for commercial or non-commercial purposes. An example is Web logs, or *blogs*, online journals where people post their thoughts, usually on a narrowly defined topic. Blogs can be about anything, from politics or golf to yoga, car repair or the latest reality television series. Today's 'blogosphere' consists of an estimated 50 million bloggers worldwide. Reviewing products and giving feedback is now the second most popular Web activity, according to a study by Universal McCann, media buyer. One source points to consumers in France, Spain, China – the world's biggest blogging market – and South Korea as being particularly keen Web critics.[32]

An increasing number of people are logging views on *social networking* websites such as MySpace, Facebook, Bebo, Friendstar, Orkut and other online communities every day. For example, at the end of 2006, MySpace boasted over 90 million unique users, with the site attracting an average of 320,000 new user profiles a day, and users from every country in the world! Similarly, Google-owned YouTube, the video-sharing site, attracts over 120 million unique users, with the site attracting a high proportion of international users (over 78 per cent) from outside the US.[33] According to ComScore, the Internet traffic measurement group, the explosive growth in popularity of sites such as MySpace, YouTube and Facebook in recent years suggests that these online destinations have made the transition from niche concepts to mass marketing appeal. Consequently, many marketers are now tapping into blogs and social networking sites as a medium for reaching carefully targeted consumers. Firms can engage with target audiences in C2C spaces in several ways. One way is to advertise on an existing blog. For example, Britain's Carphone Warehouse started blogging to promote the launch of the company's new, free broadband package for its consumer service TalkTalk. According to Thomson Intermedia, a company that tracks media advertising, IT, telecommunications, entertainment, media and leisure companies were the major sectors advertising on social networking websites. With rates for online banners on social networking websites costing 30–50 per cent lower than on Internet portals such as MSN or Yahoo!, experts predict that global ad spend on social networking sites will rise to over \$3.5bn by 2011, representing nearly 580 per cent of 2006 levels.[34]

Firms can also influence content on these sites.

> A growing number of firms have established their own pages on MySpace, to which users can link. Unilever joined a target consumers' network of friends by 'hooking up' with Christine Dolce to promote Axe, a deodorant brand. Ms Dolce, who goes by the alias ForBiddeN, boasted around 900,000 'friends' who link to her MySpace page. Unilever argued that Ms Dolce was perfect to draw in the 18- to 24-year-old lads to whom Axe is targeted. Ms Dolce hosted an interactive game, called 'Gamekillers', based around dating tips and designed to promote Axe. Some 75,000 MySpacers signed up for it.
>
> Coca-Cola set up a blog to add an online community element to its sponsorship of the 2006 Winter Olympics. It enlisted a half-dozen college students from around the world to blog about their trips to the games. Coke paid to fly and accommodate students from China, Germany, Italy, Canada and Australia, each of whom agreed to post conversations about the positive side of the games.[35]

As a marketing tool, blogs offer some advantages. They can offer a fresh, original, personal and cheap way to reach today's fragmented audiences. These sites also offer scope to users to create and share content, often free from the editorial restrictions of mainstream media. A spokesperson for Bebo says, 'The ultimate opportunity is to have a dialogue with consumers which is much richer than what you can have, say, in a 30-second television spot.[36]

" The ultimate opportunity is to have a dialogue with consumers. "

However, the 'blogosphere' is cluttered and difficult to control. There are risks inherent in manipulating a medium where individual users generate or distribute most of the content, which remains relatively uncensored. Consider the following incidents which illustrate some of the risks faced by advertisers when embracing the fast-growing genre of social networking websites.

> A spoof blog set up by 'Barry Scott', a fictional character created to sell Reckitt Benckiser's Cillit Bang household cleaner brand, backfired after the top Web searches for 'Cillit Bang' generated only bloggers attacking the campaign.[37]

In 2007, telecoms group Vodafone and First Direct, the online bank, pulled advertisements on Facebook, after discovering their campaigns appeared next to a Web page for the right-wing British National Party. The Vodafone advertisements were among several campaigns from various brands that appeared in rotation on the BNP page. 'We didn't know we had an ad next to a BNP site and we pulled it immediately. All our agencies are aware of our general criteria against supporting any political groups,' said a spokesperson for Vodafone. 'We need to make sure we have robust controls in place before we reinvest in Facebook, though it is a site we're interested in because of its popularity.'

First Direct said there appeared to be little way of screening out Facebook pages that were unsuitable for its advertising. It said it would also stay off the website until the issue of where its advertising appeared 'was resolved'.

Although advertisers are keen to tap the large youth-skewed audiences of such websites, they cannot always control the editorial context in which their advertising appears. Such advertising space is often sold through third parties, who sell anonymous bundles of space across many websites and allocate ads to slots in an automated way that pays little attention to context.[38]

'Blogs may help companies bond with consumers in exciting new ways, but they won't help them control the relationship,' says a blog expert. Such Web journals remain largely a C2C medium. 'That isn't to suggest companies can't influence the relationship or leverage blogs to engage in a meaningful relationship,' says the expert, 'but the consumer will remain in control.'[39]

In all, C2C means that online buyers don't just consume product information – increasingly, they create it. They join Internet interest groups to share information, with the result that 'word of Web' is joining 'word of mouth' as an important buying influence. Word about good companies and products travels fast. Word about bad companies and products travels even faster!

Consumer to business (C2B)

Consumer-to-business (C2B) online marketing— Online exchanges in which consumers search out sellers, learn about their offers and initiate purchases, sometimes even driving transaction terms.

The final online marketing domain is **consumer-to-business (C2B) online marketing**. Thanks to the Internet, today's consumers are finding it easier to communicate with companies. Most companies now invite prospects and customers to send in suggestions and questions via company websites. Beyond this, rather than waiting for an invitation, consumers can search out sellers on the Web, learn about their offers, initiate purchases and give feedback. Using the Web, consumers can even drive transactions with businesses, rather than the other way around. For example, using Priceline.com, would-be buyers can bid for airline tickets, hotel rooms, rental cars, cruises and vacation packages, leaving the sellers to decide whether to accept their offers.

Types of online marketers

Companies of all types are now marketing online. In this section, we first discuss the different types of online marketers shown in Figure 18.3. Then, we examine how companies go about conducting online marketing.

Click-only versus clicks-and-mortar marketers

The Internet gave birth to a new species of marketers – the *click-only* dot-coms – which operate only online without any bricks-and-mortar market presence. In addition, most traditional *bricks-and-mortar* companies have now added online marketing operations, transforming themselves into *clicks-and-mortar* competitors.

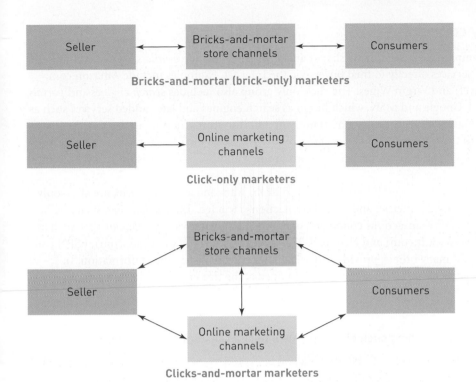

Figure 18.3 Types of online marketers

C2B e-commerce: Consumers can use websites such as PlanetFeedback.com to ask questions, offer suggestions, lodge complaints, or deliver compliments to companies.

SOURCE: planetfeedback.com.

Click-only companies

Click-only companies come in many shapes and sizes. They include *e-tailers*, dot-coms that sell products and services directly to final buyers via the Internet. Examples include Amazon.com, eBookers (travel) and Virgin Wines. The click-only group also includes *search engines* and *portals*, such as Yahoo!, Google and MSN, which began as search engines and later added services such as news, weather, stock market reports, entertainment and storefronts, hoping to become the first port of entry to the Internet. *Shopping* or *price comparison sites,* such as Shopica.com, DealTime.com, ToseekA.com and Bizrate.com, give instant product and price comparisons from thousands of vendors.

Internet service providers (*ISPs*), such as AOL, Tiscali, Wanadoo and Freeworld, are click-only companies that provide Internet and e-mail connections for a fee. *Transaction sites,* such as eBay, take commissions for transactions conducted on their sites. Finally, various *content sites,* such as Financial Times (www.ft.com) and New York Times on the Web (www.nytimes.com), ESPN.com, Virgin Media and many others, provide financial, news, research and other information. In addition, user-generated content sites such as Wikipedia, the free encyclopedia, are gaining popularity.

> The hype surrounding such click-only Web businesses reached astronomical levels during the 'dot-com gold rush'.

The hype surrounding such click-only Web businesses reached astronomical levels during the 'dot-com gold rush' of the late 1990s, when avid investors drove dot-com stock prices to dizzying heights. However, the investing frenzy collapsed in the year 2000, and many high-flying, over-valued dot-coms came crashing back to Earth. Even some of the strongest and most attractive e-tailers – Boo.com (sportswear), Clickmango (healthcare), eToys.com, Pets.com, Furniture.com, Garden.com – filed for bankruptcy. Now on firmer footing, many click-only dot-coms are surviving and even prospering in today's market space.

Electronic media are now
crashing together so allowing
agile businesses like Sky a
chance to capture customers
in several markets by offering
'TV Broadband Phone Mobile'
in one package.

SOURCE: The Advertising
Archives.

Clicks-and-mortar companies

Many established companies moved quickly to open websites providing information about their companies and products. However, most resisted adding e-commerce to their sites. They felt that this would produce *channel conflict* – that selling their products or services online would be competing with their offline retailers and agents. For example, computer manufacturers such as Toshiba, HP and Acer feared that their retailers would drop their computers if they sold the same computers directly online. Store-based booksellers including Waterstone's and Barnes & Noble delayed opening their online site to challenge Amazon.com.

These companies struggled with the question of how to conduct online sales without cannibalising the sales of their own stores, resellers or agents. However, they soon realised that the risks of losing business to online competitors were even greater than the risks of angering channel partners. If they didn't cannibalise these sales, online competitors soon would. As the Internet grew, established bricks-and-mortar companies realised that, to compete effectively with online competitors, they had to go online themselves. Thus, many established **clicks-and-mortar companies** are now prospering. For example, Tesco, a traditional bricks-and-mortar grocery retailer, became the world's biggest Web-grocer in 2002. Its success is in stark contrast to the first generation of hopeful, but unsuccessful, Internet grocery start-ups, such as Webvan, Peapod and Streamline.[40]

Many clicks-and-mortar companies are now having more online success than their click-only competitors. What gives the clicks-and-mortar companies an advantage? In the UK, for example, established companies such as Tesco, John Lewis Partnership, Marks & Spencer and Waitrose have known and trusted brand names and greater financial resources. They have large customer bases, deeper industry knowledge and experience, and good relationships with key suppliers.

 Many clicks-and-mortar companies are now having more online success than their click-only competitors.

By combining online marketing and established bricks-and-mortar operations, the clicks-and-mortar retailers can also offer customers more options. For example, consumers can choose the convenience and assortment of 24-hours-a-day online shopping, the more personal and hands-on experience of in-store shopping, or both. Customers can buy merchandise online, and then easily return unwanted goods to a nearby store. In short, their 'call, click or visit' model has enabled them to add value for consumers beyond what would be achievable for click-only or brick-only operators.

Setting up an online marketing presence

Clearly, all companies need to consider moving online. Companies can conduct online marketing in any of the four ways shown in Figure 18.4: creating a website, placing ads and promotions online, setting up or participating in Web communities, or using e-mail.

> **Clicks-and-mortar companies**—Traditional bricks-and-mortar companies that have added online marketing to their operations.

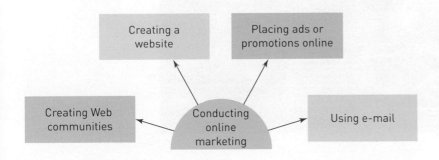

Figure 18.4 Setting up for online marketing

Corporate website—A website which carries information about the company and other features designed to answer customer questions, build customer relationships and generate excitement about the company. It aims to build goodwill rather than to sell the company's products or services directly. The site handles interactive communication initiated by the consumer.

Marketing website—A website that engages and interacts with consumers that will move them closer to a direct purchase or other marketing outcome. The site handles interactive communication initiated by the company.

Creating a website

For most companies, the first step in conducting online marketing is to create a website. However, beyond simply creating a website, marketers must design an attractive site and find ways to get consumers to visit the site, stay around and come back often.

Types of websites

Websites vary greatly in purpose and content. The most basic type is a **corporate website**. These sites are designed to build customer goodwill and to supplement other sales channels, rather than to sell the company's products directly. They handle interactive communications initiated by the consumer. For example, the corporate websites of Nestlé, Philips, Nokia and Siemens typically offer a rich variety of information and other features in an effort to answer customer questions, build closer customer relationships and generate excitement about the company. Corporate websites generally provide information about the company's history, its mission and philosophy, and the products and services that it offers. They might also tell about current events, company personnel, financial performance and employment opportunities. Many corporate websites also provide exciting entertainment features to attract and hold visitors. The site might also provide opportunities for customers to ask questions or make comments through e-mail before leaving the site.

Companies may also create a **marketing website**. These sites engage consumers in an interaction that will move them closer to a direct purchase or other marketing outcome. With a marketing website, communication and interaction are *initiated by the marketer*. Such a site might include a catalogue, shopping tips and promotional features such as coupons, sales events or contests. For example, visitors to SonyStyle.com can search through dozens of categories of Sony products, learn more about specific items and read expert product reviews. They can check out the latest hot deals, place orders online and pay by credit card, all with a few mouse clicks. B2B marketers also make good use of marketing websites. For example, FedEx's website (www.fedex.com) allows customers to schedule their own shipments, request a courier and track their packages in transit.

The MINI USA website (MINIUSA.com) does more than just provide information or sell cars; it keeps customers engaged, from designing their very own MINI to tracking it from factory to delivery.

Designing effective websites

Creating a website is one thing; getting people to *visit* the site is another. To attract visitors, companies aggressively promote their websites in offline print and broadcast advertising and through ads and links on other sites. But today's Web users are quick to abandon any website that doesn't measure up. The key is to create enough value and excitement to get consumers who come to the site to stick around and come back again. This means that companies must constantly update their sites to keep them current, fresh and useful.

For some types of products, attracting visitors is easy. Consumers buying new cars, computers or financial services will be open to information and marketing initiatives from sellers. Marketers of lower-involvement products, however, may face a difficult challenge in attracting website visitors. If you're in the market for a computer and you see a banner ad that says, 'The top 10 PCs under €800', you'll likely click on the banner. But what kind of ad would get you to visit a site like dentalfloss.com?

A key challenge is designing a website that is attractive on first view and interesting enough to encourage repeat visits. Many marketers create colourful, graphically sophisticated websites that combine text, sound and animation to capture and hold attention (for examples, see www.sonystyle.com or www.nike.com). To attract new visitors and to encourage revisits, suggests one expert, online marketers should pay close attention to the seven C's of effective website design:[41]

- *Context*: the site's layout and design.
- *Content*: the text, pictures, sound and video that the website contains.
- *Community*: the ways in which the site enables user-to-user communication.
- *Customisation*: the site's ability to tailor itself to different users or to allow users to personalise the site.
- *Communication*: the ways in which the site enables site-to-user, user-to-site or two-way communication.
- *Connection*: the degree to which the site is linked to other sites.
- *Commerce*: the site's capabilities to enable commercial transactions.

And to keep customers coming back to the site, companies need to embrace yet another 'C' – constant change.

At the very least, a website should be easy to use, professional looking and physically attractive. Ultimately, however, websites must also be *useful*. When it comes to Web surfing and shopping, most people prefer substance over style and function over flash. Thus, effective websites contain deep and useful information, interactive tools that help buyers find and evaluate products of interest, links to other related sites, changing promotional offers and entertaining features that lend relevant excitement. For example, in addition to convenient online purchasing, Clarins.com offers in-depth information about Clarins products and treatments, the latest product launches, beauty tips and advice, an interactive tool for determining the browser's skin type and promotional treats.

A company needs to review its website's attractiveness and usefulness from time to time. One way is to invite the opinion of site design experts. A better way is to get users to feed back on what they like and dislike about the site. Importantly, beyond customers, marketers have to recognise that their company's website may also serve other interest groups, including investors, job seekers, the media and society. Independent agencies exist today that offer advice to companies and organisations on their website performance. Some have also developed methodologies for benchmarking company websites. For example, the FT Bowen Craggs Index rates a company's website in terms of how well it serves major audiences (see Real Marketing 18.2).

real marketing

18.2

Corporate website performance: are you being served?

Bowen Craggs & Co. (www.bowencraggs.com), a corporate website advisory firm, developed a methodology – the Bowen Craggs Index - for examining in detail the effectiveness of a company's Web presence. The metrics used to compile the Index fall into two categories: specific and overall. Specific metrics focus on how well the site serves various groups – customers, society, investors, the media, job seekers. Overall metrics include *construction* which looks at navigation and coherence; *message*, which entails the visual and content messages the site transmits; and *contact*, which covers the efficiency of the points of contact and the effectiveness of the diversion of contacts through FAQs (frequently asked questions).

When analysing a site, expert reviewers concentrate on what should be provided and then judge how well it is provided. Using the Bowen Craggs Index, the *Financial Times* assessed the websites of companies taken from the 2006 *FT Global 500,* ranked by market capitalisation. Here's what they came up with in their assessment of the biggest 20 companies from each of Europe, the US and the rest of the world. The companies that best served each group are as follows; scores for each metric are out of 32.

- *Customers*: **Cisco Systems (score of 28); Royal Bank of Canada (28); AstraZeneca (27)**

  According to the experts, both Cisco and Royal Bank provide excellent 'journeys' for customers, leading potential customers to where they buy or make contact and providing them with excellent information. The pharmaceutical company AstraZeneca has limited opportunities to market directly. Instead it uses its site to build its brand subtly by educating customers about its products. Cisco's product demonstrations, discussion areas and videos, AstraZeneca's interactive tutorials and Royal Bank's product selection and comparison tools were particularly impressive. The experts' verdict? The sites do the job and they do it well!

- *Society*: **Petrobas (30); BHP Billiton (28); BP (28)**

  Two 'rest of the world' companies are given the thumbs up. Petrobas's site targeted financial analysts. It includes a tool showing environmental impact and gave high profile to corporate social responsibility. BHP Billiton mapped its reporting against the Global Reporting initiative, incorporating a traffic light system to indicate the extent the company is meeting its targets. BP showcased outstanding tools including the carbon footprint calculator, health, safety and environment charting tools and a plant-by-plant environmental mapping device. Notable was its use of the site for local crisis management, especially after the 2005 Texas City refinery explosion.

- *The media*: **Siemens (28); Cisco Systems (28); AstraZeneca (27); Roche (27)**

  Here Siemens scored well because it gave journalists timely, relevant information. Press releases are filtered in multiple ways and media contacts are given a great deal of attention. Cisco's high-tech Newsroom uses podcasts, videos and blogs to engage its largely high-tech audience. Roche is commended for its well-ordered press releases and invaluable stock of background material, including videos and documents. AstraZeneca's site for specialist journalists allows the user to check news by date, product or disease and to get pictures from a huge classified image library.

● *Investors*: **Vodafone (28); ENI (28); BP (27); Total (27); UBS (27)**

Here companies must serve three groups: analysts that cover the company, those that don't but want to research the company, and individual investors. Vodafone's investor section is comprehensive but simple. It gives analysts the information they need in many formats, but talks to its individual investors as though it cares about them. The experts commend the 'ENI at a glance' site, which assembles facts and figures a new analyst would want. BP's strength – an 'Interactive Analyst' charting tool – lets all three investor groups analyse historical figures which are presented in an illuminating way. Total's 'Fact Book', covering seven years, provides a rich resource for analysts, while individual shareholders are also taken seriously. UBS wins on sophistication – it lets users construct their own quarterly report.

● *Jobseekers*: **UBS (26); Microsoft (26); Siemens (24); Shell (24)**

These companies had particularly effective jobseekers' sites, which are used to list specific vacancies as well as attract graduates. In fact, jobseekers often make up the biggest group of visitors to a corporate site. According to the experts, the best graduate areas exploit technology that appeals to young people as well as tap into community features. UBS's recruitment area is impressive with its raft of videos, featuring young staff talking about their roles and responsibilities and why they joined the company, and an interactive self-assessment tool. Shell offers a tool that matches degrees with job areas. Microsoft's 'Jobs Blog' informs visitors about technical careers at the company. Siemens lets job seekers search for jobs or get an e-mail if a vacancy arises.

Thus, when designing corporate websites, a company must take on board the major interest groups it needs to serve. Global Channels communications director for Unilever, Tim Godbehere, advises, 'Work out who your audience is and what you are trying to achieve.' He stresses using online surveys for audience analysis and highlights the company's experience: Unilever.com was visited mainly by consumers although its corporate website was aiming at investors. Corporate websites can be expensive – the budget for Unilever.com plus 30 country sites is almost £1.8m a year. Thus, matching content to audience group is crucial if firms are to maximise the returns on their website investments.

In the final analysis, website effectiveness boils down to doing the job and doing it well for all of its key stakeholder groups.

SOURCES: Based on David Bowen, 'How well are we being served?', *Financial Times* (28 March 2007), p. 5; David Bowen, FT report – Digital business: 'Time to seize control', *Financial Times* (4 October 2006), p. 1. Copyright © David Bowen.

Table 18.3 Online advertising spending worldwide (in millions of US dollars)

Type of advertising	2005	2006	2007	2008	2009
Display	7,043	8,617	10,462	11,849	13,392
Search	7,833	10,610	13,993	16,803	19,711
Classified	3,291	4,578	6,169	7,532	8,856
Other (e-mail and mobile advertising)	545	649	721	742	825
Total online ad spending	18,712	24,452	31,345	36,926	42,684
Total ad spending	406,253	431,561	453,929	482,137	506,124

SOURCE: Reprinted with permission from '2007 marketing fact book', *Marketing News*, published by the American Publishing Association, Zenith Optimedia Group Ltd., December 2006, via eMarketer Inc., New York.

Placing ads and promotions online

As consumers spend more and more time on the Internet, many companies are shifting more of their marketing budget to **online advertising** to build their brands or to attract visitors to their websites.

Online advertising is becoming a major medium. Global online ad spend is forecast to grow as shown in Table 18.3. Online spending will jump from around €23bn (5 per cent of total ad spend worldwide) in 2007 to more than €31bn by 2009, representing nearly 9 per cent of total marketing ad spending across the major media (e.g., radio, TV, print, etc.).[42] Here, we discuss forms of online advertising and promotion and their future.

Online advertising— Advertising that appears while consumers are surfing the Web, including display ads (banners, interstitials, pop-ups), search-related ads, online classifieds and other forms.

Forms of online advertising

The major forms of online advertising include display ads, search-related ads and online classifieds. Online display ads currently account for around 33 per cent of online ad spend. These ads might appear anywhere on an Internet user's screen. The most common form is *banners*, banner-shaped ads found at the top, bottom, left, right or centre of a Web page. For instance, a Web surfer looking up airline schedules or fares might encounter a flashing banner that screams, 'Rent a car from Europcar and get up to two days free!' Clicking on the ad takes consumers to the Europcar website, where they can redeem the promotion.

Interstitials are online display ads that appear between screen changes on a website, especially while a new screen is loading. You may have noticed these ads, which appear as a separate window displaying a different product or service, when you visit a particular website. For example, visitors to www.msnbc.com's sports area may see a 10-second ad for a digital camera or DVD player before the home page loads.

*Pop-up*s are online ads that appear suddenly in a new window in front of the window being viewed. Such ads can multiply out of control, creating a major annoyance. As a result, Internet services and Web browser providers have developed applications that let users block most pop-ups. But not to worry. Many advertisers have now developed pop-*unders*, new windows that evade pop-up blockers by appearing *behind* the page you're viewing.

With the increase in broadband Internet access in homes, not only in Europe but worldwide, many companies are developing exciting new *rich media* display ads, which incorporate animation, video, sound and interactivity. Rich media ads attract and hold consumer attention better than traditional banner ads. They employ techniques such as float, fly and snapback – animations that jump out and sail over the Web page before retreating to their original space.

Another hot growth area for online advertising is *search-related ads* (or *contextual advertising*), in which text-based ads and links appear alongside search engine results on sites such as Google,

Microsoft's MSN and Yahoo! Internationally, search advertising currently accounts for nearly 45 per cent of all online advertising expenditures, more than any other category of online advertising.[43]

For example, search Google for 'HDTV' and you'll see inconspicuous ads for 10 or more advertisers, ranging from electrical/electronic goods retailers (e.g., Currys.co.uk, comet.co.uk) and online retailers (e.g., PriceGrabber.co.uk, PriceRunner.co.uk) to specialist suppliers (e.g. Sky.com, HDTV.theselection.co.uk). Nearly all of Google's $6.1bn in revenues worldwide comes from search advertising sales. An advertiser buys search terms from the search site and pays only if consumers click through to its site.

Search ads have grown in popularity because of their promise to reduce advertising waste – sending messages that reach the wrong audience or none at all.[44]

> " Advertisers' waste is estimated at about $220bn worldwide, or just over half of their total . . . spending. "

John Wanamaker, a Philadelphia merchant in the late nineteenth century, expounded a witticism – 'Half the money I spend on advertising is wasted. The trouble is, I don't know which half.' According to the trade association Interactive Advertising Bureau, in 2006 advertisers' waste is estimated at about $220bn (€160bn) worldwide, or just over half of their total ($431 billion) spending (see Table 18.3). Mr Wanamaker was amazingly accurate!

But thanks to Internet agencies like Google, advertisers will increasingly be able to pay only for real and measurable responses by consumers, such as clicking on a Web link, sharing a video, placing a call, printing a coupon or making a purchase.

Innovations are a factor influencing the growth in search advertising. In Google's auction-based service, AdWords, advertisers not only pay per click, but are also able to bid for keywords in an online auction. Google's AdSense service goes beyond search-results pages and places 'sponsored' advertising links on the Web pages of newspapers and other publishers signed up on Google's network. Like AdWords, these AdSense ads are 'contextual', that is, relevant only to the Web page's content, the advertiser paying only when a Web surfer clicks. This is akin to an ad agency automatically placing sponsored links and other ads on relevant third-party sites. Google's service therefore provides more flexibility and precision. Firms that want to raise brand awareness often want a higher level of control over where their ads appear. Google also offers animated ads, in addition to small, text-based ads, which are more appealing to the big-brand advertisers. Together, AdWords and AdSense generate some $6.1bn in revenues for Google. In the highly competitive UK Internet market, Google's advertising revenue of around £900m in 2006 already surpassed the $800m achieved by commercial TV Channel 4.

Because this advertising model is so lucrative, other Internet portals including Yahoo!, Microsoft's MSN and eBay want to catch up with Google. Other companies have been exploring ways of charging advertisers for consumers' actions. Start-ups like San Francisco-based ZiXXo pioneered 'pay-per-print' while others such as Ingenio bet on 'pay-per-call'. Meanwhile, Google's online payment system, Checkout, allows it to identify how many users who click on one of its ads subsequently make a purchase. Google's not alone, as new search engine start-ups such as Snap.com already offer 'cost-per-action' deals. An airline that advertises on Snap's search results would pay not when a consumer clicks but only when he or she buys a ticket.

Perhaps the age of the ultimate marketing machine has finally arrived. Thanks to the Internet, advertising may become less wasteful. And Mr Wanamaker's dictum no longer will have to seem like an economic law!

Other forms of online promotion

Other forms of online promotions include content sponsorships, alliances and affiliate programmes and viral advertising.

Using *content sponsorships,* companies gain name exposure on the Internet by sponsoring special content on various websites, such as news or financial information or special-interest topics. Sponsorships are best placed in carefully targeted sites where they can offer relevant information or service to the audience.

Internet companies can also develop *alliances and affiliate programmes,* in which they work with other companies, online and offline, to 'promote each other'. For example, BT Openworld and AOL have created many successful alliances which are mentioned on their websites.

Finally, online marketers use **viral marketing**, the Internet version of word-of-mouth marketing. As a concept, viral marketing is not new. Offline, it has been referred to as word-of-mouth influence, creating a buzz, leveraging the media, network marketing and so forth. In the online world, viral marketing involves creating a website, e-mail message or other marketing event that is so infectious that customers will want to pass it along to their friends. Because customers pass the message or promotion along to others, viral marketing can be very inexpensive. And when the information comes from a friend, the recipient is much more likely to open and read it.

Viral marketing—The Internet version of word-of-mouth marketing – e-mail messages or other marketing events that are so infectious that customers will want to pass them along to friends.

The future of online advertising

Although online advertising still accounts for only a minor portion of the total advertising and marketing expenditures of most companies, it is growing rapidly. Online advertising serves a useful purpose, especially as a supplement to other marketing efforts. As a result, it is playing an increasingly important role in the marketing mixes of many advertisers. According to forecasts by Forrester Research, spending on Internet advertising in Europe will more than double over the next five years and represent almost a fifth of total media budgets by 2012.

Analysts at Forrester predict that spending on online advertising in Europe will rise to more than €16bn in 2012. Some 18 per cent of total media budgets will go to e-mail, search, display and other online advertising, according to Forrester's survey of more than 25,000 European consumers and interviews with 24 leading European marketers.

After several slow years, overall marketing spending is growing again in Europe, Forrester said, reporting that 54 per cent of companies have set their 2007 budgets higher than for 2006. The predicted growth in online spending over the next five years parallels the rapid spread of broadband access. As the number of European consumers with high-speed Internet access rises from 47 million to 83 million over that period, Internet advertisers will increasingly expand into new formats such as video, the report predicts.

The rise in money going to Web campaigns echoes changing media habits, with more than a third of Europeans saying they watch less television because they are online, according to Forrester. Forrester also flags up the advantages of more targeted advertising. A third of online consumers said they do not mind adverts if they relate to their interests. It also found that 40 per cent of Internet consumers trust price-comparison sites and 36 per cent trust online product reviews from other users, suggesting advertisers may start to make more of online marketing, including e-mail campaigns and blog advertising. 'Over the next few years, the shift of online marketing from experiment to mainstream will force marketing organisations and processes to change,' said Forrester senior analyst Rebecca Jennings. 'As different types of social media like MySpace and peer reviews strengthen their grip on users, expect marketers to jump on the bandwagon by switching ad spend to social media forms like RSS [Web feeds], blogs and networks.'

Not surprisingly, the strong outlook for online advertising has triggered recent deals by big Internet and technology firms, keen to make the most of bigger budgets dedicated to the Web. Examples include Google's $3.1bn (€2bn) cash purchase of DoubleClick, a leading online advertising network, and Microsoft's acquisition of digital marketing specialist aQuantive for $6bn (€4bn).[45]

SOURCE: Adapted from 'Spending on internet advertising "to double"' by Katie Allen, *The Guardian*, 13 July 2007, Copyright © The Guardian News and Media Ltd 2007.

Creating or participating in Web communities

The popularity of blogs and other Web forums has resulted in a rash of commercially sponsored websites called **Web communities**, which take advantage of the C2C properties of the Internet. Such sites allow members to congregate online and exchange views on issues of common interest. They are the cyberspace equivalent to a Starbucks coffeehouse, a place where everybody knows your e-mail address.

> **Web communities—** Websites upon which members can congregate online and exchange views on issues of common interest.

Earlier, we addressed youth-skewed social networking websites. Online communities as a whole have mushroomed in the last few years. Today, people, whatever their age, gender and interests, can join online communities, ranging from sites focusing on entertainment, movies and health, to ones devoted to home and families, lifestyles, and money and investments. For example, Digg.com is a cult website for news and entertainment trend-spotters, while Flickr, a photo-sharing website, is a forum for camera and photography enthusiasts. Visitors to these Internet neighbourhoods develop a strong sense of community. Such communities are attractive to advertisers because they draw frequent, lengthy visits from consumers with common interests and well-defined demographics.

Using e-mail

E-mail has exploded onto the scene as an important online marketing tool. The company can encourage prospects and customers to send questions, suggestions and complaints to the company via e-mail. Customer service representatives can quickly respond to such messages. The company may also develop Internet-based electronic mailing lists of customers or prospects. Such lists provide an excellent opportunity to introduce the company and its offerings to new customers and to build ongoing relationships with current ones. Using the lists, online marketers can send out customer newsletters, special product or promotion offers based on customer purchasing histories, reminders of service requirements or warranty renewals, or announcements of special events.

To compete effectively in this ever-more-cluttered e-mail environment, marketers are designing 'enriched' e-mail messages – animated, interactive and personalised messages full of streaming audio and video. Then, they are targeting these attention-grabbers more carefully to those who want them and will act upon them. Consider Nintendo, a natural for e-mail-based marketing:

Young computer-savvy gaming fans actually look forward to Nintendo's monthly e-mail newsletter for gaming tips and for announcements of exciting new games. When the company launched its *Star Fox Adventure* game, it created an intensive e-mail campaign in the weeks before and after the product launch. The campaign included a variety of messages targeting potential customers. 'Each message has a different look and feel, and . . . that builds excitement for Nintendo,' notes an executive working on the account. The response? More than a third of all recipients opened the e-mails. And they did more than just glance at the messages: click-through rates averaged more than 10 per cent. Nearly two-thirds of those opening the message watched its 30-second streaming video in its entirety. Nintendo also gathered insightful customer data from the 20 per cent of people who completed an embedded survey. Although the company feared that the barrage of messages might create 'list fatigue' and irritate customers, the campaign received very few negative responses. The unsubscribe rate was under 1 per cent.[46]

As with other types of online marketing, to sustain their value, companies must be careful that they don't cause resentment among Internet users who are already overloaded with 'junk e-mail'. The explosion of 'spam' – unsolicited, unwanted, commercial e-mail messages that clog up our e-mailboxes – has produced consumer frustration and anger. Thus, e-mail marketers walk a fine line between adding value for consumers and being intrusive.

> A well-planned and executed campaign can achieve over 90 per cent messages delivered.

To avoid irritating consumers by sending unwanted marketing e-mail, companies should ask customers for permission to e-mail marketing pitches. They should also tell recipients how to 'opt in' or 'opt out' of e-mail promotions at any time. This approach, known as *permission-based marketing*, has become a standard model for e-mail marketing. A study of 890 consumers of a global cosmetics brand, who received regular permission-based e-mail messages from the company, showed that regular e-mail marketing had a positive impact on consumer brand loyalty; e-mail-activated consumers visited the retail stores and recommended the brand to friends. The study also suggested that loyal customers appreciate regular e-mail communications and relevant information content from the marketer more than mere promotional offers.[47] According to another expert, although a high proportion of e-mails are considered spam, it is still a very effective direct marketing tool. 'A well-planned and executed campaign can achieve over 90 per cent messages delivered, with about 40 per cent of delivered messages opened to display the creative content. Around 10 per cent of those delivered are clicked on. Being able to measure the individual offer that a recipient clicks through on, and then doing a digital or offline follow-up, is a direct marketer's dream,' says Dave Chaffey, an online marketing trainer at the UK's Chartered Institute of Marketing.[48]

The promise and challenges of online marketing

Online marketing continues to offer both great promise and many challenges for the future. Its most ardent apostles still envision a time when the Internet and online marketing will replace magazines, newspapers and even stores as sources for information and buying. Most marketers, however, hold a more realistic view. For most companies, online marketing serves a useful purpose, especially as a supplement to other marketing efforts in the 'offline' world. It will remain just one important approach to the marketplace that works alongside other approaches in a fully integrated communications mix.

Despite the many challenges, companies large and small are quickly integrating online marketing into their marketing strategies and mixes. As it continues to grow, online marketing will prove to be a powerful direct marketing tool for building customer relationships, improving sales, communicating company and product information and delivering products and services more efficiently and effectively. 'The key question is not whether to deploy Internet technology – companies have no choice if they want to stay competitive – but how to deploy it,' says business strategist Michael Porter. He continues: 'We need to move away from the rhetoric about "Internet industries", "e-business strategies" and a "new economy", and see the Internet for what it is: . . . a powerful set of tools that can be used, wisely or unwisely, in almost any industry and as part of almost any strategy.'[49]

Integrated direct marketing

Too often, a company's different direct-marketing efforts are not well integrated with one another or with other elements of its marketing and promotion mixes. For example, a firm's media advertising may be handled by the advertising department working with a traditional advertising agency. Meanwhile, its direct-mail and catalogue business may be handled by direct-marketing specialists, whereas its website is developed and operated by an outside Internet firm. Even within a given direct-marketing campaign, too many companies use only a 'one-shot' effort to reach and sell a prospect or a single vehicle in multiple stages to trigger purchases.

A more powerful approach is **integrated direct marketing**, which involves using carefully coordinated multiple-media, multiple-stage campaigns. Such campaigns can greatly improve response. Whereas a direct-mail piece alone might generate a 2 per cent response, adding a website and freephone number might raise the response rate by 50 per cent. Then, a well-designed outbound e-mail campaign might lift response by an additional 500 per cent. Suddenly, a 2 per cent response has grown to 15 per cent or more by adding interactive marketing channels to a regular mailing.

Integrating direct marketing channels with each other and with other media has become a top priority for marketers. For example, consider the integrated direct marketing efforts of professional services firm Ernst & Young:

> Ernst & Young is taking a decidedly integrated approach with its online, e-mail and other direct marketing. It integrates its e-mail efforts with other media, including direct mail, and tightly weaves both into interactive elements on the company's site. For example, several months ahead of an annual conference it was hosting for energy executives, it began a promotion with a 'save the date' e-mail to clients and prospects. That was followed up by a rich media e-mail. 'We created these flash movies that we e-mailed them, and the call to action was embedded there,' says an Ernst & Young marketing executive. 'There was a link built in that brought them to the website to find out details about the conference.' Next, to reinforce the online messages, the company sent out direct mail invitations, which included a registration form as well as the Web address for those who chose to register online. To ensure that Ernst & Young's direct marketing messages are well integrated, representatives from each marketing discipline meet on a regular basis. 'We all sit around the table and talk about what we've done, what's in process and what we're planning,' says the marketing executive. 'The results rely on "the whole thing". Otherwise, it's like making a cake without putting in the flour.'[50]

Public policy and ethical issues in direct marketing

Direct marketers and their customers usually enjoy mutually rewarding relationships. Occasionally, however, a darker side emerges. The aggressive and sometimes shady tactics of a few direct marketers can bother or harm consumers, giving the entire industry a black eye.

Integrated direct marketing—Direct marketing campaigns that use multiple vehicles and multiple stages to improve response rates and profits.

Abuses range from simple excesses that irritate consumers to instances of unfair practices or even outright deception and fraud. The direct marketing industry has also faced growing invasion-of-privacy concerns, and online marketers must deal with Internet security issues.

> The aggressive and sometimes shady tactics of a few direct marketers can bother or harm consumers, giving the entire industry a black eye.

Irritation, unfairness, deception and fraud

Direct-marketing excesses sometimes annoy or offend consumers. Most of us dislike direct-response TV commercials that are too loud, too long and too insistent. Our mail piles up with unwanted junk mail, our e-mail boxes fill up with unwanted spam and our computer screens fill up with unwanted pop-up or pop-under ads.

Beyond irritating consumers, some direct marketers have been accused of taking unfair advantage of impulsive or less-sophisticated buyers. TV shopping channels and programme-long 'infomercials' targeting television-addicted shoppers seem to be the worst culprits. They feature smooth-talking hosts, elaborately staged demonstrations, claims of drastic price reductions, 'while they last' time limitations and unequalled ease of purchase to inflame buyers who have low sales resistance.

Worse yet, so-called heat merchants design mailers and write copy intended to mislead buyers. Even well-known direct mailers have been accused of deceiving consumers.

Fraudulent schemes, such as investment scams or phoney collections for charity, have also multiplied in recent years. *Internet fraud*, including identity theft and financial scams, has become a serious problem. One common form of Internet fraud is *phishing*, a type of identity theft that uses deceptive e-mails and fraudulent websites to fool users into divulging their personal data. Most of us who have used the Internet have in the past received a phishing e-mail. Although many consumers are now aware of such schemes, phishing can be extremely costly to those caught in the Net. It also damages the brand identities of legitimate online marketers who have worked to build user confidence in Web and e-mail transactions.[51]

Many consumers also worry about *online security*. They fear that unscrupulous snoopers will eavesdrop on their online transactions or intercept their credit card numbers and make unauthorised purchases. In turn, companies doing business online fear that others will use the Internet to invade their computer systems for the purposes of commercial espionage or even sabotage. There appears to be an ongoing competition between the technology of Internet security systems and the sophistication of those seeking to break them.

Another Internet marketing concern is that of *access by vulnerable or unauthorised groups*. For example, marketers of adult-oriented materials have found it difficult to restrict access by minors. In a more specific example, a while back, sellers using eBay found themselves the victims of a 14-year-old boy who'd bid on and purchased more than $3m worth of high-priced antiques and rare artworks on the site. eBay has a strict policy against bidding by anyone under age 18 but works largely on the honour system. Unfortunately, this honour system did little to prevent the teenager from taking a cyberspace joyride.[52]

Invasion of privacy

Invasion of privacy is perhaps the toughest public policy issue now confronting the direct-marketing industry. Consumers often benefit from database marketing – they receive more offers that are closely matched to their interests. However, many critics worry that marketers may know *too* much about consumers' lives and that they may use this knowledge to take unfair advantage of consumers. At some point, they claim, the extensive use of databases intrudes on consumer privacy.

These days, it seems that almost every time consumers apply for a credit card, visit a website or order products by mail, telephone or the Internet, their names enter some company's already bulging database. Using sophisticated computer technologies, direct marketers can use these databases to 'micro target' their selling efforts. *Online privacy* causes special concerns. Most online marketers have become skilled at collecting and analysing detailed consumer information.

Some consumers and policy makers worry that the ready availability of information may leave consumers open to abuse if companies make unauthorised use of the information in marketing their products or exchanging databases with other companies. For example, they ask, should a telecommunications network service provider such as BT be allowed to sell marketers the names of customers who frequently call the freephone or customer-hotline numbers of catalogue companies? Should a company such as American Express be allowed to make data on its millions of cardholders worldwide available to merchants who accept AmEx cards? Is it right for credit bureaux to compile and sell lists of people who have recently applied for credit cards – people who are considered prime direct-marketing targets because of their spending behaviour?

In their drives to build databases, companies sometimes get carried away. For example, Microsoft caused substantial privacy concerns when one version of its Windows software used a 'Registration Wizard' that snooped into users' computers. When users went online to register, without their knowledge, Microsoft 'read' the configurations of their PCs to learn about the major software products they were running. Users protested loudly and Microsoft abandoned the practice.

Environmental concerns

Although direct marketing offers advantages and can be well deployed by marketers, some direct marketing forms such as mail and print catalogues have been attacked for adding to the waste paper mountain. Not surprising if one were to consider, for example, the amount of paper a catalogue business might generate. Clicking a link on the www.Quelle.com website led to a 'Did you know . . . ?' page bearing clichés which provide food for thought:

'Did you know . . . ?

- that if all the catalogues of one edition were piled on top of each other, they would be far higher than the Eiffel tower: by more than 1,030 times?

- that the total weight of one edition of Quelle's main catalogue is equivalent to 4,170 adult elephants?

- that all main catalogues of one edition placed in a row, would form a super highway 3,240 km long. It would easily stretch from Copenhagen to Palermo, or from Munich to Kiel and back.

- that the entire length of the web-fed paper required for the entire number of catalogues printed is about 395,000 kms? With this stretch of paper you could easily wrap the globe nine times over!'[53]

In the current age of eco-consumerism, unwanted junk mail (and unwanted marketing) will fuel the antipathy towards the direct marketing industry, according to the UK's Direct Marketing Association (DMA). The DMA accepts that the environmental issue is an increasing concern for the industry and has made it one of the priorities to be addressed in the years ahead.

A need for action

Access to and use of information has caused much concern and debate among companies, consumers and public policy makers. It has also led to calls for strong actions by marketers and the direct marketing industry alike to curb privacy, security and other abuses before legislators step in to do it for them.

Direct marketing activities in Europe are regulated by a combination of legislation and self-regulatory codes. For example, to build consumer confidence in shopping direct, associations for businesses practising database and interactive marketing have launched consumer privacy rules. These rules generally require that their members comply with carefully developed consumer privacy rules: members must notify customers when any personal information is rented, sold or exchanged with others; they must also honour consumer requests to 'opt out' of information exchanges with other marketers or not to receive mail, telephone or other solicitations again; and to honour consumer requests to remove their names from the company's database, when they do not wish to receive mail or telephone offers at home.

Since 2000, various 'acts', such as the Data Protection Act and the Distance Selling Directive, have come into effect. European nations implement these laws differently, with the direct marketing associations in individual countries updating members on legislation. For instance, most countries have a Mail Preference Service, MPS (or Robinson list) of consumers who don't wish to be contacted. Use of these lists is not a legal requirement, but in some countries such as the UK, the law states that telemarketers must check lists against the Telephone Preference Service, TPS. Table 18.4 provides an example of legal restrictions in several EU countries.

Updated Directives on Privacy and Electronic Communications already outlaw spam and require vendors to ask customers to 'opt-in' to receiving e-mails, failing which they can be penalised for breaking the rules. All commercial e-mail communications must also have an 'opt-out' feature. The directive also states that Web surfers must be told ahead of time about sites' cookie procedures, giving consumers the right to refuse cookie-based data collection. It also specifies that users must give explicit permission for their personal data to be included in public directories.[54]

Of special concern are the privacy rights of children. Many websites directed towards children collect personal information from children, but not all such sites may include any disclosure of their collection and use of such information. As a result, governments have passed online privacy protection laws, which require website operators targeting children to post privacy policies on their sites. In most cases, they must also notify parents about the information they're gathering and obtain parental consent before collecting personal information from children under 13. In addition, smart companies are responding to consumer privacy and security concerns with actions of their own. For example, they conduct voluntary audits of their privacy and security policies and strive to exceed government-mandated privacy regulations.

EU Directives such as Television without Frontiers 89/552/CEE has been modified by the EU Directive 97/36/CE, which lays down rules that apply to TV shopping, such as overall duration of TV shopping and exemptions, communications of content and rights to return purchased goods. The modernising of EU rules is ongoing. In early 2007, the European Commission approved proposals for a new 'Audiovisual without Frontiers' directive in response to recent technological developments and to create a new level playing field in Europe for emerging audiovisual media services, including video-on-demand, mobile TV and audio-visual services on digital TV. The directive represents a new regulatory framework for Europe's digital-era TV and TV-like services, and reaffirms EU policies ranging from consumer protection, the protection of minors and the promotion of fair and ethical business practices to advertising.[55]

More importantly, from a business sustainability perspective, some industry experts acknowledge the need for change and actions.

Table 18.4 Direct marketing: consumer protection and legislation in some EU countries

UK

- Illegal to call individuals registered with the Telephone Preference Service, TPS.

- Illegal to fax individuals or businesses registered with the Fax Preference Service, FPS.

- Voluntary consumer Mail Preference Service (MPS) for direct marketers is law under EU Distance Selling Directive.

- E-mail legislation for opt-in is covered in new EU Distance Selling Directive but UK operates a similar opt-out system for e-mails.

France

- Obligatory to add an opt-in clause to the mailing or questionnaire asking customers for permission to add their name to a mailing list.

- Not obligatory to add an opt-out clause for customers to decline further mailings.

- A Robinson list or MPS exists in France.

Germany

- Unsolicited telephone calls and faxes are not permitted to consumers.

- Telemarketing and telefaxing in business-to-business is also not permitted unless the following exception criteria are met:

    1. Prior consent from business person obtained, or

    2. Contractual relationship exists, or

    3. If caller can presume the interest of the business person called.

- Collection of names and non-sensitive data from questionnaires is permitted.

- A Robinson list or MPS exists in Germany.

- Sales promotion laws are the strictest in Europe and aim to prevent unfair competition.

- Opt-in for questionnaire respondents is not obligatory.

- Not obligatory to add an opt-out clause for customers to decline further mailings.

Spain

- Collection of names and data from questionnaires is permitted.

- A Robinson list or MPS exists in Spain.

- Not obligatory to add an opt-in clause to the mailing or questionnaire asking customers for permission to add their name to a mailing list.

- Obligatory to add an opt-out clause for customers to decline further mailings.

The Netherlands

- Mail Preference Service exists (Antwoordnummer 666).

- Consumer privacy legislation states that owners of databases must ask permission from names before rental to a third party.

Italy

- No data protection law.

- Self-regulation by the Italian DMA–AIDIM.

SOURCE: 'Legal restrictions: Summary of legal restrictions in direct marketing in Europe', published by Database and Internet Solutions, accessed online at www.dbt.co.uk, August 2007.

According to Rosemary Smith, Chair of the UK's Direct Marketing Association, 'Some people do feel targeted, in a bad sense, by parts of the industry. What is often forgotten is how often they actually respond. Something like 60 per cent of people have bought something as a result of direct marketing in the last year . . . If it didn't work, companies wouldn't use it.'

Yet although direct-marketing volumes have been falling for several years, the technique is a mainstay for financial services providers, publishers, retailers and charities. Ms Smith said: 'But the negative stories will continue to chime with the consumer if their perception of the industry is unchanged. That is what we have to change.'

Ms Smith has set the 'three E's' as her priorities. The first is environment. Under a deal with the Department for Environment, Food and Rural Affairs (DEFRA) in 2003, the industry's recycling level should have risen to at least 30 per cent of paper volumes by the end of 2005. By 2009, it should be 55 per cent and by 2013 70 per cent.

Ms Smith describes the 'environmental issue as increasingly a concern for the industry. Unfortunately, we get caught up in a lot of what we can only describe as "green fog". Our estimates are that we are responsible for 2 per cent of household waste by weight and use just over 4 per cent of the paper stock. Some 95 per cent of the paper we use is recycled.' Nevertheless, unwanted marketing, including unaddressed mail dropped through letterboxes, often tops consumers' lists of pet hates. Growth in eco-consumerism will only fuel that antipathy.

The DMA, therefore, plans to encourage use of a 'Recycle Now' logo on every mailing and a 'green accreditation' scheme for agencies. But a bigger force will be pressure from clients, Ms Smith argues. Clients will increasingly believe that being seen to support environmentalism is important for their brands and insist that agencies reduce wastage.

The DMA will continue to run the services for people to sign up to block corporate or consumer telemarketing or mailings. A similar service is also developed for door-drop mail. The organisation admits, though, that it cannot stop rogue operators, especially senders of e-mail spam, acting from abroad.

Given the sector's poor image, the second 'E' is consumer engagement. Ms Smith promises renewed effort to assure consumers of the benefits of direct marketing such as loyalty schemes, discount offers, pricing information and membership drives for groups such as charities, which make up about 10 per cent of all mailings.

The growth of Internet search engines such as Google and younger consumers' receptiveness to digital messages suggest the need for the direct marketing industry to acquire and display expertise in handling new media, hence the third of Ms Smith's 'E' priorities. Digital marketing is sometimes dubbed 'direct marketing on steroids' – both offer advertisers a straightforward way to measure responses and collect customer data. But established mail-based agencies face stiff competition from digital specialists for a share of the increasing budgets advertisers are putting into digital. Ms Smith adds: 'We have all these channels at our fingertips now. The king is what the consumer prefers and reacts to. Our job is to engage the consumer more to ensure that we are putting out what it is they want to receive.'

Whether the context is the environment, technology or a battle for better public relations, this is a message the industry forgets at its peril.

Direct marketers know that, left untended, unethical conduct will lead to increasingly negative consumer attitudes, lower response rates, and calls for more restrictive national and EU legislation. 'Privacy and customer permission have become the cornerstones of customer trust, [and] trust has become the cornerstone to a continuing relationship,' says one expert. Companies must 'become the custodians of customer trust and protect the privacy of their customers.'[56]

More importantly, most direct marketers want the same things that consumers want: honest and well-designed marketing offers targeted only towards consumers who will appreciate and respond to them. Direct marketing is just too expensive to waste on consumers who don't want it.

Reviewing the concepts

This chapter investigates direct and online marketing.

1. Define direct marketing and discuss its benefits to customers and companies

Direct marketing consists of direct connections with carefully targeted individual consumers to both obtain an immediate response and cultivate lasting customer relationships. Using detailed databases, direct marketers tailor their offers and communications to the needs of narrowly defined segments or even individual buyers.

For buyers, direct marketing is convenient, easy to use and private. It gives buyers ready access to a wealth of products and information, at home and around the globe. Direct marketing is also immediate and interactive, allowing buyers to create exactly the configuration of information, products or services they desire, then order them on the spot. For sellers, direct marketing is a powerful tool for building customer relationships. Using database marketing, today's marketers can target small groups or individual consumers, tailor offers to individual needs, and promote these offers through personalised communications. It also offers them a low-cost, efficient alternative for reaching their markets. As a result of these advantages to both buyers and sellers, direct marketing has become the fastest-growing form of marketing.

2. Identify and discuss the major forms of direct marketing

The main forms of direct marketing include personal selling, direct-mail marketing, catalogue marketing, telephone marketing, direct-response television marketing, kiosk marketing and online marketing. We discussed personal selling in the previous chapter.

Direct-mail marketing consists of the company sending an offer, announcement, reminder or other item to a person at a specific address. Recently, new forms of 'mail delivery' have become popular, such as e-mail marketing. Some marketers rely on catalogue marketing – selling through catalogues mailed to a select list of customers, made available in stores or accessed on the Web. Telephone marketing consists of using the telephone to sell directly to consumers. Direct-response television marketing has two forms: direct-response advertising (or infomercials) and home shopping channels. Kiosks are information and ordering machines that direct marketers place in stores, airports and other locations. In recent years, a number of new digital direct marketing technologies have emerged, including mobile phone marketing, podcasts, vodcasts and interactive TV. Online marketing involves online channels that digitally link sellers with consumers.

3. Explain how companies have responded to the Internet and other powerful new technologies with online marketing

Online marketing is the fastest-growing form of direct marketing. The Internet enables consumers and companies to access and share huge amounts of information with just a few

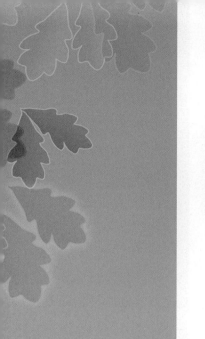

mouse clicks. In turn, the Internet has given marketers a whole new way to create value for customers and build customer relationships. Online consumer buying continues to grow at a healthy rate. Thus, smart marketers are employing integrated multi-channel strategies that use the Web to drive sales to other marketing channels.

4. Discuss how companies go about conducting online marketing to profitably deliver more value to customers

Companies of all types are now engaged in online marketing. The Internet gave birth to the *click-only* dot-coms, which operate only online. In addition, many traditional bricks-and-mortar companies have now added online marketing operations, transforming themselves into *clicks-and-mortar* competitors. Many clicks-and-mortar companies are now having more online success than their click-only competitors.

Companies can conduct online marketing in any of the following four ways: creating a website, placing ads and promotions online, setting up or participating in Web communities or using online e-mail. The first step typically is to set up a website. Beyond simply setting up a site, however, companies must make their sites engaging, easy to use and useful in order to attract visitors, hold them and bring them back again.

Online marketers can use various forms of online advertising to build their Internet brands or to attract visitors to their websites. Beyond online advertising, other forms of online promotion include online display advertising, search-related advertising, content sponsorships, alliances and affiliate programmes and viral marketing, the Internet version of word-of-mouth marketing. Online marketers can also participate in Web communities, which take advantage of the C2C properties of the Web. Finally, e-mail marketing has become a fast-growing tool for both B2C and B2B marketers. Whatever direct marketing tools they use, marketers must work hard to integrate them into a cohesive marketing effort.

5. Discuss the public policy and ethical issues presented by direct marketing

Direct marketers and their customers usually enjoy mutually rewarding relationships. Occasionally, however, direct marketing presents a darker side. The aggressive and some-times shady tactics of a few direct marketers can bother or harm consumers, giving the entire industry a bad reputation. Abuses range from simple excesses that irritate consumers to instances of unfair practices or even outright deception and fraud. The direct-marketing industry has also faced growing concerns about invasion-of-privacy and Internet security issues. Such concerns call for strong action by marketers and public policy makers to curb direct marketing abuses. In the end, most direct marketers want the same things that consumers want: honest and well-designed marketing offers targeted only towards consumers who will appreciate and respond to them.

Discussing the concepts

1. What are the benefits of direct marketing for buyers and sellers? Discuss with reference to both online and offline or traditional direct marketing approaches.

2. The backbone of a successful direct marketing campaign is the firms' customer database. Imagine that you have been approached by an online retailer that specialises

in selling ties, scarves and fashion accessories to help set up its customer database. It needs this database for direct marketing of new products and managing customer relationships. Describe the qualities and features the company must consider for an effective database.

3. Companies design websites for many purposes. Taking into account the basic types of websites, what are the major factors that marketers must consider when designing these websites?

4. Recent times have seen the emergence of new digital direct marketing technologies and online marketing techniques that enable companies to connect with target audiences and to elicit desired responses. Identify the major tools covered in this chapter. What are their key strengths and limitations in supporting firms' marketing efforts? Discuss with reference to the following companies: (a) adidas, (b) Nokia, (c) KLM (or British Airways) or (d) Sony.

5. Direct-marketing abuses are a major concern of consumers, responsible marketers and consumer protection groups alike. Identify the major consumer concerns or fears. Are these concerns (fears) usually justified? In a group, discuss and share your experience of interactions with direct marketers or previous direct marketing encounters. What actions should companies take to reduce consumers' concerns?

Applying the concepts

1. Select a company of your choice. Visit the company's website and evaluate the site:

   (a) Analyse the site and rate it on the seven C's of effective website design.

   (b) Next, assess the site's performance in relation to the key audiences (customers, the media, investors, etc.).

   (c) How might the site be improved?

2. Techno-ethical issues – the examining of ethical issues in technology – is increasingly applied to many areas of Internet marketing. Blogs are an example of a growing online marketing technology that presents some challenging ethical issues for marketers. For example, is it ethical for a company to ask consumers to blog favourably about a product? Should a company create 'fictional users' to blog about its products? Social networking websites such as MySpace have suffered problems with some users' sites re-routed to adult-content sites. Parents are concerned that their children are posting personal information when creating their profiles on the site which is accessible to millions of other visitors – including sexual predators. These are just a few examples of ethical and consumer safety issues facing firms operating in today's online world.

   (a) Is it ethical for an advertiser to pay a consumer to blog favourably about a product or service? To create 'fictional' bloggers to spread favourable stories about a product or service?

   (b) What other examples have you read or heard about recently involving ethical issues with Web-based marketing technologies or companies?

   (c) What should companies do to address these concerns and to reduce the negative public relations effects of these techno-ethical issues?

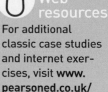

Web resources

For additional classic case studies and internet exercises, visit **www. pearsoned.co.uk/ kotler**

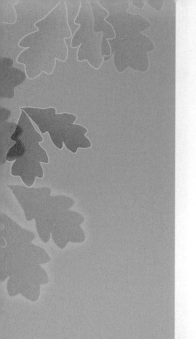

References

1. Information on annual direct marketing expenditure from 'Federation of European direct and interactive marketing – Your guiding light in unknown waters', www.fedma.org, accessed August 2007.

2. 'Pan-European: Media. Direct marketing expenditure', *The European Marketing Pocket Book* (Henley-on-Thames: World Advertising Research Centre, WARC, 2004), p. 34.

3. Juraj Sebo, 'Distance selling in an enlarged European market', www.nmoa.org/catalog/dropship.htm, accessed August 2007.

4. 'UK floods Europe with direct mail marketing demands', *Creativematch* (23 February 2006), accessed at www.creativematch.co.uk, August 2007.

5. Elizabeth Rigby, 'Eyes in the till', *FTMagazine, Technology Special* (11/12 November 2006), pp. 16–22; Daniel Lyons, 'Too much information', *Forbes* (13 December 2004), p. 110; Mike Freeman, 'Data company helps Wal-Mart, casinos, airlines analyze data', *Knight Ridder Business Tribune News* (24 February 2006), p. 1.

6. Simon London, 'Choked by a data surfeit', *Financial Times* (29 January 2004), p. 17; see also Tom Davenport and John Beck, *The Attention Economy* (Maidenhead: McGraw-Hill, 2003) and C.K. Prahalad and Venkat Ramaswamy, *The Future of Competition: Co-creating unique value with customers* (Boston, MA: Harvard Business School Publishing, 2004).

7. For more discussion of database marketing principles and practices, see Alan Tapp, *Principles of Direct and Database Marketing*, 4th edn (Harlow: FT/Prentice-Hall, 2007).

8. David Ranii, 'Compact discs, DVDs get more use as promotional tool', *Knight Ridder Tribune Business News* (5 May 2004), p. 1.

9. 'Home shopping catalogue sales overtaken by Internet', www.pindar.com/ecommerce, accessed August 2007.

10. Information on Quelle based on the company's Web communication, 'The whole world of Quelle at a glance' (2 August 2007) at www.quelle.com, accessed August 2007.

11. Jim Emerson, 'Print and the Internet go hand-in-hand', *Printing News* (30 June 2005), p. 2; 'Abacus report: Web sales soon to overtake catalog sales' (3 August 2005), accessed at http://multichannelmerchant.com/news/Abacus-trend-report-080305/.

12. Janie Curtis, 'Catalogs as portals: Why you should keep on mailing', *Multichannel Merchant* (30 November 2005), accessed at http://multichannelmerchant.com/news/catalogs_portal_1130/index.html.

13. Diane Anderson, 'HP developing retail kiosks to reach "iMoms"', *Brandweek* (6 March 2006), p. 12; Chris Jones, 'Kiosks put shopper in touch', *Knight Ridder Tribune Business News* (11 April 2006), p. 1; David Eisen, 'Hilton debuts air checkin kiosk', *Business Travel News* (1 May 2006), p. 8.

14. Based on figures for mobile advertising revenue for the region reported in '2007 Marketing Fact Book', *Marketing News* (15 July 2007), p. 28.

15. Mary Branscombe, 'What are we meant to do with all this?', *Financial Times: Digital Business* (4 October 2006), p. 9.

16. 'Mobile marketing', *Marketing News* (1 April 2006), p. 4.

17. Adapted from information in Normandy Madden, 'Cellphones spawn new "fast" promotions in Japan', *Advertising Age* (7 November 2005), p. 14.

18. Based on information provided by Dennis Timmermans, Managing Partner, OP3; for further information about OP3 and the ShotCode technology, visit www.shotcode.com.

19. Ian Limbach, 'The most personal way to reach out', *Financial Times Special Report: Digital Business* (21 June 2006), pp. 1 and 3.

20. For these and other examples, see Karyn Strauss and Derek Gale, *Hotels* (March 2006), p. 22; and 'Disneyland offers behind-the-scenes podcast', *Wireless News* (19 February 2006), p. 1.

21. Susie Haywood, 'Honda scores first with Civic "vodcast"', *Revolution* (February 2006), p. 11.

22. Alastair Ray, 'Press the red button', *Marketing Business* (April 2003), pp. 29–30.

23. Michael Svennevig, 'Press the red button', *The Marketer*, Issue 18 (November 2005), pp. 22–3.

24. Meg Carter, 'iTV's big gamble', *The Guardian* (24 November 2003), accessed at www. PiTV_Media_Guardian_200103, August 2007.

25. Internet penetration for the European Union and worldwide based on March 2007 data provided by Internet World Stats (www.InternetWorldStats.com) reported in 'Internet usage in the European Union' and 'Top 25 countries with the highest Internet penetration', in *The European Marketing Pocket Book* (Henley-on-Thames: World Advertising Research Centre, WARC, 2007), pp. 33 and 32 respectively.

26. Based on estimates provided by Computer Industry Almanac, www.c-i-a.com, reported in '2007 Marketing Fact Book', *Marketing News* (15 July 2007), p. 28.

27. 'Online sales to surpass $200 billion this year' (23 May 2006), accessed at http://www.shop.org/press/06/052306.asp; 'Jupiter Research forecasts online retail spending will reach $144 billion in 2010, a CAGR of 12% from 2005' (6 February 2006), accessed at www.jupitermedia.com/corporate/releases/06.02.06-newjupresearch.html. For other estimates, see 'Online retail sales grew in 2005' (5 January 2006), accessed at www.clickz.com; and 'Consumer Internet usage', *Interactive Marketing & Media*, a supplement to *Advertising Age* (17 April 2006), p. 28.

28. 'European e-tail tops €100 billion', Interactive Media in Retail Group (IMRG) (12 July 2006), accessed at www.imrg.org, August 2007.

29. Deidre McArdle, 'Europe's women flock to the web', ENN (ElectricNews.Net Ltd) (21 December 2004), accessed at www.enn.ie, August 2007.

30. 'China's pied piper', *The Economist* (23 September 2006), p. 80.

31. See Kim Wright Wiley, 'Meg Whitman: The $40 billion eBay sales story', *Selling Power* (November–December 2005), pp. 63–70; 'eBay Inc.', *Hoover's Company Records* (1 May 2006), p. 56307; and facts from eBay annual reports and other information accessed at www.ebay.com, September 2006.

32. Carlos Grande, 'iPhone presents a test case for media buyers', *Financial Times* (30 January 2007), p. 22; Stephen Baker and Heather Green, 'Blogs will change your business', *Business Week* (2 May 2005), pp. 57–67; Alan Scott, 'Guard your rep: Ignore blogs at the peril of brand image', *Marketing News* (15 February 2006), pp. 21–2.

33. 'MySpace doubles staff as 11 sites come online', *Financial Times* (29 January 2007), p. 19.

34. Carlos Grande, 'Facebook's popularity swells', *Financial Times* (14 August 2007), p. 3.

35. 'ForBiddeN fruit', *The Economist* (29 July 2006), p. 66; Gavin O'Malley, 'Coca-Cola sends bloggers to Olympics', *MediaPost Publications* (10 February 2006), accessed at http://pubications.mediapost.com.

36. Carlos Grande, *op. cit.*

37. Tom Braithwaite, 'Companies learn value of blogging', *Financial Times* (17 July 2006), p. 21.

38. Carlos Grande, 'Advertisers quit after Facebook's BNP gaffe', *Financial Times* (3 August 2007), p. 7.

39. Pete Blackshaw, 'Irrational exuberance? I hope we're not guilty', *Barcode Blog* (26 August 2005), accessed at www.barcodefactory.com/wordpress/?p=72.

40. 'Off their trolleys', *The Economist* (23 November 2002), pp. 80–1.

41. Jeffrey F. Rayport and Bernard J. Jaworski, *e-Commerce* (New York: McGraw-Hill, 2001), p. 116. Also see Goutam Chakraborty, 'What do customers consider important in B2B websites?', *Journal of Advertising* (March 2003), p. 50; and 'Looks are everything', *Marketing Management* (March/April 2006), p. 7.

42. Based on estimated global advertising expenditures (by medium) reported in '2007 Marketing Fact Book', *Marketing News* (15 July 2007), p. 28.

43. See Mike Shields, 'Google faces new rivals' (22 August 2005), accessed at www.mediaweek.com; and 'Internet advertising revenues grow 30% to a record $12.5 billion in '05', Internet Advertising Bureau (20 April 2006), accessed at www.iab.net.

44. Carlos Grande and Andrew Edgecliffe-Johnson, 'Google set to beat TV in race for ad revenues', *Financial Times* (2 November 2005), p. 1; 'The ultimate marketing machine', *The Economist* (8 July 2006), pp. 69–71; 'Classified calamity', *The Economist* (19 November 2005), p. 77; 'The online attack', *The Economist* (30 April 2005), pp. 63–4.

45. Katie Allen, 'Spending on internet advertising "to double"', *The Guardian* (13 July 2007), accessed at www.guardian.co.uk/technology/2007/jul/13/news.newmedia, August 2007.

46. Heidi Anderson, 'Nintendo case study: Rules are made to be broken', *E-mail Marketing Case Studies* (6 March 2003), accessed at http://www.clickz.com.

47. M. Merisavo and M. Raulas, 'The impact of e-mail marketing on brand loyalty', *Journal of Product and Brand Management*, **13**, 7 (2004), pp. 498–505.

48. Quote from Laura Mazur, 'The direct approach', *The Marketer* (18 November 2005), pp. 7–9.

49. Michael Porter, 'Strategy and the Internet', *Harvard Business Review* (March 2001), pp. 63–78.

50. Adapted from information in Carol Krol, 'E-mail marketing gains ground with integration', *BtoB* (3 April 2006), p. 1.

51. See Don Oldenburg, 'Hook, line and sinker: Personalized phishing scams use customers' names to attract attention', *The Washington Post* (2 April 2006), p. F05; and 'How not to get caught by a phishing scam', www.ftc.gov/bcp/conline/pubs/alerts/phishingalrt.htm, accessed June 2006.

52. '14-year-old bids over $3m for items in eBay auctions', *USA Today* (30 April 1999), p. 10B.

53. 'Quelle – up high and up front', www.quelle.com/en/unternehmen/1200_wussten_sie_schon, accessed August 2007.

54. Christopher Saunders, 'EU OKs spam ban, online privacy rules' (31 May 2002), accessed at www.clickz.com/news/article.php/115439, 28 March 2004.

55. Drawn from press release providing information on 'Audiovisual without Frontiers' Directive, March 2007, accessed at www.europa.eu/rapid/pressReleaseAction.do?reference=IP07/, August 2007; see also www.europa.eu/comm/avpolicy/reg/tvwf/modernisation/proposal_2005/index_en.htm.

56. Debbie A. Cannon, 'The ethics of database marketing', *Information Management Journal* (May–June 2002), pp. 42–4.

Company case 18 Viagogo goes west

Eric Baker, Viagogo chief executive, has done it and done it, but will he manage to do it again? With graduate business school buddy Jeff Fluhr, Eric did it first when they created the secondary ticketing website StubHub.com in 2000. They did it a second time when selling the operation to eBay for $307m in March 2007. Eric is working on doing it yet again with Viagogo, a European secondary ticketing agency that employs about 50 staff in London and Germany.

Viagogo is no ordinary ticket tout. The online ticket exchange allows people to trade tickets for sports games securely without resorting to illegal touts. It has succeeded by ironing out market inefficiencies that allowed ticket touts to make big profits and by facilitating customers to sell to customers safely and securely.

Eric Baker and Jeff Fluhr set up StubHub after recognising a market opportunity that many people have experienced. The story of an ageing rocker tells the tale:

As the Rolling Stones geared up for their 'A Bigger Bang' tour, Roger felt like reliving some old memories. Just because he was in his 60s didn't mean he was too old to rock. After all, he was an original Stones fan dating back to the '60s. He last saw the band at the Doncaster Odeon Cinema when they were on tour with a slew of other acts including Ike and Tina Turner. So on the day the Stones tickets went on sale, he grabbed a deck chair and headed to his local Ticketmaster outlet to 'camp out' in a queue. Roger knew that the kiosk, located inside a large chain music store, wouldn't open until 10 a.m. when tickets went on sale. He got to the store at 6 a.m. to find only three people ahead of him. 'Fantastic,' Roger thought. With so few people in front of him, getting good seats would be a snap. Maybe he would even score something close to the stage.

By the time the three people in front of him had their tickets, it was 10:13 a.m. As the clerk typed away on the Ticketmaster computer terminal, Roger couldn't believe what he heard. No tickets were available. The show was sold out. Dejected, Roger turned to leave. As he made his way out of the door, another customer said, 'You can always try StubHub.' As the fellow Stones fan explained what StubHub was, it occurred to Roger that the world had become a very different place with respect to buying tickets for the Odeon gig.

Indeed, in this Internet age, buying tickets for live events has changed dramatically since Roger's concert-going days. Originators such as Ticketmaster now sell tickets online for everything from musicals to sporting events. Increasingly, however, event tickets are resold through websites such as eBay, Craigslist, and newcomer StubHub, the fastest-growing company in the business. According to one survey conducted at a U2 concert, 29 per cent of the fans said that they had purchased their tickets from an Internet resale website, a statistic that reflects ticket buying industry-wide.

Prices are all over the place, and tickets for sold-out shows of hot events routinely sell for double or triple their face value. In some cases, the mark-up is astronomical. US prices for Coldplay in the spring of 2006 were as much as $3,000 each. And a pair of Stones tickets at New York's Madison Square Garden, close enough to see a geriatric Mick Jagger's wrinkles, went for more than $14,000. Extreme cases? Yes, but not uncommon.

When most people think of buying a ticket from a reseller, they probably envision a seedy scalper standing in the shadows near an event venue. But scalping is moving mainstream. Because the Internet and other technologies have allowed professional ticket agents to purchase event tickets in larger numbers, anyone with a computer and broadband connection can instantly become a scalper. And regular concert goers, even fans, are routinely doing so. 'Because we allowed people to buy four [tickets], if they only need two, they put the other two up for sale,' said Dave Holmes, manager for Coldplay. This dynamic, occurring for events across the board, has dramatically increased the number of ticket resellers.

StubHub enters the game

With the ticket resale market booming, StubHub started operations in 2000 under the name Liquid Seats. It all started with an idea by two business school postgraduate students. Eric Baker and Jeff Fluhr had been observing the hysteria on the ticket resale market. In their opinion, the market was economically inefficient with distorted pricing, highly fragmented and rampant with fraud. Two buyers sitting side-by-side at the same event might find they had paid wildly different prices for essentially the same product. Even with heavy hitter eBay as the biggest ticket reseller at the time, Baker and Fluhr saw an opportunity to create a system that would bring buyers and sellers together in a more efficient manner.

They entered their proposal in a new-business plan competition. Fluhr was utterly convinced the concept would work, so much so that he withdrew the proposal from the competition and dropped out of school in order to launch the business. At a time when dot-coms were dropping like flies, this might have seemed like a very poor decision. But Fluhr is now CEO of StubHub, the leader and fastest-growing company in a $10-billion-a-year industry.

Home to 200 employees, StubHub utilises 20,000 square feet of prime office space in San Francisco's pricey financial district, seven satellite offices, and two call centres. Even more telling is the company's financial performance. From 2004 to 2005, StubHub tripled its volume to $200m worth of tickets sold, generating about $50m in commissions. Most of that was profit. According to comScore Networks, a firm that tracks Web traffic, StubHub.com is the leading site among more than a dozen competitors in the ticket-resale category.

The devil is in the details

From the beginning, Baker and Fluhr set out to provide better options for both buyers and sellers by making StubHub different. Like eBay, StubHub has no ticket inventory of its own, reducing its risk. It simply provides the venue that gives buyers and sellers the opportunity to come together. But it's the differences, perhaps, that have allowed StubHub to achieve such success in such a short period of time.

One of the first differences noticed by buyers and sellers is StubHub's ticket-listing procedure. Sellers can list tickets by auction or at a fixed price, a price that declines as the event gets closer. Whereas eBay charges fees just to list tickets, StubHub lists them for free. Thus, initially, the seller has no risk whatsoever. eBay gets its revenue not only from listing fees, but from additional sliding-scale fees based on sale price. StubHub's system is simpler, and it splits the fee burden between buyer and seller. StubHub charges sellers a 15 per cent commission and buyers a 10 per cent fee.

StubHub's website structure also creates a marketplace that comes closer to pure competition than any other reseller's website. It achieves this by minimising the degree of differentiation between sellers on its site. On eBay, sellers customise their postings through a variety of details. Not only do text, graphics and conditions of sale differ from seller to seller, so do the sellers' 'trustworthiness' ratings. But with StubHub, all sellers are equal. Each posts tickets using the same template. When buyers browse, every posting looks the same. In fact, the seller's identity isn't even included. StubHub even holds the shipping method constant.

This makes the purchase process much more transparent for buyers. They can browse tickets by event, venue and section. Comparison shopping is very easy, as shoppers can simultaneously view different pairs of tickets in the same section, even in the same row. Although prices still vary, this system makes tickets more of a commodity and allows market forces to narrow the gap considerably from one seller to another. In fact, although tickets often sell for high prices, this also has the effect of pushing ticket prices down below face value.

Perhaps the biggest and most important difference between StubHub and competitors is the company's 100 per cent guarantee. Initially, it might seem more risky buying from a seller whose identity is unknown. But StubHub puts the burden of responsibility on the seller, remaining involved after the purchase where competing sites bow out. Buyers aren't charged until they confirm receipt of the tickets. 'If you open the package and it contains two squares of toilet paper instead of the tickets,' Baker explains, 'then we debit the seller's credit card for the amount of the purchase.' StubHub will also revoke site privileges for fraudulent or unreliable sellers. In contrast, the eBay system is largely self-policing and does not monitor the shipment or verification of the purchased items.

What the future holds

When StubHub was formed, it targeted primary professional ticket brokers and ordinary consumers. In examining individuals as sellers, Baker and Fluhr capitalised on the underexploited assets of sport team season ticket holders. If you have season tickets for Manchester United, that's a lot of games, Mr Baker explains, 'Unless you're unemployed or especially passionate, there's no way you're going to attend every game.' StubHub entered the equation, not only giving ticket holders a way to recoup some of their investment, but allowing them to have complete control over the process rather than selling to a ticket agent.

It quickly became apparent to StubHub's founders that the benefits of season ticket holders selling off unused tickets extended to the sports franchises as well. Being able to sell unwanted tickets encourages season ticket holders to buy again. It also puts customers in seats that would otherwise go empty – customers who buy hot dogs, souvenirs and programmes. Thus, StubHub began entering into signed agreements with professional sports teams. The teams give official reselling rights to StubHub in exchange for a fee. Originally, this was a percentage of resale profits. But because of the multiple benefits for teams, StubHub now keeps all commissions and instead pays a straight fee to each team for promoting its website and providing contact information on season tickets. This change in contract details has only increased the number of partnerships between StubHub and sports teams. The company now has signed agreements with numerous teams to be their official secondary marketplace for season ticket holders. Revenues from sporting events account for more than half of all StubHub sales.

It is not surprising that the company continues to pursue new partnerships with sports teams and even media organisations. However, it has arranged similar contractual agreements with big-name performers such as Coldplay, Britney Spears, Jewel, Christina Aguilera and Alanis Morissette. Arrangements allow StubHub to offer exclusive event packages with a portion of the proceeds supporting charities designated by the performer.

The reselling of event tickets is here to stay. Although there is more than one channel to buy or sell, StubHub's future looks bright. The company's model of entering into partnerships with event-producing organisations is establishing them as 'the official' ticket reseller. Thus, it is more than likely that StubHub's lead over the competition will only increase.

On to Viagogo

Web marketing moves so fast that yesterday's darlings of the Internet age only survive by buying into the new businesses. Just as News Corporation bought MySpace and Google bought out YouTube, eBay bought StubHub whose business model was taking business away from them.

By that time Eric Baker had already established Viagogo and signed up Manchester United and Chelsea football clubs, Peter Gabriel as well as a deal with Warner Music International who have Madonna, Green Day and the Red Hot Chili Peppers in their stable. Having had a second go at setting up the business, Eric Baker thinks he is well set to win against StubHub. To do this he has raised £14.7m (€21.6m) in London from a top-notch group of venture capitalists: Index Ventures, LVMH chairman Bernard Arnault, Lord Jacob Rothschild, Herbert Kloiber, chairman of Tele-München and other media investors.

Questions

1. Conduct a brief analysis of the marketing environment and the forces shaping the development of Viagogo.
2. Discuss StubHub's business model. What general benefits does it afford to buyers and sellers? Which benefits are most important in terms of creating value for buyers and sellers?
3. Discuss StubHub and Viagogo as new intermediaries. What effects has this new type of intermediary had on the ticket industry?
4. Apply the text's e-marketing domains framework to StubHub's business model. How has each domain played a role in the company's success?
5. What recommendations can you make for improving Viagogo's future growth and success in Europe and the US?
6. What are the legal or ethical issues, if any, for ticket-reselling websites?

SOURCES: William Grimes, 'That invisible hand guides the game of ticket hunting', *New York Times* (18 June 2004), p. E1; Henry Fountain, 'The price of admission in a material world', *New York Times* (16 April 2006), p. D5; Steve Stecklow, 'Can't get no . . . tickets?', *Wall Street Journal* (7 January 2006), p. P1; Steve Stecklow, 'StubHub's ticket to ride', *Wall Street Journal* (17 January 2006), p. B1; Bob Tedeschi, 'New era of ticket resales: Online and aboveboard', *New York Times* (29 August 2005), p. C4, and information from 'About Us'; *Wall Street Journal*, 'StubHub founder gets funds for Europe firm' (7 August 2007); Sam Hiser, FT report – Digital business: 'Winning is a high-tech game', *Financial Times* (28 February 2007); Philip Stafford, 'Ticket exchange in Warner link-up', *Financial Times* (10 May 2007); Andrew Edgecliffe-Johnson, 'Viagogo raises $30m for growth', *Financial Times* (7 August 2007); websites accessed online at stubhub.com in June 2006, and at viagogo.com and viagogo.co.uk in August 2007.

> To open a shop is easy; to keep it open is an art.
>
> CONFUCIUS (PHILOSOPHER)

Place

THE FINAL PART of this text addresses the fourth element of the marketing mix — place. It will help you to understand the decisions and actions that companies take in order to bring products and services to customers. It also considers how new information and communications technologies are transforming distribution and retailing functions.

How products and services are delivered to customers for final usage or consumption can make a difference to how customers perceive the quality and value of the overall offering. Speed of delivery, guaranteed supply and availability, convenience to shoppers and so forth can enhance buyer–seller relationships and increase customer satisfaction. Consequently, firms are increasingly paying greater attention to how they manage their distribution or marketing channels to deliver goods and services that customers want at the right time, right place and right price.

In **Chapter 19**, we address channel organisations and the functions they perform and show how firms can build more cost-effective routes to serving and satisfying their target markets.

Finally, **Chapter 20** looks at the global marketplace, which presents special challenges to marketers. Here we'll examine how marketing strategy and processes may be adapted to succeed in international markets.

PART

seven

Video Case Royal Enfield Motorcycles Europe

Royal Enfield makes India's most prestigious and largest motorcycles. The company started life as a maker of 'bone shaker' cycles in Britain in the 1850s and became Royal Enfield following a contract with the Royal Small Arms factory in Enfield, Middlesex to supply precision rifle parts. They advertise their cycles as 'Built Like A Gun', a link to military precision engineering that continues to this day.

The first Royal Enfield motorcycle appeared in 1901, with manufacturing in India starting in 1955. With the decline of the British motor cycle industry the Royal Enfield became a purely Indian machine in 1970. Now, the company is importing their classic motorcycle to Europe but with a positioning strategy that is radically different from that in India and varies hugely across Europe.

The company's websites clearly reflect the product's different positioning across the world: United Kingdom (www.royal-enfield.com), the United States (www.enfieldmotorcycles.com) and India (www.royalenfield.com).

After viewing the video, you may address the following questions:

1. Who are Royal Enfield's target customers and what core needs does the motorcycle seek to satisfy?
2. What is Royal Enfield's current competitive strategy and how successful has this been to date? Is the strategy sustainable in the long term?
3. How and why does the marketing mix strategy for Royal Enfield motorcycles differ across the European market and its home market in India?

Keep your shop and your shop will keep you.

THOMAS FULLER

Managing marketing channels

Mini Contents List

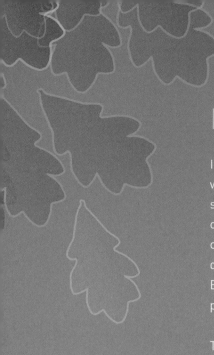

Previewing the concepts

In this chapter, we will examine the last of the marketing mix tools – place. Firms rarely work alone in bringing value to customers. Instead, most are only a single link in a larger supply chain or distribution channel. As such, an individual firm's success depends not only on how well it performs but also on how well its *entire marketing channel* competes with competitors' channels. For example, Mercedes can make the world's best cars but still not do well if its dealers perform poorly in sales and service against the dealers of Ford, Toyota, BMW or Honda. In order to bring value to customers, Mercedes must choose its channel partners carefully and practise sound partner relationship management.

The first part of this chapter addresses the nature of marketing channels and the marketer's channel design and management decisions. Then we will examine the nature and roles of two major intermediary channels, retailers and wholesalers, and the marketing decisions they make.

As mentioned earlier, most firms cannot bring value to customers by themselves. Instead, they must work closely with other firms in a larger value delivery network. Let us take a look at what is meant by a value delivery network.

After reading this chapter, you should be able to:

1. Explain why companies use marketing channels and discuss the functions these channels perform.
2. Discuss how channel members interact and how they organise to perform the work of the channel.
3. Identify the major channel alternatives open to a company and how companies select, motivate and evaluate channel members.
4. Explain the roles of retailers and wholesalers in the distribution channel.
5. Discuss the importance of marketing logistics and integrated supply chain management.

We start by looking at GHD, a small business that has grown rapidly and taken an original approach to distribution. In fact the company's products are in such demand that conventional channels are begging to sell them too.

Prelude case Good Hair Day (GHD)

Where would you go to buy hair-styling tongs? Perhaps, you'd try the obvious outlets – high street department stores, household electrical appliance stores and chemists (or pharmacies and drug stores), or you might prefer to buy from an online retailer or through one of your favourite TV shopping channels. But if you want GHD hair styling irons, then you'd be disappointed as these products are not sold in shops nor available online. Read on to find out more.

It is early January in the quiet middle reaches of Yorkshire's Aire Valley (UK), and Martin Penny is outlining one of the few downsides of being the supplier of one of Britain's most sought-after haircare products. 'We totally ran out before Christmas,' he explains. 'I had friends ringing up saying "Can you get me some irons?",' he says.

The 'irons' are GHD (Good Hair Day) styling irons, a brand so rapidly successful that GHDs have, like iPods, entered the language – particularly that of the young women who swear by them and accept no substitute.

As chief executive of the company behind GHD, Mr Penny, 53, has shown an entrepreneurial ability to maximise the opportunities that have come his way. But, much more, he followed an unusual strategy to turn his hair-styling tongs into a must-have for young women. Mr Penny's company had grown from a start-up with an untried product in 2001 to £82m (€121m) in sales and £15m in pre-tax profits by 2006. Making some counter-intuitive decisions about sales channels has helped.

In 2001, a friend, who's a hairdresser, showed him a new type of styling iron he had been sent by Tae-Cheol Kim, a South Korean inventor. Mr Penny, the friend and another acquaintance put £15,000 each into a venture to sell the irons through hair salons in the UK. Year one plans to make £300,000 of profit on £1.5m turnover failed. But in the second year, Jemella, a company set up to sell GHD, made a £4m profit on sales of £12m. The following year sales shot up to £37m and have since continued upwards.

Mr Penny says GHD succeeded because it works better than its rivals. GHD irons glide through the hair more easily and retain heat for longer. Also, some 40 design changes have continued to make further product improvements. Marketing is done through some television adverts along with fashion shows and links to celebrity stylists. The company had also used endorsements from celebrities like Gwyneth Paltrow, Madonna and Victoria Beckham. According to Mr Penny, early celebrity purchases helped make GHD, which is more expensive than rival brands, an aspirational product. Selling through salons helped win converts among professionals who passed the word on to clients.

But Mr Penny points out that selling hair irons through salons, instead of high street retailers, had some clear advantages. Hairdressers are trusted by their customers, so once GHD gained credibility in salons the knock-on effect on sales was huge. The product is sold along with professional advice, as befits a premium product. In addition, the UK's position as an international centre for training hair stylists means that visiting trainees use GHD and pass the word on back home. Mr Penny says: 'Salons have been ambassadors for the brand and we have remained loyal to them.'

GHD now claims 80 per cent of the salon market for styling irons and about 40 per cent of the total UK market. UK sales are past 3 million, but Mr Penny says there is a target market of 12 million, with saturation point still a long way off. Sales are already well beyond the £70m that were estimated.

Exports of GHD styling tongs have also started to take off. Australia, where exports began in 2003, returned about £10m of sales in 2006. Sales in Spain, Italy, the US and South Africa amounted to several million pounds each. GHD irons are also sold in Scandinavia, France and Germany.

'A lot about business is what you do not do,' he says. 'If we had decided for example to sell on QVC [the shopping channel] or through Boots [pharmacy and retail store] or whatever, it is unlikely we would ever have got the brand equity that we have now.'

But there were also drawbacks to the sales channel strategy: visits to a salon are less frequent than those to the high street and not an obvious place to buy a product. Nor do salons have the infrastructure or training to make them natural retailers. 'When we started, less than 10 per cent of a salon's income was from retailing,' says Mr Penny. Now, some hair stylists 'do 20–30 per cent of sales from retail'.

Meanwhile, the styling irons are still manufactured in South Korea, by Mr Kim, the inventor, who has also built up a successful company. Not only has he remained a loyal supplier to GHD, Mr Kim has become a friend of Mr Penny, who acknowledges that their arrangement, which is clearly very important to both businesses, is entirely based on trust. He adds, 'I find in my business life I have more trouble created by contracts than it is worth. You are far better to have a relationship based on trust than on a piece of paper.'

Today, high street retailers pester the company to let them stock GHD, with some using whatever tactics necessary to get supplies from authorised GHD distributors. Mr Penny has to consider the channel options available to GHD in order to sustain planned growth while maintaining GHD's premium image. The company plans to open two retail outlets of its own, with a salon and spa-type environment, to showcase products in London and Leeds. 'Some salons might think it will take business away but we think the reverse is true,' Mr Penny says. But for the moment, the hair salon will still be the only place most customers will be able to get their hands on this particular gadget.

Questions

1. Consider the sales channel strategy adopted by GHD. What are the advantages and disadvantages of the channel approach used by the company?
2. What are the major functions performed by its channel members? In what ways do they add value for final customers?
3. How might GHD sustain its competitive advantage as the market reaches saturation in the coming years? Recommend a channel strategy for GHD, explaining how this will enhance its value delivery network.

SOURCE: This case is based on James Wilson, 'Secrets behind a good hair day', *Financial Times* (18 January 2007), p. 12.

Supply chains and the value delivery network

Producing a product or service and making it available to buyers requires building relationships not just with customers, but also with key suppliers and resellers in the company's *supply chain*. This supply chain consists of 'upstream' and 'downstream' partners, including suppliers, intermediaries and intermediaries' customers.

Upstream from the manufacturer or service provider is the set of firms that supply the raw materials, components, parts, information, finances and expertise needed to create a product or service. Marketers, however, have traditionally focused on the downstream side of the supply chain – on the *marketing channels* or *distribution channels* that look forward towards the customer. Downstream marketing channel partners, such as wholesalers and retailers, form a vital connection between the firm and its target consumers.

Both upstream and downstream partners may also be part of other firms' supply chains. But it is the unique design of each company's supply chain that enables it to deliver superior value to customers. An individual firm's success depends not only on how well *it* performs but also on how well its entire supply chain and marketing channel competes with competitors' channels.

The term *supply chain* may be too limited – it takes a *make-and-sell* view of the business. It suggests that raw materials, productive inputs and factory capacity should serve as the starting point for market planning. A better term would be *demand chain* because it suggests a *sense-and-respond* view of the market. Under this view, planning starts with the needs of target customers, to which the company responds by organising resources with the goal of creating customer value.

Even a demand chain view of a business may be too limited, because it takes a step-by-step linear view of purchase–production–consumption activities. With the advent of the Internet, however, companies are forming more numerous and complex relationships with other firms. For example, companies such as Toyota, Mercedes and Ford manage numerous supply chains. They also sponsor or transact on many B2B websites and online purchasing exchanges as needs arise. Like these companies, many large companies today are engaged in building and managing a continuously evolving *value delivery network*.

A **value delivery network** is made up of the company, suppliers, distributors and ultimately customers who 'partner' with each other to improve the performance of the entire system. For example, Palm, the leading manufacturer of handheld devices, manages a whole community of suppliers and assemblers of semiconductor components, plastic cases, LCD displays and accessories, of offline and online resellers, and of 45,000 complementors who have created over 5,000 applications for the Palm operating systems. All of these diverse partners must work effectively together to bring superior value to Palm's customers.

This chapter focuses on the downstream side of the value delivery network. However, it is important to remember that this is only part of the full value network. To bring value to customers, companies need upstream supplier partners just as they need downstream channel partners. To provide banking services, for example, HSBC buys equipment and supplies such as automated teller machines (ATMs), printed deposit slips and computers. To make its services available to customers and obtain information about customer transactions, the bank maintains a distribution channel consisting of company-owned bank branches and websites as well as thousands of ATMs owned by other banks. Increasingly, marketers are participating in and influencing their company's upstream activities as well as its downstream activities. More than marketing channel managers, they are becoming full network managers.

Value delivery network— A network made up of the company, suppliers, distributors and customers who 'partner' with each other to improve the performance of the entire system.

The nature and importance of marketing channels

Few producers sell their goods directly to the final users. Instead, most use third parties or intermediaries to bring their products to market. They try to forge a **marketing channel** (or **distribution channel**) – a set of interdependent organisations involved in the process of making a product or service available for use or consumption by the consumer or business user.[1] The channel of distribution is therefore all those organisations through which a product must pass between its point of production and consumption.

A company's channel decisions directly affect every other marketing decision. Pricing depends on whether the company works with national discount chains, uses high-quality speciality stores, or sells directly to consumers via the Web. The firm's sales force and communications decisions depend on how much persuasion, training, motivation and support its channel partners need. Whether a company develops or acquires certain new products may depend on how well those products fit the capabilities of its channel members. Companies often pay too little attention to their distribution channels, sometimes with damaging results. As we saw in the chapter's prelude case, companies that use imaginative distribution systems can *gain* a competitive advantage.

Distribution channel decisions often involve long-term commitments to other firms. For example, companies such as BMW, Volkswagen or Nokia can easily change their advertising, pricing or promotion programmes. They can scrap old products or services and introduce new ones as market tastes demand. But when they set up distribution channels through contracts with franchises, independent dealers or large retailers, they cannot readily replace these channels with company-owned stores if conditions change. Therefore, management must design its channels carefully, with an eye on tomorrow's likely selling environment as well as today's.

How channel members add value

Why do producers give some of the selling job to intermediaries? After all, doing so means giving up some control over how and to whom the products are sold. Producers use intermediaries because they create greater efficiency in making goods available to target markets. Through their contacts, experience, specialisation and scale of operation, intermediaries usually offer the firm more than it can achieve on its own.

Figure 19.1 shows how using intermediaries can provide economies. Part (a) shows three manufacturers, each using direct marketing to reach three customers. This system requires nine

Marketing channel (or distribution channel)—A set of interdependent organisations involved in the process of making a product or service available for use or consumption by the consumer or business user.

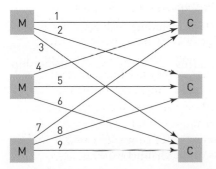

(a) Number of contacts without a distributor
$$M \times C = 3 \times 3 = 9$$
M = Manufacturer   C = Customer

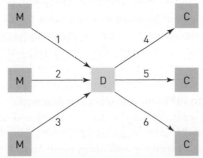

(b) Number of contacts with a distributor
$$M + C = 3 + 3 = 6$$
D = Distributor

Figure 19.1 How a marketing intermediary reduces the number of channel transactions and raises economy of effort

different contacts. Part (b) shows the three manufacturers working through one distributor, which contacts the three customers. This system requires only six contacts. In this way, intermediaries reduce the amount of work that must be done by both producers and consumers.

From the economic system's point of view, the role of marketing intermediaries is to convert the assortments of products made by producers into the assortments wanted by consumers. Producers make narrow assortments of products in large quantities, but consumers want broad assortments of products in small quantities. Marketing channel members buy the large quantities from many producers and break them down into the smaller quantities and broader assortments wanted by consumers. For example, Unilever makes millions of boxes of Persil laundry soap powder each day, but you want to buy only one box at a time. So supermarkets such as the Co-op, Tesco and Aldi buy Persil by the truckload and stock it on their store's shelves. In turn, you can buy a single box of Persil, along with a shopping trolley full of small quantities of toothpaste, shampoo and other related products as you need them. Thus, intermediaries play an important role in matching supply and demand.

The concept of marketing channels is not limited to the distribution of tangible products. Producers of services and ideas also have to make their output available to target populations. Hotels, banks, airlines and other service providers have to find ways to make their services easily available to target customers. Public service organisations and agencies develop 'education delivery systems' and 'healthcare delivery systems' for reaching sometimes widely dispersed populations. Hospitals must be located to serve various patient populations, and schools must be located close to the children who need to be taught. Communities must locate their fire stations to provide rapid response to fires, and polling stations must be placed where people can vote conveniently.

 Channel members add value by bridging the major time, place and possession gaps that separate goods and services from those who would use them.

In making products and services available to consumers, channel members add value by bridging the major time, place and possession gaps that separate goods and services from those who would use them. Members of the marketing channel perform many key functions. Some help to complete transactions:

- *Information.* Gathering and distributing marketing research and intelligence information about actors and forces in the marketing environment needed for planning and facilitating exchange.
- *Promotion.* Developing and spreading persuasive communications about an offer.
- *Contact.* Finding and communicating with prospective buyers.
- *Matching.* Shaping and fitting the offer to the buyer's needs, including such activities as manufacturing, grading, assembling and packaging.
- *Negotiation.* Reaching an agreement on price and other terms of the offer, so that ownership or possession can be transferred.

Others help to fulfil the completed transactions:

- *Physical distribution.* Transporting and storing goods.
- *Financing.* Acquiring and using funds to cover the costs of the channel work.
- *Risk taking.* Assuming the risks of carrying out the channel work.

The question is not *whether* these functions need to be performed – they must be – but rather *who* will perform them. To the extent that the manufacturer performs these functions, its costs

Large multinationals like Unilever produce millions of boxes of soap powder every day, but around Europe each supermarket stocks a small quantity of the whole. This allows consumers to buy a single box of Persil as and when they need it. Thus, intermediaries play an important role in matching supply and demand.
SOURCE: Ralph Orlowski/Getty Images.

go up and its prices have to be higher. When some of these functions are shifted to intermediaries, the producer's costs and prices may be lower, but the intermediaries must charge more to cover the costs of their work. In dividing the work of the channel, the various functions should be assigned to the channel members who can add the most value for the cost.

Number of channel levels

Companies can design their marketing channels to make products and services available to customers in different ways. Each layer of marketing intermediaries that performs some work in bringing the product and its ownership closer to the final buyer is a **channel level**. Because the producer and the final consumer both perform some work, they are part of every channel. The *number of intermediary levels* indicates the *length* of a channel. Figure 19.2(a) shows several consumer distribution channels of different lengths.

Channel 1, called a **direct-marketing channel**, has no intermediary levels; the company sells directly to consumers. For example, Avon and Tupperware sell their products door-to-door or through home and office sales parties. Wine clubs, such as Laithwaites and The Wine Society in the UK, sell their wines through mail order, telephone or at their websites. The remaining channels in Figure 19.2 are *indirect*-marketing channels containing one or more intermediaries.

Figure 19.2(b) shows some common business distribution channels. The business marketer can use its own sales force to sell directly to business customers. Or it can sell to various types of intermediaries, who in turn sell to these customers. Consumer and business marketing channels with even more levels are sometimes found, but less often. From the producer's point of view, a greater number of levels means less control and greater channel complexity. Moreover, all of the institutions in the channel are connected by several types of *flows*. These include the *physical flow* of products, the *flow of ownership*, the *payment flow*, the *information flow* and the *promotion flow*. These flows can make even channels with only one or a few levels very complex.

Channel level—A layer of intermediaries that performs some work in bringing the product and its ownership closer to the final buyer.

Direct-marketing channel—A marketing channel that has no intermediary levels.

Figure 19.2 Consumer and business marketing channels

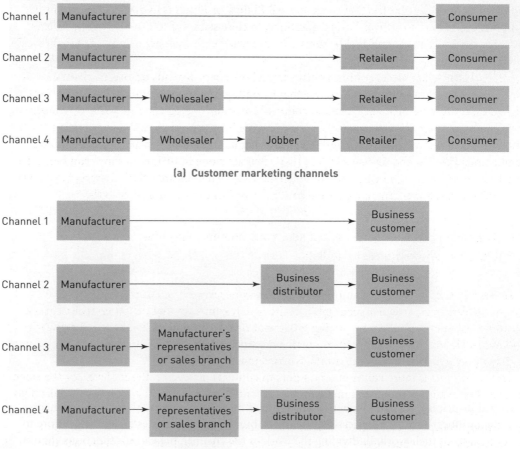

(a) Customer marketing channels

(b) Business marketing channels

Channel behaviour and organisation

Distribution channels are more than simple collections of firms tied together by various flows. They are complex behavioural systems in which people and companies interact to accomplish individual, company and channel goals. Some channel systems consist only of informal interactions among loosely organised firms. Others consist of formal interactions guided by strong organisational structures. Moreover, channel systems do not stand still – new types of intermediaries emerge and whole new channel systems evolve. Here we look at channel behaviour and at how members organise to do the work of the channel.

Channel behaviour

A marketing channel consists of firms that have partnered for their common goal. Each channel member depends on the others. For example, a Peugeot dealer depends on the manufacturer to design cars that meet consumer needs. In turn, Peugeot depends on the dealer to attract consumers, persuade them to buy Peugeot cars and service cars after the sale. The Peugeot dealer also depends on the other dealers to provide good sales and service that will uphold the reputation of Peugeot and its dealer network. In fact, the success of individual Peugeot dealers depends on how well the entire Peugeot marketing channel competes with the channels of other car manufacturers.

Each channel member plays a specialised role in the channel. For example, Philips' role is to produce consumer electronics products that consumers will like and to create demand through national, regional and worldwide advertising. The role of the specialist shops, department stores and other independent outlets that stock and sell Philips' products is to display these items in convenient locations, to answer buyers' questions, to close sales and to provide a good level of customer service. The channel will be most effective when each member assumes the tasks it can do best.

Ideally, because the success of individual channel members depends on overall channel success, all channel firms should work together smoothly. They should understand and accept their roles, coordinate their activities and cooperate to attain overall channel goals. By cooperating, they can more effectively sense, serve and satisfy the target market. But cooperating to achieve overall channel goals sometimes means giving up individual company goals. Although channel members depend on one another, they often act alone in their own short-run best interests. They often disagree on who should do what and for what rewards. Such disagreements over goals, roles and rewards generate **channel conflict**. Conflict can occur at two levels.

> Although channel members depend on one another, they often act alone in their own short-run best interests.

Channel conflict— Disagreement among marketing channel members on goals and roles – who should do what and for what rewards.

Horizontal conflict is conflict among firms at the same level of the channel. For instance, Peugeot dealers in a particular geographic territory may complain that the other dealers in the territory steal sales from them by pricing too low or by selling outside their assigned territories. Or Novotel Hotel franchisees might complain about other Novotel operators overcharging guests or giving poor service, hurting the overall Novotel image.

Vertical conflict is more common and refers to conflicts between different levels of the same channel. For example, some personal computer manufacturers created conflict with their high street dealers when they opened online stores to sell PCs directly to customers. Dealers, not surprisingly, complained. To resolve the conflict, manufacturers had to develop communication campaigns to educate dealers on how online efforts would assist dealers rather than hurt sales.

Figure 19.3 Comparison of conventional marketing channel with vertical marketing system

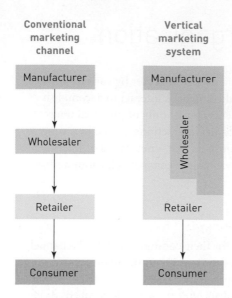

Conventional marketing channel

Manufacturer → Wholesaler → Retailer → Consumer

Vertical marketing system

Manufacturer / Wholesaler / Retailer → Consumer

Conventional distribution channel—A channel consisting of one or more independent producers, wholesalers and retailers, each a separate business seeking to maximise its own profits, even at the expense of profits for the system as a whole.

Vertical marketing system (VMS)—A distribution channel structure in which producers, wholesalers and retailers act as a unified system. One channel member owns the others, has contracts with them, or has so much power that they all cooperate.

Corporate VMS—A vertical marketing system that combines successive stages of production and distribution under single ownership – channel leadership is established through common ownership.

Channel organisation

For the channel as a whole to perform well, each channel member's role must be specified and channel conflict must be managed. The channel will perform better if it includes a firm, agency or mechanism that provides leadership and has the power to assign roles and manage conflict. Let us take a look at how channel members organise to do the work of the channel.

Historically, marketing channels have been loose collections of independent companies, each showing little concern for overall channel performance. These *conventional distribution channels* have lacked strong leadership and power, often resulting in damaging conflict and poor performance. One of the biggest recent channel developments has been the emergence of *vertical marketing systems* that provide channel leadership. Figure 19.3 compares the two types of channel arrangement.

Vertical marketing systems

A **conventional distribution channel** consists of one or more independent producers, wholesalers and retailers. Each is a separate business seeking to maximise its own profits, even at the expense of profits for the system as a whole. No channel member has much control over the other members and no formal means exists for assigning roles and resolving channel conflict. In contrast, a **vertical marketing system (VMS)** consists of producers, wholesalers and retailers acting as a unified system. One channel member owns the others, has contracts with them, or wields so much power that they must all cooperate. The VMS can be dominated by the producer, wholesaler or retailer.

We now look at the three main types of VMS: corporate, contractual and administered (see Figure 19.4). Each uses a different means for setting up leadership and power in the channel.

Corporate VMS

A **corporate VMS** combines successive stages of production and distribution under single ownership. Coordination and conflict management are attained through regular organisational channels. Italian eyewear maker Luxottica produces many famous eyewear brands – including Ray-Ban, Vogue, Anne Klein, Ferragamo and Bvlgari. It then sells these brands through two of the world's largest optical chains, LensCrafters and Sunglass Hut, which it also owns.[2]

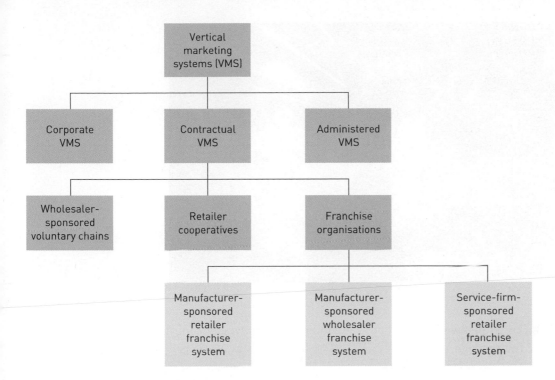

Figure 19.4 Main types of vertical marketing system

Fashion retailers have also taken advantage of corporate VMS.

By controlling the entire distribution chain, Spanish clothing chain Zara turned into the world's fastest-growing fashion retailer. The secret to Zara's success is its control over almost every aspect of the supply chain, from design and production to its own worldwide distribution network. Zara makes 40 per cent of its own fabrics and produces more than half of its own clothes, rather than relying on a hodgepodge of slow-moving suppliers. More than 11,000 new items every season take shape in Zara's own design centres, supported by real-time sales data. New designs feed into Zara manufacturing centres, which ship finished products directly to 1,100 Zara stores in 68 countries, saving time, eliminating the need for warehouses and keeping inventories low. Effective vertical integration makes Zara faster, more flexible and more efficient than international competitors such as Gap, Benetton and H&M. Its finely tuned distribution systems makes Zara seem more like Dell or Wal-Mart than Gucci or Louis Vuitton. Zara can make a new line from start to finish in less than 15 days, so a look seen on TV can be in Zara stores within a month, versus an industry average of nine months. And Zara's low costs let it offer mid-market chic at down-market prices. The company's stylish but affordable offerings have attracted a cult following, and Zara store sales have grown more than 50 per cent, from €2.3bn in 2004 to over €3.5bn by 2006.[3]

Contractual VMS

A **contractual VMS** consists of independent organisations at different levels of production and distribution who join together through contracts to obtain more economies or sales impact than each could achieve alone. Coordination and conflict management are attained through contractual agreements among channel members.

Contractual VMS—A vertical marketing system in which independent firms at different levels of production and distribution join together through contracts to obtain more economies or sales impact than they could achieve alone.

Corporate VMS: Zara's success stems from its control over almost every aspect of the supply chain, from design and production to its own worldwide distribution network.

SOURCE: Copyright © Inditex.

> " The franchise organisation is the most common type of contractual relationship. "

Franchise—A contractual association between a manufacturer, wholesaler or service organisation (a franchiser) and independent businesspeople (franchisees) who buy the right to own and operate one or more units in the franchise system.

The **franchise** organisation is the most common type of contractual relationship. Here, the channel member called a *franchiser* links several stages in the production–distribution system. The franchiser typically provides a brand identity and start-up, marketing and accounting assistance, as well as management know-how, to the *franchisee*. In return, the franchiser receives some form of compensation, such as an initial fee and a continuing royalty payment, fees for leasing equipment and a share of the profits. For example, the Hong Kong clothing group Esprit Holdings is built on a highly streamlined channel model under which it buys from third-party suppliers in China and sells to franchisees in its target markets throughout Europe, the USA and Asia, thereby minimising its own overheads.[4] Franchising has been a fast-growing retailing form in recent years. Almost every kind of business has been franchised – from furniture, fast-food restaurants and fitness centres to hotels, car rental and domestic cleaning services.

For example, all IKEA furniture and home furnishing stores worldwide operate under a franchise from Inter IKEA Systems B.V. To qualify as an IKEA franchisee, applicants must have thorough retail experience combined with extensive local market knowledge. Potential IKEA franchisees need to demonstrate an outstanding understanding of and commitment to the IKEA concept, the company's financial strength and potential as well as have identified well-located sites for the retail activity. The franchisee provides the financial investment needed to open an IKEA operation. In return, Inter IKEA Systems B.V. will continuously provide the franchisees with the support they need to operate the IKEA Concept.[5]

Franchising offers a number of benefits to both the franchiser and the franchisee. The main advantages for the franchiser are as follows:

- The franchiser secures fast distribution for its products and services without incurring the full costs of setting up and running its own operations. Franchising also enables the franchiser to expand a successful business more rapidly than by using its own capital.

"Where is the soul in a £19 bedside table? Pah! It is nowhere."

I am Van den Puup, elite designer, and I know the difference between true and fraudulent design. True design like Van den Puup's is a friend of emotion, a foe of reason, laughs with wolves and cries with angels and is priced highly as any work of brilliance should be. Fraudulent design like IKEA's can be mildly attractive but lacks spirituality and is priced so low it can have no soul. I can see it all so clearly, but then I am a genius.

Van den Puup, Elite Designer

£19
IKEA

ELITE DESIGNERS AGAINST IKEA
elitedesigners.org

The world over, IKEA provides their own well designed furniture at keen prices.
SOURCE: The Advertising Archives.

- The franchiser gets very highly motivated management as the franchisees are working for themselves rather than a salary.
- The contractual relationship ensures that franchisees operate to and maintain franchisers' standards.

The main advantages for franchisees are as follows:

- They are buying into a proven system if selling an established brand name (e.g. IKEA, Esprit, McDonald's, The Body Shop, Interflora).

- They can start a business with limited capital and benefit from the experience of the franchiser. This way they reduce the costs and risks of starting a new business.

- Franchisees also get the benefits of centralised purchasing power – since the franchisers will buy in bulk for the franchisees.

- They get instant expertise in operational issues such as advertising, promotions, accounts and legal matters, and can rely on franchisers' help should things go wrong.

Franchise systems have several disadvantages:

- Franchisers invariably have to give up some control when operating through franchisees.

- The franchisees may not all perform exactly to franchisers' operating standards, and inconsistencies in service levels can damage the brand name.

- Franchisees may not always have a good deal – they have to work extremely hard to meet sales and financial targets to make the business pay, and in addition to paying their initial fee, they must meet continuing management services or royalty payments.

There are three types of franchises. The first type is the *manufacturer-sponsored retailer franchise system*, for example BMW and its network of independent franchised dealers who are licensed to sell its cars. These dealers are independent businesspeople who agree to meet various conditions of sales and service. Shell, the oil company, adopts a franchising system on many of its petrol forecourts in countries around the world.

The second type of franchise is the *manufacturer-sponsored wholesaler franchise system*, as found in the soft-drinks industry. Coca-Cola, for example, licenses bottlers (wholesalers) in various markets, who buy Coca-Cola syrup concentrate and then bottle and sell the finished product to retailers in local markets.

The third franchise form is the *service-firm-sponsored retailer franchise system*. Here, a service firm licenses a chain of retailers to bring its service to consumers. Examples are found in the car rental business (Hertz, Avis, Europcar), the fast-food service business (Deli France, McDonald's, KFC), the hotel business (Holiday Inn, Ramada Inn), and so on.

The fact that most consumers cannot tell the difference between contractual and corporate VMSs shows how successfully the contractual organisations compete with corporate chains.

Administered VMS

Administered VMS—A vertical marketing system that coordinates successive stages of production and distribution, not through common ownership or contractual ties, but through the size and power of one of the parties.

An **administered VMS** coordinates successive stages of production and distribution, not through common ownership or contractual ties, but through the size and power of one or a few dominant channel members. Manufacturers of a top brand can obtain strong trade cooperation and support from resellers. For example, in the fast-moving consumer-goods market, companies like Nestlé, Unilever and Procter & Gamble can command unusual cooperation from resellers regarding displays, shelf space, promotions and price policies. Similarly, large retailers like Zara, IKEA and Wal-Mart can exert strong influence on their raw material suppliers and product manufacturers.

For example, IKEA grew from a single store in Sweden's backwoods to become one of the most successful international retailers in the world. Today, it has more than 237 stores in 37 countries around the world, taking over €17.6bn in annual sales. Traditionally, selling furniture was a fragmented affair, shared between department stores and small family-owned shops. All sold expensive products and delivered up to two or three months after a customer's order. IKEA, however, sells most of its furniture as knocked-down kits for customers to take home and assemble themselves. IKEA also trims costs to a minimum while still offering products that are durable and distinguished by design and quality. It does this by using global sourcing, working with key suppliers around the world that can supply high-quality raw materials at low prices. In return these suppliers get technical advice and leased equipment from the company. IKEA's designers also work closely with manufacturers to find smart ways to reduce product costs from the outset. Other savings come from the huge economies of scale from operating in cheap out-of-town stores and from enormous production runs made possible by selling the same furniture all around the world. IKEA's success also means success for its suppliers. But they must operate to IKEA's terms and enable the global firm to fulfil its promise of quality merchandise at low cost to customers worldwide.[6]

Horizontal marketing systems

Another channel development is the **horizontal marketing system**, in which two or more companies at one level join together to follow a new marketing opportunity. By working together, companies can combine their financial, production or marketing resources to accomplish more than any one company could alone.

Companies might join forces with competitors or non-competitors. They might work with each other on a temporary or permanent basis, or they may even create a separate company. For example, McDonald's now places 'express' versions of its restaurants in Wal-Mart stores. McDonald's benefits from Wal-Mart's heavy store traffic, while Wal-Mart keeps hungry shoppers from having to go elsewhere to eat. McDonald's also recently joined forces with Sinopec, China's largest gasoline retailer, to place restaurants at its more than 30,000 gas stations. The move greatly speeds McDonald's expansion into China while at the same time pulling hungry motorists into Sinopec gas stops.[7]

Such channel arrangements also work well globally. For example, because of its excellent coverage of international markets, Nestlé jointly sells General Mills' cereal brands in 80 countries outside North America. Similarly, Coca-Cola and Nestlé formed a joint venture, Beverage Partners Worldwide, to market ready-to-drink coffees, teas and flavoured milks in more than 40 countries worldwide. Nestlé contributes two established brand names – Nescafé and Nestea – while Coke provides worldwide experience in marketing and distributing beverages.[8]

Multi-channel distribution systems

In the past, many companies used a single channel to sell to a single market or market segment. These days, with the proliferation of customer segments and channel possibilities, companies, large and small, use **multi-channel distribution systems** – often called **hybrid marketing channels**. Such multi-channel marketing occurs when a single firm sets up two or more marketing channels to reach one or more customer segments.

Figure 19.5 shows a hybrid channel system. In the figure, the producer sells directly to consumer segment 1 using direct-mail catalogues, telemarketing and the Internet and reaches consumer segment 2 through retailers. It sells indirectly to business segment 1 through distributors and dealers, and to business segment 2 through its own sales force.

For example, Sony maintains a wide distribution coverage by adopting a hybrid marketing system. The company sells its consumer products through exclusive retail outlets such as the Sony Centres, through mass merchandisers like electrical chain stores (e.g. Comet, Dixons) and catalogue shops (e.g. Index, Argos) and by using direct marketing channels, such as electronic

Horizontal marketing system—A channel arrangement in which two or more companies at one level join together to follow a new marketing opportunity.

Multi-channel distribution system (or hybrid marketing channel)—A distribution system in which a single firm sets up two or more marketing channels to reach one or more customer segments. A variety of direct and indirect approaches are used to deliver the firm's goods to its customers.

Figure 19.5 Multi-channel
distribution system

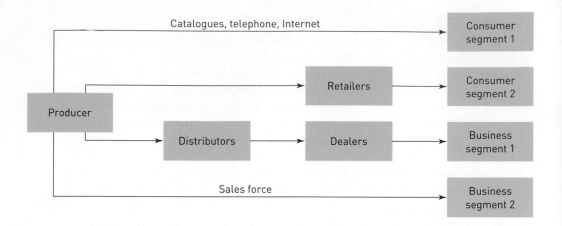

Figure 19.5 Multi-channel
distribution system

and mail-order catalogues. Hewlett-Packard uses multiple channels to serve dozens of segments and niches, ranging from large corporate and institutional buyers to small businesses and home office buyers. The HP sales force sells the company's information technology equipment and services to large and mid-sized business customers. HP also sells through a network of distributors and value-added resellers, which sell HP computers, systems and services to a variety of special business segments. Home office buyers can buy HP personal computers and printers from speciality computer stores or any of several large retailers. In addition, business, government and home office buyers can buy directly from HP by phone or online from the company's website (www.hp.com).

Multi-channel distribution systems offer many advantages to companies facing large and complex markets. With each new channel, the company expands its sales and market coverage, and gains opportunities to tailor its products and services to the specific needs of diverse customer segments. But such multi-channel, multi-market systems are harder to control, and they generate conflict as more channels compete for customers and sales. For example, when IBM began selling personal computers directly to customers at low prices through catalogues and telemarketing and its own website, many of its dealers cried 'unfair competition' and threatened to drop the IBM line or give it less emphasis. Many outside salespeople felt they were being undercut by the new 'inside channels'.[9]

Changing channel organisation

Changes in technology and the explosive growth of direct and online marketing are having a profound impact on the nature and design of marketing channels. One major trend is towards **disintermediation** – a big term with a clear message and important consequences. Disintermediation means that more and more product and service producers are bypassing intermediaries and going directly to final buyers, or that radically new types of channel intermediaries are emerging to displace traditional ones.

For example, online marketing is growing rapidly, taking business from traditional bricks-and-mortar retailers. Today, thanks to the Internet, consumers can buy clothes and accessories, books, videos, toys, jewellery, sports equipment, consumer electronics, home, garden items – in fact, almost anything – without ever stepping into a traditional retail store. And online music download services such as iTunes and Musicmatch are threatening the very existence of traditional music-store retailers (see Real Marketing 19.1).

Disintermediation presents problems and opportunities for both producers and intermediaries. To avoid being swept aside, traditional intermediaries must find new ways to *add value* in the supply chain. To remain competitive, product and service producers must develop new channel opportunities, such as the Internet and other direct channels (which we've discussed in

Disintermediation—The elimination of a layer of intermediaries from a marketing channel or the displacement of traditional resellers by radically new types of intermediaries.

real marketing 19.1

Disintermediation: the music industry dances to a new iTune

Buying music can be a pretty frustrating experience. Perhaps you can identify with the following scenario.

You whistle a happy tune as you stroll into HMV Records to do a little music shopping. But when you pick up *Essential Eels Vol. 1*, your temperature starts to rise. You should be ecstatic at the discovery of new releases by the Man called E, but instead you're furious: you can't buy them unless you spend €25.99 for the entire two-CD set that includes 24 'career-spanning classics' that you already own from his other hit records. You shove The Eels back into the display case and pick up *Close to Paradise* by Patrick Watson. It has one beautiful, tender tune that you love, called 'Man Under the Sea' – but what about those other songs? It'll cost you €16.99 to find out. Suddenly, everything seems like a roulette game. Why do they keep insisting that you buy an entire CD when you can just go online and get only the tunes you really want from iTunes or Audible for €0.99 each? Fed up, you walk away without buying anything. That is one reason why so many music stores are closing across the world and globally recorded music sales are down.

Experiences like these, coupled with revolutionary changes in the way music is being distributed and purchased, have thrown the music industry into turmoil. Today, online music download services, such as Yahoo!'s Musicmatch, AOL's MusicNow, Buy.com's BuyMusic and Apple's iTunes, offer an attractive alternative to buying over-priced standard CDs from the limited assortments of traditional music retailers. Instead, you can go online, choose from hundreds of thousands of individual tracks, digitally download one or a dozen in any of several formats, burn them onto a CD or dump them into your iPod, and listen to them wherever and whenever you please.

It seems like everyone is getting into the music download business these days. Coffee chain Starbucks opened an in-store music service – Hear Music – letting customers burn downloaded tracks onto CDs while sipping their lattes. Mobile phone makers are now unveiling music-purchase service to go with their music-playing phones that can hold thousands of downloaded songs. And fearsome competitors such as Microsoft and Sony have launched their own online music stores.

These new distribution options are great for consumers. But the new channel forms threaten the very existence of traditional music retailers. There's even a fancy word to describe this phenomenon – *disintermediation*. Strictly speaking, disintermediation means the elimination of a layer of intermediaries from a marketing channel – skipping a step between the source of a product or service and its consumers. For

example, when Dell began selling personal computers directly to consumers, it eliminated – or disintermediated – retailers from the traditional PC distribution channel.

More broadly, disintermediation includes not only the elimination of channel levels through direct marketing but also the displacement of traditional resellers by radically new types of intermediaries. For example, only a few decades ago, most recorded music was sold through independent music retailers or small chains. Many of these smaller retailers were later disintermediated by large speciality music superstores, such as Tower Records, Virgin Records and Musicland. The superstores, in turn, have faced growing competition from broadline discount retailers such as Wal-Mart and Tesco. In fact, Wal-Mart is currently the world's No.1 CD seller. Within the past decade, sales of CDs by traditional music retailers have slipped from 50 per cent to less than 32 per cent, while superstore sales have seen their share jump from 28 per cent to 54 per cent.

Now, the surge of new online music sellers is threatening to make traditional CD sellers obsolete. 'Tower Records and the other music-store chains are in a dizzying tailspin,' comments one industry expert. Overall retail CD sales have dropped nearly 20 per cent since 1999 – the year Napster (the original music download site) was launched. After five years of going in and out of bankruptcy, once-dominant Tower Records recently closed its doors for good. Musicland (No. 2) declared bankruptcy, shuttered more than two-thirds of its stores (only 345 remain), and sold out to Trans World Entertainment. Smaller chains such as National Record Mart have disappeared altogether. Things will likely get worse before they get better. One retail consultant predicts that half of today's music stores will be out of business within five years and that, eventually, 'CDs, DVDs, and other forms of physical media will become obsolete.'

How are the traditional retailers responding to the disintermediation threat? Some are following the 'if you can't beat them, join them' principle by creating their own downloading services. For example, in America Best Buy partnered with Napster to offer music downloads, as did Virgin Records. Wal-Mart offers in-store and online downloads at a bargain rate of only 88 cents a song.

Music stores do still have several advantages over their online counterparts. The stores have a larger base of existing customers, and a physical store provides a shopping experience for customers that's difficult to duplicate online. Retailers can morph their stores into comfortable, sociable gathering spots where people hang out, chat with friends, listen to music, go to album signings, and perhaps attend a live performance. Taking advantage of this notion, Musicland recently unveiled a new store-within-a-store concept called Graze, a mesh-enclosed lounge complete with couches, a video wall, a sound system, and pumped-in smells of citrus and chocolate. 'Musicland execs are betting that the new ambiance will persuade shoppers to linger, listen – and buy,' says an analyst.

But the traditional store retailers also face daunting economics. Store rents are rising while CD prices are falling. And running stores generates considerable inventory and store operating costs. New online entrants face none of those traditional distribution costs. Moreover, whereas store retailers can physically stock only a limited number of in-print titles, the music download sites can provide millions of selections and offer out-of-print songs.

What's more, whereas music stores are stuck selling pre-compiled CDs at high album prices, music download sites let customers buy only the songs they want at low per-song rates. Finally, the old retailing model of selling CDs like they were LP vinyl records doesn't work so well anymore. That was fine in an era when people had one stereo in the living room and maybe one in the kids' room. But now consumers want music in a variety of formats that they can play anywhere, anytime: on boomboxes, car stereos, computers, and digital players such as Apple's iPod, which can store thousands of songs in a nifty credit-card-sized device.

Thus, disintermediation is a big word but the meaning is clear. Disintermediation occurs only when a new channel form succeeds in serving customers better than the old channels. Marketers who continually seek new ways to create value for customers have little to fear. However, those who fall behind in adding value risk being swept aside. Will today's music-store retailers survive? Stay iTuned.

SOURCES: Opening extract adapted from Paul Keegan, 'Is the music store over?', *Business 2.0* (March 2004), pp. 114–18. Other quotes and information from Rob Levine, 'Luring MP3ers back to the mall', *Business 2.0* (January–February 2006), p. 32; Lorin Cipolla, 'Music's on the menu', *Promo* (1 May 2004); Mike Hughlett, 'More companies enter musical phone field', *Knight Ridder Tribune News* (16 June 2005), p. 1; 'How to get your music mobile', *Music Week* (25 June 2005), p. S11; Jon Ortiz, 'As big chains flail, he's got the beat', *Sacramento Bee* (9 March 2006), p. D1; Dale Kasler, 'Tower gets new leader', *Sacramento Bee* (29 July 2006), p. D1; Chris Serres, 'Buyer surfaces for bankrupt musicland', *Star Tribune* (26 February 2006), p. 1D.

Chapter 18). However, developing these new channels often brings them into direct competition with their established channels, resulting in conflict.

To ease this problem, companies often look for ways to make going direct a plus for the entire channel. For example, Black & Decker knows that many customers would prefer to buy its power tools and outdoor power equipment online. But selling directly through its website would create conflicts with important and powerful retail partners. So, although Black & Decker's website provides detailed information about the company's products, you cannot buy a Black & Decker cordless drill, laser level, leaf blower or anything else there. Instead, the Black & Decker site refers you to resellers' websites and stores. Thus, Black & Decker's direct marketing helps the company but also boosts business for its channel partners.

Channel design decisions

We now look at several channel decisions facing manufacturers. In designing marketing channels, manufacturers struggle between what is ideal and what is practical. A new firm usually starts by selling in a limited market area. Deciding on the *best* channels might not be a problem: the problem might simply be how to convince one or a few good intermediaries to handle the line.

If successful, the new firm might branch out to new markets through existing intermediaries. In smaller markets, the firm might sell directly to retailers; in larger markets, it might sell through distributors. In one part of the country, it might grant exclusive franchises; in another, it might sell through all available outlets. In one country it might use international sales agents; in another, it might partner a local firm. Or it might add a Web store that sells directly to hard-to-reach customers. In this way, channel systems often evolve to meet market opportunities and conditions. However, for maximum effectiveness, channel analysis and decision making should be more purposeful. Designing a channel system calls for:

- Analysing customer needs
- Setting channel objectives
- Identifying the major channel alternatives
- Evaluating the channel alternatives.

Analysing customer needs

As noted earlier, marketing channels are part of the overall *customer value delivery network*. Each channel member adds value for the customer. Thus designing the marketing channel starts with finding out what consumers want from the channel. Do customers want to buy from nearby locations or are they willing to travel to more distant, centralised locations? Would they rather buy in person or over the phone, through the mail or online? Do they value immediate delivery or are they willing to wait? Do they want breadth of assortment or do they prefer specialisation? Do customers want many add-on services (delivery, credit, repairs, installation) or will they obtain these elsewhere? The faster the delivery, the greater the assortment provided, and the more add-on services supplied, the greater the channel's service level.

However, providing the fastest delivery, greatest assortment and most comprehensive services may not be possible or practical. The company and its channel members may not have the resources or skills needed to provide all the desired services. Also, providing higher levels of service results in higher costs for the channel and higher prices for consumers. The company must balance consumer service needs against the feasibility and costs of meeting these needs as well as customer price preferences. Generally, customers make trade-offs between service quality and other purchase criteria, such as price. The success of discount retailing – on and off the Web – shows that consumers are often willing to accept lower service levels in exchange for lower prices.

Setting channel objectives

Channel objectives should be stated in terms of targeted levels of customer service. Usually, a company can identify several segments wanting different levels of service. The company should decide which segments to serve and the best channels to use in each case. In each segment, the company wants to minimise the total channel cost of meeting customer service requirements.

The company's channel objectives are also influenced by the nature of the company, its products, its marketing intermediaries, its competitors and the environment. For example, the company's size and financial situation determine which marketing functions it can handle itself and which it must give to intermediaries. Companies selling perishable products may require more direct marketing to avoid delays and too much handling.

In some cases, a company may want to compete in or near the same outlets that carry competitors' products. For instance, in town or city centres, Burger King wants to locate near McDonald's; Sony, Panasonic and Philips audio and video systems all compete for floor space in similar retail outlets; Nestlé and Mars confectionery brands want to be positioned side by side, and aggressively compete for shelf space, in the same grocery outlets. In other cases, producers may avoid the channels used by competitors. The Good Hair Day company featured in this chapter's prelude case does not compete with other hair-styling iron brands for shelf space in high street stores. Instead, it set up a profitable operation selling through hair salons in the home and overseas markets. Similarly, Avon Products sells direct to consumers through its corps of more than five million independent beauty sales representatives in 100 markets worldwide rather than going head-to-head with other cosmetics makers for scarce positions in retail stores.

Finally, environmental factors such as economic conditions and legal constraints may affect channel objectives and design. For example, in a depressed economy, producers want to distribute their goods in the most economical way, using shorter channels and dropping un-needed services that add to the final price of the goods.

Identifying the major channel alternatives

When the company has defined its channel objectives, it should next identify its major channel alternatives in terms of the *types* and *number* of intermediaries to use and the *responsibilities* of each channel member.

Types of channel alternatives

A firm should identify the types of channel members available to carry out its channel work. For example, suppose a manufacturer of test equipment has developed an audio device that detects poor mechanical connections in machines with moving parts. Company executives think this product would have a market in all industries in which electrical, combustion or steam engines are made or used. The company's current sales force is small, and the problem is how best to reach these different industries. The following channel alternatives might emerge:

- *Company sales force.* Expand the company's direct sales force. Assign outside salespeople to territories and have them contact all prospects in the area, or develop separate company sales forces for different industries. Or, add an inside telesales operation in which telephone sales-people handle small or mid-sized companies.

- *Manufacturer's agency.* Hire manufacturer's agents – independent firms whose sales forces handle related products from many companies – in different regions or industries to sell the new test equipment.

- *Intermediaries.* Use industrial distributors in the different regions or industries who will buy and carry the new line. Give them exclusive distribution, good margins, product training and promotional support.

Here, we will address in more depth the role of **intermediaries**, which are independent channel organisations that carry out a number of activities. They include *wholesalers* and *retailers* who buy, take title to and resell the firm's goods. We will first examine the nature and importance of wholesalers.

Wholesalers

Wholesaling includes all activities involved in selling goods and services to those buying for resale or business use. We call wholesalers those firms engaged *primarily* in wholesaling activities. Wholesalers buy mostly from producers and sell mostly to retailers, industrial consumers and

Intermediaries—
Distribution channel firms that help the company find customers or make sales to them, including wholesalers and retailers that buy and resell goods.

Wholesaler—A firm engaged primarily in selling goods and services to those buying for resale or business use.

other wholesalers. But why would a producer use wholesalers rather than selling directly to retailers or consumers? Quite simply, wholesalers add value by performing one or more of the following channel functions:

- *Selling and promoting.* Wholesalers' sales forces help manufacturers reach many small customers at a low cost. The wholesaler has many contacts and is often more trusted by the buyer than the distant manufacturer.
- *Buying and assortment building.* Wholesalers can select items and build assortments needed by their customers, thereby saving the consumers a considerable amount of work.
- *Bulk-breaking.* They save their customers money by buying in huge lots and breaking bulk (breaking large lots into small quantities).
- *Warehousing.* Wholesalers hold inventories, thereby reducing the inventory costs and risks of suppliers and customers.
- *Transportation.* Wholesalers can provide quicker delivery to buyers because they are closer than the producers.
- *Financing.* They finance their customers by giving credit, and they finance their suppliers by ordering early and paying bills on time.
- *Risk bearing.* Wholesalers absorb risk by taking title and bearing the cost of theft, damage, spoilage and obsolescence.
- *Market information.* They give information to suppliers and customers about competitors, new products and price developments.
- *Management services and advice.* Wholesalers often help retailers train their sales assistants, improve store layouts and displays, and set up accounting and inventory control systems.

There are many types of wholesaler (see Table 19.1). They fall into three major groups: *merchant wholesalers, brokers and agents* and *manufacturers' sales branches and offices.*

Merchant wholesalers include two broad types: full-service wholesalers and limited-service wholesalers. *Full-service wholesalers* provide a full set of services, whereas *limited-service wholesalers* offer fewer services to their suppliers and customers. The several different types of limited-service wholesalers perform varied specialised functions in the distribution channel.

Brokers and **agents** differ from merchant wholesalers. First, they do not take title to goods, and perform only a few functions. Like merchant wholesalers, they generally specialise by product line or customer type. A broker brings buyers and sellers together and assists in negotiation. Agents represent buyers or sellers on a more permanent basis. Manufacturers' agents, also called manufacturers' representatives, are a common type of agent wholesaler.

The third type of wholesaling is that done in manufacturers' sales branches and offices by sellers or buyers themselves rather than through independent wholesalers.

Retailers

Although wholesalers play an important channel role, **retailers** are also critical intermediaries because they provide the final link between the consumer and provider. **Retailing** includes all the activities involved in selling products or services directly to final consumers for their personal, non-business use. Many institutions – manufacturers, wholesalers and retailers – do retailing. But most retailing is done by retailers: businesses whose sales come *primarily* from retailing.

Non-store retailing has been growing much faster than has store retailing. Non-store retailing includes selling to final consumers through direct mail, catalogues, telephone, home TV shopping shows, home and office parties, door-to-door contact, vending machines, online services and the Internet, and other direct-selling approaches. We discussed such direct marketing approaches in Chapter 18. In this chapter, we will focus on store retailing.

Merchant wholesaler—Independently owned business that takes title to the merchandise it handles.

Broker—A wholesaler who does not take title to goods and whose function is to bring buyers and sellers together and assist in negotiation.

Agent—A wholesaler who represents buyers or sellers on a relatively permanent basis, performs only a few functions, and does not take title to goods.

Retailers—Businesses whose sales come primarily from retailing.

Retailing—All activities involved in selling goods and services directly to final consumers for their personal, non-business use.

Table 19.1 Major types of wholesalers

Type	Description
Merchant wholesalers	Independently owned businesses that take title to the merchandise they handle. In different trades they are called *jobbers*, *distributors* or *mill supply houses*. Include full-service wholesalers and limited-service wholesalers.
Full-service wholesalers	Provide a full line of services: carrying stock, maintaining a sales force, offering credit, making deliveries and providing management assistance. There are two types:
• Wholesale merchants	Sell primarily to retailers and provide a full range of services. *General-merchandise wholesalers* carry several merchandise lines, whereas *general-line wholesalers* carry one or two lines in greater depth. *Speciality wholesalers* specialise in carrying only part of a line. Examples are healthfood wholesalers and seafood wholesalers.
• Industrial distributors	Sell to manufacturers rather than to retailers. Provide several services, such as carrying stock, offering credit and providing delivery. May carry a broad range of merchandise, a general line or a speciality line.
Limited-service wholesalers	Offer fewer services than full-service wholesalers. Limited-service wholesalers are of several types:
• Cash-and-carry wholesalers	Carry a limited line of fast-moving goods and sell to small retailers for cash. Normally do not deliver. For example, a small fish store retailer may drive to a cash-and-carry fish wholesaler, buy fish for cash and bring the merchandise back to the store.
• Truck wholesalers (or truck jobbers)	Perform primarily a selling and delivery function. Carry a limited line of semi-perishable merchandise (such as milk, bread, snack foods), which they sell for cash as they make their rounds to supermarkets, small groceries, hospitals, restaurants, factory cafeterias and hotels.
• Drop shippers	Do not carry inventory or handle the product. On receiving an order, they select a manufacturer, who ships the merchandise directly to the customer. The drop shipper assumes title and risk from the time the order is accepted to its delivery to the customer. They operate in bulk industries, such as coal, lumber and heavy equipment.
• Rack jobbers	Serve grocery and drug retailers, mostly in non-food items. They send delivery trucks to stores, where the delivery people set up toys, paperbacks, hardware items, health and beauty aids, or other items. They price the goods, keep them fresh, set up point-of-purchase displays and keep inventory records. Rack jobbers retain title to the goods and bill the retailers only for the goods sold to consumers.
• Producers' cooperatives	Owned by farmer members and assemble farm produce to sell in local markets. The co-op's profits are distributed to members at the end of the year. They often attempt to improve product quality and promote a co-op brand name.
• Mail-order wholesalers	Send catalogues to retail, industrial and institutional customers. Orders are filled and sent by mail, truck or other transportation.
	(Continued)

Table 19.1 (Continued)

Type	Description
Brokers and agents	Do not take title to goods. Their main function is to facilitate buying and selling, for which they earn a commission on the selling price. Generally, they specialise by product line or customer types.
Brokers	Their chief function is bringing buyers and sellers together and assisting in negotiation. They are paid by the party who hired them, and do not carry inventory, get involved in financing or assume risk. Examples are food brokers, real estate brokers, insurance brokers and security brokers.
Agents	Represent either buyers or sellers on a more permanent basis than brokers do. There are several types:
• Manufacturers' agents	Represent two or more manufacturers of complementary lines. A formal written agreement with each manufacturer covers pricing, territories, order handling, delivery service and warranties, and commission rates. Often used in such lines as clothing, furniture and electrical goods. Most manufacturers' agents are small businesses, with only a few skilled salespeople as employees. They are hired by small manufacturers who cannot afford their own field sales forces, and by large manufacturers who use agents to open new territories or to cover territories that cannot support full-time salespeople.
• Selling agents	Have contractual authority to sell a manufacturer's entire output. The manufacturer either is not interested in the selling function or feels unqualified. The selling agent serves as a sales department and has significant influence over prices, terms and conditions of sale.
• Purchasing agents	Generally have a long-term relationship with buyers and make purchases for them, often receiving, inspecting, warehousing and shipping the merchandise to the buyers. They provide helpful market information to clients and help them obtain the best goods and prices available.
• Commission merchants	Take physical possession of products and negotiate sales. Normally, they are not employed on a long-term basis. Used most often by producers who do not want to sell their own output and do not belong to producers' cooperatives. The commission merchant takes a truckload of commodities to a central market, sells it for the best price, deducts a commission and expenses and remits the balance to the producer.
Manufacturers' and retailers' branches and offices	Wholesaling operations conducted by sellers or buyers themselves rather than through independent wholesalers. Separate branches and offices can be dedicated to either sales or purchasing:
Sales branches and offices	Set up by manufacturers to improve inventory control, selling and promotion. Sales branches carry inventory. Sales offices do not carry inventory.
Purchasing offices	Perform a role similar to that of brokers or agents but are part of the buyer's organisation. Retailers tend to set up purchasing offices in major market centres.

Retail stores come in all shapes and sizes, and new retail types keep emerging. Generally, they can be classified in terms of the amount of service they offer, the breadth and depth of their product lines, the relative prices charged and how they are organised.

Amount of service   Different products require *different amounts of service* and *customer service preferences* vary. Retailers may offer one of three levels of service – self-service, limited service and full service. **Self-service retailers** cater for customers who are willing to perform their own 'locate–compare–select' process to save money. Self-service is the basis of all discount operations and is typically used by sellers of convenience goods (e.g. supermarkets) and nationally branded, fast-moving shopping goods (e.g. discount stores). **Limited-service retailers**, such as department stores, provide more sales assistance because they carry more shopping goods about which customers need information. **Full-service retailers** usually carry more speciality goods for which customers like to be 'waited on'. They provide more services resulting in much higher operating costs, which are passed along to customers as higher prices.

Product line   Retailers vary in the *length and breadth of their product assortments*. A **speciality store** carries narrow product lines with a deep assortment within that line. Examples are stores selling fashion wear, outdoor leisure garments, cosmetics, books or flowers (e.g. Naf-Naf, Rohan, The Body Shop, Foyles bookstore, Interflora). Today, speciality stores are flourishing. The increasing use of market segmentation, market targeting and product specialisation has resulted in a greater need for specialist stores that focus on specific products and segments.

In contrast, **department stores** carry a wide variety of product lines. Examples include Hennes & Mauritz and Karlstadt/Quelle (both of which have stores across major European cities), Harrods and Harvey Nichols (in the United Kingdom), Takashimaya and Isetan (in Japan and south-east Asia), Saks and Bloomingdale (in the United States), El Corte Ingles (in Spain) and Galeries Lafayette (in France). In recent years, department stores have been squeezed between more focused and flexible speciality stores on the one hand, and more efficient, low-priced discounters on the other. In response, many have added promotional pricing to meet the discount threat. Others have stepped up the use of store brands and single-brand 'boutiques' and 'designer shops' (such as Prada, Dolce and Gabana, Salvatore Ferragamo or DKNY shops within department stores) to compete with speciality stores. Still others are using mail-order, telephone and Web selling. Service remains their key differentiating factor.

Supermarkets are the most frequently shopped type of retail store. Today, however, they are facing slow sales growth because of an increase in competition from convenience stores, discount food stores and superstores. Thus, supermarkets have to make improvements to attract more customers. In the battle for 'share of stomachs', some of the larger supermarkets, for example, are providing improved store environments and higher-quality food offerings, such as in-store bakeries, gourmet deli counters and fresh seafood departments. Others are cutting costs, establishing more efficient operations and lowering prices in order to compete more effectively with food discounters. Some have added Web-based sales to widen channel options for existing customers. Still others, such as Britain's Tesco and Sainsbury's, are re-establishing their presence as neighbourhood stores to compete with convenience stores (see next section).

Convenience stores are small stores that carry a limited line of high-turnover convenience goods. Typical examples are Happy Shopper, Spar, Mace and VG stores. These are located near residential areas and remain open for long hours. In countries where retail laws are more relaxed and there is less restriction on store opening hours, convenience stores may be open seven days a week. They satisfy an important consumer need in a niche segment – shoppers in this segment use convenience stores for emergency or 'fill-in' purchases outside normal hours or when time is short, and they are willing to pay for the convenience of location and opening hours.

In the UK, the convenience store market has grown between 30 and 60 per cent in the last five years. The sector is fragmented, boasting more than 50,000 stores nationwide. More and more people appear to prefer to visit their local (neighbourhood) convenience store to do top-up

---

Self-service retailers—Retailers that provide few or no services to shoppers; shoppers perform their own locate–compare–select process.

Limited-service retailers—Retailers that provide only a limited number of services to shoppers.

Full-service retailers—Retailers that provide a full range of services to shoppers.

Speciality store—A retail store that carries a narrow product line with a deep assortment within that line.

Department store—A retail organisation that carries a wide variety of product lines – each line is operated as a separate department managed by specialist buyers or merchandisers.

Supermarkets—Large, low-cost, low-margin, high-volume, self-service stores that carry a wide variety of food, laundry and household products.

Convenience store—A small store located near a residential area that is open long hours seven days a week and carries a limited line of high-turnover convenience goods.

Bullring: standing in the heart of Birmingham, Britain's second city, the Bullring shopping centre is one of Europe's largest and most innovative shopping destinations, housing two major department stores, Selfridges and Debenhams, and well over 140 shops, restaurants and bars. New shopping concepts like this offer a brand new experience for shoppers.

SOURCE: (both) Birmingham Picture Library/Jonathan Berg (www.bplphoto.co.uk).

shopping because they do not have time every day to browse endless supermarket shelves to find lunch or dinner. The major supermarket chain stores are responding to this trend.

Britain's number one grocery retailer Tesco has become a major player in the convenience sector. Its Tesco Express stores, located in convenient town centre locations, are changing the pattern of grocery retailing in the country. As opportunities for large store expansion out-of-town in the UK are declining because of planning restrictions, the industry has seen more and more 'marriages' between petrol retailers and supermarkets in recent years. Tesco operates a partnership with Esso, running 100 or more stores on the petrol retailer's forecourts. Not to be left behind, rival Sainsbury's has also gained a large slice of the growing UK convenience store market, having opened over 100 stores at Shell petrol filling stations in recent years.[10]

Superstores are much larger than regular high street supermarkets and offer a large assortment of routinely purchased food products, non-food items and services, ranging from dry cleaning, post offices and film developing and photo finishing, to cheque cashing, petrol forecourts and self-service car-washing facilities. Superstores are located out of town, frequently in retail parks, with vast free car parks. The 1990s saw the explosive growth of superstores that are actually giant speciality stores, the so-called **category killers**. They feature stores the size of aircraft hangars that carry a very deep assortment of branded products belonging to a particular line, with a knowledgeable staff. Category killers have been prevalent in a wide range of categories, including books, toys, electronics, furniture, home improvement products, sporting goods and even pet supplies. However, in recent years, many of these stores have faced declining sales growth because of an increase in competition from online stores.

Another superstore variation, **hypermarkets**, are even bigger, perhaps as large as six football fields. They carry an even larger assortment of routinely purchased food and packaged goods and non-food items such as clothing, furniture and household appliances. Carrefour, the number one grocery retailer in France, opened the world's first 'hypermarché' at Ste-Geneviève-des-Bois, near Paris, in 1963. Since then, the concept quickly took off in France and the company now operates hundreds of these giant stores in Europe, South America and Asia. Between 2006 and 2008, the French retailer plans to open 100 more hypermarkets a year. Other examples of hypermarkets include Real in Germany, Pyrca in Spain and Meijers in the Netherlands. Although hypermarkets have dominated in some countries, such as France, Italy and the Netherlands, the concept has enjoyed mixed success in the UK.[11]

Finally, for some retailers, the product line is actually a service. Service retailers include hotels and motels, banks, airlines, colleges, hospitals, movie theatres, tennis clubs, bowling alleys, restaurants, repair services, hair salons and dry cleaners. We discussed service marketing in Chapter 13.

Relative prices   Retailers can also be classified according to the prices they charge. Most retailers charge regular prices and offer normal-quality goods and customer service. Others offer higher-quality goods and services at higher prices. The retail stores that feature low prices are discount stores and off-price retailers.

A **discount store** sells standard merchandise at lower prices by accepting lower margins and selling higher volume. Examples include the German Aldi, the Danish Netto, and Matalan and Peacock in the UK. The early discount stores cut expenses by offering few services and operating in warehouse-like facilities in low-rent, heavily travelled districts. In recent years, facing intense competition from other discounters and department stores, many discount retailers have 'traded up'. They have improved their store environments and increased their services, while at the same

Superstore—A store around twice the size of a regular supermarket that carries a large assortment of routinely purchased food and non-food items and offers such services as dry cleaning, post offices, film developing, photo finishing, cheque cashing, petrol forecourts and self-service car-washing facilities.

Category killers—A modern 'breed' of exceptionally aggressive 'off-price' retailers that offer branded merchandise in clearly defined product categories at heavily discounted prices.

Hypermarkets—Huge stores that combine supermarket, discount and warehouse retailing; in addition to food, they carry furniture, appliances, clothing and many other products.

Discount store—A retail institution that sells standard merchandise at lower prices by accepting lower margins and selling at higher volume.

time keeping prices low through lean, efficient operations. For example, after 15 years of operation in the UK, Netto is changing its traditional (or earlier) hard-discounter image.

According to Mike Hinchcliffe, marketing manager at Netto Foodstores, UK, 'We've been in an unfortunate position for a number of years because we've been rejected by many potential shoppers because of stigma issues, which were pretty short-sighted really.' One major reason was that when the Danish-owned company first landed in the UK 15 years ago it chose brownfield sites for its stores, which meant that despite the quality of the fit-out there was no escaping the often grubby façades and frequently less than desirable locations of some of these buildings. 'Although we still consider specific brownfield sites, this is not our key target anymore. Instead, very many of our more recent stores are new builds and others are located on retail parks and in neighbourhood areas,' said Mr Hinchcliffe. But the changes at the company are not just about bricks and mortar. Each store now has an increased product range (1,200 lines) and a growing number of famous-name well-known brands (300-plus) including Stella Artois, Coca-Cola, Kellogg's, Heinz, Mars, Hovis and Warburtons.

'This places Netto in a very different part of the food retailing market to the hard discounters including Aldi and Lidl. Netto is not a discounter and the frequent references to it as such miss the real point of the company. They incorrectly give it a downmarket image and suggest Netto customers do not shop at its stores through choice but through necessity. What we are about is being "everyone's great value supermarket". It's about being inclusive where the only requirement of shoppers is to enjoy great value prices. But this does not mean cheap prices at the expense of quality because the Netto own-brand products are the equivalent quality to the "standard" own-label of the major supermarkets and superior to their "value" ranges. For instance, our "La Campagna" own-label baked beans are only 17p per can compared with the own-label equivalent at the major supermarkets of approaching 30p – and these are produced by the same manufacturer in Italy. What we do is strip out some of the costly overheads from our stores, so you won't see in-store cafés, an army of meeters-and-greeters, photo-processing, a dry cleaners and so-called free carrier bags. Instead, by passing on these savings we can achieve our objective of not penalising anybody by having them pay higher prices than we believe are really necessary.'[12]

Off-price retailer— Retailer that buys at less-than-regular wholesale prices and sells at less than retail.

Factory outlet— Off-price retailing operation that is owned and operated by a manufacturer and that normally carries the manufacturer's surplus, discontinued or irregular goods.

When the major discount stores traded up, a new wave of **off-price retailers** moved in to fill the low-price, high-volume gap. Ordinary discounters buy at regular wholesale prices and accept lower margins to keep prices down. In contrast, off-price retailers buy at less-than-regular wholesale prices and charge consumers less than retail. One type of off-price retailer is the **factory outlet.** Sometimes, producer-operated stores group together in *factory outlet malls* and *value-retail centres*, where dozens of outlet stores offer prices 30–50 per cent below retail on a wide range of items. Whereas outlet shopping centres consist primarily of manufacturers' outlets, value-retail centres combine manufacturers' outlets with off-price retail stores and department store clearance outlets. Some of these outlet malls are moving up-market, narrowing the gap between factory outlet and more traditional forms of retailers. For example, a growing number of outlet malls now feature brands such as Polo Ralph Lauren, Dolce & Gabbana, Esprit, Giorgio Armani, Gucci and Versace, causing department stores to protest to the manufacturers of these brands. Given their higher costs, the department stores have to charge more than the off-price outlets. Manufacturers counter that they send last year's merchandise and seconds to the factory outlet malls, not the new merchandise that they supply to the department stores. Still, the department stores are concerned about the growing number of shoppers willing to make weekend trips to stock up on branded merchandise at substantial savings.

Another off-price retail format is the **warehouse club** (also known as **wholesale club** or **membership warehouse**), which operates in huge, warehouse-like facilities and offers few frills. Customers themselves must wrestle furniture, heavy appliances and other large items to the checkout line. Such clubs make no home deliveries. The policy is 'cash and carry' as they accept no credit cards, but they do offer ultra-low prices and surprise deals on selected branded goods. For example, Costco and Makro operate vast warehouses across Europe, selling food, beverages, wines and spirits, confectionery, household goods, clothes and other assortments to members – consumers and trade (resellers/retailers) who pay a membership fee. Warehouse clubs saw tremendous growth over the 1980s, but growth has slowed considerably in the 1990s as a result of increasing competition among warehouse store chains and effective reactions by supermarkets and discount stores.

Organisational approach   Although many retail stores are independently owned, an increasing number are banding together under some form of corporate or contractual organisation. The major types of retail organisations include *corporate chains, voluntary chains* and *retailer cooperatives, franchise organisations* and *merchandising conglomerate*s.

Chain stores are two or more outlets that are commonly owned and controlled. Their size allows them to buy in large quantities at lower prices and gain promotional economies. They can hire specialists to deal with pricing, promotion, merchandising, inventory control and sales forecasting.

The great success of corporate chains caused many independents to band together in one of two forms of contractual associations. One is the *voluntary chain* – a wholesaler-sponsored group of independent retailers that engages in group-buying and common merchandising.

> One example is SPAR, established in 1932 by Adriaan van Well in Zoetermeer in the Netherlands. At that time, independent wholesalers and retailers joined together to form a voluntary chain with the aim to 'concentrate [their] strengths' in the face of ever-increasing competitive pressure. The outcome of combining these strengths was expected to benefit all the members and guarantee their commercial survival. The idea – voluntary cooperation between the wholesale and the retail trades – spread rapidly through the rest of Europe during the fifties. Today, SPAR organisations are found in Africa, the Far East, South America, Australia, Russia and China. Despite the size of the organisation, SPAR is still characterised by a high level of personal contacts.[13] Another example of a voluntary chain is the Danish Ditas, the country's largest buying organisation in the building-materials industry. Ditas is owned by some 85 independent Danish timber merchants who own some 220 of the approximately 450 outlets of building materials in Denmark. Apart from its purchasing and finance functions, Ditas operates the two building materials chains and a chain of trade shops.

The other form of contractual association is the *retailer cooperative* – a group of independent retailers that band together to set up a jointly owned, central wholesale operation and conduct joint merchandising and promotion efforts. The cooperative can enhance their purchasing power to obtain discounts from manufacturers and to share marketing investments. It is common for locally-owned food and grocery stores, hardware shops and pharmacies to participate in retailers' cooperatives. In Europe, retailer cooperatives exist, with many owned by their customers. These are called consumer cooperatives, but are sometimes referred to as retail cooperatives, but they should be distinguished from retailers' cooperatives, in terms of their ownership. Examples include the UK's Co-operative Group which owns many of its own supermarkets, as well as supplying goods wholesale to the majority of British co-operative societies, which share a common brand and logo. Italy's Coop Italia chain comprises many sub-cooperatives which together control some 18 per cent of the

Warehouse club (or wholesale club, membership warehouse)—Off-price retailer that sells a limited selection of brand-name grocery items, appliances, clothing and a hodgepodge of other goods at deep discounts to members who pay annual membership fees.

grocery market. In Finland, the S Group is owned by 22 regional cooperatives and 19 local cooperative stores. And Coop Norden, which is jointly owned by three major cooperative retail companies – Danish FDB, Swedish KF and Norwegian Coop NKL – operates around 1,000 stores across Scandinavia. By employing buying and promotion economies these organisations are better able to meet the prices of corporate chains and to offer better value for their customers.

Another form of contractual retail organisation is a franchise. The main difference between franchise organisations and other contractual systems (voluntary chains and retail cooperatives) is that franchise systems are normally based on some unique product or service, on a method of doing business, or on the trade name, goodwill or patent that the franchiser has developed. Franchising, which we discussed in an earlier section, has been prominent in fast food, fashion clothing, video stores, health and fitness centres, haircutting, vehicle hire, hotels and dozens of other product and service areas.

Finally, *merchandising conglomerates* are corporations that combine several different retailing forms under central ownership as well as integrating distribution and management of functions. For example, in the UK, Icelandic group Baugur operates a wide range of stores from toys (Hamleys), jewellery (Mappin & Webb) and shoes (Shoe Studio) to food and grocery (Iceland) and fashion clothing (Oasis, Karen Millen). The TJX Group operates across Europe, Canada and the US under various clothing and department store formats including T.J. Maxx, Marshalls and HomeGoods. The Kingfisher Group owns different DIY (do-it-yourself) and home improvement store formats, including Hornbach (DIY retailer operating across Europe including Austria, Czech Republic, Germany, Luxembourg, Netherlands, Romania, Slovakia, Sweden and Switzerland); B&Q (DIY warehouses and mini-warehouses in the UK, China, Taiwan and South Korea); Castorama (home improvement stores in Italy, Russia and Poland); Brico Depot (DIY and professional tools for the trade, in Spain and Poland); ScrewFix (direct and online hardware store aimed at the trade) and Trade Depot (building products for the trade, France and Spain). Such diversified retailing provides superior management systems and economies that benefit all the separate retail operations.

We have discussed the types of channel members. Next we look at decisions concerning the number of channels to use.

Number of marketing intermediaries

Companies must also decide on *channel breadth* – the number of channel members to use at each level. Three strategies are available: intensive distribution, exclusive distribution and selective distribution. Producers of convenience products and common raw materials typically seek **intensive distribution** – a strategy whereby they stock their products in as many outlets as possible. These goods must be available where and when consumers want them. For example, confectionery, soft drinks, personal care, household cleaning and other similar items are sold in myriad outlets to provide maximum brand exposure and consumer convenience. Nestlé, Coca-Cola, Unilever and other consumer-goods companies distribute their products in this way.

Intensive distribution— Stocking the product in as many outlets as possible.

By contrast, some producers purposely limit the number of intermediaries handling their products. The extreme form of this practice is **exclusive distribution**, in which the producer gives only a limited number of dealers the exclusive rights to distribute its products in their territories. Exclusive distribution is often found in the distribution of luxury cars (e.g. Rolls-Royce, Bentley, Jaguar) and prestige clothing for men and women (e.g. Prada, Yves St Laurent). By granting exclusive distribution, the manufacturers gain strong selling support from the outlet and more control over dealer prices, promotion, credit and services. Exclusive distribution also enhances brand image and allows for higher mark-ups.

Exclusive distribution— Giving a limited number of dealers the exclusive right to distribute the company's products in their territories.

 Exclusive distribution also enhances brand image and allows for higher mark-ups.

Exclusive distribution: Luxury car makers such as Bentley sell exclusively through a limited number of retailers. Such limited distribution enhances the car's image and generates stronger retailer support.
SOURCE: Michael Beway, Bentley Houston.

Between intensive and exclusive distribution lies **selective distribution** – the use of more than one, but fewer than all of the intermediaries that are willing to carry a company's products. Most consumer electronics products, furniture and small household appliance brands are distributed in this manner. For example, Miele, Whirlpool and AEG sell their major appliances through dealer networks and selected large retailers. By using selective distribution, they do not have to spread their efforts over many outlets, including many marginal ones. They can develop good working relationships with selected channel members and expect a better-than-average selling effort. Selective distribution gives producers good market coverage with more control and less cost than does intensive distribution.

Selective distribution—The use of more than one, but less than all of the intermediaries that are willing to carry the company's products.

Responsibilities of channel members

The producer and its intermediaries need to agree on the terms and responsibilities of each channel member. They should agree on price policies, conditions of sale, territorial rights and specific services to be performed by each party. The producer should establish a list price and a fair set of discounts for intermediaries. It must define each channel member's territory, taking care where it places new resellers. Mutual services and duties need to be spelled out carefully, especially in franchise and exclusive distribution channels. For example, as mentioned earlier, an IKEA franchisee is expected to implement the IKEA 'concept'; in return the parent firm provides the franchisee with the support it needs to operate the store. In the case of fast-food retailer McDonald's, franchisees receive promotional support, a record-keeping system, training at McDonald's Hamburger University and general management assistance. In turn, franchisees must meet company standards for physical facilities, cooperate with new promotion programmes, provide requested information and buy specified food products.

Evaluating the main channel alternatives

Once a company has identified several channel alternatives, it has to select the one that will best satisfy its long-run objectives. The firm must evaluate each alternative against *economic, control* and *adaptive* criteria.

Using economic criteria, the company compares the likely sales, costs and profitability of different channel alternatives. It estimates the investment required by each channel alternative and the likely returns for selling different volumes through each channel. The company must also consider control issues. Using intermediaries usually means giving them some control over the marketing of the product, and some intermediaries take more control than others. Other things being equal, the company prefers to keep as much control as possible. Finally, the company must apply adaptive criteria. Channels often involve long-term commitments, yet the company wants to keep the channel flexible so that it can adapt to environmental changes. Thus, to be considered, a channel involving long-term commitment should be greatly superior on economic or control grounds.

Designing international distribution channels

International marketers face many additional complexities in designing their channels. Each country has its own unique distribution system that has evolved over time and changes very slowly. For instance, in food and drinks retailing, contract distributors play a more important role in the delivery of goods from producer to retailer in the United Kingdom than in countries such as Germany, France, Spain and Italy. Also, in the grocery sector, retailer concentration is more entrenched in the United Kingdom than in the latter countries. Thus global marketers must usually adapt their channel strategies to the existing structures within each country.

In some overseas markets, the distribution system is complex and hard to penetrate, consisting of many layers and large numbers of intermediaries. For example, in Japan, the distribution system encompasses a wide range of wholesalers, agents, brokers and retailers, differing more in number than in function from their European or American counterparts. Consider the experience of two global retailers:[14]

As major store retailers within national boundaries have consolidated into corporate giants and domestic markets have become ever more crowded, the big players have been crossing borders for growth opportunities. However, store retailing is a business that is difficult to transfer across national frontiers. Even for those whose international businesses are well advanced, including Carrefour and Wal-Mart, getting things right in international markets is not easy.

Emboldened by its success in other countries, Carrefour, the world's second biggest retailer, entered Japan in 2000 and rapidly expanded its operations from one to seven outlets within 3 years. However, from the very beginning, the retail group had misread consumers and alienated wholesalers. Consumers turned away on finding low-priced Japanese fare that jarred with their expectations of French delicacies at lavish prices. It faced hostility from wholesalers with its pricing demands and refusal to accept their multi-layered distribution system, leaving the retailer often struggling to maintain stocks. Following this troubled entry, Carrefour's superstores responded by introducing French products and clustered food items to suit Japanese tastes. They offer cut-portions of fruit and a wider range of ready-to-eat meals. They developed relations with second-tier suppliers who were often blocked by the cartel-like structure of the Japanese wholesale system. Expansion then focused more on western Japan where lower prices are more likely to attract shoppers than in Tokyo.

Meanwhile, competitors such as Tesco and Wal-Mart had also entered Japan, while local market-leaders like Aeon began slashing prices and expanding aggressively with new superstore formats. Despite its efforts, the French retail group failed to recover from its troubled entry into Japan. Some analysts suggest that Carrefour should have known it could not do it alone – some of their teething problems could have been avoided had they taken the conventional route and entered through a joint venture partner or acquisition. Being too aggressive and arrogant at the beginning, Carrefour must now accept that some things work better in Japan the Japanese way. By 2006, Carrefour had withdrawn from the Japanese market.

The problems facing the world's largest retailer, America's Wal-Mart, when it entered the German market are also instructive. Through its acquisition of the Wertkauf hypermarket in 1997 and Interspar in 1998, Wal-Mart Germany became the country's fourth largest hypermarket chain. Although this move initially sent shockwaves through the European retail industry, the German venture was proving to be performing poorly, losing $200–300m (€224–333m) a year. By 2003, losses amounted to €487m ($550m). Wal-Mart acknowledges that they did make mistakes. The most serious one was disregarding the German food retailing distribution structure. To control the distribution to stores, the company centralised procurement rather than left it to suppliers. This resulted in delivery chaos and stock-out rates as high as 20 per cent compared with a 7 per cent average for the industry. Although sizeable, with 10 per cent of the hypermarket sector, Wal-Mart Germany had less than 2 per cent of the food retail market. It lacked the purchasing muscle to dictate to suppliers and distributors, unlike domestic operators. Moreover, in a sector already dominated by hard discounters, Wal-Mart's 'low-price message' was nothing new. It faced fierce competition from domestic rivals like Aldi, Lidl and Kaufland (Lidl's sister operation), who could match its price cuts. High renovation costs and the complexity of Germany's planning and social regulations have also delayed planned refurbishment of stores, with many remaining unattractive or in the wrong locations. Poor-quality staff and sloppy customer service at its Interspar stores had not helped either.

Wal-Mart also acknowledged misjudging corporate culture. Filling the top positions at the German stores with US expatriates (who spoke no German and insisted their managers spoke in English) prompted an exodus of German managers. This denied the group local expertise. The next head, an Englishman, managed the operation from England. Top management misunderstood the customers – German shoppers like to hunt for bargains on their own, without smiling assistants at their elbows. Other surprises were Germany's short shopping hours, including almost no Sunday trading.

In its early years, Wal-Mart's losses in Germany may be reconcilable. IKEA waited eight years until its US store eventually went into profit. For Wal-Mart, a turnaround never occurred. At the end of July 2006, the US giant finally withdrew from Germany, selling its 85 hypermarkets to Metro, the local market leader.

At the other extreme, distribution systems in developing countries may be scattered and inefficient, or altogether lacking. For example, China and India are huge markets, each with populations over one billion. However, because of inadequate distribution systems, most companies can profitably access only a small portion of the population located in each country's most affluent cities. 'China is a very decentralised market,' notes a China trade expert. '[It's] made up of two dozen distinct markets sprawling across 2,000 cities. Each has its own culture . . . It's like operating in an asteroid belt.' China's distribution system is so fragmented that logistics costs amount to 15 per cent of the nation's GDP, far higher than in most other countries. After 10 years of effort, even Wal-Mart executives admit that they have been unable to assemble an efficient supply chain in China.[15]

> **❝** China . . . It's like operating in an asteroid belt. **❞**

Thus international marketers face a wide range of channel alternatives. Designing efficient and effective channel systems between and within various country markets poses a difficult challenge. To succeed, like other international marketers, global retailers have to blend their products and services, quality and prices to suit local tastes. Management has to be responsive to new ideas and local systems of doing business. As a spokesperson for an Asian retail conglomerate noted, 'We considered alliances with Wal-Mart and Carrefour but they both had an attitude that their way was best. So we chose Tesco instead because we were impressed by how open its management was to new ideas.'[16]

We will address international channel decisions further in Chapter 20.

Channel management decisions

Once the company has reviewed its channel alternatives and decided on the best channel design, it must implement and manage the chosen channel. Channel management calls for selecting and motivating individual channel members and evaluating their performance over time.

Selecting channel members

When selecting intermediaries, the company should determine what characteristics distinguish the better ones. It will want to evaluate the channel members' years in business, other lines carried, growth and profit record, level of cooperation and reputation. If the intermediaries are sales agents, the company will want to evaluate the number and character of other lines carried and the size and quality of the sales force. If the intermediary is a retail store that wants exclusive or selective distribution, the company will want to evaluate the store's customers, location and future growth potential.

Managing and motivating channel members

Channel members must be continuously motivated to do their best. The company must sell not only *through* the intermediaries, but *to* and *with* them. Most companies see their intermediaries as first-line customers and partners. They practise strong *partner relationship management* (PRM) to forge long-term partnerships with channel members. This creates a marketing system that meets the needs of both the company *and* its partners.

In managing its channels, a company must convince distributors that they can succeed better by working together as a part of a cohesive value delivery system.[17] Thus, manufacturers such as Unilever and P&G work together with grocery retailers to create superior value for final consumers. They jointly plan merchandising goals and strategies, inventory levels and advertising and promotion plans. Similarly, construction equipment manufacturer JCB and car producers such as Ford and Toyota have to work closely with their dealers. They have to coordinate, support and motivate their dealers to help them to be successful in selling the company's products.

Many companies are now installing high-tech partner relationship management systems to coordinate their whole-channel marketing efforts. Just as they use customer relationship management (CRM) software systems to help manage relationships with important customers, companies use partner relationship management (PRM) and supply chain management (SCM) software to help recruit, train, organise, manage, motivate and evaluate relationships with channel partners.[18]

Evaluating channel members

The producer must regularly check channel member performance against standards such as sales quotas, average inventory levels, customer delivery time, treatment of damaged and lost goods, cooperation in company promotion and training programmes, and services to the customer. The company should recognise and reward intermediaries who are performing well and adding good value for consumers. Those who are performing poorly should be assisted or, as a last resort, replaced. A company may periodically 'requalify' its intermediaries and prune the weaker ones.

Finally, manufacturers need to be sensitive to their dealers. Those who treat their dealers poorly risk not only losing their support, but also causing legal problems. The key to profitable channel management is creating win–win outcomes for all in the value delivery network – a mutually beneficial relationship that yields cooperation, not conflict, among channel participants will result in higher channel performance.

Marketing logistics and supply chain management

In today's global marketplace, selling a product is sometimes easier than physically getting it to customers. Companies must decide on the best way to store, handle and move their products and services, so that they are available to customers in the right assortments, at the right time and in the right place. Physical distribution and logistics effectiveness will have a significant impact on both customer satisfaction and company costs. A poor distribution system can destroy an otherwise good marketing effort. Here we consider the nature and importance of *marketing logistics*, goals of the *logistics system*, *major logistics functions*, *choosing transportation modes* and the need for *integrated logistics management*.

The nature and importance of marketing logistics

To some managers, physical distribution means only trucks and warehouses. But modern logistics is much more than this. **Marketing logistics** or **physical distribution** involves planning, implementing and controlling the physical flow of goods, services and related information from points of origin to points of consumption to meet customer requirements at a profit. In short, it involves getting the right product to the right customer in the right place at the right time.

Traditional physical distribution typically started with products at the plant and then tried to find low-cost solutions to get them to customers. However, today's marketers prefer *customer-centred logistics* thinking which starts with the marketplace and works backwards to the factory or even to sources of supply. Marketing logistics addresses not only *outbound distribution* (moving products from the factory to customers), but also *inbound distribution* (moving products and materials from suppliers to the factory) and *reverse distribution* (moving broken, unwanted or excess products returned by consumers and resellers). Thus, it involves entire *supply chain management* – managing upstream and downstream value-added flows of materials, final goods and related information among suppliers, the company, resellers and final consumers, as shown in Figure 19.6. Thus the logistics manager's task is to coordinate the whole channel physical distribution system – the activities of suppliers, purchasing agents, marketers, channel members and customers. These activities include forecasting, purchasing, production planning, order processing, inventory management, warehousing and transportation planning.

Companies today are placing greater emphasis on logistics for several reasons:

● Customer service and satisfaction have become the cornerstones of marketing strategy in many businesses, and distribution is an important customer service element. Companies can gain a powerful competitive advantage by using improved logistics to give customers faster delivery, better service or lower prices.

Marketing logistics (or physical distribution)— The tasks involved in planning, implementing and controlling the physical flow of goods, services and related information from points of origin to points of consumption or use to meet customer requirements at a profit.

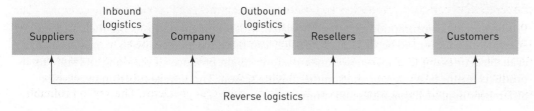

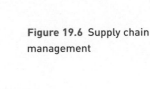
Figure 19.6 Supply chain management

- Improved logistics can yield tremendous cost savings to both the company and its customers. As much as 20 per cent of an average product's price is accounted for by shipping and transport alone. This far exceeds the cost of advertising and many other marketing costs.

- The explosion in product variety has created a need for improved logistics management. For example, 100 years ago, a typical grocery store carried only 200–300 items. The store manager could keep track of this inventory on about 10 pages of notebook paper stuffed in a shirt pocket. Today, the average store carries a bewildering stock of 20,000 or more items.

- Ordering, shipping, stocking and controlling such a variety of products presents a sizeable logistics challenge.

- Finally, improvements in information technology have created opportunities for improving distribution efficiency. Increasingly, companies use sophisticated supply chain management software, Web-based logistics systems, point-of-sale scanners, uniform product codes, satellite tracking and electronic transfer of order and payment data, to manage the flow of goods, information and finances through the supply chain quickly and efficiently.

Goals of the logistics system

The starting point for designing a marketing logistics system is to study the service needs of customers. Some companies state their logistics objective as providing *both* maximum customer service *and* least cost. Unfortunately, no logistics system can *both* maximise customer service *and* minimise distribution costs. Maximum customer service implies rapid delivery, large inventories, flexible assortments, liberal returns policies and a host of other services – all of which raise distribution costs. In contrast, minimum distribution cost implies slower delivery, small inventories and larger shipping lots – which represent a lower level of overall customer service.

> No logistics system can *both* maximise customer service *and* minimise distribution costs.

The goal of the marketing logistics system should be to provide *a targeted level of customer service at the least cost*. The company must first research the importance of various distribution services that customers require and then set desired service levels for each segment. The objective is to maximise *profits*, not sales. Therefore, the company must weigh the benefits of providing higher levels of service against the costs. Some companies offer less service than their competitors and charge a lower price. Other companies offer more service and charge higher prices to cover higher costs.

Major logistics functions

Given a set of logistics objectives, the company is ready to design a logistics system that will minimise the cost of attaining these objectives. The major logistics functions are *warehousing, inventory management* and *transportation*.

Warehousing

Production and consumption cycles rarely match. Most companies must store their tangible goods while they wait to be sold. To ensure they can meet orders speedily, they must have stock available. For example, a lawnmower manufacturer might produce all year long and store up its products for the heavy spring and summer buying season. The storage function overcomes differences in needed quantities and timing.

Warehousing: Robocom Systems specialises in providing warehouse management solutions for a variety of commercial applications.
SOURCE: Robocom Systems International (www.robocom.com).

A company must decide on *how many* and *what types* of warehouses it needs, and *where* they will be located. The company might use storage warehouses, which store goods for moderate to long periods. Or they may use **distribution centres**, which are designed to move goods rather than just store them. They are large and highly automated warehouses designed to receive goods from various plants and suppliers, take orders, fill them efficiently, and deliver goods to customers as quickly as possible.

Like almost everything else these days, warehousing has seen dramatic changes in technology in recent years. Older, multi-storey warehouses with outdated materials-handling methods are steadily being replaced by newer, single-storey *automated warehouses* with advanced, computer-controlled materials-handling systems requiring few employees. Computers and scanners read orders and direct lift trucks, electric hoists or robots to gather goods, move them to loading docks and issue invoices.

Inventory management

Inventory levels also affect customer satisfaction. The major challenge is to maintain the delicate balance between carrying too much inventory and carrying too little. With too little stock, the firm risks not having products when customers want to buy. Stock-outs lead to costly emergency shipments or production, customer dissatisfaction or lost sales as unserved customers switch to a competitor. Carrying too much inventory results in excessive inventory-carrying costs and stock obsolescence. Hence, in managing inventory, firms must balance the costs of carrying larger inventories against resulting sales and profits.

Companies can greatly reduce their inventories and related costs through *just-in-time* (JIT) logistics systems. With such systems, producers and retailers carry only small inventories of parts or merchandise, often only enough for a few days of operations. New stock arrives at the factory or retail outlet exactly when needed, rather than being stored in inventory until being used. JIT systems require accurate forecasting along with fast, frequent and flexible delivery, so that new

Distribution centre—A large, highly automated warehouse designed to receive goods from various plants and suppliers, take orders, fill them efficiently, and deliver goods to customers as quickly as possible.

supplies will be available when needed. However, these systems result in substantial savings in inventory carrying and handling costs.

Marketers are always looking for new ways to make inventory management more efficient. In the not-too-distant future, handling inventory might even become fully automated. Using RFID or 'smart tag' technology, by which small transmitter chips are embedded in or placed on products and packaging, could make the entire supply chain intelligent and automated. Companies using RFID would know, at any time, exactly where a product is located physically within the supply chain. 'Smart shelves' would not only tell them when it's time to reorder, but would also place the order automatically with their suppliers. Such exciting new information technology applications will revolutionise distribution as we know it. Many large companies, such as Wal-Mart, Tesco, Metro, Procter & Gamble, IBM and others, are investing heavily to make the full use of RFID technology a reality.[19]

Transportation

The choice of transportation carriers affects the pricing of products, delivery performance and condition of the goods when they arrive – all of which will affect customer satisfaction. In shipping goods to its warehouses, dealers and customers, the company can choose among five transportation modes: road, rail, water, pipeline and air. For digital products, firms can use an alternative distribution mode – the Internet.

Road

Trucks are highly flexible in their routing and time schedules. They are efficient for short hauls of high-value merchandise. In the EU, the bulk of goods traded is moved by road vehicles. The

Logistics technology: In the not-to-distant future, RFID or 'smart tag' technology could make the entire supply chain – which accounts for nearly 75 per cent of a product's cost – intelligent and automated.

SOURCE: Dirk Kruell/laif/Redux.

gradual deregulation and removal of restrictive practices in the road transport market in the EU has led to an increase in intra-EU haulage competition, especially from lower-cost eastern European rivals. There is also greater freedom for international hauliers to transport goods between destinations within one country, resulting in greater efficiency in the use of trucks. However, the increase in the number of trucks taking to Europe's highways has raised concerns about traffic congestion and public health.

For example, one of Europe's busiest highways is the Brenner Pass, linking Germany and Italy, via Austria. At least one in five vehicles on this highway is a truck. Moreover, since the enlargement of the EU in May 2004, increases in east–west truck movements are also compounding the long-standing controversy over trucks travelling north–south between Germany and Italy. Although public concerns in some countries like Austria were eased by the introduction of road pricing, anti-truck lobbyists such as Transitforum are not pacified. According to Transitforum, rising pollution hurts not only the local (Tyrolean) tourism, but also public health. A spokesperson for the lobby says that, 'Our doctors have sent a petition to the European parliament warning about rising lung and bronchial illnesses, especially among children.' For now, the flow of heavy trucks on the alpine gateway continues as relentlessly as the winter's driving snow.[20] In general, short of a revolution in European business to cut the volume of goods carried by road and many more initiatives to control truck traffic, road will continue to remain an important mode of intra-EU transportation.

Rail

Railroads are one of the most cost-effective modes for shipping large amounts of bulk products – coal, sand, minerals, farm and forest products – over long distances. In recent years, the EU has sped up the development of rail freight and combined road/rail transport services throughout Europe – including the opening up of networks in eastern Europe. Greater collaboration and standardisation among Europe's railways has been necessary to reinforce rail's presence on main cross-border routes.

Water

In countries favourably served by coastal and inland waterways, a large amount of goods can be moved by ships and barges. Although the cost of water transportation is very low for shipping bulky, low-value, non-perishable products such as sand, coal, grain, oil and metallic ores, water transportation is the slowest mode and is affected by the weather. In the EU, waterways' share of freight transport volume is low compared to rail and roads. Its full potential, however, will be realised through harmonisation of European shipping and port policies and pricing systems, and the removal of restrictive and unhelpful legislation.

Pipeline

Pipelines are a specialised means of shipping raw commodities such as petroleum, natural gas and chemicals from sources to markets. Most pipelines are used by their owners to ship their own products.

Air

Although the use of air carriers tends to be restricted to low-bulk goods, they are becoming more important as a transportation mode. Air-freight rates are much higher than rail or truck rates, but air freight is ideal when speed is needed or distant markets have to be reached. Among the most frequently air-freighted products are perishables (fresh fish, cut flowers) and high-value, low-bulk items (technical instruments, jewellery). Air freight is advantageous as it reduces inventory levels, packaging costs and the number of warehouses needed.

Internet

The *Internet* carries digital products from producer to customer via satellite, cable modem or telephone wire. Software firms, the media, music companies and education all make use of the Internet to transport digital products. While these firms primarily use traditional transportation to distribute CDs, DVDs, newspapers and more, the Internet holds the potential for lower product distribution costs. Whereas planes, trucks, and trains move freight and packages, digital technology moves information bits.

In choosing a transportation mode for a product, shippers must balance many considerations: speed, dependability, availability, cost, capability and others. Thus, if a shipper needs speed, air and truck are the prime choices. If the goal is low cost, then water or pipeline might be best. Moreover, transportation efficiency has become a focus of attention in view of rising oil prices and growing fears about climate change. In practice, firms meet logistics objectives cost-effectively by using a combination of transportation methods. But, as we saw earlier, there is much debate and controversy over the future of road transportation across continental Europe. Increasingly, businesses also have to consider the energy and environmental impacts of freight transport as a whole (see Real Marketing 19.2).

Logistics information management

Companies manage their supply chains through information. Channel partners often link up to share information and to make better joint logistics decisions. From a logistics perspective, information flows such as customer orders, billing, inventory levels and even customer data are closely linked to channel performance. The company should design a simple, accessible, fast and accurate process for capturing, processing and sharing channel information.

Information can be shared and managed in many ways – by mail or telephone, through salespeople, via the Internet, or through *electronic data interchange* (*EDI*), the computerised exchange of data between organisations. Retailers such as Tesco and Wal-Mart, for example, maintain EDI links with their major suppliers.

> " Companies manage their supply chains through information. "

In some cases, suppliers might actually be asked to generate orders and arrange deliveries for their customers. Large retailers are having to work closely with major suppliers to set up *vendor-managed inventory* (*VMI*) systems or *continuous inventory replenishment* systems. Using VMI, the customer shares real-time data on sales and current inventory levels with the supplier. The supplier then takes full responsibility for managing inventories and deliveries. Some retailers go so far as to shift inventory and delivery costs to the supplier. To work, however, such systems require close cooperation between the buyer and seller.

Integrated logistics management

Today, companies are increasingly adopting the concept of **integrated logistics management**. This concept recognises that providing better customer service and trimming distribution costs require *teamwork*, both inside the company and among all the marketing channel organisations. Inside the company, the various functional departments must work closely together to maximise the company's own logistics performance. Outside, the company must integrate its logistics

Integrated logistics management—The logistics concept that emphasises teamwork, both inside the company and among all the marketing channel organisations to maximise the performance of the entire distribution system.

real marketing 19.2

High-tech logistics pave way for greener trucking

Online shopping is booming. While it saves the buyer a car or bus trip to the shopping centre, someone else has to pick up the bill for order fulfilment. Products bought online still have to be moved around using physical transportation systems. With rising petrol prices and growing concerns over climate change, transport – once considered a necessary evil by retailers and shippers – is now in the spotlight. As logistics and transport companies seek to reduce their carbon footprint, they are turning to a range of solutions. Many are looking to alternative fuels and hybrid-electric vehicles. But information technology is playing an increasingly important role in making existing vehicles more efficient. Here are a few examples of how high-tech logistics can help to increase the efficiency of retailers' and carriers' supply chains.

- *Route planning software to reduce carbon emissions.* Take something as simple as reducing left-hand turns (or right-hand turns if in the UK). For drivers, this means less time idling in the middle of the road waiting for oncoming traffic to pass. 'Left-hand turns – that's a huge issue,' says Cyndi Brandt, product manager for the Roadnet transportation suite. Underlying the software is a map data base that can penalise or disable left-hand turns in the route planning process. The system is well suited to the delivery business because drivers can run circular routes, ending up where they started. Using this technique, Roadnet customers generate surprising savings on fuel and emissions. Collectively, Roadnet clients save an estimated 206 litres of fuel a year and can cut about 85,000 trucks and cars out of their logistics systems.

- *Aviation navigation.* Because aircraft are at their most fuel-efficient at cruise altitude, reducing the time spent circling at lower levels substantially cuts emissions. Automatic dependent surveillance-broadcast technology, developed by Garmin International, uses GPS to determine a plane's position and lets pilots space out their aircraft more efficiently during landing. Aircraft can use a continuous descent approach while flying in idle mode, cutting emissions by 3 per cent between cruise altitude and runway, and by 34 per cent below 1,000 metres.

  'You imagine a three-degree slope from 10,000 m down to a sea level airport, and you don't use any power on the aeroplane till you get 10 km from the runway,' says Karen Lee, a senior 747 captain at UPS. 'The savings on fuel, noise and emissions are pretty incredible.'

- *Freight matching online.* In Europe, one in three vehicles runs empty, according to some estimates. Technology can help retailers and logistics providers reduce the number of wasted return or 'backhaul' journeys – when vehicles, having delivered goods, return to base with no cargo. Online freight brokerages – like online dating – match companies that have backhaul space (i.e., empty trucks) with shippers

...19.2

that need their goods transported. 'Fleet owners are looking to fill some of their backhauls so they publish their capacity, availability and timing,' says Greg Aimi, director of supply chain research at AMR Research. He adds, 'So the network has visibility to the carriers hauling freight today that will free up tomorrow afternoon.'

- *Intermodal route optimisation.* Some modes of transport are more environmentally friendly than others. Some experts say that the real potential for cutting the freight industry's carbon emissions lies in reducing usage of trucks, especially if other modes of transport, such as rail, are available. In emissions terms, water and rail transport are the most efficient, while trucks and planes are the heaviest polluters.

The freight industry faces a greater challenge as global businesses embrace just-in-time delivery, which some believe works against fuel efficiency and carbon emissions reduction. Because speed and low inventories are the basis of just-in-time delivery, manufacturers ship goods only when retailers need them. Often, this means small, daily shipments which require extensive fleets of partially full vans, instead of a smaller number of fully loaded, larger trucks running weekly. 'What they're trading off is inventory versus oil,' says Larry Lapide, head of research at MIT's centre for transportation and logistics. 'Just-in-time is one of those concepts that makes sense while oil is cheap, but it doesn't make sense when oil is expensive.'

Demand for timely manufacturing has also limited the amount of freight transport travelling 'intermodally', using several modes of transport. Retailers like the speed and flexibility of trucks using direct routes to the shop or distribution centre, rather than the complex business of connecting their shipments with more carbon-efficient trains or ships. Getting cargo back on to these different modes of transport is the idea behind research being conducted by academics at the Rochester Institute of Technology. 'We're interested in the energy and environmental impacts of freight transport as a whole,' says RIT's James Winebrake. Professor Winebrake and his team are developing a computer model that would create commercial freight routes in the way that MapQuest or Google Maps make maps for motorists. 'But we're saying: "I want to go from point A to point B in the least carbon-heavy fashion, or emitting the least particulate matter",' Professor Winebrake says. 'We also evaluate the least cost and least time of delivery routes and make those trade-offs - because it's all about trade-offs.'

Researchers working on Gift – the geographic intermodal freight transport model – have laboriously input detailed data about roads, railways, waterways, ports and rail connections. With time and resources, Professor Winebrake says, Gift could be applied on a global basis. 'So if you want to move [shoes] from Paris, France to Paris, Texas you could see the least carbon-intensive way of doing that – our long-term goal is to have that in place.'

As we can see, the range of initiatives that are available deliver a triple benefit – lower carbon emissions, better fuel efficiency and improved overall efficiency.

...19.2

So, contrary to the belief that greening the supply chain would add costs, Jonathan Wright, a senior executive at Accenture's Global Supply Chain practice, argues that there is a direct relationship between carbon emissions and supply chain efficiency. 'Companies are becoming more environmentally conscious and so it's great if they can link this to cost and customer satisfaction.'

SOURCES: Sarah Murray, 'The green way to keep on trucking', *Financial Times* (13 March 2007), p. 12; Sarah Murray, 'It's good to go green', *Financial Times Special Report. Transport and Logistics* (27 March 2007), p. 6.

system with those of its suppliers and customers to maximise the performance of the entire channel system.

Cross-functional teamwork inside the company

In most companies, responsibility for various logistics activities is assigned to many different departments – marketing, sales, finance, manufacturing, purchasing. Too often, each function tries to optimise its own logistics performance without regard for the activities of the other functions. However, transportation, inventory, warehousing and order-processing activities interact, often in an inverse way. For example, lower inventory levels reduce inventory carrying costs. But they may also reduce customer service and increase costs from stock-outs, backorders, special production runs and costly fast-freight shipments. Because distribution activities involve strong trade-offs, decisions by different functions must be coordinated to achieve superior overall logistics performance.

Thus the goal of integrated logistics management is to harmonise all of the company's distribution decisions. Close working relationships among functions can be achieved in several ways. Some companies have created *permanent logistics committees* made up of managers responsible for different physical distribution activities and for setting policies for improving overall logistics performance.

Companies can also create *supply chain management* positions that link the logistics activities of functional areas. For example, Procter & Gamble has created supply managers, who manage all of the supply chain activities for each of its product categories. Some have a *senior executive* for logistics with cross-functional authority. Finally, companies can employ sophisticated, *system-wide supply chain management software*, now available from a wide range of software enterprises, large and small, including SAP, Oracle, CMS Worldlink and other software providers. The important thing is that the company coordinates its logistics and marketing activities to create high market satisfaction at a reasonable cost.

Building logistics partnerships

Companies must do more than improve their own logistics. They must also work with other channel members to improve whole-channel distribution. The members of a distribution channel are linked closely in delivering customer satisfaction and value. One company's distribution system is another company's supply system. The success of each channel member depends on the performance of the entire supply chain. For example, IKEA can create its stylish but affordable furniture and deliver the 'IKEA lifestyle' only if its entire supply chain – consisting of thousands of merchandise designers and suppliers, transport companies, warehouses and service providers – operates at maximum efficiency and customer-focused effectiveness.

Today, smart companies coordinate their logistics strategies and build strong partnerships with suppliers and customers to improve customer service and reduce channel costs. Many companies have created *cross-functional, cross-company teams*. For example, manufacturers such as P&G and Unilever work with key retailers to squeeze costs out of the distribution system. Working together benefits not only the manufacturer and retailer but also their shared final consumers.

Other companies partner through *shared projects*. For example, retailers such as Amsterdam's Bijenkork department store, Copenhagen's Magasin du Nord and London's Selfridges, have worked with suppliers on in-store programmes. Retailers allow key suppliers to use their stores as a testing ground for new merchandising programmes. The suppliers spend time at the test stores watching how their product sells and how customers relate to it. They then create programmes specially tailored to the retail outlet and its customers. Clearly, both the supplier and customer benefit from such partnerships. The point is that all supply chain members must work together in the process of bringing value to final consumers.

Recent research for Amsterdam's Bijenkorf department store revealed that two-thirds of its customers were female, and of those males who did enter the store many were only accompanying wives and girlfriends, not shopping for themselves.

What's a store in search of male customers to do? Observe, young retailer, observe. 'We noticed that men like to find all the things they're interested in, in the same area, whereas women like to walk around in the shop,' says Bijenkorf's Marieke Heringa. So, working with the key suppliers, the company redressed the balance by creating a stand-alone men's section, combining clothes, accessories, skincare and gadgets in one place. The Dutch store is not the only one to come up with this solution to what is, apparently, a global phenomenon.

Selfridges in London opened new men's underwear and casual wear areas as well as a 2,000 square metre enclave of formal wear. Working with suppliers, the store has specially commissioned clothes from labels ranging from Levi's to Comme des Garcons for 'Shop Like A Man', a six-week celebration that included shop-window displays and special collections from tailors such as Kilgour and Richard James.[21]

Today, more and more companies are exploiting information technology and the Internet to develop sophisticated electronic, business-to-business (B2B) marketplaces, where companies can build collaborative global procurement, trading or supply chain networks. One example is ChemConnect, a B2B exchange attracting more than 9,000 companies from over 150 countries worldwide. It connects sellers and buyers from a range of industries including chemicals, plastics, feedstocks, wire and cable, who can buy, sell and trade 24 hours a day, 7 days a week. Another example is Covisint which serves the automotive industry.[22]

Third-party logistics

Third-party logistics (3PL) provider—An independent logistics provider that performs any or all of the functions required to get its client's product to market.

Most big companies love to make and sell their products. But many loathe the associated logistics 'grunt work'. They detest the bundling, loading, unloading, sorting, storing, reloading, transporting, customs clearing and tracking required to supply their factories and to get products out to customers. They hate it so much that a growing number of firms now outsource some or all of their logistics to **third-party logistics (3PL) providers** (also called outsourced logistics or contract logistics).

> Most big companies love to make and sell their products. But many loathe the associated logistics 'grunt work'.

These '3PLs' – companies such as UPS Worldwide Logistics, DHL, FedEx Logistics and Emory Global Logistics – help clients to tighten up sluggish, overstuffed supply chains, slash inventories and get products to customers more quickly and reliably. For example, UPS's Supply Chain

Companies can outsource many of their complex logistics processes to specialists like DHL who deliver one-stop logistic services ranging from transportation and warehousing to IT-based solutions and logistics financing and consulting.
SOURCE: DHL Worldwide Network/Jung von Matt/Spree.

Services unit provides clients with a wide range of logistics services, from inventory control, warehousing and transportation management to customer service and fulfilment. Such integrated logistics companies perform any or all of the functions required to get their clients' product to market. Advanced computers and communications make it possible for companies to outsource much more than the simple delivery of physical goods, creating a wide range of services including inventory holding and after-sales services. Supply chain outsourcing is evolving from delivery of simple third-party logistics (3PL) through provision of management services (4PL) into full-blown, totally integrated logistics provision (ILP).

Companies outsource supply chain functions for several reasons. First, because getting the product to market is their main focus, these providers can often do it more efficiently and at lower cost. Outsourcing typically results in 15–30 per cent cost savings. Second, outsourcing logistics frees a company to focus more intensely on its core business. Third, integrated logistics companies understand increasingly complex logistics environments. This can be especially helpful to companies attempting to expand their global market coverage. For example, companies distributing their products across Europe face a bewildering array of environmental restrictions that affect logistics, including packaging standards, truck size and weight limits, and noise and emission pollution controls. By outsourcing its logistics, a company can gain a complete pan-European distribution system without incurring the costs, delays and risks associated with setting up its own system. Finally, globalisation trends mean that manufacturers and resellers are increasingly looking for logistics partners with international capabilities who can provide integrated supply chain services and solutions. Consider the following:[23]

The pressure to go global has seen a wave of consolidation that has swept through the industry in recent years, as logistics companies have raced to expand around the world. For example, one of the biggest deals has been Deutsche Post's £3.7bn (€5.3bn) takeover of Exel, the UK-based logistics group, in 2005. Others included the $1.1bn (€0.81bn) merger of Deutsche Bahn, the German rail operator, and US-based logistics company Bax Global, and the €490m acquisition of Paris-based ACR Logistics by Kuhne & Nagel of Switzerland. According to John Allan, chief executive of DHL Logistics, the logistics division of Deutsche Post, the world's top 10 freight forwarding companies command less than 40 per cent of the global market, but consolidation is likely to continue. 'Markets are still fairly fragmented,' he says. 'We find ourselves up against good local competition everywhere in the world. But customers are putting pressure on national players to expand so the forces behind consolidation remain strong.' For now, DHL's acquisition spree may be over. 'We've now built the scale and size we want in every major market worldwide,' he says. 'We will continue to do smaller bolt-on acquisitions. But our priority now is organic growth.'

Deutsche Post's takeover of Exel, one of the world's largest supply chain management companies, accelerated its transformation from a German mail and express delivery group into a global freight and logistics giant. The integration brought together 160,000 people in dozens of countries. John Allan says, 'We've ended up with the top 1,000 managers split almost 50/50 between DHL and Exel. This was not a British company merging with a German company. Both are active all over the world, with a very diverse, ethnically mixed group of managers. That has made it easier to bring people together.' According to Mr Allan, DHL is already reaping the rewards of the increased scale and capabilities provided by Exel. For example, DHL won a 10-year, $1.6bn contract to manage logistics for the UK's National Health Service – a deal that Mr Allan believes is the largest in the history of the logistics industry.

DHL is not alone in expanding into broader supply chain services. UPS, the world's largest parcel courier, has invested more than $2bn in about 30 acquisitions, mostly involving freight and logistics businesses, over recent years. FedEx, UPS's biggest US rival, which has a large road freight operation, is seeking to expand into higher-margin ocean freight-forwarding services, as opposed to low-margin warehousing operations.

Other groups, however, have steered clear of diversification. For example, to refocus on mail and express delivery, the Dutch TNT sold its logistics business to private equity group Apollo Management and its freight forwarding operations to Geodis, a French logistics company. David Abney, chief operating officer of UPS, says TNT's broader ambitions failed because it lacked the scale and worldwide presence of UPS. But he points out that multinational companies increasingly demand integrated transport and logistics solutions that can handle everything from the smallest package to the heaviest freight. 'We do see the synergies and the connectivity,' says Mr Abney. 'I've heard some competitors say they've never lost a single package due to not having logistics capabilities. I can't answer for them but I can say we've gained a lot of packages through also offering freight, warehousing and other services.'

Gary Hanifan, a logistics industry expert at Accenture, the consulting group, says the greatest potential for further consolidation is in emerging markets, particularly China and India, where international transport and logistics companies are seeking greater presence. One estimate puts the number of separate logistics companies in China at 18,000, while the China Logistics Club says no single competitor has more than 2 per cent of the market. Mike Eskew, chief executive of UPS, says his group's focus has shifted from acquisitions to integration. 'We feel pretty good that we have the capabilities we need to be able to take our customers anywhere they want to go,' he says, while leaving open the possibility of more bolt-on deals. 'Where we need extra capabilities faster than we can grow ourselves, we will have to speed things up through acquisitions,' he says. But size alone is not enough to guarantee success for logistics companies. 'It's a fast-changing world we live in,' says Mr Eskew. 'The winners are going to be the fast, not the large.'

Channel trends

We have examined the major channel and logistics decisions facing managers. Finally, let us look at the major changes occurring in distribution channels.

Retailing and wholesaling trends

Retailing trends

Retailers operate in a harsh and fast-changing environment, which offers threats as well as opportunities. For example, in many countries, the industry suffers from chronic overcapacity, resulting in fierce competition for customers. Consumer demographics, lifestyles and shopping patterns are changing rapidly, as are retailing technologies. To be successful, then, retailers will need to choose target segments carefully and position themselves strongly. They will have to consider the following retailing developments as they plan and execute their competitive strategies.

New retail forms and shortening retail life cycles

New retail forms continue to emerge to meet new situations and consumer needs, but the lifecycle of new retail forms is getting shorter.[24] Department stores took about 100 years to reach the mature stage of the life cycle; more recent forms, such as warehouse stores, reached maturity in about 10 years. In such an environment, seemingly solid retail positions, such as the 'category killers' of the 1990s, have crumbled quickly.

> " Department stores took about 100 years to reach the mature stage of the life cycle; more recent forms . . . reached maturity in about 10 years. "

Wheel of retailing—A concept of retailing which states that new types of retailer usually begin as low-margin, low-price, low-status operations, but later evolve into higher-priced, higher-service operations, eventually becoming like the conventional retailers they replaced.

Retailing accordion—A phenomenon describing how the width of retailers' product assortment or operations shifts over time: there tends to be a general–specific–general cycle. However, it is possible that many retailing businesses evolve along a specific–general–specific cycle.

Many retailing innovations are partially explained by the **wheel of retailing** concept. According to this concept, many new types of retailing forms begin as low-margin, low-price, low-status operations. They challenge established retailers that have become 'fat' by letting their costs and margins increase. The new retailers' success leads them to upgrade their facilities, carry higher-quality merchandise and offer more services. In turn, their costs increase, forcing them to increase their prices. Eventually, the new retailers become like the conventional retailers they replaced. The cycle begins again when still newer types of retailer evolve with lower costs and prices. The wheel of retailing concept seems to explain the initial success and later troubles of department stores, supermarkets and discount stores, and the recent success of off-price and no-frills retailers.[25] Thus retailers cannot be complacent with a successful formula. To thrive, they must keep adapting and reshaping their business accordingly.

While the wheel of retailing explains the evolution and development of new types of retail store, the concept of the **retailing accordion** can be used to explain the intermittent changes in the depth of retailers' merchandise or the breadth of their operations. Typically, retailers begin by selling a wide assortment of products. They are followed by retailers offering a narrower or more specialised range of products, which in turn are eventually superseded by broad-line mass merchandisers. The theory suggests that retailers pass through a *general–specific–general cycle*. It adequately tapped the evolution of the American retail scene, where the nineteenth-century general stores gave way to the twentieth-century specialist retailers, which were then superseded by the postwar mass merchandisers. The accordion concept may be used to describe the more recent *specific–general–specific cycle* of retailing observed in some sectors.[26]

For instance, some retailers begin by selling a narrow range or special type of goods, as in a grocery store that carries mainly food, drinks and convenience items. As sales expand, the store manager tends to add new merchandise, such as household goods, stationery, cosmetics and non-prescription drugs, to the portfolio. As it grows further, extra services and amenities – for example, delicatessen, fresh-fish-and-seafood counter, in-store bakery, credit card and cheque facilities – are added. This is the path reflected by large supermarkets, which started as narrow-line grocery retailers, stretching out over the years into broad-line superstores. More recently, further growth in edge-of-town superstores is slowing down and out-of-town shopping centres are reaching saturation point. Some of the larger supermarkets are moving back into the high streets. In the UK, Sainsbury's and Tesco reintroduced small town-centre formats, Metro and Central respectively, which are able to trade more profitably now than they could 10 years ago through the supermarkets' increased buying power and efficiency.[26]

Growth of non-store retailing

Although most retailing still takes place the old-fashioned way across store counters, consumers now have an array of alternatives, including mail order, television, phone and online shopping. Although such advances may threaten some traditional retailers, they offer exciting opportunities for others. Most store retailers are now actively exploring direct retailing channels. In fact, more online retailing is conducted by 'click-and-brick' retailers than by 'click-only' retailers. According to Nielsen/NetRatings, the leading retail websites in Europe include Germany's Tchibo, a diversified chain, OTTO, a German mail-order specialist, and Fnac, a French high-street store.[27] Moreover, in a recent ranking of the top 50 online retail sites, 35 were multi-channel retailers.[28] Far from damaging traditional retailers' businesses, the Web plays to their strengths.

Consider, for example, the growth in online retailing in the UK.[29]

At £42bn in 2007, which is predicted to reach £78bn by 2010, UK online retail sales accounted for about 6 per cent of the world's £250bn (€360bn) a year online shopping market, and about a third of total European online retail. In contrast, consumers in the US are expected to spend about £88.4bn online in 2007.

James Roper, chief executive of the Interactive Media in Retail Group, the industry body which tracks Internet sales, pointed out that more and more goods had become available online. The IMRG's figures show that spending on travel is the largest category of consumer spending, accounting for about £7bn of spending, followed by electrical goods at £5bn and clothing sales (£3.5bn). People are also buying increasingly expensive items. Just a few years ago, the average Internet transaction was a book or CD costing about £15. Today, a breed of sophisticated and Web-savvy shoppers think nothing of buying big ticket items such as sofas and fridges online.

Many of the UK's largest Internet retailers, such as Argos, Marks & Spencer, Tesco and John Lewis, have a hybrid, 'clicks-and-mortar' ('click and brick') model, in which they sell both online and in stores. They're using the Web to drive in-store sales. For example, schemes – such as Argos's 'click and collect' – which allow consumers to order online but collect in store, have proved very popular.

However, a number of 'click only' stores that exist solely on the Internet, such as Figleaves.com, the lingerie retailer, and Firebox.com, which specialises in gadgets, are thriving. With the advance of new online 'zoom and rotate' technology, retailers can make it easier for shoppers to get a good look at what they're buying. So, with a few clicks, fashionistas can snap up a pair of Chloe stilettos for £335 from upmarket online boutique Net-a-Porter.com, or order next season's trench coat from Kate Moss's Topshop collection from the website ahead of the nationwide launch. In some sectors, such as electrical goods, fierce Internet pricing and high rents have made a high street presence unsustainable. Dixons has abandoned the high street and now trades solely online. Whether others will follow this route is still unclear. 'It is too early to say which model will be dominant on the Internet,' said Mr Roper. 'Retailers are barely beginning to scratch the surface yet.'

Traditional retailers are finding many advantages in expanding their stores online: they can build virtual stores even bigger than 'bricks-and-mortar' stores and, unlike expansion offline, growth online is not constrained by planning laws or public protests; they can test-market products before making them available in their stores; more products can be offered online; and they can complement consumers' online convenience with offline experience.

Thus, hordes of niche marketers are now using the Web to reach new markets and expand their sales. As we discussed in previous chapters, today's more sophisticated search engines and comparison shopping sites put almost any e-tailer within a mouse click or two's reach of millions of customers worldwide. Still, much of the anticipated growth in online sales will go to multi-channel retailers – the clicks-and-bricks marketers who can successfully merge the virtual and physical worlds.

Retail convergence

Today's retailers are increasingly selling the same products at the same prices to the same consumers in competition with a wider variety of other retailers. For example, any consumer can buy books at outlets ranging from independent local bookstores to superstores, or websites. When it comes to brand-name appliances, department stores, discount stores, off-price retailers, electronics superstores and a slew of websites all compete for the same customers.

> " Today's retailers are increasingly selling the same products at the same prices to the same consumers. "

This merging of consumers, products, prices and retailers is called *retail convergence*: it is the coming together of shoppers, goods and prices. Customers of all income levels are shopping at the same stores, often for the same goods. Old distinctions such as discount store, speciality store and department store are losing significance. The successful store must match a host of rivals on selection, service and price.[30]

Such convergence means greater competition for retailers and greater difficulty in differentiating offerings. The competition among the hard discounters, hypermarkets, chain superstores and smaller, independently owned stores has become particularly heated. Because of their bulk buying power and high sales volume, the discounters, hypermarkets and chain stores can buy at lower costs and thrive on smaller margins. Their arrival can quickly force nearby independents out of business. For example, Carrefour, Leclerc and Auchan in France, and retailers such as Wal-Mart and Tesco in the UK, have been accused of destroying smaller independents in neighbouring towns.

Yet the news is not all bad for smaller companies. Many small, independent retailers are thriving. They are finding that sheer size and marketing muscle are often no match for the personal touch that small stores can provide or the speciality niches that small stores fill for a devoted customer base.

The rise of mega-retailers

The rise of huge mass merchandisers and speciality superstores, the formation of vertical marketing systems and buying alliances, and a rash of retail mergers and acquisitions, have created a core of superpower mega-retailers. In the grocery sector, for example, the battle for global power among the 80 large supermarket groups in Europe has created a superleague of fewer than 10 heavyweight retailers including Ahold, Aldi, Carrefour, Metro AG, Sainsbury's and Tesco. Through their superior information systems and buying power, these giant retailers are able to offer better merchandise selections, good service and strong price savings to consumers. As a result, they grow even larger by squeezing out their smaller, weaker competitors. The mega-retailers also are shifting the balance of power between retailers and producers. A relative handful of retailers now control access to enormous numbers of consumers, giving them superior bargaining power in their dealings with manufacturers.[31]

The growing importance of retail technology

Retail technologies are becoming critically important as competitive tools. Progressive retailers are using computers to produce better forecasts, control inventory costs, order electronically from suppliers, send e-mail between stores, and even sell to customers within stores. They are adopting checkout scanning systems, online transaction processing, electronic funds transfer, electronic data interchange, in-store television and improved merchandise-handling systems.

Perhaps the most startling advances in retailing technology concern the ways in which today's retailers are connecting with customers. Many retailers now routinely use technologies such as touch-screen kiosks, customer-loyalty cards, electronic shelf labels and signs, handheld shopping assistants, smartcards, self-scanning systems and virtual-reality displays to create value or to engage consumers.

Global expansion of retailers

Retailers with unique formats and strong brand positioning are increasingly moving into other countries. Many are expanding internationally to escape mature and saturated home markets. However, European and Asian retailers have led the way, with most US retailers significantly lagging behind. Ten of the world's top 20 retailers are US companies, but only two of these retailers have set up stores outside North America (Wal-Mart and Costco). Of the 10 non-US retailers in the world's top 20, nine have stores in at least 10 countries. Among foreign retailers that have gone global are Sweden's Hennes & Mauritz, France's Carrefour, Germany's Metro Group and Aldi chains, the Netherlands' Royal Ahold, Britain's Tesco, Japan's Yaohan supermarkets, and Sweden's IKEA home furnishings stores.[32]

Expansion into emerging markets is being driven heavily by the Global Top 5 – Wal-Mart, Carrefour, Metro Group, Tesco and Seven Eleven. In Western and Central Europe, Carrefour leads the pack, despite recent setbacks in its home market as well as withdrawals from several countries including Japan, Mexico and the Czech Republic. Metro Group, X5, Magnit and Auchan top the ranking in Eastern Europe, although this market as a whole continues to be dominated by local players. In all, Carrefour operates more than 12,000 stores in 29 countries in Europe, Asia and the Americas, including 926 hypermarkets. Carrefour is outpacing Wal-Mart in several emerging markets, including South America, China and the Pacific Rim. It's the leading retailer in Brazil and Argentina, where it operates close to 1,000 stores, compared to Wal-Mart's 300 units in those two countries. Carrefour is also the largest foreign retailer in China, where it operates more than 300 stores versus Wal-Mart's 60. Although no one retailer can safely claim to be in the same league with Wal-Mart as an overall retail presence, Carrefour appears to stand a better chance than most to hold its own in global retailing. According to Global Retail Bulletin, increasing consolidation, further organic expansion and a search for new markets will drive continuous expansion of the modern grocery retail sector across the European market. This drive for market concentration will almost certainly continue in many parts of the world. In particular, the top retailers will continue to target the emerging countries for future investment in their quest to gain market share.[33]

Trends in wholesaling

Today's wholesaling industry faces considerable challenges. The industry remains vulnerable to fierce resistance to price increases and the winnowing out of suppliers who are not adding value based on cost and quality. Progressive wholesalers constantly watch for better ways to meet the changing needs of their suppliers and target customers. They recognise that, in the long run, their only reason for existence comes from adding value by increasing the efficiency and effectiveness of the entire marketing channel. To achieve this goal, they must constantly improve their services and reduce their costs.

The distinction between large retailers and large wholesalers continues to blur. There are retailers that operate formats such as wholesale clubs, and hypermarkets that perform many wholesale functions. In return, many large wholesalers are setting up their own retailing operations. A prime example of this type of *hybrid* operator is the cash-and-carry self-service wholesaler Makro, which in one sense is a limited-service wholesaler, selling primarily to the trade – that is, to small shopkeepers/retailers. In another sense, Makro is also a large retailer in that many of the 'trade visitors' who purchase goods from its warehouse are not resellers but individuals bulk-buying for personal consumption.

Wholesalers will continue to increase the services they provide to retailers – retail pricing, cooperative advertising, marketing and management information reports, accounting services, online transactions and others. Rising costs on the one hand, and the demand for increased services on the other, will put the squeeze on wholesaler profits. Wholesalers who do not find efficient ways to deliver value to their customers will soon drop by the wayside. However, the

increased use of computerised, automated and Web-based systems will help wholesalers to contain the costs of ordering, shipping and inventory holding, boosting their productivity.

Facing slow growth in their domestic markets and the trend towards globalisation, many large wholesalers are going global, thus creating new challenges for the wholesaling industry worldwide. To survive, players must learn to adapt to their changing environment. Like their customers – the resellers or retailers, whose success relies on their ability to capture and retain customers by offering better value than the competition can – wholesalers must consistently add to that value-creation process.

Reviewing the concepts

1. Explain why companies use marketing channels and discuss the functions these channels perform

Most producers use intermediaries to bring their products to market. They try to forge a *marketing channel* (or *distribution channel*) – a set of interdependent organisations involved in the process of making a product or service available for use or consumption by the consumer or business user. Through their contacts, experience, specialisation and scale of operation, intermediaries usually offer the firm more than it can achieve on its own.

Marketing channels perform many key functions. Some help *complete* transactions by gathering and distributing *information* needed for planning and aiding exchange; by developing and spreading persuasive *communications* about an offer; by performing *contact* work – finding and communicating with prospective buyers; by *matching* – shaping and fitting the offer to the buyer's needs; and by entering into *negotiation* to reach an agreement on price and other terms of the offer so that ownership can be transferred. Other functions help to *fulfil* the completed transactions by offering *physical distribution* – transporting and storing goods; *financing* – acquiring and using funds to cover the costs of the channel work; and *risk taking* – assuming the risks of carrying out the channel work.

2. Discuss how channel members interact and how they organise to perform the work of the channel

The channel will be most effective when each member is assigned the tasks it can do best. Ideally, because the success of individual channel members depends on overall channel success, all channel firms should work together smoothly. They should understand and accept their roles, coordinate their goals and activities, and cooperate to attain overall channel goals. By cooperating, they can more effectively sense, serve and satisfy the target market. In a large company, the formal organisation structure assigns roles and provides needed leadership. But in a distribution channel made up of independent firms, leadership and power are not formally set. In recent years, new types of channel organisations have appeared that provide stronger leadership and improved performance.

3. Identify the major channel alternatives open to a company

Alternative ways to reach the company's market vary from direct selling to using one, two, three or more intermediary *channel levels*. Three of the most important trends are the growth of *vertical*, *horizontal* and *multi-channel marketing systems*. These trends affect channel cooperation, conflict and competition. *Channel design* begins with assessing customer channel service needs and company channel objectives and constraints. The company then identifies the major channel alternatives in terms of the *types* of intermediaries, the *number* of intermediaries and the *channel responsibilities* of each. Each channel alternative must be evaluated according to economic, control and adaptive criteria. Channel management calls for selecting qualified intermediaries and motivating them. Individual channel members must be evaluated regularly.

4. Explain how companies select, motivate and evaluate channel members

Producers vary in their ability to attract qualified marketing intermediaries. When selecting intermediaries, the company should evaluate each channel member's qualifications and select those who best fit its channel objectives. Once selected, channel members must be continuously motivated to do their best. The company must sell not only *through* the intermediaries but *to* them. It should work to forge long-term partnerships with its channel partners to create a marketing system that meets the needs of both the manufacturer *and* the partners. The company must also regularly check channel member performance against established performance standards, rewarding intermediaries who are performing well and assisting or replacing weaker ones.

5. Explain the roles of wholesalers and retailers in the distribution channel

Wholesaling and retailing consist of many organisations bringing goods and services from the point of production to the point of use. *Wholesaling* includes all the activities involved in selling goods or services to those who are buying for the purpose of resale or for business use. Wholesalers perform many functions, including selling and promoting, buying and assortment building, bulk breaking, warehousing, transporting, financing, risk bearing, supplying market information and providing management services and advice. Wholesalers fall into three groups. First, *merchant wholesalers* take possession of the goods. They include *full-service wholesalers* (wholesale merchants, industrial distributors) and *limited-service wholesalers* (cash-and-carry wholesalers, truck wholesalers, drop shippers, rack jobbers, producers' cooperatives and mail-order wholesalers). Second, *brokers* and *agents* do not take possession of the goods but are paid a commission for aiding buying and selling. Finally, *manufacturers' sales branches and offices* are wholesaling operations conducted by non-wholesalers to bypass the wholesalers.

Retailing includes all activities involved in selling goods or services directly to final consumers for their personal, non-business use. Retail stores come in all shapes and sizes, and new retail types keep emerging. Store retailers can be classified by the *amount of service* they provide (self-service, limited service or full service), *product line sold* (speciality stores, department stores, supermarkets, convenience stores, superstores and service businesses) and *relative prices* (discount stores and off-price retailers). Today, many retailers are banding together in corporate and contractual *retail organisations* (corporate chains, voluntary chains and retailer cooperatives, franchise organisations and merchandising conglomerates).

6. Discuss the importance of marketing logistics and integrated supply chain management

Just as firms are giving the marketing concept increased recognition, more business firms are paying attention to *marketing logistics* (or *physical distribution*). Logistics is an area of potentially high cost savings and improved customer satisfaction. Marketing logistics addresses not only *outbound distribution* but also *inbound distribution* and *reverse distribution*. That is, it involves entire *supply chain management* – managing value-added flows between suppliers, the company, resellers and final users. No logistics system can both maximise customer service and minimise distribution costs. Instead, logistics management aims to provide a *targeted* level of service at the least cost. The major logistics functions include *order processing*, *warehousing*, *inventory management* and *transportation*.

The *integrated supply chain management concept* recognises that improved logistics requires teamwork in the form of close working relationships across functional areas inside the company and across various organisations in the supply chain. Companies can achieve logistics harmony among functions by creating *cross-functional logistics teams*, *integrative supply manager positions* and *senior-level logistics executives* with cross-functional authority. Channel partnerships can take the form of cross-company teams, shared projects and information sharing systems. Today, some companies are outsourcing their logistics functions to third-party logistics (3PL) providers to save costs, increase efficiency and gain faster and more effective access to global markets.

Discussing the concepts

1. What do you understand to be a firm's supply chain and how is it different from its value delivery network?

2. Why do firms employ multi-channel distribution systems? Discuss the pros and cons of choosing hybrid marketing channels.

3. What are the main challenges facing retailers and wholesalers who wish to remain a viable part of the marketing channel?

4. Identify the primary challenges an organisation faces in managing its channel members. What are some of the methods companies use to motivate channel partners?

5. Many European retailers are seeking to expand globally.

   (a) What key factors might govern successful international expansion?
   (b) Thinking of examples of local retailers, explain which of these might be well positioned for global expansion.
   (c) How will online retailing affect global retail expansion?
   (d) Study Sweden's IKEA home furnishing stores (www.ikea.com). Why has IKEA been so successful in expanding into overseas markets?

Applying the concepts

1. Imagine that you are the managing director for a new company that makes award-winning exercise/fitness equipment for use in homes and the gym. What are the marketing channel alternatives available to the company? Taking into account the advantages and disadvantages of the primary marketing channels, what is your preferred option? Explain.

2. Technology is transforming the marketing logistics industry and helping managers to improve their supply chain management. Identify a company that offers software solutions for supply chain management (e.g., SAP, Oracle). Go to the company's website and explore its supply chain products. How might these offerings help managers improve their supply chain management?

Web resources

For additional classic case studies and Internet exercises, visit **www. pearsoned.co.uk/ kotler**

References

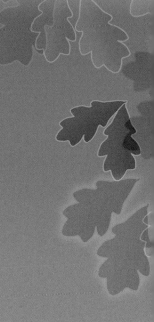

1. Louis Stern and Adel I. El-Ansary, *Marketing Channels*, 7th edn (Upper Saddle River, NJ: Prentice Hall, 2006), p. 3.

2. Information from www.luxottica.com/english/profilo_aziendale/index_keyfacts.html, accessed August 2006.

3. Miguel Helft, 'Fashion fast forward', *Business 2.0* (May 2002), p. 60; John Tagliabue, 'A rival to Gap that operates like Dell', *New York Times* (30 May 2003), p. W-1; Kasra Ferdows, Michael A. Lewis and Jose A.D. Machuca, 'Rapid-fire fulfillment', *Harvard Business Review* (November 2004), pp. 104–10; Brian Dunn, 'Inside the Zara business model', *DNR* (20 March 2006), p. 11; Rachael Tiplady, 'ZARA: Taking the lead in fast- fashion', *BusinessWeek Online* (4 April 2006), accessed at www.businessweek.com/globalbiz/content/apr2006/gb20060404_167078.htm; and annual reports and other information from www.inditex.com, August 2006.

4. Angela Mackay, 'Esprit celebrates its anniversary in style', *Financial Times* (19 September 2003), p. 31.

5. Information from www.franchisor.ikea.com/txtfranchise.html, August 2007.

6. Information on IKEA, the IKEA concept, latest facts and figures and press releases from www.ikea.com; see also Christopher Brown-Humes, 'An empire built on a flat-pack', *Financial Times* (24 November 2003), p. 12.

7. Andrew Yeh, 'McDonald's seeks heavy traffic fast-food expansion', *Financial Times* (21 June 2006), p. 12.

8. Information from www.mind-advertising.com/ch/nestea_ch.htm and www.nestle.com/Our_Brands/Breakfast_Cereals/Overview/Breakfast+Cereals.htm, September 2006. Also see Andrew McMains, 'Anomaly to introduce Gold Peak tea' (25 July 2006), accessed at www.adweek.com.

9. For a discussion of the challenges presented by multi-channel distribution systems, see Matt Hobb and Hugh Wilson, 'The multi-channel challenge', *Marketing Business* (February 2004), pp. 12–15.

10. Astrid Wendlandt, 'Sainsbury to build on deal with Shell', *Financial Times* (3 June 2003), p. 25; Alison Smith, 'Tesco steals a march on local rivals', *Financial Times* (31 October 2002), p. 25.

11. Adam Jones and Elizabeth Rigby, 'Carrefour gets competitive', *Financial Times* (10 March 2006), p. 10.

12. Mike Hinchcliffe, 'Time to take a new look at Netto', *The Retail Bulletin* (23 August 2007), accessed at www.theretailbulletin.com/print.php?

13. For more information on SPAR, visit www.spar.com and www.spar-int.com.

14. 'The bull-dozer of Bentonville slows', *The Economist* (17 February 2007), p. 70; 'Heading for exit', *The Economist* (5 August 2006), p. 54; Elizabeth Rigby, 'Carrefour gets competitive', *Financial Times* (10 March 2006), p. 10; Peggy Hollinger, 'Hypermarket hell: A price war forces Carrefour to defend the home front', *Financial Times* (25 January 2005), p. 15; Bayan Rahman, 'Carrefour begins a new era in Japan', *Financial Times* (6 October 2003), p. 26; Bertrand Benoit, 'Wal-Mart finds German failures hard to swallow', *Financial Times* (12 October 2000), p. 25; Peggy Hollinger, 'A shopping market stacked with difficulties', *Financial Times* (2 August 2000), p. 19.

15. Quotes and information from Normandy Madden, 'Two Chinas', *Advertising Age* (16 August 2004), pp. 1, 22; Dana James, 'Dark clouds should part for international marketers', *Marketing News* (7 January 2002), pp. 9, 13; Russell Flannery, 'Red tape', *Forbes* (3 March 2003), pp. 97–100; and Russell Flannery, 'China: The slow boat', *Forbes* (12 April 2004), p. 76.

16. Andrew Ward, 'An octopus in the shopping trolley', *Financial Times* (11 January 2002), p. 9.

17. For more on channel relationships, see James A. Narus and James C. Anderson, 'Rethinking distribution', *Harvard Business Review* (July–August 1996), pp. 112–20; James C. Anderson and James A. Narus, *Business Market Management* (Upper Saddle River, NJ: Prentice Hall, 1999), pp. 276–88; Jonathon D. Hibbard, Nirmalya Kumar and Louis W. Stern, 'Examining the impact of destructive acts in marketing channel relationships', *Journal of Marketing Research* (February 2001), pp. 45–61; and Stavros P. Kalafatis, 'Buyer–seller relationships among channels of distribution', *Industrial Marketing Management* (April 2002), pp. 215–28.

18. See Heather Harreld and Paul Krill, 'Channel management', *InfoWorld* (8 October 2001), pp. 46–52; and Barbara Darrow, 'Comergent revs up PRM', *CRN* (8 April 2002), p. 60.

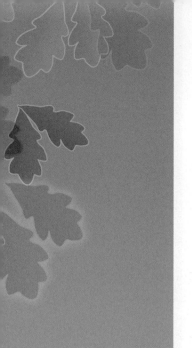

19. See Jonathan Birchall, 'Wal-Mart pushes on with product ID', *Financial Times* (22 February 2007), John Blau, 'RFID – the price must be right', *Financial Times* (30 May 2006) and Jeremy Grant, 'RFID tags take a step forward', *Financial Times* (20 April 2006), all three articles accessed at www.ft.com, September 2007; see also Ann Bednarz, 'IBM has some tall RFID plans', *Network World* (2 May 2005), pp. 17–18; and Jack Neff, 'P&G products to wear wire', *Advertising Age* (15 December 2004), pp. 1, 32.

20. Haig Simon, 'Traffic could clog up road arteries at heart of Europe', *Financial Times* (22 February 2005), p. 20.

21. Simon Brooke, 'It's different for guys', *Financial Times* (28/29 April 2007), p. 7.

22. Information on ChemConnect from www.chemconnect.com; see also www.covisint.com for information on the automotive B2B exchange.

23. Andrew Ward, 'Where winners are fast rather than large', *Financial Times Special Report* (27 March 2007), p. 2.

24. For more discussion on emerging models of retailing, see 'Reinventing the store', *The Economist* (22 November 2003), pp. 89–91.

25. Don E. Schultz, 'Another turn of the wheel', *Marketing Management* (March–April 2002), pp. 8–9.

26. S.C. Hollander, 'Notes on the retail accordion', *Journal of Retailing*, **42**, 2 (1966), p. 24; Neil Buckley, 'Still shopping as the margins drop', *Financial Times* (4 August 1994), p. 15; Cathy Hart, 'The retail accordion and assortment strategies: an exploratory study', *International Review of Retail Distribution and Consumer Research*, **9** (April 1999), pp. 111–26.

27. 'Clicks, bricks and bargains', *The Economist* (3 December 2005), pp. 59–60.

28. See 'Best of the Web – The top 50 retailing sites', *Internet Retailer* (December 2004), accessed at www.internetretailer.com; Sungwook Min and Mary Wolfinbarger, 'Market share, profit margin, and marketing efficiency of early movers, bricks and clicks, and specialists in e-commerce', *Journal of Business Research* (August 2005), pp. 1030–9; and 'Peapod and Scholastic deliver highest consistency rate', *Internet Retailer* (10 May 2006), accessed at www.internetretailer.com.

29. Maija Palmer, 'Internet shopping tops £100 billion', *Financial Times* (18 May 2007), p. 3; Elizabeth Rigby, 'Online tricks turn browsers to sales clicks', *Financial Times* (18 May 2007), p. 3; 'Clicks, bricks and bargains', *The Economist* (3 December 2005), pp. 75–6; 'Storm clouds over the mall', *The Economist* (8 October 2005), pp. 77–8.

30. Alice Z. Cuneo, 'What's in store?', *Advertising Age* (25 February 2002), pp. 1, 30–1. Also see Robert Berner, 'Dark days in white goods for Sears', *BusinessWeek* (10 March 2003), pp. 78–9.

31. See 'The Fortune 500', *Fortune* (17 April 2006), p. F1.

32. See '2006 global powers of retailing', *Stores* (January 2006), accessed at http://www.nxtbook.com/nxtbooks/nrfe/stores0106-globalretail/index.php; Nicholas George, 'Hennes to accelerate global expansion', *Financial Times* (30 January 2004), p. 31; 'H&M to expand small store concept', *Financial Times* (7 March 2003), p. 27; and Tim Craig, 'Carrefour: at the intersection of global', *Dsn Retailing Today* (18 September 2000), p. 16.

33. 'Global top 5 retailers drive expansion', www.freshplaza.com/news_detail.aso?id=1785 (23 May 2007), accessed September 2007; see also Dexter Roberts, Wendy Zellner and Carol Matlack, 'Let the retail wars begin', *BusinessWeek* (17 January 2005), pp. 44–5; 'Carrefour: at the intersection of global', *Dsn Retailing Today* (18 September 2000), p. 16; 'Top 250 global retailers', *Stores* (January 2006), accessed at http://www.nxtbook.com/nxtbooks/nrfe/stores0106-globalretail/index.php; and information from www.walmartstores.com and www.carrefour.com, accessed October 2006.

Company case 19 Zara – the fast and furious giant of fashion

One global retailer is expanding at a dizzying pace. It is on track for what appears to be world domination of its industry. Having built its own state-of-the-art distribution network, the company is leaving the competition in the dust in terms of sales and profits, not to mention speed of inventory management and turnover. Wal-Mart, you might think? No! Tesco, possibly? No! The company is Zara, the flagship speciality chain of Spain-based clothing conglomerate, Inditex. Forget football stars, the Costa del Sol and Real Madrid, they are nothing compared with Zara as Spain's most successful international export. And it has other retailers reeling as Zara's low-cost, fast fashion takes global markets by storm.

This dynamic retailer is known for selling stylish designs that resemble those of big-name fashion houses but at moderate prices. 'We sell the latest trends at low prices, but our clients value our design, quality, and constant innovation,' a company spokesman said. 'That gives us the advantage even in highly competitive, developed markets, including Britain.' More interesting is the way that Zara achieves its mission.

Fast fashion – the newest wave

A handful of European speciality clothing retailers are taking the fashion world by storm with a business model that has come to be known as 'fast-fashion'. In short, these companies can recognise and respond to fashion trends very quickly, create products that mirror the trends, and get those products onto shelves much faster and more frequently than the industry norm. Fast-fashion retailers include Sweden's Hennes & Mauritz (H&M), Britain's Top Shop, Spain's Mango and the Netherlands' Mexx. Although all of these companies are successfully employing the fast-fashion concept, Zara leads the pack in virtually every way.

For example, 'fast' at Zara means that it can take a product from concept through design, manufacturing and store shelf placement in as little as two weeks, much quicker than any of its fast-fashion competitors. For more mainstream clothing chains, such as Gap and Next, the process takes months.

This gives Zara the advantage of virtually copying fashions from the pages of *Vogue* and having them on the streets in dozens of countries before the next issue of the magazine even hits the newsstands! When Spain's Crown Prince Felipe and Letizia Ortiz Rocasolano announced their engagement in 2003, the bride-to-be wore a stylish white trouser suit. This raised some eyebrows, given that it violated royal protocol. But women loved it and within a few weeks, hundreds of them were wearing a nearly identical outfit they had purchased from Zara.

But Zara is more than just fast. It's also prolific. In a typical year, Zara launches about 11,000 new items. Compare that to the 2,000 to 4,000 items introduced by both H&M and Gap. In the fashion world, this difference is huge. Zara stores receive new merchandise two to three times each week, whereas most clothing retailers get large shipments on a seasonal basis, four to six times per year.

By introducing new products with frequency and in higher numbers, Zara produces smaller batches of items. Thus, it assumes less risk if an item doesn't sell well. But smaller batches also mean exclusivity, a unique benefit from a mass-market retailer that draws young fashionistas through Zara's doors like a magnet. When items sell out, they are not restocked with another shipment. Instead, the next Zara shipment contains something new, something different. Popular items can appear and disappear within a week. Consumers know that if they like something, they must buy it or miss out. Customers are enticed to check out store stock more often, leading to very high levels of repeat patronage. But it also means that Zara doesn't need to follow the industry pattern of marking prices down as the season progresses. Thus, Zara reaps the benefit of prices that average much closer to the list price.

The vertical secret to Zara's success

Just how does Zara achieve such mind-blowing responsiveness? The answer lies in its distribution system. In 1975, Amancio Ortega opened the first Zara store in

Spain's remote north-western town of La Coruña, home to Zara's headquarters. Having already worked in the textile industry for two decades, his experience led him to design a system in which he could control every aspect of the supply chain, from design and production to distribution and retailing. He knew, for example, that in the textile business, the biggest mark-ups were made by wholesalers and retailers. He was determined to maintain control over these activities. Ortega's original philosophy forms the heart of Zara's unique, rapid-fire supply chain today. But it's Zara's high-tech information system that has taken vertical integration in the company to an unprecedented level. According to CEO Pablo Isla, 'Our information system is absolutely avant-garde. It's what links the shop to our designers and our distribution system.'

Zara's vertically integrated system makes the starting point of a product concept hard to nail down. At Zara's headquarters, creative teams of over 300 professionals carry out the design process. But they act on information fed to them from the stores. This goes far beyond typical point-of-sales data. Store managers act as trend spotters. Every day they report hot fads to headquarters, enabling popular lines to be tweaked and slow movers to be whisked away within hours. If customers are asking for a rounded neck on a vest rather than a V neck, such an item can be in stores in seven to ten days. This process would take traditional retailers months.

Managers also consult a personal digital assistant every evening to check what new designs are available and place their orders according to what they think will sell best to their customers. Thus, store managers help shape designs by ensuring that the creative teams have real-time information based on the observed tastes of actual consumers. Mr Ortega refers to this as the democratisation of fashion.

When it comes to sourcing, Zara's supply chain is unique as well. Current conventional wisdom calls for manufacturers in all industries to outsource their goods globally to the cheapest provider. Thus, most of Zara's competitors contract manufacturing out to low-wage countries, notably Asia. But Zara makes 40 per cent of its own fabrics and produces more than half of its own clothes, rather than relying on a hodgepodge of slow-moving suppliers. Even things that are farmed out are done locally in order to maximise time efficiency. Nearly all Zara clothes for its stores worldwide are produced in its remote corner of Spain.

As it completes designs, Zara cuts fabric in-house. It then sends the designs to one of several hundred local cooperatives for sewing, minimising the time for raw material distribution. When items return to Zara's facilities, they are ironed by an assembly line of workers who specialise in a specific task (lapels, shoulders, and so on). Clothing items are wrapped in plastic and transported on conveyor belts to a group of giant warehouses.

Zara's warehouses are a vision of modern automation as swift and efficient as any automotive or consumer electronics plant. Human labour is a rare sight in these cavernous buildings. Customised machines patterned after the equipment used by overnight parcel services process up to 80,000 items an hour. The computerised system sorts, packs, labels and allocates clothing items to every one of Zara's 1,000-plus stores. For stores within a 24-hour drive, Zara delivers goods by truck, whereas it ships merchandise via cargo jet to stores farther away.

Domestic manufacturing pays off

The same philosophy that has produced such good results for Zara has led parent company Inditex to diversify. Its other chains now include underwear retailer Oysho, teen-oriented Bershka and Stradivarius, children's Kiddy's Class, menswear Massimo Duti, and casual and sportswear chain Pull & Bear. Recently, Inditex opened its first non-clothing chain, Zara Home. Each chain operates under the same style of vertical integration honed at Zara.

Making speed the main goal of its supply chain has really paid off for Inditex. In 2005, sales grew by 21 per cent over the prior year to €6bn (retail revenue growth worldwide averages single-digit increases). That puts Inditex ahead of H&M in the fast-fashion category for the first time. During the same period, profits soared by 26 per cent to $712m. Most of this performance was driven by Zara, now ranked number 73 on Interbrand's list of top 100 most valuable worldwide brands. Although Inditex has grown rapidly, it only wants more. In 2005, it opened 448 new stores (H&M added only 145) and had plans for 490 more. With more than one ribbon-cutting ceremony per day, Inditex could increase its number of stores from the current 2,900 to as many as 5,000 stores in 70 countries by the end of this decade.

After European clothing stores, including Marks & Spencer, fared badly in the US, European fast-fashion retailers have recently expanded very cautiously in the US (Zara has only 19 stores there so far). But the threat of Zara has US clothing retailers rethinking the models they have relied on for years. According to one analyst, the industry may soon experience a reversal from outsourcing to China to manufacturing in America, despite its relatively high costs:

> 'US retailers are finally looking at lost sales as lost revenue. They know that in order to capture maximum sales they need to turn their inventory much quicker. The disadvantage of importing from China is that it requires a longer lead time of between three to six months from the time an order is placed to when the inventory is stocked in stores. By then the trends may have changed and you're stuck with all the unsold inventory. If retailers want to refresh their merchandise quicker, they will have to consider sourcing at least some of the merchandise locally.'

So being the fastest of the fast-fashion retailers has not only paid off for Zara, its model has reconfigured the fashion landscape everywhere. Zara has blazed a trail for cheaper and cheaper fashion-led mass retailers, has put the squeeze on mid-priced fashion, and has forced luxury brands to scramble to find ways to set themselves apart from Zara's look-alike designs. Leadership certainly has its perks.

Questions

1. As completely as possible, sketch the supply chain for Zara from raw materials to consumer purchase.

2. Discuss the concepts of horizontal and vertical conflict as they relate to Zara.

3. Which type of vertical marketing system does Zara exhibit? List all the benefits that Zara receives by having adopted this system.

4. Does Zara incur disadvantages from its 'fast-fashion' distribution system? Are these disadvantages offset by the advantages?

5. How does Zara add value for the customer through major logistics functions?

SOURCES: 'The future of fast fashion', *The Economist* (18 June 2005); Rachel Tiplady, 'Zara: Taking the lead in fast fashion', *BusinessWeek Online* (4 April 2006); John Tagliabue, 'A rival to Gap that operates like Dell', *New York Times* (30 May 2003), p. W1; Elizabeth Nash, 'Dressed for success', *The Independent* (31 March 2006), p. 22; Parija Bhatnagar, 'Is "Made in U.S.A." back in vogue?' *CNNMoney.com* (1 March 2005); Sarah Mower, 'The Zara phenomenon', *Evening Standard* (13 January 2006), p. 30; and www.inditex.com, August 2006.

The Soundtrack to your Life
THE W800i WALKMAN™ PHONE

Carry up to 125 of your favourite tracks on your mobile with the new Sony Ericsson W800i WALKMAN™ Phone. Simply transfer songs from your computer or CDs and enjoy your music through the crystal clear stereo headset. The W800i also has a 2.0 Megapixel camera with auto focus. So you can take breathtaking shots and store them alongside your prized music collection.

Sony Ericsson

www.SonyEricsson.com/W80

The world is a stage, but the play is badly cast.

OSCAR WILDE

The global marketplace

Mini Contents List

'Drowning yourself in a world of lies
Wandering lost, until the ego dies'

From 'Deadworld' by Shadows Fall, on 'Fallout from the War', Century Media,
B000FKP5JG

Previewing the concepts

We have addressed the fundamentals of how companies develop competitive marketing strategies to create customer value and to build lasting customer relationships. In this chapter, we extend these fundamentals to global marketing. We've visited global topics in previous chapters – it's difficult to find an area of marketing that doesn't contain at least some international issues. Here, however, we'll focus on special considerations that companies face when they market their brands globally. Advances in communication, transportation and other technologies have made the world a much smaller place. Today, almost every firm, large or small, faces international marketing issues. In this chapter, we will examine the key decisions marketers make in going global: analysing the global market environment; deciding whether or not to go international; deciding which markets to enter and how to enter; deciding the global marketing programme; and determining the global marketing organisation.

After reading this chapter, you should be able to:

1. Discuss how the international trade system and the economic, political–legal and cultural environments affect a company's international marketing decisions.
2. Describe three key approaches to entering international markets.
3. Explain how companies adapt their marketing mixes for international markets.
4. Distinguish between the three major forms of international marketing organisation.

These days competing internationally is not an option, it is an imperative. If a company does not go global itself, global competitors will come to it. So, the need to globalise is not just for large businesses but part of the way of life of small to medium-sized businesses that also have resource constraints and lack experience in many of the markets they have to face. We start by looking at just such a case, Jägermeister, a medium-sized family-owned business from Germany that has to find a way of competing against huge international business with its traditional herbal schnapps.

Prelude case Jägermeister Rock'n'Race

Hasso Kaempfe and his team at Jägermeister face the unenviable task of surviving as a medium-sized family-owned outfit, in a difficult economic environment, with the help of a single product that is hardly a 'must-have'. Yet Mr Kaempfe has no reason to regret his decision, five years ago, to leave his job on the board of Tchibo, the Hamburg-based coffee roasting empire, and head to the town of Wolfenbüttel to take on the task of managing Jägermeister, the liqueur maker. At the very least, the job has provided the pleasant challenge of selling a product whose image has traditionally been more closely associated with hunting and grandmothers' after-dinner tipples than the up-and-coming, free-spending group most beverages companies like to woo. Jägermeister, which is sold in chunky green bottles emblazoned with a stag, is made to a closely guarded recipe using 56 herbs and spices. The tangy herbal taste and brown colour of this 'odd-tasting German liqueur' are more reminiscent of cough syrup than the fashionable alcopops and flavoured vodkas currently in vogue in student bars and trendy restaurants across the world. Yet the Jägermeister name is now better known than ever before in the company's 125-year history.

Mr Kaempfe's approach has differed from that generally seen in the industry. Rather than trying to enforce a single, blanket image across all its geographical markets, the company has adapted the Jägermeister brand and marketing strategy for each country. Most companies try to market products with a single image that makes them instantly recognisable anywhere in the world. 'Becks, Campari, Sol, Corona, Jack Daniels, all have a single global image carefully nurtured and pushed by their respective owners. Country-specific advertising exists, but the overall image is the same,' says Mr Kaempfe. This approach is not without merits, he says, but impractical for a niche company such as Jägermeister.

Rather than fearing that diversity could dilute brand recognition, Mr Kaempfe insists it is a vital factor in Jägermeister's success and future survival in the face of shifting tastes. 'We have slightly different images in our various key markets. This hedges the risk we have as a single-product company and means we see no need to diversify by buying in other brands,' he says.

Fifty-eight per cent of sales now go abroad (up from 46 per cent in 1998), and group sales have risen to €222m (£153m) from DM365m (€182m) in 1998. Nearly 30 per cent goes to the US, despite a name that hardly trips off the tongue and the fact that the US has little tradition of drinking schnapps. Jägermeister's initial success in the US is based on its positioning in bars in the late 1990s. Jägermeister's owes much of its US success to Sidney Frank, a colourful American octogenarian who made the 'odd-tasting German liqueur' into a major drinks brand. He is now a key figure in the remarkable rise of vodka over the past 10 years, having worked out in the mid-1990s that the world was ready and waiting for super-premium vodka – and willing to pay a super-premium price for it. In the summer of 1996, he came up with the name Grey Goose even before its distinctive bottles had been designed and before its distillery had been built.

Mr Frank succeeded in building up Jägermeister's popularity via product promotions and sponsorship. As a result, any college student in the US is likely to know the drink as something they have got drunk on at least once in the past year. Jägermeister spends no money on media advertising in the US. Instead, 'Jägerettes' girls dispense samples with a touch of raunchiness and its garish orange banners and T-shirts are common at US music events. In this way, it has become a 'college dorm joy-juice' with Jack Daniels and José Cuervo as its main competitors. The brand's youthful and somewhat aggressive US image is perpetuated through heavy metal music on jagermusic.com and Jägermeister tours featuring bands such as Shadows Fall, a Grammy-nominated heavy metal band that is 'among the most potent music forces in modern metal, melding full-on thrash power with melodic, pulverizing hooks.' Another powerful promotion is NHRA Jäger Racing, 'the fastest and most extreme of all motor sports', which pits four top professional categories (Pro Stock Car, Pro Stock Bike, Funny Car and Top Fuel) in a fast head-to-head competition down a quarter-mile track.

Ironically, few Europeans are aware that Jägermeister has attained cult status among US students, because their image of the liqueur is very different. In Italy, Jägermeister's second biggest export market, the drink is considered an upmarket, elegant version of local digestivi (after-dinner drinks) such as Ramazzotti and Averna, rather than the stuff of wild college parties. In the UK, Jägermeister is slowly gaining a foothold by targeting young adults in their twenties. Germans, meanwhile, continue to see Jägermeister as a traditional schnapps, albeit one with an increasingly cool image. The company uses Jägerettes, promotion activities and give-aways in its home country but it focuses less on universities and music sponsorship. It can also afford classic media advertising. Backed by a cheeky campaign featuring two talking wall-mounted stags, Jägermeister has undergone one of the most successful brand rejuvenations ever seen in Germany.

Beyond that, Mr Kaempfe plans to promote the brand in central and eastern Europe, Spain and Finland and, longer term, in Australia and Brazil. Judging by the speed of its growth over the past five to six years, those countries may not have long to wait. 'But we can afford to be patient,' says Mr Kaempfe. 'That is one of the advantages about being family-owned; we do not constantly have to produce rapid growth for each quarterly report.'[1]

Questions

You should attempt these questions only after completing your reading of this chapter.

1. What are the key factors that Jägermeister should consider when deciding on which new country-markets to enter?
2. What modes of market entry might Jägermeister consider when expanding into new foreign markets? Assess their merits and disadvantages.
3. What constitutes an effective global marketing programme for a company such as Jägermeister?

Global marketing today

Companies pay little attention to international trade when the home market is big and teeming with opportunities. The home market is also much safer. Managers do not need to learn other languages, deal with strange and changing currencies, face political and legal uncertainties or adapt their products to different customer needs and expectations. Jägermeister originated as a domestic product but has already shown how the fortunes of a company can be transformed by success in international markets. The company also realises that today, for itself and all other companies, the situation is different. The world is shrinking rapidly with the advent of faster communication, transportation and financial flows. The business environment is changing and firms cannot afford to ignore international markets. Products developed in one country – Gucci handbags, Sony electronics, Italian pizzas, Japanese sushi, German BMWs – are finding enthusiastic acceptance in other countries.

International trade is booming. Since 1969, the number of multinational corporations in the world has grown from 7,000 to more than 70,000. Some of these multinationals are true giants. In fact, of the largest 100 'economies' in the world, only 53 are countries. The remaining 47 are multinational corporations. Exxon Mobil, the world's largest company, has annual revenues greater than the gross domestic product of all but the world's 21 largest-GDP countries.[2]

Since 2003, total world trade has been growing at 6 to 10 per cent annually, while global gross domestic product has grown at only 2.5 to 4 per cent annually. World trade of products

Many companies have made the world their market: opening megastores in Milan, London, Los Angeles, Vienna and Tokyo.
SOURCE: Virgin Cosmetics Company.

and services was valued at over 12.4 trillion dollars in 2005, which accounted for about 28 per cent of gross domestic product worldwide. This trade growth is most visible in developing countries, such as China, which saw their share of world exports rise sharply to 24 per cent in 2005.[3] For some countries, such as The Netherlands and Hungary, exports and imports of goods and services amounted to more than 140 per cent of the country's GDP in 2006. In stark contrast, for Singapore and Hong Kong – which exist for trade – this was over 400 per cent of their GDP.[4]

Many European and US companies have long been successful at international marketing: Unilever, Philips, Royal Dutch Shell, HSBC, Mercedes, GlaxoSmithKline, Colgate, Danone, Rolls Royce, Volvo, Siemens and dozens of other western firms have made the world their market. And across the globe, names such as IKEA, Nokia, Nestlé, Gillette, Samsung, Sony, Toyota and BP have become household words.

Home markets are no longer as rich in opportunity.

But while global trade is growing, global competition is intensifying. Foreign firms are expanding aggressively into new international markets, and home markets are no longer as rich in opportunity. For example, facing declining or stagnating beer sales in traditional markets in Western Europe, Danish brewer group Carlsberg, along with other big brewing groups, are moving more to emerging markets in Russia, eastern Europe and Asia. Retailers like Tesco, Carrefour, Metro and others have expanded rapidly into countries across the globe. Few industries are now safe from foreign competition. If companies delay taking steps towards internationalising, they risk being shut out of growing markets in western and eastern Europe, India, China and the Pacific Rim, Russia and elsewhere. Firms that stay at home to play it safe not only might lose their chances to enter other markets but also risk losing their home markets. Domestic companies that never thought about foreign competitors suddenly find these competitors in their own backyards.

Ironically, although the need for companies to go abroad is greater today than in the past, so are the risks. Companies that go global may face highly unstable governments and currencies, restrictive government policies and regulations and high trade barriers. Corruption is also an increasing problem – officials in several countries often award business not to the best bidder but to the highest briber.

Still, companies selling in global industries have no choice but to internationalise their operations and strive to be a global firm. A **global industry** is one in which the strategic positions of competitors in given geographic or national markets are affected by their overall global positions. A **global firm** is one that, by operating in more than one country, gains research and development, production, marketing and financial advantages that are not available to purely domestic competitors. The global company sees the world as one market. **Global marketing** is concerned with integrating or standardising marketing actions across a number of geographic markets. This does not rule out adaptation of the marketing mix to individual countries, but suggests that the firm, where possible, takes advantage of the similarities between markets to build competitive advantage. It minimises the importance of national boundaries, and raises capital, obtains materials and components, and manufactures and markets its goods wherever it can do the best job. For example, Otis Elevator gets its elevators' door systems from France, small geared parts from Spain, electronics from Germany and special motor drives from Japan. It uses the United States only for systems integration. Thus global firms gain advantages by planning, operating and coordinating their activities on a worldwide basis. These gains are a key reason behind the recent global restructuring programmes undertaken by leading German engineering companies. Many are aggressively harnessing the opportunities offered by an interconnected global economy.

Global industry—An industry in which the strategic positions of competitors in given geographic or national markets are affected by their overall global positions.

Global firm—A firm that, by operating in more than one country, gains R&D, production, marketing and financial advantages that are not available to purely domestic competitors.

Global marketing—Marketing that is concerned with integrating or standardising marketing actions across different geographic markets.

Festo, a maker of motors for automation technology, manufactures most of its components in Germany, but assembles them locally at its 55 foreign subsidiaries. 'The growth is abroad . . . . Our company lives from globalisation,' says Eberhard Veit, the company's chief executive. Siemens-owned Flender, the gear manufacturer, has production facilities across the world, with over 80 per cent of product sales generated abroad. Manfred Egelwisse, head of Flender, says, 'We need to go where our customers are, where the demand comes from.' According to observers, German firms like these are benefiting from the current investment-driven global growth. German companies, from cars and automation components to construction machinery and machine tools, are responding to the demand for machines and vehicles that faster-growing economies need to build their factories, buildings and infrastructure.[5]

This does not mean that globalisation opportunities are only confined to large companies or that small and medium-sized firms must operate in a dozen countries to succeed. These firms can practise global niching. For example, the main German winners of globalisation in recent years have been the *Mittelstand* – small and mid-sized firms. Among the most successful are highly specialised, often dominant players in niche markets. For example, the world's largest excavator to be used for drilling two giant road tunnels under the Yangtze River is assembled in Shanghai by Black Forest-based Herrenknecht.

Global Internet enterprise is also growing rapidly. For companies that wish to go or stay global, the Internet and online services represent an easy way to get started, or to reinforce other marketing efforts. Moreover, the world is becoming smaller and every business operating in a global industry – whether large or small, online or offline – must assess and establish its place in world markets.

Increasing globalisation means that all companies have to answer some basic questions. What market position should we try to establish in our country, in our economic region (e.g. western Europe, eastern Europe, North America, Asia, Pacific Rim) and globally? Who will our global competitors be, and what are their strategies and resources? Where should we produce or source our products? What strategic alliances should we form with other firms around the world?

As shown in Figure 20.1, a company faces six major decisions in international marketing. Each decision will be discussed in detail.

Looking at the global marketing environment

Doing international business successfully requires firms to take a broad market perspective. Before deciding whether to operate internationally, a company must understand the international marketing environment. That environment has changed a great deal in the last two decades, creating both new opportunities and new problems.

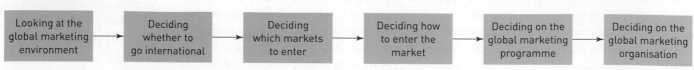

Figure 20.1 Major decisions in international marketing

The international trade system

Companies looking abroad must develop an understanding of the international trade system. When selling to another country, the firm faces various restrictions on trade between nations. Foreign government may charge **tariffs**, taxes on certain imported products designed to either raise revenue or to protect domestic firms. For example, in recent years, the US imposed an average duty of less than 4 per cent on other members of the World Trade Organization compared with India's 18 per cent.[6] Or they may set **quotas**, limits on the amount of foreign imports that they will accept in certain product categories. The purpose of a quota is to conserve foreign exchange and to protect local industry and employment. An **embargo** or boycott, which totally bans some kinds of import, is the strongest form of quota.

Firms may face **exchange controls** which limit the amount of foreign exchange and the exchange rate against other currencies. The company may also face **non-tariff trade barriers**, such as biases against company bids or restrictive product standards that favour or go against product features.

At the same time, certain forces help trade between nations. Examples are the General Agreement on Tariffs and Trade and various regional free trade agreements.

The World Trade Organization and GATT

The General Agreement on Tariffs and Trade (GATT) is designed to promote world trade by reducing tariffs and other international trade barriers. Since the treaty's inception in 1947, member nations (currently numbering 144) have met in eight rounds of GATT negotiations to reassess trade barriers and set new rules for international trade. The first seven rounds of negotiations reduced average worldwide tariffs on manufactured goods from 45 per cent to just 5 per cent.[7]

The most recently completed GATT negotiations, dubbed the Uruguay round, dragged on for seven long years before concluding in 1994. The benefits of the Uruguay round will be felt for many years as the accord promotes long-term global trade growth. It reduced the world's remaining merchandise tariffs by 30 per cent, boosting global merchandise trade by up to 10 per cent, or nearly €320bn in 2002. The agreement also extended GATT to cover trade in agriculture and a wide range of services, and it toughened international protection of copyrights, patents, trademarks and other intellectual property. Although the financial impact of such an agreement is difficult to measure, research suggests that cutting agriculture, manufacturing and services trade barriers by one-third would boost the world economy by $613bn, the equivalent of adding another Australia to the world economy.[8]

Beyond reducing trade barriers and setting international standards for trade, the Uruguay Round established the World Trade Organization (WTO) to enforce GATT rules. In general, the WTO acts as an umbrella organisation, overseeing GATT, mediating global disputes and imposing trade sanctions. The previous GATT organisation never possessed such authorities. A new round of GATT negotiations, the Doha round, began in Doha, Qatar, in late 2001 and was set to conclude in 2005, but the discussions continue.[9]

Regional free-trade zones

Some countries have formed **free-trade zones** or **economic communities** – groups of nations organised to secure common goals in the regulation of international trade. One such community is the European Union (EU). Formed in 1957, the EU set out to create a single European market by reducing barriers to the free flow of products, services, finances and labour among member countries and developing policies on trade with non-member nations. Up until 2004, the EU comprised 15 member countries. However, 10 countries from eastern and central Europe and the Mediterranean – Cyprus, the Czech Republic, Estonia, Hungary, Latvia, Lithuania, Malta, Poland,

Tariff—A tax levied by a government against certain imported products. Tariffs are designed to raise revenue or to protect domestic firms.

Quota—A limit on the amount of goods that an importing country will accept in certain product categories; it is designed to conserve on foreign exchange and to protect local industry and employment.

Embargo—A ban on the import of a certain product.

Exchange controls—Government limits on the amount of its country's foreign exchange with other countries and on its exchange rate against other currencies.

Non-tariff trade barriers—Non-monetary barriers to foreign products, such as biases against a foreign company's bids or product standards that go against a foreign company's product features.

Free-trade zones (or economic communities)—Groups of nations organised to secure common goals in the regulation of international trade.

The WTO and GATT: The General Agreement on Tariffs and Trade (GATT) promotes world trade by reducing tariffs in other international trade barriers. The WTO oversees GATT, imposes trade sanctions and mediates global disputes.

SOURCE: Stockbyte/Getty Images.

Slovakia and Slovenia – joined the EU in 2004, creating one of the world's single largest markets. Bulgaria and Romania became members in 2007. Today, the expanded 27-nation EU contains half a billion consumers and accounts for more than 20 per cent of the world's exports.[10]

European unification offers tremendous trade opportunities for non-European firms. However, it also poses threats. As a result of increased unification, European companies have grown bigger and more competitive. Perhaps an even bigger concern, however, is that lower barriers *inside* Europe will only create thicker *outside* walls. Some observers envisage a 'Fortress Europe' that heaps favours on firms from EU countries but hinders outsiders by imposing obstacles. Fears about the rise of China, India and the other Asian 'tigers' and the need to protect local workers from the impact of globalisation have led to calls to erect higher tariff barriers around the EU. For example, the temporary restraints on exports of Chinese textiles to the EU provide an example of outsiders' fears of such protectionism.[11]

Progress towards European unification, however, has been slow – many doubt that complete unification will ever be achieved. Nonetheless, on 1 January 1999, 11 of the 15 member nations (that is, all but the UK, Greece, Denmark and Sweden) took a significant step towards unification by adopting the euro as a common currency. These were joined by Greece, which became the twelfth member nation to adopt the euro, in January 2001, and Slovenia, the thirteenth, in January 2007. Many other EU countries are expected to follow within the next few years. Widespread adoption of the euro will decrease much of the currency risk associated with doing business in Europe, making member countries with previously weak currencies more attractive markets.[12]

However, even with the adoption of the euro, it is unlikely that the EU will ever go against 2,000 years of tradition and become the 'United States of Europe'. From a marketing viewpoint, creating an economic community will not create a homogeneous market. A community with two dozen different languages and cultures will always have difficulty coming together and acting as a single entity. For example, efforts to forge a single European constitution appear to have failed following French and Dutch 'no' votes in mid-2005. And economic disputes between member nations have stalled long-term budget negotiations. Still, although only partly successful so far, unification has made Europe a global force with which to reckon, with a combined annual GDP of more than €8.9 trillion.[13]

In 1994, the *North American Free Trade Agreement (NAFTA)* established a free-trade zone among the United States, Mexico and Canada. The agreement created a single market of 435 million people who produce and consume $14.4 trillion (€10.7 trillion) worth of goods and services annually. As it is implemented over a 15-year period, NAFTA will eliminate all trade barriers and investment restrictions among the three countries. Thus far, the agreement has allowed trade between the countries to flourish. In the dozen years following its establishment, trade among the NAFTA nations has risen 173 per cent. US merchandise exports to NAFTA partners grew 133 per cent, compared with exports to the rest of the world at 77 per cent. Canada and Mexico are now the nation's first and second largest trading partners.[14]

Following the apparent success of NAFTA, in 2005 the Central American Free Trade Agreement (CAFTA) established a free-trade zone between the United States and Costa Rica, the Dominican Republic, El Salvador, Guatemala, Honduras and Nicaragua. Talks have been underway since 1994 to investigate establishing a Free Trade Area of the Americas (FTAA). This mammoth free-trade zone would include 34 countries stretching from the Bering Strait to Cape Horn, with a population of 800 million and a combined gross domestic product of about $17 trillion.[15]

Other free-trade areas have formed in Latin America and South America. For example, MERCOSUR now links 10 Latin American and South American countries, and the Andean Community (CAN, for its Spanish initials) links five more. In late 2004, MERCOSUR and CAN agreed to unite, creating the South American Community of Nations (CSN), which will be modelled after the European Union. Following the achievement of complete integration between the two trade blocs by 2007, all tariffs between the nations will be eliminated by 2019. With a population of more than 370 million, a combined economy of more than $2.8 trillion a year, and exports worth $181 billion, the CSN will make up the largest trading bloc after NAFTA and the European Union.[16]

Each nation has unique features that must be understood. A country's readiness for different products and services and its attractiveness as a market to foreign firms depend on its economic, political–legal and cultural environments. We address these environmental influences next.

Economic environment

The international marketer must study each country's economy. Two economic factors reflect the country's attractiveness as a market: the country's *industrial structure* and its *income distribution*.

The country's industrial structure shapes its product and service needs, income levels and employment levels. Four types of industrial structure should be considered:

1. *Subsistence economies.* In a subsistence economy, the vast majority of people engage in simple agriculture. They consume most of their output and barter the rest for simple goods and services. They offer few market opportunities.

2. *Raw-material-exporting economies.* These economies are rich in one or more natural resources, but poor in other ways. Much of their revenue comes from exporting these resources. Examples are Chile (tin and copper), the Democratic Republic of Congo (copper, cobalt and coffee) and Saudi Arabia (oil). These countries are good markets for large

Economic environment: Many luxury brand marketers are rushing to take advantage of China's rapidly developing consumer markets.

SOURCE: Fritz Hoffmann.

equipment, tools and supplies, and trucks. If there are many foreign residents and a wealthy upper class, they are also a market for luxury goods.

3. *Industrialising economies.* In an industrialising economy, manufacturing accounts for 10–20 per cent of the country's economy. Examples include Egypt, India and Brazil. As manufacturing increases, the country needs more imports of raw textile materials, steel and heavy machinery, and fewer imports of finished textiles, paper products and motor vehicles. Industrialisation typically creates a new rich class and a small but growing middle class, both demanding new types of imported goods.

4. *Industrial economies.* Industrial economies are large exporters of manufactured goods and investment funds. They trade goods among themselves and also export them to other types of economy for raw materials and semi-finished goods. The varied manufacturing activities of these industrial nations and their large middle class make them rich markets for all sorts of goods. Asia's industrialised economies, such as Taiwan, Singapore, South Korea and Malaysia, fall into this category.

The second economic factor is the country's income distribution. Countries with subsistence economies may consist mostly of households with very low family incomes. In contrast, industrialised economies may have low-, medium- and high-income households. Still other countries may have households with only either very low or very high incomes. However, even poor or developing economies have small but wealthy segments of upper-income consumers. They may become attractive markets for all kinds of goods, including luxuries. For example, many luxury brand marketers are rushing to take advantage of China's rapidly developing consumer markets:[17]

> **"** China's booming economy is minting millionaires [yet] half of China's 1.3 billion consumers can barely afford rice. **"**

More than half of China's 1.3 billion consumers can barely afford rice, let alone luxuries. According to the World Bank, more than 400 million Chinese live on less than $2 a day. Yet posh brands – from Gucci and Cartier to BMW and Bentley – are descending on China in force. How can purveyors of €2,000 handbags, €20,000 watches and €750,000 limousines thrive in a developing economy? Easy, says a Cartier executive. 'Remember, even medium-sized cities in China . . . have populations larger than Switzerland's. So it doesn't matter if the percentage of people in those cities who can afford our products is very small.' Thus, even though China has only 0.2 millionaires per 1,000 residents, it trails only the UK, US and Germany in the total number of millionaires.

Dazzled by the pace at which China's booming economy is minting millionaires and swelling the ranks of the middle class, luxury brands are rushing to stake out shop space, tout their wares, and lay the foundations of a market they hope will eventually include as many as 100 million conspicuous consumers. 'The Chinese are a natural audience for luxury goods,' notes one analyst. After decades of socialism and poverty, China's elite are suddenly 'keen to show off their newfound wealth.'

Europe's fashion houses are happy to assist. Giorgio Armani recently hosted a star-studded fashion show to celebrate the opening of his 12,000-square-foot flagship store on Shanghai's waterfront; Armani promises 30 stores in China before the 2008 Beijing Olympics. Gucci recently opened stores in Hangzhou and Chengdu, bringing its China total to six. And it's not just clothes. Cartier, with nine stores in China and seven on the drawing board, has seen its China sales double for the past several years. Carmakers, too, are racing in. BMW recently cut the ribbon on a new Chinese factory that has the capacity to produce 50,000 BMWs a year. Audi's sleek A6 has emerged as the car of choice for the Communist Party's senior ranks, despite its €170,000 ($230,000) price tag. Bentley, whose limousines are priced at almost €1 million each, boasts three dealerships in China, as does Rolls-Royce.

Thus country and regional economic environments will affect an international marketer's decision about which global markets to enter and how.

Political–legal environment

Nations differ greatly in their political–legal environments. At least four political–legal factors should be considered in deciding whether to do business in a given country: attitudes towards international buying, government bureaucracy, political stability and monetary regulations. We will consider each of these in turn.

Attitudes towards international buying

Some nations are quite receptive to foreign firms, and others are less accommodating. Western firms have found Asian countries such as Singapore and Thailand attractive overseas investment locations. These countries court foreign investors and shower them with incentives and favourable operating conditions. In contrast, others like India are bothersome with their import quotas, currency restrictions and other limitations that make operating there a challenge.

Government bureaucracy

This is the extent to which the host government runs an efficient system for helping foreign companies: efficient customs handling, good market information, and other factors that aid in doing business.

Political stability

Political stability is another issue. Governments change hands, sometimes violently. Even without a change, a government may decide to respond to new popular feelings. For example, India's government is notoriously unstable – the country has elected 10 new governments in the past 20 years – increasing the risk of doing business there. Although most international marketers still find India's huge market attractive, the unstable political situation will affect how they handle business and financial matters.[18]

International marketers may find it profitable to do business in an unstable country, but the unsteady situation will affect how they handle business and financial matters.

Monetary regulations

Companies must also consider a country's monetary regulations. Sellers want to take their profits in a currency of value to them. Ideally, the buyer can pay in the seller's currency or in other world currencies. Short of this, sellers might accept a blocked currency – one whose removal from the country is restricted by the buyer's government – if they can buy other goods in that country that they need themselves or can sell elsewhere for a needed currency. Besides currency limits, a changing exchange rate, as mentioned earlier, creates high risks for the seller.

Most international trade involves cash transactions. Yet many nations have too little hard currency to pay for their purchases from other countries. They may want to pay with other items instead of cash, which has led to a growing practice called **countertrade**.

Countertrade takes several forms. *Barter* involves the direct exchange of goods or services. For example, British coalmining equipment has been 'sold' for Indonesian plywood; Volkswagen cars were swapped for Bulgarian dried apricots; Azerbaijan imported wheat from Romania in exchange for crude oil, and Vietnam exchanged rice for Philippine fertiliser and coconuts.

Another form is *compensation* (or *buyback*), whereby the seller sells a plant, equipment or technology to another country and agrees to take payment in the resulting products. Thus, Japan's Fukusuke Corporation sold knitting machines and raw textile materials to Shanghai clothing manufacturer Chinatex in exchange for finished textiles produced on the machines.

Another common form is *counterpurchase*. Here the seller receives full payment in cash, but agrees to spend some of the money in the other country. For example, Boeing sells aircraft to India and agrees to buy Indian coffee, rice, castor oil and other goods and sell them elsewhere.[19]

Countertrade deals can be very complex. For example, a few years back, DaimlerChrysler agreed to sell 30 trucks to Romania in exchange for 150 Romanian jeeps, which it then sold to Ecuador for bananas, which were in turn sold to a German supermarket chain for German money. Through this roundabout process, DaimlerChrysler finally obtained payment in German money.[20]

Cultural environment

Culture is defined simply as *the learned distinctive way of life of a society*. The dimensions of culture include the social organisation of society, religion, customs and rituals, values and attitudes towards domestic and international life, education provision and literacy levels, political system, aesthetic systems (e.g. folklore, music, arts, literature) and language. Each country has its own folkways, norms and taboos. When designing global marketing strategies, companies must understand how culture affects consumer reactions in each of its international markets. In turn, they must also understand how their strategies affect local cultures.

The impact of culture on marketing strategy

Companies must examine the ways consumers in different countries think about and use certain products or services before planning a marketing programme. There are often surprises.

For example, the average Frenchman uses almost twice as many cosmetics and beauty aids as does his female partner. The Germans and the French eat more packaged, branded spaghetti than do Italians. Italian children like to eat chocolate bars between slices of bread as a snack. In Belgium, do not be surprised to find that clothes for baby girls are trimmed with blue and those for baby boys with pink.

Business norms and behaviour also vary from country to country. Business executives need to be briefed on these factors before conducting business in another country. For example, American

---

Countertrade— International trade involving the direct or indirect exchange of goods for other goods instead of cash. Forms include barter compensation (buyback) and counterpurchase.

Culture—The set of basic values, perceptions, wants and behaviours learned by a member of society from family and other important institutions.

executives like to get right down to business and engage in fast and tough face-to-face bargaining. However, Japanese and other Asian businesspeople often find this behaviour offensive. They prefer to start with polite conversation, and they rarely say no in face-to-face conversations. As another example, South Americans like to sit or stand very close to each other when they talk business – in fact, almost nose-to-nose. The American business executive tends to keep backing away as the South American moves closer. Both may end up being offended. Business executives need to be briefed on these kinds of factors before conducting business in another country.[21]

Here are some examples of different global business behaviour:

- In face-to-face communications, Japanese business executives rarely say 'no' to the western business executive. Thus westerners tend to be frustrated and may not know where they stand. Where westerners come to the point quickly, Japanese business executives may find this behaviour offensive.

- In France, wholesalers tend not to promote a product. They ask their retailers what they want and deliver it. If a foreign company builds its strategy around the French wholesaler's cooperation in promotions, it is likely to fail.

- When British executives exchange business cards, each usually gives the other's card a cursory glance and stuffs it in a pocket for later reference. In Japan, however, executives dutifully study each other's cards during a greeting, carefully noting company affiliation and rank. They hand their card to the most important person first.

- In the United Kingdom and the United States, business meals are common. In Germany, these are strictly social. Foreigners are rarely invited to dinner and such an invitation suggests a very advanced association. The opposite applies in Italy where entertaining is an essential part of business life (guests should offer to pay but, in the end, should defer to their Italian host). In France, watch out. There are two kinds of business lunch – one for building up relations, without expecting anything in return, and the other to discuss a deal in the making or to celebrate a deal afterwards. Deals, however, should be concluded in the office, never over a lunch table.

- Shaking hands on meeting and on parting is common in Germany, Belgium, France and Italy. Ignoring this custom, especially in France, causes offence. In France, it is advisable to shake hands with everyone in a crowded room.

By the same token, companies that understand cultural nuances can use them to advantage when positioning products internationally. For example, consider French cosmetics giant L'Oréal:

It's a sunny afternoon outside Parkson's department store in Shanghai, and a marketing battle is raging for the attention of Chinese women. Tall, pouty models in beige skirts and sheer tops pass out flyers promoting Revlon's new spring colours. But their effort is drowned out by L'Oréal's eye-catching show for its Maybelline brand. To a pulsing rhythm, two gangly models in shimmering Lycra tops dance on a podium before a large backdrop depicting the New York City skyline. The music stops, and a makeup artist transforms a model's face while a Chinese saleswoman delivers the punch line. 'This brand comes from America. It's very trendy,' she shouts into her microphone. 'If you want to be fashionable, just choose Maybelline.' Few of the women in the crowd realise that the trendy 'New York' Maybelline brand belongs to French cosmetics giant L'Oréal. . . .

Blink an eye and L'Oréal has just sold 85 products around the world, from Redken hair care and Ralph Lauren perfumes to Helena Rubinstein cosmetics. In the battle for global beauty markets, L'Oréal has developed a winning formula: . . . conveying the allure of different cultures through its many products. Whether it's selling Italian elegance, New York street smarts, or French beauty through its brands, L'Oréal is reaching out to a vast range of people across incomes and cultures.[22]

Many US companies have developed truly global operations. Coca-Cola offers more than 400 different brands in more than 200 countries including BPM energy drink in Ireland, bitter Mare Rosso in Spain, Sprite Ice Cube in Belgium, Fanta in Chile and NaturAqua in Hungary.

Thus, the key to success for the international marketer lies in assiduously researching and understanding a country's cultural traditions, preferences and behaviours. Building *cultural empathy* in this way helps companies to avoid embarrassing mistakes and to take advantage of cross-cultural opportunities.

The impact of marketing strategy on culture

While marketers worry about the impact of culture on their global marketing strategies, others may be concerned with the impact of marketing strategies on global cultures. For example, social critics contend that large American multinationals such as McDonald's, Coca-Cola, Starbucks, Nike, Microsoft, Disney and MTV aren't just 'globalising' their brands, they are 'Americanising' the world's cultures. They worry that the more people around the world are exposed to the American culture and lifestyle in the food they eat, the stores in which they shop, and the television shows and movies they watch, the more they will lose their individual cultural identities.

> As the unrivalled global superpower, America exports its culture on an unprecedented scale. . . . Sometimes, US ideals get transmitted – such as individual rights, freedom of speech and respect for women – and local cultures are enriched. At other times, materialism or worse becomes the message and local traditions get crushed.[23]

Critics worry that, under such 'McDomination', countries around the globe are losing their individual cultural identities. Teenagers in India watch MTV and ask their parents for more westernised clothes and other symbols of American pop culture and values. Grandmothers in small

European towns no longer spend each morning visiting local meat, fish and produce markets to gather the ingredients for dinner. Instead, they now shop at Carrefour-like supercentres. Women in Saudi Arabia see American films and question their societal roles. In China, most people never drank coffee before Starbucks entered the market. Now Chinese consumers rush to Starbucks stores 'because it's a symbol of a new kind of lifestyle'.

Recently, such concerns have led to a backlash against western, especially American, globalisation. For example, well-known US brands have become the targets of boycotts and protests in some international markets. As symbols of American capitalism, companies such as Coca-Cola, McDonald's, Nike and KFC have been singled out by anti-globalisation protestors in hotspots all around the world. Despite such problems, defenders of globalisation argue that concerns of 'Americanisation' and the potential damage to American brands are overblown. US brands are doing very well internationally. In the most recent Brandz Top 100 Most Powerful Brands survey of global brands, 15 of the top 20 brands were American-owned. This echoes the ranking provided by the *BusinessWeek/*Interbrand survey of global brands, where 12 of the top 15 brands were also American-owned. And based on a recent study of 3,300 consumers in 41 countries, researchers concluded that consumers did not appear to translate anti-American sentiment into anti-brand sentiment:[24]

> **"** Although globalisation may bridge culture gaps, it does not eliminate them. **"**

Although globalisation may bridge culture gaps, it does not eliminate them. More fundamentally, most studies reveal that the cultural exchange goes both ways:[25]

Hollywood dominates the global movie market – capturing 90 per cent of audiences in some European markets. However, British TV is giving as much as it gets in serving up competition to US shows, spawning such hits as 'Who Wants to Be a Millionaire?' and 'American Idol'. And Asian and European cultural imports have increasingly influenced American childhood. Most kids know all about the Power Rangers, Tamagotchi and Pokemon, Sega and Nintendo. And J. K. Rowling's Harry Potter books are shaping the thinking of a generation of youngsters across the globe, not to mention the millions of adults who've fallen under their spell as well. For the moment, English remains cyberspace's dominant language, and having Web access often means that youths across the globe have greater exposure to 'American popular' culture. Yet these same technologies enable Balkan students studying in the United States to hear Webcast news and music from Serbia or Bosnia.

Thus, globalisation is a two-way street. If globalisation has Mickey Mouse ears, it is also wearing a Burberry jacket, talking on a Nokia mobile phone, buying furniture at IKEA, driving a Toyota Camry and watching a Sony big-screen plasma TV.

Deciding whether to go international

Not all companies need to venture into international markets to survive. Many local businesses need to market well only in the local marketplace. Operating domestically is easier and safer. Managers would not need to learn other languages and laws, deal with volatile currencies, face political and legal uncertainties, or redesign their products to suit different customer needs and expectations. However, companies that operate in global industries, where their strategic positions in specific markets are affected strongly by their overall global positions, must compete on a worldwide basis if they are to succeed.

Several factors might draw a company into the international arena. Global competitors offering better products or lower prices might attack the company's domestic market. The company might want to counterattack these competitors in their home markets to tie up their resources. Or the company's domestic market might be stagnant or shrinking and foreign markets present higher sales and profit opportunities. Alternatively, the company might want to enlarge its customer base in order to achieve economies of scale, or is seeking to reduce its dependency on any one market. Finally, the company's customers might be expanding abroad and require international servicing.

Before going abroad, the company must weigh several risks and answer many questions about its ability to operate globally. Can the company learn to understand the preferences and buyer behaviour of consumers in other countries? Can it offer competitively attractive products? Will it be able to adapt to other countries' business cultures and deal effectively with foreign nationals? Do the company's managers have the necessary international experience? Has management considered the impact of regulations and the political environments of other countries?

> **Because of the risks and difficulties of entering international markets, most companies do not act until some situation or event thrusts them into the global arena.**

Because of the risks and difficulties of entering international markets, most companies do not act until some situation or event thrusts them into the global arena. Someone – a domestic exporter, a foreign importer, a foreign government – may ask the company to sell abroad. Or the company may be saddled with overcapacity and must find additional markets for its goods.

Deciding which markets to enter

Before going abroad, the company should define its international *marketing objectives* and *policies*. It should decide what *volume* of foreign sales it wants. Most companies start small when they go abroad. Some plan to stay small, seeing foreign sales as a small part of their business. Other companies have bigger plans, seeing foreign business as equal to or even more important than their domestic business.

The company must decide *how many* countries it wants to market in and *how fast* to expand. Generally, it makes better sense to operate in fewer countries with deeper penetration in each. Companies must be careful not to spread themselves too thin or to expand beyond their capabilities by operating in too many countries too soon.

The company must also decide on the *types* of country to enter. A country's attractiveness depends on the product, geographical factors, income and population, political climate and other factors. The seller may prefer certain countries or parts of the world. In recent years, many major new markets have emerged, offering both substantial opportunities and daunting challenges. The latent needs of consumers in the developing world present huge potential markets for food, clothing, shelter, household appliances, consumer electronics and other goods. As such, many companies are now rushing into eastern and central Europe, China and India with hopes of tapping the unmet needs of these consumers.

After listing possible international markets, the company must screen and rank each one on several factors, including market size, market growth, cost of doing business, competitive

1. Demographic characteristics	4. Technological factors
Size of population	Level of technological skills
Rate of population growth	Existing production technology
Population age composition	Existing consumption technology
	Education levels
2. Geographic characteristics	5. Socio-cultural factors
Climate	Consumer lifestyles, beliefs and values
Country size	Business norms and approaches
Population density – urban, rural	Cultural and social norms
Topographical characteristics	Languages
Transportation structure and market accessibility	6. Political and legal factors
3. Economic factors	National priorities
GDP size and growth	Political stability
Income distribution	Government attitudes towards global trade
Industrial infrastructure	Government bureaucracy
Natural resources	Monetary and trade regulations
Financial and human resources	

Table 20.1 Indicators of market potential

SOURCE: Adapted from P. Douglas, et al. (1982) 'Approaches to assessing international opportunities for small and medium-sized businesses', *Columbia Journal of World Business*, 17(3) Fall, pp. 26–32.

advantage and risk level. The goal is to determine the potential of each market, using indicators like those shown in Table 20.1. Then the marketer must decide which markets offer the greatest long-run return on investment (see Real Marketing 20.1).

Deciding how to enter the market

Once a company has decided to market in a foreign country, it must determine the best mode of entry. Its choices are *exporting*, *joint venturing* and *direct investment*. Figure 20.2 shows these routes to servicing foreign markets, along with the options that each one offers. As we can see, each succeeding strategy involves more commitment and risk, but also more control and potential profits.

Exporting

The simplest way to enter a foreign market is through **exporting**. The company may passively export its surpluses from time to time, or it may make an active commitment to expand exports to a particular market. In either case, the company produces all its goods in its home country. It

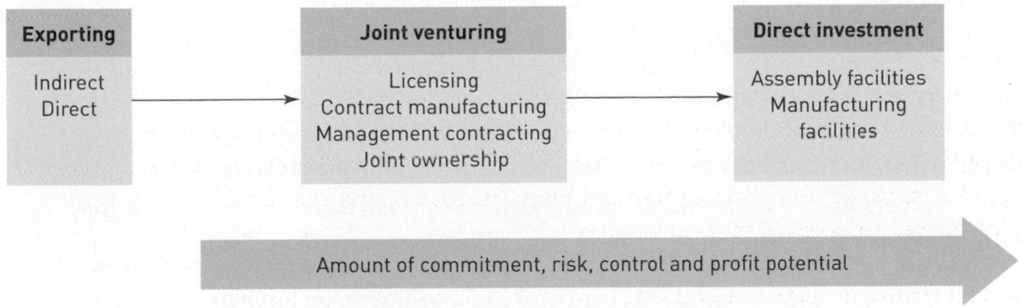

Exporting—Entering a foreign market by selling goods produced in the company's home country, often with little modification.

Figure 20.2 Market entry strategies

Exporting	Joint venturing	Direct investment
Indirect	Licensing	Assembly facilities
Direct	Contract manufacturing	Manufacturing facilities
	Management contracting	
	Joint ownership	

→ Amount of commitment, risk, control and profit potential →

20.1 real marketing

Emerging markets: elusive targets

China and India each have over a billion consumers, presenting tempting prospects for international companies. The reality is that these consumers remain an elusive target. Many dominant brands – from Unilever to Sony, from Mercedes to Ford – have all struggled to deliver on the promise of the 'billion-consumer' markets.

'Huge market out there . . . somewhere'

A common fallacy lies in the thinking that there are huge margins to be gained from skimming the 3 or 5 per cent of affluent consumers in emerging markets who have global preferences for 'luxury goods' and purchasing power. In India, Coca-Cola came in at the top and tried to trickle down. It launched pricey 350 ml bottles instead of offering cheaper, smaller ones. Rather than concentrating on the main towns, it went for the whole of India with a single size and price, using expensive and flawed distribution and advertising. Ford and other motor manufacturers also misjudged the Indian market. They started with medium-sized cars in a market dominated by small ones, and expected to compete with nearly 70 per cent overcapacity in medium-sized car manufacturing. Kellogg's offered premium-priced cereals supported by expensive marketing. They soon learnt that, although market research showed that India was the largest cereal-eating nation on earth, consumers were choosing to buy Champion's products costing a fifth the price of Kellogg's. By contrast, Akai, the Japanese consumer electronics producer, stole a march on global giant Sony by offering cheaper televisions and taking customers' old sets in part-exchange.

Defining the 'consuming class'

Despite the excitement about an 'Indian middle class' some 300 million strong, the 'consuming class', with the discretionary income to splash on Louis Vuitton handbags and Hermès scarves, remains pitifully small. True, the relatively well-off are fast rising, but they are a minority.

Analysts argue that it is important to define the Indian market not by income alone, but by consumption. A disaggregation will yield a demographic pyramid of five layers: the *destitute*, *climbers*, *aspirants*, *consumers* and the *rich* – about 1 million households earning more than Rs 1 million (€25,600) a year. The 30 million people normally identified as consumers have less disposable income than the groups below them, because they tend to spend more on education. The bottom of the pyramid, especially the aspirants, is more attractive because of rising incomes. Hindustan Lever, a 51 per cent subsidiary of Unilever, designed products for each of the five tiers. It began moving goods by road instead of rail, building a network of 40,000 wholesalers and 500,000 retailers and supplying it with credit. It also recognised that two-thirds of people live in the countryside and half work in agriculture. Of the 156 million people aged 12 to 19 that Levi Jeans sought to target, 111 million live in rural India. Aiming at the top tier gives a meagre 500,000 rich urban consumers, potentially yielding slim pickings. Recognising the potential of a market where only 15 per cent of people used shampoos, Hindustan Lever are using new ways like its 'Project Shakti' to reach the rural poor. The project extends its marketing activities by recruiting women to 'self-help' groups, which offer small loans (micro credit) to support a direct-to-home distribution network. By doing so, it now reaches 80,000 villages, and has plans to employ more than 100,000 'shakti entrepreneurs' covering half a million villages by 2010.

Segmentation's key

The key to success lies in developing products for each or most of the five consumption segments, instead of targeting the 'affluent global consumer'. But segmentation of this nature is costly and only justified if consumers are able and willing to pay for specialised products. The experience of GlaxoSmithKline (GSK) in India points to the power of targeting local consumers. But fine segmentation does not have to come at a cost. Horlicks, its flagship product in India, has long been positioned as 'the great family nourisher'. It caught on because of milk shortages and poor health conditions, and people saw a need for a nutritional supplement. GSK built its own supply chain, worked hard at paring costs and pricing, and markets its drink as a nutrient for all seasons and all types. Its supply chain now reaches 375,000 outlets across India. Horlicks refill packages and Horlicks biscuits give consumers the same nutrition at a fraction of the cost of a jar. The Horlicks brand has also been launched into new areas, from Junior Horlicks and Mothers' Horlicks for pregnant or breast-feeding women, to Horlicks for sports, convalescence, the elderly or kids during the monsoon fever period.

Unilever's early, troubled decade and a half in China culminated in recent sweeping restructuring of its Chinese operations, and careful adaptation to the vagaries of operating in this populous market. Its many joint ventures with local companies in sectors ranging from detergents, food and wine to ice-creams, toothpaste and chemicals have been consolidated under three companies: home and personal care; ice-cream; and food and beverages. It has to become more local. R&D is adapted to Chinese tastes and local remedies. Drawing from Hindustan Lever's considerable expertise on selling in rural India, Unilever now targets consumers well beyond China's largest cities and has been increasing the range of prices for its

...20.1

various brands, tapping particularly the lower end of the market. For example, Unilever sells pricier Omo laundry detergents to the wealthy, urban consumer who has a washing machine and is prepared to pay a premium for the detergent. To compete with low-priced mass-market offerings from local upstarts, it also offers its cheaper Sunlight soap to consumers with more modest means.

Increasingly, multinational companies such as Unilever, Procter & Gamble, Nestlé and Coca-Cola are discovering that consumers in emerging markets such as India and China will remain hard to get unless they develop value propositions that appeal to the mass market. Products transplanted from affluent, developed nations tend to appeal to a relatively small élite. International companies must delve deeper into the local consumer base in order to tap the potential of the 'billion-consumer' markets.

SOURCES: David Gardner, 'Slim pickings for the international brand in India', *Financial Times* (10 October 2000), p. 19; 'How Horlicks won an empire', *Financial Times* (10 October 2000), p. 19; Rahul Jacob, 'A Chinese clean-up operation', *Financial Times* (18 May 2000), p. 18; Gordon Redding, 'China: rough but ready for outsiders', *Financial Times, FT Summer School* (26 August 2003), p. 11; *The Economist*, 'From top to bottom', *Now for the hard part. A survey of business in India* (3 June 2006), pp. 16–17; Elizabeth Rigby, 'Smooth supply in high demand', *Financial Times* (14 February 2007), p. 10; Dan Ilet, 'China's very different world', *Financial Times* (12 February 2007), p. 10; *The Economist*, 'Doing business in China: An inspector calls' (24 March 2007), p. 85.

may or may not modify them for the export market. Exporting involves the least change in the company's product lines, organisation, investments or mission.

Indirect exporting

Companies typically start with *indirect exporting*, working through independent international marketing intermediaries. Indirect exporting involves less investment because the firm does not require an overseas marketing organisation or networks. It also involves less risk. International marketing intermediaries – home-based export merchants or agents, cooperative organisations, government export agencies and export-management companies – bring know-how and services to the relationship, so the seller normally makes fewer mistakes.

Direct exporting

Sellers may eventually move into *direct exporting*, whereby they handle their own exports. The investment and risk are somewhat greater in this strategy, but so is the potential return. A company can conduct direct exporting in several ways. It can set up a domestic export department that carries out export activities. Or it can set up an overseas sales branch that handles sales, distribution and perhaps promotion. The sales branch gives the seller more presence and programme control in the foreign market and often serves as a display centre and customer service centre. Or the company can send home-based salespeople abroad at certain times in order to find business. Finally, the company can do its exporting either through foreign-based distributors that buy and own the goods or through foreign-based agents that sell the goods on behalf of the company.

Today, electronic communication via the Internet enables companies, particularly small ones, to extend their reach to worldwide markets. No longer is it necessary for firms to attend overseas trade shows to exhibit their products to overseas buyers and distributors. The Internet has become an effective medium for attaining exporting information and guidelines, doing market research and enabling overseas customers to order and pay for goods.

Joint venturing

A second method of entering a foreign market is **joint venturing** – joining with foreign companies to produce or market products or services. Joint venturing differs from exporting in that the company joins with a host country partner to sell or market abroad. It differs from direct investment in that an association is formed with someone in the foreign country. There are four types of *joint venture*: *licensing*, *contract manufacturing*, *management contracting* and *joint ownership*.

Licensing

Licensing is a simple way for a manufacturer to enter international marketing. The company enters into an agreement with a *licensee* in the foreign market. For a fee or royalty, the licensee buys the right to use the company's manufacturing process, trademark, patent, trade secret or other item of value. The company thus gains entry into the market at little risk; the licensee gains production expertise or a well-known product or brand name without having to start from scratch.

> East European brewers such as the Czech Republic's Pilsner Urquell and the Budvar Company strengthened their international market positions through licensing the production of their beer brands in breweries abroad. Coca-Cola markets internationally by licensing bottlers around the world and supplying them with the syrup needed to produce the product.

Licensing has potential disadvantages, however. The firm has less control over the licensee than it would over its own production facilities. Furthermore, if the licensee is very successful, the firm has given up these profits, and if and when the contract ends, it may find it has created a competitor.

Contract manufacturing

Another option is **contract manufacturing**. The company contracts with manufacturers in the foreign market to produce its product or provide its service. International retailers may use this method in opening up stores in overseas markets, where they would work with qualified local manufacturers to produce many of the products that they sell.

The drawbacks of contract manufacturing are the decreased control over the manufacturing process and the loss of potential profits on manufacturing. The benefits are the chance to start faster, with less risk, and the later opportunity either to form a partnership with or to buy out the local manufacturer.

Management contracting

Under **management contracting**, the domestic firm supplies management know-how to a foreign company that supplies the capital. The domestic firm exports management services rather than products. Hilton uses this arrangement in managing hotels around the world. Management contracting is a low-risk method of getting into a foreign market, and it yields income from the beginning. The arrangement is even more attractive if the contracting firm has

Joint venturing—Entering foreign markets by joining with foreign companies to produce or market a product or service.

Licensing—A method of entering a foreign market in which the company enters into an agreement with a licensee in the foreign market, offering the right to use a manufacturing process, trademark, patent, trade secret or other item of value for a fee or royalty.

Contract manufacturing—A joint venture in which a company contracts with manufacturers in a foreign market to produce the product or provide its service.

Management contracting—A joint venture in which the domestic firm supplies the management know-how to a foreign company that supplies the capital; the domestic firm exports management services rather than products.

an option to buy a share in the managed company later on. The arrangement is not sensible, however, if the company can put its scarce management talent to better uses or if it can make greater profits by undertaking the whole venture. Management contracting also prevents the company from setting up its own operations for a period of time.

Joint ownership

Joint-ownership ventures consist of one company joining forces with foreign investors to create a local business in which they share joint ownership and control. A company may buy an interest in a local firm, or the two parties may form a new business venture. Joint ownership may be needed for economic or political reasons. The firm may lack the financial, physical or managerial resources to undertake the venture alone. UK distiller Diageo uses its joint-venture with the Sichuan Chengdu Quanxing group in China to help package alcohol it sells in China and to develop an international market for Chinese white spirits. Tesco has relied on joint venture partner Hymall to gain a foothold in the Chinese market.

Alternatively, a foreign government may require joint ownership as a condition for entry. For example, until the late 1990s, the Indian government usually required inward investors to team up with a local company to ensure that Indian-owned businesses would gain access to technical know-how. In the last decade, however, the government has lifted many restrictions requiring inward investors to set up joint ventures rather than taking full control of their Indian-based operations. Even so, joint ventures remain mandatory in sectors such as telecommunications, agriculture, retailing and insurance.[26]

Joint ownership has certain drawbacks. The partners may disagree over investment, marketing or other policies. Such conflicts make it hard for the two parties to work well together.

For example, in recent years, Danone's joint venture with Wahaha, the Chinese milk product and bottled water producer, turned sour due to the partner's dissatisfaction with some of the terms of the initial deal, which gave Danone control with a 51 per cent stake. Moreover, the local partner had to get approval from the joint venture to use the Wahaha name on products it launched and accused Danone of taking control of Wahaha subsidiaries which were not part of the joint venture. In turn, Danone accused the Chinese partner of setting up illegal operations to make and sell 'copy-cat' products to ones made by the joint venture.[27]

To be successful, joint ventures require 'give-and-take'. Partners must try to anticipate each other's needs and to do all they can to build a sense of trust and partnership. To enjoy partnership benefits, therefore, collaborators must clarify their expectations and objectives and work hard to secure a win–win outcome for all parties concerned.

Direct investment

The biggest involvement in a foreign market comes through **direct investment** – the development of foreign-based assembly or production facilities (or operations, in the case of a service organisation). If a company has gained experience in exporting and if the foreign market is large enough or growing rapidly, foreign production makes economic sense. For example, Nokia, the Finnish mobile handset manufacturer, initially entered the Chinese market through joint ventures. In 2003, it sought to strengthen its position in China, the world's fastest growing mobile-phone market, by merging its joint venture operations and to start local production of mobile phone handsets.[28] In 1995, Mars set up its own factory and distribution centre in

Stupino, Moscow, to produce chocolates and pet food in response to the rising demand for its products in the Russian market.[29] Foreign production facilities offer many advantages:

1. The firm may have lower costs in the form of cheaper labour or raw materials, foreign government investment incentives and freight savings.

2. The firm may improve its image in the host country because it creates jobs.

3. Generally, a firm develops a deeper relationship with government, customers, local suppliers and distributors, allowing it to adapt its products better to the local market.

4. Finally, the firm keeps full control over the investment and therefore can develop manufacturing and marketing policies that serve its long-term international objectives.

The main disadvantage of direct investment is that the firm faces many risks, such as restricted, devalued or sharply rising currencies, worsening markets or government changes.

For example, early investors in Hungary's automotive industry, such as Opel, the German subsidiary of General Motors, had to make substantial adjustments to their business plans as the economic conditions in the country proved much worse than originally anticipated. More recently, the strengthening of the Hungarian currency, the forint, has pushed labour costs up while reducing productivity growth. In response, foreign direct investors such as Philips of The Netherlands has reduced its workforce in Hungary, while others, like IBM, have closed their factories altogether.[30]

In some cases, a firm has no choice but to accept these risks if it wants to operate in the host country. This was the case with Mars, whose Stupino factory opening in 1995 coincided with the mini-rouble crash, resulting in $100m loss in sales in the year. The Russian subsidiary persevered to make a success of the investment.

By 1998, Mars's Russian operation had built up a $350m a year business. But Russia's default on domestic debt and rouble devaluation threw the business into chaos again. Says Richard Smyth, Mars's general manager for Russia and the Commonwealth of Independent States (CIS), 'We lost 70 per cent of our business in two weeks. Our entire distribution network that we had been investing in for seven years was bankrupt.'

Mars rode the crisis. It retained ownership of products sent to distributors until they were sold. The price was set at what the distributor had to sell daily based on the exchange rate, and distributors remitted immediately what they made to Mars. Thanks to steady economic growth in the last 8 years, Mars's Russian and CIS business has been transformed, with annual sales growth of $100m to $150m a year. Mr Smyth agrees that barriers to doing business remain, but after 16 years the company is used to dealing with the challenges. He contends that Russia is now an opportunity businesses cannot ignore. He adds, 'You do need to invest upfront, because it is competitive; you need to take a position on the market. But my advice is definitely get in here, and get in here now.'[31]

In summary, there are direct and indirect ways of entering a foreign market. Firms seeking to market goods and services in a foreign market should evaluate the alternative modes of entry and choose the most cost-effective path that ensures long-term performance in the selected market.

Deciding on the global marketing programme

The marketing programme for each foreign market must be carefully planned. Managers must first decide on the precise customer target or targets to be served. Then managers have to decide how, if at all, to adapt the firm's marketing mix to local conditions. To do this requires a good understanding of country market conditions as well as cultural characteristics of customers in that market. We have already addressed the need for cultural sensitivity. This section will discuss reasons for standardisation versus adaptation for the global market before highlighting specific international marketing mix decisions.

Standardisation or adaptation for international markets?

Standardised marketing mix—An international marketing strategy for using basically the same product, advertising, distribution channels and other elements of the marketing mix in all the company's international markets.

Adapted marketing mix—An international marketing strategy for adjusting the marketing-mix elements to each international target market, bearing more costs but hoping for a larger market share and return.

At one extreme are companies that use a **standardised marketing mix** worldwide, selling largely the same products and using the same marketing approaches worldwide. At the other extreme is an **adapted marketing mix**. In this case, the producer adjusts the marketing mix elements to each target market, bearing more costs but hoping for a larger market share and return.

The question of whether to adapt or standardise the marketing mix has been much debated in recent years. On the one hand, some global marketers believe that advances in communication, transportation and travel are turning the world into a common marketplace. The development of the Internet, the rapid spread of cable and satellite TV around the world, and the creation of telecommunications networks linking previously remote places have all made the world a smaller place. These marketers claim that consumers around the world are becoming more similar.

For instance, the disproportionately American programming beamed into homes in the developing nations has sparked a convergence of consumer appetites and lifestyles, particularly among youth. Fashion trends spread almost instantly, propelled by TV and Internet chat groups. Around the world, news and comment on almost any topic or product is available at the click of a mouse or twist of a dial. The resulting convergence of needs and wants has created global markets for standardised products, such as Starbucks coffee, Apple iPods and Nokia phones, particularly among the young middle-class. This paves the way for 'global brands' and standardised global marketing. Standardisation results in lower production, distribution, marketing and management costs, and thus lets the company offer consumers higher quality and more reliable products at lower prices. Thus, global branding and standardisation result in greater brand power and reduced costs from economies of scale.

> Global branding and standardisation result in greater brand power and reduced costs from economies of scale.

On the other hand, the marketing concept holds that marketing programmes will be more effective if tailored to the unique needs of each targeted customer group. If this concept applies within a country, it should apply even more in international markets. Despite global convergence, consumers in different countries have widely varied cultural backgrounds, needs and wants, spending power, product preferences and shopping patterns. Because these differences are hard to change, most marketers adapt their products, prices, channels and promotions to fit consumer desires in each country.

However, global standardisation is not an all-or-nothing proposition but rather a matter of degree. Companies may look for more standardisation to help keep down costs and prices and to build greater global brand power. Although standardisation increases efficiency, marketers must

The Italian exec...
Pirelli cam...
globa... & C. SpA.

ensure that they offer what consumers in each country want.[32] Thus, most internati...
marketers suggest that companies should 'think globally but act locally' – that t...
balance between standardisation and adaptation. The corporate level gives...
tion; regional or local units focus on individual consumer differences a...
often a mistake to set out to create a worldwide strategy,' says one ex...
from strong regional [or local] strategies brought together into a glo...

BELGIUM
Festive treat

UK
Festive treat

SWEDEN
Festive treat

Never underestimate the importance of local knowledge.

Mince pies or rice pudding at Christmas? It's just something you know when you're a local.

At HSBC, we have banks in more countries than anyone else. And each one is staffed by local people.

We have offices in 79 countries and territories; Europe, Asia-Pacific, the Americas, the Middle East, and Africa.

Being local enables them to offer insights into financial opportunities and create service initiatives that would never occur to an outsider.

It means our customers get the kind of local knowledge and personal service that you'd expect of a local bank.

And a level of global knowledge and widely sourced expertise that you wouldn't.

HSBC
The world's local bank

...e importance of 'thinking globally, but acting locally'.

...y: Lowe Worldwide. *Photographer*: Richard Pullar.

of marketing for global consumer-goods giant Unilever, puts it this way: 'We're trying to strike a balance between being mindlessly global and hopelessly local.'[33]

> " Think globally but act locally. "

Many possibilities exist between the extremes of standardisation and complete adaptation. For example, although Philips dishwashers, clothes washers and other major appliances share the same interiors worldwide, their outer styling and features are designed to meet the preferences of consumers in different countries. Global companies such as McDonald's have adapted to local cultural values and traditions rather than trying to implement a standard approach across the world. McDonald's uses the same basic fast-food operating model in its restaurants around the world but adapts the environment and menu to local tastes.[34]

In France, McDonald's visitors would be served by hosts in ties and jackets, and offered free chocolates with their coffee. iPods are also placed in restaurants in France so that people can sit and listen to music. In Britain, branches are being refurbished to look more like modish coffee shops. Lime green 'egg' chairs (called egg for the way they cocoon the body), designed by eminent Danish architect Arne Jacobsen, give the restaurants a modern and contemporary feel.

The company has taken its adaptation philosophy even further with the recent introduction of the 'McPassport', which contains details of training and language skills, enabling the holder to work in any branch in Europe. The passport is designed to appeal to Europe's mobile young. 'One of the biggest aspirations of kids is to travel around,' says Denis Hennequin, who is in charge of McDonald's restaurants in Europe. He expects the passport to get a lot of use in countries such as Greece and Italy during summer.

But while he may be happy to see his employees shift countries, he wants the restaurants to retain local customs and to serve foods that locals like. 'We're not the United States of Europe,' he says. 'We've got 41 countries at very different stages of development and we've got to respect that.'

McDonald's in France offers a range of salads and fresh fruit, as well as the Croque McDo, the classic French grilled sandwich. In Portugal, soup is on the menu and when Mr Hennequin is in London he eats the porridge that McDonald's serves for breakfast along with McBacon rolls and sausage and egg McMuffins. Its 'McCafés' in Vienna offer coffee blended to local tastes.

In Korea it sells the Bulgogi Burger, a grilled pork patty on a bun with a garlicky soy sauce. In India, where cows are considered sacred, McDonald's serves McChicken, Filet-O-Fish, McVeggie (a vegetable burger), Pizza McPuffs, McAloo Tikki (a spiced-potato burger) and the Maharaja Mac – two all-chicken patties with special sauce, lettuce, cheese, pickles and onions on a sesame-seed bun. In Japan, you can get the Tatsuta Burger; in Thailand, the McPork Burger with Thai Basil and, in Indonesia, the McTempeh Burger (made from fermented soybeans).

Similarly, South Korean electronics and appliance maker LG Electronics makes and markets its brands globally, but carefully localises its products to the needs of specific country markets (see Real Marketing 20.2).

Product

Five strategies allow for adapting product and marketing communication strategies to a global market (see Figure 20.3).[35] We first discuss the three product strategies and then turn to the two communication strategies.

20.2 real marketing

LG Electronics: think locally; succeed globally

If kimchi is in your fridge, beware. Made from fermented cabbage seasoned with garlic and chilli, kimchi is a popular condiment in Korea. However, if you keep kimchi inside a normal fridge, its strong smell contaminates all your other food.

So, 20 years ago, South Korea's leading appliance manufacturer, LG Electronics, developed a new fridge that solved the problem of the smell of kimchi. It achieved this by including a space that separates kimchi from the rest of your fridge. This product is now owned by 65 per cent of Korean homes.

The kimchi fridge has become a model for the approach that LG uses to expand into new global markets – a passionate focus on in-depth localisation. LG insists on understanding and catering to the idiosyncrasies of local markets through in-country research, manufacturing and marketing. Localisation has been a key element of LG's successful global expansion. 'Gone are the days where you could just roll out one product for the global market,' explains LG's Middle East marketing director. 'We speak to consumers individually.'

LG certainly has been successful globally. The 43,561bn Korean won (€34bn) electronics, telecommunications and appliance powerhouse now operates in more

By thinking locally, LG Electronics is succeeding globally. It makes a kimchi fridge for the Korean market, a shish kebab microwave for the Iranians, karaoke phones for the Russians, and gold-plated 71-inch flat-screen televisions for Middle Easterners with a taste for gilded opulence.

than 39 countries, and 86 per cent of its sales come from markets outside its home country. It's the world's top producer of air-conditioners and one of the top three global players in washing machines, microwaves and refrigerators. The fastest-growing unit within LG Electronics is the mobile handsets division, which has expanded rapidly in recent years and overtook Sony Ericsson towards the end of 2005 to be the world number 4. LG shipped around 55 million handsets over the year. Its mission is to 'make customers happy' worldwide by creating products that change their lives, no matter where they live.

Nowhere is the success of LG's localisation approach more evident than in India, where the company is now the clear leader in virtually every appliance and electronics category – from microwaves to televisions – despite having entered the market in 1997, two years after Samsung. With a population of more than 1 billion that spans several religions and languages, India functions like dozens of smaller regional markets. LG initially differentiated itself by introducing a line of health-oriented products, such as televisions that reduced eye-strain. By 1999, however, it had set up local research and design facilities, manufacturing plants and a network of service centres.

In India, LG launched a selection of fridges that boasted a range of innovative features: bigger water-storage compartments; power supplies that could withstand sudden surges; and brightly coloured finishes that followed local preferences (in the south, for example, consumers prefer red; in Kashmir, they prefer green). LG's marketing research showed that many Indians like to listen to music through their TV so one that can be played at high volume was built. As a result of their endeavours LG now dominates on the subcontinent, with sales of Rs 73bn (€1.3bn) in 2007.

LG is successful globally but it does not come easily. When Kwon 'the knife' Young-soo was appointed in January 2007 as the chief executive of LG Philips LCD, the world's second-largest flat-panel maker, he immediately asked his wife to leave him alone. For one year, in which he would abstain from family events, he would devote himself to saving the struggling joint venture between South Korea's LG Electronics and Philips of the Netherlands. 'I gave up enjoying my personal life and decided to live like a senior high school student ahead of a big exam because I had to find a breakthrough for turning round this company'.

Mr Kwon earned his nickname 'the knife' after, as chief financial officer of LG, he showed he was unafraid to cut costs and improve operational efficiency to turn round his embattled company's fortunes. Taking 'the knife' to LG Philips, he cut 10 per cent of the 22,000 workforce in the first eight months and plans to reduce it by a further 5 per cent by the end of the year.

Even when faced with pre-existing brand loyalties, LG has overcome inertia in emerging markets. For example, in Iran they launched a microwave oven, which at a touch of a button, reheats shish kebabs. As a result, the company claims to have 40 per cent of the Iranian microwave oven market. And, in refrigeration, LG now has fridges that include a special place to store dates, which without being kept cool, spoil easily.

In the Middle East, LG hit the headlines when it launched a 71-inch flat screen TV – plated in gold! It retails for a cool €63,000, and resonates with the region's love for lavishness. Also for the Middle East market is a mobile phone that has an alarm to call its user to prayer five times a day, as well as an in-built compass showing the direction of Mecca.

In Russia, LG's research revealed that many people entertain at home during the country's long winters, prompting the company to develop a karaoke phone that can be programmed with the top 100 Russian songs, whose lyrics scroll across the screen when they're played. The phone is a hit, selling more than 220,000 handsets.

LG will need all of their hard-won experience of adapting to meet the needs of local markets as it enters China. There it will face established domestic competitors such as Haier, the white-goods manufacturer. Replicating its model developed in India, LG has set up significant operations in China, including manufacturing plants and local marketing outfits. Since opening in Beijing in 2002, LG has increased its staff members at its main Chinese R&D offices to over 1,500 people.

They also created an 'LG Village', which reached out to local consumers by reinvigorating a decaying agricultural community and turning it into a showcase for new technology. These efforts are already working. In 2007, LG's sales in China were 60bn yuan (€5.8bn).

Not all LG's success is about going local. LG is an aggressive innovator. Faced with market fears about whether the next DVD format will be HD-DVD or Blu-ray, LG launched its SMB (Super Multi Blue) combination player that runs both. To make it even more future-proof, the machine has multi-resolution output, so if you don't yet have one of those full 1080p screens, you can still enjoy viewing at 720p. LG says, 'It will also up-res your back catalogue of standard definition DVDs to 1080p and supports myriad AV formats such as MPEG II, H.264 and Dolby Digital Plus.'

Thus, from Korean kimchi to Indian cricket mania to Russian karaoke, LG's unrelenting commitment to localisation is winning the company waves of new customers around the globe. By thinking locally, LG is succeeding globally.

SOURCES: Adapted from Elizabeth Esfahani, 'Thinking locally, succeeding globally', *Business 2.0* (December 2005), pp. 96–8. Also see Evan Ramstas, 'LG Electronics' net surges 91 percent as cell phone margins improve', *Wall Street Journal* (25 January 2006), p. B2; Song Jung-a, 'Trailblazer who is not afraid to wait', *Financial Times* (9 September 2007); 'Dominic Timms LGBH200: Early adopter', *The Guardian* (17 September 2007); www.lge.com (December 2006) and http://uk.lge.com (September 2007).

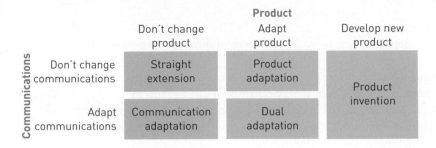

Figure 20.3 Five international product and promotion strategies

Straight product extension means marketing a product in a foreign market without any change. Straight extension has been successful in some cases. Heineken beer, Kellogg's cereals, Gillette razors and Black & Decker tools are all sold successfully in about the same form around the world. Straight extension is tempting because it involves no additional product-development costs, manufacturing changes or new promotion. But it can be costly in the long run if products fail to satisfy foreign consumers.

Product adaptation involves changing the product to meet local conditions or wants. For example, Nokia customises its mobile phones for every major market. Developers build in rudimentary voice recognition for Asia where keyboards are a problem and raise the ring volume so phones can be heard on crowded Asian streets. Philips began to make a profit in Japan only after it reduced the size of its coffee makers to fit into smaller Japanese kitchens and its shavers to fit smaller Japanese hands. Komatsu, the Japanese construction machinery maker, had to alter the design of the door handles of earthmovers sold in Finland: drivers wearing thick gloves in winter found it impossible to grasp the door handles, which were too small (obviously designed to fit the fingers of the average Japanese, but not the double-cladded ones of larger European users!).[36]

Product invention consists of creating something new for the foreign market. This strategy can take two forms. It might mean maintaining or reintroducing earlier product forms that happen to be well adapted to the needs of a given country, or a company might create a new product to meet a need in another country.

Straight product extension—Marketing a product in a foreign market without any change.

Product adaptation—Adapting a product to meet local conditions or wants in foreign markets.

Product invention—Creating new products or services for foreign markets.

Women around the world have different grooming habits. Japanese women, for example, don't just cleanse their faces once, but twice. She will brush her eyelashes with mascara 80 to 100 times, while her German counterpart will apply the wand fewer than a dozen times. Brazilians consume the most nail polish, making it integral to the beauty routine. And hairspray can be used in 12 very different ways.

'Japanese women prefer to use a compact foundation rather than a liquid,' says Eric Bone, managing director of L'Oréal's Tokyo Research Centre. 'Humidity [in Japan] is much higher and the emphasis is on long-lasting coverage.' As a result, L'Oréal develops compacts rather than liquids for the local market. And for the Japanese woman who uses so much mascara, L'Oréal makes lighter formulations than those it sells in Europe or America. According to Harvey Gedeon, executive vice-president, global research and development for cosmetics giant Estée Lauder, Asian countries are big markets for skincare products that create a more even skin tone and help diminish the appearance of brown spots. There is less demand for these products in countries like the US and UK. Estée Lauder therefore makes special skincare products that whiten and brighten the skin tone for the Asian market. It is also working with the Shanghai Innovation Centre to study the use of traditional Chinese herbs and botanicals and how they might be integrated into their products. Product invention can be costly, but the pay-offs from localised attention are worthwhile as companies increasingly look to China, where the market for cosmetics and skincare is over €350m and estimated to rise more than 54 per cent by 2009.[37]

Promotion

Companies can either adopt the same promotion strategy in different countries or change it for each local market.

Consider advertising messages. Some global companies use a standardised advertising theme around the world. For example, IBM Global Services runs virtually identical 'People Who Think. People Who Do. People Who Get It.' ads in dozens of countries around the world. Of course, even in highly standardised communications campaigns, some small changes might be required to adjust for language and minor cultural differences.

Sometimes the copy is varied in minor ways to adjust for language differences. Colours may also be changed to avoid taboos in other countries. For example, in Spain, packaging that uses red and yellow, the colours of the Spanish flag, may be seen as an offence to Spanish patriotism. In Greece, purple should be avoided as it has funeral associations. Black is an unlucky colour for the Chinese, white is a mourning colour in Japan, and green is associated with jungle sickness in Malaysia.[38]

> **Many global companies have had difficulty crossing the language barrier.**

Indeed, many global companies have had difficulty crossing the language barrier, with results ranging from mild embarrassment to outright failure. Seemingly innocuous brand names and advertising phrases can take on unintended or hidden meanings when translated into other languages. Careless translations can make a marketer look downright foolish to foreign consumers. The classic language blunders in international marketing involve standardised brand names that do not translate well. Consider the following blunders global companies have made when crossing the language barrier:

Some companies standardise their advertising around the world, adapting only to meet cultural differences. Guy Laroche uses similar ads in Europe (left) and Arab countries (right), but tones down the sensuality in the Arab version – the man is clothed and the woman barely touches him.

SOURCE: Courtesy of Bernard Matussiere.

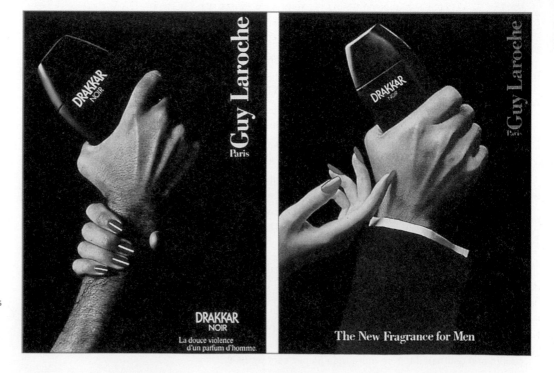

968

In Sweden, Helene Curtis changed the name of its 'Every Night Shampoo' to 'Every Day' because Swedish consumers usually wash their hair in the morning. When Coca-Cola first marketed Coke in China in the 1920s, it developed a group of Chinese characters that, when pronounced, sounded like the product name. Unfortunately, the characters actually translated to mean 'bite the wax tadpole'. Now, the characters on Chinese Coke bottles translate as 'happiness in the mouth'.

Car-maker Rolls-Royce avoided the name Silver Mist in German markets, where *Mist* means 'manure'. Sunbeam, however, entered the German market with its Mist Stick hair curling iron. As should have been expected, the Germans had little use for a 'manure wand'. A similar fate awaited Colgate when it introduced a toothpaste in France called Cue, the name of a notorious porno magazine. One well-intentioned firm sold its shampoo in Brazil under the name Evitol. It soon realised it was claiming to sell a 'dandruff contraceptive'. And IKEA marketed a children's workbench named FARTFULL (meaning speedy in Swedish) – the product was soon discontinued.

Interbrand of London, the firm that created household names such as Prozac and Acura, recently developed a brand-name 'hall of shame' list, which contained these and other foreign brand names that are unlikely to cross the English language barrier: Krapp toilet paper (Denmark), Crapsy Fruit cereal (France), Happy End toilet paper (Germany), Mukk yogurt (Italy), Zit lemonade (Germany), Poo curry powder (Argentina) and Pschitt lemonade (France).

Travellers often encounter well-intentioned advice from service firms that takes on meanings very different from those intended. The menu in one Swiss restaurant proudly stated: 'Our wines leave you nothing to hope for.' Signs in a Japanese hotel pronounced: 'You are invited to take advantage of the chambermaid.' At a laundry in Rome, it was: 'Ladies, leave your clothes here and spend the afternoon having a good time.' The brochure at a Tokyo car rental offered this sage advice: 'When passenger of foot heave in sight, tootle the horn. Trumpet him melodiously at first, but if he still obstacles your passage, tootle him with vigour.' And a Chinese grocery retailer in Kuala Lumpur offers to sell all sorts of sundry goods, although foreign visitors may be somewhat wary about stepping into the store. Why? Because it is called 'Sin Tit'.

Advertising themes often lose – or gain – something in the translation. The Coors beer slogan 'get loose with Coors' in Spanish came out as 'get the runs with Coors'. Coca-Cola's 'Coke adds life' theme in Japanese translated into 'Coke brings your ancestors back from the dead'. In Chinese, the KFC slogan 'finger lickin' good' came out as 'eat your fingers off'. Even when the language is the same, word usage may differ from country to country. Thus, the British ad line for Electrolux vacuum cleaners – 'Nothing sucks like an Electrolux' – would capture few customers in the United States. What can a company do to avoid such mistakes? One answer is to use experts (consultancies) to help dream up, identify or find appropriate brand names. They can also call in the experts to screen out the bad names and to evaluate words for language and cultural cues and miscues.[39]

Other companies follow a strategy of **communication adaptation**, fully adapting their advertising messages or techniques to local markets. Interestingly, even differences in consumer values within a local market can pose challenges to international marketers. Consider the experience of advertisers of consumer goods in the German market. Although the country has become fully unified, research shows how traditional values can still hold sway, requiring subtle adaptations.

Communication adaptation—A global communication strategy of fully adapting advertising messages to local markets.

Seventeen years after the fall of the Berlin Wall, earnings levels and political preferences may still vary between east and west, but the shelves of supermarkets in Düsseldorf and Dresden appear to be stocked with similar products. Yet significant differences remain, with consumers in the two regions often filling their shopping baskets with different brands of products as basic to German households as coffee, beer, detergent and shampoo.

Consumer product companies certainly notice the phenomenon. In particular, some companies successful in western Germany are wondering why their brands often have much lower market shares in the east. The reason, according to Alexander Mackat, joint founder of Fritzsch & Mackat, a Berlin-based advertising agency focused on eastern Germany, is not just because of the trend towards 'Ostalgie', nostalgia towards the former East Germany, which includes buying brands that date from pre-unification times. Rather, Mr Mackat believes, eastern German consumers have different underlying *values* from western Germans and that these play a role in shopping decisions. He cites the example of marketing experts at Persil, who in 1997 came to his company to better understand why the washing powder was a top-seller in the west but not the east. 'We told them that the image [in Persil's West German advertising] of a beautiful but serious-minded housewife getting upset about tiny spots of dirt turned easterners off,' he says. 'Persil was seen in the east as an élite product for rich people.'

An alternative proposal by his company, using more emotional and ironic images, was eventually adapted and used Germany-wide by Persil. Mr Mackat believes easterners have held on to what sociologists see as Germany's 'traditional values', such as community spirit, modesty and diligence, more firmly than westerners. The latter, in turn, from the late 1960s onwards switched to more 'modern values' such as individualism, creativity and adventure. Such values are not static. Almost two decades after German unity, Mr Mackat has been keen to find out what 'values mix', if any, is common to east and west. 'Companies need Germany-wide advertising campaigns, but are unsure which values to focus on,' he says. Two years of research involving interviews with marketing directors and tests with hundreds of consumers in Leipzig, Hamburg and elsewhere, have produced a surprising result: western Germans are becoming more like their eastern cousins in their outlook on life. 'The western values that dominated immediately after reunification are now being mixed with eastern values – the hedonism in much western advertising is more controlled,' he says.

For example, for Lavazza, the Italian coffee, he found that an advertising image the company was using, which showed a highly-stylised model and a man in chains, was seen by eastern consumers as artificially erotic and unreal, and by westerners as exaggerated. An alternative concept, showing an elderly man sucking a finger, had 'pan-German appeal', Mr Mackat says, stirring positive reactions of authenticity and humour in both east and west.

Helmut Sailer, marketing vice-president for household goods at Bosch, the German appliances maker, says he had been impressed by Mr Mackat's work. 'German advertising for engineering-based products is traditionally very cool and technical, so the degree to which emotional elements and community now play an important role even in the west was surprising,' says Mr Sailer. Aptly, he concludes, 'We have to be open to new trends, whether from east or west.[40]

Media also need to be adapted internationally because media use and media availability vary from country to country. TV advertising time is very limited in Europe, for instance, ranging from four hours a day in France to none in Scandinavian countries, where print advertising is preferred to TV ads. Advertisers must buy time months in advance, and they have little control over airtimes. Magazines also vary in effectiveness. For example, magazines are a major medium in Italy but a minor one in Austria. Newspapers are national in the United Kingdom but are only local in Spain.[41]

Companies adopt a dual adaptation strategy when both the product and communication messages have to be modified to meet the needs and expectations of target customers in different country markets.

> For example, the French food multinational, Danone, not only had to bring its products closer to consumer tastes, but also adapted advertising messages to suit different European market expectations. In France, yoghurt is typically sold as plain yoghurt, a symbol of good health. Fruit and flavourings come later. Advertising emphasises the health logic. In the UK, the product is associated with pleasure, of a sort enjoyed by adults. Fruits add to the pleasure of eating yoghurt. Plain, flavoured yoghurt (without the fruit) is considered a lesser yoghurt, one without the pleasure. In Spain or Portugal, where fruit is abundant, consumers prefer plain yoghurt, eaten as much by children as by adults. In Italy, consumers prefer blended yoghurt, while flavoured varieties are positioned for very young children. Advertising messages are therefore adjusted accordingly to reflect these preferences.

Even sales promotion techniques have to be adapted to different countries. As discussed in Chapter 17, European countries differ in the extent to which they have enforced regulations preventing or restricting the use of sales promotion tools such as rebates, coupons, premiums and games of chance. Variation in national rules and the enforcement of EU regulations on advertising and direct and online marketing by member states within the community, also mean that companies must adapt their communications strategy when marketing to different countries within the EU.

Price

Companies also face several problems when setting their international prices.

For example, how might Bosch price its power tools globally? It could set a uniform price all around the world, but this amount would be too high a price in poor countries and not high enough in rich ones. It could charge what consumers in each country would bear, but this strategy ignores differences in the actual costs from country to country. Finally, the company could use a standard mark-up of its costs everywhere, but this approach might price Bosch out of the market in some countries where costs are high.

Companies selling their products abroad may face a *price escalation* problem due to the need to add the cost of transportation, tariffs, importer margin, wholesaler margin and retailer margin to their factory price. For example, a Gucci handbag may sell for €150 in Italy and the equivalent of €350 in Singapore. Depending on these added costs, the product may have to sell for two to five times as much in another country to make the same profit.

Another problem involves setting a *transfer price* – that is, the price that a company charges for goods that it ships to its foreign subsidiaries. If the company charges a foreign subsidiary too much, it may end up paying higher tariff duties even while paying lower income taxes in the foreign country. If the company charges its subsidiary too little, it can be charged with *dumping* – that is, pricing exports at levels less than their costs or less than the prices charged in its home market.

Recent technological and economic forces have had an impact on global pricing. For example, in the European Union, the transition to the euro is reducing the amount of price differentiation. As consumers recognise price differentiation by country, companies are being forced to harmonise prices throughout the countries that have adopted the single currency. Companies and marketers that offer the most unique or necessary products or services will be least affected by such 'price transparency'.

For Marie-Claude Lang, a 72-year-old retired Belgian postal worker, the euro is the best thing since bottled water – or French country sausage. Always on the prowl for bargains, Ms Lang is stalking the wide aisles of an Auchan hypermarket in Roncq, France, a 15-minute drive from her Wervick home. . . . Ms Lang has been coming to France every other week for years to stock up on bottled water, milk and yoghurt. But the euro . . . has opened her eyes to many more products that she now sees cost less across the border. Today she sees that 'saucisse de campagne' is cheaper 'by about five euro cents', a saving she didn't notice when she had to calculate the difference between Belgian and French francs. At Europe's borders, the euro is turning into the coupon clipper's delight. Sure, price-conscious Europeans have long crossed into foreign territory to find everything from cheaper television sets to bargain bottles of Perona. But the new transparency is making comparisons a whole lot easier.[42]

The Internet will also make global price differences more obvious. When firms sell their wares over the Internet, customers can see how much products sell for in different countries. They might even be able to order a given product directly from the company location or dealer offering the lowest price. This will force companies towards more standardised international pricing.

Distribution channels

The international company must take a *whole-channel* view of the problem of distributing products to final consumers. Figure 20.4 shows the three major links between the *seller* and the *final buyer*. The first link, the *seller's headquarters organisation*, supervises the channels and is part of the channel itself. The second link, *channels between nations*, moves the products to the borders of the foreign nations. The third link, *channels within nations*, moves the products from their foreign entry point to the final consumers. Some manufacturers may think their job is done once the product leaves their hands, but they would do well to pay more attention to its handling within foreign countries.

Channels of distribution within countries vary greatly from nation to nation. First, there are the large differences in the *numbers and types of intermediaries* serving each foreign market.

For example, a foreign company marketing in China must operate through a frustrating maze of state-controlled wholesalers and retailers. Chinese distributors often carry competitors' products and frequently refuse to share even basic sales and marketing information with their suppliers. Hustling for sales is an alien concept to Chinese distributors, who are used to selling all

Figure 20.4 Whole-channel concept for international marketing

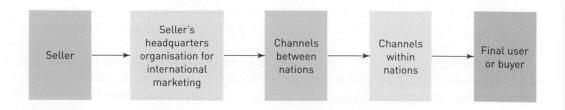

they can obtain. Working with or getting around this system sometimes requires substantial time and investment.

> When Coke first entered China, for example, customers bicycled up to bottling plants to get their soft drinks. Many shopkeepers still don't have enough electricity to run soft-drink coolers. Now, Coca-Cola sets up direct-distribution channels, investing heavily in refrigerators and trucks, and upgrading wiring so that more retailers can install coolers. The company has also built an army of more than 10,000 sales representatives that makes regular visits on resellers, often on foot or bicycle, to check on stocks and record sales. 'Coke and its bottlers have been trying to map every supermarket, restaurant, barbershop, or market stall where a can of soda might be consumed,' notes an industry observer. 'Those data help Coke get closer to its customers, whether they are in large hypermarkets, Spartan noodle shops, or schools.' Still, to reach the most isolated spots in the country, Coca-Cola relies on some pretty unlikely business partners – teams of delivery donkeys. 'Massive advertising budgets can drum up demand,' says another observer, 'but if the distribution network doesn't exist properly or doesn't work, the potential of China's vast market cannot be realized.'[43]

Another difference lies in the size and character of retail units abroad. Whereas large-scale retail chains dominate the British and US scene, most retailing in the rest of Europe and other countries, such as Japan and India, is done by many small independent retailers. For example, in India, millions of retailers operate tiny shops or sell in open markets. Their mark-ups are high, but the actual price is lowered through haggling. Supermarkets could offer lower prices, but supermarkets are difficult to build and open because of many economic and cultural barriers. Incomes are low, and people prefer to shop daily for small amounts rather than weekly for large amounts. They also lack storage and refrigeration to keep food for several days. Packaging is not well developed because it would add too much to the cost. These factors have kept large-scale retailing from spreading rapidly in developing countries.

Getting to grips with a foreign country's distribution structure is often crucial to achieving effective market access. The international firm must therefore invest in acquiring knowledge about each foreign market's channel features and decide on how best to break into complex or entrenched distribution systems. In addition, when first entering a foreign market, the company must select the most appropriate distributors, working with them to determine and agree on mutually beneficial distribution targets and performance goals.[44]

Deciding on the global marketing organisation

The key to success in any marketing strategy is the firm's ability to implement the chosen strategy. The firm's distance from its foreign markets poses particular difficulties for international marketing strategy implementation. The firm must have an organisational structure that fits with the international environment.

Export department—A form of international marketing organisation that comprises a sales manager and a few assistants whose job is to organise the shipping out of the company's goods to foreign markets.

International division— A form of international marketing organisation in which the division handles all of the firm's international activities. Marketing, manufacturing, research, planning and specialist staff are organised into operating units according to geography or product groups, or as an international subsidiary responsible for its own sales and profitability.

Global organisation— A form of international organisation whereby top corporate management and staff plan worldwide manufacturing or operational facilities, marketing policies, financial flows and logistical systems. The global operating unit reports directly to the chief executive, not to an international divisional head.

Companies manage their international marketing activities in at least three different ways. Most companies first organise an export department, then create an international division and finally become a global organisation.

Export department

A firm normally gets into international marketing by simply shipping out its goods. If its international sales expand, the company organises an **export department** with a sales manager and a few assistants. As sales increase, the export department can then expand to include various marketing services, so that it can actively go after business. If the firm moves into joint ventures or direct investment, the export department will no longer be adequate.

International division

Many companies get involved in several international markets and ventures. A company may export to one country, license to another, have a joint-ownership venture in a third and own a subsidiary in a fourth. Sooner or later it will create an **international division** or subsidiary to handle all its international activities.

International divisions are organised in a variety of ways. An international division's corporate staff consists of marketing, manufacturing, research, finance, planning and personnel specialists. It plans for and provides services to various operating units, which can be organised in one of three ways. They may be *geographical* organisations, with country managers who are responsible for salespeople, sales branches, distributors and licensees in their respective countries. Or the operating units may be *world product groups*, each responsible for worldwide sales of different product groups. Finally, operating units may be *international subsidiaries*, each responsible for its own sales and profits.

Global organisation

Many firms have passed beyond the international division stage and become truly **global organisations**. They stop thinking of themselves as national marketers that sell abroad and start thinking of themselves as global marketers. The top corporate management and staff plan worldwide manufacturing facilities, marketing policies, financial flows and logistical systems. The global operating units report directly to the chief executive or executive committee of the organisation, not to the head of an international division. Executives are trained in worldwide operations, not just domestic or international. The company recruits management from many countries, buys components and supplies where they cost the least, and invests where the expected returns are greatest.

Today, major companies must become more global if they hope to compete. As foreign companies successfully invade the domestic market, domestic companies must move more aggressively into foreign markets. They will have to change from companies that treat their foreign operations as secondary concerns, to companies that view the entire world as a single borderless market.[45]

Reviewing the concepts

In this chapter, we looked at why companies today can no longer afford to pay attention only to their domestic market, regardless of its size. Many industries are global industries, and those firms that operate globally achieve lower costs and higher brand awareness. At the same time, *global marketing* is risky because of variable exchange rates, unstable governments, protectionist tariffs and trade barriers, and several other factors. Given the potential gains and risks of international marketing, companies need to adopt a systematic approach to make their global marketing decisions. Here, we review the major global marketing concepts covered in this chapter.

1. Discuss how the international trade system and the economic, political–legal and cultural environments affect a company's international marketing decisions

A company must understand the *global marketing environment*, especially the *international trade system*. It must assess each foreign market's *economic*, *political–legal* and *cultural characteristics*. The company must then decide whether to go international based on a consideration of the potential risks and benefits. It must decide on the volume of international sales it wants, how many countries it wants to market in, and which specific *country markets* it *wants to enter*. This decision calls for weighing the probable rate of return on investment against the level of risk.

2. Describe three key approaches to entering international markets

The company has to *decide how to enter* each chosen market – whether through *exporting*, *joint venturing* or *direct investment*. Many companies start as exporters, move to joint ventures and finally make a direct investment in foreign markets. Increasingly, however, firms – domestic or international – use joint ventures and even direct investments to enter a new country market for the first time. In *exporting*, the company enters a foreign market by sending and selling products through international marketing intermediaries (indirect exporting) or the company's own department, branch, or sales representative or agents (direct exporting). When establishing a *joint venture*, a company enters foreign markets by joining with foreign companies to produce or market a product or service. In *licensing*, the company enters a foreign market by contracting with a licensee in the foreign market, offering the right to use a manufacturing process, trademark, patent, trade secret or other item of value for a fee or royalty. In *direct investment*, the company enters a foreign market by developing foreign-based assembly or production facilities.

3. Explain how companies adapt their marketing mixes for international markets

When selling goods or services abroad, the company must decide on its global marketing programme. Managers must decide on the level of *adaptation* or *standardisation* of their *product*, *promotion*, *price* and *distribution channels* for each foreign market. At one extreme, global companies use a *standardised marketing mix* worldwide. Others use an *adapted marketing mix*, in which they adjust the marketing mix to each target market, bearing more costs but hoping for a larger market share and return.

4. Identify the three major forms of international marketing organisation

Finally, the firm must develop an effective organisation for international marketing. Most firms start with an *export department* and graduate to an *international division*. A few become *global organisations*, with worldwide marketing planned and managed by the top officers of the company, who view the entire world as a single borderless market.

Discussing the concepts

1. With all the problems facing companies that 'go global', why are so many companies choosing to expand internationally? What are the major factors contributing to the intensity of today's global competition?

2. What must a company consider when it decides whether to expand globally?

3. Discuss the advantages and disadvantages of direct investment in a foreign market. Identify two overseas markets in which a household appliance manufacturer would be interested in investing and two overseas markets in which it would have no interest in doing so. Discuss.

4. Assume that you are a product manager for a company that sells intelligent supply chain software systems. The company currently operates in the UK, Ireland and several countries in northern Europe. Outline a plan for expanding your operations and marketing efforts into eastern and central Europe. Would you recommend that the company standardise or adapt its marketing mix?

5. What do you understand by the concept of a 'whole-channel view' of international distribution? Would a company require the full range of international channel intermediaries for distributing products to final consumers in international markets? Explain.

Applying the concepts

1. In 1911, Nivea introduced a revolutionary product, Nivea Crème, in a simple blue tin. Still in its signature blue tin, today the Crème is the centrepiece of a wide range of personal care products Nivea markets, including everything from soap, shampoo and shaving products to baby care products, deodorant and sunscreen. And despite its small beginnings, today the company's products are sold in more than 150 countries worldwide. Most Nivea consumers believe that the products they buy are produced and marketed locally. Although Nivea looks for commonalities between consumers around the globe, the company's marketers also recognise the differences between consumers in different markets. So Nivea adapts its marketing mix to reach local consumers while keeping its message consistent everywhere products are sold. This globally consistent, locally customised marketing strategy has sold more than 11 billion tins of the traditional Nivea Crème.

   (a) Which of the five strategies for adapting products and promotion for the global market does Nivea employ?

   (b) Visit Nivea's website, www.nivea.com, and tour the sites for several different countries. How does Nivea market its products differently in different countries? How does the company maintain the consistency of its brand?

Web resources

For additional classic case studies and Internet exercises, visit **www. pearsoned.co.uk/ kotler**

2. Form teams of four students. Suppose you work for a European company that makes medical diagnostic equipment such as heart rate and blood pressure monitors and a range of blood diagnostic equipment. The company's products are aimed at users in hospitals and public and private medical clinics. It also offers a range of heart rate and blood pressure monitors for use by individuals in the home. Discuss how the company might adapt its marketing strategy and marketing mixes when entering (a) the Chinese market; (b) the Indian market.

References

1. This case is a reproduction of Bettina Wassener, 'Schnapps goes to college', *Financial Times* (4 September 2003), p. 15; also see 'Hot shots', *Irish Times* (6 August 2005); Jenny Wiggins, 'Mixing its drinks could be wrong policy for Diageo', *Financial Times* (20 July 2007); www.shadowsfall.com and www.jagermusic.com, accessed September 2007.

2. Data from 'Fortune 500', *Fortune* (17 April 2006), p. F-1; United Nations Conference on Trade and Development, *World Investment Report 2005* (New York and Geneva: United Nations, 2005); World Bank, *Total GDP 2004*, World Development Indicators Database, www.worldbank.org, accessed 2 April 2006; and 'List of countries by GDP', in *Wikipedia*, accessed at http://en.wikipedia.org/wiki/List_of_countries_by_GDP_%28nominal%29, July 2006.

3. World Bank, *Global Economic Prospects 2006* (3 June 2005), accessed at www.worldbank.org; CIA, *The World Factbook*, www.cia.gov, accessed June 2006; and World Trade Organization, 'World trade picks up in mid-2005; but 2006 picture is uncertain', press release (11 April 2006), accessed at www.wto.org/english/news_e/pres06_e/pr437_e.htm.

4. 'Trade and output', *The Economist* (10 February 2007), p. 114.

5. Bertrand Benoit and Richard Milne, 'Germany's best-kept secret: how its exporters are beating the world', *Financial Times* (19 May 2006), p. 13.

6. Information on tariffs for countries from www.economist.com/indicators.

7. 'What is the WTO?', www.wto.org/english/thewto_e/whatis_e/whatis_e.htm, accessed September 2006.

8. See World Trade Organization, *WTO Annual Report 2005*, accessed at www.wto.org, September 2006, and '10 benefits of the WTO trading system', accessed at www.wto.org/english/thewto_e/whatis_e/whatis_e.htm, September 2006.

9. 'Finance and Economics: In the rough; world trade talks', *The Economist* (5 November 2005), p. 102; Peter Coy, 'Why free-trade talks are in free fall', *BusinessWeek* (22 May 2006), p. 44; 'The real world economic forum', *The Economist* (27 January 2007), pp. 11–12.

10. 'The European Union at a glance', http://europa.eu.int, accessed September 2006.

11. 'Europe's new protectionism', *The Economist* (2 July 2005), p. 42.

12. 'Overviews of European Union activities: Economic and monetary affairs', http://europa.eu.int/pol/emu/overview_en.htm, accessed September 2006.

13. See 'European Union's heated budget negotiations collapse', *New York Times* (18 June 2005), p. A3; 'Europe: Desperately seeking a policy; France and the European Union', *The Economist* (21 January 2006); CIA, *The World Factbook*, www.cia.gov, accessed June 2006; and Vito Breda, 'A European constitution in a multinational Europe or a multinational constitution for Europe?', *European Law Journal* (May 2006), pp. 330–44.

14. Statistics and other information from 'List of countries by GDP', in *Wikipedia*, accessed at http://en.wikipedia.org/wiki/List_of_countries_by_GDP_%28nominal%29, July 2006; 'Area and population of countries', in *Infoplease*, accessed at www.infoplease.com/ipa/A0004379.html, July 2006; and 'Trade facts: NAFTA – A strong record of success', Office of the United States Trade Representative, March 2006, accessed at www.ustr.gov/assets/Document_Library/Fact_Sheets/2006/asset_upload_file242_9156.pdf.

15. See Angela Greiling Keane, 'Counting on CAFTA', *Traffic World* (8 August 2005), p. 1; Gilberto Meza, 'Is the FTAA floundering?', *Business Mexico* (February 2005), pp. 46–8; Peter Robson, 'Integrating the Americas: FTAA and beyond', *Journal of Common Market Studies* (June 2005), p. 430; Diana Kinch,

'Latin America: Mercosul boosted', *Metal Bulletin Monthly* (February 2006), p. 1; 'Foreign trade statistics', www.census.gov, accessed June 2006; and Kevin Z. Jiang, 'Americas: Trading up?', *Harvard International Review* (Spring 2006), pp. 10–12.

16. Richard Lapper, 'South American unity still a distant dream', *Financial Times* (9 December 2004), accessed at www.news.ft.com; Alan Clendenning, 'Venezuela's entry may shake up Mercosur', *AP Financial Wire* (30 November 2005), p. 1; Mary Turck, 'South American community of nations', Resource Center of the Americas.org, accessed at www.americas.org, August 2006.

17. Adapted from information from Clay Chandler, 'China deluxe', *Fortune* (26 July 2004), pp. 148–56. Also see 'Selling to China's rich and not so rich', *Strategic Directions* (June 2005), pp. 5–8; Lisa Movius, 'Luxury's China puzzle', *WWD* (15 June 2005), p. 1; Normandy Madden, 'After slow start, Porsche cranks its Chinese marketing plan into top gear', *Advertising Age* (8 May 2006), p. 28; William McEwen, Xiaoguang Fang, Chuanping Zhang and Richard Burkholder, 'Inside the mind of the Chinese consumer', *Harvard Business Review* (March–April 2006), p. 76.

18. See Om Malik, 'The new land of opportunity', *Business 2.0* (July 2004), pp. 72–9; and 'India economy: South Asia's worst business environment', *EIU ViewsWire* (January 2006).

19. Ricky Griffin and Michael Pustay, *International Business*, 4th edn (Upper Saddle River, NJ: Prentice Hall, 2005), pp. 522–3.

20. Dalia Marin and Monika Schnitzer, 'The economic institution of international barter', *The Economic Journal* (April 2002), pp. 293–316.

21. For other examples and discussion, see www.executiveplanet.com, December 2006; *Dun & Bradstreet's Guide to Doing Business Around the World* (Upper Saddle River, NJ: Prentice Hall, 2000); Ellen Neuborne, 'Bridging the culture gap', *Sales & Marketing Management* (July 2003), p. 22; Richard Pooley, 'When cultures collide', *Management Services* (Spring 2005), pp. 28–31; and Helen Deresky, *International Management*, 5th edn (Upper Saddle River, NJ: Prentice Hall, 2006).

22. Gail Edmondson, 'The beauty of global branding', *BusinessWeek* (28 June 1999), pp. 70–5.

23. Adapted from Mark Rice-Oxley, 'In 2,000 years, will the world remember Disney or Plato?', *Christian Science Monitor* (15 January 2004), p. 16.

24. 'How the ranking is compiled', *Financial Times Special Report: Global Brands* (23 April 2007), p. 2; Robert Berner and David Kiley, 'Global brands', *BusinessWeek* (1 August 2005), pp. 86–94.

25. Portions adapted from information from Mark Rice-Oxley, *op. cit.*

26. Peter Marsh, 'Partnerships feel the Indian heat', *Financial Times* (22 June 2006), p. 11.

27. Geoff Dyer, 'How Danone's China venture turned sour', *Financial Times* (12 April 2007), p. 26.

28. Christopher Brown-Humes, 'Nokia plans to launch new Chinese venture', *Financial Times* (1 April 2003), p. 27.

29. Neil Buckley, 'Petfoods overtake sweet success', *Financial Times Special Report: Investing in Russia* (10 October 2006), p. 6.

30. Robert Wright, 'Fresh investors sought', *Financial Times Special Report: Hungary* (27 May 2003), p. VI.

31. Neil Buckley, *op. cit.*

32. David M. Szymanski, Sundar G. Bharadwaj and Rajan Varadarajan, 'Standardization versus adaptation of international marketing strategy: An empirical investigation', *Journal of Marketing* (October 1993), pp. 1–17; Jeryl Whitelock and Carole Pimblett, 'The standardization debate in international marketing', *Journal of Global Marketing* (1997), p. 22; David A. Aaker and Ericj Joachimsthaler, 'The lure of global branding', *Harvard Business Review* (November–December 1999), pp. 137–44.

33. Quotes from Pankaj Ghemawat, 'Regional strategies for global leadership', *Harvard Business Review* (December 2005), pp. 97–108; Douglas B. Holt, John A. Quelch and Earl L. Taylor, 'How global brands compete', *Harvard Business Review* (September 2004), pp. 68–75; and Simon Sherwood, 'Building an advertising factory', www.internationalist.com/commentary/commentary%2020+21%202-18.1.pdf, 16 June 2006.

34. Jenny Wiggins, 'Burger, fries and a shake-up', *Financial Times* (27 February 2007), p. 12.

35. Warren J. Keegan, *Global Marketing Management*, 7th edn (Upper Saddle River, NJ: Prentice Hall, 2002), pp. 346–51. Also see Philip Kotler and Kevin Lane Keller, *Marketing Management*, 12th edn (Upper Saddle River, NJ: Prentice Hall, 2006), pp. 677–84.

36. See Andrew Kupfer, 'How to be a global manager', *Fortune* (14 March 1988), pp. 52–8; Jack Neff, 'Test it in Paris, France, launch it in Paris, Texas', *Advertising Age* (31 May 1999), p. 28.

37. Beatrice Aidin, 'Big brands are watching you', *Financial Times Weekend* (4–5 November 2007), p. W6.

38. For further information on colour and culture, see Mubeen M. Aslam, 'Are you selling the right colour? A cross-cultural review of colour as a marketing cue', *Journal of Marketing Communications* (March 2006), pp. 15–20.

39. Based on examples and quotes from 'Naming products is no game', *BusinessWeek Online* (9 April 2004), accessed at www.businessweekonline.com. See also David A. Ricks, 'Perspectives: Translation blunders in international business', *Journal of Language for International Business*, **7**, 2 (1996), pp. 50–5; Sam Solley, 'Developing a name to work worldwide', *Marketing* (21 December 2000), p. 27; Thomas T. Sermon, 'Cutting corners in language is a risky business', *Marketing News* (23 April 2001), p. 9; Martin Croft, 'Mind your language', *Marketing* (19 June 2003), pp. 35–9; Mark Lasswell, 'Lost in translation', *Business 2.0* (August 2004), pp. 68–70; 'Lost in translation', *Hispanic* (May 2005), p. 12; and 'Striking a chord in Tamil', *Businessline* (19 January 2006), p. 1.

40. Hugh Williams, 'Advertisers try to bridge Germany's consumer divide', *Financial Times* (27 July 2007), p. 12; Alexander Mackat, *Das Deutsch-Deutsche Geheimnis* [The inner German secret] (Berlin: SuperIllu Verlag, 2007).

41. See Alicia Clegg, 'One ad one world?', *Marketing Week* (20 June 2002), pp. 51–2; and George E. Belch and Michael A. Belch, *Advertising and Promotion: An integrated marketing communications perspective*, 7th edn (New York: McGraw-Hill, 2007), Ch. 20.

42. Sarah Ellison, 'Revealing price disparities, the euro aids bargain-hunters', *Wall Street Journal* (30 January 2002), p. A15. *Wall Street Journal* (Central Edition) by Sarah Ellison. Copyright 2002 by Dow Jones & Company, Inc. Reproduced with permission of Dow Jones & Company, Inc. in the format Textbook via Copyright Clearance Center.

43. See Patrick Powers, 'Distribution in China: The end of the beginning', *China Business Review* (July–August 2001), pp. 8–12; Drake Weisert, 'Coca-Cola in China: Quenching the thirst of a billion', *op. cit.*, pp. 52–5; Gabriel Kahn, 'Coke works harder at being the real thing in hinterland', *Wall Street Journal* (26 November 2002), p. B1; Leslie Chang, Chad Terhune and Betsy McKay, 'A global journal report; Rural Thing – Coke's big gamble in Asia', *Wall Street Journal* (11 August 2004), p. A1; and Ann Chen and Vijay Vishwanath, 'Expanding in China', *Harvard Business Review* (1 March 2005).

44. David Arnold, 'Seven rules of international distribution', *Harvard Business Review* (November–December 2000), pp. 131–7.

45. John A. Byrne and Kathleen Kerwin, 'Borderless management', *BusinessWeek* (23 May 1994), pp. 24–6; see also Christopher A. Bartlett and Sumantra Goshal, *Managing Across Borders* (Cambridge, MA: Harvard Business School Press, 1989).

Company case 20 The global wine SCAM: soil, climate, aspect and mystique

'A few decades ago it was not difficult to know about wine,' explained Ivor Trink, one of Australia's new breed of flash, flying wine makers. 'There was claret, burgundy, champagne, port, sherry and loads of gut rot.' Dr Trink had been invited, and paid a fat fee, to talk to a gathering of some of Bordeaux's 12,000 wine producers. He continued, 'You are the guardians of the *terrier*, that combination of soil, climate and aspect shaped by two millennia of expertise that signal a wine's excellence. Australian wine producers are resigned to French producers continuing to dominate the great heights of wine making, trophy wines selling for hundreds of euros a bottle.' 'Of course,' heckled one distinguished wine grower, 'but we don't need you to tell us that.'

Undeterred, Dr Trink continued and started to win over his sceptical audience. He projected a chart (Exhibit 20.1) that showed how the main European suppliers, which he called the 'old world', are still dominating the world's wine production. 'You have the advantage,' he continued, 'as your own Baroness Philippine de Rothschild told me, "Winemaking is easy. Only the first 200 years are difficult." And you certainly have experience. The museum at Château Mouton Rothschild traces wine making back to Roman times and has a cellar devoted to mid-nineteenth-century vintages. The whole place reeks as much of history as wine.'

In a market that is very fragmented, the world market leader – France's luxury goods giant LVHM – has less than 1 per cent of the world market, and the number of 'old world' winemakers swamp those from the new world. Italy alone has 1 million winemakers and this region, Bordeaux, makes more wine than the whole of Australia.

'You have the mystique beloved of wine enthusiasts. As the author and wine guru Hugh Johnson proclaims: "Why is wine so fascinating? Because there are so many different kinds, and every single one is different." The prices of the world's most costly wines show France's dominance. While Château d'Yquem (1811) sauternes has sold for $26,500 (€20,000), Moët & Chandon Esprit de Siècle champagne for $10,000 and Château Mouton Rothschild (1945) for $4,200, the best that the rest of the world can manage is $1,400 for Australian Grange (1955) and $1,000 for Californian Screaming Eagle (1995).'

'In addition you have the *appellation contrôlée* that protects your wine's identity through a plethora of rigidly enforced regulations covering the grapes that can be used in a region's blend, the way they are picked, the way the wines are planted, their irrigation, the wine's alcoholic content, the labelling and much more. Your "brands", if you will excuse my use of the word, are the most protected in the world.'

'You also have amazingly loyal customers. For example, France is one of the world's greatest consumers of wine and yet imports account for less than 5 per cent of sales. As Françoise Brugière, of the Office National Intreprofessionel des Vins, explained to me, "It's no accident that Chauvin was a Frenchman." And the French are not alone in their loyalty. Italian and Spanish wine drinkers are just as loyal to wine made in their own country. Even in Australia over 90 per cent of the wine consumed is home grown.'

'Your position in the wine world is pre-eminent. Through your combined strength you have already given bloody noses to the big conglomerates moving into your markets. Remember the fanfare when Coca-Cola introduced their new beverage category, wine, in 1976. It took them four years of losses to learn that Coke is no Grand Cru and make an ignominious exit in 1980. Having not learned from your victory over Coca-Cola, Nestlé, Philip Morris and RJR Nabisco all entered the wine trade, lost their shirts and quit the wine trade in the 1980s. True,

Exhibit 20.1 Regional share of world production (2006)

Region	% share
Main European exporters: France, Italy, Portugal and Spain	51
Second-tier European producers (Germany, Portugal, Romania)	9
Other major southern hemisphere exporters: Argentina, Chile, New Zealand and South Africa	10
Australia	5
US	8
Rest of world	17

some global companies are still dabbling in wine but they are finding it tough. Seagram has just sold off its champagne brands. Only Diageo is hanging on but they are dismissive of the role of wine in their overall strategy. As one manager joked: "Two millennia ago a miracle changes water into wine. We're still waiting for the second miracle: turning wine into profits!".'

The audience was getting to like Dr Tipple but their mood was about to change. 'Yes, you are confidently on top of the pile now but, unless you shape up, Bordeaux will be as much a wine-making joke as Britain. For too long you have ignored customers. You think you are so special, custodians of a grand heritage that defines your nation. You are wrong. You are mostly outdated business, yes business, who for generations have operated more for your own convenience than that of the customers.'

'You may have 95 per cent of the French market but the market is, literally, dying on you and you are losing ground elsewhere. Over the past 30 years France's wine consumption has halved and the average age of the regular wine consumer, who drinks at least a glass a day, has risen from 35 to 55. You have lost touch with the youth market. Go to Paris and you will find the bars full of young people drinking. Drinking, yes, but not French wine or wine from any other country. Their drink is foreign beer or whisky.'

'The situation in your traditional export markets is equally dire. In the late 1980s, France and Europe's other three big exporters accounted for 85 per cent of the world's exports. They are now down to about 70 per cent. The British market is a good example of what is happening outside the wine-producing countries. Only six years ago, French, German and Italian wines accounted for two-thirds of the wine the Brits consumed. Their combined share is now less than 50 per cent and declining. In 2003 Australia overtook France as Britain's largest wine supplier.'

'France, Italy and Spain may be holding on to their share of their declining markets but, elsewhere, new-world wines are driving out the old. And it is in these non-wine-growing areas that wine consumption is growing. While the share of world exports, excluding intra-EU trade, of the main European exporters has slipped from 75 per cent to 55 per cent over the last 10 years, sales of new-world exporters have soared. This table (Exhibit 20.2) shows how percentage points in world production is forecast to change. And the pain is not over yet. Australia is planning to increase its sales from A\$26bn (€15.6bn) to A \$30bn by 2010 by increasing the volume and the price that their wine can command.'

'Your political parties are now competing in thinking of ways of bolstering up your flagging industry. The

Exhibit 20.2 Change in wine production (2001–2006)

Region	% point change in share
Chile	+24
Australia	+20
Spain	+14
US	+11
France	+6
Italy	−4

Socialists have proposed classing wine as an agricultural product so that it avoids the ban on advertising on alcoholic beverages. Your agriculture minister is also proposing to rationalise the numerous national and regional committees that control wine research. This government assistance may help but it is you, the wine makers, who have to change or wither on the vine with your unwanted grapes.'

'There are signs that the European Commission already knows that the battle is lost for many wine growers. Europe's wine lake is to be drained and millions of its vines uprooted in an effort to tackle the onslaught from producers in the New World. Mariann Fischer Boel, the farm commissioner, said reforms would put European wine "back . . . on top of the world" by driving out low-quality products. She explained it was "indefensible" that Brussels spent more than €300m a year buying unsold stocks. She wants to use the Commission's annual €1.3bn budget for the wine industry to avert a crisis. The plan faces opposition from France, Spain, Portugal and Italy but they are likely to amend rather than block the reforms. There will be less money for intervention methods after 2013, when Common Agricultural Policy funding will be cut.'

'You may claim that the new world's gains have been made because of their heavy advertising but that is only part of the story. New-world wine producers are producing brands but a large part of their success is because they understand what brands are. For a brand to succeed consumers have got to recognise and enjoy what they are getting. For a long time, that has not been true of old-world wines. The quality of old-world wines can be outstanding but often it is not. One old-world wine buff was close to the truth when he joked: "It costs £20 (€33) for a good bottle of burgundy, but to enjoy a great bottle of burgundy it cost £200 plus £1,800 for the other nine bottles that were not."'

'The old world are still trying to use the old SCAM of Soil, Climate, Aspect and Mystique but are losing out to the new world's appliance of science and professionalism. That is what accounted for the "Judgement of

Paris" as long ago as 1976. On that occasion the Paris-based wine merchant Steven Spurrier brought together 15 of the most influential French wine critics to compare Californian and French wines in a blind test. These critics were shocked and there was a national outcry when, without the benefit of labels and bottles to guide them, the critics chose the Californian wine over the French. After cries that the test was rigged it was rerun two years later and, once again, gave the same results!'

'It seems that your great wine heritage now accounts for little, according to the world's leading wine critics. Australia's Grange, first produced in 1950, "has replaced Bordeaux's Pétrus as the world's most exotic and concentrated wine" and it is argued that New Zealand sauvignon blanc, first produced in 1970, is "arguably, the best in the world". Price comparisons in the UK market show how consumers are voting. Besides gaining sales, new-world wines carry higher prices than European producers: the average price paid for a bottle of New Zealand wine is over £5, for Australian and US wines over £4 a bottle, the average French bottle is about £3.50 and the average German bottle a little over £2.50.'

'How has the new world achieved this success? The answer is the appliance of science in wine making and marketing. As John Worontschak, a fellow Australian who lives in Bordeaux, so eloquently explains: "It's because we're open to new ideas, and we're not full of pretentious bullshit." Australia, California and New Zealand do not strive to uphold wine-making traditions supported by state subsidies, but strive to make good, consistent, keenly priced wines, carefully crafted to fit consumers' tastes and expectations. An indication of their scientific endeavour is the production of scientific papers on wine making. Although Australia and New Zealand have only a fraction of the world market, they already produce 20 per cent of the scientific papers on wine making. That investment has made them good but also means they are getting better.'

'The new world's more enlightened regulations enable them to make both consistent and excellent wines in a way that your *appellation contrôlée* blocks. Their wines are consistent because they can use different irrigation methods and take grapes from different areas to make the taste right. If in one year the conditions are perfect to produce an excellent strong vintage, they will do it and win international prizes for their efforts; your *appellation contrôlée* would prevent you making the superb wines above the regulated strength. If the vintage needs it, they will put oak chips in a barrel to bring out the flavour

while you would have to hope for the vagaries of the oak barrel and your variable climate. Yes, your love of the old ways, cottage industries and *appellation contrôlée* are great gifts to the new world.'

'Our final great advantage is marketing, but that is more than big budgets. It is finding out what people want and respecting their views. For instance we know that, once people have decided not to buy the cheapest wine, their choice is influenced by four main factors: past experience of wines, the country of origin of the wine, the variety of grape and brand. Too often the wine labels in the old world are designed to look grand and regulate, rather than elucidate. As Hugh Johnson comments on German wine labels: ". . . laws have introduced ambiguities which only the most dogged use of a reference book can elucidate. Whether there was a publisher on the committee that framed them I don't know. But there can't have been a customer."'

'In pandering to customers, not custom, new-world growers understand the importance of consistency and rewarding customers with a taste they like. You may find it amazing but many potential customers are attracted to the sophistication of wine drinking but don't like the taste. Rather than rejecting these lost causes, Californians have invested in wine coolers (a mixture of wine and fruit juices) and fruit-flavoured wines. It is consistently giving customers what they want that allows inexpensively produced new-world wines to sell at a higher price than old-world bottles.'

'It is also important to recognise the importance of country of origin. Many of the new-world wines come from young countries with a youthful, fun-loving image. There are also linguistic and historic links with the new world. To English-speaking people, Screaming Eagle is a lot easier to remember and sounds more fun than Veuve Clicquot-Ponsardin or Regierungsbezirk. These links really do matter in the wine trade. For example, the historical links are helping South African wines in the Netherlands, while "brand Australia" is struggling in Germany. Eventually Australia will have to do in Germany what they did for the UK market, use focus groups to come up with attractive Australian-sounding names – like Barramundi – that appeal to the local consumer.'

'Certainly some French producers have responded with English-sounding names, but are they the right names to build an attack against the young competition? Names like Fat Bastard, Old Git and Old Tart are certainly Anglo-Saxon and memorable, but they sound to me more like an expression of disdain for modern wine consumers than names that will build loyalty and prestige.'

'Californians started putting grape varieties on their wine to help give consumers a clue to taste. It is a trick that has since been adopted from New Zealand's superb sauvignon blanc to Chile's merlot. The grape variety constrains the taste that can be constructed but is a useful shorthand valued by mid-range consumers. South Africa is even marketing a Goats do Roam but I believe your Institut National des Appellations d'Origine is trying to ban it since it sounds too similar to Côtes du Rhône!'

'Branding is the real spirit of new-world wines. It demands the simple labelling, consistency and quality that new-world wines give. In using these marketing techniques, the scale of new-world wine makers gives them an advantage. Although globally no single wine-grower has the dominance of Diageo in the spirits market or Coca-Cola in soft drinks, new-world producers are huge compared with Europe's fragmented industry. In Australia four companies have 80 per cent of wine production and in the huge US market the five biggest producers account for 62 per cent of the market. Like it or not, the big brands are coming. Yes, wine is special to the producers and drinkers, but no more special than globally marketed Highland Park malt whisky or Guinness beer. As the wine journalist Andrew Jefford complained, Australian brands, like Jacob's Creek and Nottage Hill, are "becoming the equivalent of cans of lager; standardised, consistent, reliable, risk-free, challenge-free". Why does he complain? What's wrong with that? The longer you and he fight the march of progress, the sooner you'll die.'

Wine is a product like any other, and like any other industry it is 'innovate or die'. Take the packaging. New world wines now come with plastic or even screwtops. Not because it is cheap, but because it works better than plugging the bottle with a lump of bark. Cordier, the Bordeaux merchant, is now trialling the idea in Belgium of selling wine with straws in containers like milk cartons a third the size of a wine bottle. It fits the needs of today's casual drinkers.

Not everyone agrees with such 'awful ideas'. As one traditionalist explained: 'I don't think it is a hugely good idea. Part of the pleasure of wine is the aroma, the bouquet when you pour it in to a glass. If you drink it through a straw you lose that. It also brings wine to the level of fruit juices and I don't think you want to bring young people in to wine in that way.'

Questions

1. What accounts for the new world's recent success over the old world's wine producers?

The remaining questions for this case ask you to evaluate alternative courses of action suggested in a discussion by the Bordeaux winemakers following Dr Tipple's presentation.

2. Stick to what we have always been doing and build upon our unique *terrier*. Great wines are beyond the marketing babble of the multinationals. We have defeated Coca-Cola, Nestlé and the like, and will defeat this new challenge from much smaller new-world wine makers who are a fraction of the size of those we have already beaten. After all, the world's wine critics, wine enthusiasts the world over and our local customers remain discerning and are loyal to our wines.

3. Adopt Australian methods of wine production and branding for international markets, like several local wine-makers have done. We must be humble and learn from British Diageo in developing an accessible French brand, such as their Le Piat d'Or, or American Australian Southcorp with Vichon.

4. Follow the lead taken by France's LVMH and Pernod Ricard and buy into the new-world wines' positioning and expertise. LVMH own Australian Green Point and Californian Domaine Chandon while Pernod Ricard owns Australian Jacob's Creek and South African Long Mountain.

5. Seek the disestablishment of *appellation contrôlée* for many of our wine-growing areas so that we can develop the global French brands we need.

6. Follow the lead shown by our farming colleagues to protect our consumers from practices that undermine our European heritage. We have fought against hormones in American beef, genetically modified soya beans and bananas from the Windward Islands. We need to use our political clout in the EU as well as our own parliament.

SOURCES: Giles MacDonogh, 'French take to terrier in battle with brands', *Financial Times Survey: World Wine Industry* (15 December 2000), p. I; Stephen Brook, 'The long road from Hirondelle to here', *Financial Times Survey: World Wine Industry* (15 December 2000), p. IV; Adam Jones, 'Rivalries bubble out in the world of wine', *Finamcial Times* (19 August 2003), p. 24; *La Tribune*, 'French socialists propose wine-advertising rescue' (19 February 2004); *La Tribune*, 'French wine sector: New World challenge' (24 November 2003); Carrie LaFrenz, 'Aust wine industry sets $4 bln sales target over 5 yrs', *AAP News* (2 May 2007); *The Independent*, 'Wine Anthony Rose clutching at straws' (8 September 2007); David Gow and Ian Traynor, 'Grown in Italy, pressed in Sweden, sold as chianti. Europlonk nouveau has arrived: Backstory: Europe's wine industry', *The Guardian* (5 July 2007).

GLOSSARY

Actual product—A product's parts, quality level, features, design, brand name, packaging and other attributes that combine to deliver core product benefits.

Adapted marketing mix—An international marketing strategy for adjusting the marketing-mix elements to each international target market, bearing more costs but hoping for a larger market share and return.

Administered VMS—A vertical marketing system that coordinates successive stages of production and distribution, not through common ownership or contractual ties, but through the size and power of one of the parties.

Adoption—The decision by an individual to become a regular user of the product.

Adoption process—The mental process through which an individual passes from first hearing about an innovation to final adoption.

Advertising—Any paid form of non-personal presentation and promotion of ideas, goods or services by an identified sponsor.

Advertising media—The vehicle through which advertising messages are delivered to their intended audiences.

Advertising objective—A specific communication task to be accomplished with a specific target audience during a specific period of time.

Advertising specialities—Useful articles imprinted with an advertiser's name, given as gifts to consumers.

Affordable method—Setting the promotion budget at the level management thinks the company can afford.

Age segmentation—see Life-cycle segmentation.

Agent—A wholesaler who represents buyers or sellers on a relatively permanent basis, performs only a few functions, and does not take title to goods.

Allowance—(1) Reduction in price on damaged goods. (2) Promotional money paid by manufacturers to retailers in return for an agreement to feature the manufacturer's product in some way.

Alternative evaluation—The stage of the buyer decision process in which the consumer uses information to evaluate alternative brands in the choice set.

Annual plan—A short-term plan that describes the company's current situation, its objectives, the strategy, action programme and budgets for the year ahead, and controls.

Approach—The step in the selling process in which the salesperson meets and greets the buyer to get the relationship off to a good start.

Aspirational group—A group to which an individual wishes to belong.

Atmospheres—Designed environments that create or reinforce the buyer's leanings towards consumption of a product.

Attitude—A person's consistently favourable or unfavourable evaluations, feelings and tendencies towards an object or idea.

Augmented product—Additional consumer services and benefits built around the core and actual products.

Baby boomers—Consumers born between 1946 and 1964.

Balance sheet—A financial statement that shows assets, liabilities and net worth of a company at a given time.

Basing-point pricing—A geographic pricing strategy in which the seller designates some city as a basing point and charges all customers the freight cost from that city to the customer location, regardless of the city from which the goods are actually shipped.

Behavioural segmentation—Dividing a market into groups based on consumer knowledge, attitude, use or response to a product.

Belief—A descriptive thought that a person holds about something.

Benchmarking—The process of comparing the company's products and processes to those of competitors or leading firms in other industries to find ways to improve quality and performance.

Brand—A name, term, sign, symbol or design, or a combination of these that identifies the goods or services of one seller or group of sellers and differentiates them from those of competitors.

Brand equity—The positive differential effect that knowing the brand name has on customer response to the product or service.

Brand extension—Extending an existing brand name to new product categories.

Brand image—The set of beliefs that consumers hold about a particular brand.

Break-even pricing—Setting price to break even on the costs of making and marketing a product.

Broker—A wholesaler who does not take title to goods and whose function is to bring buyers and sellers together and assist in negotiation.

Business analysis—A review of the sales, costs and profit projections for a new product to find out whether these factors satisfy the company's objectives.

Business buying process—The decision-making process by which business buyers establish the need for purchased products and services, and identify, evaluate and choose among alternative brands and suppliers.

Business market—All the organisations that buy goods and services to use in the production of other products and services, or for the purpose of reselling or renting them to others at a profit.

Business portfolio—The collection of businesses and products that make up the company.

Business promotion—Sales promotion designed to generate business leads, stimulate purchase, reward business customers and motivate the salesforce.

Business-to-business (B2B) online marketing—Using B2B websites, e-mail, online product catalogues, online trading networks, barter sites and other online resources to reach new business customers, serve current customers more effectively and obtain buying efficiencies and better prices.

Business-to-consumer (B2C) online marketing—The online selling of goods and services to final consumers.

Buyer—The person who makes an actual purchase.

Buyer-readiness stages—The stages that consumers normally pass through on their way to purchase, including awareness, knowledge, liking, preference, conviction and purchase.

Buying centre—All the individuals and units that play a role in the business purchase decision-making process.

Buzz marketing—Cultivating opinion leaders and getting them to spread information about a product or service to others in their communities.

By-product pricing—Setting a price for by-products in order to make the main product's price more competitive.

By-products—Items produced as a result of the main factory process, such as waste and reject items.

Capital items—Industrial goods that partly enter the finished product, including installations and accessory equipment.

Captive-product pricing—Setting a price for products that must be used along with a main product, such as blades for a razor and film for a camera.

Cash cows—Low-growth, high-share businesses or products; established and successful units that generate cash that the company uses to pay its bills and support other business units that need investment.

Cash discount—A price reduction to buyers who pay their bills promptly.

Cash refund offers (or rebates)—Offers to refund part of the purchase price of a product to consumers who send a 'proof of purchase' to the manufacturer.

Catalogue marketing—Direct marketing through print, video or electronic catalogues that are mailed to selected customers, made available in stores or presented online.

Category killers—A modern 'breed' of exceptionally aggressive 'off-price' retailers that offer branded merchandise in clearly defined product categories at heavily discounted prices.

Causal research—Marketing research to test hypotheses about cause-and-effect relationships.

Channel conflict—Disagreement among marketing channel members on goals and roles – who should do what and for what rewards.

Channel level—A layer of intermediaries that performs some work in bringing the product and its ownership closer to the final buyer.

Click-only companies—The so-called dot-coms which operate only online without any bricks-and-mortar market presence.

Clicks-and-mortar companies—Traditional bricks-and-mortar companies that have added online marketing to their operations.

Closing—The step in the selling process in which the salesperson asks the customer for an order.

Co-brand—The practice of using the established brand names of two different companies on the same product.

Cognitive dissonance—Buyer discomfort caused by postpurchase conflict.

Commercialisation—Introducing a new product into the market.

Communication adaptation—A global communication strategy of fully adapting advertising messages to local markets.

Company and individual branding strategy—A branding approach that focuses on the company name and individual brand name.

Comparison advertising (or 'knocking copy')—Advertising that compares one brand directly or indirectly to one or more other brands.

Competitions, sweepstakes, lotteries and games—Promotions that offer customers the chance to win something – cash, goods or trips – by luck or extra effort.

Competitive advantage—An advantage over competitors gained by offering consumers greater value, either through lower prices or by providing more benefits that justify higher prices.

Competitive marketing strategies—Strategies that strongly position the company against competitors and that give the company the strongest possible strategic advantage.

Competitive-parity method—Setting the promotion budget to match competitors' outlays.

Competitor analysis—The process of identifying key competitors; assessing their objectives, strategies, strengths and weaknesses, and reaction patterns; and selecting which competitors to attack or avoid.

Competitor-centred company—A company whose moves are mainly based on competitors' actions and reactions; it spends most of its time tracking competitors' moves and market shares and trying to find strategies to counter them.

Competitor intelligence—Information gathered that informs on what the competition is doing or is about to do.

Complex buying behaviour—Consumer buying behaviour in situations characterised by high consumer involvement in a purchase and significant perceived differences among brands.

Concentrated marketing (or niche marketing)—A market-coverage strategy in which a firm goes after a large share of one or a few submarkets.

Concept testing—Testing new-product concepts with a group of target consumers to find out whether the concepts have strong consumer appeal.

Consumer buying behaviour—The buying behaviour of final consumers – individuals and households who buy goods and services for personal consumption.

Consumer market—All the individuals and households who buy or acquire goods and services for personal consumption.

Consumer-oriented marketing—The philosophy of enlightened marketing that holds that the company should view and organise its marketing activities from the consumers' point of view.

Consumer product—A product bought by final consumers for personal consumption.

Consumer promotion—Sales promotion designed to stimulate consumer purchasing, including samples, coupons, rebates, prices-off, premiums, patronage rewards, displays, and contests and sweepstakes.

Consumer relationship-building promotions—Sales promotions that promote the product's positioning and include a selling message along with the deal.

Consumer-to-business (C2B) online marketing—Online exchanges in which consumers search out sellers, learn about their offers and initiate purchases, sometimes even driving transaction terms.

Consumer-to-consumer (C2C) online marketing—Online exchanges of goods and information between final consumers.

Consumerism—An organised movement of citizens and government agencies to improve the rights and power of buyers in relation to sellers.

Continuity—Scheduling ads evenly within a given period.

Contract manufacturing—A joint venture in which a company contracts with manufacturers in a foreign market to produce the product or provide its service.

Contractual VMS—A vertical marketing system in which independent firms at different levels of production and distribution join together through contracts to obtain more economies or sales impact than they could achieve alone.

Convenience product—A consumer product that the customer usually buys frequently, immediately, and with a minimum of comparison and buying effort.

Convenience store—A small store located near a residential area that is open long hours seven days a week and carries a limited line of high-turnover convenience goods.

Conventional distribution channel—A channel consisting of one or more independent producers, wholesalers and retailers, each a separate business seeking to maximise its own profits, even at the expense of profits for the system as a whole.

Core product—The core problem-solving services or benefits that consumers are really buying when they obtain a product.

Corporate brand licensing—A form of licensing whereby a firm rents a corporate trademark or logo made famous in one product or service category and uses it in a related category.

Corporate branding strategy—A brand strategy whereby the firm makes its company name the dominant brand identity across all of its products.

Corporate VMS—A vertical marketing system that combines successive stages of production and distribution under single ownership – channel leadership is established through common ownership.

Corporate website—A website which carries information about the company and other features designed to answer customer questions, build customer relationships and generate excitement about the company. It aims to build goodwill rather than to sell the company's products or services directly. The site handles interactive communication initiated by the consumer.

Cost-based pricing—Setting prices based on the costs of producing, distributing and selling the product plus a fair rate of return for effort and risk.

Cost-plus pricing—Adding a standard mark-up to the cost of the product.

Countertrade—International trade involving the direct or indirect exchange of goods for other goods instead of cash. Forms include barter compensation (buyback) and counterpurchase.

Coupons—Certificates that give buyers a saving when they purchase a product.

Creative concept—The compelling 'big idea' that will bring the advertising message strategy to life in a distinctive and memorable way.

Critical success factors—The strengths and weaknesses that most critically affect an organisation's success. These are measured relative to competition.

CRM—see Customer relationship management.

Cultural environment—Institutions and other forces that affect society's basic values, perceptions, preferences and behaviours.

Culture—The set of basic values, perceptions, wants and behaviours learned by a member of society from family and other important institutions.

Current marketing situation—The section of a marketing plan that describes the target market and the company's position in it.

Customer-centred company—A company that focuses on customer developments in designing its marketing strategies and on delivering superior value to its target customers.

Customer-centred new-product development—New-product development that focuses on finding new ways to solve customer problems and create more customer-satisfying experiences.

Customer database—An organised collection of comprehensive data about individual customers or prospects, including geographic, demographic, psychographic and buying behaviour data.

Customer defections—The loss of customers to alternative suppliers of a similar or the same service.

Customer delivered value—The difference between total customer value and total customer cost of a marketing offer – 'profit' to the customer.

Customer equity—The total combined customer lifetime values of all of the company's customers.

Customer lifetime value—The value of the entire stream of purchases that a customer would make over a lifetime of patronage.

Customer perceived value—The customer's evaluation of the difference between all the benefits and all the costs of a market offering relative to those of competing offers.

Customer relationship management (CRM)—The overall process of building and maintaining profitable customer relationships by delivering superior customer value and satisfaction.

Customer sales force structure—A sales force organisation under which salespeople specialise in selling only to certain customers or industries.

Customer satisfaction—The extent to which a product's perceived performance matches a buyer's expectations.

Customer value—The consumer's assessment of the product's overall capacity to satisfy his or her needs.

Customer value analysis—Analysis conducted to determine what benefits target customers value and how they rate the relative value of various competitors' offers.

Customer value delivery system—The system made up of the value chains of the company and its suppliers, distributors and ultimately customers, who work together to deliver value to customers.

Customer-value marketing—A principle of enlightened marketing that holds that a company should put most of its resources into customer value-building marketing investments.

Decider—The person who ultimately makes a buying decision or any part of it – whether to buy, what to buy, how to buy, or where to buy.

Deciders—People in the organisation's buying centre who have formal or informal powers to select or approve the final suppliers.

Decision-making unit (DMU)—All the individuals who participate in, and influence, the consumer buying-decision process.

Decline stage—The product life-cycle stage at which a product's sales decline.

Defects—Non-conformity of a product or service to its specifications.

Deficient products—Products that have neither immediate appeal nor long-term benefits.

Demands—Human wants that are backed by buying power.

Demarketing—Marketing to reduce demand temporarily or permanently – the aim is not to destroy demand, but only to reduce or shift it.

Demographic segmentation—Dividing the market into groups based on demographic variables such as age, gender, family size, family life cycle, income, occupation, education, religion, race, generation and nationality.

Demography—The study of human populations in terms of size, density, location, age, sex, race, occupation and other statistics.

Department store—A retail organisation that carries a wide variety of product lines – each line is operated as a separate department managed by specialist buyers or merchandisers.

Derived demand—Business demand that ultimately comes (derives) from the demand for consumer goods.

Descriptive research—Marketing research to better describe marketing problems, situations or markets, such as the market potential for a product or the demographics and attitudes of consumers.

Desirable products—Products that give both high immediate satisfaction and high long-run benefits.

Differentiated marketing (or segmented marketing)—A market-coverage strategy in which a firm decides to target several market segments and designs separate offers for each.

Differentiation—Differentiating the firm's market offering to create superior customer value.

Direct investment—Entering a foreign market by developing foreign-based assembly or production facilities.

Direct-mail marketing—Direct marketing through mailings that include letters, catalogues, ads, CDs, DVDs, samples, fold-outs and other 'salespeople on wings' sent to prospects on mailing lists.

Direct marketing—Direct communications with carefully targeted individual consumers both to obtain an immediate response and to cultivate lasting customers.

Direct-marketing channel—A marketing channel that has no intermediary levels.

Direct-response television (DRTV) marketing—The marketing of products or services via television commercials and programmes which involve a responsive element, typically the use of a freephone number that allows consumers to phone for more information or to place an order for the goods advertised.

Discount—A straight reduction in price on purchases during a stated period of time.

Discount store—A retail institution that sells standard merchandise at lower prices by accepting lower margins and selling at higher volume.

Disintermediation—The elimination of a layer of intermediaries from a marketing channel or the displacement of traditional resellers by radically new types of intermediaries.

Dissonance-reducing buying behaviour—Consumer buying behaviour in situations characterised by high involvement but few perceived differences among brands.

Distribution centre—A large, highly automated warehouse designed to receive goods from various plants and suppliers, take orders, fill them efficiently, and deliver goods to customers as quickly as possible.

Distribution channel—see Marketing channel.

Distributor brand—see Private brand.

Diversification—A strategy for company growth through starting up or acquiring businesses outside the company's current products and markets.

DMU—see Decision-making unit.

Dogs—Low-growth, low-share businesses and products that may generate enough cash to maintain themselves, but do not promise to be large sources of cash.

Downsizing—Reducing the business portfolio by eliminating products of business units that are not profitable or that no longer fit the company's overall strategy.

Drive—see Motive.

DRTV marketing—see Direct-response television marketing.

Durable product—A consumer product that is usually used over an extended period of time and that normally survives many uses.

Dynamic pricing—Charging different prices depending on individual customers and situations.

Economic communities—see Free-trade zones.

Economic environment—Factors that affect consumer buying power and spending patterns.

Embargo—A ban on the import of a certain product.

Emotional appeals—Message appeals that attempt to stir up negative or positive emotions that will motivate purchase; examples are fear, guilt, shame, love, humour, pride and joy appeals.

Engel's laws—Differences noted over a century ago by Ernst Engel in how people shift their spending across food, housing, transportation, healthcare and other goods and services categories as family income rises.

Enlightened marketing—A marketing philosophy holding that a company's marketing should support the best long-run performance of the marketing system; its five principles are consumer-oriented marketing, innovative marketing, value marketing, sense-of-mission marketing and societal marketing.

Environmental sustainability—A management approach that involves developing strategies that both sustain the environment and produce profits for the company.

Environmentalism—An organised movement of concerned citizens and government agencies to protect and improve people's living environment.

Ethnographic research—A form of observational research that involves sending trained observers to watch and interact with consumers in their 'natural habitat'.

Events—Occurrences staged to communicate messages to target audiences; examples are news conferences and grand openings.

Exchange—The act of obtaining a desired object from someone by offering something in return.

Exchange controls—Government limits on the amount of its country's foreign exchange with other countries and on its exchange rate against other currencies.

Exclusive distribution—Giving a limited number of dealers the exclusive right to distribute the company's products in their territories.

Execution style—The approach, style, tone, words and format used for executing an advertising message.

Experience curve (or **learning curve**)—The drop in the average per-unit production cost that comes with accumulated production experience.

Experimental research—The gathering of primary data by selecting matched groups of subjects, giving them different treatments, controlling related factors and checking for differences in group responses.

Exploratory research—Marketing research to gather preliminary information that will help to better define problems and suggest hypotheses.

Export department—A form of international marketing organisation that comprises a sales manager and a few assistants whose job is to organise the shipping out of the company's goods to foreign markets.

Exporting—Entering a foreign market by selling goods produced in the company's home country, often with little modification.

External audit—A detailed examination of the markets, competition, business and economic environment in which the organisation operates.

Externality—The effect of a purchase by one party on others who do not have a choice and whose interests are not taken into account.

Factory outlet—Off-price retailing operation that is owned and operated by a manufacturer and that normally carries the manufacturer's surplus, discontinued or irregular goods.

Fad—A temporary period of unusually high sales driven by consumer enthusiasm and immediate product or brand popularity.

Family life cycle—The stages through which families might pass as they mature over time.

Fashion—A currently accepted or popular style in a given field.

Field sales force—see Outside sales force.

Financial intermediaries—Banks, credit companies, insurance companies and other businesses that help finance transactions or insure against the risks associated with the buying and selling of goods.

Fixed costs—Costs that do not vary with production or sales level.

FOB-origin pricing—A geographic pricing strategy in which goods are placed free on board a carrier; the customer pays the freight from the factory to the destination.

Focus group—A small sample of typical consumers under the direction of a group leader who elicits their reaction to a stimulus such as an ad or product concept.

Follow-up—The last step in the selling process, in which the salesperson follows up after the sale to ensure customer satisfaction and repeat business.

Franchise—A contractual association between a manufacturer, wholesaler or service organisation (a franchiser) and independent businesspeople (franchisees) who buy the right to own and operate one or more units in the franchise system.

Free riders—People who consume more than their fair share of a resource, or shoulder less than a fair share of the costs of its production.

Free-trade zones (or **economic communities**)—Groups of nations organised to secure common goals in the regulation of international trade.

Freight-absorption pricing—A geographic pricing strategy in which the company absorbs all or part of the actual freight charges in order to get the desired business.

Frequency—The number of times the average person in the target market is exposed to an advertising message during a given period.

Full-service retailers—Retailers that provide a full range of services to shoppers.

Functional discount—see Trade discount.

Gatekeepers—People in the organisation's buying centre who control the flow of information to others.

Gender segmentation—Dividing a market into different groups based on gender.

General need description—The stage in the business buying process in which the company describes the general characteristics and quantity of a needed item.

GenXers—Consumers born between 1965 and 1976.

Geodemographics—The study of the relationship between geographical location and demographics.

Geographic segmentation—Dividing the market into different geographical units such as nations, regions, states, counties, cities or neighbourhoods.

Geographical pricing—Setting prices for customers located in different parts of the country or world.

Global firm—A firm that, by operating in more than one country, gains R&D, production, marketing and financial advantages that are not available to purely domestic competitors.

Global industry—An industry in which the strategic positions of competitors in given geographic or national markets are affected by their overall global positions.

Global marketing—Marketing that is concerned with integrating or standardising marketing actions across different geographic markets.

Global organisation—A form of international organisation whereby top corporate management and staff plan worldwide manufacturing or operational facilities, marketing policies, financial flows and logistical systems. The global operating unit reports directly to the chief executive, not to an international divisional head.

Good-value pricing—Offering just the right combination of quality and good service at a fair price.

Governance—The action of developing and managing consistent and cohesive policies, processes, policies and decision rights for areas of responsibility within a business.

Government market—Governmental units – national and local – that purchase or rent goods and services for carrying out the main functions of government.

Growth stage—The product life-cycle stage at which a product's sales start climbing quickly.

Habitual buying behaviour—Consumer buying behaviour in situations characterised by low consumer involvement and few significant perceived brand differences.

Handling objections—The step in the selling process in which the salesperson seeks out, clarifies and overcomes customer objections to buying.

Horizontal marketing system—A channel arrangement in which two or more companies at one level join together to follow a new marketing opportunity.

Hybrid marketing channel—see Multi-channel distribution system.

Hypermarkets—Huge stores that combine supermarket, discount and warehouse retailing; in addition to food, they carry furniture, appliances, clothing and many other products.

Idea generation—The systematic search for new-product ideas.

Idea screening—Screening new-product ideas in order to spot good ideas and drop poor ones as soon as possible.

IMC—see Integrated marketing communications.

Income segmentation—Dividing a market into different income groups.

Income statement—see Operating statement.

Individual marketing—Tailoring products and marketing programmes to the needs and preferences of individual customers.

Industrial product—A product bought by individuals and organisations for further processing or for use in conducting a business.

Inelastic demand—Total demand for a product that is not much affected by price changes, especially in the short run.

Influencer—A person whose views or advice carry some weight in making a final buying decision.

Information search—The stage of the buyer decision process in which the consumer is aroused to search for more information; the consumer may simply have heightened attention or may go into active information search.

Informative advertising—Advertising used to inform consumers about a new product or feature and to build primary demand.

Initiator—The person who first suggests or thinks of the idea of buying a particular product or service.

Innovative marketing—A principle of enlightened marketing which requires that a company seek real product and marketing improvements.

Inside sales force—Salespeople who conduct business from their offices via telephone, the Internet or visits from prospective customers.

Institutional market—Schools, hospitals, nursing homes, prisons and other institutions that provide goods and services to people in their care.

Integrated direct marketing—Direct marketing campaigns that use multiple vehicles and multiple stages to improve response rates and profits.

Integrated logistics management—The logistics concept that emphasises teamwork, both inside the company and among all the marketing channel organisations to maximise the performance of the entire distribution system.

Integrated marketing communications (IMC)—The concept under which a company carefully integrates and coordinates its many communications channels to deliver a clear, consistent and compelling message about the organisation and its products.

Intensive distribution—Stocking the product in as many outlets as possible.

Interactive marketing—Marketing by a service firm that recognises that perceived service quality depends heavily on the quality of buyer–seller interaction.

Intermarket segmentation—Forming segments of consumers who have similar needs and buying behaviour even though they are from different countries.

Intermediaries—Distribution channel firms that help the company find customers or make sales to them, including wholesalers and retailers that buy and resell goods.

Internal audit—An evaluation of the firm's entire value chain.

Internal databases—Information sources that exist within the company.

Internal marketing—Marketing by a service firm to train and effectively motivate its customer-contact employees and all the supporting service people to work as a team to provide customer satisfaction.

International division—A form of international marketing organisation in which the division handles all of the firm's international activities. Marketing, manufacturing, research, planning and specialist staff are organised into operating units according to geography or product groups, or as an international subsidiary responsible for its own sales and profitability.

Internet (the Net)—A vast public web of computer networks connecting users of all types all around the world to each other and to a large 'information repository'.

Introduction stage—The product life-cycle stage when the new product is first distributed and made available for purchase.

Joint ownership—A joint venture in which a company joins investors in a foreign market to create a local business in which the company shares joint ownership and control.

Joint venturing—Entering foreign markets by joining with foreign companies to produce or market a product or service.

'Knocking copy'—see Comparison advertising.

Law of Unintended Consequences—The recognition that almost all human actions have *unforeseen* outcomes.

Learning—Changes in an individual's behaviour arising from experience.

Learning curve—see Experience curve.

Licensed brand—A product or service using a brand name offered by the brand owner to the licensee for an agreed fee or royalty.

Licensing—A method of entering a foreign market in which the company enters into an agreement with a licensee in the foreign market, offering the right to use

a manufacturing process, trademark, patent, trade secret or other item of value for a fee or royalty.

Life-cycle segmentation (or age segmentation)—Offering products or marketing approaches that recognise the consumer's changing needs at different stages of their life.

Lifestyle—A person's pattern of living as expressed in his or her activities, interests and opinions.

Limited-service retailers—Retailers that provide only a limited number of services to shoppers.

Line extension—Extending an existing brand name to new forms, colours, sizes, ingredients or flavours of an existing product category.

Local marketing—Marketing that involves tailoring brands and promotions to the needs and wants of local customer groups.

Long-range plan—A plan that describes the principal factors and forces affecting the organisation during the next several years, including long-term objectives, the chief marketing strategies used to attain them and the resources required.

Macroenvironment—The larger societal forces that affect the whole microenvironment – demographic, economic, natural, technological, political and cultural forces.

Management contracting—A joint venture in which the domestic firm supplies the management know-how to a foreign company that supplies the capital; the domestic firm exports management services rather than products.

Manufacturer's brand (or national brand)—A brand created and owned by the producer of a product or service.

Market—The set of all actual and potential buyers of a product or service.

Market-centred company—A company that pays balanced attention to both customers and competitors in designing its marketing strategies.

Market challenger—A runner-up firm in an industry that is fighting hard to increase its market share.

Market development—A strategy for company growth by identifying and

developing new market segments for current company products.

Market follower—A runner-up firm in an industry that wants to hold its share without rocking the boat.

Market leader—The firm in an industry with the largest market share; it usually leads other firms in price changes, new product introductions, distribution coverage and promotion spending.

Market nicher—A firm in an industry that serves small segments that the other firms overlook or ignore.

Market offering—Some combination of products, services, information or experiences offered to a market to satisfy a need or want.

Market penetration—A strategy for company growth by increasing sales of current products to current market segments without changing the product.

Market-penetration pricing—Setting a low price for a new product in order to attract large numbers of buyers and a large market share.

Market positioning—Arranging for a product to occupy a clear, distinctive and desirable place relative to competing products in the minds of target consumers. Formulating competitive positioning for a product and a detailed marketing mix.

Market segmentation—Dividing a market into distinct groups of buyers who have distinct needs, characteristics or behaviour and who might require separate products or marketing programmes.

Market-skimming pricing—Setting a high price for a new product to skim maximum revenues layer by layer from the segments willing to pay the high price; the company makes fewer but more profitable sales.

Market targeting—The process of evaluating each market segment's attractiveness and selecting one or more segments to enter.

Marketing—A social and managerial process by which individuals and groups obtain what they need and want through creating and exchanging products and value with others.

Marketing audit—A comprehensive, systematic, independent and periodic examination of a company's environment, objectives, strategies and activities to determine problem areas and opportunities, and to recommend a plan of action to improve the company's marketing performance.

Marketing channel (or distribution channel)—A set of interdependent organisations involved in the process of making a product or service available for use or consumption by the consumer or business user.

Marketing communications mix—see Promotion mix.

Marketing concept—The marketing management philosophy which holds that achieving organisational goals depends on determining the needs and wants of target markets and delivering the desired satisfactions more effectively and efficiently than competitors do.

Marketing control—The process of measuring and evaluating the results of marketing strategies and plans, and taking corrective action to ensure that marketing objectives are attained.

Marketing environment—The actors and forces outside marketing that affect marketing management's ability to develop and maintain successful relationships with its target customers.

Marketing implementation—The process that turns marketing strategies and plans into marketing actions in order to accomplish strategic marketing objectives.

Marketing information system (MIS)—People, equipment and procedures to gather, sort, analyse, evaluate and distribute needed, timely and accurate information to marketing decision makers.

Marketing intelligence—Everyday information about developments in the marketing environment that helps managers prepare and adjust marketing plans.

Marketing intermediaries—Firms that help the company to promote, sell and distribute its goods to final buyers; they include physical distribution firms, marketing service agencies and financial intermediaries.

Marketing logistics (or physical distribution)—The tasks involved in planning, implementing and controlling the physical flow of goods, services and related information from points of origin to points of consumption or use to meet customer requirements at a profit.

Marketing management—The art and science of choosing target markets and building profitable relationships with them.

Marketing mix—The set of controllable tactical marketing tools – product, price, place and promotion – that the firm blends to produce the response it wants in the target market.

Marketing process—The process of (1) analysing marketing opportunities; (2) selecting target markets; (3) developing the marketing mix; and (4) managing the marketing effort.

Marketing research—The function that links the consumer, customer and public to the marketer through information that is used to identify and define marketing opportunities and problems, to generate, refine and evaluate marketing actions, to monitor marketing performance, and to improve understanding of the marketing process.

Marketing ROI—see Return on marketing investment.

Marketing services agencies—Marketing research firms, advertising agencies, media firms, marketing consulting firms and other service providers that help a company to target and promote its products to the right markets.

Marketing strategy—The marketing logic by which the business unit hopes to achieve its marketing objectives.

Marketing strategy development—Designing an initial marketing strategy for a new product based on the product concept.

Marketing strategy statement—A statement of the planned strategy for a new product that outlines the intended target market, the planned product positioning, and the sales, market share and profit goals for the first few years.

Marketing website—A website that engages and interacts with consumers that will move them closer to a direct purchase or other marketing outcome. The site handles interactive communication initiated by the company.

Mark-up/mark-down—The difference between selling price and cost as a percentage of selling price or cost.

Mass-marketing—see Undifferentiated marketing.

Materials and parts—Industrial products that enter the manufacturer's product completely, including raw materials and manufactured materials and parts.

Maturity stage—The stage in the product life cycle where sales growth slows or levels off.

Measurability—The degree to which the size, purchasing power and profits of a market segment can be measured.

Media—Non-personal communications channels including print media (newspapers, magazines, direct mail), broadcast media (radio, television), and display media (billboards, signs, posters).

Media impact—The qualitative value of an exposure through a given medium.

Media vehicles—Specific media within each general media type, such as specific magazines, television shows or radio programmes.

Membership groups—Groups that have a direct influence on a person's behaviour and to which a person belongs.

Membership warehouse—see Warehouse club.

Merchant wholesaler—Independently owned business that takes title to the merchandise it handles.

Message source—The company, the brand name, the salesperson of the brand, or the actor in the ad who endorses the product.

Microenvironment—The actors close to the company that affect its ability to serve its customers – the company, suppliers, marketing intermediaries, customer markets, competitors and publics.

Micromarketing—A form of target marketing in which companies tailor their marketing programmes to the needs and wants of narrowly defined geographic, demographic, psychographic or behavioural segments.

Middleman brand—see Private brand.

MIS—see Marketing information system.

Mission statement—A statement of the organisation's purpose – what it wants to accomplish in the wider environment.

Modified rebuy—A business buying situation in which the buyer wants to modify product specifications, prices, terms or suppliers.

Monopolistic competition—A market in which many buyers and sellers trade over a range of prices rather than a single market price.

Moral appeals—Message appeals that are directed to the audience's sense of what is right and proper.

Motive (or drive)—A need that is sufficiently pressing to direct the person to seek satisfaction of the need.

Multibrand strategy—A brand strategy under which a seller develops two or more brands in the same product category.

Multi-channel distribution system (or hybrid marketing channel)—A distribution system in which a single firm sets up two or more marketing channels to reach one or more customer segments. A variety of direct and indirect approaches are used to deliver the firm's goods to its customers.

Multiple niching—Adopting a strategy of having several independent offerings that appeal to several different sub-segments of customers.

National brand—see Manufacturer's brand.

Natural environment—Natural resources that are needed as inputs by marketers or that are affected by marketing activities.

Need recognition—The first stage of the buyer decision process in which the consumer recognises a problem or need.

Needs—States of felt deprivation.

Net—see Internet.

Net profit—The difference between the income from goods sold and all expenses incurred.

Neuromarketing—The use of neuro-technology to improve marketing decision making.

New product—A good, service or idea that is perceived by some potential customers as new.

New-product development—The development of original products, product improvements, product modifications and new brands through the firm's own R&D efforts.

New task—A business buying situation in which the buyer purchases a product or service for the first time.

Niche marketing—see Concentrated marketing.

Non-durable product—A consumer product that is normally consumed in one or a few uses.

Non-personal communication channels—Media that carry messages without personal contact or feedback, including media, atmospheres and events.

Non-tariff trade barriers—Non-monetary barriers to foreign products, such as biases against a foreign company's bids or product standards that go against a foreign company's product features.

Objective-and-task method—Developing the promotion budget by (1) defining specific objectives, (2) determining the tasks that must be performed to achieve these objectives, and (3) estimating the costs of performing these tasks. The sum of these costs is the proposed promotion budget.

Observational research—The gathering of primary data by observing relevant people, actions and situations.

Occasion segmentation—Dividing the market into groups according to occasions when buyers get the idea to buy, actually make their purchase or use the purchased item.

Off-price retailer—Retailer that buys at less-than-regular wholesale prices and sells at less than retail.

Oligopolistic competition—A market in which there are a few sellers that are highly sensitive to each other's pricing and marketing strategies.

Online advertising—Advertising that appears while consumers are surfing the Web, including display ads (banners, interstitials, pop-ups), search-related ads, online classifieds and other forms.

Online databases—Computerised collections of information available from online commercial sources or via the Internet.

Online marketing—Company efforts to market products and services and build customer relationships over the Internet.

Online marketing research—Internet-based research using online surveys, panels, experiments, focus groups, etc.

Online trading networks—Huge online marketplaces in which B2B buyers and sellers find each other online, share information and complete transactions efficiently.

Operating statement (profit-and-loss statement or income statement)—A financial statement that shows company sales, cost of goods sold and expenses during a given period of time.

Opinion leaders—People within a reference group who, because of special skiils, knowledge, personality or other characteristics, exert influence on others.

Optional-product pricing—The pricing of optional or accessory products along with a main product.

Order-routine specification—The stage of the business buying process in which the buyer writes the final order with the chosen supplier(s), listing the technical specifications, quantity needed, expected time of delivery, return policies and warranties.

Outside sales force (or field sales force)—Outside salespeople who travel to call on customers in the field.

Packaging—The activities of designing and producing the container or wrapper for a product.

Patronage rewards—Cash or other awards for the regular use of a certain company's products or services.

Percentage-of-sales method—Setting the promotion budget at a certain percentage of current or forecasted sales or as a percentage of the unit sales price.

Perception—The process by which people select, organise and interpret information to form a meaningful picture of the world.

Performance review—The stage of the business buying process in which the buyer rates its satisfaction with suppliers, deciding whether to continue, modify or drop them.

Personal communication channels—Channels through which two or more people communicate directly with each other, including face to face, person to audience, on the phone, through mail or e-mail or through an Internet 'chat'.

Personal selling—Personal presentation by the firm's sales force for the purpose of making sales and building customer relationships.

Personality—A person's distinguishing psychological characteristics that lead to relatively consistent and lasting responses to his or her own environment.

Persuasive advertising—Advertising used to build selective demand for a brand by persuading consumers that it offers the best quality for their money.

Physical distribution—see Marketing logistics.

Physical distribution firms—Warehouse, transportation and other firms that help a company to stock and move goods from their points of origin to their destinations.

Place—All the company activities that make the product or service available to target customers.

Planned obsolescence—A strategy of causing products to become obsolete before they actually need replacement.

PLC—see Product life cycle.

Pleasing products—Products that give high immediate satisfaction but may hurt consumers in the long run.

Podcast—An audio file downloaded from the Internet to an Apple iPod or other handheld device.

Point-of-purchase (POP) promotions—Displays and demonstrations that take place at the point of purchase or sale.

Political environment—Laws, government agencies and pressure groups that influence and limit various organisations and individuals in a given society.

POP—see Point-of-purchase.

Portfolio analysis—A tool by which management identifies and evaluates the various businesses that make up the company.

Positioning—Arranging for a product to occupy a clear, distinctive and desirable place relative to competing products in the minds of target consumers.

Positioning statement—A statement that summarises company or brand positioning. It takes this form: To (target segment and need) our (brand) is (concept) that (point of difference).

Postpurchase behaviour—The stage of the buyer decision process in which consumers take further action after purchase based on their satisfaction or dissatisfaction.

Pre-approach—The step in the selling process in which the salesperson learns as much as possible about a prospective customer before making a sales call.

Premiums—Goods offered either free or at low cost as an incentive to buy a product.

Presentation—The step in the selling process in which the salesperson tells the product 'story' to the buyer, highlighting customer benefits.

Price—The amount of money charged for a product or service, or the sum of the values that consumers exchange for the benefits of having or using the product or service.

Price elasticity—A measure of the sensitivity of demand to changes in price.

Price packs—Reduced prices that are marked by the producer directly on the label or package.

Primary data—Information collected for the specific purpose at hand.

Private brand (or **middleman, retailer, distributor** or **store brand**)—A brand created and owned by a reseller of a product or service.

Problem recognition—The first stage of the business buying process in which someone in the company recognises a problem or need that can be met by acquiring a good or a service.

Product—Anything that can be offered to a market for attention, acquisition, use or consumption that might satisfy a want or need. It includes physical objects, services, persons, places, organisations and ideas.

Product adaptation—Adapting a product to meet local conditions or wants in foreign markets.

Product assortment—see Product mix.

Product-bundle pricing—Combining several products and offering the bundle at a reduced price.

Product concept—The idea that consumers will favour products that offer the most quality, performance and features, and that the organisation should therefore devote its energy to making continuous product improvements.

Product development—A strategy for company growth by offering modified new products to current market segments.

Product idea—An idea for a possible product that the company can see itself offering to the market.

Product image—The way consumers perceive an actual or potential product.

Product invention—Creating new products or services for foreign markets.

Product life cycle (PLC)—The course of a product's sales and profits over its lifetime. It involves five distinct stages: product development, introduction, growth, maturity and decline.

Product line—A group of products that are closely related because they function in a similar manner, are sold to the same customer groups, are marketed through the same types of outlet, or fall within given price ranges.

Product line filling—Increasing the product line by adding more items within the present range of the line.

Product line pricing—Setting the price steps between various products in a product line based on cost differences between the products, customer evaluations of different features and competitors' prices.

Product line stretching—Increasing the product line by lengthening it beyond its current range.

Product/market expansion grid—A portfolio-planning tool foridentifying company growth opportunities through market penetration, market development, new product development or diversification.

Product mix (or **product portfolio, product assortment**)—The set of all product lines and items that a particular seller offers for sale to buyers.

Product portfolio—see Product mix.

Product sales force structure—A sales force organisation under which salespeople specialise in selling only a portion of the company's products or lines.

Product specification—The stage of the business buying process in which the buying organisation decides on and specifies the best technical product characteristics for a needed item.

Product-support services—Services that augment actual products.

Product's position—The way the product is defined by consumers on important attributes – the place the product occupies in consumers' minds relative to competing products.

Production concept—The philosophy that consumers will favour products that are available and highly affordable, and that management should therefore focus on improving production and distribution efficiency.

Profit-and-loss statement—see Operating statement.

Profitable customer—A person, household or company whose revenues over time exceed, by an acceptable amount, the company's costs of attracting, selling and servicing that customer.

Promotion—Activities that communicate the product or service and its merits to target customers and persuade them to buy.

Promotion mix (or marketing communications mix)—The specific mix of advertising, sales promotion, public relations, personal selling and direct marketing tools that the company uses to persuasively communicate customer value and build customer relationships.

Promotional allowance—A payment or price reduction to reward dealers for participating in advertising and sales-support programmes.

Promotional pricing—Temporarily pricing products below the list price, and sometimes even below cost, to increase short-run sales.

Proposal solicitation—The stage of the business buying process in which the buyer invites qualified suppliers to submit proposals.

Prospecting—The step in the selling process in which the salesperson identifies qualified potential customers.

PR—see Public relations.

Psychographic segmentation—Dividing a market into different groups based on social class, lifestyle or personality characteristics.

Psychographics—The technique of measuring lifestyles and developing lifestyle classifications; it involves measuring the chief AIO dimensions (activities, interests, opinions).

Psychological pricing—A pricing approach that considers the psychology of prices and not simply the economics; the price is used to say something about the product.

Public—Any group that has an actual or potential interest in or impact on an organisation's ability to achieve its objectives.

Public relations (PR)—Building good relations with the company's various publics by obtaining favourable publicity, building up a good corporate image, and handling or heading off unfavourable rumours, stories and events. Major PR functions include press relations, product publicity, public affairs, lobbying, investor relations and development.

Pull strategy—A promotion strategy that calls for spending a lot on advertising and consumer promotion to induce final consumers to buy the product. If the strategy is effective, consumers will then demand the product from channel members, who will in turn demand it from producers.

Pulsing—Scheduling ads unevenly, in bursts, over a certain time period.

Purchase decision—The stage of the buyer decision process in which the consumer actually buys the product.

Pure competition—A market in which many buyers and sellers trade in a uniform commodity – no single buyer or seller has much effect on the going market price.

Pure monopoly—A market in which there is a single seller – it may be a government monopoly, a private regulated monopoly or a private non-regulated monopoly.

Push strategy—A promotion strategy that calls for using the sales force and trade promotion to push the product through channels. The producer promotes the product to channel members to induce them to carry the product and to promote it to final consumers.

Quality—The totality of features and characteristics of a product or service that bear on its ability to satisfy stated or implied needs.

Quantity discount—A price reduction to buyers who buy large volumes.

Quantity premium—A surcharge paid by buyers who purchase high volumes of a product.

Question marks—Low-share business units in high-growth markets that require a lot of cash in order to hold their share or become stars.

Quota—A limit on the amount of goods that an importing country will accept in certain product categories; it is designed to conserve on foreign exchange and to protect local industry and employment.

Range branding strategy—A brand strategy whereby the firm develops separate product range names for different families of product.

Rational appeals—Message appeals that relate to the audience's self-interest and show that the product will produce the claimed benefits; examples are appeals of product quality, economy, value or performance.

Reach—The percentage of people in the target market exposed to an ad campaign during a given period.

Rebates—see Cash refund offers.

Reference groups—Groups that have a direct (face-to-face) or indirect influence on the person's attitudes or behaviour.

Reference prices—Prices that buyers carry in their minds and refer to when they look at a given product.

Relationship marketing—The process of creating, maintaining and enhancing strong, value-laden relationships with customers and other stakeholders.

Reminder advertising—Advertising used to maintain customer relationships and keep consumers thinking about a product.

Resellers—The individuals and organisations that buy goods and services to resell at a profit.

Retailer brand—see Private brand.

Retailer promotion—see Trade promotion.

Retailers—Businesses whose sales come primarily from retailing.

Retailing—All activities involved in selling goods and services directly to final consumers for their personal, non-business use.

Retailing accordion—A phenomenon describing how the width of retailers' product assortment or operations shifts over time: there tends to be a general–specific–general cycle. However, it is possible that many retailing businesses evolve along a specific–general–specific cycle.

Return on advertising investment—The net return on advertising investment divided by the costs of the advertising investment.

Return on marketing investment (or marketing ROI)—The net return from a marketing investment divided by the costs of the marketing investment.

Role—The activities a person is expected to perform according to the people around him or her.

Sales force management—The analysis, planning, implementation and control of sales force activities. It includes designing sales force strategy and structure and recruiting, selecting, training, supervising and evaluating the firm's salespeople.

Sales force promotion—Sales promotion designed to motivate the sales force and make sales force selling efforts more effective, including bonuses, contests and sales rallies.

Sales promotion—Short-term incentives to encourage purchase or sale of a product or service.

Sales quotas—Standards set for salespeople, stating the amount they should sell and how sales should be divided among the company's products.

Salesperson—An individual representing a company to customers by performing one or more of the following activities: prospecting, communicating, selling, servicing, information gathering and relationship building.

Salutary products—Products that have low appeal but may benefit consumers in the long run.

Sample—A segment of the population selected for market research to represent the population as a whole.

Samples—Offers to consumers of a trial amount of a product.

SBU—see Strategic business unit.

Seasonal discount—A price reduction to buyers who buy merchandise or services out of season.

Secondary data—Information that already exists somewhere, having been collected for another purpose.

Segmented marketing—see Differentiated marketing.

Segmented pricing—Selling a product or service at two or more prices that allows for differences in customers, products and locations, rather than based on differences in costs.

Selective attention—The tendency of people to screen out most of the information to which they are exposed.

Selective distortion—The tendency of people to adapt information to personal meanings.

Selective distribution—The use of more than one, but less than all of the intermediaries that are willing to carry the company's products.

Selective retention—The tendency of people to retain only part of the information to which they are exposed, usually information that supports their attitudes or beliefs.

Self-concept (or self-image)—The complex mental picture that people have of themselves.

Self-service retailers—Retailers that provide few or no services to shoppers; shoppers perform their own locate–compare–select process.

Selling concept—The idea that consumers will not buy enough of the organisation's products unless the organisation undertakes a large-scale selling and promotion effort.

Selling process—The steps that the salesperson follows when selling, which include prospecting and qualifying, pre-approach, approach, presentation and demonstration, handling objections, closing and follow-up.

Sense-of-mission marketing—A principle of enlightened marketing which holds that a company should define its mission in broad social terms rather than narrow product terms.

Service—Any activity or benefit that one party can offer to another which is essentially intangible and does not result in the ownership of anything.

Service inseparability—A major characteristic of services – they are produced and consumed at the same time and cannot be separated from their providers, whether the providers are people or machines.

Service intangibility—A major characteristic of services – they cannot be seen, tasted, felt, heard or smelt before they are bought.

Service perishability—A major characteristic of services – they cannot be stored for later sale or use.

Service variability—A major characteristic of services – their quality may vary greatly depending on who provides them and when, where and how.

Services—Activities, benefits or satisfactions offered for sale that are essentially intangible and do not result in the ownership of anything.

Share of customer—The share of the customer's purchasing that a company gets in its product categories.

Shopping product—A consumer product that the customer, in the process of selection and purchase, characteristically compares on such bases as suitability, quality, price and style.

Six Sigma—A set of practices to systematically improve processes by eliminating defects.

Social classes—Relatively permanent and ordered divisions in a society whose members share similar values, interests and behaviours.

Social networking—Social interaction carried out over Internet media.

Societal marketing concept—A principle of enlightened marketing which holds that an organisation should make good marketing decisions by considering consumers' wants, the company's requirements, consumers' long-run interests and society's long-run interests.

'Spam'—Unsolicited, unwanted, commercial e-mail messages.

Speciality product—A consumer product with unique characteristics or brand identification for which a significant group of buyers is willing to make a special purchase effort.

Speciality store—A retail store that carries a narrow product line with a deep assortment within that line.

Standardised marketing mix—An international marketing strategy for using basically the same product, advertising, distribution channels and other elements of the marketing mix in all the company's international markets.

Stars—High-growth, high-share businesses or products that often require heavy investment to finance their rapid growth.

Status—The general esteem given to a role by society.

Store brand—see Private brand.

Straight product extension—Marketing a product in a foreign market without any change.

Straight rebuy—A business buying situation in which the buyer routinely reorders something without any modifications.

Strategic business unit (SBU)—A unit of the company that has a separate mission and objectives and that can be planned independently from other company businesses. An SBU can be a company division, a product line within a division, or sometimes just a single product or brand

Strategic group—A group of firms in an industry following the same or a similar strategy.

Strategic plan—A plan that describes how a firm will adapt to take advantage of opportunities in its constantly changing environment, thereby maintaining a strategic fit between the firm's goals and capabilities and its changing market opportunities.

Style—A basic and distinctive mode of expression.

Subculture—A group of people with shared value systems based on common life experiences and situations.

Supermarkets—Large, low-cost, low-margin, high-volume, self-service stores that carry a wide variety of food, laundry and household products.

Superstore—A store around twice the size of a regular supermarket that carries a large assortment of routinely purchased food and non-food items and offers such services as dry cleaning, post offices, film developing, photo finishing, cheque cashing, petrol forecourts and self-service car-washing facilities.

Supplier search—The stage of the business buying process in which the buyer tries to find the best vendors.

Supplier selection—The stage of the business buying process in which the buyer reviews proposals and selects a supplier or suppliers.

Suppliers—Firms and individuals that provide the resources needed by the company and its competitors to produce goods and services.

Supplies and services—Industrial products that do not enter the finished product at all.

Survey research—The gathering of primary data by asking people questions about their knowledge, attitudes, preferences and buying behaviour.

Sustainable marketing concept—A principle of marketing that holds that an organisation should meet the needs of its present consumers without compromising the ability of future generations to fulfil their own needs.

SWOT analysis—A distillation of the findings of the internal and external audits which draws attention to the critical organisational strengths and weaknesses and the opportunities and threats facing the company.

Systems selling—Selling a packaged solution to a problem, without all the separate decisions involved.

Target costing—A technique to support pricing decisions, which starts with deciding a target cost for a new product and works back to designing the product.

Target market—A set of buyers sharing common needs or characteristics that the company decides to serve.

Target marketing—Directing a company's marketing effort towards serving one or more groups of customers sharing common needs or characteristics.

Target profit pricing—Setting price to make a target profit.

Targeting—The process of evaluating each market segment's attractiveness and selecting one or more segments to enter.

Tariff—A tax levied by a government against certain imported products. Tariffs are designed to raise revenue or to protect domestic firms.

Team selling—Using teams of people from sales, marketing, production, finance, technical support, and even upper management to service large, complex accounts.

Team-based new-product development—An approach to developing new products in which various company departments work closely together, overlapping the steps in the product development process to save time and increase effectiveness.

Technological environment—Forces that create new technologies, creating new product and market opportunities.

Telephone marketing (or telemarketing)—Using the telephone to sell directly to consumers.

Territorial sales force structure—A sales force organisation that assigns each salesperson to an exclusive geographic territory in which that salesperson sells the company's full line.

Test marketing—The stage of new product development where the product and marketing programme are tested in more realistic market settings.

Third-party logistics (3PL) provider—An independent logistics provider that performs any or all of the functions required to get its client's product to market.

Total costs—The sum of the fixed and variable costs for any given level of production.

Total customer cost—The total of all the monetary, time, energy and psychic costs associated with a marketing offer.

Total customer value—The total of the entire product, services, personnel and image values that a buyer receives from a marketing offer.

Total quality management (TQM)—Programmes designed to constantly improve the quality of products, services and marketing processes.

Trade discount (or functional discount)—A price reduction offered by the seller to trade channel members that perform certain functions, such as selling, storing and record keeping.

Trade promotion (or retailer promotion)—Sales promotion designed to gain reseller support and to improve reseller selling efforts, including discounts, allowances, free goods, cooperative advertising, push money, and conventions and trade shows.

Trade-in allowance—A price reduction given for turning in an old item when buying a new one.

The Tragedy of the Commons—Free access to finite resource ultimately dooms the resource by over-exploitation.

Transaction—A trade between two parties that involves at least two things of value, agreed-upon conditions, a time of agreement and a place of agreement.

Two-part pricing—A strategy for pricing services in which price is broken into a fixed fee plus a variable usage rate.

Undifferentiated marketing (or mass-marketing)—A market-coverage strategy in which a firm decides to ignore market segment differences and go after the whole market with one offer.

Uniform delivered pricing—A geographic pricing strategy in which the company charges the same price plus freight to all customers, regardless of their location.

Unsought product—A consumer product that the consumer either does not know about or knows about but does not normally think of buying.

User—The person who consumes or uses a product or service.

Users—Members of the organisation who will use the product or service; users often initiate the buying proposal and help define product specifications.

Value analysis—An approach to cost reduction in which components are studied carefully to determine whether they can be redesigned, standardised or made by less costly methods of production.

Value-based pricing—Setting price based on buyers' perceptions of product values rather than on cost.

Value chain—A major tool for identifying ways to create more customer value; the series of departments that carry out value-creating activities to design, produce, market, deliver and support a firm's products.

Value-delivery network—The network made up of the company, suppliers, distributors and ultimately customers who 'partner' with each other to improve the performance of the entire system.

Value positioning—A range of positioning alternatives based on the value an offering delivers and its price.

Variable costs—Costs that vary directly with the level of production.

Variety-seeking buying behaviour—Consumer buying behaviour in situations characterised by low consumer involvement, but significant perceived brand differences.

Vertical marketing system (VMS)—A distribution channel structure in which producers, wholesalers and retailers act as a unified system. One channel member owns the others, has contracts with them, or has so much power that they all cooperate.

Viral marketing—The Internet version of word-of-mouth marketing – e-mail messages or other marketing events that are so infectious that customers will want to pass them along to friends.

VMS—see Vertical marketing system.

Vodcast—A video file downloaded from the Internet to an Apple iPod or other handheld device.

Wants—The form that human needs take as shaped by culture and individual personality.

Warehouse club (or wholesale club, membership warehouse)—Off-price retailer that sells a limited selection of brand-name grocery items, appliances, clothing and a hodgepodge of other goods at deep discounts to members who pay annual membership fees.

Web communities—Web sites upon which members can congregate online and exchange views on issues of common interest.

Wheel of retailing—A concept of retailing which states that new types of retailer usually begin as low-margin, low-price, low-status operations, but later evolve into higher-priced, higher-service operations, eventually becoming like the conventional retailers they replaced.

Wholesale club—see Warehouse club.

Wholesaler—A firm engaged primarily in selling goods and services to those buying for resale or business use.

Word-of-mouth influence—Personal communication about a product between target buyers and neighbours, friends, family members and associates.

Workload approach—An approach to setting sales force size, whereby the company groups accounts into different classes according to size, account status or other factors related to the effort required to maintain them, and then determines how many salespeople are needed to call on them the desired number of times.

Zone pricing—A geographic pricing strategy in which the company sets up two or more zones. All customers within a zone pay the same total price; the more distant the zone, the higher the price.

SUBJECT INDEX

Note: items in bold are included in the glossary

COMPANY INDEX